COLLEGE
ACCOUNTING

18TH EDITION

JAMES A. HEINTZ, DBA, CPA
Professor of Accounting
University of Kansas
Lawrence, Kansas

ROBERT W. PARRY, JR., PhD
Professor of Accounting
Indiana University
Bloomington, Indiana

THOMSON

SOUTH-WESTERN

Australia · Canada · Mexico · Singapore · Spain · United Kingdom · United States

THOMSON

SOUTH-WESTERN

College Accounting, 18e, Chapters 1-29
By James A. Heintz and Robert W. Parry

Vice President/Editorial Director
Jack Calhoun

Vice President/Editor-in-Chief
George Werthman

Publisher
Rob Dewey

Acquisitions Editor
Jennifer Codner

Sr. Developmental Editor
Sara Wilson

Sr. Marketing Manager
Larry Qualls

Marketing Channel Manager
Brian Joyner

Sr. Production Editor
Tim Bailey

Manager of Technology Solutions
Jim Rice

Technology Project Editor
Sally Nieman

Media Editor
Robin Browning

Editorial Assistant
Janice Hughes

Sr. Design Project Manager
Michelle Kunkler

Manufacturing Coordinator
Doug Wilke

Cover and Internal Design
Lisa Albonetti,
Cincinnati, OH

Cover Images
© PhotoDisc, Inc.

Production
Navta Associates, Inc.

Printer
Quebecor World
Versailles, KY

LEADING THE REST—THE BEST COLLEGE ACCOUNTING TEXT

Edition after edition, Heintz & Parry's *College Accounting* has been the leader in providing solid, tested content to hundreds of thousands of students. The 18th edition continues that tradition of excellence. We've kept intact everything that has made *College Accounting* so successful, then added new features, supplements, and technology to ensure it remains **the best text** on the market. Our main objective has and always will be to make accounting understandable to every student and to do so without sacrificing crucial substance and technical correctness. Our step-by-step, straightforward approach helps build practical accounting skills that are needed when entering the world of work. The text presents basic topics first and builds to more advanced coverage so that learners are never overwhelmed. Likewise, the narrative approach covers a simpler example of a service business before moving on to a merchandising business and then to a manufacturing environment. In the end, *College Accounting, 18e,* combines an easily readable style throughout the text with helpful reinforcement through its unparalleled learning package. By building practical accounting skills and developing an understanding of concepts, students will be prepared for success in the business world. We're confident that this new edition represents a text that achieves our goals and continues its tradition of fundamental excellence.

PROVEN TO BE THE BEST!

The Best Approach

Heintz & Parry has proven that students excel when they're not rushed into financial statements or overloaded with theory. This text presents concepts simply and ensures the best, most accurate coverage, which allows students to build on their foundation of knowledge one topic at a time.

The Best Enhancements

The 18th edition refines the many improvements of earlier editions that were made in response to both instructors' feedback and our own commitment to meet the evolving needs of the learning environment. Newly revised and expanded *Computers and Accounting* coverage and enhanced technology opportunities encourage students to understand how the computerized environment enhances the world of accounting. Choices of coverage increase teaching flexibility to allow subject matter to be taught with or without special journals. We also have enriched Comprehensive Problem 1 to provide students the opportunity to see the impact of transactions on more than one financial period and Comprehensive Problem 2 by offering the option of completing it with or without special journals.

The Best Pedagogy

College Accounting, 18e, employs time-tested, classroom-proven educational techniques.

Repetition of key topics, a continuing topic example, and relevant demonstration problems are some of the methods used to ensure—and enhance—student progress.

The Best Supporting Products

A helpful instructor's resource manual, colorful teaching transparencies tied to the text as well as transparencies of assignment solutions, and excellent PowerPoint® slides are just a few of the features that constitute the extensive supplement package. See descriptions of these and other ancillary products below under "Supplements For Instructors."

The Best Technology

Our expanded WebTutor Advantage™ and revised Personal Trainer® offer exceptional technology tools for high-impact assistance to students and instructors.

The Best Service

You have our commitment to always provide you with the best of everything accompanying our products. From your ITP sales representative, to the Academic Resource Center staff, to the authors themselves, our professional resources and support team is committed to helping you.

**Take a closer look at *College Accounting, 18e,*
and see for yourself why it's THE BEST!**

PROVEN TO BE THE BEST!

WHAT MAKES OUR APPROACH THE BEST?

Quality and creative suggestions and other feedback from instructors and students provide excellent opportunities for our ongoing refinement and enhancement of each edition. As always, we listened and responded in this new edition. Skill development and mastery are encouraged and assisted by a number of features.

College Accounting, 18e, presents simple concepts first and builds to more advanced content. In each chapter students focus on only one major topic or procedure, ensuring that they master each new concept before moving on.

- **Real-world skills** are developed to help students get jobs after graduation.

- **Careful development of topics** prevents "information overload."

- **Repetition of key topics** throughout helps students master important concepts and procedures.

- **Narrative approach** covers the simpler example of a service business before moving on to a merchandising business and later a manufacturing business. Along the way, the company structure moves from sole proprietorship to partnership to corporation.

- **Demonstration problems** can be used as study aids or in-class examples.

- **Comprehensive problems** provide important opportunities to review skills.

- **Three versions** of the text (10, 16, or 29 chapters) create a custom fit for your course.

- **An optional alternative version** of Chapters 11 and 12 expand the presentation of special journals for those wanting more coverage in that area.

WHAT'S NEW WITH THIS EDITION?

Flexible Coverage of Special Journals

Continuing the approach introduced in the 17th edition, Chapters 11 (Sales and Cash Receipts) and 12 (Purchases and Cash Payments) guide the student through these topics using the general journal for recording all transactions. Chapter 13 combines those topics and teaches how special journals can be used to assist the recording process. In the 18th edition, instructors may choose to bundle, free of charge with the text, a two-chapter soft-cover book (*College Accounting: Special Journals, an Alternative to Chapters 11–13, 0-324-29160-4*) to use instead of Chapters 11–13 in the text. The two alternative chapters cover the same topics but use both the general journal and special journals together. Thus, *Special Journals* allow instructors to easily skip Chapter 13 in the text without concern that students will miss key content.

H&P PROVEN TO BE THE BEST!

Computers and Accounting *(continued)*

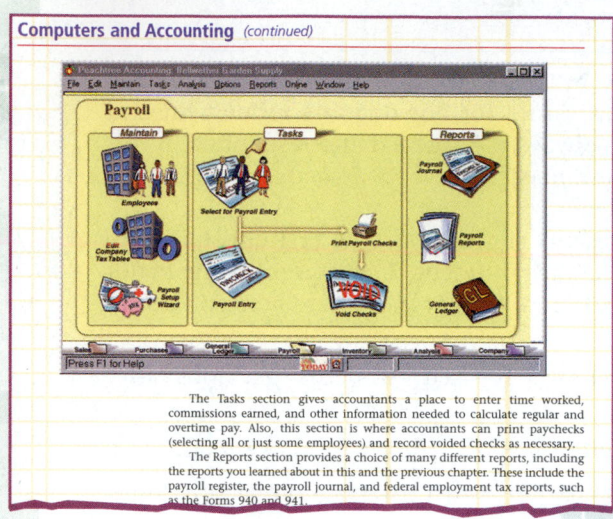

The Tasks section gives accountants a place to enter time worked, commissions earned, and other information needed to calculate regular and overtime pay. Also, this section is where accountants can print paychecks (selecting all or just some employees) and record voided checks as necessary.

The Reports section provides a choice of many different reports, including the reports you learned about in this and the previous chapter. These include the payroll register, the payroll journal, and federal employment tax reports, such as the Forms 940 and 941.

Completely Revised and Expanded!

Computers and Accounting, written by Gary Schneider of the University of San Diego, puts computers in the context of their importance to accounting in the real world. This coverage, which has been increased, now appears in Chapters 2, 6, 9, 13, 26 and 29. The coverage:

- Describes the computer skills that are used in accounting.
- Explains how computer software aids bookkeeping.
- Examines the use of the computer in payroll accounting.
- Tells how the computer helps process cash receipt, cash payment, sales, and purchase transactions through a special journal environment.
- Explains the purpose of computer languages.
- Explores the computer's company-wide influence in the manufacturing environment.

Where helpful, screen captures from Peachtree® software are shown to assist understanding.

GENERALLY ACCEPTED ACCOUNTING PRINCIPLES (GAAP)

LO3 Define GAAP and describe the process used to develop these principles.

Financial Accounting Series

Statement of Financial Accounting Standards No. 148

Soon after the stock market crash of 1929, the federal government established the Securities and Exchange Commission (SEC). The purpose of this government agency is to help develop standards for reporting financial information to stockholders. The SEC currently has authority over 12,000 companies listed on the major stock exchanges (New York Stock, American, and NASDAQ). It has the power to require these firms to follow certain rules when preparing their financial statements. These rules are referred to as **generally accepted accounting principles** (GAAP).

Rather than developing GAAP on its own, the SEC encouraged the creation of a private standard-setting body. It did so because it believed the private sector had better access to the resources and talent necessary to develop these standards. Since 1973, the Financial Accounting Standards Board (FASB) has filled this role. In developing accounting standards, FASB follows a specific process and relies on the advice of many organizations. When an accounting issue is identified, the following steps are followed.

1. The issue is placed on FASB's agenda. This lets everyone know that the Board plans to develop a standard addressing this issue.

Enhanced Coverage of Content

- In Chapter 1, the coverage of generally accepted accounting principles (GAAP) and the process used by the Financial Accounting Standards Board has been expanded. (See page 3.)
- A basic introduction to perpetual inventory has been added to Chapter 15 to help students have a better understanding of accounting for inventory in a retail setting. This earlier coverage also helps prepare students for the later discussion of inventory in Chapter 19. (See page 563.)
- Expanded coverage of notes receivable and notes payable appears in Chapter 18.
- The coverage of accounting for corporate organization costs and stock subscriptions has been updated in Chapter 22.

Self-Study Problems as Pre-Tests

In each chapter, the Self-Study Problems have been repositioned so that they can more easily be used by the student to test their knowledge *before* they work on chapter assignments. As before, the solutions to the Self-Study Problems are located at the end of the text.

New Location for Challenge Problems

Now following the Mastery Problem in each chapter, the Challenge Problem contains a reminder, in the margin, that this problem is intended to challenge students to think a step beyond the chapter's coverage.

H&P PROVEN TO BE THE BEST!

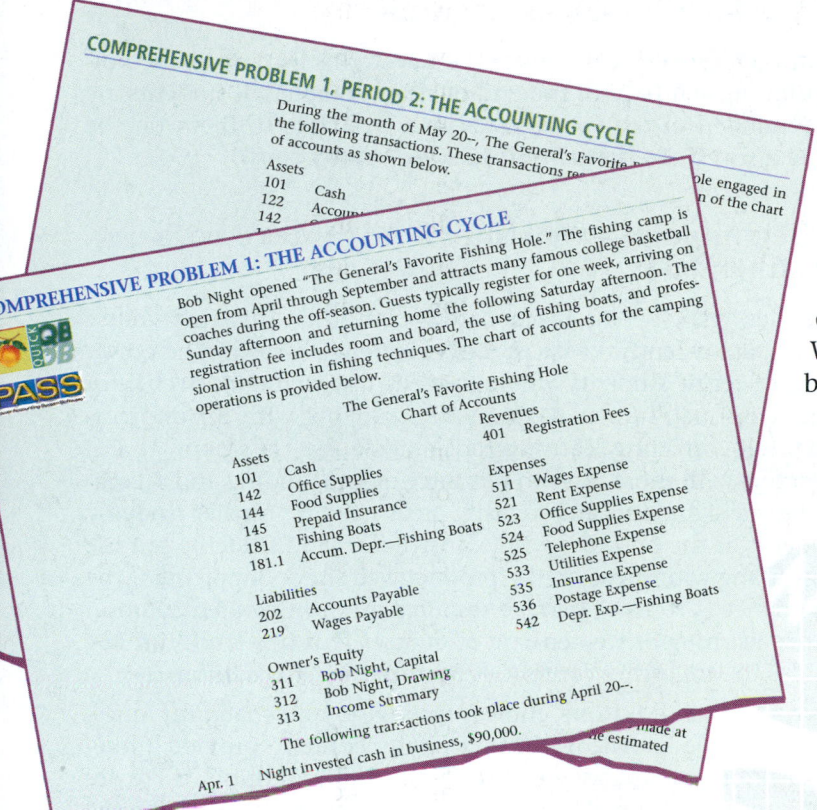

Expansion and Enhanced Flexibility of the Comprehensive Problems

Comprehensive Problems 1 and 2 each contain a "Part 2" that takes students into a second period. In addition, Comprehensive Problem 2 can be assigned using only a general journal or using special journals, depending on the instructor's preference. (The Solutions Manual and the Working Papers contain complete coverage of both versions of Comprehensive Problem 2.)

New Assignment Numbering System

To provide easy designation of assignments, the set "A" assignments (exercises and problems) are now numbered consecutively. The set "B" assignments follow the same pattern and, as before, parallel the set "A" counterpart. This numbering system is also followed in the Study Guide, the Working Papers, and the Solutions Manual.

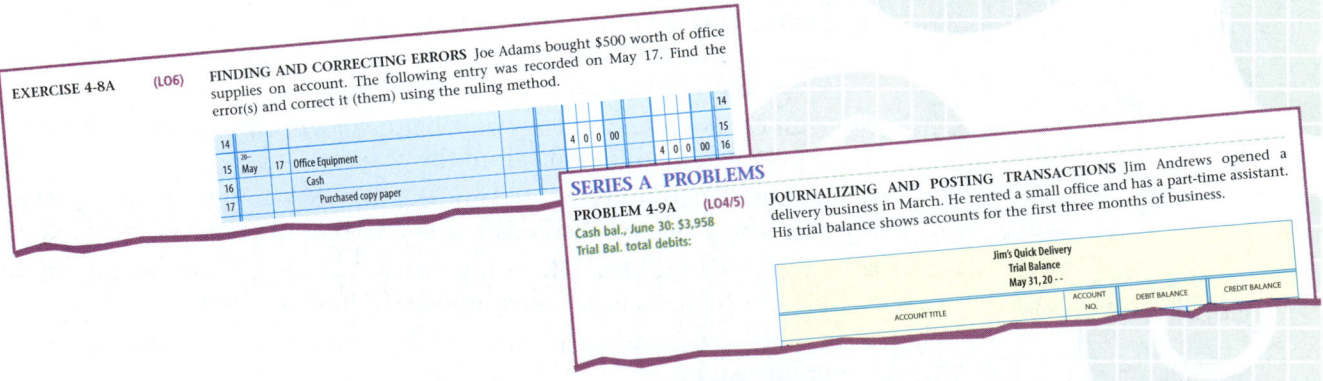

Check Figures

These helpful benchmarks are now provided in the text's margin by applicable assignments.

PROVEN TO BE THE BEST!

Web Site Resources Reminder

In each chapter, just before the Key Terms list and at the bottom of each page of the end-of-chapter material, students are reminded of the valuable resource available to them on the text's web site (**http://heintz.swlearning.com**).

Enhanced Technology—WebTutor® Advantage with Personal Trainer® 3.0

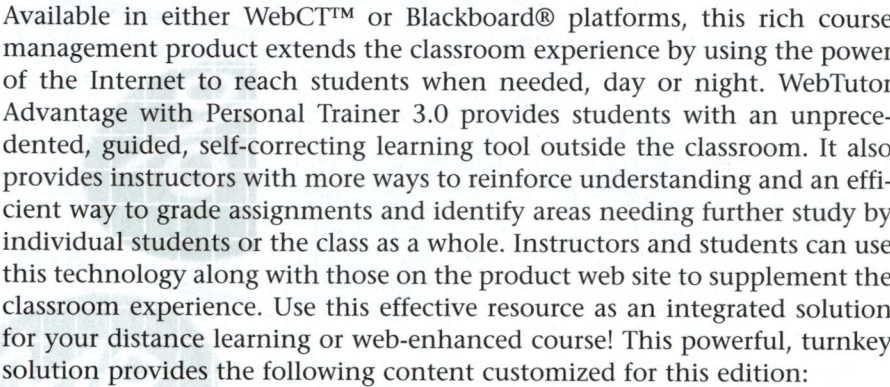

Available in either WebCT™ or Blackboard® platforms, this rich course management product extends the classroom experience by using the power of the Internet to reach students when needed, day or night. WebTutor Advantage with Personal Trainer 3.0 provides students with an unprecedented, guided, self-correcting learning tool outside the classroom. It also provides instructors with more ways to reinforce understanding and an efficient way to grade assignments and identify areas needing further study by individual students or the class as a whole. Instructors and students can use this technology along with those on the product web site to supplement the classroom experience. Use this effective resource as an integrated solution for your distance learning or web-enhanced course! This powerful, turnkey solution provides the following content customized for this edition:

- **Interactive Quizzes**—Multiple choice, true/false, and matching questions, which test the knowledge of the chapter content, provide immediate feedback on the accuracy of the response. In addition, there are specific quizzes in Chapters 2–6 that reinforce understanding of the accounting cycle. All of the quizzes help students pinpoint areas needing more study.

- **Problem Demonstrations**—The chapter demonstration problem is presented and an audio step-by-step explanation of the solution is provided to guide student understanding.

- **Practice Exercises**—These practice exercises provide students an opportunity to further test their knowledge and receive immediate feedback.

- **Learning Objectives & Chapter Review**—To reinforce and remind students of the objectives of each chapter, the learning objectives are provided and tied to a brief review of the chapter.

- **Flashcards**—A terminology quiz helps students gain a complete understanding of the key terms from the chapter.

- **Spanish Dictionary of Accounting Terms**—To aid Spanish-speaking students, a Spanish dictionary of key accounting terms is provided.

- **Crossword Puzzles**—These interactive puzzles provide an alternative tool for students to test their understanding of terminology.

- **Games**—Students can review chapter content and terminology using online games.

- **Personal Trainer 3.0**—This Internet-based homework tutor is a rich tool for students and instructors. With the help of warm-ups and hints, students can complete exercise and problem assignments or practice by completing unassigned homework online. Instructors receive the

H&P   PROVEN TO BE THE BEST!

results, which can be automatically entered into a grade book for the assigned homework, and can view the efforts of the unassigned work completed by students. Unlike any other tutorial on the market, students receive the pedagogical benefits of the completion of homework assignments and instructors have more time to devote to other classroom activities. (Personal Trainer 3.0 is also available as a standalone product for those instructors not using WebTutor Advantage.)

WHY IS OUR PEDAGOGY THE BEST?

This text facilitates student learning by employing a classroom-proven pedagogy.

- A **narrative approach** uses a continuing example to help students understand topics.
- **Repetition of key topics** benefits students by repeated exposure to important concepts and techniques.
- **Learning objectives** preview the skills that will be studied and mastered in that chapter.
- **Chapter openers** present the topic in context and pose a question that is answered at the end of the chapter.
- **Margin notes** enrich student understanding of concepts and terms beyond what is contained in the text narrative.
- **Learning Keys** emphasize important new points and help students gain a clearer understanding of the key coverage in each chapter.
- A **Broader View** provides students with interesting examples of actual events or situations that tie to accounting.

- **Profiles in Accounting** feature real people successfully working and using their College Accounting skills.
- **Arrow pointers** and **text pointers** emphasize the sources and calculations of numbers.
- **Key steps** demonstrate steps to accomplish specific objectives, such as how to prepare a bank reconciliation or work sheet.
- **Accounting forms** are presented on rulings to emphasize structure and help students quickly learn how to prepare these documents.
- The **statement of cash flows coverage** reflects its importance today.
- **Depreciation methods** are introduced in Chapter 5 with some detailing in that chapter's appendix.
- The most current **payroll information** is presented in two chapters (Chapters 8 and 9).
- The **combination journal** is featured in Chapter 10 and provides flexibility for those instructors not wishing to cover this topic.
- The topics of **sales and cash receipts** and **purchases and cash payments** in a general

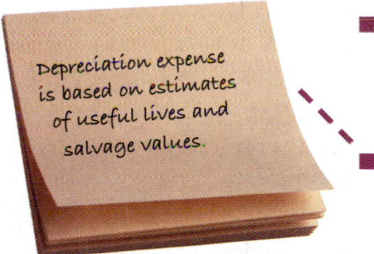
Depreciation expense is based on estimates of useful lives and salvage values.

LEARNING KEY: The business entity's assets and liabilities are separate from the owner's nonbusiness assets and liabilities.

A BROADER VIEW
Fraud—A Real Threat to Small Business

The bookkeeper for Kramer Iron, Inc., in Hamden, Connecticut, embezzled $213,539 from the company over a four-year period. She used two schemes. One was to alter the number of the dollar amount printed on checks payable to her. The other technique involved putting her own name on the "pay to" line on checks intended for other parties.

This fraud shows the importance of two procedures described in this chapter: (1) Make sure that all aspects of a check are correct before signing it. (2) In preparing the bank reconciliation, compare canceled checks with the accounting records.

H&P   PROVEN TO BE THE BEST!

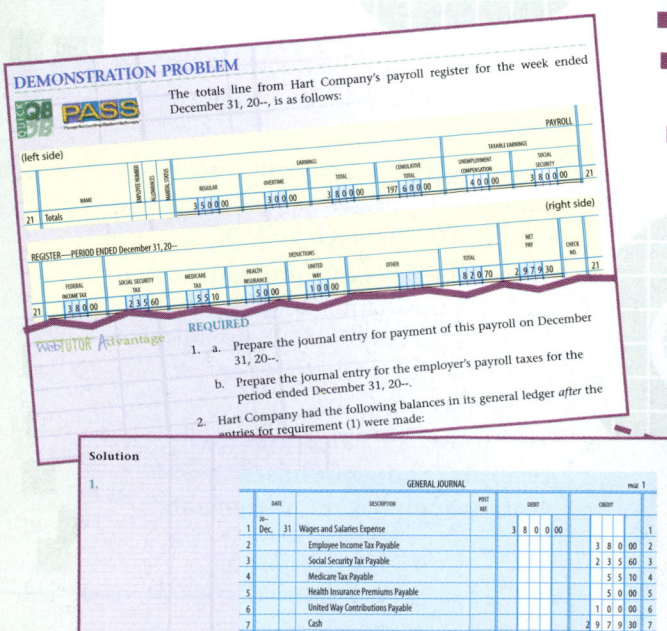

Jessie Jane's Campus Delivery Trial Balance June 30, 20 - -													
ACCOUNT TITLE		DEBIT BALANCE					CREDIT BALANCE						
Cash			3	7	0	00							
Accounts Receivable			6	5	0	00							
Supplies				8	0	00							
Prepaid Insurance			2	0	0	00							
Delivery Equipment		3	6	0	0	00							
Accounts Payable								1	8	0	0	00	
Jessica Jane, Capital								2	0	0	0	00	
Jessica Jane, Drawing			1	5	0	00							
Delivery Fees								2	1	5	0	00	
Rent Expense			2	0	0	00							
Telephone Expense				5	0	00							
Wages Expense			6	5	0	00							
		5	9	5	0	00		5	9	5	0	00	

Jessie Jane's Campus Delivery Income Statement For Month Ended June 30, 20 --											
Revenue:											
Delivery fees							$2	1	5	0	00
Expenses:											
Wages expense	$	6	5	0	00						
Rent expense		2	0	0	00						
Telephone expense			5	0	00						
Total expenses								9	0	0	00
Net income							$1	2	5	0	00

journal system are presented consecutively in Chapters 11 and 12.

- **Special journals system** coverage (Chapter 13) immediately follows the sales and cash receipts and purchases and cash payments chapters. (For those instructors wanting to cover these topics, in two chapters, using special journals, a special journals book is available bundled with the text, upon request, at no additional cost.)

- **Color-coding** enhances understanding by highlighting accounts in a consistent color scheme. Assets are shown in blue, liabilities in yellow, ownership equity in purple, revenues in green, expenses in light red, and drawing accounts in mauve. All journals are on blue rulings to differentiate those chronological records from ledgers and other processing documents, which are shown in yellow. Financial statements are white. Source documents vary in color, in the same manner as real-life documents.

- The **voucher system** (Chapter 14) coverage illustrates this system as a natural expansion of accounting for purchases with a special journal.

- **Accounts receivable** and **notes receivable** are presented in a more logical order with the simpler subject of accounts receivable covered first (Chapter 17).

- **Text & Supplements carefully verified** to guarantee an accurate and error-free text and package.

Some additional specific examples include:

- Transactions reflected in the accounting equation (Page 18)
- The interaction of the key financial statements (Page 29)
- Owner's equity umbrella (Page 50)
- Source documents (Page 90)
- General journal and general ledger relationship (Page 99)
  - Work sheet development (Page 142G)
  - Linkages between the work sheet and the financial statements (Pages 177 and 178)
  - Tax forms (Pages 266–268 and 305–310)

Chapter-ending activities reinforce learning.

- **Key Points** provide an effective review of important information covered in each chapter.
- **Reflection: Answering the Opening Question** provides the answer to the question posed in the opening scenario.
- **Key Terms** are defined at the end of each chapter, and the page of their first appearance is listed.
- **Demonstration Problems** bring together key concepts and principles. Students can work through the problems and solutions independently to gain confidence before

PROVEN TO BE THE BEST!

working the homework assignments. The problems are also effective for in-class examples.

- **Review Questions** for each chapter help students understand and assimilate the important points covered and determine where additional review is required.

- **Managing Your Writing**, introduced in a Chapter 1 module and written by Ken Davis of Indiana University—Purdue University, guides students through an easy-to-follow, 12-step process for honing writing skills. An assignment at the end of each chapter allows students to apply critical thinking and writing skills to issues raised by material in that chapter.

MANAGING YOUR WRITING

The current month's bank statement for your account arrives in the mail. In reviewing the statement, you notice a deposit listed for $400.00 that you did not make. It has been credited in error to your account.
Discuss whether you have an ethical or legal obligation to inform the bank of the error. What action should you take?

- **Ethics Cases** help students think through what they would do in various situations. Case problems for individual and group use allow students to weigh the merits of various ethical considerations related to accounting.

WEB WORK

Your business will, at some point in time, need to write a check to pay a vendor or an employee, or to cover an unforeseen expense. What do you need to do to open an account? What are some of the costs and restrictions a business owner needs to be aware of? Visit the Interactive Study Center on our web site at **http://heintz.swlearning.com** for special hotlinks to assist you in this assignment.

- **Web Work** assignments, identified by an icon, begin in Chapter 7. Web Work assignments expose students to the business applications of the Internet by directing them to Internet sites, where they obtain information to complete an assignment.

- **Self-Study Test Questions**, consisting of multiple choice and true/false items, allow students to assess their understanding of chapter material to determine if further study is required before proceeding to the exercises and problems. Answers to the questions are provided at the end of the text.

- **A & B Exercises and Problems**, keyed to chapter learning objectives, provide a range of instructional choices. One set can be used in class and the other for assignments. Alternatively, both sets can be used for practice for students needing extra assistance.

MASTERY PROBLEM

Adjusted Trial Bal. total: $58,500;
Net income: $13,630

Kristi Williams offers family counseling services specializing in financial and marital problems. A chart of accounts and a trial balance taken on December 31, 20-1, follow.

KRISTI WILLIAMS FAMILY COUNSELING SERVICES CHART OF ACCOUNTS

Assets		Revenue	
		401	Client Fees
101	Cash		
142	Office Supplies	Expenses	
145	Prepaid Insurance	511	Wages Expense
181	Office Equipment	521	Rent Expense
181.1	Accumulated Depr.—	523	Office Supplies Expense
	Office Equipment	533	Utilities Expense
187	Computer Equipment	535	Insurance Expense
	Accumulated Depr.—	541	Depr. Expense—
	Computer Equipment		Office Equipment

- **Mastery Problems** challenge students to apply the essential elements introduced in the chapter. Selected assignments may be solved using the PASS, Peachtree®, or QuickBooks® software. These are designated by icons shown here.

- **Challenge Problems**—Perhaps the most important measure of student understanding is the ability to apply newly learned concepts to new and unfamiliar situations. At the end of each chapter, the Challenge Problem tests the ability of more advanced or ambitious students to apply concepts to transactions, events, or economic conditions one step beyond what is laid out in the text.

CHALLENGE PROBLEM

This problem challenges you to apply your cumulative accounting knowledge to move a step beyond the material in the chapter.

2. Item 4: Dr. Depositor Accounts, $350.00

Susan Panera is preparing the June 30 bank reconciliation for Panera Bakery. She discovers the following items that explain the difference between the cash balance on her books and the balance as reported by Lawrence Bank.

1. An ATM withdrawal of $200.00 for personal use was not recorded by Susan.
2. A deposit of $850.00 was recorded by Susan but has not been received by Lawrence Bank as of June 30.
3. A check written in payment on account to Jayhawk Supply for $340.00 was recorded by Susan as $430.00 and by Lawrence Bank as $530.00.
4. An ATM deposit of $350.00 was recorded twice by Lawrence Bank.
5. An electronic funds transfer of $260.00 to Sunflower Mills as a payment on account was not recorded by Susan.
6. Check No. 103 for $235.00 and No. 110 for $127.00 had not cleared Lawrence Bank as of June 30.

REQUIRED

1. Prepare the journal entries required to correct Panera Bakery's books as of June 30.
2. Prepare the journal entries required to correct Lawrence Bank's books as of June 30.

PROVEN TO BE THE BEST!

■ **Comprehensive Problems**—Comprehensive review problems are built directly into the text, providing an opportunity to review topics from multiple chapters. These appear after Chapters 6, 16, and 21.

WHAT MAKES OUR SERVICE THE BEST?

The entire Heintz & Parry team is ready to help instructors. Your South-Western representative is always available to provide individualized assistance. The Heintz & Parry web site at **http://heintz.swlearning.com** gives you access to supplement downloads, a help line, teaching ideas, hot links, and more.

The Product Web Site Is a Rich Resource.

The Heintz & Parry web site **(http://heintz.swlearning.com)** provides easy access assistance to both students and instructors. Links for Web Work assignments provide a helpful way to connect with assignment resources. Online quizzes with solutions help students test themselves as they study. Instructors have online access to many other resources, such as the solutions and instructor's manuals in Microsoft® Word, which are all password protected.

■ Call the Academic Resource Center for desk copies and product information: Career College Customers: 800-477-3692 Community College or University Customers: 800-423-0563

■ Call the Preferred Accounting Customer Hotline for special requests: 800-342-8798

■ E-mail the authors or the publisher through the hot link at **http://heintz.swlearning.com**

DEDICATION

We are grateful to our wives, Celia Heintz and Jane Parry, and our children, Andrea Heintz, John Heintz, Jessica Jane Parry, and Mitch Parry, for their love, support, and assistance during the creation of this eighteenth edition. We especially appreciate Jessie Parry's willingness to let us use her name throughout the first six chapters.

H&P PROVEN TO BE THE BEST!

ACKNOWLEDGMENTS

We thank the following individuals for their helpful contributions in assisting us in the revision of *College Accounting*.

Julia L. Angel, *North Arkansas College*
Catherine A. Arp, *Treasure Valley Community College*
Lelia Austin, *Lake City Community College*
John Babich, CPA, *Kankakee Community College*
Ann Bikofsky, *Westchester Business Institute*
Suzanne R. Bradford, *Angelina College*
Madeline Brogan, *North Harris College*
Teresa K. Burkett, *Tiffin University*
Bruce A. Cassel, *Dutchess Community College*
Diana V. Cole, *UNM-Valencia Campus*
Karen G. Collins, *MPA, Georgetown Technical College*
Charles R. Faust, *San Joaquin Valley College*
Cheryl Fries, *Guilford Technical College*
Jon Gartman MS, *Texas State Technical College*
Ken Haling, *Gateway Technical College*
Sueann Hely, *Paducah Community College*
Mary L. Hollars, *Vincennes University*
Bill R. Huerter, *Northeast Iowa Community College*
Gregory P. Iwaniuk, *Lake Michigan College*
Betty Jording, *Newcastle Community Education*
Judith Kizzie, *Clinton Community College*
Michael S. Manis, Assoc. Prof., *College of the Desert*
Paul A. Martin, *Muscatine Community College*
Sandy Martin, *Albuquerque TV-I Community College*
Betty Jo McKie, *Morgan Community College*
Roger K. McMillian, Department Chair, *Mineral Area College*

Wanda Metzgar, Senior Instructor, *Boise State* University, Larry G. Selland *College of Applied Technology*
Jeanette B. Morrison, *Hinds Community College*
Paul Muller, *Western Nevada Community College*
Mary Etta Naftel, Ph.D., *Hinds Community College*
William A. Padley, *Madison Area Technical College*
Michelle Parker, *Altamaha Technical College*
Linda H. Pates, *Hind Community College*
Ned E. Perri, *Gateway Technical College*
Vickie L. Petritz, *Montana Tech of The University of Montana College of Technology*
Alan F. Rainford, CPA, *Greenfield Community College*
Betsy Ray, *Indiana Business College*
Mary Beth Robbins, *Herzing College*
Luis Quiros, *Westchester Business Institute*
B. Blan Santito, *Community College of Denver*
Carolyn M. Seefer, *Diablo Valley College*
Del Spencer, *Trinity Valley Community College*
Ronald Strittmater, Accounting Instructor, *North Hennepin Community College*
Linda H. Tarrago, CPA, *Hillsborough Community College*
Donna Ulmer, *St. Louis Community College at Meramec*
Marcia F. Williams, *Fergus Falls Community College*
Mary Wilsey, *Finger Lakes Community College*
Barry D. Woosley, CPA, CRM, *Western Kentucky University*
David L. Zagorodney, *Heald College*

In addition, we would like to thank all who have assisted in providing the supporting materials. These individuals are listed in the supplements tables that follow. We thank Sheila Viel, of the University of Wisconsin-Milwaukee, for her diligent verification.

Special thanks to Jane Parry and Andrea Heintz for assistance in the development of this text. Finally, we thank Tina McCarty, owner of Pass It On Pet Supplies **(http://www.passitonpetsupplies.com)** in Cincinnati, Ohio, for providing the location site for the Parkway Pet Supplies store photos.

Through 18 editions, *College Accounting* has helped millions of students understand and employ basic accounting skills. But we know we can't rest on past success. The business world continues to change, and so do we. To prepare today's generation for a lifetime of accounting skills, the solution is simple. Depend on the text that's simply better than ever.

College Accounting, 18e. From the leader in college accounting, you expect the best.

Jim Heintz
Rob Parry

PROVEN TO BE THE BEST!

Supplements for Students	ISBN	Authors, Affiliations, Description
Accounting Workbook for Peachtree® 2004 (with Data & Software on CD) for Chapters 4–29	0-324-22368-4	**Donna Ulmer, St. Louis Community College, James Heintz, and Robert Parry** Available for use with selected problems (marked by an icon in the main text). A student instruction book accompanies the software. The data files and a student version of the software are included on the CD. This product assists students in learning how to use real-world accounting software. Can also be used as a stand-alone ancillary.
Accounting Workbook for QuickBooks® 2003 (with Data CD) for Chapters 4–29	0-324-29171-X	**Carol Fischer, University of Wisconsin –Waukesha, James Heintz, and Robert Parry** Available for use with selected problems (marked by an icon in the main text). A student instruction book and the data files, which are on a CD in the book, provide guidance to students in learning how to use real-world accounting software. Can also be used as a stand-alone ancillary.
Power Accounting Software System (PASS) and Data Files CD for Chapters 2–29	0-324-22180-0	**Warren Allen, Mary Allen, James Heintz, and Robert Parry** Available for use with selected problems found in the main text (identified by icons). As students use the opening balances, chart of accounts, and set-up functions to complete problems, they gain valuable, hands-on experience with full-functioning general ledger software.
R&K UltraGlo Practice Set	0-324-22339-0	**Janet Caruso, Briarcliffe College** This practice set is a sole-proprietorship service business simulation for use after text Chapter 7. It reviews the accounting cycle and accounting for cash.
Laurel Appliance Center Practice Set	0-324-22340-4	**Toni Hartley, Laurel Business Institute** This practice set contains information about a sole-proprietorship merchandising business. It can be completed by using either the general journal alone or special journals. It is appropriate for use after text Chapter 16.
Lake Side Lawn Products Practice Set	0-324-22341-2	**Richard Dugger, Kilgore College** This practice set gives students hands-on experience with a small departmentalized wholesaler operating as a corporation. Includes preparation of financial statements and ratio analysis. For use after text Chapter 27.
Study Guide with Working Papers for Chapters 1–10 & Chapters 11–16 (package) **Study Guide with Working Papers** for Chapters 17–29	0-324-29161-2 0-324-22183-5	**James Heintz and Robert Parry** A study guide and the working papers for the text assignments are provided together in one convenient resource. Students are able to reinforce their learning experience with chapter outlines that are linked to learning objectives and a set "C" of assignments consisting of review questions, exercises, and problems. The working papers are tailored to the text's end-of-chapter assignments. (The text solutions manual contains the solutions to the working papers. The solutions to the study guide assignments are available separately.)
On the Internet: Web site WebTutor Advantage on WebCT for Chapters 1–29 WebTutor Advantage on Blackboard for Chapters 1–29 Personal Trainer 3.0 for Chapters 1–29	0-324-22159-2 0-324-22336-6 0-324-22338-2 0-324-22189-4	Please see the preface for descriptions of these products.

Supplements for Instructors	ISBN	Authors, Affiliations, Description
Solutions Manual to Accompany the Accounting Workbooks for Peachtree® 2004 (Chapters 4–29)	0-324-22396-X	**Donna Ulmer, St. Louis Community College**
Solutions Manual to Accompany the Accounting Workbooks for QuickBooks® 2003 (Chapters 4–29)	0-324-29173-6	**Carol Fischer, University of Wisconsin-Waukesha**

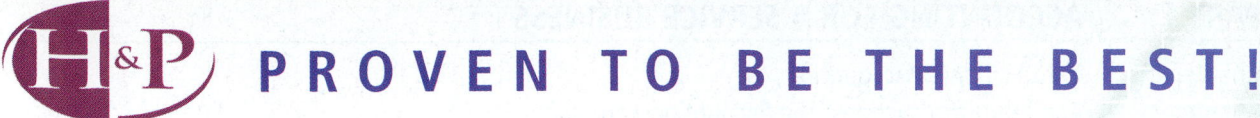

PROVEN TO BE THE BEST!

PASS Inspector Disk for Chapters 2–29   0-324-22170-3   **Warren Allen, Mary Allen**
This disk contains the electronic solutions to PASS.

R&K UltraGlo Practice Set Key
with Inspector Disk   0-324-29175-2   **Janet Caruso, Briarcliffe College**

Laurel Appliance Center Practice Set Key
with Inspector Disk   0-324-29178-7   **Toni Hartley, Laurel Business Institute**

Lake Side Lawn Products Practice Set Key
with Inspector Disk   0-324-29181-7   **Richard Dugger, Kilgore College**
Printed and electronic solution to the practice set.

Achievement Tests
–version A, Chapters 1–16	0-324-22171-1	These tests, grouped in "A" and "B" sets, allow for maximum flexibility in assigning in-class
–version A, Chapters 17–29	0-324-22172-x	and out-of-class work for students.
–version B, Chapters 1–16	0-324-22173-8	
–version B, Chapters 17–29	0-324-22174-6	

Achievement Test Keys
–version A, Chapters 1–16	0-324-22175-4	Solutions for the Achievement tests.
–version A, Chapters 17–29	0-324-22176-2	
–version B, Chapters 1–16	0-324-22177-0	
–version B, Chapters 17–29	0-324-22178-9	

Instructor Resource Guide
for Chapters 1–16   0-324-22162-2
Instructor Resource Guide
for Chapters 17–29   0-324-22163-0

William CK. Alberts, National Business College
This guide contains a wealth of resources to help instructors create an exciting and productive classroom experience. Included are enhanced chapter outlines and teaching tips; references to exhibits, PowerPoint® slides, and teaching transparencies; suggested enrichments and activities; check figures for text assignments; pretests tied to learning objectives; and Ten Questions Your Students Will Always Ask to help anticipate student learning needs.

Solutions Manual for Chapters 1–16   0-324-22164-9
Solutions Manual for Chapters 17–29   0-324-22165-7

James Heintz and Robert Parry
The complete, carefully verified solutions for all text assignments. Accounting rulings are used where appropriate. (Note: These are also the solutions to the working papers.)

Study Guide Solutions for Chapters 1–16   0-324-22185-1
Study Guide Solutions for Chapters 17–29   0-324-22186-x

James Heintz and Robert Parry
Solutions to all study guide set "C" assignments found in the study guide. This may be packaged with the study guide at the instructor's discretion.

Solutions Transparencies
for Chapters 1–16   0-324-22166-5
Solutions Transparencies
for Chapters 17–29   0-324-22167-3

James Heintz and Robert Parry
Contains solutions for the Series A & B Exercises and Problems, Mastery Problems, Challenge Problems, and Comprehensive Problems in the text. Where appropriate, solutions appear on accounting rulings.

Teaching Transparencies
for Chapters 1–16   0-324-22168-1
Teaching Transparencies
for Chapters 17–29   0-324-22169-X

James Heintz and Robert Parry
Colorful teaching transparencies of many of the text illustrations for use in classroom presentations.

Test Bank for Chapters 1–16   0-324-22160-6
Test Bank for Chapters 17–29   0-324-22161-4

Lee Moore, South Plains College
These tests have been revised and carefully verified. The electronic test bank (ExamView) is available on the Instructor's Resource CD-ROM, described below.

Instructor's CD-ROM with ExamView   0-324-22157-6
ExamView 4.0 is an enhanced, easy to use electronic test bank that contains the content found in the two printed test banks; also: (a) A complete set of PowerPoint® presentations, by Donna Larner of Davenport College, reinforce text content by using extremely engaging visuals that are paced well for student comprehension; (b) The solutions manual, instructor's manual, and check figures are provided in Microsoft® Word files.

CONTENTS IN BRIEF

Accounting for a Service Business

© DIGITAL IMAGING GROUP

Introduction to Accounting

So, you have decided to study accounting. Good decision. A solid foundation in accounting concepts and techniques will be helpful. This is true whether you take a professional position in accounting or business, or simply want to better understand your personal finances and dealings with businesses.

Throughout Chapters 2 through 6, we will introduce Jessie Jane's Campus Delivery service. By studying Jessie's business transactions and accounting techniques, you will learn about business and accounting. This is a major advantage of studying accounting. While studying accounting, you also learn a lot about business.

Knowledge of how accounting works will help you evaluate the financial health of businesses and other organizations. It will also give you a solid approach to dealing with financial and business transactions in your personal life. How do you plan to use the accounting skills developed in this class?

Careful study of this chapter should enable you to:

LO1 Describe the purpose of accounting.

LO2 Describe the accounting process.

LO3 Define GAAP and describe the process used to develop these principles.

LO4 Define three types of business ownership structures.

LO5 Classify different types of businesses by activities.

LO6 Identify career opportunities in accounting.

Accounting is the language of business. You must learn this language to understand the impact of economic events on a specific company. Common, everyday terms have very precise meanings when used in accounting. For example, you have probably heard terms like asset, liability, revenue, expense, and net income. Take a moment to jot down how you would define each of these terms. After reading and studying Chapter 2, compare your definitions with those developed in this text. This comparison will show whether you can trust your current understanding of accounting terms. Whether you intend to pursue a career in accounting or simply wish to understand the impact of business transactions, you need a clear understanding of this language.

THE PURPOSE OF ACCOUNTING

LO1 Describe the purpose of accounting.

The purpose of accounting is to provide financial information about the current operations and financial condition of a business to individuals, agencies, and organizations. As shown in Figure 1-1, owners, managers, creditors, and government agencies all need accounting information. Other users of accounting information include customers, clients, labor unions, stock exchanges, and financial analysts.

USER	INFORMATION NEEDED	DECISIONS MADE BY USERS
Owners— Present and future	Company's profitability and current financial condition.	If business is good, owners may consider making additional investments for growth. If business is poor, they may want to talk to management to find out why and may consider closing the business.
Managers— May or may not own business	Detailed measures of business performance.	Managers need to make operating decisions. How much and what kinds of inventory should be carried? Is business strong enough to support higher wages for employees?
Creditors— Present and future	Company's profitability, debt outstanding, and assets that could be used to secure debt.	Should a loan be granted to this business? If so, what amount of debt can the business support and what interest rate should be charged?
Government Agencies— National, state, and local	Company's profitability, cash flows, and overall financial condition.	The IRS will decide how much income tax the business must pay. Local governments may be willing to adjust property taxes paid by the business to encourage it to stay in town.

FIGURE 1-1 Users of Accounting Information

THE ACCOUNTING PROCESS

LO2 Describe the accounting process.

Accounting is a system of gathering financial information about a business and reporting this information to users. The six major steps of the accounting process are analyzing, recording, classifying, summarizing, reporting, and interpreting (Figure 1-2). Computers are often used in the recording, classifying, summarizing, and reporting steps. Whether or not computers are used, the accounting concepts and techniques are the same. Information entered into the computer system must reflect a proper application of these concepts. Otherwise, the output will be meaningless.

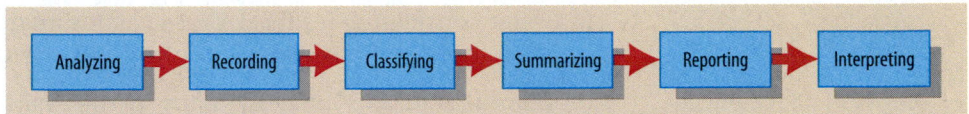

FIGURE 1-2   The Accounting Process

■ **Analyzing** is looking at events that have taken place and thinking about how they affect the business.

■ **Recording** is entering financial information about events into the accounting system. Although this can be done with paper and pencil, most businesses use computers to perform routine record-keeping operations.

■ **Classifying** is sorting and grouping similar items together rather than merely keeping a simple, diary-like record of numerous events.

■ **Summarizing** is bringing the various items of information together to determine a result.

■ **Reporting** is telling the results. In accounting, it is common to use tables of numbers to report results.

■ **Interpreting** is deciding the meaning and importance of the information in various reports. This may include ratio analysis to help explain how pieces of information relate to one another.

GENERALLY ACCEPTED ACCOUNTING PRINCIPLES (GAAP)

LO3 Define GAAP and describe the process used to develop these principles.

Soon after the stock market crash of 1929, the federal government established the Securities and Exchange Commission (SEC). The purpose of this government agency is to help develop standards for reporting financial information to stockholders. The SEC currently has authority over 12,000 companies listed on the major stock exchanges (New York Stock, American, and NASDAQ). It has the power to require these firms to follow certain rules when preparing their financial statements. These rules are referred to as **generally accepted accounting principles** (GAAP).

Rather than developing GAAP on its own, the SEC encouraged the creation of a private standard-setting body. It did so because it believed the private sector had better access to the resources and talent necessary to develop these standards. Since 1973, the Financial Accounting Standards Board (FASB) has filled this role. In developing accounting standards, FASB follows a specific process and relies on the advice of many organizations. When an accounting issue is identified, the following steps are followed.

1. The issue is placed on FASB's agenda. This lets everyone know that the Board plans to develop a standard addressing this issue.

2. After researching an issue, FASB issues a **discussion memorandum**. This document identifies the pros and cons of various accounting treatments for an event.

3. To gather additional views on the issue, the Board will often hold **public hearings** around the country. Interested parties are invited to express their opinions at these hearings.

4. Following these hearings, the Board issues an **exposure draft**. This document explains the rules that FASB believes firms should follow in accounting for this event.

5. After considering feedback on the exposure draft, the Board issues a final **statement of financial accounting standards** (SFAS).

Throughout this process, many parties participate by testifying at public hearings, or by sending letters to the Board explaining why they agree or disagree with the proposed standard. These parties include the American Institute of Certified Public Accountants (AICPA), the American Accounting Association (AAA), Institute of Management Accountants (IMA), Financial Executives Institute (FEI), corporate executives and accountants, representatives from the investment community, analysts, bankers, industry associations, and the SEC and other government agencies. Clearly, FASB considers the views of a wide range of parties. By doing so, it maximizes the likelihood of developing and gaining acceptance of the most appropriate accounting and disclosure requirements.

THREE TYPES OF OWNERSHIP STRUCTURES

LO4 **Define three types of business ownership structures.**

One or more persons may own a business. Businesses are classified according to who owns them and the specific way they are organized. Three types of ownership structures are (1) sole proprietorship, (2) partnership, and (3) corporation (Figure 1-3). Accountants provide information to owners of all three types of ownership structures.

Sole Proprietorship

A **sole proprietorship** is owned by one person. The owner is often called a proprietor. The proprietor often manages the business. The owner assumes all risks for the business, and personal assets can be taken to pay creditors. The advantage of a sole proprietorship is that the owner can make all decisions.

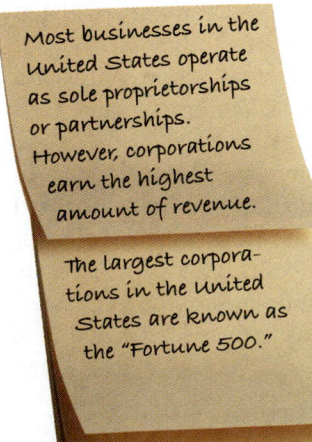

Most businesses in the United States operate as sole proprietorships or partnerships. However, corporations earn the highest amount of revenue.

The largest corporations in the United States are known as the "Fortune 500."

TYPES OF OWNERSHIP STRUCTURES		
Sole Proprietorship	**Partnership**	**Corporation**
• One owner	• Two or more partners	• Stockholders
• Owner assumes all risk	• Partners share risks	• Stockholders have limited risk
• Owner makes all decisions	• Partners may disagree on how to run business	• Stockholders may have little influence on business decisions

FIGURE 1-3 Types of Ownership Structures—Advantages and Disadvantages

Partnership

A **partnership** is owned by more than one person. One or more partners may manage the business. Like proprietors, partners assume the risks for the business, and their assets may be taken to pay creditors. An advantage of a partnership is that owners share risks and decision making. A disadvantage is that partners may disagree about the best way to run the business.

Corporation

A **corporation** is owned by stockholders (or shareholders). Corporations may have many owners, and they usually employ professional managers. The owners' risk is usually limited to their initial investment, and they often have very little influence on the business decisions.

TYPES OF BUSINESSES

LO5 Classify different types of businesses by activities.

Businesses are classified according to the type of service or product provided. Some businesses provide a service. Others sell a product. A business that provides a service is called a **service business**. A business that buys a product from another business to sell to customers is called a **merchandising business**. A business that makes a product to sell is called a **manufacturing business**. You will learn about all three types of businesses in this book. Figure 1-4 lists examples of types of businesses organized by activity.

SERVICE	MERCHANDISING	MANUFACTURING
Travel Agency	Department Store	Automobile Manufacturer
Computer Consultant	Pharmacy	Furniture Maker
Physician	Jewelry Store	Toy Factory

FIGURE 1-4 Types and Examples of Businesses Organized by Activities

A BROADER VIEW

All Kinds of Businesses Need Accounting Systems

Even small businesses like those that provide guided horseback tours of the Rocky Mountains need good accounting systems. Proper records must be maintained for the cost of the horses, feed, food served, tour guides' salaries, and office expenses. Without this information, the company would not know how much to charge and whether a profit is made on these trips.

© BLY/GETTY IMAGES

CAREER OPPORTUNITIES IN ACCOUNTING

LO6 Identify career opportunities in accounting.

Accounting offers many career opportunities. The positions described below require varying amounts of education, experience, and technological skill.

Accounting Clerks

Businesses with large quantities of accounting tasks to perform daily often employ **accounting clerks** to record, sort, and file accounting information. Often accounting clerks will specialize in cash, payroll, accounts receivable, accounts payable, inventory, or purchases. As a result, they are involved with only a small portion of the total accounting responsibilities for the firm. Accounting clerks usually have at least one year of accounting education.

Bookkeepers and Para-Accountants

Bookkeepers generally supervise the work of accounting clerks, help with daily accounting work, and summarize accounting information. In small-to-medium-sized businesses, the bookkeeper may also help managers and owners interpret the accounting information. Bookkeepers usually have one to two years of accounting education and experience as an accounting clerk.

Para-accountants provide many accounting, auditing, or tax services under the direct supervision of an accountant. A typical para-accountant has a two-year degree or significant accounting and bookkeeping experience.

Accountants

The difference between accountants and bookkeepers is not always clear, particularly in smaller companies where bookkeepers also help interpret the accounting information. In large companies, the distinction is clearer. Bookkeepers focus on the processing of accounting data. **Accountants** design the accounting information system and focus on analyzing and interpreting information. They also look for important trends in the data and study the impact of alternative decisions.

Most accountants enter the field with a college degree in accounting. Accountants are employed in public accounting, private (managerial) accounting, and in governmental and not-for-profit accounting (Figure 1-5).

ACCOUNTING CLERK
Travel agency is looking for an accounting clerk to handle bookkeeping tasks. 1–3 years experience with an automated accounting system required.

BOOKKEEPING/ACCOUNTING
Service company has an opening for a full charge bookkeeper/accountant. Previous accounting experience with an associate degree preferred. Salary commensurate with experience. Excellent knowledge of LOTUS 1-2-3® or Excel® required.

ACCOUNTANT
Responsibilities include accounts receivable, accounts payable, and general ledger. Familiarity with computerized systems a must. Supervisory experience a plus.

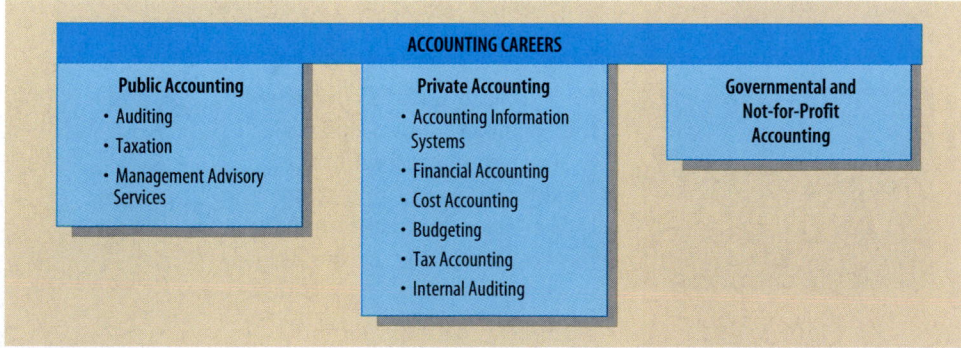

FIGURE 1-5   Accounting Careers

Public Accounting. Public accountants offer services in much the same way as doctors and lawyers. The public accountant can achieve professional recognition as a **Certified Public Accountant** (CPA). This is done by meeting certain educational and experience requirements as determined by each state, and passing a uniform examination prepared by the American Institute of Certified Public Accountants.

Many CPAs work alone, while others work for local, regional, or national accounting firms that vary in scope and size. The largest public accounting firms in the United States are known as the "Big Four." They are Deloitte and Touche, Ernst & Young, KPMG, and PricewaterhouseCoopers.

Services offered by public accountants are listed below.

■ **Auditing.** Auditing involves the application of standard review and testing procedures to be certain that proper accounting policies and practices have been followed. The purpose of the audit is to provide an independent opinion that the financial information about a business is fairly presented in a manner consistent with generally accepted accounting principles.

■ **Taxation.** Tax specialists advise on tax planning, prepare tax returns, and represent clients before governmental agencies such as the Internal Revenue Service.

■ **Management Advisory Services.** Given the financial training and business experience of public accountants, many businesses seek their advice on a wide variety of managerial issues. Often, accounting firms are involved in designing computerized accounting systems.

Private (Managerial) Accounting. Many accountants are employees of private business firms. The **controller** oversees the entire accounting process and is the principal accounting officer of the company. Private or managerial accountants perform a wide variety of services for the business. These services are listed below.

■ **Accounting Information Systems.** Accountants in this area design and implement manual and computerized accounting systems.

■ **Financial Accounting.** Based on the accounting data prepared by the bookkeepers and accounting clerks, accountants prepare various reports and financial statements and help in analyzing operating, investing, and financing decisions.

■ **Cost Accounting.** The cost of producing specific products or providing services must be measured. Further analysis is also done to determine whether the products and services are produced in the most cost-effective manner.

■ **Budgeting.** In the budgeting process, accountants help managers develop a financial plan.

■ **Tax Accounting.** Instead of hiring a public accountant, a company may have its own accountants. They focus on tax planning, preparation of tax returns, and dealing with the Internal Revenue Service and other governmental agencies.

■ **Internal Auditing.** Internal auditors review the operating and accounting control procedures adopted by management to make sure the controls are adequate and are being followed. They also monitor the accuracy and timeliness of the reports provided to management and to external parties.

A managerial accountant can achieve professional status as a **Certified Management Accountant** (CMA). This is done by passing a uniform examination offered by the Institute of Management Accountants. An internal auditor can achieve professional recognition as a **Certified Internal Auditor** (CIA) by passing the uniform examination offered by the Institute of Internal Auditors.

Governmental and Not-for-Profit Accounting. Thousands of governmental and not-for-profit organizations (states, cities, schools, churches, and hospitals) gather and report financial information. These organizations employ a large number of accountants. Since these entities are not profit-oriented, the rules are somewhat different for governmental and not-for-profit organizations. However, many accounting procedures are similar to those found in profit-seeking enterprises.

CONTROLLER
$45,000–$50,000
Service company seeks financial manager to oversee all general accounting and financial reporting. PC skills important. 4+ years in corporate or public accounting will qualify.

ACCOUNTANT
Assist fiscal officer in not-for-profit accounting. Experience in payroll, payroll taxes, and LOTUS 1-2-3 or Excel helpful. Qualifications: accounting degree or equivalent. $25–$28K.

Job Opportunities

Job growth in some areas will be much greater than in others. Newspaper advertisements often indicate that accountants and accounting clerks are expected to have computer skills. Computer skills definitely increase the opportunities available to you in your career. Almost every business needs accountants, accounting clerks, and bookkeepers. Figure 1-6 shows the expected growth for different types of businesses. Notice that growth will be greatest in the service businesses. Chapters 2 through 10 introduce accounting skills that you will need to work in a service business. Chapter 11 begins the discussion of merchandising businesses. Accounting for manufacturing businesses is addressed in the last chapters of the book.

Figure 1-7 shows the expected demand for accounting skills. Although a small drop in demand is expected for bookkeeping, accounting, and auditing clerks, these types of positions will offer the highest number of job opportunities over the next several years. The next highest demand is for accountants and auditors and this demand is expected to increase over the next several years.

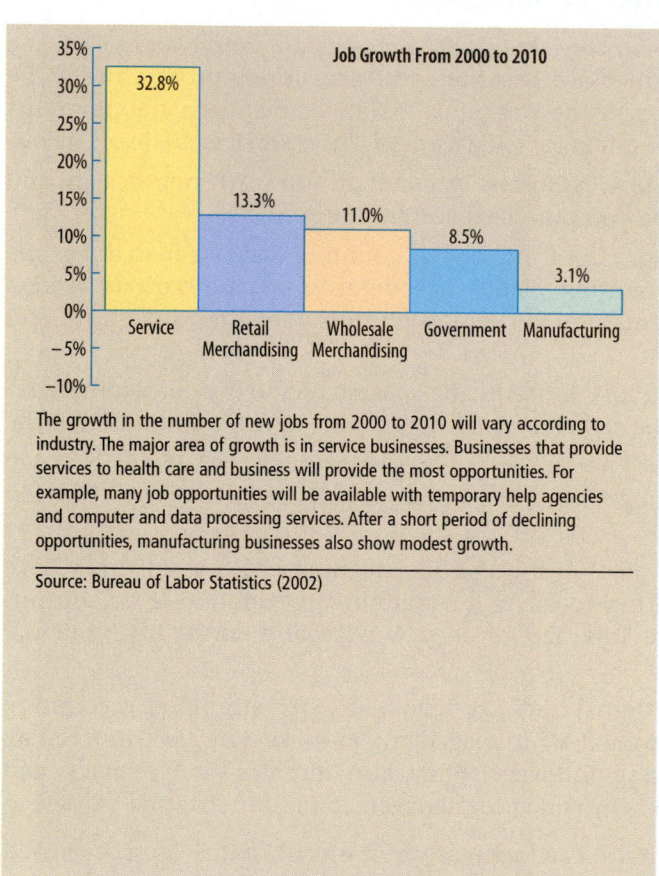

The growth in the number of new jobs from 2000 to 2010 will vary according to industry. The major area of growth is in service businesses. Businesses that provide services to health care and business will provide the most opportunities. For example, many job opportunities will be available with temporary help agencies and computer and data processing services. After a short period of declining opportunities, manufacturing businesses also show modest growth.

Source: Bureau of Labor Statistics (2002)

FIGURE 1-6 Expected Growth

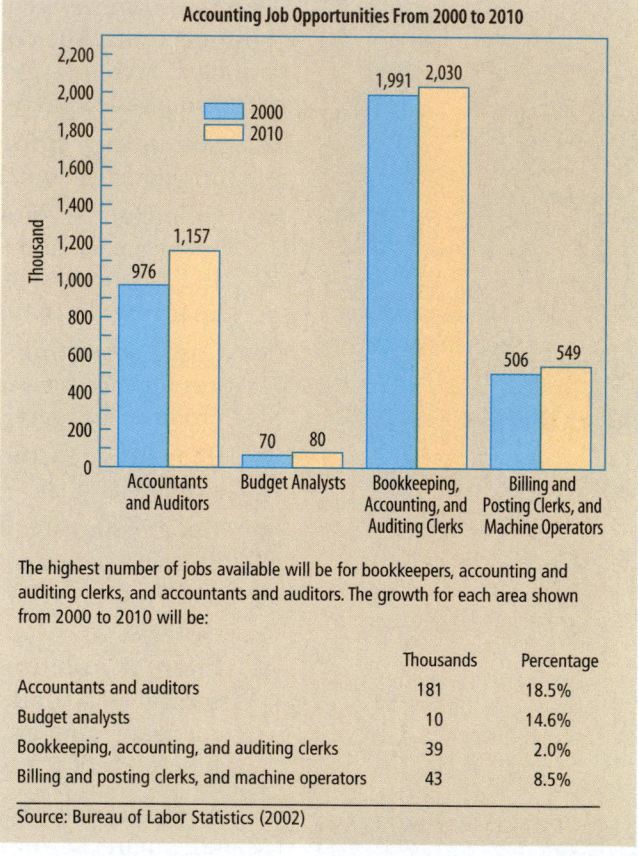

The highest number of jobs available will be for bookkeepers, accounting and auditing clerks, and accountants and auditors. The growth for each area shown from 2000 to 2010 will be:

	Thousands	Percentage
Accountants and auditors	181	18.5%
Budget analysts	10	14.6%
Bookkeeping, accounting, and auditing clerks	39	2.0%
Billing and posting clerks, and machine operators	43	8.5%

Source: Bureau of Labor Statistics (2002)

FIGURE 1-7 Expected Demand

Regardless of the type of career you desire, writing skills are important in business and your personal life. Becoming a good writer requires practice and a strategy for the process used to prepare memos, letters, and other documents. On pages 9 and 10, Ken Davis offers an excellent approach to managing your writing. Take a moment to read Ken's tips. Then, practice his approach by completing the writing assignments as you finish each chapter.

Managing Your Writing

—Ken Davis

Here's a secret: the business writing that you and I do—the writing that gets the world's work done—requires no special gift. It can be managed, like any other business process.

Managing writing is largely a matter of managing time. Writing is a process, and like any process it can be done efficiently or inefficiently. Unfortunately, most of us are pretty inefficient writers. That's because we try to get each word, each sentence, right the first time. Given a letter to write, we begin with the first sentence. We think about that sentence, write it, revise it, even check its spelling, before going on to the second sentence. In an hour of writing, we might spend 45 or 50 minutes doing this kind of detailed drafting. We spend only a few minutes on overall planning at the beginning and only a few minutes on overall revising at the end.

That approach to writing is like building a house by starting with the front door: planning, building, finishing—even washing the windows—before doing anything with the rest of the house. No wonder most of us have so much trouble writing.

Efficient, effective writers take better charge of their writing time. They *manage* their writing. Like building contractors, they spend time planning before they start construction. Once construction has started, they don't try to do all of the finishing touches as they go.

As the following illustration shows, many good writers break their writing process into three main stages: planning, drafting, and revising. They spend more time at the first and third stages than at the second. They also build in some "management" time at the beginning and the end, and some break time in the middle. To manage *your* writing time, try the following steps.

At the **MANAGING** stage (perhaps two or three minutes for a one-hour writing job), remind yourself that writing *can* be managed and that it's largely a matter of managing time. Plan your next hour.

At the **PLANNING** stage (perhaps 20 minutes out of the hour):

1. **Find the "we."** Define the community to which you and your reader belong. Then ask, "How are my reader and I alike and different?"—in knowledge, attitudes, and circumstances.

2. **Define your purpose.** Remember the advice a consultant once gave Stanley Tool executives: "You're not in the business of making drills: you're in the business of making holes." Too many of us lose sight of the difference between making drills and making holes when we write letters and memos. We focus on the piece of writing—the tool itself—not its purpose. The result: our writing often misses the chance to be as effective as it could be. When you're still at the planning stage, focus on the outcome you want, not on the means you will use to achieve it.

3. **Get your stuff together.** Learn from those times when you've turned a one-hour home-improvement project into a three- or four-hour job by having to make repeated trips to the hardware store for tools or parts. Before you start the drafting stage of writing, collect the information you need.

4. **Get your ducks in a row.** Decide on the main points you want to make. Then, make a list or rough outline placing your points in the most logical order.

At the **DRAFTING STAGE** (perhaps 5 minutes out of the hour):

5. **Do it wrong the first time.** Do a "quick and dirty" draft, without editing. Think of your draft as a "prototype," written not for the end user but for your own testing and improvement. Stopping to edit while you draft breaks your train of thought and keeps you from being a good writer. (Hint: If you are writing at a computer, try turning off the monitor during the drafting stage.)

At the **BREAK STAGE** (perhaps 5 minutes):

6. **Take a break and change hats.** Get away from your draft, even if for only a few minutes. Come back with a fresh perspective—the reader's perspective.

At the **REVISING STAGE** (perhaps 25 minutes):

7. **Signal your turns.** Just as if you were driving a car, you're leading your reader through new territory. Use "turn signals"—*and, in addition, but, however, or, therefore, because, for example*—to guide your reader from sentence to sentence.

8. **Say what you mean.** Put the point of your sentences in the subjects and verbs. For example, revise "There are drawbacks to using this accounting method" to "This accounting method has some drawbacks." You'll be saying what you mean, and you'll be a more effective communicator.

9. **Pay by the word.** Reading your memo requires work. If your sentences are wordy and you are slow to get to the point, the reader may decide that it is not worth the effort. Pretend you are paying the reader by the word to read your memo. Then, revise your memo to make it as short and to the point as possible.

10. **Translate into English.** Keep your words simple. (Lee Iacocca put both these tips in one "commandment of good management": "Say it in English and keep it short.") Remember that you write to express, not impress.

11. **Finish the job.** Check your spelling, punctuation, and mechanics.

Finally, at the **MANAGING STAGE** again (2 to 3 minutes):

12. **Evaluate your writing process.** Figure out how to improve it next time.

By following these 12 steps, you can take charge of your writing time. Begin today to *manage your writing.* As a United Technologies Corporation advertisement in *The Wall Street Journal* admonished, "If you want to manage somebody, manage yourself. Do that well and you'll be ready to stop managing and start leading."

Dr. Kenneth W. Davis is Professor of English and Adjunct Professor of Communication Studies at Indiana University-Purdue University, Indianapolis. He is also president of Komei, Inc., a communication consulting and training company.

Learning Objectives	Key Points to Remember
1 **Describe the purpose of accounting.**	The purpose of accounting is to provide financial information about a business to individuals and organizations.
2 **Describe the accounting process.**	The six major steps of the accounting process are analyzing, recording, classifying, summarizing, reporting, and interpreting.
3 **Define GAAP and describe the process used by FASB to develop these principles.**	Generally accepted accounting principles (GAAP) are the rules that businesses must follow when preparing financial statements. FASB takes the following steps to develop an accounting standard: 1. The issue is placed on the Board's agenda. 2. After researching the issue, a discussion memorandum is issued. 3. Public hearings are held. 4. An exposure draft is issued. 5. The statement of financial accounting standards is issued.
4 **Define three types of business ownership structures.**	Three types of business ownership structures are sole proprietorship, partnership, and corporation.
5 **Classify different types of businesses by activities.**	Different types of businesses classified by activities are a service business, a merchandising business, and a manufacturing business.
6 **Identify career opportunities in accounting.**	Career opportunities in accounting include work in public accounting, private accounting, and governmental and not-for-profit accounting.

REFLECTION

Reflection: Answering the Opening Question

Of course, your answer to the opening question depends on your specific plans. In general, though, accounting skills are helpful in all kinds of business, nonprofit, and personal activities. As discussed in the chapter, accounting knowledge is important when working in all types of businesses: service, merchandising, and manufacturing. It is also helpful regardless of the ownership structure: sole proprietorship, partnership, or corporation.

On-Line Learning Tools

For more information, visit: http://heintz.swlearning.com

The Heintz & Parry product web site is designed specifically for **COLLEGE ACCOUNTING, 18e.** The features include downloadable student resources and an interactive study center, organized by chapter, which contains learning objectives, web links, on-line quizzes with automatic feedback, and more.

Interactive Learning: http://heintz.swlearning.com

KEY TERMS

accountant, (6)   Designs the accounting information system and focuses on analyzing and interpreting information.

accounting, (3)   A system of gathering financial information about a business and reporting this information to users.

accounting clerk, (6)   Records, sorts, and files accounting information.

accounting information systems, (7)   Accountants in this area design and implement manual and computerized accounting systems.

analyzing, (3)   Looking at events that have taken place and thinking about how they affect the business.

auditing, (7)   Reviewing and testing to be certain that proper accounting policies and practices have been followed.

bookkeeper, (6)   Generally supervises the work of accounting clerks, helps with daily accounting work, and summarizes accounting information.

budgeting, (7)   The process in which accountants help managers develop a financial plan.

Certified Internal Auditor, (7)   An internal auditor who has achieved professional recognition by passing the uniform examination offered by the Institute of Internal Auditors.

Certified Management Accountant, (7)   An accountant who has passed an examination offered by the Institute of Management Accountants.

Certified Public Accountant, (6)   A public accountant who has met certain educational and experience requirements and has passed an examination prepared by the American Institute of Certified Public Accountants.

classifying, (3)   Sorting and grouping similar items together rather than merely keeping a simple, diary-like record of numerous events.

controller, (7)   The accountant who oversees the entire accounting process and is the principal accounting officer of a company.

corporation, (5)   A type of ownership structure in which stockholders own the business. The owners' risk is usually limited to their initial investment, and they usually have very little influence on the business decisions.

cost accounting, (7)   Determining the cost of producing specific products or providing services and analyzing for cost effectiveness.

discussion memorandum, (4)   The first document issued by FASB when developing an accounting standard. This document identifies the pros and cons of various accounting treatments for an event.

exposure draft, (4)   This document explains the rules that FASB believes firms should follow in accounting for a particular event. Based on the responses to the exposure draft, the Board will decide if any changes are necessary before issuing a final standard.

financial accounting, (7)   Includes preparing various reports and financial statements and analyzing operating, investing, and financing decisions.

generally accepted accounting principles (GAAP), (3)   Procedures and guidelines developed by the Financial Accounting Standards Board to be followed in the accounting and reporting process.

internal auditing, (7)   Reviewing the operating and accounting control procedures adopted by management to make sure the controls are adequate and being followed; assuring that accurate and timely information is provided.

interpreting, (3)   Deciding the meaning and importance of the information in various reports.

management advisory services, (7)   Providing advice to businesses on a wide variety of managerial issues.

manufacturing business, (5)   A business that makes a product to sell.

merchandising business, (5)   A business that buys products to sell.

para-accountant, (6)   A paraprofessional who provides many accounting, auditing, or tax services under the direct supervision of an accountant.

partnership, (5)   A type of ownership structure in which more than one person owns the business.

public hearing, (4)   Following the issuance of a discussion memorandum, FASB often holds public hearings to gather opinions on the accounting issue.

recording, (3)   Entering financial information about events affecting the company into the accounting system.

reporting, (3)   Telling the results of the financial information.

service business, (5)   A business that provides a service.

sole proprietorship, (4)   A type of ownership structure in which one person owns the business.

statement of financial accounting standards, (4)   A standard issued by the Financial Accounting Standards Board. These standards must be followed when preparing financial statements.

summarizing, (3)   Bringing the various items of information together to determine a result.

tax accounting, (7)   Focusing on tax planning, preparing tax returns, and dealing with the Internal Revenue Service and other governmental agencies.

taxation, (7)   See tax accounting.

REVIEW QUESTIONS

(LO1)   1. What is the purpose of accounting?

(LO1)   2. Identify four user groups normally interested in financial information about a business.

(LO2)   3. Identify the six major steps of the accounting process and explain each step.

(LO3)   4. What are generally accepted accounting principles (GAAP)?

(LO3)   5. Describe the steps followed by the Financial Accounting Standards Board when developing an accounting standard.

(LO4)   6. Identify the three types of ownership structures and discuss the advantages and disadvantages of each.

(LO5)   7. Identify three types of businesses according to activities.

(LO6)   8. What are the main functions of an accounting clerk?

(LO6)   9. Name and describe three areas of specialization for a public accountant.

(LO6)   10. Name and describe six areas of specialization for a managerial accountant.

MANAGING YOUR WRITING

1. Prepare a one-page memo to your instructor that explains what you hope to learn in this course and how this knowledge will be useful to you.

2. If you started a business, what would it be? Prepare a one-page memo that describes the type of business you would enjoy the most. Would it be a service, merchandising, or manufacturing business? Explain what form of ownership you would prefer and why.

SERIES A EXERCISES

EXERCISE 1-1A   **(LO1)**   **PURPOSE OF ACCOUNTING** Match the following users with the information needed.

1. Owners	a. Whether the firm can pay its bills on time
2. Managers	b. Detailed, up-to-date information to measure business performance (and plan for future operations)
3. Creditors	
4. Government agencies	c. To determine taxes to be paid and whether other regulations are met
	d. The firm's current financial condition

EXERCISE 1-2A   **(LO2)**   **ACCOUNTING PROCESS** List the six major steps of the accounting process in order (1–6) and define each.

_____ Recording

_____ Summarizing

_____ Reporting

_____ Analyzing

_____ Interpreting

_____ Classifying

SERIES B EXERCISES

EXERCISE 1-1B   **(LO1)**   **PURPOSE OF ACCOUNTING** Describe the kind of information needed by the users listed.

Owners (present and future)

Managers

Creditors (present and future)

Government agencies

EXERCISE 1-2B   **(LO2)**   **ACCOUNTING PROCESS** Match the following steps of the accounting process with their definitions.

Analyzing	a. Telling the results
Recording	b. Looking at events that have taken place and thinking about how they affect the business
Classifying	c. Deciding the importance of the various reports
Summarizing	d. Bringing together information to explain a result
Reporting	e. Sorting and grouping like items together
Interpreting	f. Entering financial information into the accounting system

©DIGITAL IMAGING GROUP

Analyzing Transactions:
The Accounting Equation

Have you ever heard the expression "garbage in, garbage out"? Computer users commonly use it to mean that if input to the computer system is not correctly entered, the output from the system will be worthless. The same expression applies in accounting. In this chapter Jessica Jane enters into many transactions while running her delivery business. For example, she purchases a motor scooter to make deliveries. To understand the impact of this event, Jessie needs to know how to properly measure the cost of the asset, estimate its useful life, and keep records of whether she paid cash or promised to make payments in the future. If Jessie does not understand the economic events affecting her delivery business and their impact on the accounting equation, the events will not be correctly entered into the accounting system. This will make the outputs from the system (the financial statements) worthless. What kinds of questions do you think Jessie should ask herself to improve her understanding of an event and its impact on the business?

Careful study of this chapter should enable you to:

LO1 Define the accounting elements.

LO2 Construct the accounting equation.

LO3 Analyze business transactions.

LO4 Show the effects of business transactions on the accounting equation.

LO5 Prepare and describe the purposes of a simple income statement, statement of owner's equity, and balance sheet.

LO6 Define the three basic phases of the accounting process.

The entire accounting process is based on one simple equation, called the accounting equation. In this chapter, you will learn how to use this equation to analyze business transactions. You also will learn how to prepare financial statements that report the effect of these transactions on the financial condition of a business.

THE ACCOUNTING ELEMENTS

LO1 Define the accounting elements.

Before the accounting process can begin, the entity to be accounted for must be defined. A **business entity** is an individual, association, or organization that engages in economic activities and controls specific economic resources. This definition allows the personal and business finances of an owner to be accounted for separately.

Three basic accounting elements exist for every business entity: assets, liabilities, and owner's equity. These elements are defined below.

LEARNING KEY: Pay close attention to the definitions for the basic accounting elements. A clear understanding of these definitions will help you analyze even the most complex business transactions.

Assets

Assets are items that are owned by a business and will provide future benefits. Examples of assets include cash, merchandise, furniture, fixtures, machinery, buildings, and land. Businesses may also have an asset called **accounts receivable**. This asset represents the amount of money owed to the business by its customers as a result of making sales "on account," or "on credit." Making sales on account simply means that the customers have promised to pay sometime in the future.

Liabilities

Liabilities represent something owed to another business entity. The amount owed represents a probable future outflow of assets as a result of a past event or transaction. Liabilities are debts or obligations of the business that can be paid with cash, goods, or services.

The most common liabilities are accounts payable and notes payable. An **account payable** is an unwritten promise to pay a supplier for assets purchased or services received. Acquiring assets or services by promising to make payments in the future is referred to as making a purchase "on account," or "on credit." Formal written promises to pay suppliers or lenders specified sums of money at definite future times are known as **notes payable**.

Owner's Equity

Owner's equity is the amount by which the business assets exceed the business liabilities. Other terms used for owner's equity include **net worth** and **capital**. If there are no business liabilities, the owner's equity is equal to the total assets.

The owner of a business may have business assets and liabilities as well as nonbusiness assets and liabilities. For example, the business owner probably owns a home, clothing, and a car, and perhaps owes the dentist for dental service. These are personal, nonbusiness assets and liabilities. According to the **business entity concept**, nonbusiness assets and liabilities are not included in the business entity's accounting records.

If the owner invests money or other assets in the business, the item invested is reclassified from a nonbusiness asset to a business asset. If the owner withdraws money or other assets from the business for personal use, the item withdrawn is reclassified from a business asset to a nonbusiness asset. These distinctions are important and allow the owner to make decisions based on the financial condition and results of the business apart from nonbusiness activities.

LEARNING KEY: The business entity's assets and liabilities are separate from the owner's nonbusiness assets and liabilities.

A BROADER VIEW

Assets and the Cost of Products We Buy

© SUPERSTOCK

Next time you buy something, think of all the assets that a company needs to produce that product. If the product comes from a capital-intensive industry, one that requires heavy investments in assets, the company must price the product high enough to cover the cost of using the assets and replacing them when they wear out. For example, General Motors recently reported that the cost of property, plant, and equipment used for operating purposes came to over $60 billion.

THE ACCOUNTING EQUATION

LO2 Construct the accounting equation.

> The accounting equation is a very important tool to help in understanding and analyzing transactions.

The relationship between the three basic accounting elements—assets, liabilities, and owner's equity—can be expressed in the form of a simple equation known as the **accounting equation**.

Assets	=	Liabilities	+	Owner's Equity

This equation reflects the fact that both outsiders and insiders have an interest in the assets of a business. *Liabilities represent the outside interests of creditors. Owner's equity represents the inside interests of owners. Or, viewed another way, the left side of the equation shows the assets. The right side of the equation shows where the money came from to buy the assets. When two elements are known, the third can always be calculated.* For example, assume that assets on December 31 total $60,400. On that same day, the business liabilities consist of $5,400 owed for equipment. Owner's equity is calculated by subtracting total liabilities from total assets, $60,400 − $5,400 = $55,000.

> The left side of the equation represents the assets. The right side of the equation shows where the money came from to buy the assets.

Assets	=	Liabilities	+	Owner's Equity
$60,400	=	$5,400	+	$55,000
$60,400	=		$60,400	

LEARNING KEY: If you know two accounting elements, you can calculate the third element.

Total assets	$60,400
Total liabilities	−5,400
Owner's equity	$55,000

ANALYZING BUSINESS TRANSACTIONS

LO3 Analyze business transactions.

A **business transaction** is an economic event that has a direct impact on the business. A business transaction almost always requires an exchange between the business and another outside entity. We must be able to measure this exchange in dollars. Examples of business transactions include buying goods and services, selling goods and services, buying and selling assets, making loans, and borrowing money.

All business transactions affect the accounting equation through specific accounts. An **account** is a separate record used to summarize changes in each asset, liability, and owner's equity of a business. **Account titles** provide a description of the particular type of asset, liability, or owner's equity affected by a transaction.

Three basic questions must be answered when analyzing the effects of a business transaction on the accounting equation. These questions help address the steps in the accounting process discussed in Chapter 1.

1. **What happened?**

   ■ Make certain you understand the event that has taken place.

2. **Which accounts are affected?**

   ■ Identify the accounts that are affected.

   ■ Classify these accounts as assets, liabilities, or owner's equity.

3. **How is the accounting equation affected?**

   ■ Determine which accounts have increased or decreased.

   ■ Make certain that the accounting equation remains in balance after the transaction has been entered.

EFFECT OF TRANSACTIONS ON THE ACCOUNTING EQUATION

LO4 Show the effects of business transactions on the accounting equation.

Each transaction affects at least two accounts and one or more of the three basic accounting elements. A transaction increases or decreases specific asset, liability, or owner's equity accounts. Assume that the following transactions occurred during June 20--, the first month of operations for Jessie Jane's Campus Delivery.

Remember, capital does not mean cash. The cash is shown in the cash account.

Transaction (a): Investment by owner

An Increase in an Asset Offset by an Increase in Owner's Equity. Jessica Jane opened a bank account with a deposit of $2,000 for her business. The new business now has $2,000 of the asset Cash. Since Jessie contributed the asset, the owner's equity element, Jessica Jane, Capital, increases by the same amount.

Assets (Items Owned)	=	Liabilities (Amounts Owed)	+	Owner's Equity (Owner's Investment)
Cash	=			Jessica Jane, Capital
(a) $2,000	=			$2,000

Transaction (b): Purchase of an asset for cash

An Increase in an Asset Offset by a Decrease in Another Asset. Jessie decided that the fastest and easiest way to get around campus and find parking is on a motor scooter. Thus, she bought a motor scooter (delivery equipment) for $1,200 cash. Jessie exchanged one asset, cash, for another, delivery equipment. This transaction reduces Cash and creates a new asset, Delivery Equipment.

Assets (Items Owned)		=	Liabilities (Amounts Owed)	+	Owner's Equity (Owner's Investment)
Cash	+ Delivery Equipment	=			Jessica Jane, Capital
$2,000					$2,000
(b) −1,200	+$1,200				
$ 800 +	$1,200				$2,000
$2,000		=			$2,000

LEARNING KEY: If transactions are entered correctly, the accounting equation always remains in balance.

Transaction (c): Purchase of an asset on account

An Increase in an Asset Offset by an Increase in a Liability. Jessie hired a friend to work for her, which meant that a second scooter would be needed. Given Jessie's limited cash, she bought the dealer's demonstration model for $900. The seller agreed to allow Jessie to spread the payments over the next three months. This transaction increased an asset, Delivery Equipment, by $900 and increased the liability, Accounts Payable, by an equal amount.

	Assets (Items Owned)		=	Liabilities (Amounts Owed)	+	Owner's Equity (Owner's Investment)
	Cash	+ Delivery Equipment	=	Accounts Payable	+	Jessica Jane, Capital
	$ 800	$1,200				$2,000
(c)		+900		+$900		
	$ 800 +	$2,100	=	$900	+	$2,000
	$2,900			$2,900		

Transaction (d): Payment on a loan

A Decrease in an Asset Offset by a Decrease in a Liability. Jessie paid the first installment on the scooter of $300 (see transaction (c)). This payment decreased the asset, Cash, and the liability, Accounts Payable, by $300.

	Assets (Items Owned)		=	Liabilities (Amounts Owed)	+	Owner's Equity (Owner's Investment)
	Cash	+ Delivery Equipment	=	Accounts Payable	+	Jessica Jane, Capital
	$ 800	$2,100		$900		$2,000
(d)	−300			−300		
	$ 500 +	$2,100	=	$600	+	$2,000
	$2,600		=	$2,600		

Expanding the Accounting Equation: Revenues, Expenses, and Withdrawals

In the preceding sections, three key accounting elements of every business entity were defined and explained: assets, liabilities, and owner's equity. To complete the explanation of the accounting process, three additional elements must be added to the discussion: revenues, expenses, and withdrawals.

Revenues. **Revenues** represent the amount a business charges customers for products sold or services performed. Customers generally pay with cash or a credit card, or they promise to pay at a later date. Most businesses recognize revenues when earned, even if cash has not yet been received. Separate accounts are used to recognize different types of revenue. Examples include Delivery Fees; Consulting Fees; Rent Revenue, if the business rents space to others; Interest Revenue, for interest earned on bank deposits; and Sales, for sales of merchandise. *Revenues increase both assets and owner's equity.*

Expenses. **Expenses** represent the decrease in assets (or increase in liabilities) as a result of efforts made to produce revenues. Common examples of expenses are rent, salaries, supplies consumed, and taxes. As with revenues, separate accounts are used to maintain records for each different type of expense. Expenses are "incurred" as assets are consumed (such as supplies), cash is paid for services performed for the business, or a promise is made to pay cash at a future date for services performed for the business (such as wages). The promise to pay in the future represents a liability. *Expenses either decrease assets or increase liabilities. Expenses always reduce owner's equity.*

LEARNING KEY: It is important to remember that expenses do not always reduce cash and revenues do not always increase cash right away.

The main purposes of recognizing an expense are to keep track of the amount and types of expenses incurred and to show the reduction in owner's equity. Note that an expense can cause a reduction in assets or an increase in liabilities. Wages earned by employees is a good example. If paid, the expense reduces an asset, Cash. If not paid, it increases a liability, Wages Payable. Either way, owner's equity is reduced.

If total revenues exceed total expenses of the period, the excess is the **net income** or net profit for the period.

Revenues Greater than Expenses = Net Income

On the other hand, if expenses exceed revenues of the period, the excess is a **net loss** for the period.

Expenses Greater than Revenues = Net Loss

The owner can determine the time period used in the measurement of net income or net loss. It may be a month, a quarter (three months), a year, or some other time period. The concept that income determination can be made on a periodic basis is known as the **accounting period concept**. Any accounting period of twelve months is called a **fiscal year**. The fiscal year frequently coincides with the calendar year.

Withdrawals. **Withdrawals**, or **drawing**, reduce owner's equity as a result of the owner taking cash or other assets out of the business for personal use. Since earnings are expected to offset withdrawals, this reduction is viewed as temporary.

The accounting equation is expanded to include revenues, expenses, and withdrawals. Note that revenues increase owner's equity, while expenses and drawing reduce owner's equity.

LEARNING KEY:

Owner's Equity	
Decrease	Increase
Expenses	Revenues
Drawing	Investments

	Assets (Items Owned)		=	Liabilities (Amounts Owed)	+	Owner's Equity (Owner's Investment + Earnings)				
	Cash	+ Delivery Equipment	=	Accounts Payable	+	Jessica Jane, Capital	– Jessica Jane, Drawing	+ Revenues	– Expenses
Balance	$ 500	+ $2,100	=	$600	+	$2,000			
		$2,600	=				$2,600		

Effect of Revenue, Expense, and Withdrawal Transactions on the Accounting Equation

To show the effects of revenue, expense, and withdrawal transactions, the example of Jessie Jane's Campus Delivery will be continued. Assume that the following transactions took place in Jessie's business during June 20--.

Transaction (e): Delivery revenues earned in cash

An Increase in an Asset Offset by an Increase in Owner's Equity Resulting from Revenue. Jessie received $500 cash from clients for delivery services. This transaction increased the asset, Cash, and increased owner's equity by $500. The increase in owner's equity is shown by increasing the revenue account, Delivery Fees, by $500.

Assets (Items Owned)		=	Liabilities (Amounts Owed)	+	Owner's Equity (Owner's Investment + Earnings)				
Cash +	Delivery Equipment	=	Accounts Payable	+	Jessica Jane, Capital −	Jessica Jane, Drawing	+ Revenues	− Expenses	Description
$ 500	$2,100		$600		$2,000				
(e) +500							+$500		Deliv. Fees
$1,000 +	$2,100	=	$600	+	$2,000		+	$500	
$3,100		=				$3,100			

Transaction (f): Paid rent for month

A Decrease in an Asset Offset by a Decrease in Owner's Equity Resulting from an Expense. Jessie rents a small office on campus. She paid $200 for office rent for June. This transaction decreased both Cash and owner's equity by $200. The decrease in owner's equity is shown by increasing an expense called Rent Expense by $200. An increase in an expense decreases owner's equity.

Assets (Items Owned)		=	Liabilities (Amounts Owed)	+	Owner's Equity (Owner's Investment + Earnings)				
Cash +	Delivery Equipment	=	Accounts Payable	+	Jessica Jane, Capital −	Jessica Jane, Drawing	+ Revenues	− Expenses	Description
$1,000	$2,100		$600		$2,000		$500		
(f) −200								+200	Rent Exp.
$ 800 +	$2,100	=	$600	+	$2,000		+	$500 −	$200
$2,900		=				$2,900			

Transaction (g): Paid telephone bill

A Decrease in an Asset Offset by a Decrease in Owner's Equity Resulting from an Expense. Jessie paid $50 in cash for telephone service. This transaction, like the previous one, decreased both Cash and owner's equity. This decrease in owner's equity is shown by increasing an expense called Telephone Expense by $50.

Assets (Items Owned)		=	Liabilities (Amounts Owed)	+	Owner's Equity (Owner's Investment + Earnings)				
Cash	+ Delivery Equipment	=	Accounts Payable	+ Jessica Jane, Capital	− Jessica Jane, Drawing	+ Revenues	− Expenses	Description	
$ 800	$2,100		$600	$2,000		$500	$200		
(g) − 50								+ 50	Tel. Expense
$ 750 +	$2,100 =		$600 +	$2,000		+ $500 −	$250		
$2,850		=			$2,850				

Transaction (h): Delivery revenues earned on account

An Increase in an Asset Offset by an Increase in Owner's Equity Resulting from Revenue. Jessie extends credit to regular customers. Often delivery services are performed for which payment will be received later. Since revenues are recognized when earned, an increase in owner's equity must be reported by increasing the revenue account. Since no cash is received at this time, Cash cannot be increased. Instead, an increase is reported for another asset, Accounts Receivable. *The total of Accounts Receivable at any point in time reflects the amount owed to Jessie by her customers.* Deliveries made on account amounted to $600. Accounts Receivable and Delivery Fees are increased.

Assets (Items Owned)			=	Liabilities (Amounts Owed)	+	Owner's Equity (Owner's Investment + Earnings)				
Cash	+ Accounts Receivable	+ Delivery Equipment	=	Accounts Payable	+ Jessica Jane, Capital	− Jessica Jane, Drawing	+ Revenues	− Expenses	Description	
$ 750		$2,100		$600	$2,000		$ 500	$250		
(h)	+ 600						+ 600		Deliv. Fees	
$ 750 +	$ 600 +	$2,100 =		$600 +	$2,000		+ $1,100 −	$250		
$3,450			=			$3,450				

LEARNING KEY: Revenue is recognized when it is earned even though cash is not received.

Transaction (i): Purchase of supplies

An Increase in an Asset Offset by a Decrease in an Asset. Jessie bought pens, paper, delivery envelopes, and other supplies for $80 cash. These supplies should last for several months. Since they will generate future benefits, the supplies should be recorded as an asset. The accounting equation will show an increase in an asset, Supplies, and a decrease in Cash.

Assets (Items Owned)				=	Liabilities (Amounts Owed)	+	Owner's Equity (Owner's Investment + Earnings)				
Cash	+ Accounts Receivable	+ Supplies	+ Delivery Equipment	=	Accounts Payable	+ Jessica Jane, Capital	− Jessica Jane, Drawing	+ Revenues	− Expenses	Description	
$ 750	$ 600		$2,100		$600	$2,000		$1,100	$250		
(i) − 80		+$80									
$ 670 +	$ 600 +	$80 +	$2,100 =		$600 +	$2,000		+ $1,100 −	$250		
$3,450				=			$3,450				

Transaction (j): Payment of insurance premium

An Increase in an Asset Offset by a Decrease in an Asset. Since Jessie plans to graduate and sell the business next January, she paid $200 for an eight-month liability insurance policy. Insurance is paid in advance and will provide future benefits. Thus, it is treated as an asset. We must expand the equation to include another asset, Prepaid Insurance, and show that Cash has been reduced.

	Assets (Items Owned)				=	Liabilities (Amounts Owed)	+	Owner's Equity (Owner's Investment + Earnings)				
Cash +	Accounts Receivable +	Supplies +	Prepaid Insurance +	Delivery Equipment =		Accounts Payable	+	Jessica Jane, Capital	− Jessica Jane, Drawing	+ Revenues	− Expenses	Description
$ 670	$ 600	$80		$2,100		$600		$2,000		$1,100	$250	
(j) − 200			+$200									
$ 470 +	$ 600 +	$80 +	$200 +	$2,100	=	$600	+	$2,000		+ $1,100	− $250	
	$3,450				=			$3,450				

LEARNING KEY: Both supplies and insurance are recorded as assets because they will provide benefits for several months.

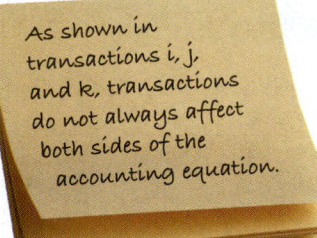

As shown in transactions i, j, and k, transactions do not always affect both sides of the accounting equation.

Transaction (k): Cash receipts from prior sales on account

An Increase in an Asset Offset by a Decrease in an Asset. Jessie received $570 in cash for delivery services performed for customers earlier in the month (see transaction (h)). Receipt of this cash increases the cash account and reduces the amount due from customers reported in the accounts receivable account. *Notice that owner's equity is not affected in this transaction. Owner's equity increased in transaction (h) when revenue was recognized as it was earned, rather than now when cash is received.*

	Assets (Items Owned)				=	Liabilities (Amounts Owed)	+	Owner's Equity (Owner's Investment + Earnings)				
Cash +	Accounts Receivable +	Supplies +	Prepaid Insurance +	Delivery Equipment =		Accounts Payable	+	Jessica Jane, Capital	− Jessica Jane, Drawing	+ Revenues	− Expenses	Description
$ 470	$ 600	$80	$200	$2,100		$600		$2,000		$1,100	$250	
(k) +570	− 570											
$1,040 +	$ 30 +	$80 +	$200 +	$2,100	=	$600	+	$2,000		+ $1,100	− $250	
	$3,450				=			$3,450				

Transaction (l): Purchase of an asset on account making a partial payment

An Increase in an Asset Offset by a Decrease in an Asset and an Increase in a Liability. With business increasing, Jessie hired a second employee and bought a third motor scooter. The scooter cost $1,500. Jessie paid $300 in cash and will spread the remaining payments over the next four months. The asset Delivery

Equipment increases by $1,500, Cash decreases by $300, and the liability Accounts Payable increases by $1,200. *Note that this transaction changes three accounts. Even so, the accounting equation remains in balance.*

	Assets (Items Owned)				=	Liabilities (Amounts Owed)	+	Owner's Equity (Owner's Investment + Earnings)				
Cash +	Accounts Receivable +	Supplies +	Prepaid Insurance +	Delivery Equipment =		Accounts Payable +		Jessica Jane, Capital –	Jessica Jane, Drawing +	Revenues –	Expenses	Description
$1,040	$30	$80	$200	$2,100		$ 600		$2,000		$1,100	$250	
(l) –300				+1,500		+1,200						
$ 740 +	$30 +	$80 +	$200 +	$3,600 =		$1,800	+	$2,000		+ $1,100 –	$250	
	$4,650				=			$4,650				

Transaction (m): Payment of wages

A Decrease in an Asset Offset by a Decrease in Owner's Equity Resulting from an Expense. Jessie paid her part-time employees $650 in wages. This represents an additional business expense. As with other expenses, Cash is reduced and owner's equity is reduced by increasing an expense.

	Assets (Items Owned)				=	Liabilities (Amounts Owed)	+	Owner's Equity (Owner's Investment + Earnings)				
Cash +	Accounts Receivable +	Supplies +	Prepaid Insurance +	Delivery Equipment =		Accounts Payable +		Jessica Jane, Capital –	Jessica Jane, Drawing +	Revenues –	Expenses	Description
$740	$30	$80	$200	$3,600		$1,800		$2,000		$1,100	$250	
(m) – 650											+650	Wages Exp.
$ 90 +	$30 +	$80 +	$200 +	$3,600 =		$1,800	+	$2,000		+ $1,100 –	$900	
	$4,000				=			$4,000				

Transaction (n): Deliveries made for cash and on account

An Increase in Two Assets Offset by an Increase in Owner's Equity. Total delivery fees for the remainder of the month amounted to $1,050: $430 in cash and $620 on account. Since all of these delivery fees have been earned, the revenue account increases by $1,050. Also, Cash increases by $430 and Accounts Receivable increases by $620. Thus, revenues increase assets and owner's equity. Note, once again, that one event impacts three accounts while the equation remains in balance.

	Assets (Items Owned)				=	Liabilities (Amounts Owed)	+	Owner's Equity (Owner's Investment + Earnings)				
Cash +	Accounts Receivable +	Supplies +	Prepaid Insurance +	Delivery Equipment =		Accounts Payable +		Jessica Jane, Capital –	Jessica Jane, Drawing +	Revenues –	Expenses	Description
$ 90	$ 30	$80	$200	$3,600		$1,800		$2,000		$1,100	$900	
(n) + 430	+ 620									+1,050		Deliv. Fees
$520 +	$650 +	$80 +	$200 +	$3,600 =		$1,800	+	$2,000		+ $2,150 –	$900	
	$5,050				=			$5,050				

Transaction (o): Withdrawal of cash from business

A Decrease in an Asset Offset by a Decrease in Owner's Equity Resulting from a Withdrawal by the Owner. At the end of the month, Jessie took $150 in cash from the business to purchase books for her classes. Since the books are not business related, this is a withdrawal. Withdrawals can be viewed as the opposite of investments by the owner. Both owner's equity and Cash decrease.

	Cash	+	Accounts Receivable	+	Supplies	+	Prepaid Insurance	+	Delivery Equipment	=	Accounts Payable	+	Jessica Jane, Capital	−	Jessica Jane, Drawing	+	Revenues	−	Expenses	Description
	\$ 520		\$650		\$80		\$200		\$3,600		\$1,800		\$2,000				\$2,150		\$900	
(o)	− 150														+\$150					
	\$370	+	\$650	+	\$80	+	\$200	+	\$3,600	=	\$1,800	+	\$2,000	−	\$150	+	\$2,150	−	\$900	

Assets (Items Owned) = \$4,900   Liabilities (Amounts Owed) + Owner's Equity (Owner's Investment + Earnings) = \$4,900

LEARNING KEY: Withdrawals by the owner are reported in the drawing account. Withdrawals are the opposite of investments by the owner. Recall the business entity concept. The owner of the business and the business are separate economic entities. Thus, personal transactions must not be included with those of the business. If this is allowed, it will be very difficult to evaluate the performance of the business.

Figure 2-1 shows a summary of the transactions. Use this summary to test your understanding of transaction analysis by describing the economic event represented by each transaction. At the bottom of Figure 2-1, the asset accounts and their totals are compared with the liability and owner's equity accounts and their totals.

Trans-action	Cash +	Accounts Receivable +	Supplies +	Prepaid Insurance +	Delivery Equipment =	Accounts Payable +	Jessica Jane, Capital –	Jessica Jane, Drawing +	Revenues –	Expenses	Description
Assets (Items Owned)						**= Liabilities + (Amounts Owed)**	**Owner's Equity (Owner's Investment + Earnings)**				
Balance											
(a)	2,000						2,000				
Balance	2,000						2,000				
(b)	(1,200)				1,200						
Balance	800				1,200		2,000				
(c)					900	900					
Balance	800				2,100	900	2,000				
(d)	(300)					(300)					
Balance	500				2,100	600	2,000				
(e)	500								500		Deliv. Fees
Balance	1,000				2,100	600	2,000		500		
(f)	(200)									200	Rent Exp.
Balance	800				2,100	600	2,000		500	200	
(g)	(50)									50	Tele. Exp.
Balance	750				2,100	600	2,000		500	250	
(h)		600							600		Deliv. Fees
Balance	750	600			2,100	600	2,000		1,100	250	
(i)	(80)		80								
Balance	670	600	80		2,100	600	2,000		1,100	250	
(j)	(200)			200							
Balance	470	600	80	200	2,100	600	2,000		1,100	250	
(k)	570	(570)									
Balance	1,040	30	80	200	2,100	600	2,000		1,100	250	
(l)	(300)				1,500	1,200					
Balance	740	30	80	200	3,600	1,800	2,000		1,100	250	
(m)	(650)									650	Wages Exp.
Balance	90	30	80	200	3,600	1,800	2,000		1,100	900	
(n)	430	620							1,050		Deliv. Fees
Balance	520	650	80	200	3,600	1,800	2,000		2,150	900	
(o)	(150)							150			
Balance	**370 +**	**650 +**	**80 +**	**200 +**	**3,600 =**	**1,800 +**	**2,000 –**	**150 +**	**2,150 –**	**900**	

Cash	$ 370	Accounts Payable	$ 1,800
Accounts Receivable	650	Jessica Jane, Capital	2,000
Supplies	80	Jessica Jane, Drawing	(150)
Prepaid Insurance	200	Delivery Fees	2,150
Delivery Equipment	3,600	Rent Expense	(200)
Total assets	$ 4,900	Telephone Expense	(50)
		Wages Expense	(650)
		Total liabilities and owner's equity	$ 4,900

Amounts in ( ) are subtracted

FIGURE 2-1   Summary of Transactions Illustrated

LEARNING KEY: As with the running totals in the table, the listing immediately below the table provides proof that the accounting equation is in balance.

FINANCIAL STATEMENTS

LO5 Prepare and describe the purposes of a simple income statement, statement of owner's equity, and balance sheet.

Three financial statements commonly prepared by a business entity are the income statement, statement of owner's equity, and balance sheet. The transaction information gathered and summarized in the accounting equation may be used to prepare these financial statements. Figure 2-2 shows the following:

1. A summary of the specific revenue and expense transactions and the ending totals for the asset, liability, capital, and drawing accounts from the accounting equation.

2. The financial statements and their linkages with the accounting equation and each other.

Note that each of the financial statements in Figure 2-2 has a heading consisting of:

HEADING FOR FINANCIAL STATEMENTS	
1. The name of the company	Jessie Jane's Campus Delivery
2. The title of the statement	Income Statement, Statement of Owner's Equity, or Balance Sheet
3. The time period covered or the date of the statement	For Month Ended June 30, 20--, or June 30, 20--

The income statement and statement of owner's equity provide information concerning events covering a period of time, in this case, *the month ended* June 30, 20--. The balance sheet, on the other hand, offers a picture of the business *on a specific date*, June 30, 20--.

The Income Statement

The income statement reports the following:
Revenues   xxx
Expenses   (xx)
Net income   xx

The **income statement**, sometimes called the **profit and loss statement** or **operating statement**, reports the profitability of business operations for a specific period of time. Jessie's income statement shows the revenues earned for the month of June. Next, the expenses incurred as a result of the efforts made to earn these revenues are deducted. If the revenues are greater than the expenses, net income is reported. If the expenses are greater than the revenue, a net loss is reported.

LEARNING KEY:	Income Statement		Income Statement	
	Revenues	$500	Revenues	$500
	Expenses	400	Expenses	700
	Net income	$100	Net loss	$200

By carefully studying the income statement, it is clear that Jessie earns revenues in only one way: by making deliveries. If other types of services were offered, these revenues would also be identified on the statement. Further, the reader can see the kinds of expenses that were incurred. The reader can make a judgment as to whether these seem reasonable given the amount of revenue earned. Finally, the most important number on the statement is the net income. This is known as the "bottom line."

	Assets (Items Owned)				=	**Liabilities** (Amounts Owed)	+	**Owner's Equity** (Owner's Investment + Earnings)				
Trans-action	Cash +	Accounts Receivable +	Supplies +	Prepaid Insurance +	Delivery Equipment =	Accounts Payable +	Jessica Jane, Capital −	Jessica Jane, Drawing +	Revenues −	Expenses	Description
(e)									500		Deliv. Fees
(f)										200	Rent Exp.
(g)										50	Tele. Exp.
(h)									600		Deliv. Fees
(m)										650	Wages Exp.
(n)									1,050		Deliv. Fees
Balance	370 +	650 +	80 +	200 +	3,600 =	1,800 +	2,000 −	150 +	2,150 −	900	

Jessie Jane's Campus Delivery
Income Statement
For Month Ended June 30, 20 --

Revenues		
Delivery fees		$2 1 5 0 00
Expenses		
Wages expense	$ 6 5 0 00	
Rent expense	2 0 0 00	
Telephone expense	5 0 0 00	
Total expenses		9 0 0 00
Net income		$1 2 5 0 00

$ at top of columns
Subtotal underline

Jessie Jane's Campus Delivery
Statement of Owner's Equity
For Month Ended June 30, 20 - -

Jessica Jane, capital, June 1, 20 - -		$2 0 0 0 00
Net income for June	$1 2 5 0 00	
Less withdrawals for June	1 5 0 00	
Increase in capital		1 1 0 0 00
Jessica Jane, capital, June 30, 20 - -		$3 1 0 0 00

$ on total

Jessie Jane's Campus Delivery
Balance Sheet
June 30, 20 - -

Assets		Liabilities	
Cash	$ 3 7 0 00	Accounts payable	$1 8 0 0 00
Accounts receivable	6 5 0 00		
Supplies	8 0 00	Owner's Equity	
Prepaid insurance	2 0 0 00	Jessica Jane, capital	3 1 0 0 00
Delivery equipment	3 6 0 0 00		
		Total liabilities and	
Total assets	$4 9 0 0 00	owner's equity	$4 9 0 0 00

Double underline totals

FIGURE 2-2 Summary and Financial Statements

The Statement of Owner's Equity

The **statement of owner's equity** illustrated in Figure 2-2 reports on these activities for the month of June. Jessie started her business with an investment of $2,000. During the month of June she earned $1,250 in net income and withdrew $150 for personal expenses. This resulted in a net increase in Jessie's capital of $1,100. Jessie's $2,000 original investment, plus the net increase of $1,100, results in her ending capital of $3,100.

Note that Jessie's original investment and later withdrawal are taken from the accounting equation. *The net income figure could have been computed from information in the accounting equation. However, it is easier to simply transfer net income as reported on the income statement to the statement of owner's equity.* This is an important linkage between the income statement and statement of owner's equity.

If Jessie had a net loss of $500 for the month, the statement of owner's equity would be prepared as shown in Figure 2-3.

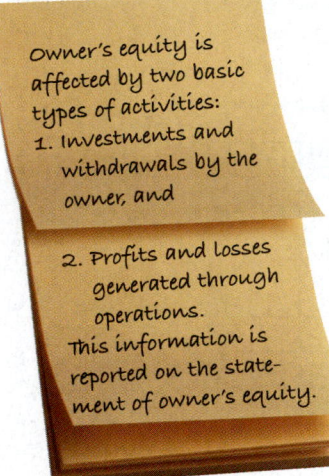

Owner's equity is affected by two basic types of activities:
1. Investments and withdrawals by the owner, and
2. Profits and losses generated through operations.
This information is reported on the statement of owner's equity.

Jessie Jane's Campus Delivery Statement of Owner's Equity For Month Ended June 30, 20 - -									
Jessica Jane, capital, June 1, 20 - -						$2	0	0	0	00
Less: Net loss for June	$	5	0	0	00				
Withdrawals for June		1	5	0	00				
Decrease in capital							6	5	0	00
Jessica Jane, capital, June 30, 20 - -						$1	3	5	0	00

FIGURE 2-3   Statement of Owner's Equity with Net Loss

The Balance Sheet

Balance Sheet

Assets   Liabilities + Owner's Equity

xxx   xxx

The **balance sheet** reports a firm's assets, liabilities, and owner's equity on a specific date. It is called a balance sheet because it confirms that the accounting equation has remained in balance. It is also referred to as a **statement of financial position** or **statement of financial condition**.

As illustrated in Figure 2-2, the asset and liability accounts are taken from the accounting equation and reported on the balance sheet. *The total of Jessie's capital account on June 30 could have been computed from the owner's equity accounts in the accounting equation ($2,000 – $150 + $2,150 – $900). However, it is simpler to take the June 30, 20--, capital as computed on the statement of owner's equity and transfer it to the balance sheet.* This is an important linkage between these two statements.

GUIDELINES FOR PREPARING FINANCIAL STATEMENTS

1. Financial statements are prepared primarily for users not associated with the company. To make a good impression and enhance understanding, financial statements must follow a standard form with careful attention to placement, spacing, and indentations.

2. All statements have a heading with the name of the company, name of the statement, and accounting period or date.

3. Single rules (lines) indicate that the numbers above the line have been added or subtracted. Double rules (double underlines) indicate a total.

4. Dollar signs are used at the top of columns and for the first amount entered in a column beneath a ruling.

5. On the income statement, a common practice is to list expenses from highest to lowest dollar amount, with miscellaneous expense listed last.

6. On the balance sheet, assets are listed from most liquid to least liquid. **Liquidity** measures the ease with which the asset will be converted to cash. Liabilities are listed from most current to least current.

Most firms also prepare a statement of cash flows. Given the complexity of this statement, we will postpone its discussion until later in this text.

OVERVIEW OF THE ACCOUNTING PROCESS

LO6 **Define the three basic phases of the accounting process.**

Figure 2-4 shows the three basic phases of the accounting process in terms of input, processing, and output.

- *Input.* Business transactions provide the necessary **input**.
- *Processing.* Recognizing the effect of these transactions on the assets, liabilities, owner's equity, revenues, and expenses of a business is the **processing** function.
- *Output.* The financial statements are the **output**.

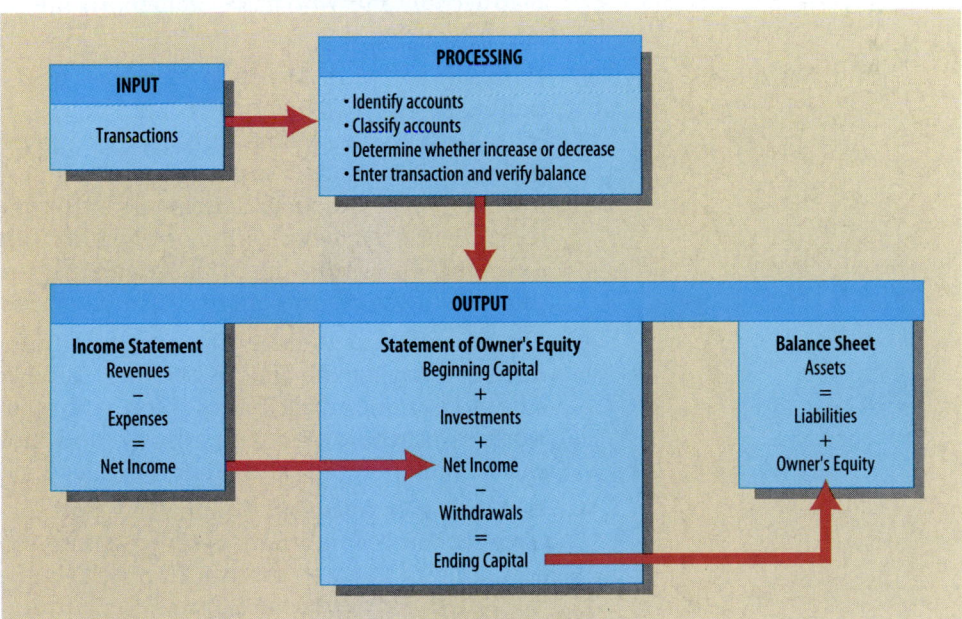

FIGURE 2-4   Input, Processing, and Output

Computers and Accounting

Computer Skills for Accountants—Gary P. Schneider, University of San Diego

In recent years, accountants and others increasingly use computers in their daily work activities. Most accountants find themselves using word-processing, spreadsheet, presentation, database, e-mail, and web browser software on a regular basis. Being a skilled computer user is important for accountants who want to obtain good jobs in the field. The specific skills needed by accountants include:

- **Word-processing software**. Accountants are frequently required to prepare reports for management or outside parties. Having good writing skills is important, but knowing how to use computers to design and format interesting, informative documents is also important.

- **Spreadsheet software**. This is an important tool for accountants. Most accountants find themselves using spreadsheet software daily. Accountants use spreadsheet software to analyze the details of accounts, to project costs and revenues, to create budgets, to perform "what-if" analyses of proposed business strategies, and to calculate the likely return on invested funds. Most spreadsheet software packages include chart-building features. Accountants must know how to use these features to create informative charts and integrate them into reports and memos.

- **Presentation software**. Increasingly, accountants are called upon to deliver their results to company management, lenders, and investors in the form of personal presentations. This requires good oral communication skills and the ability to create and use effective visual aids. One of the most commonly used visual aids is the computer presentation. Accountants must know how to build an effective presentation that incorporates the results of their work. Presentation software is an important tool that can help accountants who make oral reports full of facts and figures compelling and interesting.

- **Database software**. Database software is used by all types of businesses and not-for-profit organizations to keep track of their activities. Companies often keep databases for customers, employees, suppliers, and even competitors. Accountants use database software to extract the information they need to prepare financial statements. Auditors need to know how to access their clients' databases so they can gather evidence to support their opinions on their clients' financial statements. In large organizations, most of the accounting records are stored in databases.

- **E-mail software**. A large percentage of business communication is conducted using e-mail. This is another software tool that accountants use daily to ask questions, gather information, and report the results of their work to others. Accountants must know how to attach reports, spreadsheets, presentations, and other files they have created to e-mail messages.

- **Web browser software**. The Internet and the World Wide Web (the Web) have become important resources for accountants. The Web offers accountants a way to stay current with the field of accounting by providing access to the business press, accounting journals, and information about their industry.

In addition to these five types of general office productivity software, many companies have their own software for specific functions, including accounting. Although companies usually provide training to new employees who need to use specific software products, most companies expect newly hired accountants to have basic skills in using word-processing, spreadsheet, presentation, database, e-mail, and web browser software. Many employers expect new accounting employees to have considerable skills in some of these software tools, particularly spreadsheet and database software.

Learning Objectives	Key Points to Remember
1 **Define the accounting elements.**	The three key accounting elements are assets, liabilities, and owner's equity. Owner's equity is expanded to include revenues, expenses, and drawing.
2 **Construct the accounting equation.**	The accounting equation is: Assets = Liabilities + Owner's Equity
3 **Analyze business transactions.**	Three questions must be answered in analyzing business transactions: 1. What happened? 2. Which accounts are affected? 3. How is the accounting equation affected?
4 **Show the effects of business transactions on the accounting equation.**	Each transaction affects at least two accounts and one or more of the three basic accounting elements. The transactions described in this chapter can be classified into five groups: 1. Increase in an asset offset by an increase in owner's equity. 2. Increase in an asset offset by a decrease in another asset. 3. Increase in an asset offset by an increase in a liability. 4. Decrease in an asset offset by a decrease in a liability. 5. Decrease in an asset offset by a decrease in owner's equity.
5 **Prepare and describe the purposes of a simple income statement, statement of owner's equity, and balance sheet.**	The purposes of the income statement, statement of owner's equity, and balance sheet can be summarized as follows: **STATEMENT** — **PURPOSE** Income statement — Reports net income or loss; Revenues – Expenses = Net Income or Loss Statement of owner's equity — Shows changes in the owner's capital account; Beginning Capital + Investments + Net Income – Withdrawals = Ending Capital Balance sheet — Verifies balance of accounting equation; Assets = Liabilities + Owner's Equity
6 **Define the three basic phases of the accounting process.**	The three basic phases of the accounting process are shown below. ▶ **Input.** Business transactions provide the necessary input. ▶ **Processing.** Recognizing the effect of these transactions on the assets, liabilities, owner's equity, revenues, and expenses of a business is the processing function. ▶ **Output.** The financial statements are the output.

Reflection: Answering the Opening Question

1. What happened?

2. Which accounts are affected?

3. How is the accounting equation affected?

DEMONSTRATION PROBLEM

Power Accounting System Software®

WebTUTOR Advantage

Damon Young has started his own business, Home and Away Inspections. He inspects property for buyers and sellers of real estate. Young rents office space and has a part-time assistant to answer the phone and help with inspections. The transactions for the month of September are as follows:

(a) On the first day of the month, Young invested cash by making a deposit in a bank account for the business, $15,000.

(b) Paid rent for September, $300.

(c) Bought a used truck for cash, $8,000.

(d) Purchased tools on account from Crafty Tools, $3,000.

(e) Paid electricity bill, $50.

(f) Paid two-year premium for liability insurance on truck, $600.

(g) Received cash from clients for services performed, $2,000.

(h) Paid part-time assistant (wages) for first half of month, $200.

(i) Performed inspection services for clients on account, $1,000.

(j) Paid telephone bill, $35.

(k) Bought office supplies costing $300. Paid $100 cash and will pay the balance next month, $200.

(l) Received cash from clients for inspections performed on account in (i), $300.

(m) Paid part-time assistant (wages) for last half of month, $250.

(n) Made partial payment on tools bought in (d), $1,000.

(o) Earned additional revenues amounting to $2,000: $1,400 in cash and $600 on account.

(p) Young withdrew cash at the end of the month for personal expenses, $500.

REQUIRED

1. Enter the transactions in an accounting equation similar to the one illustrated on the following page. After each transaction, show the new amount for each account.

	Assets (Items Owned)						= Liabilities (Amounts Owed)	+ Owner's Equity (Owner's Investment + Earnings)				
	Cash +	Accounts Receivable +	Supplies +	Prepaid Insurance +	Tools +	Truck =	Accounts Payable	+ Damon Young, Capital	− Damon Young, Drawing	+ Revenues	− Expenses	Description

2. Compute the ending balances for all accounts.

3. Prepare an income statement for Home and Away Inspections for the month of September 20--.

4. Prepare a statement of owner's equity for Home and Away Inspections for the month of September 20--.

5. Prepare a balance sheet for Home and Away Inspections as of September 30, 20--.

Solution

1, 2.

	Assets (Items Owned)						= Liabilities (Amounts Owed)	+ Owner's Equity (Owner's Investment + Earnings)				
	Cash +	Accounts Receivable +	Supplies +	Prepaid Insurance +	Tools +	Truck =	Accounts Payable	+ Damon Young, Capital	− Damon Young, Drawing	+ Revenues	− Expenses	Description
Bal.												
(a)	15,000							15,000				
Bal.	15,000							15,000				
(b)	(300)										300	Rent Exp.
Bal.	14,700							15,000			300	
(c)	(8,000)					8,000						
Bal.	6,700					8,000		15,000			300	
(d)					3,000		3,000					
Bal.	6,700				3,000	8,000	3,000	15,000			300	
(e)	(50)										50	Utilities Exp.
Bal.	6,650				3,000	8,000	3,000	15,000			350	
(f)	(600)		600									
Bal.	6,050		600		3,000	8,000	3,000	15,000			350	
(g)	2,000									2,000		Inspect. Fees
Bal.	8,050		600		3,000	8,000	3,000	15,000		2,000	350	
(h)	(200)										200	Wages Exp.
Bal.	7,850		600		3,000	8,000	3,000	15,000		2,000	550	
(i)		1,000								1,000		Inspect. Fees
Bal.	7,850	1,000	600		3,000	8,000	3,000	15,000		3,000	550	
(j)	(35)										35	Tele. Exp.
Bal.	7,815	1,000	600		3,000	8,000	3,000	15,000		3,000	585	
(k)	(100)		300				200					
Bal.	7,715	1,000	300	600	3,000	8,000	3,200	15,000		3,000	585	
(l)	300	(300)										
Bal.	8,015	700	300	600	3,000	8,000	3,200	15,000		3,000	585	
(m)	(250)										250	Wages Exp.
Bal.	7,765	700	300	600	3,000	8,000	3,200	15,000		3,000	835	
(n)	(1,000)						(1,000)					
Bal.	6,765	700	300	600	3,000	8,000	2,200	15,000		3,000	835	
(o)	1,400	600								2,000		Inspect. Fees
Bal.	8,165	1,300	300	600	3,000	8,000	2,200	15,000		5,000	835	
(p)	(500)								500			
Bal.	7,665 +	1,300 +	300 +	600 +	3,000 +	8,000 =	2,200	+ 15,000	− 500	+ 5,000	− 835	

3.

Home and Away Inspections Income Statement For Month Ended September 30, 20 --										
Revenues										
Inspection fees							$5	0	0	0	00
Expenses										
Wages expense		$	4	5	0	00				
Rent expense			3	0	0	00				
Utilities expense				5	0	00				
Telephone expense				3	5	00				
Total expenses								8	3	5	00
Net income							$4	1	6	5	00

4.

Home and Away Inspections Statement of Owner's Equity For Month Ended September 30, 20 - -										
Damon Young, capital, September 1, 20 - -							$15	0	0	0	00
Net income for September	$4	1	6	5	00					
Less withdrawals for September		5	0	0	00					
Increase in capital							3	6	6	5	00
Damon Young, capital, September 30, 20 - -							$18	6	6	5	00

5.

Home and Away Inspections Balance Sheet September 30, 20 - -											
Assets						Liabilities					
Cash	$ 7	6	6	5	00	Accounts payable	$ 2	2	0	0	00
Accounts receivable	1	3	0	0	00						
Supplies		3	0	0	00	Owner's Equity					
Prepaid insurance		6	0	0	00	Damon Young, capital	18	6	6	5	00
Tools	3	0	0	0	00						
Truck	8	0	0	0	00	Total liabilities and					
Total assets	$20	8	6	5	00	owner's equity	$20	8	6	5	00

KEY TERMS

account, (18)   A separate record used to summarize changes in each asset, liability, and owner's equity of a business.

account payable, (17)   An unwritten promise to pay a supplier for assets purchased or services received.

accounts receivable, (16)   An amount owed to a business by its customers as a result of the sale of goods or services.

account title, (18)   Provides a description of the particular type of asset, liability, owner's equity, revenue, or expense.

accounting equation, (18)   The accounting equation consists of the three basic accounting elements: assets = liabilities + owner's equity.

accounting period concept, (21)   The concept that income determination can be made on a periodic basis.

asset, (16)   An item that is owned by a business and will provide future benefits.

balance sheet, (30)   Reports assets, liabilities, and owner's equity on a specific date. It is called a balance sheet because it confirms that the accounting equation is in balance.

business entity, (16)   An individual, association, or organization that engages in economic activities and controls specific economic resources.

business entity concept, (17)   The concept that nonbusiness assets and liabilities are not included in the business entity's accounting records.

business transaction, (18)   An economic event that has a direct impact on the business.

capital, (17)   Another term for owner's equity, the amount by which the business assets exceed the business liabilities.

drawing, (21)   Withdrawals that reduce owner's equity as a result of the owner taking cash or other assets out of the business for personal use.

expenses, (20)   The decrease in assets (or increase in liabilities) as a result of efforts to produce revenues.

fiscal year, (21)   Any accounting period of twelve months' duration.

income statement, (28)   Reports the profitability of business operations for a specific period of time.

input, (31)   Business transactions provide the necessary input for the accounting information system.

liability, (16)   Something owed to another business entity.

liquidity, (31)   A measure of the ease with which an asset will be converted to cash.

net income, (21)   The excess of total revenues over total expenses for the period.

net loss, (21)   The excess of total expenses over total revenues for the period.

net worth, (17)   Another term for owner's equity, the amount by which the business assets exceed the business liabilities.

notes payable, (17)   A formal written promise to pay a supplier or lender a specified sum of money at a definite future time.

operating statement, (28)   Another name for the income statement, which reports the profitability of business operations for a specific period of time.

output, (31)   The financial statements are the output of the accounting information system.

owner's equity, (17)   The amount by which the business assets exceed the business liabilities.

processing, (31)   Recognizing the effect of transactions on the assets, liabilities, owner's equity, revenues, and expenses of a business.

profit and loss statement, (28) Another name for the income statement, which reports the profitability of business operations for a specific period of time.

revenues, (20) The amount a business charges customers for products sold or services performed.

statement of financial condition, (30) Another name for the balance sheet, which reports assets, liabilities, and owner's equity on a specific date.

statement of financial position, (30) Another name for the balance sheet, which reports assets, liabilities, and owner's equity on a specific date.

statement of owner's equity, (30) Reports beginning capital plus net income less withdrawals to compute ending capital.

withdrawals, (21) Reduce owner's equity as a result of the owner taking cash or other assets out of the business for personal use.

REVIEW QUESTIONS

(LO1) 1. Why is it necessary to distinguish between business assets and liabilities and nonbusiness assets and liabilities of a single proprietor?

(LO1) 2. Name and define the six major elements of the accounting equation.

(LO3) 3. List the three basic questions that must be answered when analyzing the effects of a business transaction on the accounting equation.

(LO5) 4. What is the function of an income statement?

(LO5) 5. What is the function of a statement of owner's equity?

(LO5) 6. What is the function of a balance sheet?

(LO6) 7. What are the three basic phases of the accounting process?

Self-Study Test Questions

True/False

1. Assets are items that are owned by the business and are expected to provide future benefits. _____

2. Accounts Payable is an example of an asset account. _____

3. According to the business entity concept, nonbusiness assets and liabilities are not included in the business's accounting records. _____

4. The accounting equation (assets = liabilities + owner's equity) must always be in balance. _____

5. When an asset increases, a liability must also increase. _____

6. When total revenues exceed total expenses, the difference is called net loss. _____

7. Expenses represent outflows of assets or increases in liabilities as a result of efforts to produce revenues. _____

Interactive Learning: **http://heintz.swlearning.com**

Multiple Choice

1. An increase to which of these accounts will increase owner's equity? _____

   (a) Accounts Payable
   (b) Drawing
   (c) Client Fees
   (d) Rent Expense

2. When delivery revenue is earned in cash, which accounts increase or decrease? _____

   (a) Cash increases; Revenue increases.
   (b) Cash decreases; Revenue increases.
   (c) Cash decreases; Revenue decreases.
   (d) Cash does not change; owner's equity increases.

3. When delivery revenue is earned on account, which accounts increase or decrease? _____

   (a) Cash increases; Revenue increases.
   (b) Accounts Receivable increases; Revenue increases.
   (c) Accounts Receivable increases; Revenue decreases.
   (d) Accounts Receivable decreases; Revenue decreases.

4. When payment is made on an existing debt, which accounts increase or decrease? _____

   (a) Cash increases; Accounts Receivable increases.
   (b) Cash decreases; Accounts Payable increases.
   (c) Cash increases; Accounts Payable increases.
   (d) Cash decreases; Accounts Payable decreases.

5. Which of the following accounts does not appear on the income statement? _____

   (a) Delivery fees
   (b) Wages expense
   (c) Drawing
   (d) Rent expense

The answers to the Self-Study Test Questions are at the end of the text.

MANAGING YOUR WRITING

Write a brief memo that explains the differences and similarities between expenses and withdrawals.

SERIES A EXERCISES

EXERCISE 2-1A   (LO1)   ACCOUNTING ELEMENTS Label each of the following accounts as an asset (A), a liability (L), or owner's equity (OE), using the following format.

Item	Account	Classification
Money in bank	Cash	
Office supplies	Supplies	
Money owed	Accounts Payable	
Office chairs	Office Furniture	
Net worth of owner	John Smith, Capital	
Money withdrawn by owner	John Smith, Drawing	
Money owed by customers	Accounts Receivable	

EXERCISE 2-2A **(LO2)** **THE ACCOUNTING EQUATION** Using the accounting equation, compute the missing elements.

Assets	=	Liabilities	+	Owner's Equity
_____	=	$24,000	+	$10,000
$25,000	=	$18,000	+	_____
$40,000	=	_____	+	$15,000

EXERCISE 2-3A **(LO3/4)**
Assets following (d): $22,000

EFFECTS OF TRANSACTIONS (BALANCE SHEET ACCOUNTS) Alice Stern started a business. During the first month (February 20--), the following transactions occurred. Show the effect of each transaction on the accounting equation: *Assets = Liabilities + Owner's Equity.* After each transaction, show the new account totals.

(a) Invested cash in the business, $20,000.

(b) Bought office equipment on account, $3,500.

(c) Bought office equipment for cash, $1,200.

(d) Paid cash on account to supplier in (b), $1,500.

EXERCISE 2-4A **(LO3/4)**
Assets following (k): $23,427

EFFECTS OF TRANSACTIONS (REVENUE, EXPENSE, WITHDRAWALS) Assume Alice Stern completed the following additional transactions during February. Show the effect of each transaction on the basic elements of the expanded accounting equation: *Assets = Liabilities + Owner's Equity [Capital – Drawing + Revenues – Expenses].* After each transaction show the new account totals.

(e) Received cash from a client for professional services, $2,500.

(f) Paid office rent for February, $900.

(g) Paid February telephone bill, $73.

(h) Withdrew cash for personal use, $500.

(i) Performed services for clients on account, $1,000.

(j) Paid wages to part-time employee, $600.

(k) Received cash for services performed on account in (i), $600.

EXERCISE 2-5A **(LO1/5)** **FINANCIAL STATEMENT ACCOUNTS** Label each of the following accounts as an asset (A), liability (L), owner's equity (OE), revenue (R), or expense (E). Indicate the financial statement on which the account belongs—income statement (IS), statement of owner's equity (SOE), or balance sheet (BS)—in a format similar to the following.

Account	Classification	Financial Statement
Cash		
Rent Expense		
Accounts Payable		
Service Fees		
Supplies		
Wages Expense		
Ramon Martinez, Drawing		
Ramon Martinez, Capital		
Prepaid Insurance		
Accounts Receivable		

EXERCISE 2-6A   **(LO5)**
Capital, 6/30: $22,000

STATEMENT OF OWNER'S EQUITY REPORTING NET INCOME Betsy Ray started an accounting service on June 1, 20--, by investing $20,000. Her net income for the month was $10,000 and she withdrew $8,000. Prepare a statement of owner's equity for the month of June.

EXERCISE 2-7A   **(LO5)**
Capital, 6/30: $9,000

STATEMENT OF OWNER'S EQUITY REPORTING NET LOSS Based on the information provided in Exercise 2-6A, prepare a statement of owner's equity assuming Ray had a net loss of $3,000.

SERIES A PROBLEMS

PROBLEM 2-8A   **(LO1/2)**
3: $34,920 = $12,570 + $22,350

THE ACCOUNTING EQUATION Dr. John Schleper is a chiropractor. As of December 31, he owned the following property that related to his professional practice.

Cash	$ 4,750
Office Equipment	$ 6,200
X-ray Equipment	$11,680
Laboratory Equipment	$ 7,920

He also owes the following business suppliers:

Chateau Gas Company	$2,420
Aloe Medical Supply Company	$3,740

REQUIRED

1. From the preceding information, compute the accounting elements and enter them in the accounting equation shown as follows.

Assets	=	Liabilities	+	Owner's Equity
_____	=	_____	+	_____

2. During January, the assets increase by $7,290, and the liabilities increase by $4,210. Compute the resulting accounting equation.
3. During February, the assets decrease by $2,920, and the liabilities increase by $2,200. Compute the resulting accounting equation.

PROBLEM 2-9A   **(LO3/4)**
Total cash following (g): $12,950

PASS
Power Accounting System Software®

EFFECT OF TRANSACTIONS ON ACCOUNTING EQUATION Jay Pembroke started a business. During the first month (April 20--), the following transactions occurred.

(a) Invested cash in business, $18,000.
(b) Bought office supplies for $4,600: $2,000 in cash and $2,600 on account.
(c) Paid one-year insurance premium, $1,200.
(d) Earned revenues totaling $3,300: $1,300 in cash and $2,000 on account.
(e) Paid cash on account to the company that supplied the office supplies in (b), $2,300.
(f) Paid office rent for the month, $750.
(g) Withdrew cash for personal use, $100.

REQUIRED

Show the effect of each transaction on the individual accounts of the expanded accounting equation: *Assets = Liabilities + Owner's Equity [Capital – Drawing + Revenues – Expenses]*. After each transaction, show the new account totals.

PROBLEM 2-10A   **(LO5)**   **INCOME STATEMENT** Based on Problem 2-9A, prepare an income statement for
Net income: $2,550   Jay Pembroke for the month of April 20--.

PROBLEM 2-11A   **(LO5)**   **STATEMENT OF OWNER'S EQUITY** Based on Problem 2-9A, prepare a statement
Capital, 4/30: $20,450   of owner's equity for Jay Pembroke for the month of April 20--.

PROBLEM 2-12A   **(LO5)**   **BALANCE SHEET** Based on Problem 2-9A, prepare a balance sheet for Jay
Total assets, 4/30: $20,750   Pembroke as of April 30, 20--.

SERIES B EXERCISES

EXERCISE 2-1B   **(LO1)**   **ACCOUNTING ELEMENTS** Label each of the following accounts as an asset (A),
liability (L), or owner's equity (OE) using the following format.

Account	Classification
Cash	
Accounts Payable	
Supplies	
Bill Jones, Drawing	
Prepaid Insurance	
Accounts Receivable	
Bill Jones, Capital	

EXERCISE 2-2B   **(LO2)**   **THE ACCOUNTING EQUATION** Using the accounting equation, compute the
missing elements.

Assets	=	Liabilities	+	Owner's Equity
_____	=	$20,000	+	$5,000
$30,000	=	$15,000	+	_____
$20,000	=	_____	+	$10,000

EXERCISE 2-3B   **(LO3/4)**   **EFFECTS OF TRANSACTIONS (BALANCE SHEET ACCOUNTS)** Jon Wallace
Assets following (d): $32,500   started a business. During the first month (March 20--), the following transactions
occurred. Show the effect of each transaction on the accounting equation: *Assets
= Liabilities + Owner's Equity*. After each transaction, show the new account
totals.

(a) Invested cash in the business, $30,000.

(b) Bought office equipment on account, $4,500.

(c) Bought office equipment for cash, $1,600.

(d) Paid cash on account to supplier in (b), $2,000.

EXERCISE 2-4B   **(LO3/4)**
Assets following (k): $34,032

EFFECTS OF TRANSACTIONS (REVENUE, EXPENSE, WITHDRAWALS) Assume Jon Wallace completed the following additional transactions during March. Show the effect of each transaction on the basic elements of the expanded accounting equation: *Assets = Liabilities + Owner's Equity [Capital – Drawing + Revenues – Expenses].* After each transaction show the new account totals.

(e) Performed services and received cash, $3,000.

(f) Paid rent for March, $1,000.

(g) Paid March telephone bill, $68.

(h) Jon Wallace withdrew cash for personal use, $800.

(i) Performed services for clients on account, $900.

(j) Paid wages to part-time employee, $500.

(k) Received cash for services performed on account in (i), $500.

EXERCISE 2-5B   **(LO1/5)**

FINANCIAL STATEMENT ACCOUNTS Label each of the following accounts as an asset (A), liability (L), owner's equity (OE), revenue (R), or expense (E). Indicate the financial statement on which the account belongs—income statement (IS), statement of owner's equity (SOE), or balance sheet (BS)—in a format similar to the following.

Account	Classification	Financial Statement
Cash		
Rent Expense		
Accounts Payable		
Service Fees		
Supplies		
Wages Expense		
Amanda Wong, Drawing		
Amanda Wong, Capital		
Prepaid Insurance		
Accounts Receivable		

EXERCISE 2-6B   **(LO5)**
Capital, 6/30: $14,000

STATEMENT OF OWNER'S EQUITY REPORTING NET INCOME Efran Lopez started a financial consulting service on June 1, 20--, by investing $15,000. His net income for the month was $6,000 and he withdrew $7,000 for personal use. Prepare a statement of owner's equity for the month of June.

EXERCISE 2-7B   **(LO5)**
Capital, 6/30: $6,000

STATEMENT OF OWNER'S EQUITY REPORTING NET LOSS Based on the information provided in Exercise 2-6B, prepare a statement of owner's equity assuming Lopez had a net loss of $2,000.

SERIES B PROBLEMS

PROBLEM 2-8B   **(LO1/2)**
3: $25,235 = $10,165 + $15,070

THE ACCOUNTING EQUATION Dr. Patricia Parsons is a dentist. As of January 31, Parsons owned the following property that related to her professional practice:

Cash	$3,560
Office Equipment	$4,600
X-ray Equipment	$8,760
Laboratory Equipment	$5,940

She also owes the following business suppliers:

Cupples Gas Company	$1,815
Swan Dental Lab	$2,790

REQUIRED

1. From the preceding information, compute the accounting elements and enter them in the accounting equation as shown below.

Assets	=	Liabilities	+	Owner's Equity
_____	=	_____	+	_____

2. During February, the assets increase by $4,565, and the liabilities increase by $3,910. Compute the resulting accounting equation.

3. During March, the assets decrease by $2,190, and the liabilities increase by $1,650. Compute the resulting accounting equation.

PROBLEM 2-9B   **(LO3/4)**

Total cash following (g): $11,300

EFFECT OF TRANSACTIONS ON ACCOUNTING EQUATION David Segal started a business. During the first month (October 20--), the following transactions occurred.

(a) Invested cash in the business, $15,000.

(b) Bought office supplies for $3,800: $1,800 in cash and $2,000 on account.

(c) Paid one-year insurance premium, $1,000.

(d) Earned revenues amounting to $2,700: $1,700 in cash and $1,000 on account.

(e) Paid cash on account to the company that supplied the office supplies in (b), $1,800.

(f) Paid office rent for the month, $650.

(g) Withdrew cash for personal use, $150.

REQUIRED

Show the effect of each transaction on the individual accounts of the expanded accounting equation: *Assets = Liabilities + Owner's Equity [Capital – Drawing + Revenues – Expenses].* After each transaction, show the new account totals.

PROBLEM 2-10B   **(LO5)**

Net income: $2,050

INCOME STATEMENT Based on Problem 2-9B, prepare an income statement for David Segal for the month of October 20--.

PROBLEM 2-11B   **(LO5)**

Capital, 10/31: $16,900

STATEMENT OF OWNER'S EQUITY Based on Problem 2-9B, prepare a statement of owner's equity for David Segal for the month of October 20--.

PROBLEM 2-12B   **(LO5)**

Total assets, 10/31: $17,100

BALANCE SHEET Based on Problem 2-9B, prepare a balance sheet for David Segal as of October 31, 20--.

MASTERY PROBLEM

Cash following (p): $3,105;
Revenue following (p): $2,100

Lisa Vozniak started her own business, We Do Windows. She offers interior and exterior window cleaning for local area residents. Lisa rents a garage to store her tools and cleaning supplies and has a part-time assistant to answer the phone and handle third-story work. (Lisa is afraid of heights.) The transactions for the month of July are as follows:

(a) On the first day of the month, Vozniak invested cash by making a deposit in a bank account for the business, $8,000.

(b) Paid rent for July, $150.

(c) Purchased a used van for cash, $5,000.

(d) Purchased tools on account from Clean Tools, $600.

(e) Purchased cleaning supplies that cost $300. Paid $200 cash and will pay the balance next month, $100.

(f) Paid part-time assistant (wages) for first half of month, $100.

(g) Paid for advertising, $75.

(h) Paid two-year premium for liability insurance on van, $480.

(i) Received cash from clients for services performed, $800.

(j) Performed cleaning services for clients on account, $500.

(k) Paid telephone bill, $40.

(l) Received cash from clients for window cleaning performed on account in (j), $200.

(m) Paid part-time assistant (wages) for last half of month, $150.

(n) Made partial payment on tools purchased in (d), $200.

(o) Earned additional revenues amounting to $800: $600 in cash and $200 on account.

(p) Vozniak withdrew cash at the end of the month for personal expenses, $100.

REQUIRED

1. Enter the above transactions in an accounting equation similar to the one illustrated below. After each transaction, show the new amount for each account.

Assets (Items Owned)						=	Liabilities (Amounts Owed)	+	Owner's Equity (Owner's Investment + Earnings)				
Cash	+ Accounts Receivable	+ Supplies	+ Prepaid Insurance	+ Tools	+ Van	=	Accounts Payable	+	Lisa Vozniak Capital	– Lisa Vozniak Drawing	+ Revenues	– Expenses	Description

2. Compute the ending balances for all accounts.

3. Prepare an income statement for We Do Windows for the month of July 20--.

4. Prepare a statement of owner's equity for We Do Windows for the month of July 20--.

5. Prepare a balance sheet for We Do Windows as of July 31, 20--.

CHALLENGE PROBLEM

This problem challenges you to apply your cumulative accounting knowledge to move a step beyond the material in the chapter.

Cash from operating activities: $2,165

In this chapter you learned about three important financial statements: the income statement, statement of owner's equity, and balance sheet. As mentioned in the margin note on page 31, most firms also prepare a statement of cash flows. Part of this statement reports the **cash received** from customers, and **cash paid** for goods and services.

REQUIRED

Take another look at the Demonstration Problem for Damon Young's "Home and Away Inspections." Note that when revenues are measured based on the amount earned, and expenses are measured based on the amount incurred, net income for the period was $4,165. Now, compute the difference between cash received from customers and cash paid to suppliers of goods and services by completing the form provided below. Are these measures different? Which provides a better measure of profitability?

Cash from customers _____

Cash paid for wages _____

Cash paid for rent _____

Cash paid for utilities _____

Cash paid for insurance _____

Cash paid for supplies _____

Cash paid for telephone _____

Total cash paid for operating items _____

Difference between cash received from
    customers and cash paid for goods
    and services _____

©DIGITAL IMAGING GROUP

The Double-Entry Framework

How do you keep track of your personal finances? Perhaps you make a list of your earnings and other cash inflows. Then you prepare a list of how the money was spent. Jessie needs to do this, too. However, since businesses earn and spend money in many different ways, and enter thousands of transactions, a systematic approach must be followed. This is called the double-entry framework. Could you use this double-entry system for your personal finances, or for a small business that you might start?

Careful study of this chapter should enable you to:

LO1 Define the parts of a T account.

LO2 Foot and balance a T account.

LO3 Describe the effects of debits and credits on specific types of accounts.

LO4 Use T accounts to analyze transactions.

LO5 Prepare a trial balance and explain its purposes and linkages with the financial statements.

The terms asset, liability, owner's equity, revenue, and expense were explained in Chapter 2. Examples showed how individual business transactions change one or more of these basic accounting elements. Each transaction had a dual effect. An increase or decrease in any asset, liability, owner's equity, revenue, or expense was *always* accompanied by an offsetting change within the basic accounting elements. The fact that each transaction has a dual effect upon the accounting elements provides the basis for what is called **double-entry accounting**. To understand double-entry accounting, it is important to learn how T accounts work and the role of debits and credits in accounting.

THE T ACCOUNT

LO1 Define the parts of a T account.

The assets of a business may consist of a number of items, such as cash, accounts receivable, equipment, buildings, and land. The liabilities may consist of one or more items, such as accounts payable and notes payable. Similarly, owner's equity may consist of the owner's investments and various revenue and expense items. A separate account is used to record the increases and decreases in each type of asset, liability, owner's equity, revenue, and expense.

The T account gets its name from the fact that it resembles the letter T. As shown below, there are three major parts of an account:

1. the title,

2. the debit, or left side, and

3. the credit, or right side.

Title	
Debit = Left	Credit = Right

The debit side is always on the left and the credit side is always on the right. This is true for all types of asset, liability, owner's equity, revenue, and expense accounts.

 LEARNING KEY: Debit means left and credit means right.

BALANCING A T ACCOUNT

LO2 Foot and balance a T account.

To determine the balance of a T account at any time, simply total the dollar amounts on the debit and credit sides. These totals are known as **footings**. The difference between the footings is called the **balance** of the account. This amount is then written on the side with the larger footing.

In Chapter 2, the accounting equation was used to analyze business transactions. This required columns in which to record the increases and decreases in various accounts. Let's compare this approach with the use of a T account for the transactions affecting cash. When a T account is used, increases in cash are recorded on the debit side and decreases are recorded on the credit side. Transactions for Jessie Jane's Campus Delivery are shown in Figure 3-1.

COLUMNAR SUMMARY (From Chapter 2, page 27)		T ACCOUNT FORM	
Transaction	**Cash**		
(a)	2,000		
(b)	(1,200)		
(d)	(300)		
(e)	500		
(f)	(200)		
(g)	(50)		
(i)	(80)		
(j)	(200)		
(k)	570		
(l)	(300)		
(m)	(650)		
(n)	430		
(o)	(150)		
Balance	**370**		

Cash

	Debit		Credit
(a)	2,000	(b)	1,200
(e)	500	(d)	300
(k)	570	(f)	200
(n)	430	(g)	50
footing →	**3,500**	(i)	80
		(j)	200
		(l)	300
		(m)	650
Balance →	370	(o)	150
			3,130 ← footing

FIGURE 3-1   Cash T Account

DEBITS AND CREDITS

LO3 Describe the effects of debits and credits on specific types of accounts.

Abbreviations:
Often debit and credit are abbreviated as:
Dr. = Debit
Cr. = Credit
(based on the Latin terms "debere" and "credere")

To **debit** an account means to enter an amount on the left or debit side of the account. To **credit** an account means to enter an amount on the right or credit side of the account. *Debits may increase* **or** *decrease the balances of specific accounts. This is also true for credits. To learn how to use debits and credits, it is best to reflect on the accounting equation.*

Assets		=	Liabilities		+	Owner's Equity	
Debit	**Credit**		**Debit**	**Credit**		**Debit**	**Credit**
+	–		–	+		–	+

Assets

Assets are on the left side of the accounting equation. Therefore, increases are entered on the left (debit) side of an asset account and decreases are entered on the right (credit) side.

Liabilities and Owner's Equity

Liabilities and owner's equity are on the right side of the equation. Therefore, increases are entered on the right (credit) side and decreases are entered on the left (debit) side.

LEARNING KEY: Debits increase assets and decrease liabilities and owner's equity. Credits decrease assets and increase liabilities and owner's equity.

Normal Balances

A **normal balance** is the side of an account that is increased. Since assets are debited for increases, these accounts normally have **debit balances**. Since liability and owner's equity accounts are credited for increases, these accounts normally have **credit balances**. Figure 3-2 shows the relationship between normal balances and debits and credits.

ACCOUNT	SIDE OF ACCOUNTING EQUATION	INCREASE	DECREASE	NORMAL BALANCE
Assets	Left	Debit	Credit	Debit
Liabilities	Right	Credit	Debit	Credit
Owner's Equity	Right	Credit	Debit	Credit

FIGURE 3-2 Normal Balances

Expanding the accounting equation helps illustrate the use of debits and credits for revenue, expense, and drawing accounts. Since these accounts affect owner's equity, they are shown under the "umbrella" of owner's equity in the accounting equation in Figure 3-3.

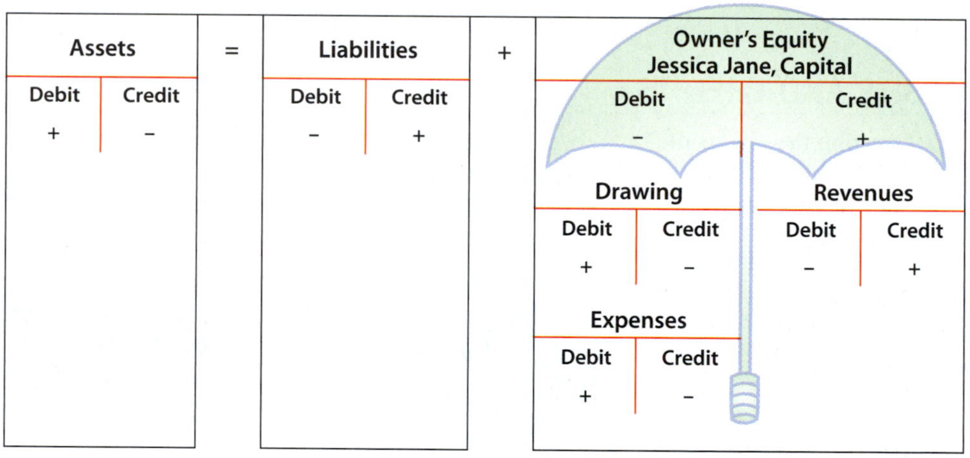

FIGURE 3-3 The Accounting Equation and the Owner's Equity Umbrella

Revenues

Revenues increase owner's equity. Revenues could be recorded directly on the credit side of the owner's capital account. However, readers of financial statements are interested in the specific types of revenues earned. Therefore, specific revenue accounts, like Delivery Fees, Sales, and Service Fees, are used. These specific accounts are credited when revenue is earned.

Expenses

Expenses decrease owner's equity. Expenses could be recorded on the debit side of the owner's capital account. However, readers of financial statements want to see the types of expenses incurred during the accounting period. Thus, specific expense accounts are maintained for items like rent, wages, advertising, and utilities. These specific accounts are debited as expenses are incurred.

 LEARNING KEY: You could credit the owner's capital account for revenues and debit the capital account for expenses and withdrawals. However, this is not a good idea. Using specific accounts provides additional information. Remember: an increase in an expense decreases owner's equity.

Drawing

Withdrawals of cash and other assets by the owner for personal reasons decrease owner's equity. Withdrawals could be debited directly to the owner's capital account. However, readers of financial statements want to know the amount of withdrawals for the accounting period. Thus, this information is kept in a separate account.

Normal Balances for the Owner's Equity Umbrella

Since expense and drawing accounts are debited for increases, these accounts normally have debit balances. Since revenue accounts are credited for increases, these accounts normally have credit balances. Figure 3-4 shows the normal balances for the owner's equity accounts.

ACCOUNT	SIDE OF OWNER'S EQUITY UMBRELLA	INCREASE	DECREASE	NORMAL
Revenues	Right	Credit	Debit	Credit
Expenses	Left	Debit	Credit	Debit
Drawing	Left	Debit	Credit	Debit

FIGURE 3-4 Normal Balances for the Owner's Equity Umbrella

TRANSACTION ANALYSIS

LO4 **Use T accounts to analyze transactions.**

In Chapter 2, you learned how to analyze transactions by using the accounting equation. Here, we continue to use the accounting equation, but add debits and credits by using T accounts. As shown in Figure 3-5, the three basic questions that must be answered when analyzing a transaction are essentially the same, but are expanded slightly to address the use of the owner's equity umbrella and T accounts. You must determine the location of the account within the accounting equation and/or the owner's equity umbrella. You must also determine whether the accounts should be debited or credited.

1. **What happened?**
   Make certain you understand the event that has taken place.

2. **Which accounts are affected?**
   Once you have determined what happened, you must:
   ■ Identify the accounts that are affected.
   ■ Classify these accounts as assets, liabilities, owner's equity, revenues, or expenses.
   ■ Identify the location of the accounts in the accounting equation and/or the owner's equity umbrella—left or right.

3. **How is the accounting equation affected?**
   ■ Determine whether the accounts have increased or decreased.
   ■ Determine whether the accounts should be debited or credited.
   ■ Make certain that the accounting equation remains in balance after the transaction has been entered.
   (1) Assets = Liabilities + Owner's Equity.
   (2) Debits = Credits for every transaction.

FIGURE 3-5   Steps in Transaction Analysis

LEARNING KEY: If you have a debit, you must always have at least one credit. If you have a credit, you must always have at least one debit.

Debits and Credits: Asset, Liability, and Owner's Equity Accounts

Transactions (a) through (d) from Jessie Jane's Campus Delivery (Chapter 2) demonstrate the double-entry process for transactions affecting asset, liability, and owner's equity accounts.

As you study each transaction, answer the three questions: (1) What happened? (2) Which accounts are affected? and (3) How is the accounting equation affected? The transaction statement tells you what happened. The analysis following the illustration of each transaction tells which accounts are affected. The illustration shows you how the accounting equation is affected.

Transaction (a): Investment by owner
Jessica Jane opened a bank account with a deposit of $2,000 for her business (Figure 3-6).

Analysis: As a result of this transaction, the business acquired an asset, Cash. In exchange for the asset, the business gave Jessica Jane owner's equity. The owner's equity account is called Jessica Jane, Capital. The transaction is entered as an increase in an asset and an increase in owner's equity. Debit Cash and credit Jessica Jane, Capital for $2,000.

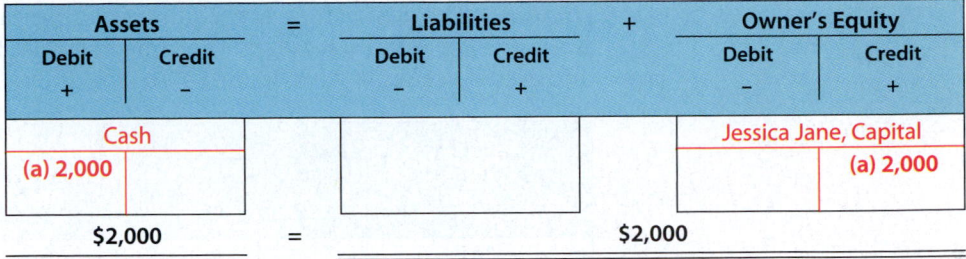

ACCOUNT AFFECTED	CLASSIFICATION	LOCATION IN EQUATION	INCREASE OR DECREASE	DEBIT OR CREDIT
Cash	Asset	Left	Increase	Debit
Capital	Owner's Equity	Right	Increase	Credit

FIGURE 3-6 Transaction (a): Investment by Owner

Transaction (b): Purchase of an asset for cash

Jessie bought a motor scooter (delivery equipment) for $1,200 cash (Figure 3-7).

Analysis: Jessie exchanged one asset, Cash, for another, Delivery Equipment. Debit Delivery Equipment and credit Cash for $1,200. Notice that the total assets are still $2,000 as they were following transaction (a). Transaction (b) shifted assets from cash to delivery equipment, but total assets remained the same.

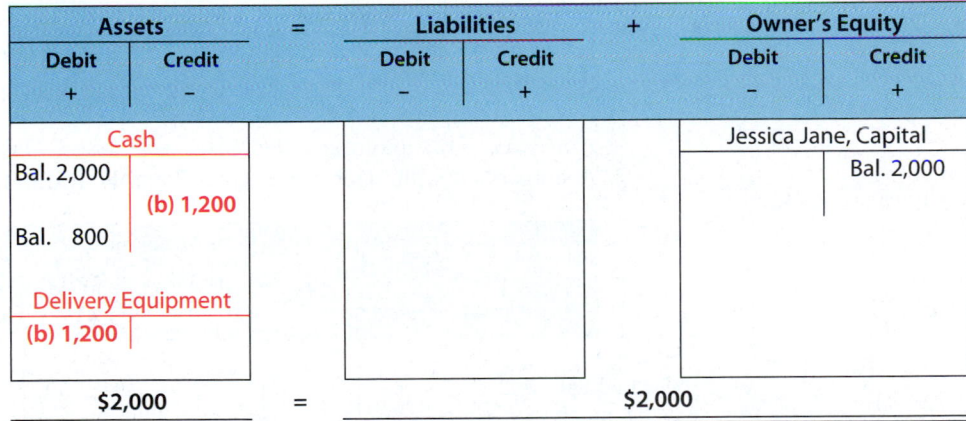

ACCOUNT AFFECTED	CLASSIFICATION	LOCATION IN EQUATION	INCREASE OR DECREASE	DEBIT OR CREDIT
Delivery Equipment	Asset	Left	Increase	Debit
Cash	Asset	Left	Decrease	Credit

FIGURE 3-7 Transaction (b): Purchase of an Asset for Cash

Transaction (c): Purchase of an asset on account

Jessie bought a second motor scooter on account for $900 (Figure 3-8).

Analysis: The asset, Delivery Equipment, increases by $900 and the liability, Accounts Payable, increases by the same amount. Thus, debit Delivery Equipment and credit Accounts Payable for $900.

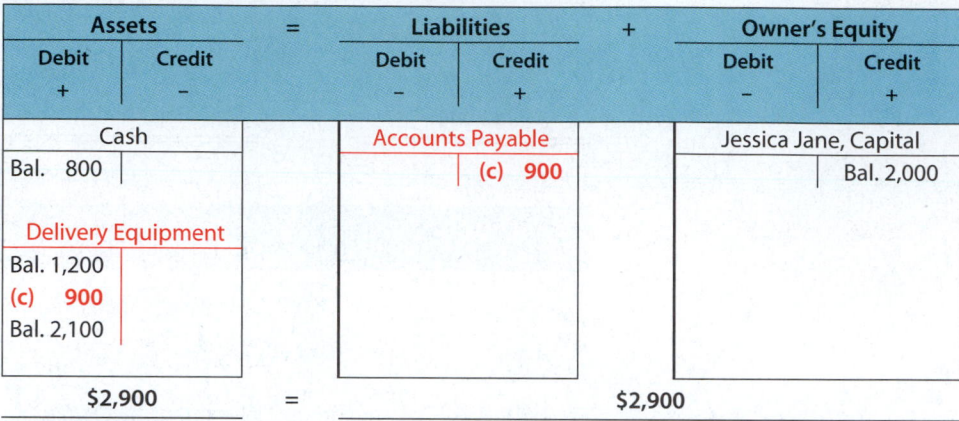

ACCOUNT AFFECTED	CLASSIFICATION	LOCATION IN EQUATION	INCREASE OR DECREASE	DEBIT OR CREDIT
Delivery Equipment	Asset	Left	Increase	Debit
Accounts Payable	Liability	Right	Increase	Credit

FIGURE 3-8 Transaction (c): Purchase of an Asset on Account

Transaction (d): Payment on a loan

Jessie made the first $300 payment on the scooter purchased in transaction (c) (Figure 3-9).

Analysis: This payment decreases the asset, Cash, and decreases the liability, Accounts Payable. Debit Accounts Payable and credit Cash for $300.

Assets	=	Liabilities	+	Owner's Equity

Cash: Bal. 800 / (d) 300 / Bal. 500; Delivery Equipment Bal. 2,100. Accounts Payable: (d) 300 / Bal. 900 / Bal. 600. Jessica Jane, Capital Bal. 2,000.

$2,600 = $2,600

ACCOUNT AFFECTED	CLASSIFICATION	LOCATION IN EQUATION	INCREASE OR DECREASE	DEBIT OR CREDIT
Accounts Payable	Liability	Right	Decrease	Debit
Cash	Asset	Left	Decrease	Credit

FIGURE 3-9   Transaction (d): Payment on a Loan

Notice that for transactions (a) through (d), the debits equal credits and the accounting equation is in balance. Review transactions (a) through (d). Again, identify the accounts that were affected and how they were classified (assets, liabilities, or owner's equity). Finally, note each account's location within the accounting equation.

Debits and Credits: Including Revenues, Expenses, and Drawing

Transactions (a) through (d) involved only assets, liabilities, and the owner's capital account. To complete the illustration of Jessie Jane's Campus Delivery, the equation is expanded to include revenues, expenses, and drawing. Remember, revenues increase owner's equity and are shown under the credit side of the capital account. Expenses and drawing decrease owner's equity and are shown under the debit side of the capital account. The expanded equation is shown in Figure 3-10.

LEARNING KEY: Credits increase the capital account. Revenues increase capital. Thus, revenues are shown under the credit side of the capital account. Debits decrease the capital account. Expenses and drawing reduce owner's equity. Thus, they are shown under the debit side of the capital account.

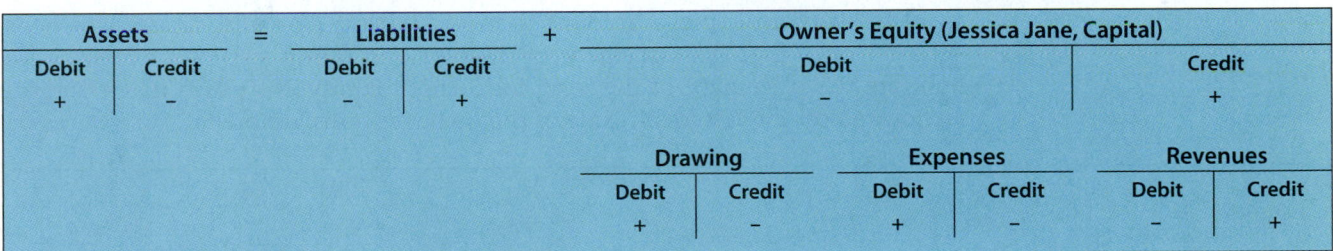

FIGURE 3-10   The Expanded Accounting Equation

Transaction (e): Delivery revenues earned in cash
Jessie made deliveries and received $500 cash from clients (Figure 3-11).

Analysis: The asset, Cash, and the revenue, Delivery Fees, increase. Debit Cash and credit Delivery Fees for $500.

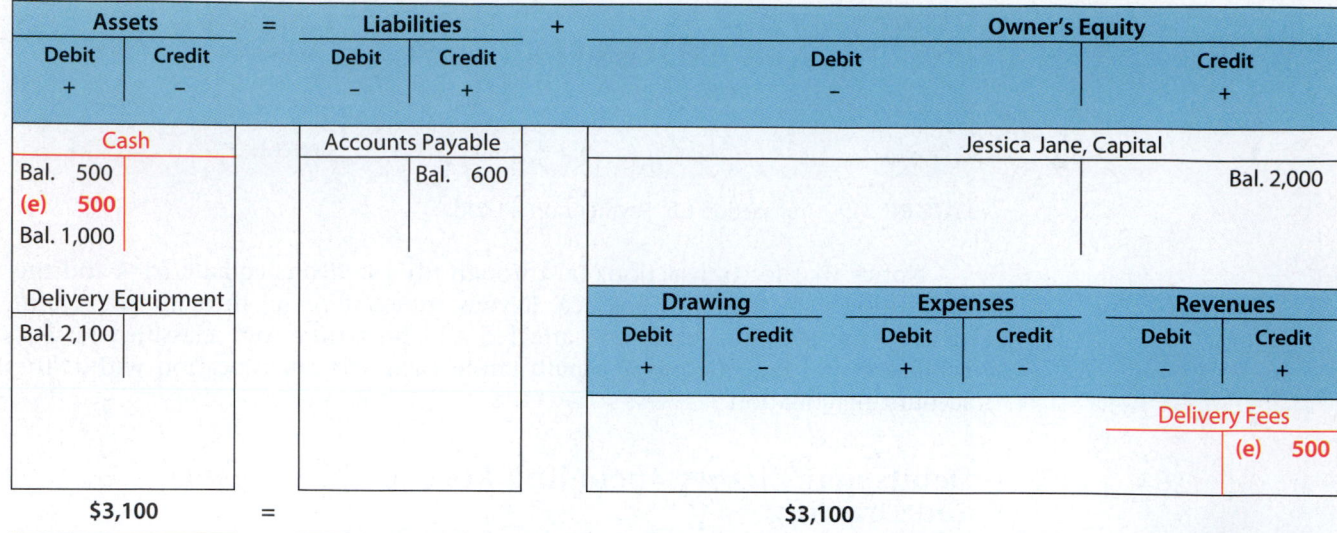

ACCOUNT AFFECTED	CLASSIFICATION	LOCATION IN EQUATION	INCREASE OR DECREASE	DEBIT OR CREDIT
Cash	Asset	Left	Increase	Debit
Delivery Fees	Revenue	Right O.E.—Right Side	Increase	Credit

FIGURE 3-11   Transaction (e): Delivery Revenues Earned in Cash

Transaction (f): Paid rent for month

Jessie paid $200 for office rent for June (Figure 3-12).

Analysis: Rent Expense increases and Cash decreases. Debit Rent Expense and credit Cash for $200.

A debit to an expense account *increases* that expense and *decreases* owner's equity. Notice that the placement of the plus and minus signs for expenses are opposite the placement of the signs for owner's equity. Note also that expenses are located on the left (debit) side of the owner's equity umbrella.

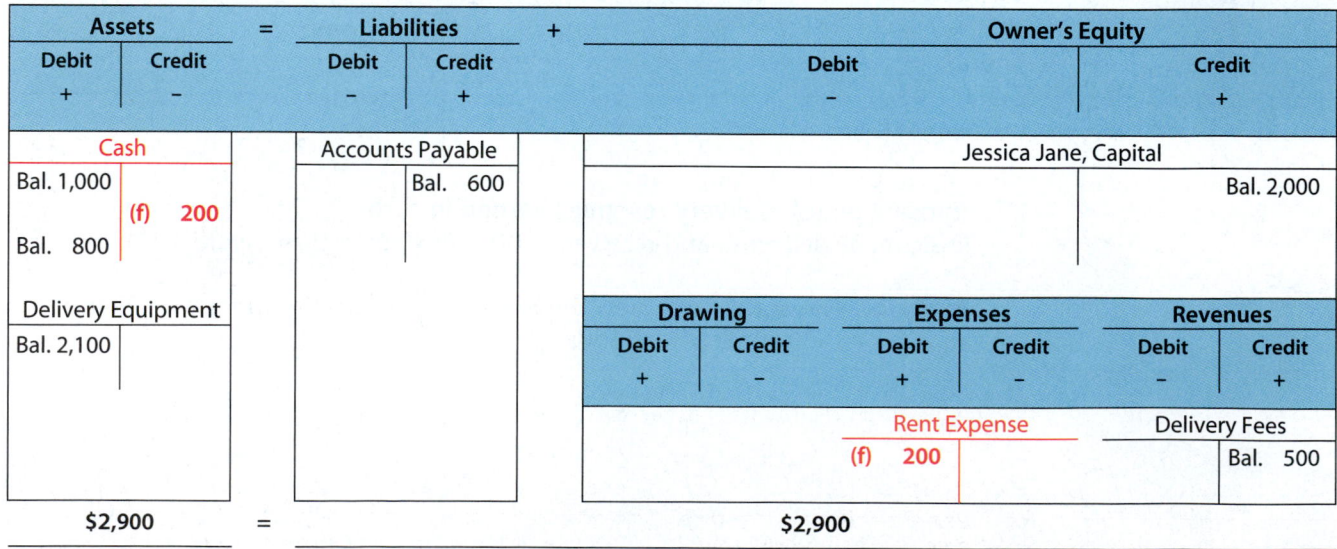

ACCOUNT AFFECTED	CLASSIFICATION	LOCATION IN EQUATION	INCREASE OR DECREASE	DEBIT OR CREDIT
Rent Expense	Expense	Right O.E.—Left Side	Exp.— Increases; O.E.— Decreases	Debit
Cash	Asset	Left	Decrease	Credit

FIGURE 3-12   Transaction (f): Paid Rent for Month

Transaction (g): Paid telephone bill

Jessie paid for telephone service, $50 (Figure 3-13).

Analysis: This transaction, like the previous one, increases an expense and decreases an asset. Debit Telephone Expense and credit Cash for $50.

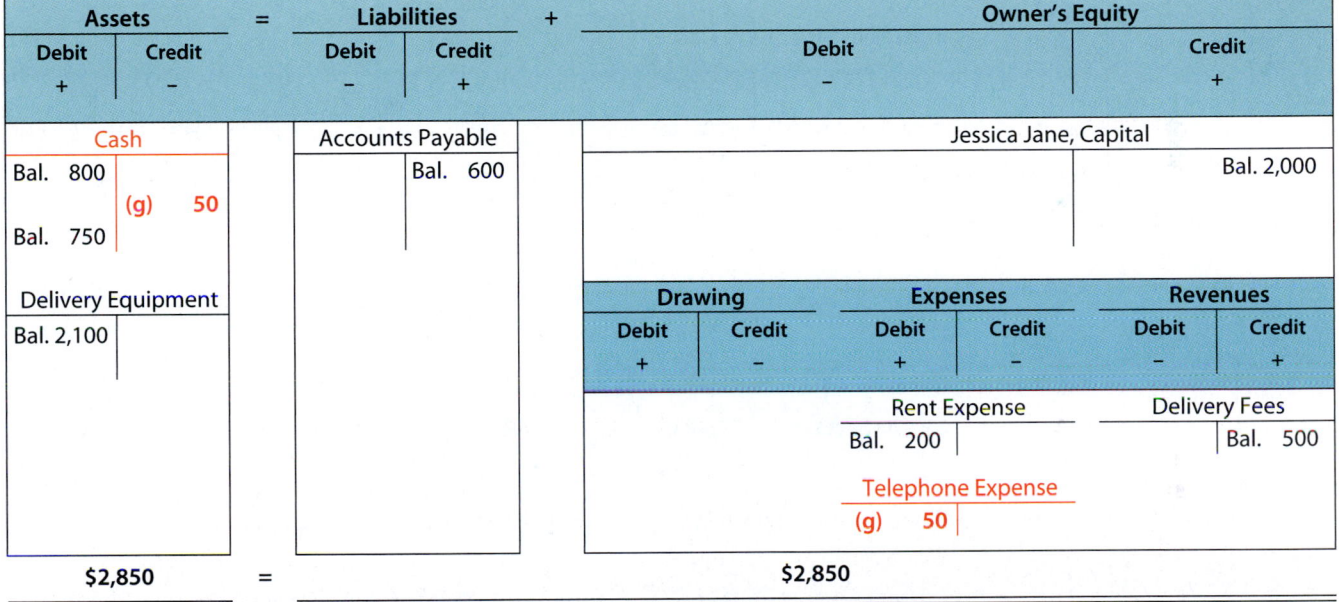

ACCOUNT AFFECTED	CLASSIFICATION	LOCATION IN EQUATION	INCREASE OR DECREASE	DEBIT OR CREDIT
Tele. Expense	Expense	Right O.E.—Left Side	Exp.— Increases; O.E.— Decreases	Debit
Cash	Asset	Left	Decrease	Credit

FIGURE 3-13   Transaction (g): Paid Telephone Bill

Transaction (h): Delivery revenues earned on account

Jessie made deliveries on account for $600 (Figure 3-14).

Analysis: As discussed in Chapter 2, delivery services are performed for which payment will be received later. This is called offering services "on account" or "on credit." Instead of receiving cash, Jessie receives a promise that her customers will pay cash in the future. Therefore, the asset, Accounts Receivable, increases. Since revenues are recognized when earned, the revenue account, Delivery Fees, also increases. Debit Accounts Receivable and credit Delivery Fees for $600.

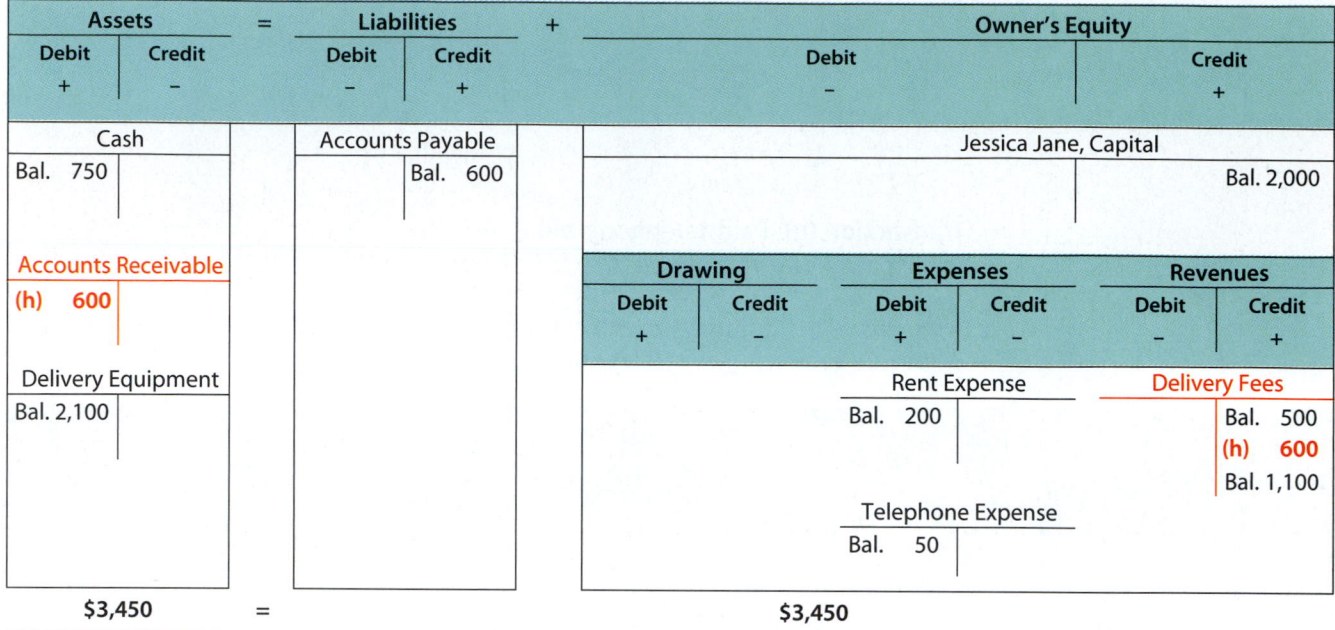

ACCOUNT AFFECTED	CLASSIFICATION	LOCATION IN EQUATION	INCREASE OR DECREASE	DEBIT OR CREDIT
Accounts Rec.	Asset	Left	Increase	Debit
Delivery Fees	Revenue	Right O.E.—Right Side	Increase	Credit

FIGURE 3-14   Transaction (h): Delivery Revenues Earned on Account

Review transactions (e) through (h). Two of these transactions are expenses and two are revenue transactions. Each of these transactions affected the owner's equity umbrella. Three transactions affected Cash and one transaction affected Accounts Receivable. Keep in mind that expense and revenue transactions do not always affect cash.

Notice that the debits equal credits and the accounting equation is in balance after each transaction. As you review transactions (e) through (h), identify the accounts that were affected and classify each account (assets, liabilities, owner's equity, revenue, or expense). Notice each account's location within the accounting equation and the owner's equity umbrella.

Upcoming transactions (i) and (j) both involve an exchange of cash for another asset. As you analyze these two transactions and answer the three questions about these transactions, you may wonder why prepaid insurance and supplies are assets while the rent and telephone bill in transactions (f) and (g) are expenses. Prepaid insurance and supplies are assets because they will provide benefits for more than one month. Jessie pays her rent and her telephone bill each month so they are classified as expenses. If Jessie paid her rent only once every three months, she would need to set up an asset account called Prepaid Rent. She would debit this account when she paid the rent.

Transaction (i): Purchase of supplies
Jessie bought pens, paper, delivery envelopes, and other supplies for $80 cash (Figure 3-15).

Analysis: These supplies will last for several months. Since they will generate future benefits, the supplies should be recorded as an asset. An asset, Supplies, increases, and an asset, Cash, decreases. Debit Supplies and credit Cash for $80.

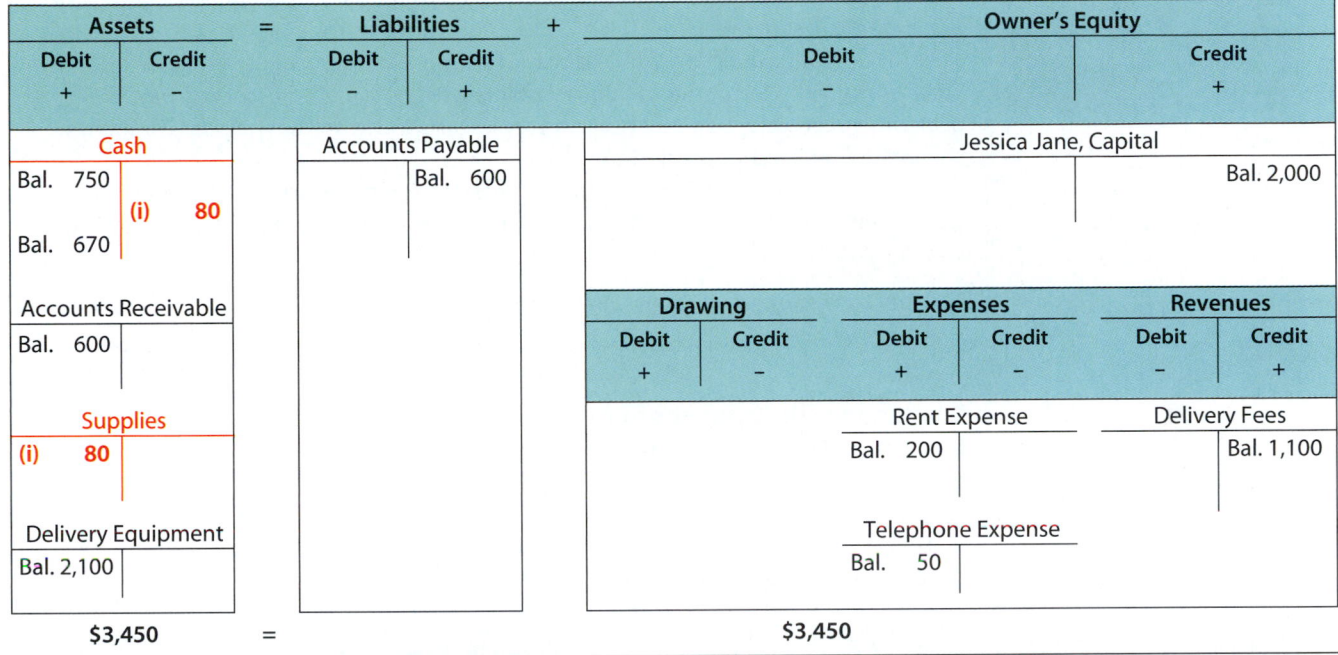

ACCOUNT AFFECTED	CLASSIFICATION	LOCATION IN EQUATION	INCREASE OR DECREASE	DEBIT OR CREDIT
Supplies	Asset	Left	Increase	Debit
Cash	Asset	Left	Decrease	Credit

FIGURE 3-15   Transaction (i): Purchase of Supplies

A BROADER VIEW
Supplies—Asset or Expense?

When businesses buy office supplies from Staples or other suppliers, the supplies are initially recorded as assets. This is done because the supplies will provide future benefits. Those still remaining at the end of the accounting period are reported on the balance sheet as assets. Supplies actually used during the period are recognized as an expense on the income statement. We will discuss how to account for the expense in Chapter 5.

PROFILES IN ACCOUNTING

Jeanette Anderson, Factory Accounting Clerk

Jeanette Anderson earned a 4.0 GPA and membership in Phi Theta Kappa while completing her Associate Degree in Business at Eastern Wyoming College. While on campus, she held a work-study job as an Instructor Assistant. In this position Jeanette demonstrated a sound work ethic, an ability to get along well with others, and competence.

After graduation, she went to work for Imperial/Holly Sugar Corp. in Torrington, WY. Her duties include working with automated accounts payable, accounts receivable, and inventory control. During the annual harvest campaign, she supervises data entry clerks.

Jeanette believes the key to her success has been her understanding of double-entry accounting combined with her computer skills. Possessing problem-solving skills and being flexible are also important.

Source: Jack Kappeler, Eastern Wyoming College

Transaction (j): Payment of insurance premium

Jessie paid $200 for an eight-month liability insurance policy (Figure 3-16).

Analysis: Since insurance is paid in advance and will provide future benefits, it is treated as an asset. Therefore, one asset, Prepaid Insurance, increases and another, Cash, decreases. Debit Prepaid Insurance and credit Cash for $200.

Assets		=	Liabilities		+	Owner's Equity			
Debit	Credit		Debit	Credit		Debit			Credit
+	–		–	+		–			+

Cash
Bal. 670
(j) 200
Bal. 470

Accounts Receivable
Bal. 600

Supplies
Bal. 80

Prepaid Insurance
(j) 200

Delivery Equipment
Bal. 2,100

Accounts Payable
Bal. 600

Jessica Jane, Capital
Bal. 2,000

Drawing		Expenses		Revenues	
Debit	Credit	Debit	Credit	Debit	Credit
+	–	+	–	–	+

Rent Expense
Bal. 200

Delivery Fees
Bal. 1,100

Telephone Expense
Bal. 50

$3,450 = $3,450

ACCOUNT AFFECTED	CLASSIFICATION	LOCATION IN EQUATION	INCREASE OR DECREASE	DEBIT OR CREDIT
Prepaid Insurance	Asset	Left	Increase	Debit
Cash	Asset	Left	Decrease	Credit

FIGURE 3-16   Transaction (j): Payment of Insurance Premium

Transaction (k): Cash receipts from prior sales on account

Jessie received $570 in cash for delivery services performed for customers earlier in the month (see transaction (h)) (Figure 3-17).

Analysis: This transaction increases Cash and reduces the amount due from customers reported in Accounts Receivable. Debit Cash and credit Accounts Receivable $570.

As you analyze transaction (k), notice which accounts are affected and the location of these accounts in the accounting equation. Jessie received cash, but this transaction did not affect revenue. The revenue was recorded in transaction (h). Transaction (k) is an exchange of one asset (Accounts Receivable) for another asset (Cash).

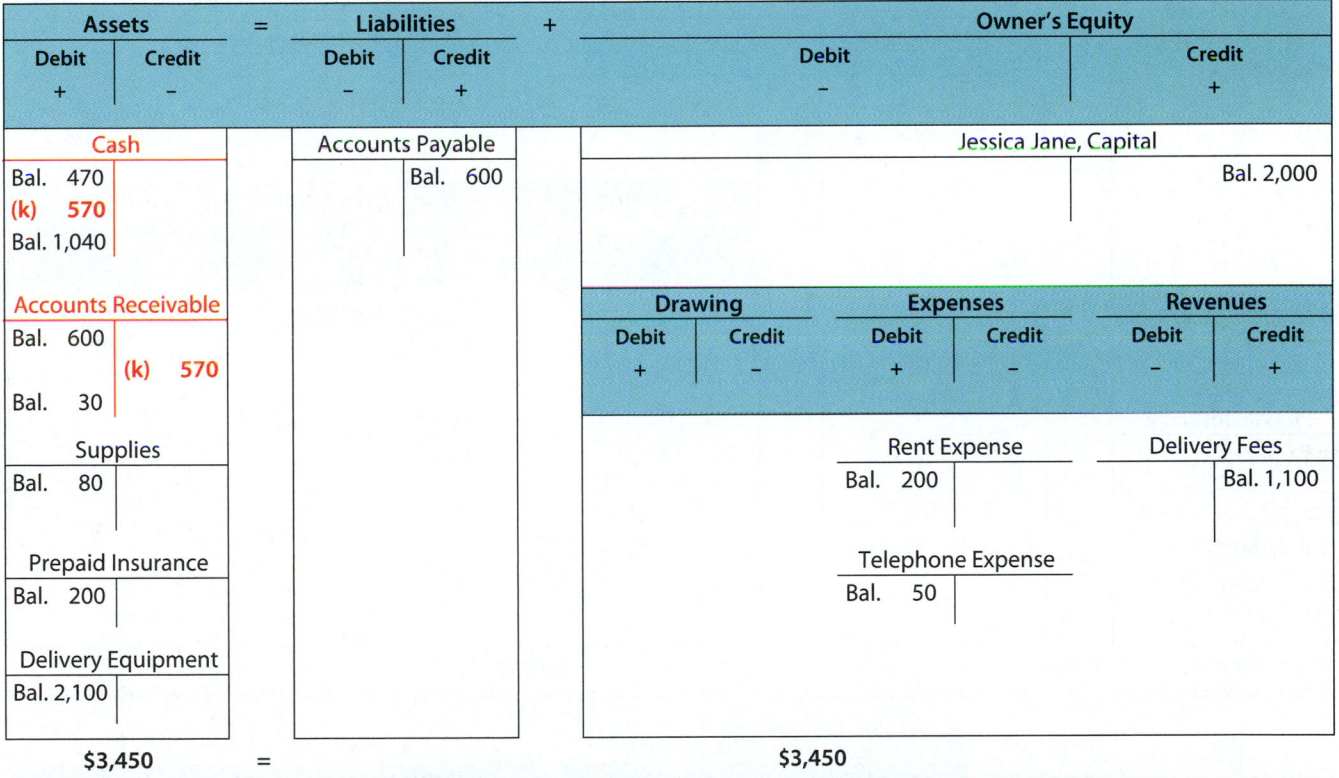

ACCOUNT AFFECTED	CLASSIFICATION	LOCATION IN EQUATION	INCREASE OR DECREASE	DEBIT OR CREDIT
Cash	Asset	Left	Increase	Debit
Accounts Rec.	Asset	Left	Decrease	Credit

FIGURE 3-17   Transaction (k): Cash Receipts from Prior Sales on Account

As you analyze transactions (l) through (o), make certain that you understand what has happened in each transaction. Identify the accounts that are affected and the locations of these accounts within the accounting equation. Notice that the accounting equation remains in balance after every transaction and debits equal credits for each transaction.

Transaction (l): Purchase of an asset on credit making a partial payment

Jessie bought a third motor scooter for $1,500. Jessie made a down payment of $300 and spread the remaining payments over the next four months (Figure 3-18).

Analysis: The asset, Delivery Equipment, increases by $1,500, Cash decreases by $300, and the liability, Accounts Payable, increases by $1,200. Thus, debit Delivery Equipment for $1,500, credit Cash for $300, and credit Accounts Payable for $1,200. This transaction requires one debit and two credits. Even so, total debits ($1,500) equal the total credits ($1,200 + $300) and the accounting equation remains in balance.

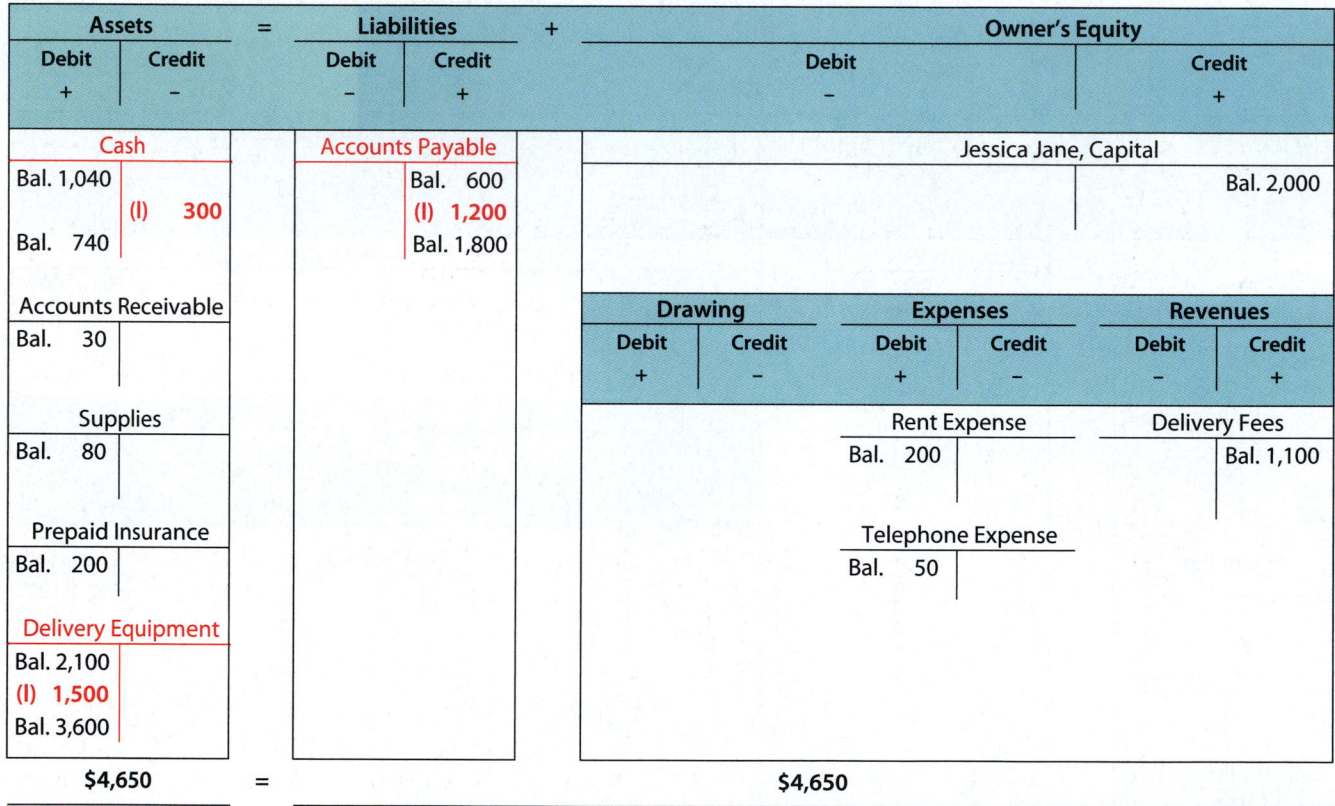

ACCOUNT AFFECTED	CLASSIFICATION	LOCATION IN EQUATION	INCREASE OR DECREASE	DEBIT OR CREDIT
Delivery Equip.	Asset	Left	Increase	Debit
Cash	Asset	Left	Decrease	Credit
Accounts Payable	Liability	Right	Increase	Credit

FIGURE 3-18   Transaction (l): Purchase of an Asset on Credit Making a Partial Payment

Transaction (m): Payment of wages

Jessie paid her part-time employees $650 in wages (Figure 3-19).

Analysis: This is an additional business expense. Wages Expense increases and Cash decreases. Debit Wages Expense and credit Cash for $650.

Assets		=	Liabilities		+	Owner's Equity		
Debit	Credit		Debit	Credit		Debit		Credit
+	–		–	+		–		+

Cash			Accounts Payable			Jessica Jane, Capital	
Bal. 740				Bal. 1,800			Bal. 2,000
	(m) 650						
Bal. 90							

Accounts Receivable	
Bal. 30	

	Drawing		Expenses		Revenues	
	Debit	Credit	Debit	Credit	Debit	Credit
	+	–	+	–	–	+

Supplies	
Bal. 80	

Rent Expense		Delivery Fees	
Bal. 200			Bal. 1,100

Prepaid Insurance	
Bal. 200	

Telephone Expense	
Bal. 50	

Delivery Equipment	
Bal. 3,600	

Wages Expense	
(m) 650	

$4,000   =   **$4,000**

ACCOUNT AFFECTED	CLASSIFICATION	LOCATION IN EQUATION	INCREASE OR DECREASE	DEBIT OR CREDIT
Wages Expense	Expense	Right O.E.— Left Side	Exp.— Increases; O.E.— Decreases	Debit
Cash	Asset	Left	Decrease	Credit

FIGURE 3-19   Transaction (m): Payment of Wages

Transaction (n): Deliveries made for cash and credit

Total delivery fees for the remainder of the month amounted to $1,050: $430 in cash and $620 on account (Figure 3-20).

Analysis: Since the delivery fees have been earned, the revenue account increases by $1,050. Also, Cash increases by $430 and Accounts Receivable increases by $620. Note once again that one event impacts three accounts. This time we have debits of $430 to Cash and $620 to Accounts Receivable, and a credit of $1,050 to Delivery Fees. As before, the total debits ($430 + $620) equal the total credits ($1,050) and the accounting equation remains in balance.

Assets		=	Liabilities		+	Owner's Equity		
Debit	**Credit**		**Debit**	**Credit**		**Debit**		**Credit**
+	−		−	+		−		+

Cash			Accounts Payable			Jessica Jane, Capital		
Bal. 90				Bal. 1,800				Bal. 2,000
(n) 430								
Bal. 520								

Accounts Receivable	
Bal. 30	
(n) 620	
Bal. 650	

Drawing		Expenses		Revenues	
Debit	**Credit**	**Debit**	**Credit**	**Debit**	**Credit**
+	−	+	−	−	+

Supplies	
Bal. 80	

Rent Expense		Delivery Fees	
Bal. 200			Bal. 1,100
			(n) 1,050
			Bal. 2,150

Prepaid Insurance	
Bal. 200	

Telephone Expense	
Bal. 50	

Delivery Equipment	
Bal. 3,600	

Wages Expense	
Bal. 650	

$$\$5,050 \quad = \quad \$5,050$$

ACCOUNT AFFECTED	CLASSIFICATION	LOCATION IN EQUATION	INCREASE OR DECREASE	DEBIT OR CREDIT
Cash	Asset	Left	Increase	Debit
Accounts Rec.	Asset	Left	Increase	Debit
Delivery Fees	Revenue	Right O.E.—Right Side	Increase	Credit

FIGURE 3-20   Transaction (n): Deliveries Made for Cash and Credit

Transaction (o): Withdrawal of cash from business

At the end of the month, Jessie withdrew $150 in cash from the business to purchase books for her classes (Figure 3-21).

Analysis: Cash withdrawals decrease owner's equity and decrease cash. Debit Jessica Jane, Drawing and credit Cash for $150.

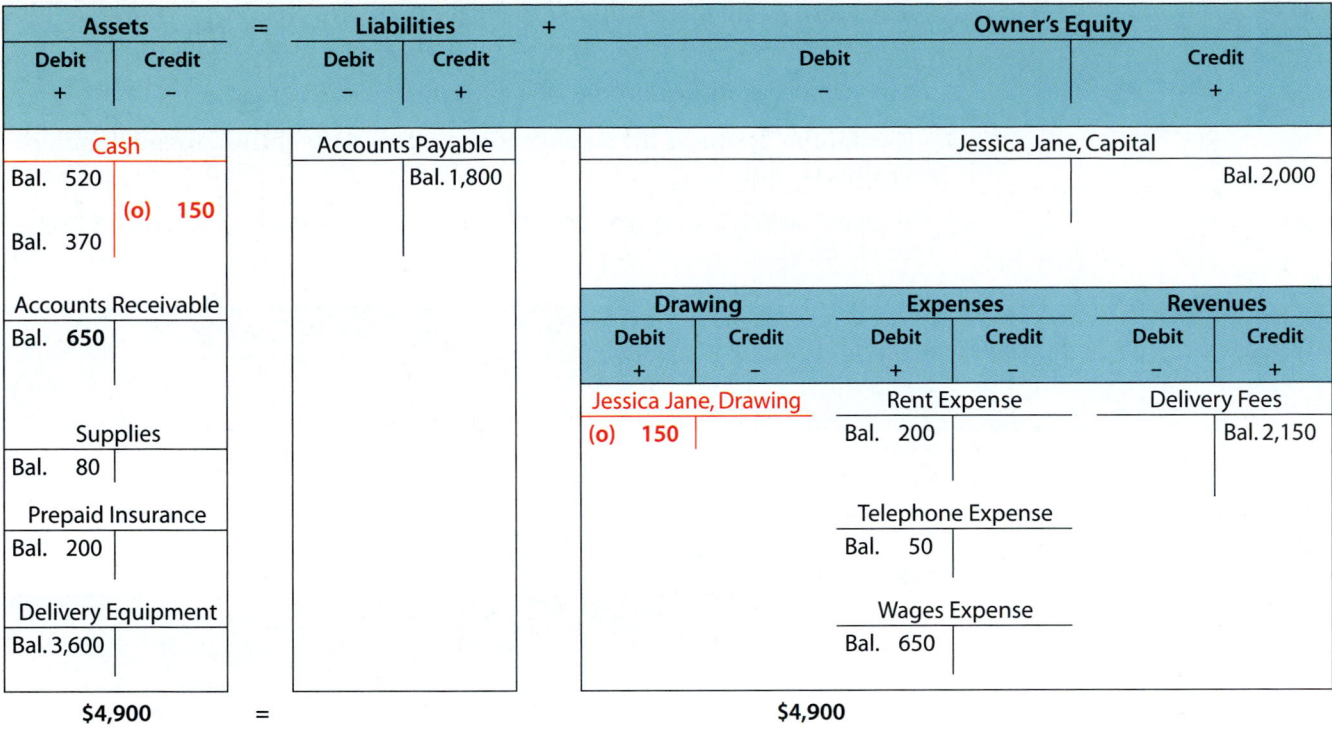

ACCOUNT AFFECTED	CLASSIFICATION	LOCATION IN EQUATION	INCREASE OR DECREASE	DEBIT OR CREDIT
Drawing	Drawing	Right O.E.— Left Side	Drawing— Increases; O.E.— Decreases	Debit
Cash	Asset	Left	Decrease	Credit

FIGURE 3-21   Transaction (o): Withdrawal of Cash from Business

Withdrawals are reported in the drawing account. Withdrawals by an owner are the opposite of an investment. You could debit the owner's capital account for withdrawals. However, using a specific account tells the user of the accounting information how much was withdrawn for the period.

Summary of Transactions

In illustrating transactions (a) through (o), each T account for Jessie Jane's Campus Delivery shows a balance before and after each transaction. To focus your attention on the transaction being explained, only a single entry was shown. In practice, this is not done. Instead, each account gathers all transactions for a period. Jessie's accounts, with all transactions listed, are shown in Figure 3-22. Note the following:

1. The footings are directly under the debit (left) and credit (right) sides of the T account for those accounts with more than one debit or credit.

2. The balance is shown on the side with the larger footing.

3. The footing serves as the balance for accounts with entries on only one side of the account.

4. If an account has only a single entry, it is not necessary to enter a footing or balance.

Assets		=	Liabilities		+	Owner's Equity	
Debit	Credit		Debit	Credit		Debit	Credit
+	–		–	+		–	+

Cash

(a) 2,000	(b) 1,200
(e) 500	(d) 300
(k) 570	(f) 200
(n) 430	(g) 50
3,500	(i) 80
	(j) 200
	(l) 300
	(m) 650
	(o) 150
	3,130
Bal. 370	

Accounts Receivable

(h) 600	(k) 570
(n) 620	
1,220	
Bal. 650	

Supplies

(i) 80	

Prepaid Insurance

(j) 200	

Delivery Equipment

(b) 1,200	
(c) 900	
(l) 1,500	
Bal. 3,600	

Accounts Payable

(d) 300	(c) 900
	(l) 1,200
	2,100
	Bal. 1,800

Jessica Jane, Capital

	(a) 2,000

Drawing		Expenses		Revenues	
Debit	Credit	Debit	Credit	Debit	Credit
+	–	+	–	–	+

Jessica Jane, Drawing		Rent Expense		Delivery Fees	
(o) 150		(f) 200			(e) 500
					(h) 600
					(n) 1,050
					Bal. 2,150

Telephone Expense

(g) 50	

Wages Expense

(m) 650	

$4,900	=	**$4,900**

FIGURE 3-22 Summary of Transactions (a) Through (o)

THE TRIAL BALANCE

LO5 Prepare a trial balance and explain its purposes and linkages with the financial statements.

Recall the two very important rules in double-entry accounting:

1. The sum of the debits must equal the sum of the credits. This means that at least two accounts are affected by each transaction. This rule is so important that many computer accounting programs will not permit a transaction to be entered into the accounting system unless the debits equal the credits.

2. The accounting equation must remain in balance.

In illustrating the transactions for Jessie Jane's Campus Delivery, the equality of the accounting equation was verified after each transaction. Because of the large number of transactions entered each day, this is not done in practice. Instead, a trial balance is prepared periodically to determine the equality of the debits and credits. A **trial balance** is a list of all accounts showing the title and balance of each account. By totaling the debits and credits, their equality can be tested.

A trial balance of Jessie's accounts, taken on June 30, 20--, is shown in Figure 3-23. This date is shown on the third line of the heading. The trial balance shows that the debit and credit totals are equal in amount. This is proof that (1) in entering transactions (a) through (o), the total of the debits was equal to the total of the credits, and (2) the accounting equation has remained in balance.

 LEARNING KEY: A trial balance provides proof that total debits equal total credits and shows that the accounting equation is in balance.

A trial balance is not a formal statement or report. Normally, only the accountant sees it. As shown in Figure 3-24, a trial balance can be used as an aid in preparing the financial statements.

Since a trial balance is not a formal statement, dollar signs are not used.

Jessie Jane's Campus Delivery Trial Balance June 30, 20 - -											
ACCOUNT TITLE	\multicolumn{5}{c}{DEBIT BALANCE}	\multicolumn{6}{c}{CREDIT BALANCE}
Cash		3	7	0	00						
Accounts Receivable		6	5	0	00						
Supplies			8	0	00						
Prepaid Insurance		2	0	0	00						
Delivery Equipment	3	6	0	0	00						
Accounts Payable							1	8	0	0	00
Jessica Jane, Capital							2	0	0	0	00
Jessica Jane, Drawing		1	5	0	00						
Delivery Fees							2	1	5	0	00
Rent Expense		2	0	0	00						
Telephone Expense			5	0	00						
Wages Expense		6	5	0	00						
	5	9	5	0	00	5	9	5	0	00	

FIGURE 3-23 Trial Balance

Jessie Jane's Campus Delivery
Trial Balance
June 30, 20 - -

ACCOUNT TITLE	DEBIT BALANCE				CREDIT BALANCE			
Cash		3	7	0	00				
Accounts Receivable		6	5	0	00				
Supplies			8	0	00				
Prepaid Insurance			2	0	0	00				
Delivery Equipment	3	6	0	0	00				
Accounts Payable						1	8	0	0	00
Jessica Jane, Capital						2	0	0	0	00
Jessica Jane, Drawing		1	5	0	00				
Delivery Fees						2	1	5	0	00
Rent Expense		2	0	0	00				
Telephone Expense			5	0	00				
Wages Expense		6	5	0	00				
	5	9	5	0	00	5	9	5	0	00

Jessie Jane's Campus Delivery
Income Statement
For Month Ended June 30, 20 --

Revenue:									
Delivery fees						$2	1	5	0	00
Expenses:									
Wages expense	$	6	5	0	00				
Rent expense		2	0	0	00				
Telephone expense			5	0	00				
Total expenses							9	0	0	00
Net income						$1	2	5	0	00

Jessie Jane's Campus Delivery
Statement of Owner's Equity
For Month Ended June 30, 20 - -

Jessica Jane, capital, June 1, 20 - -						$2	0	0	0	00
Net income for June	$1	2	5	0	00				
Less withdrawals for June		1	5	0	00				
Increase in capital						1	1	0	0	00
Jessica Jane, capital, June 30, 20 - -						$3	1	0	0	00

Jessie Jane's Campus Delivery
Balance Sheet
June 30, 20 - -

Assets						Liabilities					
Cash	$	3	7	0	00	Accounts payable	$1	8	0	0	00
Accounts receivable		6	5	0	00						
Supplies			8	0	00	Owner's Equity					
Prepaid insurance		2	0	0	00	Jessica Jane, capital	3	1	0	0	00
Delivery equipment	3	6	0	0	00						
						Total liabilities and					
Total assets	$4	9	0	0	00	owner's equity	$4	9	0	0	00

FIGURE 3-24 Linkages Between the Trial Balance and Financial Statements

Learning Objectives	Key Points to Remember
1 **Define the parts of a T account.**	The parts of a T account are: 　1.　the title, 　2.　the debit or left side, and 　3.　the credit or right side. **Title** Debit = Left ｜ Credit = Right
2 **Foot and balance a T account.**	Rules for footing and balancing T accounts are: 　1.　The footings are directly under the debit (left) and credit (right) sides of the T account for those accounts with more than one debit or credit. 　2.　The balance is shown on the side with the larger footing. 　3.　The footing serves as the balance for accounts with entries on only one side of the account. 　4.　If an account has only a single entry, it is not necessary to enter a footing or balance.
3 **Describe the effects of debits and credits on specific types of accounts.**	Rules for debits and credits. (See illustration below.) 　1.　Assets are on the left side of the accounting equation. Therefore, increases are entered on the left (debit) side of an asset account and decreases are entered on the right (credit) side. 　2.　Liabilities and owner's equity are on the right side of the accounting equation. Therefore, increases are entered on the right (credit) side and decreases are entered on the left (debit) side. 　3.　Revenues are on the right side of the owner's equity umbrella. Therefore, increases are entered on the right (credit) side and decreases are entered on the left (debit) side. 　4.　Expenses and drawing are on the left side of the owner's equity umbrella. Therefore, increases are entered on the left (debit) side and decreases are entered on the right (credit) side. Accounting Equation with Owner's Equity Umbrella
4 **Use T accounts to analyze transactions.**	Picture the accounting equation in your mind as you analyze transactions. When entering transactions in T accounts: 　1.　The sum of the debits must equal the sum of the credits. 　2.　At least two accounts are affected by each transaction. 　3.　When finished, the accounting equation must remain in balance.
5 **Prepare a trial balance and explain its purposes and linkages with the financial statements.**	A trial balance shows that the debit and credit totals are equal. A trial balance also can be used in preparing the financial statements.

Reflection: Answering the Opening Question

The beauty of the double-entry system illustrated in this chapter is that it can be used for businesses of all kinds (service, merchandising, and manufacturing), ownership interests (proprietorship, partnership, corporation), and sizes, including your own personal finances.

DEMONSTRATION PROBLEM

WebTUTOR Advantage

Celia Pints opened We-Buy, You-Pay Shopping Services. For a fee that is based on the amount of research and shopping time required, Pints and her associates will shop for almost anything from groceries to home furnishings. Business is particularly heavy around Christmas and in early summer. The business operates from a rented store front. The associates receive a commission based on the revenues they produce and a mileage reimbursement for the use of their personal automobiles for shopping trips. Pints decided to use the following accounts to record transactions.

Assets	Owner's Equity
Cash	Celia Pints, Capital
Accounts Receivable	Celia Pints, Drawing
Office Equipment	Revenue
Computer Equipment	Shopping Fees
Liabilities	Expenses
Accounts Payable	Rent Expense
Notes Payable	Telephone Expense
	Commissions Expense
	Utilities Expense
	Travel Expense

The following transactions are for the month of December 20--.

(a) Pints invested cash in the business, $30,000.

(b) Bought office equipment for $10,000. Paid $2,000 in cash and promised to pay the balance over the next four months.

(c) Paid rent for December, $500.

(d) Provided shopping services for customers on account, $5,200.

(e) Paid telephone bill, $90.

(f) Borrowed cash from the bank by signing a note payable, $5,000.

(g) Bought a computer and printer, $4,800.

(h) Collected cash from customers for services performed on account, $4,000.

(i) Paid commissions to associates for revenues generated during the first half of the month, $3,500.

(j) Paid utility bill, $600.

(k) Paid cash on account for the office equipment purchased in transaction (b), $2,000.

(l) Earned shopping fees of $13,200: $6,000 in cash and $7,200 on account.

(m) Paid commissions to associates for last half of month, $7,000.

(n) Paid mileage reimbursements for the month, $1,500.

(o) Paid cash on note payable to bank, $1,000.

(p) Pints withdrew cash for personal use, $2,000.

REQUIRED

1. Enter the transactions for December in T accounts. Use the accounting equation as a guide for setting up the T accounts.

2. Foot the T accounts and determine their balances as necessary.

3. Prepare a trial balance of the accounts as of December 31 of the current year.

4. Prepare an income statement for the month ended December 31 of the current year.

5. Prepare a statement of owner's equity for the month ended December 31 of the current year.

6. Prepare a balance sheet as of December 31 of the current year.

(continued)

Solution

1, 2.

Assets	=	Liabilities	+	Owner's Equity

Assets			=	**Liabilities**		+	**Owner's Equity**	
Debit	Credit			Debit	Credit		Debit	Credit
+	−			−	+		−	+

Cash

Debit (+)	Credit (−)
(a) 30,000	(b) 2,000
(f) 5,000	(c) 500
(h) 4,000	(e) 90
(l) 6,000	(g) 4,800
45,000	(i) 3,500
	(j) 600
	(k) 2,000
	(m) 7,000
	(n) 1,500
	(o) 1,000
	(p) 2,000
	24,990
Bal. 20,010	

Accounts Receivable

Debit	Credit
(d) 5,200	(h) 4,000
(l) 7,200	
12,400	
Bal. 8,400	

Office Equipment

Debit	Credit
(b) 10,000	

Computer Equipment

Debit	Credit
(g) 4,800	

$43,210

Accounts Payable

Debit (−)	Credit (+)
(k) 2,000	(b) 8,000
	Bal. 6,000

Notes Payable

Debit	Credit
(o) 1,000	(f) 5,000
	Bal. 4,000

Celia Pints, Capital

Debit	Credit
	(a) 30,000

	Drawing		**Expenses**		**Revenues**	
	Debit	Credit	Debit	Credit	Debit	Credit
	+	−	+	−	−	+

Celia Pints, Drawing

Debit	Credit
(p) 2,000	

Rent Expense

Debit	Credit
(c) 500	

Shopping Fees

Debit	Credit
	(d) 5,200
	(l) 13,200
	Bal. 18,400

Telephone Expense

Debit	Credit
(e) 90	

Commissions Expense

Debit	Credit
(i) 3,500	
(m) 7,000	
Bal. 10,500	

Utilities Expense

Debit	Credit
(j) 600	

Travel Expense

Debit	Credit
(n) 1,500	

=   **$43,210**

3.

	We-Buy, You-Pay Shopping Services Trial Balance December 31, 20 - -									
ACCOUNT TITLE		DEBIT BALANCE					CREDIT BALANCE			
Cash	20	0	1	0	00					
Accounts Receivable	8	4	0	0	00					
Office Equipment	10	0	0	0	00					
Computer Equipment	4	8	0	0	00					
Accounts Payable							6	0	0	0	00
Notes Payable							4	0	0	0	00
Celia Pints, Capital							30	0	0	0	00
Celia Pints, Drawing	2	0	0	0	00					
Shopping Fees							18	4	0	0	00
Rent Expense		5	0	0	00					
Telephone Expense			9	0	00					
Commissions Expense	10	5	0	0	00					
Utilities Expense		6	0	0	00					
Travel Expense	1	5	0	0	00					
	58	4	0	0	00		58	4	0	0	00

4.

We-Buy, You-Pay Shopping Services Income Statement For Month Ended December 31, 20 - -										
Revenue:										
Shopping fees						$18	4	0	0	00
Expenses:										
Commissions expense	$10	5	0	0	00					
Travel expense	1	5	0	0	00					
Utilities expense		6	0	0	00					
Rent expense		5	0	0	00					
Telephone expense			9	0	00					
Total expenses						13	1	9	0	00
Net income						$ 5	2	1	0	00

5.

We-Buy, You-Pay Shopping Services Statement of Owner's Equity For Month Ended December 31, 20 - -										
Celia Pints, capital, December 1, 20 - -						$30	0	0	0	00
Net income for December	$5	2	1	0	00					
Less withdrawals for December	2	0	0	0	00					
Increase in capital						3	2	1	0	00
Celia Pints, capital, December 31, 20 - -						$33	2	1	0	00

(continued)

6.

We-Buy, You-Pay Shopping Services
Balance Sheet
December 31, 20 - -

Assets						Liabilities					
Cash	$ 20	0	1	0	00	Accounts payable	$ 6	0	0	0	00
Accounts receivable	8	4	0	0	00	Notes payable	4	0	0	0	00
Office equipment	10	0	0	0	00	Total liabilities	$10	0	0	0	00
Computer equipment	4	8	0	0	00						
						Owner's Equity					
						Celia Pints, capital	33	2	1	0	00
						Total liabilities and					
Total assets	$43	2	1	0	00	owner's equity	$43	2	1	0	00

On-Line Learning Tools

For more information, visit: http://heintz.swlearning.com

The Heintz & Parry product web site is designed specifically for **COLLEGE ACCOUNTING, 18e.** The features include downloadable student resources and an interactive study center, organized by chapter, which contains learning objectives, web links, on-line quizzes with automatic feedback, and more.

KEY TERMS

balance, (48)   The difference between the footings of an account.

credit, (49)   To enter an amount on the right side of an account.

credit balance, (50)   The normal balance of liability, owner's equity, and revenue accounts.

debit, (49)   To enter an amount on the left side of an account.

debit balance, (50)   The normal balance of asset, expense, and drawing accounts.

double-entry accounting, (48)   A system in which each transaction has a dual effect on the accounting elements.

footings, (48)   The total dollar amounts on the debit and credit sides of an account.

normal balance, (50)   The side of an account that is increased.

trial balance, (67)   A list of all accounts, showing the title and balance of each account, used to prove that the sum of the debits equals the sum of the credits.

REVIEW QUESTIONS

(LO1)   1.   What are the three major parts of a T account?

(LO1)   2.   What is the left side of the T account called? the right side?

(LO2)   3.   What is a footing?

(LO3)   4.   What is the relationship between the revenue and expense accounts and the owner's equity account?

(LO5)   5.   What is the function of the trial balance?

Self-Study Test Questions

True/False

1.   To debit an account is to enter an amount on the left side of the account. _____

2.   Liability accounts normally have debit balances. _____

3.   Increases in owner's equity are entered as credits. _____

4.   Revenue accounts normally have debit balances. _____

5.   To credit an account is to enter an amount on the right side of the account. _____

6.   A debit to an asset account will decrease it. _____

Multiple Choice

1.   A common example of an asset is _____

   (a) Professional Fees.   (c) Accounts Receivable.
   (b) Rent Expense.   (d) Accounts Payable.

2.   To record the payment of rent expense, an accountant would _____

   (a) debit Cash; credit Rent Expense.   (c) debit Rent Expense; credit Cash.
   (b) debit Rent Expense; debit Cash.   (d) credit Rent Expense; credit Cash.

3.   The accounting equation may be expressed as _____

   (a) Assets = Liabilities – Owner's Equity.   (c) Liabilities = Owner's Equity – Assets.
   (b) Assets = Liabilities + Owner's Equity.   (d) all of the above.

4.   Liability, owner's equity, and revenue accounts normally have _____

   (a) debit balances.   (c) negative balances.
   (b) large balances.   (d) credit balances.

5.   An investment of cash by the owner will _____

   (a) increase assets and owner's equity.   (c) increase liabilities and owner's equity.
   (b) increase assets and liabilities.   (d) increase owner's equity; decrease liabilities.

The answers to the Self-Study Test Questions are at the end of the text.

MANAGING YOUR WRITING

Write a one-page memo to your instructor explaining how you could use the double-entry system to maintain records of your personal finances. What types of accounts would you use for the accounting elements?

Interactive Learning: **http://heintz.swlearning.com**

SERIES A EXERCISES

EXERCISE 3-1A   **(LO2)**   **FOOT AND BALANCE A T ACCOUNT** Foot and balance the cash T account shown.
Cash bal.: $1,200 (Dr.)

Cash	
500	100
400	200
600	

EXERCISE 3-2A   **(LO3)**   **DEBIT AND CREDIT ANALYSIS** Complete the following questions using either "debit" or "credit."

(a) The Cash account is increased with a _____.

(b) The owner's capital account is increased with a _____.

(c) The Delivery Equipment account is increased with a _____.

(d) The Cash account is decreased with a _____.

(e) The liability account Accounts Payable is increased with a _____.

(f) The revenue account Delivery Fees is increased with a _____.

(g) The asset account Accounts Receivable is increased with a _____.

(h) The Rent Expense account is increased with a _____.

(i) The owner's drawing account is increased with a _____.

EXERCISE 3-3A   **(LO2/3/4)**   **ANALYSIS OF T ACCOUNTS** Jim Arnold began a business called Arnold's Shoe Repair.
Cash bal. after (c): $2,700 (Dr.)

1.   Create T accounts for Cash; Supplies; Jim Arnold, Capital; and Utilities Expense. Identify the following transactions by letter and place them on the proper side of the T accounts.

   (a)   Arnold invested cash in the business, $5,000.

   (b)   Purchased supplies for cash, $800.

   (c)   Paid utility bill, $1,500.

2.   Foot the T account for cash and enter the ending balance.

EXERCISE 3-4A   **(LO3)**   **NORMAL BALANCE OF ACCOUNT** Indicate the normal balance (debit or credit) for each of the following accounts.

1.   Cash

2.   Wages Expense

3.   Accounts Payable

4.   Owner's Drawing

5.   Supplies

6.   Owner's Capital

7.   Equipment

EXERCISE 3-5A   **(LO4)**   **TRANSACTION ANALYSIS** Sheryl Hansen started a business on May 1, 20--. Analyze the following transactions for the first month of business using T accounts. Label each T account with the title of the account affected and then place the transaction letter and the dollar amount on the debit or credit side.

(a) Hansen invested cash in the business, $4,000.

(b) Bought equipment for cash, $500.

(c) Bought equipment on account, $800.

(d) Paid cash on account for equipment purchased in transaction (c), $300.

(e) Hansen withdrew cash for personal use, $700.

EXERCISE 3-6A   (LO2)
Cash bal. after (e): $2,500 (Dr.)

FOOT AND BALANCE A T ACCOUNT Foot and balance the cash T account prepared in Exercise 3-5A.

EXERCISE 3-7A   (LO2/4)
Cash bal. after (k): $24,400 (Dr.)

ANALYSIS OF TRANSACTIONS Charles Chadwick opened a business called Charlie's Detective Service in January 20--. Set up T accounts for the following accounts: Cash; Accounts Receivable; Office Supplies; Computer Equipment; Office Furniture; Accounts Payable; Charles Chadwick, Capital; Charles Chadwick, Drawing; Professional Fees; Rent Expense; and Utilities Expense.

The following transactions occurred during the first month of business. Record these transactions in T accounts. After all transactions are recorded, foot and balance the accounts if necessary.

(a) Chadwick invested cash in the business, $30,000.

(b) Bought office supplies for cash, $300.

(c) Bought office furniture for cash, $5,000.

(d) Purchased computer and printer on account, $8,000.

(e) Received cash from clients for services, $3,000.

(f) Paid cash on account for computer and printer purchased in transaction (d), $4,000.

(g) Earned professional fees on account during the month, $9,000.

(h) Paid cash for office rent for January, $1,500.

(i) Paid utility bills for the month, $800.

(j) Received cash from clients billed in transaction (g), $6,000.

(k) Chadwick withdrew cash for personal use, $3,000.

EXERCISE 3-8A   (LO5)
Trial bal. total debits: $46,000

TRIAL BALANCE Based on the transactions recorded in Exercise 3-7A, prepare a trial balance for Charlie's Detective Service as of January 31, 20--.

EXERCISE 3-9A   (LO5)
Trial bal. total debits: $21,400

TRIAL BALANCE The following accounts have normal balances. Prepare a trial balance for Juanita's Delivery Service as of September 30, 20--.

Cash	$ 5,000
Accounts Receivable	3,000
Supplies	800
Prepaid Insurance	600
Delivery Equipment	8,000
Accounts Payable	2,000
Juanita Raye, Capital	10,000
Juanita Raye, Drawing	1,000
Delivery Fees	9,400
Wages Expense	2,100
Rent Expense	900

EXERCISE 3-10A   **(LO5)**
Net income: $6,400

INCOME STATEMENT From the information in Exercise 3-9A, prepare an income statement for Juanita's Delivery Service for the month ended September 30, 20--.

EXERCISE 3-11A   **(LO5)**
Capital, 9/30: $15,400

STATEMENT OF OWNER'S EQUITY From the information in Exercise 3-9A, prepare a statement of owner's equity for Juanita's Delivery Service for the month ended September 30, 20--.

EXERCISE 3-12A   **(LO5)**
Total assets, 9/30: $17,400

BALANCE SHEET From the information in Exercise 3-9A, prepare a balance sheet for Juanita's Delivery Service as of September 30, 20--.

SERIES A PROBLEMS

PROBLEM 3-13A (LO2/4/5)
Cash bal. after (p): $14,820 (Dr.);
Trial bal. total debits: $38,200

T ACCOUNTS AND TRIAL BALANCE Harold Long started a business in May 20-- called Harold's Home Repair. Long hired a part-time college student as an assistant. Long has decided to use the following accounts for recording transactions.

Assets	Owner's Equity
Cash	Harold Long, Capital
Accounts Receivable	Harold Long, Drawing
Office Supplies	Revenue
Prepaid Insurance	Service Fees
Equipment	Expenses
Van	Rent Expense
Liabilities	Wages Expense
Accounts Payable	Telephone Expense
	Gas and Oil Expense

The following transactions occurred during May.

(a) Long invested cash in the business, $20,000.

(b) Purchased a used van for cash, $7,000.

(c) Purchased equipment on account, $5,000.

(d) Received cash for services rendered, $6,000.

(e) Paid cash on account owed from transaction (c), $2,000.

(f) Paid rent for the month, $900.

(g) Paid telephone bill, $200.

(h) Earned revenue on account, $4,000.

(i) Purchased office supplies for cash, $120.

(j) Paid wages to student, $600.

(k) Purchased insurance, $1,200.

(l) Received cash from services performed in transaction (h), $3,000.

(m) Paid cash for gas and oil expense on the van, $160.

(n) Purchased additional equipment for $3,000, paying $1,000 cash and spreading the remaining payments over the next 10 months.

(o) Service fees earned for the remainder of the month amounted to $3,200: $1,800 in cash and $1,400 on account.

(p) Long withdrew cash at the end of the month, $2,800.

REQUIRED

1. Enter the transactions in T accounts, identifying each transaction with its corresponding letter.

2. Foot and balance the accounts where necessary.

3. Prepare a trial balance as of May 31, 20--.

PROBLEM 3-14A   **(LO5)**

Net income: $11,340
Owner's equity, 5/31: $28,540
Total assets, 5/31: $33,540

NET INCOME AND CHANGE IN OWNER'S EQUITY Refer to the trial balance of Harold's Home Repair in Problem 3-13A to determine the following information. Use the format provided below.

1. a. Total revenue for the month   _____

    b. Total expenses for the month   _____

    c. Net income for the month   _____

2. a. Harold Long's original investment   _____
        in the business

        + the net income for the month   _____

        – owner's drawing   _____

        Increase (decrease) in capital   _____

        = ending owner's equity   _____

    b. End of month accounting equation:

Assets	=	Liabilities	+	Owner's Equity
_____	=	_____	+	_____

PROBLEM 3-15A   **(LO5)**

NI: $11,340; Capital, 5/31/20--:
$28,540; Total assets: $33,540

FINANCIAL STATEMENTS Refer to the trial balance in Problem 3-13A and to the analysis of the change in owner's equity in Problem 3-14A.

REQUIRED

1. Prepare an income statement for Harold's Home Repair for the month ended May 31, 20--.

2. Prepare a statement of owner's equity for Harold's Home Repair for the month ended May 31, 20--.

3. Prepare a balance sheet for Harold's Home Repair as of May 31, 20--.

SERIES B EXERCISES

EXERCISE 3-1B **(LO2)**
Accts. Pay: $400 (Cr.)

FOOT AND BALANCE A T ACCOUNT Foot and balance the accounts payable T account shown.

Accounts Payable	
300	450
250	350
	150

EXERCISE 3-2B **(LO3)**

DEBIT AND CREDIT ANALYSIS Complete the following questions using either "debit" or "credit."

(a) The asset account Prepaid Insurance is increased with a _____.

(b) The owner's drawing account is increased with a _____.

(c) The asset account Accounts Receivable is decreased with a _____.

(d) The liability account Accounts Payable is decreased with a _____.

(e) The owner's capital account is increased with a _____.

(f) The revenue account Professional Fees is increased with a _____.

(g) The expense account Repair Expense is increased with a _____.

(h) The asset account Cash is decreased with a _____.

(i) The asset account Delivery Equipment is decreased with a _____.

EXERCISE 3-3B **(LO2/3/4)**
Cash bal. after (c): $3,900 (Dr.)

ANALYSIS OF T ACCOUNTS Roberto Alvarez began a business called Roberto's Fix-It Shop.

1. Create T accounts for Cash; Supplies; Roberto Alvarez, Capital; and Utilities Expense. Identify the following transactions by letter and place them on the proper side of the T accounts.

   (a) Alvarez invested cash in the business, $6,000.

   (b) Purchased supplies for cash, $1,200.

   (c) Paid utility bill, $900.

2. Foot the T account for cash and enter the ending balance.

EXERCISE 3-4B **(LO3)**

NORMAL BALANCE OF ACCOUNT Indicate the normal balance (debit or credit) for each of the following accounts.

1. Cash

2. Rent Expense

3. Notes Payable

4. Owner's Drawing

5. Accounts Receivable

6. Owner's Capital

7. Tools

EXERCISE 3-5B **(LO4)**

TRANSACTION ANALYSIS George Atlas started a business on June 1, 20--. Analyze the following transactions for the first month of business using T accounts. Label each T account with the title of the account affected and then place the transaction letter and the dollar amount on the debit or credit side.

(a) Atlas invested cash in the business, $7,000.

(b) Purchased equipment for cash, $900.

(c) Purchased equipment on account, $1,500.

(d) Paid cash on account for equipment purchased in transaction (c), $800.

(e) Atlas withdrew cash for personal use, $1,100.

EXERCISE 3-6B   (LO2)
Cash bal. after (e): $4,200 (Dr.)

FOOT AND BALANCE A T ACCOUNT Foot and balance the cash T account prepared in Exercise 3-5B.

EXERCISE 3-7B   (LO2/4)
Cash bal. after (k): $9,000 (Dr.)

ANALYSIS OF TRANSACTIONS Nicole Lawrence opened a business called Nickie's Neat Ideas in January 20--. Set up T accounts for the following accounts: Cash; Accounts Receivable; Office Supplies; Computer Equipment; Office Furniture; Accounts Payable; Nicole Lawrence, Capital; Nicole Lawrence, Drawing; Professional Fees; Rent Expense; and Utilities Expense.

The following transactions occurred during the first month of business. Record these transactions in T accounts. After all transactions have been recorded, foot and balance the accounts if necessary.

(a) Lawrence invested cash in the business, $18,000.

(b) Purchased office supplies for cash, $500.

(c) Purchased office furniture for cash, $8,000.

(d) Purchased computer and printer on account, $5,000.

(e) Received cash from clients for services, $4,000.

(f) Paid cash on account for computer and printer purchased in transaction (d), $2,000.

(g) Earned professional fees on account during the month, $7,000.

(h) Paid office rent for January, $900.

(i) Paid utility bills for the month, $600.

(j) Received cash from clients that were billed previously in transaction (g), $3,000.

(k) Lawrence withdrew cash for personal use, $4,000.

EXERCISE 3-8B   (LO5)
Trial bal. total debits: $32,000

TRIAL BALANCE Based on the transactions recorded in Exercise 3-7B, prepare a trial balance for Nickie's Neat Ideas as of January 31, 20--.

EXERCISE 3-9B   (LO5)
Trial bal. total debits: $27,500

TRIAL BALANCE The following accounts have normal balances. Prepare a trial balance for Bill's Delivery Service as of September 30, 20--.

Cash	$ 7,000
Accounts Receivable	4,000
Supplies	600
Prepaid Insurance	900
Delivery Equipment	9,000
Accounts Payable	3,000
Bill Swift, Capital	12,000
Bill Swift, Drawing	2,000
Delivery Fees	12,500
Wages Expense	3,000
Rent Expense	1,000

EXERCISE 3-10B   **(LO5)**
Net income: $8,500

INCOME STATEMENT From the information in Exercise 3-9B, prepare an income statement for Bill's Delivery Service for the month ended September 30, 20--.

EXERCISE 3-11B   **(LO5)**
Capital, 9/30: $18,500

STATEMENT OF OWNER'S EQUITY From the information in Exercise 3-9B, prepare a statement of owner's equity for Bill's Delivery Service for the month ended September 30, 20--.

EXERCISE 3-12B   **(LO5)**
Total assets, 9/30: $21,500

BALANCE SHEET From the information in Exercise 3-9B, prepare a balance sheet for Bill's Delivery Service as of September 30, 20--.

SERIES B PROBLEMS

PROBLEM 3-13B (LO2/4/5)
Cash bal. after (p): $20,200 (Dr.);
Trial bal. total debits: $44,300

T ACCOUNTS AND TRIAL BALANCE Sue Jantz started a business in August 20-- called Jantz Plumbing Service. Jantz hired a part-time college student as an administrative assistant. Jantz has decided to use the following accounts.

Assets	Owner's Equity
Cash	Sue Jantz, Capital
Accounts Receivable	Sue Jantz, Drawing
Office Supplies	Revenue
Prepaid Insurance	Service Fees
Plumbing Equipment	Expenses
Van	Rent Expense
Liabilities	Wages Expense
Accounts Payable	Telephone Expense
	Advertising Expense

The following transactions occurred during August.

(a) Jantz invested cash in the business, $30,000.

(b) Purchased a used van for cash, $8,000.

(c) Purchased plumbing equipment on account, $4,000.

(d) Received cash for services rendered, $3,000.

(e) Paid cash on account owed from transaction (c), $1,000.

(f) Paid rent for the month, $700.

(g) Paid telephone bill, $100.

(h) Earned revenue on account, $4,000.

(i) Purchased office supplies for cash, $300.

(j) Paid wages to student, $500.

(k) Purchased insurance, $800.

(l) Received cash from services performed in transaction (h), $3,000.

(m) Paid cash for advertising expense, $2,000.

(n) Purchased additional plumbing equipment for $2,000, paying $500 cash and spreading the remaining payments over the next six months.

(o) Revenue earned from services for the remainder of the month amounted to $2,800: $1,100 in cash and $1,700 on account.

(p) Jantz withdrew cash at the end of the month, $3,000.

REQUIRED

1. Enter the transactions in T accounts, identifying each transaction with its corresponding letter.

2. Foot and balance the accounts where necessary.

3. Prepare a trial balance as of August 31, 20--.

PROBLEM 3-14B   (LO5)
Net income: $6,500
Owner's equity, 8/31: $33,500
Total assets, 8/31: $38,000

NET INCOME AND CHANGE IN OWNER'S EQUITY Refer to the trial balance of Jantz Plumbing Service in Problem 3-13B to determine the following information. Use the format provided below.

1. a. Total revenue for the month _____
   b. Total expenses for the month _____
   c. Net income for the month _____

2. a. Sue Jantz's original investment in the business _____
   + the net income for the month _____
   – owner's drawing _____
   Increase (decrease) in capital _____
   = ending owner's equity _____

   b. End of month accounting equation:

Assets	=	Liabilities	+	Owner's Equity
_____	=	_____	+	_____

PROBLEM 3-15B   (LO5)
NI: $6,500; Capital, 8/31/20--:
$33,500; Total assets: $38,000

FINANCIAL STATEMENTS Refer to the trial balance in Problem 3-13B and to the analysis of the change in owner's equity in Problem 3-14B.

REQUIRED

1. Prepare an income statement for Jantz Plumbing Service for the month ended August 31, 20--.

2. Prepare a statement of owner's equity for Jantz Plumbing Service for the month ended August 31, 20--.

3. Prepare a balance sheet for Jantz Plumbing Service as of August 31, 20--.

MASTERY PROBLEM

Cash bal. after (p): $1,980;
Trial bal. debit total: $5,840;
Net income: $500;
Total assets: $4,300

Craig Fisher started a lawn service called Craig's Quick Cut to earn money over the summer months. Fisher has decided to use the following accounts for recording transactions.

Assets
    Cash
    Accounts Receivable
    Mowing Equipment
    Lawn Tools
Liabilities
    Accounts Payable
    Notes Payable
Owner's Equity
    Craig Fisher, Capital
    Craig Fisher, Drawing

Revenue
    Lawn Fees
Expenses
    Rent Expense
    Wages Expense
    Telephone Expense
    Gas and Oil Expense
    Transportation Expense

Transactions for the month of June are listed below.

(a) Fisher invested cash in the business, $3,000.

(b) Bought mowing equipment for $1,000: paid $200 in cash and promised to pay the balance over the next four months.

(c) Paid garage rent for June, $50.

(d) Provided lawn services for customers on account, $520.

(e) Paid telephone bill, $30.

(f) Borrowed cash from the bank by signing a note payable, $500.

(g) Bought lawn tools, $480.

(h) Collected cash from customers for services performed on account in transaction (d), $400.

(i) Paid associates for lawn work done during the first half of the month, $350.

(j) Paid for gas and oil for the equipment, $60.

(k) Paid cash on account for the mowing equipment purchased in transaction (b), $200.

(l) Earned lawn fees of $1,320: $600 in cash and $720 on account.

(m) Paid associates for last half of month, $700.

(n) Reimbursed associates for expenses associated with using their own vehicles for transportation, $150.

(o) Paid on note payable to bank, $100.

(p) Fisher withdrew cash for personal use, $200.

REQUIRED

1. Enter the transactions for June in T accounts. Use the accounting equation as a guide for setting up the T accounts.

2. Foot and balance the T accounts where necessary.

3. Prepare a trial balance of the accounts as of June 30, 20--.

4. Prepare an income statement for the month ended June 30, 20--.

5. Prepare a statement of owner's equity for the month ended June 30, 20--.

6. Prepare a balance sheet as of June 30, 20--.

CHALLENGE PROBLEM

This problem challenges you to apply your cumulative accounting knowledge to move a step beyond the material in the chapter.

Capital, 8/31/20--: $600

Your friend, Chris Stevick, started a part-time business in June and has been keeping her own accounting records. She has been preparing monthly financial statements. At the end of August, she stopped by to show you her performance for the most recent month. She prepared the following income statement and balance sheet.

Income Statement		Balance	End of	Beginning
		Sheet	Month	of Month
Revenues	$500	Cash	$600	$400
Expenses	200	Capital	$600	$400
Net Income	$300			

Chris has also heard that there is a statement of owner's equity, but is not familiar with that statement. She asks if you can help her prepare one. After confirming that she has no assets other than cash, no liabilities, and made no additional investments in the business in August, you agree.

REQUIRED

1. Prepare the statement of owner's equity for your friend's most recent month.

2. What suggestions might you make to Chris that would make her income statement more useful?

CHAPTER

4

©DIGITAL IMAGING GROUP

Journalizing and Posting Transactions

With business picking up, Jessie realized that she needed help maintaining records of her business transactions. Since she has not studied accounting and prefers to spend her time making deliveries and meeting with new clients, she hired an accounting student, Mitch, to help her "keep the books." After a few days on the job, Mitch and Jessie sat down to discuss the business events that had taken place and the entries made by Mitch. As might be expected, Mitch had misunderstood a few transactions and had entered them improperly. Jessie suggested that they go through the journal and ledger to erase the errors and make the corrections. Is this the best way to make corrections?

Careful study of this chapter should enable you to:

LO1 Describe the flow of data from source documents through the trial balance.

LO2 Describe the chart of accounts as a means of classifying financial information.

LO3 Describe and explain the purpose of source documents.

LO4 Journalize transactions.

LO5 Post to the general ledger and prepare a trial balance.

LO6 Explain how to find and correct errors.

The double-entry framework of accounting was explained and illustrated in Chapter 3. To demonstrate the use of debits and credits, business transactions were entered directly into T accounts. Now we will take a more detailed look at the procedures used to account for business transactions.

FLOW OF DATA

LO1 Describe the flow of data from source documents through the trial balance.

This chapter traces the flow of financial data from the source documents through the accounting information system. This process includes the following steps:

1. Analyze what happened by using information from source documents and the firm's chart of accounts.

2. Enter business transactions in the general journal in the form of journal entries.

3. Post these journal entries to the accounts in the general ledger.

4. Prepare a trial balance.

The flow of data from the source documents through the preparation of a trial balance is shown in Figure 4-1.

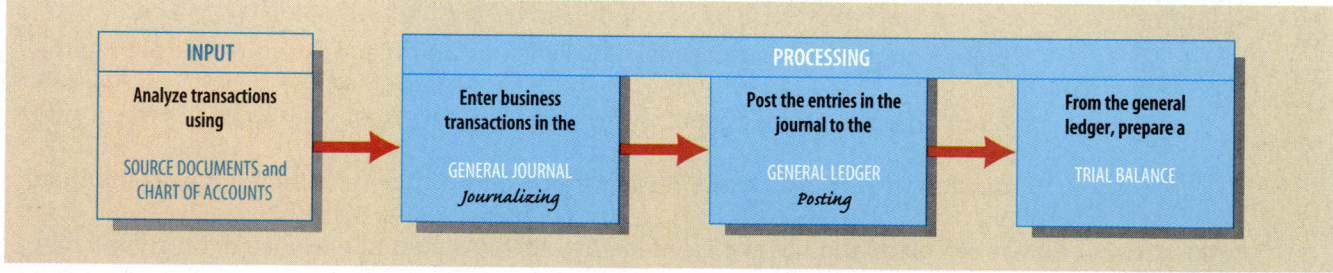

FIGURE 4-1 Flow of Data from Source Documents through Trial Balance

THE CHART OF ACCOUNTS

LO2 Describe the chart of accounts as a means of classifying financial information.

You learned in Chapters 2 and 3 that there are three basic questions that must be answered when analyzing transactions:

1. What happened?

2. Which accounts are affected?

3. How is the accounting equation affected?

To determine which accounts are affected (step 2), the accountant must know the accounts being used by the business. A list of all accounts used by a business is called a **chart of accounts.**

The chart of accounts includes the account titles in numeric order for all assets, liabilities, owner's equity, revenues, and expenses. The numbering should follow a consistent pattern. In Jessie Jane's Campus Delivery, asset accounts begin with "1," liability accounts begin with "2," owner's equity accounts begin with "3," revenue accounts begin with "4," and expense accounts begin with "5." Jessie uses three-digit numbers for all accounts.

A chart of accounts for Jessie Jane's Campus Delivery is shown in Figure 4-2. Jessie would not need many accounts initially because the business is new. Additional accounts can easily be added as needed. Note that the accounts are arranged according to the accounting equation.

JESSIE JANE'S CAMPUS DELIVERY CHART OF ACCOUNTS			
Assets	**(100–199)**	**Revenues**	**(400–499)**
101	Cash	401	Delivery Fees
122	Accounts Receivable		
141	Supplies	**Expenses**	**(500–599)**
145	Prepaid Insurance	511	Wages Expense
185	Delivery Equipment	521	Rent Expense
		525	Telephone Expense
Liabilities	**(200–299)**		
202	Accounts Payable		
Owner's Equity	**(300–399)**		
311	Jessica Jane, Capital		
312	Jessica Jane, Drawing		

Assets begin with 1 · Liabilities begin with 2 · Owner's Equity begin with 3 · Revenues begin with 4 · Expenses begin with 5

FIGURE 4-2 Chart of Accounts

SOURCE DOCUMENTS

LO3 Describe and explain the purpose of source documents.

Almost any document that provides information about a business transaction can be called a **source document**. A source document triggers the analysis of what happened. It begins the process of entering transactions in the accounting system. Examples of source documents are shown in Figure 4-3. These source documents provide information that is useful in determining the effect of business transactions on specific accounts.

In addition to serving as input for transaction analysis, source documents serve as objective evidence of business transactions. If anyone questions the accounting records, these documents may be used as objective, verifiable evidence of the accuracy of the accounting records. For this reason, source documents are filed for possible future reference. *Having objective, verifiable evidence that a transaction occurred is an important accounting concept.*

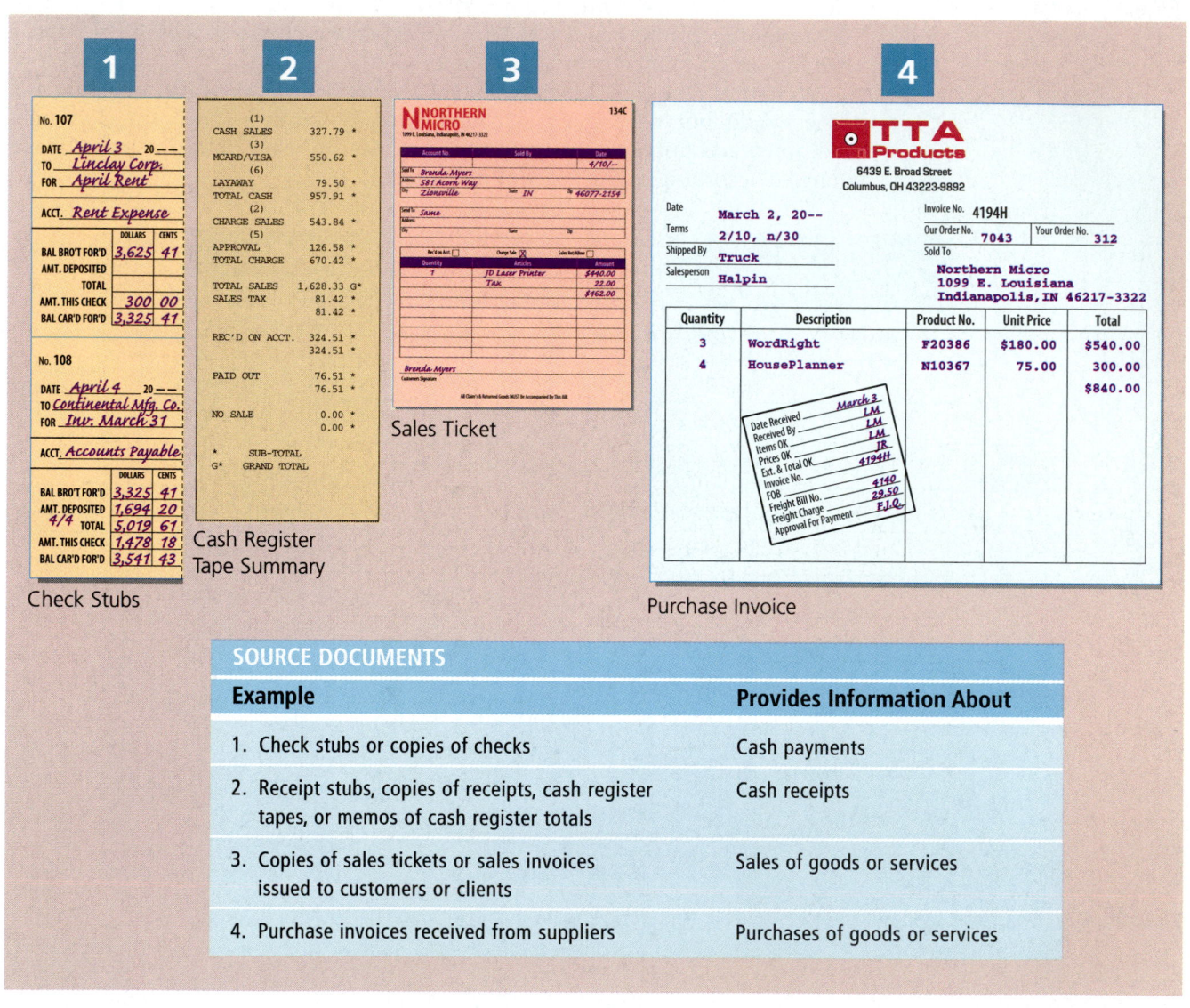

Check Stubs

Cash Register Tape Summary

Sales Ticket

Purchase Invoice

SOURCE DOCUMENTS	
Example	**Provides Information About**
1. Check stubs or copies of checks	Cash payments
2. Receipt stubs, copies of receipts, cash register tapes, or memos of cash register totals	Cash receipts
3. Copies of sales tickets or sales invoices issued to customers or clients	Sales of goods or services
4. Purchase invoices received from suppliers	Purchases of goods or services

FIGURE 4-3 Source Documents

A BROADER VIEW

Electronic Source Documents

With the ability to go shopping in cyberspace, more transactions are being initiated electronically. Even Sears, known for its low prices and excellent in-store service, has "online" shopping at www.sears.com. Customers can place orders and these orders can be filled, all based on electronic communications. This means that more and more "source documents" will be in an electronic form.

THE GENERAL JOURNAL

LO4 Journalize transactions.

A day-by-day listing of the transactions of a business is called a **journal.** The purpose of a journal is to provide a record of all transactions completed by the business. The journal shows the date of each transaction, titles of the accounts to be debited and credited, and the amounts of the debits and credits.

> **LEARNING KEY:** A journal provides a day-by-day listing of all transactions completed by the business.

A journal is commonly referred to as a **book of original entry** because it is here that the first formal accounting record of a transaction is made. Although many types of journals are used in business, the simplest journal form is a two-column general journal (Figure 4-4). Any kind of business transaction may be entered into a general journal.

A **two-column general journal** is so-named because it has only two amount columns, one for debit amounts and one for credit amounts. Journal pages are numbered in the upper right-hand corner. The five column numbers in Figure 4-4 are explained in Figure 4-5.

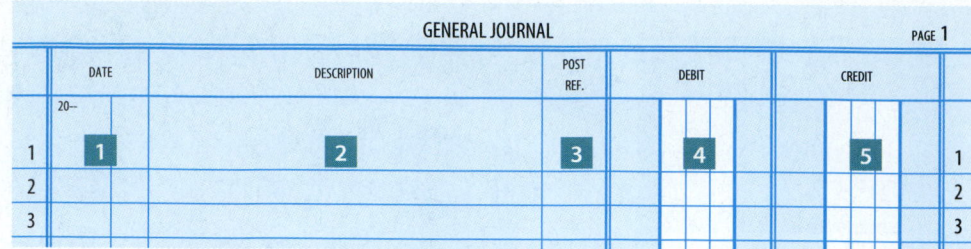

FIGURE 4-4 Two-Column General Journal

Column 1 Date	The year is entered in small figures at the top of the column immediately below the column heading. The year is repeated only at the top of each new page. The month is entered for the first entry on the page and for the first transaction of the month. The day of the month is recorded for every transaction, even if it is the same as the prior entry.
Column 2 Description	The *Description* or *Explanation* column is used to enter the titles of the accounts affected by each transaction, and to provide a very brief description of the transaction. Each transaction affects two or more accounts. The account(s) to be debited are entered first at the extreme left of the column. The account(s) to be credited are listed after the debits and indented. The description should be entered immediately following the last credit entry with an additional indentation.
Column 3 Posting Reference	No entries are made in the *Posting Reference* column during journalizing. Entries are made in this column when the debits and credits are copied to the proper accounts in the ledger. This process will be explained in detail later in this chapter.
Column 4 Debit Amount	The *Debit amount column* is used to enter the amount to be debited to an account. The amount should be entered on the same line as the title of that account.
Column 5 Credit Amount	The *Credit amount column* is used to enter the amount to be credited to an account. The amount should be entered on the same line as the title of that account.

FIGURE 4-5 The Columns in a Two-Column General Journal

Journalizing

Entering the transactions in a journal is called **journalizing**. For every transaction, the entry should include the date, the title of each account affected, the amounts, and a brief description.

To illustrate the journalizing process, transactions for the first month of operations of Jessie Jane's Campus Delivery will be journalized. The transactions are listed in Figure 4-6. Since you analyzed these transactions in Chapters 2 and 3, the journalizing process should be easier to understand. Let's start with a close look at the steps followed when journalizing the first transaction, Jessie's initial investment of $2,000.

LEARNING KEY: When journalizing, the exact account titles shown in the chart of accounts must be used. Refer to the chart of accounts in Figure 4-2 as you review the entries for Jessie Jane's Campus Delivery.

	SUMMARY OF TRANSACTIONS JESSIE JANE'S CAMPUS DELIVERY	

	Transaction	
(a)	June 1	Jessica Jane invested cash in her business, $2,000.
(b)	3	Bought delivery equipment for cash, $1,200.
(c)	5	Bought delivery equipment on account from Big Red Scooters, $900.
(d)	6	Paid first installment from transaction (c) to Big Red Scooters, $300.
(e)	6	Received cash for delivery services rendered, $500.
(f)	7	Paid cash for June office rent, $200.
(g)	15	Paid telephone bill, $50.
(h)	15	Made deliveries on account for a total of $600: Accounting Department ($400) and the School of Music ($200).
(i)	16	Bought supplies for cash, $80.
(j)	18	Paid cash for an eight-month liability insurance policy, $200. Coverage began on June 1.
(k)	20	Received $570 in cash for services performed in transaction (h): $400 from the Accounting Department and $170 from the School of Music.
(l)	25	Bought a third scooter from Big Red Scooters, $1,500. Paid $300 cash, with the remaining payments expected over the next four months.
(m)	27	Paid wages of part-time employees, $650.
(n)	30	Earned delivery fees for the remainder of the month amounting to $1,050: $430 in cash and $620 on account. Deliveries on account: Accounting Department ($250) and Athletic Ticket Office ($370).
(o)	30	Jessie withdrew cash for personal use, $150.

FIGURE 4-6 Summary of Transactions

Transaction (a)

June 1   Jessica Jane opened a bank account with a deposit of $2,000 for her business.

STEP 1   **Enter the date.** Since this is the first entry on the journal page, the year is entered on the first line of the Date column (in small print at the top of the line). The month and day are entered on the same line, below the year, in the Date column.

STEP 2   **Enter the debit.** Cash is entered on the first line at the extreme left of the Description column. The amount of the debit, $2,000, is entered on the same line in the Debit column. Since this is not a formal financial statement, dollar signs are not used.

In Chapter 3, we simply debited the T account.

Cash

(a) $2,000

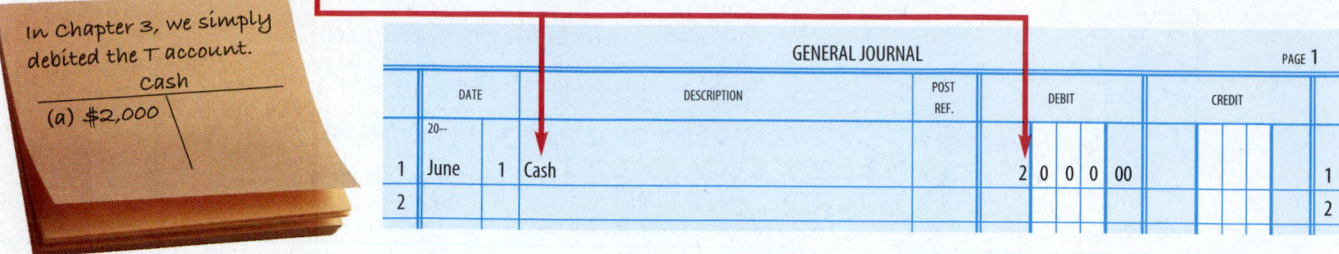

STEP 3   **Enter the credit.** The title of the account to be credited, Jessica Jane, Capital, is entered on the second line, indented one-half inch from the left side of the Description column. The amount of the credit, $2,000, is entered on the same line in the Credit column.

In Chapter 3, we simply credited the T account.

Jessica Jane, Capital

(a) $2,000

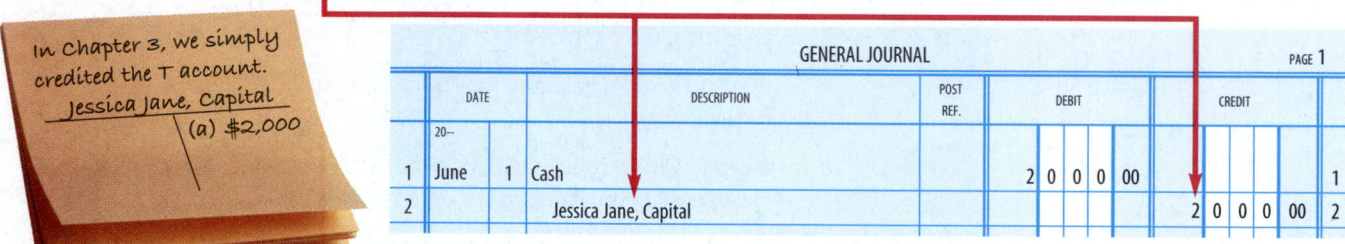

STEP 4   **Enter the explanation.** The explanation of the entry is entered on the next line, indented an additional one-half inch. The second line of the explanation, if needed, is also indented the same distance as the first.

	DATE		DESCRIPTION	POST REF.	DEBIT	CREDIT	
	20--						
1	June	1	Cash		2 0 0 0 00		1
2			Jessica Jane, Capital			2 0 0 0 00	2
3			Owner's original investment in				3
4			delivery business				4

GENERAL JOURNAL   PAGE 1

To enter transaction (b), the purchase of a motor scooter for $1,200 cash, we skip a line and follow the same four steps. *To help prevent inappropriate changes to entries, you probably would not skip a line in practice.* Note that the month and year do not need to be repeated. The day of the month must, however, be entered.

GENERAL JOURNAL   PAGE 1

	DATE		DESCRIPTION	POST REF.	DEBIT	CREDIT	
	20--						
1	June	1	Cash		2 0 0 0 00		1
2			Jessica Jane, Capital			2 0 0 0 00	2
3			Owner's original investment in				3
4			delivery business				4
5							5
6		3	Delivery Equipment		1 2 0 0 00		6
7			Cash			1 2 0 0 00	7
8			Purchased delivery equipment for cash				8

Skip a line → (points to line 5)

The journal entries for the month of June are shown in Figure 4-7. Note that the entries on June 25 and June 30 affect more than two accounts. Entries requiring more than one debit and/or one credit are called **compound entries**. The entry on June 25 has two credits. The credits are listed after the debit, indented and listed one under the other. The entry on June 30 has two debits. They are aligned with the left margin of the Description column and listed one under the other. In both cases, the debits equal the credits.

GENERAL JOURNAL   PAGE 1

	DATE		DESCRIPTION	POST REF.	DEBIT	CREDIT	
	20--						
1	June	1	Cash *(List debits first)*		2 0 0 0 00		1
2			Jessica Jane, Capital			2 0 0 0 00	2
3			Owner's original investment in				3
4			delivery business				4
5							5
6			Delivery Equipment		1 2 0 0 00		6
7			Cash			1 2 0 0 00	7
8			Purchased delivery equipment for cash				8
9							9
10		5	Delivery Equipment		9 0 0 00		10
11			Accounts Payable			9 0 0 00	11
12			Purchased delivery equipment on account				12
13			from Big Red Scooters				13
14							14
15		6	Accounts Payable		3 0 0 00		15
16			Cash			3 0 0 00	16
17			Made partial payment to Big Red Scooters				17
18							18
19		6	Cash		5 0 0 00		19
20			Delivery Fees			5 0 0 00	20
21			Received cash for delivery services				21

Annotations: *List credits second and indented.* (points to line 2); *Explanation is third and indented.* (points to line 3); *Space to make entries easier to read. To prevent improper changes to entries, the extra spacing might not be used in practice.* (points to line 5)

FIGURE 4-7 General Journal Entries

GENERAL JOURNAL — PAGE 1

	DATE	DESCRIPTION	POST REF.	DEBIT	CREDIT	
23	7	Rent Expense		2 0 0 00		23
24		Cash			2 0 0 00	24
25		Paid office rent for June				25
26						26
27	15	Telephone Expense		5 0 00		27
28		Cash			5 0 00	28
29		Paid telephone bill for June				29
30						30
31	15	Accounts Receivable		6 0 0 00		31
32		Delivery Fees			6 0 0 00	32
33		Deliveries made on account for Accounting				33
34		Department ($400) and School of Music ($200)				34
35						35

GENERAL JOURNAL — PAGE 2

	DATE	DESCRIPTION	POST REF.	DEBIT	CREDIT	
	20--					
1	June 16	Supplies		8 0 00		1
2		Cash			8 0 00	2
3		Purchased supplies for cash				3
4						4
5	18	Prepaid Insurance		2 0 0 00		5
6		Cash			2 0 0 00	6
7		Paid premium for eight-month				7
8		insurance policy				8
9						9
10	20	Cash		5 7 0 00		10
11		Accounts Receivable			5 7 0 00	11
12		Received cash on account from Accounting				12
13		Department ($400) and School of Music ($170)				13
14						14
15	25	Delivery Equipment — *Compound entry*		1 5 0 0 00		15
16		Accounts Payable — *Line up credits* — *Debits = Credits*			1 2 0 0 00	16
17		Cash			3 0 0 00	17
18		Purchased scooter with down payment;				18
19		balance on account with Big Red Scooters				19
20						20
21	27	Wages Expense		6 5 0 00		21
22		Cash			6 5 0 00	22
23		Paid employees				23
24						24

FIGURE 4-7 General Journal Entries *(continued)*

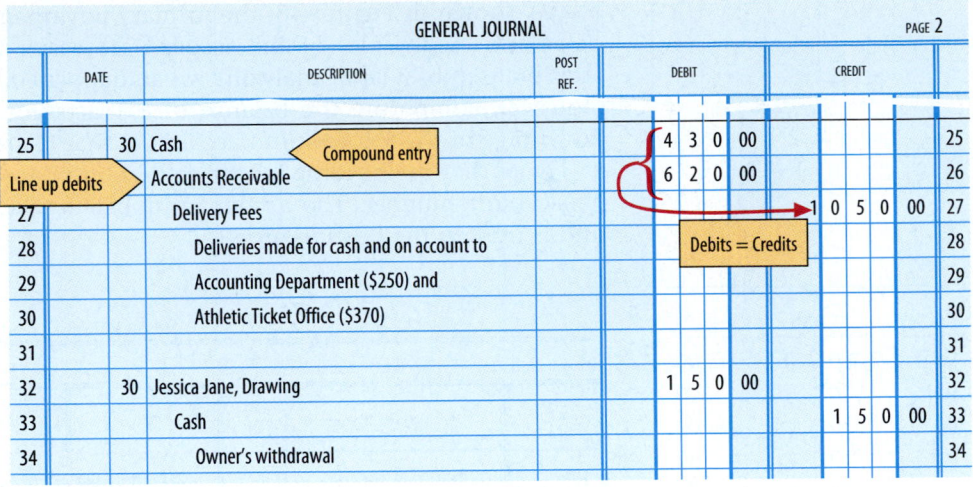

FIGURE 4-7   General Journal Entries *(continued)*

THE GENERAL LEDGER

LO5 Post to the general ledger and prepare a trial balance.

The journal provides a day-by-day record of business transactions. To determine the current balance of specific accounts, however, the information in the journal must be transferred to accounts similar to the T accounts illustrated in Chapter 3. This process is called posting.

A complete set of all the accounts used by a business is known as the **general ledger**. The general ledger accumulates a complete record of the debits and credits made to each account as a result of entries made in the journal. The accounts are numbered and arranged in the same order as the chart of accounts. That is, accounts are numbered and grouped by classification: assets, liabilities, owner's equity, revenues, and expenses.

LEARNING KEY: While the journal provides a day-by-day record of business transactions, the ledger provides a record of the transactions entered in each account.

Four-Column Account

For purposes of illustration, the T account was introduced in Chapter 3. In practice, businesses are more likely to use a version of the account called the **four-column account**. Figure 4-8 compares the cash T account from Chapter 3 for Jessie Jane's Campus Delivery and a four-column cash account summarizing the same cash transactions. A four-column account contains columns for the debit or credit transaction and columns for the debit or credit running balance. In addition, there are columns for the date, description of the item, and posting reference. The Item column is used to provide descriptions of special entries. For example, "Balance" is written in this column when the balance of an account is transferred to a new page. The Posting Reference column is used to indicate the journal page from which an entry was posted, or a check mark (✔) is inserted to indicate that no posting was required.

As shown in Figure 4-8, the primary advantage of the T account is that the debit and credit sides of the account are easier to identify. Thus, for demonstration purposes and analyzing what happened, T accounts are very helpful. However, computing the balance of a T account is cumbersome. The primary advantage of the four-column account is that it maintains a running balance.

Note that the heading for the four-column account has the account title and an account number. The account number is taken from the chart of accounts and is used in the posting process.

Cash (T Account)

(a)	2,000	(b)	1,200
(e)	500	(d)	300
(k)	570	(f)	200
(n)	430	(g)	50
	3,500	(i)	80
		(j)	200
		(l)	300
		(m)	650
		(o)	150
Bal.	370		**3,130**

GENERAL LEDGER

ACCOUNT: Cash   ACCOUNT NO. 101

DATE	ITEM	POST REF.	DEBIT	CREDIT	BALANCE DEBIT	BALANCE CREDIT
20-- June 1			2 0 0 0 00		2 0 0 0 00	
3				1 2 0 0 00	8 0 0 00	
6				3 0 0 00	5 0 0 00	
6			5 0 0 00		1 0 0 0 00	
7				2 0 0 00	8 0 0 00	
15				5 0 00	7 5 0 00	
16				8 0 00	6 7 0 00	
18				2 0 0 00	4 7 0 00	
20			5 7 0 00		1 0 4 0 00	
25				3 0 0 00	7 4 0 00	
27				6 5 0 00	9 0 00	
30			4 3 0 00		5 2 0 00	
30				1 5 0 00	3 7 0 00	

└── Transaction Amount ──┘ └── Running Balance ──┘

FIGURE 4-8 Comparison of T Account and Four-Column Account

LEARNING KEY: The four-column account is similar to the T account, but makes it easier to maintain a running balance.

Posting to the General Ledger

The process of copying the debits and credits from the journal to the ledger accounts is known as **posting.** All amounts entered in the journal must be posted to the general ledger accounts.

LEARNING KEY: Posting is simply the copying of the exact dates and dollar amounts from the journal to the ledger.

Posting from the journal to the ledger is done daily or at frequent intervals. There are five steps.

Steps in the Posting Process

In the ledger account:

STEP 1   Enter the date of the transaction in the Date column. There is no need to repeat the month and year, but the day must be entered even if it is the same date as in the previous transaction.

STEP 2   Enter the amount of the debit or credit in the Debit or Credit column.

STEP 3   Enter the new balance in the Balance columns under Debit or Credit. If the balance of the account is zero, draw a line through the debit and credit columns.

STEP 4   Enter the journal page number from which each transaction is posted in the Posting Reference column.

In the journal:

STEP 5   Enter the ledger account number in the Posting Reference column of the journal for each transaction that is posted.

Step 5 is the last step in the posting process. After this step is completed, the posting references will indicate which journal entries have been posted to the ledger accounts. This is very helpful, particularly if you are interrupted during the posting process. The information in the Posting Reference columns of the journal and ledger provides a link between the journal and ledger known as a **cross-reference**.

 LEARNING KEY: Posting references indicate that a journal entry has been posted to the general ledger.

To illustrate the posting process, the first journal entry for Jessie Jane's Campus Delivery will be posted step-by-step. First, let's post the debit to Cash (Figure 4-9).

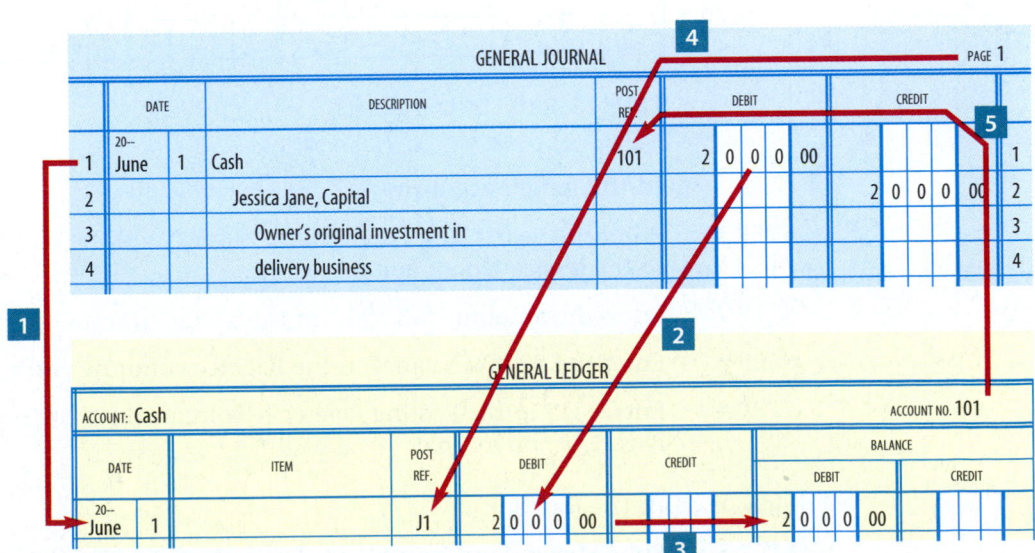

FIGURE 4-9   Posting a Debit

In the ledger account:

STEP 1   Enter the year, "20--," the month, "June," and the day, "1," in the Date column of the cash account.

STEP 2   Enter the amount, "$2,000," in the Debit column. Again, since this is not a formal financial statement, dollar signs are not used.

STEP 3   Enter the $2,000 balance in the Balance columns under Debit.

STEP 4   Enter "J1" in the Posting Reference column since the posting came from page 1 of the *Journal*.

       The Item column is left blank, except for special reasons such as indicating the beginning balance.

In the journal:

STEP 5   Enter the account number for Cash, 101 (see chart of accounts in Figure 4-2 on page 89), in the Posting Reference column of the journal on the same line as the debit to Cash for $2,000.

       Now let's post the credit portion of the first entry (Figure 4-10).

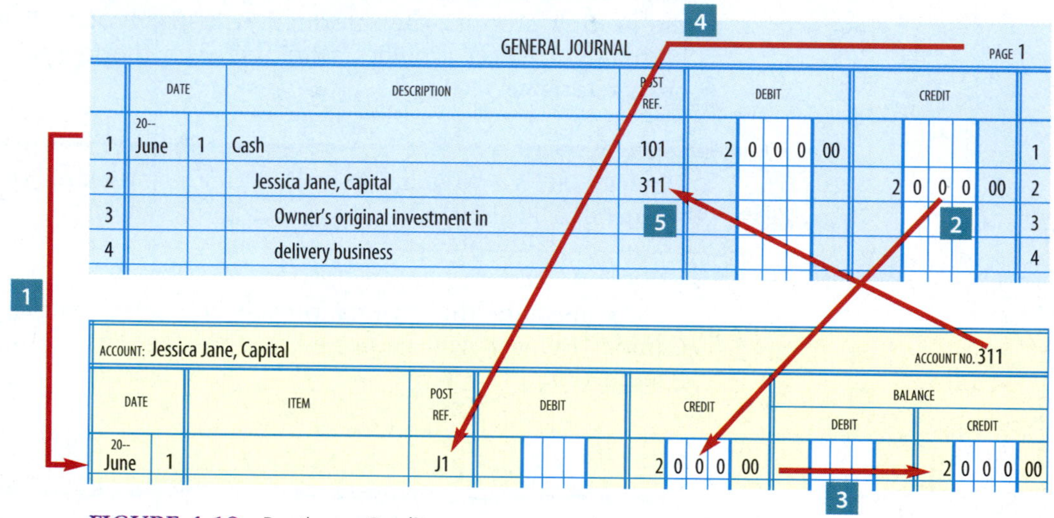

FIGURE 4-10   Posting a Credit

In the ledger account:

STEP 1   Enter the year, "20--," the month, "June," and the day, "1," in the Date column of the Jessica Jane, Capital account.

STEP 2   Enter the amount, "$2,000," in the Credit column.

STEP 3   Enter the $2,000 balance in the Balance columns under Credit.

STEP 4   Enter "J1" in the Posting Reference column since the posting came from Page 1 of the *Journal*.

In the journal:

STEP 5   Enter the account number for Jessica Jane, Capital, 311, in the Posting Reference column.

After posting the journal entries for Jessie Jane's Campus Delivery for the month of June, the general journal and general ledger should appear as illustrated in Figures 4-11 and 4-12 on pages 101–104. *Note that the Posting Reference column of the journal has been filled in because the entries have been posted.*

	DATE		DESCRIPTION	POST REF.	DEBIT					CREDIT					
	20--		GENERAL JOURNAL											PAGE 1	
1	June	1	Cash	101	2	0	0	0	00						1
2			Jessica Jane, Capital	311						2	0	0	0	00	2
3			Owner's original investment in												3
4			delivery business												4
5															5
6		3	Delivery Equipment	185	1	2	0	0	00						6
7			Cash	101						1	2	0	0	00	7
8			Purchased delivery equipment for cash												8
9															9
10		5	Delivery Equipment	185		9	0	0	00						10
11			Accounts Payable	202							9	0	0	00	11
12			Purchased delivery equipment on account												12
13			from Big Red Scooters												13
14															14
15		6	Accounts Payable	202		3	0	0	00						15
16			Cash	101							3	0	0	00	16
17			Made partial payment to Big Red Scooters												17
18															18
19		6	Cash	101		5	0	0	00						19
20			Delivery Fees	401							5	0	0	00	20
21			Received cash for delivery services												21
22															22
23		7	Rent Expense	521		2	0	0	00						23
24			Cash	101							2	0	0	00	24
25			Paid office rent for June												25
26															26
27		15	Telephone Expense	525			5	0	00						27
28			Cash	101								5	0	00	28
29			Paid telephone bill for June												29
30															30
31		15	Accounts Receivable	122		6	0	0	00						31
32			Delivery Fees	401							6	0	0	00	32
33			Deliveries made on account for Accounting												33
34			Department ($400) and School of Music ($200)												34
35															35

FIGURE 4-11   General Journal After Posting

	DATE		DESCRIPTION	POST REF.	DEBIT				CREDIT				
	20--												
1	June	16	Supplies	141		8	0	00					1
2			Cash	101						8	0	00	2
3			Purchased supplies for cash										3
4													4
5		18	Prepaid Insurance	145	2	0	0	00					5
6			Cash	101					2	0	0	00	6
7			Paid premium for eight-month										7
8			insurance policy										8
9													9
10		20	Cash	101	5	7	0	00					10
11			Accounts Receivable	122					5	7	0	00	11
12			Received cash on account from Accounting										12
13			Department ($400) and School of Music ($170)										13
14													14
15		25	Delivery Equipment	185	1 5	0	0	00					15
16			Accounts Payable	202					1 2	0	0	00	16
17			Cash	101					3	0	0	00	17
18			Purchased scooter with down payment;										18
19			balance on account with Big Red Scooters										19
20													20
21		27	Wages Expense	511	6	5	0	00					21
22			Cash	101					6	5	0	00	22
23			Paid employees										23
24													24
25		30	Cash	101	4	3	0	00					25
26			Accounts Receivable	122	6	2	0	00					26
27			Delivery Fees	401					1 0	5	0	00	27
28			Deliveries made for cash and on account to										28
29			Accounting Department ($250) and										29
30			Athletic Ticket Office ($370)										30
31													31
32		30	Jessica Jane, Drawing	312	1	5	0	00					32
33			Cash	101					1	5	0	00	33
34			Owner's withdrawal										34

GENERAL JOURNAL   PAGE 2

FIGURE 4-11   General Journal After Posting *(continued)*

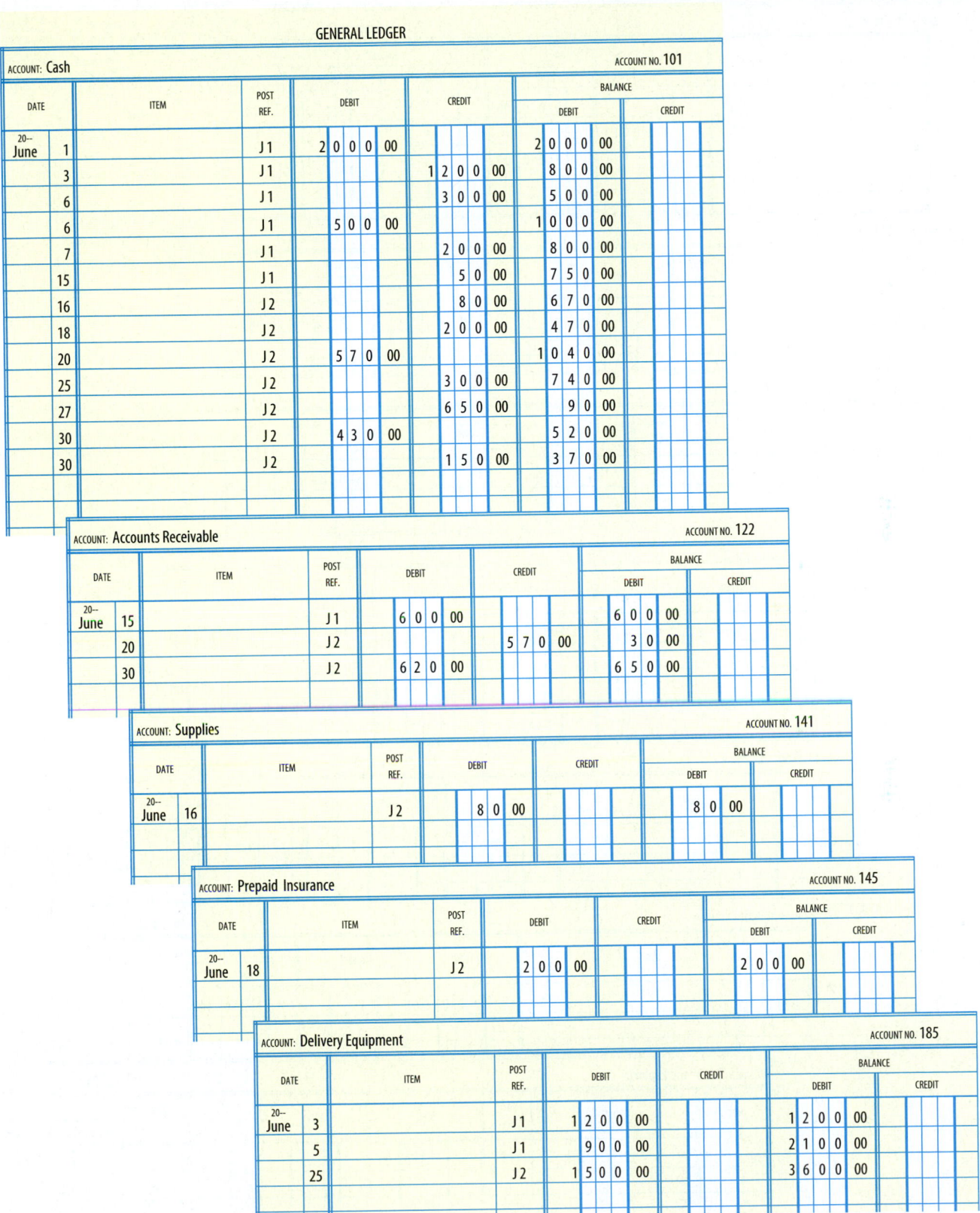

GENERAL LEDGER

ACCOUNT: Cash   ACCOUNT NO. 101

DATE		ITEM	POST REF.	DEBIT	CREDIT	BALANCE DEBIT	BALANCE CREDIT
20-- June	1		J1	2 0 0 0 00		2 0 0 0 00	
	3		J1		1 2 0 0 00	8 0 0 00	
	6		J1		3 0 0 00	5 0 0 00	
	6		J1	5 0 0 00		1 0 0 0 00	
	7		J1		2 0 0 00	8 0 0 00	
	15		J1		5 0 00	7 5 0 00	
	16		J2		8 0 00	6 7 0 00	
	18		J2		2 0 0 00	4 7 0 00	
	20		J2	5 7 0 00		1 0 4 0 00	
	25		J2		3 0 0 00	7 4 0 00	
	27		J2		6 5 0 00	9 0 00	
	30		J2	4 3 0 00		5 2 0 00	
	30		J2		1 5 0 00	3 7 0 00	

ACCOUNT: Accounts Receivable   ACCOUNT NO. 122

DATE		ITEM	POST REF.	DEBIT	CREDIT	BALANCE DEBIT	BALANCE CREDIT
20-- June	15		J1	6 0 0 00		6 0 0 00	
	20		J2		5 7 0 00	3 0 00	
	30		J2	6 2 0 00		6 5 0 00	

ACCOUNT: Supplies   ACCOUNT NO. 141

DATE		ITEM	POST REF.	DEBIT	CREDIT	BALANCE DEBIT	BALANCE CREDIT
20-- June	16		J2	8 0 00		8 0 00	

ACCOUNT: Prepaid Insurance   ACCOUNT NO. 145

DATE		ITEM	POST REF.	DEBIT	CREDIT	BALANCE DEBIT	BALANCE CREDIT
20-- June	18		J2	2 0 0 00		2 0 0 00	

ACCOUNT: Delivery Equipment   ACCOUNT NO. 185

DATE		ITEM	POST REF.	DEBIT	CREDIT	BALANCE DEBIT	BALANCE CREDIT
20-- June	3		J1	1 2 0 0 00		1 2 0 0 00	
	5		J1	9 0 0 00		2 1 0 0 00	
	25		J2	1 5 0 0 00		3 6 0 0 00	

FIGURE 4-12 General Ledger After Posting

PART 1   Accounting for a Service Business

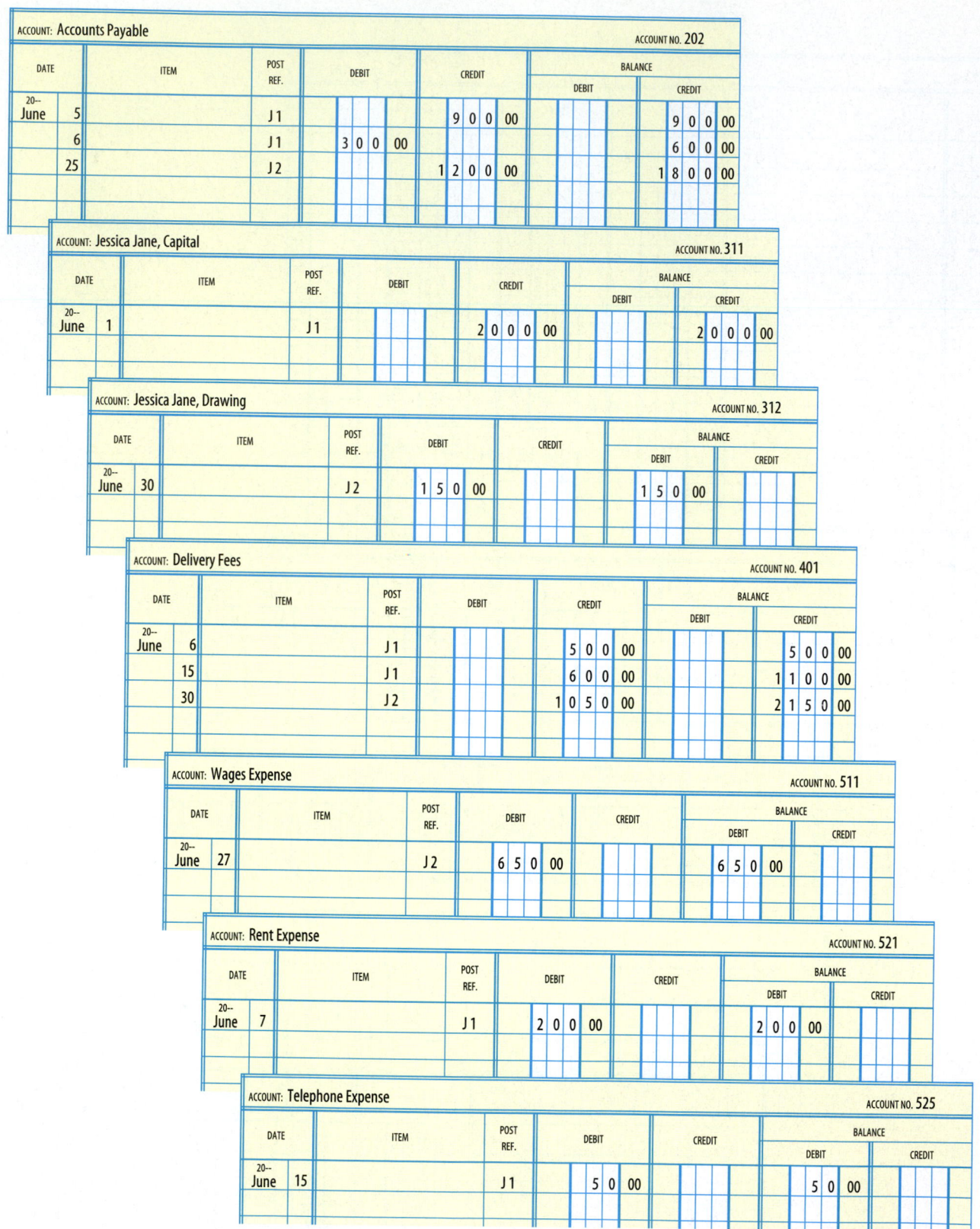

ACCOUNT: Accounts Payable   ACCOUNT NO. **202**

DATE		ITEM	POST REF.	DEBIT	CREDIT	BALANCE	
						DEBIT	CREDIT
20-- June	5		J 1		9 0 0 00		9 0 0 00
	6		J 1	3 0 0 00			6 0 0 00
	25		J 2		1 2 0 0 00		1 8 0 0 00

ACCOUNT: Jessica Jane, Capital   ACCOUNT NO. **311**

DATE		ITEM	POST REF.	DEBIT	CREDIT	BALANCE	
						DEBIT	CREDIT
20-- June	1		J 1		2 0 0 0 00		2 0 0 0 00

ACCOUNT: Jessica Jane, Drawing   ACCOUNT NO. **312**

DATE		ITEM	POST REF.	DEBIT	CREDIT	BALANCE	
						DEBIT	CREDIT
20-- June	30		J 2	1 5 0 00		1 5 0 00	

ACCOUNT: Delivery Fees   ACCOUNT NO. **401**

DATE		ITEM	POST REF.	DEBIT	CREDIT	BALANCE	
						DEBIT	CREDIT
20-- June	6		J 1		5 0 0 00		5 0 0 00
	15		J 1		6 0 0 00		1 1 0 0 00
	30		J 2		1 0 5 0 00		2 1 5 0 00

ACCOUNT: Wages Expense   ACCOUNT NO. **511**

DATE		ITEM	POST REF.	DEBIT	CREDIT	BALANCE	
						DEBIT	CREDIT
20-- June	27		J 2	6 5 0 00		6 5 0 00	

ACCOUNT: Rent Expense   ACCOUNT NO. **521**

DATE		ITEM	POST REF.	DEBIT	CREDIT	BALANCE	
						DEBIT	CREDIT
20-- June	7		J 1	2 0 0 00		2 0 0 00	

ACCOUNT: Telephone Expense   ACCOUNT NO. **525**

DATE		ITEM	POST REF.	DEBIT	CREDIT	BALANCE	
						DEBIT	CREDIT
20-- June	15		J 1	5 0 00		5 0 00	

FIGURE 4-12 General Ledger After Posting *(continued)*

The Trial Balance

In Chapter 3, a **trial balance** was used to prove that the totals of the debit and credit balances in the T accounts were equal. In this chapter, a trial balance is used to prove the equality of the debits and credits in the ledger accounts. A trial balance can be prepared daily, weekly, monthly, or whenever desired. Before preparing a trial balance, all transactions should be journalized and posted so that the effect of all transactions will be reflected in the ledger accounts.

The trial balance for Jessie Jane's Campus Delivery shown in Figure 4-13 was prepared from the balances in the general ledger in Figure 4-12. The accounts are listed in the order used in the chart of accounts. This order is also often used when preparing financial statements. In Chapter 2, we pointed out that many firms list expenses from highest to lowest amounts. Some firms list expenses according to the chart of accounts, which is the method we will follow.

LEARNING KEY: The chart of accounts determines the order for listing accounts in the general ledger and trial balance. This order may also be used when preparing financial statements.

Jessie Jane's Campus Delivery Trial Balance June 30, 20 - -			
ACCOUNT TITLE	ACCOUNT NO.	DEBIT BALANCE	CREDIT BALANCE
Cash	101	3 7 0 00	
Accounts Receivable	122	6 5 0 00	
Supplies	141	8 0 00	
Prepaid Insurance	145	2 0 0 00	
Delivery Equipment	185	3 6 0 0 00	
Accounts Payable	202		1 8 0 0 00
Jessica Jane, Capital	311		2 0 0 0 00
Jessica Jane, Drawing	312	1 5 0 00	
Delivery Fees	401		2 1 5 0 00
Wages Expense	511	6 5 0 00	
Rent Expense	521	2 0 0 00	
Telephone Expense	525	5 0 00	
		5 9 5 0 00	5 9 5 0 00

FIGURE 4-13 Trial Balance

Even though the trial balance indicates that the ledger is in balance, the ledger can still contain errors. For example, if a journal entry was made debiting or crediting the wrong accounts, or if an item was posted to the wrong account, the ledger will still be in balance. It is important, therefore, to be very careful in preparing the journal entries and in posting them to the ledger accounts.

FINDING AND CORRECTING ERRORS IN THE TRIAL BALANCE

LO6 Explain how to find and correct errors.

Tips are available to help if your trial balance has an error. Figure 4-14 offers hints for finding the error when your trial balance does not balance.

1. Double check your addition. Review balances to see if they are too large or small, relative to other accounts, or entered in the wrong column.

2. Find the difference between the debits and the credits.

   a. If the difference is equal to the amount of a specific transaction, perhaps you forgot to post the debit or credit portion of this transaction.

   b. Divide the difference by 2. If the difference is evenly divisible by 2, you may have posted two debits or two credits for a transaction. If a debit were posted as a credit, it would mean that one transaction had two credits and no debits. The difference between the total debits and credits would be twice the amount of the debit that was posted as a credit.

   c. Divide the difference by 9. If the difference is evenly divisible by 9, you may have committed a **slide error** or a **transposition error**. A slide occurs when debit or credit amounts "slide" a digit or two to the left or right when entered. For example, if $250 was entered as $25:

   | $250 | – | 25 | = | $225 |
   | $225 | ÷ | 9 | = | $25 |

   The difference is evenly divisible by 9.

   A transposition occurs when two digits are reversed. For example, if $250 was entered as $520:

   | $520 | – | 250 | = | $270 |
   | $270 | ÷ | 9 | = | $30 |

   Again, the difference is evenly divisible by 9.

FIGURE 4-14   Tips for Finding Errors in the Trial Balance

If the tips in Figure 4-14 don't work, you must retrace your steps through the accounting process. Double check your addition for the ledger accounts. Also trace all postings. Be patient as you search for your error. Use this process as an opportunity to reinforce your understanding of the flow of information through the accounting system. Much can be learned while looking for an error.

Once you have found an error, there are two methods of making the correction. Although you may want to erase when correcting your homework, this is not acceptable in practice. An erasure may suggest that you are trying to hide something. You should use the ruling method or make a correcting entry instead.

Ruling Method

The **ruling method** should be used to correct two types of errors:

1. When an incorrect journal entry has been made, but not yet posted.

2. When a proper entry has been made but posted to the wrong account or for the wrong amount.

When using the ruling method, draw a single line through the incorrect account title or amount and write the correct information directly above the line. Corrections should be initialed by someone authorized to make such changes. This is done so the source and reason for the correction can be traced. This type of correction may be made in the journal or ledger accounts, as shown in Figure 4-15.

FIGURE 4-15 Ruling Method of Making a Correction

Correcting Entry Method

If an incorrect entry has been journalized and posted to the wrong account, a **correcting entry** should be made. For example, assume that a $400 payment for Rent Expense was incorrectly debited to Repair Expense and correctly credited to Cash. This requires a correcting entry and explanation as shown in Figure 4-16. Figure 4-17 shows the effects of the correcting entry on the ledger accounts. Generally, "Correcting" is written in the Item column of the general ledger account.

	DATE		DESCRIPTION	POST REF.	DEBIT	CREDIT	
1	20-- Sept.	25	Rent Expense	521	4 0 0 00		1
2			Repair Expense	537		4 0 0 00	2
3			To correct error in which payment for rent				3
4			was debited to Repair Expense				4
5							5

GENERAL JOURNAL — PAGE 6

FIGURE 4-16 Correcting Entry Method

GENERAL LEDGER

ACCOUNT: Rent Expense — ACCOUNT NO. 521

DATE		ITEM	POST REF.	DEBIT	CREDIT	BALANCE DEBIT	BALANCE CREDIT
20-- Sept.	25	Correcting	J 6	4 0 0 00		4 0 0 00	

ACCOUNT: Repair Expense — ACCOUNT NO. 537

DATE		ITEM	POST REF.	DEBIT	CREDIT	BALANCE DEBIT	BALANCE CREDIT
20-- Sept.	10		J 5	5 0 00		5 0 00	
	15		J 5	4 0 0 00		4 5 0 00	
	25	Correcting	J 6		4 0 0 00	5 0 00	

FIGURE 4-17 Effects of Correcting Entry on Ledger Accounts

Learning Objectives	Key Points to Remember
1 Describe the flow of data from source documents through the trial balance.	The flow of data from the source documents through the trial balance is: 1. Analyze business transactions. 2. Journalize transactions in the general journal. 3. Post journal entries to the general ledger. 4. Prepare a trial balance. **INPUT** — Analyze transactions using SOURCE DOCUMENTS and CHART OF ACCOUNTS → **PROCESSING** — Enter business transactions in the GENERAL JOURNAL *Journalizing* → Post the entries in the journal to the GENERAL LEDGER *Posting* → From the general ledger, prepare a TRIAL BALANCE
2 Describe the chart of accounts as a means of classifying financial information.	The chart of accounts includes the account titles in numerical order for all assets, liabilities, owner's equity, revenues, and expenses. The chart of accounts is used in classifying information about transactions.
3 Describe and explain the purpose of source documents.	Source documents trigger the analysis of business transactions and the entries into the accounting system.
4 Journalize transactions.	A journal provides a day-by-day listing of transactions. The journal shows the date, titles of the accounts to be debited or credited, and the amounts of the debits and credits. The steps in the journalizing process are: 1. Enter the date. 2. Enter the debit. Accounts to be debited are entered first. 3. Enter the credit. Accounts to be credited are entered after the debits and are indented one-half inch. 4. Enter the explanation. A brief explanation of the transaction should be entered in the description column on the line following the last credit. The explanation should be indented an additional one-half inch.
5 Post to the general ledger and prepare a trial balance.	The general ledger is a complete set of all accounts used by the business. The steps in posting from the general journal to the general ledger are: In the general ledger: 1. Enter the date of each transaction. 2. Enter the amount of each debit or credit in the Debit or Credit column. 3. Enter the new balance. 4. Enter the journal page number from which each transaction is posted in the Posting Reference column. In the journal: 5. Enter the account number to which each transaction is posted in the Posting Reference column. The trial balance provides a check to make sure the total of all debit balances in the ledger accounts equals the total of all credit balances in the ledger accounts.
6 Explain how to find and correct errors.	Errors may be found by verifying your addition, by dividing the difference between the debits and credits by 2 or 9, and by retracing your steps through the accounting process. Use the ruling method or the correcting entry method to correct the error.

Reflection: Answering the Opening Question

Corrections should not be made by erasing the original entry. Erasing could create suspicion over what was changed and the reasons for the change. Instead, use the ruling method or make a correcting entry as discussed in the chapter.

DEMONSTRATION PROBLEM

George Fielding is a financial planning consultant. He provides budgeting, estate planning, tax planning, and investing advice for professional golfers. He developed the following chart of accounts for his business.

Assets	Revenues
101 Cash	401 Professional Fees
142 Office Supplies	

Liabilities	Expenses
202 Accounts Payable	511 Wages Expense
	521 Rent Expense
	525 Telephone Expense
Owner's Equity	533 Utilities Expense
311 George Fielding, Capital	534 Charitable Contributions Expense
312 George Fielding, Drawing	538 Automobile Expense

The following transactions took place during the month of December of the current year.

Dec. 1	Fielding invested cash to start the business, $20,000.
3	Paid Bollhorst Real Estate for December office rent, $1,000.
4	Received cash from Aaron Patton, a client, for services, $2,500.
6	Paid T. Z. Anderson Electric for December heating and light, $75.
7	Received cash from Andrew Conder, a client, for services, $2,000.
12	Paid Fichter's Super Service for gasoline and oil purchases for the company car, $60.
14	Paid Hillenburg Staffing for temporary secretarial services during the past two weeks, $600.
17	Bought office supplies from Bowers Office Supply on account, $280.
20	Paid Mitchell Telephone Co. for business calls during the past month, $100.
21	Fielding withdrew cash for personal use, $1,100.
24	Made donation to the National Multiple Sclerosis Society, $100.
27	Received cash from Billy Walters, a client, for services, $2,000.

28   Paid Hillenburg Staffing for temporary secretarial services during the past two weeks, $600.

29   Made payment on account to Bowers Office Supply, $100.

REQUIRED

1. Record the preceding transactions in a general journal.

2. Post the entries to the general ledger.

3. Prepare a trial balance.

Solution

1, 2.

		GENERAL JOURNAL					PAGE 1
	DATE	DESCRIPTION	POST REF.	DEBIT	CREDIT	
	20--					
1	Dec. 1	Cash	101	20 0 0 0 00		1
2		George Fielding, Capital	311		20 0 0 0 00	2
3		Owner's original investment in				3
4		consulting business				4
5						5
6	3	Rent Expense	521	1 0 0 0 00		6
7		Cash	101		1 0 0 0 00	7
8		Paid rent for December				8
9						9
10	4	Cash	101	2 5 0 0 00		10
11		Professional Fees	401		2 5 0 0 00	11
12		Received cash for services rendered				12
13						13
14	6	Utilities Expense	533	7 5 00		14
15		Cash	101		7 5 00	15
16		Paid utilities				16
17						17
18	7	Cash	101	2 0 0 0 00		18
19		Professional Fees	401		2 0 0 0 00	19
20		Received cash for services rendered				20
21						21
22	12	Automobile Expense	538	6 0 00		22
23		Cash	101		6 0 00	23
24		Paid for gas and oil				24
25						25
26	14	Wages Expense	511	6 0 0 00		26
27		Cash	101		6 0 0 00	27
28		Paid temporary secretaries				28
29						29
30	17	Office Supplies	142	2 8 0 00		30
31		Accounts Payable	202		2 8 0 00	31
32		Purchased office supplies on account from				32
33		Bowers Office Supply				33
34						34
35						35

(continued)

GENERAL JOURNAL
PAGE 2

	DATE	DESCRIPTION	POST REF.	DEBIT	CREDIT	
1	20-- Dec. 20	Telephone Expense	525	1 0 0 00		1
2		Cash	101		1 0 0 00	2
3		Paid telephone bill				3
4						4
5	21	George Fielding, Drawing	312	1 1 0 0 00		5
6		Cash	101		1 1 0 0 00	6
7		Owner's withdrawal				7
8						8
9	24	Charitable Contributions Expense	534	1 0 0 00		9
10		Cash	101		1 0 0 00	10
11		Contribution to National Multiple				11
12		Sclerosis Society				12
13						13
14	27	Cash	101	2 0 0 0 00		14
15		Professional Fees	401		2 0 0 0 00	15
16		Received cash for services rendered				16
17						17
18	28	Wages Expense	511	6 0 0 00		18
19		Cash	101		6 0 0 00	19
20		Paid temporary secretaries				20
21						21
22	29	Accounts Payable	202	1 0 0 00		22
23		Cash	101		1 0 0 00	23
24		Payment on account to Bowers Office Supply				24

2.

GENERAL LEDGER

ACCOUNT: Cash   ACCOUNT NO. 101

DATE	ITEM	POST REF.	DEBIT	CREDIT	BALANCE DEBIT	BALANCE CREDIT
20-- Dec. 1		J 1	20 0 0 0 00		20 0 0 0 00	
3		J 1		1 0 0 0 00	19 0 0 0 00	
4		J 1	2 5 0 0 00		21 5 0 0 00	
6		J 1		7 5 00	21 4 2 5 00	
7		J 1	2 0 0 0 00		23 4 2 5 00	
12		J 1		6 0 00	23 3 6 5 00	
14		J 1		6 0 0 00	22 7 6 5 00	
20		J 2		1 0 0 00	22 6 6 5 00	
21		J 2		1 1 0 0 00	21 5 6 5 00	
24		J 2		1 0 0 00	21 4 6 5 00	
27		J 2	2 0 0 0 00		23 4 6 5 00	
28		J 2		6 0 0 00	22 8 6 5 00	
29		J 2		1 0 0 00	22 7 6 5 00	

ACCOUNT: Office Supplies   ACCOUNT NO. 142

DATE	ITEM	POST REF.	DEBIT	CREDIT	BALANCE DEBIT	BALANCE CREDIT
20-- Dec. 17		J1	2 8 0 00		2 8 0 00	

ACCOUNT: Accounts Payable   ACCOUNT NO. 202

DATE	ITEM	POST REF.	DEBIT	CREDIT	BALANCE DEBIT	BALANCE CREDIT
20-- Dec. 17		J1		2 8 0 00		2 8 0 00
29		J2	1 0 0 00			1 8 0 00

ACCOUNT: George Fielding, Capital   ACCOUNT NO. 311

DATE	ITEM	POST REF.	DEBIT	CREDIT	BALANCE DEBIT	BALANCE CREDIT
20-- Dec. 1		J1		20 0 0 0 00		20 0 0 0 00

ACCOUNT: George Fielding, Drawing   ACCOUNT NO. 312

DATE	ITEM	POST REF.	DEBIT	CREDIT	BALANCE DEBIT	BALANCE CREDIT
20-- Dec. 21		J2	1 1 0 0 00		1 1 0 0 00	

ACCOUNT: Professional Fees   ACCOUNT NO. 401

DATE	ITEM	POST REF.	DEBIT	CREDIT	BALANCE DEBIT	BALANCE CREDIT
20-- Dec. 4		J1		2 5 0 0 00		2 5 0 0 00
7		J1		2 0 0 0 00		4 5 0 0 00
27		J2		2 0 0 0 00		6 5 0 0 00

ACCOUNT: Wages Expense   ACCOUNT NO. 511

DATE	ITEM	POST REF.	DEBIT	CREDIT	BALANCE DEBIT	BALANCE CREDIT
20-- Dec. 14		J1	6 0 0 00		6 0 0 00	
28		J2	6 0 0 00		1 2 0 0 00	

ACCOUNT: Rent Expense   ACCOUNT NO. 521

DATE	ITEM	POST REF.	DEBIT	CREDIT	BALANCE DEBIT	BALANCE CREDIT
20-- Dec. 3		J1	1 0 0 0 00		1 0 0 0 00	

(continued)

ACCOUNT: Telephone Expense   ACCOUNT NO. 525

DATE	ITEM	POST REF.	DEBIT	CREDIT	BALANCE DEBIT	BALANCE CREDIT
20-- Dec. 20		J 2	1 0 0 00		1 0 0 00	

ACCOUNT: Utilities Expense   ACCOUNT NO. 533

DATE	ITEM	POST REF.	DEBIT	CREDIT	BALANCE DEBIT	BALANCE CREDIT
20-- Dec. 6		J 1	7 5 00		7 5 00	

ACCOUNT: Charitable Contributions Expense   ACCOUNT NO. 534

DATE	ITEM	POST REF.	DEBIT	CREDIT	BALANCE DEBIT	BALANCE CREDIT
20-- Dec. 24		J 2	1 0 0 00		1 0 0 00	

ACCOUNT: Automobile Expense   ACCOUNT NO. 538

DATE	ITEM	POST REF.	DEBIT	CREDIT	BALANCE DEBIT	BALANCE CREDIT
20-- Dec. 12		J 1	6 0 00		6 0 00	

3.

George Fielding, Financial Planning Consultant
Trial Balance
December 31, 20 - -

ACCOUNT TITLE	ACCOUNT NO.	DEBIT BALANCE	CREDIT BALANCE
Cash	101	22 7 6 5 00	
Office Supplies	142	2 8 0 00	
Accounts Payable	202		1 8 0 00
George Fielding, Capital	311		20 0 0 0 00
George Fielding, Drawing	312	1 1 0 0 00	
Professional Fees	401		6 5 0 0 00
Wages Expense	511	1 2 0 0 00	
Rent Expense	521	1 0 0 0 00	
Telephone Expense	525	1 0 0 00	
Utilities Expense	533	7 5 00	
Charitable Contributions Expense	534	1 0 0 00	
Automobile Expense	538	6 0 00	
		26 6 8 0 00	26 6 8 0 00

On-Line Learning Tools

For more information, visit: http://heintz.swlearning.com

The Heintz & Parry product web site is designed specifically for **COLLEGE ACCOUNTING, 18e.** The features include downloadable student resources and an interactive study center, organized by chapter, which contains learning objectives, web links, on-line quizzes with automatic feedback, and more.

KEY TERMS

book of original entry, (91)   The journal or the first formal accounting record of a transaction.

chart of accounts, (89)   A list of all accounts used by a business.

compound entry, (95)   A general journal entry that affects more than two accounts.

correcting entry, (108)   An entry to correct an incorrect entry that has been journalized and posted to the wrong account.

cross-reference, (99)   The information in the Posting Reference columns of the journal and ledger that provides a link between the journal and ledger.

four-column account, (97)   An account with columns for the debit or credit transaction and columns for the debit or credit running balance.

general ledger, (97)   A complete set of all the accounts used by a business. The general ledger accumulates a complete record of the debits and credits made to each account as a result of entries made in the journal.

journal, (91)   A day-by-day listing of the transactions of a business.

journalizing, (92)   Entering the transactions in a journal.

posting, (98)   Copying the debits and credits from the journal to the ledger accounts.

ruling method, (107)   A method of correcting an entry in which a line is drawn through the error and the correct information is placed above it.

slide error, (106)   An error that occurs when debit or credit amounts "slide" a digit or two to the left or right.

source document, (90)   Any document that provides information about a business transaction.

transposition error, (106)   An error that occurs when two digits are reversed.

trial balance, (105)   A list used to prove that the totals of the debit and credit balances in the ledger accounts are equal.

two-column general journal, (91)   A journal with only two amount columns, one for debit amounts and one for credit amounts.

REVIEW QUESTIONS

(LO1)   1. Trace the flow of accounting information through the accounting system.

(LO2)   2. Explain the purpose of a chart of accounts.

(LO2)   3. Name the five types of financial statement classifications for which it is ordinarily desirable to keep separate accounts.

(LO3)   4. Name a source document that provides information about each of the following types of business transactions:
     a. Cash payment
     b. Cash receipt
     c. Sale of goods or services
     d. Purchase of goods or services

(LO4)   5. Where is the first formal accounting record of a business transaction usually made?

(LO4)   6. Describe the four steps required to journalize a business transaction in a general journal.

(LO5)   7. In what order are the accounts customarily placed in the ledger?

(LO5)   8. Explain the primary advantage of a four-column ledger account.

(LO5)   9. Explain the five steps required when posting the journal to the ledger.

(LO5)   10. What information is entered in the Posting Reference column of the journal as an amount is posted to the proper account in the ledger?

(LO6)   11. Explain why the ledger can still contain errors even though the trial balance is in balance. Give examples of two such types of errors.

(LO6)   12. What is a slide error?

(LO6)   13. What is a transposition error?

(LO6)   14. What is the ruling method of correcting an error?

(LO6)   15. What is the correcting entry method?

Self-Study Test Questions

True/False

1. Source documents serve as historical evidence of business transactions.   _____

2. No entries are made in the Posting Reference column at the time of journalizing.   _____

3. When entering the credit item in a general journal, it should be listed after all debits and indented.   _____

4. The chart of accounts lists capital accounts first, followed by liabilities, assets, expenses, and revenue.   _____

5. When an incorrect entry has been journalized and posted to the wrong account, a correcting entry should be made.   _____

Multiple Choice

1. The process of copying debits and credits from the journal to the ledger is called

   (a) journalizing.   (c) cross-referencing.
   (b) posting.   (d) sliding.

2. To purchase an asset such as office equipment on account, you would credit which account?

   (a) Cash   (c) Accounts Payable
   (b) Accounts Receivable   (d) Capital

3. When fees are earned but will be paid later, which account is debited?

   (a) Cash   (c) Accounts Payable
   (b) Accounts Receivable   (d) Capital

4. When the correct numbers are used but are in the wrong order, the error is called a

   (a) transposition.   (c) ruling.
   (b) slide.   (d) correcting entry.

5. A revenue account will begin with the number _____ in the chart of accounts.

   (a) 1   (c) 3
   (b) 2   (d) 4

The answers to the Self-Study Test Questions are at the end of the text.

MANAGING YOUR WRITING

You are a public accountant with many small business clients. During a recent visit to a client's business, the bookkeeper approached you with a problem. The columns of the trial balance were not equal. You helped the bookkeeper find and correct the error, but believe you should go one step further. Write a memo to all of your clients that explains the purpose of the double-entry framework, the importance of maintaining the equality of the accounting equation, the errors that might cause an inequality, and suggestions for finding the errors.

SERIES A EXERCISES

EXERCISE 4-1A   **(LO3)**   **SOURCE DOCUMENTS** Source documents trigger the analysis of events requiring an accounting entry. Match the following source documents with the type of information they provide.

1. Check stubs or check register   a. A good or service has been sold.

2. Purchase invoice from   b. Cash has been received by the
   suppliers (vendors)   business.

3. Sales tickets or invoices to   c. Cash has been paid by the business.
   customers
                                           d. Goods or services have been
4. Receipts or cash register tapes   purchased by the business.

EXERCISE 4-2A **(LO4)** **GENERAL JOURNAL ENTRIES** For each of the following transactions, list the account to be debited and the account to be credited in the general journal.

1. Invested cash in the business, $5,000.

2. Paid office rent, $500.

3. Purchased office supplies on account, $300.

4. Received cash for services rendered (fees), $400.

5. Paid cash on account, $50.

6. Rendered services on account, $300.

7. Received cash for an amount owed by a customer, $100.

EXERCISE 4-3A **(LO5)**
Final cash bal.: $4,950

GENERAL LEDGER ACCOUNTS Set up T accounts for each of the general ledger accounts needed for Exercise 4-2A and post debits and credits to the accounts. Foot the accounts and enter the balances. Prove that total debits equal total credits.

EXERCISE 4-4A **(LO4)** **GENERAL JOURNAL ENTRIES** Jean Jones has opened Jones Consulting. Journalize the following transactions that occurred during January of the current year. Use the following journal pages: January 1–10, page 1, and January 11–29, page 2. Use the following chart of accounts.

Chart of Accounts

Assets	Revenues
101 Cash	401 Consulting Fees
142 Office Supplies	
181 Office Equipment	Expenses
	511 Wages Expense
Liabilities	521 Rent Expense
202 Accounts Payable	525 Telephone Expense
	533 Utilities Expense
Owner's Equity	549 Miscellaneous Expense
311 Jean Jones, Capital	
312 Jean Jones, Drawing	

Jan. 1 Jones invested cash in the business, $10,000.

2 Paid office rent, $500.

3 Purchased office equipment on account, $1,500.

5 Received cash for services rendered, $750.

8 Paid telephone bill, $65.

10 Paid for a magazine subscription (miscellaneous expense), $15.

11 Purchased office supplies on account, $300.

15 Made a payment on account (see Jan. 3 transaction), $150.

18 Paid part-time employee, $500.

21 Received cash for services rendered, $350.

25 Paid utilities bill, $85.

27 Jones withdrew cash for personal use, $100.

29 Paid part-time employee, $500.

EXERCISE 4-5A   **(LO5)**
Final cash bal.: $9,185;
Trial Bal. total debits: $12,750

GENERAL LEDGER ACCOUNTS; TRIAL BALANCE Set up four-column general ledger accounts using the chart of accounts provided in Exercise 4-4A. Post the transactions from Exercise 4-4A to the general ledger accounts and prepare a trial balance.

EXERCISE 4-6A   **(LO5)**
Total assets, Jan. 31: $10,985

FINANCIAL STATEMENTS From the information in Exercises 4-4A and 4-5A, prepare an income statement, a statement of owner's equity, and a balance sheet.

EXERCISE 4-7A   **(LO5)**
Total assets, July 31: $7,100

FINANCIAL STATEMENTS From the following trial balance taken after one month of operation, prepare an income statement, a statement of owner's equity, and a balance sheet. Assume that TJ Ulza made no additional investments in the business during the month.

TJ's Paint Service
Trial Balance
July 31, 20 - -

ACCOUNT TITLE	ACCOUNT NO.	DEBIT BALANCE	CREDIT BALANCE
Cash	101	4 3 0 0 00	
Accounts Receivable	122	1 1 0 0 00	
Supplies	141	8 0 0 00	
Paint Equipment	183	9 0 0 00	
Accounts Payable	202		2 1 5 0 00
TJ Ulza, Capital	311		3 2 0 5 00
TJ Ulza, Drawing	312	5 0 0 00	
Painting Fees	401		3 6 0 0 00
Wages Expense	511	9 0 0 00	
Rent Expense	521	2 5 0 00	
Telephone Expense	525	5 0 00	
Transportation Expense	526	6 0 00	
Utilities Expense	533	7 0 00	
Miscellaneous Expense	549	2 5 00	
		8 9 5 5 00	8 9 5 5 00

EXERCISE 4-8A   **(LO6)**

FINDING AND CORRECTING ERRORS Joe Adams bought $500 worth of office supplies on account. The following entry was recorded on May 17. Find the error(s) and correct it (them) using the ruling method.

15	May	17	Office Equipment	4 0 0 00	
16			Cash		4 0 0 00
17			Purchased copy paper		

On May 25, after the transactions had been posted, Adams discovered that the following entry contains an error. The cash received represents a collection on account, rather than new service fees. Correct the error in the general journal using the correcting entry method.

23	May	23	Cash	101	1 0 0 0 00	
24			Service Fees	401		1 0 0 0 00
25			Received cash for services previously earned			

SERIES A PROBLEMS

PROBLEM 4-9A   (LO4/5)
Cash bal., June 30: $3,958
Trial Bal. total debits: $22,358

JOURNALIZING AND POSTING TRANSACTIONS Jim Andrews opened a delivery business in March. He rented a small office and has a part-time assistant. His trial balance shows accounts for the first three months of business.

ACCOUNT TITLE	ACCOUNT NO.	DEBIT BALANCE	CREDIT BALANCE
Jim's Quick Delivery Trial Balance May 31, 20 - -			
Cash	101	3 8 2 6 00	
Accounts Receivable	122	1 2 1 2 00	
Office Supplies	142	6 4 8 00	
Office Equipment	181	2 1 0 0 00	
Delivery Truck	185	8 0 0 0 00	
Accounts Payable	202		6 0 0 0 00
Jim Andrews, Capital	311		4 4 7 8 00
Jim Andrews, Drawing	312	1 8 0 0 00	
Delivery Fees	401		9 8 8 0 00
Wages Expense	511	1 2 0 0 00	
Advertising Expense	512	9 0 00	
Rent Expense	521	9 0 0 00	
Telephone Expense	525	1 2 6 00	
Electricity Expense	533	9 8 00	
Charitable Contributions Expense	534	6 0 00	
Gas and Oil Expense	538	1 8 6 00	
Miscellaneous Expense	549	1 1 2 00	
		20 3 5 8 00	20 3 5 8 00

Andrews' transactions for the month of June are as follows:

June 1   Paid rent, $300.

2   Performed delivery services for $300: $100 in cash and $200 on account.

4   Paid for newspaper advertising, $15.

6   Purchased office supplies on account, $180.

7   Received cash for delivery services rendered, $260.

9   Paid cash on account (truck payment), $200.

10   Purchased a copier (office equipment) for $700: paid $100 in cash and put $600 on account.

11   Made a contribution to the Red Cross (charitable contributions), $20.

12   Received cash for delivery services rendered, $380.

13   Received cash on account for services previously rendered, $100.

15   Paid a part-time worker, $200.

16   Paid electric bill, $36.

18   Paid telephone bill, $46.

19   Received cash on account for services previously rendered, $100.

20	Andrews withdrew cash for personal use, $200.
21	Paid for gas and oil, $32.
22	Made payment on account (for office supplies), $40.
24	Received cash for services rendered, $340.
26	Paid for a magazine subscription (miscellaneous expense), $15.
27	Received cash for services rendered, $180.
27	Received cash on account for services previously rendered, $100.
29	Paid for gasoline, $24.
30	Paid a part-time worker, $200.

REQUIRED

1. Set up four-column general ledger accounts by entering the balances as of June 1.

2. Journalize the transactions for June in a two-column general journal. Use the following journal pages: June 1–10, page 7; June 11–20, page 8; June 21–30, page 9.

3. Post the entries from the general journal.

4. Prepare a trial balance.

PROBLEM 4-10A   (LO4/5)

Cash bal., Jan. 31: $10,021
Trial Bal. total debits: $13,460

JOURNALIZING AND POSTING TRANSACTIONS Annette Creighton opened Creighton Consulting. She rented a small office and paid a part-time worker to answer the telephone and make deliveries. Her chart of accounts is as follows:

Chart of Accounts

Assets	Revenues
101 Cash	401 Consulting Fees
142 Office Supplies	
181 Office Equipment	**Expenses**
	511 Wages Expense
Liabilities	512 Advertising Expense
202 Accounts Payable	521 Rent Expense
	525 Telephone Expense
	526 Transportation Expense
Owner's Equity	533 Utilities Expense
311 Annette Creighton, Capital	549 Miscellaneous Expense
312 Annette Creighton, Drawing	

Creighton's transactions for the first month of business are as follows:

Jan. 1	Creighton invested cash in the business, $10,000.
1	Paid rent, $500.
2	Purchased office supplies on account, $300.
4	Purchased office equipment on account, $1,500.
6	Received cash for services rendered, $580.
7	Paid telephone bill, $42.
8	Paid utilities bill, $38.
10	Received cash for services rendered, $360.

(continued)

12   Made payment on account, $50.

13   Paid for car rental while visiting an out-of-town client (transportation expense), $150.

15   Paid part-time worker, $360.

17   Received cash for services rendered, $420.

18   Creighton withdrew cash for personal use, $100.

20   Paid for a newspaper ad, $26.

22   Reimbursed part-time employee for cab fare incurred delivering materials to clients (transportation expense), $35.

24   Paid for books on consulting practices (miscellaneous expense), $28.

25   Received cash for services rendered, $320.

27   Made payment on account for office equipment purchased, $150.

29   Paid part-time worker, $360.

30   Received cash for services rendered, $180.

REQUIRED

1. Set up four-column general ledger accounts from the chart of accounts.

2. Journalize the transactions for January in a two-column general journal. Use the following journal page numbers: January 1–10, page 1; January 12–24, page 2; January 25–30, page 3.

3. Post the transactions from the general journal.

4. Prepare a trial balance.

5. Prepare an income statement and a statement of owner's equity for the month of January, and a balance sheet as of January 31, 20--.

PROBLEM 4-11A   **(LO6)**   **CORRECTING ERRORS** Assuming that all entries have been posted, prepare correcting entries for each of the following errors.

1. The following entry was made to record the purchase of $500 in supplies on account.

Supplies	142	500	
Cash	101		500

2. The following entry was made to record the payment of $300 in wages.

Rent Expense	521	300	
Cash	101		300

3. The following entry was made to record a $200 payment to a supplier on account.

Supplies	142	100	
Cash	101		100

SERIES B EXERCISES

EXERCISE 4-1B   **(LO3)**   **SOURCE DOCUMENTS** What type of information is found on each of the following source documents?

1. Cash register tape

2. Sales ticket (issued to customer)

3. Purchase invoice (received from supplier or vendor)

4. Check stub

EXERCISE 4-2B   **(LO4)**   **GENERAL JOURNAL ENTRIES** For each of the following transactions, list the account to be debited and the account to be credited in the general journal.

1. Invested cash in the business, $1,000.

2. Performed services on account, $200.

3. Purchased office equipment on account, $500.

4. Received cash on account for services previously rendered, $200.

5. Made a payment on account, $100.

EXERCISE 4-3B   **(LO5)**
Final cash bal.: $1,100

GENERAL LEDGER ACCOUNTS Set up T accounts for each of the general ledger accounts needed for Exercise 4-2B and post debits and credits to the accounts. Foot the accounts and enter the balances. Prove that total debits equal total credits.

EXERCISE 4-4B   **(LO4)**   **GENERAL JOURNAL ENTRIES** Sengel Moon opened The Bike Doctor. Journalize the following transactions that occurred during the month of October of the current year. Use the following journal pages: October 1–12, page 1, and October 14–29, page 2. Use the following chart of accounts.

Chart of Accounts

Assets	Revenues
101 Cash	401 Repair Fees
141 Bicycle Parts	
142 Office Supplies	Expenses
	511 Wages Expense
Liabilities	521 Rent Expense
202 Accounts Payable	525 Telephone Expense
	533 Utilities Expense
Owner's Equity	549 Miscellaneous Expense
311 Sengel Moon, Capital	
312 Sengel Moon, Drawing	

Oct. 1   Moon invested cash in the business, $15,000.

2   Paid shop rental for the month, $300.

3   Purchased bicycle parts on account, $2,000.

5   Purchased office supplies on account, $250.

8   Paid telephone bill, $38.

9   Received cash for services, $140.

11   Paid a sports magazine subscription (miscellaneous expense), $15.

12   Made payment on account (see Oct. 3 transaction), $100.

(continued)

14   Paid part-time employee, $300.

15   Received cash for services, $350.

16   Paid utilities bill, $48.

19   Received cash for services, $250.

23   Moon withdrew cash for personal use, $50.

25   Made payment on account (see Oct. 5 transaction), $50.

29   Paid part-time employee, $300.

EXERCISE 4-5B   (LO5)
Final cash bal.: $14,539;
Trial Bal. total debits: $17,840

GENERAL LEDGER ACCOUNTS; TRIAL BALANCE Set up four-column general ledger accounts using the chart of accounts provided in Exercise 4-4B. Post the transactions from Exercise 4-4B to the general ledger accounts and prepare a trial balance.

EXERCISE 4-6B   (LO5)
Total assets, Oct. 31: $16,789

FINANCIAL STATEMENTS From the information in Exercises 4-4B and 4-5B, prepare an income statement, a statement of owner's equity, and a balance sheet.

EXERCISE 4-7B   (LO5)
Total assets, Mar. 31: $11,900

FINANCIAL STATEMENTS From the following trial balance taken after one month of operation, prepare an income statement, a statement of owner's equity, and a balance sheet. Assume that no additional investments were made during the month.

AT's Speaker's Bureau
Trial Balance
March 31, 20 - -

ACCOUNT TITLE	ACCOUNT NO.	DEBIT BALANCE	CREDIT BALANCE
Cash	101	6 6 0 0 00	
Accounts Receivable	122	2 8 0 0 00	
Office Supplies	142	1 0 0 0 00	
Office Equipment	181	1 5 0 0 00	
Accounts Payable	202		3 0 0 0 00
AT Speaker, Capital	311		6 0 9 8 00
AT Speaker, Drawing	312	8 0 0 00	
Speaking Fees	401		4 8 0 0 00
Wages Expense	511	4 0 0 00	
Rent Expense	521	2 0 0 00	
Telephone Expense	525	3 5 00	
Travel Expense	526	4 5 0 00	
Utilities Expense	533	8 8 00	
Miscellaneous Expense	549	2 5 00	
		13 8 9 8 00	13 8 9 8 00

EXERCISE 4-8B   (LO6)

FINDING AND CORRECTING ERRORS Mary Smith purchased $350 worth of office equipment on account. The following entry was recorded on April 6. Find the error(s) and correct it (them) using the ruling method.

7						7
8	20-- Apr.	6	Office Supplies	5 3 0 00		8
9			Cash		5 3 0 00	9
10			Purchased office equipment			10

On April 25, after the transactions had been posted, Smith discovered the following entry contains an error. When her customer received services, Cash was debited, but no cash was received. Correct the error in the journal using the correcting entry method.

27										27
28	20-- Apr.	21	Cash	101	3 0 0 00					28
29			Service Fees	401			3 0 0 00	29
30			Revenue earned from services							30
31			previously rendered							31

SERIES B PROBLEMS

PROBLEM 4-9B   (LO4/5)
Cash bal., Nov. 30: $7,012;
Trial Bal. total debits: $16,105

PASS
Power Accounting System Software®

JOURNALIZING AND POSTING TRANSACTIONS Ann Tailor owns a suit tailoring shop. She opened business in September. She rented a small work space and has an assistant to receive job orders and process claim tickets. Her trial balance shows her account balances for the first two months of business.

Tailor Tailoring Trial Balance October 31, 20 - -			
ACCOUNT TITLE	ACCOUNT NO.	DEBIT BALANCE	CREDIT BALANCE
Cash	101	6 2 1 1 00	
Accounts Receivable	122	4 8 4 00	
Tailoring Supplies	141	1 0 0 0 00	
Tailoring Equipment	183	3 8 0 0 00	
Accounts Payable	202		4 1 2 5 00
Ann Tailor, Capital	311		6 1 3 0 00
Ann Tailor, Drawing	312	8 0 0 00	
Tailoring Fees	401		3 6 0 0 00
Wages Expense	511	8 0 0 00	
Advertising Expense	512	3 4 00	
Rent Expense	521	6 0 0 00	
Telephone Expense	525	6 0 00	
Electricity Expense	533	4 4 00	
Miscellaneous Expense	549	2 2 00	
		13 8 5 5 00	13 8 5 5 00

Tailor's transactions for November are as follows:

Nov. 1   Paid rent, $300.

2   Purchased tailoring supplies on account, $150.

3   Purchased a new button hole machine on account, $300.

5   Earned first week's revenue, $400: $100 in cash and $300 on account.

8   Paid for newspaper advertising, $13.

9   Paid telephone bill, $28.

10   Paid electric bill, $21.

11   Received cash on account from customers, $200.

(continued)

12 Earned second week's revenue, $450: $200 in cash and $250 on account.

15 Paid assistant, $400.

16 Made payment on account, $100.

17 Paid for magazine subscription (miscellaneous expense), $12.

19 Earned third week's revenue, $450: $300 in cash, $150 on account.

23 Received cash on account from customers, $300.

24 Paid for newspaper advertising, $13.

26 Paid for postage (miscellaneous expense), $12.

27 Earned fourth week's revenue, $600: $200 in cash and $400 on account.

30 Received cash on account from customers, $400.

REQUIRED

1. Set up four-column general ledger accounts by entering the balances as of November 1, 20--.

2. Journalize the transactions for November in a two-column general journal. Use the following journal page numbers: November 1–11, page 7; November 12–24, page 8; November 26–30, page 9.

3. Post the entries from the general journal.

4. Prepare a trial balance.

PROBLEM 4-10B **(LO4/5)**

**Cash bal., May 31: $4,500;
Trial Bal. total debits: $8,790**

JOURNALIZING AND POSTING TRANSACTIONS Benito Mendez opened Mendez Appraisals. He rented office space and has a part-time secretary to answer the telephone and make appraisal appointments. His chart of accounts is as follows:

Chart of Accounts

Assets	Revenues
101 Cash	401 Appraisal Fees
122 Accounts Receivable	
142 Office Supplies	Expenses
181 Office Equipment	511 Wages Expense
	512 Advertising Expense
Liabilities	521 Rent Expense
202 Accounts Payable	525 Telephone Expense
	526 Transportation Expense
Owner's Equity	533 Electricity Expense
311 Benito Mendez, Capital	549 Miscellaneous Expense
312 Benito Mendez, Drawing	

Mendez's transactions for the first month of business are as follows:

May 1 Mendez invested cash in the business, $5,000.

2 Paid rent, $500.

3 Purchased office supplies, $100.

4 Purchased office equipment on account, $2,000.

5 Received cash for services rendered, $280.

8 Paid telephone bill, $38.

9   Paid electric bill, $42.

10   Received cash for services rendered, $310.

13   Paid part-time employee, $500.

14   Paid car rental for out-of-town trip, $200.

15   Paid for newspaper ad, $30.

18   Received cash for services rendered, $620.

19   Paid mileage reimbursement for part-time employee's use of personal car for business deliveries (transportation expense), $22.

21   Mendez withdrew cash for personal use, $50.

23   Made payment on account for office equipment purchased earlier, $200.

24   Earned appraisal fee, which will be paid in a week, $500.

26   Paid for newspaper ad, $30.

27   Paid for local softball team sponsorship (miscellaneous expense), $15.

28   Paid part-time employee, $500.

29   Received cash on account, $250.

30   Received cash for services rendered, $280.

31   Paid cab fare (transportation expense), $13.

REQUIRED

1. Set up four-column general ledger accounts from the chart of accounts.

2. Journalize the transactions for May in a two-column general journal. Use the following journal page numbers: May 1–10, page 1; May 13–24, page 2; May 26–31, page 3.

3. Post the transactions from the general journal.

4. Prepare a trial balance.

5. Prepare an income statement and a statement of owner's equity for the month of May, and a balance sheet as of May 31, 20--.

PROBLEM 4-11B   (LO6)   CORRECTING ERRORS Assuming that all entries have been posted, prepare correcting entries for each of the following errors.

1. The following entry was made to record the purchase of $400 in equipment on account.

Supplies	142	400	
Cash	101		400

2. The following entry was made to record the payment of $200 for advertising.

Repair Expense	537	200	
Cash	101		200

3. The following entry was made to record a $600 payment to a supplier on account.

Prepaid Insurance	145	400	
Cash	101		400

MASTERY PROBLEM

Cash bal., June 30: $45,495;
Trial Bal. total debits: $96,200

Barry Bird opened the Barry Bird Basketball Camp for children ages 10 through 18. Campers typically register for one week in June or July, arriving on Sunday and returning home the following Saturday. College players serve as cabin counselors and assist the local college and high school coaches who run the practice sessions. The registration fee includes a room, meals at a nearby restaurant, and basketball instruction. In the off-season, the facilities are used for weekend retreats and coaching clinics. Bird developed the following chart of accounts for his service business.

Chart of Accounts

Assets	Revenues
101 Cash	401 Registration Fees
142 Office Supplies	
183 Athletic Equipment	Expenses
184 Basketball Facilities	511 Wages Expense
	512 Advertising Expense
Liabilities	524 Food Expense
202 Accounts Payable	525 Telephone Expense
	533 Utilities Expense
Owner's Equity	536 Postage Expense
311 Barry Bird, Capital	
312 Barry Bird, Drawing	

The following transactions took place during the month of June.

June 1   Bird invested cash in the business, $10,000.

1   Purchased basketballs and other athletic equipment, $3,000.

2   Paid Hite Advertising for flyers that had been mailed to prospective campers, $5,000.

2   Collected registration fees, $15,000.

2   Rogers Construction completed work on a new basketball court that cost $12,000. Arrangements were made to pay the bill in July.

5   Purchased office supplies on account from Gordon Office Supplies, $300.

6   Received bill from Magic's Restaurant for meals served to campers on account, $5,800.

7   Collected registration fees, $16,200.

10   Paid wages to camp counselors, $500.

14   Collected registration fees, $13,500.

14   Received bill from Magic's Restaurant for meals served to campers on account, $6,200.

17   Paid wages to camp counselors, $500.

18   Paid postage, $85.

21   Collected registration fees, $15,200.

22   Received bill from Magic's Restaurant for meals served to campers on account, $6,500.

24   Paid wages to camp counselors, $500.

28   Collected registration fees, $14,000.

30   Received bill from Magic's Restaurant for meals served to campers on account, $7,200.

30   Paid wages to camp counselors, $500.

30   Paid Magic's Restaurant on account, $25,700.

30   Paid utility bill, $500.

30   Paid telephone bill, $120.

30   Bird withdrew cash for personal use, $2,000.

REQUIRED

1. Enter the transactions in a general journal. Use the following journal pages: June 1–6, page 1; June 7–22, page 2; June 24–30, page 3.

2. Post the entries to the general ledger.

3. Prepare a trial balance.

CHALLENGE PROBLEM

This problem challenges you to apply your cumulative accounting knowledge to move a step beyond the material in the chapter.

Total debits: $19,150

Journal entries and a trial balance for Fred Phaler Consulting follow. As you will note, the trial balance does not balance, suggesting that there are errors. Recall that the chapter offers tips on identifying individual posting errors. These techniques are not as effective when there are two or more errors. Thus, you will need to first carefully inspect the trial balance to see if you can identify any obvious errors either due to amounts that look out of proportion or simply reported in the wrong place. Then, you will need to carefully evaluate the other amounts by using the techniques offered in the text, or tracing the journal entries to the amounts reported on the trial balance. (Hint: Four errors were made in the posting process and preparation of the trial balance.)

(continued)

	DATE		DESCRIPTION	POST REF.	DEBIT					CREDIT					
	20--														
1	June	1	Cash	101	10	0	0	0	00						1
2			Fred Phaler, Capital	311						10	0	0	0	00	2
3															3
4		2	Rent Expense	521		5	0	0	00						4
5			Cash	101							5	0	0	00	5
6															6
7		3	Cash	101	4	0	0	0	00						7
8			Professional Fees	401						4	0	0	0	00	8
9															9
10		4	Utilities Expense	533		1	0	0	00						10
11			Cash	101							1	0	0	00	11
12															12
13		7	Cash	101	3	0	0	0	00						13
14			Professional Fees	401						3	0	0	0	00	14
15															15
16		12	Automobile Expense	526			5	0	00						16
17			Cash	101								5	0	00	17
18															18
19		14	Wages Expense	511		5	0	0	00						19
20			Cash	101							5	0	0	00	20
21															21
22		14	Office Supplies	142		2	5	0	00						22
23			Accounts Payable	202							2	5	0	00	23
24															24
25		20	Telephone Expense	525		1	0	0	00						25
26			Cash	101							1	0	0	00	26
27															27
28		21	Fred Phaler, Drawing	312	1	2	0	0	00						28
29			Cash	101						1	2	0	0	00	29
30															30
31		24	Accounts Receivable	122	2	0	0	0	00						31
32			Professional Fees	401						2	0	0	0	00	32
33															33
34		25	Accounts Payable	202		1	0	0	00						34
35			Cash	101							1	0	0	00	35
36															36
37		30	Wages Expense	511		3	0	0	00						37
38			Cash	101							3	0	0	00	38

GENERAL JOURNAL   PAGE 1

Fred Phaler Consulting Trial Balance June 30, 20 - -											
ACCOUNT TITLE	ACCOUNT NO.	DEBIT BALANCE					CREDIT BALANCE				
Cash	101						13	9	0	0	00
Accounts Receivable	122	2	0	0	0	00					
Office Supplies	142		2	5	0	00					
Accounts Payable	202		1	0	0	00					
Fred Phaler, Capital	311						10	0	0	0	00
Fred Phaler, Drawing	312	2	1	0	0	00					
Professional Fees	401						9	0	0	0	00
Wages Expense	511		8	0	0	00					
Rent Expense	521		5	0	0	00					
Telephone Expense	525		1	0	0	00					
Automobile Expense	526	50	0	0	0	00					
Utilities Expense	533		1	0	0	00					
		55	9	5	0	00	32	9	0	0	00

REQUIRED

1. Find the errors.

2. Explain what caused the errors.

3. Prepare a corrected trial balance.

©DIGITAL IMAGING GROUP

Adjusting Entries and the Work Sheet

At the end of the first month of operations, Jessie and Mitch were looking over the trial balance. "These accounts don't look right," said Jessie. "Don't worry, I just need to make a few adjustments before we prepare the financial statements," replied Mitch. Does it seem appropriate to make adjustments prior to issuing financial statements?

Careful study of this chapter should enable you to:

LO1 Prepare end-of-period adjustments.

LO2 Prepare a work sheet.

LO3 Describe methods for finding errors on the work sheet.

LO4 Journalize adjusting entries.

LO5 Post adjusting entries to the general ledger.

Up to this point, you have learned how to journalize business transactions, post to the ledger, and prepare a trial balance. Now it is time to learn how to make end-of-period adjustments to the accounts listed in the trial balance. This chapter explains the need for adjustments and illustrates how they are made using a work sheet.

END-OF-PERIOD ADJUSTMENTS

LO1 Prepare end-of-period adjustments.

Transactions are entered as they occur throughout the year. Adjustments are made to reflect changes in account balances that are not the direct result of an exchange with an outside party. Adjustments are made at the end of the accounting period.

Throughout the accounting period, business transactions are entered in the accounting system. These transactions are based on exchanges between the business and other companies and individuals. During the accounting period, other changes occur that affect the business's financial condition. For example, equipment is wearing out, prepaid insurance and supplies are being used up, and employees are earning wages that have not yet been paid. Since these events have not been entered into the accounting system, **adjusting entries** must be made prior to the preparation of financial statements.

The **matching principle** in accounting requires the matching of revenues earned during an accounting period with the expenses incurred to produce the revenues. This approach offers the best measure of net income. The income statement reports earnings for a specific period of time and the balance sheet reports the assets, liabilities, and owner's equity on a specific date. Thus, to follow the matching principle, the accounts must be brought up to date before financial statements are prepared. This requires adjusting some of the accounts listed in the trial balance. Figure 5-1 lists reasons to adjust the trial balance.

 LEARNING KEY: Matching revenues earned with expenses incurred as a result of efforts to produce those revenues offers the best measure of net income.

1. To report all revenues earned during the accounting period.

2. To report all expenses incurred to produce the revenues earned in this accounting period.

3. To accurately report the assets on the balance sheet date. Some assets may have been used up during the accounting period.

4. To accurately report the liabilities on the balance sheet date. Expenses may have been incurred but not yet paid.

FIGURE 5-1 Reasons to Adjust the Trial Balance

Generally, adjustments are made and financial statements prepared at the end of a twelve-month period called a **fiscal year**. This period does not need to be the same as a calendar year. In fact, many businesses schedule their fiscal year end for a time when business is slow. In this chapter we continue the illustration of Jessie Jane's Campus Delivery and will prepare adjustments at the end of the first month of operations. We will focus on the following accounts: Supplies, Prepaid Insurance, Delivery Equipment, and Wages Expense.

Supplies

During June, Jessie purchased supplies consisting of paper, pens, and delivery envelopes for $80. *Since these supplies were expected to provide future benefits, Supplies, an asset, was debited at the time of the purchase.* No other entries were made to the supplies account during June. As reported on the trial balance in Figure 5-2, the $80 balance remains in the supplies account at the end of the month.

As supplies are used, an expense is incurred. However, it is not practical to make a journal entry to recognize this expense and the reduction in the supplies account every time someone uses an envelope. It is more efficient to wait until the end of the accounting period to make one adjusting entry to reflect the expense incurred for the use of supplies for the entire month.

A BROADER VIEW
Adjusting Entries

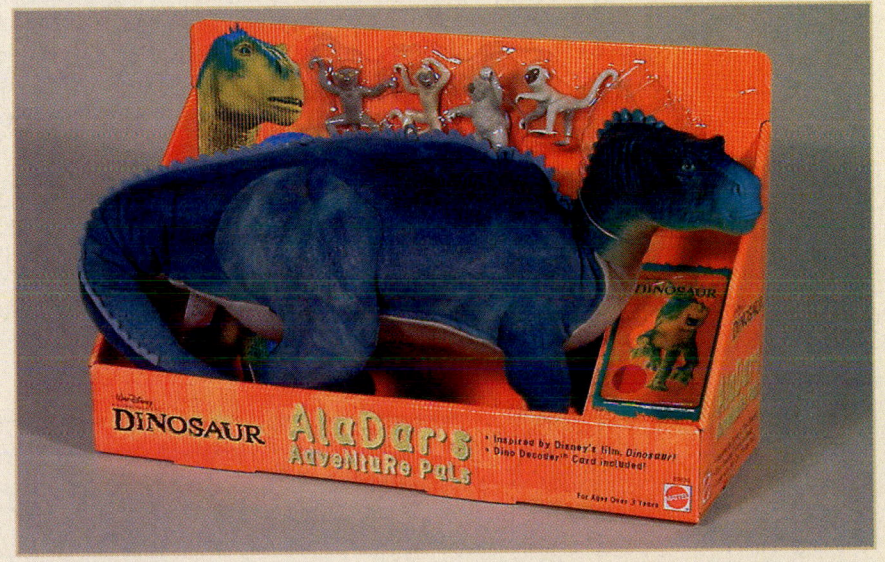

PHOTO BY CARY BENBOW

Are adjusting entries important? The Walt Disney Company and Mattel, Inc. probably think so. The Walt Disney Company granted Mattel, Inc. the right to make and sell toys based on Disney characters. In return, Mattel agreed to make payments to Disney as the toys were sold. One of the issues in a court case was whether Mattel should have made an adjusting entry when it fell behind on these payments. The entry would have been:

Royalty Expense on Disney Characters	17,000,000	
Accounts Payable (Disney)		17,000,000

This adjusting entry would have reduced Mattel's fourth quarter earnings for that year by more than 15%. Following an investigation by the Securities and Exchange Commission, Mattel eventually agreed to make an adjustment to later financial statements.

Jessie Jane's Campus Delivery Trial Balance June 30, 20 - -													
ACCOUNT TITLE	ACCOUNT NO.	\multicolumn{6}{c}{DEBIT BALANCE}	\multicolumn{6}{c}{CREDIT BALANCE}
Cash	101		3	7	0	00						
Accounts Receivable	122		6	5	0	00						
Supplies	141			8	0	00						
Prepaid Insurance	145		2	0	0	00						
Delivery Equipment	185	3	6	0	0	00						
Accounts Payable	202							1	8	0	0	00
Jessica Jane, Capital	311							2	0	0	0	00
Jessica Jane, Drawing	312		1	5	0	00						
Delivery Fees	401							2	1	5	0	00
Wages Expense	511		6	5	0	00						
Rent Expense	521		2	0	0	00						
Telephone Expense	525			5	0	00						
		5	9	5	0	00	5	9	5	0	00		

FIGURE 5-2 Trial Balance

At the end of the month, an inventory, or physical count, of the remaining supplies is taken. The inventory shows that supplies costing $20 were still unused at the end of June. Since Jessie bought supplies costing $80, and only $20 worth remain, supplies costing $60 must have been used ($80 – $20 = $60). Thus, supplies expense for the month is $60. (Trial balance is abbreviated as TB in Figure 5-3 and other T account illustrations.)

Since $60 worth of supplies have been used, Supplies Expense is debited and Supplies (asset) is credited for $60 (Figure 5-3). Thus, as shown in Figure 5-4, supplies with a cost of $20 will be reported as an asset on the balance sheet and a supplies expense of $60 will be reported on the income statement. The adjusting entry affected an income statement account (Supplies Expense) and a balance sheet account (Supplies).

LEARNING KEY: Since it is not practical to make a journal entry for supplies expense each time supplies are used, one adjusting entry is made at the end of the accounting period.

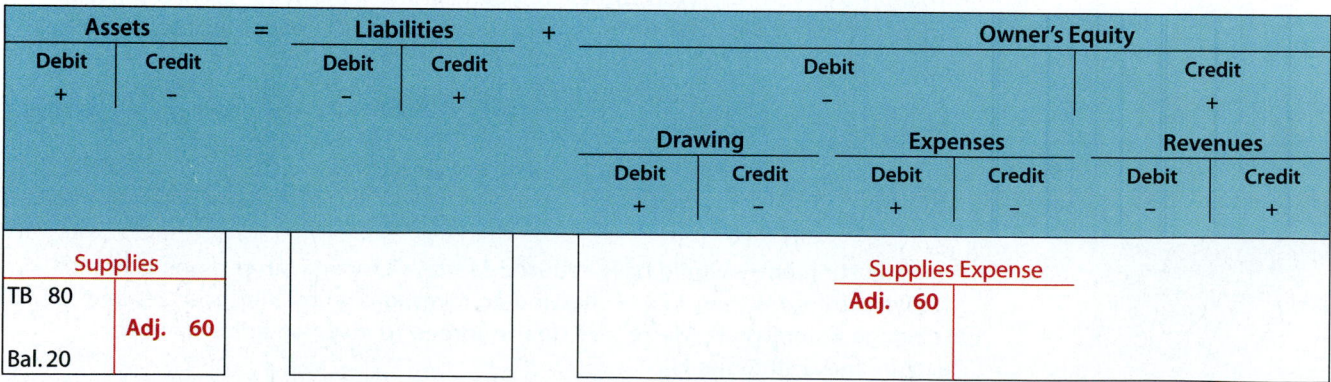

FIGURE 5-3 Adjustment for Supplies

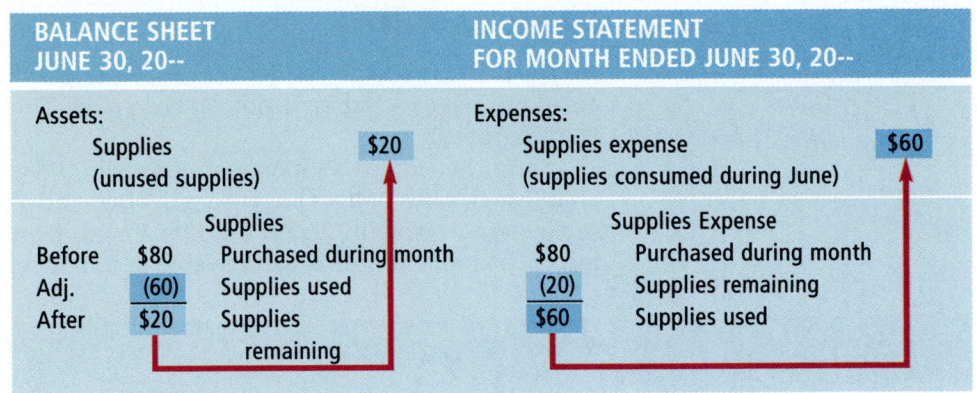

FIGURE 5-4   Effect of Adjusting Entry for Supplies on Financial Statements

Prepaid Insurance

On June 18, Jessie paid $200 for an eight-month liability insurance policy with coverage beginning on June 1. *Prepaid Insurance, an asset, was debited because the insurance policy is expected to provide future benefits.* The $200 balance is reported on the trial balance. As the insurance policy expires with the passage of time, the asset should be reduced and an expense recognized.

Since the $200 premium covers eight months, the cost of the expired coverage for June is $25 ($200 ÷ 8 months). As shown in Figure 5-5, the adjusting entry is to debit Insurance Expense for $25 and credit Prepaid Insurance for $25. Figure 5-6 shows that the unexpired portion of the insurance premium will be reported on the balance sheet as Prepaid Insurance of $175. The expired portion will be reported on the income statement as Insurance Expense of $25.

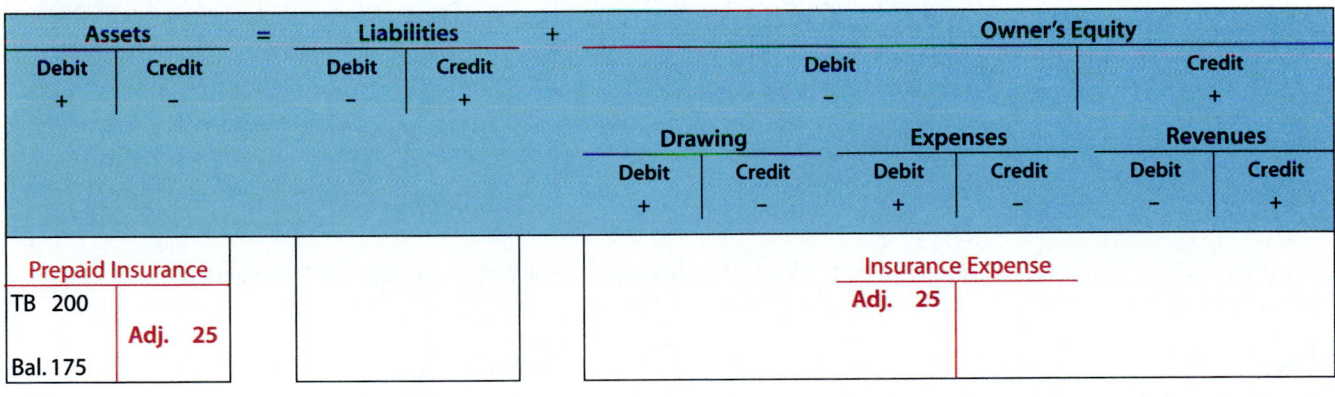

FIGURE 5-5   Adjustment for Expired Insurance

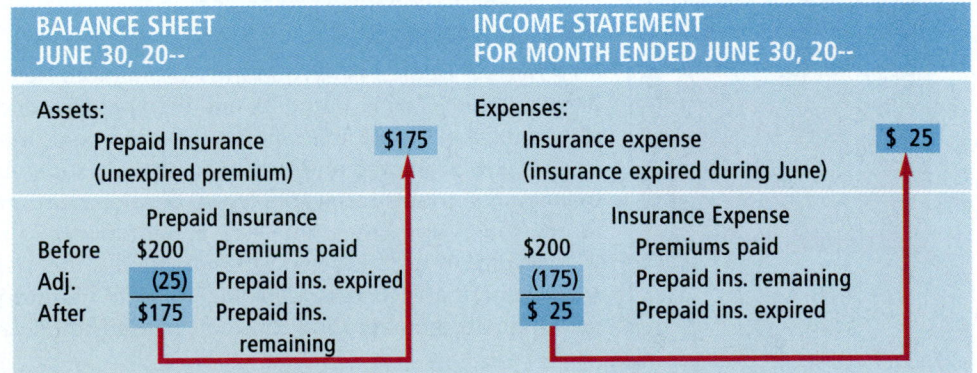

FIGURE 5-6   Effect of Adjusting Entry for Prepaid Insurance on Financial Statements

Wages Expense

Jessie paid her part-time employees $650 on June 27. Since then, they have earned an additional $50, but have not yet been paid. The additional wages expense must be recognized.

Since the employees have not been paid, Wages Payable, a liability, should be established. Thus, Wages Expense is debited and Wages Payable is credited for $50 in Figure 5-7. Note in Figure 5-8 that Wages Expense of $700 is reported on the income statement and Wages Payable of $50 is reported on the balance sheet.

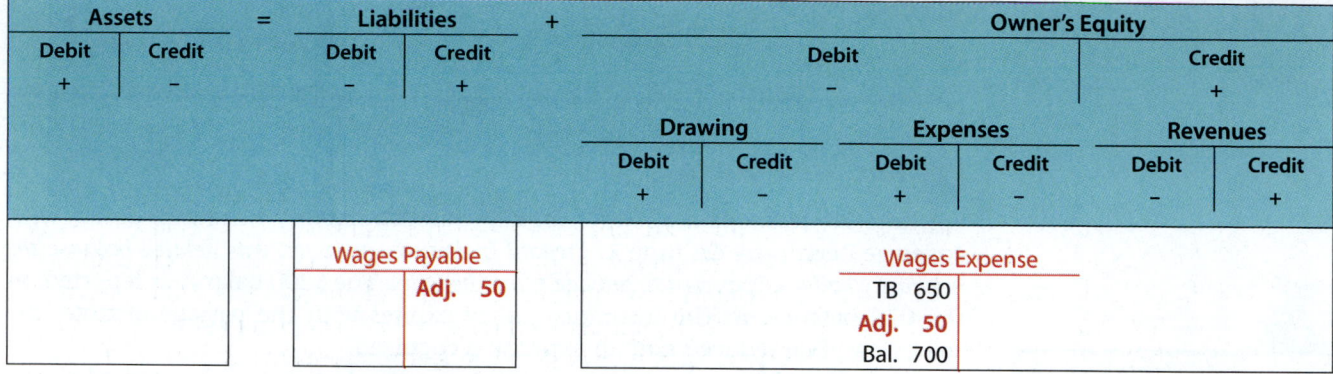

FIGURE 5-7　Adjustment for Unpaid Wages

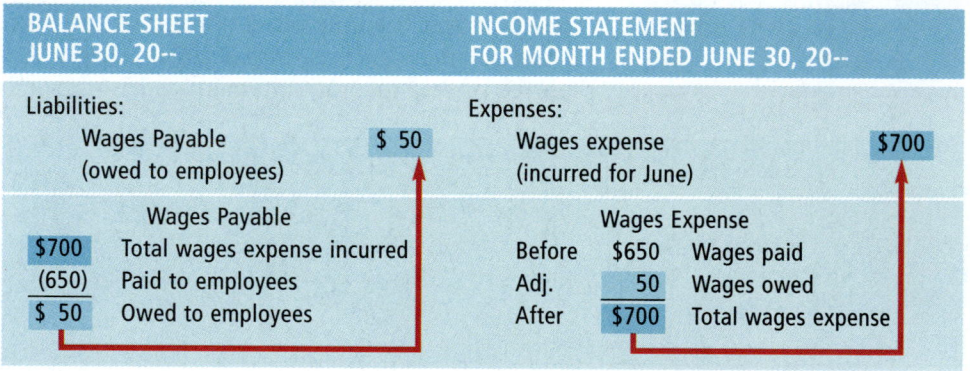

FIGURE 5-8　Effect of Adjusting Entry for Wages on Financial Statements

PROFILES IN ACCOUNTING

Jeff Clifton, Account Supervisor

Jeff Clifton maintained a 4.0 GPA with nearly perfect attendance while earning an Associate Degree in Accounting Automation. He performed an externship with Brooke County Taxing Authority and then began working as an accounts receivable clerk with the DeBartolo Properties Management, Inc., in Youngstown, Ohio.

He was promoted and is now an account supervisor. His duties include managing accounts receivable for 20 development properties across the United States, supervising five employees, and interviewing prospective employees.

According to Jeff, being self-motivated is the main key to success. You need to work hard and success will come. Accounting interested Jeff because he enjoys working with numbers and considers himself to be very analytical.

Depreciation Expense

During the month of June, Jessie purchased three motor scooters. Since the scooters will provide future benefits, they were recorded as assets in the delivery equipment account. Under the **historical cost principle**, assets are recorded at their actual cost, in this case $3,600. This cost remains on the books as long as the business owns the asset. No adjustments are made for changes in the market value of the asset. It does not matter whether the firm got a "good buy" or paid "too much" when the asset was purchased.

LEARNING KEY: The historical cost principle is an important accounting concept. Assets are recorded at their actual cost. This historical cost is not adjusted for changes in market values.

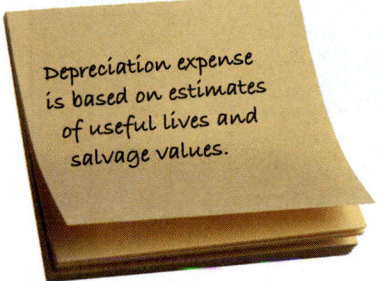

Depreciation expense is based on estimates of useful lives and salvage values.

The period of time that an asset is expected to help produce revenues is called its **useful life**. The asset's useful life expires as a result of wear and tear or because it no longer satisfies the needs of the business. For example, as Jessie adds miles to her scooters, they will become less reliable and will eventually fail to run. As this happens, depreciation expense should be recognized and the value of the asset should be reduced. **Depreciation** is a method of *matching* an asset's original cost against the revenues produced over its useful life. There are many depreciation methods. In our example, we will use the **straight-line method**.

Let's assume that Jessie's motor scooters have estimated useful lives of three years and will have no salvage value at the end of that time period. **Salvage value** (also called scrap value, or residual value) is the expected **market value** or selling price of the asset at the end of its useful life. The **depreciable cost** of these scooters is the original cost, less salvage value, or $3,600. It is this amount that is subject to depreciation. Let's also assume that a full month's depreciation is recognized in the month in which an asset is purchased.

The depreciable cost is spread over 36 months (3 years × 12 months). Thus, the straight-line depreciation expense for the month of June is $100 ($3,600 ÷ 36 months).

Straight-Line Depreciation				
Original Cost	−	Salvage Value	=	Depreciable Cost
$\dfrac{\text{Depreciable Cost}}{\text{Estimated Useful Life}}$	=	$\dfrac{\$3,600}{36 \text{ months}}$	=	$100 per month

When we made adjustments for supplies and prepaid insurance, the asset accounts were credited to show that they had been consumed. Assets of a durable nature that are expected to provide benefits over several years or more, called **plant assets**, require a different approach. The business maintains a record of the original cost and the amount of depreciation taken since the asset was acquired. By comparing these two amounts, the reader can estimate the relative age of the assets. Thus, instead of crediting Delivery Equipment for the amount of depreciation, a contra-asset account, Accumulated Depreciation—Delivery Equipment, is credited. "Contra" means opposite or against. Thus, a **contra-asset** has a credit balance (the opposite of an asset) and is deducted from the related asset account on the balance sheet.

LEARNING KEY: Depreciable assets provide benefits over more than one year. Therefore, the historical cost of the asset remains in the asset account. To show that it has been depreciated, a *contra-asset* account is used.

As shown in Figure 5-9, the appropriate adjusting entry consists of a debit to Depreciation Expense—Delivery Equipment and a credit to Accumulated Depreciation—Delivery Equipment. Note the position of the accumulated depreciation account in the accounting equation. It is shown in the asset section, directly beneath Delivery Equipment. Contra-asset accounts should always be shown along with the related asset account. Therefore, Delivery Equipment and Accumulated Depreciation—Delivery Equipment are shown together.

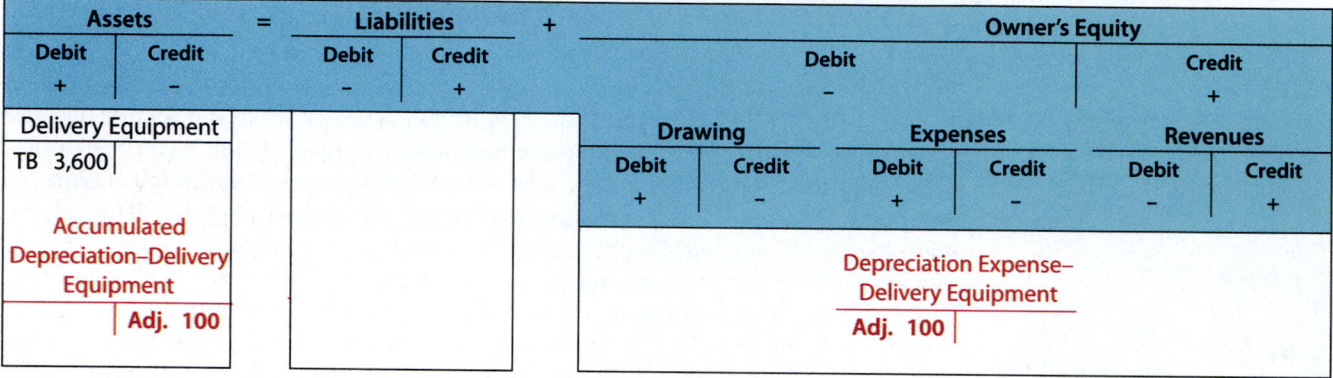

FIGURE 5-9 Adjustment for Depreciation of Delivery Equipment

The same concept is used on the balance sheet. Note in Figure 5-10 that Accumulated Depreciation is reported immediately beneath Delivery Equipment as a deduction. The difference between these accounts is known as the **book value**, or **undepreciated cost**, of the delivery equipment. Book value simply means the value carried on the books or in the accounting records. It does *not* represent the market value, or selling price, of the asset.

LEARNING KEY: Book Value = Cost of Plant Assets – Accumulated Depreciation. There is no individual account that reports book value. It must be computed as shown below.

BALANCE SHEET JUNE 30, 20--			INCOME STATEMENT FOR MONTH ENDED JUNE 30, 20--	
Assets:			Expenses:	
Delivery equipment	$3,600		Depreciation expense	$100
Less: Accumulated			(Expired cost for June)	
depreciation	100	$3,500		
		(Book value)		

FIGURE 5-10 Effect of Adjusting Entry for Depreciation on Financial Statements for June

If no delivery equipment is bought or sold during the next month, the same adjusting entry would be made at the end of July. If an income statement for the month of July and a balance sheet as of July 31 were prepared, the amounts shown in Figure 5-11 would be reported for the delivery equipment.

BALANCE SHEET JULY 31, 20--			INCOME STATEMENT FOR MONTH ENDED JULY 31, 20--	
Assets:			Expenses:	
Delivery equipment	$3,600		Depreciation expense	$100
Less: Accumulated			(Expired cost for July)	
depreciation	200	$3,400		
		(Book value)		

FIGURE 5-11   Effect of Adjusting Entry for Depreciation on Financial Statements for July

The cost ($3,600) remains unchanged, but the accumulated depreciation has increased to $200. This represents *the depreciation that has accumulated* since the delivery equipment was purchased ($100 in June and $100 in July). The depreciation expense for July is $100, the same as reported for June. Depreciation expense is reported for a specific time period. It does not accumulate across reporting periods.

Expanded Chart of Accounts

Several new accounts were needed to make the adjusting entries. New accounts are easily added to the chart of accounts, as shown in Figure 5-12. Note the close relationship between assets and contra-assets in the numbering of the accounts. Contra-accounts carry the same number as the related asset account with a ".1" suffix. For example, Delivery Equipment is account number 185 and the contra-asset account, Accumulated Depreciation—Delivery Equipment, is account number 185.1.

JESSIE JANE'S CAMPUS DELIVERY CHART OF ACCOUNTS			
Assets		**Revenue**	
101	Cash	401	Delivery Fees
122	Accounts Receivable		
141	Supplies	**Expenses**	
145	Prepaid Insurance	511	Wages Expense
185	Delivery Equipment	521	Rent Expense
185.1	Accumulated Depr.—	523	Supplies Expense
	Delivery Equipment	525	Telephone Expense
		535	Insurance Expense
		541	Depr. Expense—
Liabilities			Delivery Equipment
202	Accounts Payable		
219	Wages Payable		
Owner's Equity			
311	Jessica Jane, Capital		
312	Jessica Jane, Drawing		

FIGURE 5-12   Expanded Chart of Accounts

THE WORK SHEET

LO2 Prepare a work sheet.

A **work sheet** pulls together all of the information needed to enter adjusting entries and prepare the financial statements. Work sheets are not financial statements and are not a formal part of the accounting system. Ordinarily, only the accountant uses a work sheet. For this reason, a work sheet is usually prepared in pencil or as a spreadsheet on a computer.

The Ten-Column Work Sheet

Although a work sheet can take several forms, a common format has a column for account titles and ten amount columns grouped into five pairs. The work sheet format and the five steps in preparing the work sheet are illustrated in Figure 5-13. As with financial statements, the work sheet has a heading consisting of the name of the company, name of the working paper, and the date of the accounting period just ended. The five major column headings for the work sheet are Trial Balance, Adjustments, Adjusted Trial Balance, Income Statement, and Balance Sheet.

Preparing the Work Sheet

Let's apply the five steps required for the preparation of a work sheet to Jessie Jane's Campus Delivery.

STEP 1

Prepare the Trial Balance. As shown in Figure 5-14, the first pair of amount columns is for the trial balance. The trial balance assures the equality of the debits and credits before the adjustment process begins. The columns should be double ruled to show that they are equal.

You are already familiar with a trial balance. Here we are simply copying a trial balance to a different form, called a work sheet.

Note that all accounts listed in the expanded chart of accounts are included in the Trial Balance columns of the work sheet. This is done even though some accounts have zero balances. The accounts with zero balances could be added to the bottom of the list as they are needed for adjusting entries. However, it is easier to include them now, especially if preparing the work sheet on an electronic spreadsheet. Listing the accounts within their proper classifications (assets, liabilities, etc.) also makes it easier to extend the amounts to the proper columns.

STEP 2

Prepare the Adjustments. As shown in Figure 5-15, the second pair of amount columns is used to prepare the adjusting entries. Enter the adjustments directly in these columns. When an account is debited or credited, the amount is entered on the same line as the name of the account and in the appropriate Adjustments Debit or Credit column. A small letter in parentheses identifies each adjusting entry made on the work sheet.

LEARNING KEY: For adjustments (a), (b), and (d), we are simply recognizing that assets have been used. When this happens, the asset must be decreased and an expense recognized. Note that the reported amount for delivery equipment is reduced by crediting a contra-asset.

ADJUSTMENT (a):
Supplies costing $60 were used during June.

	Debit	Credit
Supplies Expense	60	
Supplies		60

FIGURE 5-13 Steps in Preparing the Work Sheet

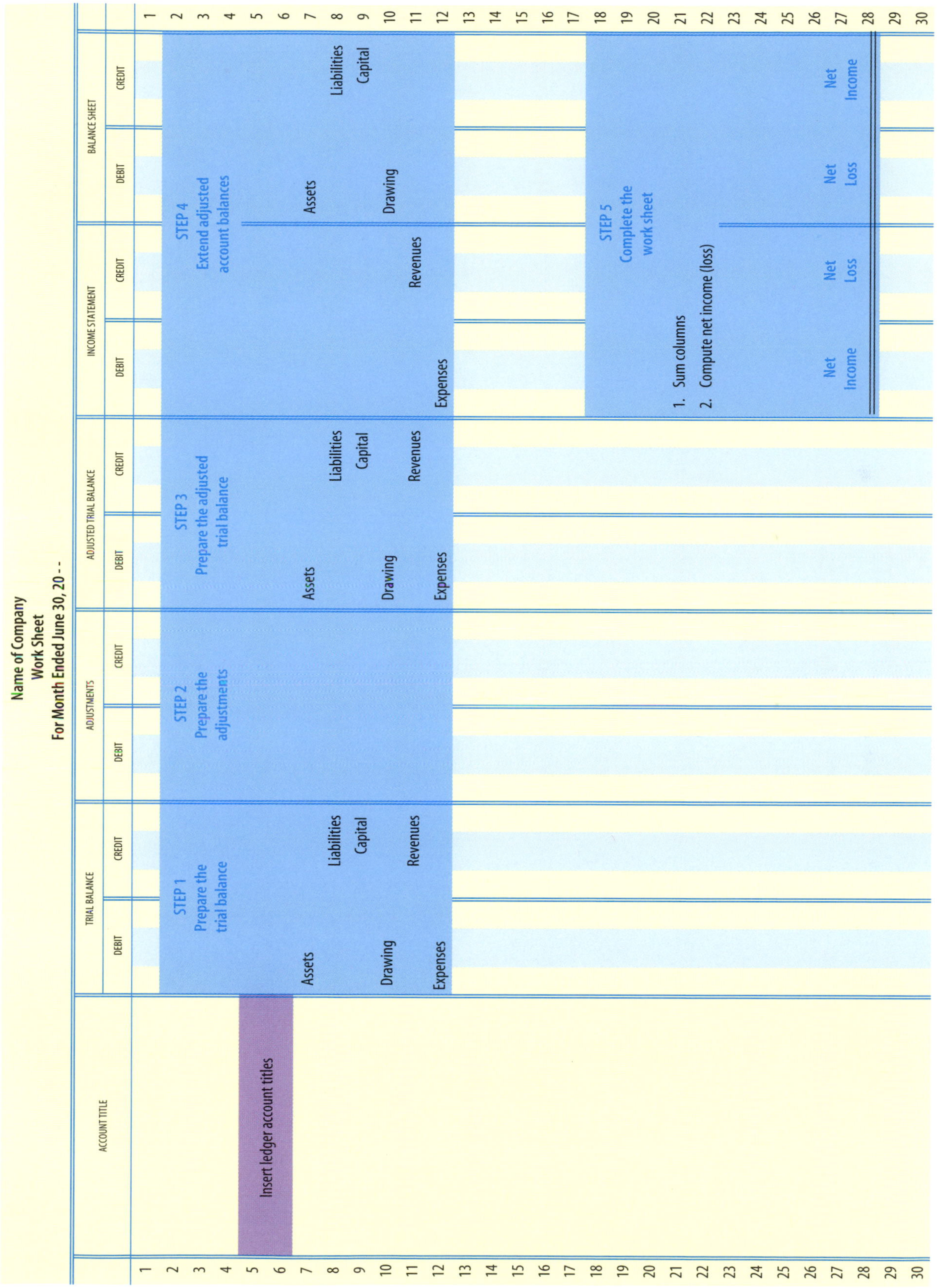

Name of Company
Work Sheet
For Month Ended June 30, 20 - -

ACCOUNT TITLE	TRIAL BALANCE		ADJUSTMENTS		ADJUSTED TRIAL BALANCE		INCOME STATEMENT		BALANCE SHEET	
	DEBIT	CREDIT	DEBIT	CREDIT	DEBIT	CREDIT	DEBIT	CREDIT	DEBIT	CREDIT
Insert ledger account titles	STEP 1 Prepare the trial balance		STEP 2 Prepare the adjustments		STEP 3 Prepare the adjusted trial balance		STEP 4 Extend adjusted account balances			
	Assets	Liabilities			Assets	Liabilities			Assets	Liabilities
		Capital				Capital				Capital
	Drawing				Drawing				Drawing	
		Revenues				Revenues		Revenues		
	Expenses				Expenses		Expenses			
							STEP 5 Complete the work sheet 1. Sum columns 2. Compute net income (loss)			
							Net Income	Net Loss	Net Loss	Net Income

FIGURE 5-14 Step 1—Prepare the Trial Balance

Jessica Jane's Campus Delivery
Work Sheet
For Month Ended June 30, 20 - -

	ACCOUNT TITLE	TRIAL BALANCE		ADJUSTMENTS		ADJUSTED TRIAL BALANCE		INCOME STATEMENT		BALANCE SHEET		
		DEBIT	CREDIT	DEBIT	CREDIT	DEBIT	CREDIT	DEBIT	CREDIT	DEBIT	CREDIT	
1	Cash	3 7 0 0 00										1
2	Accounts Receivable	6 5 0 00										2
3	Supplies	8 0 00										3
4	Prepaid Insurance	2 0 0 00										4
5	Delivery Equipment	3 6 0 0 00										5
6	Accum. Depr.—Delivery Equipment											6
7	Accounts Payable		1 8 0 0 00									7
8	Wages Payable											8
9	Jessica Jane, Capital		2 0 0 0 00									9
10	Jessica Jane, Drawing	1 5 0 00										10
11	Delivery Fees		2 1 5 0 00									11
12	Wages Expense	6 5 0 00										12
13	Rent Expense	2 0 0 00										13
14	Supplies Expense											14
15	Telephone Expense	5 0 00										15
16	Insurance Expense											16
17	Depr. Expense—Delivery Equipment											17
18		5 9 5 0 00	5 9 5 0 00									18
19												19
20												20
21												21
22												22
23												23
24												24
25												25
26												26
27												27
28												28
29												29
30												30

STEP 1

Preparing the Work Sheet

STEP 1 **Prepare the Trial Balance.**

- Write the heading, account titles, and the debit and credit amounts from the general ledger.
- Place a single rule across the Trial Balance columns and total the debit and credit amounts.
- Place a double rule under the totals for each column.
- Total debits must equal total credits.

STEP 2 **Prepare the Adjustments.**

- Record the adjustments.
  Hint: Make certain that each adjustment is on the same line as the account name and in the appropriate column.
  Hint: Identify each adjusting entry by a letter in parentheses.
- Rule the Adjusted Trial Balance columns.
- Total the debit and credit columns and double rule the columns.
- Total debits must equal total credits.

STEP 3 **Prepare the Adjusted Trial Balance.**

- Extend those debits and credits that are not adjusted directly to the appropriate Adjusted Trial Balance column.
- Enter the adjusted balances in the appropriate Adjusted Trial Balance column.
  Hint: If an account has a debit and a credit, subtract the adjustment. If an account has two debits or two credits, add the adjustment.
- Single rule the Adjusted Trial Balance columns.
- Total and double rule the debit and credit columns.
- Total debits must equal total credits.

STEP 4 **Extend Adjusted Balances to the Income Statement and Balance Sheet Columns.**

- Extend all revenue accounts to the Income Statement Credit column.
- Extend all expense accounts to the Income Statement Debit column.
- Extend the asset and drawing accounts to the Balance Sheet Debit column.
- Extend the liability and owner's capital accounts to the Balance Sheet Credit column.

STEP 5 **Complete the Work Sheet.**

- Rule and total the Income Statement and Balance Sheet columns.
- Calculate the difference between the Income Statement Debit and Credit columns.
- Calculate the difference between the Balance Sheet Debit and Credit columns.
  Hint: If the Income Statement credits exceed debits, net income has occurred; otherwise a net loss has occurred. If the Balance Sheet debits exceed the credits, the difference is net income; otherwise a net loss has occurred.
  Hint: The difference between the Balance Sheet columns should be the same as the difference between the Income Statement columns.
- Add the net income to the Income Statement Debit column or add the net loss to the Income Statement Credit column. Add the net income to the Balance Sheet Credit column or the net loss to the Balance Sheet Debit column.
- Total and double rule the columns.

ADJUSTMENT (b):

One month's insurance premium has expired.

	Debit	Credit
Insurance Expense	25	
Prepaid Insurance		25

ADJUSTMENT (c):

Employees earned $50 that has not yet been paid.

	Debit	Credit
Wages Expense	50	
Wages Payable		50

> **LEARNING KEY:** Adjustment (c) recognizes an economic event that has not required an actual transaction yet. Employees earned wages, but have not been paid. The adjustment recognizes an expense and a liability.

ADJUSTMENT (d):

Depreciation on the motor scooters is recognized.

	Debit	Credit
Depreciation Expense—Delivery Equipment	100	
Accumulated Depreciation—Delivery Equipment		100

When all adjustments have been entered on the work sheet, each column should be totaled to assure that the debits equal the credits for all entries. After balancing the columns, they should be double ruled.

STEP 3   **Prepare the Adjusted Trial Balance.** As shown in Figure 5-16, the third pair of amount columns on the work sheet are the **Adjusted Trial Balance columns.** When an account balance is not affected by entries in the Adjustments columns, the amount in the Trial Balance columns is extended directly to the Adjusted Trial Balance columns. *When affected by an entry in the Adjustments columns, the balance to be entered in the Adjusted Trial Balance columns increases or decreases by the amount of the adjusting entry.*

For example, in Jessica Jane's business, Supplies is listed in the Trial Balance Debit column as $80. Since the entry of $60 is in the Adjustments Credit column, the amount extended to the Adjusted Trial Balance Debit column is $20 ($80 – $60).

Wages Expense is listed in the Trial Balance Debit column as $650. Since $50 is in the Adjustments Debit column, the amount extended to the Adjusted Trial Balance Debit column is $700 ($650 + $50).

After all extensions have been made, the Adjusted Trial Balance columns are totaled to prove the equality of the debits and the credits. Once balanced, the columns are double ruled.

STEP 4   **Extend Adjusted Balances to the Income Statement and Balance Sheet Columns.** As shown in Figure 5-17, each account listed in the Adjusted Trial Balance must be extended to either the Income Statement or Balance Sheet columns. The **Income Statement columns** show the amounts that will be reported in the income statement. All revenue accounts are extended to the Income Statement Credit column and expense accounts are extended to the Income Statement Debit column.

The asset, liability, drawing, and capital accounts are extended to the **Balance Sheet columns.** Although called the Balance Sheet columns, these columns of the work sheet show the amounts that will be reported in the balance sheet and the statement of owner's equity. The asset and drawing accounts are extended to the Balance Sheet Debit column. The liability and owner's capital accounts are extended to the Balance Sheet Credit column.

> **LEARNING KEY:** The Balance Sheet columns show the amounts for both the balance sheet and the statement of owner's equity.

STEP 5 **Complete the Work Sheet.** To complete the work sheet, first total the Income Statement columns. If the total of the credits (revenues) exceeds the total of the debits (expenses), the difference represents net income. If the total of the debits exceeds the total of the credits, the difference represents a net loss.

The Income Statement columns of Jessie's work sheet in Figure 5-18 show total credits of $2,150 and total debits of $1,135. The difference, $1,015, is the net income for the month of June. This amount should be added to the debit column to balance the Income Statement columns. "Net Income" should be written on the same line in the Account Title column. If the business had a net loss, the amount of the loss would be added to the Income Statement Credit column and the words "Net Loss" would be written in the Account Title column. Once balanced, the columns should be double ruled.

Finally, the Balance Sheet columns are totaled. The difference between the totals of these columns also is the amount of net income or net loss for the accounting period. If the total debits exceed the total credits, the difference is net income. If the total credits exceed the total debits, the difference is a net loss. This difference should be the same as the difference we found for the Income Statement columns.

> **LEARNING KEY:** In the Balance Sheet columns of the work sheet, total debits minus total credits equals net <u>income</u> if greater than zero and equals net <u>loss</u> if less than zero.

The Balance Sheet columns of Jessie's work sheet show total debits of $4,965 and total credits of $3,950. The difference of $1,015 represents the amount of net income for the month. This amount is added to the credit column to balance the Balance Sheet columns. If the business had a net loss, this amount would be added to the Balance Sheet Debit column. Once balanced, the columns should be double ruled.

A trick for remembering the appropriate placement of the net income and net loss is the following: Net Income *apart*; Net Loss *together*. Figure 5-19 illustrates this learning aid.

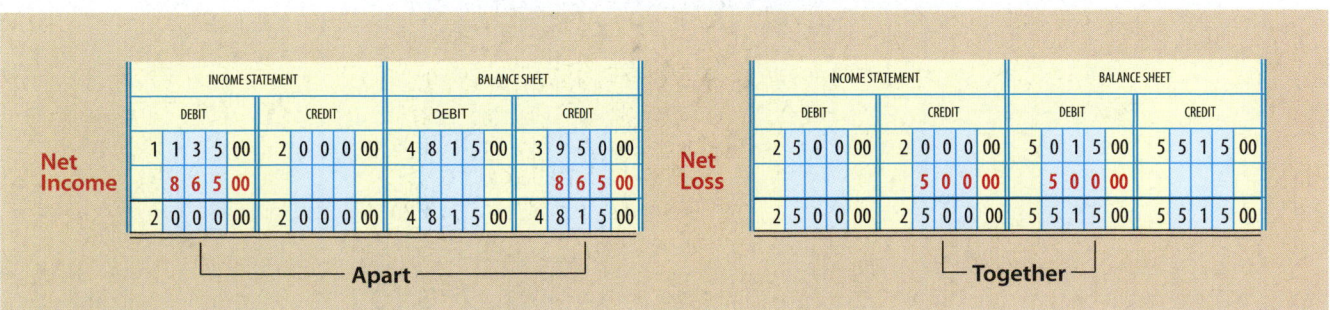

FIGURE 5-19 Net Income Apart, Net Loss Together

FINDING ERRORS ON THE WORK SHEET

LO3 Describe methods for finding errors on the work sheet.

If any of the columns on the work sheet do not balance, you must find the error before you continue. Once you are confident that the work sheet is accurate, you are ready to journalize the adjusting entries and prepare financial statements. Figure 5-20 offers tips for finding errors on the work sheet.

TIPS FOR FINDING ERRORS ON THE WORK SHEET
1. Check the addition of all columns.
2. Check the addition and subtraction required when extending to the Adjusted Trial Balance columns.
3. Make sure the adjusted account balances have been extended to the appropriate columns.
4. Make sure that the net income or net loss has been added to the appropriate columns.

FIGURE 5-20   Finding Errors on the Work Sheet

JOURNALIZING ADJUSTING ENTRIES

LO4 Journalize adjusting entries.

Keep in mind that the work sheet simply helps the accountant organize the end-of-period work. *Writing the adjustments on the work sheet has no effect on the ledger accounts in the accounting system. The only way to change the balance of a ledger account is to make a journal entry.* Once the adjustments have been entered on the work sheet, simply copy the adjustments from the work sheet to the journal.

Jessie's adjusting entries are illustrated in Figure 5-21 as they would appear in a general journal. Note that the last day of the accounting period, June 30, has been entered in the date column and *"Adjusting Entries"* is written in the Description column prior to the first adjusting entry. No explanation is required in the Description column for individual adjusting entries. We simply label them as adjusting entries.

POSTING ADJUSTING ENTRIES

LO5 Post adjusting entries to the general ledger.

Adjusting entries are posted to the general ledger in the same manner as all other entries, except that *"Adjusting"* is written in the Item column of the general ledger. Figure 5-22 shows the posting of the adjusting entry for supplies. The posting reference numbers are inserted as each entry is posted.

	DATE		DESCRIPTION	POST REF.	DEBIT			CREDIT			
1			**Adjusting Entries**								1
2	20-- June	30	Supplies Expense	523	6 0	00					2
3			Supplies	141				6 0	00		3
4											4
5		30	Insurance Expense	535	2 5	00					5
6			Prepaid Insurance	145				2 5	00		6
7											7
8		30	Wages Expense	511	5 0	00					8
9			Wages Payable	219				5 0	00		9
10											10
11		30	Depr. Expense — Delivery Equipment	541	1 0 0	00					11
12			Accum. Depr. — Delivery Equipment	185.1				1 0 0	00		12

GENERAL JOURNAL   PAGE 3

FIGURE 5-21   Adjusting Entries

GENERAL LEDGER

ACCOUNT: Supplies   ACCOUNT NO. 141

DATE		ITEM	POST REF.	DEBIT	CREDIT	BALANCE DEBIT	BALANCE CREDIT
20-- June	16		J1	8 0 00		8 0 00	
	30	Adjusting	J3		6 0 00	2 0 00	

ACCOUNT: Supplies Expense   ACCOUNT NO. 523

DATE		ITEM	POST REF.	DEBIT	CREDIT	BALANCE DEBIT	BALANCE CREDIT
20-- June	30	Adjusting	J3	6 0 00		6 0 00	

FIGURE 5-22   Posting the Adjusting Entry for Supplies

Learning Objectives	Key Points to Remember
1 Prepare end-of-period adjustments.	End-of-period adjustments are necessary to bring the general ledger accounts up to date prior to preparing financial statements. Reasons to adjust the trial balance are: 1. To report all revenues earned during the accounting period. 2. To report all expenses incurred to produce the revenues during the accounting period. 3. To accurately report the assets on the balance sheet. Some assets may have expired, depreciated, or been used up during the accounting period. 4. To accurately report the liabilities on the balance sheet date. Expenses may have been incurred, but not yet paid.
2 Prepare a work sheet.	Steps in preparing the work sheet are: 1. Prepare the trial balance. 2. Prepare the adjustments. 3. Prepare the adjusted trial balance. 4. Extend the adjusted account balances to the Income Statement and Balance Sheet columns. 5. Total the Income Statement and Balance Sheet columns to compute the net income or net loss.
3 Describe methods for finding errors on the work sheet.	Tips for finding errors on the work sheet include: 1. Check the addition of all columns. 2. Check the addition and subtraction required when extending to the Adjusted Trial Balance columns. 3. Make sure the adjusted account balances have been extended to the appropriate columns. 4. Make sure that the net income or net loss has been added to the appropriate columns.
4 Journalize adjusting entries.	The adjustments are copied from the work sheet to the journal. The last day of the accounting period is entered in the Date column and "Adjusting Entries" is written in the Description column.
5 Post adjusting entries to the general ledger.	Adjusting entries are posted to the general ledger in the same manner as all other entries, except that "Adjusting" is written in the Item column of the general ledger.

Reflection: Answering the Opening Question

As discussed in the chapter, it is essential to make appropriate adjustments prior to the preparation of financial statements.

DEMONSTRATION PROBLEM

WebTUTOR Advantage

Justin Park is a lawyer specializing in corporate tax law. He began his practice on January 1. A chart of accounts and trial balance taken on December 31, 20-- are provided below.

Information for year-end adjustments:

(a) Office supplies on hand at year end amounted to $300.

(b) On January 1, 20--, Park purchased office equipment costing $15,000 with an expected life of five years and no salvage value.

(c) Computer equipment costing $6,000 with an expected life of three years and no salvage value was purchased on July 1, 20--. Assume that Park computes depreciation to the nearest full month.

(d) A premium of $1,200 for a one-year insurance policy was paid on December 1, 20--.

(e) Wages earned by Park's part-time secretary, which have not yet been paid, amount to $300.

REQUIRED

1. Prepare the work sheet for the year ended December 31, 20--.

2. Prepare adjusting entries in a general journal.

JUSTIN PARK LEGAL SERVICES CHART OF ACCOUNTS				
Assets			**Revenue**	
101	Cash		401	Client Fees
142	Office Supplies			
145	Prepaid Insurance		**Expenses**	
181	Office Equipment		511	Wages Expense
181.1	Accumulated Depr.—		521	Rent Expense
	Office Equipment		523	Office Supplies Expense
187	Computer Equipment		525	Telephone Expense
187.1	Accumulated Depr.—		533	Utilities Expense
	Computer Equipment		535	Insurance Expense
Liabilities			541	Depr. Expense—
201	Notes Payable			Office Equipment
202	Accounts Payable		542	Depr. Expense—
219	Wages Payable			Computer Equipment
Owner's Equity				
311	Justin Park, Capital			
312	Justin Park, Drawing			

(continued)

		Justin Park Legal Services Trial Balance December 31, 20 - -							
ACCOUNT TITLE	ACCOUNT NO.	DEBIT BALANCE				CREDIT BALANCE			
Cash	101	7	0	0	0	00				
Office Supplies	142		8	0	0	00				
Prepaid Insurance	145	1	2	0	0	00				
Office Equipment	181	15	0	0	0	00				
Computer Equipment	187	6	0	0	0	00				
Notes Payable	201						5	0	0	0	00
Accounts Payable	202							5	0	0	00
Justin Park, Capital	311						11	4	0	0	00
Justin Park, Drawing	312	5	0	0	0	00				
Client Fees	401						40	0	0	0	00
Wages Expense	511	12	0	0	0	00				
Rent Expense	521	5	0	0	0	00				
Telephone Expense	525	1	0	0	0	00				
Utilities Expense	533	3	9	0	0	00				
		56	9	0	0	00	56	9	0	0	00

Solution

1.

Justin Park Legal Services
Work Sheet
For Year Ended December 31, 20 - -

#	ACCOUNT TITLE	Trial Balance DEBIT	Trial Balance CREDIT	Adjustments DEBIT	Adjustments CREDIT	Adjusted Trial Balance DEBIT	Adjusted Trial Balance CREDIT	Income Statement DEBIT	Income Statement CREDIT	Balance Sheet DEBIT	Balance Sheet CREDIT
1	Cash	7 0 0 0 00				7 0 0 0 00				7 0 0 0 00	
2	Office Supplies	8 0 0 00			(a) 5 0 0 00	3 0 0 00				3 0 0 00	
3	Prepaid Insurance	1 2 0 0 00			(d) 1 0 0 00	1 1 0 0 00				1 1 0 0 00	
4	Office Equipment	15 0 0 0 00				15 0 0 0 00				15 0 0 0 00	
5	Accum. Depr.—Office Equip.				(b) 3 0 0 00		3 0 0 00				3 0 0 00
6	Computer Equipment	6 0 0 0 00				6 0 0 0 00				6 0 0 0 00	
7	Accum. Depr.—Computer Equip.				(c) 1 0 0 0 00		1 0 0 0 00				1 0 0 0 00
8	Notes Payable		5 0 0 0 00				5 0 0 0 00				5 0 0 0 00
9	Accounts Payable		5 0 0 00				5 0 0 00				5 0 0 00
10	Wages Payable				(e) 3 0 0 00		3 0 0 00				3 0 0 00
11	Justin Park, Capital		11 4 0 0 00				11 4 0 0 00				11 4 0 0 00
12	Justin Park, Drawing	5 0 0 0 00				5 0 0 0 00				5 0 0 0 00	
13	Client Fees		40 0 0 0 00				40 0 0 0 00		40 0 0 0 00		
14	Wages Expense	12 0 0 0 00		(e) 3 0 0 00		12 3 0 0 00		12 3 0 0 00			
15	Rent Expense	5 0 0 0 00				5 0 0 0 00		5 0 0 0 00			
16	Office Supplies Expense			(a) 5 0 0 00		5 0 0 00		5 0 0 00			
17	Telephone Expense	1 0 0 0 00				1 0 0 0 00		1 0 0 0 00			
18	Utilities Expense	3 9 0 0 00				3 9 0 0 00		3 9 0 0 00			
19	Insurance Expense			(d) 1 0 0 00		1 0 0 00		1 0 0 00			
20	Depr. Expense—Office Equip.			(b) 3 0 0 00		3 0 0 00		3 0 0 00			
21	Depr. Expense—Computer Equip.			(c) 1 0 0 0 00		1 0 0 0 00		1 0 0 0 00			
22		56 9 0 0 00	56 9 0 0 00	4 9 0 0 00	4 9 0 0 00	61 2 0 0 00	61 2 0 0 00	26 8 0 0 00	40 0 0 0 00	34 4 0 0 00	21 2 0 0 00
23	Net Income							13 2 0 0 00			13 2 0 0 00
24								40 0 0 0 00	40 0 0 0 00	34 4 0 0 00	34 4 0 0 00

(continued)

2.

	DATE		DESCRIPTION	POST. REF.	DEBIT					CREDIT					
			GENERAL JOURNAL						PAGE 11						
1			Adjusting Entries												1
2	20-- Dec.	31	Office Supplies Expense			5	0	0	00						2
3			Office Supplies								5	0	0	00	3
4															4
5		31	Depr. Expense—Office Equipment		3	0	0	0	00						5
6			Accum. Depr.—Office Equipment							3	0	0	0	00	6
7															7
8		31	Depr. Expense—Computer Equipment		1	0	0	0	00						8
9			Accum. Depr.—Computer Equipment							1	0	0	0	00	9
10															10
11		31	Insurance Expense			1	0	0	00						11
12			Prepaid Insurance								1	0	0	00	12
13															13
14		31	Wages Expense			3	0	0	00						14
15			Wages Payable								3	0	0	00	15

On-Line Learning Tools

For more information, visit: http://heintz.swlearning.com

The Heintz & Parry product web site is designed specifically for *COLLEGE ACCOUNTING, 18e.* The features include downloadable student resources and an interactive study center, organized by chapter, which contains learning objectives, web links, on-line quizzes with automatic feedback, and more.

KEY TERMS

Adjusted Trial Balance columns, (142H)   The third pair of amount columns on the work sheet. They are used to prove the equality of the debits and credits in the general ledger accounts after making all end-of-period adjustments.

adjusting entries, (134)   Journal entries made at the end of an accounting period to reflect changes in account balances that are not the direct result of an exchange with an outside party.

Balance Sheet columns, (142H)   The work sheet columns that show the amounts that will be reported in the balance sheet and the statement of owner's equity.

book value, (140)   The difference between the asset account and its related accumulated depreciation account. The value reflected by the accounting records.

contra-asset, (139)   An account with a credit balance that is deducted from the related asset account on the balance sheet.

depreciable cost, (139)   The cost of an asset that is subject to depreciation.

depreciation, (139)   A method of matching an asset's original cost against the revenues produced over its useful life.

fiscal year, (134)   A twelve-month period for which financial reports are prepared.

historical cost principle, (139)   A principle that requires assets to be recorded at their actual cost.

Income Statement columns, (142H)   The work sheet columns that show the amounts that will be reported in the income statement.

market value, (139)   The amount an item can be sold for under normal economic conditions.

matching principle, (134)   A principle that requires the matching of revenues earned during an accounting period with the expenses incurred to produce the revenues.

plant assets, (139)   Assets of a durable nature that will be used for operations over several years. Examples include buildings and equipment.

salvage value, (139)   The expected market value of an asset at the end of its useful life.

straight-line method, (139)   A depreciation method in which the depreciable cost is divided by the estimated useful life.

undepreciated cost, (140)   The difference between the asset account and its related accumulated depreciation account. Also known as book value.

useful life, (139)   The period of time that an asset is expected to help produce revenues.

work sheet, (142)   A form used to pull together all of the information needed to enter adjusting entries and prepare the financial statements.

REVIEW QUESTIONS

(LO1)	1. Explain the matching principle.
(LO1)	2. Explain the historical cost principle.
(LO1)	3. Describe a plant asset.
(LO1)	4. What is a contra-asset?
(LO1)	5. What is the useful life of an asset?
(LO1)	6. What is the purpose of depreciation?
(LO1)	7. What is an asset's depreciable cost?
(LO1)	8. What is the book value of an asset?
(LO2)	9. Explain the purpose of the work sheet.
(LO2)	10. Identify the five major column headings on a work sheet.
(LO2)	11. List the five steps taken in preparing a work sheet.
(LO3)	12. Describe four tips for finding errors on the work sheet.

Self-Study Test Questions

True/False

1. The matching principle in accounting requires the matching of debits and credits. _____

2. Adjusting entries are required at the end of the accounting period because of mistakes in the journal and ledger. _____

3. As part of the adjustment of supplies, an expense account is debited and Supplies is credited for the amount of supplies used during the accounting period. _____

4. Depreciable cost is the difference between the original cost of the asset and its accumulated depreciation. _____

5. The purpose of depreciation is to record the asset's market value in the accounting records. _____

Multiple Choice

1. The purpose of depreciation is to _____

   (a) spread the cost of an asset over its useful life.
   (b) show the current market value of an asset.
   (c) set up a reserve fund to purchase a new asset.
   (d) expense the asset in the year it was purchased.

2. Depreciable cost is the _____

   (a) difference between original cost and accumulated depreciation.
   (b) difference in actual cost and true market value.
   (c) difference between original cost and estimated salvage value.
   (d) difference between estimated salvage value and the actual salvage value.

3. Book value is the _____

   (a) difference between market value and estimated value.
   (b) difference between market value and historical cost.
   (c) difference between original cost and salvage value.
   (d) difference between original cost and accumulated depreciation.

4. The adjustment for wages earned but not yet paid is _____

   (a) debit Wages Payable and credit Wages Expense.
   (b) debit Wages Expense and credit Cash.
   (c) debit Wages Expense and credit Wages Payable.
   (d) debit Wages Expense and credit Accounts Receivable.

5. The first step in preparing a work sheet is to _____

   (a) prepare the trial balance.
   (b) prepare the adjustments.
   (c) prepare the adjusted trial balance.
   (d) extend the amounts from the Adjusted Trial Balance to the Income Statement and Balance Sheet columns.

The answers to the Self-Study Test Questions are at the end of the text.

MANAGING YOUR WRITING

Delia Alvarez, owner of Delia's Lawn Service, wants to borrow money to buy new lawn equipment. A local bank has asked for financial statements. Alvarez has asked you to prepare financial statements for the year ended December 31, 20--. You have been given the unadjusted trial balance shown below and suspect that Alvarez expects you to base your statements on this information. You are concerned, however, that some of the account balances may need to be adjusted. Write a memo to Alvarez explaining what additional information you need before you can prepare the financial statements. Alvarez is not familiar with accounting issues. Therefore, explain in your memo why you need this information, the potential impact of this information on the financial statements, and the importance of making these adjustments before approaching the bank for a loan.

Delia's Lawn Service Trial Balance December 31, 20 - -												
ACCOUNT TITLE	ACCOUNT NO.	DEBIT BALANCE					CREDIT BALANCE					
Cash	101		7	7	0	00						
Accounts Receivable	122	1	7	0	0	00						
Supplies	142		2	8	0	00						
Prepaid Insurance	145		4	0	0	00						
Lawn Equipment	183	13	8	0	0	00						
Accounts Payable	202							2	2	0	0	00
Delia Alvarez, Capital	311							3	0	0	0	00
Delia Alvarez, Drawing	312		3	5	0	00						
Lawn Cutting Fees	401							52	4	0	0	00
Wages Expense	511	35	8	5	0	00						
Rent Expense	521	1	2	0	0	00						
Gas and Oil Expense	538	3	2	5	0	00						
		57	6	0	0	00		57	6	0	0	00

SERIES A EXERCISES

EXERCISE 5-1A   **(LO1)**   **ADJUSTMENT FOR SUPPLIES** On December 31, the trial balance indicates that the supplies account has a balance, prior to the adjusting entry, of $320. A physical count of the supplies inventory shows that $90 of supplies remain. Analyze this adjustment for supplies using T accounts, and then formally enter this adjustment in the general journal.

EXERCISE 5-2A   **(LO1)**   **ADJUSTMENT FOR INSURANCE** On December 1, a six-month liability insurance policy was purchased for $900. Analyze the required adjustment as of December 31 using T accounts, and then formally enter this adjustment in the general journal.

EXERCISE 5-3A   **(LO1)**   **ADJUSTMENT FOR WAGES** On December 31, the trial balance shows wages expense of $600. An additional $200 of wages was earned by the employees, but has not yet been paid. Analyze this adjustment for wages, and then formally enter this adjustment in the general journal.

EXERCISE 5-4A   **(LO1)**   **ADJUSTMENT FOR DEPRECIATION OF ASSET** On December 1, delivery equipment was purchased for $7,200. The delivery equipment has an estimated useful life of four years (48 months) and no salvage value. Using the straight-line depreciation method, prepare the necessary adjusting entry as of December 31 (one month), and then formally enter this adjustment in the general journal.

EXERCISE 5-5A   **(LO1)**   **CALCULATION OF BOOK VALUE** On June 1, 20--, a depreciable asset was acquired for $5,400. The asset has an estimated useful life of five years (60 months) and no salvage value. Using the straight-line depreciation method, calculate the book value as of December 31, 20--.

EXERCISE 5-6A   **(LO1)**   **ANALYSIS OF ADJUSTING ENTRY FOR SUPPLIES** Analyze each situation and indicate the correct dollar amount for the adjusting entry. (Trial balance is abbreviated as TB.)

1. Ending inventory of supplies is $130.

(Balance Sheet) Supplies	(Income Statement) Supplies Expense
TB 460	
Adj. _____	Adj. _____
Bal. _____	

2. Amount of supplies used is $320.

(Balance Sheet) Supplies	(Income Statement) Supplies Expense
TB 545	
Adj. _____	Adj. _____
Bal. _____	

EXERCISE 5-7A   **(LO1)**   **ANALYSIS OF ADJUSTING ENTRY FOR INSURANCE** Analyze each situation and indicate the correct dollar amount for the adjusting entry.

1. Amount of insurance expired is $900.

(Balance Sheet) Prepaid Insurance	(Income Statement) Insurance Expense
TB 1,300	
Adj. _____	Adj. _____
Bal. _____	

2. Amount of unexpired insurance is $185.

(Balance Sheet) Prepaid Insurance	(Income Statement) Insurance Expense
TB 860	
Adj. _____	Adj. _____
Bal. _____	

EXERCISE 5-8A   (LO2)
Adjustments col. total: $1,550

WORK SHEET AND ADJUSTING ENTRIES A partial work sheet for Jim Jacob's furniture repair is shown as follows. Indicate by letters (a) through (d) the four adjustments in the Adjustments columns of the work sheet, properly matching each debit and credit. Complete the Adjustments columns.

Jim Jacob's Furniture Repair
Work Sheet (Partial)
For Year Ended December 31, 20 - -

	ACCOUNT TITLE	TRIAL BALANCE DEBIT	TRIAL BALANCE CREDIT	ADJUSTMENTS DEBIT	ADJUSTMENTS CREDIT	ADJUSTED TRIAL BALANCE DEBIT	ADJUSTED TRIAL BALANCE CREDIT	
1	Cash	1 0 0 00				1 0 0 00		1
2	Supplies	8 5 0 00				2 0 0 00		2
3	Prepaid Insurance	9 0 0 00				3 0 0 00		3
4	Delivery Equipment	3 6 0 0 00				3 6 0 0 00		4
5	Accum. Depr.— Delivery Equipment		6 0 0 00				8 0 0 00	5
6	Wages Payable						1 0 0 00	6
7	Jim Jacob, Capital		4 0 0 0 00				4 0 0 0 00	7
8	Repair Fees		1 6 5 0 00				1 6 5 0 00	8
9	Wages Expense	6 0 0 00				7 0 0 00		9
10	Advertising Expense	2 0 0 00				2 0 0 00		10
11	Supplies Expense					6 5 0 00		11
12	Insurance Expense					6 0 0 00		12
13	Depr. Expense—Delivery Equipment					2 0 0 00		13
14		6 2 5 0 00	6 2 5 0 00			6 5 5 0 00	6 5 5 0 00	14

EXERCISE 5-9A   (LO4)

JOURNALIZING ADJUSTING ENTRIES From the adjustments columns in Exercise 5-8A, journalize the four adjusting entries, as of December 31, in proper general journal format.

EXERCISE 5-10A   (LO2)

EXTENDING ADJUSTED BALANCES TO THE INCOME STATEMENT AND BALANCE SHEET COLUMNS Indicate with an "x" whether each account total should be extended to the Income Statement Debit or Credit or to the Balance Sheet Debit or Credit columns on the work sheet.

	Income Statement Debit	Income Statement Credit	Balance Sheet Debit	Balance Sheet Credit
Cash	_____	_____	_____	_____
Accounts Receivable	_____	_____	_____	_____
Supplies	_____	_____	_____	_____
Prepaid Insurance	_____	_____	_____	_____
Delivery Equipment	_____	_____	_____	_____
Accum. Depr.—Delivery Equipment	_____	_____	_____	_____
Accounts Payable	_____	_____	_____	_____
Wages Payable	_____	_____	_____	_____
Owner, Capital	_____	_____	_____	_____
Owner, Drawing	_____	_____	_____	_____
Delivery Fees	_____	_____	_____	_____
Wages Expense	_____	_____	_____	_____
Rent Expense	_____	_____	_____	_____
Supplies Expense	_____	_____	_____	_____
Insurance Expense	_____	_____	_____	_____
Depr. Exp.—Delivery Equipment	_____	_____	_____	_____

EXERCISE 5-11A   **(LO2)**   **ANALYSIS OF NET INCOME OR NET LOSS ON THE WORK SHEET** Indicate with an "x" in which columns, Income Statement Debit or Credit or Balance Sheet Debit or Credit, a net income or a net loss would appear on a work sheet.

	Income Statement		Balance Sheet	
	Debit	Credit	Debit	Credit
Net Income	_____	_____	_____	_____
Net Loss	_____	_____	_____	_____

EXERCISE 5-12A   **(LO5)**   **POSTING ADJUSTING ENTRIES** Two adjusting entries are in the following general journal. Post these adjusting entries to the four general ledger accounts. The following account numbers were taken from the chart of accounts: 141, Supplies; 219, Wages Payable; 511, Wages Expense; and 523, Supplies Expense. If you are not using the working papers that accompany this text, enter the following balances before posting the entries: Supplies, $200 Dr.; Wages Expense, $1,200 Dr.

GENERAL JOURNAL   PAGE 9

	DATE		DESCRIPTION	POST REF.	DEBIT	CREDIT	
1			Adjusting Entries				1
2	20-- Dec.	31	Supplies Expense		8 5 00		2
3			Supplies			8 5 00	3
4							4
5		31	Wages Expense		2 2 0 00		5
6			Wages Payable			2 2 0 00	6

SERIES A PROBLEMS

PROBLEM 5-13A   **(LO1/2)**

Adjustments col. total: $1,895;
Net income: $1,060

ADJUSTMENTS AND WORK SHEET SHOWING NET INCOME The trial balance after one month of operation for Mason's Delivery Service as of September 30, 20--, is shown on page 157. Data to complete the adjustments are as follows:

(a) Supplies inventory as of September 30, $165.
(b) Insurance expired (used), $800.
(c) Depreciation on delivery equipment, $400.
(d) Wages earned by employees but not paid as of September 30, $225.

REQUIRED

1. Enter the adjustments in the Adjustments columns of the work sheet.

2. Complete the work sheet.

Mason's Delivery Service
Work Sheet
For Month Ended September 30, 20 - -

	ACCOUNT TITLE	TRIAL BALANCE DEBIT	TRIAL BALANCE CREDIT	ADJUSTMENTS DEBIT	ADJUSTMENTS CREDIT	
1	Cash	1 6 0 0 00				1
2	Accounts Receivable	9 4 0 00				2
3	Supplies	6 3 5 00				3
4	Prepaid Insurance	1 2 0 0 00				4
5	Delivery Equipment	6 4 0 0 00				5
6	Accum. Depr.—Delivery Equipment					6
7	Accounts Payable		1 2 2 0 00			7
8	Wages Payable					8
9	Jill Mason, Capital		8 0 0 0 00			9
10	Jill Mason, Drawing	1 4 0 0 00				10
11	Delivery Fees		6 2 0 0 00			11
12	Wages Expense	1 5 0 0 00				12
13	Advertising Expense	4 6 0 00				13
14	Rent Expense	8 0 0 00				14
15	Supplies Expense					15
16	Telephone Expense	1 6 5 00				16
17	Insurance Expense					17
18	Repair Expense	2 3 0 00				18
19	Oil and Gas Expense	9 0 00				19
20	Depr. Expense—Delivery Equipment					20
21		15 4 2 0 00	15 4 2 0 00			21

PROBLEM 5-14A   **(LO1/2)**
Adjustments col. total: $1,380;
Net loss: $2,495

ADJUSTMENTS AND WORK SHEET SHOWING A NET LOSS Jason Armstrong started a business called Campus Escort Service. After the first month of operations, the trial balance as of November 30, 20--, is as shown on the next page.

REQUIRED

1. Analyze the following adjustments and enter them on the work sheet.

   (a) Ending inventory of supplies on November 30, $185.

   (b) Unexpired (remaining) insurance as of November 30, $800.

   (c) Depreciation expense on van, $300.

   (d) Wages earned but not paid as of November 30, $190.

2. Complete the work sheet.

(continued)

	ACCOUNT TITLE	TRIAL BALANCE				ADJUSTMENTS				
		DEBIT		CREDIT		DEBIT		CREDIT		
1	Cash	9 8 0 00								1
2	Accounts Receivable	5 9 0 00								2
3	Supplies	5 7 5 00								3
4	Prepaid Insurance	1 3 0 0 00								4
5	Van	5 8 0 0 00								5
6	Accum. Depr.—Van									6
7	Accounts Payable			9 6 0 00						7
8	Wages Payable									8
9	Jason Armstrong, Capital			10 0 0 0 00						9
10	Jason Armstrong, Drawing	6 0 0 00								10
11	Escort Fees			2 6 0 0 00						11
12	Wages Expense	1 8 0 0 00								12
13	Advertising Expense	3 8 0 00								13
14	Rent Expense	9 0 0 00								14
15	Supplies Expense									15
16	Telephone Expense	2 2 0 00								16
17	Insurance Expense									17
18	Repair Expense	3 1 5 00								18
19	Oil and Gas Expense	1 0 0 00								19
20	Depr. Expense—Van									20
21		13 5 6 0 00		13 5 6 0 00						21

Campus Escort Service
Work Sheet
For Month Ended November 30, 20 - -

PROBLEM 5-15A **(LO4/5)**

JOURNALIZE AND POST ADJUSTING ENTRIES FROM THE WORK SHEET
Refer to Problem 5-14A and the following additional information.

Account Name	Account Number	Balance in Account Before Adjusting Entry
Supplies	141	$ 575
Prepaid Insurance	145	1,300
Accum. Depr.—Van	185.1	0
Wages Payable	219	0
Wages Expense	511	1,800
Supplies Expense	523	0
Insurance Expense	535	0
Depr. Expense—Van	541	0

REQUIRED

1. Journalize the adjusting entries on page 5 of the general journal.

2. Post the adjusting entries to the general ledger. (If you are not using the working papers that accompany this text, enter the balances provided in this problem before posting the adjusting entries.)

PROBLEM 5-16A   **(LO3)**
Adjustments col. total: $1,160;
Net income: $1,575

CORRECTING WORK SHEET WITH ERRORS A beginning accounting student tried to complete a work sheet for Joyce Lee's Tax Service. The following adjusting entries were to have been analyzed and entered onto the work sheet. The work sheet is shown on page 160.

(a) Ending inventory of supplies as of March 31, $160.

(b) Unexpired insurance as of March 31, $520.

(c) Depreciation of office equipment, $275.

(d) Wages earned, but not paid as of March 31, $110.

REQUIRED

The accounting student made a number of errors. Review the work sheet for addition mistakes, transpositions, and other errors and make all necessary corrections.

SERIES B EXERCISES

EXERCISE 5-1B   **(LO1)**

ADJUSTMENT FOR SUPPLIES On July 31, the trial balance indicates that the supplies account has a balance, prior to the adjusting entry, of $430. A physical count of the supplies inventory shows that $120 of supplies remain. Analyze the adjustment for supplies using T accounts, and then formally enter this adjustment in the general journal.

EXERCISE 5-2B   **(LO1)**

ADJUSTMENT FOR INSURANCE On July 1, a six-month liability insurance policy was purchased for $750. Analyze the required adjustment as of July 31 using T accounts, and then formally enter this adjustment in the general journal.

EXERCISE 5-3B   **(LO1)**

ADJUSTMENT FOR WAGES On July 31, the trial balance shows wages expense of $800. An additional $150 of wages was earned by the employees but has not yet been paid. Analyze the required adjustment using T accounts, and then formally enter this adjustment in the general journal.

EXERCISE 5-4B   **(LO1)**

ADJUSTMENT FOR DEPRECIATION OF ASSET On July 1, delivery equipment was purchased for $4,320. The delivery equipment has an estimated useful life of three years (36 months) and no salvage value. Using the straight-line depreciation method, prepare the necessary adjusting entry as of July 31 (one month), and then formally enter this adjustment in the general journal.

EXERCISE 5-5B   **(LO1)**

CALCULATION OF BOOK VALUE On January 1, 20--, a depreciable asset was acquired for $5,760. The asset has an estimated useful life of four years (48 months) and no salvage value. Use the straight-line depreciation method to calculate the book value as of July 1, 20--.

PROBLEM 5-16A

Joyce Lee's Tax Service
Work Sheet
For Month Ended March 31, 20--

This work sheet contains errors.

#	Account Title	Trial Balance Debit	Trial Balance Credit	Adjustments Debit	Adjustments Credit	Adjusted Trial Balance Debit	Adjusted Trial Balance Credit	Income Statement Debit	Income Statement Credit	Balance Sheet Debit	Balance Sheet Credit
1	Cash	1 725 00				1 725 00				1 725 00	
2	Accounts Receivable	960 00				960 00				960 00	
3	Supplies	525 00			(a) 160 00	365 00				365 00	
4	Prepaid Insurance	930 00			(b) 410 00	540 00				540 00	
5	Office Equipment	5 450 00			(c) 275 00	5 175 00				5 175 00	
6	Accum. Depr.—Office Equipment		480 00				480 00				480 00
7	Accounts Payable										
8	Wages Payable				(d) 110 00		110 00		110 00		
9	Joyce Lee, Capital		7 500 00				7 500 00				7 500 00
10	Joyce Lee, Drawing	1 125 00				1 125 00		1 125 00			
11	Professional Fees		5 700 00				5 700 00		5 700 00		
12	Wages Expense	1 420 00		(d) 110 00		1 420 00		1 420 00			
13	Advertising Expense	350 00				350 00		350 00			
14	Rent Expense	700 00				700 00		700 00			
15	Supplies Expense			(a) 160 00		160 00		160 00			
16	Telephone Expense	130 00				130 00		130 00			
17	Utilities Expense	190 00				190 00		190 00			
18	Insurance Expense			(b) 410 00		410 00		410 00			
19	Depr. Expense—Office Equipment			(c) 275 00		275 00		275 00			
20	Miscellaneous Expense	175 00				175 00		175 00			
21											
22		13 680 00	13 680 00	955 00	955 00	13 160 00	13 790 00	4 566 00	5 810 00	9 508 00	7 980 00
23								1 244 00			1 528 00
24								5 810 00	5 810 00	9 508 00	9 508 00

EXERCISE 5-6B   (LO1)   **ANALYSIS OF ADJUSTING ENTRY FOR SUPPLIES** Analyze each situation and indicate the correct dollar amount for the adjusting entry.

1. Ending inventory of supplies is $95.

(Balance Sheet) Supplies	(Income Statement) Supplies Expense
TB 540	
Adj. _____	Adj. _____
Bal. _____	

2. Amount of supplies used is $280.

(Balance Sheet) Supplies	(Income Statement) Supplies Expense
TB 330	
Adj. _____	Adj. _____
Bal. _____	

EXERCISE 5-7B   (LO1)   **ANALYSIS OF ADJUSTING ENTRY FOR INSURANCE** Analyze each situation and indicate the correct dollar amount for the adjusting entry.

1. Amount of insurance expired (used) is $830.

(Balance Sheet) Prepaid Insurance	(Income Statement) Insurance Expense
TB 960	
Adj. _____	Adj. _____
Bal. _____	

2. Amount of unexpired (remaining) insurance is $340.

(Balance Sheet) Prepaid Insurance	(Income Statement) Insurance Expense
TB 1,135	
Adj. _____	Adj. _____
Bal. _____	

EXERCISE 5-8B   (LO2)
Adjustments col. total: $1,530

WORK SHEET AND ADJUSTING ENTRIES Page 162 shows a partial work sheet for Jasmine Kah's Auto Detailing. Indicate by letters (a) through (d) the four adjustments in the Adjustments columns of the work sheet, properly matching each debit and credit. Complete the Adjustments columns.

(continued)

Jasmine Kah's Auto Detailing
Work Sheet (Partial)
For Month Ended June 30, 20 - -

	ACCOUNT TITLE	TRIAL BALANCE DEBIT	TRIAL BALANCE CREDIT	ADJUSTMENTS DEBIT	ADJUSTMENTS CREDIT	ADJUSTED TRIAL BALANCE DEBIT	ADJUSTED TRIAL BALANCE CREDIT	
1	Cash	1 5 0 0 00				1 5 0 0 00		1
2	Supplies	5 2 0 00				9 0 00		2
3	Prepaid Insurance	7 5 0 00				2 0 0 00		3
4	Cleaning Equipment	5 4 0 0 00				5 4 0 0 00		4
5	Accum. Depr.— Cleaning Equipment		8 5 0 00				1 1 5 0 00	5
6	Wages Payable						2 5 0 00	6
7	Jasmine Kah, Capital		4 6 0 0 00				4 6 0 0 00	7
8	Detailing Fees		2 2 2 0 00				2 2 2 0 00	8
9	Wages Expense	7 0 0 00				9 5 0 00		9
10	Advertising Expense	1 5 0 00				1 5 0 00		10
11	Supplies Expense					4 3 0 00		11
12	Insurance Expense					5 5 0 00		12
13	Depr. Expense—Cleaning Equipment					3 0 0 00		13
14		7 6 7 0 00	7 6 7 0 00			8 2 2 0 00	8 2 2 0 00	14

EXERCISE 5-9B (LO4) **JOURNALIZING ADJUSTING ENTRIES** From the Adjustments columns in Exercise 5-8B, journalize the four adjusting entries as of June 30, in proper general journal format.

EXERCISE 5-10B (LO2) **EXTENDING ADJUSTED BALANCES TO THE INCOME STATEMENT AND BALANCE SHEET COLUMNS** Indicate with an "x" whether each account total should be extended to the Income Statement Debit or Credit or to the Balance Sheet Debit or Credit columns on the work sheet.

	Income Statement Debit	Income Statement Credit	Balance Sheet Debit	Balance Sheet Credit
Cash				
Accounts Receivable				
Supplies				
Prepaid Insurance				
Automobile				
Accum. Depr.—Automobile				
Accounts Payable				
Wages Payable				
Owner, Capital				
Owner, Drawing				
Service Fees				
Wages Expense				
Supplies Expense				
Utilities Expense				
Insurance Expense				
Depr. Exp.—Automobile				

EXERCISE 5-11B   **(LO2)**   **ANALYSIS OF NET INCOME OR NET LOSS ON THE WORK SHEET** Insert the dollar amounts where the net income or net loss would appear on the work sheet.

	Income Statement		Balance Sheet	
	Debit	Credit	Debit	Credit
Net Income: $2,500	_____	_____	_____	_____
Net Loss: $1,900	_____	_____	_____	_____

EXERCISE 5-12B   **(LO5)**   **POSTING ADJUSTING ENTRIES** Two adjusting entries are shown in the following general journal. Post these adjusting entries to the four general ledger accounts. The following account numbers were taken from the chart of accounts: 145, Prepaid Insurance; 183.1, Accumulated Depreciation—Cleaning Equipment; 541, Depreciation Expense—Cleaning Equipment; and 535, Insurance Expense. If you are not using the working papers that accompany this text, enter the following balances before posting the entries: Prepaid Insurance, $960 Dr.; Accumulated Depr.—Cleaning Equip., $870 Cr.

	GENERAL JOURNAL			PAGE 7
DATE	DESCRIPTION	POST REF.	DEBIT	CREDIT
	Adjusting Entries			
20-- July 31	Insurance Expense		320 00	
	Prepaid Insurance			320 00
31	Depr. Expense—Cleaning Equipment		145 00	
	Accum. Depr.—Cleaning Equipment			145 00

SERIES B PROBLEMS

PROBLEM 5-13B   (LO1/2)
Adjustments col. total: $805;
Net income: $2,410

ADJUSTMENTS AND WORK SHEET SHOWING NET INCOME Louie Long started a business called Louie's Lawn Service. The trial balance as of March 31, after the first month of operation, is as follows:

Louie's Lawn Service
Work Sheet
For Month Ended March 31, 20 - -

	ACCOUNT TITLE	TRIAL BALANCE DEBIT	TRIAL BALANCE CREDIT	ADJUSTMENTS DEBIT	ADJUSTMENTS CREDIT	
1	Cash	1 3 7 5 00				1
2	Accounts Receivable	8 8 0 00				2
3	Supplies	4 9 0 00				3
4	Prepaid Insurance	8 0 0 00				4
5	Lawn Equipment	5 7 0 0 00				5
6	Accum. Depr.—Lawn Equipment					6
7	Accounts Payable		7 8 0 00			7
8	Wages Payable					8
9	Louie Long, Capital		6 5 0 0 00			9
10	Louie Long, Drawing	1 2 5 0 00				10
11	Lawn Service Fees		6 1 0 0 00			11
12	Wages Expense	1 1 4 5 00				12
13	Advertising Expense	5 4 0 00				13
14	Rent Expense	7 2 5 00				14
15	Supplies Expense					15
16	Telephone Expense	1 6 0 00				16
17	Insurance Expense					17
18	Repair Expense	2 5 0 00				18
19	Depr. Expense—Lawn Equipment					19
20	Miscellaneous Expense	6 5 00				20
21		13 3 8 0 00	13 3 8 0 00			21

REQUIRED

1. Analyze the following adjustments and enter them on a work sheet.
   (a) Ending supplies inventory as of March 31, $165.
   (b) Insurance expired (used), $100.
   (c) Depreciation of lawn equipment, $200.
   (d) Wages earned but not paid as of March 31, $180.
2. Complete the work sheet.

PROBLEM 5-14B   (LO1/2)
Adjustments col. total: $990;
Net loss: $1,625

ADJUSTMENTS AND WORK SHEET SHOWING A NET LOSS Val Nolan started a business called Nolan's Home Appraisals. The trial balance as of October 31, after the first month of operations, is as follows:

Nolan's Home Appraisals
Work Sheet
For Month Ended October 31, 20 - -

	ACCOUNT TITLE	TRIAL BALANCE		ADJUSTMENTS		
		DEBIT	CREDIT	DEBIT	CREDIT	
1	Cash	8 3 0 00				1
2	Accounts Receivable	7 6 0 00				2
3	Supplies	6 2 5 00				3
4	Prepaid Insurance	9 5 0 00				4
5	Automobile	6 5 0 0 00				5
6	Accum. Depr.—Automobile					6
7	Accounts Payable		1 5 0 0 00			7
8	Wages Payable					8
9	Val Nolan, Capital		9 9 0 0 00			9
10	Val Nolan, Drawing	1 1 0 0 00				10
11	Appraisal Fees		3 0 0 0 00			11
12	Wages Expense	1 5 6 0 00				12
13	Advertising Expense	4 2 0 00				13
14	Rent Expense	1 0 5 0 00				14
15	Supplies Expense					15
16	Telephone Expense	2 5 5 00				16
17	Insurance Expense					17
18	Repair Expense	2 7 0 00				18
19	Oil and Gas Expense	8 0 00				19
20	Depr. Expense—Automobile					20
21		14 4 0 0 00	14 4 0 0 00			21

REQUIRED

1. Analyze the following adjustments and enter them on the work sheet.

    (a) Supplies inventory as of October 31, $210.

    (b) Unexpired (remaining) insurance as of October 31, $800.

    (c) Depreciation of automobile, $250.

    (d) Wages earned but not paid as of October 31, $175.

2. Complete the work sheet.

PROBLEM 5-15B   **(LO4/5)**

JOURNALIZE AND POST ADJUSTING ENTRIES FROM THE WORK SHEET
Refer to Problem 5-14B and the following additional information.

Account Name	Account Number	Balance in Account Before Adjusting Entry
Supplies	141	$ 625
Prepaid Insurance	145	950
Accum. Depr.—Automobile	185.1	0
Wages Payable	219	0
Wages Expense	511	1,560
Supplies Expense	523	0
Insurance Expense	535	0
Depr. Expense—Automobile	541	0

REQUIRED

1. Journalize the adjusting entries on page 3 of the general journal.

2. Post the adjusting entries to the general ledger. (If you are not using the working papers that accompany this text, enter the balances provided in this problem before posting the adjusting entries.)

PROBLEM 5-16B   **(LO3)**
Adjustments col. total: $1,640;
Net income: $1,405

CORRECTING WORK SHEET WITH ERRORS A beginning accounting student tried to complete a work sheet for Dick Ady's Bookkeeping Service. The following adjusting entries were to have been analyzed and entered in the work sheet.

(a) Ending inventory of supplies on July 31, $130.

(b) Unexpired insurance on July 31, $420.

(c) Depreciation of office equipment, $325.

(d) Wages earned, but not paid as of July 31, $95.

REQUIRED

Review the work sheet shown on page 167 for addition mistakes, transpositions, and other errors and make all necessary corrections.

PROBLEM 5-16B

Dick Ady's Bookkeeping Service
Work Sheet
For Month Ended July 31, 20 - -

#	ACCOUNT TITLE	TRIAL BALANCE Debit	TRIAL BALANCE Credit	ADJUSTMENTS Debit	ADJUSTMENTS Credit	ADJUSTED TRIAL BALANCE Debit	ADJUSTED TRIAL BALANCE Credit	INCOME STATEMENT Debit	INCOME STATEMENT Credit	BALANCE SHEET Debit	BALANCE SHEET Credit
1	Cash	1 3 6 5 00				1 3 6 5 00				1 3 5 6 00	
2	Accounts Receivable	8 4 5 00				8 4 5 00					
3	Supplies	6 2 0 00			(a) 4 9 0 00	1 3 0 00				1 3 0 00	
4	Prepaid Insurance	1 1 5 0 00			(b) 4 2 0 00	7 3 0 00				7 3 0 00	
5	Office Equipment	6 4 0 0 00			(c) 3 2 5 00	6 7 2 5 00				6 7 2 5 00	
6	Accum. Depr.—Office Equipment								8 4 5 00		
7	Accounts Payable		7 3 5 00				7 3 5 00				7 3 5 00
8	Wages Payable				(d) 9 5 00		9 5 00				5 9 00
9	Dick Ady, Capital		7 8 0 0 00				7 8 0 0 00				7 8 0 0 00
10	Dick Ady, Drawing	1 2 0 0 00				1 2 0 0 00				1 2 0 0 00	
11	Professional Fees		6 3 5 0 00				6 3 5 0 00		6 3 5 0 00		
12	Wages Expense	1 4 9 5 00		(d) 9 5 00		1 5 9 0 00		1 5 9 0 00			
13	Advertising Expense	3 8 0 00				3 8 0 00		3 8 0 00			
14	Rent Expense	8 5 0 00				8 5 0 00		8 5 0 00			
15	Supplies Expense			(a) 4 9 0 00		4 9 0 00		4 9 0 00			
16	Telephone Expense	2 0 5 00				2 0 5 00		2 5 0 00			
17	Utilities Expense	2 8 5 00				2 8 5 00		2 8 5 00			
18	Insurance Expense			(b) 4 2 0 00		4 2 0 00		4 2 0 00			
19	Depr. Expense—Office Equipment			(c) 3 2 5 00		3 2 5 00		3 2 5 00			
20	Miscellaneous Expense	9 0 00				9 0 00		9 0 00			
21	Net Income	14 8 8 5 00	14 8 8 5 00	1 3 3 0 00	1 3 3 0 00	15 6 3 0 00	14 9 8 0 00	4 8 8 0 00	7 1 9 5 00	10 1 4 1 00	8 5 9 4 00
22								2 3 1 5 00			1 5 4 7 00
23								7 1 9 5 00	7 1 9 5 00	10 1 4 1 00	10 1 4 1 00

MASTERY PROBLEM

Adjusted Trial Bal. total: $58,500;
Net income: $13,630

Kristi Williams offers family counseling services specializing in financial and marital problems. A chart of accounts and a trial balance taken on December 31, 20-1, follow.

KRISTI WILLIAMS FAMILY COUNSELING SERVICES CHART OF ACCOUNTS			
Assets		**Revenue**	
101	Cash	401	Client Fees
142	Office Supplies		
145	Prepaid Insurance	**Expenses**	
181	Office Equipment	511	Wages Expense
181.1	Accumulated Depr.—	521	Rent Expense
	Office Equipment	523	Office Supplies Expense
187	Computer Equipment	533	Utilities Expense
187.1	Accumulated Depr.—	535	Insurance Expense
	Computer Equipment	541	Depr. Expense—
			Office Equipment
Liabilities		542	Depr. Expense—
201	Notes Payable		Computer Equipment
202	Accounts Payable	549	Miscellaneous Expense
Owner's Equity			
311	Kristi Williams, Capital		
312	Kristi Williams, Drawing		

Kristi Williams Family Counseling Services Trial Balance December 31, 20 - 1			
ACCOUNT TITLE	ACCOUNT NO.	DEBIT BALANCE	CREDIT BALANCE
Cash	101	8 7 3 0 00	
Office Supplies	142	7 0 0 00	
Prepaid Insurance	145	6 0 0 00	
Office Equipment	181	18 0 0 0 00	
Computer Equipment	187	6 0 0 0 00	
Notes Payable	201		8 0 0 0 00
Accounts Payable	202		5 0 0 00
Kristi Williams, Capital	311		11 4 0 0 00
Kristi Williams, Drawing	312	3 0 0 0 00	
Client Fees	401		35 8 0 0 00
Wages Expense	511	9 5 0 0 00	
Rent Expense	521	6 0 0 0 00	
Utilities Expense	533	2 1 7 0 00	
Miscellaneous Expense	549	1 0 0 0 00	
		55 7 0 0 00	55 7 0 0 00

Information for year-end adjustments:

(a) Office supplies on hand at year end amounted to $100.

(b) On January 1, 20-1, Williams purchased office equipment that cost $18,000. It has an expected useful life of ten years and no salvage value.

(c) On July 1, 20-1, Williams purchased computer equipment costing $6,000. It has an expected useful life of three years and no salvage value. Assume that Williams computes depreciation to the nearest full month.

(d) On December 1, 20-1, Williams paid a premium of $600 for a six-month insurance policy.

REQUIRED

1. Prepare the work sheet for the year ended December 31, 20-1.

2. Prepare adjusting entries in a general journal.

CHALLENGE PROBLEM

This problem challenges you to apply your cumulative accounting knowledge to move a step beyond the material in the chapter.

Your friend, Diane Kiefner, teaches elementary school and operates her own wilderness kayaking tours in the summers. She thinks she has been doing fine financially, but has never really measured her profits. Until this year, her business has always had more money at the end of the summer than at the beginning. She enjoys kayaking and as long as she came out a little ahead, that was fine. Unfortunately, Diane had to dip into her savings to make up for "losses" on her kayaking tours this past summer. Hearing that you have been studying accounting, she brought a list of cash receipts and expenditures and would like you to try to figure out what happened.

Cash balance beginning of summer		$15,000
Cash receipts from kayakers over the summer	$10,000	
Cash expenditures over the summer	13,500	
Amount taken from savings		($3,500)
Cash balance end of summer		$11,500

When asked for more details on the expenditures and the kayaking gear that you saw in her garage, Diane provided the following information.

Expenditures were made on the following items:

Brochures used to advertise her services (Diane only used about 1/4 of them and plans to use the remainder over the next three summers.)	$1,000
Food for trips (nothing left)	2,000
Rent on equipment used by kayakers on trips	3,000
Travel expenses	4,000
A new kayak and paddles (At the beginning of the summer, Diane bought a new kayak and paddles. Up to this time, she had always borrowed her father's. Diane expects to use the equipment for about five years. At that time she expects it to have no value.)	3,500

A trial balance based on this information follows. As you will note, Diane's trial balance is not consistent with some of the concepts discussed in this chapter.

(continued)

Diane Kiefner's Wilderness Kayaking Tours
Work Sheet
For Summer Ended 20 - -

	ACCOUNT TITLE	TRIAL BALANCE		ADJUSTMENTS		ADJUSTED TRIAL BALANCE		INCOME STATEMENT		BALANCE SHEET		
		DEBIT	CREDIT	DEBIT	CREDIT	DEBIT	CREDIT	DEBIT	CREDIT	DEBIT	CREDIT	
1	Cash	11 5 0 0 00										1
2	Diane Kiefner, Capital		15 0 0 0 00									2
3	Tour Revenue		10 0 0 0 00									3
4	Advertising Supplies Expense	1 0 0 0 00										4
5	Food Expense	2 0 0 0 00										5
6	Equipment Rental Expense	3 0 0 0 00										6
7	Travel Expense	4 0 0 0 00										7
8	Kayak Expense	3 5 0 0 00										8
9		25 0 0 0 00	25 0 0 0 00									9

REQUIRED

1. Complete Diane's work sheet by making appropriate adjustments and extensions. Note: (a) You may need to add new accounts. (b) Some of the adjustments you need to make are actually "corrections of errors" Diane has made in classifying certain items.

2. What is your best measure of Diane's net income for the summer of 20--?

Careful study of this chapter should enable you to:

LO1 Prepare a depreciation schedule using the straight-line method.

LO2 Prepare a depreciation schedule using the sum-of-the-years'-digits method.

LO3 Prepare a depreciation schedule using the double-declining-balance method.

LO4 Prepare a depreciation schedule for tax purposes using the Modified Accelerated Cost Recovery System.

Chapter 5 Appendix
Depreciation Methods

In Chapter 5, we introduced the straight-line method of depreciation. Here, we will review this method and illustrate three others: sum-of-the-years'-digits; double-declining-balance; and, for tax purposes, the Modified Accelerated Cost Recovery System. For all illustrations, we will assume that a delivery van was purchased for $40,000. It has a five-year useful life and salvage value of $4,000.

STRAIGHT-LINE METHOD

LO1 Prepare a depreciation schedule using the straight-line method.

Under the straight-line method, an equal amount of depreciation will be taken each period. First, compute the depreciable cost by subtracting the salvage value from the cost of the asset. This is done because we expect to sell the asset for $4,000 at the end of its useful life. Thus, the total cost to be recognized as an expense over the five years is $36,000, not $40,000.

Cost	–	Salvage Value	=	Depreciable Cost
$40,000	–	$4,000	=	$36,000

Next, we divide the depreciable cost by the expected life of the asset, five years.

Depreciation Expense per Year	=	Depreciable Cost / Years of Life
$7,200 per year	=	$36,000 / 5 years

When preparing a depreciation schedule, it is often convenient to use a depreciation rate per year. In this case it would be 20% (100% ÷ 5 years of life). Figure 5A-1 shows the depreciation expense, accumulated depreciation, and book value for each of the five years.

	STRAIGHT-LINE DEPRECIATION					
Year	Depreciable Cost[a]	×	Rate[b]	=	Depreciation Expense	Accumulated Depreciation (End of Year)	Book Value[c] (End of Year)
1	$36,000		20%		$7,200	$ 7,200	$32,800
2	36,000		20%		7,200	14,400	25,600
3	36,000		20%		7,200	21,600	18,400
4	36,000		20%		7,200	28,800	11,200
5	36,000		20%		7,200	36,000	4,000

[a] Depreciable Cost = Cost − Salvage Value ($40,000 − $4,000 = $36,000)
[b] Rate = 1 year ÷ 5 years of life × 100 = 20%
[c] Book Value = Cost ($40,000) − Accumulated Depreciation

FIGURE 5A-1 Depreciation Schedule Using Straight-Line Method

SUM-OF-THE-YEARS'-DIGITS

LO2 Prepare a depreciation schedule using the sum-of-the-years'-digits method.

Under the sum-of-the-years'-digits method, depreciation is determined by multiplying the depreciable cost by a schedule of fractions. The numerator of the fraction for a specific year is the number of years of remaining useful life for the asset, measured from the beginning of the year. The denominator for all fractions is determined by adding the digits that represent the years of the estimated life of the asset. The calculation for our delivery van with a five-year useful life is shown below.

Sum-of-the-Years'-Digits = 5 + 4 + 3 + 2 + 1 = 15

A depreciation schedule using these fractions is shown in Figure 5A-2.

	SUM-OF-THE-YEARS' DIGITS					
Year	Depreciable Cost[a]	×	Rate[b]	=	Depreciation Expense	Accumulated Depreciation (End of Year)	Book Value[c] (End of Year)
1	$36,000		5/15		$12,000	$12,000	$28,000
2	36,000		4/15		9,600	21,600	18,400
3	36,000		3/15		7,200	28,800	11,200
4	36,000		2/15		4,800	33,600	6,400
5	36,000		1/15		2,400	36,000	4,000

[a] Depreciable Cost = Cost − Salvage Value ($40,000 − $4,000 = $36,000)
[b] Rate = Number of Years of Remaining Useful Life ÷ Sum-of-the-Years'-Digits
[c] Book Value = Cost ($40,000) − Accumulated Depreciation

FIGURE 5A-2 Depreciation Schedule Using Sum-of-the-Years'-Digits Method

DOUBLE-DECLINING-BALANCE METHOD

LO3 Prepare a depreciation schedule using the double-declining-balance method.

Under this method, the book value is multiplied by a fixed rate, often double the straight-line rate. The van has a five-year life, so the straight-line rate is $1 \div 5$, or 20%. Double the straight-line rate is $2 \times 20\%$, or 40%. The double-declining-balance depreciation schedule is shown in Figure 5A-3. Note that the rate is applied to the book value of the asset. Once the book value is reduced to the expected salvage value, $4,000, no more depreciation may be recognized.

LEARNING KEY:
Double means double the straight-line rate. Declining-balance means that the rate is multiplied by the *book value* (not depreciable cost) at the beginning of each year. This amount is *declining* each year.

DOUBLE-DECLINING-BALANCE METHOD

Year	Book Value[a] (Beginning of Year)	×	Rate[b]	=	Depreciation Expense	Accumulated Depreciation (End of Year)	Book Value[a] (End of Year)
1	$40,000		40%		$16,000	$16,000	$24,000
2	24,000		40%		9,600	25,600	14,400
3	14,400		40%		5,760	31,360	8,640
4	8,640		40%		3,456	34,816	5,184
5	5,184				1,184	36,000	4,000

[a] Book Value = Cost ($40,000) − Accumulated Depreciation
[b] Rate = Double the straight-line rate (1/5 × 2 = 2/5 or 40%)

FIGURE 5A-3   Depreciation Schedule Using Double-Declining-Balance Method

MODIFIED ACCELERATED COST RECOVERY SYSTEM

LO4 Prepare a depreciation schedule for tax purposes using the Modified Accelerated Cost Recovery System.

For assets purchased since 1986, many firms use the Modified Accelerated Cost Recovery System (MACRS) for tax purposes. Under this method, the Internal Revenue Service (IRS) classifies various assets according to useful life and sets depreciation rates for each year of the asset's life. These rates are then multiplied by the cost of the asset. Even though the van is expected to have a useful life of five years, and a salvage value of $4,000, the IRS schedule, shown in Figure 5A-4, spreads the depreciation over a six-year period and assumes no salvage value.

MODIFIED ACCELERATED COST RECOVERY SYSTEM

Year	Cost	×	Rate[a]	=	Depreciation Expense	Accumulated Depreciation (End of Year)	Book Value[b] (End of Year)
1	$40,000		20.00%		$ 8,000	$ 8,000	$32,000
2	40,000		32.00%		12,800	20,800	19,200
3	40,000		19.20%		7,680	28,480	11,520
4	40,000		11.52%		4,608	33,088	6,912
5	40,000		11.52%		4,608	37,696	2,304
6	40,000		5.76%		2,304	40,000	0

[a] Rates set by IRS
[b] Book Value = Cost ($40,000) − Accumulated Depreciation

FIGURE 5A-4   Depreciation Schedule Using Modified Accelerated Cost Recovery System

SERIES A EXERCISES

EXERCISE 5Apx-1A **(LO1)**
Accum. depr. end of Yr. 2: $10,000

STRAIGHT-LINE DEPRECIATION A small delivery truck was purchased on January 1 at a cost of $25,000. It has an estimated useful life of four years and an estimated salvage value of $5,000. Prepare a depreciation schedule showing the depreciation expense, accumulated depreciation, and book value for each year under the straight-line method.

EXERCISE 5Apx-2A **(LO2)**
Accum. depr. end of Yr. 2: $14,000

SUM-OF-THE-YEARS'-DIGITS DEPRECIATION Using the information given in Exercise 5Apx-1A, prepare a depreciation schedule showing the depreciation expense, accumulated depreciation, and book value for each year under the sum-of-the-years'-digits method.

EXERCISE 5Apx-3A **(LO3)**
Accum. depr. end of Yr. 2: $18,750

DOUBLE-DECLINING-BALANCE DEPRECIATION Using the information given in Exercise 5Apx-1A, prepare a depreciation schedule showing the depreciation expense, accumulated depreciation, and book value for each year under the double-declining-balance method.

EXERCISE 5Apx-4A **(LO4)**
Accum. depr. end of Yr. 2: $13,000

MODIFIED ACCELERATED COST RECOVERY SYSTEM Using the information given in Exercise 5Apx-1A and the rates shown in Figure 5A-4, prepare a depreciation schedule showing the depreciation expense, accumulated depreciation, and book value for each year under the Modified Accelerated Cost Recovery System. For tax purposes, assume that the truck has a useful life of five years. (The IRS schedule will spread depreciation over six years.)

SERIES B EXERCISES

EXERCISE 5Apx-1B **(LO1)**
Accum. depr. end of Yr. 2: $1,800

STRAIGHT-LINE DEPRECIATION A computer was purchased on January 1 at a cost of $5,000. It has an estimated useful life of five years and an estimated salvage value of $500. Prepare a depreciation schedule showing the depreciation expense, accumulated depreciation, and book value for each year under the straight-line method.

EXERCISE 5Apx-2B **(LO2)**
Accum. depr. end of Yr. 2: $2,700

SUM-OF-THE-YEARS'-DIGITS DEPRECIATION Using the information given in Exercise 5Apx-1B, prepare a depreciation schedule showing the depreciation expense, accumulated depreciation, and book value for each year under the sum-of-the-years'-digits method.

EXERCISE 5Apx-3B **(LO3)**
Accum. depr. end of Yr. 2: $3,200

DOUBLE-DECLINING-BALANCE DEPRECIATION Using the information given in Exercise 5Apx-1B, prepare a depreciation schedule showing the depreciation expense, accumulated depreciation, and book value for each year under the double-declining-balance method.

EXERCISE 5Apx-4B **(LO4)**
Accum. depr. end of Yr. 2: $2,600

MODIFIED ACCELERATED COST RECOVERY SYSTEM Using the information given in Exercise 5Apx-1B and the rates shown in Figure 5A-4, prepare a depreciation schedule showing the depreciation expense, accumulated depreciation, and book value for each year under the Modified Accelerated Cost Recovery System. For tax purposes, assume that the computer has a useful life of five years. (The IRS schedule will spread depreciation over six years.)

© SUPERSTOCK

Financial Statements and the Closing Process

"Come on Jessie, let's get busy. We have to close the books before we go to the New Year's Eve party," said Mitch. But after seeing the disappointed look on Jessie's face, Mitch changed his mind. "What the heck. Let's do it on the 2nd, while we recover from watching all of those bowl games." "Great," said Jessie, "let's get out of here." Will Mitch and Jessie be in trouble for not closing the books before the end of the year?

The work sheet, introduced in Chapter 5, is used for three major end-of-period activities:

1. journalizing adjusting entries,

2. preparing financial statements, and

3. journalizing closing entries.

This chapter illustrates the use of the work sheet for preparing financial statements and closing entries. In addition, the post-closing trial balance is explained and illustrated. All of these activities take place at the end of the firm's fiscal year. However, to continue our illustration of Jessie Jane's Campus Delivery, we demonstrate these activities at the end of the first month of operations.

THE FINANCIAL STATEMENTS

LO1 Prepare financial statements with the aid of a work sheet.

Since Jessie made no additional investments during the month, the work sheet prepared in Chapter 5 supplies all of the information needed to prepare an income statement, a statement of owner's equity, and a balance sheet. The statements and work sheet columns from which they are derived for Jessie Jane's Campus Delivery are shown in Figures 6-1 and 6-2.

As you refer to the financial statements in Figures 6-1 and 6-2, notice the placement of dollar signs, single rulings, and double rulings. Dollar signs are placed at the top of each column and beneath rulings. Single rulings indicate addition or subtraction, and double rulings are placed under totals. Notice that each statement heading contains three lines: (1) company name, (2) statement title, and (3) period ended or date.

The Income Statement

Figure 6-1 shows how the Income Statement columns of the work sheet provide the information needed to prepare an income statement. Revenue is shown first, followed by an itemized and totaled list of expenses. Then, net income is calculated to double check the accuracy of the work sheet. It is presented with a double ruling as the last item in the statement.

The expenses could be listed in the same order that they appear in the chart of accounts or in descending order by dollar amount. The second approach helps the reader identify the most important expenses.

The Statement of Owner's Equity

Figure 6-2 shows that the Balance Sheet columns of the work sheet provide the information needed to prepare a statement of owner's equity. Jessie's capital account balance and the drawing account balance are in the Balance Sheet columns of the work sheet. The net income for the year can be found either on the work sheet at the bottom of the Income Statement (see Figure 6-1) and Balance Sheet columns or on the income statement. With these three items of information, the statement of owner's equity can be prepared.

Multiple columns are used on the financial statements to make them easier to read. There are no debit or credit columns on the financial statements.

FIGURE 6-1   Linkages Between the Work Sheet and Income Statement

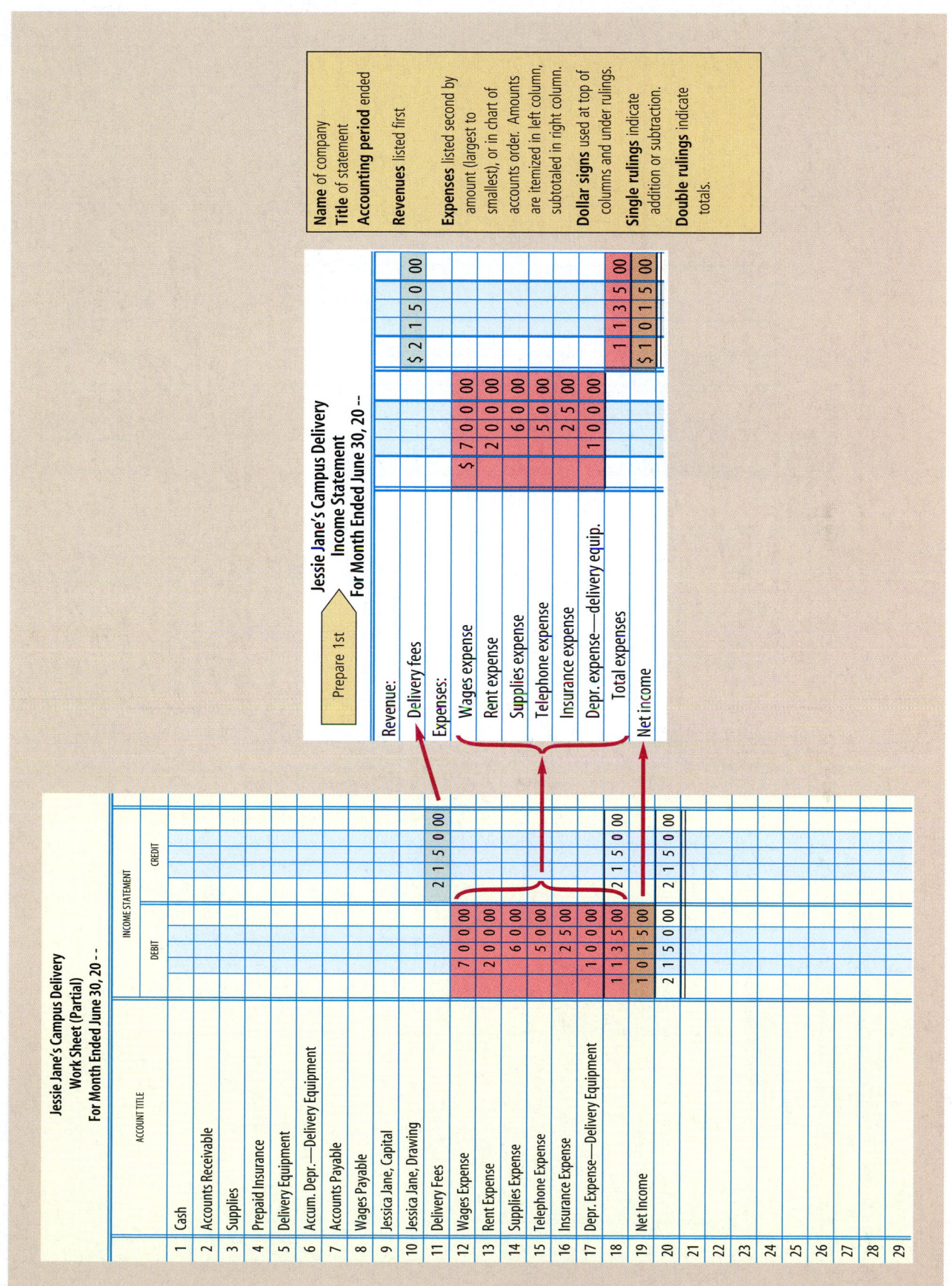

FIGURE 6-2 Linkages Between the Work Sheet, Statement of Owner's Equity, and Balance Sheet

Note: The statement of owner's equity is prepared before the balance sheet. The S.O.E. is shown below the B.S. to enhance the illustration of the linkages between the work sheet and financial statements.

Name of company
Title of statement
Accounting period ended

Current assets: cash and items that will be converted to cash or consumed within a year.

Property, plant, and equipment: durable assets that will help produce revenues for several years.

Current liabilities: amounts owed that will be paid within a year (will require the use of current assets).

Ending capital is not taken from the work sheet. It is computed on the statement of owner's equity.

Dollar signs used at top of columns and beneath rulings.

Single rulings indicate addition or subtraction.

Double rulings indicate totals.

Prepare 3rd

Jessie Jane's Campus Delivery
Balance Sheet
June 30, 20 --

Assets

Current assets:		
Cash	$ 3 7 0 00	$1 2 1 5 00
Accounts receivable	6 5 0 00	
Supplies	2 0 00	
Prepaid insurance	1 7 5 00	
Total current assets		$1 2 1 5 00
Property, plant, and equipment:		
Delivery equipment	$3 6 0 0 00	
Less accumulated depreciation	1 0 0 00	3 5 0 0 00
Total assets		$4 7 1 5 00

Liabilities

Current liabilities:		
Accounts payable	$1 8 0 0 00	
Wages payable	5 0 00	
Total current liabilities		$1 8 5 0 00
Owner's Equity		
Jessica Jane, capital		2 8 6 5 00
Total liabilities and owner's equity		$4 7 1 5 00

Prepare 2nd

Jessie Jane's Campus Delivery
Statement of Owner's Equity
For Month Ended June 30, 20--

Jessica Jane, capital, June 1, 20--		$ 2 0 0 0 00
Net income for June	$1 0 1 5 00	
Less withdrawals for June	1 5 0 00	
Increase in capital		8 6 5 00
Jessica Jane, capital, June 30, 20--		$ 2 8 6 5 00

Jessie Jane's Campus Delivery
Work Sheet (Partial)
For Month Ended June 30, 20 --

	ACCOUNT TITLE	BALANCE SHEET DEBIT	BALANCE SHEET CREDIT
1	Cash	3 7 0 00	
2	Accounts Receivable	6 5 0 00	
3	Supplies	2 0 00	
4	Prepaid Insurance	1 7 5 00	
5	Delivery Equipment	3 6 0 0 00	
6	Accum. Depr.—Delivery Equip.		1 0 0 00
7	Accounts Payable		1 8 0 0 00
8	Wages Payable		5 0 00
9	Jessie Jane, Capital		2 0 0 0 00
10	Jessie Jane, Drawing	1 5 0 00	
11	Delivery Fees		
12	Wages Expense		
13	Rent Expense		
14	Supplies Expense		
15	Telephone Expense		
16	Insurance Expense		
17	Depr. Expense—Delivery Equip.		
18		4 9 6 5 00	3 9 5 0 00
19	Net Income		1 0 1 5 00
20		4 9 6 5 00	4 9 6 5 00
21			

Be careful when using the capital account balance reported in the Balance Sheet columns of the work sheet. This account balance is the beginning balance *plus any additional investments made during the period.* Since Jessie made no additional investments during June, the $2,000 balance may be used as the beginning balance on the statement of owner's equity.

The Balance Sheet

As shown in Figure 6-2, the work sheet and the statement of owner's equity are used to prepare Jessie's balance sheet. The asset and liability amounts can be found in the Balance Sheet columns of the work sheet. The ending balance in Jessica Jane, Capital has been computed on the statement of owner's equity. This amount should be copied from the statement of owner's equity to the balance sheet.

Two important features of the balance sheet in Figure 6-2 should be noted. First, it is a **report form of balance sheet**, which means that the liabilities and owner's equity sections are shown below the assets section. It differs from an **account form of balance sheet** in which the assets are on the left and the liabilities and owner's equity sections are on the right. (See Jessie's balance sheet illustrated in Figure 2-2 on page 29 in Chapter 2.)

Second, it is a **classified balance sheet**, which means that similar items are grouped together on the balance sheet. Assets are classified as current assets and property, plant, and equipment. Similarly, liabilities are broken down into current and long-term sections. The following major balance sheet classifications are generally used.

Current Assets. **Current assets** include cash and assets that will be converted into cash or consumed within either one year or the normal operating cycle of the business, whichever is longer. Examples include cash, accounts receivable, supplies, and prepaid insurance. An **operating cycle** is the period of time required to purchase supplies and services and convert them back into cash.

Property, Plant, and Equipment. **Property, plant, and equipment**, also called **plant assets** or **long-term assets**, represent assets that are expected to serve the business for many years. Examples include land, buildings, and equipment.

Current Liabilities. **Current liabilities** are due within either one year or the normal operating cycle of the business, whichever is longer. They will be paid out of current assets. Accounts payable and wages payable are classified as current liabilities.

Long-Term Liabilities. **Long-term liabilities**, or **long-term debt**, are obligations that are not expected to be paid within a year and do not require the use of current assets. A mortgage on an office building is an example of a long-term liability. Jessie has no long-term debts. If she did, they would be listed on the balance sheet in the long-term liabilities section immediately following the current liabilities.

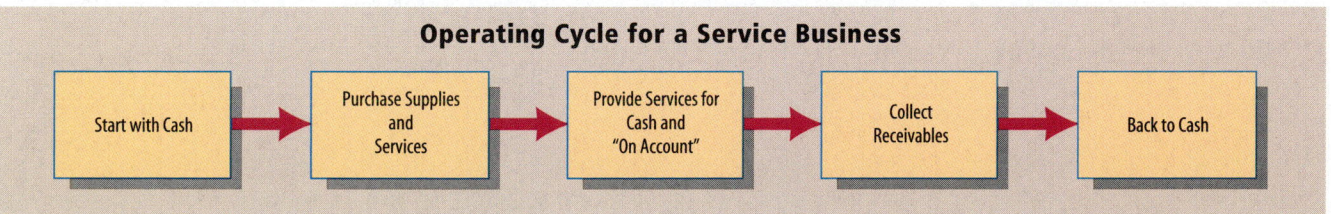

Operating Cycle for a Service Business

Start with Cash → Purchase Supplies and Services → Provide Services for Cash and "On Account" → Collect Receivables → Back to Cash

Additional Investments by the Owner

If the owner of a business made additional investments during the accounting period, the owner's capital reported in the Balance Sheet columns of the work sheet would represent the beginning balance plus any additional investments made during the accounting period. If this amount were used as the beginning balance on the statement of owner's equity, it would not equal the ending balance from last period and would create confusion for those comparing the two statements. In addition, the statement would not reflect all of the activities affecting the owner's capital account during the period.

Thus, we must also review the owner's capital account in the general ledger to get the information needed to prepare the statement of owner's equity. Figure 6-3 illustrates this situation for another business, Ramon's Shopping Service. The $5,000 balance of July 1, 20--, in Ramon Balboa's general ledger capital account is used as the beginning balance on the statement of owner's equity. Note that this is also the ending balance on June 30, 20--. The additional investment of $3,000 made on July 5 and posted to Balboa's general ledger capital account is reported by writing "add additional investments" on the line immediately after the beginning balance. The beginning balance plus the additional investment equals the total investment by the owner in the business and is the amount reported in the Balance Sheet columns of the work sheet. From this point, the preparation of the statement is the same as for businesses without additional investments.

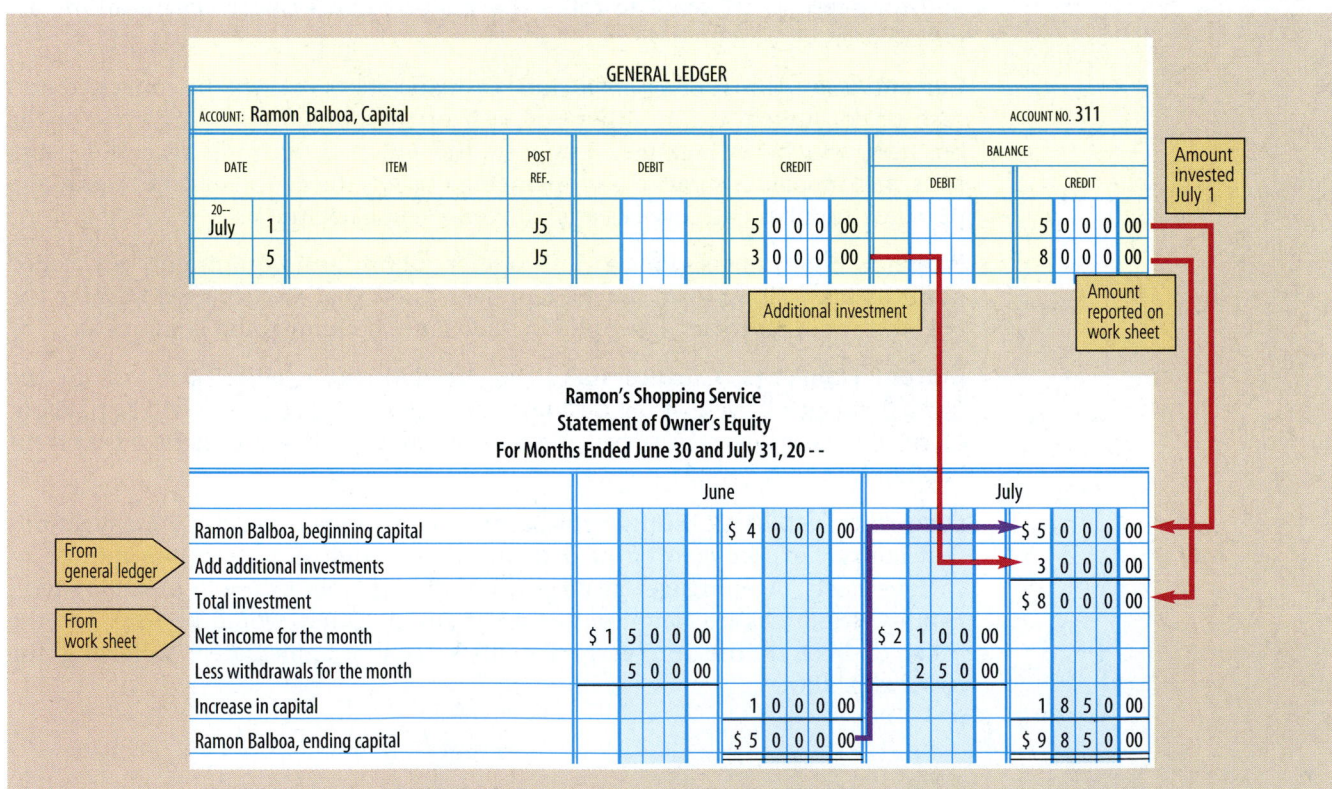

FIGURE 6-3   Statement of Owner's Equity with Additional Investment

THE CLOSING PROCESS

LO2 Journalize and post closing entries.

Assets, liabilities, and the owner's capital account accumulate information across accounting periods. Their balances are brought forward for each new period. For example, the amount of cash at the end of one accounting period must be the same as the amount of cash at the beginning of the next period. Thus, the balance reported for Cash is a result of all cash transactions since the business first opened. This is true for all accounts reported on the balance sheet. For this reason, they are called **permanent accounts**.

> **LEARNING KEY:** Permanent accounts contain the results of all transactions since the business started. Their balances are carried forward to each new accounting period.

Revenue, expense, and drawing accounts accumulate information *for a specific accounting period*. At the end of the fiscal year, these accounts must be *closed*. The **closing process** gives these accounts zero balances so they are prepared to accumulate new information for the next accounting period. Since these accounts do not accumulate information across accounting periods, they are called **temporary accounts**. The drawing account and all accounts reported in the income statement are temporary accounts and must be closed at the end of each accounting period.

> **LEARNING KEY:** Temporary accounts contain information for one accounting period. These accounts are closed at the end of each accounting period.

The income summary account is not really needed for the closing process. Some businesses simply close the revenue and expense accounts directly to the owner's capital account. One benefit of using the income summary account is that its balance before closing to the capital account equals

the net income or net loss for the period. Thus, it can serve as a check of the accuracy of the closing entries for revenues and expenses. Of course, computer programs post the closing entries to the owner's capital account automatically.

The closing process is most clearly demonstrated by returning to the accounting equation and T accounts. As shown in Figure 6-4, revenue, expense, and drawing accounts impact owner's equity and should be considered "under the umbrella" of the capital account. The effect of these accounts on owner's equity is formalized at the end of the accounting period when the balances of the temporary accounts are transferred to the owner's capital account (a permanent account) during the closing process.

The four basic steps in the closing process are illustrated in Figure 6-4. As you can see, a new account, **Income Summary**, is used in the closing process. This account may also be called *Expense and Revenue Summary*. This temporary account is used to close the revenue and expense accounts. After closing the revenues and expenses to Income Summary, the balance of this account is equal to the net income. This is why it is called Income Summary. Income Summary is opened during the closing process. Then it is closed to the owner's capital account. It does not appear on any financial statement. The four steps in the closing process are explained on page 182.

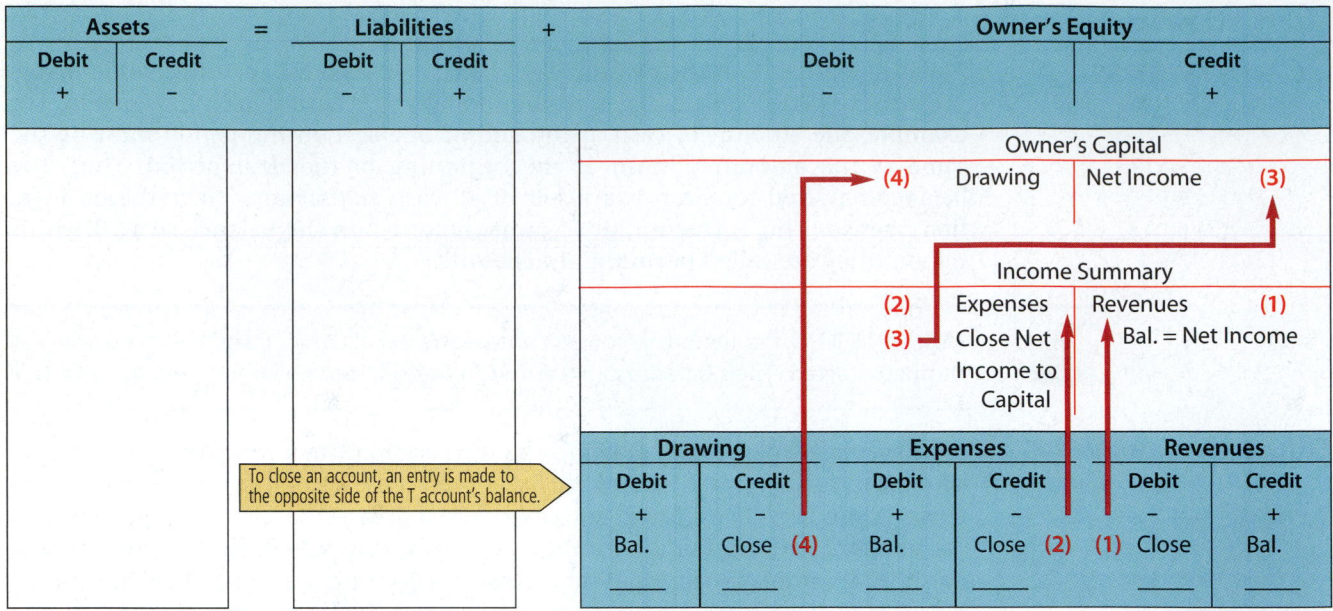

FIGURE 6-4 The Closing Process

STEPS IN THE CLOSING PROCESS

STEP 1   **Close Revenue Accounts to Income Summary.** Revenues have credit balances and increase owner's equity. Therefore, the revenue account is debited to create a zero balance. Income Summary is credited for the same amount.

STEP 2   **Close Expense Accounts to Income Summary.** Expenses have debit balances and reduce owner's equity. Therefore, the expense accounts are credited to create a zero balance. Income Summary must be debited for the total of the expenses.

STEP 3   **Close Income Summary to Capital.** The balance in Income Summary represents the net income (credit balance) or net loss (debit balance) for the period. This balance is transferred to the owner's capital account. If net income has been earned, Income Summary is debited to create a zero balance, and the owner's capital account is credited. If a net loss has been incurred, the owner's capital account is debited and Income Summary is credited to create a zero balance. Figure 6-5 shows examples for closing net income and net loss.

STEP 4   **Close Drawing to Capital.** Drawing has a debit balance and reduces owner's equity. Therefore, it is credited to create a zero balance. The owner's capital account is debited.

LEARNING KEY: The owner can make withdrawals from the business for any amount and at any time, as long as the assets are available. These withdrawals are for personal reasons and have nothing to do with measuring the profitability of the firm. Thus, they are closed directly to the owner's capital account.

NET INCOME

Capital

	1,000	STEP 3
		(Net Income)

Income Summary

(Expenses)	4,000	5,000	(Revenues)
STEP 3 to close	1,000	1,000	(Bal. before closing)

NET LOSS

Capital

STEP 3	2,000	
(Net Loss)		

Income Summary

(Expenses)	6,000	4,000	(Revenues)
(Bal. before closing)	2,000	2,000	STEP 3 to close

FIGURE 6-5 Step 3: Closing Net Income and Closing Net Loss

Upon completion of these four steps, all temporary accounts have zero balances. The earnings and withdrawals for the period have been transferred to the owner's capital account.

Journalize Closing Entries

Of course, to actually change the ledger accounts, the closing entries must be journalized and posted to the general ledger. As shown in Figure 6-6, the balances of the accounts to be closed are readily available from the Income Statement and Balance Sheet columns of the work sheet. These balances are used to illustrate the

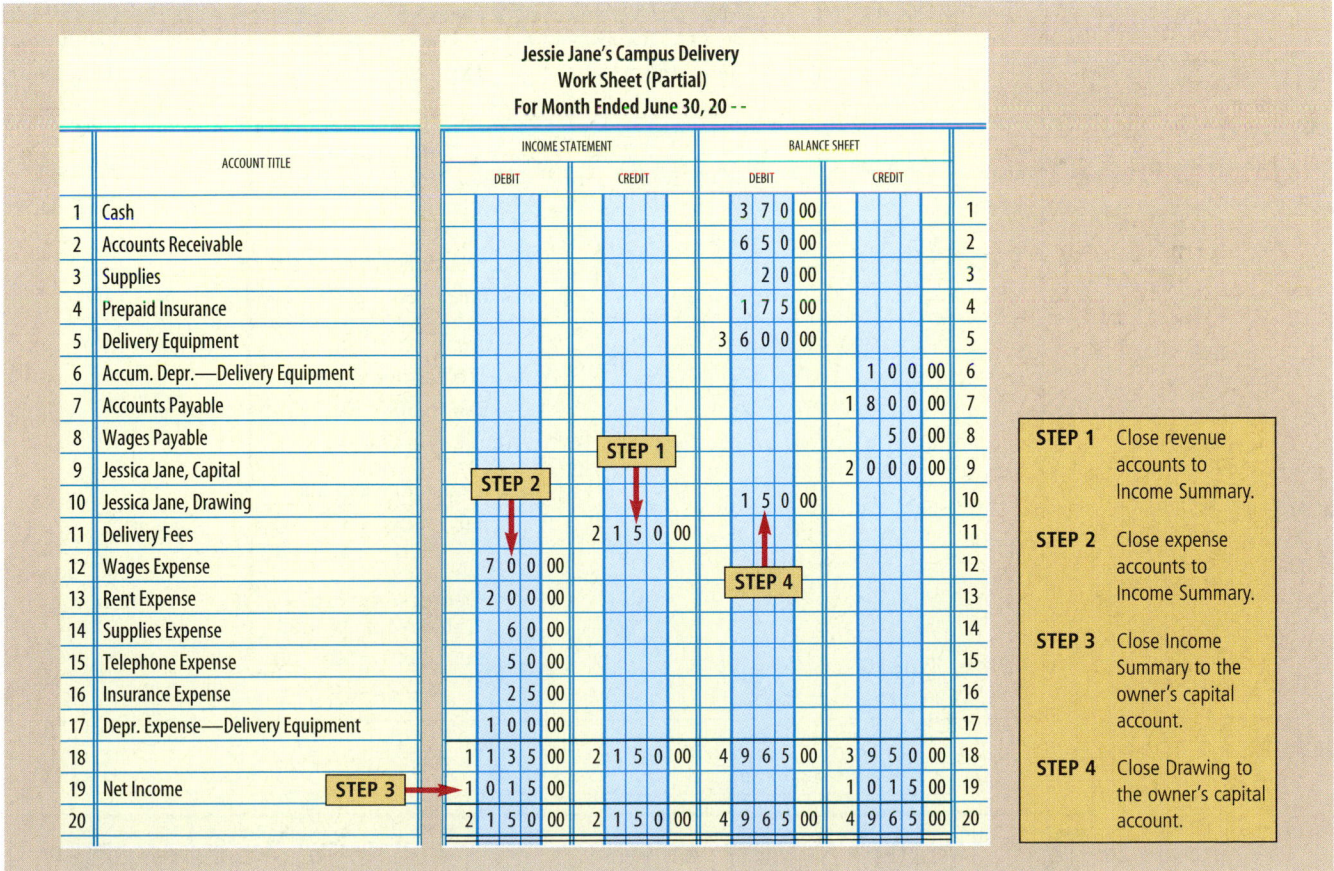

FIGURE 6-6 Role of the Work Sheet in the Closing Process

Rulings are entered on the debit and credit sides of the T accounts to indicate a zero balance.

closing entries for Jessie Jane's Campus Delivery, in T account and general journal form, in Figures 6-7 and 6-8, respectively. Remember: Closing entries are made at the end of the *fiscal year*. Closing entries made at the end of June are illustrated here so you can see the completion of the accounting cycle for Jessie Jane's Campus Delivery.

Like adjusting entries, the closing entries are made on the last day of the accounting period. "Closing Entries" is written in the Description column before the first entry and no explanations are required. Note that it is best to make one compound entry to close the expense accounts.

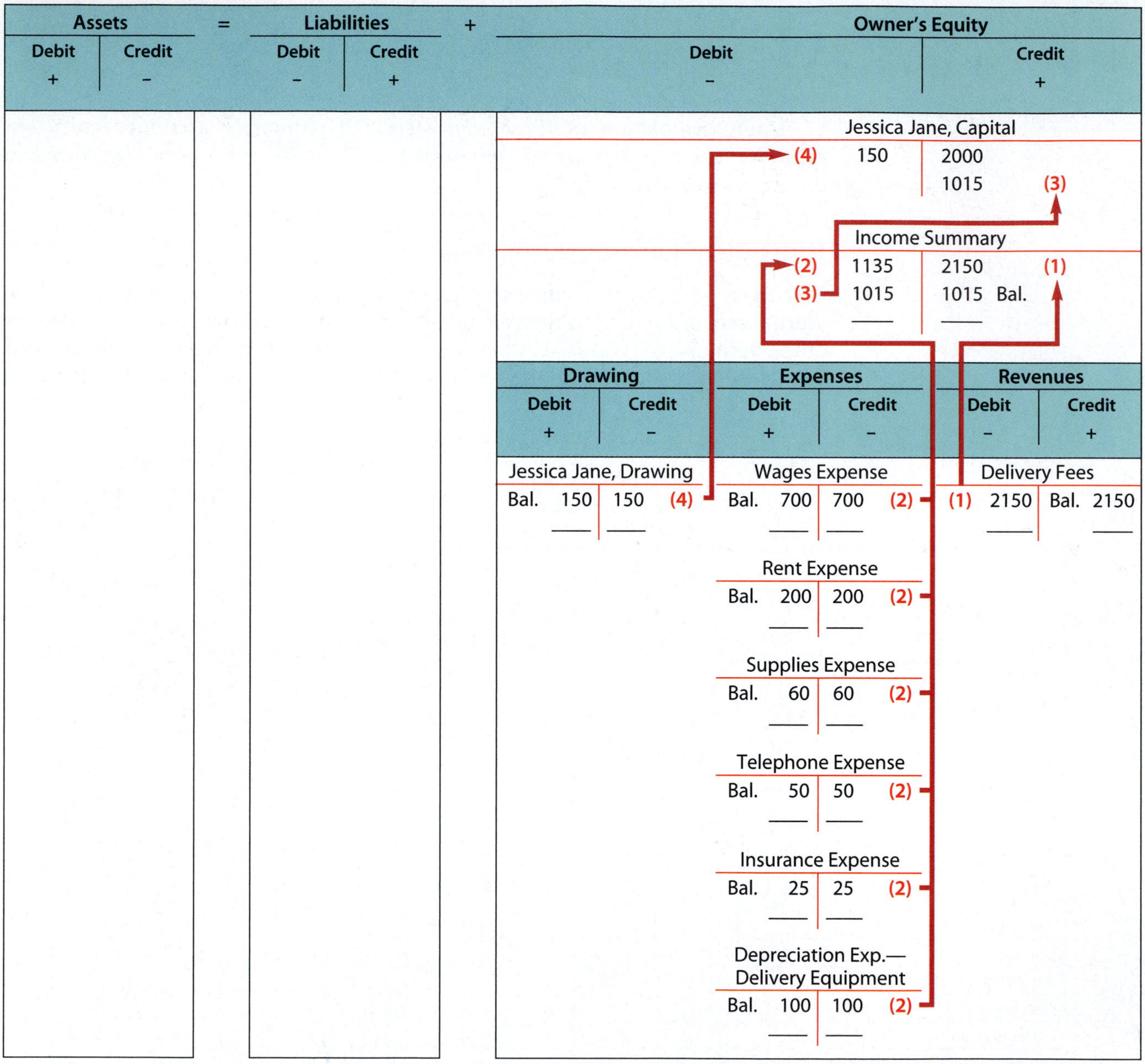

Assets		=	Liabilities		+	Owner's Equity	
Debit	**Credit**		**Debit**	**Credit**		**Debit**	**Credit**
+	−		−	+		−	+

Jessica Jane, Capital

(4) 150	2000
	1015 **(3)**

Income Summary

(2) 1135	2150 **(1)**
(3) 1015	1015 Bal.

Drawing		Expenses		Revenues	
Debit	**Credit**	**Debit**	**Credit**	**Debit**	**Credit**
+	−	+	−	−	+

Jessica Jane, Drawing		Wages Expense		Delivery Fees	
Bal. 150	150 **(4)**	Bal. 700	700 **(2)**	**(1)** 2150	Bal. 2150

Rent Expense	
Bal. 200	200 **(2)**

Supplies Expense	
Bal. 60	60 **(2)**

Telephone Expense	
Bal. 50	50 **(2)**

Insurance Expense	
Bal. 25	25 **(2)**

Depreciation Exp.—Delivery Equipment	
Bal. 100	100 **(2)**

FIGURE 6-7 Closing Entries in T Account Form

LEARNING KEY: Each individual revenue, expense, and drawing account must be closed.

A BROADER VIEW

Importance of Earnings to the Stock Market

Investors in the stock market pay close attention to earnings reported on the income statement. This information is so important that corporate officials often announce expected earnings before the financial statements are actually distributed to the public. If the announcement is different from what investors are expecting, the price of the stock may go up or down. For example, when Aetna, a leader in the managed health care industry, warned that earnings would be about 27 percent lower than expected by stock analysts, its stock price fell more than 10 percent.

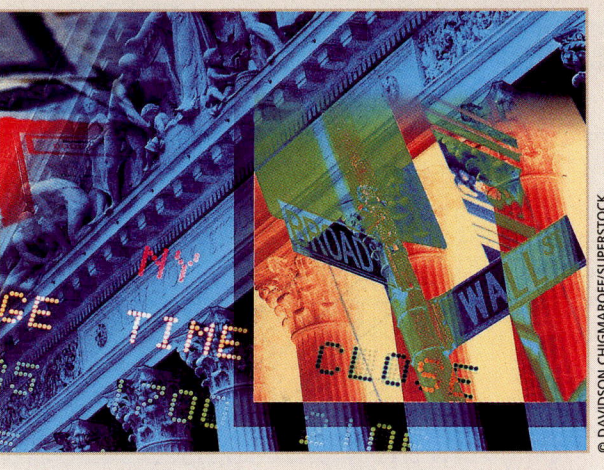

© DAVIDSON CHIGMAROFF/SUPERSTOCK

			GENERAL JOURNAL												PAGE 4	
		DATE	DESCRIPTION	POST REF.	DEBIT					CREDIT						
	1		**Closing Entries**													1
STEP 1	2	20-- June 30	Delivery Fees	401	2	1	5	0	00							2
	3		Income Summary	313						2	1	5	0	00		3
	4															4
STEP 2	5	30	Income Summary	313	1	1	3	5	00							5
	6		Wages Expense	511							7	0	0	00		6
Compund Entry	7		Rent Expense	521							2	0	0	00		7
	8		Supplies Expense	523								6	0	00		8
	9		Telephone Expense	525								5	0	00		9
	10		Insurance Expense	535								2	5	00		10
	11		Depr. Expense—Delivery Equipment	541							1	0	0	00		11
	12															12
STEP 3	13	30	Income Summary	313	1	0	1	5	00							13
	14		Jessica Jane, Capital	311						1	0	1	5	00		14
	15															15
STEP 4	16	30	Jessica Jane, Capital	311		1	5	0	00							16
	17		Jessica Jane, Drawing	312							1	5	0	00		17
No explanations are necessary	18															18
	19															19

FIGURE 6-8   Closing Entries in General Journal

Post the Closing Entries

The account numbers have been entered in the Posting Reference column of the journal to show that the entries have been posted to the ledger accounts illustrated in Figure 6-9. Note that "Closing" has been written in the Item column of each account to identify the closing entries. Zero account balances are recorded by drawing a line in both the debit and credit Balance columns.

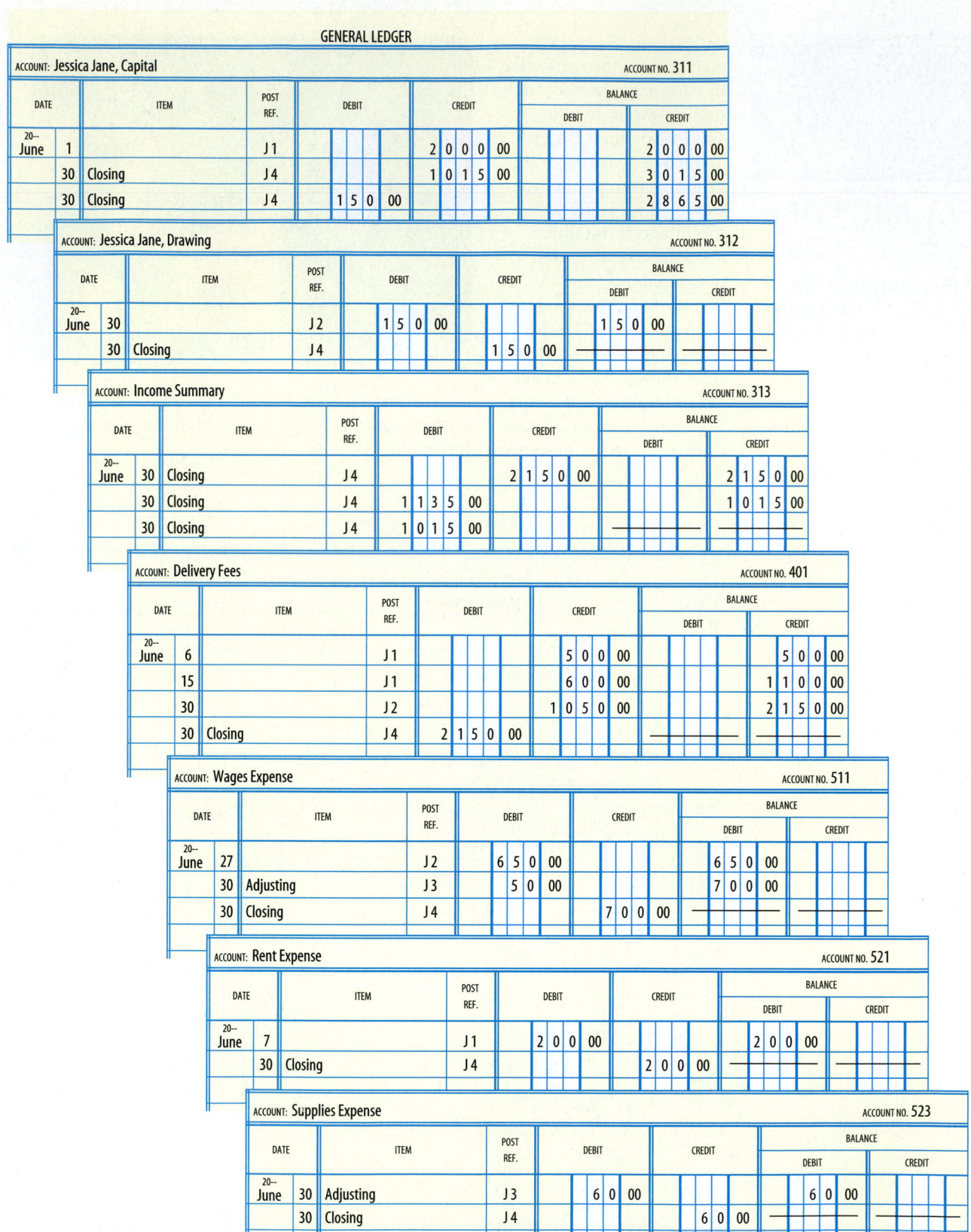

FIGURE 6-9 Closing Entries Posted to the General Ledger

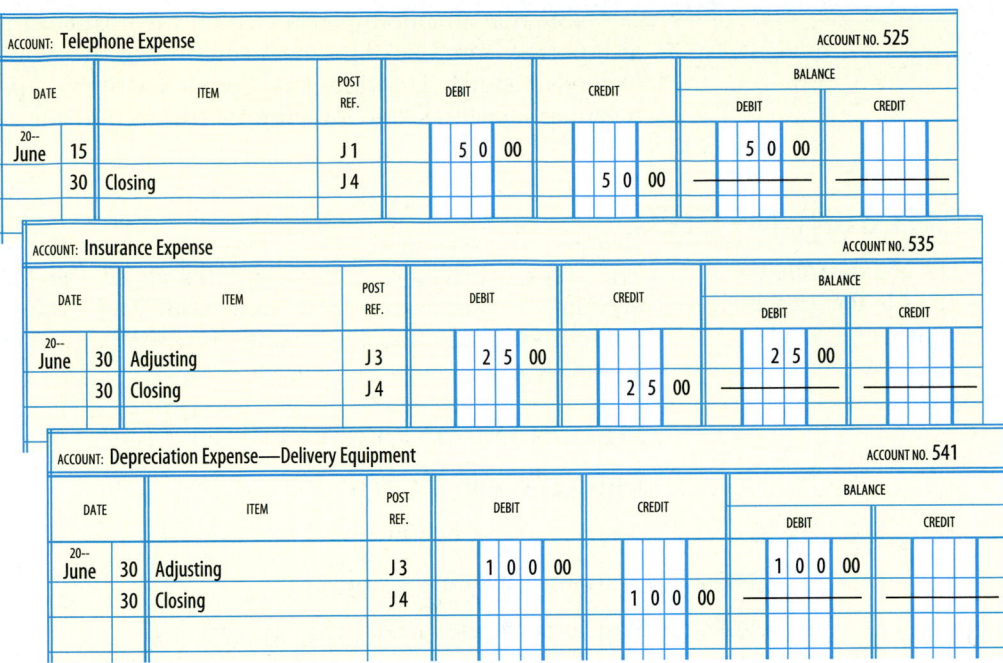

FIGURE 6-9   Closing Entries Posted to the General Ledger *(continued)*

 LEARNING KEY: Once the closing entries are posted, the general ledger account balances will agree with the amounts reported on the balance sheet.

POST-CLOSING TRIAL BALANCE

LO3 Prepare a post-closing trial balance.

After posting the closing entries, a **post-closing trial balance** should be prepared to prove the equality of the debit and credit balances in the general ledger accounts. The ending balance of each general ledger account that remains open at the end of the year is listed. Remember: Only the permanent accounts remain open after the closing process is completed. Figure 6-10 shows the post-closing trial balance for Jessie's ledger.

Jessie Jane's Campus Delivery **Post-Closing Trial Balance** **June 30, 20 - -**									
ACCOUNT TITLE	ACCOUNT NO.	DEBIT BALANCE				CREDIT BALANCE			
Cash	101	3	7	0	00				
Accounts Receivable	122	6	5	0	00				
Supplies	141		2	0	00				
Prepaid Insurance	145	1	7	5	00				
Delivery Equipment	185	3 6	0	0	00				
Accumulated Depreciation—Delivery Equipment	185.1					1	0	0	00
Accounts Payable	202					1 8	0	0	00
Wages Payable	219						5	0	00
Jessica Jane, Capital	311					2	8 6	5	00
		4	8	1 5	00	4	8	1 5	00

FIGURE 6-10   Post-Closing Trial Balance

Note that all amounts reflected on the post-closing trial balance are the same as reported in the Balance Sheet columns of the work sheet except Drawing and Owner's Capital. Drawing was closed. Owner's Capital was updated to reflect revenues, expenses, and drawing for the accounting period.

THE ACCOUNTING CYCLE

LO4 List and describe the steps in the accounting cycle.

The steps involved in accounting for all of the business activities during an accounting period are called the **accounting cycle**. The cycle begins with the analysis of source documents and ends with a post-closing trial balance. A brief summary of the steps in the cycle follows.

STEPS IN THE ACCOUNTING CYCLE

During Accounting Period

STEP 1   Analyze source documents.

STEP 2   Journalize the transactions.

STEP 3   Post to the ledger accounts.

End of Accounting Period

STEP 4   Prepare a trial balance.

STEP 5   Determine and prepare the needed adjustments on the work sheet.

STEP 6   Complete an end-of-period work sheet.

STEP 7   Prepare an income statement, statement of owner's equity, and balance sheet.

STEP 8   Journalize and post the adjusting entries.

STEP 9   Journalize and post the closing entries.

STEP 10   Prepare a post-closing trial balance.

 LEARNING KEY: Properly analyzing and journalizing transactions is very important. A mistake made in step 1 is carried through the entire accounting cycle.

Steps 4 through 10 in the preceding list are performed *as of* the last day of the accounting period. This does not mean that they are actually done on the last day. The accountant may not be able to do any of these things until the first few days (sometimes weeks) of the next period. Nevertheless, the work sheet, statements, and entries are prepared as of the closing date.

COMPUTERS AND ACCOUNTING

Accounting Software—Gary P. Schneider, University of San Diego

People use computers to help them do many common tasks in business, at school, and in everyday life. For example, instead of writing a homework assignment using pen and paper or a typewriter, many students use software on a personal computer to create the homework assignment. If the homework requires calculations, students might use spreadsheet software to perform those calculations and paste the results into the document. If the homework requires a figure or other artwork, students might use a graphics program to create the art and, again, paste the results into the document. Some students will print the assignment and carry it to class. Other students may use the computer to handle the delivery chore. They can use their e-mail software to attach the document file to an e-mail message and send it to their instructor's e-mail account.

Similarly, accountants use computers to make their jobs easier. They use the types of software that other office workers use: word processing, spreadsheet, presentation, database, e-mail, and web browser software. Although it is possible to create journals and ledgers for a small business using spreadsheet software, most accountants use software that is designed to help them perform the accounting tasks you have learned about thus far in this book. Most of these accounting software packages include databases or are built on database software.

Many different companies develop accounting software. Some companies develop more than one accounting software package. The needs of a small business are quite different from the needs of a major international company. Thus, different accounting software products are available for businesses of different sizes. Although the accounting software used by larger companies is often more complex and can do more things than the software used by smaller companies, remember that the basic accounting tasks that the software must accomplish are very much the same in any size company. Also, keep in mind that accounting software does not change any of the fundamental principles that you have learned in this book. It just makes the work easier for accountants. Larger companies often write their own accounting software. In the past, this software was written in a procedural language, such as COBOL. Today, most custom-written accounting software is built using the tools and features that are a part of large database software products sold by companies such as IBM, Microsoft, and Oracle.

Good software can make accountants' jobs easier in two ways: (1) The software can do some tasks automatically, and (2) it can reduce the likelihood of errors in tasks that accountants must still do themselves, for example, making adjusting journal entries such as those you learned about in Chapter 5. At the end of the accounting period, the accountant must adjust the amount of prepaid insurance to reflect the insurance expense that has expired during the period. In a manual bookkeeping system, the accountant would debit insurance expense and credit prepaid insurance for the amount of the prepaid insurance that is used up in the period. The accountant would make this entry in the general journal. Figure A shows how one popular accounting software package, Peachtree®, accomplishes this task.

Figure A

Clicking this button instructs the software to create the same entry each accounting period.

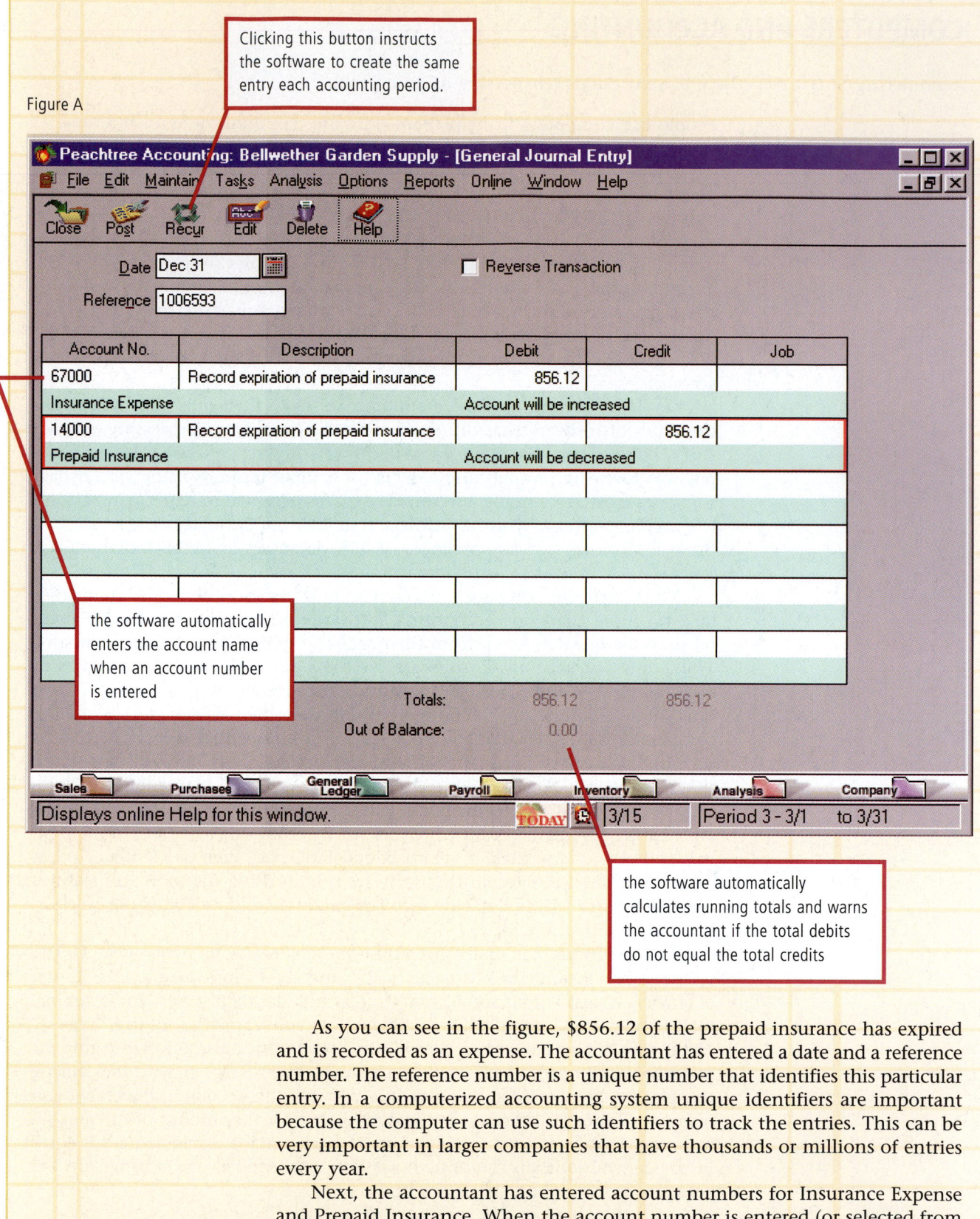

the software automatically enters the account name when an account number is entered

the software automatically calculates running totals and warns the accountant if the total debits do not equal the total credits

As you can see in the figure, $856.12 of the prepaid insurance has expired and is recorded as an expense. The accountant has entered a date and a reference number. The reference number is a unique number that identifies this particular entry. In a computerized accounting system unique identifiers are important because the computer can use such identifiers to track the entries. This can be very important in larger companies that have thousands or millions of entries every year.

Next, the accountant has entered account numbers for Insurance Expense and Prepaid Insurance. When the account number is entered (or selected from a drop-down list), the computer displays and enters the corresponding account names. This is an important error-reduction feature. It can help the accountant catch a mistaken account number entry. Finally, the accountant enters the amounts of the debit and credit for the two accounts. The software keeps a running total of the debits and credits entered and displays an Out of Balance amount if the debits and credits do not equal. Once again, the software helps prevent errors.

If an entry is one that occurs regularly, such as a monthly depreciation expense entry, the accountant can click the Recur button near the top of the form to have the software create the entry automatically every period. When the accountant has reviewed the entry and made sure that the accounts are correct and the debits and credits balance, he or she can click the Post button to record the debits and credits in the general ledger. Figure B shows the general ledger task and report options in the Peachtree accounting software package.

Figure B

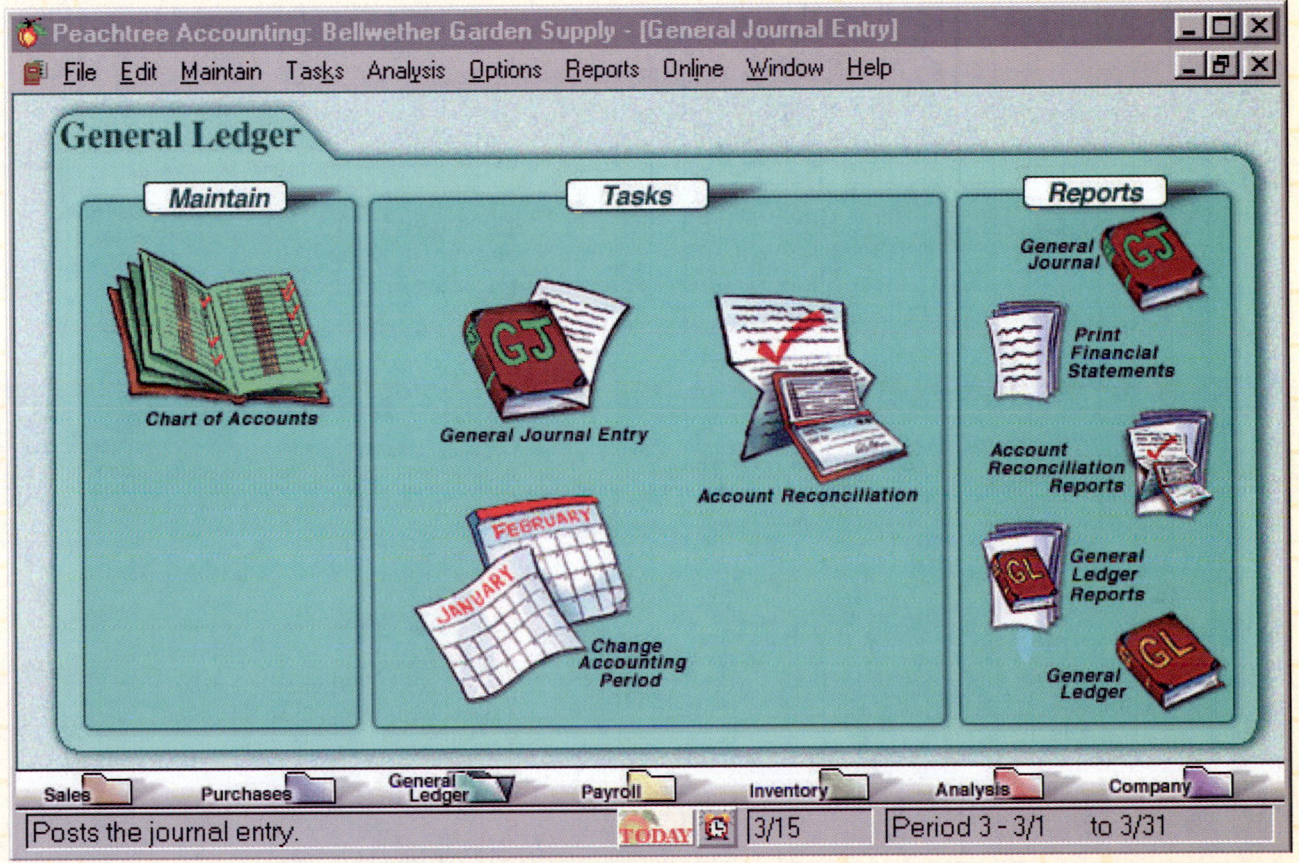

By clicking on the icons that appear in Figure B, the accountant can use the software to perform the same kinds of tasks that are necessary in any accounting system, manual or computerized. In every accounting system, someone must create and maintain the chart of accounts and make entries in the general journal. Although accountants rarely change the accounting periods of their companies, it is something that the software must be capable of doing. Finally, the reports that the software can produce include printouts of the general journal and the general ledger, along with the standard financial statements. This software package also gives the accountant the ability to create reconciliation reports and customized reports based on numbers in the general ledger.

Learning Objectives	Key Points to Remember

1 **Prepare financial statements with the aid of a work sheet.**	The work sheet is used as an aid in preparing:
	  1. adjusting entries,
	  2. financial statements, and
	  3. closing entries
	
	The following classifications are used for accounts reported on the balance sheet.
	■ *Current assets* include cash and assets that will be converted into cash or consumed within either one year or the normal operating cycle of the business, whichever is longer. An *operating cycle* is the time required to purchase supplies and services and convert them back into cash.
	■ *Property, plant, and equipment*, also called *plant assets* or *long-term assets*, represent assets that are expected to serve the business for many years.
	■ *Current liabilities* are liabilities that are due within either one year or the normal operating cycle of the business, whichever is longer, and that are to be paid out of current assets.
	■ *Long-term liabilities*, or *long-term debt*, are obligations that are not expected to be paid within a year and do not require the use of current assets.

2 **Journalize and post closing entries.**	Steps in the closing process are:
	  1. Close revenue accounts to Income Summary.
	  2. Close expense accounts to Income Summary.
	  3. Close Income Summary to Capital.
	  4. Close Drawing to Capital.

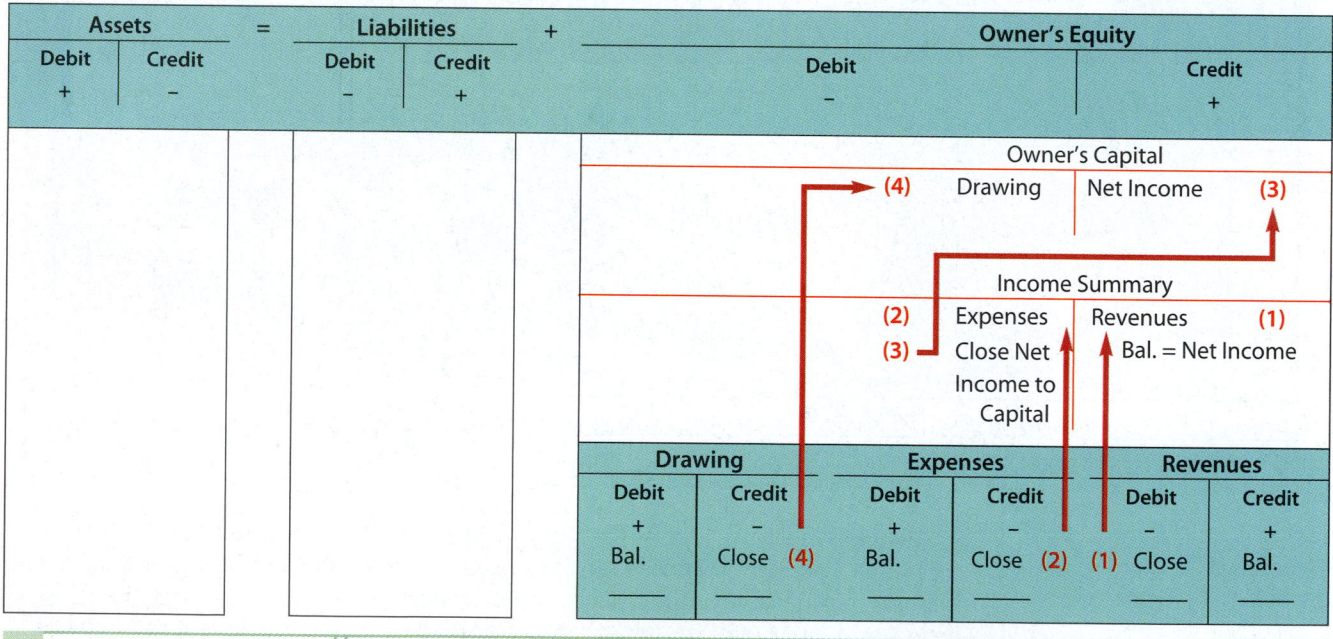

3 **Prepare a post-closing trial balance.**	After posting the closing entries, a post-closing trial balance should be prepared to prove the equality of the debit and credit balances in the general ledger accounts. The accounts shown in the post-closing trial balance are the permanent accounts.

Learning Objectives	Key Points to Remember
4 List and describe the steps in the accounting cycle.	Steps in the accounting cycle are: *During Accounting Period* 1. Analyze source documents. 2. Journalize the transactions. 3. Post to the ledger accounts. *End of Accounting Period* 4. Prepare a trial balance. 5. Determine and prepare the needed adjustments on the work sheet. 6. Complete an end-of-period work sheet. 7. Prepare an income statement, statement of owner's equity, and balance sheet. 8. Journalize and post the adjusting entries. 9. Journalize and post the closing entries. 10. Prepare a post-closing trial balance.

Reflection: Answering the Opening Question

The accounting records are closed "as of" December 31, or another fiscal year end chosen by the firm. The actual adjustments, closing entries, and financial statements are generally prepared several weeks after the official closing date. However, it is important to include all transactions occurring prior to year end in the current year's financial statements. Similarly, transactions taking place after year end must be included in the next year's financial statements. Improper timing of the recognition of transactions taking place around the end of the year can have major effects on the reported profits. For example, some firms have been found to "leave the books open" for a few days to include a major sale, or other profitable transactions, that actually took place after the end of the year. If undetected, the good news could be reported on the current year's statements, rather than in the following year. Similarly, a firm could be tempted to "close early" to avoid recognizing unprofitable events occurring during the last few days of the year. Thus, proper treatment of transactions taking place around the end of the year is carefully monitored by auditors.

DEMONSTRATION PROBLEM

Timothy Chang owns and operates Hard Copy Printers. A work sheet for the year ended December 31, 20--, is provided on the next page. Chang made no additional investments during the year.

REQUIRED

1. Prepare financial statements.
2. Prepare closing entries.

(continued)

Hard Copy Printers
Work Sheet
For Year Ended December 31, 20 - -

#	ACCOUNT TITLE	TRIAL BALANCE DEBIT	TRIAL BALANCE CREDIT	ADJUSTMENTS DEBIT	ADJUSTMENTS CREDIT	ADJUSTED TRIAL BALANCE DEBIT	ADJUSTED TRIAL BALANCE CREDIT	INCOME STATEMENT DEBIT	INCOME STATEMENT CREDIT	BALANCE SHEET DEBIT	BALANCE SHEET CREDIT
1	Cash	1 180 00				1 180 00				1 180 00	
2	Paper Supplies	3 600 00			(a) 3 550 00	50 00				50 00	
3	Prepaid Insurance	1 000 00			(b) 505 00	495 00				495 00	
4	Printing Equipment	5 800 00				5 800 00				5 800 00	
5	Accum. Depr.—Printing Equipment				(d) 1 200 00		1 200 00				1 200 00
6	Accounts Payable		500 00				500 00				500 00
7	Wages Payable				(c) 30 00		30 00				30 00
8	Timothy Chang, Capital		10 000 00				10 000 00				10 000 00
9	Timothy Chang, Drawing	13 000 00				13 000 00				13 000 00	
10	Printing Fees		35 100 00				35 100 00		35 100 00		
11	Wages Expense	11 970 00		(c) 30 00		12 000 00		12 000 00			
12	Rent Expense	7 500 00				7 500 00		7 500 00			
13	Paper Supplies Expense			(a) 3 550 00		3 550 00		3 550 00			
14	Telephone Expense	550 00				550 00		550 00			
15	Utilities Expense	1 000 00				1 000 00		1 000 00			
16	Insurance Expense			(b) 505 00		505 00		505 00			
17	Depr. Expense—Printing Equipment			(d) 1 200 00		1 200 00		1 200 00			
18		45 600 00	45 600 00	5 285 00	5 285 00	46 830 00	46 830 00	26 305 00	35 100 00	20 525 00	11 730 00
19	Net Income							8 795 00			8 795 00
20								35 100 00	35 100 00	20 525 00	20 525 00
21											
22											
23											
24											
25											
26											
27											
28											
29											
30											

Solution

1.

Hard Copy Printers Income Statement For Year Ended December 31, 20 - -													
Revenue:													
Printing fees								$ 35	1	0	0	00
Expenses:												
Wages expense	$ 12	0	0	0	00							
Rent expense	7	5	0	0	00							
Paper supplies expense	3	5	5	0	00							
Telephone expense		5	5	0	00							
Utilities expense	1	0	0	0	00							
Insurance expense		5	0	5	00							
Depreciation expense—printing equipment	1	2	0	0	00							
Total expenses							26	3	0	5	00
Net income							$ 8	7	9	5	00

Hard Copy Printers Statement of Owner's Equity For Year Ended December 31, 20 - -												
Timothy Chang, capital, Jan. 1, 20 - -						$ 10	0	0	0	00
Net income for 20 - -	$ 8	7	9	5	00					
Less withdrawals for 20 - -	13	0	0	0	00					
Decrease in capital						(4	2	0	5	00)
Timothy Chang, capital, Dec. 31, 20 - -						$ 5	7	9	5	00

Hard Copy Printers Balance Sheet December 31, 20 - -												
Assets											
Current assets:											
Cash	$ 1	1	8	0	00					
Paper supplies			5	0	00					
Prepaid insurance		4	9	5	00					
Total current assets						$ 1	7	2	5	00
Property, plant and equipment:											
Printing equipment	$ 5	8	0	0	00					
Less accumulated depreciation	1	2	0	0	00	4	6	0	0	00
Total assets						$ 6	3	2	5	00
Liabilities											
Current liabilities:											
Accounts payable	$	5	0	0	00					
Wages payable			3	0	00					
Total current liabilities						$	5	3	0	00
Owner's Equity											
Timothy Chang, capital						5	7	9	5	00
Total liabilities and owner's equity						$ 6	3	2	5	00

2.

	DATE		DESCRIPTION	POST REF.	DEBIT					CREDIT					
1			Closing Entries												1
2	20-- Dec.	31	Printing Fees		35	1	0	0	00						2
3			Income Summary							35	1	0	0	00	3
4															4
5		31	Income Summary		26	3	0	5	00						5
6			Wages Expense							12	0	0	0	00	6
7			Rent Expense							7	5	0	0	00	7
8			Paper Supplies Expense							3	5	5	0	00	8
9			Telephone Expense								5	5	0	00	9
10			Utilities Expense							1	0	0	0	00	10
11			Insurance Expense								5	0	5	00	11
12			Depr. Expense—Printing Equipment							1	2	0	0	00	12
13															13
14		31	Income Summary		8	7	9	5	00						14
15			Timothy Chang, Capital							8	7	9	5	00	15
16															16
17		31	Timothy Chang, Capital		13	0	0	0	00						17
18			Timothy Chang, Drawing							13	0	0	0	00	18
19															19

GENERAL JOURNAL   PAGE 4

On-Line Learning Tools

For more information, visit: http://heintz.swlearning.com

The Heintz & Parry product web site is designed specifically for **COLLEGE ACCOUNTING, 18e.** The features include downloadable student resources and an interactive study center, organized by chapter, which contains learning objectives, web links, on-line quizzes with automatic feedback, and more.

KEY TERMS

account form of balance sheet, (179)   A balance sheet in which the assets are on the left and the liabilities and the owner's equity sections are on the right.

accounting cycle, (188)   The steps involved in accounting for all of the business activities during an accounting period.

classified balance sheet, (179)   A balance sheet with separate categories for current assets; property, plant, and equipment; current liabilities; and long-term liabilities.

closing process, (181)   The process of giving zero balances to the temporary accounts so that they can accumulate information for the next accounting period.

current assets, (179)   Cash and assets that will be converted into cash or consumed within either one year or the normal operating cycle of the business, whichever is longer.

current liabilities, (179)   Liabilities that are due within either one year or the normal operating cycle of the business, whichever is longer, and that are to be paid out of current assets.

Income Summary, (181)   A temporary account used in the closing process to summarize the effects of all revenue and expense accounts.

long-term assets, (179)   See property, plant, and equipment.

long-term debt, (179)   See long-term liabilities.

long-term liabilities, (179)   Obligations that are not expected to be paid within a year and do not require the use of current assets. Also called long-term debt.

operating cycle, (179)   The period of time required to purchase supplies and services and convert them back into cash.

permanent accounts, (181)   Accounts that accumulate information across accounting periods; all accounts reported on the balance sheet.

plant assets, (179)   See property, plant, and equipment.

post-closing trial balance, (187)   Prepared after posting the closing entries to prove the equality of the debit and credit balances in the general ledger accounts.

property, plant, and equipment, (179)   Assets that are expected to serve the business for many years. Also called plant assets or long-term assets.

report form of balance sheet, (179)   A balance sheet in which the liabilities and the owner's equity sections are shown below the assets section.

temporary accounts, (181)   Accounts that do not accumulate information across accounting periods but are closed, such as the drawing account and all income statement accounts.

REVIEW QUESTIONS

(LO1)   1. Identify the source of the information needed to prepare the income statement.

(LO1)   2. Describe two approaches to listing the expenses in the income statement.

(LO1)   3. Identify the sources of the information needed to prepare the statement of owner's equity.

(LO1)   4. If additional investments were made during the year, what information in addition to the work sheet would be needed to prepare the statement of owner's equity?

(LO1)   5. Identify the sources of the information needed to prepare the balance sheet.

(LO2)   6. What is a permanent account? On which financial statement are permanent accounts reported?

(LO2)   7. Name three types of temporary accounts.

(LO2)   8. List the four steps for closing the temporary accounts.

(LO2)   9. Describe the net effect of the four closing entries on the balance of the owner's capital account. Where else is this same amount calculated?

(LO3)   10. What is the purpose of the post-closing trial balance?

(LO4)   11. List the ten steps in the accounting cycle.

Self-Study Test Questions

True/False

1. Expenses are listed on the income statement as they appear in the chart of accounts or in descending order (by dollar amount). _____

2. Additional investments of capital during the month are not reported on the statement of owner's equity. _____

3. The income statement cannot be prepared using the work sheet alone. _____

4. A classified balance sheet groups similar items together such as current assets. _____

5. Temporary accounts are closed at the end of each accounting period. _____

Multiple Choice

1. Which of these types of accounts is considered a "permanent" account? _____

   (a) Revenue   (c) Drawing
   (b) Asset   (d) Expense

2. Which of these accounts is considered a "temporary" account? _____

   (a) Cash   (c) J. Jones, Capital
   (b) Accounts Payable   (d) J. Jones, Drawing

3. Which of these is the first step in the closing process? _____

   (a) Close revenue account(s).
   (b) Close expense accounts.
   (c) Close the income summary account.
   (d) Close the drawing account.

4. The _____ is prepared after closing entries are posted to prove the equality of debit and credit balances. _____

   (a) balance sheet   (c) post-closing trial balance
   (b) income statement   (d) statement of owner's equity

5. Steps that begin with analyzing source documents and conclude with the post-closing trial balance are called the _____ . _____

   (a) closing process.   (c) adjusting entries.
   (b) accounting cycle.   (d) posting process.

The answers to the Self-Study Test Questions are at the end of the text.

MANAGING YOUR WRITING

At lunch, two bookkeepers got into a heated discussion about whether closing entries should be made before or after preparing the financial statements. They have come to you to resolve this issue and have agreed to accept your position. Write a memo explaining the purpose of closing entries and whether they should be made before or after preparing the financial statements.

SERIES A EXERCISES

EXERCISE 6-1A   (LO1)   **INCOME STATEMENT** From the partial work sheet for Case Advising, prepare an
Net income: $1,990   income statement.

	Case Advising Work Sheet (Partial) For Month Ended January 31, 20 - -						
		INCOME STATEMENT		BALANCE SHEET			
	ACCOUNT TITLE	DEBIT	CREDIT	DEBIT	CREDIT		
1	Cash			1 2 1 2 00			1
2	Accounts Receivable			8 9 6 00			2
3	Supplies			4 8 2 00			3
4	Prepaid Insurance			9 0 0 00			4
5	Office Equipment			3 0 0 0 00			5
6	Accum. Depr.—Office Equipment				1 0 0 00		6
7	Accounts Payable				1 0 0 0 00		7
8	Wages Payable				2 0 0 00		8
9	Bill Case, Capital				4 0 0 0 00		9
10	Bill Case, Drawing			8 0 0 00			10
11	Advising Fees		3 7 9 3 00				11
12	Wages Expense	8 0 0 00					12
13	Advertising Expense	8 0 00					13
14	Rent Expense	5 0 0 00					14
15	Supplies Expense	1 2 0 00					15
16	Telephone Expense	5 8 00					16
17	Electricity Expense	4 4 00					17
18	Insurance Expense	3 0 00					18
19	Gas and Oil Expense	3 8 00					19
20	Depr. Expense—Office Equipment	1 0 0 00					20
21	Miscellaneous Expense	3 3 00					21
22		1 8 0 3 00	3 7 9 3 00	7 2 9 0 00	5 3 0 0 00		22
23	Net Income	1 9 9 0 00			1 9 9 0 00		23
24		3 7 9 3 00	3 7 9 3 00	7 2 9 0 00	7 2 9 0 00		24

EXERCISE 6-2A   (LO1)   **STATEMENT OF OWNER'S EQUITY** From the partial work sheet in Exercise
Capital 1/31: $5,190   6-1A, prepare a statement of owner's equity, assuming no additional investment
                               was made by the owner.

EXERCISE 6-3A   (LO1)   **BALANCE SHEET** From the partial work sheet in Exercise 6-1A, prepare a balance
Total assets: $6,390   sheet.

EXERCISE 6-4A   (LO2)   **CLOSING ENTRIES (NET INCOME)** Set up T accounts for Case Advising based
Capital 1/31: $5,190   on the work sheet in Exercise 6-1A and the chart of accounts provided below.
                               Enter the existing balance for each account. Prepare closing entries in general
                               journal form. Then post the closing entries to the T accounts.

Chart of Accounts

Assets		Revenues	
101	Cash	401	Advising Fees
122	Accounts Receivable		
141	Supplies	Expenses	
145	Prepaid Insurance	511	Wages Expense
181	Office Equipment	512	Advertising Expense
181.1	Accum. Depr.—Office Equip.	521	Rent Expense

(continued)

	Liabilities
202	Accounts Payable
219	Wages Payable
	Owner's Equity
311	Bill Case, Capital
312	Bill Case, Drawing
313	Income Summary

524	Supplies Expense
525	Telephone Expense
533	Electricity Expense
535	Insurance Expense
538	Gas and Oil Expense
541	Depr. Exp.—Office Equip.
549	Miscellaneous Expense

EXERCISE 6-5A
Capital 1/31: $2,597

(LO2)

CLOSING ENTRIES (NET LOSS) Using the following T accounts, prepare closing entries in general journal form dated January 31, 20--. Then post the closing entries to the T accounts.

Accum. Depr.—Del. Equip. 185.1
Bal. 100

Wages Expense 511
Bal. 1,800

Electricity Expense 533
Bal. 44

Wages Payable 219
Bal. 200

Advertising Expense 512
Bal. 80

Insurance Expense 535
Bal. 30

Saburo Goto, Capital 311
Bal. 4,000

Rent Expense 521
Bal. 500

Gas and Oil Expense 538
Bal. 38

Saburo Goto, Drawing 312
Bal. 800

Supplies Expense 523
Bal. 120

Depr. Exp.—Del. Equip. 541
Bal. 100

Income Summary 313

Telephone Expense 525
Bal. 58

Miscellaneous Expense 549
Bal. 33

Delivery Fees 401
Bal. 2,200

SERIES A PROBLEMS

PROBLEM 6-6A
Net income: $1,400;
Capital 1/31: $7,400;
Total assets: $8,650

(LO1)

FINANCIAL STATEMENTS Page 201 shows a work sheet for Monte's Repairs. No additional investments were made by the owner during the month.

REQUIRED

1. Prepare an income statement.
2. Prepare a statement of owner's equity.
3. Prepare a balance sheet.

Monte's Repairs
Work Sheet
For Month Ended January 31, 20--

	ACCOUNT TITLE	TRIAL BALANCE DEBIT	TRIAL BALANCE CREDIT	ADJUSTMENTS DEBIT	ADJUSTMENTS CREDIT	ADJUSTED TRIAL BALANCE DEBIT	ADJUSTED TRIAL BALANCE CREDIT	INCOME STATEMENT DEBIT	INCOME STATEMENT CREDIT	BALANCE SHEET DEBIT	BALANCE SHEET CREDIT	
1	Cash	3 0 8 0 00				3 0 8 0 00				3 0 8 0 00		1
2	Accounts Receivable	1 2 0 0 00				1 2 0 0 00				1 2 0 0 00		2
3	Supplies	8 0 0 00			(a) 2 0 0 00	6 0 0 00				6 0 0 00		3
4	Prepaid Insurance	9 0 0 00			(b) 1 0 0 00	8 0 0 00				8 0 0 00		4
5	Delivery Equipment	3 0 0 0 00				3 0 0 0 00				3 0 0 0 00		5
6	Accum. Depr.—Delivery Equipment				(d) 3 0 00		3 0 00				3 0 00	6
7	Accounts Payable		1 1 0 0 00				1 1 0 0 00				1 1 0 0 00	7
8	Wages Payable				(c) 1 5 0 00		1 5 0 00				1 5 0 00	8
9	Monte Eli, Capital		7 0 0 0 00				7 0 0 0 00				7 0 0 0 00	9
10	Monte Eli, Drawing	1 0 0 0 00				1 0 0 0 00				1 0 0 0 00		10
11	Repair Fees		4 2 3 0 00				4 2 3 0 00		4 2 3 0 00			11
12	Wages Expense	1 6 5 0 00		(c) 1 5 0 00		1 8 0 0 00		1 8 0 0 00				12
13	Advertising Expense	1 7 0 00				1 7 0 00		1 7 0 00				13
14	Rent Expense	4 2 0 00				4 2 0 00		4 2 0 00				14
15	Supplies Expense			(a) 2 0 0 00		2 0 0 00		2 0 0 00				15
16	Telephone Expense	4 9 00				4 9 00		4 9 00				16
17	Insurance Expense			(b) 1 0 0 00		1 0 0 00		1 0 0 00				17
18	Gas and Oil Expense	3 3 00				3 3 00		3 3 00				18
19	Depr. Expense—Delivery Equipment			(d) 3 0 00		3 0 00		3 0 00				19
20	Miscellaneous Expense	2 8 00				2 8 00		2 8 00				20
21		12 3 3 0 00	12 3 3 0 00	4 8 0 00	4 8 0 00	12 5 1 0 00	12 5 1 0 00	2 8 3 0 00	4 2 3 0 00	9 6 8 0 00	8 2 8 0 00	21
22	Net Income							1 4 0 0 00			1 4 0 0 00	22
23								4 2 3 0 00	4 2 3 0 00	9 6 8 0 00	9 6 8 0 00	23
24												24
25												25
26												26
27												27
28												28
29												29
30												30

(PROBLEM 6-6A)

PROBLEM 6-7A   **(LO1)**   **STATEMENT OF OWNER'S EQUITY** The capital account for Autumn Chou,
Capital 1/31: $6,820   including an additional investment, and a partial work sheet are shown below.

REQUIRED

Prepare a statement of owner's equity.

GENERAL LEDGER

ACCOUNT: Autumn Chou, Capital   ACCOUNT NO. 311

DATE		ITEM	POST REF.	DEBIT	CREDIT	BALANCE DEBIT	BALANCE CREDIT
20-- Jan.	1	Balance	✔				4 8 0 0 00
	18		J 1		1 2 0 0 00		6 0 0 0 00

Autumn's Home Designs
Work Sheet (Partial)
For Month Ended January 31, 20 - -

	ACCOUNT TITLE	INCOME STATEMENT DEBIT	INCOME STATEMENT CREDIT	BALANCE SHEET DEBIT	BALANCE SHEET CREDIT	
1	Cash			3 2 0 0 00		1
2	Accounts Receivable			1 6 0 0 00		2
3	Supplies			8 0 0 00		3
4	Prepaid Insurance			9 0 0 00		4
5	Office Equipment			2 5 0 0 00		5
6	Accum. Depr.—Office Equipment				5 0 00	6
7	Accounts Payable				1 9 5 0 00	7
8	Wages Payable				1 8 0 00	8
9	Autumn Chou, Capital				6 0 0 0 00	9
10	Autumn Chou, Drawing			1 0 0 0 00		10
11	Design Fees		4 8 6 6 00			11
12	Wages Expense	1 9 0 0 00				12
13	Advertising Expense	2 1 00				13
14	Rent Expense	6 0 0 00				14
15	Supplies Expense	2 0 0 00				15
16	Telephone Expense	8 5 00				16
17	Electricity Expense	4 8 00				17
18	Insurance Expense	6 0 00				18
19	Gas and Oil Expense	3 2 00				19
20	Depr. Expense—Office Equipment	5 0 00				20
21	Miscellaneous Expense	5 0 00				21
22		3 0 4 6 00	4 8 6 6 00	10 0 0 0 00	8 1 8 0 00	22
23	Net Income	1 8 2 0 00			1 8 2 0 00	23
24		4 8 6 6 00	4 8 6 6 00	10 0 0 0 00	10 0 0 0 00	24

PROBLEM 6-8A   **(LO2/3)**

Capital 1/31: $7,400;
Post-closing Trial Bal.
total debits: $8,680

CLOSING ENTRIES AND POST-CLOSING TRIAL BALANCE Refer to the work sheet in Problem 6-6A for Monte's Repairs. The trial balance amounts (before adjustments) have been entered in the ledger accounts provided in the working papers. If you are not using the working papers that accompany this book, set up ledger accounts and enter these balances as of January 31, 20--. A chart of accounts is provided below.

Monte's Repairs
Chart of Accounts

Assets
101   Cash
122   Accounts Receivable
141   Supplies
145   Prepaid Insurance
185   Delivery Equipment
185.1 Accum. Depr.—Delivery Equip.

Liabilities
202   Accounts Payable
219   Wages Payable

Owner's Equity
311   Monte Eli, Capital
312   Monte Eli, Drawing
313   Income Summary

Revenues
401   Repair Fees

Expenses
511   Wages Expense
512   Advertising Expense
521   Rent Expense
523   Supplies Expense
525   Telephone Expense
535   Insurance Expense
538   Gas and Oil Expense
541   Depr. Exp.—Delivery Equip.
549   Miscellaneous Expense

REQUIRED

1.   Journalize (page 10) and post the adjusting entries

2.   Journalize (page 11) and post the closing entries.

3.   Prepare a post-closing trial balance.

SERIES B EXERCISES

EXERCISE 6-1B   **(LO1)**
Net income: $1,826

INCOME STATEMENT From the partial work sheet for Adams' Shoe Shine on the next page, prepare an income statement.

EXERCISE 6-2B   **(LO1)**
Capital 6/30: $5,826

STATEMENT OF OWNER'S EQUITY From the partial work sheet in Exercise 6-1B, prepare a statement of owner's equity, assuming no additional investment was made by the owner.

EXERCISE 6-3B   **(LO1)**
Total assets: $7,936

BALANCE SHEET From the partial work sheet in Exercise 6-1B, prepare a balance sheet for Adams' Shoe Shine.

(EXERCISE 6-1B)

Adams' Shoe Shine
Work Sheet (Partial)
For Month Ended June 30, 20 - -

	ACCOUNT TITLE	INCOME STATEMENT DEBIT	INCOME STATEMENT CREDIT	BALANCE SHEET DEBIT	BALANCE SHEET CREDIT	
1	Cash			3 2 6 2 00		1
2	Accounts Receivable			1 2 4 4 00		2
3	Supplies			8 0 0 00		3
4	Prepaid Insurance			6 4 0 00		4
5	Office Equipment			2 1 0 0 00		5
6	Accum. Depr.—Office Equipment				1 1 0 00	6
7	Accounts Payable				1 8 5 0 00	7
8	Wages Payable				2 6 0 00	8
9	Mary Adams, Capital				6 0 0 0 00	9
10	Mary Adams, Drawing			2 0 0 0 00		10
11	Service Fees		4 8 1 3 00			11
12	Wages Expense	1 0 8 0 00				12
13	Advertising Expense	3 4 00				13
14	Rent Expense	9 0 0 00				14
15	Supplies Expense	3 2 2 00				15
16	Telephone Expense	1 3 3 00				16
17	Utilities Expense	1 0 2 00				17
18	Insurance Expense	1 2 0 00				18
19	Gas and Oil Expense	8 8 00				19
20	Depr. Expense—Office Equipment	1 1 0 00				20
21	Miscellaneous Expense	9 8 00				21
22		2 9 8 7 00	4 8 1 3 00	10 0 4 6 00	8 2 2 0 00	22
23	Net Income	1 8 2 6 00			1 8 2 6 00	23
24		4 8 1 3 00	4 8 1 3 00	10 0 4 6 00	10 0 4 6 00	24

EXERCISE 6-4B   **(LO2)**

Capital 6/30: $5,826

CLOSING ENTRIES (NET INCOME) Set up T accounts for Adams' Shoe Shine based on the work sheet in Exercise 6-1B and the chart of accounts provided below. Enter the existing balance for each account. Prepare closing entries in general journal form. Then, post the closing entries to the T accounts.

Chart of Accounts

Assets
101   Cash
122   Accounts Receivable
141   Supplies
145   Prepaid Insurance
181   Office Equipment
181.1   Accum. Depr.—Office Equip.

Liabilities
202   Accounts Payable
219   Wages Payable

Owner's Equity
311   Mary Adams, Capital
312   Mary Adams, Drawing
313   Income Summary

Revenues
401   Service Fees

Expenses
511   Wages Expense
512   Advertising Expense
521   Rent Expense
523   Supplies Expense
525   Telephone Expense
533   Utilities Expense
535   Insurance Expense
538   Gas and Oil Expense
542   Depr. Exp.—Office Equip.
549   Miscellaneous Expense

EXERCISE 6-5B   **(LO2)**   **CLOSING ENTRIES (NET LOSS)** Using the following T accounts, prepare closing entries in general journal form dated June 30, 20--. Then post the closing entries to the T accounts.

Capital 6/30: $3,826

Accum. Depr.— Office Equip. 181.1		Wages Expense 511		Utilities Expense 533
Bal. 110	Bal. 1,080		Bal. 102	

Wages Payable 219		Advertising Expense 512		Insurance Expense 535
Bal. 260	Bal. 34		Bal. 120	

Raquel Zapata, Capital 311		Rent Expense 521		Gas and Oil Expense 538
Bal. 6,000	Bal. 900		Bal. 88	

Raquel Zapata, Drawing 312		Supplies Expense 523		Depr. Exp.— Office Equip. 541
Bal. 2,000	Bal. 322		Bal. 110	

Income Summary 313		Telephone Expense 525		Miscellaneous Expense 549
	Bal. 133		Bal. 98	

Referral Fees 401
Bal. 2,813

SERIES B PROBLEMS

PROBLEM 6-6B   **(LO1)**   **FINANCIAL STATEMENTS** A work sheet for Juanita's Consulting is shown on the following page. There were no additional investments made by the owner during the month.

Net income: $1,450;
Capital 1/31: $7,650;
Total assets: $9,350

REQUIRED

1. Prepare an income statement.

2. Prepare a statement of owner's equity.

3. Prepare a balance sheet.

(continued)

Juanita's Consulting
Work Sheet
For Month Ended June 30, 20- -

	ACCOUNT TITLE	TRIAL BALANCE DEBIT	TRIAL BALANCE CREDIT	ADJUSTMENTS DEBIT	ADJUSTMENTS CREDIT	ADJUSTED TRIAL BALANCE DEBIT	ADJUSTED TRIAL BALANCE CREDIT	INCOME STATEMENT DEBIT	INCOME STATEMENT CREDIT	BALANCE SHEET DEBIT	BALANCE SHEET CREDIT	
1	Cash	5 2 8 5 00				5 2 8 5 00				5 2 8 5 00		1
2	Accounts Receivable	1 0 7 5 00				1 0 7 5 00				1 0 7 5 00		2
3	Supplies	7 5 0 00			(a) 2 5 0 00	5 0 0 00				5 0 0 00		3
4	Prepaid Insurance	5 0 0 00			(b) 1 0 0 00	4 0 0 00				4 0 0 00		4
5	Office Equipment	2 2 0 0 00				2 2 0 0 00				2 2 0 0 00		5
6	Accum. Depr.—Office Equipment				(d) 1 1 0 00		1 1 0 00				1 1 0 00	6
7	Accounts Payable		1 5 0 0 00				1 5 0 0 00				1 5 0 0 00	7
8	Wages Payable				(c) 2 0 0 00		2 0 0 00				2 0 0 00	8
9	Juanita Alvarez, Capital		7 0 0 0 00				7 0 0 0 00				7 0 0 0 00	9
10	Juanita Alvarez, Drawing	8 0 0 00				8 0 0 00				8 0 0 00		10
11	Consulting Fees		4 2 0 4 00				4 2 0 4 00		4 2 0 4 00			11
12	Wages Expense	1 4 0 0 00		(c) 2 0 0 00		1 6 0 0 00		1 6 0 0 00				12
13	Advertising Expense	6 0 00				6 0 00		6 0 00				13
14	Rent Expense	5 0 0 00				5 0 0 00		5 0 0 00				14
15	Supplies Expense			(a) 2 5 0 00		2 5 0 00		2 5 0 00				15
16	Telephone Expense	4 6 00				4 6 00		4 6 00				16
17	Electricity Expense	3 9 00				3 9 00		3 9 00				17
18	Insurance Expense			(b) 1 0 0 00		1 0 0 00		1 0 0 00				18
19	Gas and Oil Expense	2 8 00				2 8 00		2 8 00				19
20	Depr. Expense—Office Equipment			(d) 1 1 0 00		1 1 0 00		1 1 0 00				20
21	Miscellaneous Expense	2 1 00				2 1 00		2 1 00				21
22		12 7 0 4 00	12 7 0 4 00	6 6 0 00	6 6 0 00	13 0 1 4 00	13 0 1 4 00	2 7 5 4 00	4 2 0 4 00	10 2 6 0 00	8 8 1 0 00	22
23	Net Income							1 4 5 0 00			1 4 5 0 00	23
24								4 2 0 4 00	4 2 0 4 00	10 2 6 0 00	10 2 6 0 00	24
25												25
26												26
27												27
28												28
29												29
30												30

(PROBLEM 6-6B)

PROBLEM 6-7B   **(LO1)**   **STATEMENT OF OWNER'S EQUITY** The capital account for Minta's Editorial
Capital 1/31: $9,975   Services, including an additional investment, and a partial work sheet are shown
below.

GENERAL LEDGER

ACCOUNT: Minta Berry, Capital   ACCOUNT NO. 311

DATE	ITEM	POST REF.	DEBIT	CREDIT	BALANCE DEBIT	BALANCE CREDIT
20-- Jan. 1	Balance	✔				3 6 0 0 00
22		J1		2 9 0 0 00		6 5 0 0 00

Minta's Editorial Services
Work Sheet (Partial)
For Month Ended January 31, 20 - -

	ACCOUNT TITLE	INCOME STATEMENT DEBIT	INCOME STATEMENT CREDIT	BALANCE SHEET DEBIT	BALANCE SHEET CREDIT	
1	Cash			3 8 0 0 00		1
2	Accounts Receivable			2 2 0 0 00		2
3	Supplies			1 0 0 0 00		3
4	Prepaid Insurance			9 5 0 00		4
5	Computer Equipment			4 5 0 0 00		5
6	Accum. Depr.—Computer Equipment				2 2 5 00	6
7	Accounts Payable				2 1 0 0 00	7
8	Wages Payable				1 5 0 00	8
9	Minta Berry, Capital				6 5 0 0 00	9
10	Minta Berry, Drawing			1 7 0 0 00		10
11	Editing Fees		7 0 1 2 00			11
12	Wages Expense	6 0 0 00				12
13	Advertising Expense	4 9 00				13
14	Rent Expense	4 5 0 00				14
15	Supplies Expense	2 8 8 00				15
16	Telephone Expense	4 4 00				16
17	Utilities Expense	3 8 00				17
18	Insurance Expense	1 2 5 00				18
19	Depr. Expense—Computer Equipment	2 2 5 00				19
20	Miscellaneous Expense	1 8 00				20
21		1 8 3 7 00	7 0 1 2 00	14 1 5 0 00	8 9 7 5 00	21
22	Net Income	5 1 7 5 00			5 1 7 5 00	22
23		7 0 1 2 00	7 0 1 2 00	14 1 5 0 00	14 1 5 0 00	23

REQUIRED

Prepare a statement of owner's equity.

PROBLEM 6-8B   (LO2/3)

Capital 6/30: $7,650;
Post-closing Trial Bal.
total debits: $9,460

CLOSING ENTRIES AND POST-CLOSING TRIAL BALANCE Refer to the work sheet for Juanita's Consulting in Problem 6-6B. The trial balance amounts (before adjustments) have been entered in the ledger accounts provided in the working papers. If you are not using the working papers that accompany this book, set up ledger accounts and enter these balances as of June 30, 20--. A chart of accounts is provided below.

Juanita's Consulting
Chart of Accounts

Assets		Revenues	
101	Cash	401	Consulting Fees
122	Accounts Receivable		
141	Supplies	Expenses	
145	Prepaid Insurance	511	Wages Expense
181	Office Equipment	512	Advertising Expense
181.1	Accum. Depr.—Office Equip.	521	Rent Expense
		523	Supplies Expense
Liabilities		525	Telephone Expense
202	Accounts Payable	533	Electricity Expense
219	Wages Payable	535	Insurance Expense
		538	Gas and Oil Expense
Owner's Equity		541	Depr. Exp.—Office Equip.
311	Juanita Alvarez, Capital	549	Miscellaneous Expense
312	Juanita Alvarez, Drawing		
313	Income Summary		

REQUIRED

1. Journalize (page 10) and post the adjusting entries.

2. Journalize (page 11) and post the closing entries.

3. Prepare a post-closing trial balance.

MASTERY PROBLEM

Total assets: $4,740;
E. Soltis, capital, Dec. 31: $4,475

Elizabeth Soltis owns and operates Aunt Ibby's Styling Salon. A year-end work sheet is provided on the next page. Using this information, prepare financial statements and closing entries. Soltis made no additional investments during the year.

(continued)

Aunt Ibby's Styling Salon
Work Sheet
For Year Ended December 31, 20 - -

	ACCOUNT TITLE	TRIAL BALANCE DEBIT	TRIAL BALANCE CREDIT	ADJUSTMENTS DEBIT	ADJUSTMENTS CREDIT	ADJUSTED TRIAL BALANCE DEBIT	ADJUSTED TRIAL BALANCE CREDIT	INCOME STATEMENT DEBIT	INCOME STATEMENT CREDIT	BALANCE SHEET DEBIT	BALANCE SHEET CREDIT	
1	Cash	9 4 0 00				9 4 0 00				9 4 0 00		1
2	Styling Supplies	1 5 0 0 00			(a) 1 4 5 0 00	5 0 00				5 0 00		2
3	Prepaid Insurance	8 0 0 00			(b) 6 5 0 00	1 5 0 00				1 5 0 00		3
4	Salon Equipment	4 5 0 0 00				4 5 0 0 00				4 5 0 0 00		4
5	Accum. Depr.—Salon Equipment				(d) 9 0 0 00		9 0 0 00				9 0 0 00	5
6	Accounts Payable		2 2 5 00				2 2 5 00				2 2 5 00	6
7	Wages Payable				(c) 4 0 00		4 0 00				4 0 00	7
8	Elizabeth Soltis, Capital		2 7 6 5 00				2 7 6 5 00				2 7 6 5 00	8
9	Elizabeth Soltis, Drawing	12 0 0 0 00				12 0 0 0 00				12 0 0 0 00		9
10	Styling Fees		32 0 0 0 00				32 0 0 0 00		32 0 0 0 00			10
11	Wages Expense	8 0 0 0 00		(c) 4 0 00		8 0 4 0 00		8 0 4 0 00				11
12	Rent Expense	6 0 0 0 00				6 0 0 0 00		6 0 0 0 00				12
13	Styling Supplies Expense			(a) 1 4 5 0 00		1 4 5 0 00		1 4 5 0 00				13
14	Telephone Expense	4 5 0 00				4 5 0 00		4 5 0 00				14
15	Utilities Expense	8 0 0 00				8 0 0 00		8 0 0 00				15
16	Insurance Expense			(b) 6 5 0 00		6 5 0 00		6 5 0 00				16
17	Depr. Expense—Salon Equipment			(d) 9 0 0 00		9 0 0 00		9 0 0 00				17
18		34 9 9 0 00	34 9 9 0 00	3 0 4 0 00	3 0 4 0 00	35 9 3 0 00	35 9 3 0 00	18 2 9 0 00	32 0 0 0 00	17 6 4 0 00	3 9 3 0 00	18
19	Net Income							13 7 1 0 00			13 7 1 0 00	19
20								32 0 0 0 00	32 0 0 0 00	17 6 4 0 00	17 6 4 0 00	20

CHALLENGE PROBLEM

This problem challenges you to apply your cumulative accounting knowledge to move a step beyond the material in the chapter.

Net Loss: $2,100;
Capital, 1/31/20--: ($700)

Provided below is a partial work sheet for Ardery Advising.

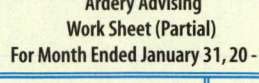

Ardery Advising
Work Sheet (Partial)
For Month Ended January 31, 20 - -

	ACCOUNT TITLE	INCOME STATEMENT DEBIT	INCOME STATEMENT CREDIT	BALANCE SHEET DEBIT	BALANCE SHEET CREDIT	
1	Cash			2 4 1 2 00		1
2	Accounts Receivable			8 9 6 00		2
3	Supplies			4 8 2 00		3
4	Prepaid Insurance			9 0 0 00		4
5	Office Equipment			3 0 0 0 00		5
6	Accum. Depr.—Office Equipment				2 0 0 0 00	6
7	Accounts Payable				2 1 9 0 00	7
8	Wages Payable				1 2 0 0 00	8
9	Notes Payable				3 0 0 0 00	9
10	Sam Ardery, Capital				2 2 0 0 00	10
11	Sam Ardery, Drawing			8 0 0 00		11
12	Advising Fees		3 8 0 2 00			12
13	Wages Expense	1 8 0 0 00				13
14	Advertising Expense	4 0 0 00				14
15	Rent Expense	1 5 0 0 00				15
16	Supplies Expense	1 2 0 00				16
17	Telephone Expense	3 0 0 00				17
18	Electricity Expense	4 4 00				18
19	Insurance Expense	2 0 0 00				19
20	Gas and Oil Expense	3 8 00				20
21	Depr. Expense—Office Equipment	1 0 0 0 00				21
22	Miscellaneous Expense	5 0 0 00				22
23		5 9 0 2 00	3 8 0 2 00	8 4 9 0 00	10 5 9 0 00	23
24	Net Income Loss		2 1 0 0 00	2 1 0 0 00		24
25		5 9 0 2 00	5 9 0 2 00	10 5 9 0 00	10 5 9 0 00	25

REQUIRED

During January, Ardery made an additional investment of $1,200. Prepare an income statement, statement of owner's equity, and balance sheet for Ardery Advising.

Careful study of this appendix should enable you to:

LO1 Classify business trans-actions as operating, investing, or financing.

LO2 Prepare a statement of cash flows by analyzing and categorizing a series of business transactions.

Chapter 6 Appendix
Statement of Cash Flows

Thus far, we have discussed three financial statements: the income statement, the statement of owner's equity, and the balance sheet. A fourth statement, the statement of cash flows, is also very important. It explains what the business did to generate cash and how the cash was used. This is done by categorizing all cash transactions into three types of activities: operating, investing, and financing.

TYPES OF BUSINESS ACTIVITIES

LO1 Classify business trans-actions as operating, investing, or financing.

Cash flows from **operating activities** are related to the revenues and expenses reported on the income statement. Examples include cash received for services performed and the payment of cash for expenses.

LEARNING KEY: There are three types of business activities: operating, investing, and financing.

Investing activities are those transactions involving the purchase and sale of long-term assets, lending money, and collecting the principal on the related loans.

Financing activities are those transactions dealing with the exchange of cash between the business and its owners and creditors. Examples include cash received from the owner to finance the operations and cash paid to the owner as withdrawals. Financing activities also include borrowing cash and repaying the loan principal.

LEARNING KEY: Lending money to another entity is an outflow of cash from investing activities. The collection of the principal when the loan is due is an inflow of cash from investing activities. Borrowing cash is an inflow from financing activities. Repayment of the loan principal is an outflow from financing activities.

Figure 6A-1 provides a review of the transactions for Jessie Jane's Campus Delivery for the month of June. The transactions are classified as operating, investing, or financing, and an explanation for the classification is provided.

SUMMARY OF TRANSACTIONS FOR JESSIE JANE'S CAMPUS DELIVERY	TYPE OF TRANSACTION	EXPLANATION
(a) Jessica Jane invested cash in her business, $2,000.	Financing	Cash received from the owner is an inflow from financing activities. Don't be fooled by the word "invested." From the company's point of view, this is a way to *finance* the business.
(b) Purchased delivery equipment for cash, $1,200.	Investing	Purchases of long-term assets are investments.
(c) Purchased delivery equipment on account from Big Red Scooters, $900. (Note: Big Red has loaned Jane $900.)	No cash involved	This transaction will not affect the main sections of the statement of cash flows. (This is a noncash investing and financing activity.)
(d) Paid first installment to Big Red Scooters, $300. (See transaction (c).)	Financing	Repayments of loans are financing activities.
(e) Received cash for delivery services rendered, $500.	Operating	Cash received as a result of providing services is classified as an operating activity.
(f) Paid cash for June office rent, $200.	Operating	Cash payments for expenses are classified as operating activities.
(g) Paid telephone bill, $50.	Operating	Cash payments for expenses are classified as operating activities.
(h) Made deliveries on account for a total of $600: $400 for the Accounting Department and $200 for the School of Music.	No cash involved	This transaction will not affect the statement of cash flows.
(i) Purchased supplies for cash, $80.	Operating	Cash payments for expenses are classified as operating activities. Most of these supplies were used up. Those that remain will be used in the near future. These are not long-term assets and, thus, do not qualify as investments.
(j) Paid cash for an eight-month liability insurance policy, $200. Coverage began on June 1.	Operating	Cash payments for expenses are classified as operating activities. Prepaid Insurance is not considered a long-term asset and, thus, does not qualify as an investment.
(k) Received $570 in cash for services performed in transaction (h): $400 from the Accounting Department and $170 from the School of Music.	Operating	Cash received as a result of providing services is classified as an operating activity.
(l) Purchased a third scooter from Big Red Scooters, $1,500. A down payment of $300 was made with the remaining payments expected over the next four months.	Investing	Purchases of long-term assets are investments. Only the $300 cash paid will be reported on the statement of cash flows.
(m) Paid wages of part-time employees, $650.	Operating	Cash payments for expenses are classified as operating activities.
(n) Earned delivery fees for the remainder of the month amounting to $1,050: $430 in cash and $620 on account. Deliveries on account: $250 for the Accounting Department and $370 for the Athletic Ticket Office.	Operating	Cash received ($430) as a result of providing services is classified as an operating activity.
(o) Jane withdrew cash for personal use, $150.	Financing	Cash payments to owners are classified as a financing activity.

FIGURE 6A-1   Summary of Transactions for Jessie Jane's Campus Delivery

PREPARING THE STATEMENT OF CASH FLOWS

LO2 Prepare a statement of cash flows by analyzing and categorizing a series of business transactions.

The classifications of the cash transactions for Jessie Jane's Campus Delivery are summarized in the expanded cash T account shown in Figure 6A-2. Using this information, we can prepare a statement of cash flows. As shown in Figure 6A-3, the heading is similar to that used for the income statement. Since the statement of cash flows reports on the flow of cash for a period of time, the statement is dated for the month ended June 30, 20--.

CASH

Event	Classification	Amount	Amount	Classification	Event
(a) Investment by Jessie.	Financing	2,000	1,200	Investing	Purchased delivery equipment. (b)
(e) Cash received for services.	Operating	500	300	Financing	Made payment on loan. (d)
(k) Cash received for services.	Operating	570	200	Operating	Paid office rent. (f)
(n) Cash received for services.	Operating	430	50	Operating	Paid telephone bill. (g)
		3,500	80	Operating	Purchased supplies. (i)
			200	Operating	Paid for insurance. (j)
			300	Investing	Purchased delivery equipment. (l)
			650	Operating	Paid wages. (m)
			150	Financing	Withdrawal by owner. (o)
			3,130		
	Bal.	370			

FIGURE 6A-2   Cash T Account for Jessie Jane's Campus Delivery with Classifications of Cash Transactions

Jessie Jane's Campus Delivery
Statement of Cash Flows
For Month Ended June 30, 20 - -

Cash flows from operating activities:			
Cash received from customers for delivery services			$1 5 0 0 00
Cash paid for wages	$ (6 5 0 00)		
Cash paid for rent	(2 0 0 00)		
Cash paid for supplies	(8 0 00)		
Cash paid for telephone	(5 0 00)		
Cash paid for insurance	(2 0 0 00)		
Total cash paid for operations		(1 1 8 0 00)	
Net cash provided by operating activities			$ 3 2 0 00
Cash flows from investing activities:			
Cash paid for delivery equipment	$(1 5 0 0 00)		
Net cash used for investing activities		(1 5 0 0 00)	
Cash flows from financing activities:			
Cash investment by owner	$2 0 0 0 00		
Cash withdrawal by owner	(1 5 0 00)		
Payment made on loan	(3 0 0 00)		
Net cash provided by financing activities		1 5 5 0 00	
Net increase in cash		$ 3 7 0 00	

FIGURE 6A-3   Statement of Cash Flows for Jessie Jane's Campus Delivery

The main body of the statement is arranged in three sections: operating, investing, and financing activities. First, cash received from customers is listed under operating activities. Then, cash payments for operating activities are listed and totaled. The net amount is reported as net cash provided by operating activities. Since this is the main purpose of the business, it is important to be able to generate positive cash flows from operating activities.

The next two sections list the inflows and outflows from investing and financing activities. Debits to the cash account are inflows and credits are outflows. Note that there was an outflow, or net use of cash, from investing activities resulting from the purchase of the motor scooters. In addition, cash was provided from financing activities because Jessie's initial investment more than covered her withdrawal and the payment on the loan. These investing and financing activities are typical for a new business.

The sum of the inflows and outflows from operating, investing, and financing activities equals the net increase (or decrease) in the cash account during the period. Since this is a new business, the cash account had a beginning balance of zero. The ending balance is $370. This agrees with the net increase in cash of $370 reported on the statement of cash flows.

LEARNING KEY: To prove the accuracy of the statement of cash flows, compare the net increase or decrease reported on the statement with the change in the balance of the cash account.

This appendix introduces you to the purpose and format of the statement of cash flows. Here, we classified entries made to the cash account as operating, investing, or financing. These classifications were then used to prepare the statement. Businesses have thousands of entries to the cash account. Thus, this approach to preparing the statement is not really practical. Other approaches to preparing the statement will be discussed in Chapter 25. However, the purpose and format of the statements are the same.

Learning Objectives	Key Points to Remember
1 **Classify business transactions as operating, investing, or financing.**	The purpose of the statement of cash flows is to report what the firm did to generate cash and how the cash was used. Business transactions are classified as operating, investing, and financing activities. *Operating activities* are those transactions related to the revenues and expenses reported on the income statement. *Investing activities* are those transactions involving the purchase and sale of long-term assets, lending money, and collecting the principal on the related loans. *Financing activities* are those transactions dealing with the exchange of cash between the business and its owners and creditors.
2 **Prepare a statement of cash flows by analyzing and categorizing a series of business transactions.**	The main body of the statement of cash flows consists of three sections: operating, investing, and financing activities.

Name of Business
Statement of Cash Flows
For Period Ended Date

Cash flows from operating activities:		
Cash received from customers		$ x x x x xx
List cash paid for various expenses	$ (x x x x xx)	
Total cash paid for operations		(x x x x xx)
Net cash provided by (used for) operating activities		$ x x x x xx
Cash flows from investing activities:		
List cash received from the sale of long-term assets and other investing activities	$ x x x x xx	
List cash paid for the purchase of long-term assets and other investing activities	(x x x x xx)	
Net cash provided by (used for) investing activities		x x x x xx
Cash flows from financing activities:		
List cash received from owners and creditors	$ x x x x xx	
List cash paid to owners and creditors	(x x x xx)	
Net cash provided by (used for) financing activities		x x x x xx
Net increase (decrease) in cash		$ x x x xx

KEY TERMS

financing activities, (211)   Those transactions dealing with the exchange of cash between the business and its owners and creditors.

investing activities, (211)   Those transactions involving the purchase and sale of long-term assets, lending money, and collecting the principal on the related loans.

operating activities, (211)   Those transactions related to the revenues and expenses reported on the income statement.

REVIEW QUESTIONS

(LO1)   1. Explain the purpose of the statement of cash flows.

(LO1)   2. Define and provide examples of the three types of business activities.

SERIES A EXERCISE

EXERCISE 6Apx-1A (LO1)

CLASSIFYING BUSINESS TRANSACTIONS Dolores Lopez opened a new consulting business. The following transactions occurred during January of the current year. Classify each transaction as an operating, investing, or financing activity.

(a) Invested cash in the business, $10,000.

(b) Paid office rent, $500.

(c) Purchased office equipment. Paid $1,500 cash and agreed to pay the balance of $2,000 in four monthly installments.

(d) Received cash for services rendered, $900.

(e) Paid telephone bill, $65.

(f) Made payment on loan in transaction (c), $500.

(g) Paid wages to part-time employee, $500.

(h) Received cash for services rendered, $800.

(i) Paid electricity bill, $85

(j) Withdrew cash for personal use, $100.

(k) Paid wages to part-time employee, $500.

SERIES A PROBLEM

PROBLEM 6Apx-2A (LO2)
Operating activities: $50;
Investing activities: ($1,500);
Financing activities: $9,400

PREPARING A STATEMENT OF CASH FLOWS Prepare a statement of cash flows based on the transactions reported in Exercise 6Apx-1A.

SERIES B EXERCISE

EXERCISE 6Apx-1B (LO1)

CLASSIFYING BUSINESS TRANSACTIONS Bob Jacobs opened an advertising agency. The following transactions occurred during January of the current year. Classify each transaction as an operating, investing, or financing activity.

(a) Invested cash in the business, $5,000.

(b) Purchased office equipment. Paid $2,500 cash and agreed to pay the balance of $2,000 in four monthly installments.

(c) Paid office rent, $400.

(d) Received cash for services rendered, $700.

(e) Paid telephone bill, $95.

(f) Received cash for services rendered, $600.

(g) Made payment on loan in transaction (b), $500.

(h) Paid wages to part-time employee, $800.

(i) Paid electricity bill, $100.

(j) Withdrew cash for personal use, $500.

(k) Paid wages to part-time employee, $600.

SERIES B PROBLEM

PROBLEM 6Apx-2B (LO2)
Operating activities: ($695);
Investing activities: ($2,500);
Financing activities: $4,000

PREPARING A STATEMENT OF CASH FLOWS Prepare a statement of cash flows based on the transactions reported in Exercise 6Apx-1B.

COMPREHENSIVE PROBLEM 1: THE ACCOUNTING CYCLE

Bob Night opened "The General's Favorite Fishing Hole." The fishing camp is open from April through September and attracts many famous college basketball coaches during the off-season. Guests typically register for one week, arriving on Sunday afternoon and returning home the following Saturday afternoon. The registration fee includes room and board, the use of fishing boats, and professional instruction in fishing techniques. The chart of accounts for the camping operations is provided below.

The General's Favorite Fishing Hole
Chart of Accounts

Assets		Revenues	
101	Cash	401	Registration Fees
142	Office Supplies		
144	Food Supplies		Expenses
145	Prepaid Insurance	511	Wages Expense
181	Fishing Boats	521	Rent Expense
181.1	Accum. Depr.—Fishing Boats	523	Office Supplies Expense
		524	Food Supplies Expense
Liabilities		525	Telephone Expense
202	Accounts Payable	533	Utilities Expense
219	Wages Payable	535	Insurance Expense
		536	Postage Expense
Owner's Equity		542	Depr. Exp.—Fishing Boats
311	Bob Night, Capital		
312	Bob Night, Drawing		
313	Income Summary		

The following transactions took place during April 20--.

Apr. 1	Night invested cash in business, $90,000.
1	Paid insurance premium for camping season, $9,000.
2	Paid rent for lodge and campgrounds for the month of April, $40,000.
2	Deposited registration fees, $35,000.
2	Purchased ten fishing boats on account for $60,000. The boats have estimated useful lives of five years, at which time they will be donated to a local day camp. Arrangements were made to pay for the boats in July.
3	Purchased food supplies from Acme Super Market on account, $7,000.
5	Purchased office supplies from Gordon Office Supplies on account, $500.
7	Deposited registration fees, $38,600.
10	Purchased food supplies from Acme Super Market on account, $8,200.
10	Paid wages to fishing guides, $10,000.
14	Deposited registration fees, $30,500.
16	Purchased food supplies from Acme Super Market on account, $9,000.
17	Paid wages to fishing guides, $10,000.
18	Paid postage, $150.
21	Deposited registration fees, $35,600.

24	Purchased food supplies from Acme Super Market on account, $8,500.
24	Paid wages to fishing guides, $10,000.
28	Deposited registration fees, $32,000.
29	Paid wages to fishing guides, $10,000.
30	Purchased food supplies from Acme Super Market on account, $6,000.
30	Paid Acme Super Market on account, $32,700.
30	Paid utilities bill, $2,000.
30	Paid telephone bill, $1,200.
30	Bob Night withdrew cash for personal use, $6,000.

Adjustment information for the end of April is provided below.

(a) Office supplies remaining on hand, $100.

(b) Food supplies remaining on hand, $8,000.

(c) Insurance expired during the month of April, $1,500.

(d) Depreciation on the fishing boats for the month of April, $1,000.

(e) Wages earned, but not yet paid, at the end of April, $500.

REQUIRED

1. Enter the transactions in a general journal. Enter transactions from April 1–5 on page 1, April 7–18 on page 2, April 21–29 and the first two entries for April 30 on page 3, and the remaining entries for April 30 on page 4.

2. Post the entries to the general ledger. (If you are not using the working papers that accompany this text, you will need to enter the account titles and account numbers in the general ledger accounts.)

3. Prepare a trial balance on a work sheet.

4. Complete the work sheet.

5. Prepare the income statement.

6. Prepare the statement of owner's equity.

7. Prepare the balance sheet.

8. Journalize the adjusting entries (page 5).

9. Post the adjusting entries to the general ledger.

10. Journalize the closing entries (pages 5 and 6).

11. Post the closing entries to the general ledger.

12. Prepare a post-closing trial balance.

COMPREHENSIVE PROBLEM 1, PERIOD 2: THE ACCOUNTING CYCLE

During the month of May 20--, The General's Favorite Fishing Hole engaged in the following transactions. These transactions required an expansion of the chart of accounts as shown below.

Assets		Revenues	
101	Cash	401	Registration Fees
122	Accounts Receivable	404	Vending Revenue
142	Office Supplies		
144	Food Supplies	Expenses	
145	Prepaid Insurance	511	Wages Expense
146	Prepaid Subscriptions	512	Advertising Expense
161	Land	521	Rent Expense
171	Building	523	Office Supplies Expense
171.1	Accum. Depr.—Buildings	524	Food Supplies Expense
181	Fishing Boats	525	Telephone Expense
181.1	Accum. Depr.—Fishing Boats	533	Utilities Expense
182	Surround Sound System	535	Insurance Expense
182.1	Accum. Depr.—Surround Sound Sys.	536	Postage Expense
183	Big Screen TV	537	Repair Expense
183.1	Accum. Depr.—Big Screen TV	540	Depr. Exp.—Buildings
		541	Depr. Exp.—Surround Sound Sys.
Liabilities		542	Depr. Exp.—Fishing Boats
202	Accounts Payable	543	Depr. Exp.—Big Screen TV
219	Wages Payable	546	Satellite Programming Exp.
		548	Subscriptions Expense
Owner's Equity			
311	Bob Night, Capital		
312	Bob Night, Drawing		
313	Income Summary		

May 1 In order to provide snacks for guests on a 24-hour basis, Night signed a contract with Snack Attack. Snack Attack will install vending machines with food and drinks and pay a 10% commission on all sales. Estimated payments are made at the beginning of each month. Night received a check for $200, the estimated commission on sales for May.

2 Night purchased a surround sound system and big screen TV with a Digital Satellite System for the guest lounge. The surround sound system cost $3,600 and has an estimated useful life of five years and no salvage value. The TV cost $8,000, has an estimated useful life of eight years, and a salvage value of $800. Night paid cash for both items.

2 Paid for May's programming on the new Digital Satellite System, $125.

3 Night's office manager returned $100 worth of office supplies to Gordon Office Supply. Night received a $100 reduction on the account.

3 Deposited registration fees, $52,700.

3 Paid rent for lodge and campgrounds for the month of May, $40,000.

3 In preparation for the purchase of a nearby campground, Night invested an additional $600,000.

4 Paid Gordon Office Supply on account, $400.

4   Purchased the assets of a competing business and paid cash for the following: land, $100,000; lodge, $530,000; and fishing boats, $9,000. The lodge has a remaining useful life of 50 years and a $50,000 salvage value. The boats have remaining lives of 5 years and no salvage value.

5   Paid May's insurance premium for the new camp, $1,000.

5   Purchased food supplies from Acme Super Market on account, $22,950.

5   Purchased office supplies from Gordon Office Supplies on account, $1,200.

7   Night paid $40 each for one-year subscriptions to Fishing Illustrated, Fishing Unlimited, and Fish Master.

10   Deposited registration fees, $62,750.

13   Paid wages to fishing guides, $30,000.

14   A guest became ill and was unable to stay for the entire week. A refund was issued in the amount of $1,000.

17   Deposited registration fees, $63,000.

19   Purchased food supplies from Acme Super Market on account, $18,400.

21   Deposited registration fees, $63,400.

23   Paid $2,500 for advertising spots on National Sports Talk Radio.

25   Paid repair fee for damaged boat, $850.

27   Paid wages to fishing guides, $30,000.

28   Paid $1,800 for advertising spots on billboards.

29   Purchased food supplies from Acme Super Market on account, $14,325.

30   Paid utilities bill, $3,300.

30   Paid telephone bill, $1,800.

30   Paid Acme Super Market on account, $47,350.

31   Bob Night withdrew cash for personal use, $7,500.

Adjustment information at the end of May is provided below.

(a) Total vending machine sales were $2,300 for the month of May.

(b) Straight-line depreciation is used for the ten boats purchased on April 2 for $60,000. The useful life for these assets is five years and there is no salvage value. A full month's depreciation was taken in April on these boats.

(c) Straight-line depreciation is used for the two boats purchased in May.

(d) Straight-line depreciation is used to depreciate the surround sound system.

(e) Straight-line depreciation is used to depreciate the big screen TV.

(f) Straight-line depreciation is used for the building purchased in May.

(g) On April 2 Night paid $9,000 for insurance during the six-month camping season. May's portion of this premium was used up during this month.

(h) Night received his May issues of Fishing Illustrated, Fishing Unlimited, and Fish Master.

(i) Office supplies remaining on hand, $150.

(j)   Food supplies remaining on hand, $5,925.

(k)   Wages earned, but not yet paid, at the end of May, $6,000.

REQUIRED

1. Enter the transactions in a general journal. Enter transactions from May 1–4 on page 5, May 5–28 on page 6, and the remaining entries on page 7.

2. Post the entries to the general ledger. (If you are not using the working papers that accompany this text, you will need to enter the account titles and account numbers in the general ledger accounts.)

3. Prepare a trial balance on a work sheet.

4. Complete the work sheet.

5. Prepare the income statement.

6. Prepare the statement of owner's equity.

7. Prepare the balance sheet.

8. Journalize the adjusting entries on page 8 of the general journal.

9. Post the adjusting entries to the general ledger.

10. Journalize the closing entries on page 9 of the general journal.

11. Post the closing entries to the general ledger.

12. Prepare a post-closing trial balance.

Accounting for Cash, Payroll and Service Businesses

©GETTY IMAGES/PHOTODISC

DIGITAL IMAGING GROUP

Accounting for Cash

Evan Taylor recently opened his own retail business called Parkway Pet Supplies. To protect and properly manage cash, Evan uses a checking account. All cash and checks received from customers are deposited promptly. All bills are paid by check. In this way, Evan can use the deposit slips and monthly bank statement to verify his records of cash received. Similarly, canceled checks and the monthly bank statement can be used to verify Evan's records of cash payments. Complete and accurate records of cash receipts and cash payments help Evan control this important asset and plan for future cash needs.

At the end of the month, the balance in the cash account in the store's books differs from the cash balance shown on the bank statement. In trying to reconcile the two amounts, how should Evan treat the checks he wrote during the month that have not yet been presented to the bank for payment?

Careful study of this chapter should enable you to:

LO1 Describe how to open and use a checking account.

LO2 Prepare a bank reconciliation and related journal entries.

LO3 Establish and use a petty cash fund.

LO4 Establish a change fund and use the cash short and over account.

Cash is an asset that is quite familiar and important to all of us. We generally think of **cash** as the currency and coins in our pockets and the money we have in our checking accounts. To a business, cash also includes checks received from customers, money orders, and bank cashier's checks.

Because it plays such a central role in operating a business, cash must be carefully managed and controlled. A business should have a system of **internal control**—a set of procedures designed to ensure proper accounting for transactions. For good internal control of cash transactions, all cash received should be deposited daily in a bank. All disbursements, except for payments from petty cash, should be made by check.

CHECKING ACCOUNT

LO1 Describe how to open and use a checking account.

The key documents and forms required in opening and using a checking account are the signature card, deposit tickets, checks, and bank statements.

Opening a Checking Account

To open a checking account, each person authorized to sign checks must complete and sign a **signature card** (Figure 7-1). The bank uses this card to verify the depositor's signature on any banking transactions. The taxpayer identification number (TIN) is the depositor's social security number or employer identification number (EIN). This number is shown on the card to identify the depositor for income tax purposes. An EIN can be obtained from the Internal Revenue Service.

Making Deposits

A **deposit ticket** (Figure 7-2) is a form showing a detailed listing of items being deposited. Currency, coins, and checks are listed separately. Each check should be identified by its **ABA (American Bankers Association) Number**. This number is the small fraction printed in the upper right-hand corner of each check (Figure 7-5). The number also appears in **magnetic ink character recognition (MICR) code** on the lower left side of the front of each check. The code is used to sort and route checks throughout the U.S. banking system. Normally, only the numerator of the fraction is used in identifying checks on the deposit ticket.

The depositor delivers or mails the deposit ticket and all items being deposited to the bank. The bank then gives or mails a receipt to the depositor.

Endorsements. Each check being deposited must be endorsed by the depositor. The **endorsement** consists of stamping or writing the depositor's name and sometimes other information on the back of the check, in the space provided near the left end. There are two basic types of endorsements:

1. **Blank endorsement**—the depositor simply signs the back of the check. This makes the check payable to any bearer.

2. **Restrictive endorsement**—the depositor adds words such as "For deposit," "Pay to any bank," or "Pay to Daryl Beck only" to restrict the payment of the check.

ACCOUNT OWNER NAME & ADDRESS

ACCOUNT NUMBER

Number of signatures required for withdrawal _____   ☐ This is a temporary account agreement.

SIGNATURE(S) - THE UNDERSIGNED AGREE(S) TO THE TERMS STATED ON PAGES 1 AND 2 OF THIS FORM, AND ACKNOWLEDGE(S) RECEIPT OF A COMPLETED COPY ON TODAY'S DATE. THE UNDERSIGNED ALSO ACKNOWLEDGE(S) RECEIPT OF A COPY OF AND AGREE(S) TO THE TERMS OF THE FOLLOWING DISCLOSURE(S):

☐ Funds Availability Disclosure   ☐ Truth-In-Savings Disclosure

☐ Electronic Funds Transfer Disclosure   ☐ _____

Signature(s)   Identifying Info.

(1) _____

(2) _____

(3) _____

(4) _____

☐ AUTHORIZED SIGNER (name) _____
   Individual Accounts Only

X _____

ADDITIONAL INFORMATION:

BACKUP WITHHOLDING CERTIFICATIONS

TIN: _____

☐ TAXPAYER I.D. NUMBER - The Taxpayer Identification Number shown above (TIN) is my correct taxpayer identification number.

☐ BACKUP WITHHOLDING - I am not subject to backup withholding either because I have not been notified that I am subject to backup withholding as a result of a failure to report all interest or dividends, or the Internal Revenue Service has notified me that I am no longer subject to backup withholding.

☐ EXEMPT RECIPIENTS - I am an exempt recipient under the Internal Revenue Service Regulations.

SIGNATURE - I certify under penalties of perjury the statements checked in this section.

X _____
                                                              (Date)

© 1983, 1988, 1990, 1991 Bankers Systems, Inc., St. Cloud, MN Form MPSC-KS 3/15/99   ♻   (page 1 of 2)

FIGURE 7-1 Signature Card

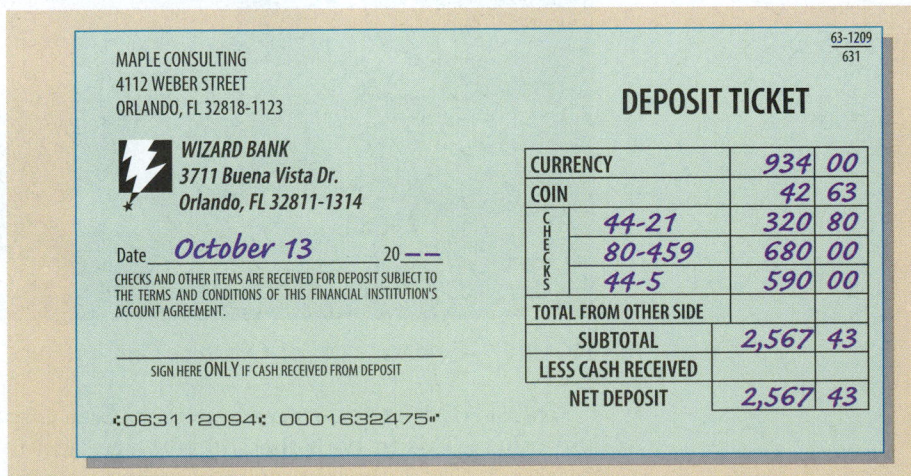

FIGURE 7-2 Deposit Ticket

Businesses commonly use a rubber stamp to endorse checks for deposit. The check shown in Figure 7-3 has been stamped with a restrictive endorsement.

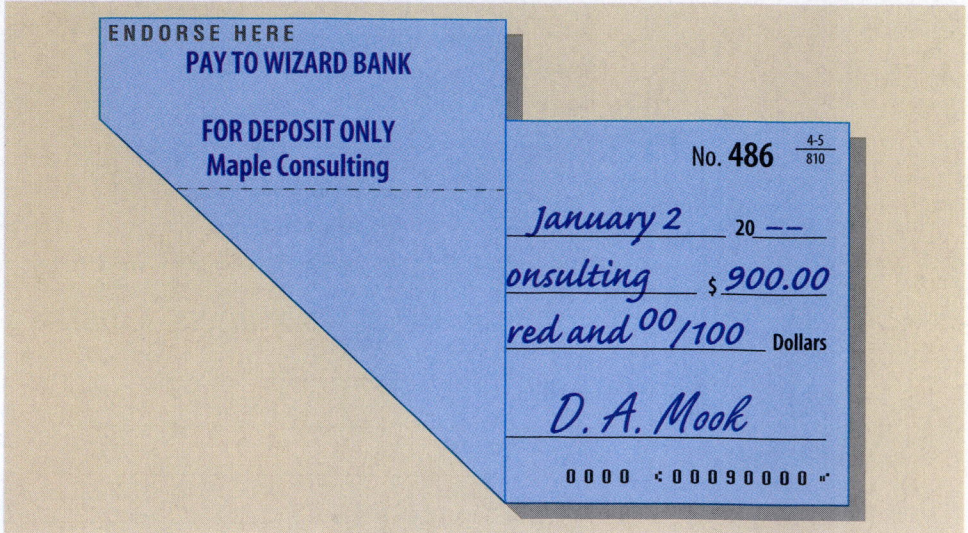

FIGURE 7-3   Restrictive Endorsement

Automated Teller Machines. Most banks now make **automated teller machines (ATMs)** available at all times to depositors for making deposits or withdrawals. Each depositor has a plastic card (Figure 7-4) and a personal identification number (PIN). The depositor inserts the card, keys in the PIN, indicates whether the transaction is a withdrawal or a deposit, and enters the amount. The machine has a drawer or door for the withdrawal or deposit.

FIGURE 7-4   Automated Teller Machine Card

Most ATMs are now on a system such as Cirrus that allows noncustomers to use other ATMs in both the United States and foreign countries. There are also "cash machines" that supply only cash and do not take deposits. These are often found at airports and convenience stores.

It is important for the depositor to keep an accounting record of ATM withdrawals and deposits. This is done on the check stub or register described in the following section, and with an appropriate journal entry.

Writing Checks

A **check** is a document ordering a bank to pay cash from a depositor's account. There are three parties to every check:

1. **Drawer**—the depositor who orders the bank to pay the cash.

2. **Drawee**—the bank on which the check is drawn.

3. **Payee**—the person being paid the cash.

Checks used by businesses are usually bound in the form of a book. In some checkbooks, each check is attached to a **check stub** (Figure 7-5) that contains space to record all relevant information about the check. Other checkbooks are accompanied by a small register book in which the relevant information is noted. If a financial computer software package is used, both the check and the register can be prepared electronically.

Use the following three steps in preparing a check.

STEP 1   Complete the check stub or register.

STEP 2   Enter the date, payee name, and amount on the check.

STEP 3   Sign the check.

The check stub is completed first so that the drawer retains a record of each check issued. This information is needed to determine the proper journal entry for the transaction.

The payee name is entered on the first long line on the check, followed by the amount in figures. The amount in words is then entered on the second long line. If the amount in figures does not agree with the amount in words, the bank usually contacts the drawer for the correct amount or returns the check unpaid.

The most critical point in preparing a check is signing it, and this should be done last. The signature authorizes the bank to pay cash from the drawer's account. The check signer should make sure that all other aspects of the check are correct before signing it.

LEARNING KEY: The check should not be signed until the check signer has verified that all aspects of the check are correct.

Note that the check stubs in Figure 7-5 contain space to record amounts deposited. It generally is a good idea also to indicate the date of the deposit, as shown on check stub No. 108.

The payee and amount written in words should be followed by something, such as a line, to make it difficult to alter the payee or the amount.

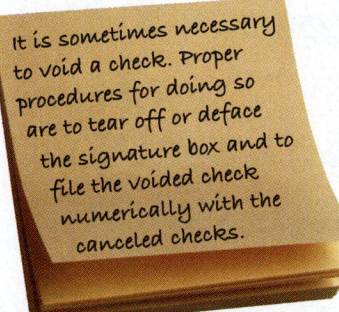

It is sometimes necessary to void a check. Proper procedures for doing so are to tear off or deface the signature box and to file the voided check numerically with the canceled checks.

PROFILES IN ACCOUNTING

Lisa Davis, Legal Coordinator

Lisa Davis began working as a part-time legal secretary with Zegarelli Associates. Lisa continued her career with this company after earning an Associate Degree in Legal Office Management.

After graduation, Lisa was hired as a legal assistant and later promoted to legal coordinator. Her duties include budgeting, accounts receivable, supervising two employees, coordinating schedules, researching, and dealing with clients on a daily basis.

According to Lisa, dependability, initiative, and loyalty lead to success. Lisa chose the legal field because she always had an interest in law and wanted to work in a fast-paced environment.

No. 107

DATE *April 3* 20 — —
TO *Linclay Corp.*
FOR *April Rent*

ACCT. *Rent Expense*

	DOLLARS	CENTS
BAL BRO'T FOR'D	3,625	41
AMT. DEPOSITED		
TOTAL		
AMT. THIS CHECK	300	00
BAL CAR'D FOR'D	3,325	41

MAPLE CONSULTING
4112 WEBER STREET
ORLANDO, FL 32818-1123

No. 107 63-1209/631

April 3 20 — —

PAY TO THE ORDER OF *Linclay Corporation* ———— $ *300.00*

Three Hundred 00/100 ———— Dollars

⚡ **WIZARD BANK**
3711 Buena Vista Dr.
Orlando, FL 32811-1314

FOR CLASSROOM USE ONLY

MEMO _____   BY *James Maple*

⑆063112094⑆ 0001632475⑈

No. 108

DATE *April 4* 20 — —
TO *Continental Mfg. Co.*
FOR *Inv. March 31*

ACCT. *Accounts Payable*

	DOLLARS	CENTS
BAL BRO'T FOR'D	3,325	41
AMT. DEPOSITED	1,694	20
4/4 TOTAL	5,019	61
AMT. THIS CHECK	1,478	18
BAL CAR'D FOR'D	3,541	43

MAPLE CONSULTING
4112 WEBER STREET
ORLANDO, FL 32818-1123

No. 108 63-1209/631

April 4 20 — —

PAY TO THE ORDER OF *Continental Mfg. Co.* ———— $ *1,478.18*

One Thousand Four Hundred Seventy-Eight 18/100 Dollars

⚡ **WIZARD BANK**
3711 Buena Vista Dr.
Orlando, FL 32811-1314

FOR CLASSROOM USE ONLY

MEMO _____   BY *James Maple*

⑆063112094⑆ 0001632475⑈

FIGURE 7-5 Checks and Check Stubs

Bank Statement

A statement of account issued by a bank to each depositor once a month is called a **bank statement**. Figure 7-6 is a bank statement for a checking account. The statement shows:

1. The balance at the beginning of the period.

2. Deposits and other amounts added during the period.

3. Checks and other amounts subtracted during the period.

4. The balance at the end of the period.

With the bank statement, the bank normally sends to the depositor:

1. **Canceled checks**—the depositor's checks paid by the bank during the period. The bank may send the checks themselves, "imaged" sheets showing only the faces of the checks, or simply a listing of the checks on the bank statement.

2. Any other forms representing items added to or subtracted from the account.

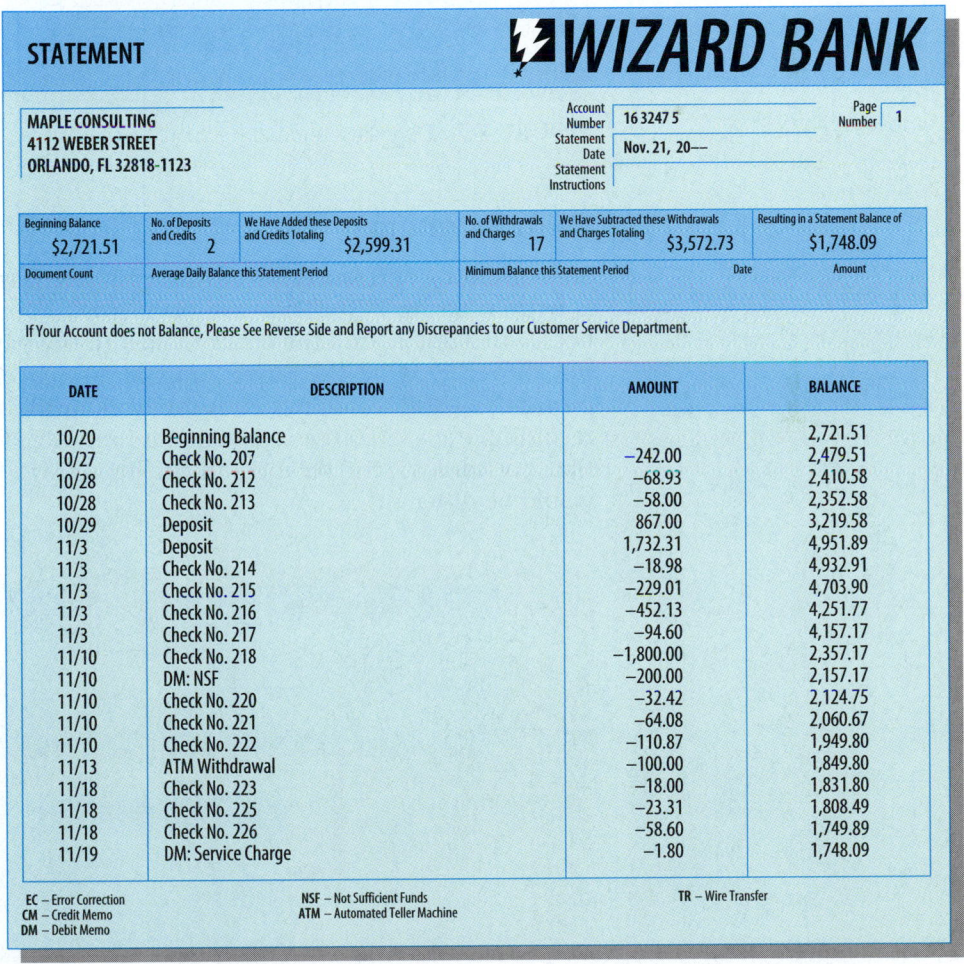

FIGURE 7-6   Bank Statement

RECONCILING THE BANK STATEMENT

LO2 Prepare a bank reconciliation and related journal entries.

On any given day, the balance in the cash account on the depositor's books (the book balance) is unlikely to be the same as that on the bank's books (the bank balance). This difference can be due to errors, but it usually is caused by timing. Transactions generally are recorded by the business at a time that is different from when the bank records them.

Deposits

Suppose there are cash receipts of $600.00 on April 30. These cash receipts would be recorded on the depositor's books on April 30 and a deposit of $600.00 would be sent to the bank. The deposit would not reach the bank, however, until at least the following day, May 1. This timing difference in recording the $600.00 of cash receipts is illustrated in Figure 7-7. Notice that on April 30, the balances in the depositor's books and in the bank's books would be different.

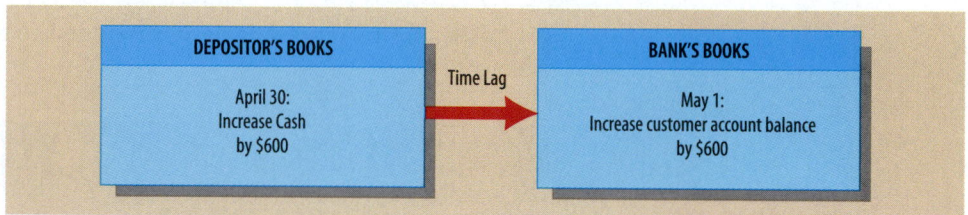

FIGURE 7-7 Depositor and Bank Records—Deposits

Cash Payments

Similar timing differences occur with cash payments. Suppose a check for $350.00 is written on April 30. This cash payment would be recorded on the depositor's books on April 30 and the check mailed to the payee. The check probably would not be received by the payee until May 3. If the payee deposited the check promptly, it still would not clear the bank until May 4. This timing difference in recording the $350.00 cash payment is illustrated in Figure 7-8. Notice once again that on April 30, the balances in the depositor's books and in the bank's books would be different.

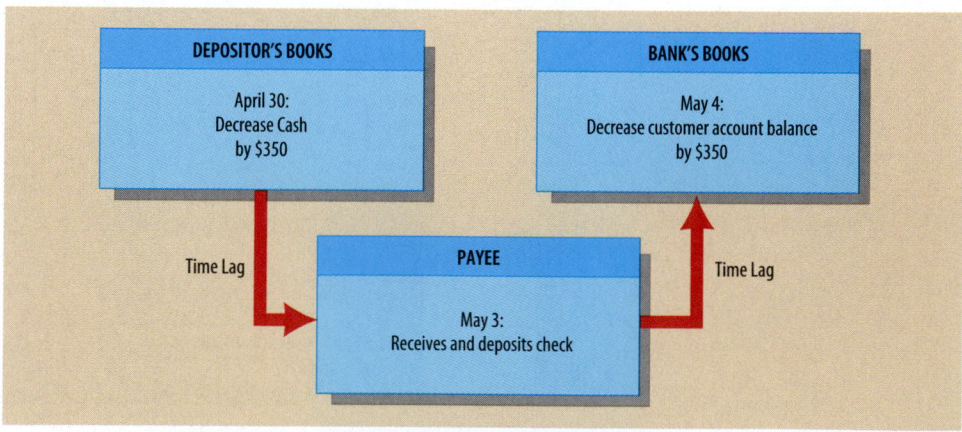

FIGURE 7-8 Depositor and Bank Records—Cash Payments

Reasons for Differences Between Bank and Book Balances

When the bank statement is received, the depositor examines the records to identify the items that explain the difference between the book and bank balances. This process of bringing the book and bank balances into agreement is called preparing a **bank reconciliation**.

The most common reasons for differences between the book and bank balances are the following:

1. **Outstanding checks.** Checks issued that have not been presented to the bank for payment before the statement is prepared.

2. **Deposits in transit.** Deposits that have not reached or been recorded by the bank before the statement is prepared.

3. **Service charges.** Bank charges for services such as check printing and processing.

4. **Collections.** Collections of promissory notes or charge accounts made by the bank on behalf of the depositor.

5. **Not sufficient funds (NSF) checks.** Checks deposited by the depositor that are not paid because the drawer did not have sufficient funds.

6. **Errors.** Errors made by the bank or the depositor in recording cash transactions.

Steps in Preparing the Bank Reconciliation

Use the following three steps in preparing the bank reconciliation.

STEP 1   Identify deposits in transit and any related errors.

STEP 2   Identify outstanding checks and any related errors.

STEP 3   Identify additional reconciling items.

Deposits in Transit and Related Errors. Follow these steps:

STEP 1   Compare deposits listed on the bank statement with deposits in transit on last month's bank reconciliation. All of last month's deposits in transit should appear on the current month's bank statement.

STEP 2   Compare the remaining deposits on the bank statement with deposits listed in the accounting records. Any deposits listed in the accounting records but not on the bank statement are deposits in transit on the current bank reconciliation.

STEP 3   Compare the individual deposit amounts on the bank statement and in the accounting records. If they differ, the error needs to be corrected.

Outstanding Checks and Related Errors. Follow these steps:

STEP 1   Compare canceled checks with the bank statement and the accounting records. If the amounts differ, the error needs to be corrected.

STEP 2   As each canceled check is compared with the accounting records, place a check mark on the check stub or other accounting record to indicate that the check has cleared.

STEP 3   Any checks written that have not been checked off represent outstanding checks on the bank reconciliation. This includes outstanding checks from last month's bank reconciliation that have not yet cleared.

Additional Reconciling Items. Compare any additions and deductions on the bank statement that are not deposits or checks with the accounting records. Items that the bank adds to the account are called **credit memos**. Items that the bank deducts from the account are called **debit memos**. Remember that a depositor's account is a liability to the bank. Thus, a credit memo increases this liability; a debit memo reduces the liability. Any of these items not appearing in the accounting records represent additional items on the bank reconciliation.

Illustration of a Bank Reconciliation

A general format for the bank reconciliation is shown in Figure 7-9. Not every item shown in this illustration would be in every bank reconciliation, but this format is helpful in determining where to put items. A bank reconciliation form also can be found on the back of most bank statements.

BANK RECONCILIATION		
Bank statement balance		$xxxx
Add: Deposits in transit	$xxxx	
Bank errors	xxxx	xxxx
		$xxxx
Deduct: Outstanding checks	$xxxx	
Bank errors	xxxx	xxxx
Adjusted bank balance		$xxxx
Book balance		$xxxx
Add: Bank credit memos	$xxxx	
Book errors	xxxx	xxxx
		$xxxx
Deduct: Bank debit memos	$xxxx	
Book errors	xxxx	xxxx
Adjusted book balance		$xxxx

FIGURE 7-9 Bank Reconciliation Format

To illustrate the preparation of a bank reconciliation, we will use the Maple Consulting bank statement shown in Figure 7-6. That statement shows a balance of $1,748.09 as of November 21. The balance in Maple's check stubs and general ledger cash account is $2,393.23. The three steps described on page 233 were used to identify the following items, and the reconciliation in Figure 7-10 was prepared.

1. A deposit of $637.02 recorded on November 21 had not been received by the bank. Maple has received the funds but the amount has not yet been counted by the bank. This deposit in transit is added to the bank statement balance.

2. Check numbers 219, 224, and 227 are outstanding. The funds have been disbursed by Maple but have not yet been paid out by the bank. The amount of these outstanding checks is subtracted from the bank statement balance.

3. Check number 214 was written for $18.98, but was entered on the check stub and on the books as $19.88. This $.90 error is added to the book balance because $.90 too much had been deducted from the book balance.

4. Maple made an ATM withdrawal of $100.00 on November 13 for personal use but did not record the withdrawal on the books. The bank has reduced Maple's balance by this amount. Thus, this amount is deducted from the book balance.

5. The bank returned an NSF check of $200.00. This was a check received by Maple from a customer. The bank has reduced Maple's balance by $200.00 but Maple has not yet recorded it. This amount is deducted from the book balance.

6. The bank service charge was $1.80. The bank has reduced Maple's balance by this amount but Maple has not yet recorded it. This amount is deducted from the book balance.

Maple Consulting Bank Reconciliation November 21, 20 - -				
Bank statement balance, November 21			$1 7 4 8 09	
Add deposit in transit			6 3 7 02	
			$2 3 8 5 11	
Deduct outstanding checks:				
No. 219	$ 2 0 0 00			
No. 224	2 5 00			
No. 227	6 7 78	2 9 2 78		
Adjusted bank balance			$2 0 9 2 33	←
Book balance, November 21			$2 3 9 3 23	
Add error on check no. 214			90	
			$2 3 9 4 13	Reconciled balances
Deduct:				
Unrecorded ATM withdrawal	$ 1 0 0 00			
NSF check	2 0 0 00			
Bank service charge	1 80	3 0 1 80		
Adjusted book balance			$2 0 9 2 33	←

Requires journal entry → (Add error on check no. 214)

Require journal entries → (Unrecorded ATM withdrawal, NSF check, Bank service charge)

FIGURE 7-10 Bank Reconciliation

Journal Entries

Only two kinds of items appearing on a bank reconciliation require journal entries:

1. Errors in the books.

2. Bank additions and deductions that do not already appear in the books.

LEARNING KEY: Journal entries are needed to correct errors in the books and to record bank additions and deductions that are not in the books.

A BROADER VIEW

Fraud—A Real Threat to Small Business

The bookkeeper for Kramer Iron, Inc., in Hamden, Connecticut, embezzled $213,539 from the company over a four-year period. She used two schemes. One was to alter the number of the dollar amount printed on checks payable to her. The other technique involved putting her own name on the "pay to" line on checks intended for other parties.

This fraud shows the importance of two procedures described in this chapter: (1) Make sure that all aspects of a check are correct before signing it. (2) In preparing the bank reconciliation, compare canceled checks with the accounting records.

Figure 7-11 contains a detailed list of items that require journal entries.

ADDITIONS TO CASH BALANCE	DEDUCTIONS FROM CASH BALANCE

* Unrecorded deposits (including ATM)
* Note collected by bank
* Interest earned
* Errors:
  1. Added too little as a deposit
  2. Deducted too much as a check
	* Unrecorded ATM withdrawals
	* NSF checks
	* Bank service charges
	* Deposits recorded twice
	* Unrecorded checks
	* Loan payments
	* Interest payments
	* Errors:
	  1. Added too much as a deposit
	  2. Deducted too little as a check

FIGURE 7-11   Bank Reconciliation Items that Require Journal Entries

Note the four items in the lower portion of the bank reconciliation in Figure 7-10. A journal entry always is required for each item in this book balance portion of the bank reconciliation.

The $.90 item is an error in the accounting records that occurred when the check amount was incorrectly entered. Assume the $18.98 was in payment of an account payable which had been incorrectly debited for $19.88. The entry to correct this error is:

4		Cash			90		4
5		Accounts Payable				90	5
6		Error in recording check					6

The $100.00 ATM withdrawal has been deducted from Maple's account by the bank. Maple has not yet recorded the withdrawal. Maple withdrew the funds for personal use, so the following journal entry is required.

8		James Maple, Drawing			1	0	0	00								8
9		Cash									1	0	0	00		9
10		Unrecorded ATM withdrawal														10

The \$200.00 NSF check is a deduction by the bank for a check deposited by Maple that proved to be worthless. This amount must be deducted from the book balance. Assuming the \$200.00 was received from a customer on account, the following journal entry is required.

12		Accounts Receivable			2	0	0	00								12
13		Cash									2	0	0	00		13
14		Unrecorded NSF check														14

The \$1.80 bank service charge is a fee for bank services received by Maple. The bank has deducted this amount from Maple's account. Bank service charges are usually small and are charged to Miscellaneous Expense.

16		Miscellaneous Expense					1	80								16
17		Cash											1	80		17
18		Bank service charge														18

Electronic Funds Transfer

Electronic funds transfer (EFT) uses a computer rather than paper checks to complete transactions with the bank. This technique is being used increasingly today. Applications of EFT include payrolls, social security payments, retail purchases, mortgage payments, and the ATM transactions described earlier in the chapter.

Heavy use of EFT can present a challenge in preparing bank reconciliations. Many of the documents handled in a purely manual environment disappear when EFT is used. Bank accounts are just one of many areas where computers require accountants to think in new ways. Regardless of what system is used, the key point to remember is that the accounting records must be correctly updated.

THE PETTY CASH FUND

LO3 Establish and use a petty cash fund.

For good control over cash, payments generally should be made by check. Unfortunately, payments of very small amounts by check can be both inconvenient and inefficient. For example, the time and cost required to write a check for \$.70 to mail a letter might be greater than the cost of the postage. Therefore, businesses customarily establish a **petty cash fund** to pay for small items with cash. "Petty" means small, and both the amount of the fund and the maximum amount of any bill that can be paid from the fund are small.

Establishing a Petty Cash Fund

To establish a petty cash fund, a check is written to the petty cash custodian for the amount to be set aside in the fund. The amount may be \$50.00, \$100.00, \$200.00, or any amount considered necessary. The journal entry to establish a petty cash fund of \$100.00 would be as follows:

4		Petty Cash			1	0	0	00								4
5		Cash									1	0	0	00		5
6		Establish petty cash fund														6

Petty Cash is an asset that is listed immediately below Cash on the balance sheet.

The custodian cashes the check and places the money in a petty cash box. For good control, the custodian should be the only person authorized to make payments from the fund. The custodian should be able to account for the full amount of the fund at any time.

Making Payments from a Petty Cash Fund

A receipt called a **petty cash voucher** (Figure 7-12) should be prepared for every payment from the fund. The voucher shows the name of the payee, the purpose of the payment, and the account to be charged for the payment. Each voucher should be signed by the custodian and by the person receiving the cash. The vouchers should be numbered consecutively so that all vouchers can be accounted for.

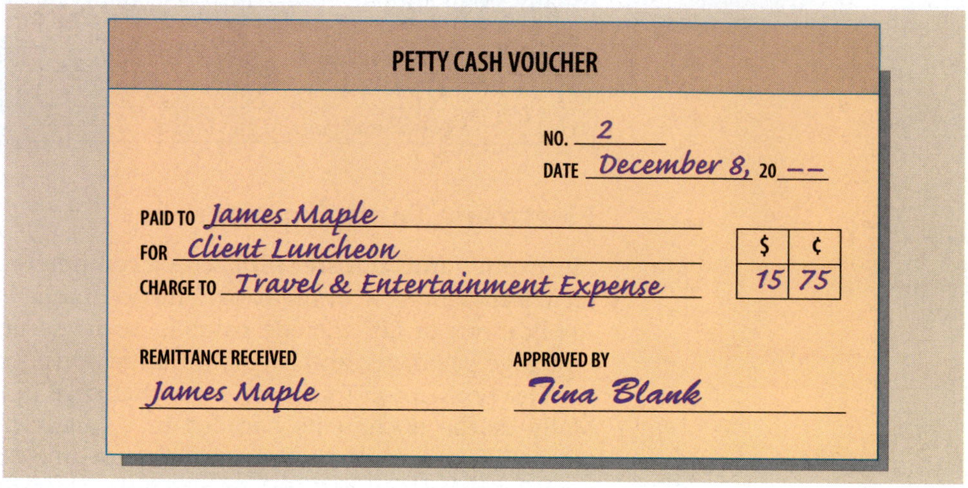

PETTY CASH VOUCHER

NO. 2
DATE December 8, 20 —

PAID TO James Maple
FOR Client Luncheon
CHARGE TO Travel & Entertainment Expense — $ 15 ¢ 75

REMITTANCE RECEIVED
James Maple

APPROVED BY
Tina Blank

FIGURE 7-12   Petty Cash Voucher

Petty Cash Payments Record

When a petty cash fund is maintained, a formal record is often kept of all payments from the fund. The **petty cash payments record** (Figure 7-13) is a special multi-column record that supplements the regular accounting records. It is not a journal. The headings of the Distribution of Payments columns may vary, depending upon the types of expenditures.

The petty cash payments record of Maple Consulting is shown in Figure 7-13. A narrative of the petty cash transactions shown in Figure 7-13 is as follows:

Dec. 1   Maple issued a check for $200.00 payable to Tina Blank, Petty Cash Custodian. Blank cashed the check and placed the money in a secure cash box.

A notation of the amount received is made in the Description column of the petty cash payments record. In addition, this transaction is entered in the journal as follows:

8	Dec. 1	Petty Cash		2 0 0 00		8
9		Cash			2 0 0 00	9
10		Establish petty cash fund				10

During the month of December, the following payments were made from the petty cash fund.

Dec. 5   Paid $32.80 to Jerry's Auto for servicing the company automobile. Voucher No. 1.

8   Reimbursed Maple $15.75 for the amount spent for lunch with a client. Voucher No. 2.

9   Gave Maple $30.00 for personal use. Voucher No. 3.

There is no special Distribution column for entering amounts withdrawn by the owner for personal use. Therefore this payment is entered by writing the account name in the Account column and $30.00 in the Amount column at the extreme right of the petty cash payments record.

15   Paid $38.25 for printer repairs. Voucher No. 4.

17   Reimbursed Maple $14.50 for travel expenses. Voucher No. 5.

19   Paid $8.00 to Big Red Car Care for washing the company automobile. Voucher No. 6.

22   Paid $9.50 for mailing a package. Voucher No. 7.

29   Paid $30.00 for postage stamps. Voucher No. 8.

Replenishing the Petty Cash Fund

The petty cash fund should be replenished whenever the fund runs low and at the end of each accounting period, so that the accounts are brought up to date. The amount columns of the petty cash payments record are totaled to verify that the total of the Total Amount column equals the total of the Distribution columns. The amount columns are then ruled as shown in Figure 7-13.

The information in the petty cash payments record is then used to replenish the petty cash fund. On December 31, a check for $178.80 is issued to the petty cash custodian. The journal entry to record the replenishment of the fund is as follows:

18	Dec.	31	Automobile Expense				4	0	80							18
19			Postage Expense				3	9	50							19
20			Travel and Entertainment Expense				3	0	25							20
21			Miscellaneous Expense				3	8	25							21
22			James Maple, Drawing				3	0	00							22
23			Cash							1	7	8	80			23
24			Replenishment of petty cash fund													24

Note two important aspects of the functioning of a petty cash fund:

1. Once the fund is established by debiting Petty Cash and crediting Cash, no further entries are made to Petty Cash. Notice in the journal entry to replenish the fund that the debits are to appropriate expense accounts and the credit is to Cash. Only if the amount of the fund itself is being changed would there be a debit or credit to Petty Cash.

2. The petty cash payments record is strictly a supplement to the regular accounting records. Because it is not a journal, no posting is done from this record. A separate entry must be made in the journal to replenish the fund and update the expense accounts.

FIGURE 7-13   Maple Consulting's Petty Cash Payments Record

PETTY CASH PAYMENTS FOR THE MONTH OF December 20—

PAGE 1

DAY		DESCRIPTION	VOU. NO.	TOTAL AMOUNT	DISTRIBUTION OF PAYMENTS					
					AUTO EXP.	POST. EXP.	TRAVEL/ ENTERT. EXP.	MISC. EXP.	ACCOUNT	AMOUNT
1	1	Received in fund 200.00								
2	5	Automobile repairs	1	32 80	32 80					
3	8	Client luncheon	2	15 75			15 75			
4	9	James Maple, personal use	3	30 00					James Maple, Drawing	30 00
5	15	Printer repairs	4	38 25				38 25		
6	17	Traveling expenses	5	14 50			14 50			
7	19	Washing automobile	6	8 00	8 00					
8	22	Postage expense	7	9 50		9 50				
9	29	Postage stamps	8	30 00		30 00				
10				178 80	40 80	39 50	30 25	38 25		30 00
11	31	Balance 21.20								
12	31	Replenished fund 178.80								
13		Total 200.00								
14										
15										
16										
17										
18										
19										
20										
21										
22										
23										
24										
25										
26										
27										
28										

Debits to replenish petty cash fund

Credit to replenish petty cash fund

THE CHANGE FUND AND CASH SHORT AND OVER

LO4 Establish a change fund and use the cash short and over account.

Businesses generally must be able to make change when customers use cash to pay for goods or services received. To do so, generally it is a good idea to establish a **change fund**. A change fund is a supply of currency and coins kept in a cash register or cash drawer for use in handling cash sales.

Establishing and Operating the Change Fund

The journal entries for establishing and maintaining a change fund are very similar to the ones just used for petty cash. To establish a change fund of $200.00 on June 1, the following entry would be made.

8	June 1	Change Fund		2 0 0 00		8
9		Cash			2 0 0 00	9
10		Establish change fund				10

At the end of the day, cash received during the day is deposited, but the change fund is held back for use the following business day. For example, if cash sales of $1,250.00 were made on June 3, the cash drawer would contain $1,450.00, as follows:

Change fund	$ 200.00
Cash sales	1,250.00
Total cash on hand	$1,450.00

The $1,250 would be deposited in the bank and the following journal entry would be made.

12	June 3	Cash		1 2 5 0 00		12
13		Sales			1 2 5 0 00	13
14		Cash Sales				14

Notice the additional similarity between the change fund and the petty cash fund. Once the change fund is established by a debit to Change Fund and a credit to Cash, no further entries are made to the change fund. Only if the amount of the change fund itself is being changed would there be a debit or credit to Change Fund.

Cash Short and Over

An unavoidable part of the change-making process is that errors can occur. It is important to know whether such errors have occurred and how to account for them.

Businesses commonly use cash registers with tapes that accumulate a record of the day's receipts. The amount of cash according to the tapes plus the amount of the change fund can be compared with the amount of cash in the register to determine any error. For example, assume a cash shortage is identified for June 19.

Change fund	$ 200.00
Receipts per register tapes	963.00
Total	1,163.00
Cash count	1,161.00
Cash shortage	$ 2.00

Similarly, assume a cash overage is identified for June 20.

Change fund	$ 200.00
Receipts per register tapes	814.00
Total	1,014.00
Cash count	1,015.00
Cash overage	$ 1.00

We account for such errors by using an account called Cash Short and Over. In T account form, Cash Short and Over appears as follows:

Cash Short and Over

Shortage (Expense)	Overage (Revenue)

The register tapes on June 19 showed receipts of $963.00 and the change fund was $200.00, but only $1,161.00 in cash was counted. The journal entry on June 19 to record the revenues and cash shortage (remember that we hold back the change fund) would be:

18	June	19	Cash			9 6 1 00			18
19			Cash Short and Over			2 00			19
20			Service Fees				9 6 3 00		20
21			Record service fees and cash shortage						21

The entry on June 20 to record the revenues and cash overage (holding back the change fund) would be:

23	June	20	Cash			8 1 5 00			23
24			Service Fees				8 1 4 00		24
25			Cash Short and Over				1 00		25
26			Record service fees and cash overage						26

The cash short and over account is used to accumulate cash shortages and overages throughout the accounting period. At the end of the period, a debit balance in the account (a net shortage) is treated as an expense. A credit balance in the account (a net overage) is treated as revenue.

Learning Objectives	Key Points to Remember
1 **Describe how to open and use a checking account.**	Three steps to follow in preparing a check are: 1. Complete the check stub or register. 2. Enter the date, payee name, and amount on the check. 3. Sign the check.
2 **Prepare a bank reconciliation and related journal entries.**	The most common reasons for differences between the book and bank cash balances are: 1. Outstanding checks 2. Deposits in transit 3. Bank service charges 4. Bank collections for the depositor 5. NSF checks 6. Errors by the bank or the depositor Three steps to follow in preparing a bank reconciliation are: 1. Identify deposits in transit and any related errors. 2. Identify outstanding checks and any related errors. 3. Identify additional reconciling items. Only two kinds of items on a bank reconciliation require journal entries: 1. Errors in the depositor's books. 2. Bank additions and deductions that do not already appear in the books.
3 **Establish and use a petty cash fund.**	Two important aspects of the functioning of a petty cash fund are: 1. Once the fund is established, subsequent entries do not affect the petty cash account balance, unless the size of the fund itself is being changed. 2. The petty cash payments record is supplemental to the regular accounting records. No posting is done from this record.
4 **Establish a change fund and use the cash short and over account.**	A change fund is established by debiting Change Fund and crediting Cash. Cash shortages and overages are accounted for using the cash short and over account. A debit balance in this account represents expense; a credit balance represents revenue.

REFLECTION

Reflection: Answering the Opening Question

Checks Evan wrote that have not been presented to the bank for payment are considered outstanding checks. When reconciling the book and bank balances, Evan should subtract outstanding checks from the bank statement balance to determine the adjusted bank balance. If the outstanding checks are not subtracted correctly on the bank reconciliation, Evan could overstate the store's cash balance and risk writing a check for funds Parkway does not have in the bank. This would harm the store's credibility with both its creditors and the bank.

DEMONSTRATION PROBLEM

Power Accounting System Software®

WebTUTOR Advantage

Jason Kuhn's check stubs indicated a balance of $4,673.12 for Kuhn's Wilderness Outfitters on March 31. This included a record of a deposit of $926.10 mailed to the bank on March 30, but not credited to Kuhn's account until April 1. In addition, the following checks were outstanding on March 31.

No. 462,	$524.26
No. 465,	$213.41
No. 473,	$543.58
No. 476,	$351.38
No. 477,	$197.45

The bank statement showed a balance of $5,419.00 as of March 31. The bank statement included a service charge of $4.10 with the date of March 29. In matching the canceled checks and record of deposits with the stubs, it was discovered that check no. 456, to Office Suppliers, Inc., for $93.00 was erroneously recorded on the stub as $39.00. This caused the bank balance on that stub and those following to be $54.00 too large. It was also discovered that an ATM withdrawal of $100.00 for personal use was not recorded on the books.

Kuhn maintains a $200.00 petty cash fund. His petty cash payments record showed the following totals at the end of March of the current year.

Automobile expense	$ 32.40
Postage expense	27.50
Charitable contributions expense	35.00
Telephone expense	6.20
Travel and entertainment expense	38.60
Miscellaneous expense	17.75
Jason Kuhn, Drawing	40.00
Total	$197.45

This left a balance of $2.55 in the petty cash fund, and the fund was replenished.

REQUIRED

1. Prepare a bank reconciliation for Jason Kuhn as of March 31, 20--.

2. Journalize the entries that should be made by Kuhn on his books as of March 31, 20--, (a) as a result of the bank reconciliation and (b) to replenish the petty cash fund.

3. Show proof that, after these entries, the total of the cash and petty cash account balances equals $4,715.02.

Solution

1.

Kuhn's Wilderness Outfitters Bank Reconciliation March 31, 20 - -				
Bank statement balance, March 31			$5 4 1 9 00
Add deposit in transit			9 2 6 10
			$6 3 4 5 10
Deduct outstanding checks:			
No. 462	$ 5 2 4 26		
No. 465	2 1 3 41		
No. 473	5 4 3 58		
No. 476	3 5 1 38		
No. 477	1 9 7 45	1 8 3 0 08	
Adjusted bank balance		$4 5 1 5 02	
Book balance, March 31		$4 6 7 3 12	
Deduct: Bank service charge	$ 4 10		
Error on check no. 456	5 4 00		
Unrecorded ATM withdrawal	1 0 0 00	1 5 8 10	
Adjusted book balance		$4 5 1 5 02	

2a.

3						3
4	20-- Mar.	31	Miscellaneous Expense	4 10		4
5			Accounts Payable—Office Supp., Inc	5 4 00		5
6			Jason Kuhn, Drawing	1 0 0 00		6
7			Cash		1 5 8 10	7
8			Bank transactions for March			8
9						9

b.

10		31	Automobile Expense	3 2 40		10
11			Postage Expense	2 7 50		11
12			Charitable Contributions Expense	3 5 00		12
13			Telephone Expense	6 20		13
14			Travel and Entertainment Expense	3 8 60		14
15			Miscellaneous Expense	1 7 75		15
16			Jason Kuhn, Drawing	4 0 00		16
17			Cash		1 9 7 45	17
18			Replenishment of petty cash			18
19			fund			19
20						20
21						21

3. Cash in bank:

Check stub balance, March 31	$4,673.12
Less bank charges	158.10
Adjusted cash in bank	$4,515.02

Cash on hand:

Petty cash fund	$ 2.55
Add replenishment	197.45
Adjusted cash on hand	$ 200.00
Total cash in bank and petty cash on hand	$4,715.02

On-Line Learning Tools

For more information, visit: http://heintz.swlearning.com

The Heintz & Parry product web site is designed specifically for **COLLEGE ACCOUNTING**, *18e.* The features include downloadable student resources and an interactive study center, organized by chapter, which contains learning objectives, web links, on-line quizzes with automatic feedback, and more.

KEY TERMS

ABA (American Bankers Association) Number, (226)   The small fraction printed in the upper right-hand corner of each check.

automated teller machine (ATM), (228)   A machine used by depositors to make withdrawals or deposits at any time.

bank reconciliation, (233)   A report used to bring the book and bank balances into agreement.

bank statement, (231)   A statement of account issued by a bank to each depositor once a month.

blank endorsement, (226)   An endorsement where the depositor simply signs the back of the check, making the check payable to any bearer.

canceled check, (231)   A depositor's check paid by the bank during the bank statement period.

cash, (226)   To a business, cash includes currency, coins, checks received from customers, money orders, and bank cashier's checks.

change fund, (241)   A supply of currency and coins kept in a cash register or cash drawer for use in handling cash sales.

check, (229)   A document ordering a bank to pay cash from a depositor's account.

check stub, (229)   In some checkbooks, a document attached to a check that contains space for relevant information about the check.

credit memo, (234)   An item that the bank adds to the account.

debit memo, (234)   An item that the bank deducts from the account.

deposit ticket, (226)   A form showing a detailed listing of items being deposited.

deposits in transit, (233)   Deposits that have not reached or been recorded by the bank before the bank statement is prepared.

drawee, (229)   The bank on which the check is drawn.

drawer, (229)   The depositor who orders the bank to pay the cash.

electronic funds transfer (EFT), (237)   A process using a computer rather than paper checks to complete transactions with the bank.

endorsement, (226)   Stamping or writing the depositor's name and sometimes other information on the back of the check.

internal control, (226)   A set of procedures designed to ensure proper accounting for transactions.

magnetic ink character recognition (MICR) code, (226)   The character code used to print identifying information on the lower left front side of each check.

not sufficient funds (NSF) check, (233)   A check deposited by the depositor that is not paid because the drawer did not have sufficient funds.

outstanding check, (233)   A check issued that has not been presented to the bank for payment before the statement is prepared.

payee, (229)   The person being paid the cash.

petty cash fund, (237)   A fund established to pay for small items with cash.

petty cash payments record, (238)   A special multi-column record that supplements the regular accounting records.

petty cash voucher, (238)   A receipt that is prepared for every payment from the petty cash fund.

restrictive endorsement, (226)   An endorsement where the depositor adds words such as "For deposit" to restrict the payment of the check.

service charge, (233)   A bank charge for services such as check printing and processing.

signature card, (226)   A card that is completed and signed by each person authorized to sign checks.

REVIEW QUESTIONS

(LO1)   1. Why must a signature card be filled out and signed to open a checking account?

(LO1)   2. Explain the difference between a blank endorsement and a restrictive endorsement.

(LO1)   3. Who are the three parties to every check?

(LO1)   4. What are the three steps to follow in preparing a check?

(LO2)   5. What are the most common reasons for differences between the book and bank cash balances?

(LO2)   6. What are the three steps to follow in preparing a bank reconciliation?

(LO2)   7. What two kinds of items on a bank reconciliation require journal entries?

(LO2)   8. Name five applications of electronic funds transfer in current use.

(LO3)   9. What is the purpose of a petty cash fund?

(LO3)   10. What should be prepared every time a petty cash payment is made?

(LO3)   11. At what two times should the petty cash fund be replenished?

(LO3)   12. From what source is the information obtained for issuing a check to replenish the petty cash fund?

(LO4)   13. At what two times would an entry be made affecting the change fund?

(LO4)   14. What does a debit balance in the cash short and over account represent? What does a credit balance in this account represent?

Self-Study Test Questions

True/False

1. The primary purpose of a bank reconciliation is to detect and correct errors made by the bank in its records.   _____

2. NSF checks are subtracted from the bank's ending balance on the bank reconciliation.   _____

3. The bank service charge requires a journal entry to record its effects on the cash account.   _____

4. Unrecorded ATM withdrawals are added to the checkbook balance on the bank reconciliation.   _____

5. The petty cash record is a journal of original entry (entries are posted from it to the general ledger accounts).   _____

Multiple Choice

1. To establish a petty cash fund, which account is debited?   _____

   (a) Cash
   (b) Petty Cash
   (c) Miscellaneous Expense
   (d) Revenue

2. When the cash short and over account has a debit balance at the end of the month, it is considered   _____

   (a) an expense.
   (b) an asset.
   (c) revenue.
   (d) a liability.

3. Which of these could be *added* to the ending checkbook balance?   _____

   (a) service charges
   (b) NSF check
   (c) checkbook errors
   (d) outstanding checks

4. Which of these is *subtracted* from the ending checkbook balance?   _____

   (a) deposits in transit
   (b) service charges
   (c) note collection
   (d) bank errors

5. Which of these is *added* to the ending bank statement balance?   _____

   (a) outstanding checks
   (b) service charges
   (c) checkbook errors
   (d) deposits in transit

The answers to the Self-Study Test Questions are at the end of the text.

MANAGING YOUR WRITING

The current month's bank statement for your account arrives in the mail. In reviewing the statement, you notice a deposit listed for $400.00 that you did not make. It has been credited in error to your account.

Discuss whether you have an ethical or legal obligation to inform the bank of the error. What action should you take?

ETHICS CASE

Ben Thomas works as a teller for First National Bank. When he arrived at work on Friday, the branch manager, Frank Mills, asked him to get his cash drawer out early because the head teller, Naomi Ray, was conducting a surprise cash count for all the tellers. Surprise cash counts are usually done four or five times a year by the branch manager or the head teller and once or twice a year by internal auditors. Ben's drawer was $100.00 short and his reconciliation tape showed that he was in balance on Thursday night. Naomi asked Ben for an explanation, and Ben immediately took $100.00 out of his pocket and handed it to her. He went on to explain he needed the cash to buy prescriptions for his son and pay for groceries and intended to put the $100.00 back in his cash drawer on Monday, which was pay day. He also told Naomi that this was the first time he had ever "borrowed" money from his cash drawer and that he would never do it again.

1. What are the ethical considerations in this case from both Ben's and Naomi's perspectives?

2. What options does Naomi have to address this problem?

3. Assume Naomi chooses to inform the branch manager. Write a short incident report describing the findings.

4. In small groups come up with as many ideas as possible on how to safeguard cash on hand in a bank (petty cash, teller drawer cash, and vault cash) from employee theft and mismanagement.

WEB WORK

Your business will, at some point in time, need to write a check to pay a vendor or an employee, or to cover an unforeseen expense. What do you need to do to open an account? What are some of the costs and restrictions a business owner needs to be aware of? Visit the Interactive Study Center on our web site at **http://heintz.swlearning.com** for special hotlinks to assist you in this assignment.

SERIES A EXERCISES

EXERCISE 7-1A   (LO1)   CHECKING ACCOUNT TERMS Match the following words with their definitions.

1. An endorsement where the depositor simply signs on the back of the check

2. An endorsement that contains words like "For Deposit Only" together with the signature

3. A card filled out and signed by each person authorized to sign checks on an account

4. The depositor who orders the bank to pay cash from the depositor's account

5. The bank on which the check is drawn

6. The person being paid the cash

7. A check that has been paid by the bank and is being returned to the depositor

a. signature card

b. canceled check

c. blank endorsement

d. drawer

e. restrictive endorsement

f. drawee

g. payee

EXERCISE 7-2A
Total deposit: $817.00

(LO1)   **PREPARE DEPOSIT TICKET** Based on the following information, prepare a deposit ticket.

Date:		January 15, 20--
Currency:		$334.00
Coin:		26.00
Checks:	No. 4-11	311.00
	No. 80-322	108.00
	No. 3-9	38.00

EXERCISE 7-3A   **(LO1)**   **PREPARE CHECK AND STUB** Based on the following information, prepare a check and stub.

Date:	January 15, 20--
Balance brought forward:	$2,841.50
Deposit:	(from Exercise 7-2A)
Check to:	J.M. Suppliers
Amount:	$150.00
For:	Office Supplies
Signature:	Sign your name

EXERCISE 7-4A   **(LO2)**   **BANK RECONCILIATION PROCEDURES** In a format similar to the following, indicate whether the action at the left will result in an addition to (+) or subtraction from (–) the ending bank balance or the ending checkbook balance.

	Ending Bank Balance	Ending Checkbook Balance
1. Deposits in transit to the bank	_____	_____
2. Error in checkbook: check recorded as $32.00 but was actually for $23.00	_____	_____
3. Service fee charged by bank	_____	_____
4. Outstanding checks	_____	_____
5. NSF check deposited earlier	_____	_____
6. Error in checkbook: check recorded as $22.00 but was actually for $220.00	_____	_____
7. Bank credit memo advising they collected a note for us	_____	_____

EXERCISE 7-5A   (LO2)
NSF check: Dr. Accounts
Receivable, $390.00

PREPARE JOURNAL ENTRIES FOR BANK RECONCILIATION   Based on the following bank reconciliation, prepare the journal entries.

Lisa Choy Associates			
Bank Reconciliation			
July 31, 20 - -			
Bank statement balance, July 31			$2 7 6 4 40
Add deposits in transit	$ 2 5 0 00		
	9 8 00	3 4 8 00	
		$3 1 1 2 40	
Deduct outstanding checks:			
No. 387	$ 3 5 3 50		
No. 393	1 7 80		
No. 398	3 3 20	4 0 4 50	
Adjusted bank balance		$2 7 0 7 90	
Book balance, July 31		$3 1 3 0 90	
Deduct: Error on check no. 394*	$ 2 3 00		
NSF check	3 9 0 00		
Bank service charge	1 0 00	4 2 3 00	
Adjusted book balance		$2 7 0 7 90	
*Accounts Payable was debited in original entry.			

EXERCISE 7-6A   (LO3)
Replenishment: Cr. Cash, $197.00

PETTY CASH JOURNAL ENTRIES Based on the following petty cash information, prepare (a) the journal entry to establish a petty cash fund, and (b) the journal entry to replenish the petty cash fund.

On January 1, 20--, a check was written in the amount of $200.00 to establish a petty cash fund. During January, the following vouchers were written for cash removed from the petty cash drawer.

Voucher No.	Account Debited	Amount
1	Telephone Expense	$17.50
2	Automobile Expense	33.00
3	Joseph Levine, Drawing	70.00
4	Postage Expense	12.50
5	Charitable Contributions Expense	15.00
6	Miscellaneous Expense	49.00

EXERCISE 7-7A   (LO4)
Apr. 16: Cr. Cash Short and Over, $1.75

CASH SHORT AND OVER ENTRIES Based on the following information, prepare the weekly entries for cash receipts from service fees and cash short and over. A change fund of $100.00 is maintained.

Date	Change Fund	Cash Register Receipt Amount	Actual Cash Counted
April 2	$100.00	$268.50	$366.50
9	100.00	237.75	333.50
16	100.00	309.25	411.00
23	100.00	226.50	324.00
30	100.00	318.00	422.00

SERIES A PROBLEMS

PROBLEM 7-8A **(LO2)**

Adjusted book balance:
$4,182.00

BANK RECONCILIATION AND RELATED JOURNAL ENTRIES The balance in the checking account of Violette Enterprises as of October 31 is $4,765.00. The bank statement shows an ending balance of $4,235.00. The following information is discovered by (1) comparing last month's deposits in transit and outstanding checks with this month's bank statement, (2) comparing deposits and checks written per books and per bank in the current month, and (3) noting service charges and other debit and credit memos shown on the bank statement.

Deposits in transit:	10/29	$175.00
	10/30	334.00
Outstanding checks:	No. 1764	$ 47.00
	No. 1767	146.00
	No. 1781	369.00
Unrecorded ATM withdrawal*:		180.00
Bank service charge:		43.00
NSF check:		370.00

Error on check no. 1754   Checkbook shows it was for $72.00, but it was actually written for $62.00. Accounts Payable was debited.

*Funds were withdrawn by Guy Violette for personal use.

REQUIRED

1. Prepare a bank reconciliation as of October 31, 20--.

2. Prepare the required journal entries.

PROBLEM 7-9A **(LO2)**

Adjusted bank balance:
$3,069.95

BANK RECONCILIATION AND RELATED JOURNAL ENTRIES The balance in the checking account of Lyle's Salon as of November 30 is $3,282.95. The bank statement shows an ending balance of $2,127.00. By examining last month's bank reconciliation, comparing the deposits and checks written per books and per bank in November, and noting the service charges and other debit and credit memos shown on the bank statement, the following were found.

a. An ATM withdrawal of $150.00 on November 18 by Lyle for personal use was not recorded on the books.

b. A bank debit memo issued for an NSF check from a customer of $19.50.

c. A bank credit memo issued for interest of $19.00 earned during the month.

d. On November 30, a deposit of $1,177.00 was made, which is not shown on the bank statement.

e. A bank debit memo issued for $17.50 for bank service charges.

f. Checks No. 549, 561, and 562 for the amounts of $185.00, $21.00, and $9.40, respectively, were written during November but have not yet been received by the bank.

g. The reconciliation from the previous month showed outstanding checks of $271.95. One of those checks, No. 471 for $18.65, has not yet been received by the bank.

h. Check No. 523 written to a creditor in the amount of $372.90 was recorded in the books as $327.90.

REQUIRED

1. Prepare a bank reconciliation as of November 30.

2. Prepare the required journal entries.

PROBLEM 7-10A   (LO3)
Replenishment: Cr. Cash, $138.00

PETTY CASH RECORD AND JOURNAL ENTRIES On May 1, a petty cash fund was established for $150.00. The following vouchers were issued during May.

Date	Voucher No.	Purpose	Amount
May 1	1	postage due	$ 3.50
3	2	office supplies	11.00
5	3	auto repair (miscellaneous)	22.00
7	4	drawing (Joy Adams)	25.00
11	5	donation (Red Cross)	10.00
15	6	travel expenses	28.00
22	7	postage stamps	3.50
26	8	telephone call	5.00
30	9	donation (Boy Scouts)	30.00

REQUIRED

1. Prepare the journal entry to establish the petty cash fund.

2. Record the vouchers in the petty cash record. Total and rule the petty cash record.

3. Prepare the journal entry to replenish the petty cash fund. Make the appropriate entry in the petty cash record.

PROBLEM 7-11A   (LO4)
July 23: Dr. Cash Short and Over, $2.50

CASH SHORT AND OVER ENTRIES Listed below are the weekly cash register tape amounts for service fees and the related cash counts during the month of July. A change fund of $100.00 is maintained.

Date	Change Fund	Cash Register Receipt Amount	Actual Cash Counted
July 2	$100.00	$289.50	$387.00
9	100.00	311.50	411.50
16	100.00	306.00	408.50
23	100.00	317.50	415.00
30	100.00	296.00	399.50

REQUIRED

1. Prepare the journal entries to record the cash service fees and cash short and over for each of the five weeks.

2. Post to the cash short and over account (use account no. 516).

3. Determine the ending balance of the cash short and over account. Does it represent an expense or revenue?

SERIES B EXERCISES

EXERCISE 7-1B   (LO1)   CHECKING ACCOUNT TERMS Match the following words with their definitions.

1. Banking number used to identify checks for deposit tickets

2. A card filled out to open a checking account

3. A machine from which withdrawals can be taken or deposits made to accounts

4. A place where relevant information is recorded about a check

5. A set of procedures designed to ensure proper accounting for transactions

6. A statement of account issued to each depositor once a month

7. A detailed listing of items being deposited to an account

a. bank statement
b. deposit ticket
c. signature card
d. internal control
e. check stub
f. ATM
g. ABA number

EXERCISE 7-2B   (LO1)
Total deposit: $645.00

PREPARE DEPOSIT TICKET Based on the following information, prepare a deposit ticket.

Date:		November 15, 20--
Currency:		$283.00
Coin:		19.00
Checks:	No. 3-22	201.00
	No. 19-366	114.00
	No. 3-2	28.00

EXERCISE 7-3B   (LO1)   PREPARE CHECK AND STUB Based on the following information, prepare a check and stub.

Date:	November 15, 20--
Balance brought forward:	$3,181.00
Deposit:	(from Exercise 7-2B)
Check to:	R.J. Smith Co.
Amount:	$120.00
For:	Payment on account
Signature:	Sign your name

EXERCISE 7-4B   (LO2)   BANK RECONCILIATION PROCEDURES In a format similar to the following, indicate whether the action at the left will result in an addition to (+) or subtraction from (–) the ending bank balance or the ending checkbook balance.

	Ending Bank Balance	Ending Checkbook Balance
1. Service fee of $12 charged by bank	_____	_____
2. Outstanding checks	_____	_____
3. Error in checkbook: check recorded as $36.00 was actually for $28.00	_____	_____

4. NSF check deposited earlier   _____ _____

5. Bank credit memo advising they
   collected a note for us   _____ _____

6. Deposits in transit to the bank   _____ _____

7. Error in checkbook: check recorded as
   $182.00 was actually for $218.00   _____ _____

EXERCISE 7-5B   (LO2)

NSF check: Dr. Accounts
Receivable, $66.00

PREPARE JOURNAL ENTRIES FOR BANK RECONCILIATION Based on the following bank reconciliation, prepare the journal entries.

Regina D'Alfonso Associates Bank Reconciliation July 31, 20 - -		
Bank statement balance, July 31		$1,784.00
Add deposits in transit	$418.50	
	100.50	519.00
		$2,303.00
Deduct outstanding checks:		
No. 185	$206.50	
No. 203	317.40	
No. 210	56.10	580.00
Adjusted bank balance		$1,723.00
Book balance, July 31		$1,794.00
Add error on check no. 191*		10.00
		$1,804.00
Deduct: NSF check	$66.00	
Bank service charge	15.00	81.00
Adjusted book balance		$1,723.00
*Accounts Payable was debited in original entry.		

EXERCISE 7-6B   (LO3)

Replenishment: Cr. Cash, $190.00

PETTY CASH JOURNAL ENTRIES Based on the following petty cash information, prepare (a) the journal entry to establish a petty cash fund, and (b) the journal entry to replenish the petty cash fund.

On October 1, 20--, a check was written in the amount of $200.00 to establish a petty cash fund. During October, the following vouchers were written for cash taken from the petty cash drawer:

Voucher No.	Account Debited	Amount
1	Postage Expense	$13.00
2	Miscellaneous Expense	17.00
3	John Flanagan, Drawing	45.00
4	Telephone Expense	36.00
5	Charitable Contributions Expense	50.00
6	Automobile Expense	29.00

EXERCISE 7-7B   (LO4)
June 15: Dr. Cash Short and Over,
$2.00

CASH SHORT AND OVER ENTRIES Based on the following information, prepare the weekly entries for cash receipts from service fees and cash short and over. A change fund of $100.00 is maintained.

Date	Change Fund	Cash Register Receipt Amount	Actual Cash Counted
June 1	$100.00	$330.00	$433.00
8	100.00	297.00	400.00
15	100.00	233.00	331.00
22	100.00	302.00	396.50
29	100.00	316.00	412.00

SERIES B PROBLEMS

PROBLEM 7-8B   (LO2)
Adjusted book balance:
$2,674.00

BANK RECONCILIATION AND RELATED JOURNAL ENTRIES The balance in the checking account of Kyros Enterprises as of November 30 is $3,004.00. The bank statement shows an ending balance of $2,525.00. The following information is discovered by (1) comparing last month's deposits in transit and outstanding checks with this month's bank statement, (2) comparing deposits and checks written per books and per bank in the current month, and (3) noting service charges and other debit and credit memos shown on the bank statement.

Deposits in transit:	11/29	$125.00
	11/30	200.00
Outstanding checks:	No. 322	17.00
	No. 324	105.00
	No. 327	54.00
Unrecorded ATM withdrawal*:		100.00
Bank service charge:		25.00
NSF check:		185.00
Error on check no. 321	Checkbook shows it was for $44.00, but it was actually written for $64.00. Accounts Payable was debited.	

*Funds were withdrawn by Steve Kyros for personal use.

REQUIRED

1. Prepare a bank reconciliation as of November 30, 20--.
2. Prepare the required journal entries.

PROBLEM 7-9B   (LO2)

Adjusted bank balance:
$4,518.70

BANK RECONCILIATION AND RELATED JOURNAL ENTRIES The balance in the checking account of Tori's Health Center as of April 30 is $4,690.30. The bank statement shows an ending balance of $3,275.60. By examining last month's bank reconciliation, comparing the deposits and checks written per books and per bank in April, and noting the service charges and other debit and credit memos shown on the bank statement, the following were found.

a. An ATM withdrawal of $200.00 on April 20 by Tori for personal use was not recorded on the books.
b. A bank debit memo issued for an NSF check from a customer of $29.10.
c. A bank credit memo issued for interest of $28.00 earned during the month.

d. On April 30, a deposit of $1,592.00 was made, which is not shown on the bank statement.

e. A bank debit memo issued for $24.50 for bank service charges.

f. Checks No. 481, 493, and 494 for the amounts of $215.00, $71.00, and $24.30, respectively, were written during April but have not yet been received by the bank.

g. The reconciliation from the previous month showed outstanding checks of $418.25. One of these checks, No. 397 for $38.60, has not yet been received by the bank.

h. Check No. 422 written to a creditor in the amount of $217.90 was recorded in the books as $271.90.

REQUIRED

1. Prepare a bank reconciliation as of April 30.

2. Prepare the required journal entries.

PROBLEM 7-10B   (LO3)

Replenishment: Cr. Cash, $87.00

PETTY CASH RECORD AND JOURNAL ENTRIES On July 1, a petty cash fund was established for $100.00. The following vouchers were issued during July.

Date	Voucher No.	Purpose	Amount
July 1	1	office supplies	$ 3.00
3	2	donation (Goodwill)	15.00
5	3	travel expenses	5.00
7	4	postage due	2.00
8	5	office supplies	4.00
11	6	postage due	3.50
15	7	telephone call	5.00
21	8	travel expenses	11.00
25	9	withdrawal by owner (L. Ortiz)	20.00
26	10	copier repair (miscellaneous)	18.50

REQUIRED

1. Prepare the journal entry to establish the petty cash fund.

2. Record the vouchers in the petty cash record. Total and rule the petty cash record.

3. Prepare the journal entry to replenish the petty cash fund. Make the appropriate entry in the petty cash record.

PROBLEM 7-11B   (LO4)

Aug. 8: Dr. Cash Short and Over, $3.50

CASH SHORT AND OVER ENTRIES Listed below are the weekly cash register tape amounts for service fees and the related cash counts during the month of July. A change fund of $200.00 is maintained.

Date	Change Fund	Cash Register Receipt Amount	Actual Cash Counted
Aug. 1	$200.00	$292.50	$495.00
8	200.00	305.00	501.50

(continued)

	15	200.00	286.00	486.00
	22	200.00	330.25	532.75
	29	200.00	298.50	495.00

REQUIRED

1. Prepare the journal entries to record the cash service fees and cash short and over for each of the five weeks.

2. Post to the cash short and over account. (Use account no. 516.)

3. Determine the ending balance of the cash short and over account. Does it represent an expense or revenue?

MASTERY PROBLEM

Adjusted bank balance:
$4,324.05

Turner Excavation maintains a checking account and has decided to open a petty cash fund. The following petty cash fund transactions occurred during July.

July 2   Established a petty cash fund by issuing Check No. 301 for $100.00.

5   Paid $25.00 from the petty cash fund for postage. Voucher No. 1.

7   Paid $30.00 from the petty cash fund for delivery of flowers (Miscellaneous Expense). Voucher No. 2.

8   Paid $20.00 from the petty cash fund to repair a tire on the company truck. Voucher No. 3.

12   Paid $22.00 from the petty cash fund for a newspaper advertisement. Voucher No. 4.

13   Issued Check No. 303 to replenish the petty cash fund. (Total and rule the petty cash payments record. Record the balance and the amount needed to replenish the fund in the Description column of the petty cash payments record.)

20   Paid $26.00 from the petty cash fund to reimburse an employee for expenses incurred to repair the company truck. Voucher No. 5.

24   Paid $12.50 from the petty cash fund for telephone calls made from a phone booth. Voucher No. 6.

28   Paid $25.00 from the petty cash fund as a contribution to the YMCA. Voucher No. 7.

31   Issued Check No. 308 to replenish the petty cash fund. (Total and rule the petty cash payments record. Record the balance and the amount needed to replenish the fund in the Description column of the petty cash payments record.)

The following additional transactions occurred during July.

July 5   Issued Check No. 302 to pay office rent, $650.00.

15   Issued Check No. 304 for office equipment, $525.00.

17   Issued Check No. 305 for the purchase of supplies, $133.00.

18   Issued Check No. 306 to pay attorney fees, $1,000.00.

30   Issued Check No. 307 to pay newspaper for an advertisement, $200.20.

REQUIRED

1. Record the petty cash transactions in a petty cash payments record.

2. Make all required general journal entries for the cash transactions. (Note: The petty cash fund was established and replenished twice during July.)

3. The following bank statement (Figure 7-14) was received in the mail. Deposits were made on July 6 for $3,500.00 and on July 29 for $2,350.00. The checkbook balance on July 31 is $4,331.55. Notice the discrepancy in Check No. 302 that cleared the bank for $655.00. This check was written on July 5 for rent expense, but was incorrectly entered on the check stub and in the journal as $650.00. Prepare a bank reconciliation and make any necessary journal entries as of July 31.

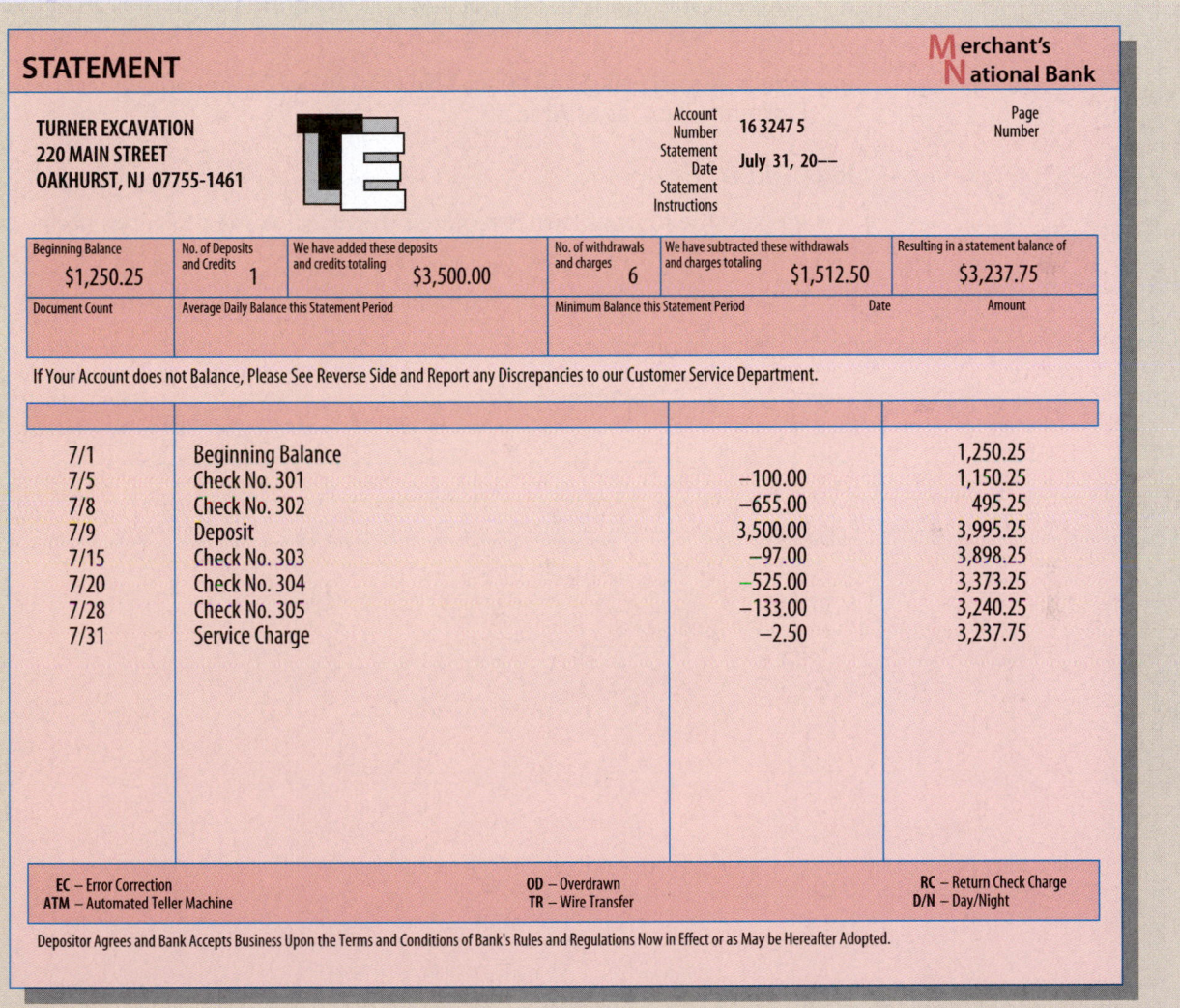

FIGURE 7-14   Bank Statement

CHALLENGE PROBLEM

This problem challenges you to apply your cumulative accounting knowledge to move a step beyond the material in the chapter.

2. Item 4: Dr. Depositor Accounts, $350.00

Susan Panera is preparing the June 30 bank reconciliation for Panera Bakery. She discovers the following items that explain the difference between the cash balance on her books and the balance as reported by Lawrence Bank.

1. An ATM withdrawal of $200.00 for personal use was not recorded by Susan.

2. A deposit of $850.00 was recorded by Susan but has not been received by Lawrence Bank as of June 30.

3. A check written in payment on account to Jayhawk Supply for $340.00 was recorded by Susan as $430.00 and by Lawrence Bank as $530.00.

4. An ATM deposit of $350.00 was recorded twice by Lawrence Bank.

5. An electronic funds transfer of $260.00 to Sunflower Mills as a payment on account was not recorded by Susan.

6. Check No. 103 for $235.00 and No. 110 for $127.00 had not cleared Lawrence Bank as of June 30.

REQUIRED

1. Prepare the journal entries required to correct Panera Bakery's books as of June 30.

2. Prepare the journal entries required to correct Lawrence Bank's books as of June 30.

DIGITAL IMAGING GROUP

Payroll Accounting: Employee Earnings and Deductions

Six months after opening his Parkway Pet Supplies store described at the beginning of Chapter 7, Evan Taylor is pleased to find that the business is doing very well. Evan has hired a student, who is studying accounting at the local college, as a part-time bookkeeper. He also has added an employee to help in the store during peak periods and to keep the inventory organized. Evan knows he needs to keep a record of each employee's work hours so he can compute the employees' earnings. His new bookkeeper says Evan also needs to withhold certain taxes from the wages. What taxes must Evan withhold from his employees' wages? How does he determine the correct amounts to withhold?

Careful study of this chapter should enable you to:

LO1 Distinguish between employees and independent contractors.

LO2 Calculate employee earnings and deductions.

LO3 Describe and prepare payroll records.

LO4 Account for employee earnings and deductions.

LO5 Describe various payroll record-keeping methods.

The only contact most of us have with payroll is receiving a paycheck. Few of us have seen the large amount of record keeping needed to produce that paycheck.

Employers maintain complete payroll accounting records for two reasons. First, payroll costs are major expenditures for most companies. Payroll accounting records provide data useful in analyzing and controlling these expenditures. Second, federal, state, and local laws require employers to keep payroll records. Companies must accumulate payroll data both for the business as a whole and for each employee.

There are two major types of payroll taxes: those paid by the employee and those paid by the employer. In this chapter we discuss employee taxes. In Chapter 9 we address payroll taxes paid by the employer.

EMPLOYEES AND INDEPENDENT CONTRACTORS

LO1 Distinguish between employees and independent contractors.

Not every person who performs services for a business is considered an employee. An **employee** works under the control and direction of an employer. Examples include secretaries, maintenance workers, salesclerks, and plant supervisors. In contrast, an **independent contractor** performs a service for a fee and does not work under the control and direction of the company paying for the service. Examples of independent contractors include public accountants, real estate agents, and lawyers.

The distinction between an employee and an independent contractor is important for payroll purposes. Government laws and regulations regarding payroll are much more complex for employees than for independent contractors. Employers must deduct certain taxes, maintain payroll records, and file numerous reports for all employees. Only one form (Form 1099) must be filed for independent contractors. The payroll accounting procedures described in this chapter apply only to employer/employee relationships.

EMPLOYEE EARNINGS AND DEDUCTIONS

LO2 Calculate employee earnings and deductions.

Three steps are required to determine how much to pay an employee for a pay period:

1. Calculate total earnings.

2. Determine the amounts of deductions.

3. Subtract deductions from total earnings to compute net pay.

Salaries and Wages

Compensation for managerial or administrative services usually is called **salary**. A salary normally is expressed in biweekly (every two weeks), monthly, or annual terms. Compensation for skilled or unskilled labor usually is referred to as **wages**. Wages ordinarily are expressed in terms of hours, weeks, or units produced. The terms "salaries" and "wages" often are used interchangeably in practice.

The **Fair Labor Standards Act (FLSA)** requires employers to pay overtime at 1½ times the regular rate to any hourly employee who works over 40 hours in a week. Some companies pay a higher rate for hours worked on Saturday or Sunday, but this is not required by the FLSA. Some salaried employees are exempt from the FLSA rules and are not paid overtime.

Computing Total Earnings

Compensation usually is based on the time worked during the payroll period. Sometimes earnings are based on sales or units of output during the period. When compensation is based on time, a record must be kept of the time worked by each employee. Time cards (Figure 8-1) are helpful for this purpose. In large businesses with computer-based timekeeping systems, plastic cards or badges with special magnetic strips or barcodes (Figure 8-2) can be used. Employees use the cards to clock in and out at terminals with card readers. For increased security, these terminals also are available with fingerprint readers.

Westly, Inc.
Time Card — Hourly Payroll

Emp. Name **Kuzmik, Helen**   Base Dept.: **Sales**

Emp. ID: **359-47-1138**   Pay Per. End: **12/19/20--**

Date	Time In	Time Out	Time In	Time Out	Reg	OT	DT	Total
12/13	8:00	12:30	13:00	17:30	8	1		9
12/14	8:00	12:30	13:00	17:30	8	1		9
12/15	8:00	12:30	13:00	17:30	8	1		9
12/16	8:00	12:30	13:00	17:30	8	1		9
12/17	8:00	12:30	13:00	17:30	8	1		9
12/18	10:00	16:00				6		6
12/19	13:00	17:00					4	4
TOTAL					40	11	4	55

Remarks _____

Approval _____ TM _____
Dept. Head

FIGURE 8-1 Time Card

FIGURE 8-2 Time Cards and Clock Terminal

To illustrate the computation of total earnings, look at the time card of Helen Kuzmik in Figure 8-1. The card shows that Kuzmik worked 55 hours for the week.

Regular hours	40 hours
Overtime	11
Double time	4
Total hours worked	55 hours

Kuzmik's regular rate of pay is $12 per hour. She is paid 1½ times the regular rate for hours in excess of 8 on Monday through Friday and any hours worked on Saturday, and twice the regular rate for hours on Sunday. Kuzmik's total earnings for the week ended December 19 are computed as follows:

40 hours × $12	$480
11 hours × $18 (1½ × $12 = $18)	198
4 hours (on Sunday) × $24 (2 × $12 = $24)	96
Total earnings for the week	$774

An employee who is paid a salary may also be entitled to premium pay for overtime. If this is the case, it is necessary to compute the regular hourly rate of pay before computing the overtime rate. To illustrate, assume that Linda Swaney has a salary of $2,288 a month plus 1½ times the regular hourly rate for hours in excess of 40 per week. Swaney's overtime rate of pay is computed as follows:

$2,288 × 12 months	$27,456 annual pay
$27,456 ÷ 52 weeks	$528.00 pay per week
$528.00 ÷ 40 hours	$13.20 pay per regular hour
$13.20 × 1½	$19.80 overtime pay per hour

There are 52 weeks in each year but not 4 weeks in each month. That is why monthly salaries must be annualized in order to determine the hourly rate.

If Swaney worked 50 hours during the week ended December 19, her total earnings for the week would be computed as follows:

40 hours × $13.20	$528.00
10 hours × $19.80	198.00
Total earnings for the week	$726.00

Deductions from Total Earnings

An employee's total earnings are called **gross pay**. Various deductions are made from gross pay to yield take-home or **net pay**. Deductions from gross pay fall into three major categories:

1. Federal (and possibly state and city) income tax withholding

2. Employee FICA tax withholding

3. Voluntary deductions

Income Tax Withholding. Federal law requires employers to withhold certain amounts from the total earnings of each employee. These withholdings are applied toward the payment of the employee's federal income tax. Four factors determine the amount to be withheld from an employee's gross pay each pay period:

1. Total earnings

2. Marital status

3. Number of withholding allowances claimed

4. Length of the pay period

Withholding Allowances. Each employee is required to furnish the employer an Employee's Withholding Allowance Certificate, Form W-4 (Figure 8-3). The marital status of the employee and the number of allowances claimed on Form W-4 determine the dollar amount of earnings subject to withholding. A **withholding allowance** exempts a specific dollar amount of an employee's gross pay from federal income tax withholding. In general, each employee is permitted one personal withholding allowance, one for a spouse who does not also claim an allowance, and one for each dependent.

A withholding certificate completed by Ken Istone is shown in Figure 8-3. Istone is married, has a spouse who does not claim an allowance, and has four dependent children. On line 5 of the W-4 form, Istone claims 6 allowances, calculated as follows:

Personal allowance	1
Spouse allowance	1
Allowances for dependents	4
Total withholding allowances	6

Form **W-4**	**Employee's Withholding Allowance Certificate**	OMB No. 1545-0010

Form **W-4**
Department of the Treasury
Internal Revenue Service

Employee's Withholding Allowance Certificate

► **For Privacy Act and Paperwork Reduction Act Notice, see page 2.**

OMB No. 1545-0010

20 - -

1 Type or print your first name and middle initial   Last name
Ken M.   **Istone**

2 Your social security number
393 : 58 : 8194

Home address (number and street or rural route)
1546 Swallow Drive

3 ☐ Single ☒ Married ☐ Married, but withhold at higher Single rate.
Note: If married, but legally separated, or spouse is a nonresident alien, check the "Single" box.

City or town, state, and ZIP code
St. Louis, MO 63144-4752

4 If your last name differs from that shown on your social security card, check here. You must call 1-800-772-1213 for a new card. ► ☐

5 Total number of allowances you are claiming (from line **H** above **or** from the applicable worksheet on page 2) . . . . . . **5** | **6**

6 Additional amount, if any, you want withheld from each paycheck . . . . **6** $

7 I claim exemption from withholding for 20--, and I certify that I meet **both** of the following conditions for exemption:
● Last year I had a right to a refund of **all** Federal income tax withheld because I had **no** tax liability **and**
● This year I expect a refund of **all** Federal income tax withheld because I expect to have **no** tax liability.
If you meet both conditions, write "Exempt" here . . . . ► **7**

Under penalties of perjury, I certify that I am entitled to the number of withholding allowances claimed on this certificate, or I am entitled to claim exempt status.

Employee's signature
(Form is not valid
unless you sign it.) ► ***Ken M. Istone***   Date ***January 3, 20--***

8 Employer's name and address (Employer: Complete lines 8 and 10 only if sending to the IRS.)

9 Office code (optional)

10 Employer identification number

Cat. No. 10220Q

FIGURE 8-3   Employee's Withholding Allowance Certificate (Form W-4)

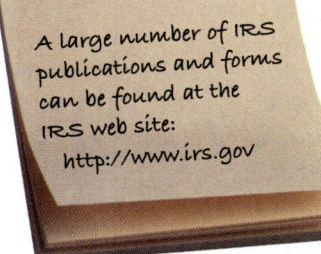

A large number of IRS publications and forms can be found at the IRS web site: http://www.irs.gov

Wage-Bracket Method. Employers generally use the **wage-bracket method** to determine the amount of tax to be withheld from an employee's pay. The employee's gross pay for a specific time period is traced into the appropriate wage-bracket table provided by the Internal Revenue Service (IRS). These tables cover various time periods, and there are separate tables for single and married taxpayers. Copies are provided in *Circular E—Employer's Tax Guide*, which may be obtained from any local IRS office or at the IRS Internet Site.

Portions of weekly income tax wage-bracket withholding tables for single and married persons are illustrated in Figure 8-4. Assume that Ken Istone (who claims 6 allowances) had gross earnings of $545 for the week ending December 19, 20--. The table for married persons is used as follows:

1. Find the row for wages of "at least $540, but less than $550."

2. Find the column headed "6 withholding allowances."

3. Where the row and column cross, $7.00 is given as the amount to be withheld.

> **LEARNING KEY:**
> 1. Find the row for wages.
> 2. Find the column for withholding allowances.
> 3. Find the amount where they cross.

For state or city income taxes, withholding generally is handled in one of two ways: (1) forms and tables similar to those provided by the IRS are used or (2) an amount equal to a percentage of the federal withholding amount is withheld.

SINGLE Persons—WEEKLY Payroll Period

(For Wages Paid in 2003)

If the wages are—		And the number of withholding allowances claimed is—										
At least	But less than	0	1	2	3	4	5	6	7	8	9	10
		The amount of income tax to be withheld is—										
200	210	17	10	4	0	0	0	0	0	0	0	0
210	220	19	11	5	0	0	0	0	0	0	0	0
220	230	20	12	6	0	0	0	0	0	0	0	0
230	240	22	13	7	1	0	0	0	0	0	0	0
240	250	23	15	8	2	0	0	0	0	0	0	0
250	260	25	16	9	3	0	0	0	0	0	0	0
260	270	26	18	10	4	0	0	0	0	0	0	0
270	280	28	19	11	5	0	0	0	0	0	0	0
280	290	29	21	12	6	0	0	0	0	0	0	0
290	300	31	22	13	7	1	0	0	0	0	0	0
300	310	32	24	15	8	2	0	0	0	0	0	0
310	320	34	25	16	9	3	0	0	0	0	0	0
320	330	35	27	18	10	4	0	0	0	0	0	0
330	340	37	28	19	11	5	0	0	0	0	0	0
340	350	38	30	21	12	6	0	0	0	0	0	0
350	360	40	31	22	14	7	1	0	0	0	0	0
360	370	41	33	24	15	8	2	0	0	0	0	0
370	380	43	34	25	17	9	3	0	0	0	0	0
380	390	44	36	27	18	10	4	0	0	0	0	0
390	400	46	37	28	20	11	5	0	0	0	0	0
400	410	47	39	30	21	12	6	0	0	0	0	0
410	420	49	40	31	23	14	7	1	0	0	0	0
420	430	50	42	33	24	15	8	2	0	0	0	0
430	440	52	43	34	26	17	9	3	0	0	0	0
440	450	53	45	36	27	18	10	4	0	0	0	0
450	460	55	46	37	29	20	11	5	0	0	0	0
460	470	56	48	39	30	21	12	6	0	0	0	0
470	480	58	49	40	32	23	14	7	1	0	0	0
480	490	59	51	42	33	24	15	8	2	0	0	0
490	500	61	52	43	35	26	17	9	3	0	0	0
500	510	62	54	45	36	27	18	10	4	0	0	0
510	520	64	55	46	38	29	20	11	5	0	0	0
520	530	65	57	48	39	30	21	13	6	0	0	0
530	540	67	58	49	41	32	23	14	7	1	0	0
540	550	68	60	51	42	33	24	16	8	2	0	0
550	560	70	61	52	44	35	26	17	9	3	0	0
560	570	71	63	54	45	36	27	19	10	4	0	0
570	580	73	64	55	47	38	29	20	11	5	0	0
580	590	75	66	57	48	39	30	22	13	6	1	0
590	600	78	67	58	50	41	32	23	14	7	2	0
600	610	81	69	60	51	42	33	25	16	8	3	0
610	620	83	70	61	53	44	35	26	17	9	4	0
620	630	86	72	63	54	45	36	28	19	10	5	0
630	640	89	73	64	56	47	38	29	20	12	6	0
640	650	91	76	66	57	48	39	31	22	13	7	1
650	660	94	78	67	59	50	41	32	23	15	8	2
660	670	97	81	69	60	51	42	34	25	16	9	3
670	680	99	84	70	62	53	44	35	26	18	10	4
680	690	102	86	72	63	54	45	37	28	19	11	5
690	700	105	89	73	65	56	47	38	29	21	12	6
1,200	1,210	243	227	211	195	179	163	148	132	116	100	84
1,210	1,220	245	229	214	198	182	166	150	134	119	103	87
1,220	1,230	248	232	216	200	185	169	153	137	121	105	90
1,230	1,240	251	235	219	203	187	171	156	140	124	108	92
1,240	1,250	253	238	222	206	190	174	158	143	127	111	95

FIGURE 8-4   Federal Withholding Tax Table: Single Persons

MARRIED Persons—WEEKLY Payroll Period
(For Wages Paid in 2003)

If the wages are—		And the number of withholding allowances claimed is—										
At least	But less than	0	1	2	3	4	5	6	7	8	9	10
		The amount of income tax to be withheld is—										
200	210	8	2	0	0	0	0	0	0	0	0	0
210	220	9	3	0	0	0	0	0	0	0	0	0
220	230	10	4	0	0	0	0	0	0	0	0	0
230	240	11	5	0	0	0	0	0	0	0	0	0
240	250	12	6	0	0	0	0	0	0	0	0	0
250	260	13	7	1	0	0	0	0	0	0	0	0
260	270	14	8	2	0	0	0	0	0	0	0	0
270	280	15	9	3	0	0	0	0	0	0	0	0
280	290	16	10	4	0	0	0	0	0	0	0	0
290	300	17	11	5	0	0	0	0	0	0	0	0
300	310	18	12	6	1	0	0	0	0	0	0	0
310	320	19	13	7	2	0	0	0	0	0	0	0
320	330	20	14	8	3	0	0	0	0	0	0	0
330	340	21	15	9	4	0	0	0	0	0	0	0
340	350	22	16	10	5	0	0	0	0	0	0	0
350	360	23	17	11	6	0	0	0	0	0	0	0
360	370	25	18	12	7	1	0	0	0	0	0	0
370	380	26	19	13	8	2	0	0	0	0	0	0
380	390	28	20	14	9	3	0	0	0	0	0	0
390	400	29	21	15	10	4	0	0	0	0	0	0
400	410	31	22	16	11	5	0	0	0	0	0	0
410	420	32	23	17	12	6	0	0	0	0	0	0
420	430	34	25	18	13	7	1	0	0	0	0	0
430	440	35	26	19	14	8	2	0	0	0	0	0
440	450	37	28	20	15	9	3	0	0	0	0	0
450	460	38	29	21	16	10	4	0	0	0	0	0
460	470	40	31	22	17	11	5	0	0	0	0	0
470	480	41	32	24	18	12	6	0	0	0	0	0
480	490	43	34	25	19	13	7	1	0	0	0	0
490	500	44	35	27	20	14	8	2	0	0	0	0
500	510	46	37	28	21	15	9	3	0	0	0	0
510	520	47	38	30	22	16	10	4	0	0	0	0
520	530	49	40	31	23	17	11	5	0	0	0	0
530	540	50	41	33	24	18	12	6	0	0	0	0
540	550	52	43	34	25	19	13	7	1	0	0	0
550	560	53	44	36	27	20	14	8	2	0	0	0
560	570	55	46	37	28	21	15	9	3	0	0	0
570	580	56	47	39	30	22	16	10	4	0	0	0
580	590	58	49	40	31	23	17	11	5	0	0	0
590	600	59	50	42	33	24	18	12	6	0	0	0
600	610	61	52	43	34	25	19	13	7	1	0	0
610	620	62	53	45	36	27	20	14	8	2	0	0
620	630	64	55	46	37	28	21	15	9	3	0	0
630	640	65	56	48	39	30	22	16	10	4	0	0
640	650	67	58	49	40	31	23	17	11	5	0	0
650	660	68	59	51	42	33	24	18	12	6	0	0
660	670	70	61	52	43	34	26	19	13	7	1	0
670	680	71	62	54	45	36	27	20	14	8	2	0
680	690	73	64	55	46	37	29	21	15	9	3	0
690	700	74	65	57	48	39	30	22	16	10	4	0
1,300	1,310	201	186	170	154	138	122	113	104	95	86	78
1,310	1,320	204	188	172	157	141	125	114	106	97	88	79
1,320	1,330	207	191	175	159	143	128	116	107	98	89	81
1,330	1,340	209	194	178	162	146	130	117	109	100	91	82
1,340	1,350	212	196	181	165	149	133	119	110	101	92	84
1,350	1,360	215	199	183	167	152	136	120	112	103	94	85
1,360	1,370	218	202	186	170	154	138	123	113	104	95	87
1,370	1,380	220	204	189	173	157	141	125	115	106	97	88
1,380	1,390	223	207	191	175	160	144	128	116	107	98	90
1,390	1,400	226	210	194	178	162	147	131	118	109	100	91

FIGURE 8-4 Federal Withholding Tax Table: *(continued)* Married Persons

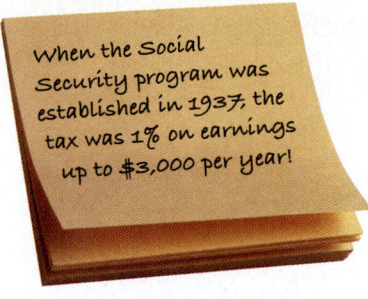

Employee FICA Tax Withholding. The Federal Insurance Contributions Act requires employers to withhold **FICA taxes** from employees' earnings. FICA taxes include amounts for both Social Security and Medicare programs. Social Security provides pensions and disability benefits. Medicare provides health insurance.

Congress has frequently changed the tax rates and the maximum amounts of earnings subject to FICA taxes. For this text, we assume the Social Security rate is 6.2% on maximum earnings of $87,000. The Medicare rate is 1.45% on all earnings; there is no maximum.

To illustrate the calculation of FICA taxes, assume the following earnings for Sarah Cadrain:

| | Earnings | |
Pay Period	Week	Year-to-Date
Dec. 6–12	$1,600	$86,340
Dec. 13–19	$1,660	$88,000

For the week of December 6–12, FICA taxes on Cadrain's earnings would be:

Gross Pay ×	Tax Rate	=	Tax
$1,600	Social Security 6.2%		$99.20
	Medicare 1.45%		23.20
			$122.40

During the week of December 13–19, Cadrain's earnings for the calendar year went over the $87,000 Social Security maximum by $1,000 ($88,000 – $87,000). Therefore, $1,000 of her $1,660 earnings for the week would not be subject to the Social Security tax.

Year-to-date earnings	$88,000
Social Security maximum	87,000
Amount not subject to Social Security tax	$ 1,000

The Social Security tax on Cadrain's December 13–19 earnings would be:

Gross pay	$1,660.00
Amount not subject to Social Security tax	1,000.00
Amount subject to Social Security tax	660.00
Tax rate	6.2%
Social Security tax	$ 40.92

Since there is no Medicare maximum, all of Cadrain's December 13–19 earnings would be subject to the Medicare tax.

Gross pay	$1,660.00
Tax rate	1.45%
Medicare tax	$ 24.07

The total FICA tax would be:

Social Security tax	$40.92
Medicare tax	24.07
Total FICA tax	$64.99

For the rest of the calendar year through December 31, Cadrain's earnings would be subject only to Medicare taxes.

Voluntary Deductions. In addition to the mandatory deductions from employee earnings for income and FICA taxes, many other deductions are possible. These deductions are usually voluntary and depend on specific agreements between the employee and employer. Examples of voluntary deductions are:

1. United States savings bond purchases

2. Health insurance premiums

3. Credit union deposits

4. Pension plan payments

5. Charitable contributions

Computing Net Pay

To compute an employee's net pay for the period, subtract all tax withholdings and voluntary deductions from the gross pay. Ken Istone's net pay for the week ended December 19 would be calculated as follows:

Gross pay		$545.00
Deductions:		
Federal income tax withholding	$ 7.00	
Social Security tax withholding	33.79	
Medicare tax withholding	7.90	
Health insurance premiums	10.00	
Total deductions		58.69
Net pay		$486.31

PAYROLL

	NAME	ALLOWANCES	MARITAL STATUS	EARNINGS						TAXABLE EARNINGS			
				REGULAR	OVERTIME	TOTAL	CUMULATIVE TOTAL	UNEMPLOYMENT COMPENSATION	SOCIAL SECURITY	
1	Cadrain, Sarah	4	M	1 600 00	60 00	1 660 00	88 000 00		660 00	1
2	Guder, James	1	S	760 00	140 00	900 00	43 400 00		900 00	2
3	Istone, Ken	6	M	545 00		545 00	27 025 00		545 00	3
4	Kuzmik, Helen	2	M	480 00	294 00	774 00	31 000 00		774 00	4
5	Lee, Hoseoup	3	M	440 00		440 00	22 340 00		440 00	5
6	Swaney, Linda	2	S	528 00	198 00	726 00	27 500 00		726 00	6
7	Tucci, Paul	5	M	490 00		490 00	25 050 00		490 00	7
8	Wiles, Harry	1	S	300 00		300 00	6 300 00	300 00	300 00	8
9				5 143 00	692 00	5 835 00	270 615 00	300 00	4 835 00	9

Time cards, pay rates

Prior period total + current period earnings

Current below $7,000 cumul. total

Current below $87,000 cumul. total

FIGURE 8-5 Payroll Register (left side)

PAYROLL RECORDS

LO3 Describe and prepare payroll records.

Payroll records should provide the following information for each employee.

1. Name, address, occupation, social security number, marital status, and number of withholding allowances

2. Gross amount of earnings, date of payment, and period covered by each payroll

3. Gross amount of earnings accumulated for the year

4. Amounts of taxes and other items withheld

Three types of payroll records are used to accumulate this information:

1. The payroll register

2. The payroll check with earnings statement attached

3. The employee earnings record

These records can be prepared by either manual or automated methods. The illustrations in this chapter are based on a manual system. The forms and procedures illustrated are equally applicable to both manual and automated systems.

Payroll Register

A **payroll register** is a form used to assemble the data required at the end of each payroll period. Figure 8-5 illustrates Westly, Inc.'s payroll register for the payroll period ended December 19, 20--. Detailed information on earnings, taxable earnings, deductions, and net pay is provided for each employee. Column headings for deductions may vary, depending on which deductions are commonly used by a particular business. The sources of key information in the register are indicated in Figure 8-5.

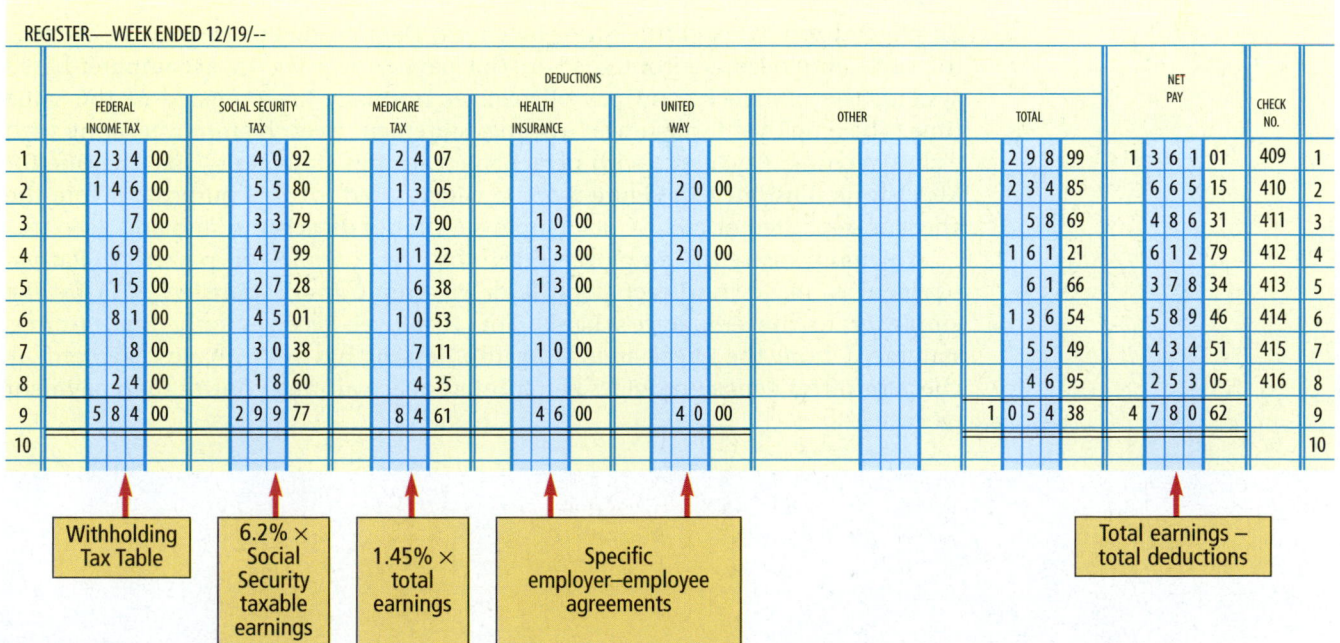

FIGURE 8-5   Payroll Register (right side)

Westly, Inc., has eight employees. The first $87,000 of earnings of each employee is subject to Social Security tax. The Cumulative Total column, under the Earnings category, shows that Sarah Cadrain has exceeded this limit during the period. Thus only $660 of her earnings for this pay period is subject to Social Security tax, as shown in the Taxable Earnings columns. The Taxable Earnings columns are needed for determining the Social Security tax and the employer's payroll taxes. Employers must pay unemployment tax on the first $7,000 of employee earnings and Social Security tax on the first $87,000. Employer payroll taxes are discussed in Chapter 9.

Regular deductions are made from employee earnings for federal income tax and Social Security and Medicare taxes. In addition, voluntary deductions are made for health insurance and United Way contributions, based on agreements with individual employees.

After the data for each employee have been entered, the amount columns in the payroll register should be totaled and the totals verified as follows:

Regular earnings		$5,143.00
Overtime earnings		692.00
Gross earnings		$5,835.00
Deductions:		
Federal income tax	$584.00	
Social Security tax	299.77	
Medicare tax	84.61	
Health insurance premiums	46.00	
United Way	40.00	1,054.38
Net amount of payroll		$4,780.62

In a computerized accounting system, the payroll software performs this proof. An error in the payroll register could cause the payment of an incorrect amount to an employee. It also could result in sending an incorrect amount to the government or other agencies for whom funds are withheld.

Payroll Check

Employees may be paid in cash or by check. Data needed to prepare a paycheck for each employee are contained in the payroll register. In a computer-based system, the paychecks and payroll register normally are prepared at the same time. The employer furnishes an earnings statement to each employee along with each paycheck. Paychecks with detachable earnings statements, like the one for Ken Istone illustrated in Figure 8-6, are widely used for this purpose. Before the check is deposited or cashed, the employee should detach the stub and keep it.

In many cases, the employee does not even handle the paycheck. Rather, payment is made by **direct deposit** or electronic funds transfer (EFT) by the employer to the employee's bank. The employee receives only the earnings statement from the check indicating the deposit has been made. Payment by check or direct deposit provides better internal accounting control than payment by cash.

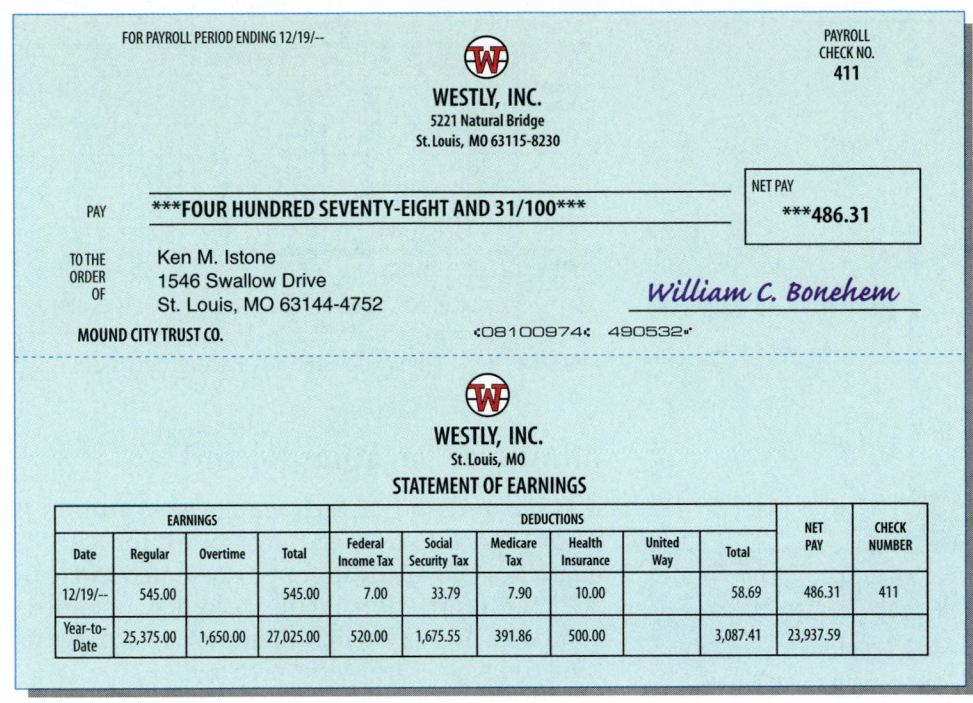

FIGURE 8-6   Paycheck and Earnings Statement

A BROADER VIEW

Payroll Fraud— Paying for Ghosts

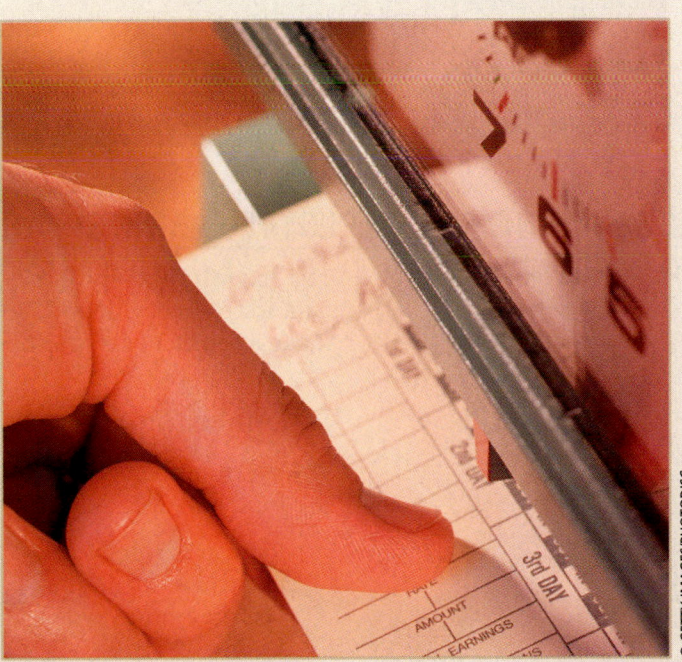

A supervisor at Haas Transfer Warehouse embezzled $12,000 from the company by collecting paychecks for former employees. When an employee left the company, the supervisor continued to submit a department time report for the employee. This caused a paycheck to be generated for the "ghost" employee. The supervisor then simply kept this paycheck when others were distributed to actual employees.

This fraud shows the importance of two procedures that appear in this chapter: (1) a time card, plastic card, or badge should be used for each employee to keep an accurate record of time worked and (2) payment by direct deposit or electronic funds transfer to the employee's bank is a good internal control.

	EARNINGS				TAXABLE EARNINGS		EMPLOYEE EARNINGS RECORD
PERIOD ENDED	REGULAR	OVERTIME	TOTAL	CUMULATIVE TOTAL	UNEMPLOYMENT COMPENSATION	SOCIAL SECURITY	
11/28	545 00	75 00	620 00	25 240 00		620 00	
12/5	545 00	75 00	620 00	25 860 00		620 00	
12/12	545 00	75 00	620 00	26 480 00		620 00	
12/19	545 00		545 00	27 025 00		545 00	

GENDER	DEPARTMENT	OCCUPATION	SOCIAL SECURITY NUMBER	MARITAL STATUS	ALLOWANCES
M ✓ / F	Maintenance	Service	393-58-8194	M	6

FIGURE 8-7 Employee Earnings Record (left side)

Employee Earnings Record

A separate record of each employee's earnings is called an **employee earnings record**. An employee earnings record for Ken M. Istone for a portion of the last quarter of the calendar year is illustrated in Figure 8-7.

The information in this record is obtained from the payroll register. In a computer-based system, the employee earnings record can be updated at the same time the payroll register is prepared.

Istone's earnings for four weeks of the last quarter of the year are shown on this form. Note that the entry for the pay period ended December 19 is the same as that in the payroll register illustrated in Figure 8-5. This linkage between the payroll register and the employee earnings record always exists. The payroll register provides a summary of the earnings of all employees for each pay period. The earnings record provides a summary of the annual earnings of an individual employee.

The earnings record illustrated in Figure 8-7 is designed to accumulate both quarterly and annual totals. The employer needs this information to prepare several reports. These reports will be discussed in Chapter 9.

ACCOUNTING FOR EMPLOYEE EARNINGS AND DEDUCTIONS

LO4 Account for employee earnings and deductions.

The payroll register described in the previous section provides complete payroll data for each pay period. But the payroll register is not a journal. We still need to make a journal entry for payroll.

Journalizing Payroll Transactions

The totals at the bottom of the columns of the payroll register in Figure 8-5 show the following information.

Regular earnings		$5,143.00
Overtime earnings		692.00
Gross earnings		$5,835.00
Deductions:		
Federal income tax	$584.00	
Social Security tax	299.77	
Medicare tax	84.61	
Health insurance premiums	46.00	
United Way contributions	40.00	1,054.38
Net amount of payroll		$4,780.62

FOR PERIOD ENDED															20--												

DEDUCTIONS

FEDERAL INCOME TAX			SOCIAL SECURITY TAX			MEDICARE TAX			HEALTH INSURANCE			UNITED WAY			OTHER			TOTAL			CHECK NO.	AMOUNT		
1 5	00		3 8	44		8	99		1 0	00								7 2	43		387	5 4 7	57	
1 5	00		3 8	44		8	99		1 0	00								7 2	43		395	5 4 7	57	
1 5	00		3 8	44		8	99		1 0	00								7 2	43		403	5 4 7	57	
7	00		3 3	79		7	90		1 0	00								5 8	69		411	4 8 6	31	

PAY RATE	DATE OF BIRTH	DATE HIRED	NAME/ADDRESS	EMPLOYEE NUMBER
$545/wk	8/17/64	1/3/87	Ken M. Istone 1546 Swallow Drive St. Louis, MO 63144-4752	3

FIGURE 8-7 Employee Earnings Record (right side)

The payroll register column totals thus provide the basis for recording the payroll. If the employee paychecks are written from the regular bank account, the following journal entry is made.

5	Dec.	19	Wages and Salaries Expense			5 8 3 5	00						5
6			Employee Income Tax Payable						5 8 4	00			6
7			Social Security Tax Payable						2 9 9	77			7
8			Medicare Tax Payable						8 4	61			8
9			Health Insurance Premiums Payable						4 6	00			9
10			United Way Contributions Payable						4 0	00			10
11			Cash					4 7 8 0	62				11
12			Payroll for week ended Dec. 19										12

Employee paychecks also can be written from a special payroll bank account. Large businesses with many employees commonly use a payroll bank account. If Westly used a payroll bank account, it first would have made the following entry on December 19 to transfer funds from the regular bank account to the payroll bank account.

5	Dec.	19	Payroll Cash			4 7 8 0	62						5
6			Cash						4 7 8 0	62			6
7			Cash for Dec. 19 payroll										7

Then, the payroll entry shown above would be made, except that the credit of $4,780.62 would be to Payroll Cash rather than Cash.

If a payroll bank account is used, individual checks totaling $4,780.62 are written to the employees from that account. Otherwise, individual checks totaling that amount are written to the employees from the regular bank account.

Notice two important facts about the payroll entry. First, Wages and Salaries Expense is debited for the gross pay of the employees. The expense to the employer is the gross pay, not the employees' net pay after deductions. Second, a separate account is kept for each deduction.

LEARNING KEY: Wages and Salaries Expense is debited for the gross pay. A separate account is kept for each earnings deduction. Cash is credited for the net pay.

The accounts needed in entering deductions depend upon the deductions involved. To understand the accounting for these deductions, consider what the employer is doing. By deducting amounts from employees' earnings, the employer is simply serving as an agent for the government and other groups. Amounts that are deducted from an employee's gross earnings must be paid by the employer to these groups. Therefore, a separate account should be kept for the liability for each type of deduction.

To help us understand the journal entry for payroll, let's use the accounting equation to examine the accounts involved. The seven accounts affected by the payroll entry on page 275 are shown in the accounting equation in Figure 8-8.

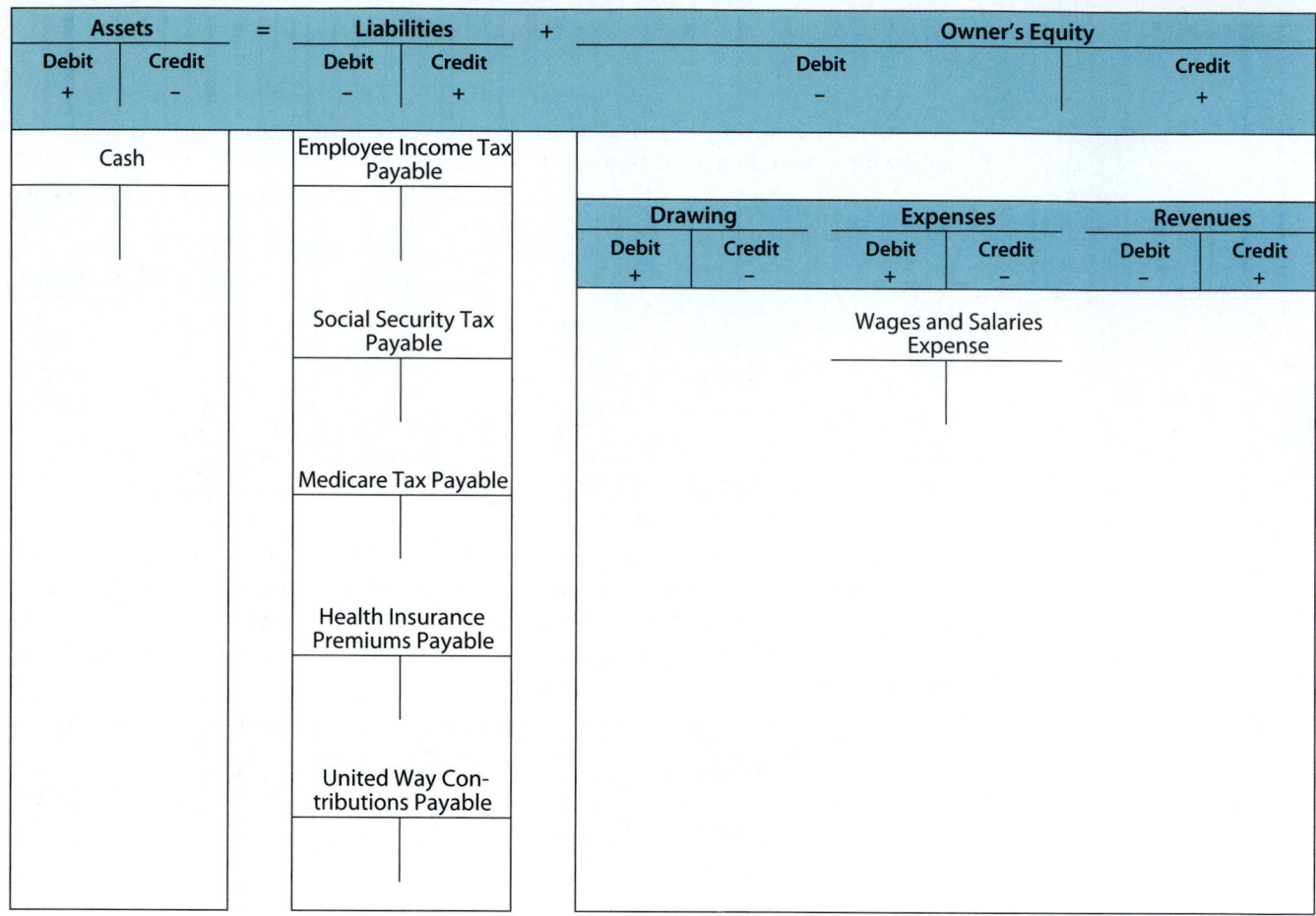

FIGURE 8-8 Accounting for Payroll

Wages and Salaries Expense

This account is debited for the gross pay of all employees for each pay period. Sometimes separate expense accounts are kept for the employees of different departments. Thus separate accounts may be kept for Office Salaries Expense, Sales Salaries Expense, and Factory Wages Expense.

Wages and Salaries Expense

Debit gross pay of employees for each pay period	Credit

Employee Income Tax Payable

This account is credited for the total federal income tax withheld from employees' earnings. The account is debited for amounts paid to the IRS. When all of the income taxes withheld have been paid, the account will have a zero balance. A state or city income tax payable account is used in a similar manner.

Employee Income Tax Payable

Debit	Credit
payment of income tax previously withheld	federal income tax withheld from employees' earnings

Social Security and Medicare Taxes Payable

These accounts are credited for (1) the Social Security and Medicare tax withheld from employees' earnings and (2) the Social Security and Medicare taxes imposed on the employer. Social Security and Medicare taxes imposed on the employer are discussed in Chapter 9. The accounts are debited for amounts paid to the IRS. When all of the Social Security and Medicare taxes have been paid, the accounts will have zero balances.

Social Security Tax Payable

Debit	Credit
payment of Social Security tax previously withheld or imposed	Social Security taxes (1) withheld from employees' earnings and (2) imposed on the employer

Medicare Tax Payable

Debit	Credit
payment of Medicare tax previously withheld or imposed	Medicare taxes (1) withheld from employees' earnings and (2) imposed on the employer

Other Deductions

Health Insurance Premiums Payable is credited for health insurance contributions deducted from an employee's pay. The account is debited for the subsequent payment of these amounts to the health insurer. United Way Contributions Payable is handled in a similar manner.

PAYROLL RECORD-KEEPING METHODS

LO5 Describe various payroll record-keeping methods.

Payroll typically is one of the first functions to be computerized by businesses.

You probably noticed that the same information appears in several places in the payroll records—in the payroll register, paycheck and stub, and employee earnings records. If all records are prepared by hand (a **manual system**), the same information would be recorded several times. Unless an employer has only a few employees, this can be very inefficient. Various approaches are available to make payroll accounting more efficient and accurate.

Both medium- and large-size businesses commonly use two approaches for payroll record keeping: payroll processing centers and electronic systems. A **payroll processing center** is a business that sells payroll record-keeping services. The employer provides the center with all basic employee data and each period's report of hours worked. The processing center maintains all payroll records and prepares each period's payroll checks. Payroll processing center fees tend to be much less than the cost to an employer of handling payroll internally.

An **electronic system** is a computer system based on a software package that performs all payroll record keeping and prepares payroll checks. In this system, only the employee number and hours worked need to be entered into a computer each pay period, as shown in Figure 8-9. All other payroll data needed to prepare the payroll records can be stored in the computer. The computer uses the employee number and hours worked to determine the gross pay, deductions, and net pay. The payroll register, checks, and employee earnings records are provided as outputs.

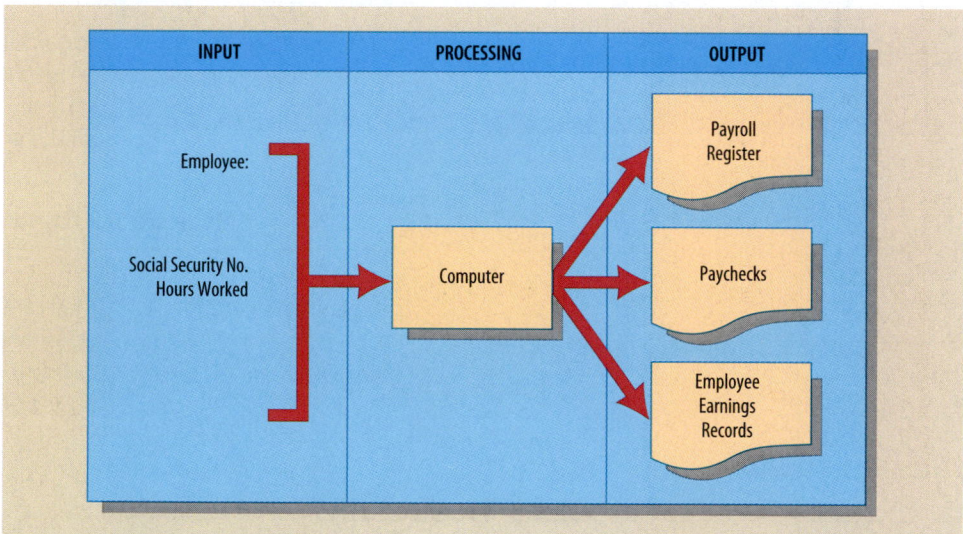

FIGURE 8-9 Electronic Payroll System

The same inputs and outputs are required in all payroll systems. Even with a computer, the data required for payroll processing have to be entered into the system at some point. The outputs—the payroll register, paychecks, and employee earnings records—are basically the same under each system.

Learning Objectives	Key Points to Remember
1 **Distinguish between employees and independent contractors.**	Employees work under the control and direction of an employer. Independent contractors perform a service for a fee and do not work under the control and direction of the company paying for the service. Payroll accounting procedures apply only to employees, not to independent contractors.
2 **Calculate employee earnings and deductions.**	Three steps are required to determine how much to pay an employee for a pay period: 1. Calculate total earnings. 2. Determine the amounts of deductions. 3. Subtract deductions from total earnings to compute net pay. Deductions from gross pay fall into three categories: 1. Income tax withholding. 2. Employee Social Security and Medicare taxes withholding. 3. Voluntary deductions. Four factors determine the amount to be withheld from an employee's gross pay each pay period: 1. Total earnings 2. Marital status 3. Number of withholding allowances claimed 4. Length of the pay period
3 **Describe and prepare payroll records.**	The payroll register and the employee earnings record are linked. The payroll register provides a summary of earnings of all employees for each pay period. The earnings record provides a summary of the annual earnings of an individual employee.
4 **Account for employee earnings and deductions.**	The totals at the bottom of the columns of the payroll register provide the basis for the journal entry for payroll. Amounts withheld or deducted by the employer from employee earnings are credited to liability accounts. The employer must pay these amounts to the proper government groups and other appropriate groups.
5 **Describe various payroll record-keeping methods.**	In a manual payroll system, the same information needs to be recorded several times. An electronic payroll system is much more efficient.

R E F L E C T I O N

Reflection: Answering the Opening Question

Evan must withhold amounts for federal (and possibly city and state) income taxes and for FICA taxes (Social Security and Medicare). To determine the correct amount of income tax withholding, each employee must complete Form W-4. Based on the number of withholding allowances claimed, Evan can use the withholding tables to determine the amount to withhold. These tables are provided in *Circular E—Employer's Tax Guide*. FICA tax should be withheld at a rate of 6.2% for Social Security and 1.45% for Medicare. *Circular E* also provides guidance regarding FICA taxes. Evan's bookkeeper should be able to handle all of these payroll matters.

DEMONSTRATION PROBLEM

WebTUTOR Advantage

Carole Vohsen operates a pet grooming salon called Canine Coiffures. She has five employees, all of whom are paid on a weekly basis. Canine Coiffures uses a payroll register, individual employee earnings records, a journal, and a general ledger.

The payroll data for each employee for the week ended January 21, 20--, are given below. Employees are paid 1½ times the regular rate for work over 40 hours a week and double time for work on Sunday.

Name	Employee No.	No. of Allowances	Marital Status	Total Hours Worked Jan. 15–21	Rate	Total Earnings Jan. 1–14
DeNourie, Katie	1	2	S	44	$11.50	$1,058.00
Garriott, Pete	2	1	M	40	12.00	1,032.00
Martinez, Sheila	3	3	M	39	12.50	987.50
Parker, Nancy	4	4	M	42	11.00	957.00
Shapiro, John	5	2	S	40	11.50	931.50

Sheila Martinez is the manager of the Shampooing Department. Her Social Security number is 500-88-4189, and she was born April 12, 1969. She lives at 46 Darling Crossing, Norwich, CT 06360. Martinez was hired September 1 of last year.

Canine Coiffures uses a federal income tax withholding table. A portion of this weekly table is provided in Figure 8-4 on pages 267 and 268. Social Security tax is withheld at the rate of 6.2% of the first $87,000 earned. Medicare tax is withheld at the rate of 1.45%, and city earnings tax at the rate of 1%, both applied to gross pay. Garriott and Parker each have $14.00 and DeNourie and Martinez each have $4.00 withheld for health insurance. DeNourie, Martinez, and Shapiro each have $15.00 withheld to be invested in the groomers' credit union. Garriott and Shapiro each have $18.75 withheld under a savings bond purchase plan.

Canine Coiffures' payroll is met by drawing checks on its regular bank account. This week, the checks were issued in sequence, beginning with no. 811.

REQUIRED

1. Prepare a payroll register for Canine Coiffures for the week ended January 21, 20--. (In the Taxable Earnings/Unemployment Compensation column, enter the same amounts as in the Social Security column.) Total the amount columns, verify the totals, and rule with single and double lines.

2. Prepare an employee earnings record for Sheila Martinez for the week ended January 21, 20--.

3. Assuming that the wages for the week ended January 21 were paid on January 23, prepare the journal entry for the payment of this payroll.

4. Post the entry in requirement 3 to the affected accounts in the ledger of Canine Coiffures. Do not enter any amounts in the Balance columns. Use account numbers as follows: Cash—101; Employee Income Tax Payable—211; Social Security Tax Payable—212; Medicare Tax Payable—213; City Earnings Tax Payable—215; Health Insurance Premiums Payable—216; Credit Union Payable—217; Savings Bond Deductions Payable—218; Wages and Salaries Expense—511.

Solution

1.

PAYROLL

	NAME	EMPLOYEE NO.	ALLOWANCES	MARITAL STATUS	EARNINGS REGULAR	EARNINGS OVERTIME	EARNINGS TOTAL	CUMULATIVE TOTAL	TAXABLE EARNINGS UNEMPLOYMENT COMPENSATION	TAXABLE EARNINGS SOCIAL SECURITY	
1	DeNourie, Katie	1	2	S	460 00	69 00	529 00	1587 00	529 00	529 00	1
2	Garriott, Pete	2	1	M	480 00		480 00	1512 00	480 00	480 00	2
3	Martinez, Sheila	3	3	M	487 50		487 50	1475 00	487 50	487 50	3
4	Parker, Nancy	4	4	M	440 00	33 00	473 00	1430 00	473 00	473 00	4
5	Shapiro, John	5	2	S	460 00		460 00	1391 50	460 00	460 00	5
6					2327 50	102 00	2429 50	7395 50	2429 50	2429 50	6
7											7

REGISTER—WEEK ENDED January 21, 20--

	DEDUCTIONS FEDERAL INCOME TAX	SOCIAL SECURITY TAX	MEDICARE TAX	CITY TAX	HEALTH INSURANCE	CREDIT UNION	OTHER		TOTAL	NET PAY	CHECK NO.	
1	48 00	32 80	7 67	5 29	4 00	15 00			112 76	416 24	811	1
2	34 00	29 76	6 96	4 80	14 00		U.S. Savings Bond	18 75	108 27	371 73	812	2
3	19 00	30 23	7 07	4 88	4 00	15 00			80 18	407 32	813	3
4	12 00	29 33	6 86	4 73	14 00				66 92	406 08	814	4
5	39 00	28 52	6 67	4 60		15 00	U.S. Savings Bond	18 75	112 54	347 46	815	5
6	152 00	150 64	35 23	24 30	36 00	45 00		37 50	480 67	1948 83		6
7												7

2.

EMPLOYEE EARNINGS RECORD

20-- PERIOD ENDED	EARNINGS REGULAR	EARNINGS OVERTIME	EARNINGS TOTAL	CUMULATIVE TOTAL	TAXABLE EARNINGS UNEMPLOYMENT COMPENSATION	TAXABLE EARNINGS SOCIAL SECURITY
1/7						
1/14						
1/21	487 50		487 50	1475 00	487 50	487 50
1/28						

GENDER	DEPARTMENT	OCCUPATION	SOCIAL SECURITY NUMBER	MARITAL STATUS	ALLOWANCES
M F ✔	Shampooing	Manager	500-88-4189	M	3

FOR PERIOD ENDED   20--

DEDUCTIONS FEDERAL INCOME TAX	SOCIAL SECURITY TAX	MEDICARE TAX	CITY TAX	HEALTH INSURANCE	CREDIT UNION	OTHER		TOTAL	CHECK NO.	AMOUNT
19 00	30 23	7 07	4 88	4 00	15 00			80 18	813	407 32

PAY RATE	DATE OF BIRTH	DATE HIRED	NAME/ADDRESS	EMPLOYEE NUMBER
$12.50	4/12/69	9/1/--	Sheila Martinez 46 Darling Crossing Norwich, CT 06360	3

(continued)

3.

	DATE		DESCRIPTION	POST REF.	DEBIT	CREDIT	
1	20-- Jan.	23	Wages and Salaries Expense	511	2 4 2 9 50		1
2			Employee Income Tax Payable	211		1 5 2 00	2
3			Social Security Tax Payable	212		1 5 0 64	3
4			Medicare Tax Payable	213		3 5 23	4
5			City Earnings Tax Payable	215		2 4 30	5
6			Health Insurance Premiums Payable	216		3 6 00	6
7			Credit Union Payable	217		4 5 00	7
8			Savings Bond Deductions Payable	218		3 7 50	8
9			Cash	101		1 9 4 8 83	9
10			Payroll for week ended Jan. 21				10

GENERAL JOURNAL — PAGE 1

4.

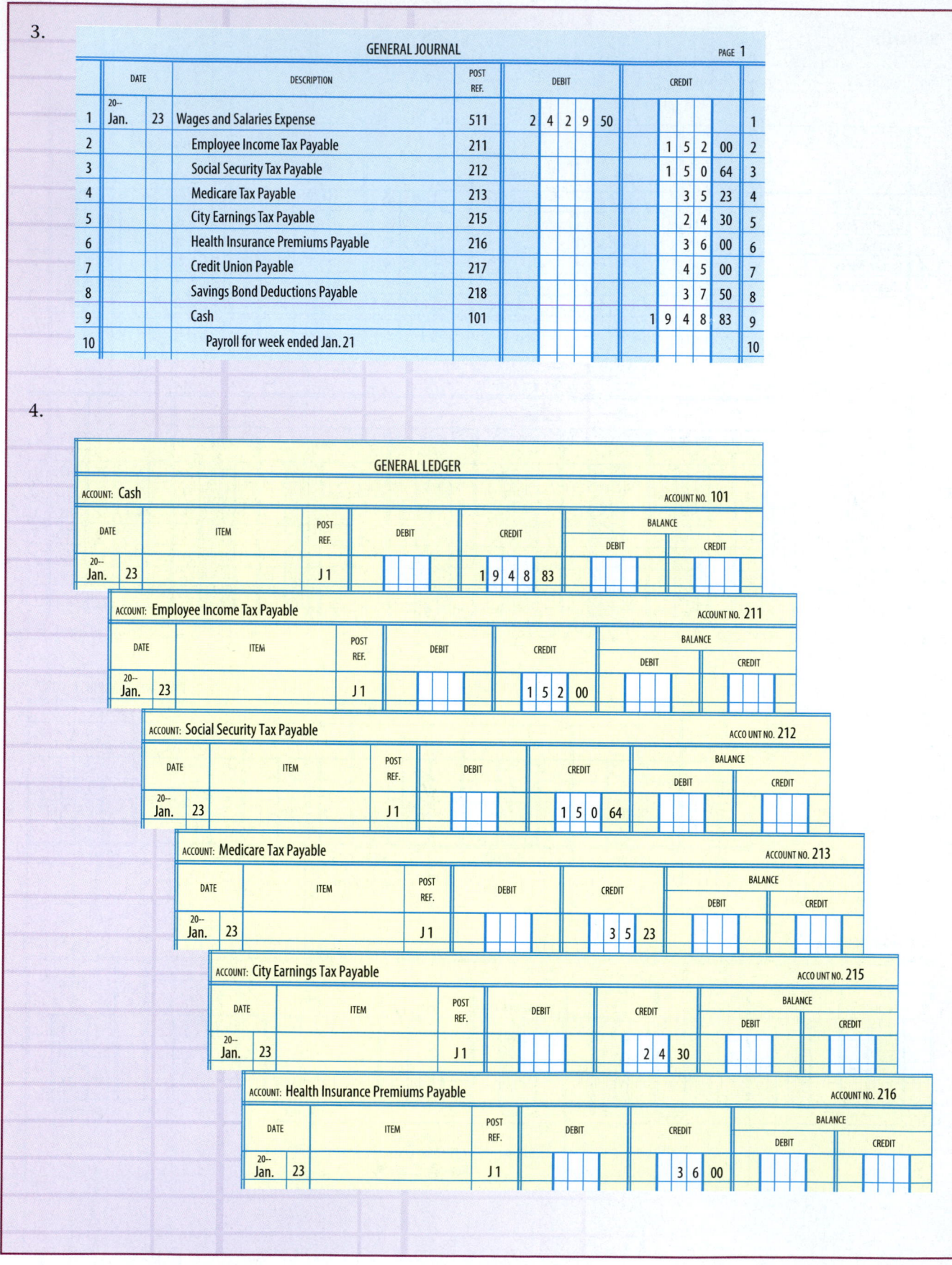

GENERAL LEDGER

ACCOUNT: Cash — ACCOUNT NO. 101

DATE	ITEM	POST REF.	DEBIT	CREDIT	BALANCE DEBIT	BALANCE CREDIT
20-- Jan. 23		J 1		1 9 4 8 83		

ACCOUNT: Employee Income Tax Payable — ACCOUNT NO. 211

DATE	ITEM	POST REF.	DEBIT	CREDIT	BALANCE DEBIT	BALANCE CREDIT
20-- Jan. 23		J 1		1 5 2 00		

ACCOUNT: Social Security Tax Payable — ACCOUNT NO. 212

DATE	ITEM	POST REF.	DEBIT	CREDIT	BALANCE DEBIT	BALANCE CREDIT
20-- Jan. 23		J 1		1 5 0 64		

ACCOUNT: Medicare Tax Payable — ACCOUNT NO. 213

DATE	ITEM	POST REF.	DEBIT	CREDIT	BALANCE DEBIT	BALANCE CREDIT
20-- Jan. 23		J 1		3 5 23		

ACCOUNT: City Earnings Tax Payable — ACCOUNT NO. 215

DATE	ITEM	POST REF.	DEBIT	CREDIT	BALANCE DEBIT	BALANCE CREDIT
20-- Jan. 23		J 1		2 4 30		

ACCOUNT: Health Insurance Premiums Payable — ACCOUNT NO. 216

DATE	ITEM	POST REF.	DEBIT	CREDIT	BALANCE DEBIT	BALANCE CREDIT
20-- Jan. 23		J 1		3 6 00		

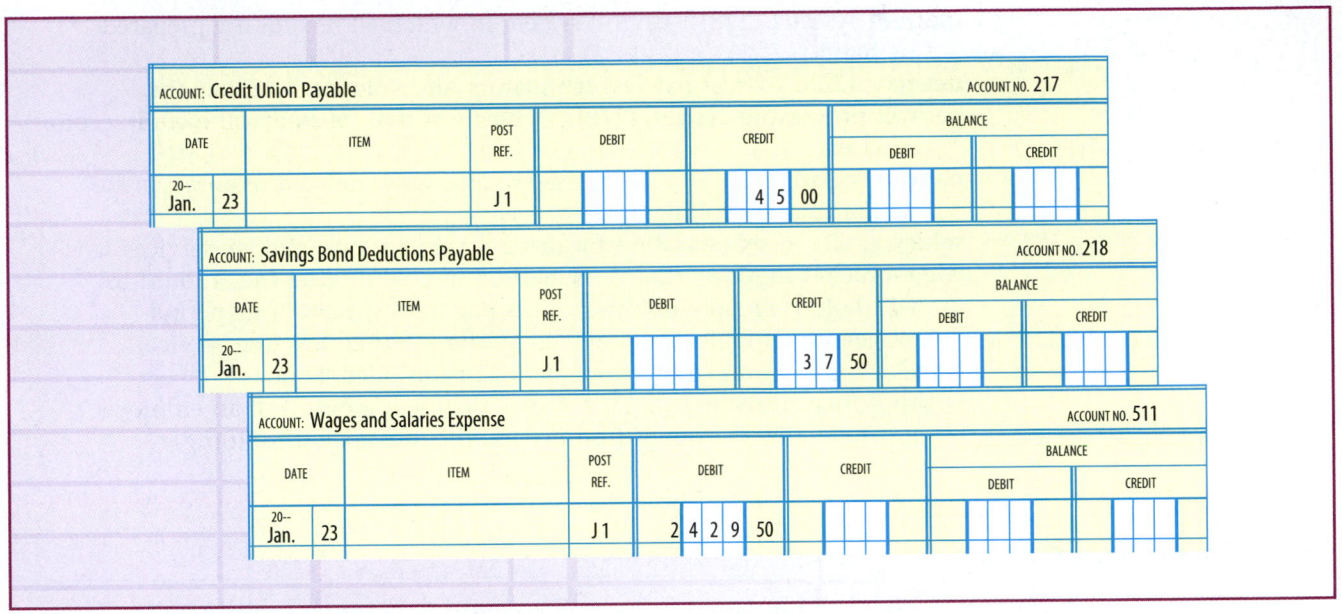

ACCOUNT: Credit Union Payable							ACCOUNT NO. 217	
DATE	ITEM	POST REF.	DEBIT	CREDIT	BALANCE			
					DEBIT		CREDIT	
20-- Jan. 23		J 1		4 5 00				

ACCOUNT: Savings Bond Deductions Payable							ACCOUNT NO. 218	
DATE	ITEM	POST REF.	DEBIT	CREDIT	BALANCE			
					DEBIT		CREDIT	
20-- Jan. 23		J 1		3 7 50				

ACCOUNT: Wages and Salaries Expense							ACCOUNT NO. 511	
DATE	ITEM	POST REF.	DEBIT	CREDIT	BALANCE			
					DEBIT		CREDIT	
20-- Jan. 23		J 1	2 4 2 9 50					

On-Line Learning Tools

For more information, visit: http://heintz.swlearning.com

The Heintz & Parry product web site is designed specifically for **COLLEGE ACCOUNTING, 18e.** The features include downloadable student resources and an interactive study center, organized by chapter, which contains learning objectives, web links, on-line quizzes with automatic feedback, and more.

KEY TERMS

direct deposit, (272)   A payroll method in which the employee does not handle the paycheck; payment is made by the employer directly to the employee's bank.

electronic system, (278)   A computer system based on a software package that performs all payroll record keeping and prepares payroll checks.

employee, (262)   Someone who works under the control and direction of an employer.

employee earnings record, (274)   A separate record of each employee's earnings.

Fair Labor Standards Act (FLSA), (263)   A law that requires employers to pay overtime at 1½ times the regular rate to any hourly employee who works over 40 hours in a week.

FICA taxes, (269)   Payroll taxes withheld to provide Social Security and Medicare benefits.

gross pay, (265)   An employee's total earnings.

independent contractor, (262)   Someone who performs a service for a fee and does not work under the control and direction of the company paying for the service.

manual system, (278)   Payroll system in which all records are prepared by hand.

net pay, (265)   Gross pay less mandatory and voluntary deductions.

payroll processing center, (278)   A business that sells payroll record-keeping services.

payroll register, (271)   A form used to assemble the data required at the end of each payroll period.

salary, (263)   Compensation for managerial or administrative services.

wage-bracket method, (266)   A method of determining the amount to withhold from an employee's gross pay for a specific time period. Wage-bracket tables are provided by the Internal Revenue Service.

wages, (263)   Compensation for skilled or unskilled labor.

withholding allowance, (265)   A specific dollar amount of an employee's gross pay that is exempt from federal income tax withholding.

REVIEW QUESTIONS

(LO1)   1. Why is it important for payroll accounting purposes to distinguish between an employee and an independent contractor?

(LO2)   2. Name three major categories of deductions from an employee's gross pay.

(LO2)   3. Identify the four factors that determine the amount of federal income tax that is withheld from an employee's pay each pay period.

(LO2)   4. In general, an employee is entitled to withholding allowances for what purposes?

(LO3)   5. Identify the three payroll records usually needed by an employer.

(LO3)   6. Describe the information contained in the payroll register.

(LO3)   7. Why is it important to total and verify the totals of the payroll register after the data for each employee have been entered?

(LO3)   8. Distinguish between the payroll register and the employee earnings record.

(LO4)   9. Explain what an employer does with the amounts withheld from an employee's pay.

(LO5)   10. Explain why payroll processing centers and electronic systems are commonly used in payroll accounting.

Self-Study Test Questions

True/False

1. An independent contractor is one who works under the control and direction of an employer. _____

2. Government laws and regulations regarding payroll are more complex for employees than for independent contractors. _____

3. Compensation for skilled or unskilled labor expressed in terms of hours, weeks, or units is called salary. _____

4. An employee's total earnings is called gross pay. _____

5. A payroll register is a multi-column form used to assemble the data required at the end of each payroll period. _____

Multiple Choice

1. Jack Smith is married, has a spouse who is not employed, has five dependent children, and does not anticipate large itemized deductions. How many withholding allowances is Smith entitled to? _____

    (a) 5   (c) 7
    (b) 6   (d) 8

2. A separate record of each employee's earnings is called a(n) _____

    (a) payroll register.   (c) W-4.
    (b) employee earnings record. (d) earnings statement.

3. Nancy Summers worked 44 hours during the past week. She is entitled to 1½ times her regular pay for all hours worked in excess of 40 during the week. Her regular rate of pay is $12.00. Social Security tax is withheld at the rate of 6.2% and Medicare tax is withheld at the rate of 1.45%; federal income tax withheld is $68; and $5 of union dues are withheld. Her net pay for the week is _____

    (a) $440.89.   (c) $552.00.
    (b) $472.00.   (d) $436.78.

4. Social Security Tax Payable and Medicare Tax Payable are classified as _____

    (a) liabilities.   (c) owner's equity.
    (b) assets.   (d) expenses.

5. Which of the following is *not* a factor that determines the amount of federal income tax to be withheld from an employee's gross pay? _____

    (a) marital status   (c) total earnings
    (b) number of withholding allowances claimed (d) age of employee

The answers to the Self-Study Test Questions are at the end of the text.

MANAGING YOUR WRITING

The minimum wage originally was only 25 cents an hour. Today it is $5.15 an hour. Assume that Congress is considering raising the minimum wage again and your United States representative is asking for public opinion on this issue. Write a letter to your representative with arguments for and against a higher minimum wage.

ETHICS CASE

Maura Lowe is a payroll accountant for N & L Company. She prepares and processes the company's payroll on a weekly basis and has been at N & L for only three months. All employees are paid on Friday. On Wednesday afternoon, Simon Lentz, one of the company's top sales associates, asks Maura to not take out any payroll deductions from his pay this week. He explains that he is short of cash and needs the full amount of his gross salary just to put food on the table and make his past-due car payment. He promises Maura that she can catch up on the deductions over the next month. The deductions include employee income tax, Social Security tax, Medicare tax, and health insurance premiums.

1. Is Simon's request of Maura ethical? Why or why not?

2. If this were the first pay period of the year and Maura agreed not to take out deductions from Simon's pay, what effect would this have on the liabilities section of the balance sheet?

3. Write a short paragraph from Maura to Simon explaining how omitting deductions from a pay period will cause errors in the company's financial statements.

4. In small groups, discuss what action Maura should take regarding Simon's request.

WEB WORK

Most people receive paychecks; they don't issue them. The bottom line and the benefits are noted and grumbled about, but what really goes into a person's paycheck? What are various benefits and compensation strategies? Visit the Interactive Study Center on our web site at **http://heintz.swlearning.com** for special hotlinks to assist you in this assignment.

SERIES A EXERCISES

EXERCISE 8-1A   (LO2)   **COMPUTING NET PAY** Mary Sue Guild works for a company that pays its
Net pay: $438.51   employees 1½ times the regular rate for all hours worked in excess of 40 per week. Guild's pay rate is $10.00 per hour. Her wages are subject to deductions for federal income tax, Social Security tax, and Medicare tax. She is married and claims 4 withholding allowances. Guild has a ½-hour lunch break during an 8½-hour day. Her time card is shown on the next page.

Name	Mary Sue Guild					
Week Ending	March 30, 20--					
Day	In	Out	In	Out	Hours Worked	
					Regular	Overtime
M	7:57	12:05	12:35	4:33	8	
T	7:52	12:09	12:39	5:05	8	½
W	7:59	12:15	12:45	5:30	8	1
T	8:00	12:01	12:30	6:31	8	2
F	7:56	12:05	12:34	4:30	8	
S	8:00	10:31				2½

Complete the following:

a) _____ regular hours × $10.00 per hour $_____

b) _____ overtime hours × $15.00 per hour $_____

c) Total gross wages $_____

d) Federal income tax withholding (from tax tables in Figure 8-4, pages 000 and 000) $_____

e) Social Security withholding at 6.2% $_____

f) Medicare withholding at 1.45% $_____

g) Total withholding $_____

h) Net pay $_____

EXERCISE 8-2A   **(LO2)**
Gross pay: $795.00

COMPUTING WEEKLY GROSS PAY Ryan Lawrence's regular hourly rate is $15.00. He receives 1½ times the regular rate for any hours worked over 40 a week and double the rate for work on Sunday. During the past week, Lawrence worked 8 hours each day Monday through Thursday, 10 hours on Friday, and 5 hours on Sunday. Compute Lawrence's gross pay for the past week.

EXERCISE 8-3A   **(LO2)**
b: $712.50

COMPUTING OVERTIME RATE OF PAY AND GROSS WEEKLY PAY Rebecca Huang receives a regular salary of $2,600 a month and is paid 1½ times the regular hourly rate for hours worked in excess of 40 per week.

a) Calculate Huang's overtime rate of pay.

b) Calculate Huang's total gross weekly pay if she works 45 hours during the week.

EXERCISE 8-4A   **(LO2)**
e: $13.00

COMPUTING FEDERAL INCOME TAX Using the table in Figure 8-4 on pages 267 and 268, determine the amount of federal income tax an employer should withhold weekly for employees with the following marital status, earnings, and withholding allowances.

	Marital Status	Total Weekly Earnings	Number of Allowances	Amount of Withholding
a)	S	$327.90	2	_____
b)	S	$410.00	1	_____
c)	M	$438.16	5	_____
d)	S	$518.25	0	_____
e)	M	$603.98	6	_____

EXERCISE 8-5A   (LO2)
3d row, Soc. Sec. tax: $161.20

CALCULATING SOCIAL SECURITY AND MEDICARE TAXES Assume a Social Security tax rate of 6.2% is applied to maximum earnings of $87,000 and a Medicare tax rate of 1.45% is applied to all earnings. Calculate the Social Security and Medicare tax for the following situations.

Cumul. Pay Before Current Weekly Payroll	Current Gross Pay	Year-to-Date Earnings	Soc. Sec. Maximum	Amount Over Max. Soc. Sec.	Amount Subject to Soc. Sec.	Soc. Sec. Tax Withheld	Medicare Tax Withheld
$22,000	$1,200	_____	$87,000	_____	_____	_____	_____
$54,000	$4,200	_____	$87,000	_____	_____	_____	_____
$84,400	$3,925	_____	$87,000	_____	_____	_____	_____
$86,400	$4,600	_____	$87,000	_____	_____	_____	_____

EXERCISE 8-6A   (LO4)
Med. tax: $126.15

JOURNALIZING PAYROLL TRANSACTIONS   On December 31, the payroll register of Hamstreet Associates indicated the following information.

Wages and Salaries Expense	$8,700.00
Employee Income Tax Payable	920.00
United Way Contributions Payable	200.00
Earnings subject to Social Security tax	8,000.00

Determine the amount of Social Security and Medicare taxes to be withheld and record the journal entry for the payroll, crediting Cash for the net pay.

EXERCISE 8-7A   (LO4)
Cr. Cash: $4,756.49

PAYROLL JOURNAL ENTRY Journalize the following data taken from the payroll register of University Printing as of April 15, 20--.

Regular earnings	$5,418.00
Overtime earnings	824.00
Deductions:	
Federal income tax	593.00
Social Security tax	387.00
Medicare tax	90.51
Pension plan	90.00
Health insurance premiums	225.00
United Way contributions	100.00

SERIES A PROBLEMS

PROBLEM 8-8A   (LO2/4)
Net pay: $179.19

GROSS PAY, DEDUCTIONS, AND NET PAY Donald Chin works for Northwest Supplies. His rate of pay is $8.50 per hour, and he is paid 1½ times the regular rate for all hours worked in excess of 40 per week. During the last week of January of the current year he worked 48 hours. Chin is married and claims 4 withholding allowances on his W-4 form. His weekly wages are subject to the following deductions.

a)   Employee income tax (use Figure 8-4 on pages 267 and 268)

b)   Social Security tax at 6.2%

c)   Medicare tax at 1.45%

d)   Health insurance premium, $85.00

e)   Credit union, $125.00

f)   United Way contribution, $10.00

REQUIRED

1. Compute Chin's regular pay, overtime pay, gross pay, and net pay.

2. Journalize the payment of his wages for the week ended January 31, crediting Cash for the net amount.

PROBLEM 8-9A   (LO2/3/4)

Cr. Cash: $1,799.01

PAYROLL REGISTER AND PAYROLL JOURNAL ENTRY Don McCullum operates a travel agency called Don's Luxury Travel. He has five employees, all of whom are paid on a weekly basis. The travel agency uses a payroll register, individual employee earnings records, and a general journal.

Don's Luxury Travel uses a weekly federal income tax withholding table. The payroll data for each employee for the week ended March 22, 20--, are given below. Employees are paid 1½ times the regular rate for working over 40 hours a week.

Name	No. of Allowances	Marital Status	Total Hours Worked Mar. 16–22	Rate	Total Earnings Jan. 1–Mar. 15
Ali, Loren	4	M	45	$11.00	$5,280.00
Carson, Judy	1	S	40	12.00	5,760.00
Hernandez, Maria	3	M	43	9.50	4,560.00
Knox, Wayne	1	S	39	11.00	5,125.50
Paglione, Jim	2	M	40	10.50	4,720.50

Social Security tax is withheld from the first $87,000 of earnings at the rate of 6.2%. Medicare tax is withheld at the rate of 1.45%, and city earnings tax at the rate of 1%, both applied to gross pay. Ali and Knox have $15.00 withheld and Carson and Hernandez have $5.00 withheld for health insurance. Ali and Knox have $20.00 withheld to be invested in the travel agency's credit union. Carson has $38.75 withheld and Hernandez has $18.75 withheld under a savings bond purchase plan.

Don's Luxury Travel's payroll is met by drawing checks on its regular bank account. The checks were issued in sequence, beginning with check no. 423.

REQUIRED

1. Prepare a payroll register for Don's Luxury Travel for the week ended March 22, 20--. (In the Taxable Earnings/Unemployment Compensation column, enter the same amounts as in the Social Security column.) Total the amount columns, verify the totals, and rule with single and double lines.

2. Assuming that the wages for the week ended March 22 were paid on March 24, prepare the journal entry for the payment of the payroll.

PROBLEM 8-10A   (LO3)

Soc. Sec. tax: $29.76

EMPLOYEE EARNINGS RECORD Don's Luxury Travel in Problem 8-9A keeps employee earnings records. Judy Carson, employee number 62, is employed as a manager in the ticket sales department. She was born on May 8, 1959, and was hired on June 1 of last year. Her Social Security number is 544-67-1283. She lives at 28 Quarry Drive, Vernon, CT 06066.

REQUIRED

For the week ended March 22, complete an employee earnings record for Judy Carson. (Insert earnings data only for the week of March 22.)

SERIES B EXERCISES

EXERCISE 8-1B   **(LO2)**
Net pay: $518.70

COMPUTING NET PAY Tom Hallinan works for a company that pays its employees $1\frac{1}{2}$ times the regular rate for all hours worked in excess of 40 per week. Hallinan's pay rate is $12.00 per hour. His wages are subject to deductions for federal income tax, Social Security tax, and Medicare tax. He is married and claims 5 withholding allowances. Hallinan has a $\frac{1}{2}$-hour lunch break during an $8\frac{1}{2}$-hour day. His time card is shown below.

Name	Tom Hallinan					
Week Ending	March 30, 20--					
					Hours Worked	
Day	In	Out	In	Out	Regular	Overtime
M	7:55	12:02	12:32	5:33	8	1
T	7:59	12:04	12:34	6:05	8	1½
W	7:59	12:05	12:35	4:30	8	
T	8:00	12:01	12:30	5:01	8	½
F	7:58	12:02	12:31	5:33	8	1
S	7:59	9:33				1½

Complete the following:

a) _____ regular hours × $12.00 per hour $_____

b) _____ overtime hours × $18.00 per hour $_____

c) Total gross wages $_____

d) Federal income tax withholding (from tax
    tables in Figure 8-4, pages 267 and 268) $_____

e) Social Security withholding at 6.2% $_____

f) Medicare withholding at 1.45% $_____

g) Total withholding $_____

h) Net pay $_____

EXERCISE 8-2B   **(LO2)**
Gross pay: $678.00

COMPUTING WEEKLY GROSS PAY Manuel Soto's regular hourly rate is $12.00. He receives $1\frac{1}{2}$ times the regular rate for hours worked in excess of 40 a week and double the rate for work on Sunday. During the past week, Soto worked 8 hours each day Monday through Thursday, 11 hours on Friday, and 6 hours on Sunday. Compute Soto's gross pay for the past week.

EXERCISE 8-3B   **(LO2)**
b: $918.75

COMPUTING OVERTIME RATE OF PAY AND GROSS WEEKLY PAY Mike Fritz receives a regular salary of $3,250 a month and is paid $1\frac{1}{2}$ times the regular hourly rate for hours worked in excess of 40 per week.

a) Calculate Fritz's overtime rate of pay. (Compute to the nearest half cent.)

b) Calculate Fritz's total gross weekly pay if he works 46 hours during the week.

EXERCISE 8-4B   (LO2)
e: $83.00

COMPUTING FEDERAL INCOME TAX Using the table in Figure 8-4 on pages 267 and 268, determine the amount of federal income tax an employer should withhold weekly for employees with the following marital status, earnings, and withholding allowances.

	Marital Status	Total Weekly Earnings	Number of Allowances	Amount of Withholding
a)	M	$546.00	4	_____
b)	M	$390.00	3	_____
c)	S	$461.39	2	_____
d)	M	$522.88	6	_____
e)	S	$612.00	0	_____

EXERCISE 8-5B   (LO2)
3d row, Soc. Sec. tax: $179.80

CALCULATING SOCIAL SECURITY AND MEDICARE TAXES Assume a Social Security tax rate of 6.2% is applied to maximum earnings of $87,000 and a Medicare tax rate of 1.45% is applied to all earnings. Calculate the Social Security and Medicare tax for the following situations.

Cumul. Pay Before Current Weekly Payroll	Current Gross Pay	Year-to-Date Earnings	Soc. Sec. Maximum	Amount Over Max. Soc. Sec.	Amount Subject to Soc. Sec.	Soc. Sec. Tax Withheld	Medicare Tax Withheld
$31,000	$1,500	____	$87,000	____	____	____	____
$53,000	$2,860	____	$87,000	____	____	____	____
$84,100	$3,140	____	$87,000	____	____	____	____
$86,400	$2,920	____	$87,000	____	____	____	____

EXERCISE 8-6B   (LO4)
Med. tax: $136.30

JOURNALIZING PAYROLL TRANSACTIONS On November 30, the payroll register of Webster & Smith indicated the following information:

Wages and Salaries Expense	$9,400.00
Employee Income Tax Payable	985.00
United Way Contributions Payable	200.00
Earnings subject to Social Security tax	9,400.00

Determine the amount of Social Security and Medicare taxes to be withheld and record the journal entry for the payroll, crediting Cash for the net pay.

EXERCISE 8-7B   (LO4)
Cr. Cash: $5,696.54

PAYROLL JOURNAL ENTRY Journalize the following data taken from the payroll register of Himes Bakery as of June 12, 20--.

Regular earnings	$6,520.00
Overtime earnings	950.00
Deductions:	
Federal income tax	782.00
Social Security tax	463.14
Medicare tax	108.32
Pension plan	80.00
Health insurance premiums	190.00
United Way contributions	150.00

SERIES B PROBLEMS

PROBLEM 8-8B   (LO2/4)
Net pay: $191.27

GROSS PAY, DEDUCTIONS, AND NET PAY Elyse Lin works for Columbia Industries. Her rate of pay is $9.00 per hour, and she is paid 1½ times the regular rate for all hours worked in excess of 40 per week. During the last week of January of the current year she worked 46 hours. Lin is married and claims 4 withholding allowances on her W-4 form. Her weekly wages are subject to the following deductions.

a)   Employee income tax (use Figure 8-4 on pages 267 and 268)

b)   Social Security tax at 6.2%

c)   Medicare tax at 1.45%

d)   Health insurance premium, $92.00

e)   Credit union, $110.00

f)   United Way contribution, $5.00

REQUIRED

1.   Compute Lin's regular pay, overtime pay, gross pay, and net pay.

2.   Journalize the payment of her wages for the week ended January 31, crediting Cash for the net amount.

PROBLEM 8-9B   (LO2/3/4)

Cr. Cash: $1,746.40

PAYROLL REGISTER AND PAYROLL JOURNAL ENTRY Karen Jolly operates a bakery called Karen's Cupcakes. She has five employees, all of whom are paid on a weekly basis. Karen's Cupcakes uses a payroll register, individual employee earnings records, and a general journal.

Karen's Cupcakes uses a weekly federal income tax withholding table. The payroll data for each employee for the week ended February 15, 20--, are given below. Employees are paid 1½ times the regular rate for working over 40 hours a week.

Name	No. of Allowances	Marital Status	Total Hours Worked Feb. 9–15	Rate	Total Earnings Jan. 1–Feb. 8
Barone, William	1	S	40	$10.00	$2,400.00
Hastings, Gene	4	M	45	12.00	3,360.00
Nitobe, Isako	3	M	46	8.75	2,935.00
Smith, Judy	4	M	42	11.00	2,745.00
Tarshis, Dolores	1	S	39	10.50	2,650.75

Social Security tax is withheld from the first $87,000 of earnings at the rate of 6.2%. Medicare tax is withheld at the rate of 1.45%, and city earnings tax at the rate of 1%, both applied to gross pay. Hastings and Smith have $35.00 withheld and Nitobe and Tarshis have $15.00 withheld for health insurance. Nitobe and Tarshis have $25.00 withheld to be invested in the bakers' credit union. Hastings has $18.75 withheld and Smith has $43.75 withheld under a savings bond purchase plan.

Karen's Cupcakes' payroll is met by drawing checks on its regular bank account. The checks were issued in sequence, beginning with no. 365.

REQUIRED

1.   Prepare a payroll register for Karen's Cupcakes for the week ended February 15, 20--. (In the Taxable Earnings/Unemployment Compensation column,

enter the same amounts as in the Social Security column.) Total the amount columns, verify the totals, and rule with single and double lines.

2. Assuming that the wages for the week ended February 15 were paid on February 17, prepare the journal entry for the payment of this payroll.

PROBLEM 8-10B   (LO3)
Soc. Sec. tax: $24.80

EMPLOYEE EARNINGS RECORD Karen's Cupcakes in Problem 8-9B keeps employee earnings records. William Barone, employee number 19, is employed as a baker in the desserts department. He was born on August 26, 1959, and was hired on October 1 of last year. His Social Security number is 342-73-4681. He lives at 30 Timber Lane, Willington, CT 06279.

REQUIRED

For the week ended February 15, complete an employee earnings record for William Barone. (Insert earnings data only for the week of February 15.)

MASTERY PROBLEM

Cr. Cash: $4,133.52

Abigail Trenkamp owns and operates the Trenkamp Collection Agency. Listed below are the name, number of allowances claimed, marital status, information from time cards on hours worked each day, and the hourly rate of each employee. All hours worked in excess of 40 hours for Monday through Friday are paid at 1½ times the regular rate. All weekend hours are paid at double the regular rate.

Trenkamp uses a weekly federal income tax withholding table (see Figure 8-4 on pages 267 and 268). Social Security tax is withheld at the rate of 6.2% for the first $87,000 earned. Medicare tax is withheld at 1.45% and state income tax at 3.5%. Each employee has $5.00 withheld for health insurance. All employees use payroll deduction to the credit union for varying amounts as listed below.

Trenkamp Collection Agency
Payroll Information for the Week Ended November 18, 20--

Name	Employee No.	No. of Allow.	Marital Status	Regular Hours Worked S	S	M	T	W	T	F	Hourly Rate	Credit Union Deposit	Total Earnings 1/1–11/11
Berling, James	1	3	M	2	2	9	8	8	9	10	$12.00	$149.60	$24,525.00
Merz, Linda	2	4	M	4	3	8	8	8	8	11	10.00	117.00	20,480.00
Goetz, Ken	3	5	M	0	0	6	7	8	9	10	11.00	91.30	21,500.00
Menick, Judd	4	2	S	8	8	0	0	8	8	9	11.00	126.50	22,625.00
Morales, Eva	5	3	M	0	0	8	8	8	6	8	13.00	117.05	24,730.00
Heimbrock, Jacob	6	2	M	0	0	8	8	8	8	8	34.00	154.25	86,040.00
Townsley, Sarah	7	2	M	4	0	6	6	6	6	4	9.00	83.05	21,425.00
Salzman, Ben	8	4	M	6	2	8	8	6	6	6	11.00	130.00	6,635.00
Layton, Esther	9	4	M	0	0	8	8	8	8	8	11.00	88.00	5,635.00
Thompson, David	10	5	M	0	2	10	9	7	7	10	11.00	128.90	21,635.00
Vadillo, Carmen	11	2	S	8	0	4	8	8	8	9	13.00	139.11	24,115.00

The Trenkamp Collection Agency follows the practice of drawing a single check for the net amount of the payroll and depositing the check in a special payroll account at the bank. Individual checks issued were numbered consecutively, beginning with no. 331.

(continued)

REQUIRED

1. Prepare a payroll register for Trenkamp Collection Agency for the week ended November 18, 20--. (In the Taxable Earnings/Unemployment Compensation column, enter $365 for Salzman and $440 for Layton. Leave this column blank for all other employees.) Total the amount columns, verify the totals, and rule with single and double lines.

2. Assuming that the wages for the week ended November 18 were paid on November 21, prepare the journal entry for the payment of this payroll.

3. The current employee earnings record for Ben Salzman is provided in the working papers. Update Salzman's earnings record to reflect the November 18 payroll. Although this information should have been entered earlier, complete the required information on the earnings record. The necessary information is provided below.

Name	Ben F. Salzman
Address	12 Windmill Lane
	Trumbull, CT 06611
Employee No.	8
Gender	Male
Department	Administration
Occupation	Office Manager
Social Security No.	446-46-6321
Marital Status	Married
Allowances	4
Pay Rate	$11.00 per hour
Date of Birth	4/5/64
Date Hired	7/22/--

CHALLENGE PROBLEM

This problem challenges you to apply your cumulative accounting knowledge to move a step beyond the material in the chapter.

Dr. Wages and Salaries Expense: $1,596

Irina Company pays its employees weekly. The last pay period for 20-1 was on December 28. From December 28 through December 31, the employees earned $1,754.00, so the following adjusting entry was made.

5	20-1 Dec.	31	Wages and Salaries Expense	1 7 5 4 00				5
6			Wages and Salaries Payable		1 7 5 4 00			6
7			To record accrued wages and salaries					7

The first pay period in 20-2 was on January 4. The totals line from Irina Company's payroll register for the week ended January 4, 20-2 was as follows:

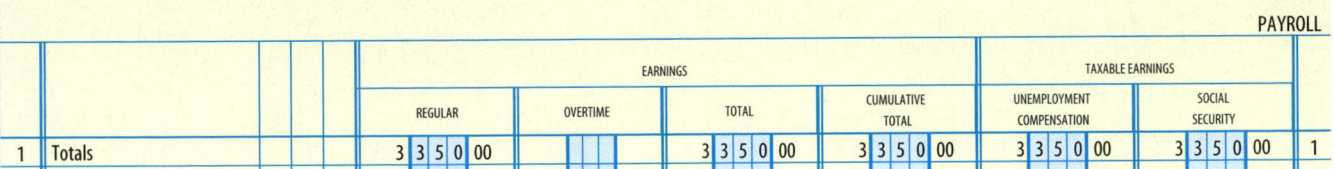

PAYROLL

				EARNINGS				TAXABLE EARNINGS		
				REGULAR	OVERTIME	TOTAL	CUMULATIVE TOTAL	UNEMPLOYMENT COMPENSATION	SOCIAL SECURITY	
1	Totals			3 3 5 0 00		3 3 5 0 00	3 3 5 0 00	3 3 5 0 00	3 3 5 0 00	1

REGISTER—WEEK ENDED January 4, 20-2

		DEDUCTIONS							NET PAY	
		FEDERAL INCOME TAX	SOCIAL SECURITY TAX	MEDICARE TAX	HEALTH INSURANCE	UNITED WAY	OTHER	TOTAL		
1		3 4 2 00	2 0 7 70	4 8 58	5 0 00	8 0 00		7 2 8 28	2 6 2 1 72	1

REQUIRED

1. Prepare the journal entry for the payment of the payroll on January 4, 20-2.

2. Prepare T accounts for Wages and Salaries Expense and Wages and Salaries Payable showing the beginning balance, January 4, 20-2 entry, and ending balance as of January 4, 20-2.

DIGITAL IMAGING GROUP

Payroll Accounting: Employer Taxes and Reports

Evan Taylor's new shop assistant has worked out extremely well. Parkway Pet Supplies is better organized, and customers receive more direct attention. Having worked in a store in another state, the new hire also was able to help Evan obtain accounts with two new vendors. The only negative feature of having the new employee has been the cost. Based on 25 hours per week at $8 an hour, Evan had budgeted a cost of $200 per week for help. In fact, as Evan's bookkeeper had warned him, the cost is substantially higher. In simple terms, Evan has discovered that he must pay numerous payroll taxes, in addition to the basic wages of the employee. What payroll taxes must Evan pay as an employer? Assuming the employee works a full year and is paid $10,400 (52 weeks × $200), what is the total payroll cost to Evan of having this employee?

Careful study of this chapter
should enable you to:

LO1 **Describe and calculate
employer payroll taxes.**

LO2 **Account for employer
payroll taxes expense.**

LO3 **Describe employer
reporting and payment
responsibilities.**

LO4 **Describe and account
for workers' compen-
sation insurance.**

The taxes we discussed in Chapter 8 had one thing in common—they all were levied on the employee. The employer withheld them from employees' earnings and paid them to the government. They did not add anything to the employer's payroll expenses.

In this chapter, we will examine several taxes that are imposed directly on the employer. All of these taxes represent additional payroll expenses.

EMPLOYER PAYROLL TAXES

LO1 Describe and calculate employer payroll taxes.

Most employers must pay FICA, FUTA (Federal Unemployment Tax Act), and SUTA (state unemployment tax) taxes.

Employer FICA Taxes

Employer FICA taxes are levied on employers at the same rates and on the same earnings bases as the employee FICA taxes. As explained in Chapter 8, we are assuming the Social Security component is 6.2% on maximum earnings of $87,000 for each employee. Since there is no maximum on the Medicare component, this tax is 1.45% on all earnings.

The payroll register we saw in Chapter 8 is a key source of information for computing employer payroll taxes. That payroll register is reproduced in Figure 9-1. The Taxable Earnings Social Security column shows that $4,835 of employee earnings were subject to Social Security tax for the pay period. The employer's Social Security tax on these earnings is computed as follows:

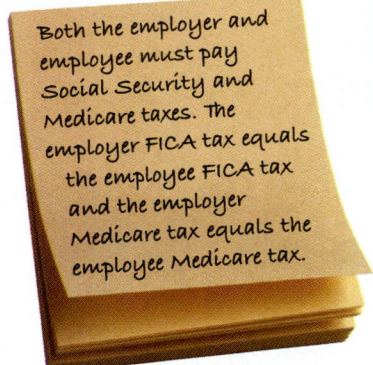

Both the employer and employee must pay Social Security and Medicare taxes. The employer FICA tax equals the employee FICA tax and the employer Medicare tax equals the employee Medicare tax.

PAYROLL

	NAME	ALLOWANCES	MARITAL STATUS	EARNINGS							TAXABLE EARNINGS		
				REGULAR	OVERTIME	TOTAL	CUMULATIVE TOTAL	UNEMPLOYMENT COMPENSATION	SOCIAL SECURITY	
1	Cadrain, Sarah	4	M	1 6 0 0 00	6 0 00	1 6 6 0 00	88 0 0 0 00		6 6 0 00	1
2	Guder, James	1	S	7 6 0 00	1 4 0 00	9 0 0 00	43 4 0 0 00		9 0 0 00	2
3	Istone, Ken	6	M	5 4 5 00		5 4 5 00	27 0 2 5 00		5 4 5 00	3
4	Kuzmik, Helen	2	M	4 8 0 00	2 9 4 00	7 7 4 00	31 0 0 0 00		7 7 4 00	4
5	Lee, Hoseoup	3	M	4 4 0 00		4 4 0 00	22 3 4 0 00		4 4 0 00	5
6	Swaney, Linda	2	S	5 2 8 00	1 9 8 00	7 2 6 00	27 5 0 0 00		7 2 6 00	6
7	Tucci, Paul	5	M	4 9 0 00		4 9 0 00	25 0 5 0 00		4 9 0 00	7
8	Wiles, Harry	1	S	3 0 0 00		3 0 0 00	6 3 0 0 00	3 0 0 00	3 0 0 00	8
9				5 1 4 3 00	6 9 2 00	5 8 3 5 00	270 6 1 5 00	3 0 0 00	4 8 3 5 00	9

Time cards, pay rates

Prior period total + current period earnings

Current below $7,000 cumul. total

Current below $87,000 cumul. total

FIGURE 9-1 Payroll Register (left side)

Social Security Taxable Earnings	×	Tax Rate	=	Tax
$4,835		.062		$299.77

> **LEARNING KEY:** Use the information in the payroll register to compute employer payroll taxes.

The Medicare tax applies to the total earnings of $5,835. The employer's Medicare tax on these earnings is computed as follows:

Total Earnings	×	Tax Rate	=	Tax
$5,835		.0145		$84.61

These amounts plus the employees' Social Security and Medicare taxes withheld must be paid by the employer to the Internal Revenue Service (IRS).

Self-Employment Tax

Individuals who own and run their own business are considered self-employed. These individuals can be viewed as both employer and employee. They do not receive salary or wages from the business, but they do have earnings in the form of the business net income. **Self-employment income** is the net income of a trade or business run by an individual. Currently, persons earning net self-employment income of $400 or more must pay a **self-employment tax**. Self-employment tax is a contribution to the FICA program. The tax rates are double the Social Security and Medicare rates. They are applied to the same income bases as those used for the Social Security and Medicare taxes.

One half of the self-employment tax is a personal expense of the owner of the business. The other half is similar to the employer Social Security and Medicare taxes paid for each employee. This portion of the tax is considered a business expense and is debited to Self-Employment Tax.

The self-employment tax rate is double the employee and employer Social Security and Medicare rates because the self-employed person is considered both the employer and employee.

REGISTER—WEEK ENDED 12/19/--

	FEDERAL INCOME TAX	SOCIAL SECURITY TAX	MEDICARE TAX	HEALTH INSURANCE	UNITED WAY	OTHER	TOTAL	NET PAY	CHECK NO.	
1	234 00	40 92	24 07				298 99	1 361 01	409	1
2	146 00	55 80	13 05		20 00		234 85	665 15	410	2
3	7 00	33 79	7 90	10 00			58 69	486 31	411	3
4	69 00	47 99	11 22	13 00	20 00		161 21	612 79	412	4
5	15 00	27 28	6 38	13 00			61 66	378 34	413	5
6	81 00	45 01	10 53				136 54	589 46	414	6
7	8 00	30 38	7 11	10 00			55 49	434 51	415	7
8	24 00	18 60	4 35				46 95	253 05	416	8
9	584 00	299 77	84 61	46 00	40 00		1 054 38	4 780 62		9

Withholding Tax Table — 6.2% × Social Security taxable earnings — 1.45% × total earnings — Specific employer–employee agreements — Total earnings – total deductions

FIGURE 9-1 Payroll Register (right side)

Employer FUTA Tax

The **FUTA (Federal Unemployment Tax Act) tax** is levied only on employers. It is not deducted from employees' earnings. The purpose of this tax is to raise funds to administer the combined federal/state unemployment compensation program. The maximum amount of earnings subject to the FUTA tax and the tax rate can be changed by Congress. The current rate is 6.2% applied to maximum earnings of $7,000 for each employee, but employers are allowed a credit of up to 5.4% for participation in state unemployment programs. Thus, the effective federal rate is commonly 0.8%.

Gross FUTA rate	6.2%
Credit for state unemployment taxes	5.4%
Net FUTA rate	0.8%

To illustrate the computation of the FUTA tax, refer to Figure 9-1. The Taxable Earnings Unemployment Compensation column shows that only $300 of employee earnings were subject to the FUTA tax. This amount is so low because the payroll period is late in the calendar year (December 19, 20--). It is common for most employees to exceed the $7,000 earnings limit by this time. The FUTA tax is computed as shown in Figure 9-2.

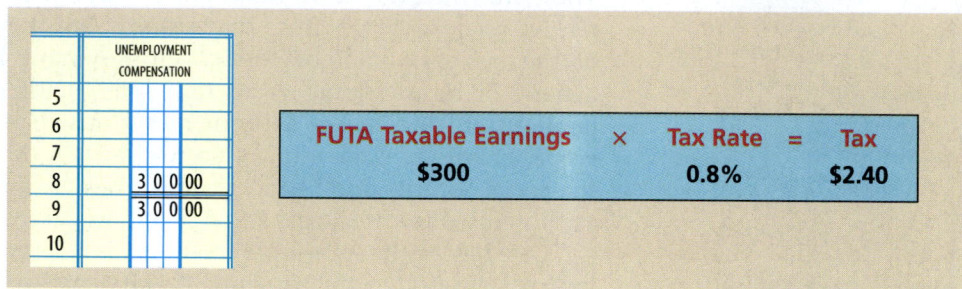

FIGURE 9-2   Computation of FUTA Tax

Employer SUTA Tax

The **SUTA (state unemployment tax) tax** is also levied only on employers in most states. The purpose of this tax is to raise funds to pay unemployment benefits. Tax rates and unemployment benefits vary among the states. A common rate is 5.4% applied to maximum earnings of $7,000 for each employee. Most states have a **merit-rating system** to encourage employers to provide regular employment to workers. If an employer has very few former employees receiving unemployment compensation, the employer qualifies for a lower state unemployment tax rate. If an employer qualifies for a lower state rate, the full credit of 5.4% would still be allowed in computing the federal unemployment tax due.

Refer to the payroll register in Figure 9-1. As we saw with the FUTA tax, only $300 of employee earnings for this pay period are subject to the state unemployment tax. The tax is computed as shown in Figure 9-3.

State unemployment tax rates and maximum earnings amounts vary greatly. Current rates range from 4.5% to 10%. Maximum earnings amounts are $7,000 to $29,300.

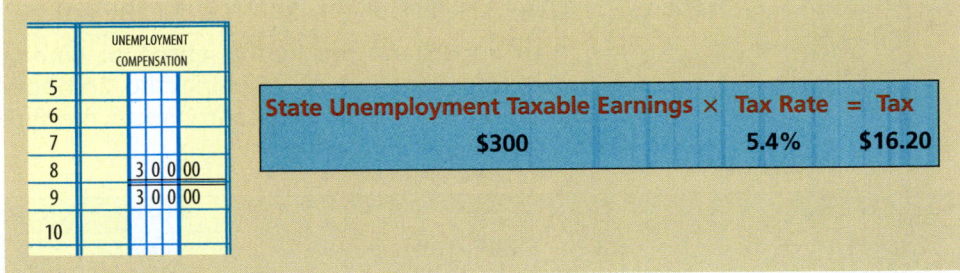

FIGURE 9-3 Computation of SUTA Tax

ACCOUNTING FOR EMPLOYER PAYROLL TAXES

LO2 Account for employer payroll taxes expense.

Now that we have computed the employer payroll taxes, we need to journalize them. It is common to debit all employer payroll taxes to a single account—Payroll Taxes Expense. However, we usually credit separate liability accounts for Social Security, Medicare, FUTA, and SUTA taxes payable.

Journalizing Employer Payroll Taxes

The employer payroll taxes computed in the previous section can be summarized as follows:

Employer's Social Security tax	$299.77
Employer's Medicare tax	84.61
FUTA tax	2.40
SUTA tax	16.20
Total employer payroll taxes	$402.98

These amounts provide the basis for the following journal entry.

5	Dec.	19	Payroll Taxes Expense	4 0 2 98				5
6			Social Security Tax Payable		2 9 9 77			6
7			Medicare Tax Payable		8 4 61			7
8			FUTA Tax Payable		2 40			8
9			SUTA Tax Payable		1 6 20			9
10			Employer payroll taxes for week ended Dec. 19					10

The steps needed to prepare this journal entry for employer payroll taxes are:

STEP 1 Obtain the total earnings and taxable earnings amounts from the Earnings—Total and Taxable Earnings columns of the payroll register. In this case, total earnings were $5,835; Social Security taxable earnings were $4,835; and Unemployment Compensation taxable earnings were $300.

STEP 2 Compute the amount of employer Social Security tax by multiplying the Social Security taxable earnings by 6.2%.

STEP 3 Compute the amount of employer Medicare tax by multiplying total earnings by 1.45%.

STEP 4 Compute the amount of FUTA tax by multiplying the Unemployment Taxable earnings by 0.8%.

STEP 5 Compute the amount of SUTA tax by multiplying the Unemployment Taxable earnings by 5.4%.

STEP 6   Prepare the appropriate journal entry using the amounts computed in steps 2–5.

To understand the journal entry for employer payroll taxes, let's use the accounting equation to examine the accounts involved. The five accounts affected by the payroll taxes entry above are shown in the accounting equation in Figure 9-4.

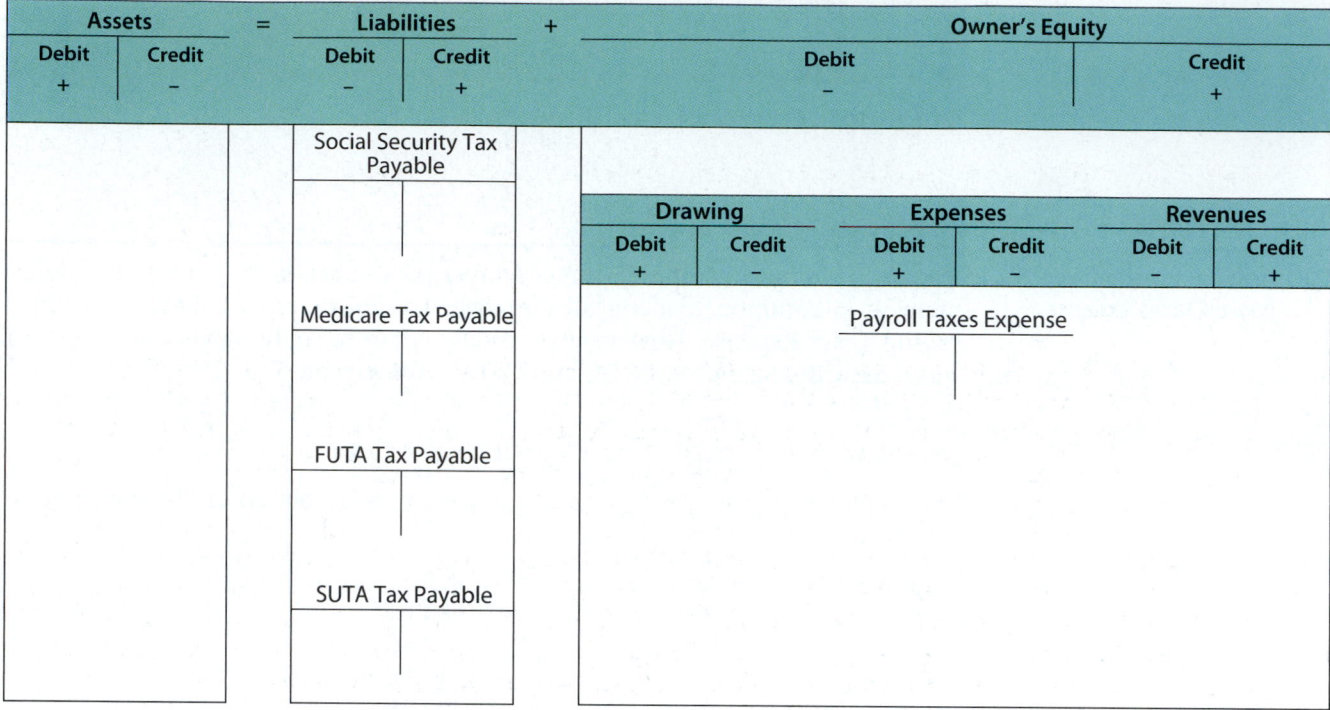

FIGURE 9-4   Accounting for Payroll Taxes

Payroll Taxes Expense

The Social Security, Medicare, FUTA, and SUTA taxes imposed on the employer are expenses of doing business. Each of the employer taxes is debited to Payroll Taxes Expense.

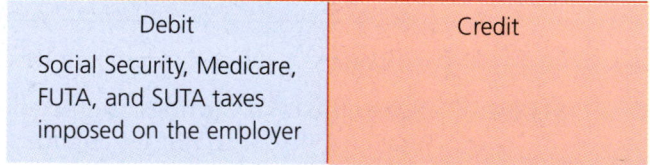

Social Security and Medicare Taxes Payable

These are the same liability accounts used in Chapter 8 to record the Social Security and Medicare taxes withheld from employees' earnings. The accounts are credited to enter the Social Security and Medicare taxes imposed on the employer. They are debited when the taxes are paid to the IRS. When all of the Social Security and Medicare taxes have been paid, the accounts will have zero balances.

Social Security Tax Payable

Debit	Credit
payment of Social Security tax	Social Security taxes (1) withheld from employees' earnings and (2) imposed on the employer

Medicare Tax Payable

Debit	Credit
payment of Medicare tax	Medicare taxes (1) withheld from employees' earnings and (2) imposed on the employer

 LEARNING KEY: Employer and employee Social Security and Medicare taxes are credited to the same liability accounts because both of these taxes are due and will be paid to the IRS.

FUTA Tax Payable

A separate liability account entitled FUTA Tax Payable is kept for the employer's FUTA tax. This account is credited for the tax imposed on employers under the Federal Unemployment Tax Act. The account is debited when this tax is paid. When all of the FUTA taxes have been paid, the account will have a zero balance.

FUTA Tax Payable

Debit	Credit
payment of FUTA tax	FUTA tax imposed on the employer

SUTA Tax Payable

A separate liability account entitled SUTA Tax Payable is kept for the state unemployment tax. This account is credited for the tax imposed on employers under the state unemployment compensation laws. The account is debited when this tax is paid. When all of the state unemployment taxes have been paid, the account will have a zero balance.

SUTA Tax Payable

Debit	Credit
payment of SUTA tax	SUTA tax imposed on the employer

Total Payroll Cost of an Employee

It is interesting to note what it really costs to employ a person. The employer must, of course, pay the gross wages of an employee. In addition, the employer must pay payroll taxes on employee earnings up to certain dollar limits.

To illustrate, assume that an employee earns $26,000 a year. The total cost of this employee to the employer is calculated as follows:

Gross wages	$26,000
Employer Social Security tax, 6.2% of $26,000	1,612
Employer Medicare tax, 1.45% of $26,000	377
State unemployment tax, 5.4% of $7,000	378
FUTA tax, 0.8% of $7,000	56
	$28,423

Thus, the total payroll cost of employing a person whose stated compensation is $26,000 is $28,423. Employer payroll taxes clearly are a significant cost of doing business. Employer-paid medical insurance and pension plans can further increase total payroll costs.

REPORTING AND PAYMENT RESPONSIBILITIES

LO3 **Describe employer reporting and payment responsibilities.**

Employer payroll reporting and payment responsibilities fall into five areas:

1. Federal income tax withholding and Social Security and Medicare taxes

2. FUTA taxes

3. SUTA taxes

4. Employee Wage and Tax Statement (Form W-2)

5. Summary of employee wages and taxes

Federal Income Tax Withholding and Social Security and Medicare Taxes

Three important aspects of employer reporting and payment responsibilities for federal income tax withholding and Social Security and Medicare taxes are:

1. Determining when payments are due

2. Use of Form 8109, Federal Tax Deposit Coupon

3. Use of Form 941, Employer's Quarterly Federal Tax Return

When Payments are Due. The date by which federal income tax withholding and Social Security and Medicare taxes must be paid depends on the amount of these taxes. Figure 9-5 summarizes the deposit rules stated in *Circular E—Employer's Tax Guide*. In general, the larger the amount that needs to be deposited, the more frequently payments must be made. For simplicity, we will assume that deposits must be made 15 days after the end of each month.

ACCUMULATED TAX LIABILITY	DEPOSIT DUE
1. Less than $2,500 at the end of the current quarter	1. Pay with Form 941 at end of the month following end of the quarter
2. $2,500 or more at the end of the current quarter and $50,000 or less in total during the lookback period*	2. Deposit 15 days after end of the month
3. $2,500 or more at the end of the current quarter and more than $50,000 in total during the lookback period*	3. Deposit every other Wednesday or Friday, depending on day of the week payroll payments are made
4. $100,000 or more on any day during the current quarter	4. Deposit by the end of the next banking day

*Lookback period is the four quarters beginning July 1, two years ago, and ending June 30, one year ago.

FIGURE 9-5 Summary of Deposit Rules

Form 8109. Deposits may be made using either the **Electronic Federal Tax Payment System (EFTPS)** or Form 8109. The EFTPS is an electronic funds transfer system for making federal tax deposits. Any taxpayer whose deposits in the prior year exceeded $200,000 is required to use this system. Deposits other than EFTPS are made at an authorized commercial bank using Form 8109, Federal Tax Deposit Coupon (Figure 9-6). The **Employer Identification Number (EIN)** shown on this form is obtained by the employer from the IRS. This number identifies the employer and must be shown on all payroll forms and reports filed with the IRS.

Taxpayers who are not required to make electronic deposits may voluntarily participate in EFTPS.

FIGURE 9-6 Federal Tax Deposit Coupon (Form 8109)

The $5,850.88 deposit shown in Figure 9-6 for Westly, Inc. was for the following taxes.

Employees' income tax withheld from wages		$2,526.80
Social Security tax:		
Withheld from employees' wages	$1,346.24	
Imposed on employer	1,346.24	2,692.48
Medicare tax:		
Withheld from employees' wages	$ 315.80	
Imposed on employer	315.80	631.60
Amount of check		$5,850.88

The journal entry for this deposit would be:

5	Feb.	15	Employee Income Tax Payable	2 5 2 6 80		5
6			Social Security Tax Payable	2 6 9 2 48		6
7			Medicare Tax Payable	6 3 1 60		7
8			Cash		5 8 5 0 88	8
9			Deposit of employee federal income tax and			9
10			Social Security and Medicare taxes			10

Form 941. Form 941, Employer's Quarterly Federal Tax Return, must be filed with the IRS at the end of the month following each calendar quarter. This form reports the following taxes for the quarter.

1. Employee federal income tax withheld

2. Employee Social Security and Medicare taxes withheld

3. Employer Social Security and Medicare taxes

A completed form for Westly, Inc. for the first quarter of the calendar year is shown in Figure 9-7. Instructions for completing the form are provided with the form and in *Circular E*.

FUTA Taxes

Federal unemployment taxes must be calculated on a quarterly basis. If the accumulated liability exceeds $100, the total must be paid to an authorized commercial bank. The total is due by the end of the month following the close of the quarter. If the liability is $100 or less, no deposit is necessary. The amount is simply added to the amount to be deposited for the next quarter. FUTA taxes are deposited using either EFTPS or Form 8109 (Figure 9-6).

Assume that Westly, Inc.'s accumulated FUTA tax liability for the first quarter of the calendar year is $408. Westly would use Form 8109 to deposit this amount on April 30. The journal entry for this transaction would be as follows:

15	Apr.	30	FUTA Tax Payable	4 0 8 00		15
16			Cash		4 0 8 00	16
17			Paid federal unemployment tax			17

Form 941
(Rev. January 2003)
Department of the Treasury
Internal Revenue Service (99)

Employer's Quarterly Federal Tax Return
See separate instructions revised January 2003 for information on completing this return.
Please type or print.

OMB No. 1545-0029

Enter state code for state in which deposits were made **only** if different from state in address to the right ▶ (see page 2 of separate instructions).

Name (as distinguished from trade name)

Date quarter ended
March 30, 20–

Trade name, if any
Westly, Inc.

Employer identification number
43-0211630

Address (number and street)
5221 Natural Bridge

City, state, and ZIP code
St. Louis, MO 63115-8230

T	
FF	
FD	
FP	
I	
T	

If address is different from prior return, check here ▶

IRS Use

| 1 1 1 1 1 1 1 1 1 1 | 2 | 3 3 3 3 3 3 3 | 4 4 4 | 5 5 5 |
| 6 7 8 9 8 8 8 8 9 8 8 | | 9 9 9 | 10 10 10 10 10 10 10 10 10 10 | |

A If you **do not have to file** returns in the future, check here ▶ ☐ and enter date final wages paid ▶

B If you are a seasonal employer, see **Seasonal employers** on page 1 of the instructions and check here ▶ ☐

1	Number of employees in the pay period that includes March 12th . ▶	1	8	
2	Total wages and tips, plus other compensation		**2**	65,160 00
3	Total income tax withheld from wages, tips, and sick pay		**3**	7,595 80
4	Adjustment of withheld income tax for preceding quarters of **this calendar year**		**4**	0
5	Adjusted total of income tax withheld (line 3 as adjusted by line 4)		**5**	7,595 80
6	Taxable social security wages	6a 65,160 00	12.4% (.124) =	**6b**	8,079 84
	Taxable social security tips	6c 0	12.4% (.124) =	**6d**	0
7	Taxable Medicare wages and tips . . .	7a 65,160 00	2.9% (.029) =	**7b**	1,889 64
8	Total social security and Medicare taxes (add lines 6b, 6d, and 7b). **Check here if wages are not subject to social security and/or Medicare tax** . . . . ▶ ☐		**8**	9,969 48
9	Adjustment of social security and Medicare taxes (see instructions for required explanation) Sick Pay $ _____ Fractions of Cents $ _____ Other $ _____ =		**9**	0
10	Adjusted total of social security and Medicare taxes (line 8 as adjusted by line 9)		**10**	9,969 48
11	**Total taxes** (add lines 5 and 10)		**11**	17,565 28
12	Advance earned income credit (EIC) payments made to employees (see instructions) . . .		**12**	0
13	Net taxes (subtract line 12 from line 11. **If $2,500 or more, this must equal line 17, column (d) below (or line D of Schedule B (Form 941))**		**13**	17,565 28
14	Total deposits for quarter, including overpayment applied from a prior quarter		**14**	17,565 28
15	**Balance due** (subtract line 14 from line 13). See instructions		**15**	0
16	**Overpayment.** If line 14 is more than line 13, enter excess here ▶ $ _____ and check if to be: ☐ Applied to next return **or** ☐ Refunded.			

- **All filers:** If line 13 is less than $2,500, **do not** complete line 17 or Schedule B (Form 941).
- **Semiweekly schedule depositors:** Complete Schedule B (Form 941) and check here . . . . ▶ ☐
- **Monthly schedule depositors:** Complete line 17, columns (a) through (d), and check here. . . . . ▶ ☒

17	Monthly Summary of Federal Tax Liability. (Complete **Schedule B (Form 941)** instead, if you were a semiweekly schedule depositor.)			
	(a) First month liability	**(b)** Second month liability	**(c)** Third month liability	**(d)** Total liability for quarter
	5,850.88	5,690.77	6,023.63	17,565.28

Third Party Designee

Do you want to allow another person to discuss this return with the IRS (see separate instructions)? ☐ **Yes.** Complete the following. ☐ **No**

Designee's name ▶

Phone no. ▶ ( )

Personal identification number (PIN)

Sign Here

Under penalties of perjury, I declare that I have examined this return, including accompanying schedules and statements, and to the best of my knowledge and belief, it is true, correct, and complete.

Signature ▶ *William P. Jones*

Print Your Name and Title ▶ *William P. Jones* Treasurer

Date ▶ 4/30/--

For Privacy Act and Paperwork Reduction Act Notice, see back of Payment Voucher.

Cat. No. 17001Z

Form **941** (Rev. 1-2003)

FIGURE 9-7 Employer's Quarterly Federal Tax Return (Form 941)

Form **940-EZ**

Department of the Treasury
Internal Revenue Service (99)

Employer's Annual Federal
Unemployment (FUTA) Tax Return

See separate Instructions for Form 940-EZ for information on completing this form.

OMB No. 1545-1110

20**02**

T	
FF	
FD	
FP	
I	
T	

You must complete this section. ▶

Name (as distinguished from trade name)

Calendar year

Trade name, if any
Westly, Inc.

Address and ZIP code
5221 Natural Bridge, St. Louis, MO 63115-8230

Employer identification number
43 : 0211630

Answer the questions under **Who May Use Form 940-EZ** *on page 2. If you cannot use Form 940-EZ, you must use Form 940.*

A Enter the amount of contributions paid to your state unemployment fund. (see separate instructions) . . . ▶ $ _____ 3,007.80

B (1) Enter the name of the state where you have to pay contributions . . . . ▶ _____ MO

(2) Enter your state reporting number as shown on your state unemployment tax return ▶ _____ 36112

If you will not have to file returns in the future, check here (see **Who Must File** in separate instructions) **and complete and sign the return.** ▶ ☐

If this is an Amended Return, check here (see **Amended Returns** on page 2 of the separate instructions) . . . . ▶ ☐

Part I   Taxable Wages and FUTA Tax

1	Total payments (including payments shown on lines 2 and 3) during the calendar year for services of employees	1	258,954.00
2	Exempt payments. (Explain all exempt payments, attaching additional sheets if necessary.)	2	
3	Payments of more than $7,000 for services. Enter only amounts over the first $7,000 paid to each employee. **(see separate instructions)**	3	203,254.00
4	Add lines 2 and 3	4	203,254.00
5	**Total taxable wages** (subtract line 4 from line 1) . . . . ▶	5	55,700.00
6	**FUTA tax.** Multiply the wages on line 5 by .008 and enter here. **(If the result is over $100, also complete Part II.)**	6	445.60
7	Total FUTA tax deposited for the year, including any overpayment applied from a prior year	7	427.60
8	**Balance due** (subtract line 7 from line 6). Pay to the "United States Treasury." . . . . ▶	8	18.00
	If you owe more than $100, see **Depositing FUTA tax** in separate instructions.		
9	**Overpayment** (subtract line 6 from line 7). Check if it is to be: ☐ **Applied to next return** or ☐ **Refunded** ▶	9	

Part II   Record of Quarterly Federal Unemployment Tax Liability (Do not include state liability.) **Complete only if line 6 is over $100.**

Quarter	First (Jan. 1 – Mar. 31)	Second (Apr. 1 – June 30)	Third (July 1 – Sept. 30)	Fourth (Oct. 1 – Dec. 31)	Total for year
Liability for quarter	408.00	26.00	5.60	6.00	445.60

Third Party Designee

Do you want to allow another person to discuss this return with the IRS (see instructions page 5)? ☐ **Yes.** Complete the following. ☐ **No**

Designee's name ▶ _____ Phone no. ▶ ( ) Personal identification number (PIN) ☐☐☐☐☐

Under penalties of perjury, I declare that I have examined this return, including accompanying schedules and statements, and, to the best of my knowledge and belief, it is true, correct, and complete, and that no part of any payment made to a state unemployment fund claimed as a credit was, or is to be, deducted from the payments to employees.

Signature ▶ *William P. Jones*   Title (Owner, etc.) ▶ *Treasurer*   Date ▶ *1/31/--*

For Privacy Act and Paperwork Reduction Act Notice, see separate instructions.   **DETACH HERE**   Cat. No. 10983G   Form **940-EZ** (2002)

- -

Form **940-EZ(V)**

Department of the Treasury
Internal Revenue Service

Form 940-EZ Payment Voucher

Use this voucher only when making a payment with your return.

OMB No. 1545-1110

20**02**

Complete boxes 1, 2, and 3. Do not send cash, and do not staple your payment to this voucher. Make your check or money order payable to the "United States Treasury." Be sure to enter your employer identification number, "Form 940-EZ," and "2002" on your payment.

1 Enter your employer identification number.

2 Enter the amount of your payment. ▶ | Dollars | Cents |

3 Enter your business name (individual name for sole proprietors).

Enter your address.

Enter your city, state, and ZIP code.

FIGURE 9-8   Employer's Annual Federal Unemployment (FUTA) Tax Return (Form 940-EZ)

Form 940. In addition to making quarterly deposits, employers are required to file an annual report of federal unemployment tax using Form 940 or 940-EZ, a simplified version of Form 940. Form 940-EZ may be used by employers who pay unemployment contributions in only one state and have made all the payments by January 31. This form must be filed with the IRS by January 31 following the end of the calendar year. Figure 9-8 shows a completed Form 940-EZ for Westly, Inc. Instructions for completing the form are provided with the form and in *Circular E*.

SUTA Taxes

Deposit rules and forms for state unemployment taxes vary among the states. Deposits usually are required on a quarterly basis. Assume that Westly's accumulated state unemployment liability for the first quarter of the calendar year is $2,754. The journal entry for the deposit of this amount with the state on April 30 would be:

19	Apr.	30	SUTA Tax Payable		2 7 5 4 00			19
20			Cash			2 7 5 4 00		20
21			Paid state unemployment tax					21

Employee Wage and Tax Statement

By January 31 of each year, employers must furnish each employee with a Wage and Tax Statement, Form W-2 (Figure 9-9). This form shows the total amount of wages paid to the employee and the amounts of taxes withheld during the preceding taxable year. The employee earnings record contains the information needed to complete this form.

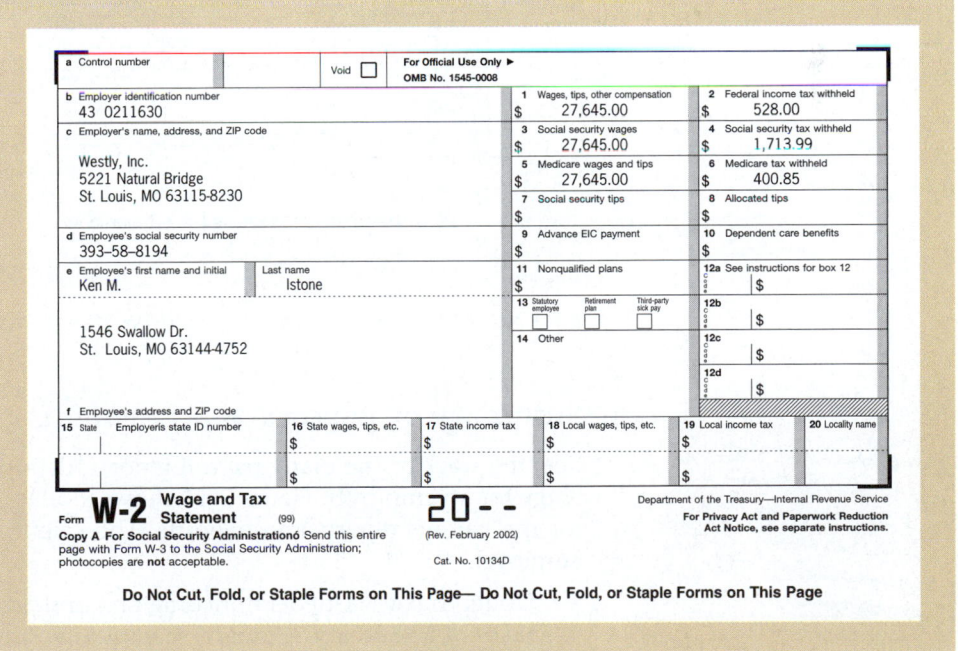

FIGURE 9-9   Wage and Tax Statement (Form W-2)

Multiple copies of Form W-2 are needed for the following purposes.

- Copy A—Employer sends to Social Security Administration
- Copy B—Employee attaches to federal income tax return
- Copy C—Employee retains for his or her own records
- Copy D—Employer retains for business records
- Copy 1—Employer sends to state or local tax department
- Copy 2—Employee attaches to state, city, or local income tax return

Summary of Employee Wages and Taxes

Employers send Form W-3, Transmittal of Wage and Tax Statements (Figure 9-10), with Copy A of Forms W-2 to the Social Security Administration. Form W-3 must be filed by February 28 following the end of each taxable year. This form summarizes the employee earnings and tax information presented on Forms W-2 for the year. Information needed to complete Form W-3 is contained in the employee earnings records.

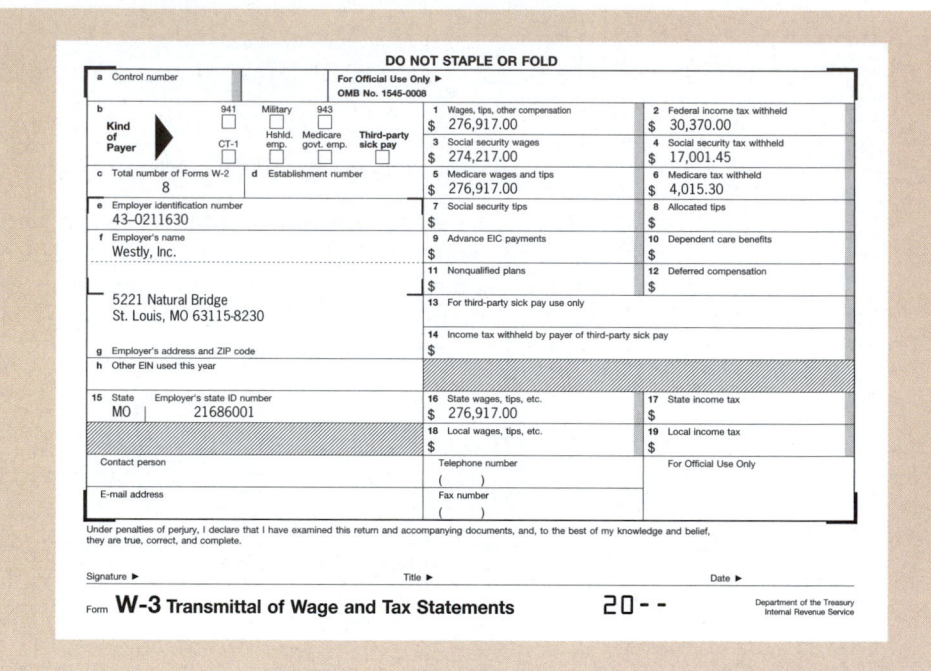

FIGURE 9-10   Transmittal of Wage and Tax Statements (Form W-3)

Summary of Reports and Payments

Keeping track of the many payroll reports, deposits, and due dates can be a challenge for an employer. Figure 9-11 shows a calendar that highlights the due dates for the various reports and deposits. The calendar assumes the following for an employer.

The complexity of payroll reports, deposit rules, and due dates is a major reason that small businesses often hire an accountant or an outside company to handle payroll.

1. Undeposited FIT (federal income tax) and Social Security and Medicare taxes of $2,500 at the end of each quarter and less than $50,000 during the lookback period.

2. Undeposited FUTA taxes of more than $100 at the end of each quarter.

3. SUTA taxes deposited quarterly.

Color Key

File Forms 940, 941, state unemployment tax report, and send W-2 to employees.	File form W-3 with Copy A of W-2s.	File Form 941 and make FUTA and SUTA tax deposits.	Deposit FIT and Social Security and Medicare taxes from previous month.

January
S	M	T	W	T	F	S
			1	2	3	4
5	6	7	8	9	10	11
12	13	14	15	16	17	18
19	20	21	22	23	24	25
26	27	28	29	30	31	

February
S	M	T	W	T	F	S
						1
2	3	4	5	6	7	8
9	10	11	12	13	14	15
16	17	18	19	20	21	22
23	24	25	26	27	28	29

March
S	M	T	W	T	F	S
1	2	3	4	5	6	7
8	9	10	11	12	13	14
15	16	17	18	19	20	21
22	23	24	25	26	27	28
29	30	31				

April
S	M	T	W	T	F	S
			1	2	3	4
5	6	7	8	9	10	11
12	13	14	15	16	17	18
19	20	21	22	23	24	25
26	27	28	29	30		

May
S	M	T	W	T	F	S
				1	2	
3	4	5	6	7	8	9
10	11	12	13	14	15	16
17	18	19	20	21	22	23
24	25	26	27	28	29	30
31						

June
S	M	T	W	T	F	S
	1	2	3	4	5	6
7	8	9	10	11	12	13
14	15	16	17	18	19	20
21	22	23	24	25	26	27
28	29	30				

July
S	M	T	W	T	F	S
			1	2	3	4
5	6	7	8	9	10	11
12	13	14	15	16	17	18
19	20	21	22	23	24	25
26	27	28	29	30	31	

August
S	M	T	W	T	F	S
						1
2	3	4	5	6	7	8
9	10	11	12	13	14	15
16	17	18	19	20	21	22
23	24	25	26	27	28	29
30	31					

September
S	M	T	W	T	F	S
		1	2	3	4	5
6	7	8	9	10	11	12
13	14	15	16	17	18	19
20	21	22	23	24	25	26
27	28	29	30			

October
S	M	T	W	T	F	S
				1	2	3
4	5	6	7	8	9	10
11	12	13	14	15	16	17
18	19	20	21	22	23	24
25	26	27	28	29	30	31

November
S	M	T	W	T	F	S
1	2	3	4	5	6	7
8	9	10	11	12	13	14
15	16	17	18	19	20	21
22	23	24	25	26	27	28
29	30					

December
S	M	T	W	T	F	S
		1	2	3	4	5
6	7	8	9	10	11	12
13	14	15	16	17	18	19
20	21	22	23	24	25	26
27	28	29	30	31		

FIGURE 9-11   Payroll Calendar

A BROADER VIEW

Dealing with Payroll Complexity—Let Someone Else Do It

A common way for both small and large businesses to deal with the complexity of payroll reports, deposit rules, and due dates is to hire an outside company to handle the payroll. Payroll processing companies have combined payroll expertise with the power of computers to create a major business enterprise based on the efficient and effective provision of payroll services.

To give you some idea of the extent to which businesses have turned to outside companies to handle payroll, consider Automatic Data Processing, Inc. (ADP), the world's largest provider of payroll services. ADP currently processes payrolls for more than 450,000 employers, with over 30 million employees in 26 countries. ADP prepares employee paychecks, journals, and summary reports; collects and remits funds for federal, state, and local payroll taxes; and files all required forms with government taxing authorities.

WORKERS' COMPENSATION INSURANCE

LO4 Describe and account for workers' compensation insurance.

Most states require employers to carry workers' compensation insurance. **Workers' compensation insurance** provides insurance for employees who suffer a job-related illness or injury.

The employer usually pays the entire cost of workers' compensation insurance. The cost of the insurance depends on the number of employees, riskiness of the job, and the company's accident history. For example, the insurance premium for workers in a chemical plant could be higher than for office workers. Employers generally obtain the insurance either from the state in which they operate or from a private insurance company.

The employer usually pays the premium at the beginning of the year, based on the estimated payroll for the year. At the end of the year, after the actual amount of payroll is known, an adjustment is made. If the employer has overpaid, a credit is received from the state or insurance company. If the employer has underpaid, an additional premium is paid.

To illustrate the accounting for workers' compensation insurance, assume that Lockwood Co. expects its payroll for the year to be $210,000. If Lockwood's insurance premium rate is 0.2%, its payment for workers' compensation insurance at the beginning of the year would be $420:

Estimated Payroll	×	Rate	=	Estimated Insurance Premium
$210,000		.002		$420.00

The journal entry for the payment of this $420 premium would be:

7			Workers' Compensation Insurance Expense		4 2 0 00		7
8			Cash			4 2 0 00	8
9			Paid insurance premium				9

If Lockwood's actual payroll for the year is $220,000, Lockwood would owe an additional premium of $20 at year end:

Actual Payroll	×	Rate	=	Insurance Premium
$220,000		.002		$440.00
Less premium paid				420.00
Additional premium due				$ 20.00

The adjusting entry at year end for this additional expense would be:

11	Dec.	31	Workers' Compensation Insurance Expense		2 0 00		11
12			Workers' Compensation Insurance Payable			2 0 00	12
13			Adjustment for insurance premium				13

In T account form, the total Workers' Compensation Insurance Expense of $440.00 would look like this:

Workers' Compensation Insurance Expense

Debit	Credit
420.00	
20.00	
440.00	

If Lockwood's actual payroll for the year is only $205,000, Lockwood would be due a refund of $10:

Payroll	×	Rate	=	Insurance Premium
$205,000		.002		$410.00
Less premium paid				420.00
Refund due				$ (10.00)

The adjusting entry at year end for this refund due would be:

16	Dec.	31	Insurance Refund Receivable			1 0 00			16
17			Workers' Compensation Insurance Expense				1 0 00		17
18			Adjustment for insurance premium						18

In T account form, the total Workers' Compensation Insurance Expense of $410 would look like this:

Workers' Compensation Insurance Expense

Debit	Credit
420.00	10.00
410.00	

Computers and Accounting

Computerized Payroll Systems—Gary P. Schneider, University of San Diego

Payroll, as you have learned in this and the previous chapter, is one of the most detailed and computation-laden parts of accounting. For this reason, payroll was one of the first accounting activities that companies computerized. All payroll systems divide the work into four main parts: (1) maintaining basic records about employees and tax rates, (2) recording employee activities such as time worked or commissions earned, (3) calculating net pay and payroll taxes, and (4) reporting the results of those calculations in a variety of formats. You can see parts (1), (2), and (4) illustrated in the accompanying figure (in a computerized payroll system, the part (3) calculations are done by the computer behind the scenes). The figure shows the main payroll module screen for Peachtree®, a popular accounting software package for small and medium-sized businesses.

As you can see in the figure, the Peachtree payroll module is organized into three sections, Maintain, Tasks, and Reports. The program performs the payroll calculations based on information that accountants enter in the Maintain and Tasks sections and makes the results of those calculations available in the Reports section.

The Maintain section allows accountants to enter information about employees and tax rates. Employee information includes names, addresses, social security numbers, pay rates, marital status and number of tax exemptions claimed. The Edit Company Tax Tables part lets accountants keep the payroll module updated to reflect changes in federal and state tax laws. Payroll Setup Wizard helps accountants specify the general ledger accounts in which payroll information will be recorded. It also sets up the payroll module to apply the company's rules about such things as vacation pay and sick leave.

Computers and Accounting (continued)

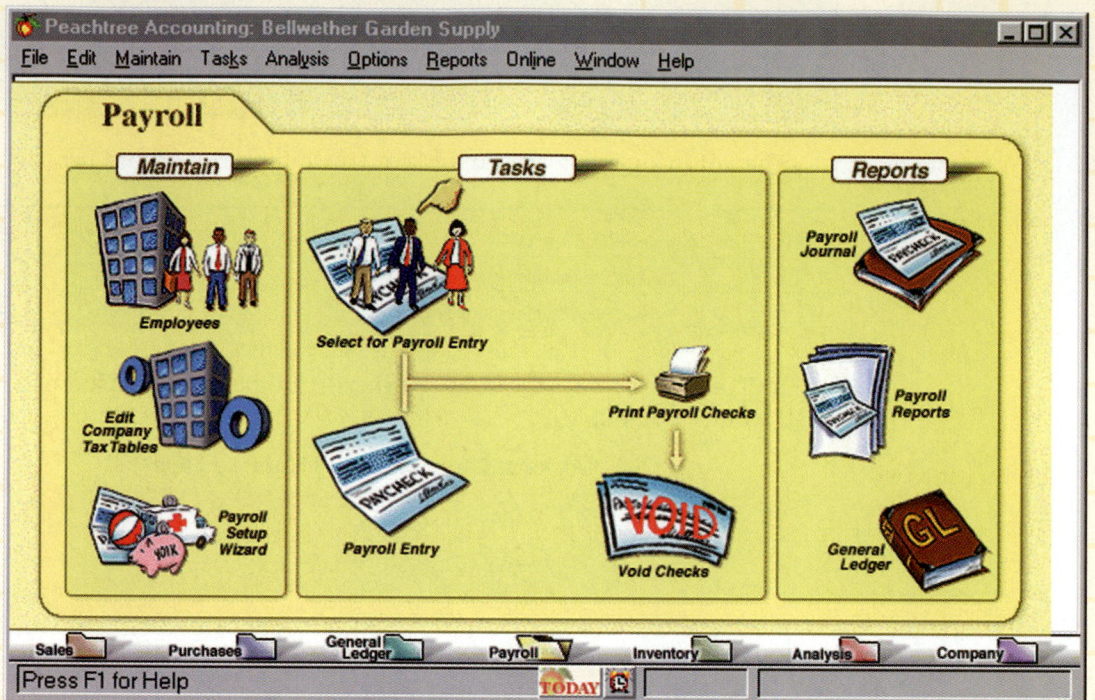

The Tasks section gives accountants a place to enter time worked, commissions earned, and other information needed to calculate regular and overtime pay. Also, this section is where accountants can print paychecks (selecting all or just some employees) and record voided checks as necessary.

The Reports section provides a choice of many different reports, including the reports you learned about in this and the previous chapter. These include the payroll register, the payroll journal, and federal employment tax reports, such as the Forms 940 and 941.

In smaller companies, the payroll module can provide all of the information that managers need to track the people they hire, promote, and fire. It also can do a good job of recording raises. However, as the business grows, hires more employees, and introduces more complex benefit plans, the company's information needs can exceed the capabilities of accounting software payroll modules.

When they grow to this point, many companies buy or create separate human resource management (HRM) information systems to keep track of hirings, firings, promotions, and benefit plan participation. Most of these HRM systems can share information with the payroll module of the accounting software. Virtually all of the information stored in the employee records section of a payroll module (for example, employee names, addresses, social security numbers, pay rates) is the same information a company will want to have in its HRM. It is more efficient to keep that information stored in one format and in one place. The employee information can then be shared effectively by the payroll and human resources departments.

Learning Objectives	Key Points to Remember
1 **Describe and calculate employer payroll taxes.** **2** **Account for employer payroll taxes expense.**	Employer payroll taxes include FICA, FUTA, and SUTA taxes. These taxes represent additional payroll expenses of the employer. The journal entry for payroll taxes is

8		Payroll Taxes Expense	x x x xx				8
9		Social Security Tax Payable			x x x xx		9
10		Medicare Tax Payable			x x x xx		10
11		FUTA Tax Payable			x x x xx		11
12		SUTA Tax Payable			x x x xx		12

The steps to be followed in preparing this journal entry are:

1. Obtain the total earnings and taxable earnings amounts from the Earnings—Total and Taxable Earnings columns of the payroll register.
2. Compute the amount of employer Social Security tax by multiplying the Social Security taxable earnings by 6.2%.
3. Compute the amount of employer Medicare tax by multiplying total earnings by 1.45%.
4. Compute the amount of FUTA tax by multiplying the Unemployment Taxable earnings by 0.8%.
5. Compute the amount of SUTA tax by multiplying the Unemployment Taxable earnings by 5.4%.
6. Prepare the appropriate journal entry using the amounts computed in steps 2–5.

3 **Describe employer reporting and payment responsibilities.**

Employer payroll reporting and payment responsibilities fall into five areas:

1. Federal income tax withholding and Social Security and Medicare taxes
2. FUTA taxes
3. SUTA taxes
4. Employee Wage and Tax Statement (Form W-2)
5. Summary of employee wages and taxes

Key forms needed in reporting and paying employer payroll taxes are:

1. Form 8109, Federal Tax Deposit Coupon
2. Form 941, Employer's Quarterly Federal Tax Return
3. Form 940, Employer's Annual Federal Unemployment Tax Return

By January 31 of each year, employers must provide each employee with a Wage and Tax Statement, Form W-2.

By February 28 of each year, employers must file Form W-3 and Copy A of Forms W-2 with the Social Security Administration.

4 **Describe and account for workers' compensation insurance.**

Workers' compensation insurance provides insurance for employees who suffer a job-related illness or injury. Employers generally are required to carry and pay the entire cost of this insurance.

Reflection: Answering the Opening Question

Evan must pay employer Social Security and Medicare taxes, SUTA tax, and FUTA tax. The total payroll cost of this employee is:

Gross wages	$10,400.00
Social Security tax (6.2% of $10,400)	644.80
Medicare tax (1.45% of $10,400)	150.80
SUTA tax (5.4% of $7,000)	378.00
FUTA tax (0.8% of $7,000)	56.00
Total cost	$11,629.60

DEMONSTRATION PROBLEM

Power Accounting System Software®

The totals line from Hart Company's payroll register for the week ended December 31, 20--, is as follows:

(left side)

PAYROLL

	NAME	EMPLOYEE NUMBER	ALLOWANCES	MARITAL STATUS	EARNINGS REGULAR	EARNINGS OVERTIME	EARNINGS TOTAL	CUMULATIVE TOTAL	TAXABLE EARNINGS UNEMPLOYMENT COMPENSATION	TAXABLE EARNINGS SOCIAL SECURITY	
21	Totals				3 5 0 0 00	3 0 0 00	3 8 0 0 00	197 6 0 0 00	4 0 0 00	3 8 0 0 00	21

REGISTER—PERIOD ENDED December 31, 20--   (right side)

	DEDUCTIONS FEDERAL INCOME TAX	SOCIAL SECURITY TAX	MEDICARE TAX	HEALTH INSURANCE	UNITED WAY	OTHER	TOTAL	NET PAY	CHECK NO.	
21	3 8 0 00	2 3 5 60	5 5 10	5 0 00	1 0 0 00		8 2 0 70	2 9 7 9 30		21

WebTUTOR Advantage

Payroll taxes are imposed as follows: Social Security, 6.2%; Medicare, 1.45%; FUTA, 0.8%; and SUTA, 5.4%.

REQUIRED

1. a. Prepare the journal entry for payment of this payroll on December 31, 20--.

   b. Prepare the journal entry for the employer's payroll taxes for the period ended December 31, 20--.

2. Hart Company had the following balances in its general ledger *after* the entries for requirement (1) were made:

Employee Income Tax Payable	$1,520.00
Social Security Tax Payable	1,847.00
Medicare Tax Payable	433.00
FUTA Tax Payable	27.20
SUTA Tax Payable	183.60

   a. Prepare the journal entry for payment of the liabilities for employee federal income taxes and Social Security and Medicare taxes on January 15, 20--.

b. Prepare the journal entry for payment of the liability for FUTA tax on January 31, 20--.

c. Prepare the journal entry for payment of the liability for SUTA tax on January 31, 20--.

3. Hart Company paid a premium of $280 for workers' compensation insurance based on estimated payroll as of the beginning of the year. Based on actual payroll as of the end of the year, the premium is $298. Prepare the adjusting entry to reflect the underpayment of the insurance premium.

Solution

1.

GENERAL JOURNAL — PAGE 1

	DATE		DESCRIPTION	POST REF.	DEBIT	CREDIT	
1	20-- Dec.	31	Wages and Salaries Expense		3 8 0 0 00		1
2			Employee Income Tax Payable			3 8 0 00	2
3			Social Security Tax Payable			2 3 5 60	3
4			Medicare Tax Payable			5 5 10	4
5			Health Insurance Premiums Payable			5 0 00	5
6			United Way Contributions Payable			1 0 0 00	6
7			Cash			2 9 7 9 30	7
8			To record Dec. 31 payroll				8
9							9
10	Dec.	31	Payroll Taxes Expense		3 1 5 50		10
11			Social Security Tax Payable			2 3 5 60	11
12			Medicare Tax Payable			5 5 10	12
13			FUTA Tax Payable			3 20	13
14			SUTA Tax Payable			2 1 60	14
15			Employer payroll taxes for week ended Dec. 31				15

2, 3.

	DATE		DESCRIPTION	POST REF.	DEBIT	CREDIT	
18	Jan.	15	Employee Income Tax Payable		1 5 2 0 00		18
19			Social Security Tax Payable		1 8 4 7 00		19
20			Medicare Tax Payable		4 3 3 00		20
21			Cash			3 8 0 0 00	21
22			Deposit of employee federal income tax and				22
23			Social Security and Medicare taxes				23
24							24
25	Jan.	31	FUTA Tax Payable		2 7 20		25
26			Cash			2 7 20	26
27			Paid FUTA tax				27
28							28
29	Jan.	31	SUTA Tax Payable		1 8 3 60		29
30			Cash			1 8 3 60	30
31			Paid SUTA tax				31
32							32
33	Dec.	31	Workers' Compensation Insurance Expense		1 8 00		33
34			Workers' Compensation Insurance Payable			1 8 00	34
35			Adjustment for insurance premium				35

On-Line Learning Tools

For more information, visit: http://heintz.swlearning.com

The Heintz & Parry product web site is designed specifically for **COLLEGE ACCOUNTING, 18e.** The features include downloadable student resources and an interactive study center, organized by chapter, which contains learning objectives, web links, on-line quizzes with automatic feedback, and more.

KEY TERMS

Electronic Federal Tax Payment System (EFTPS), (305)   An electronic funds transfer system for making federal tax deposits.

employer FICA taxes, (298)   Taxes levied on employers at the same rates and on the same earnings bases as the employee FICA taxes.

Employer Identification Number (EIN), (305)   A number that identifies the employer on all payroll forms and reports filed with the IRS.

FUTA (Federal Unemployment Tax Act) tax, (300)   A tax levied on employers to raise funds to administer the federal/state unemployment compensation program.

merit-rating system, (300)   A system to encourage employers to provide regular employment to workers.

self-employment income, (299)   The net income of a trade or business run by an individual.

self-employment tax, (299)   A contribution to the FICA program.

SUTA (state unemployment tax) tax, (300)   A tax levied on employers to raise funds to pay unemployment benefits.

workers' compensation insurance, (312)   Provides insurance for employees who suffer a job-related illness or injury.

REVIEW QUESTIONS

(LO1)   1. Why do employer payroll taxes represent an additional expense to the employer, whereas the various employee payroll taxes do not?

(LO1)   2. At what rate and on what earnings base is the employer's Social Security tax levied?

(LO1)   3. What is the purpose of the FUTA tax and who must pay it?

(LO1)   4. What is the purpose of the state unemployment tax and who must pay it?

(LO2)   5. What accounts are affected when employer payroll tax expenses are properly recorded?

(LO2)   6. Identify all items that are debited or credited to Social Security Tax Payable and to Medicare Tax Payable.

(LO2)   7. Explain why an employee whose gross salary is $20,000 costs an employer more than $20,000 to employ.

(LO3)   8. What is the purpose of Form 8109, Federal Tax Deposit Coupon?

(LO3)   9. What is the purpose of Form 941, Employer's Quarterly Federal Tax Return?

(LO3)   10. What is the purpose of Form 940, Employer's Annual Federal Unemployment Tax Return?

(LO3)   11. What information appears on Form W-2, the employee's Wage and Tax Statement?

(LO4)   12. What is the purpose of workers' compensation insurance and who must pay for it?

Self-Study Test Questions

True/False

1. Employer payroll taxes are deducted from the employee's pay. _____

2. The payroll register is a key source of information for computing employer payroll taxes. _____

3. Self-employment income is the net income of a trade or business owned and run by an individual. _____

4. The FUTA tax is levied only on the employees. _____

5. The W-4, which shows total annual earnings and deductions for federal and state income taxes, must be completed by the employer and given to the employee by January 31. _____

Multiple Choice

1. The general ledger accounts commonly used to record the employer's Social Security, Medicare, FUTA, and SUTA taxes are classified as _____

   (a) assets.   (c) expenses.
   (b) liabilities.   (d) owner's equity.

2. Joyce Lee earns $30,000 a year. Her employer pays a matching Social Security tax of 6.2% on the first $87,000 in earnings, a Medicare tax of 1.45% on gross earnings, and a FUTA tax of 0.8% and a SUTA tax of 5.4%, both on the first $7,000 in earnings. What is the total cost of Joyce Lee to her employer? _____

   (a) $32,250   (c) $30,434
   (b) $30,000   (d) $32,729

3. The Form 941 tax deposit includes which of the following types of taxes withheld from the employee and paid by the employer? _____

   (a) Federal income tax and FUTA tax
   (b) Federal income tax and Social Security and Medicare taxes
   (c) Social Security and Medicare taxes and SUTA tax
   (d) FUTA tax and SUTA tax

(continued)

Self-Study Test Questions *(continued)*

4. Workers' compensation provides insurance for employees who   _____

    (a) are unemployed due to a layoff.
    (b) are unemployed due to a plant closing.
    (c) are underemployed and need additional compensation.
    (d) suffer a job-related illness or injury.

5. The journal entry at the end of the year that recognizes an additional premium   _____
    owed under workers' compensation insurance will include a

    (a) debit to Workers' Compensation Insurance Expense.
    (b) debit to Cash.
    (c) debit to Workers' Compensation Insurance Payable.
    (d) credit to Workers' Compensation Insurance Expense.

The answers to the Self-Study Test Questions are at the end of the text.

MANAGING YOUR WRITING

The Director of the Art Department, Wilson Watson, wants to hire new office staff. His boss tells him that to do so he must find in his budget not only the base salary for this position but an additional 30% for "fringe benefits." Wilson explodes: "How in the world can there be 30% in fringe benefits?" Write a memo to Wilson Watson explaining the costs that probably make up these fringe benefits.

ETHICS CASE

Bob Estes works at Cliffrock Company in the central receiving department. He unpacks incoming shipments and verifies quantities of goods received. Over the weekend, Bob pulled a muscle in his back while playing basketball. When he came to work on Monday and started unpacking shipments, his back started to hurt again. Bob called the Human Resources Department and told them he hurt his back lifting a package at work. He was told to fill out an accident report and sent to an orthopedic clinic with a workers' compensation form. The doctor at the clinic told Bob not to lift anything heavy for two weeks and to stay home from work for at least one week.

1. Is Bob entitled to workers' compensation? Why or why not?

2. What effect will Bob's claim have on Cliffrock Company's workers' compensation insurance premium?

3. Write a short memo from the Human Resources Department to Cliffrock Company's employees explaining the purpose of workers' compensation.

4. In small groups discuss the job-related illness or injury risks of a computer input operator and measures an employer might take to minimize these risks.

WEB WORK

How long are employers required to keep employment tax records? Visit the Interactive Study Center on our web site at **http://heintz.swlearning.com** for special hotlinks to assist you in this assignment.

Interactive Learning: **http://heintz.swlearning.com**

SERIES A EXERCISES

EXERCISE 9-1A   (LO1/2)
Payroll taxes expense:
$1,584.30

CALCULATION AND JOURNAL ENTRY FOR EMPLOYER PAYROLL TAXES
Portions of the payroll register for Barney's Bagels for the week ended July 15 are shown below. The SUTA tax rate is 5.4% and the FUTA tax rate is 0.8%, both of which are levied on the first $7,000 of earnings. The Social Security tax rate is 6.2% on the first $87,000 of earnings. The Medicare rate is 1.45% on gross earnings.

Barney's Bagels
Payroll Register
Total Taxable Earnings of All Employees

Total Earnings	Unemployment Compensation	Social Security
$12,200	$10,500	$12,200

Calculate the employer's payroll taxes expense and prepare the journal entry to record the employer's payroll taxes expense for the week ended July 15 of the current year.

EXERCISE 9-2A   (LO1/2)
Payroll taxes expense: $350.02

CALCULATION AND JOURNAL ENTRY FOR EMPLOYER PAYROLL TAXES
Earnings for several employees for the week ended March 12, 20--, are as follows:

		Taxable Earnings	
Employee Name	Total Earnings	Unemployment Compensation	Social Security
Aus, Glenn E.	$ 700	$200	$ 700
Diaz, Charles K.	350	350	350
Knapp, Carol S.	1,200	—	1,200
Mueller, Deborah F.	830	125	830
Yeager, Jackie R.	920	35	920

Calculate the employer's payroll taxes expense and prepare the journal entry as of March 12, 20--, assuming that FUTA tax is 0.8%, SUTA tax is 5.4%, Social Security tax is 6.2%, and Medicare tax is 1.45%.

EXERCISE 9-3A   (LO1/2)
Payroll taxes expense: $886.86

CALCULATION OF TAXABLE EARNINGS AND EMPLOYER PAYROLL TAXES AND PREPARATION OF JOURNAL ENTRY Selected information from the payroll register of Raynette's Boutique for the week ended September 14, 20--, is as follows. Social Security tax is 6.2% on the first $87,000 of earnings for each employee. Medicare tax is 1.45% of gross earnings. FUTA tax is 0.8% and SUTA tax is 5.4% on the first $7,000 of earnings.

	Cumulative Pay Before Current Earnings	Current Gross Pay	Taxable Earnings	
Employee Name			Unemployment Compensation	Social Security
Burgos, Juan	$ 6,800	$1,250		
Ellis, Judy A.	6,300	1,100		
Lewis, Arlene S.	54,200	2,320		
Mason, Jason W.	53,900	2,270		
Yates, Ruby L.	27,650	1,900		
Zielke, Ronald M.	85,130	2,680		

Calculate the amount of taxable earnings for unemployment, Social Security, and Medicare taxes, and prepare the journal entry to record the employer's payroll taxes as of September 14, 20--.

EXERCISE 9-4A   **(LO1/2)**
Total cost: $34,882.00

TOTAL COST OF EMPLOYEE J. B. Kenton employs Sharla Knox at a salary of $32,000 a year. Kenton is subject to employer Social Security taxes at a rate of 6.2% and Medicare taxes at a rate of 1.45% on Knox's salary. In addition, Kenton must pay SUTA tax at a rate of 5.4% and FUTA tax at a rate of 0.8% on the first $7,000 of Knox's salary.

Compute the total cost to Kenton of employing Knox for the year.

EXERCISE 9-5A   **(LO3)**
941 deposit: $6,900.00

JOURNAL ENTRIES FOR PAYMENT OF EMPLOYER PAYROLL TAXES Angel Ruiz owns a business called Ruiz Construction Co. He does his banking at Citizens National Bank in Portland, Oregon. The amounts in his general ledger for payroll taxes and the employees' withholding of Social Security, Medicare, and federal income tax payable as of April 15 of the current year are as follows:

Social Security tax payable (includes both employer and employee)	$3,750
Medicare tax payable (includes both employer and employee)	875
FUTA tax payable	200
SUTA tax payable	1,350
Employee income tax payable	2,275

Journalize the payment of the Form 941 deposit (i.e., Social Security, Medicare, and federal income tax) on April 15, 20-- and the payments of the FUTA and SUTA taxes on April 30, 20--.

EXERCISE 9-6A   **(LO4)**
2. Additional premium due: $14.00

WORKERS' COMPENSATION INSURANCE AND ADJUSTMENT General Manufacturing estimated that its total payroll for the coming year would be $425,000. The workers' compensation insurance premium rate is 0.2%.

REQUIRED

1. Calculate the estimated workers' compensation insurance premium and prepare the journal entry for the payment as of January 2, 20--.

2. Assume that General Manufacturing's actual payroll for the year is $432,000. Calculate the total insurance premium owed and prepare a journal entry as of December 31, 20--, to record the adjustment for the underpayment. The actual payment of the additional premium will take place in January of the next year.

SERIES A PROBLEMS

PROBLEM 9-7A   **(LO1/2)**
Payroll taxes expense: $662.06

CALCULATING PAYROLL TAXES EXPENSE AND PREPARING JOURNAL ENTRY Selected information from the payroll register of Anderson's Dairy for the week ended July 7, 20--, is shown below. The SUTA tax rate is 5.4% and the FUTA tax rate is 0.8%, both on the first $7,000 of earnings. Social Security tax on the employer is 6.2% on the first $87,000 of earnings and Medicare tax is 1.45% on gross earnings.

			Taxable Earnings	
Employee Name	Cumulative Pay Before Current Earnings	Current Weekly Earnings	Unemployment Compensation	Social Security
Barnum, Alex	$ 6,750	$ 820		
Duel, Richard	6,340	725		
Hunt, J. B.	23,460	1,235		
Larson, Susan	6,950	910		
Mercado, Denise	85,650	3,520		
Swan, Judy	25,470	1,125		
Yates, Keith	28,675	1,300		

REQUIRED

1. Calculate the total employer payroll taxes for these employees.

2. Prepare the journal entry to record the employer payroll taxes as of July 7, 20--.

PROBLEM 9-8A   (LO2/3)

Payroll taxes expense: $1,104.00

JOURNALIZING AND POSTING PAYROLL ENTRIES The Cascade Company has four employees. All are paid on a monthly basis. The fiscal year of the business is May 1 to April 30. Payroll taxes are imposed as follows:

1. Social Security tax of 6.2% withheld from employees' wages on the first $87,000 of earnings and Medicare tax withheld at 1.45% of gross earnings.

2. Social Security tax of 6.2% imposed on the employer on the first $87,000 of earnings and Medicare tax of 1.45% on gross earnings.

3. SUTA tax of 5.4% imposed on the employer on the first $7,000 of earnings.

4. FUTA tax of 0.8% imposed on the employer on the first $7,000 of earnings.

The accounts kept by Cascade include the following:

Account Number	Title	Balance on June 1
101	Cash	$50,200
211	Employee Income Tax Payable	1,015
212	Social Security Tax Payable	1,458
213	Medicare Tax Payable	342
218	Savings Bond Deductions Payable	350
221	FUTA Tax Payable	164
222	SUTA Tax Payable	810
511	Wages and Salaries Expense	0
530	Payroll Taxes Expense	0

The following transactions relating to payrolls and payroll taxes occurred during June and July.

June 15	Paid $2,815 covering the following May taxes:		
	Social Security tax		$ 1,458
	Medicare tax		342
	Employee income tax withheld		1,015
	Total		$ 2,815
30	June payroll:		
	Total wages and salaries expense		$12,000
	Less amounts withheld:		
	Social Security tax	$ 744	
	Medicare tax	174	
	Employee income tax	1,020	
	Savings bond deductions	350	2,288
	Net amount paid		$ 9,712
30	Purchased savings bonds for employees, $700		
30	Data for completing employer's payroll taxes expense for June:		
	Social Security taxable wages		$12,000
	Unemployment taxable wages		3,000
July 15	Paid $2,856 covering the following June taxes:		
	Social Security tax		$ 1,488
	Medicare tax		348
	Employee income tax withheld		1,020
	Total		$ 2,856
31	Paid SUTA tax for the quarter, $972		
31	Paid FUTA tax, $188		

(continued)

REQUIRED

1. Journalize the preceding transactions using a general journal.
2. Open T accounts for the payroll expenses and liabilities. Enter the beginning balances and post the transactions recorded in the journal.

PROBLEM 9-9A (LO4)
3. Refund due: $48.00

WORKERS' COMPENSATION INSURANCE AND ADJUSTMENT Willamette Manufacturing estimated that its total payroll for the coming year would be $650,000. The workers' compensation insurance premium rate is 0.3%.

REQUIRED

1. Calculate the estimated workers' compensation insurance premium and prepare the journal entry for the payment as of January 2, 20--.
2. Assume that Willamette Manufacturing's actual payroll for the year was $672,000. Calculate the total insurance premium owed and prepare a journal entry as of December 31, 20--, to record the adjustment for the underpayment. The actual payment of the additional premium will take place in January of the next year.
3. Assume instead that Willamette Manufacturing's actual payroll for the year was $634,000. Prepare a journal entry as of December 31, 20--, for the total amount that should be refunded. The refund will not be received until the next year.

SERIES B EXERCISES

EXERCISE 9-1B (LO1/2)
Payroll taxes expense: $1,962.74

CALCULATION AND JOURNAL ENTRY FOR EMPLOYER PAYROLL TAXES Portions of the payroll register for Kathy's Cupcakes for the week ended June 21 are shown below. The SUTA tax rate is 5.4% and the FUTA tax rate is 0.8%, both on the first $7,000 of earnings. The Social Security tax rate is 6.2% on the first $87,000 of earnings. The Medicare rate is 1.45% on gross earnings.

Kathy's Cupcakes
Payroll Register
Total Taxable Earnings of All Employees

Total Earnings	Unemployment Compensation	Social Security
$15,680	$12,310	$15,680

Calculate the employer's payroll taxes expense and prepare the journal entry to record the employer's payroll taxes expense for the week ended June 21 of the current year.

EXERCISE 9-2B (LO1/2)
Payroll taxes expense: $503.63.00

CALCULATION AND JOURNAL ENTRY FOR EMPLOYER PAYROLL TAXES Earnings for several employees for the week ended April 7, 20--, are as follows:

Employee Name	Total Earnings	Taxable Earnings Unemployment Compensation	Social Security
Boyd, Glenda L.	$ 850	$300	$ 850
Evans, Sheryl N.	970	225	970
Fox, Howard J.	830	830	830
Jacobs, Phyllis J.	1,825	—	1,825
Roh, William R.	990	25	990

Calculate the employer's payroll taxes expense and prepare the journal entry as of April 7, 20--, assuming that FUTA tax is 0.8%, SUTA tax is 5.4%, Social Security tax is 6.2%, and Medicare tax is 1.45%.

EXERCISE 9-3B   (LO1/2)
Payroll taxes expense: $788.04

CALCULATION OF TAXABLE EARNINGS AND EMPLOYER PAYROLL TAXES, AND PREPARATION OF JOURNAL ENTRY Selected information from the payroll register of Howard's Cutlery for the week ended October 7, 20--, is presented below. Social Security tax is 6.2% on the first $87,000 of earnings for each employee. Medicare tax is 1.45% on gross earnings. FUTA tax is 0.8% and SUTA tax is 5.4% on the first $7,000 of earnings.

| | | | Taxable Earnings | |
Employee Name	Cumulative Pay Before Current Earnings	Current Gross Pay	Unemployment Compensation	Social Security
Carlson, David J.	$ 6,635	$ 950		
Delgado, Luisa	6,150	1,215		
Lewis, Arlene S.	54,375	2,415		
Nixon, Robert R.	53,870	1,750		
Shippe, Lance W.	24,830	1,450		
Watts, Brandon Q.	85,600	2,120		

Calculate the amount of taxable earnings for unemployment, Social Security, and Medicare taxes, and prepare the journal entry to record the employer's payroll taxes as of October 7, 20--.

EXERCISE 9-4B   (LO1/2)
Total cost: $49,953.00

TOTAL COST OF EMPLOYEE B. F. Goodson employs Eduardo Gonzales at a salary of $46,000 a year. Goodson is subject to employer Social Security taxes at a rate of 6.2% and Medicare taxes at a rate of 1.45% on Gonzales' salary. In addition, Goodson must pay SUTA tax at a rate of 5.4% and FUTA tax at a rate of 0.8% on the first $7,000 of Gonzales' salary.

Compute the total cost to Goodson of employing Gonzales for the year.

EXERCISE 9-5B   (LO3)
941 deposit: $12,705.00

JOURNAL ENTRIES FOR PAYMENT OF EMPLOYER PAYROLL TAXES Francis Baker owns a business called Baker Construction Co. She does her banking at the American National Bank in Seattle, Washington. The amounts in her general ledger for payroll taxes and employees' withholding of Social Security, Medicare, and federal income tax payable as of July 15 of the current year are as follows:

Social Security tax payable (includes both employer and employee)	$6,375
Medicare tax payable (includes both employer and employee)	1,500
FUTA tax payable	336
SUTA tax payable	2,268
Employee federal income tax payable	4,830

Journalize the payment of the Form 941 deposit (i.e., Social Security, Medicare, and federal income tax) on July 15, 20-- and the payments of the FUTA and state unemployment taxes on July 31, 20--.

EXERCISE 9-6B   (LO4)
2. Additional premium due: $22.00

WORKERS' COMPENSATION INSURANCE AND ADJUSTMENT Columbia Industries estimated that its total payroll for the coming year would be $385,000. The workers' compensation insurance premium rate is 0.2%.

REQUIRED

1. Calculate the estimated workers' compensation insurance premium and prepare the journal entry for the payment as of January 2, 20--.

2. Assume that Columbia Industries' actual payroll for the year is $396,000. Calculate the total insurance premium owed and prepare a journal entry as of December 31, 20--, to record the adjustment for the underpayment. The actual payment of the additional premium will take place in January of the next year.

SERIES B PROBLEMS

PROBLEM 9-7B   **(LO1/2)**

Payroll taxes expense: $738.34

CALCULATING PAYROLL TAXES EXPENSE AND PREPARING JOURNAL ENTRY Selected information from the payroll register of Wray's Drug Store for the week ended July 14, 20--, is shown below. The SUTA tax rate is 5.4% and the FUTA tax rate is 0.8%, both on the first $7,000 of earnings. Social Security tax on the employer is 6.2% on the first $87,000 of earnings and Medicare tax is 1.45% on gross earnings.

Employee Name	Cumulative Pay Before Current Earnings	Current Weekly Earnings	Taxable Earnings	
			Unemployment Compensation	Social Security
Ackers, Alice	$ 6,460	$ 645		
Conley, Dorothy	27,560	1,025		
Davis, James	6,850	565		
Lawrence, Kevin	52,850	2,875		
Rawlings, Judy	16,350	985		
Tanaka, Sumio	22,320	835		
Vadillo, Raynette	85,160	3,540		

REQUIRED

1.   Calculate the total employer payroll taxes for these employees.

2.   Prepare the journal entry to record the employer payroll taxes as of July 14, 20--.

PROBLEM 9-8B   **(LO2/3)**

Payroll taxes expense: $1,403.55

JOURNALIZING AND POSTING PAYROLL ENTRIES The Oxford Company has five employees. All are paid on a monthly basis. The fiscal year of the business is June 1 to May 31. Payroll taxes are imposed as follows:

1.   Social Security tax of 6.2% to be withheld from employees' wages on the first $87,000 of earnings and Medicare tax of 1.45% on gross earnings.

2.   Social Security tax of 6.2% imposed on the employer on the first $87,000 of earnings and Medicare tax of 1.45% on gross earnings.

3.   SUTA tax of 5.4% imposed on the employer on the first $7,000 of earnings.

4.   FUTA tax of 0.8% imposed on the employer on the first $7,000 of earnings.

The accounts kept by the Oxford Company include the following:

Account Number	Title	Balance on June 1
101	Cash	$48,650
211	Employee Income Tax Payable	1,345
212	Social Security Tax Payable	1,823
213	Medicare Tax Payable	427
218	Savings Bond Deductions Payable	525
221	FUTA Tax Payable	360
222	SUTA Tax Payable	920
511	Wages and Salaries Expense	0
530	Payroll Taxes Expense	0

The following transactions relating to payrolls and payroll taxes occurred during June and July.

June 15	Paid $3,595.00 covering the following May taxes:		
	Social Security tax		$ 1,823.00
	Medicare tax		427.00
	Employee income tax withheld		1,345.00
	Total		$ 3,595.00

30	June payroll:		
	Total wages and salaries expense		$14,700.00
	Less amounts withheld:		
	Social Security tax	$ 911.40	
	Medicare tax	213.15	
	Employee income tax	1,280.00	
	Savings bond deductions	525.00	2,929.55
	Net amount paid		$11,770.45

30   Purchased savings bonds for employees, $1,050.00

30	Data for completing employer's payroll taxes expense for June:	
	Social Security taxable wages	$14,700.00
	Unemployment taxable wages	4,500.00

July 15	Paid $3,529.10 covering the following June taxes:	
	Social Security tax	$ 1,822.80
	Medicare tax	426.30
	Employee income tax withheld	1,280.00
	Total	$ 3,529.10

31   Paid SUTA tax for the quarter, $1,163.00

31   Paid FUTA tax, $396.00

REQUIRED

1. Journalize the preceding transactions using a general journal.

2. Open T accounts for the payroll expenses and liabilities. Enter the beginning balances and post the transactions recorded in the journal.

PROBLEM 9-9B   **(LO4)**
3. Refund due: $16.00

WORKERS' COMPENSATION INSURANCE AND ADJUSTMENT Multnomah Manufacturing estimated that its total payroll for the coming year would be $540,000. The workers' compensation insurance premium rate is 0.2%.

REQUIRED

1. Calculate the estimated workers' compensation insurance premium and prepare the journal entry for the payment as of January 2, 20--.

2. Assume that Multnomah Manufacturing's actual payroll for the year was $562,000. Calculate the total insurance premium owed and prepare a journal entry as of December 31, 20--, to record the adjustment for the underpayment. The actual payment of the additional premium will take place in January of the next year.

3. Assume instead that Multnomah Manufacturing's actual payroll for the year was $532,000. Prepare a journal entry as of December 31, 20--, for the total amount that should be refunded. The refund will not be received until the next year.

MASTERY PROBLEM

The totals line from Nix Company's payroll register for the week ended March 31, 20--, is as follows:

(left side)

PAYROLL

	NAME	EMPLOYEE NUMBER	ALLOWANCES	MARITAL STATUS	EARNINGS			CUMULATIVE TOTAL	TAXABLE EARNINGS		
					REGULAR	OVERTIME	TOTAL		UNEMPLOYMENT COMPENSATION	SOCIAL SECURITY	
21	Totals				5 4 0 0 00	1 0 0 00	5 5 0 0 00	71 5 0 0 00	5 0 0 0 00	5 5 0 0 00	21

(right side)

REGISTER—PERIOD ENDED March 31, 20--

	DEDUCTIONS							NET PAY	CHECK NO.	
	FEDERAL INCOME TAX	SOCIAL SECURITY TAX	MEDICARE TAX	HEALTH INSURANCE	LIFE INSURANCE	OTHER	TOTAL			
21	5 0 0 00	3 4 1 00	7 9 75	1 6 5 00	2 0 0 00		1 2 8 5 75	4 2 1 4 25		21

Payroll taxes expense: $730.75

Payroll taxes are imposed as follows: Social Security tax, 6.2%; Medicare tax, 1.45%; FUTA tax 0.8%, and SUTA tax, 5.4%.

REQUIRED

1. a. Prepare the journal entry for payment of this payroll on March 31, 20--.

    b. Prepare the journal entry for the employer's payroll taxes for the period ended March 31, 20--.

2. Nix Company had the following balances in its general ledger before the entries for requirement (1) were made.

Employee income tax payable	$2,500
Social Security tax payable	2,008
Medicare tax payable	470
FUTA tax payable	520
SUTA tax payable	3,510

    a. Prepare the journal entry for payment of the liabilities for federal income taxes and Social Security and Medicare taxes on April 15, 20--.

    b. Prepare the journal entry for payment of the liability for FUTA tax on April 30, 20--.

    c. Prepare the journal entry for payment of the liability for SUTA tax on April 30, 20--.

3. Nix Company paid a premium of $420 for workers' compensation insurance based on the estimated payroll as of the beginning of the year. Based on actual payroll as of the end of the year, the premium is only $400. Prepare the adjusting entry to reflect the overpayment of the insurance premium at the end of the year (December 31, 20--).

CHALLENGE PROBLEM

This problem challenges you to apply your cumulative accounting knowledge to move a step beyond the material in the chapter.

Payroll taxes expense: $1,306.25

Payrex Co. has six employees. All are paid on a weekly basis. For the payroll period ending January 7, total employee earnings were $12,500, all of which were subject to SUTA, FUTA, Social Security, and Medicare taxes. The SUTA tax rate in Payrex's state is 5.4%, but Payrex qualifies for a rate of 2.0% because of its good record of providing regular employment to its employees. Other employer payroll taxes are at the rates described in the chapter.

REQUIRED

1. Calculate Payrex's FUTA, SUTA, Social Security, and Medicare taxes for the week ended January 7.

2. Prepare the journal entry for Payrex's payroll taxes for the week ended January 7.

3. What amount of payroll taxes did Payrex save because of its good employment record?

© ERIC FOWKE / PHOTO EDIT

Accounting for a Professional Service Business: The Combination Journal

Betty Jenkins, Evan's bookkeeper, was comparing notes with a college classmate who recently accepted a bookkeeping position in a doctor's office. The classmate has been observing general office procedures and is a bit confused about the accounting methods employed. Recording revenues is a good example. Some patients pay cash as they leave the office. Others submit forms that are filed with insurance companies. Sometimes the insurance companies pay the entire amount. Other times, insurance companies pay only a portion of the bill, and the balance is billed to the patient. Generally, the patients pay the balance, but occasionally they don't. Finally, there are some patients that never seem to pay. It appears that the doctor's office simply waits until cash is collected before recognizing any revenue. This seems contrary to the accrual method of accounting. Is this an acceptable procedure, or should Betty's friend seek employment elsewhere?

Careful study of this chapter should enable you to:

LO1 Explain the cash, modified cash, and accrual bases of accounting.

LO2 Describe special records for a professional service business using the modified cash basis.

LO3 Describe and use a combination journal to record transactions of a professional service business.

LO4 Post from the combination journal to the general ledger.

LO5 Prepare a work sheet, financial statements, and adjusting and closing entries for a professional service business.

The accrual basis of accounting offers the best matching of revenues and expenses and is required under generally accepted accounting principles. Throughout the first nine chapters, the accrual basis was demonstrated for a service business. For simplicity, we used a general journal as the book of original entry.

GAAP financial statements prepared using the accrual method are particularly important when major businesses want to raise large amounts of money. Investors and creditors expect GAAP financial statements and generally will not invest or make loans without them.

However, many small professional service organizations are not concerned with raising large amounts of money from investors and creditors. These organizations include CPAs, doctors, dentists, lawyers, engineers, and architects. Since these organizations do not need to prepare GAAP financial statements, they often use the cash or modified cash basis. Further, instead of using a general journal, a manual or computerized specialized journal is employed. These methods simplify the accounting process and provide results similar to GAAP if receivables and payables are minimal. Further, if one of these organizations needs to borrow money from a bank that requires GAAP financial statements, an accountant can convert the financial statements to the accrual basis.

In this chapter we explain the cash basis and modified cash basis of accounting. In addition, we demonstrate the advantages of using a combination journal as the book of original entry.

ACCRUAL BASIS VERSUS CASH BASIS

LO1 Explain the cash, modified cash, and accrual bases of accounting.

Under the **accrual basis of accounting**, revenues are recorded when earned. Revenues are considered earned when a service is provided or a product sold, regardless of whether cash is received. If cash is not received, a receivable is set up. The accrual basis also assumes that expenses are recorded when incurred. Expenses are incurred when a service is received or an asset consumed, regardless of when cash is paid. If cash is not paid when a service is received, a payable is set up. When assets are consumed, prepaid assets are decreased or long-term assets are depreciated. Since the accrual basis accounts for long-term assets, prepaid assets, receivables, and payables, it is the most comprehensive system and best method of measuring income for the vast majority of businesses.

LEARNING KEY:

Accrual Basis

Accounting for:

Revenues and Expenses	Assets and Liabilities	
Record revenue when earned.	Accounts receivable:	Yes
Record expenses when incurred.	Accounts payable:	Yes
	Prepaid assets:	Yes
	Long-term assets:	Yes

Under the **cash basis of accounting**, revenues are recorded when cash is received and expenses are recorded when cash is paid. This method will provide results that are similar to the accrual basis if there are few receivables, payables, and assets. However, as shown in Figure 10-1, the cash and accrual bases can result in very different measures of net income if a business has significant amounts of receivables, payables, and assets.

RECOGNITION OF REVENUES AND EXPENSES: ACCRUAL BASIS VS. CASH BASIS

Transaction	Accrual Basis Expense	Accrual Basis Revenue	Cash Basis Expense	Cash Basis Revenue
(a) Provided services on account, $600.		$600		
(b) Paid wages, $300.	$300		$300	
(c) Received cash for services performed on account last month, $200.				$200
(d) Received cleaning bill for month, $250.	250			
(e) Paid on account for last month's advertising, $100.			100	
(f) Purchase of supplies, $50.			50	
(g) Supplies used during month, $40.	40			
	$590	$600	$450	$200
Revenue		$600		$200
Expense		590		450
Net Income (Loss)		$ 10		($250)
Revenues are recognized when:		earned		cash is received
Expenses are recognized when:		incurred		cash is paid

FIGURE 10-1   Cash Versus Accrual Accounting

The modified cash basis is the same as the accrual basis, except receivables and payables are not recognized for revenues and operating expenses.

A third method of accounting combines aspects of the cash and accrual methods. With the **modified cash basis**, a business uses the cash basis for recording revenues and most expenses. Exceptions are made when cash is paid for assets with useful lives greater than one accounting period. For example, under a strict cash basis, if cash is paid for equipment, buildings, supplies, or insurance, the amount is immediately recorded as an expense. This approach could cause major distortions when measuring net income. Under the modified cash basis, cash payments like these are recorded as assets, and adjustments are made each period as under the accrual basis. Liabilities associated with the acquisition of these assets are also recognized.

Although similar to the accrual basis, the modified cash basis does not account for receivables or for payables for services received. Thus, the modified cash basis is a combination of the cash and accrual methods of accounting. The differences and similarities among the cash, modified cash, and accrual methods of accounting are demonstrated in Figure 10-2.

If all businesses were the same, only one method of accounting would be needed. However, businesses vary in their need for major assets like buildings and

ENTRIES MADE UNDER EACH ACCOUNTING METHOD

Event	Cash	Modified Cash	Accrual
Revenues: Perform services for cash	Cash Professional Fees	Cash Professional Fees	Cash Professional Fees
Perform services on account	No entry	No entry	Accounts Receivable Professional Fees
Expenses: Pay cash for operating expenses: wages, advertising, rent, telephone, etc.	Expense Cash	Expense Cash	Expense Cash
Pay cash for prepaid items: insurance, supplies, etc.	Expense Cash	Prepaid Asset Cash	Prepaid Asset Cash
Pay cash for property, plant, and equipment (PP&E)	Expense Cash	PP&E Asset Cash	PP&E Asset Cash
Receive bill for services received	No entry	No entry	Expense Accounts Payable
End-of-period adjustments: Wages earned by employees but not paid	No entry	No entry	Wages Expense Wages Payable
Prepaid items used	No entry	Expense Prepaid Asset	Expense Prepaid Asset
Depreciation on property, plant, and equipment	No entry	Depreciation Expense Accumulated Depreciation	Depreciation Expense Accumulated Depreciation
Other: Purchase of assets on account	No entry	Asset Accounts Payable	Asset Accounts Payable
Payments for assets purchased on account	Expense Cash	Accounts Payable Cash	Accounts Payable Cash

FIGURE 10-2 Comparison of Cash, Modified Cash, and Accrual Methods

LEARNING KEY: Shaded area shows that sometimes the modified cash basis is the same as the cash basis and sometimes it is the same as the accrual basis. For some transactions, all methods are the same.

A BROADER VIEW

The Modified Cash Basis

Many professional and small service businesses use the modified cash basis of accounting. Doctors do this because it permits the recognition of medical equipment as assets that are depreciated as services are provided. Further, it simplifies accounting for revenues. Doctors are somewhat uncertain about the actual amount of revenue earned at the time a visit with a

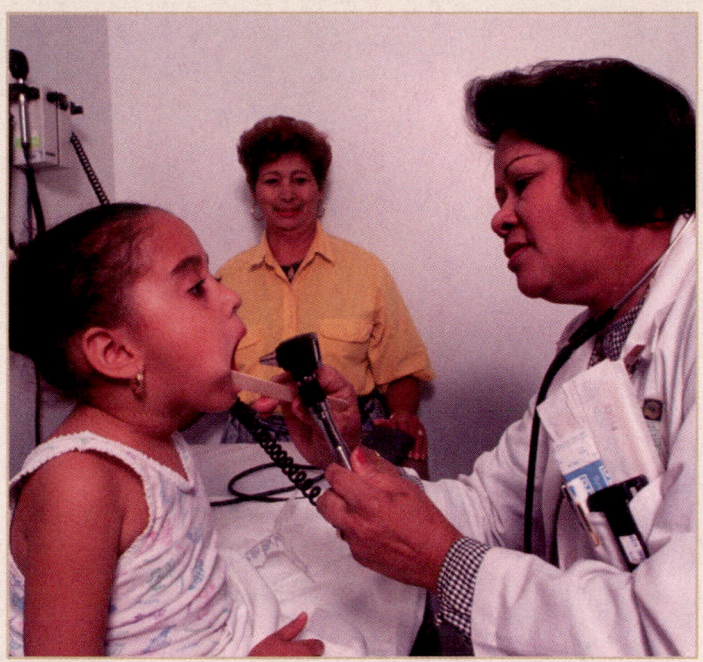

patient has been completed. Insurance companies pay different amounts for various procedures. Sometimes this is the same as the amount charged by the doctor, but not always. Some doctors simply accept what the insurance company pays. Others bill the patient for the difference. And, of course, not all patients pay their bills. Thus, it is easier to wait until cash is received to recognize revenue.

equipment, the amount of customer receivables, and payables to suppliers. For example, if a business were rather small with no major assets, receivables, or payables, it would be simpler to use the cash basis of accounting. In addition, under these circumstances, the difference in net income under the accrual and cash bases of accounting would be small. Most individuals fit this description and use the cash basis on their tax returns.

Businesses with buildings and equipment, but few receivables and payables, might use the modified cash basis. Again, the accounting would be a little simpler and differences between net income computed under the modified cash and accrual bases would be small.

Finally, businesses with buildings and equipment, and receivables and payables, should use the accrual basis of accounting to achieve the best matching of revenues and expenses. The following sections will focus primarily on the modified cash basis of accounting.

ACCOUNTING FOR A PROFESSIONAL SERVICE BUSINESS

LO2 Describe special records for a professional service business using the modified cash basis.

Many small professional service businesses use the modified cash basis of accounting. Professional service businesses include law, dentistry, medicine, optometry, architecture, engineering, and accounting.

Look again at Figure 10-2. There are two primary differences between the accrual basis and the modified cash basis. First, under the modified cash basis, no adjusting entries are made for accrued wages expense. Second, under the modified cash basis, revenues from services performed on account are not

Date: 6/4/--

Time	Patient	Medical Service	Fees	Payments
8:00	Dennis Rogan	OV	40.00	40.00
15				
30	Rick Cosier	OV;EKG	120.00	
45				
9:00	George Hettenhouse	OV;MISC	50.00	
15				
30	Sam Frumer	OV;LAB	75.00	75.00
45				
10:00	Dan Dalton	OV	40.00	
15				
30	Louis Biagioni	OV;X	65.00	
45				
11:00	Mike Groomer	X	40.00	40.00
15				
30				
45				
12:00				
15				
30				
45				
1:00	Mike Tiller	OV;LAB	80.00	
15				
30	Peggy Hite	OV;PHYS	190.00	
45				
2:00				
15				
30				
45				
3:00	Vivian Winston	OV;MISC	40.00	
15				
30				
45				
4:00	Hank Davis	OV	40.00	40.00
15				
30				
45				
	Bill Sharp			150.00
	Phil Jones			80.00
	Diane Gallagher			200.00
			780.00	625.00

FIGURE 10-3 Appointment Record

recorded until cash is received. Thus, no accounts receivable are entered in the accounting system. This means that other records must be maintained to keep track of amounts owed by clients and patients. These records generally include an appointment record and a client or patient ledger record. These records are illustrated in Figures 10-3 and 10-4.

The appointment record is used to schedule appointments and to maintain a record of the services rendered, fees charged, and payments received. It also serves as a source document for the patient ledger records, which show the amount owed by each client or patient for services performed. A copy of this record may also be used for billing purposes.

Patient Name	Dennis Rogan				
Address	1542 Hamilton Avenue Cincinnati OH 45240-5524				
Phone Number	555-1683				

Date	Service Rendered	Time	Debit	Credit	Balance
20-- June 4	Office Visit	8:00	40.00		40.00
4				40.00	—

FIGURE 10-4   Client or Patient Ledger Account

THE COMBINATION JOURNAL

LO3 Describe and use a combination journal to record transactions of a professional service business.

The two-column general journal illustrated in Chapter 4 can be used to enter every transaction of a business. However, in most businesses, there are many similar transactions that involve the same account or accounts. Cash receipts and payments are good examples. Suppose that in a typical month there are 30 transactions that result in an increase in cash and 40 transactions that cause a decrease in cash. In a two-column general journal, this would require entering the account Cash 70 times, using a journal line each time.

A considerable amount of time and space is saved if a journal contains **special columns** for cash debits and cash credits. At the end of the month, the special columns for cash debits and credits are totaled. The total of the Cash Debit column is posted as one amount to the debit side of the cash account and the total of the Cash Credit column is posted as one amount to the credit side of the cash account. Thus, instead of receiving 70 postings, Cash receives only two: one debit and one credit. This method requires much less time and reduces the risk of making posting errors.

LEARNING KEY: The totals of special journal columns are posted as one amount to the account. This saves time and reduces the possibility of posting errors.

If other accounts are used frequently, special columns can be added for these accounts. **General Debit** and **General Credit columns** are used for accounts not affected by many transactions. A journal with such special and general columns is called a **combination journal**.

Many small professional enterprises use a combination journal to record business transactions. To demonstrate the use of a combination journal, let's consider the medical practice of Dr. Ray Bonita. Bonita uses the modified cash basis of accounting. The chart of accounts for his medical practice is shown in Figure 10-5. The transactions for the month of June, his first month in practice, are provided in Figure 10-6.

A combination journal for Bonita's medical practice is illustrated in Figure 10-7 on page 340. Note that special columns were set up for Cash (Debit and Credit), Medical Fees (Credit), Wages Expense (Debit), Laboratory Expense (Debit), Medical Supplies (Debit), and Office Supplies (Debit). Special columns were set up for these accounts because they will be used frequently in this business. Other businesses might set up special columns for different accounts depending on the frequency of their use. Of course, General Debit and Credit columns for transactions affecting other accounts are also needed.

LEARNING KEY: Set up special columns for the most frequently used accounts.

RAY BONITA, M.D. CHART OF ACCOUNTS

Assets			Revenue	
101	Cash		401	Medical Fees
141	Medical Supplies			
142	Office Supplies		**Expenses**	
145	Prepaid Insurance		511	Wages Expense
182	Office Furniture		521	Rent Expense
182.1	Accum. Depr. —Office Furn.		523	Office Supplies Expense
185	Medical Equipment		524	Medical Supplies Expense
185.1	Accum. Depr.—Med. Equip.		525	Telephone Expense
			526	Laboratory Expense
Liabilities			535	Insurance Expense
202	Accounts Payable		541	Depr. Exp.—Office Furn.
			542	Depr. Exp.—Med. Equip.
Owner's Equity				
311	Ray Bonita, Capital			
312	Ray Bonita, Drawing			
313	Income Summary			

FIGURE 10-5   Chart of Accounts

June 1	Ray Bonita invested cash to start a medical practice, $50,000.
2	Paid for a one-year liability insurance policy, $6,000. Coverage began on June 1.
3	Purchased medical equipment for cash, $22,000.
4	Paid bill for laboratory work, $300.
5	Purchased office furniture on credit from Bittle's Furniture, $9,000.
6	Received cash from patients and insurance companies for medical services rendered, $5,000.
7	Paid June office rent, $2,000.
8	Paid part-time wages, $3,000.
9	Purchased medical supplies for cash, $250.
15	Paid telephone bill, $150.
15	Received cash from patients and insurance companies for medical services rendered, $10,000.
16	Paid bill for laboratory work, $280.
17	Paid part-time wages, $3,000.
19	Purchased office supplies for cash, $150.
20	Received cash from patients and insurance companies for medical services rendered, $3,200.
22	Paid the first installment to Bittle's Furniture, $3,300.
23	Purchased medical supplies for cash, $200.
24	Paid bill for laboratory work, $400.
25	Purchased additional furniture from Bittle's Furniture, $4,000. A down payment of $500 was made, with the remaining payments expected over the next four months.
27	Paid part-time wages, $2,500.
30	Received cash from patients and insurance companies for medical services rendered, $7,000.
30	Bonita withdrew cash for personal use, $10,000.

FIGURE 10-6   Summary of Transactions for Ray Bonita's Medical Practice

Journalizing in a Combination Journal

The following procedures were used to enter the transactions for Bonita for June.

General Columns. Enter transactions in the *general columns* in a manner similar to that used for the *general journal.* Look at the entry for June 5 in Figure 10-7.

a.   Enter the name of the debited account (Office Furniture) first at the extreme left of the Description column.

b.   Enter the amount in the General Debit column.

c.   Enter the name of the account credited (Accounts Payable—Bittle's Furniture) on the next line, indented.

d.   Enter the amount in the General Credit column.

General and Special Accounts. Some transactions affect both a *general account and a special account.* Look at the entry for June 1 in Figure 10-7.

a.   Enter the name of the general account in the Description column.

b.   Enter the amount in the General Debit or Credit column.

c.   Enter the amount of the debit or credit for the special account in the appropriate special column.

Enter all of this information on the same line.

Special Accounts. Many transactions affect only *special accounts.* Look at the entry for June 6 in Figure 10-7.

a.   Enter the amounts in the appropriate special debit and credit columns.

b.   Do not enter anything in the Description column.

c.   Place a dash in the Posting Reference column to indicate that this amount is not posted individually. It will be posted as part of the total of the special column at the end of the month. (The posting process is described later in this chapter.)

Description Column. In general, the **Description column** is used for the following:

a.   To enter the account titles for the General Debit and General Credit columns.

b.   To identify specific creditors when assets are purchased on account (see entry for June 5).

   NOTE: For firms using the accrual basis of accounting, this column also would be used to identify specific customers receiving services on account (accounts receivable) and specific businesses that provided services on account (accounts payable).

c.   To identify specific creditors when payments are made on account (see entry for June 22).

d.   To identify adjusting and closing entries.

COMBINATION JOURNAL

PAGE 1

Line	DATE	CASH DEBIT	CASH CREDIT	POST REF.	DESCRIPTION	GENERAL DEBIT	GENERAL CREDIT	MEDICAL FEES CREDIT	WAGES EXPENSE DEBIT	LABORATORY EXPENSE DEBIT	MEDICAL SUPPLIES DEBIT	OFFICE SUPPLIES DEBIT
1	20— June 1	50 0 0 0 00		311	Ray Bonita, Capital		50 0 0 0 00					
2	2		6 0 0 0 00	145	Prepaid Insurance	6 0 0 0 00						
3	3		22 0 0 0 00	185	Medical Equipment	22 0 0 0 00						
4	4		3 0 0 00	—						3 0 0 00		
5	5			182	Office Furniture	9 0 0 0 00						
6			9 0 0 0 00	202	Accounts Payable—Bittle's Furn.		9 0 0 0 00					
7	6	5 0 0 0 00		—				5 0 0 0 00				
8	7		2 0 0 0 00	521	Rent Expense	2 0 0 0 00						
9	8		3 0 0 0 00	—					3 0 0 0 00			
10	9		2 5 0 00	—							2 5 0 00	
11	10	10 0 0 0 00		—				10 0 0 0 00				
12	11		1 5 0 00	525	Telephone Expense	1 5 0 00						
13	15		2 8 0 00	—						2 8 0 00		
14	16		3 0 0 0 00	—					3 0 0 0 00			
15	17	3 2 0 0 00		—				3 2 0 0 00				
16	19		1 5 0 00	—								1 5 0 00
17	20		3 3 0 0 00	202	Accounts Payable—Bittle's Furniture	3 3 0 0 00						
18	22		2 0 0 00	—							2 0 0 00	
19	23		4 0 0 00	—						4 0 0 00		
20	24		5 0 0 00	182	Office Furniture	4 0 0 0 00						
21				202	Accounts Payable—Bittle's Furn.		3 5 0 0 00					
22	25		2 5 0 0 00	—					2 5 0 0 00			
23	27	7 0 0 0 00		—				7 0 0 0 00				
24	30		10 0 0 0 00	312	Ray Bonita, Drawing	10 0 0 0 00						
25		75 2 0 0 00	54 0 3 0 00			56 4 5 0 00	62 5 0 0 00	25 2 0 0 00	8 5 0 0 00	9 8 0 00	4 5 0 00	1 5 0 00
26		(1 0 1)	(1 0 1)			(✓)	(✓)	(4 0 1)	(5 1 1)	(5 2 6)	(1 4 1)	(1 4 2)

Proving the Combination Journal

Debit Columns		Credit Columns	
Cash	75,200	Cash	54,030
General	56,450	General	62,500
Wages Expense	8,500	Medical Fees	25,200
Laboratory Expense	980		141,730
Medical Supplies	450		
Office Supplies	150		
	141,730		

> **Note:** The account numbers in the Posting Reference Column and at the bottom of the Special Columns are inserted as posting is completed. The same is true for the (✓) at the bottom of the General Debit and Credit Columns.

FIGURE 10-7 Combination Journal: Modified Cash Basis

e. To identify amounts forwarded. When more than one page is required during an accounting period, amounts from the previous page are brought forward. In this situation, "Amounts Forwarded" is entered in the Description column on the first line.

Proving the Combination Journal

At the end of the accounting period, all columns of the combination journal should be totaled and ruled. The sum of the debit columns should be compared with the sum of the credit columns to verify that they are equal. The proving of Bonita's combination journal for the month of June is shown at the bottom of Figure 10-7 on page 340.

POSTING FROM THE COMBINATION JOURNAL

LO4 Post from the combination journal to the general ledger.

The procedures for posting a special column are different from the procedures used when posting a general column. Accounts debited or credited in the general columns are posted individually throughout the month in the same manner followed for the general journal. A different procedure is used for special columns. Figure 10-8 describes the procedures to follow in posting from the combination journal.

GENERAL COLUMNS	Since a combination journal is being used, enter "CJ" and the page number in each general ledger account's **Posting Reference column**. Once the amount has been posted to the general ledger account, the account number is entered in the Posting Reference column of the combination journal. Accounts in the general column should be posted daily. The check marks at the bottom of the General Debit and Credit columns are entered at the end of the month and serve as a reminder that these totals should not be posted.
SPECIAL COLUMNS	1. Post the totals of the special columns to the appropriate general ledger accounts.
	2. Once posted, enter the account number (in parentheses) beneath the column and "CJ" and the page number in each general ledger account's Posting Reference column.

FIGURE 10-8   Posting from a Combination Journal

LEARNING KEY: Amounts in the General column are posted individually. Only the totals of the special columns are posted.

Portions of the combination journal in Figure 10-7 and general ledger accounts for Cash, Office Furniture, Accounts Payable, and Medical Fees are shown in Figure 10-9 to illustrate the effects of this posting process. Note that the individual debits and credits in the General Columns are posted individually throughout the month. Only the totals of the Special Columns are posted at the end of the month.

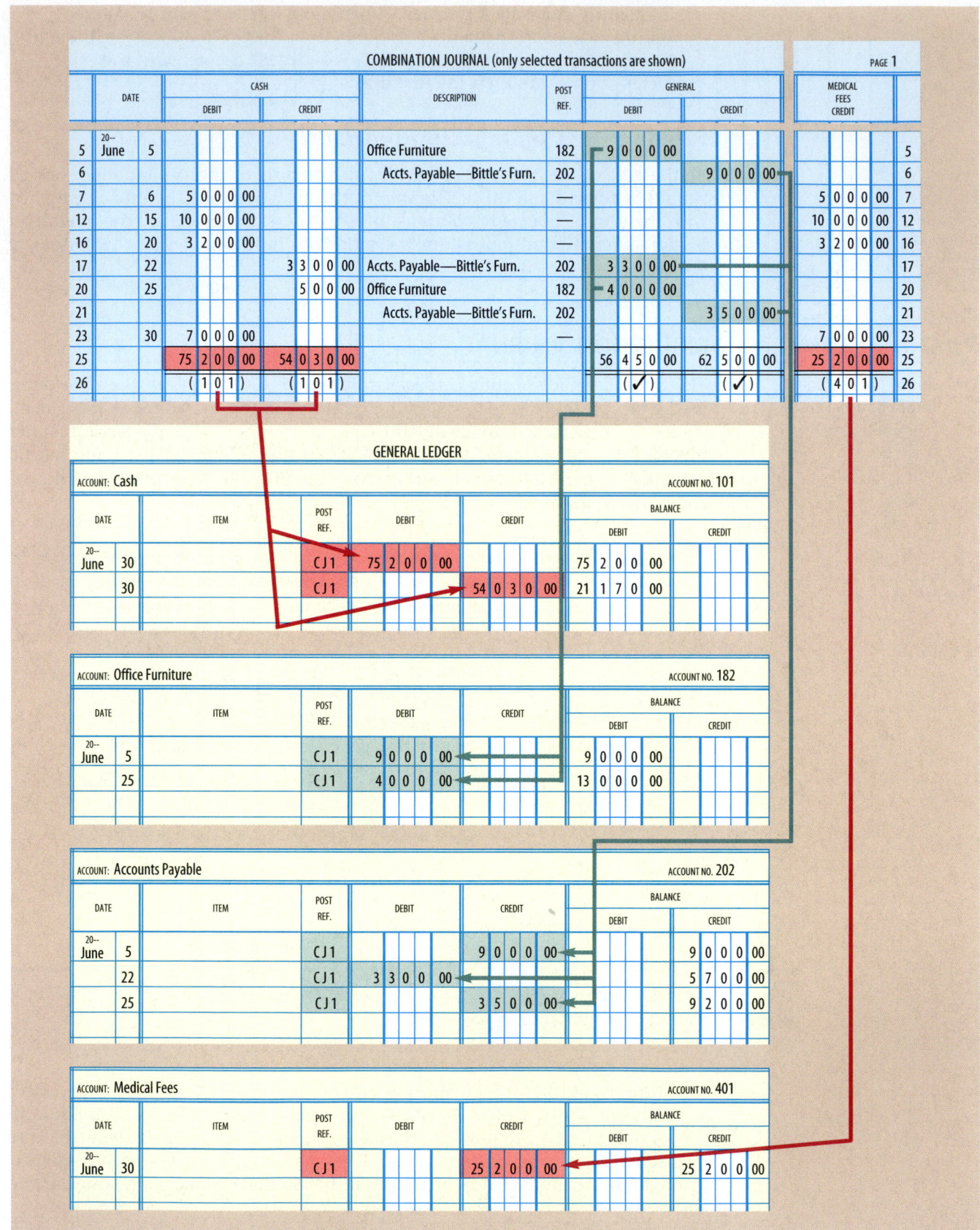

FIGURE 10-9 Posting the Combination Journal

To see the advantages of posting a combination journal compared with the general journal, simply compare the accounts in Figure 10-9 with the same accounts in Chapter 4, Figure 4-12. Note the number of postings required for the general journal and combination journal.

	Number of Postings		
	General Journal	Combination Journal	
Cash	13	2	(Special columns for cash)
Delivery Equip./Office Furniture	3	2	(No special column)
Accounts Payable	3	3	(No special column)
Delivery/Medical Fees	3	1	(Special column for Medical Fees)

Clearly, using the combination journal can be quite efficient.

Determining the Cash Balance

The debits and credits to Cash are not posted until the end of the accounting period. Therefore, the cash balance must be computed when this information is needed. The cash balance may be computed at any time during the month by taking the beginning balance and adding total cash debits and subtracting total cash credits to date. Figure 10-10 shows the calculation of Bonita's cash balance on June 15.

LEARNING KEY:

Beginning cash balance
+ Cash debits to date
– Cash credits to date
Current cash balance

PERFORMING END-OF-PERIOD WORK FOR A PROFESSIONAL SERVICE BUSINESS

LO5 Prepare a work sheet, financial statements, and adjusting and closing entries for a professional service business.

Once the combination journal has been posted to the general ledger, the end-of-period work sheet is prepared in the same way as described in Chapter 5. Recall that financial statements are prepared and end-of-period work is normally performed at the end of the fiscal year. For illustration purposes, we will perform these activities at the end of Bonita's first month of operations.

Preparing the Work Sheet

Bonita's work sheet is illustrated in Figure 10-11 on page 345. Adjustments were made for the following items:

(a) Medical supplies remaining on June 30, $350.

(b) Office supplies remaining on June 30, $100.

(c) Prepaid insurance expired during June, $500.

(d) Depreciation on office furniture for June, $200.

(e) Depreciation on medical equipment for June, $300.

COMBINATION JOURNAL

PAGE 1

	DATE		CASH DEBIT	CASH CREDIT	DESCRIPTION	POST REF.	GENERAL DEBIT	GENERAL CREDIT	MEDICAL FEES CREDIT	WAGES EXPENSE DEBIT	LABORATORY EXPENSE DEBIT	MEDICAL SUPPLIES DEBIT	OFFICE SUPPLIES DEBIT	
1	20-- June	1	50000 00		Ray Bonita, Capital	311		50000 00						1
2		2		6000 00	Prepaid Insurance	145	6000 00							2
3		3		22000 00	Medical Equipment	185	22000 00							3
4		4		300 00		—					300 00			4
5		5			Office Furniture	182	9000 00							5
6					Accounts Payable—Bittle's Furn.	202		9000 00						6
7		6	5000 00			—			5000 00					7
8		7		2000 00	Rent Expense	521	2000 00							8
9		8		3000 00		—				3000 00				9
10		9		250 00		—						250 00		10
11		15		150 00	Telephone Expense	525	150 00							11
12		15	10000 00			—			10000 00					12
13			65000 00	33700 00										13

Beginning balance	$ 0
Add cash debits	65,000
Total	$65,000
Less cash credits	33,700
Cash balance, June 15	$31,300

FIGURE 10-10 Determining the Cash Balance

Ray Bonita, M.D.
Worksheet
For Month Ended June 30, 20 - -

	Trial Balance Debit	Trial Balance Credit	Adjustments Debit	Adjustments Credit	Adjusted Trial Balance Debit	Adjusted Trial Balance Credit	Income Statement Debit	Income Statement Credit	Balance Sheet Debit	Balance Sheet Credit	
1 Cash	21 1 7 0 00				21 1 7 0 00				21 1 7 0 00		1
2 Medical Supplies	4 5 0 00			(a) 1 0 0 00	3 5 0 00				3 5 0 00		2
3 Office Supplies	1 5 0 00			(b) 5 0 00	1 0 0 00				1 0 0 00		3
4 Prepaid Insurance	6 0 0 0 00			(c) 5 0 0 00	5 5 0 0 00				5 5 0 0 00		4
5 Office Furniture	13 0 0 0 00				13 0 0 0 00				13 0 0 0 00		5
6 Accum. Depr.—Office Furniture				(d) 2 0 0 00		2 0 0 00				2 0 0 00	6
7 Medical Equipment	22 0 0 0 00				22 0 0 0 00				22 0 0 0 00		7
8 Accum. Depr.—Medical Equipment				(e) 3 0 0 00		3 0 0 00				3 0 0 00	8
9 Accounts Payable		9 2 0 0 00				9 2 0 0 00				9 2 0 0 00	9
10 Ray Bonita, Capital		50 0 0 0 00				50 0 0 0 00				50 0 0 0 00	10
11 Ray Bonita, Drawing	10 0 0 0 00				10 0 0 0 00				10 0 0 0 00		11
12 Medical Fees		25 2 0 0 00				25 2 0 0 00		25 2 0 0 00			12
13 Wages Expense	8 5 0 0 00				8 5 0 0 00		8 5 0 0 00				13
14 Rent Expense	2 0 0 0 00				2 0 0 0 00		2 0 0 0 00				14
15 Office Supplies Expense			(b) 5 0 00		5 0 00		5 0 00				15
16 Medical Supplies Expense			(a) 1 0 0 00		1 0 0 00		1 0 0 00				16
17 Telephone Expense	1 5 0 00				1 5 0 00		1 5 0 00				17
18 Laboratory Expense	9 8 0 00				9 8 0 00		9 8 0 00				18
19 Insurance Expense			(c) 5 0 0 00		5 0 0 00		5 0 0 00				19
20 Depr. Expense—Office Furniture			(d) 2 0 0 00		2 0 0 00		2 0 0 00				20
21 Depr. Expense—Medical Equipment			(e) 3 0 0 00		3 0 0 00		3 0 0 00				21
22	84 4 0 0 00	84 4 0 0 00	1 1 5 0 00	1 1 5 0 00	84 9 0 0 00	84 9 0 0 00	12 7 8 0 00	25 2 0 0 00	72 1 2 0 00	59 7 0 0 00	22
23 Net Income							12 4 2 0 00			12 4 2 0 00	23
24							25 2 0 0 00	25 2 0 0 00	72 1 2 0 00	72 1 2 0 00	24
25											25
26											26
27											27
28											28
29											29
30											30

FIGURE 10-11 Work Sheet for Ray Bonita, M.D.

Preparing Financial Statements

Dr. Bonita made no additional investment during June. Thus, as we saw in Chapter 6, the financial statements can be prepared directly from the work sheet. Recall that if Bonita had made an additional investment, this amount would be identified by reviewing Bonita's capital account and would need to be reported in the statement of owner's equity. Bonita's financial statements are illustrated in Figure 10-12.

Ray Bonita, M.D.
Income Statement
For Month Ended June 30, 20 - -

Revenue:									
Medical fees						$ 25	2	0 0	00
Expenses:									
Wages expense	$ 8	5	0 0	00					
Rent expense	2	0	0 0	00					
Office supplies expense			5 0	00					
Medical supplies expense		1	0 0	00					
Telephone expense		1	5 0	00					
Laboratory expense		9	8 0	00					
Insurance expense		5	0 0	00					
Depreciation expense—office furniture		2	0 0	00					
Depreciation expense—medical equipment		3	0 0	00					
Total expenses						12	7	8 0	00
Net income						$12	4	2 0	00

Ray Bonita, M.D.
Statement of Owner's Equity
For Month Ended June 30, 20 - -

Ray Bonita, capital, June 1, 20 - -						$50	0	0 0	00
Net income for June	$12	4	2 0	00					
Less withdrawals for June	10	0	0 0	00					
Increase in capital						2	4	2 0	00
Ray Bonita, capital, June 30, 20 - -						$52	4	2 0	00

Ray Bonita, M.D.
Balance Sheet
June 30, 20 - -

Assets									
Current assets:									
Cash	$21	1	7 0	00					
Medical supplies		3	5 0	00					
Office supplies		1	0 0	00					
Prepaid insurance	5	5	0 0	00					
Total current assets						$27	1	2 0	00
Property, plant, and equipment:									
Office furniture	$13	0	0 0	00					
Less accumulated depreciation		2	0 0	00		12	8	0 0	00
Medical equipment	$22	0	0 0	00					
Less accumulated depreciation		3	0 0	00		21	7	0 0	00
Total assets						$61	6	2 0	00
Liabilities									
Current liabilities:									
Accounts payable						$ 9	2	0 0	00
Owner's Equity									
Ray Bonita, capital						52	4	2 0	00
Total liabilities and owner's equity						$61	6	2 0	00

FIGURE 10-12 Financial Statements for Ray Bonita, M.D.

PROFILES IN ACCOUNTING
Amy Butler, Office Manager

Amy Butler earned an Associate Degree in Travel/Hospitality Management. After completing her externship with the Clubhouse Inn, Amy worked for Design Coatings as a receptionist. After eight months, she accepted an office manager's position with EMI, a database consulting firm.

Amy's duties include accounts payable and receivable, payroll, word processing, filing, and supervising and training eight employees.

She considers being professional at all times the key to success.

Preparing Adjusting and Closing Entries

Adjusting and closing entries are made in the combination journal in the same manner demonstrated for the general journal in Chapter 6. We simply use the Description and General Debit and Credit columns. These posted entries are illustrated in Figures 10-13 and 10-14.

COMBINATION JOURNAL

	DATE	CASH DEBIT	CASH CREDIT	DESCRIPTION	POST REF.	GENERAL DEBIT	GENERAL CREDIT	
1				Adjusting Entries				1
2	20-- June 30			Medical Supplies Expense	524	1 0 0 00		2
3				Medical Supplies	141		1 0 0 00	3
4	30			Office Supplies Expense	523	5 0 00		4
5				Office Supplies	142		5 0 00	5
6	30			Insurance Expense	535	5 0 0 00		6
7				Prepaid Insurance	145		5 0 0 00	7
8	30			Depr. Expense—Office Furniture	541	2 0 0 00		8
9				Accum. Depr.—Office Furn.	182.1		2 0 0 00	9
10	30			Depr. Expense—Medical Equip.	542	3 0 0 00		10
11				Accum. Depr.—Medical Equip.	185.1		3 0 0 00	11

FIGURE 10-13   Adjusting Entries

COMBINATION JOURNAL

	DATE	CASH DEBIT	CASH CREDIT	DESCRIPTION	POST REF.	GENERAL DEBIT	GENERAL CREDIT	
12								12
13				Closing Entries				13
14	20-- June 30			Medical Fees	401	25 2 0 0 00		14
15				Income Summary	313		25 2 0 0 00	15
16	30			Income Summary	313	12 7 8 0 00		16
17				Wages Expense	511		8 5 0 0 00	17
18				Rent Expense	521		2 0 0 0 00	18
19				Office Supplies Expense	523		5 0 00	19
20				Medical Supplies Expense	524		1 0 0 00	20
21				Telephone Expense	525		1 5 0 00	21
22				Laboratory Expense	526		9 8 0 00	22
23				Insurance Expense	535		5 0 0 00	23
24				Depr. Expense—Office Furn.	541		2 0 0 00	24
25				Depr. Expense—Med. Equip.	542		3 0 0 00	25
26	30			Income Summary	313	12 4 2 0 00		26
27				Ray Bonita, Capital	311		12 4 2 0 00	27
28	30			Ray Bonita, Capital	311	10 0 0 0 00		28
29				Ray Bonita, Drawing	312		10 0 0 0 00	29

FIGURE 10-14   Closing Entries

Learning Objectives	Key Points to Remember
1 **Explain the cash, modified cash, and accrual bases of accounting.**	There are three bases of accounting: cash, modified cash, and accrual. Differences in the recording of revenues, expenses, assets, and liabilities are listed below.

Recording revenues

Cash:	when cash is received
Modified cash:	when cash is received
Accrual:	when earned

Recording expenses

Cash:	when cash is paid
Modified cash:	when cash is paid, except for property, plant, and equipment and prepaid items
Accrual:	when incurred

Recording assets and liabilities

	Cash Basis	Modified Cash Basis	Accrual Basis
Accounts receivable	No	No	Yes
Payables			
for purchase of assets	No	Yes	Yes
for services received (wages payable)	No	No	Yes
Prepaid assets	No	Yes	Yes
Long-term assets	No	Yes	Yes

Learning Objectives	Key Points to Remember
2 **Describe special records for a professional service business using the modified cash basis.**	Special records are required for a professional service business using the modified cash basis. Since accounts receivable are not entered in the accounting system, other records must be maintained to keep track of amounts owed by clients and patients. These records generally include an appointment record and a client or patient ledger record.
3 **Describe and use a combination journal to record transactions of a professional service business.**	A combination journal is used by some businesses to improve the efficiency of recording and posting transactions. It includes general and special columns. The headings for a typical combination journal for a doctor's office are shown below.

COMBINATION JOURNAL   PAGE 1

DATE	CASH DEBIT	CASH CREDIT	DESCRIPTION	POST REF.	GENERAL DEBIT	GENERAL CREDIT	MEDICAL FEES CREDIT	WAGES EXPENSE DEBIT	LABORATORY EXPENSE DEBIT	MEDICAL SUPPLIES DEBIT	OFFICE SUPPLIES DEBIT

Learning Objectives	Key Points to Remember
4 **Post from the combination journal to the general ledger.**	Rules for posting a combination journal: 1. Amounts entered in the general columns are posted individually to the general ledger on a daily basis. 2. The totals of the special columns are posted to the general ledger at the end of the month.
5 **Prepare a work sheet, financial statements, and adjusting and closing entries for a professional service business.**	The work sheet, financial statements, adjusting entries, and closing entries are prepared in the same manner as discussed in Chapters 5 and 6. Remember, however, that under the modified cash basis, adjustments are made only for prepaid items and depreciation of plant and equipment.

Reflection: Answering the Opening Question

To comply with generally accepted accounting principles (GAAP), all firms should use the accrual basis. As you recall, this means that revenues should be recognized when earned, regardless of when cash is received, and expenses should be recognized when incurred, regardless of when cash is paid. Investors and creditors expect GAAP financial statements when major companies seek to raise funds. Thus, if the doctor wants GAAP financial statements, revenues should be recorded when the doctor provides the service. (Later, in Chapter 17, we will discuss what should be done about differences between the amount charged by the doctor and the amount finally paid by the patient, or insurance company.)

Many small professional service businesses are not concerned with raising large amounts of money from investors and creditors. These firms include CPAs, doctors, dentists, lawyers, engineers, and architects. Since these firms do not need to prepare GAAP financial statements, they often use the cash or modified cash basis. This simplifies the accounting process and provides results similar to GAAP if receivables and payables are minimal. Further, if one of these organizations needs to borrow money from a bank that requires GAAP financial statements, an accountant can convert the financial statements to the accrual basis.

DEMONSTRATION PROBLEM

Maria Vietor is a financial planning consultant. She developed the following chart of accounts for her business.

Vietor Financial Planning
Chart of Accounts

Assets	Revenues
101 Cash	401 Professional Fees
142 Office Supplies	
	Expenses
Liabilities	511 Wages Expense
202 Accounts Payable	521 Rent Expense
	523 Office Supplies Expense
	525 Telephone Expense
Owner's Equity	526 Automobile Expense
311 Maria Vietor, Capital	533 Utilities Expense
312 Maria Vietor, Drawing	534 Charitable Contributions Expense
313 Income Summary	

Vietor completed the following transactions during the month of December of the current year.

Dec. 1	Vietor invested cash to start a consulting business, $20,000.
3	Paid December office rent, $1,000.
4	Received a check from Aaron Bisno, a client, for services, $2,500.
6	Paid Union Electric for December heating and light, $75.
7	Received a check from Will Carter, a client, for services, $2,000.
12	Paid Smith's Super Service for gasoline and oil purchases, $60.

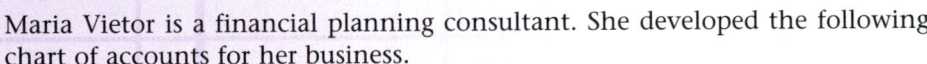

(continued)

14 Paid Comphelp for temporary secretarial services obtained through them during the past two weeks, $600.

17 Purchased office supplies on account from Cleat Office Supply, $280.

20 Paid Cress Telephone Co. for local and long-distance business calls during the past month, $100.

21 Vietor withdrew cash for personal use, $1,100.

24 Made donation to the National Multiple Sclerosis Society, $100.

27 Received a check from Ellen Thaler, a client, for services, $2,000.

28 Paid Comphelp for temporary secretarial services obtained through them during the past two weeks, $600.

29 Made payment on account to Cleat Office Supply, $100.

REQUIRED

1. Enter the transactions in a combination journal. Establish special columns for Professional Fees, Wages Expense, and Automobile Expense. Vietor uses the modified cash basis of accounting. (Refer to the Chapter 4 Demonstration Problem to see how similar transactions were recorded in a general journal. Notice that the combination journal is much more efficient.)

2. Prove the combination journal.

3. Post these transactions to a general ledger.

4. Prepare a trial balance.

Solution

1, 2.

COMBINATION JOURNAL   PAGE 1

#	DATE	CASH DEBIT	CASH CREDIT	DESCRIPTION	POST REF.	GENERAL DEBIT	GENERAL CREDIT	PROFESSIONAL FEES CREDIT	WAGES EXPENSE DEBIT	AUTOMOBILE EXPENSE DEBIT
1	20-- Dec. 1	20 0 0 0 00		Maria Vietor, Capital	311		20 0 0 0 00			
2	3		1 0 0 0 00	Rent Expense	521	1 0 0 0 00				
3	4	2 5 0 0 00			—			2 5 0 0 00		
4	6		7 5 00	Utilities Expense	533	7 5 00				
5	7	2 0 0 0 00			—			2 0 0 0 00		
6	12		6 0 0 00		—				6 0 0 00	
7	14		6 0 00		—					6 0 00
8	17			Office Supplies	142	2 8 0 00				
9				Accounts Payable—Cleat Office Supply	202		2 8 0 00			
10	20		1 0 0 00	Telephone Expense	525	1 0 0 00				
11	21		1 0 0 0 00	Maria Vietor, Drawing	312	1 0 0 0 00				
12	24		1 0 0 00	Charitable Contributions Expense	534	1 0 0 00				
13	27	2 0 0 0 00			—			2 0 0 0 00		
14	28		6 0 0 00		—				6 0 0 00	
15	29		2 0 0 00	Accounts Payable—Cleat Office Supply	202	2 0 0 00				
16		26 5 0 0 00	3 7 3 5 00			2 7 5 5 00	20 2 8 0 00	6 5 0 0 00	12 0 0 00	6 0 00
17		(1 0 1)	(1 0 1)			(✓)	(✓)	(4 0 1)	(5 1 1)	(5 2 6)
18										

Proving the Combination Journal

Debit Columns		Credit Columns	
Cash	26,500	Cash	3,735
General	2,755	General	20,280
Wages Expense	1,200	Professional Fees	6,500
Auto. Expense	60		30,515
	30,515		

(continued)

3.

GENERAL LEDGER

ACCOUNT: Cash   ACCOUNT NO. 101

DATE		ITEM	POST REF.	DEBIT	CREDIT	BALANCE	
						DEBIT	CREDIT
20-- Dec.	31		C J 1	26 500 00		26 500 00	
	31		C J 1		3 735 00	22 765 00	

ACCOUNT: Office Supplies   ACCOUNT NO. 142

DATE		ITEM	POST REF.	DEBIT	CREDIT	BALANCE	
						DEBIT	CREDIT
20-- Dec.	17		C J 1	280 00		280 00	

ACCOUNT: Accounts Payable   ACCOUNT NO. 202

DATE		ITEM	POST REF.	DEBIT	CREDIT	BALANCE	
						DEBIT	CREDIT
20-- Dec.	17		C J 1		280 00		280 00
	29		C J 1	100 00			180 00

ACCOUNT: Maria Vietor, Capital   ACCOUNT NO. 311

DATE		ITEM	POST REF.	DEBIT	CREDIT	BALANCE	
						DEBIT	CREDIT
20-- Dec.	1		C J 1		20 000 00		20 000 00

ACCOUNT: Maria Vietor, Drawing   ACCOUNT NO. 312

DATE		ITEM	POST REF.	DEBIT	CREDIT	BALANCE	
						DEBIT	CREDIT
20-- Dec.	21		C J 1	1 100 00		1 100 00	

ACCOUNT: Income Summary   ACCOUNT NO. 313

DATE	ITEM	POST REF.	DEBIT	CREDIT	BALANCE	
					DEBIT	CREDIT
20--						

ACCOUNT: Professional Fees   ACCOUNT NO. 401

DATE		ITEM	POST REF.	DEBIT	CREDIT	BALANCE	
						DEBIT	CREDIT
20-- Dec.	31		C J 1		6 500 00		6 500 00

ACCOUNT: Wages Expense   ACCOUNT NO. 511

DATE		ITEM	POST REF.	DEBIT	CREDIT	BALANCE	
						DEBIT	CREDIT
20-- Dec.	31		C J 1	1 200 00		1 200 00	

3.

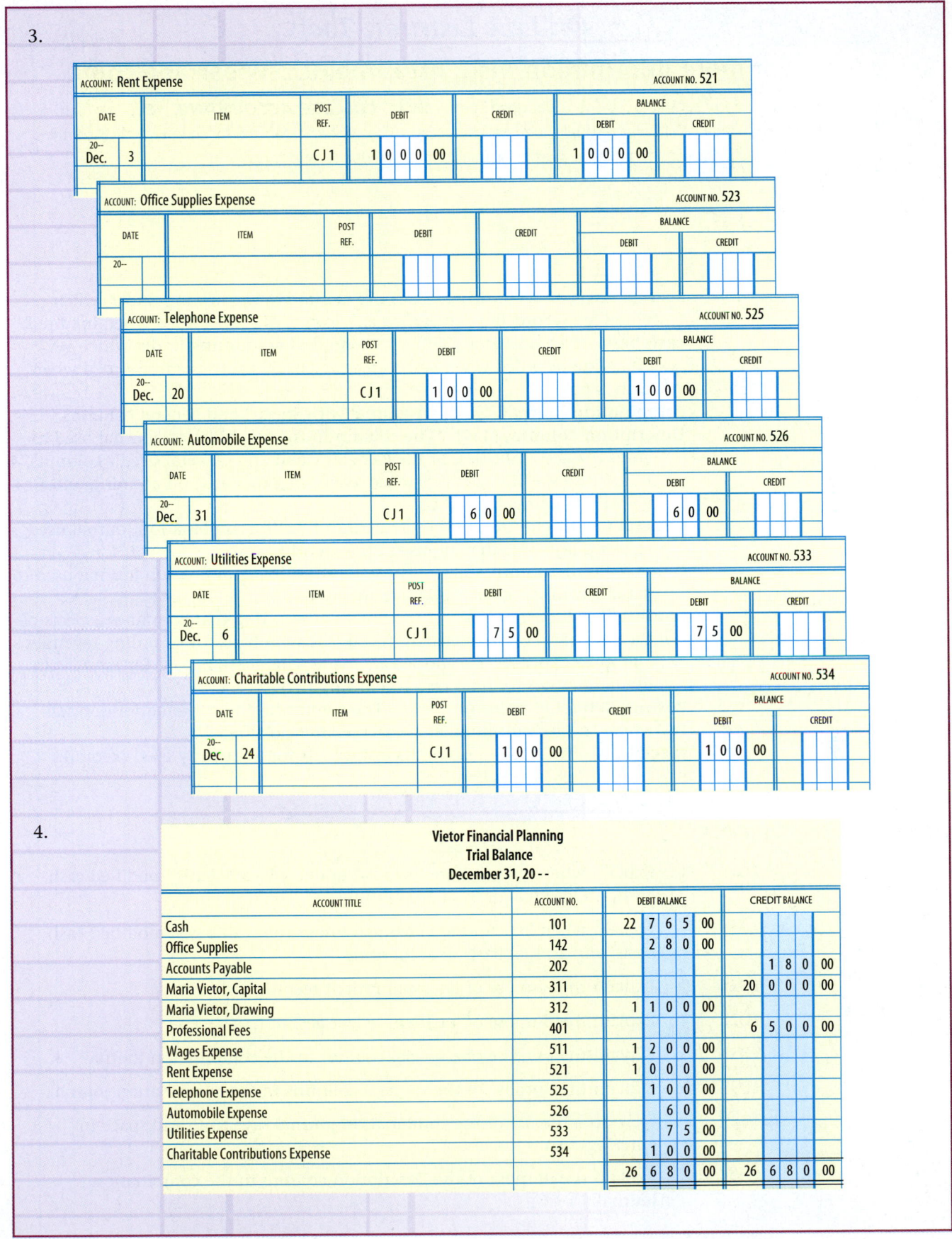

ACCOUNT: Rent Expense   **ACCOUNT NO.** 521

DATE	ITEM	POST REF.	DEBIT	CREDIT	BALANCE DEBIT	BALANCE CREDIT
20-- Dec. 3		CJ1	1 0 0 0 00		1 0 0 0 00	

ACCOUNT: Office Supplies Expense   **ACCOUNT NO.** 523

DATE	ITEM	POST REF.	DEBIT	CREDIT	BALANCE DEBIT	BALANCE CREDIT
20--						

ACCOUNT: Telephone Expense   **ACCOUNT NO.** 525

DATE	ITEM	POST REF.	DEBIT	CREDIT	BALANCE DEBIT	BALANCE CREDIT
20-- Dec. 20		CJ1	1 0 0 00		1 0 0 00	

ACCOUNT: Automobile Expense   **ACCOUNT NO.** 526

DATE	ITEM	POST REF.	DEBIT	CREDIT	BALANCE DEBIT	BALANCE CREDIT
20-- Dec. 31		CJ1	6 0 00		6 0 00	

ACCOUNT: Utilities Expense   **ACCOUNT NO.** 533

DATE	ITEM	POST REF.	DEBIT	CREDIT	BALANCE DEBIT	BALANCE CREDIT
20-- Dec. 6		CJ1	7 5 00		7 5 00	

ACCOUNT: Charitable Contributions Expense   **ACCOUNT NO.** 534

DATE	ITEM	POST REF.	DEBIT	CREDIT	BALANCE DEBIT	BALANCE CREDIT
20-- Dec. 24		CJ1	1 0 0 00		1 0 0 00	

4.

Vietor Financial Planning
Trial Balance
December 31, 20 - -

ACCOUNT TITLE	ACCOUNT NO.	DEBIT BALANCE	CREDIT BALANCE
Cash	101	22 7 6 5 00	
Office Supplies	142	2 8 0 00	
Accounts Payable	202		1 8 0 00
Maria Vietor, Capital	311		20 0 0 0 00
Maria Vietor, Drawing	312	1 1 0 0 00	
Professional Fees	401		6 5 0 0 00
Wages Expense	511	1 2 0 0 00	
Rent Expense	521	1 0 0 0 00	
Telephone Expense	525	1 0 0 00	
Automobile Expense	526	6 0 00	
Utilities Expense	533	7 5 00	
Charitable Contributions Expense	534	1 0 0 00	
		26 6 8 0 00	26 6 8 0 00

On-Line Learning Tools

For more information, visit: http://heintz.swlearning.com

The Heintz & Parry product web site is designed specifically for **COLLEGE ACCOUNTING, 18e.** The features include downloadable student resources and an interactive study center, organized by chapter, which contains learning objectives, web links, on-line quizzes with automatic feedback, and more.

KEY TERMS

accrual basis of accounting, (332)   A method of accounting under which revenues are recorded when earned and expenses are recorded when incurred.

cash basis of accounting, (332)   A method of accounting under which revenues are recorded when cash is received and expenses are recorded when cash is paid.

combination journal, (337)   A journal with special and general columns.

Description column, (339)   The column in the combination journal used to enter the account titles for the General Debit and General Credit columns, to identify specific creditors when assets are purchased on account, and to identify amounts forwarded.

General Credit column, (337)   The column in the combination journal used to credit accounts that are used infrequently.

General Debit column, (337)   The column in the combination journal used to debit accounts that are used infrequently.

modified cash basis, (333)   A method of accounting that combines aspects of the cash and accrual methods. It uses the cash basis for recording revenues and most expenses. Exceptions are made when cash is paid for assets with useful lives greater than one accounting period.

Posting Reference column, (341)   The column in the combination journal where the account number is entered after posting.

special columns, (337)   Columns in journals for frequently used accounts.

REVIEW QUESTIONS

(LO1)   1. Explain when revenues are recorded under the cash basis, modified cash basis, and accrual basis of accounting.

(LO1)   2. Explain when expenses are recorded under the cash basis, modified cash basis, and accrual basis of accounting.

(LO2)   3. Explain the purpose of an appointment record.

(LO2)   4. Explain the purpose of a patient ledger account.

(LO3)   5. Explain the purpose of a special column in the combination journal.

(LO3)   6. Explain the purpose of the General columns in the combination journal.

(LO3/4)   7. How does the use of the combination journal save time and space in entering cash transactions?

(LO3)   8. Explain the purpose of the Description column in the combination journal.

(LO3)   9. What is the purpose of proving the totals in the combination journal?

(LO4)   10. When an entry is posted from the combination journal to a ledger account, what information is entered in the Posting Reference column of the combination journal? in the Posting Reference column of the ledger account?

Self-Study Test Questions

True/False

1. Under the accrual basis of accounting, revenues are recorded when earned.   _____

2. The cash basis of accounting is used by most large businesses.   _____

3. The modified cash basis uses the accrual basis when recording revenues and expenses.   _____

4. The modified cash basis is a combination of the cash and accrual methods of accounting.   _____

5. Many small professional service businesses use the modified cash basis.   _____

Multiple Choice

1. Which of these would make the best "special column" in a combination journal?   _____

    (a) Office Equipment   (c) Revenue
    (b) Prepaid Insurance   (d) Telephone Expense

2. Verifying that debit column totals equal credit column totals is the process of   _____

    (a) debiting.   (c) closing.
    (b) proving.   (d) adjusting.

3. Posting from the combination journal is accomplished by placing a " _____ " and page number in the Posting Reference column of the general ledger account.   _____

    (a) G   (c) J
    (b) DJ   (d) CJ

4. Using the modified cash basis, when a business provides services on account, _____ is debited.   _____

    (a) no entry   (c) Cash
    (b) Accounts Receivable   (d) Owner's Equity

5. Using the modified cash basis, when wages are earned but not paid, _____ is debited.   _____

    (a) Wages Expense   (c) Wages Payable
    (b) no entry   (d) Accrued Wages

The answers to the Self-Study Test Questions are at the end of the text.

MANAGING YOUR WRITING

Your friend is planning to start her own business and has asked you for advice. In particular, she is concerned about which method of accounting she should use. She has heard about the cash, modified cash, and accrual methods of accounting. However, she does not really understand the differences. Write a memo that explains each method and the type of business for which each method is most appropriate.

ETHICS CASE

Nancy Bowles, the owner of Bowles Services, a sole proprietorship, rushed into the office late Monday morning carrying a deposit receipt from the bank. Upon handing the receipt to Sarah, the accountant, she instructed her to debit Cash and credit Professional Fees for the full $10,000. When Sarah examined the source document she saw that the cash had come from the account of Richard Bowles, Nancy's father. Nancy explained to Sarah that she was applying for a bank loan and needed to "show that her company earned more year-to-date income than it actually had." Nancy used the rationale that the company would earn at least $10,000 in revenue during the next few months but the financial statements the bank required were as of the end of this month.

1. Does Nancy's explanation make sense? Is it ethical?

2. How should this transaction be entered in Bowles Services' books? Does it matter whether the cash basis or accrual basis of accounting is used?

3. Make a written list of all the consequences Nancy might face as a result of recording this transaction as a debit to Cash and a credit to Professional Fees.

4. Break up into groups of two and role play Nancy and Sarah's points of view in this situation.

WEB WORK

For some other views on accrual and cash accounting, check out these web pages. What are some differences between cash and accrual accounting? Can businesses use one method for internal record keeping and another method for tax reporting?

Visit the Interactive Study Center on our web site at **http://heintz.swlearning.com** for special hotlinks to assist you in this assignment.

SERIES A EXERCISES

EXERCISE 10-1A **(LO1)**
See Figure 10-2 in text

CASH, MODIFIED CASH, AND ACCRUAL BASES OF ACCOUNTING Prepare the entry for each of the following transactions, using the (a) cash basis, (b) modified cash basis, and (c) accrual basis of accounting.

1. Purchase supplies on account.

2. Make payment on asset previously purchased.

3. Purchase supplies for cash.

4. Purchase insurance for cash.

5. Pay cash for wages.

6. Pay cash for telephone expense.

7. Pay cash for new equipment.

End-of-Period Adjusting Entries:

8. Wages earned but not paid.

9. Prepaid item purchased, partly used.

10. Depreciation on long-term assets.

EXERCISE 10-2A   **(LO1/3)**
General Debit total: $2,715;
Cash debit total: $11,100

JOURNAL ENTRIES Jean Akins opened a consulting business. Journalize the following transactions that occurred during the month of January of the current year using the modified cash basis and a combination journal. Set up special columns for Consulting Fees (credit) and Wages Expense (debit).

Jan. 1   Invested cash in the business, $10,000.

2   Paid office rent, $500.

3   Purchased office equipment on account from Business Machines, Inc., $1,500.

5   Received cash for services rendered, $750.

8   Paid telephone bill, $65.

10   Paid for a magazine subscription (miscellaneous expense), $15.

11   Purchased office supplies on account from Leo's Office Supplies, $300.

15   Paid for one-year liability insurance policy, $150.

18   Paid part-time help, $500.

21   Received cash for services rendered, $350.

25   Paid electricity bill, $85.

27   Withdrew cash for personal use, $100.

29   Paid part-time help, $500.

EXERCISE 10-3A   **(LO1/3)**
Total debits: $19,191

JOURNAL ENTRIES Bill Rackes opened a bicycle repair shop. Journalize the following transactions that occurred during the month of October of the current year. Use the modified cash basis and a combination journal with special columns for Repair Fees (credit) and Wages Expense (debit). Prove the combination journal.

Oct. 1   Invested cash in the business, $15,000.

2   Paid shop rental for the month, $300.

3   Purchased bicycle parts on account from Tracker's Bicycle Parts, $2,000.

5   Purchased office supplies on account from Downtown Office Supplies, $250.

8   Paid telephone bill, $38.

9   Received cash for services, $140.

11   Paid for a sports magazine subscription (miscellaneous expense), $15.

12   Made payment on account for parts previously purchased, $100.

14   Paid part-time help, $300.

15   Received cash for services, $350.

(continued)

16	Paid electricity bill, $48.
19	Received cash for services, $250.
23	Withdrew cash for personal use, $50.
25	Made payment on account for office supplies previously purchased, $50.
29	Paid part-time help, $300.

SERIES A PROBLEMS

PROBLEM 10-4A (LO3/4/5)

Power Accounting System Software®

Cash bal., 1/12: $10,310;
Total journal credits: $15,499;
Trial Bal. total debits: $13,460

JOURNALIZING AND POSTING TRANSACTIONS AND PREPARING A TRIAL BALANCE Angela McWharton opened an on-call nursing services business. She rented a small office space and pays a part-time worker to answer the telephone. Her chart of accounts is shown below.

Angela McWharton Nursing Services
Chart of Accounts

Assets		Revenues	
101	Cash	401	Nursing Care Fees
142	Office Supplies		
181	Office Equipment	Expenses	
		511	Wages Expense
Liabilities		512	Advertising Expense
202	Accounts Payable	521	Rent Expense
		525	Telephone Expense
		526	Transportation Expense
Owner's Equity		533	Electricity Expense
311	Angela McWharton, Capital	549	Miscellaneous Expense
312	Angela McWharton, Drawing		
313	Income Summary		

McWharton's transactions for the first month of business are as follows:

Jan. 1	Invested cash in the business, $10,000.
1	Paid January rent, $500.
2	Purchased office supplies on account from Crestline Office Supplies, $300.
4	Purchased office equipment on account from Office Technology, Inc., $1,500.
6	Received cash for nursing services rendered, $580.
7	Paid telephone bill, $42.
8	Paid electricity bill, $38.
10	Received cash for nursing services rendered, $360.
12	Made payment on account for office supplies previously purchased, $50.
13	Reimbursed part-time worker for use of personal automobile (transportation expense), $150.
15	Paid part-time worker, $360.
17	Received cash for nursing services rendered, $420.
18	Withdrew cash for personal use, $100.
20	Paid for newspaper advertising, $26.

22   Paid for gas and oil, $35.

24   Paid subscription for journal on nursing care practices (miscellaneous expense), $28.

25   Received cash for nursing services rendered, $320.

27   Made payment on account for office equipment previously purchased, $150.

29   Paid part-time worker, $360.

30   Received cash for nursing services rendered, $180.

REQUIRED

1. Journalize the transactions for January using the modified cash basis and page 1 of a combination journal. Set up special columns for Nursing Care Fees (credit), Wages Expense (debit), and Transportation Expense (debit).

2. Determine the cash balance as of January 12 (using the combination journal).

3. Prove the combination journal.

4. Set up four-column general ledger accounts from the chart of accounts and post the transactions from the combination journal.

5. Prepare a trial balance.

PROBLEM 10-5A (LO3/4/5)

Cash bal., 11/12: $5,949;
Total journal credits: $6,499;
Trial Bal. total debits: $18,155;
Adjusted Trial Bal. total debits: $18,455; Net income: $1,842;
Capital, 11/30: $6,772;
Total assets, 11/30: $13,947

JOURNALIZING AND POSTING TRANSACTIONS AND PREPARING FINANCIAL STATEMENTS Sue Reyton owns a suit tailoring shop. She opened her business in September. She rents a small work space and has an assistant to receive job orders and process claim tickets. Her trial balance shows her account balances for the first two months of business (September and October). No adjustments were made in September or October.

		Sue Reyton Tailors											
		Trial Balance											
		October 31, 20 - -											
ACCOUNT TITLE	ACCOUNT NO.	DEBIT BALANCE						CREDIT BALANCE					
Cash	101	5	7	1	1	00							
Tailoring Supplies	141	1	0	0	0	00							
Office Supplies	142		4	8	5	00							
Prepaid Insurance	145		1	0	0	00							
Tailoring Equipment	188	3	8	0	0	00							
Accumulated Depreciation—Tailoring Equipment	188.1												
Accounts Payable	202							4	1	2	5	00	
Sue Reyton, Capital	311							5	4	3	0	00	
Sue Reyton, Drawing	312		5	0	0	00							
Tailoring Fees	401							3	6	0	0	00	
Wages Expense	511		8	0	0	00							
Advertising Expense	512			3	3	00							
Rent Expense	521		6	0	0	00							
Telephone Expense	525			6	0	00							
Electricity Expense	533			4	4	00							
Miscellaneous Expense	549			2	2	00							
		13	1	5	5	00		13	1	5	5	00	

Reyton's transactions for November are as follows:

Nov. 1   Paid November rent, $300.

(continued)

2   Purchased tailoring supplies on account from Sew Easy Supplies, $150.

3   Purchased a new button hole machine on account from Seam's Sewing Machines, $3,000.

5   Earned first week's revenue: $400 in cash.

8   Paid for newspaper advertising, $13.

9   Paid telephone bill, $28.

10 Paid electricity bill, $21.

12 Earned second week's revenue: $200 in cash, $300 on account.

15 Paid part-time worker, $400.

16 Made payment on account for tailoring supplies, $100.

17 Paid for magazine subscription (miscellaneous expense), $12.

19 Earned third week's revenue: $450 in cash.

21 Paid for prepaid insurance for the year, $500.

23 Received cash from customers (previously owed), $300.

24 Paid for newspaper advertising, $13.

26 Paid for special delivery fee (miscellaneous expense), $12.

29 Earned fourth week's revenue: $600 in cash.

Additional accounts needed are as follows:

313   Income Summary
523   Office Supplies Expense
524   Tailoring Supplies Expense
535   Insurance Expense
542   Depreciation Expense—Tailoring Equipment

Nov. 30 Adjustments:

(a) Tailoring supplies on hand, $450.

(b) Office supplies on hand, $285.

(c) Prepaid insurance expired over past three months, $150.

(d) Depreciation on tailoring equipment for the last three months, $300.

REQUIRED

1. Journalize the transactions for November using the modified cash basis and page 5 of a combination journal. Set up special columns for Tailoring Fees (credit), Wages Expense (debit), and Advertising Expense (debit).

2. Determine the cash balance as of November 12.

3. Prove the combination journal.

4. Set up four-column general ledger accounts, including the additional accounts listed above, entering the balances as of November 1, 20--. Post the entries from the combination journal.

5. Prepare a work sheet for the three months ended November 30, 20--.

6. Prepare an income statement and statement of owner's equity for the three months ended November 30, and a balance sheet as of November 30, 20--. (Assume that Reyton made an investment of $5,430 on September 1, 20--.)

7. Record the adjusting and closing entries on page 6 of the combination journal and post to the general ledger accounts.

SERIES B EXERCISES

EXERCISE 10-1B   (LO1)
See Figure 10-2 in text

CASH, MODIFIED CASH, AND ACCRUAL BASES OF ACCOUNTING For each journal entry shown below, indicate the accounting method(s) for which the entry would be appropriate. If the journal entry is not appropriate for a particular accounting method, explain the proper accounting treatment for that method.

1. Office Equipment
    Cash
        Purchased equipment for cash

2. Office Equipment
    Accounts Payable
        Purchased equipment on account

3. Cash
    Revenue
        Cash receipts for week

4. Accounts Receivable
    Revenue
        Services performed on account

5. Prepaid Insurance
    Cash
        Purchased prepaid asset

6. Supplies
    Accounts Payable
        Purchased prepaid asset

7. Telephone Expense
    Cash
        Paid telephone bill

8. Wages Expense
    Cash
        Paid wages for month

9. Accounts Payable
    Cash
        Payment on account

Adjusting Entries:

10. Supplies Expense
    Supplies

11. Wages Expense
    Wages Payable

12. Depreciation Expense—Office Equipment
    Accumulated Depreciation—Office Equipment

EXERCISE 10-2B **(LO1/3)**
General Debit total: $2,129;
Cash debit total: $9,400

JOURNAL ENTRIES Bill Miller opened a bookkeeping service business. Journalize the following transactions that occurred during the month of March of the current year. Use the modified cash basis and a combination journal with special columns for Bookkeeping Fees (credit) and Wages Expense (debit).

Mar. 1   Invested cash in the business, $7,500.

3   Paid March office rent, $500.

5   Purchased office equipment on account from Desk Top Office Equipment, $800.

6   Received cash for services rendered, $400.

8   Paid telephone bill, $48.

10   Paid for a magazine subscription (miscellaneous expense), $25.

11   Purchased office supplies, $200.

14   Received cash for services rendered, $520.

16   Paid for a one-year insurance policy, $200.

18   Paid part-time worker, $400.

21   Received cash for services rendered, $380.

22   Made payment on account for office equipment previously purchased, $100.

24   Paid electricity bill, $56.

27   Withdrew cash for personal use, $200.

29   Paid part-time worker, $400.

30   Received cash for services rendered, $600.

EXERCISE 10-3B **(LO1/3)**
Total debits: $14,349

JOURNAL ENTRIES Amy Anjelo opened a delivery service. Journalize the following transactions that occurred in January of the current year. Use the modified cash basis and a combination journal with special columns for Delivery Fees (credit) and Wages Expense (debit). Prove the combination journal.

Jan. 1   Invested cash in the business, $10,000.

2   Paid shop rental for the month, $400.

3   Purchased a delivery cart on account from Walt's Wheels, $1,000.

5   Purchased office supplies, $250.

6   Paid telephone bill, $51.

8   Received cash for delivery services, $428.

11   Paid electricity bill, $37.

12   Paid part-time employee, $480.

13   Paid for postage stamps (miscellaneous expense), $29.

15   Received cash for delivery services, $382.

18   Made payment on account for delivery cart previously purchased, $90.

21   Withdrew cash for personal use, $250.

24   Paid for a one-year liability insurance policy, $180.

26   Received cash for delivery services, $292.

29   Paid part-time employee, $480.

SERIES B PROBLEMS

PROBLEM 10-4B (LO3/4/5)

Cash bal., 7/14: $4,786;
Total journal credits: $9,472;
Trial Bal. total debits: $8,190

JOURNALIZING AND POSTING TRANSACTIONS AND PREPARING A TRIAL BALANCE J. B. Hoyt opened a training center at the marina where he provides private water-skiing lessons. He rented a small building at the marina and has a part-time worker to assist him. His chart of accounts is shown below.

Water Walking by Hoyt
Chart of Accounts

Assets
101 Cash
142 Office Supplies
183 Skiing Equipment

Liabilities
202 Accounts Payable

Owner's Equity
311 J. B. Hoyt, Capital
312 J. B. Hoyt, Drawing
313 Income Summary

Revenues
401 Training Fees

Expenses
511 Wages Expense
521 Rent Expense
525 Telephone Expense
526 Transportation Expense
533 Electricity Expense
537 Repair Expense
549 Miscellaneous Expense

Transactions for the first month of business are as follows:

July 1	Invested cash in the business, $5,000.
2	Paid rent for the month, $250.
3	Purchased office supplies, $150.
4	Purchased skiing equipment on account from Water Fun, Inc., $2,000.
6	Paid telephone bill, $36.
7	Received cash for skiing lessons, $200.
10	Paid electricity bill, $28.
12	Paid part-time worker, $250.
14	Received cash for skiing lessons, $300.
16	Paid for gas and oil (transportation expense), $60.
17	Received cash for skiing lessons, $250.
20	Paid for repair to ski rope, $20.
21	Made payment on account for skiing equipment previously purchased, $100.
24	Received cash for skiing lessons, $310.
26	Paid for award certificates (miscellaneous expense), $18.
28	Paid part-time worker, $250.
30	Received cash for skiing lessons, $230.
31	Paid for repair to life jacket, $20.

(continued)

REQUIRED

1. Journalize the transactions for July using the modified cash basis and page 1 of a combination journal. Set up special columns for Training Fees (credit), Wages Expense (debit), and Repair Expense (debit).

2. Determine the cash balance as of July 14, 20--.

3. Prove the combination journal.

4. Set up four-column general ledger accounts from the chart of accounts and post the transactions from the combination journal.

5. Prepare a trial balance.

PROBLEM 10-5B (LO3/4/5)

Cash bal., 6/12: $4,832;
Total journal credits:
$4,587; Trial Bal.
total debits: $13,023;
Adjusted Trial Bal.
total debits: $13,283;
Net income: $2,928;
Capital, 6/30: $7,028;
Total assets, 6/30: $9,008

JOURNALIZING AND POSTING TRANSACTIONS AND PREPARING FINANCIAL STATEMENTS Molly Claussen owns a lawn care business. She opened her business in April. She rents a small shop area where she stores her equipment and has an assistant to receive orders and process accounts. Her trial balance shows her account balances for the first two months of business (April and May). No adjustments were made at the end of April or May.

ACCOUNT TITLE	ACCOUNT NO.	DEBIT BALANCE	CREDIT BALANCE
Molly Claussen's Green Thumb Trial Balance May 31, 20 - -			
Cash	101	4 6 0 4 00	
Lawn Care Supplies	141	5 8 8 00	
Office Supplies	142	2 4 3 00	
Prepaid Insurance	145	1 5 0 00	
Lawn Care Equipment	189	2 4 0 8 00	
Accumulated Depreciation—Lawn Care Equipment	189.1		
Accounts Payable	202		1 0 8 0 00
Molly Claussen, Capital	311		5 0 0 0 00
Molly Claussen, Drawing	312	8 0 0 00	
Lawn Care Fees	401		4 0 3 3 00
Wages Expense	511	6 0 0 00	
Rent Expense	521	4 0 0 00	
Telephone Expense	525	8 8 00	
Electricity Expense	533	6 2 00	
Repair Expense	537	5 0 00	
Gas and Oil Expense	538	1 2 0 00	
		10 1 1 3 00	10 1 1 3 00

Transactions for June are as follows:

June 1   Paid shop rent, $200.

   2   Purchased office supplies, $230.

   3   Purchased new landscaping equipment on account from Earth Care, Inc., $1,000.

   5   Paid telephone bill, $31.

   6   Received cash for lawn care fees, $640.

   8   Paid electricity bill, $31.

10   Paid part-time worker, $300.

11   Received cash for lawn care fees, $580.

12   Paid for a one-year insurance policy, $200.

14   Made payment on account for landscaping equipment previously purchased, $100.

15   Paid for gas and oil, $40.

19   Paid for mower repairs, $25.

21   Received $310 cash for lawn care fees and earned $480 on account.

24   Withdrew cash for personal use, $100.

26   Paid for edging equipment repairs, $20.

28   Received cash from customers (previously owed), $480.

29   Paid part-time worker, $300.

Additional accounts needed are as follows:

313   Income Summary
523   Office Supplies Expense
524   Lawn Care Supplies Expense
535   Insurance Expense
542   Depreciation Expense—Lawn Care Equipment

June 30 Adjustments:

(a) Office supplies on hand, $273.

(b) Lawn care supplies on hand, $300.

(c) Prepaid insurance expired over past three months, $100.

(d) Depreciation on lawn care equipment for past three months, $260.

REQUIRED

1. Journalize the transactions for June using the modified cash basis and page 5 of a combination journal. Set up special columns for Lawn Care Fees (credit), Repair Expense (debit), and Wages Expense (debit).

2. Determine the cash balance as of June 12.

3. Prove the combination journal.

4. Set up four-column general ledger accounts including the additional accounts listed above, entering balances as of June 1, 20--. Post the entries from the combination journal.

5. Prepare a work sheet for the three months ended June 30, 20--.

6. Prepare an income statement and statement of owner's equity for the three months ended June 30, and a balance sheet as of June 30, 20--. Assume that Claussen invested $5,000 on April 1, 20--.

7. Record the adjusting and closing entries on page 6 of the combination journal and post to the general ledger accounts.

MASTERY PROBLEM

Total debits to General Dr. col. of CJ: $112,705; Total debits of CJ: $305,305; Total debits on Trial Bal.: $232,200

John McRoe opened a tennis resort in June 20--. Most guests register for one week, arriving on Sunday afternoon and returning home the following Saturday afternoon. Guests stay at an adjacent hotel. The tennis resort provides lunch and dinner. Dining and exercise facilities are provided in a building rented by McRoe. A dietitian, masseuse, physical therapist, and athletic trainers are on call to assure the proper combination of diet and exercise. The chart of accounts and transactions for the month of June are provided below. McRoe uses the modified cash basis of accounting.

McRoe Tennis Resort
Chart of Accounts

Assets		Revenue	
101	Cash	401	Registration Fees
142	Office Supplies		
144	Food Supplies	**Expenses**	
184	Tennis Facilities	511	Wages Expense
184.1	Accum. Depr.—Tennis Facilities	521	Rent Expense
186	Exercise Equipment	523	Office Supplies Expense
186.1	Accum. Depr.—Exercise Equip.	524	Food Supplies Expense
		525	Telephone Expense
Liabilities		533	Utilities Expense
202	Accounts Payable	535	Insurance Expense
		536	Postage Expense
Owner's Equity		541	Depr. Exp.—Tennis Facilities
311	John McRoe, Capital	542	Depr. Exp.—Exercise Equip.
312	John McRoe, Drawing		
313	Income Summary		

June 1	McRoe invested cash in the business, $90,000.
1	Paid for new exercise equipment, $9,000.
2	Deposited registration fees in the bank, $15,000.
2	Paid rent for month of June on building and land, $2,500.
2	Rogers Construction completed work on new tennis courts that cost $70,000. The estimated useful life of the facility is five years, at which time the courts will have to be resurfaced. Arrangements were made to pay the bill in July.
3	Purchased food supplies on account from Au Naturel Foods, $5,000.
5	Purchased office supplies on account from Gordon Office Supplies, $300.
7	Deposited registration fees in the bank, $16,200.
10	Purchased food supplies on account from Au Naturel Foods, $6,200.
10	Paid wages to staff, $500.
14	Deposited registration fees in the bank, $13,500.
16	Purchased food supplies on account from Au Naturel Foods, $4,000.
17	Paid wages to staff, $500.
18	Paid postage, $85.
21	Deposited registration fees in the bank, $15,200.
24	Purchased food supplies on account from Au Naturel Foods, $5,500.

24	Paid wages to staff, $500.

24   Paid wages to staff, $500.

28   Deposited registration fees in the bank, $14,000.

30   Purchased food supplies on account from Au Naturel Foods, $6,000.

30   Paid wages to staff, $500.

30   Paid Au Naturel Foods on account, $28,700.

30   Paid utility bill, $500.

30   Paid telephone bill, $120.

30   McRoe withdrew cash for personal use, $1,500.

REQUIRED

1. Enter the transactions in a combination journal (page 1). Establish special columns for Registration Fees (credit), Wages Expense (debit), and Food Supplies (debit).

2. Prove the combination journal.

3. Post these transactions to a general ledger.

4. Prepare a trial balance as of June 30.

CHALLENGE PROBLEM

This problem challenges you to apply your cumulative accounting knowledge to move a step beyond the material in the chapter.

**NI cash basis: $6,000;
NI modified cash basis: $7,000;
NI accrual basis: $7,300**

Gerald Resler recently opened a financial consulting business. Summary transactions for the month of June, his second month of operation, are provided below.

1. Cash collected from clients for consulting fees, $10,000. $1,500 of the $10,000 was for consulting fees earned in May, but received in June.

2. Consulting fees earned in June, but to be received in July, $2,000.

3. Supplies on hand at the beginning of June amounted to $500. All purchases of supplies are made on account. Supplies purchased during June, $1,000. At the end of June, $600 worth of supplies remained unused.

4. Paid cash on account to suppliers during June, $800. $200 of the $800 was for purchases of supplies made in May.

5. Wages paid to an assistant, $2,000. Of this $2,000, $300 had been earned in May. In addition, the assistant earned $500 in June, which will be paid next month.

6. Purchased a laptop. Paid $1,200 cash in June and will pay the balance of $1,200 in July. Gerald expects to use the laptop for two years at which time he expects that it will be obsolete and have a zero salvage value.

REQUIRED

Prepare income statements for the month of June using the cash, modified cash, and accrual bases.

©GETTY IMAGES/PHOTODISC

Accounting for a Merchandising Business

DIGITAL IMAGING GROUP

Accounting for Sales and Cash Receipts

When Evan Taylor opened Parkway Pet Supplies, he accepted only cash and personal checks from customers. Soon he had several customers asking to make large purchases of merchandise on account. Evan refused because he thought his business was too small to carry such receivables, and he was unsure about the credit risk of some customers. Evan had a similar attitude toward bank credit cards, such as MasterCard and Visa. A friend with a similar store in Lawrence, Kansas, encouraged Evan to reconsider. He said bank credit card sales are "just like cash" and can provide a major boost in sales. How are bank credit card sales "just like cash"? How should Evan's bookkeeper account for such sales?

LO1 Describe merchandise sales transactions.

LO2 Describe and use merchandise sales accounts.

LO3 Describe and use the accounts receivable ledger.

LO4 Prepare a schedule of accounts receivable.

Over the last ten chapters, we have learned how to account for a service business. We are now ready to consider accounting for a different kind of business—merchandising. A **merchandising business** purchases merchandise such as clothing, furniture, or computers, and sells that merchandise to customers. For example, John Zenith buys shirts from vendors and manufacturers and sells them to his customers at Be A Sport.

This chapter examines how to account for the sale of merchandise using the accrual basis of accounting. We will learn how to use four new accounts and a subsidiary ledger.

MERCHANDISE SALES TRANSACTIONS

LO1 Describe merchandise sales transactions.

A **sale** is a transfer of merchandise from one business or individual to another in exchange for cash or a promise to pay cash. Sales procedures and documents vary greatly, depending on the nature and size of the business.

Retailer

Retail businesses generally sell to customers who enter the store, select the merchandise they want, and bring it to a salesclerk. The salesclerk enters the sale in some type of electronic cash register that generates a receipt for the customer. A copy of the receipt is retained in the register. Most registers can print a summary of the day's sales activity, like the one in Figure 11-1. This summary can be used to journalize sales in the accounting records.

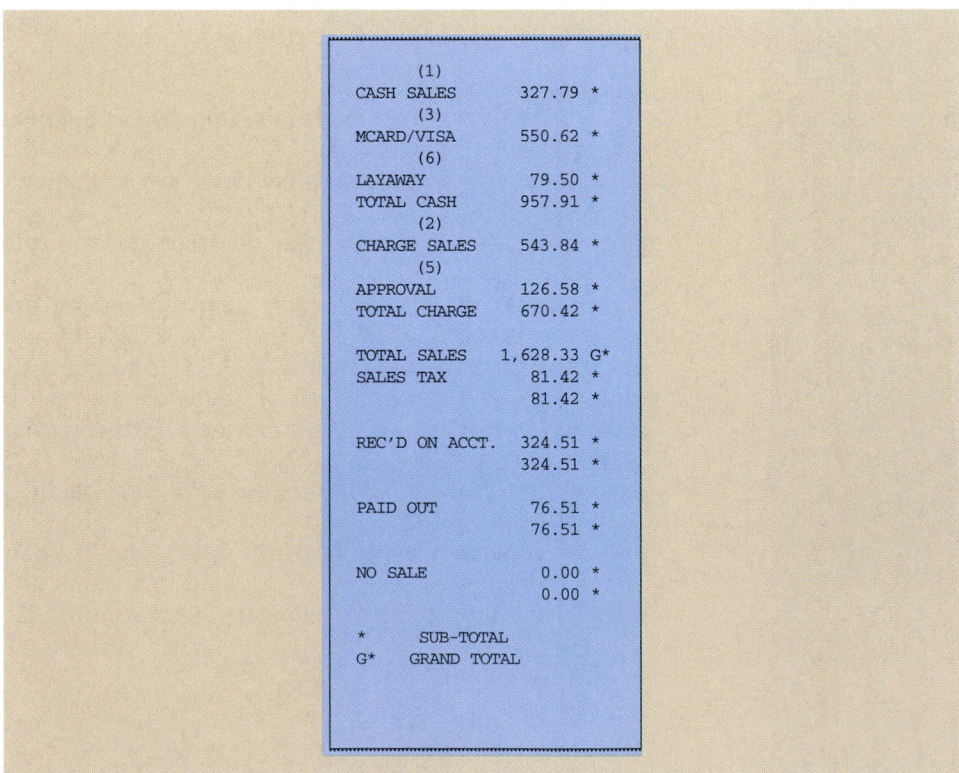

```
            (1)
CASH  SALES        327.79 *
            (3)
MCARD/VISA         550.62 *
            (6)
LAYAWAY             79.50 *
TOTAL  CASH        957.91 *
            (2)
CHARGE  SALES      543.84 *
            (5)
APPROVAL           126.58 *
TOTAL  CHARGE      670.42 *

TOTAL  SALES     1,628.33 G*
SALES  TAX          81.42 *
                    81.42 *

REC'D ON ACCT.     324.51 *
                   324.51 *

PAID  OUT           76.51 *
                    76.51 *

NO  SALE             0.00 *
                     0.00 *

  *       SUB-TOTAL
  G*      GRAND TOTAL
```

FIGURE 11-1 Cash Register Tape Summary

An additional document often created as evidence of a sale in a retail business is a **sales ticket** (Figure 11-2). One copy of the sales ticket is given to the customer and the other copy is sent to accounting.

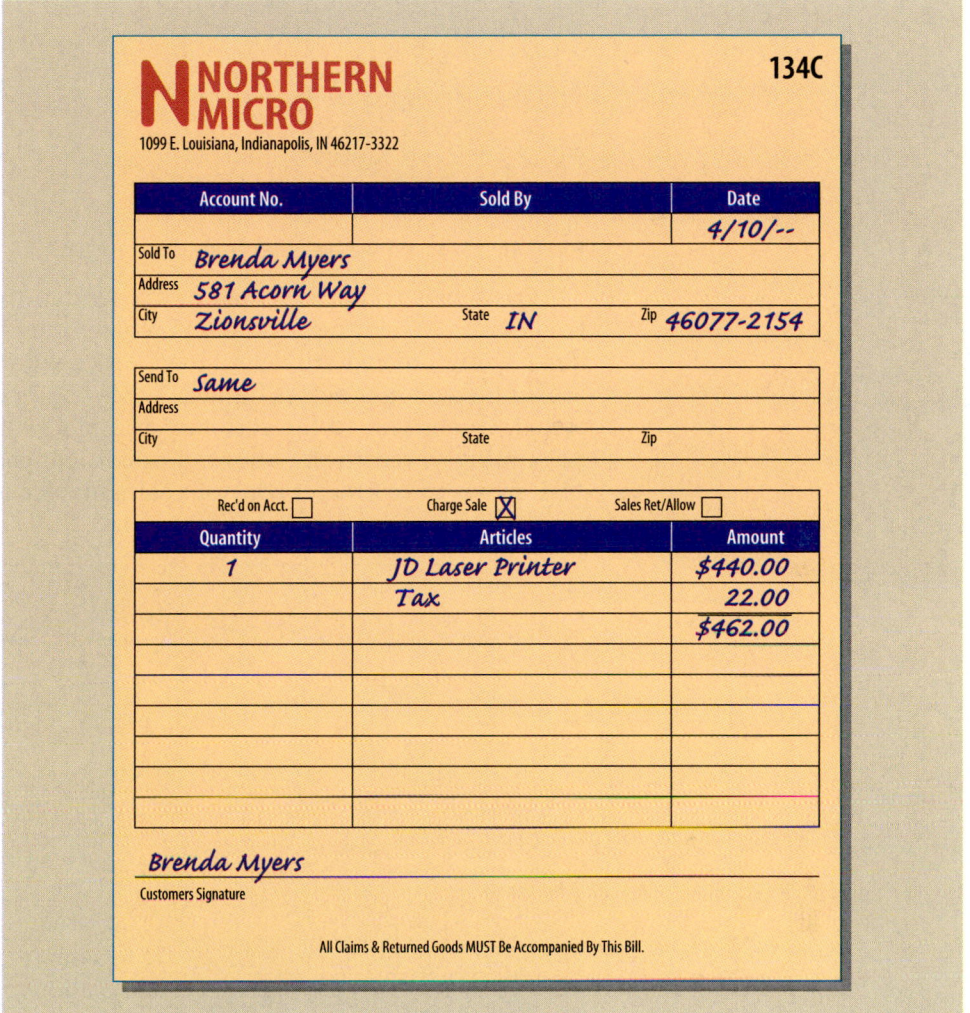

FIGURE 11-2 Sales Ticket

Wholesaler

Figure 11-3 shows how the wholesaler plays a different role than the retailer in the marketing chain. Retailers usually sell to final consumers, whereas wholesalers tend to sell to retailers. This causes the wholesale sales transaction process to differ, as shown in Figure 11-4.

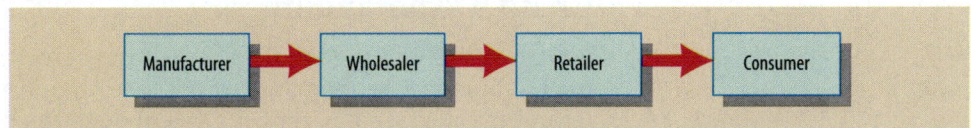

FIGURE 11-3 Marketing Chain

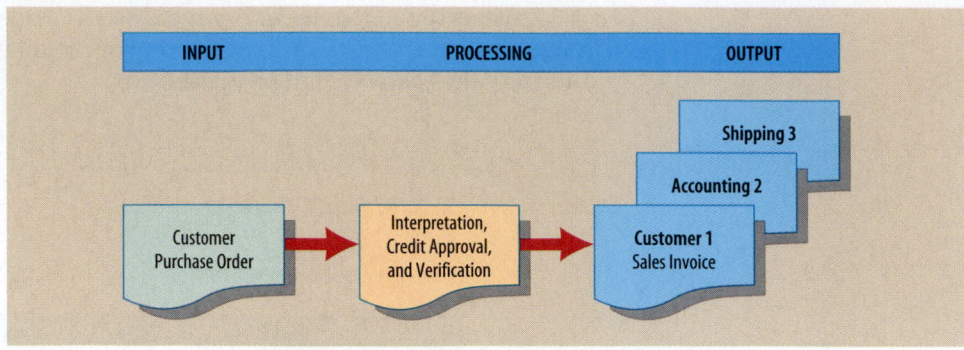

FIGURE 11-4 Wholesale Sales Transaction Process

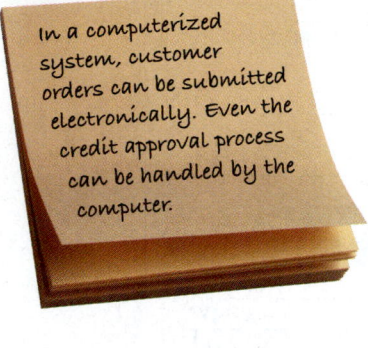

In a computerized system, customer orders can be submitted electronically. Even the credit approval process can be handled by the computer.

Customers commonly mail or fax written orders to buy merchandise from wholesalers. When the customer purchase order arrives, the customer name and items being ordered are determined. Since wholesalers typically make sales on account, credit approval is needed. Three copies of a **sales invoice** are then generated. One is sent to the customer as a bill for the merchandise, one is sent to accounting to record the sale, and one is shipped with the merchandise. Figure 11-5 shows the customer copy of a sales invoice for Aladdin Electric Supply.

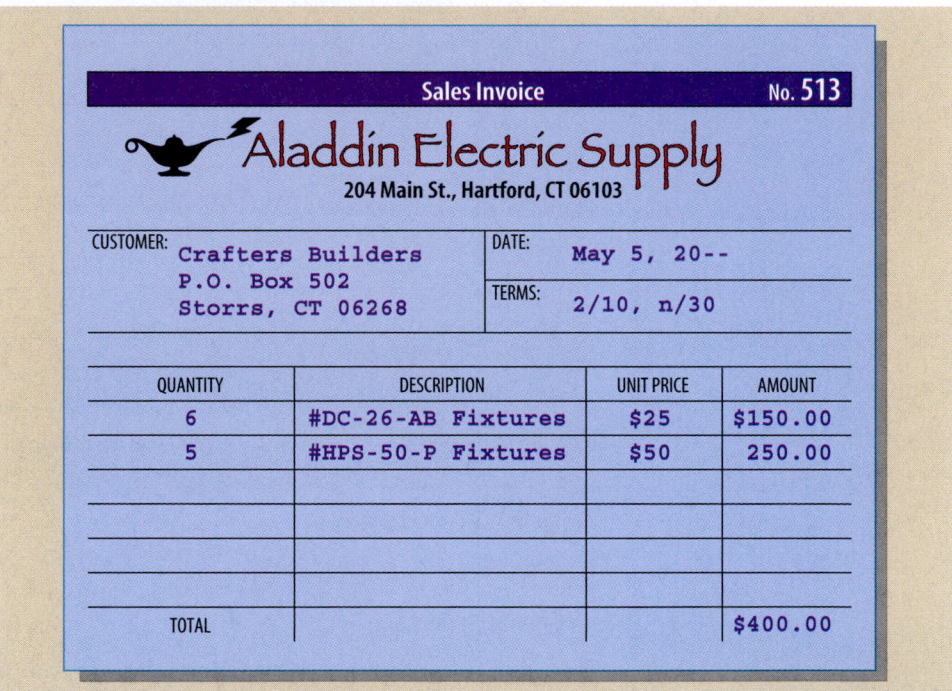

FIGURE 11-5 Sales Invoice

Credit Memorandum

Both retailers and wholesalers sometimes have customers return goods or seek price reductions for damaged goods. Merchandise returned by a customer for a refund is called a **sales return**. Price reductions granted by the seller because of defects or other problems with the merchandise are called **sales allowances**. When credit is given for merchandise returned or for an allowance, a **credit memo** is issued for the amount involved. This document is called a credit memo because the customer's account receivable is *credited* to reduce the amount the customer owes. One copy of the credit memo is given to the customer and one copy is sent to accounting. Figure 11-6 shows a credit memo issued by Northern Micro for merchandise returned by a customer.

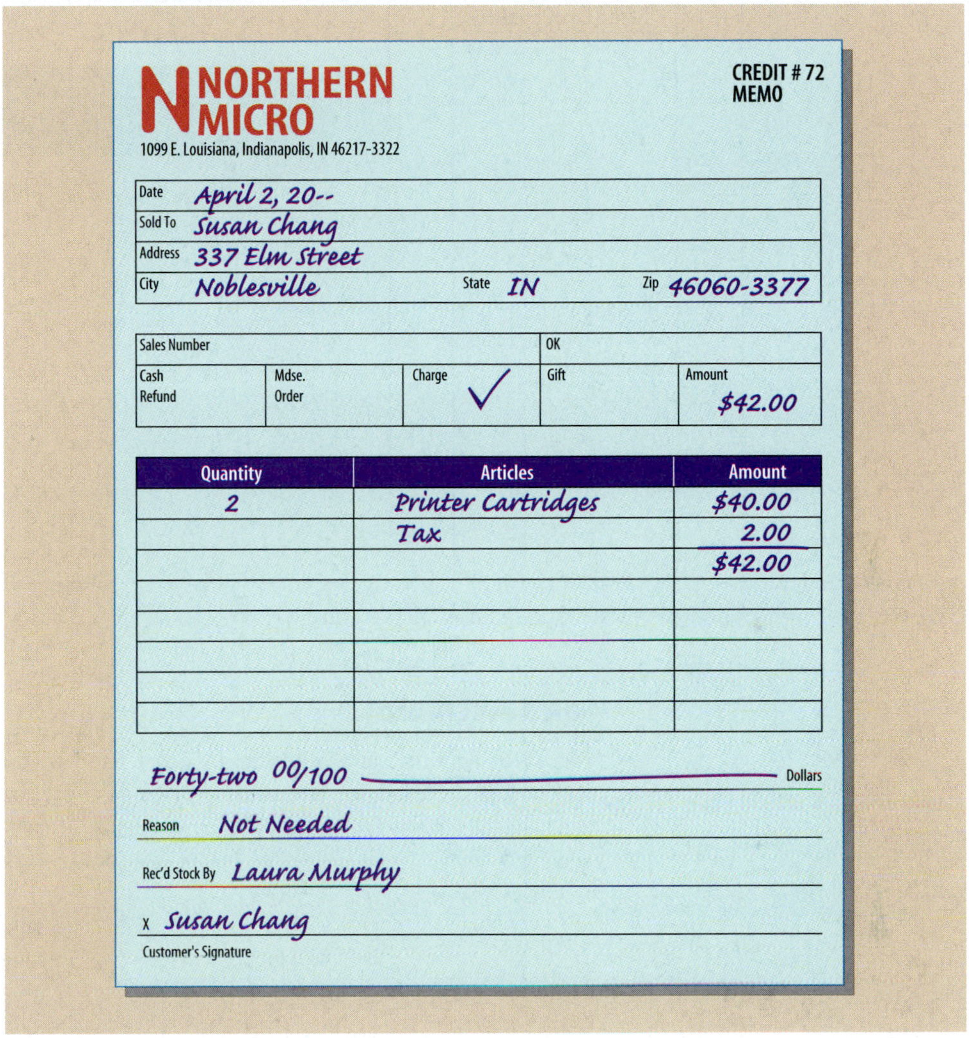

NORTHERN MICRO
1099 E. Louisiana, Indianapolis, IN 46217-3322

CREDIT # 72
MEMO

Date April 2, 20--
Sold To Susan Chang
Address 337 Elm Street
City Noblesville State IN Zip 46060-3377

Sales Number			OK	
Cash Refund	Mdse. Order	Charge ✓	Gift	Amount $42.00

Quantity	Articles	Amount
2	Printer Cartridges	$40.00
	Tax	2.00
		$42.00

Forty-two 00/100 Dollars
Reason Not Needed
Rec'd Stock By Laura Murphy
X Susan Chang
Customer's Signature

FIGURE 11-6 Credit Memo

MERCHANDISE SALES ACCOUNTS

LO2 Describe and use merchandise sales accounts.

To account for merchandise sales transactions, we will use four new accounts:

1. Sales
2. Sales Tax Payable
3. Sales Returns and Allowances
4. Sales Discounts

The position of these accounts in the accounting equation and their normal balances are shown in Figure 11-7.

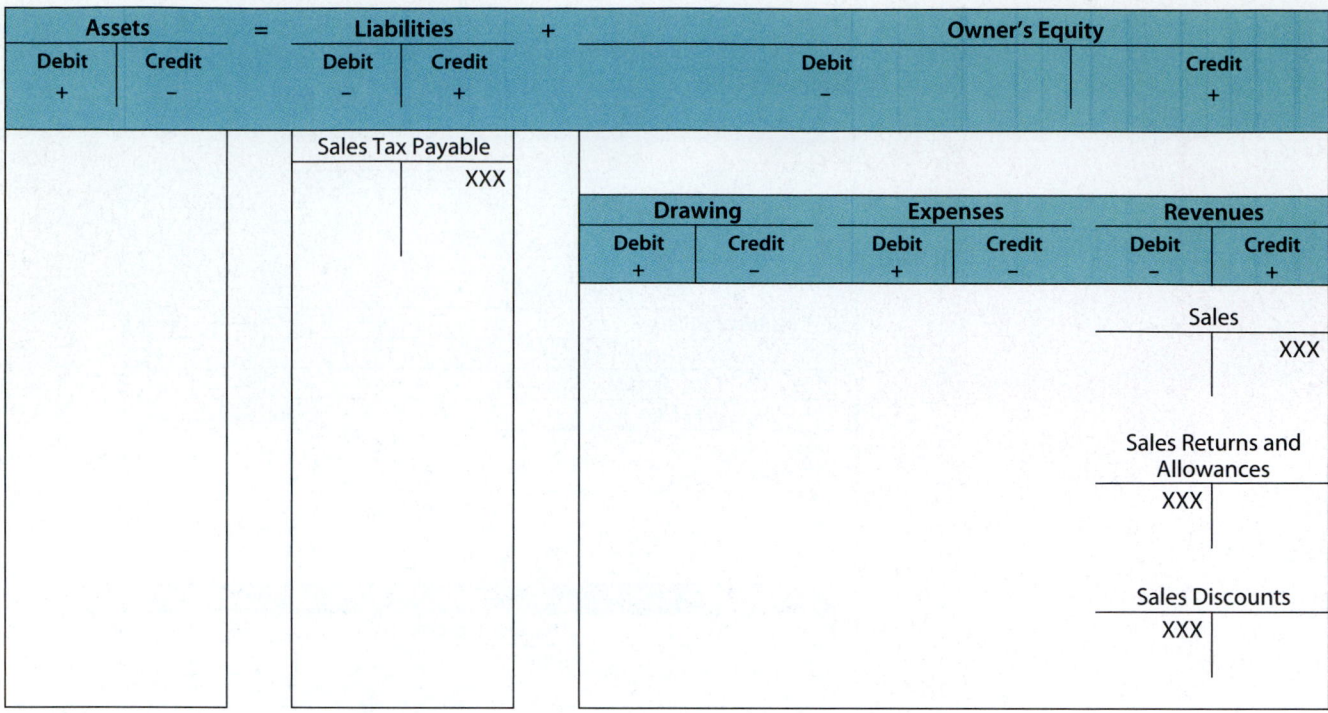

FIGURE 11-7 Accounting for Merchandise Sales Transactions

Sales Account

The sales account is a revenue account used to record sales of merchandise. The account is credited for the selling price of merchandise sold during the period.

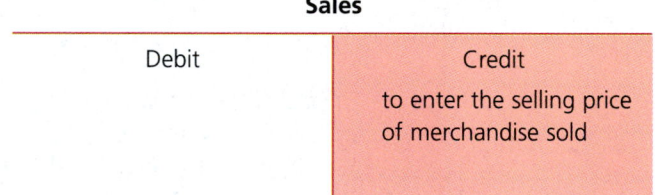

If a $100 sale is made for cash, the following entry is made.

5		Cash			1 0 0 00			5
6		Sales				1 0 0 00		6
7		Made cash sale						7

If the same sale is made on account, the entry is:

5		Accounts Receivable/Customer			1 0 0 00			5
6		Sales				1 0 0 00		6
7		Made credit sale						7

Accounts Receivable is followed by a slash (/) and the name of the specific customer who owes the money.

Sales Tax Payable Account

When sales tax is imposed on merchandise sold, a separate account for Sales Tax Payable is kept. This is a liability account that is credited for the taxes imposed on sales. The account is debited for sales taxes paid to the proper taxing authority or for sales taxes on merchandise returned by customers. A credit balance in the account indicates the amount owed to the taxing authority for taxes collected.

Sales Tax Payable

Debit	Credit
to enter payment of tax to taxing authority or adjustment of tax on merchandise returned by customers	to enter tax imposed on sales

If a cash sale for $100 plus 5% sales tax (5% × $100 = $5) occurs, the following entry is made.

10	Cash	1 0 5 00			10
11	Sales		1 0 0 00		11
12	Sales Tax Payable		5 00		12
13	Made cash sale				13

If the same sale is made on account, the entry is:

10	Accounts Receivable/Customer	1 0 5 00			10
11	Sales		1 0 0 00		11
12	Sales Tax Payable		5 00		12
13	Made credit sale				13

The debit to Accounts Receivable indicates that the amount owed by customers to the business has increased. Since the buyer has accepted the merchandise and promised to pay for it, revenue is recognized by crediting Sales. Sales Tax Payable is credited because the amount of sales tax owed to the taxing authority has increased.

Sales Returns and Allowances Account

Sales Returns and Allowances is a contra-revenue account to which sales returns and sales allowances are debited. As shown in Figure 11-8, this account is reported as a deduction from Sales on the income statement. Returns and allowances are debited to a separate account rather than directly to Sales so that the business can more readily keep track of this activity.

Sales Returns and Allowances

Debit	Credit
to enter returns and allowances	

Look at the credit memo in Figure 11-6 on page 000. The entry for the return of these printer cartridges by Susan Chang would be:

19		Sales Returns and Allowances		4 0 00			19
20		Sales Tax Payable		2 00			20
21		Accounts Receivable/Susan Chang			4 2 00		21
22		Returned merchandise — Credit Memo #72					22

Note carefully the parts of this entry. Sales Returns and Allowances is debited for the amount of the sale, *excluding* the sales tax. Sales Tax Payable is debited separately for the sales tax on the original sale amount. Accounts Receivable is credited for the total amount originally billed to Chang.

Sales	$38,500.00
Less sales returns and allowances	200.00
Net sales	$38,300.00

FIGURE 11-8   Sales Returns and Allowances on the Income Statement

LEARNING KEY: To record returns and allowances, debit Sales Returns and Allowances for the amount of the sale excluding the sales tax.

Sales Discounts Account

Some businesses offer **cash discounts** to encourage prompt payment by customers who buy merchandise on account. Some possible credit terms are shown in Figure 11-9.

TERMS	MEANING
2/10, n/30*	2% discount off sales price if paid within 10 days Total amount due within 30 days
1/10, n/30	Same as 2/10, n/30, except 1% discount instead of 2%
2/eom, n/60	2% discount if paid before end of month Total amount due within 60 days
3/10 eom, n/60	3% discount if paid within 10 days after end of month Total amount due within 60 days

* See Figure 11-5. A discount of $8 (2% × $400) is allowed if this invoice is paid by May 15 (invoice date of May 5 + 10 days).

FIGURE 11-9   Credit Terms

To the seller, cash discounts are considered **sales discounts**. Sales Discounts is a contra-revenue account to which cash discounts allowed are debited. Like Sales Returns and Allowances, this account is reported as a deduction from Sales on the income statement, as shown in Figure 11-10.

Sales Discounts

Debit	Credit
to enter cash discounts	

If merchandise is sold for $100 with credit terms of 2/10, n/30, and cash is received within the discount period, the following entries are made.

At time of sale:

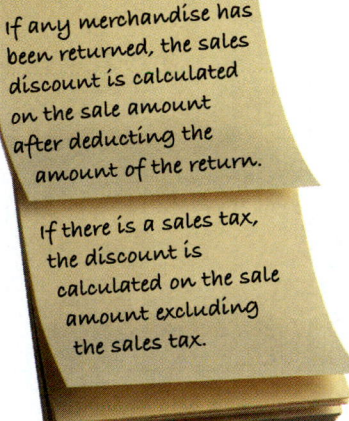

If any merchandise has been returned, the sales discount is calculated on the sale amount after deducting the amount of the return.

If there is a sales tax, the discount is calculated on the sale amount excluding the sales tax.

26		Accounts Receivable/Customer		1 0 0 00			26
27		Sales			1 0 0 00		27
28		Made sale on account					28

At time of collection:

30		Cash		9 8 00			30
31		Sales Discounts		2 00			31
32		Accounts Receivable/Customer			1 0 0 00		32
33		Received cash on account					33

Sales		$38,500.00
Less: Sales returns and allowances	$200.00	
Sales discounts	140.00	340.00
Net sales		$38,160.00

FIGURE 11-10 Sales Discounts on the Income Statement

JOURNALIZING AND POSTING SALES AND CASH RECEIPTS TRANSACTIONS

LO3 Describe and use the accounts receivable ledger.

To illustrate the journalizing and posting of sales and cash receipts transactions, we use Northern Micro, a retail computer business.

Sales

Assume the following sales transactions occurred during April, 20--.

April 4   Made sale no. 133C on account to Enrico Lorenzo, $1,520 plus $76 sales tax.

10   Made sale no. 134C on account to Brenda Myers, $440 plus $22 sales tax.

18   Made sale no. 105D on account to Edith Walton, $980 plus $49 sales tax.

21   Made sale no. 202B on account to Susan Chang, $620 plus $31 sales tax.

24   Made sale no. 162A on account to Heidi Schwitzer, $1,600 plus $80 sales tax.

These transactions are entered in a general journal as shown in Figure 11-11.

4	Apr.	4	Accounts Receivable/E. Lorenzo		1	5	9	6	00									4
5			Sales								1	5	2	0	00			5
6			Sales Tax Payable										7	6	00			6
7			Sale No. 133C															7
8																		8
9		10	Accounts Receivable/B. Meyers			4	6	2	00									9
10			Sales									4	4	0	00			10
11			Sales Tax Payable										2	2	00			11
12			Sale No. 134C															12
13																		13
14		18	Accounts Receivable/E. Walton		1	0	2	9	00									14
15			Sales									9	8	0	00			15
16			Sales Tax Payable										4	9	00			16
17			Sale No. 105D															17
18																		18
19		21	Accounts Receivable/S. Chang			6	5	1	00									19
20			Sales									6	2	0	00			20
21			Sales Tax Payable										3	1	00			21
22			Sale No. 202B															22
23																		23
24		24	Accounts Receivable/H. Schwitzer		1	6	8	0	00									24
25			Sales								1	6	0	0	00			25
26			Sales Tax Payable										8	0	00			26
27			Sale No. 162A															27

FIGURE 11-11 Sales Entered in General Journal

Posting to the General Ledger

Sales transactions are posted from the general journal to the general ledger in the same manner as was illustrated in Chapter 4. The following steps are used, as indicated in Figure 11-12 for Northern Micro's April 4 and 10 sales transactions.

In the ledger account:

STEP 1   Enter the date of the transaction in the Date column.

STEP 2   Enter the amount of the debit or credit in the Debit or Credit column.

STEP 3   Enter the new balance in the Balance columns under Debit or Credit.

STEP 4   Enter the journal page number from which each transaction is posted in the Posting Reference column.

In the journal:

STEP 5   Enter the ledger account number in the Posting Reference column of the journal for each transaction that is posted.

Other sales transactions would be posted in the same manner.

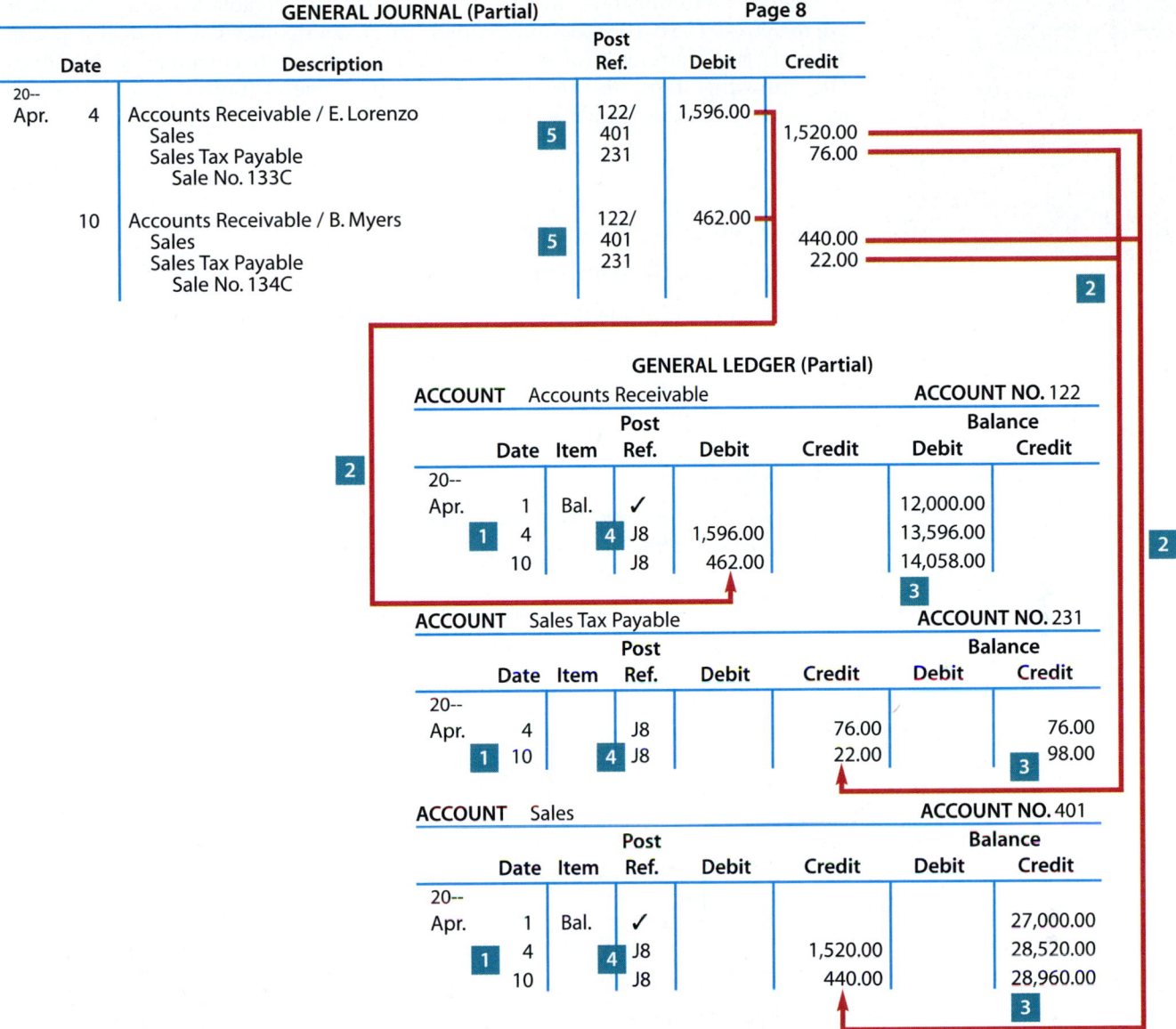

FIGURE 11-12 Posting Sales to the General Ledger

The accounts receivable ledger also can be posted from the source document used to make the general journal entry. For example, sales ticket #134C (see Figure 11-2) could be used

to post that sale to Brenda Myers' account in the accounts receivable ledger. In this case, 134C would be inserted in the Posting Reference column of her account.

Posting to the Accounts Receivable Ledger

After all posting to the general ledger is completed, the Accounts Receivable, Sales Tax Payable, and Sales accounts in the general ledger are up to date. But at this point Northern Micro has no complete record of the account receivable from *individual customers*. To run the business properly, Northern Micro needs this information.

A common approach to keeping a record of each customer's account receivable is to use a subsidiary **accounts receivable ledger**. This is a separate ledger containing an individual account receivable for each customer. If there are many customer accounts, it is good practice to assign each customer an account number. The subsidiary ledger accounts are kept in either alphabetical or numerical order, depending on whether customer accounts are identified by number. A summary accounts receivable account called a **controlling account** is still maintained in the general ledger. The accounts receivable ledger is "subsidiary" to this account.

A 3-column account form is commonly used for customer accounts. Only one balance column is needed because the normal balance is a debit. If a credit balance occurs, the amount may be bracketed.

Figure 11-13 illustrates the use of the accounts receivable ledger for Northern Micro's April 4 and 10 sales transactions. The accounts receivable ledger is posted *daily* so that current information is available for each customer at all times. The following steps are used to post from the general journal to the accounts receivable ledger, as shown in Figure 11-13.

In the accounts receivable ledger account:

STEP 1 Enter the date of the transaction in the Date column.

STEP 2 Enter the amount of the debit or credit in the Debit or Credit column.

STEP 3 Enter the new balance in the Balance column.

STEP 4 Enter the journal page number from which each transaction is posted in the Posting Reference column.

In the journal:

STEP 5 Enter a slash (/) followed by a check mark (✓) in the Posting Reference column of the journal for each transaction that is posted.

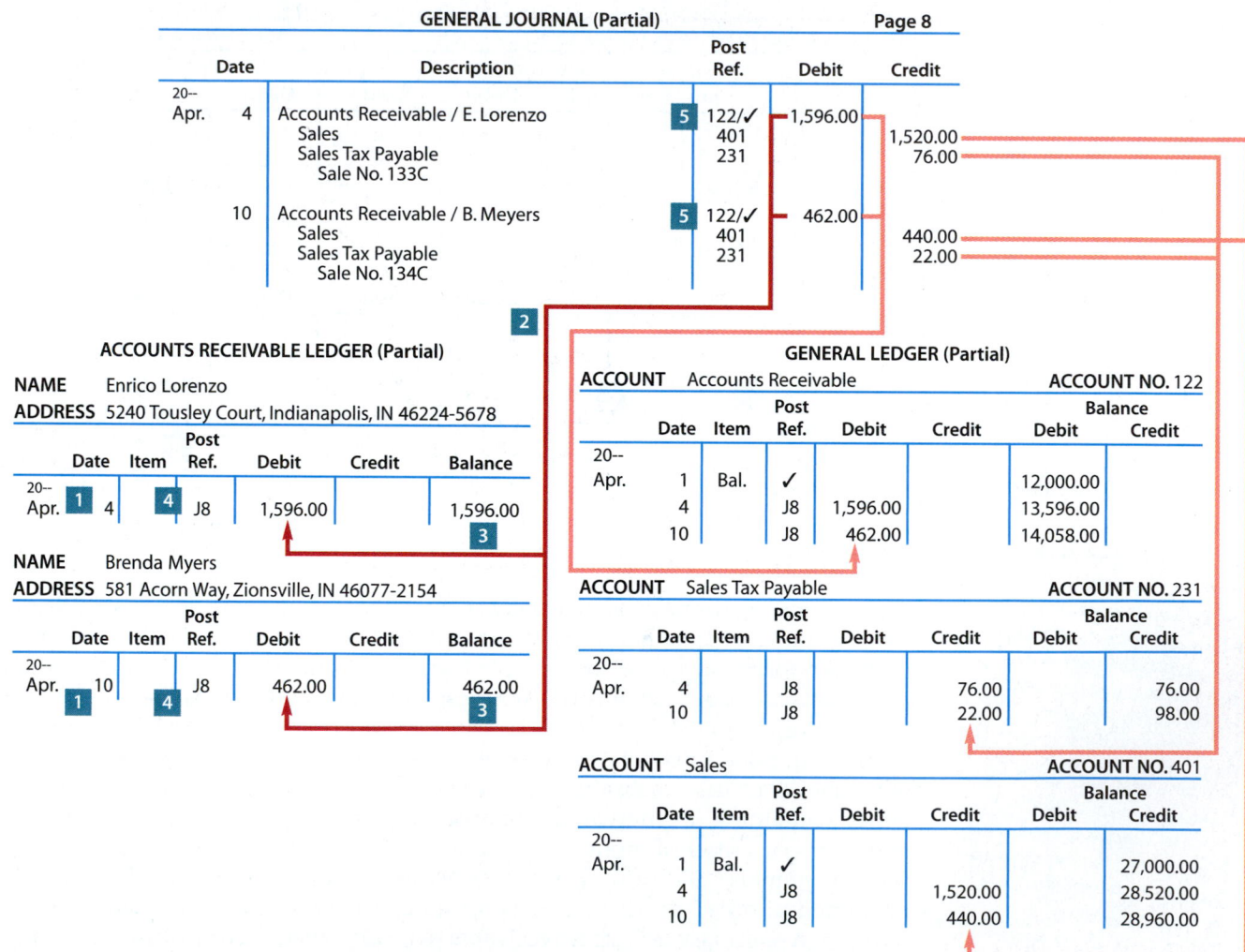

FIGURE 11-13 Posting Sales to the Accounts Receivable Ledger

LEARNING KEY: When an accounts receivable ledger is used, the posting reference column in the general journal serves two purposes. (1) The account number is inserted to indicate the general ledger account has been posted. (2) A slash (/) and a check mark (✓) are inserted to indicate the accounts receivable ledger account has been posted.

LEARNING KEY: The total of the accounts receivable ledger balances must equal the Accounts Receivable balance in the general ledger.

Note the relationship between the general journal, accounts receivable ledger, and general ledger. All entries in the general journal are posted to the general ledger and accounts receivable ledger. After the posting of the accounts receivable ledger and the general ledger is completed, the total of the accounts receivable ledger balances should equal the Accounts Receivable balance in the general ledger. Remember, the accounts receivable ledger is simply a detailed listing of the same information that is summarized in Accounts Receivable in the general ledger.

Sales Returns and Allowances

If a customer returns merchandise or is given an allowance for damaged merchandise, a general journal entry is required. On May 5, Susan Chang returned two printer cartridges costing $40 plus $2 sales tax (Figure 11-6, page 000). Figure 11-14 shows the general journal entry, general ledger posting, and accounts receivable ledger posting for this transaction.

The general journal entry is made in the usual manner. The general ledger is posted using the same five steps as were illustrated for sales transactions in Figure 11-12. The accounts receivable ledger is posted using the following five steps, as illustrated in Figure 11-14.

In the accounts receivable ledger account:

STEP 1   Enter the date of the transaction in the Date column.

STEP 2   Enter the amount of the debit or credit in the Debit or Credit column.

STEP 3   Enter the new balance in the Balance column.

STEP 4   Enter the journal page number from which each transaction is posted in the Posting Reference column.

In the journal:

STEP 5   Enter a slash (/) followed by a check mark (✓) in the Posting Reference column of the journal for each transaction that is posted.

Cash Receipts

Like sales transactions, cash receipt transactions occur frequently in most businesses. Sales on account lead to cash receipts, which are entered in the general journal. For example, assume that Northern Micro receives cash from Enrico Lorenzo for sale no. 133C on April 14. The transaction is recorded in the general journal as follows:

25	Apr.	14	Cash		1 5 9 6 00		25
26			Accounts Receivable/E. Lorenzo			1 5 9 6 00	26
27			Received cash on account				27

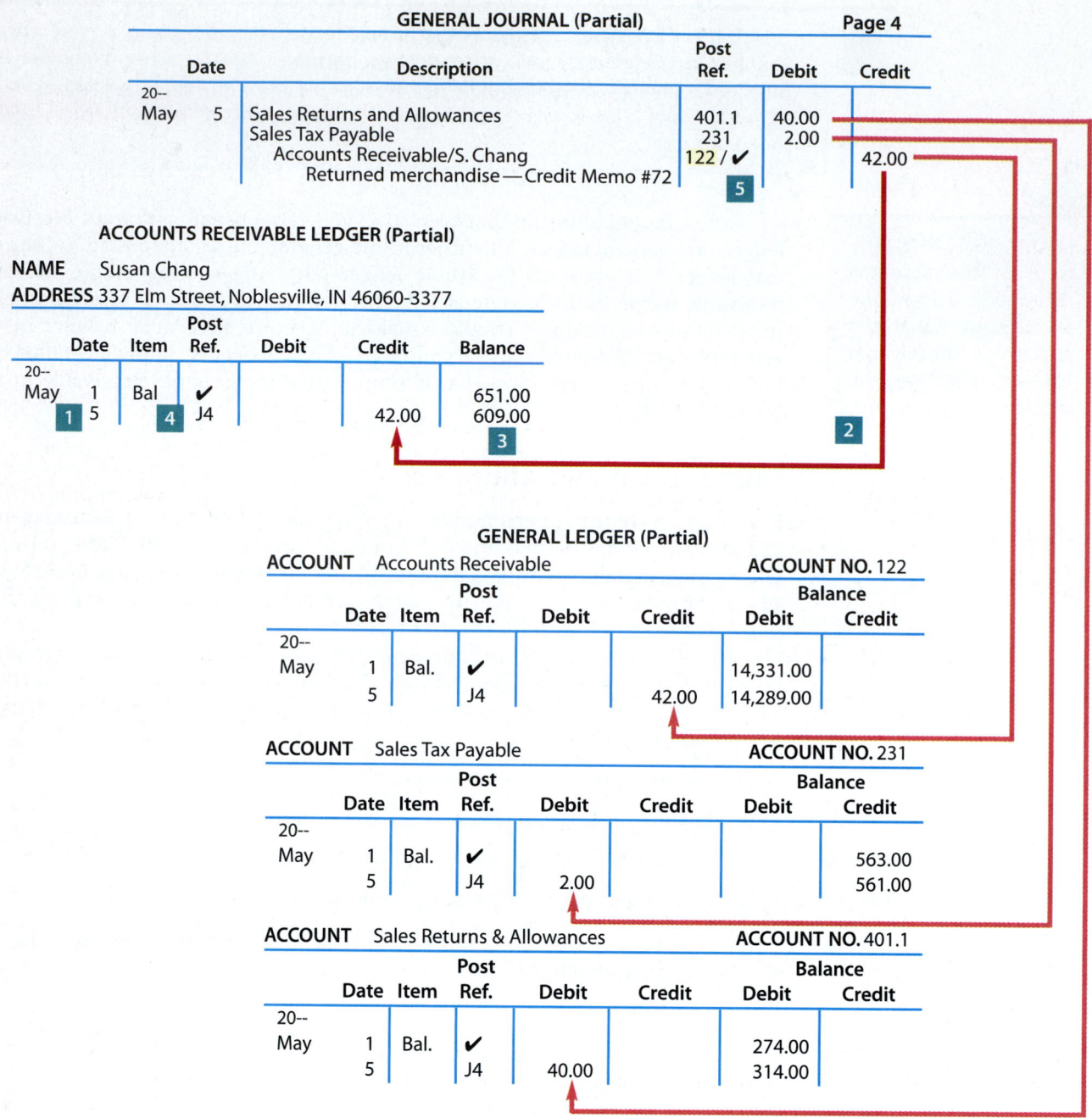

FIGURE 11-14 Accounting for Sales Returns and Allowances

Most businesses also regularly make cash sales. The following entry shows cash sales of $500 recorded in the general journal on May 5.

3	May	5	Cash				5 0 0 00					3
4			Sales					5 0 0 00	4
5			Made cash sales						5

In addition, an increasing amount of sales today are made using bank credit cards. Bank credit card sales are similar to cash sales because the cash is available to the business as soon as an electronic deposit is made at the end of the day. The credit card company makes the electronic deposit to the merchandiser's bank account for the gross amount of credit card sales less a processing fee. The fee is based on the gross amount of the sale, including the sales tax. Thus, on a sale of $100 plus sales tax of $5, the credit card fee at 4% would be $4.20 (4% × $105). The following entry shows this credit card sale recorded on May 6.

8	May	6	Cash					1	0	0	80									8
9			Bank Credit Card Expense							4	20									9
10			Sales										1	0	0	00				10
11			Sales Tax Payable												5	00				11
12			Made credit card sale																	12

To illustrate the journalizing and posting of cash receipts transactions, we continue to use Northern Micro. Assume the following cash receipts transactions related to sales occurred during April 20--. (To simplify the illustration, cash sales and bank credit card sales for the month are summarized as a single transaction at the end of the month.)

Apr. 14   Received cash on account from Enrico Lorenzo for sale no. 133C, $1,596.

20   Received cash on account from Brenda Myers for sale no. 134C, $462.

28   Received cash on account from Edith Walton for sale no. 105D, $1,029.

30   Cash sales for the month are $3,600 plus tax of $180.

30   Bank credit card sales for the month are $2,500 plus tax of $125. Bank credit card expenses on these sales are $100.

These transactions are entered in a general journal as shown in Figure 11-15.

4	Apr.	14	Cash					1	5	9	6	00								4
5			Accounts Receivable/E. Lorenzo										1	5	9	6	00			5
6			Received cash on account																	6
7																				7
8		20	Cash						4	6	2	00								8
9			Accounts Receivable/B. Myers											4	6	2	00			9
10			Received cash on account																	10
11																				11
12		28	Cash					1	0	2	9	00								12
13			Accounts Receivable/E. Walton										1	0	2	9	00			13
14			Received cash on account																	14
15																				15
16		30	Cash					3	7	8	0	00								16
17			Sales										3	6	0	0	00			17
18			Sales Tax Payable											1	8	0	00			18
19			Made cash sales																	19
20																				20
21		30	Cash					2	5	2	5	00								21
22			Bank Credit Card Expense						1	0	0	00								22
23			Sales										2	5	0	0	00			23
24			Sales Tax Payable											1	2	5	00			24
25			Made credit card sales																	25

FIGURE 11-15   Cash Receipts Entered in General Journal

A BROADER VIEW

Is This Sale for Real?

U.S. businesses lose billions of dollars annually because of credit card fraud and bad checks. To reduce credit card fraud, cashiers should do two things: (1) Watch the customer sign the credit card slip and match it to the signature on the card. (2) Obtain an approval code on all credit card transactions. To reduce bad check losses, cashiers should accept only a driver's license as identification. They should compare the picture with the customer, watch the check being signed, and match the check signature with that on the driver's license.

Posting to the General Ledger and Accounts Receivable Ledger

Cash receipts transactions are posted to the general ledger in the same manner as was illustrated for sales transactions in Figure 11-12. To post cash receipts to the accounts receivable ledger, the following steps are used, as illustrated in Figure 11-16 for Northern Micro's April 14 and 20 cash receipts transactions.

In the accounts receivable ledger account:

STEP 1   Enter the date of the transaction in the Date column.

STEP 2   Enter the amount of the debit or credit in the Debit or Credit column.

STEP 3   Enter the new balance in the Balance column.

STEP 4   Enter the journal page number from which each transaction is posted in the Posting Reference column.

In the journal:

STEP 5   Enter a slash (/) followed by a check mark (✓) in the Posting Reference column of the journal for each transaction that is posted.

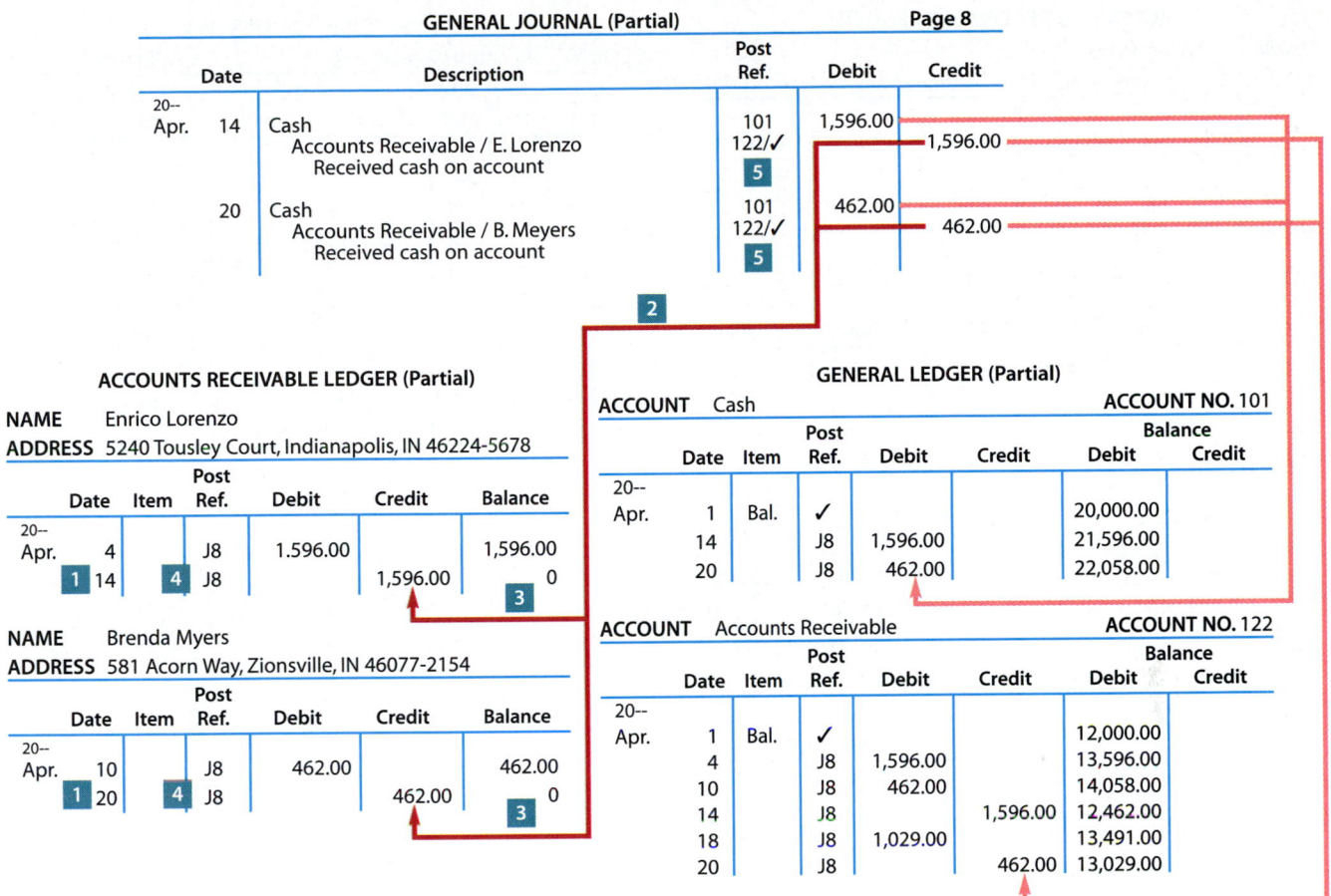

FIGURE 11-16 Posting Cash Receipts to the General Ledger and Accounts Receivable Ledger

SCHEDULE OF ACCOUNTS RECEIVABLE

LO4 Prepare a schedule of accounts receivable.

At the end of the month, all postings to Accounts Receivable in the general ledger and to the accounts receivable ledger should be complete, as shown in Figure 11-17. At this point, the Accounts Receivable balance in the general ledger should equal the sum of the customer balances in the accounts receivable ledger.

To verify that the sum of the accounts receivable ledger balances equals the Accounts Receivable balance, a **schedule of accounts receivable** is prepared. This is an alphabetical or numerical listing of customer accounts and balances, usually prepared at the end of the month. Note that customers whose account balance is zero are not included. The schedule of accounts receivable for Northern Micro as of April 30 is illustrated in Figure 11-18.

ACCOUNTS RECEIVABLE LEDGER

NAME Helen Avery
ADDRESS 1739 Woodsage Trace, Indianapolis, IN 46237-1199

Date	Item	Post Ref.	Debit	Credit	Balance
20-- Apr. 1	Bal.	✔			2,302.00

NAME Susan Chang
ADDRESS 337 Elm Street, Noblesville, IN 46060-3377

Date	Item	Post Ref.	Debit	Credit	Balance
20-- Apr. 21		J9	651.00		651.00

NAME Enrico Lorenzo
ADDRESS 5240 Tousley Court, Indianapolis, IN 46224-5678

Date	Item	Post Ref.	Debit	Credit	Balance
20-- Apr. 4		J8	1,596.00		1,596.00
14		J8		1,596.00	0

NAME Brenda Myers
ADDRESS 581 Acorn Way, Zionsville, IN 46077-2154

Date	Item	Post Ref.	Debit	Credit	Balance
20-- Apr. 10		J8	462.00		462.00
20		J8		462.00	0

NAME Heidi Schwitzer
ADDRESS 5858 Wildflower Cir., Bloomington, IN 47401-6209

Date	Item	Post Ref.	Debit	Credit	Balance
20-- Apr. 1	Bal.	✓			1,883.00
24		J9	1,680.00		3,563.00

NAME Ken Ulmet
ADDRESS 5260 Eagle Creek, Indianapolis, IN 46254-8275

Date	Item	Post Ref.	Debit	Credit	Balance
20-- Apr. 1	Bal.	✓			3,315.00

NAME Edith Walton
ADDRESS 1113 Stones Crossing, Zionsville, IN 46077-6601

Date	Item	Post Ref.	Debit	Credit	Balance
20-- Apr. 18		J8	1,029.00		1,029.00
28		J9		1,029.00	0

NAME Vivian Winston
ADDRESS 124 Main St., Zionsville, IN 46077-1358

Date	Item	Post Ref.	Debit	Credit	Balance
20-- Apr. 1	Bal.	✔			4,500.00

GENERAL LEDGER (Partial)

ACCOUNT Accounts Receivable **ACCOUNT NO.** 122

Date	Item	Post Ref.	Debit	Credit	Balance Debit	Balance Credit
20-- Apr. 1	Bal.	✔			12,000.00	
4		J8	1,596.00		13,596.00	
10		J8	462.00		14,058.00	
14		J8		1,596.00	12,462.00	
18		J8	1,029.00		13,491.00	
20		J8		462.00	13,029.00	
21		J9	651.00		13,680.00	
24		J9	1,680.00		15,360.00	
28		J9		1,029.00	14,331.00	

FIGURE 11-17 General Ledger and Accounts Receivable Ledger after Posting

Northern Micro Schedule of Accounts Receivable April 30, 20--					
Helen Avery	$ 2	3	0	2	00
Susan Chang		6	5	1	00
Heidi Schwitzer		3	5	6	3	00
Ken Ulmet		3	3	1	5	00
Vivian Winston		4	5	0	0	00
Total	$14	3	3	1	00

FIGURE 11-18   Schedule of Accounts Receivable

This schedule is prepared from the list of customer accounts in the accounts receivable ledger. The total calculated in the schedule is compared with the balance in Accounts Receivable in the general ledger. Note that the $14,331 total listed in the schedule equals the Accounts Receivable balance shown in Figure 11-17. If the schedule total and the Accounts Receivable balance do not agree, the error must be located and corrected. To find the error, use the following procedures.

STEP 1   Verify the total of the schedule.

STEP 2   Verify the postings to the accounts receivable ledger.

STEP 3   Verify the postings to Accounts Receivable in the general ledger.

Learning Objectives	Key Points to Remember
1 **Describe merchandise sales transactions.**	A merchandising business buys and sells merchandise. Retailers generally make sales in the store. Important accounting documents are cash register tapes and sales tickets. Wholesalers generally ship merchandise to retailers. A key accounting document is the sales invoice. When customers return merchandise or obtain price adjustments, a credit memo is issued.
2 **Describe and use merchandise sales accounts.**	Four accounts are used in accounting for merchandise sales transactions: 1. Sales 2. Sales Tax Payable 3. Sales Returns and Allowances 4. Sales Discounts
3 **Describe and use the accounts receivable ledger.**	To post sales transactions to the general ledger: **In the ledger account:** STEP 1 Enter the date of the transaction in the Date column. STEP 2 Enter the amount of the debit or credit in the Debit or Credit column. STEP 3 Enter the new balance in the Balance columns under Debit or Credit. STEP 4 Enter the journal page number from which each transaction is posted in the Posting Reference column. **In the journal:** STEP 5 Enter the ledger account number in the Posting Reference column of the journal for each transaction that is posted.

(continued)

Learning Objectives	Key Points to Remember
3 (continued)	An accounts receivable ledger is a separate ledger containing an individual account receivable for each customer. To post sales transactions to the accounts receivable ledger:
	In the accounts receivable ledger account:
	STEP 1 Enter the date of the transaction in the Date column.
	STEP 2 Enter the amount of the debit or credit in the Debit or Credit column.
	STEP 3 Enter the new balance in the Balance column.
	STEP 4 Enter the journal page number from which each transaction is posted in the Posting Reference column.
	In the journal:
	STEP 5 Enter a slash (/) followed by a check mark (✓) in the Posting Reference column of the journal for each transaction that is posted.
	To post cash receipts transactions to the general ledger:
	In the ledger account:
	STEP 1 Enter the date of the transaction in the Date column.
	STEP 2 Enter the amount of the debit or credit in the Debit or Credit column.
	STEP 3 Enter the new balance in the Balance columns under Debit or Credit.
	STEP 4 Enter the journal page number from which each transaction is posted in the Posting Reference column.
	In the journal:
	STEP 5 Enter the ledger account number in the Posting Reference column of the journal for each transaction that is posted.
	To post cash receipts transactions to the accounts receivable ledger:
	In the accounts receivable ledger account:
	STEP 1 Enter the date of the transaction in the Date column.
	STEP 2 Enter the amount of the debit or credit in the Debit or Credit column.
	STEP 3 Enter the new balance in the Balance column.
	STEP 4 Enter the journal page number from which each transaction is posted in the Posting Reference column.
	In the journal:
	STEP 5 Enter a slash (/) followed by a check mark (✓) in the Posting Reference column of the journal for each transaction that is posted.
4 **Prepare a schedule of accounts receivable.**	The schedule of accounts receivable is used to verify that the sum of the accounts receivable ledger balances equals the Accounts Receivable balance.

Reflection: Answering the Opening Question

Bank credit card sales are similar to cash sales because the cash is available to the business as soon as an electronic deposit is made to the merchandiser's bank account by the credit card company at the end of the day. The cash available is the gross amount of the sale less a processing fee. The bookkeeper should account for such sales by crediting Sales for the gross amount of the sale, debiting Bank Credit Card Expense for the bank fee, and debiting Cash for the net proceeds.

DEMONSTRATION PROBLEM

Karen Hunt operates Hunt's Audio-Video Store. The books include a general journal, general ledger, and accounts receivable ledger. The following transactions related to sales on account and cash receipts occurred during April 20--.

April 3	Sold merchandise on account to Susan Haberman, $159.50 plus tax of $11.17. Sale no. 41.
4	Sold merchandise on account to Goro Kimura, $299.95 plus tax of $21.00. Sale no. 42.
6	Received payment from Tera Scherrer on account, $69.50.
7	Issued credit memo no. 48 to Kenneth Watt for merchandise returned that had been sold on account, $42.75 including tax of $2.80.
10	Received payment from Kellie Cokley on account, $99.95.
11	Sold merchandise on account to Victor Cardona, $499.95 plus tax of $35.00. Sale no. 43.
14	Received payment from Kenneth Watt in full settlement of account, $157.00.
17	Sold merchandise on account to Susan Haberman, $379.95 plus tax of $26.60. Sale no. 44.
19	Sold merchandise on account to Tera Scherrer, $59.95 plus tax of $4.20. Sale no. 45.
21	Issued credit memo no. 49 to Goro Kimura for merchandise returned that had been sold on account, $53.45 including tax of $3.50.
24	Received payment from Victor Cardona on account, $299.95.
25	Sold merchandise on account to Kellie Cokley, $179.50 plus tax of $12.57. Sale no. 46.
26	Received payment from Susan Haberman on account, $250.65.
28	Sold merchandise on account to Kenneth Watt, $49.95 plus tax of $3.50. Sale no. 47.
30	Bank credit card sales for the month, $1,220.00 plus tax of $85.40. Bank credit card expense on these sales, $65.27.
30	Cash sales for the month, $2,000.00 plus tax of $140.00.

(continued)

Hunt had the following general ledger account balances as of April 1.

Account Title	Account No.	General Ledger Balance on April 1
Cash	101	$5,000.00
Accounts Receivable	122	1,208.63
Sales Tax Payable	231	72.52
Sales	401	8,421.49
Sales Returns and Allowances	401.1	168.43
Bank Credit Card Expense	513	215.00

Hunt also had the following accounts receivable ledger account balances as of April 1.

Customer	Accounts Receivable Balance
Victor Cardona 6300 Washington Blvd. St. Louis, MO 63130-9523	$299.95
Kellie Cokley 4220 Kingsbury Blvd. St. Louis, MO 63130-1645	$99.95
Susan Haberman 9421 Garden Ct. Kirkwood, MO 63122-1878	$79.98
Goro Kimura 6612 Arundel Pl. Clayton, MO 63150-9266	$379.50
Tera Scherrer 315 W. Linden St. Webster Groves, MO 63119-9881	$149.50
Kenneth Watt 11742 Fawnridge Dr. St. Louis, MO 63131-1726	$199.75

REQUIRED

1. Open four-column general ledger accounts and three-column accounts receivable ledger accounts for Hunt's Audio-Video Store as of April 1, 20--. Enter the April 1 balance in each of the accounts.

2. Enter each transaction in a general journal (page 7).

3. Post directly from the journal to the proper customers' accounts in the accounts receivable ledger. Each subsidiary ledger account should show the initial "J," followed by the appropriate journal page number as a posting reference for each transaction.

4. Post from the journal to the proper general ledger accounts. Each general ledger account should show the initial "J," followed by the appropriate journal page number as a posting reference for each transaction.

5. Prove the balance of the summary accounts receivable account by preparing a schedule of accounts receivable as of April 30, based on the accounts receivable ledger.

Solution

1, 3, 4.

ACCOUNTS RECEIVABLE LEDGER

NAME: Victor Cardona

DATE		ITEM	POST REF.	DEBIT	CREDIT	BALANCE
20-- Apr.	1	Bal.	✔			2 9 9 95
	11		J7	5 3 4 95		8 3 4 90
	24		J8		2 9 9 95	5 3 4 95

NAME: Kellie Cokley

DATE		ITEM	POST REF.	DEBIT	CREDIT	BALANCE
20-- Apr.	1	Bal.	✔			9 9 95
	10		J7		9 9 95	--
	25		J8	1 9 2 07		1 9 2 07

NAME: Susan Haberman

DATE		ITEM	POST REF.	DEBIT	CREDIT	BALANCE
20-- Apr.	1	Bal.	✔			7 9 98
	3		J7	1 7 0 67		2 5 0 65
	17		J7	4 0 6 55		6 5 7 20
	26		J8		2 5 0 65	4 0 6 55

NAME: Goro Kimura

DATE		ITEM	POST REF.	DEBIT	CREDIT	BALANCE
20-- Apr.	1	Bal.	✔			3 7 9 50
	4		J7	3 2 0 95		7 0 0 45
	21		J8		5 3 45	6 4 7 00

NAME: Tera Scherrer

DATE		ITEM	POST REF.	DEBIT	CREDIT	BALANCE
20-- Apr.	1	Bal.	✔			1 4 9 50
	6		J7		6 9 50	8 0 00
	19		J8	6 4 15		1 4 4 15

(continued)

NAME: Kenneth Watt

DATE		ITEM	POST REF.	DEBIT	CREDIT	BALANCE
20-- Apr.	1	Bal.	✔			1 9 9 75
	7		J7		4 2 75	1 5 7 00
	14		J7		1 5 7 00	--
	28		J8	5 3 45		5 3 45

2, 3, 4.

			GENERAL JOURNAL				PAGE 7	
	DATE		DESCRIPTION	POST REF.	DEBIT	CREDIT		
1	20-- Apr.	3	Accounts Receivable / Susan Haberman	122/✔	1 7 0 67			1
2			Sales	401		1 5 9 50		2
3			Sales Tax Payable	231		1 1 17		3
4			Sale No. 41					4
5								5
6		4	Accounts Receivable / Goro Kimura	122/✔	3 2 0 95			6
7			Sales	401		2 9 9 95		7
8			Sales Tax Payable	231		2 1 00		8
9			Sale No. 42					9
10								10
11		6	Cash	101	6 9 50			11
12			Accounts Receivable / Tera Scherrer	122/✔		6 9 50		12
13			Received cash on account					13
14								14
15		7	Sales Returns and Allowances	401.1	3 9 95			15
16			Sales Tax Payable	231	2 80			16
17			Accounts Receivable / Kenneth Watt	122/✔		4 2 75		17
18			Returned merchandise					18
19								19
20		10	Cash	101	9 9 95			20
21			Accounts Receivable / Kellie Cokley	122/✔		9 9 95		21
22			Received cash on account					22
23								23
24		11	Accounts Receivable / Victor Cardona	122/✔	5 3 4 95			24
25			Sales	401		4 9 9 95		25
26			Sales Tax Payable	231		3 5 00		26
27			Sale No. 43					27
28								28
29		14	Cash	101	1 5 7 00	1 5 7 00		29
30			Accounts Receivable / Kenneth Watt	122/✔		1 5 7 00		30
31			Received cash on account					31
32								32
33		17	Accounts Receivable / Susan Haberman	122/✔	4 0 6 55			33
34			Sales	401		3 7 9 95		34
35			Sales Tax Payable	231		2 6 60		35
36			Sale No. 44					36

2, 3, 4.

	DATE		DESCRIPTION	POST REF.	DEBIT					CREDIT					
	20--														
1	Apr.	19	Accounts Receivable / Tera Scherrer	122/✓		6	4	15							1
2			Sales	401							5	9	95		2
3			Sales Tax Payable	231								4	20		3
4			Sale No. 45												4
5															5
6		21	Sales Returns and Allowances	401.1		4	9	95							6
7			Sales Tax Payable	231		3		50							7
8			Accounts Receivable / Goro Kimura	122/✓							5	3	45		8
9			Returned merchandise—Credit memo #49												9
10															10
11		24	Cash	101	2	9	9	95							11
12			Accounts Receivable / Victor Cardona	122/✓						2	9	9	95		12
13			Received cash on account												13
14															14
15		25	Accounts Receivable / Kellie Cokley	122/✓	1	9	2	07							15
16			Sales	401						1	7	9	50		16
17			Sales Tax Payable	231							1	2	57		17
18			Sale No. 46												18
19															19
20		26	Cash	101	2	5	0	65							20
21			Accounts Receivable / Susan Haberman	122/✓						2	5	0	65		21
22			Received cash on account												22
23															23
24		28	Accounts Receivable / Kenneth Watt	122/✓		5	3	45							24
25			Sales	401							4	9	95		25
26			Sales Tax Payable	231								3	50		26
27			Sale No. 47												27
28															28
29		30	Cash	101	1	2	4	0	13						29
30			Bank Credit Card Expense	513		6	5	27							30
31			Sales	401						1	2	2	0	00	31
32			Sales Tax Payable	231							8	5	40		32
33			Credit card sales												33
34															34
35		30	Cash	101	2	1	4	0	00						35
36			Sales	401						2	0	0	0	00	36
37			Sales Tax Payable	231							1	4	0	00	37
38			Made cash sales												38

GENERAL JOURNAL   PAGE 8

1, 3, 4.

ACCOUNT: Cash   ACCOUNT NO. 101

DATE		ITEM	POST REF.	DEBIT					CREDIT					BALANCE DEBIT					BALANCE CREDIT				
20--																							
Apr.	1	Balance	✓											5	0	0	0	00					
	6		J7		6	9	50							5	0	6	9	50					
	10		J7		9	9	95							5	1	6	9	45					
	14		J7	1	5	7	00							5	3	2	6	45					
	24		J8	2	9	9	95							5	6	2	6	40					
	26		J8	2	5	0	65							5	8	7	7	05					
	30		J8	1	2	4	0	13						7	1	1	7	18					
	30		J8	2	1	4	0	00						9	2	5	7	18					

(continued)

1, 3, 4.

ACCOUNT: Accounts Receivable   ACCOUNT NO. 122

DATE		ITEM	POST REF.	DEBIT	CREDIT	BALANCE DEBIT	BALANCE CREDIT
20-- Apr.	1	Balance	✓			1 2 0 8 63	
	3		J7	1 7 0 67		1 3 7 9 30	
	4		J7	3 2 0 95		1 7 0 0 25	
	6		J7		6 9 50	1 6 3 0 75	
	7		J7		4 2 75	1 5 8 8 00	
	10		J7		9 9 95	1 4 8 8 05	
	11		J7	5 3 4 95		2 0 2 3 00	
	14		J7		1 5 7 00	1 8 6 6 00	
	17		J7	4 0 6 55		2 2 7 2 55	
	19		J8	6 4 15		2 3 3 6 70	
	21		J8		5 3 45	2 2 8 3 25	
	24		J8		2 9 9 95	1 9 8 3 30	
	25		J8	1 9 2 07		2 1 7 5 37	
	26		J8		2 5 0 65	1 9 2 4 72	
	28		J8		5 3 45	1 9 7 8 17	

ACCOUNT: Sales Tax Payable   ACCOUNT NO. 231

DATE		ITEM	POST REF.	DEBIT	CREDIT	BALANCE DEBIT	BALANCE CREDIT
20-- Apr.	1	Balance	✓				7 2 52
	3		J7		1 1 17		8 3 69
	4		J7		2 1 00		1 0 4 69
	7		J7	2 80			1 0 1 89
	11		J7		3 5 00		1 3 6 89
	17		J7		2 6 60		1 6 3 49
	19		J8		4 20		1 6 7 69
	21		J8	3 50			1 6 4 19
	25		J8		1 2 57		1 7 6 76
	28		J8		3 50		1 8 0 26
	30		J8		8 5 40		2 6 5 66
	30		J8		1 4 0 00		4 0 5 66

ACCOUNT: Sales   ACCOUNT NO. 401

DATE		ITEM	POST REF.	DEBIT	CREDIT	BALANCE DEBIT	BALANCE CREDIT
20-- Apr.	1	Balance	✓				8 4 2 1 49
	3		J7		1 5 9 50		8 5 8 0 99
	4		J7		2 9 9 95		8 8 8 0 94
	11		J7		4 9 9 95		9 3 8 0 89
	17		J7		3 7 9 95		9 7 6 0 84
	19		J8		5 9 95		9 8 2 0 79
	25		J8		1 7 9 50		10 0 0 0 29
	28		J8		4 9 95		10 0 5 0 24
	30		J8		1 2 2 0 00		11 2 7 0 24
	30		J8		2 0 0 0 00		13 2 7 0 24

1, 3, 4.

ACCOUNT: Sales Returns and Allowances ACCOUNT NO. 401.1

DATE	ITEM	POST REF.	DEBIT	CREDIT	BALANCE DEBIT	BALANCE CREDIT
20-- Apr. 1	Balance	✓			1 6 8 43	
7		J7	3 9 95		2 0 8 38	
21		J8	4 9 95		2 5 8 33	

ACCOUNT: Bank Credit Card Expense ACCOUNT NO. 513

DATE	ITEM	POST REF.	DEBIT	CREDIT	BALANCE DEBIT	BALANCE CREDIT
20-- Apr. 1	Balance	✓			2 1 5 00	
30		J8	6 5 27		2 8 0 27	

5.

Hunt's Audio-Video Store
Schedule of Accounts Receivable
April 30, 20--

Victor Cardona	5 3 4 95
Kellie Cokley	1 9 2 07
Susan Haberman	4 0 6 55
Goro Kimura	6 4 7 00
Tera Scherrer	1 4 4 15
Kenneth Watt	5 3 45
Total	1 9 7 8 17

On-Line Learning Tools

For more information, visit: http://heintz.swlearning.com

The Heintz & Parry product web site is designed specifically for **COLLEGE ACCOUNTING, 18e.** The features include downloadable student resources and an interactive study center, organized by chapter, which contains learning objectives, web links, on-line quizzes with automatic feedback, and more.

KEY TERMS

accounts receivable ledger, (381) A separate ledger containing an individual account receivable for each customer, kept in either alphabetical or numerical order.

cash discounts, (378) Discounts to encourage prompt payment by customers who buy merchandise on account.

controlling account, (381) A summary account maintained in the general ledger with a subsidiary ledger (for example, the accounts receivable ledger).

credit memo, (374) A document issued when credit is given for merchandise returned or for an allowance.

(continued)

merchandising business, (372)   A business that purchases merchandise such as clothing, furniture, or computers, and sells that merchandise to its customers.

sale, (372)   A transfer of merchandise from one business or individual to another in exchange for cash or a promise to pay cash.

sales allowances, (374)   Reductions in the price of merchandise granted by the seller because of defects or other problems with the merchandise.

sales discounts, (379)   To the seller, cash discounts are considered sales discounts.

sales invoice, (374)   A document that is generated to bill the customer to whom the sale was made.

sales return, (374)   Merchandise returned by a customer for a refund.

sales ticket, (373)   A document created as evidence of a sale in a retail business.

schedule of accounts receivable, (387)   An alphabetical or numerical listing of customer accounts and balances, usually prepared at the end of the month.

REVIEW QUESTIONS

(LO1)   1. Identify the sales documents commonly used in retail and wholesale businesses.

(LO1)   2. What is the purpose of a credit memo?

(LO2)   3. Describe how each of the following accounts is used: (1) Sales, (2) Sales Tax Payable, (3) Sales Returns and Allowances, and (4) Sales Discounts.

(LO3)   4. What steps are followed in posting sales from the general journal to the general ledger?

(LO3)   5. What steps are followed in posting sales from the general journal to the accounts receivable ledger?

(LO3)   6. What steps are followed in posting sales returns and allowances from the general journal to the general ledger and accounts receivable ledger?

(LO3)   7. What steps are followed in posting cash receipts from the general journal to the general ledger?

(LO3)   8. What steps are followed in posting cash receipts from the general journal to the accounts receivable ledger?

(LO4)   9. If the total of the schedule of accounts receivable does not agree with the Accounts Receivable balance, what procedures should be used to search for the error?

Self-Study Test Questions

True/False

1. All sales, for cash or on credit, can be recorded in the general journal. _____

2. Reductions in the price of merchandise granted by the seller because of defects or other problems with the merchandise are called sales allowances. _____

3. Sales Tax Payable is a liability account that is credited for the amount of tax imposed on sales. _____

4. Sales Returns and Allowances is debited for the amount of the sale, including the sales tax on that amount. _____

5. Cash discounts are offered to encourage prompt payment by customers who buy on account. _____

Multiple Choice

1. A credit sale of $250 plus a 6 percent sales tax would require a debit to Accounts Receivable of _____

   (a) $15.   (c) $30.
   (b) $280.   (d) $265.

2. When $25 of merchandise is returned for a credit on account, what is the amount of the credit to Accounts Receivable, assuming a 6 percent sales tax rate? _____

   (a) $1.50   (c) $26.50
   (b) $25.00   (d) $31.00

3. When $300, plus sales tax of 6 percent, is received for an amount previously owed, Cash is debited for what amount? _____

   (a) $18   (c) $300
   (b) $318   (d) $282

4. When credit sales are $325 plus sales tax of 5 percent, and there is a bank credit card fee of 3 percent, what is the debit to Bank Credit Card Expense? _____

   (a) $16.25   (c) $341.25
   (b) $10.24   (d) $331.01

5. Cash receipts should be posted to customer accounts _____

   (a) daily.   (c) end of month.
   (b) weekly.   (d) not posted.

The answers to the Self-Study Test Questions are at the end of the text.

MANAGING YOUR WRITING

You and your spouse have separate charge accounts at a local department store. When you tried to use your card last week, you were told that you were over your credit limit. This puzzled you because you had paid the entire account balance several weeks ago. When the monthly statements arrived yesterday, the error was clear. The store had credited your payment to your spouse's account.

Your account was treated as over the limit, and the store charged you interest on the unpaid balance. You suspect that part of the problem is that you and your spouse use the same last name (Morales) and have similar first names (Carmen and Carmelo).

Write a letter to the store requesting correction of your accounts and suggesting a way to identify your accounts so that this error does not happen again.

ETHICS CASE

Wholesale Health Supply sells a variety of medical equipment and supplies to retailers. When a new retailer is approved for credit, one of the criteria is that the retailer must have been in business for at least six months. Good Earth Foods placed a large order with Wholesale Health Supply and requested credit terms. Wholesale Health Supply faxed a credit request form to Good Earth Foods and the buyer at Good Earth Foods faxed the completed form back to Wholesale Health Supply. Robin Sylvester, the Sales Manager at Wholesale Health Supply, saw the credit application and noticed Good Earth Foods had only been in business for two months. Thinking she might lose the order if Good Earth Foods wasn't extended credit, Robin authorized the shipment. She figured by the time the credit department rejected the application, Good Earth Foods would have received the order and the Vice President would override the rejection to keep a new customer. Robin was sure that everything would turn out alright.

1. Do you think Robin's decision to ship the order was unethical? Why or why not?

2. What would you have done if you were in Robin's position?

3. Write a memo from the Credit Department Manager to Robin Sylvester explaining the reasoning behind requiring a new credit customer to be in business for at least six months.

4. In small groups discuss ways to prevent a situation like this from happening.

WEB WORK

1. Not only is mail order big business, but Internet retailing is expanding at a tremendous rate. Companies like Sears, J. C. Penney and L.L. Bean are on the Internet, as are millions of other retailers. How would their sales journals differ, if at all, for Internet sales versus mail order? What new challenges or problems might Internet sales present for record keeping?

2. E-business is not just for major players. Check out an example by linking to it from our text web site.

Visit the Interactive Study Center on our web site at **http://heintz.swlearning .com** for special hotlinks to assist you in this assignment.

SERIES A EXERCISES

EXERCISE 11-1A   **(LO1)**   **SALES DOCUMENTS** For each document or procedure listed below, indicate whether it would be used for a retail business or a wholesale business, as described in the chapter.

1. sales ticket
2. sales invoice
3. credit approval
4. cash register tape summary
5. credit memo
6. customer purchase order

EXERCISE 11-2A   **(LO2)**

3(d):

Sales Ret. & Allow   35
   Accts. Rec.   35

SALES TRANSACTIONS AND T ACCOUNTS Using T accounts for Cash, Accounts Receivable, Sales Tax Payable, Sales, Sales Returns and Allowances, and Sales Discounts, enter the following sales transactions. Use a new set of accounts for each part, 1–5.

1. No sales tax.

    (a)   Merchandise is sold for $300 cash.

    (b)   Merchandise is sold on account for $285.

    (c)   Payment is received for merchandise sold on account.

2. 5% sales tax.

    (a)   Merchandise is sold for $300 cash plus sales tax.

    (b)   Merchandise is sold on account for $285 plus sales tax.

    (c)   Payment is received for merchandise sold on account.

3. Cash and credit sales, with returned merchandise.

    (a)   Merchandise is sold for $325 cash.

    (b) $25 of merchandise sold for $325 is returned for refund.

    (c)   Merchandise is sold on account for $350.

    (d) $35 of merchandise sold for $350 is returned for a credit.

    (e)   Payment is received for balance owed on merchandise sold on account.

4. 5% sales tax, with returned merchandise.

    (a)   Merchandise is sold on account for $400 plus sales tax.

    (b)   Merchandise totaling $40 is returned for a credit.

    (c)   Balance on account is paid in cash.

    (d)   Merchandise is sold for $280 cash plus sales tax.

    (e) $20 of merchandise sold for $280 cash is returned for a refund.

5. Sales on account, with 2/10, n/30 cash discount terms.

    (a)   Merchandise is sold on account for $350.

    (b)   The balance is paid within the discount period.

    (c)   Merchandise is sold on account for $290.

    (d)   The balance is paid after the discount period.

EXERCISE 11-3A   (LO2)
Net sales: $3,079

COMPUTING NET SALES Based on the following information, compute net sales.

Gross sales	$3,580
Sales returns and allowances	428
Sales discounts	73

EXERCISE 11-4A   (LO3)

JOURNALIZING SALES TRANSACTIONS Enter the following transactions in a general journal. Use a 6% sales tax rate.

May 1:
Accts. Rec./J. Adams 2,120
  Sales   2,000
  Sales Tax Payable   120

May 1   Sold merchandise on account to J. Adams, $2,000 plus sales tax. Sale no. 488.

4   Sold merchandise on account to B. Clark, $1,800 plus sales tax. Sale no. 489.

8   Sold merchandise on account to A. Duck, $1,500 plus sales tax. Sale no. 490.

11   Sold merchandise on account to E. Hill, $1,950 plus sales tax. Sale no. 491.

EXERCISE 11-5A   (LO3)
Ending Accts. Rec.
balance: $4,059

JOURNALIZING SALES RETURNS AND ALLOWANCES Enter the following transactions in a general journal and post them to the appropriate general ledger and accounts receivable ledger accounts. Use account numbers as shown in the chapter. Beginning balance in Accounts Receivable is $4,200. Beginning balances in customer accounts are Abramowitz, $850; Perez, $1,018; and Gruder, $428.

June 1   John B. Abramowitz returned merchandise previously purchased on account (sale no. 329), $73.

6   Marie L. Perez returned merchandise previously purchased on account (sale no. 321), $44.

8   L. B. Gruder returned merchandise previously purchased on account (sale no. 299), $24.

EXERCISE 11-6A   (LO3)
July 6:
Cash   643
  Accts.Rec./J. Adler 643

JOURNALIZING CASH RECEIPTS Enter the following transactions in a general journal.

July 6   James Adler made payment on account, $643.

10   Cash sales for the week, $2,320.

14   Betty Havel made payment on account, $430.

15   J. L. Borg made payment on account, $117.

17   Cash sales for the week, $2,237.

EXERCISE 11-7A   (LO4)
Accts. Rec. balance: $4,586

SCHEDULE OF ACCOUNTS RECEIVABLE From the accounts receivable ledger shown, prepare a schedule of accounts receivable for Pheng Co. as of August 31, 20--.

ACCOUNTS RECEIVABLE LEDGER						
NAME B & G Distributors						
ADDRESS 2628 Burlington Avenue, Chicago, IL 60604-1329						
DATE	ITEM	POST REF.	DEBIT	CREDIT	BALANCE	
20-- Aug. 3		J1	1 3 8 0 00		1 3 8 0 00	
8		J1		1 4 0 00	1 2 4 0 00	

NAME	M. Chang															
ADDRESS	1422 SW Pacific, Chicago, IL 60603-8596															
DATE	ITEM	POST REF.	DEBIT					CREDIT					BALANCE			
20-- Aug. 5		J1	2	1	3	6	00						2	1	3	6	00
11		J2						2	1	3	6	00					

NAME	B. J. Hinschliff & Co.															
ADDRESS	133 College Blvd., Des Plaines, IL 60611-4431															
DATE	ITEM	POST REF.	DEBIT					CREDIT					BALANCE			
20-- Aug. 15		J2	1	1	0	6	00						1	1	0	6	00
21		J3		3	8	4	00						1	4	9	0	00

NAME	Sally M. Pitts															
ADDRESS	213 East 29th Place, Chicago, IL 60601-6287															
DATE	ITEM	POST REF.	DEBIT					CREDIT					BALANCE			
20-- Aug. 21		J3		8	3	8	00							8	3	8	00

NAME	Trendsetter, Inc.															
ADDRESS	29 Industrial Way, Chicago, IL 60600-5918															
DATE	ITEM	POST REF.	DEBIT					CREDIT					BALANCE			
20-- Aug. 28		J4	1	0	1	8	00						1	0	1	8	00

SERIES A PROBLEMS

PROBLEM 11-8A   **(LO3)**

Accts. Rec. balance:
$16,345.20

SALES TRANSACTIONS J. K. Bijan owns a retail business and made the following sales on account during the month of August 20--. There is a 6% sales tax on all sales.

Aug. 1   Sale no. 213 to Jung Manufacturing Co., $1,200 plus sales tax.

3   Sale no. 214 to Hassad Co., $3,600 plus sales tax.

7   Sale no. 215 to Helsinki, Inc., $1,400 plus sales tax. (Open a new account for this customer. Address is 125 Fishers Dr., Noblesville, IN 47870-8867.)

11   Sale no. 216 to Ardis Myler, $1,280 plus sales tax.

18   Sale no. 217 to Hassad Co., $4,330 plus sales tax.

22   Sale no. 218 to Jung Manufacturing Co., $2,000 plus sales tax.

30   Sale no. 219 to Ardis Myler, $1,610 plus sales tax.

REQUIRED

1. Record the transactions in a general journal.

2. Post from the journal to the general ledger and accounts receivable ledger accounts. Use account numbers as shown in the chapter.

PROBLEM 11-9A   **(LO3)**   **CASH RECEIPTS TRANSACTIONS** Zebra Imaginarium, a retail business, had the following cash receipts during December 20--. The sales tax is 6%.

Accts. Rec. balance:
$3,533.08

Dec. 1   Received payment on account from Michael Anderson, $1,360.

2   Received payment on account from Ansel Manufacturing, $382.

7   Cash sales for the week, $3,160 plus tax. Bank credit card sales for the week, $1,000 plus tax. Bank credit card fee is 3%.

8   Received payment on account from J. Gorbea, $880.

11   Michael Anderson returned merchandise for a credit, $60 plus tax.

14   Cash sales for the week, $2,800 plus tax. Bank credit card sales for the week, $800 plus tax. Bank credit card fee is 3%.

20   Received payment on account from Tom Wilson, $1,110.

21   Ansel Manufacturing returned merchandise for a credit, $22 plus tax.

21   Cash sales for the week, $3,200 plus tax.

24   Received payment on account from Rachel Carson, $2,000.

Beginning general ledger account balances were:

Cash	$9,862
Accounts Receivable	$9,352

Beginning customer account balances were:

M. Anderson	$2,480
Ansel Manufacturing	982
J. Gorbea	880
R. Carson	3,200
T. Wilson	1,810

REQUIRED

1.   Record the transactions in a general journal.

2.   Post from the journal to the general ledger and accounts receivable ledger accounts. Use account numbers as shown in the chapter.

PROBLEM 11-10A   **(LO3)**   **SALES AND CASH RECEIPTS TRANSACTIONS** Owens Distributors is a retail business. The following sales, returns, and cash receipts occurred during March 20--. There is an 8% sales tax. Beginning general ledger account balances were Cash, $9,741.00; and Accounts Receivable, $1,058.25. Beginning customer account balances were Thompson Group, $1,058.25.

Accts. Rec. balance:
$8,133.33

March 1   Sale no. 33C to Able & Co., $1,800 plus sales tax.

3   Sale no. 33D to R. J. Kalas, Inc., $2,240 plus sales tax.

5   Able & Co. returned merchandise from sale no. 33C for a credit (credit memo no. 66), $30 plus sales tax.

7   Cash sales for the week, $3,160 plus sales tax.

10   Received payment from Able & Co. for sale no. 33C less credit memo no. 66.

11   Sale no. 33E to Blevins Bakery, $1,210 plus sales tax.

13   Received payment from R. J. Kalas for sale no. 33D.

14	Cash sales for the week, $4,200 plus sales tax.
16	Blevins Bakery returned merchandise from sale no. 33E for a credit (credit memo no. 67), $44 plus sales tax.
18	Sale no. 33F to R. J. Kalas, Inc., $2,620 plus sales tax.
20	Received payment from Blevins Bakery for sale no. 33E less credit memo no. 67.
21	Cash sales for the week, $2,400 plus sales tax.
25	Sale no. 33G to Blevins Bakery, $1,915 plus sales tax.
27	Sale no. 33H to Thompson Group, $2,016 plus sales tax.
28	Cash sales for the week, $3,500 plus sales tax.

REQUIRED

1. Record the transactions in a general journal.

2. Post from the journal to the general ledger and accounts receivable ledger accounts. Use account numbers as shown in the chapter.

PROBLEM 11-11A   (LO4)
Accts. Rec. balance,
Thompson Group: $3,235.53

SCHEDULE OF ACCOUNTS RECEIVABLE Based on the information provided in Problem 11-10A, prepare a schedule of accounts receivable for Owens Distributors as of March 31, 20--. Verify that the accounts receivable account balance in the general ledger agrees with the schedule of accounts receivable total.

SERIES B EXERCISES

EXERCISE 11-1B   (LO1)

SALES DOCUMENTS Indicate whether each of the following documents or procedures is for a retail business or for a wholesale business, as described in the chapter.

1. A cash register receipt is given to the customer.
2. Credit approval is required since sales are almost always "on account."
3. Three copies of the sales invoice are prepared: one for shipping, one for the customer (as a bill), and one for accounting.
4. A sales ticket is given to a customer and another copy is sent to accounting.
5. The sales process begins with a customer purchase order.
6. The sales invoice itemizes what is sold, its cost, and the total amount owed.

EXERCISE 11-2B   (LO2)
3(d):
Sales Ret. & Allow.   24
 Accts. Rec.   24

SALES TRANSACTIONS AND T ACCOUNTS Using T accounts for Cash, Accounts Receivable, Sales Tax Payable, Sales, Sales Returns and Allowances, and Sales Discounts, enter the following sales transactions. Use a new set of accounts for each part, 1–5.

1. No sales tax.
   (a) Merchandise is sold for $250 cash.
   (b) Merchandise is sold on account for $225.
   (c) Payment is received for merchandise sold on account.

(continued)

2. 6% sales tax.

   (a)   Merchandise is sold for $250 cash plus sales tax.

   (b)   Merchandise is sold on account for $225 plus sales tax.

   (c)   Payment is received for merchandise sold on account.

3. Cash and credit sales, with returned merchandise.

   (a)   Merchandise is sold for $481 cash.

   (b) $18 of merchandise sold for $481 is returned for a refund.

   (c)   Merchandise is sold on account for $388.

   (d) $24 of merchandise sold for $388 is returned for a credit.

   (e)   Payment is received for balance owed on merchandise sold on account.

4. 6% sales tax, with returned merchandise.

   (a)   Merchandise is sold on account for $480 plus sales tax.

   (b)   Merchandise totaling $30 is returned.

   (c)   The balance on the account is paid in cash.

   (d)   Merchandise is sold for $300 cash plus sales tax.

   (e) $30 of merchandise sold for $300 cash is returned for a refund.

5. Sales on account, with 2/10, n/30 cash discount terms.

   (a)   Merchandise is sold on account for $280.

   (b)   The balance is paid within the discount period.

   (c)   Merchandise is sold on account for $203.

   (d)   The balance is paid after the discount period.

EXERCISE 11-3B   **(LO2)**
Net sales: $2,502

COMPUTING NET SALES Based on the following information, compute net sales.

Gross sales	$2,880
Sales returns and allowances	322
Sales discounts	56

EXERCISE 11-4B   **(LO3)**

JOURNALIZING SALES TRANSACTIONS Enter the following transactions in a general journal. Use a 5% sales tax rate.

Sept. 1:
Accts. Rec./K. Smith 1,890
  Sales   1,800
  Sales Tax Payable   90

Sept. 1   Sold merchandise on account to K. Smith, $1,800 plus sales tax. Sale no. 228.

3   Sold merchandise on account to J. Arnes, $3,100 plus sales tax. Sale no. 229.

5   Sold merchandise on account to M. Denison, $2,800 plus sales tax. Sale no. 230.

7   Sold merchandise on account to B. Marshall, $1,900 plus sales tax. Sale no. 231.

EXERCISE 11-5B   **(LO3)**
Ending Accts. Rec.
balance: $3,777

JOURNALIZING SALES RETURNS AND ALLOWANCES Enter the following transactions in a general journal and post them to the appropriate general ledger and accounts receivable ledger accounts. Use account numbers as shown in the chapter. Beginning balance in Accounts Receivable is $3,900. Beginning balances in customer accounts are Phillips, $1,018; Adams, $850; and Green, $428.

June 1   Marie L. Phillips returned merchandise previously purchased on account (sale no. 33), $43.

     11   John B. Adams returned merchandise previously purchased on account (sale no. 34), $59.

     15   L. B. Greene returned merchandise previously purchased on account (sale no. 35), $21.

EXERCISE 11-6B   **(LO3)**   **JOURNALIZING CASH RECEIPTS** Enter the following transactions in a general journal.

Nov. 1:
Cash   750
   Accts. Rec./J. Haghighat 750

Nov. 1   Jean Haghighat made payment on account, $750.

     12   Marc Antonoff made payment on account, $464.

     15   Cash sales, $3,763.

     18   Will Mossein made payment on account, $241.

     25   Cash sales, $2,648.

EXERCISE 11-7B   **(LO4)**
Accts. Rec. balance: $6,402

SCHEDULE OF ACCOUNTS RECEIVABLE From the accounts receivable ledger shown, prepare a schedule of accounts receivable for Gelph Co. as of November 30, 20--.

ACCOUNTS RECEIVABLE LEDGER

NAME James L. Adams Co.

ADDRESS 24481 McAdams Road, Dallas, TX 77001-3465

DATE	ITEM	POST REF.	DEBIT	CREDIT	BALANCE
20-- Nov. 1		J1	3 1 8 0 00		3 1 8 0 00
5		J1		1 8 0 00	3 0 0 0 00
7		J2	2 0 0 00		3 2 0 0 00

NAME Trish Berens

ADDRESS 34 West 55th Avenue, Fort Worth, TX 76310-8182

DATE	ITEM	POST REF.	DEBIT	CREDIT	BALANCE
20-- Nov. 3		J1	1 3 6 0 00		1 3 6 0 00

NAME M and T Jenkins, Inc.

ADDRESS 100 NW Richfield, Austin, TX 78481-3791

DATE	ITEM	POST REF.	DEBIT	CREDIT	BALANCE
20-- Nov. 5		J1	2 6 2 8 00		2 6 2 8 00
12		J2		2 6 2 8 00	--

NAME R & J Travis

ADDRESS 288 Beacon Street, Dallas, TX 79301-6642

DATE	ITEM	POST REF.	DEBIT	CREDIT	BALANCE
20-- Nov. 22		J3	1 8 4 2 00		1 8 4 2 00

SERIES B PROBLEMS

PROBLEM 11-8B   **(LO3)**

Accts. Rec. balance:
$13,072.50

SALES TRANSACTIONS   T. M. Maxwell owns a retail business and made the following sales on account during the month of July 20--. There is a 5% sales tax on all sales.

July 1   Sale no. 101 to Saga, Inc., $1,200 plus sales tax.

8   Sale no. 102 to Vinnie Ward, $2,100 plus sales tax.

15   Sale no. 103 to Dvorak Manufacturing, $4,300 plus sales tax.

21   Sale no. 104 to Vinnie Ward, $1,800 plus sales tax.

24   Sale no. 105 to Zapata Co., $1,600 plus sales tax. (Open a new account for this customer. Address is 789 N. Stafford Dr., Bloomington, IN 47401-6201.)

29   Sale no. 106 to Saga, Inc., $1,450 plus sales tax.

REQUIRED

1. Record the transactions in a general journal.

2. Post from the journal to the general ledger and accounts receivable ledger accounts. Use account numbers as shown in the chapter.

PROBLEM 11-9B   **(LO3)**

Accts. Rec. balance:
$2,744.45

CASH RECEIPTS TRANSACTIONS Color Florists, a retail business, had the following cash receipts during January 20--. The sales tax is 5%.

Jan. 1   Received payment on account from Ray Boyd, $880.

3   Received payment on account from Clint Hassell, $271.

5   Cash sales for the week, $2,800 plus tax. Bank credit card sales for the week, $1,200 plus tax. Bank credit card fee is 3%.

8   Received payment on account from Jan Sowada, $912.

11   Ray Boyd returned merchandise for a credit, $40 plus tax.

12   Cash sales for the week, $3,100 plus tax. Bank credit card sales for the week, $1,900 plus tax. Bank credit card fee is 3%.

15   Received payment on account from Robert Zehnle, $1,100.

18   Robert Zehnle returned merchandise for a credit, $31 plus tax.

19   Cash sales for the week, $2,230 plus tax.

25   Received payment on account from Dazai Manufacturing, $318.

Beginning general ledger account balances were:

Cash	$2,890.75
Accounts Receivable	6,300.00

Beginning customer account balances were:

R. Boyd	$1,400
Dazai Manufacturing	318
C. Hassell	815
J. Sowada	1,481
R. Zehnle	2,286

REQUIRED

1. Record the transactions in a general journal.

2. Post from the journal to the general ledger and accounts receivable ledger accounts. Use account numbers as shown in the chapter.

PROBLEM 11-10B   (LO3)

Accts. Rec. balance:
$8,290.25

SALES AND CASH RECEIPTS TRANSACTIONS Paul Jackson owns a retail business. The following sales, returns, and cash receipts are for April 20--. There is a 7% sales tax.

April 1 Sale no. 111 to O. L. Meyers, $2,100 plus sales tax.

3 Sale no. 112 to Andrew Plaa, $1,000 plus sales tax.

6 O. L. Meyers returned merchandise from sale no. 111 for a credit (credit memo no. 42), $50 plus sales tax.

7 Cash sales for the week, $3,240 plus sales tax.

9 Received payment from O. L. Meyers for sale no. 111 less credit memo no. 42.

12 Sale no. 113 to Melissa Richfield, $980 plus sales tax.

14 Cash sales for the week, $2,180 plus sales tax.

17 Melissa Richfield returned merchandise from sale no. 113 for a credit (credit memo no. 43), $40 plus sales tax.

19 Sale no. 114 to Kelsay Munkres, $1,020 plus sales tax.

21 Cash sales for the week, $2,600 plus sales tax.

24 Sale no. 115 to O. L. Meyers, $920 plus sales tax.

27 Sale no. 116 to Andrew Plaa, $1,320 plus sales tax.

28 Cash sales for the week, $2,800 plus sales tax.

Beginning general ledger account balances were:

| Cash | $2,864.54 |
| Accounts Receivable | 2,726.25 |

Beginning customer account balances were:

O. L. Meyers	$2,186.00
K. Munkres	482.00
M. Richfield	58.25

REQUIRED

1. Record the transactions in a general journal.

2. Post from the journal to the general ledger and accounts receivable ledger accounts. Use account numbers as shown in the chapter.

PROBLEM 11-11B   (LO4)
Accts. Rec. balance,
Melissa Richfield: $1,064.05

SCHEDULE OF ACCOUNTS RECEIVABLE Based on the information provided in Problem 11-10B, prepare a schedule of accounts receivable for Paul Jackson as of April 30, 20--. Verify that the accounts receivable account balance in the general ledger agrees with the schedule of accounts receivable total.

MASTERY PROBLEM

Accts. Rec. balance: $1,900.54

Geoff and Sandy Harland own and operate Wayward Kennel and Pet Supply. Their motto is, "If your pet is not becoming to you, he should be coming to us." The Harlands maintain a sales tax payable account throughout the month to account for the 6% sales tax. They use a general journal, general ledger, and accounts receivable ledger. The following sales and cash collections took place during the month of September.

Sept. 2 Sold a fish aquarium on account to Ken Shank, $125.00 plus tax of $7.50, terms n/30. Sale no. 101.

3 Sold dog food on account to Nancy Truelove, $68.25 plus tax of $4.10, terms n/30. Sale no. 102.

5 Sold a bird cage on account to Jean Warkentin, $43.95 plus tax of $2.64, terms n/30. Sale no. 103.

8 Cash sales for the week, $2,332.45 plus tax of $139.95.

10 Received cash for boarding and grooming services, $625.00 plus tax of $37.50.

11 Jean Warkentin stopped by the store to point out a minor defect in the bird cage purchased in sale no. 103. The Harlands offered a sales allowance of $10.00 plus tax on the price of the cage which satisfied Warkentin.

12 Sold a cockatoo on account to Tully Shaw, $1,200.00 plus tax of $72.00, terms n/30. Sale no. 104.

14 Received cash on account from Rosa Alanso, $256.00

15 Rosa Alanso returned merchandise, $93.28 including tax of $5.28.

15 Cash sales for the week, $2,656.85 plus tax of $159.41.

16 Received cash on account from Nancy Truelove, $58.25.

18 Received cash for boarding and grooming services, $535.00 plus tax of $32.10.

19 Received cash on account from Ed Cochran, $63.25.

20 Sold pet supplies on account to Susan Hays, $83.33 plus tax of $5.00, terms n/30. Sale no. 105.

21 Sold three Labrador Retriever puppies to All American Day Camp, $375.00 plus tax of $22.50, terms n/30. Sale no. 106.

22 Cash sales for the week, $3,122.45 plus tax of $187.35.

23 Received cash for boarding and grooming services, $515.00 plus tax of $30.90.

25 Received cash on account from Ken Shank, $132.50.

26 Received cash on account from Nancy Truelove, $72.35.

27 Received cash on account from Joe Gloy, $273.25.

28 Borrowed cash to purchase a pet limousine, $11,000.00.

29 Cash sales for the week, $2,835.45 plus tax of $170.13.

30 Received cash for boarding and grooming services, $488.00 plus tax of $29.28.

Wayward had the following general ledger account balances as of September 1.

Account Title	Account No.	General Ledger Balance on Sept. 1
Cash	101	$23,500.25
Accounts Receivable	122	850.75
Notes Payable	201	2,500.00
Sales Tax Payable	231	909.90
Sales	401	13,050.48
Sales Returns and Allowances	401.1	86.00
Boarding and Grooming Revenue	402	2,115.00

Wayward also had the following accounts receivable ledger balances as of September 1.

Customer	Accounts Receivable Balance
Rosa Alanso 2541 East 2nd Street Bloomington, IN 47401-5356	$456.00
Ed Cochran 2669 Windcrest Drive Bloomington, IN 47401-5446	$63.25
Joe Gloy 1458 Parnell Avenue Muncie, IN 47304-2682	$273.25
Nancy Truelove 2300 E. National Road Cumberland, IN 46229-4824	$58.25

New customers opening accounts during September were:

All American Day Camp
3025 Old Mill Run
Bloomington, IN 47408-1080

Tully Shaw
3315 Longview Avenue
Bloomington, IN 47401-7223

Susan Hays
1424 Jackson Creek Road
Nashville, IN 47448-2245

Jean Warkentin
1813 Deep Well Court
Bloomington, IN 47401-5124

Ken Shank
6422 E. Bender Road
Bloomington, IN 47401-7756

REQUIRED

1. Enter the transactions for the month of September in a general journal. (Begin with page 7.)

2. Post the entries to the general and subsidiary ledgers. Open new accounts for any customers who did not have a balance as of September 1.

3. Prepare a schedule of accounts receivable.

4. Compute the net sales for the month of September.

CHALLENGE PROBLEM

This problem challenges you to apply your cumulative accounting knowledge to move a step beyond the material in the chapter.

Enter the following transactions in a general journal.

June 14: Dr. Sales Discounts, $12

June 4	Sold merchandise on account to T. Allen, $1,500.00 plus 6% sales tax, with 1/10, n/30 cash discount terms.
7	Sold merchandise on account to K. Bryant, $1,800.00 plus 6% sales tax, with 1/10, n/30 cash discount terms.
11	T. Allen returned merchandise totaling $300.00 from the June 4 sale, for credit.
14	T. Allen paid the balance due from the June 4 sale, less discount.
17	K. Bryant paid the balance due from the June 7 sale, less discount.

DIGITAL IMAGING GROUP

Accounting for Purchases and Cash Payments

In the early months of operating Parkway Pet Supplies, Evan Taylor paid for his purchases by issuing a check to the vendors who delivered the items to his store. His store was new, so manufacturers and vendors would not sell to him on account. Accounting for such purchases was simple. As the business succeeded, Evan was able to buy on account and have merchandise shipped to his store. He had to pay the freight charges on such shipments. He also found that he was eligible for various discounts on his purchases and could return items for credit on his account. Accounting for purchases has become much more complicated. How should Evan's bookkeeper account for items like freight charges, discounts, and credits for purchases that he returns to the manufacturer or vendor?

LO1 Define merchandise purchases transactions.

LO2 Describe and use merchandise purchases accounts and compute gross profit.

LO3 Describe and use the accounts payable ledger.

LO4 Prepare a schedule of accounts payable.

Chapter 11 demonstrated how to account for sales in a merchandising business. This chapter continues the study of the merchandising business by examining how to account for merchandise purchases. We will learn how to use four new accounts and another subsidiary ledger.

MERCHANDISE PURCHASES TRANSACTIONS

LO1 Define merchandise purchases transactions.

In everyday language, purchases can refer to almost anything we have bought. For a merchandising business, however, **purchases** refers to merchandise acquired for resale. These are the goods a business buys for the sole purpose of selling them to its customers.

Purchasing procedures and documents vary, depending on the nature and size of a business. For example, in a small business, the owner or an employee might do the buying on a part-time basis. In a large business, there might be a separate purchasing department with a full-time manager and staff. In addition, the procedures and documents used can be affected by whether purchases are made on account or for cash.

The flowchart in Figure 12-1 shows some of the major documents used in the purchasing process of a merchandising business. In discussing the purchasing process, we will assume that the business makes purchases on account and has a purchasing department.

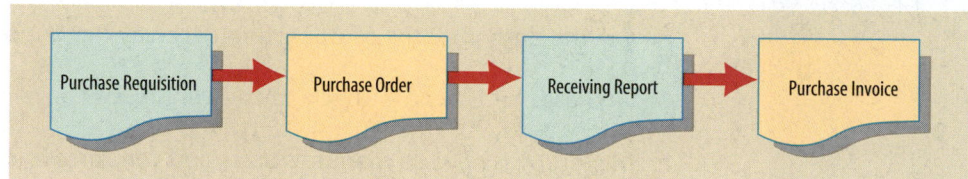

FIGURE 12-1 Purchasing Process Documents

Purchase Requisition

A **purchase requisition** is a form used to request the purchase of merchandise or other property. Any authorized person or department can prepare this form and submit it to the purchasing department. Figure 12-2 shows a purchase requisition used by Northern Micro. One copy of this form is sent to the purchasing department, one to the accounting department, and one is kept by the department that prepared the requisition.

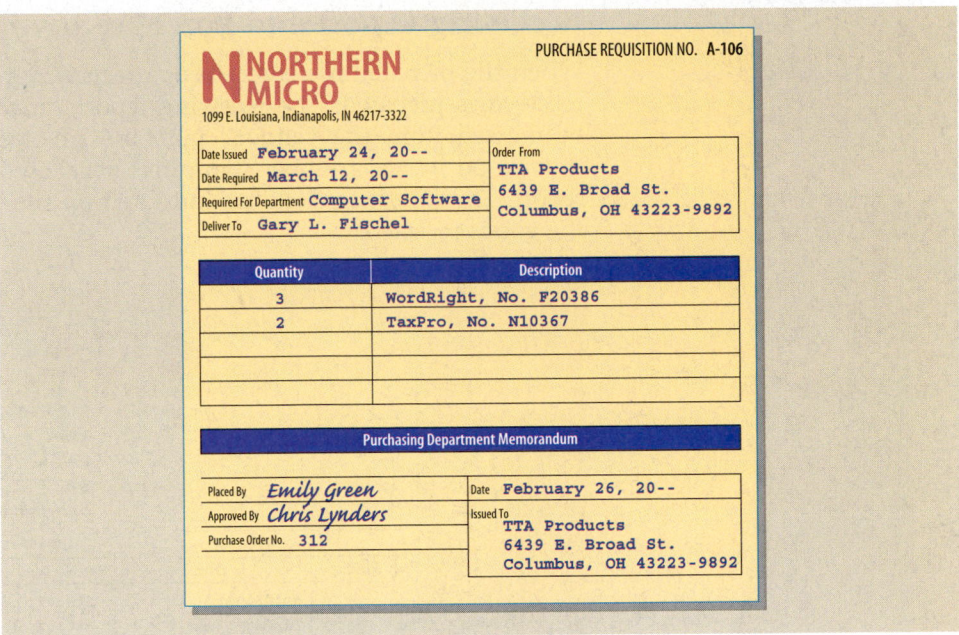

FIGURE 12-2   Purchase Requisition

Purchase Order

In a computerized system, purchase orders can be submitted electronically. Signals are sent to the vendor and the accounting and purchasing departments at the same time.

The purchasing department reviews and approves the purchase requisition and prepares a purchase order. A **purchase order** is a written order to buy goods from a specific vendor (supplier). Figure 12-3 shows a purchase order prepared by Northern Micro based on the purchase requisition in Figure 12-2. One copy of the purchase order is sent to the vendor to order the goods, one to the accounting department, and one copy is kept in the purchasing department. Other copies may be sent to the department that prepared the purchase requisition and to the receiving area.

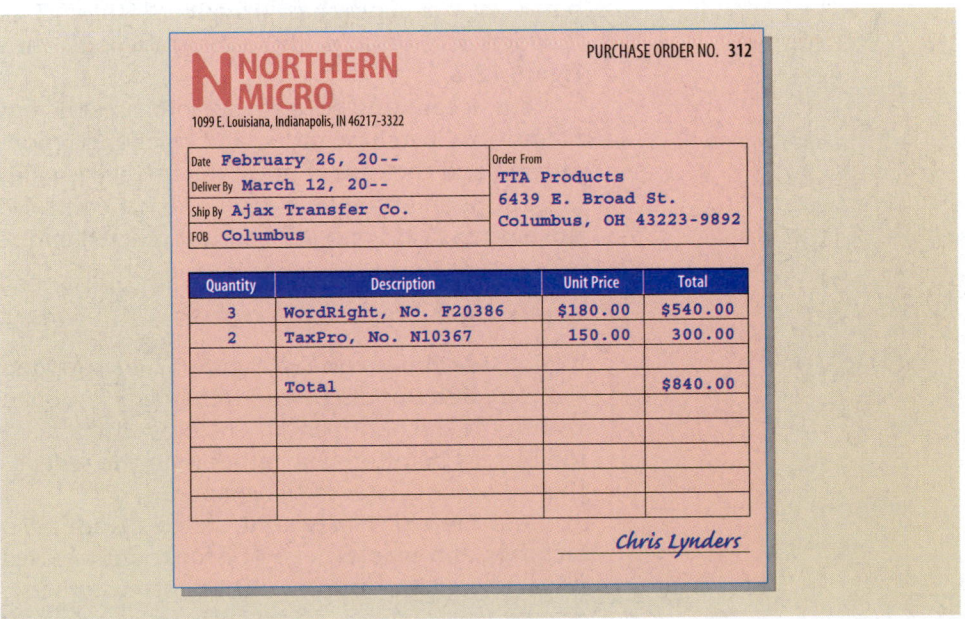

FIGURE 12-3   Purchase Order

Receiving Report and Purchase Invoice

When the merchandise is received, a **receiving report** indicating what has been received is prepared. The receiving report can be a separate form, or one can be created from the vendor's purchase invoice. Figure 12-4 shows a vendor invoice on which a rubber stamp has been used to imprint a type of receiving report. The receiving clerk has indicated on the form the date and condition of the goods received.

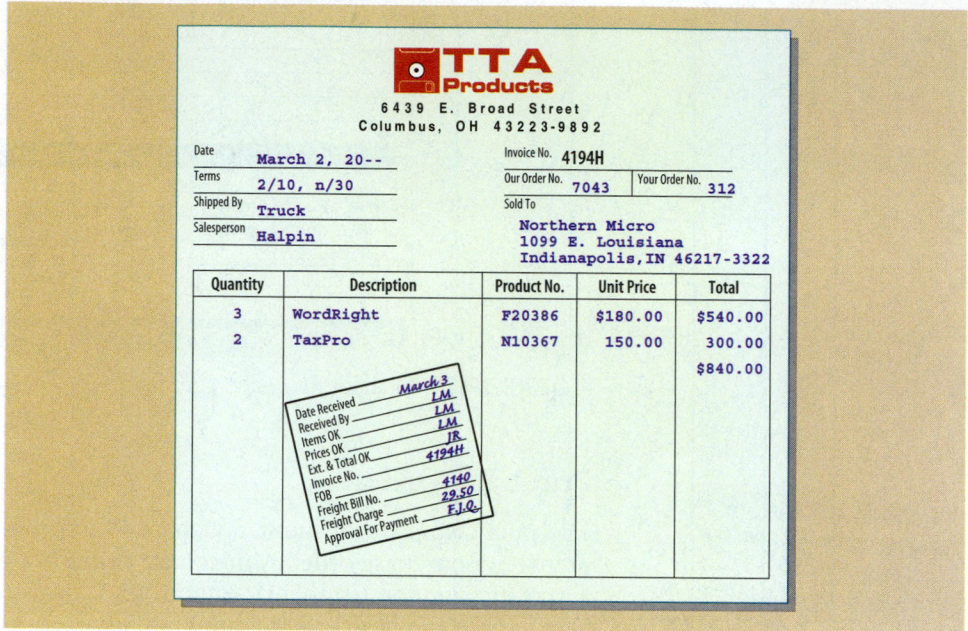

FIGURE 12-4   Purchase Invoice

An **invoice** is a document prepared by the seller as a bill for the merchandise shipped. To the seller, this is a sales invoice, as explained in Chapter 11. To the buyer, this is a **purchase invoice**. Figure 12-4 shows an invoice sent by TTA Products to Northern Micro for the goods ordered with the purchase order in Figure 12-3.

The accounting department compares the purchase invoice with the purchase requisition, purchase order, and receiving report. If the invoice is for the goods ordered and the correct price, the invoice is paid by the due date.

This is an example of good internal control. The procedure helps ensure that the business pays only for goods it ordered and received, and at the correct price.

Cash and Trade Discounts

Notice that the invoice in Figure 12-4 shows terms of 2/10, n/30. These are the same credit terms discussed in Chapter 11. A discount is available if the bill is paid within the discount period. The only difference is that we are now looking from the buyer's point of view rather than the seller's. We will see how to account for these discounts later in the chapter.

Another type of discount, called a **trade discount**, is often offered by manufacturers and wholesalers. This discount is a reduction from the list or catalog price offered to different classes of customers. By simply adjusting the trade discount percentages, companies can avoid the cost of reprinting catalogs every time there is a change in prices. Trade discounts are usually shown as a deduction from the total amount of the invoice. For example, the invoice in Figure 12-5 includes a trade discount of 10%. The amount to be entered in the accounting records for this invoice is $756, the net amount after deducting the trade discount of $84. Trade discounts represent a reduction in the price of the merchandise and should not be entered in the accounts of either the seller or the buyer.

 LEARNING KEY: Purchases and sales subject to trade discounts should be recorded in the accounting records at the *net amount* after deducting the trade discounts.

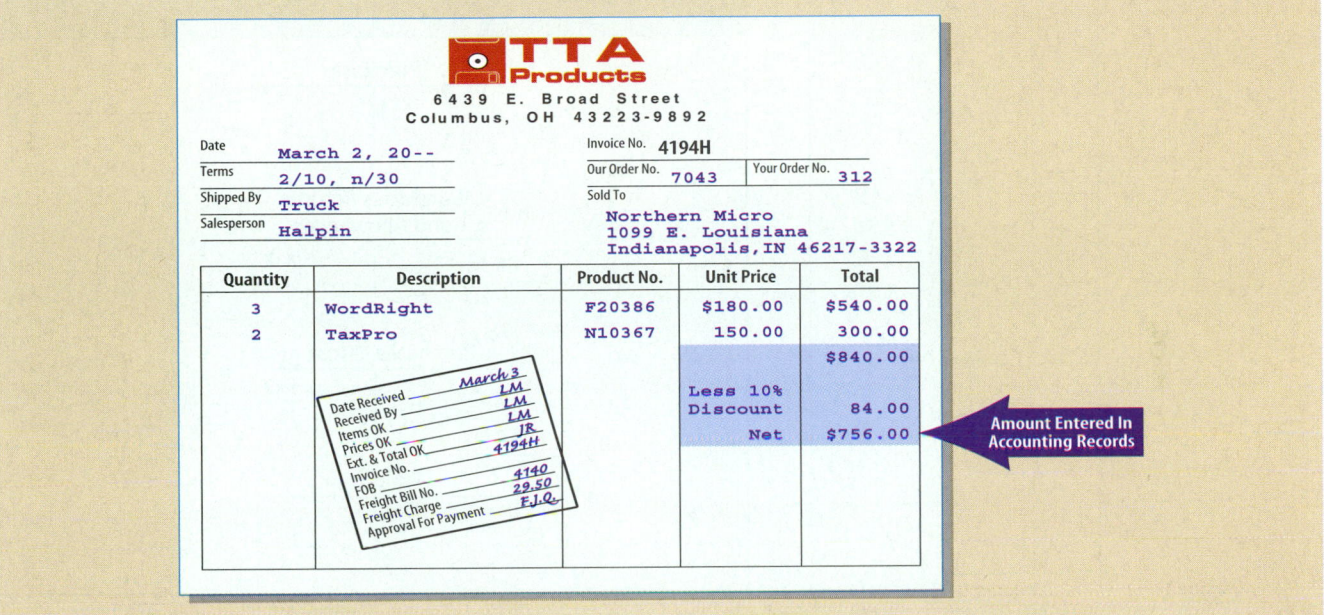

FIGURE 12-5 Purchase Invoice with Trade Discount

We need to be careful in computing the cash discount when an invoice has both cash and trade discounts. The cash discount applies to the *net amount* after deducting the trade discount. For example, the cash discount and amount to be paid on the invoice in Figure 12-5 would be calculated as follows:

Gross amount	$840.00
Less 10% trade discount	84.00
Net amount	$756.00
Less 2% cash discount	15.12
Amount to be paid	$740.88

MERCHANDISE PURCHASES ACCOUNTS

LO2 Describe and use merchandise purchases accounts and compute gross profit.

To account for merchandise purchases transactions, we will use four new accounts:

1. Purchases
2. Purchases Returns and Allowances
3. Purchases Discounts
4. Freight-In

The position of these accounts in the accounting equation and their normal balances are shown in Figure 12-6.

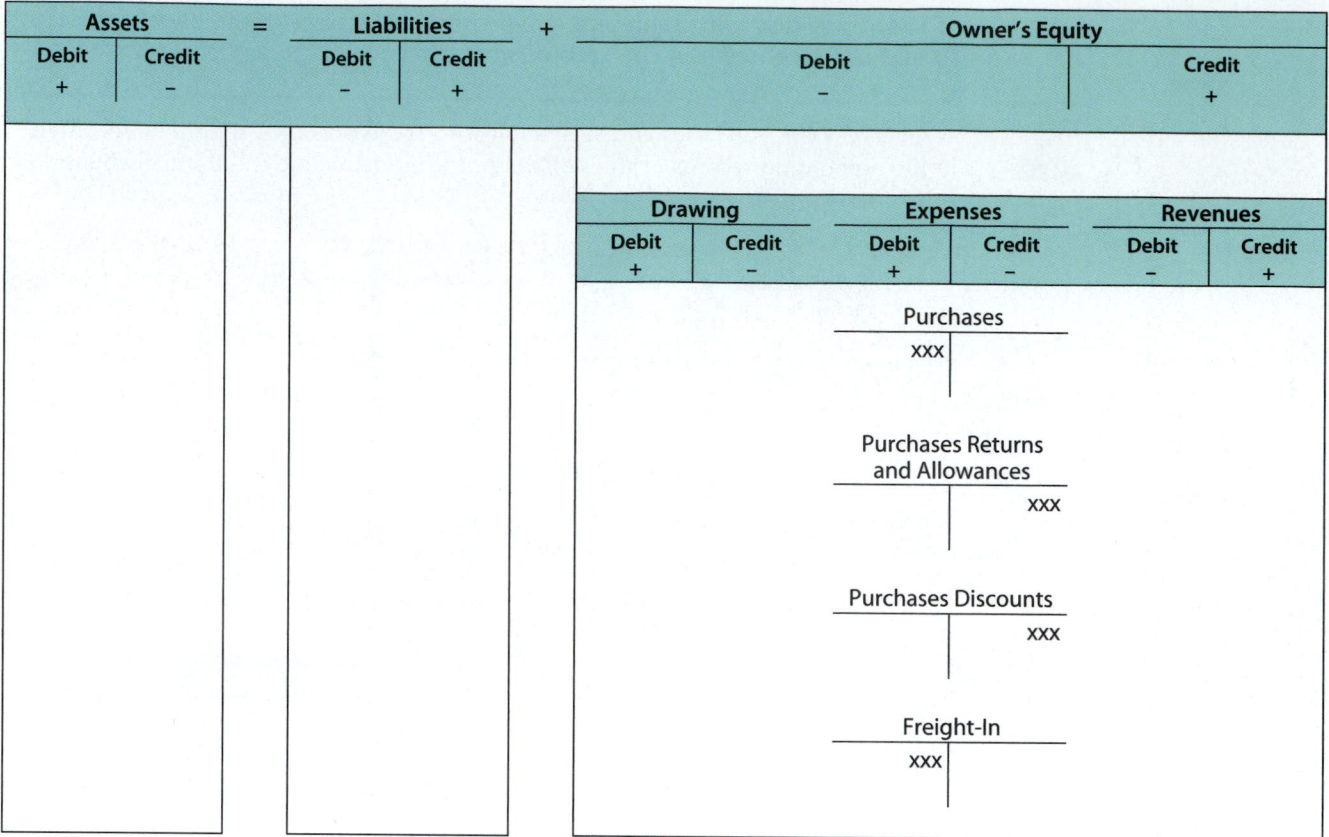

FIGURE 12-6 Accounting for Merchandise Purchases Transactions

Purchases Account

The purchases account is used to record the cost of merchandise purchased.

Purchases	
Debit	Credit
to enter the cost of merchandise purchased	

If a $100 purchase is made for cash, the following entry is made.

5	Purchases		1 0 0 00		5
6	Cash			1 0 0 00	6
7	Made cash purchase				7

If the same purchase is made on account, the entry is:

5	Purchases		1 0 0 00		5
6	Accounts Payable / Vendor			1 0 0 00	6
7	Made purchase on account				7

Accounts Payable is followed by a slash (/) and the name of the specific vendor to whom the purchaser owes money.

Purchases Returns and Allowances Account

Purchases Returns and Allowances is a contra-purchases account used to record purchases returns and purchases allowances. It is reported as a deduction from Purchases on the income statement (see Figure 12-7).

Purchases returns and allowances are similar to the sales returns and allowances we discussed in Chapter 11. We are simply looking at returns and allowances from the buyer's point of view. If merchandise is returned to a sup-plier, or the supplier grants a price reduction because of defects or other problems with merchandise purchased, Purchases Returns and Allowances is credited.

Purchases Returns and Allowances

Debit	Credit
	to enter returns and allowances

If merchandise that was purchased on account for $200 is defective and is returned to the supplier, the following entry is made.

9		Accounts Payable / Vendor	2 0 0 00		9
10		Purchases Returns and Allowances		2 0 0 00	10
11		Returned merchandise			11

If the same merchandise is retained but the supplier grants a price reduction of $45 because of the defects, the entry is:

9		Accounts Payable / Vendor	4 5 00		9
10		Purchases Returns and Allowances		4 5 00	10
11		Allowance for defective merchandise			11

Purchases Discounts Account

Purchases Discounts is a contra-purchases account used to record cash discounts allowed on purchases. Like Purchases Returns and Allowances, it is reported as a deduction from Purchases on the income statement (see Figure 12-7).

Purchases Discounts

Debit	Credit
	for cash discounts taken

If merchandise is purchased for $100 on account, with credit terms of 2/10, n/30, the following entry is made.

14		Purchases	1 0 0 00		14
15		Accounts Payable / Vendor		1 0 0 00	15
16		Made purchase on account			16

If payment for the merchandise is subsequently made within the discount period, the entry is:

18	Accounts Payable / Vendor		1	0	0	00						18
19	Cash								9	8	00	19
20	Purchases Discounts									2	00	20
21	Made payment on account											21

This approach to accounting for purchases discounts is known as the "gross-price method." The "net-price method" is described in the Appendix.

Note the parts of this entry. Accounts Payable is debited for $100, the full amount of the invoice, because the entire debt has been satisfied. Cash is credited for only $98 because that is all that was required to pay the debt. The difference of $2 ($100 – $98) is credited to Purchases Discounts, which represents a reduction in the purchase price of the merchandise. That is why Purchases Discounts is deducted from Purchases on the income statement.

Freight-In Account

Freight-In is an adjunct-purchases account used to record transportation charges on merchandise purchases. It is added to Purchases on the income statement (see Figure 12-7).

Freight-In

Debit	Credit
for transportation charges on merchandise purchases	

Transportation charges are expressed in FOB (free on board) terms that indicate who is responsible for paying the freight costs. **FOB shipping point** means that transportation charges are paid by the buyer. **FOB destination** means that transportation charges are paid by the seller.

When the terms are FOB shipping point, either the freight charges will be listed separately on the purchase invoice or a separate freight bill will be sent. Assume Northern Micro receives an invoice for $400 plus freight charges of $38. The entry for this purchase is:

25	Purchases		4	0	0	00						25
26	Freight-In		3	8	00							26
27	Accounts Payable / Vendor							4	3	8	00	27
28	Made purchase on account											28

Assume instead that Northern Micro receives an invoice for $400 for the same merchandise, shipped FOB shipping point. Northern Micro then receives a separate bill from the transportation company for $38. These two transactions are entered as follows:

30	Purchases		4	0	0	00						30
31	Accounts Payable / Vendor							4	0	0	00	31
32	Made purchase on account											32
33												33
34	Freight-In		3	8	00							34
35	Accounts Payable / Vendor								3	8	00	35
36	Freight charges on merchandise purchase											36

When the terms are FOB destination, generally no freight charges appear on the purchase invoice. The buyer simply records the purchase at the amount of the invoice. The freight-in account is not used in recording this purchase.

Computation of Gross Profit

An important step in determining net income for a merchandising business is the calculation of its gross profit. **Gross profit** (also called **gross margin**) is the difference between net sales and cost of goods sold. **Cost of goods sold** (also called **cost of merchandise sold**) is the difference between the goods available for sale and the ending inventory. It indicates the cost of the goods sold during the period. Gross profit provides very important information. It tells management the amount of sales dollars available to cover expenses, after covering the cost of the goods sold.

> *Goods available for sale include beginning inventory plus the cost of all goods purchased during the year.*

LEARNING KEY: Net sales – cost of goods sold = gross profit.

To compute gross profit, we use two of the four new accounts described in Chapter 11, the four new accounts described above, and the merchandise inventory balances. Assume that Northern Micro has the following sales, purchases, and merchandise inventory balances for the year ended December 31, 20--.

From Chapter 11 Sales	$200,500
Sales returns and allowances	1,200
From Chapter 12 Purchases	105,000
Purchases returns and allowances	800
Purchases discounts	1,000
Freight-In	300
Merchandise inventory, January 1, 20--	26,000
Merchandise inventory, December 31, 20--	18,000

A BROADER VIEW

Cash Management— Those Discounts Matter

> *In Chapter 18 we discuss how to compute interest. There you will learn to compute the exact interest rate.*

If a business makes a $2,000 purchase on account, with terms of 2/10, n/30, the available discount is only $40 ($2,000 × .02). On the surface, this seems unimportant, like "small change." But take a closer look. If the business does not pay $1,960 ($2,000 – $40) within 10 days, it must pay $2,000 within 30 days. This means that the business would pay $40 for the use of $1,960 for 20 more days. If we assume a 360-day year, the approximate annual interest rate for using the $1,960 for 20 days is 36%.

The innocent looking 2% cash discount represents a very high rate of interest. If a business regularly misses cash discount opportunities, the annual dollar cost can be substantial. For sound cash management, take advantage of discounts.

©GETTY IMAGES/PHOTODISC

Figure 12-7 uses these balances to compute net sales, net purchases, cost of goods sold, and gross profit. The following four steps in computing gross profit are labeled in the figure.

STEP 1 Compute net sales.

> (Sales – sales returns and allowances)

STEP 2 Compute goods available for sale.

> (Beginning inventory + cost of goods purchased)

STEP 3 Compute cost of goods sold.

> (Goods available for sale – ending inventory)

STEP 4 Compute gross profit.

> (Net sales – cost of goods sold)

Sales		$200 5 0 0 00	
Less sales returns and allowances		1 2 0 0 00	
Net sales (Step 1)			$199 3 0 0 00
Cost of goods sold:			
Merchandise inventory, Jan. 1		$ 26 0 0 0 00	
Purchases	$105 0 0 0 00		
Less: Purchases returns and allowances	$ 8 0 0 00		
Purchases discounts	1 0 0 0 00 1 8 0 0 00		
Net purchases	$103 2 0 0 00		
Add freight-in	3 0 0 00		
Cost of goods purchased		103 5 0 0 00	
Goods available for sale (Step 2)		$129 5 0 0 00	
Less merchandise inventory, Dec. 31		18 0 0 0 00	
Cost of goods sold (Step 3)			111 5 0 0 00
Gross profit (Step 4)			$ 87 8 0 0 00

FIGURE 12-7 Computation of Gross Profit

JOURNALIZING AND POSTING PURCHASES AND CASH PAYMENTS TRANSACTIONS

LO3 Describe and use the accounts payable ledger.

To illustrate the journalizing and posting of purchases transactions, we will continue with the transactions of Northern Micro.

Purchases

Assume the following purchases on account occurred during the month of April.

April 4	Purchased merchandise from Compucraft, Inc., $3,300. Invoice no. 631, dated April 2, terms, n/30.
8	Purchased merchandise from Datasoft, $2,500. Invoice no. 927D, dated April 6, terms, n/30.
11	Purchased merchandise from EZX Corp., $8,700. Invoice no. 804, dated April 9, terms, 1/15, n/30.
17	Purchased merchandise from Printpro Corp., $800. Invoice no. 611, dated April 16, terms, n/30.
23	Purchased merchandise from Televax, Inc., $5,300. Invoice no. 1465, dated April 22, terms, 1/10, n/30.

These transactions are entered in a general journal as shown in Figure 12-8.

GENERAL JOURNAL   PAGE 6

	DATE	DESCRIPTION	POST REF.	DEBIT	CREDIT	
1	20-- Apr. 4	Purchases		3 3 0 0 00		1
2		Accounts Payable/Compucraft			3 3 0 0 00	2
3		Invoice no. 631				3
4						4
5	8	Purchases		2 5 0 0 00		5
6		Accounts Payable/Datasoft			2 5 0 0 00	6
7		Invoice no. 927D				7
8						8
9	11	Purchases		8 7 0 0 00		9
10		Accounts Payable/EZX			8 7 0 0 00	10
11		Invoice no. 804				11
12						12
13	17	Purchases		8 0 0 00		13
14		Accounts Payable/Printpro			8 0 0 00	14
15		Invoice no. 611				15
16						16
17	23	Purchases		5 3 0 0 00		17
18		Accounts Payable/Televax			5 3 0 0 00	18
19		Invoice no. 1465				19

FIGURE 12-8 Purchases Entered in General Journal

Posting to the General Ledger

Purchases transactions are posted from the general journal to the general ledger in the same manner as was illustrated for sales in Chapter 11. The following steps are used, as indicated in Figure 12-9 for Northern Micro's April 4 and 8 purchases transactions.

In the ledger account:

STEP 1   Enter the date of the transaction in the Date column.

STEP 2   Enter the amount of the debit or credit in the Debit or Credit column.

STEP 3   Enter the new balance in the Balance columns under Debit or Credit.

STEP 4   Enter the journal page number from which each transaction is posted in the Posting Reference column.

In the journal:

STEP 5   Enter the ledger account number in the Posting Reference column of the journal for each transaction that is posted.

Other purchases transactions would be posted in the same manner.

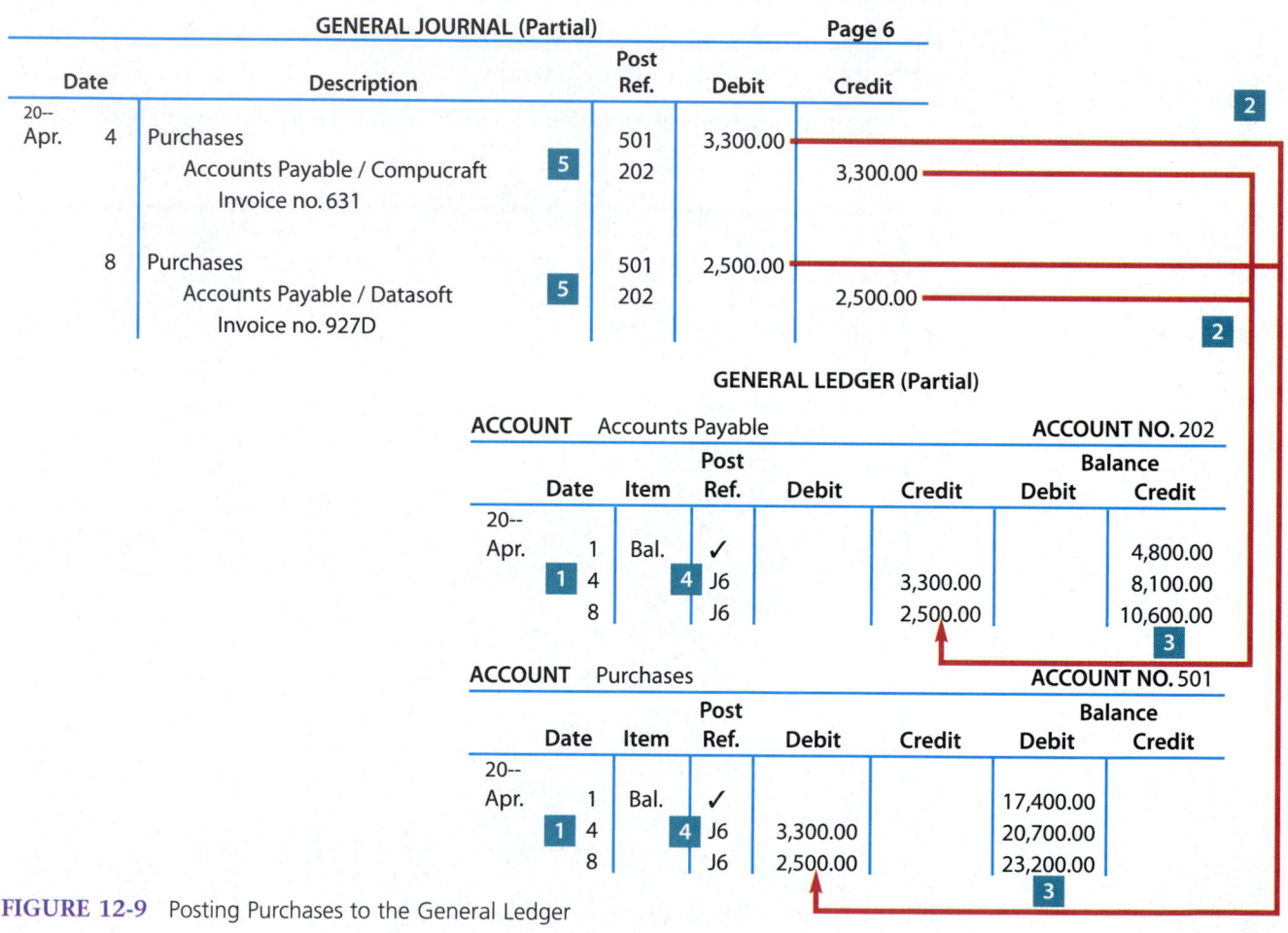

FIGURE 12-9 Posting Purchases to the General Ledger

Posting to the Accounts Payable Ledger

The Purchases and Accounts Payable resulting from merchandise purchases on account are now up to date in the general ledger. A record can be kept of the amount owed to each supplier by using a subsidiary **accounts payable ledger.** This is a separate ledger containing an individual account payable for each

A 3-column account form is commonly used for supplier accounts. Only one balance column is needed because the normal balance is a credit. If a debit balance occurs, the amount may be bracketed.

supplier. If there are many supplier accounts, it is a good practice to assign each supplier an account number. The subsidiary ledger accounts are kept in either alphabetical or numerical order, depending on whether the supplier accounts are identified by number. A summary accounts payable account called a controlling account is maintained in the general ledger. The accounts payable ledger is "subsidiary" to this account.

Figure 12-10 illustrates the use of the accounts payable ledger for Northern Micro's April 4 and 8 purchases transactions. The following steps are used to post from the general journal to the accounts payable ledger, as shown in Figure 12-10.

In the accounts payable ledger account:

STEP 1   Enter the date of the transaction in the Date column.

STEP 2   Enter the amount of the debit or credit in the Debit or Credit column.

STEP 3   Enter the new balance in the Balance column.

STEP 4   Enter the journal page number from which each transaction is posted in the Posting Reference column.

In the journal:

STEP 5   Enter a slash (/) followed by a check mark (✓) in the Posting Reference column of the journal for each transaction that is posted.

LEARNING KEY: When an accounts payable ledger is used, the posting reference column in the general journal serves two purposes. (1) The account number is inserted to indicate the general ledger account has been posted. (2) A slash (/) and a check mark (✓) are inserted to indicate the accounts payable ledger account has been posted.

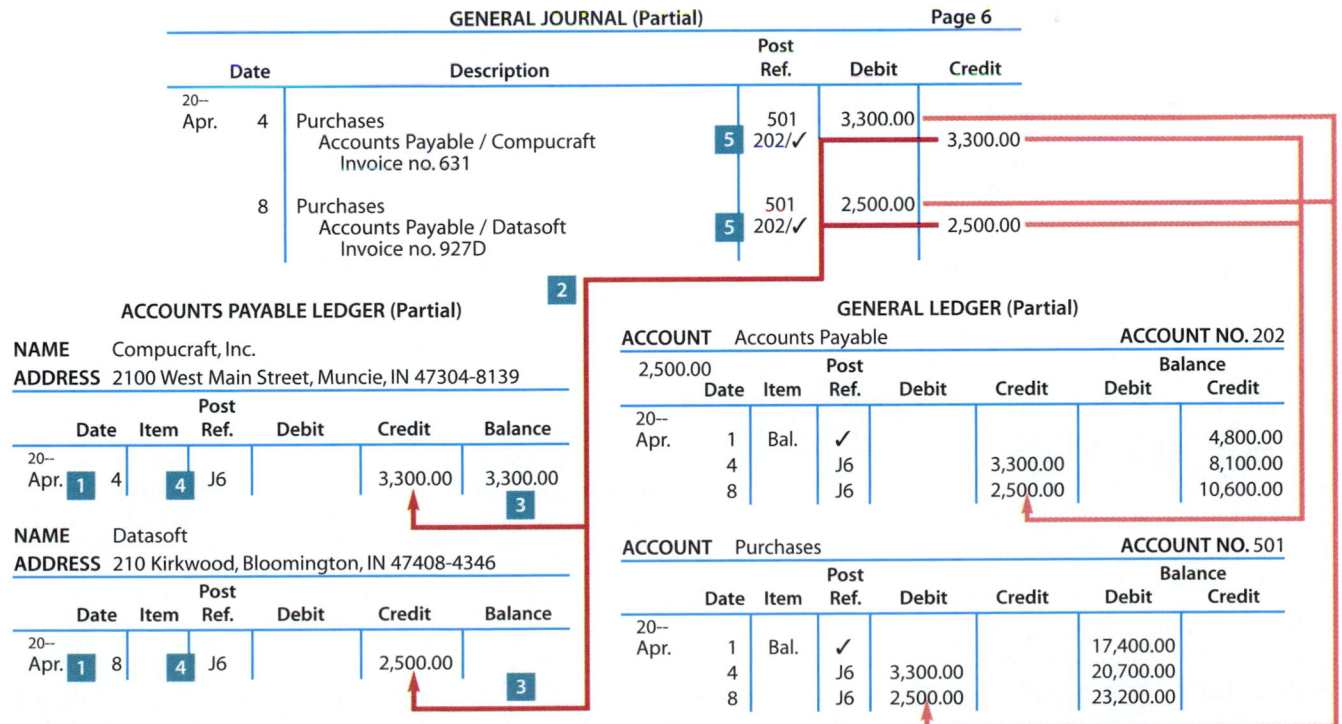

FIGURE 12-10   Posting Purchases to the Accounts Payable Ledger

Note the relationship between the general journal, accounts payable ledger, and general ledger. All general journal entries are posted to both the general ledger and the accounts payable ledger. After the posting of the accounts payable ledger and general ledger is completed, the total of the accounts payable ledger balances should equal the Accounts Payable balance in the general ledger.

Purchases Returns and Allowances

If a buyer returns merchandise or is given an allowance for damaged merchandise, a general journal entry is required. Assume that on May 4, Northern Micro returns $200 of merchandise to Televax, Inc. These goods were part of a purchase made on April 23. Figure 12-11 shows the general journal entry, general ledger posting, and accounts payable ledger posting for this transaction.

The general journal entry is made in the usual manner. The general ledger is posted using the same five steps as were illustrated for purchases transactions in Figure 12-9. The accounts payable ledger is posted using the following five steps, as illustrated in Figure 12-11.

In the accounts payable ledger account:

STEP 1   Enter the date of the transaction in the Date column.

STEP 2   Enter the amount of the debit or credit in the Debit or Credit column.

STEP 3   Enter the new balance in the Balance column.

STEP 4   Enter the journal page number from which each transaction is posted in the Posting Reference column.

In the journal:

STEP 5   Enter a slash (/) followed by a check mark (✓) in the Posting Reference column of the journal for each transaction that is posted.

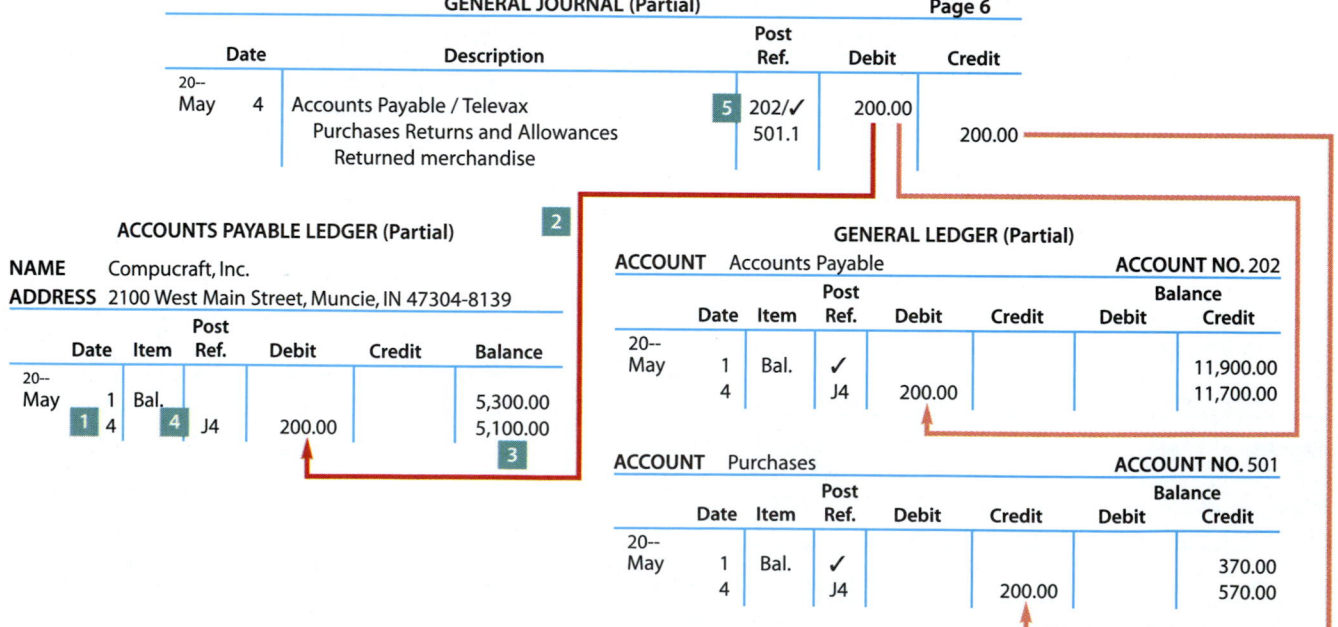

FIGURE 12-11   Accounting for Purchases Returns and Allowances

Cash Payments

To illustrate the journalizing and posting of cash payments, we will use Northern Micro's cash payment transactions. Assume Northern Micro made the following two payments on account during the month of April.

April 10   Paid B.B. Small $4,800 for purchases made on account.

24   Paid EZX Corp. $8,700 less discount of 1% for purchases made on account.

These transactions are entered in a general journal as shown in Figure 12-12.

30	Apr.	10	Accounts Payable / B.B. Small	4 8 0 0 00		30
31			Cash		4 8 0 0 00	31
32			Made payment on account			32
33						33
34		24	Accounts Payable / EZX Corp.	8 7 0 0 00		34
35			Cash		8 6 1 3 00	35
36			Purchases Discounts		8 7 00	36
37			Made payment less discount on account			37

FIGURE 12-12   Cash Payments Entered in a General Journal

Posting to the General Ledger and Accounts Payable Ledger

Cash payment transactions are posted to the general ledger in the same manner as was illustrated for purchases transactions in Figure 12-9. To post cash payments to the accounts payable ledger, the following steps are used, as indicated in Figure 12-13 for Northern Micro's April 10 and 24 cash payment transactions.

In the accounts payable ledger account:

STEP 1   Enter the date of the transaction in the Date column.

STEP 2   Enter the amount of the debit or credit in the Debit or Credit column.

STEP 3   Enter the new balance in the Balance column.

STEP 4   Enter the journal page number from which each transaction is posted in the Posting Reference column.

In the journal:

STEP 5   Enter a slash (/) followed by a check mark (✔) in the Posting Reference column of the journal for each transaction that is posted.

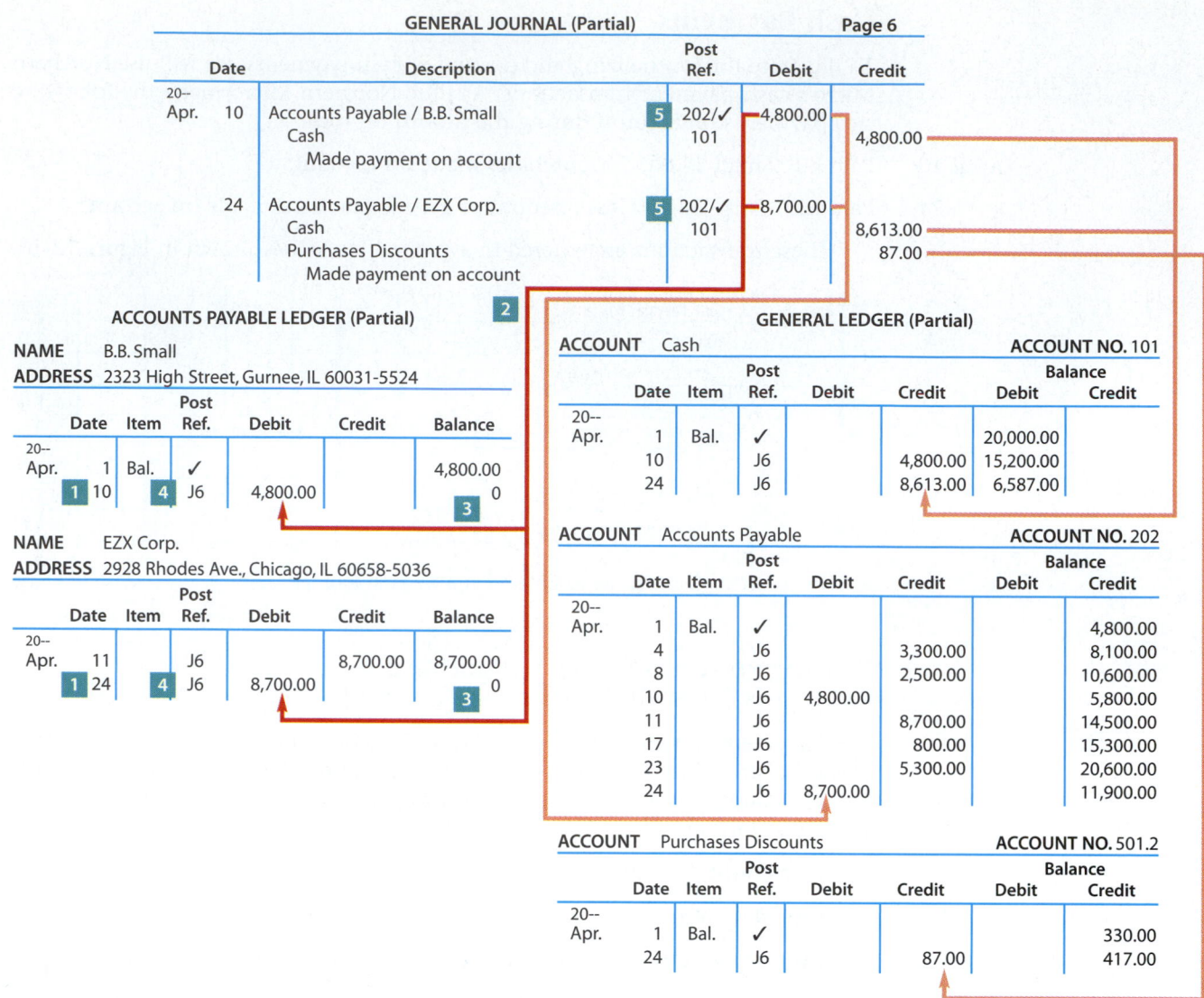

FIGURE 12-13 Posting Cash Payments to the General Ledger and Accounts Payable Ledger

SCHEDULE OF ACCOUNTS PAYABLE

LO4 **Prepare a schedule of accounts payable.**

At the end of the month, all postings to Accounts Payable in the general ledger and to the accounts payable ledger should be complete, as shown in Figure 12-14. At this point, the Accounts Payable balance in the general ledger should equal the sum of the supplier balances in the accounts payable ledger.

ACCOUNTS PAYABLE LEDGER

NAME   B.B. Small
ADDRESS 2323 High Street, Gurnee, IL 60031-5524

Date		Item	Post Ref.	Debit	Credit	Balance
20--						
Apr.	1	Bal.	✓			4,800.00
	10		J6	4,800.00		0

NAME   Compucraft, Inc.
ADDRESS 2100 West Main Street, Muncie, IN 47304-8139

Date		Item	Post Ref.	Debit	Credit	Balance
20--						
Apr.	4		J6		3,300.00	3,300.00

NAME   Datasoft
ADDRESS 210 Kirkwood, Bloomington, IN 47408-4346

Date		Item	Post Ref.	Debit	Credit	Balance
20--						
Apr.	8		J6		2,500.00	2,500.00

NAME   EZX Corp.
ADDRESS 2928 Rhodes Ave., Chicago, IL 60658-5036

Date		Item	Post Ref.	Debit	Credit	Balance
20--						
Apr.	11		J6		8,700.00	8,700.00
	24		J6	8,700.00		0

NAME   Printpro Corp.
ADDRESS 1200 Chambers Pike, Lincolnwood, IL 60648-2417

Date		Item	Post Ref.	Debit	Credit	Balance
20--						
Apr.	17		J6		800.00	800.00

NAME   Televax, Inc.
ADDRESS 1500 North Walnut Street, Addison, IL 60101-2417

Date		Item	Post Ref.	Debit	Credit	Balance
20--						
Apr.	23		J6		5,300.00	5,300.00

GENERAL LEDGER (Partial)

ACCOUNT Accounts Payable   **ACCOUNT NO. 202**

Date		Item	Post Ref.	Debit	Credit	Balance Debit	Balance Credit
20--							
Apr.	1	Bal.	✓				4,800.00
	4		J6		3,300.00		8,100.00
	8		J6		2,500.00		10,600.00
	10		J6	4,800.00			5,800.00
	11		J6		8,700.00		14,500.00
	17		J6		800.00		15,300.00
	23		J6		5,300.00		20,600.00
	24		J6	8,700.00			11,900.00

FIGURE 12-14   General Ledger and Accounts Payable Ledger after Posting

To verify that the sum of the accounts payable ledger balances equals the Accounts Payable balance, a **schedule of accounts payable** is prepared. This is an alphabetical or numerical listing of supplier accounts and balances, usually prepared at the end of the month. Note that suppliers whose account balance is zero are not included. Figure 12-15 shows the schedule of accounts payable for Northern Micro as of April 30.

Northern Micro Schedule of Accounts Payable April 30, 20--						
Compucraft, Inc.	$ 3	3	0	0	00
Datasoft	2	5	0	0	00
Printpro Corp.		8	0	0	00
Televax, Inc.	5	3	0	0	00
	$11	9	0	0	00

FIGURE 12-15   Schedule of Accounts Payable

This schedule is prepared from the list of supplier accounts in the accounts payable ledger. The total calculated in the schedule is compared with the balance in Accounts Payable in the general ledger. Note that the $11,900 total listed in the schedule equals the Accounts Payable balance shown in Figure 12-14. If the schedule total and the Accounts Payable balance do not agree, the error must be located and corrected. To find the error, use the following procedures.

STEP 1   Verify the total of the schedule.

STEP 2   Verify the postings to the accounts payable ledger.

STEP 3   Verify the postings to Accounts Payable in the general ledger.

PROFILES IN ACCOUNTING

Christy Rankin, Accounts Payable Representative

Christy Rankin credits good training and a willingness to continue to learn for her success as an accounts payable representative for a home builder. After 18 months at Davis Homes LLC, Christy finds her job challenging and rewarding. She uses what she learned in her college accounting classes, including computer accounting, every day at work.

This is Christy's first job since graduating with an Associate Degree in Business Management. She firmly believes her degree, along with the skills she learned in college, has helped her earn a better salary and will continue to pay off in the future.

Christy believes her college education provided her with a foundation and she feels that she is building her skills each day. Asked if she had any advice for today's students, Christy said "stick with it."

Learning Objectives	Key Points to Remember
1 **Define merchandise purchases transactions.**	For a merchandising business, purchases refers to merchandise acquired for resale. Major documents used in the purchasing process are the purchase requisition, purchase order, receiving report, and purchase invoice.
2 **Describe and use merchandise purchases accounts and compute gross profit.**	Four accounts are used in accounting for merchandise purchases transactions: 1. Purchases 2. Purchases Returns and Allowances 3. Purchases Discounts 4. Freight-In Cost of goods sold = beginning inventory + net purchases – ending inventory. Gross profit = net sales – cost of goods sold.
3 **Describe and use the accounts payable ledger.**	To post purchases transactions to the general ledger: **In the ledger account:** STEP 1 Enter the date of the transaction in the Date column. STEP 2 Enter the amount of the debit or credit in the Debit or Credit column. STEP 3 Enter the new balance in the Balance columns under Debit or Credit. STEP 4 Enter the journal page number from which each transaction is posted in the Posting Reference column. **In the journal:** STEP 5 Enter the ledger account number in the Posting Reference column of the journal for each transaction that is posted. An accounts payable ledger is a separate ledger containing an individual account payable for each supplier. To post from the general journal to the accounts payable ledger: **In the accounts payable ledger account:** STEP 1 Enter the date of the transaction in the Date column. STEP 2 Enter the amount of the debit or credit in the Debit or Credit column. STEP 3 Enter the new balance in the Balance column. STEP 4 Enter the journal page number from which each transaction is posted in the Posting Reference column. **In the journal:** STEP 5 Enter a slash (/) followed by a check mark (✓) in the Posting Reference column of the journal for each transaction that is posted. To post cash payments transactions to the general ledger: **In the ledger account:** STEP 1 Enter the date of the transaction in the Date column. STEP 2 Enter the amount of the debit or credit in the Debit or Credit column. STEP 3 Enter the new balance in the Balance columns under Debit or Credit. STEP 4 Enter the journal page number from which each transaction is posted in the Posting Reference column. **In the journal:** STEP 5 Enter the ledger account number in the Posting Reference column of the journal for each transaction that is posted.

Learning Objectives	Key Points to Remember
3 (continued)	To post cash payments transactions to the accounts payable ledger:
	In the accounts payable ledger account:
	STEP 1 Enter the date of the transaction in the Date column.
	STEP 2 Enter the amount of the debit or credit in the Debit or Credit column.
	STEP 3 Enter the new balance in the Balance column.
	STEP 4 Enter the journal page number from which each transaction is posted in the Posting Reference column.
	In the journal:
	STEP 5 Enter a slash (/) followed by a check mark (✓) in the Posting Reference column of the journal for each transaction that is posted.
4 **Prepare a schedule of accounts payable.**	The schedule of accounts payable is used to verify that the sum of the accounts payable ledger balances equals the Accounts Payable balance.

Reflection: Answering the Opening Question

Freight charges should be debited to Freight-In and added to the cost of the purchases. Trade discounts should not be entered in the accounts. Purchases should be debited for the net amount paid for the items after deducting trade discounts. Cash discounts should be credited to Purchases Discounts and deducted from the cost of the purchases. The amount of returned purchases should be credited to Purchases Returns and Allowances and deducted from the cost of the purchases.

DEMONSTRATION PROBLEM

Jodi Rutman operates a retail pharmacy called Rutman Pharmacy. The books of original entry include a general journal, general ledger, and accounts payable ledger. The following are the transactions related to purchases and cash payments for the month of June 20--.

June 1	Purchased merchandise from Sullivan Co. on account, $234.20. Invoice no. 71 dated June 1, terms 2/10, n/30.
2	Issued check no. 536 for payment of June rent (Rent Expense), $1,000.00.
5	Purchased merchandise from Amfac Drug Supply on account, $562.40. Invoice no. 196 dated June 2, terms 1/15, n/30.
7	Purchased merchandise from University Drug Co. on account, $367.35. Invoice no. 914A dated June 5, terms 3/10 eom, n/30.
9	Issued check no. 537 to Sullivan Co. in payment of invoice no. 71 less 2% discount.

12   Received a credit memo from Amfac Drug Supply for merchandise returned that was purchased on June 5, $46.20.

14   Purchased merchandise from Mutual Drug Co. on account, $479.40. Invoice no. 745 dated June 14, terms 2/10, n/30.

15   Received a credit memo from University Drug Co. for merchandise returned that was purchased on June 7, $53.70.

16   Issued check no. 538 to Amfac Drug Supply in payment of invoice no. 196 less the credit memo of June 12 and less 1% discount.

23   Issued check no. 539 to Mutual Drug Co. in payment of invoice no. 745 less 2% discount.

27   Purchased merchandise from Flites Pharmaceuticals on account, $638.47. Invoice no. 675 dated June 27, terms 2/10 eom, n/30.

29   Issued check no. 540 to Dolgin Candy Co. for a cash purchase of merchandise, $270.20.

30   Issued check no. 541 to Vashon Medical Supply in payment of invoice no. 416, $1,217.69. No discount allowed.

REQUIRED

1.   Enter the transactions in a general journal (Page 7).

2.   Post from the journal to the general ledger accounts and the accounts payable ledger. Account numbers and June 1 balances are as indicated in the accounts presented below. Then, update the account balances.

3.   Prepare a schedule of accounts payable from the accounts payable ledger in the problem. Verify that the total of accounts payable in the schedule equals the June 30 balance of Accounts Payable in the general ledger.

Solution

1.

GENERAL JOURNAL					PAGE 7
	DATE	DESCRIPTION	POST REF.	DEBIT	CREDIT
1	20— June 1	Purchases	501	2 3 4 20		1
2		Accounts Payable / Sullivan Co.	202/✓		2 3 4 20	2
3		Invoice No. 71				3
4						4
5	2	Rent Expense	521	1 0 0 0 00		5
6		Cash	101		1 0 0 0 00	6
7		Check No. 536				7
8						8
9	5	Purchases	501	5 6 2 40		9
10		Accounts Payable / Amfac Drug Supply	202/✓		5 6 2 40	10
11		Invoice No. 196				11
12						12
13	7	Purchases	501	3 6 7 35		13
14		Accounts Payable / University Drug Co.	202/✓		3 6 7 35	14
15		Invoice No. 914A				15
16						16

(continued)

1. (continued)

	Date	Description	Post. Ref.	Debit				Credit				
17	9	Accounts Payable / Sullivan Co.	202/✓	2	3	4	20					17
18		Cash	101					2	2	9	52	18
19		Purchases Discounts	501.2							4	68	19
20		Check No. 537										20
21												21
22	12	Accounts Payable / Amfac Drug Supply	202/✓		4	6	20					22
23		Purchases Returns and Allowances	501.1						4	6	20	23
24		Returned merchandise										24
25												25
26	14	Purchases	501		4	7	9	40				26
27		Accounts Payable / Mutual Drug Co.	202/✓					4	7	9	40	27
28		Invoice No. 745										28
29												29

GENERAL JOURNAL   PAGE 8

	Date		Description	Post. Ref.	Debit				Credit				
1	20-- June	15	Accounts Payable / University Drug Co.	202/✓		5	3	70					1
2			Purchases Returns and Allowances	501.1						5	3	70	2
3			Returned merchandise										3
4													4
5		16	Accounts Payable / Amfac Drug Supply	202/✓		5	1	6	20				5
6			Cash	101					5	1	1	04	6
7			Purchases Discounts	501.2							5	16	7
8			Check No. 538										8
9													9
10		23	Accounts Payable / Mutual Drug Co.	202/✓		4	7	9	40				10
11			Cash	101					4	6	9	81	11
12			Purchases Discounts	501.2							9	59	12
13			Check No. 539										13
14													14
15		27	Purchases	501		6	3	8	47				15
16			Accounts Payable / Flites Pharmaceuticals	202/✓					6	3	8	47	16
17			Invoice No. 675										17
18													18
19		29	Purchases	501		2	7	0	20				19
20			Cash	101					2	7	0	20	20
21			Check No. 540										21
22													22
23		30	Accounts Payable / Vashon Medical Supply	202/✓	1	2	1	7	69				23
24			Cash	101					1	2	1	7	69	24
25			Check No. 541										25
26													26

2.

ACCOUNT: Cash ACCOUNT NO. 101

DATE		ITEM	POST REF.	DEBIT	CREDIT	BALANCE DEBIT	BALANCE CREDIT
20-- June	1	Balance	✓			9 1 8 0 00	
	2		J7		1 0 0 0 00	8 1 8 0 00	
	9		J7		2 2 9 52	7 9 5 0 48	
	16		J8		5 1 1 04	7 4 3 9 44	
	23		J8		4 6 9 81	6 9 6 9 63	
	29		J8		2 7 0 20	6 6 9 9 43	
	30		J8		1 2 1 7 69	5 4 8 1 74	

ACCOUNT: Accounts Payable ACCOUNT NO. 202

DATE		ITEM	POST REF.	DEBIT	CREDIT	BALANCE DEBIT	BALANCE CREDIT
20-- June	1	Balance	✓				1 2 1 7 69
	1		J7		2 3 4 20		1 4 5 1 89
	5		J7		5 6 2 40		2 0 1 4 29
	7		J7		3 6 7 35		2 3 8 1 64
	9		J7	2 3 4 20			2 1 4 7 44
	12		J7	4 6 20			2 1 0 1 24
	14		J7		4 7 9 40		2 5 8 0 64
	15		J8	5 3 70			2 5 2 6 94
	16		J8	5 1 6 20			2 0 1 0 74
	23		J8	4 7 9 40			1 5 3 1 34
	27		J8		6 3 8 47		2 1 6 9 81
	30		J8	1 2 1 7 69			9 5 2 12

ACCOUNT: Purchases ACCOUNT NO. 501

DATE		ITEM	POST REF.	DEBIT	CREDIT	BALANCE DEBIT	BALANCE CREDIT
20-- June	1	Balance	✓			13 8 2 6 25	
	1		J7	2 3 4 20		14 0 6 0 45	
	5		J7	5 6 2 40		14 6 2 2 85	
	7		J7	3 6 7 35		14 9 9 0 20	
	14		J7	4 7 9 40		15 4 6 9 60	
	27		J8	6 3 8 47		16 1 0 8 07	
	29		J8	2 7 0 20		16 3 7 8 27	

ACCOUNT: Purchases Returns and Allowances ACCOUNT NO. 501.1

DATE		ITEM	POST REF.	DEBIT	CREDIT	BALANCE DEBIT	BALANCE CREDIT
20-- June	1	Balance	✓				3 1 2 63
	12		J7		4 6 20		3 5 8 83
	15		J8		5 3 70		4 1 2 53

(continued)

PART 3   Accounting for a Merchandising Business

2. (continued)

ACCOUNT: Purchases Discounts ACCOUNT NO. 501.2

DATE	ITEM	POST REF.	DEBIT	CREDIT	BALANCE DEBIT	BALANCE CREDIT
June 1	Balance	✔				2 1 1 45
9		J7		4 68		2 1 6 13
16		J8		5 16		2 2 1 29
23		J8		9 59		2 3 0 88

ACCOUNT: Rent Expense ACCOUNT NO. 521

DATE	ITEM	POST REF.	DEBIT	CREDIT	BALANCE DEBIT	BALANCE CREDIT
June 1	Balance	✔			5 0 0 0 00	
2		J7	1 0 0 0 00		6 0 0 0 00	

ACCOUNTS PAYABLE LEDGER

NAME: Amfac Drug Supply

DATE	ITEM	POST REF.	DEBIT	CREDIT	BALANCE
June 5		J7		5 6 2 40	5 6 2 40
12		J7	4 6 20		5 1 6 20
16		J8	5 1 6 20		--

NAME: Flites Pharmaceuticals

DATE	ITEM	POST REF.	DEBIT	CREDIT	BALANCE
June 27		J8		6 3 8 47	6 3 8 47

NAME: Mutual Drug Co.

DATE	ITEM	POST REF.	DEBIT	CREDIT	BALANCE
June 14		J7		4 7 9 40	4 7 9 40
23		J8	4 7 9 40		--

NAME: Sullivan Co.

DATE	ITEM	POST REF.	DEBIT	CREDIT	BALANCE
June 1		J7		2 3 4 20	2 3 4 20
9		J7	2 3 4 20		--

NAME: University Drug Co.

DATE	ITEM	POST REF.	DEBIT	CREDIT	BALANCE
June 7		J7		3 6 7 35	3 6 7 35
15		J8	5 3 70		3 1 3 65

NAME: Vashon Medical Supply

DATE	ITEM	POST REF.	DEBIT	CREDIT	BALANCE
June 1	Balance	✔			1 2 1 7 69
30		J8	1 2 1 7 69		--

3.

Rutman Pharmacy					
Schedule of Accounts Payable					
June 30, 20--					
Flites Pharmaceuticals	$	6	3	8	47
University Drug Co.		3	1	3	65
	$	9	5	2	12
Proof					
Balance of Accounts Payable, June 30	$	9	5	2	12

On-Line Learning Tools

For more information, visit: http://heintz.swlearning.com

The Heintz & Parry product web site is designed specifically for **COLLEGE ACCOUNTING, 18e.** The features include downloadable student resources and an interactive study center, organized by chapter, which contains learning objectives, web links, on-line quizzes with automatic feedback, and more.

KEY TERMS

accounts payable ledger, (424)   A separate ledger containing an individual account payable for each supplier.

cost of goods sold, (421)   The difference between the goods available for sale and the ending inventory.

cost of merchandise sold, (421)   See cost of goods sold.

FOB destination, (420)   Shipping terms indicating that transportation charges are paid by the seller.

FOB shipping point, (420)   Shipping terms indicating that transportation charges are paid by the buyer.

gross margin, (421)   See gross profit.

gross profit, (421)   The difference between net sales and cost of goods sold.

invoice, (416)   A document prepared by the seller as a bill for the merchandise shipped. To the seller, this is a sales invoice. To the buyer, this is a purchase invoice.

purchase invoice, (416)   A document prepared by the seller as a bill for the merchandise shipped. To the buyer, this is a purchase invoice.

purchase order, (415)   A written order to buy goods from a specific vendor (supplier).

purchase requisition, (414)   A form used to request the purchase of merchandise or other property.

purchases, (414)   Merchandise acquired for resale to customers.

receiving report, (416)   A report indicating what has been received.

schedule of accounts payable, (430)   An alphabetical or numerical listing of supplier accounts and balances, usually prepared at the end of the month.

trade discount, (416)   A reduction from the list or catalog price offered to different classes of customers.

REVIEW QUESTIONS

(LO1)   1. Identify the major documents commonly used in the purchasing process.

(LO1)   2. Distinguish between a cash discount and a trade discount.

(LO2)   3. Describe how each of the following accounts is used: (1) Purchases, (2) Purchases Returns and Allowances, (3) Purchases Discounts, and (4) Freight-In.

(LO2)   4. How are cost of goods sold and gross profit computed?

(LO3)   5. What steps are followed in posting purchases from the general journal to the general ledger?

(LO3)   6. What steps are followed in posting purchases from the general journal to the accounts payable ledger?

(LO3)   7. What steps are used to post Purchases Returns and Allowances from the general journal to the general ledger and accounts payable ledger?

(LO3)   8. What steps are followed in posting cash payments from the general journal to the general ledger?

(LO3)   9. What steps are followed in posting cash payments from the general journal to the accounts payable ledger?

(LO4)   10. If the total of the schedule of accounts payable does not agree with the Accounts Payable balance, what procedures should be used to search for the error?

Self-Study Test Questions

True/False

1. In the purchasing process, the purchase invoice is the first document prepared. _____

2. A sales invoice prepared by the seller is called a purchase invoice by the buyer. _____

3. A trade discount is a reduction from the list or catalog price offered to different classes of customers. _____

4. Purchases Returns and Allowances is debited when merchandise is returned for credit. _____

5. FOB shipping point means that transportation charges are paid by the seller. _____

Multiple Choice

1. A purchase of merchandise for $300 with a trade discount of 10% would require a debit to purchases of _____

   (a) $330.   (c) $297.
   (b) $300.   (d) $270.

Self-Study Test Questions *(continued)*

2. In the income statement, Freight-In is   _____

   (a) added to purchases.
   (b) subtracted from purchases.
   (c) added to sales.
   (d) subtracted from cost of goods sold.

3. The difference between net sales and cost of goods sold is called   _____

   (a) gross profit.
   (b) net purchases.
   (c) goods available for sale.
   (d) the bottom line.

4. The difference between merchandise available for sale and the end-of-period merchandise   _____
   inventory is called

   (a) gross profit.
   (b) net purchases.
   (c) net sales.
   (d) cost of goods sold.

5. A purchase invoice for $1,200 with credit terms 2/10, n/30, and a return of $300   _____
   received by the seller prior to payment, is paid within the discount period. A check
   should be sent for

   (a) $1,200.
   (b) $882.
   (c) $900.
   (d) $810.

The answers to the Self-Study Test Questions are at the end of the text.

MANAGING YOUR WRITING

You are working as a summer intern at a rapidly growing organic food distributor. Part of your responsibility is to assist in the accounts payable department. You notice that most bills from suppliers are not paid within the discount period. The manager of accounts payable says the bills are organized by vendor, like the accounts payable ledger, and she is too busy to keep track of the discount periods. Besides, the owner has told her that the 1% and 2% discounts available are not worth worrying about.

Write a memo to the owner explaining why it is expensive not to take advantage of cash discounts on credit purchases. In addition, suggest a way to file (organize) supplier invoices so that they are paid within the discount period.

ETHICS CASE

Bob's Discount Auto Parts receives a cash discount of 2% from Auto Warehouse if they pay an invoice within 10 days. Bob, the owner, consistently sends payments 15 to 20 days after receiving the invoice and still deducts the amount of the discount. Last week Bob received a call from Auto Warehouse reminding him that in order to get the discount, an invoice must be paid within 10 days. When Bob received the next invoice, he dated the check exactly 10 days from the date of the invoice but didn't mail the check for another week. The Receivables Manager from Auto Warehouse called Bob and again reminded him that the check should be mailed by the 10th day in order to receive the 2% discount. When Bob received the next invoice he mailed it on time but post-dated the check for the following week.

(continued)

1. Are Bob's attempts to extend the discount period unethical?

2. What alternatives can Auto Warehouse take to prevent Bob's Discount Auto Parts from stretching the discount period?

3. Write a short note from Auto Warehouse to Bob's Discount Auto Parts explaining cash discounts and credit terms.

4. In small groups make a list of the advantages and disadvantages of offering cash discounts.

WEB WORK

As mentioned in the Chapter 11 question, many retailers are going on-line. More banks are on-line too. Many paychecks are direct deposited and people are seeing less and less physical currency. What happens to cash accounting when there is no more cash? If this sounds farfetched, take a look at the PNC Bank site. PNC Bank is only one of many banks that offers on-line banking.

Visit the Interactive Study Center on our web site at **http://heintz. swlearning.com** for special hotlinks to assist you in this assignment.

SERIES A EXERCISES

EXERCISE 12-1A **(LO1)** **PURCHASING DOCUMENTS AND FLOWCHART LABELING** A partially completed flowchart showing some of the major documents commonly used in the purchasing function of a merchandise business is presented below. Identify documents 1, 3, and 4.

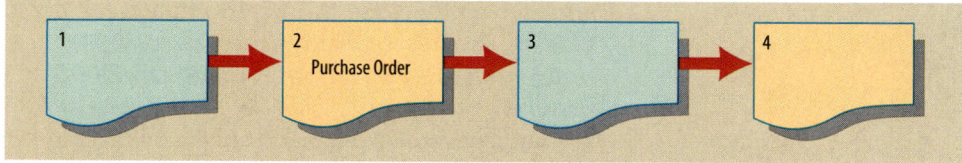

EXERCISE 12-2A **(LO1/2)**
2: $1,764

TRADE DISCOUNT AND CASH DISCOUNTS Merchandise was purchased on account from Jacob's Distributors on May 17. The purchase price was $2,000, subject to a 10% trade discount and credit terms of 2/10, n/30.

1. Calculate the net amount to record the invoice, subject to the 10% trade discount.

2. Calculate the amount to be paid on this invoice within the discount period.

3. Journalize the purchase of the merchandise on May 17 in a general journal. Journalize the payment on May 27 (within the discount period).

EXERCISE 12-3A **(LO2)**
3(c): Purchases Discounts: $70

PURCHASE TRANSACTIONS AND T ACCOUNTS Using T accounts for Cash, Accounts Payable, Purchases, Purchases Returns and Allowances, Purchases Discounts, and Freight-In, enter the following purchase transactions. Identify each transaction with its corresponding letter. Use a new set of T accounts for each set of transactions, 1–4.

1. Purchase of merchandise with cash.

    (a) Merchandise is purchased for cash, $1,500.

    (b) Merchandise listed at $3,500, subject to a trade discount of 15%, is purchased for cash.

2. Purchase of merchandise on account with credit terms.

   (a) Merchandise is purchased on account, credit terms 2/10, n/30, $2,000.

   (b) Merchandise is purchased on account, credit terms 3/10, n/30, $1,200.

   (c) Payment is made on invoice (a) within the discount period.

   (d) Payment is made on invoice (b) too late to receive the cash discount.

3. Purchase of merchandise on account with return of merchandise.

   (a) Merchandise is purchased on account, credit terms 2/10, n/30, $4,000.

   (b) Merchandise is returned for credit before payment is made, $500.

   (c) Payment is made within the discount period.

4. Purchase of merchandise with freight-in.

   (a) Merchandise is purchased on account, $2,500 plus freight charges of $100. Terms of the sale were FOB shipping point.

   (b) Payment is made for the cost of merchandise and the freight charge.

EXERCISE 12-4A   **(LO2)**
Cost of goods sold: $74,500

COMPUTING GROSS PROFIT The following data were taken from the accounts of Delhi Hardware, a small retail business. Determine the gross profit.

Sales	$113,000
Sales returns and allowances	800
Merchandise inventory, January 1	34,000
Purchases during the period	76,000
Purchases returns and allowances during the period	4,000
Purchases discounts taken during the period	3,000
Freight-in on merchandise purchased during the period	1,500
Merchandise inventory, December 31	30,000

EXERCISE 12-5A   **(LO3)**
May 9: Dr. Purchases, $2,300

JOURNALIZING PURCHASES TRANSACTIONS
Journalize the following transactions in a general journal.

May 3   Purchased merchandise from Cintron, $6,500. Invoice no. 321, dated May 1, terms n/30.

9   Purchased merchandise from Mitsui, $2,300. Invoice no. 614, dated May 8, terms 2/10, n/30.

18   Purchased merchandise from Aloha Distributors, $4,200. Invoice no. 180, dated May 15, terms 1/15, n/30.

23   Purchased merchandise from Soto, $6,300. Invoice no. 913, dated May 22, terms 1/10, n/30.

EXERCISE 12-6A   **(LO3)**
Ending Accounts Payable balance: $8,600

JOURNALIZING PURCHASES RETURNS AND ALLOWANCES AND POSTING TO GENERAL LEDGER AND ACCOUNTS PAYABLE LEDGER Using page 3 of a general journal and the following general ledger and accounts payable ledger accounts, journalize and post the following transactions.

July 7   Merchandise returned to Starcraft Industries, $700.

15   Merchandise returned to XYZ, Inc., $450.

27   Merchandise returned to Datamagic, $900.

(continued)

General Ledger

Account No.	Account	Balance July 1, 20--
202	Accounts Payable	$10,650
501.1	Purchases Returns and Allowances	

Accounts Payable Ledger

Name	Balance, July 1, 20--
Datamagic	$2,600
Starcraft Industries	4,300
XYZ, Inc.	3,750

EXERCISE 12-7A   **(LO3)**
Sept. 12: Cr. Cash, $6,930

JOURNALIZING CASH PAYMENTS TRANSACTIONS Enter the following cash payments transactions in a general journal.

Sept. 5   Issued check no. 318 to Clinton Corp. for merchandise purchased August 28, $6,000, terms 2/10, n/30. Payment is made within the discount period.

12   Issued check no. 319 to Mitchell Company for merchandise purchased September 2, $7,500, terms 1/10, n/30. A credit memo had been received on September 8 from Mitchell Company for merchandise returned, $500. Payment is made within the discount period after deduction for the return dated September 8.

19   Issued check no. 320 to Expert Systems for merchandise purchased August 19, $4,100, terms n/30.

27   Issued check no. 321 to Graphic Data for merchandise purchased September 17, $9,000, terms 2/10, n/30. Payment is made within the discount period.

EXERCISE 12-8A   **(LO4)**
Total Accounts Payable: $14,370

SCHEDULE OF ACCOUNTS PAYABLE Ryan's Express, a retail business, had the following beginning balances and purchases and payments activity in its accounts payable ledger during October. Prepare a schedule of accounts payable for Ryan's Express as of October 31, 20--.

Accounts Payable Ledger

Name	Balance Oct. 1, 20--	Purchases	Payments
Columbia Products	$4,350	$3,060	$2,060
Favorite Fashions	4,910	1,970	2,600
Rustic Legends	5,130	2,625	3,015

SERIES A PROBLEMS

PROBLEM 12-9A   **(LO3)**
Purchases balance: $20,790

PURCHASES TRANSACTIONS J. B. Speck, owner of Speck's Galleria, made the following purchases of merchandise on account during the month of September.

Sept. 3   Purchase invoice no. 415, $2,650, from Smith Distributors.

8   Purchase invoice no. 132, $3,830, from Michaels Wholesaler.

11   Purchase invoice no. 614, $3,140, from J. B. Sanders & Co.

18   Purchase invoice no. 329, $2,250, from Bateman & Jones, Inc.

23   Purchase invoice no. 767, $4,160, from Smith Distributors.

27   Purchase invoice no. 744, $1,980, from Anderson Company.

30   Purchase invoice no. 652, $2,780, from Michaels Wholesaler.

REQUIRED

1. Record the transactions in a general journal.

2. Post from the general journal to the general ledger accounts and to the accounts payable ledger accounts. Use account numbers as shown in the chapter.

PROBLEM 12-10A   **(LO3)**
Accounts Payable balance:
$1,900

CASH PAYMENTS TRANSACTIONS Sam Santiago operates a retail variety store. The books include a general journal and an accounts payable ledger.

Selected account balances on May 1 are as follows:

General Ledger

Cash	$40,000
Accounts Payable	20,000

Accounts Payable Ledger

Fantastic Toys	$5,200
Goya Outlet	3,800
Mueller's Distributors	3,600
Van Kooning	7,400

The following are the transactions related to cash payments for the month of May.

May 1	Issued check no. 426 in payment of May rent (Rent Expense), $2,400.
3	Issued check no. 427 to Mueller's Distributors in payment of merchandise purchased on account, $3,600 less a 3% discount. Check was written for $3,492.
7	Issued check no. 428 to Van Kooning in partial payment of merchandise purchased on account, $5,500. A cash discount was not allowed.
12	Issued check no. 429 to Fantastic Toys for merchandise purchased on account, $5,200, less a 1% discount. Check was written for $5,148.
15	Issued check no. 430 to City Power and Light (Utilities Expense), $1,720.
18	Issued check no. 431 to A-1 Warehouse for a cash purchase of merchandise, $4,800.
26	Issued check no. 432 to Goya Outlet for merchandise purchased on account, $3,800, less a 2% discount. Check was written for $3,724.
30	Issued check no. 433 to Mercury Transit Company for freight charges on merchandise purchased (Freight-In), $1,200.
31	Issued check no. 434 to Town Merchants for a cash purchase of merchandise, $3,000.

REQUIRED

1. Enter the transactions in a general journal.

2. Post from the general journal to the general ledger and the accounts payable ledger. Use general ledger account numbers as shown in the chapter.

PROBLEM 12-11A   **(LO3)**

Cash balance: $8,830

PURCHASES AND CASH PAYMENTS TRANSACTIONS Freddy Flint owns a small retail business called Flint's Fantasy. The cash account has a balance of $20,000 on July 1. The following transactions occurred during July.

July 1	Issued check no. 414 in payment of July rent, $1,500.
1	Purchased merchandise on account from Tang's Toys, invoice no. 311, $2,700, terms 2/10, n/30.
3	Purchased merchandise on account from Sillas & Company, invoice no. 812, $3,100, terms 1/10, n/30.
5	Returned merchandise purchased from Tang's Toys, receiving a credit memo on the amount owed, $500.
8	Purchased merchandise on account from Daisy's Dolls, invoice no. 139, $1,900, terms 2/10, n/30.
11	Issued check no. 415 to Tang's Toys for merchandise purchased on account, less return of July 5 and less 2% discount.
13	Issued check no. 416 to Sillas & Company for merchandise purchased on account, less 1% discount.
15	Returned merchandise purchased from Daisy's Dolls, receiving a credit memo on the amount owed, $400.
18	Issued check no. 417 to Daisy's Dolls for merchandise purchased on account, less return of July 15 and less 2% discount.
25	Purchased merchandise on account from Allied Business, invoice no. 489, $2,450, terms n/30.
26	Purchased merchandise on account from Tang's Toys, invoice no. 375, $1,980, terms 2/10, n/30.
29	Purchased merchandise on account from Sillas & Company, invoice no. 883, $3,460, terms 1/10, n/30.
31	Freddy Flint withdrew cash for personal use, $2,000. Issued check no. 418.
31	Issued check no. 419 to Glisan Distributors for a cash purchase of merchandise, $975.

REQUIRED

1. Enter the transactions in a general journal.

2. Post from the journal to the general ledger and accounts payable ledger accounts. Use general ledger account numbers as shown in the chapter.

PROBLEM 12-12A   **(LO4)**

Accounts Payable balance,
Tang's Toys: $1,980

SCHEDULE OF ACCOUNTS PAYABLE Based on the information provided in Problem 12-11A, prepare a schedule of accounts payable for Flint's Fantasy as of July 31, 20--. Verify that the accounts payable account balance in the general ledger agrees with the schedule of accounts payable total.

SERIES B EXERCISES

EXERCISE 12-1B   **(LO1)**   **PURCHASING DOCUMENTS AND FLOWCHART LABELING** A flowchart showing some of the major documents commonly used in the purchasing function of a merchandise business is presented below. Briefly describe each document.

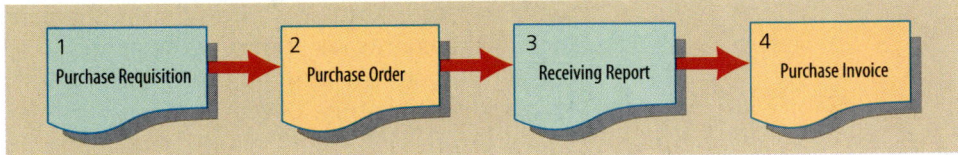

EXERCISE 12-2B   **(LO1)**
2: $4,365

TRADE DISCOUNT AND CASH DISCOUNTS Merchandise was purchased on account from Grant's Distributors on June 12. The purchase price was $5,000, subject to a 10% trade discount and credit terms of 3/10, n/30.

1. Calculate the net amount to record the invoice, subject to the 10% trade discount.

2. Calculate the amount to be paid on this invoice within the discount period.

3. Journalize the purchase of the merchandise on June 12 and the payment on June 22 (within the discount period) in a general journal.

EXERCISE 12-3B   **(LO2)**
3(c): Purchases Discounts, $100

PURCHASE TRANSACTIONS AND T ACCOUNTS Using T accounts for Cash, Accounts Payable, Purchases, Purchases Returns and Allowances, Purchases Discounts, and Freight-In, enter the following purchase transactions. Identify each transaction with its corresponding letter. Use a new set of T accounts for each set of transactions, 1–4.

1. Purchase of merchandise with cash.

    (a)   Merchandise is purchased for cash, $2,300.

    (b)   Merchandise listed at $4,000, subject to a trade discount of 10%, is purchased for cash.

2. Purchase of merchandise on account with credit terms.

    (a)   Merchandise is purchased on account, credit terms 2/10, n/30, $4,000.

    (b)   Merchandise is purchased on account, credit terms 3/10, n/30, $2,800.

    (c)   Payment is made on invoice (a) within the discount period.

    (d)   Payment is made on invoice (b) too late to receive the cash discount.

3. Purchase of merchandise on account with return of merchandise.

    (a)   Merchandise is purchased on account, credit terms 2/10, n/30, $5,600.

    (b)   Merchandise is returned for credit before payment is made, $600.

    (c)   Payment is made within the discount period.

4. Purchase of merchandise with freight-in.

    (a)   Merchandise is purchased on account, $3,800 plus freight charges of $200. Terms of the sale were FOB shipping point.

    (b)   Payment is made for the cost of merchandise and the freight charge.

EXERCISE 12-4B   (LO2)
Cost of goods sold: $76,700

COMPUTING GROSS PROFIT The following data were taken from the accounts of Burnside Bedknobs, a retail business. Determine the gross profit.

Sales	$116,500
Sales returns and allowances	1,100
Merchandise inventory, January 1	30,000
Purchases during the period	100,000
Purchases returns and allowances during the period	2,000
Purchases discounts taken during the period	2,800
Freight-in on merchandise purchased during the period	1,500
Merchandise inventory, December 31	50,000

EXERCISE 12-5B   (LO3)
Jan. 12: Dr. Purchases, $9,000

JOURNALIZING PURCHASES TRANSACTIONS

Journalize the following transactions in a general journal.

Jan. 3   Purchased merchandise from Feng, $6,000. Invoice no. 416, dated January 1, terms 2/10, n/30.

12   Purchased merchandise from Miranda, $9,000. Invoice no. 624, dated January 10, terms n/30.

19   Purchased merchandise from J. B. Barba, $6,400. Invoice no. 190, dated January 18, terms 1/10, n/30.

26   Purchased merchandise from Ramirez, $3,700. Invoice no. 923, dated January 25, terms 1/15, n/30.

EXERCISE 12-6B   (LO3)
Ending Accounts Payable balance: $6,950

JOURNALIZING PURCHASES RETURNS AND ALLOWANCES AND POSTING TO GENERAL LEDGER AND ACCOUNTS PAYABLE LEDGER Using page 3 of a general journal and the following general ledger accounts and accounts payable ledger accounts, journalize and post the following transactions.

Mar. 5   Merchandise returned to Tower Industries, $500.

11   Merchandise returned to A & D Arms, $625.

23   Merchandise returned to Mighty Mansion, $275.

General Ledger

Account No.	Account	Balance Mar. 1, 20--
202	Accounts Payable	$8,350
501.1	Purchases Returns and Allowances	

Accounts Payable Ledger

Name	Balance, Mar. 1, 20--
A & D Arms	$2,300
Mighty Mansion	1,450
Tower Industries	4,600

EXERCISE 12-7B   (LO3)
Apr. 19: Cr. Cash, $4,950

JOURNALIZING CASH PAYMENTS TRANSACTIONS Enter the following cash payments transactions in a general journal.

April 5   Issued check no. 429 to Standard Industries for merchandise purchased April 3, $8,000, terms 2/10, n/30. Payment is made within the discount period.

19   Issued check no. 430 to Finest Company for merchandise purchased April 10, $5,300, terms 1/10, n/30. A credit memo had been received on April 12 from Finest Company for merchandise returned, $300. Payment is made within the discount period after deduction for the return dated April 12.

21 Issued check no. 431 to Funny Follies for merchandise purchased March 21, $3,250, terms n/30.

29 Issued check no. 432 to Classic Data for merchandise purchased April 20, $7,000, terms 2/10, n/30. Payment is made within the discount period.

EXERCISE 12-8B **(LO4)**
Total accounts payable: $10,565

SCHEDULE OF ACCOUNTS PAYABLE Crystal's Candles, a retail business, had the following balances and purchases and payments activity in its accounts payable ledger during November. Prepare a schedule of accounts payable for Crystal's Candles as of November 30, 20--.

Accounts Payable Ledger

Name	Balance Nov. 1, 20--	Purchases	Payments
Carl's Candle Wax	$4,135	$ 955	$1,610
Handy Supplies	3,490	1,320	1,850
Wishy Wicks	3,300	1,905	1,080

SERIES B PROBLEMS

PROBLEM 12-9B **(LO3)**
Purchases balance: $18,515

PURCHASES TRANSACTIONS Ann Benton, owner of Benton's Galleria, made the following purchases of merchandise on account during the month of October.

Oct. 2 Purchase invoice no. 321, $1,950, from Boggs Distributors.

7 Purchase invoice no. 152, $2,915, from Wolfs Wholesaler.

10 Purchase invoice no. 634, $3,565, from Komuro & Co.

16 Purchase invoice no. 349, $2,845, from Fritz & McCord, Inc.

24 Purchase invoice no. 587, $3,370, from Boggs Distributors.

26 Purchase invoice no. 764, $2,240, from Sanderson Company.

31 Purchase invoice no. 672, $1,630, from Wolfs Wholesaler.

REQUIRED

1. Record the transactions in a general journal.

2. Post from the general journal to the general ledger accounts and to the accounts payable ledger accounts. Use account numbers as shown in the chapter.

PROBLEM 12-10B **(LO3)**
Accounts Payable balance: $600

CASH PAYMENTS TRANSACTIONS Kay Zembrowski operates a retail variety store. The books include a general journal and an accounts payable ledger. Selected account balances on May 1 are as follows:

General Ledger

Cash	$40,000
Accounts Payable	20,000

Accounts Payable Ledger

Cortez Distributors	$4,200
Indra & Velga	6,800
Toy Corner	4,600
Troutman Outlet	4,400

(continued)

The following are the transactions related to cash payments for the month of May.

May 1   Issued check no. 326 in payment of May rent (Rent Expense), $2,600.

4   Issued check no. 327 to Cortez Distributors in payment of merchandise purchased on account, $4,200 less a 3% discount. Check was written for $4,074.

7   Issued check no. 328 to Indra & Velga in partial payment of merchandise purchased on account, $6,200. A cash discount was not allowed.

11   Issued check no. 329 to Toy Corner for merchandise purchased on account, $4,600 less a 1% discount. Check was written for $4,554.

15   Issued check no. 330 to County Power and Light (Utilities Expense), $1,500.

19   Issued check no. 331 to Builders Warehouse for a cash purchase of merchandise, $3,500.

25   Issued check no. 332 to Troutman Outlet for merchandise purchased on account, $4,400 less a 2% discount. Check was written for $4,312.

30   Issued check no. 333 to Rapid Transit Company for freight charges on merchandise purchased (Freight-In), $800.

31   Issued check no. 334 to City Merchants for a cash purchase of merchandise, $2,350.

REQUIRED

1. Enter the transactions in a general journal.

2. Post from the general journal to the general ledger and the accounts payable ledger. Use general ledger account numbers as shown in the chapter.

PROBLEM 12-11B   **(LO3)**

Cash balance: $9,240

PURCHASES AND CASH PAYMENTS TRANSACTIONS Debbie Mueller owns a small retail business called Debbie's Doll House. The cash account has a balance of $20,000 on July 1. The following transactions occurred during July.

July 1   Issued check no. 314 for July rent, $1,400.

1   Purchased merchandise on account from Topper's Toys, invoice no. 211, $2,500, terms 2/10, n/30.

3   Purchased merchandise on account from Jones & Company, invoice no. 812, $2,800, terms 1/10, n/30.

5   Returned merchandise purchased from Topper's Toys receiving a credit memo on the amount owed, $400.

8   Purchased merchandise on account from Downtown Merchants, invoice no. 159, $1,600, terms 2/10, n/30.

11   Issued check no. 315 to Topper's Toys for merchandise purchased on account, less return of July 5 and less 2% discount.

13   Issued check no. 316 to Jones & Company for merchandise purchased on account, less 1% discount.

15   Returned merchandise purchased from Downtown Merchants receiving a credit memo on the amount owed, $600.

18   Issued check no. 317 to Downtown Merchants for merchandise purchased on account, less return of July 15 and less 2% discount.

25   Purchased merchandise on account from Columbia Products, invoice no. 468, $3,200, terms n/30.

26   Purchased merchandise on account from Topper's Toys, invoice no. 395, $1,430, terms 2/10, n/30.

29   Purchased merchandise on account from Jones & Company, invoice no. 853, $2,970 terms 1/10, n/30.

31   Mueller withdrew cash for personal use, $2,500. Issued check no. 318.

31   Issued check no. 319 to Burnside Warehouse for a cash purchase of merchandise, $1,050.

REQUIRED

1.   Enter the transactions in a general journal.

2.   Post from the journal to the general ledger and accounts payable ledger accounts. Use general ledger account numbers as shown in the chapter.

PROBLEM 12-12B   (LO4)
Accounts Payable balance,
Topper's Toys: $1,430

SCHEDULE OF ACCOUNTS PAYABLE Based on the information provided in Problem 12-11B, prepare a schedule of accounts payable for Debbie's Doll House as of July 31, 20--. Verify that the accounts payable account balance in the general ledger agrees with the schedule of accounts payable total.

MASTERY PROBLEM

Accounts Payable balance:
$10,000

Michelle French owns and operates Books and More, a retail book store. Selected account balances on June 1 are as follows:

General Ledger

Cash	$32,200.00
Accounts Payable	2,000.00
Michelle French, Drawing	18,000.00
Purchases	67,021.66
Purchases Returns and Allowances	2,315.23
Purchases Discounts	905.00
Freight-In	522.60
Rent Expense	3,125.00
Utilities Expense	1,522.87

Accounts Payable Ledger

North-Eastern Publishing Co.	$2,000.00

The following purchases and cash payment transactions took place during the month of June.

June 1   Purchased books on account from Irving Publishing Company, $2,100. Invoice no. 101, terms 2/10, n/30, FOB destination.

2   Issued check no. 300 to North-Eastern Publishing Company for goods purchased on May 23, terms 2/10, n/30, $1,960 (the $2,000 invoice amount less the 2% discount).

3   Purchased books on account from Broadway Publishing, Inc., $2,880. Invoice no. 711, subject to 20% trade discount, and invoice terms of 3/10, n/30, FOB shipping point.

(continued)

3   Issued check no. 301 to Mayday Shipping for delivery from Broadway Publishing Company, $250.

4   Issued check no. 302 for June rent, $625.

8   Purchased books on account from North-Eastern Publishing Company, $5,825. Invoice no. 268, terms 2/eom, n/60, FOB destination.

10   Received a credit memo from Irving Publishing Company, $550. Books had been returned because the covers were on upside down.

13   Issued check no. 304 to Broadway Publishing, Inc., for the purchase made on June 3. (Check no. 303 was voided because an error was made in preparing it.)

28   Made the following purchases:

Invoice No.	Company	Amount	Terms
579	Broadway Publishing, Inc.	$2,350	2/10, n/30 FOB destination
406	North-Eastern Publishing Co.	4,200	2/eom, n/60 FOB destination
964	Riley Publishing Co.	3,450	3/10, n/30 FOB destination

30   Issued check no. 305 to Taylor County Utility Co., for June utilities, $325.

30   French withdrew cash for personal use, $4,500. Issued check no. 306.

30   Issued check no. 307 to Irving Publishing Company for purchase made on June 1 less returns made on June 10.

30   Issued check no. 308 to North-Eastern Publishing Company for purchase made on June 8.

30   Issued check no. 309 for books purchased at an auction, $1,328.

REQUIRED

1. Enter the transactions in a general journal. (Begin with page 16.)

2. Post from the journal to the general ledger accounts and the accounts payable ledger. Use account numbers as indicated in the chapter.

3. Prepare a schedule of accounts payable.

4. If merchandise inventory was $35,523 on January 1 and $42,100 as of June 30, prepare the cost of goods sold section of the income statement for the six months ended June 30, 20--.

CHALLENGE PROBLEM

This problem challenges you to apply your cumulative accounting knowledge to move a step beyond the material in the chapter.

May 14: Cr. Purchases Discounts, $9

Record the following transactions in a general journal.

May 4   Merchandise listed at $2,900, subject to a trade discount of 10%, is purchased on account, credit terms of 1/10, n/30, shipping terms FOB destination.

8   Merchandise purchased on May 4, listed at $520, is returned for credit.

14   Partial payment is made for the merchandise purchased on May 4, listed at $1,000, less 1% discount.

June 3   Payment is made of the balance due on the May 4 purchase.

Chapter 12 Appendix
The Net-Price Method
of Recording Purchases

OBJECTIVES

Careful study of this appendix should enable you to:

LO1 Describe the net-price method of recording purchases.

LO2 Record purchases and cash payments using the net-price method.

NET-PRICE METHOD

LO1 Describe the net-price method of recording purchases.

In this chapter, purchases were recorded using the **gross-price method**. Under this method, purchases are recorded at the gross amount, regardless of available cash discounts. An alternative approach to accounting for purchases is the **net-price method**. Under this method, purchases are recorded at the net amount, assuming that all available cash discounts will be taken.

RECORDING WITH THE NET-PRICE METHOD

LO2 Record purchases and cash payments using the net-price method.

To compare the two methods, reconsider the purchase for $100 on account, with credit terms of 2/10, n/30, on page 419. At the time of the purchase, the following entries are made under the two methods:

Gross-Price			Net-Price		
Purchases	100.00		Purchases	98.00*	
Accounts Payable		100.00	Accounts Payable		98.00

*$100 – $2 (2% cash discount)

If the payment for the merchandise is made within the discount period, the entries are:

Gross-Price			Net-Price		
Accounts Payable	100.00		Accounts Payable	98.00	
Cash		98.00	Cash		98.00
Purchases Discounts		2.00			

If payment for the merchandise is not made until after the discount period, the entries are:

Gross-Price			Net-Price		
Accounts Payable	100.00		Accounts Payable	98.00	
Cash		100.00	Purchases Discounts Lost	2.00	
			Cash		100.00

Note that under the net-price method a new account, Purchases Discounts Lost, is used. Purchases Discounts Lost is a temporary owners' equity account used to record cash discounts lost on purchases.

Purchases Discounts Lost

Debit	Credit
for discounts lost because of late payment of invoices	

Purchases Discounts Lost represents a finance charge for postponing the payment for merchandise. If the balance in this account is large relative to the amount of gross purchases, management should review its cash payment procedures. Purchases Discounts Lost is reported as an expense on the income statement.

Learning Objectives	Key Points to Remember
1 Describe the net-price method of recording purchases.	Under the net-price method, purchases are recorded at the net amount, assuming all available cash discounts will be taken.
2 Record purchases and cash payments using the net-price method.	Assume a purchase is made for $100 on account, with credit terms of 2/10, n/30. Under the net-price method, the entry at the time of purchase is:

Purchases   98.00
  Accounts Payable   98.00

If payment is made within the discount period, the entry is:

Accounts Payable   98.00
  Cash   98.00

If payment is not made until after the discount period, the entry is:

Accounts Payable   98.00
Purchases Discounts Lost 2.00
  Cash   100.00

KEY TERMS

gross-price method, (451)   Under this method, purchases are recorded at the gross amount.

net-price method, (451)   Under this method, purchases are recorded at the net amount, assuming all available cash discounts are taken.

SERIES A EXERCISE

EXERCISE 12Apx-1A (LO2)
1. Apr. 11: Dr. Purchases
Discounts, $20

PURCHASES TRANSACTIONS—GROSS-PRICE AND NET-PRICE METHODS
Romero's Heating and Cooling had the following transactions during April.

April 2   Purchased merchandise on account from Alanon Valve for $1,000, terms 2/10, n/30.

5   Purchased merchandise on account from Leon's Garage for $1,400, terms 1/10, n/30.

11   Paid the amount due to Alanon Valve for the purchase on April 2.

25   Paid the amount due to Leon's Garage for the purchase on April 5.

1.   Prepare general journal entries for these transactions using the gross-price method.

2.   Prepare general journal entries for these transactions using the net-price method.

SERIES B EXERCISE

EXERCISE 12Apx-1B (LO2)
2. May 27: Dr. Purchases
Discounts Lost, $12

PURCHASES TRANSACTIONS—GROSS-PRICE AND NET-PRICE METHODS
Gloria's Repair Shop had the following transactions during May.

May 2   Purchased merchandise on account from Delgado's Supply for $900, terms 2/10, n/30.

6   Purchased merchandise on account from Goro's Auto Care for $1,200, terms 1/10, n/30.

11   Paid the amount due to Delgado's Supply for the purchase on May 2.

27   Paid the amount due to Goro's Auto Care for the purchase on May 6.

1.   Prepare general journal entries for these transactions using the gross-price method.

2.   Prepare general journal entries for these transactions using the net-price method.

DIGITAL IMAGING GROUP

Special Journals

As Evan Taylor's business has grown, the hours required for his part-time bookkeeper, Betty Jenkins, to maintain the books for Parkway Pet Supplies have grown substantially. Recently, she informed Evan that the increased hours were starting to affect her college studies, so they needed to adopt more efficient accounting methods. She seemed particularly annoyed about the sales, cash receipts, purchases, and cash payments transactions. Each week, she has to write the same account names in the general journal and then post to the same accounts in the general ledger hundreds of times for these transactions. Betty suggested that one way to improve the recording process would be to use the special journals she has studied in her accounting classes. What are special journals? How would they make the record keeping more efficient?

Careful study of this chapter should enable you to:

LO1 Describe, explain the purpose of, and identify transactions recorded in special journals.

LO2 Describe and use the sales journal.

LO3 Describe and use the cash receipts journal.

LO4 Describe and use the purchases journal.

LO5 Describe and use the cash payments journal.

Chapters 11 and 12 demonstrated how to account for sales, cash receipts, purchases, and cash payments in a merchandising business. We also saw how to use accounts receivable and accounts payable ledgers to keep track of individual customer and supplier accounts. In this chapter, we continue to study how to account for sales, cash receipts, purchases, and cash payments, but our objective is to find a way to be more efficient. We will learn how to use four special journals that enable us to achieve this objective.

SPECIAL JOURNALS

LO1 Describe, explain the purpose of, and identify transactions recorded in special journals.

A **special journal** is a journal designed for recording only certain kinds of transactions. A special journal can be created for almost any kind of transaction. The types of special journals a business uses should depend on the types of transactions that occur most frequently for a business. The more transactions of a specific type that occur, the more likely a special journal of that type would be useful for the business.

The primary purpose of using special journals is to save time journalizing and posting transactions. In a general journal, we recorded transactions by writing the account names, debit and credit amounts, and an explanation for each transaction on several lines in the journal. In contrast, most transactions are entered in a special journal on a single line, with the debit and credit amounts indicated in special columns provided for each account. This enables substantial time saving. The posting process also is more efficient. Using the general journal, each transaction is posted separately to the appropriate general ledger accounts. With a special journal, summary postings of column totals are made to appropriate accounts on a periodic basis.

Of course, even if a business uses special journals, there still is a need for a general journal. For example, transactions that occur infrequently, and adjusting and closing entries, usually are recorded in the general journal.

LEARNING KEY: The special journals and general journal all are books of original entry. Each transaction is recorded in only <u>one</u> of these journals.

Four special journals commonly used by businesses are as follows:

- Sales journal
- Cash receipts journal
- Purchases journal
- Cash payments journal

Figure 13-1 identifies the types of transactions recorded in each of the four special journals and the general journal. You might find it helpful to refer back to Figure 13-1 as the four special journals are introduced in this chapter.

Type of Journal	Type of Transactions Recorded
Sales journal	All sales of merchandise on account
Cash receipts journal	All cash receipts
Purchases journal	All purchases of merchandise on account
Cash payments journal	All cash payments
General journal	All other transactions

FIGURE 13-1 Types of Journals and Transactions

In the following sections, we will examine the journalizing and posting process using each of the four special journals.

SALES JOURNAL

LO2 Describe and use the sales journal.

A **sales journal** is a special journal used to record only sales of merchandise on account. To illustrate the journalizing and posting of sales transactions in the sales journal, the sales transactions and general journal entries for Northern Micro from Chapter 11 are reproduced below.

April 4   Made sale no. 133C on account to Enrico Lorenzo, $1,520 plus $76 sales tax.

10   Made sale no. 134C on account to Brenda Myers, $440 plus $22 sales tax.

18   Made sale no. 105D on account to Edith Walton, $980 plus $49 sales tax.

21   Made sale no. 202B on account to Susan Chang, $620 plus $31 sales tax.

24   Made sale no. 162A on account to Heidi Schwitzer, $1,600 plus $80 sales tax.

4	Apr.	4	Accounts Receivable/E. Lorenzo		1	5	9	6	00									4
5			Sales								1	5	2	0	00			5
6			Sales Tax Payable										7	6	00			6
7			Sale No. 133C															7
8																		8
9		10	Accounts Receivable/B. Myers			4	6	2	00									9
10			Sales									4	4	0	00			10
11			Sales Tax Payable										2	2	00			11
12			Sale No. 134C															12
13																		13
14		18	Accounts Receivable/E. Walton		1	0	2	9	00									14
15			Sales										9	8	0	00		15
16			Sales Tax Payable										4	9	00			16
17			Sale No. 105D															17
18																		18
19		21	Accounts Receivable/S. Chang			6	5	1	00									19
20			Sales									6	2	0	00			20
21			Sales Tax Payable										3	1	00			21
22			Sale No. 202B															22
23																		23
24		24	Accounts Receivable/H. Schwitzer		1	6	8	0	00									24
25			Sales								1	6	0	0	00			25
26			Sales Tax Payable										8	0	00			26
27			Sale No. 162A															27

FIGURE 13-2 Sales Entered in General Journal

Notice that each of these five entries involved the same three accounts. The same account titles were recorded five times. Similarly, to post these entries to the general ledger, five separate postings would be made to each of the three accounts, a total of fifteen postings.

LEARNING KEY: Use a sales journal only for recording sales of merchandise on account.

Remember that sales returns and allowances are recorded in the general journal, as illustrated in Chapter 11, not in the sales journal.

These transactions can be recorded more efficiently by using a sales journal. To illustrate, reconsider the five sales made on account by Northern Micro. They are entered in the sales journal in Figure 13-3. The sales journal provides separate columns for Accounts Receivable Debit, Sales Credit, and Sales Tax Payable Credit, the three accounts used repeatedly in the general journal in Figure 13-2. A sale is recorded in the sales journal by entering the following information:

1. Date

2. Sale number

3. Customer

4. Dollar amounts

There is no need to enter any general ledger account titles, since they appear in the column headings.

	DATE	SALE NO.	TO WHOM SOLD	POST REF.	ACCOUNTS RECEIVABLE DEBIT	SALES CREDIT	SALES TAX PAYABLE CREDIT	
1	20-- Apr. 4	133C	Enrico Lorenzo		1 5 9 6 00	1 5 2 0 00	7 6 00	1
2	10	134C	Brenda Myers		4 6 2 00	4 4 0 00	2 2 00	2
3	18	105D	Edith Walton		1 0 2 9 00	9 8 0 00	4 9 00	3
4	21	202B	Susan Chang		6 5 1 00	6 2 0 00	3 1 00	4
5	24	162A	Heidi Schwitzer		1 6 8 0 00	1 6 0 0 00	8 0 00	5

SALES JOURNAL — PAGE 6

FIGURE 13-3   Northern Micro Sales Journal

The illustrations of posting sales here and of posting other transactions later in the chapter are for a manual accounting system. With a computerized system, the journal, general ledger, and any subsidiary ledger can be updated simultaneously when a transaction is entered. (See pp. 474–477)

The sales journal in Figure 13-3 is designed for a company, like Northern Micro, that charges sales tax. For a wholesaler or any other company that does not charge sales tax, a sales journal like that in Figure 13-4 would be sufficient. In this case, there is only a single amount column headed Accounts Receivable Debit/Sales Credit. With no sales tax, the Accounts Receivable Debit and Sales Credit amounts are identical for each sale. Thus only a single column is needed.

DATE	SALE NO.	TO WHOM SOLD	POST REF.	ACCOUNTS RECEIVABLE DEBIT/ SALES CREDIT

SALES JOURNAL — PAGE 1

FIGURE 13-4   Sales Journal Without Sales Tax

Posting from the Sales Journal

Posting from the sales journal also is very efficient. Each general ledger account used in the sales journal requires only one posting each period. Figure 13-5 illustrates the general ledger posting process for Northern Micro's sales journal for the month of April.

The following steps are used to post from the sales journal to the general ledger at the end of each month, as indicated in Figure 13-5.

In the sales journal:

STEP 1   Total the amount columns, verify that the total of the debit column equals the total of the credit columns, and rule the columns.

In the ledger account:

STEP 2   Enter the date of the transaction in the Date column.

STEP 3   Enter the amount of the debit or credit in the Debit or Credit column.

STEP 4   Enter the new balance in the Balance columns under Debit or Credit.

STEP 5   Enter the initial "S" and the journal page number in the Posting Reference column.

In the sales journal:

STEP 6   Enter the ledger account number immediately below the column totals for each account that is posted.

> The main difference between posting the sales journal and posting the general journal to the general ledger is step 1—totaling and verifying the amount columns. The remaining steps 2–6 are essentially the same as steps 1–5 used to post the general journal.

SALES JOURNAL   Page 6

Date	Sale No.	To Whom Sold	Post Ref.	Accounts Receivable Debit	Sales Credit	Sales Tax Payable Credit
20--						
Apr. 4	133C	Enrico Lorenzo		1,596.00	1,520.00	76.00
10	134C	Brenda Myers		462.00	440.00	22.00
18	105D	Edith Walton		1,029.00	980.00	49.00
21	202B	Susan Chang		651.00	620.00	31.00
24	162A	Heidi Schwitzer		1,680.00	1,600.00	80.00
				5,418.00	5,160.00	258.00	**1**
				(122)	(401)	(231)	**6** **3**

1 Debit total: $5,418

Credit total: $5,160
                       258
                    $5,418

GENERAL LEDGER (Partial)

ACCOUNT   Accounts Receivable   ACCOUNT NO. 122

Date	Item	Post Ref.	Debit	Credit	Balance Debit	Balance Credit
20--						
Apr. 1	Bal.	✔			12,000.00	
2 30	**5**	S6	5,418.00		17,418.00 **4**	

ACCOUNT   Sales Tax Payable   ACCOUNT NO. 231

Date	Item	Post Ref.	Debit	Credit	Balance Debit	Balance Credit
20--						
2 Apr. 30	**5**	S6		258.00		258.00 **4**

ACCOUNT   Sales   ACCOUNT NO. 401

Date	Item	Post Ref.	Debit	Credit	Balance Debit	Balance Credit
20--						
Apr. 1	Bal.	✔				27,000.00
2 30	**5**	S6		5,160.00		32,160.00 **4**

FIGURE 13-5   Posting the Sales Journal to the General Ledger

As we saw in Chapter 11, Northern Micro also needs a record of the accounts receivable from *individual customers*. Figure 13-6 illustrates the use of the accounts receivable ledger. The accounts receivable ledger is posted *daily* so that current information is available for each customer at all times. The following steps are used to post from the sales journal to the accounts receivable ledger, as shown in Figure 13-6.

In the accounts receivable ledger account:

STEP 1 Enter the date of the transaction in the Date column.

STEP 2 Enter the amount of the debit or credit in the Debit or Credit column.

STEP 3 Enter the new balance in the Balance column.

STEP 4 Enter the initial "S" and the journal page number in the Posting Reference column.

In the sales journal:

STEP 5 Enter a check mark (✓) in the Posting Reference column of the journal for each transaction that is posted.

Note the relationship between the sales journal, accounts receivable ledger, and general ledger. All individual entries in the sales journal are posted to the accounts receivable ledger. The totals of all entries in the sales journal are posted to the general ledger accounts. After the posting of the accounts receivable ledger and the general ledger is completed, the total of the accounts receivable ledger balances should equal the Accounts Receivable balance in the general ledger.

> *The accounts receivable ledger also can be posted from the source document used to make the sales journal entry. For example, sales ticket #134C (see Figure 11-2) could be used to post that sale to Brenda Myers' account in the accounts receivable ledger. In this case, 134C would be inserted in the Posting Reference column of her account.*

> *Note what happens if the accounts receivable ledger is posted daily and the general ledger is posted at the end of the month. The accounts receivable ledger total will equal the general ledger Accounts Receivable total only at the end of the month.*

LEARNING KEY: The total of the accounts receivable ledger balances must equal the Accounts Receivable balance in the general ledger.

CASH RECEIPTS JOURNAL

LO3 Describe and use the cash receipts journal.

A **cash receipts journal** is a special journal used to record only cash receipts transactions. To illustrate its use, we continue with the transactions of Northern Micro. Northern Micro's cash receipts journal for the month of April is shown in Figure 13-7, with the following transactions.

Apr. 14 Received cash on account from Enrico Lorenzo for sale no. 133C, $1,596.

20 Received cash on account from Brenda Myers for sale no. 134C, $462.

28 Received cash on account from Edith Walton for sale no. 105D, $1,029.

30 Cash sales for the month are $3,600 plus tax of $180.

30 Bank credit card sales for the month are $2,500 plus tax of $125. Bank credit card expenses on these sales are $100.

30 Received cash for rent revenue, $600.

30 Borrowed cash from the bank by signing a note, $3,000.

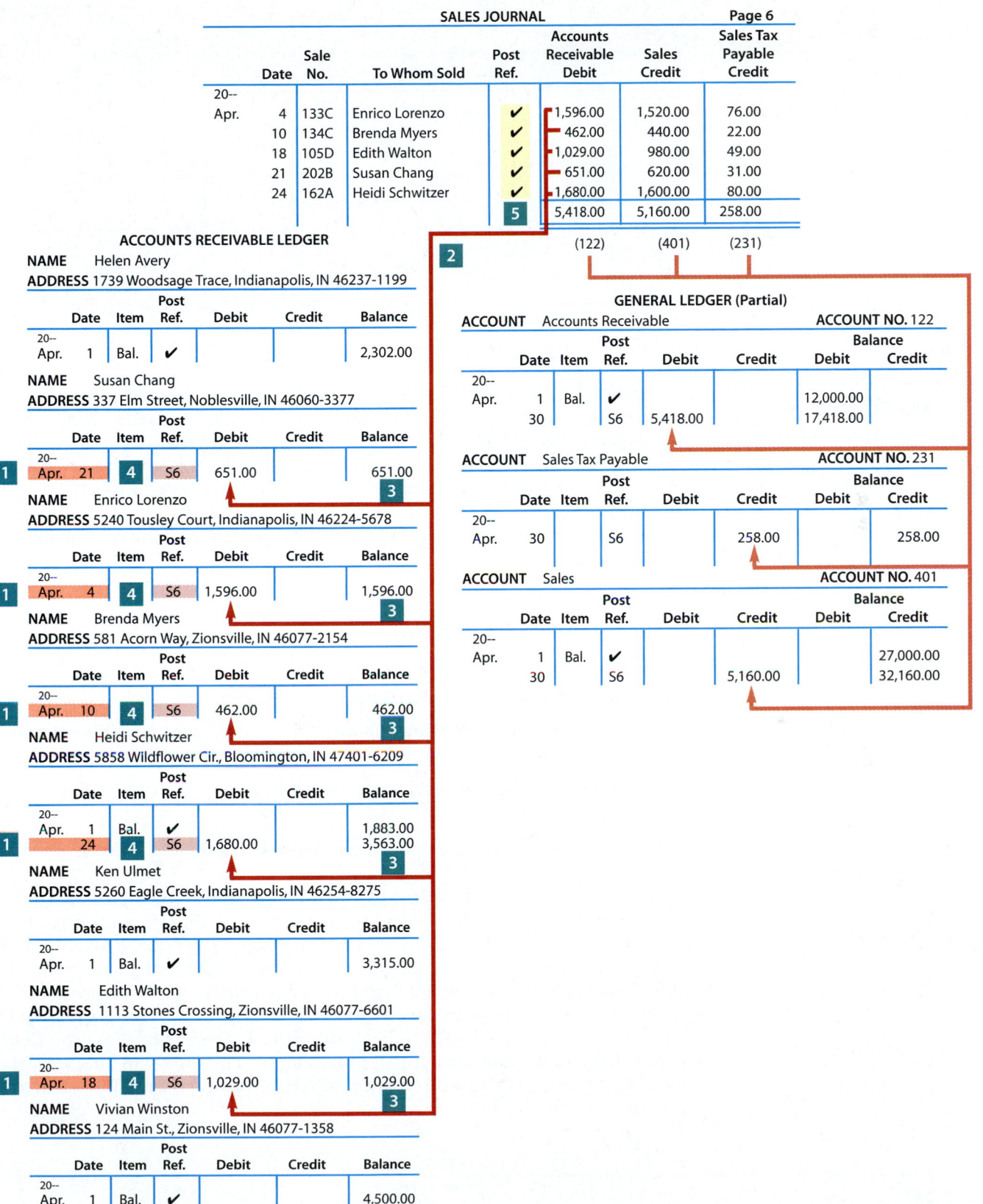

FIGURE 13-6   Posting the Sales Journal to the Accounts Receivable Ledger

	CASH RECEIPTS JOURNAL					
	DATE		ACCOUNT CREDITED	POST REF.	GENERAL CREDIT	
	20--					
1	Apr.	14	Enrico Lorenzo			1
2		20	Brenda Myers			2
3		28	Edith Walton			3
4		30				4
5		30				5
6		30	Rent Revenue		6 0 0 00	6
7		30	Notes Payable		3 0 0 0 00	7
8						8

FIGURE 13-7 Northern Micro Cash Receipts Journal (left side)

LEARNING KEY: Use a cash receipts journal to streamline journalizing and posting of cash receipts.

Northern Micro's cash receipts journal provides separate columns for Accounts Receivable Credit, Sales Credit, Sales Tax Payable Credit, Bank Credit Card Expense Debit, and Cash Debit. These are the accounts most frequently affected by Northern Micro's cash receipts transactions. In addition, a General Credit column is provided for credits to any other accounts affected by cash receipts transactions.

A cash receipt is recorded in the cash receipts journal by entering the following information.

1. Date
2. Account credited (if applicable)
3. Dollar amounts

The Account Credited column is used for two purposes:

1. To identify the customer name for any collection on account. This column is used whenever the Accounts Receivable Credit column is used.
2. To enter the appropriate account name whenever the General Credit column is used.

The Account Credited column is left blank whenever the entry is for cash sales or bank credit card sales.

The cash receipts journal in Figure 13-7 is designed for a company like Northern Micro, which charges sales tax, makes bank credit card sales, and offers no cash discounts. For a wholesaler who does not charge sales tax, makes no bank credit card sales, and offers cash discounts, a cash receipts journal like the one in Figure 13-8 would be used. Recall that a special journal should be designed with column headings for frequently used accounts. Thus, the cash receipts journal in Figure 13-8 has no Sales Tax Payable Credit or Bank Credit Card Expense Debit column. Instead, a Sales Discounts Debit column is provided. In this way, the common cash receipts transactions of the wholesaler can be easily and efficiently recorded.

SALES JOURNAL PAGE 1

	DATE		ACCOUNT CREDITED	POST REF.	GENERAL CREDIT	ACCOUNTS RECEIVABLE CREDIT	SALES CREDIT	SALES DISCOUNTS DEBIT	CASH DEBIT	
1										1

FIGURE 13-8 Cash Receipts Journal Without Sales Tax

	ACCOUNTS RECEIVABLE CREDIT				SALES CREDIT				SALES TAX PAYABLE CREDIT			BANK CREDIT CARD EXPENSE DEBIT			CASH DEBIT					
																				PAGE 7
1	1	5	9	6	00											1	5	9	6	00	1
2		4	6	2	00												4	6	2	00	2
3	1	0	2	9	00											1	0	2	9	00	3
4						3	6	0	0	00	1	8	0	00			3	7	8	0	00	4
5						2	5	0	0	00	1	2	5	00	1	0	0	00	2	5	2	5	00	5
6																	6	0	0	00	6
7																	3	0	0	0	00	7
8																					8

FIGURE 13-7   Northern Micro Cash Receipts Journal (right side)

Posting from the Cash Receipts Journal

The cash receipts journal is posted to the general ledger in two stages, as illustrated in Figure 13-9. First, on a daily basis, the individual amounts in the General Credit column are posted. Second, at the end of the month, the totals of each of the other amount columns are posted.

A BROADER VIEW

Improving Efficiency— The Power of Computerized Bookkeeping

In this chapter, we see many examples of the ways in which special journals can make the bookkeeping process more efficient. Yet these efficiency gains pale by comparison with the power of computerized bookkeeping. By means of a single keyboard entry, journals, general and subsidiary ledgers, customer and supplier accounts, periodic financial reports, and more can be updated. You can even pay bills when due electronically as part of the system.

A good example of computerized bookkeeping software is Peachtree.® This software utilizes the one entry–many reports feature. The system makes entries using the keyboard, then tracks the effects on the financial status of the business. Software like Peachtree can produce income statements, balance sheets, reports of expenses by vendor or revenues by customer, and many other types of reports and graphs.

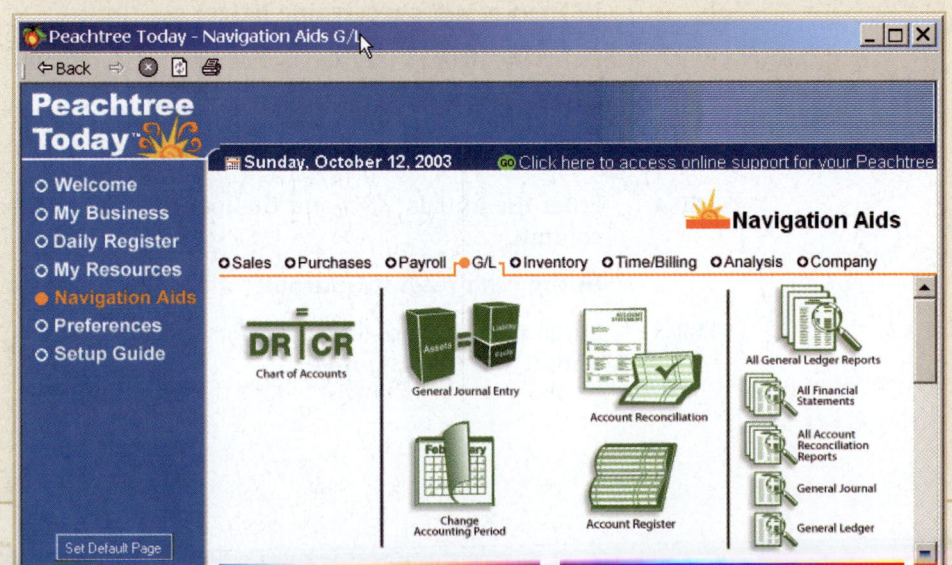

To post the General Credit column, on a daily basis:

In the ledger account:

STEP 1   Enter the date of the transaction in the Date column.

STEP 2   Enter the amount of the debit or credit in the Debit or Credit column.

STEP 3   Enter the new balance in the Balance columns under Debit or Credit.

STEP 4   Enter the initials "CR" and the journal page number in the Posting Reference column.

In the cash receipts journal:

STEP 5   Enter the ledger account number in the Posting Reference column for each account that is posted.

To post the other amount columns, at the end of the month:

In the cash receipts journal:

STEP 6   Total the amount columns, verify that the total of the debit columns equals the total of the credit columns, and rule the columns.

In the ledger account:

STEP 7   Enter the date in the Date column.

STEP 8   Enter the amount of the debit or credit in the Debit or Credit column.

STEP 9   Enter the new balance in the Balance columns under Debit or Credit.

STEP 10   Enter the initials "CR" and the journal page number in the Posting Reference column.

In the cash receipts journal:

STEP 11   Enter the ledger account number immediately below the column totals for each account that is posted.

STEP 12   Enter a check mark (✓) in the Posting Reference column for the cash sales and bank credit card sales, and immediately below the General Credit column.

The general ledger accounts affected by the cash receipts transactions are now up to date. Postings to the accounts receivable ledger also must be made. These postings are made daily. Figure 13-10 illustrates the posting procedures, as follows:

In the accounts receivable ledger account:

STEP 1   Enter the date of the transaction in the Date column.

STEP 2   Enter the amount of the debit or credit in the Debit or Credit column.

STEP 3   Enter the new balance in the Balance column.

STEP 4   Enter the initials "CR" and the journal page number in the Posting Reference column.

In the cash receipts journal:

STEP 5   Enter a check mark (✓) in the Posting Reference column of the journal for each transaction that is posted.

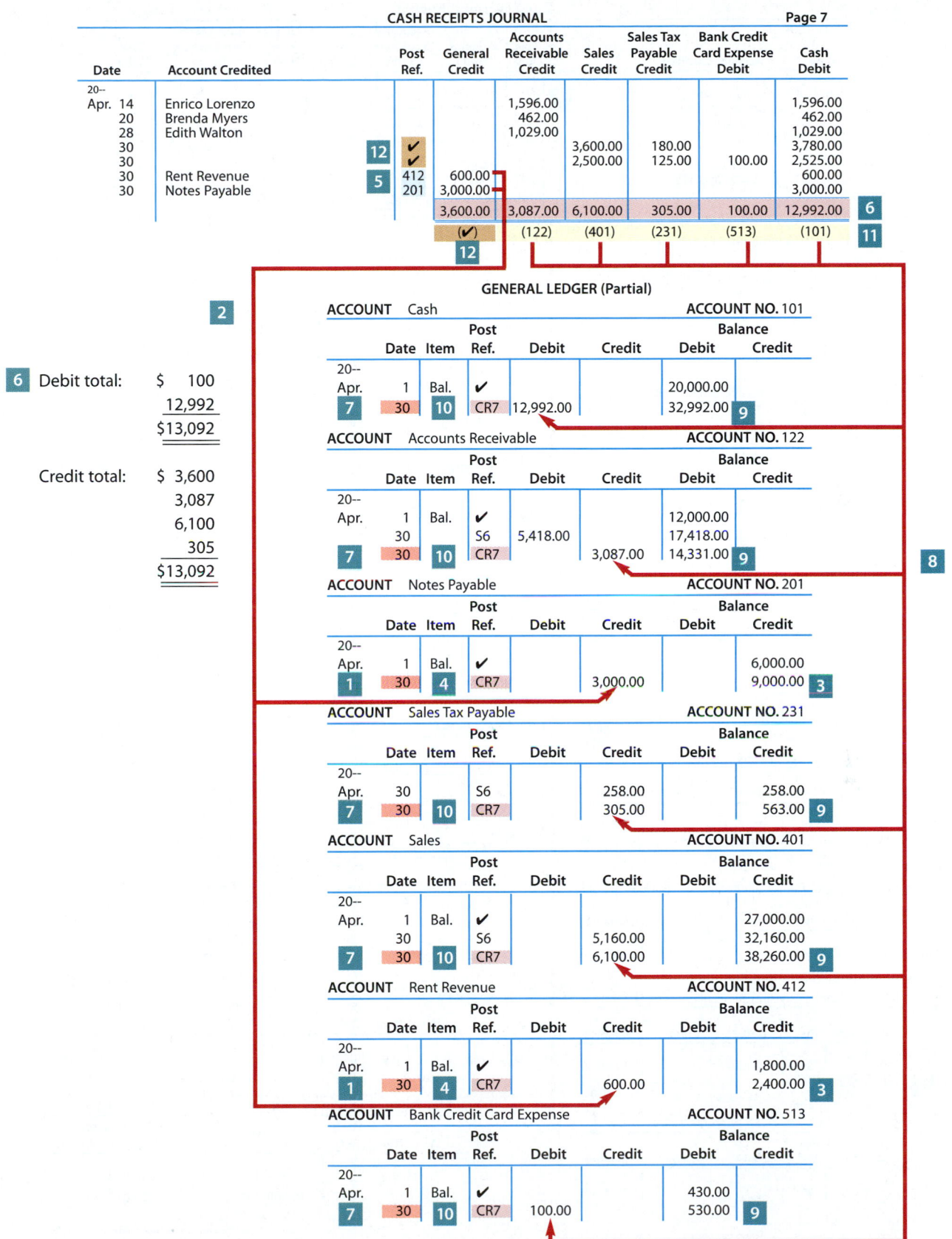

FIGURE 13-9   Posting the Cash Receipts Journal to the General Ledger

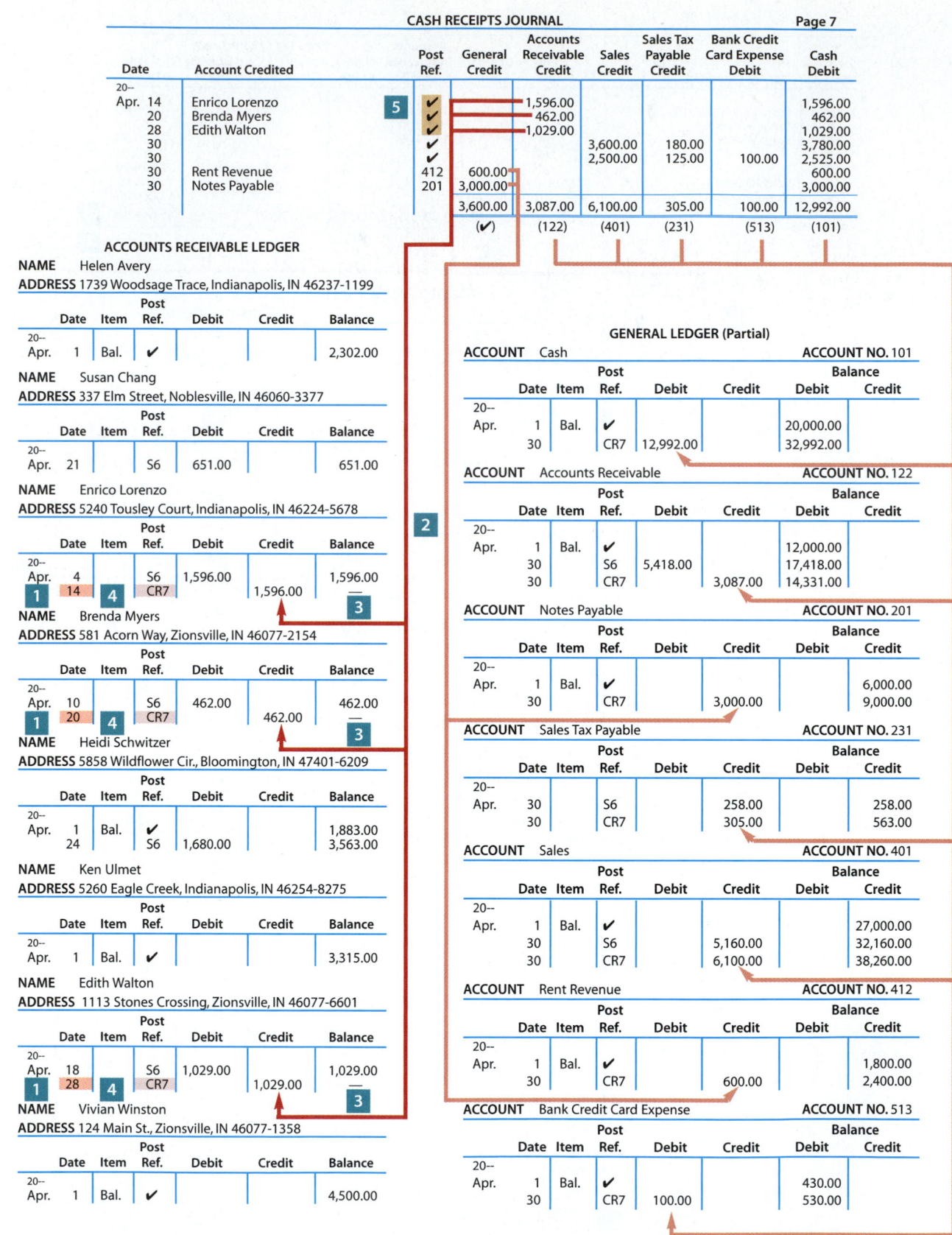

FIGURE 13-10 Posting the Cash Receipts Journal to the Accounts Receivable Ledger

PURCHASES JOURNAL

LO4 Describe and use the purchases journal.

A **purchases journal** is a special journal used to record only purchases of merchandise on account. To illustrate the journalizing and posting of purchases transactions in the purchases journal, we will continue with the transactions of Northern Micro. The following purchases on account are reproduced from Chapter 12.

April 4	Purchased merchandise from Compucraft, Inc., $3,300. Invoice no. 631, dated April 2, terms, n/30.
8	Purchased merchandise from Datasoft, $2,500. Invoice no. 927D, dated April 6, terms, n/30.
11	Purchased merchandise from EZX Corp., $8,700. Invoice no. 804, dated April 9, terms, 1/15, n/30.
17	Purchased merchandise from Printpro Corp., $800. Invoice no. 611, dated April 16, terms, n/30.
23	Purchased merchandise from Televax, Inc., $5,300. Invoice no. 1465, dated April 22, terms, 1/10, n/30.

 LEARNING KEY: Use a purchases journal only for recording purchases of merchandise on account.

Remember that purchases returns and allowances are recorded in the general journal, as illustrated in Chapter 12, not in the purchases journal.

As we saw with sales transactions, these purchases transactions can be recorded efficiently in a special journal, in this case a purchases journal. To illustrate, the five purchases on account of Northern Micro are entered in the purchases journal in Figure 13-11. Northern Micro's purchases journal has a single column for Purchases Debit/Accounts Payable Credit, the two accounts used repeatedly when these transactions are recorded in a general journal. A purchase is recorded in the purchases journal by entering the following information.

1. Date
2. Invoice number
3. Supplier (from whom purchased)
4. Dollar amount

There is no need to enter any general ledger account titles, since they appear in the column heading.

			PURCHASES JOURNAL		PAGE 8	
	DATE	INVOICE NO.	FROM WHOM PURCHASED	POST REF.	PURCHASES DEBIT/ACCOUNTS PAYABLE CREDIT	
1	20-- Apr. 4	631	Compucraft, Inc.		3 3 0 0 00	1
2	8	927D	Datasoft		2 5 0 0 00	2
3	11	804	EZX Corp.		8 7 0 0 00	3
4	17	611	Printpro Corp.		8 0 0 00	4
5	23	1465	Televax, Inc.		5 3 0 0 00	5
6					20 6 0 0 00	6

FIGURE 13-11 Northern Micro Purchases Journal

The purchases journal in Figure 13-11 is designed for a company like Northern Micro, whose suppliers generally pay freight charges. For a company that frequently pays freight charges as part of the purchase price of merchandise, a purchases journal like the one in Figure 13-12 would be used. In this case, there are three columns: (1) Purchases Debit, (2) Freight-In Debit, and (3) Accounts Payable Credit.

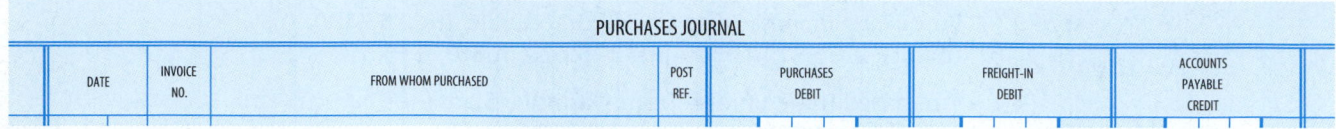

		PURCHASES JOURNAL				
DATE	INVOICE NO.	FROM WHOM PURCHASED	POST REF.	PURCHASES DEBIT	FREIGHT-IN DEBIT	ACCOUNTS PAYABLE CREDIT

FIGURE 13-12 Purchases Journal with Freight-In Column

Posting the Purchases Journal

Each general ledger account used in the purchases journal requires only one posting each period. Figure 13-13 illustrates the general ledger posting process for Northern Micro's purchases journal for the month of April.

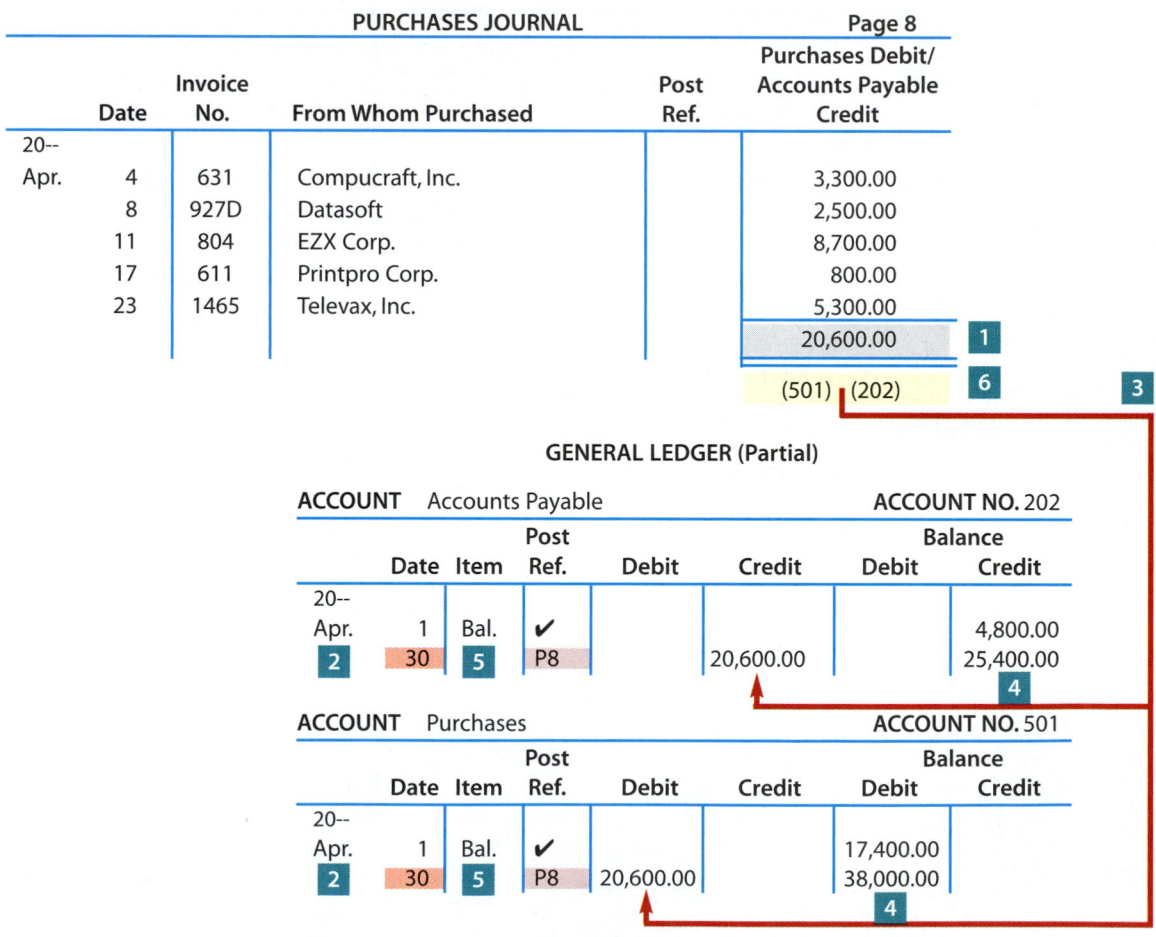

PURCHASES JOURNAL　　　　　　　　　　　　　　**Page 8**

Date	Invoice No.	From Whom Purchased	Post Ref.	Purchases Debit/ Accounts Payable Credit
20--				
Apr. 4	631	Compucraft, Inc.		3,300.00
8	927D	Datasoft		2,500.00
11	804	EZX Corp.		8,700.00
17	611	Printpro Corp.		800.00
23	1465	Televax, Inc.		5,300.00
				20,600.00
				(501) (202)

GENERAL LEDGER (Partial)

ACCOUNT Accounts Payable　　　　　　　　　　　**ACCOUNT NO.** 202

			Post			Balance	
Date	Item	Ref.	Debit	Credit	Debit	Credit
20--						
Apr. 1	Bal.	✔				4,800.00
30		P8		20,600.00		25,400.00

ACCOUNT Purchases　　　　　　　　　　　　　　**ACCOUNT NO.** 501

			Post			Balance	
Date	Item	Ref.	Debit	Credit	Debit	Credit
20--						
Apr. 1	Bal.	✔			17,400.00	
30		P8	20,600.00		38,000.00	

FIGURE 13-13 Posting the Purchases Journal to the General Ledger

The following steps are used to post from the purchases journal to the general ledger at the end of each month, as indicated in Figure 13-13.

In the purchases journal:

STEP 1   Total and rule the amount column.

In the ledger account:

STEP 2   Enter the date in the Date column.

STEP 3   Enter the amount of the debit or credit in the Debit or Credit column.

STEP 4   Enter the new balance in the Balance columns under Debit or Credit.

STEP 5   Enter the initial "P" and the journal page number in the Posting Reference column.

In the purchases journal:

STEP 6   Enter the Purchases and Accounts Payable account numbers immediately below the column total.

To maintain a record of the amount owed to each supplier, an accounts payable ledger is used. Figure 13-14 illustrates the use of the accounts payable ledger. The following steps are used to post from the purchases journal to the accounts payable ledger daily, as shown in Figure 13-14.

In the accounts payable ledger account:

STEP 1   Enter the date of the transaction in the Date column.

STEP 2   Enter the amount of the debit or credit in the Debit or Credit column.

STEP 3   Enter the new balance in the Balance column.

STEP 4   Enter the initial "P" and the journal page number in the Posting Reference column.

In the purchases journal:

STEP 5   Enter a check mark (✓) in the Posting Reference column of the journal for each transaction that is posted.

After the posting of the accounts payable ledger and general ledger is completed, the total of the accounts payable ledger balances should equal the Accounts Payable balance in the general ledger.

The main difference between posting the sales journal and posting the general journal to the general ledger is step 1—totaling and verifying the amount columns. The remaining steps 2–6 are essentially the same as steps 1–5 used to post the general journal.

Note what happens if the accounts payable ledger is posted daily and the general ledger is posted at the end of the month. The accounts payable ledger total will equal the general ledger Accounts Payable total only at the end of the month.

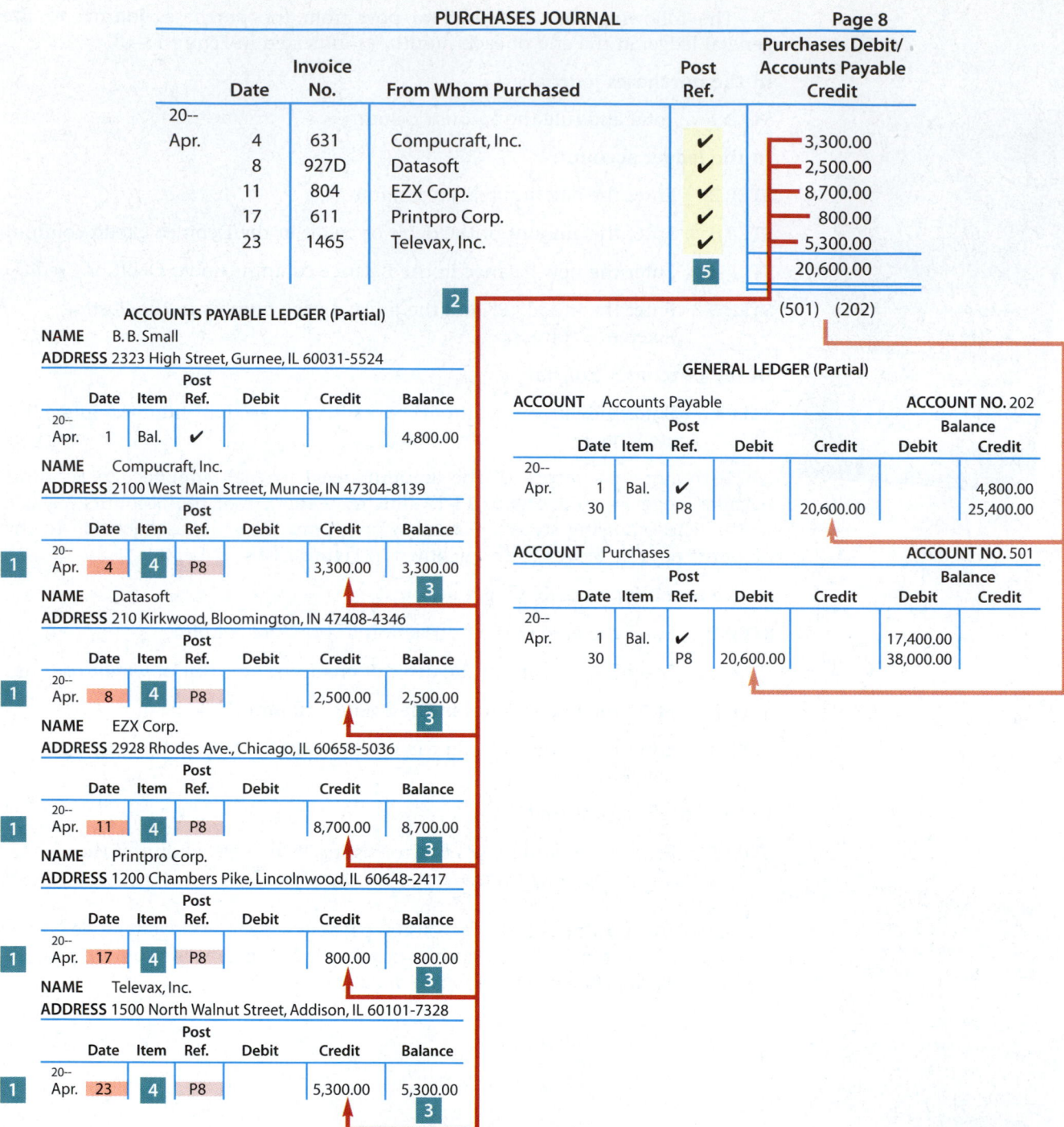

FIGURE 13-14   Posting the Purchases Journal to the Accounts Payable Ledger

CASH PAYMENTS JOURNAL

LO5 **Describe and use the cash payments journal.**

A **cash payments journal** is a special journal used to record only cash payments transactions. To illustrate its use, we will record the cash payments transactions of Northern Micro. Northern Micro's cash payments journal for the month of April is shown in Figure 13-15. Five types of cash payments transactions are shown:

1. Payment of an expense (April 2)

2. Cash purchase (April 4)

3. Payment of an account payable (April 10 and 24)

4. Payment of a note payable (April 14)

5. Withdrawal by the owner (April 22)

CASH PAYMENTS JOURNAL

	DATE		CK. NO.	ACCOUNT DEBITED	POST REF.	GENERAL DEBIT	
1	Apr.	2	307	Rent Expense		2 4 0 0 00	1
2		4	308				2
3		10	309	B. B. Small			3
4		14	310	Notes Payable		2 0 0 0 00	4
5		22	311	Gary L. Fishel, Drawing		1 6 0 0 00	5
6		24	312	EZX Corp.			6
7						6 0 0 0 00	7

FIGURE 13-15   Northern Micro Cash Payments Journal (left side)

	ACCOUNTS PAYABLE DEBIT	PURCHASES DEBIT	PURCHASES DISCOUNTS CREDIT	CASH CREDIT	
1				2 4 0 0 00	1
2		1 4 0 0 00		1 4 0 0 00	2
3	4 8 0 0 00			4 8 0 0 00	3
4				2 0 0 0 00	4
5				1 6 0 0 00	5
6	8 7 0 0 00		8 7 00	8 6 1 3 00	6
7	13 5 0 0 00	1 4 0 0 00	8 7 00	20 8 1 3 00	7

FIGURE 13-15   Northern Micro Cash Payments Journal (right side)

Northern Micro's cash payments journal provides separate columns for Accounts Payable Debit, Purchases Debit, Purchases Discounts Credit, and Cash Credit. These are the accounts most frequently affected by Northern Micro's cash payments transactions. In addition, a General Debit column is provided for

LEARNING KEY: Use a cash payments journal to streamline journalizing and posting of cash payments.

debits to any other accounts affected by cash payments transactions. For good internal control over cash payments, all payments (except out of petty cash) should be made by check. Therefore, the cash payments journal also includes a Check No. column.

A cash payment is recorded in the cash payments journal by entering the following information.

1. Date

2. Check number

3. Account debited (if applicable)

4. Dollar amounts

The Account Debited column is used for two purposes:

1. To identify the supplier name for any payment on account. This column is used whenever the Accounts Payable Debit column is used.

2. To enter the appropriate account name whenever the General Debit column is used.

Note that the column is left blank if the entry is for cash purchases.

Posting the Cash Payments Journal

The cash payments journal is posted to the general ledger in two stages, as illustrated in Figure 13-16. First, on a daily basis, the individual amounts in the General Debit column are posted. Second, at the end of the month, the totals of each of the other amount columns are posted.

To post the General Debit column, on a daily basis:

In the ledger account:

STEP 1   Enter the date of the transaction in the Date column.

STEP 2   Enter the amount of the debit or credit in the Debit or Credit column.

STEP 3   Enter the new balance in the Balance columns under Debit or Credit.

STEP 4   Enter the initials "CP" and the journal page number in the Posting Reference column.

In the cash payments journal:

STEP 5   Enter the ledger account number in the Posting Reference column for each account that is posted.

To post the other amount columns, at the end of the month:

In the cash payments journal:

STEP 6   Total the amount columns, verify that the total of the debit columns equals the total of the credit columns, and rule the columns.

In the ledger account:

STEP 7   Enter the date in the Date column.

STEP 8   Enter the amount of the debit or credit in the Debit or Credit column.

STEP 9   Enter the new balance in the Balance columns under Debit or Credit.

STEP 10   Enter the initials "CP" and the journal page number in the Posting Reference column.

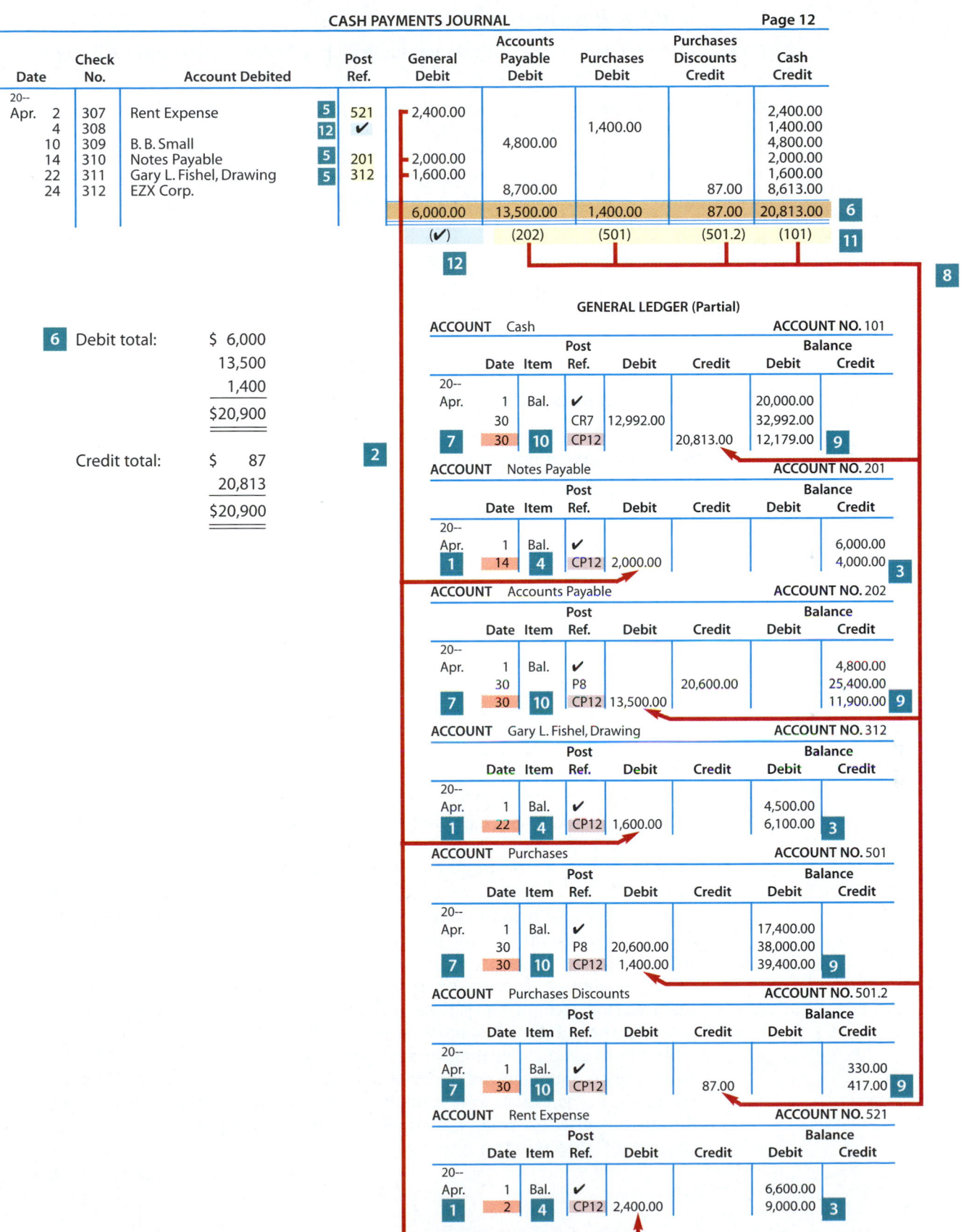

FIGURE 13-16 Posting the Cash Payments Journal to the General Ledger

In the cash payments journal:

STEP 11   Enter the ledger account number immediately below the column totals for each account that is posted.

STEP 12   Enter a check mark (✓) in the Posting Reference column for the cash purchases, and immediately below the General Debit column.

Postings from the cash payments journal to the accounts payable ledger also must be made. These postings are made daily. Posting procedures are as follows, as shown in Figure 13-17.

In the accounts payable ledger account:

STEP 1   Enter the date of the transaction in the Date column.

STEP 2   Enter the amount of the debit or credit in the Debit or Credit column.

STEP 3   Enter the new balance in the Balance column.

STEP 4   Enter the initials "CP" and the journal page number in the Posting Reference column.

In the cash payments journal:

STEP 5   Enter a check mark (✓) in the Posting Reference column of the journal for each transaction that is posted.

Computers and Accounting

Special Journals in Computerized Accounting Systems—Gary P. Schneider, University of San Diego

Special journals are an important part of manual accounting systems because they make it easy for accountants to record the types of transactions that occur most frequently in businesses. The common special journals are those used to record sales, cash receipts, purchases, and cash payments (also called cash disbursements). When working with an accounting system that uses special journals, accountants use the general journal to record the relatively few transactions that are not recorded in special journals.

Computerized accounting systems are organized somewhat differently than manual accounting systems. Instead of recording transactions directly in journals, they often use specialized entry screens designed to make recording transactions even easier than in a manual system with special journals. These entry screens are organized into modules. Each module is devoted to a specific transaction type, much as a manual system uses special journals to organize things. Figure A on page 476 shows the modular organization of a typical computerized accounting system.

(continued on page 476)

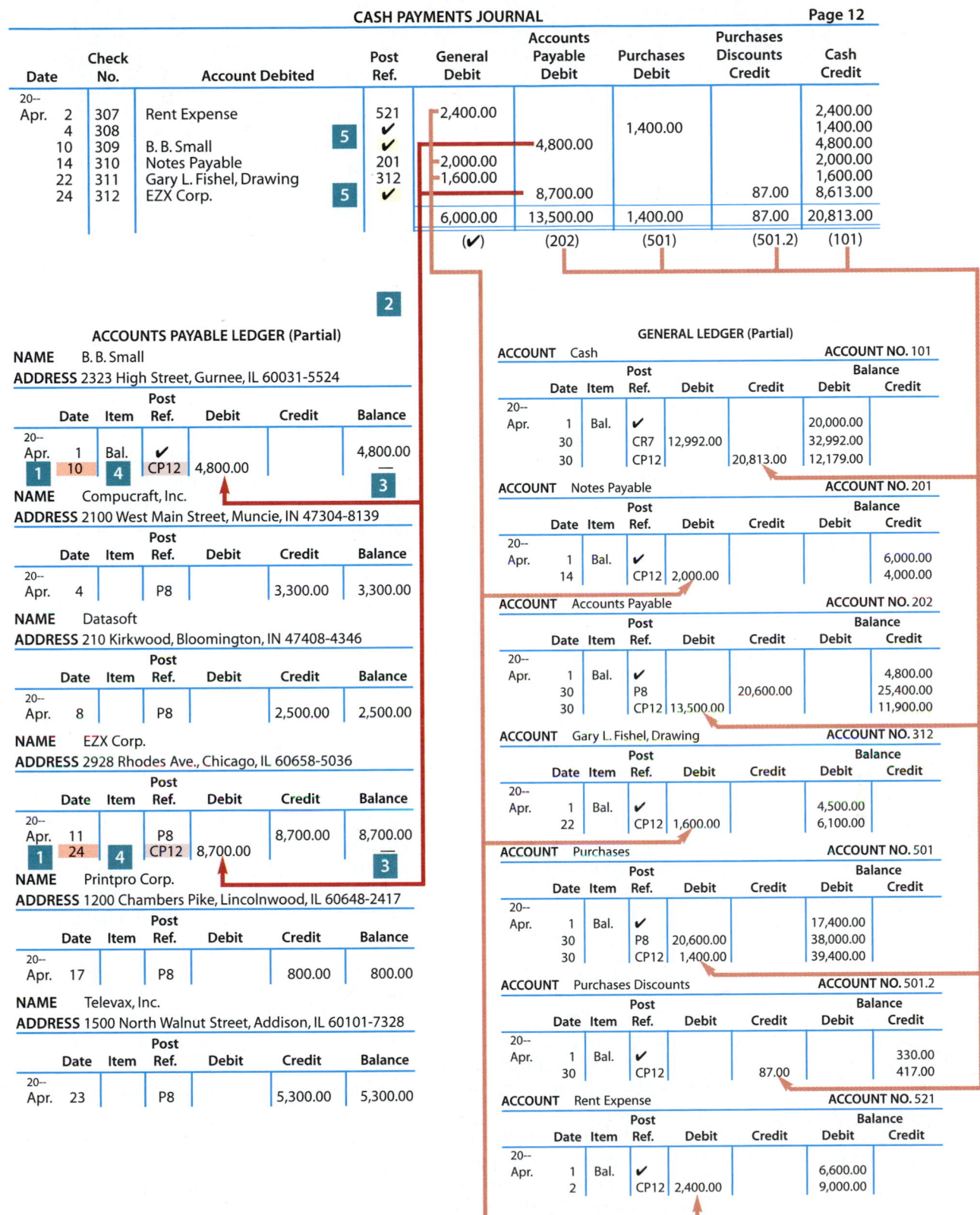

FIGURE 13-17 Posting the Cash Payments Journal to the Accounts Payable Ledger

Figure A

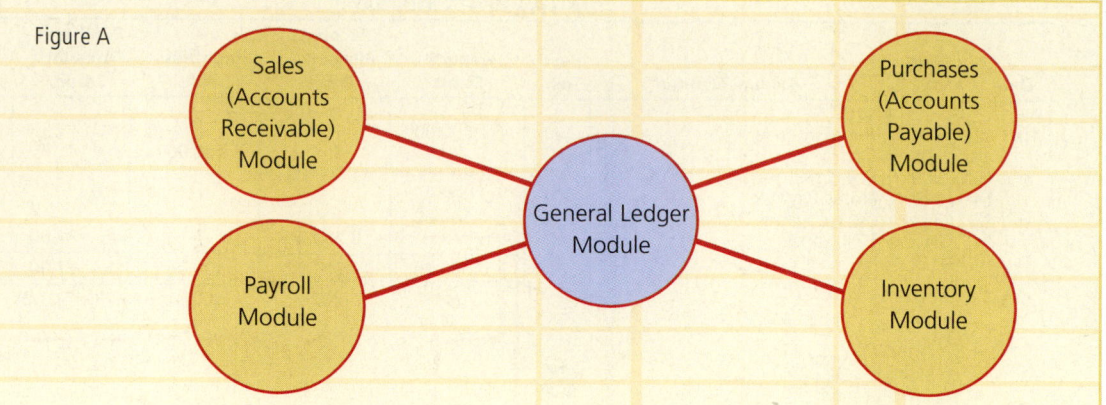

As you can see in the figure, this accounting system includes five modules: general ledger, sales (accounts receivable), purchases (accounts payable), payroll, and inventory. The general ledger module includes tools that accountants can use to record any type of transaction. In fact, some simple computerized accounting systems have only this module. Each of the other modules includes tools that accountants can use to record transactions of a specific type. For example, the sales module will have data entry screens for invoices and cash receipts. The details of the sales module for Peachtree®, a popular accounting software package, appear in Figure B.

To enter information into the Peachtree sales module, the accountant clicks one of the icons in the Tasks area to open the appropriate data entry screen. For example, an accountant can click the cash register icon to enter cash receipts from customers. The Reports section of the module includes both the sales journal and the cash receipts journal.

Unlike a manual accounting system, in which the accountant would enter the sales in the sales journal, computerized systems have the accountant enter sales using a specific data entry screen (in this case, the Sales/Invoicing screen). The accounting software stores this sales information in its internal database. This differs from a manual accounting system, which would store the information in a sales journal. To obtain a printed sales journal from the computerized accounting system, the accountant clicks the Sales Journal icon in the Reports area. the software searches its database, collects the sales information, and then prints the sales journal in a format that resembles a manual accounting system's sales journal.

By storing the sales information in a database, instead of a pen-and-ink journal, a computerized accounting system records the information only once. Accountants can then extract information from the database to create journals, subsidiary ledgers, and even the entire general ledger at any time. The computerized accounting system, in effect, updates all of the accounting records simultaneously when transaction information is entered. This updating occurs immediately.

The purchases module of the computerized accounting system is similar. It helps accountants perform purchase-related functions such as issuing purchase orders and writing checks to pay vendors. Figure C shows details of the Peachtree Purchases module. This module includes icons in its Tasks area that accountants can click to enter purchase orders, record the receipt of inventory, and write checks to pay vendors.

Figure B

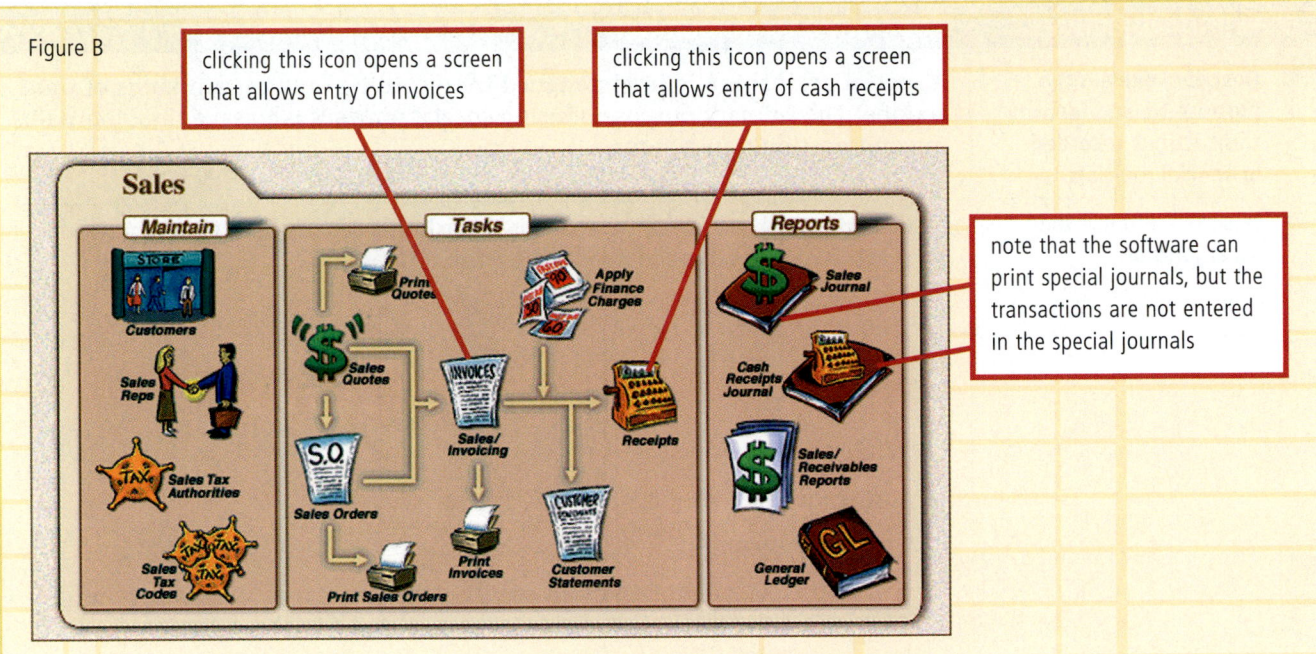

clicking this icon opens a screen that allows entry of invoices

clicking this icon opens a screen that allows entry of cash receipts

note that the software can print special journals, but the transactions are not entered in the special journals

Most accounting software packages include the ability to calculate payroll and print the necessary reports and government-required forms. You learned about these computerized payroll modules at the end of Chapter 9. Peachtree also includes an inventory module to help accountants track inventory that the company buys. More complex accounting software includes additional modules to record inventory movements from one warehouse to another and to record the manufacturing activities that some businesses undertake.

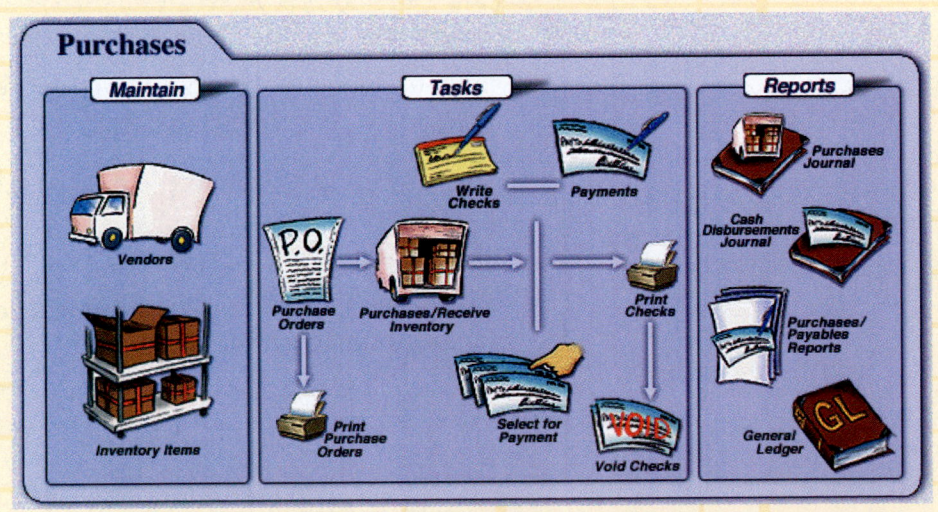

Figure C

Learning Objectives	Key Points to Remember
1 Describe, explain the purpose of, and identify transactions recorded in special journals.	A special journal is a journal designed for recording only certain kinds of transactions. The primary purpose of using special journals is to save time journalizing and posting transactions.
2 Describe and use the sales journal.	A sales journal is a special journal for recording sales of merchandise on account. A sale is recorded by entering the following:

      1. Date

      2. Sale number

      3. Customer

      4. Dollar amounts

To post from the sales journal to the general ledger:

In the sales journal:

STEP 1 Total the amount columns, verify that the total of the debit column equals the total of the credit columns, and rule the columns.

In the ledger account:

STEP 2 Enter the date of the transaction in the Date column.

STEP 3 Enter the amount of the debit or credit in the Debit or Credit column.

STEP 4 Enter the new balance in the Balance columns under Debit or Credit.

STEP 5 Enter the initial "S" and the journal page number in the Posting Reference column.

In the sales journal:

STEP 6 Enter the ledger account number immediately below the column totals for each account that is posted.

To post from the sales journal to the accounts receivable ledger:

In the accounts receivable ledger account:

STEP 1 Enter the date of the transaction in the Date column.

STEP 2 Enter the amount of the debit or credit in the Debit or Credit column.

STEP 3 Enter the new balance in the Balance column.

STEP 4 Enter the initial "S" and the journal page number in the Posting Reference column.

In the sales journal:

STEP 5 Enter a check mark (✓) in the Posting Reference column of the journal for each transaction that is posted.

3 Describe and use the cash receipts journal.	A cash receipts journal is a special journal for recording cash receipts. A cash receipt is recorded by entering the following:

      1. Date

      2. Account credited (if applicable)

      3. Dollar amounts

Learning Objectives	Key Points to Remember

To post from the cash receipts journal to the general ledger:

To post the General Credit column, on a daily basis:

In the ledger account:

STEP 1 Enter the date of the transaction in the Date column.

STEP 2 Enter the amount of the debit or credit in the Debit or Credit column.

STEP 3 Enter the new balance in the Balance columns under Debit or Credit.

STEP 4 Enter the initials "CR" and the journal page number in the Posting Reference column.

In the cash receipts journal:

STEP 5 Enter the ledger account number in the Posting Reference column for each account that is posted.

To post the other amount columns, at the end of the month:

In the cash receipts journal:

STEP 6 Total the amount columns, verify that the total of the debit columns equals the total of the credit columns, and rule the columns.

In the ledger account:

STEP 7 Enter the date in the Date column.

STEP 8 Enter the amount of the debit or credit in the Debit or Credit column.

STEP 9 Enter the new balance in the Balance columns under Debit or Credit.

STEP 10 Enter the initials "CR" and the journal page number in the Posting Reference column.

In the cash receipts journal:

STEP 11 Enter the ledger account number immediately below the column totals for each account that is posted.

STEP 12 Enter a check mark (✓) in the Posting Reference column for the cash sales and bank credit card sales, and immediately below the General Credit column.

To post from the cash receipts journal to the accounts receivable ledger:

In the accounts receivable ledger account:

STEP 1 Enter the date of the transaction in the Date column.

STEP 2 Enter the amount of the debit or credit in the Debit or Credit column.

STEP 3 Enter the new balance in the Balance column.

STEP 4 Enter the initials "CR" and the journal page number in the Posting Reference column.

In the cash receipts journal:

STEP 5 Enter a check mark (✓) in the Posting Reference column of the journal for each transaction that is posted.

Learning Objectives	Key Points to Remember
4 Describe and use the purchases journal.	A purchases journal is a special journal for recording purchases of merchandise on account. A purchase is recorded by entering the following: 1. Date 2. Invoice number 3. Supplier 4. Dollar amount To post from the purchases journal to the general ledger: **In the purchases journal:** STEP 1 Total and rule the amount column. **In the ledger account:** STEP 2 Enter the date in the Date column. STEP 3 Enter the amount of the debit or credit in the Debit or Credit column. STEP 4 Enter the new balance in the Balance columns under Debit or Credit. STEP 5 Enter the initial "P" and the journal page number in the Posting Reference column. **In the purchases journal:** STEP 6 Enter the Purchases and Accounts Payable account numbers immediately below the column total. To post from the purchases journal to the accounts payable ledger: **In the accounts payable ledger account:** STEP 1 Enter the date of the transaction in the Date column. STEP 2 Enter the amount of the debit or credit in the Debit or Credit column. STEP 3 Enter the new balance in the Balance column. STEP 4 Enter the initial "P" and the journal page number in the Posting Reference column. **In the purchases journal:** STEP 5 Enter a check mark (✓) in the Posting Reference column of the journal for each transaction that is posted.
5 Describe and use the cash payments journal.	A cash payments journal is a special journal for recording cash payments. A cash payment is recorded by entering the following: 1. Date 2. Check number 3. Account debited (if applicable) 4. Dollar amounts

Learning Objectives	Key Points to Remember

To post from the cash payments journal to the general ledger:

To post the General Debit column, on a daily basis:

In the ledger account:

STEP 1   Enter the date of the transaction in the Date column.

STEP 2   Enter the amount of the debit or credit in the Debit or Credit column.

STEP 3   Enter the new balance in the Balance columns under Debit or Credit.

STEP 4   Enter the initials "CP" and the journal page number in the Posting Reference column.

In the cash payments journal:

STEP 5   Enter the ledger account number in the Posting Reference column for each account that is posted.

To post the other amount columns, at the end of the month:

In the cash payments journal:

STEP 6   Total the amount columns, verify that the total of the debit columns equals the total of the credit columns, and rule the columns.

In the ledger account:

STEP 7   Enter the date in the Date column.

STEP 8   Enter the amount of the debit or credit in the Debit or Credit column.

STEP 9   Enter the new balance in the Balance columns under Debit or Credit.

STEP 10   Enter the initials "CP" and the journal page number in the Posting Reference column.

In the cash payments journal:

STEP 11   Enter the ledger account number immediately below the column totals for each account that is posted.

STEP 12   Enter a check mark (✔) in the Posting Reference column for the cash purchases, and immediately below the General Debit column.

To post from the cash payments journal to the accounts payable ledger:

In the accounts payable ledger account:

STEP 1   Enter the date of the transaction in the Date column.

STEP 2   Enter the amount of the debit or credit in the Debit or Credit column.

STEP 3   Enter the new balance in the Balance column.

STEP 4   Enter the initials "CP" and the journal page number in the Posting Reference column.

In the cash payments journal:

STEP 5   Enter a check mark (✔) in the Posting Reference column of the journal for each transaction that is posted.

Reflection: Answering the Opening Question

Special journals are journals designed for recording only certain kinds of transactions. The special journals Betty Jenkins had in mind are the sales, cash receipts, purchases, and cash payments journals. By using these journals, the bookkeeper would eliminate the need to write account titles when journalizing most sales, cash receipts, purchases, and cash payments transactions. In addition, summary postings to the related accounts could be made only once a month. Time savings for the bookkeeper should be substantial.

DEMONSTRATION PROBLEM

WebTUTOR Advantage

During the month of May, 20--, David's Specialty Shop engaged in the following transactions.

May 1	Sold merchandise on account to Molly Mac, $2,000 plus tax of $100. Sale no. 533.
2	Issued check no. 750 to Kari Co. in partial payment of May 1 balance, $800 less 2% discount.
3	Purchased merchandise on account from Scanlan Wholesalers $2,000. Invoice no. 621, dated May 3, terms 2/10, n/30.
4	Purchased merchandise on account from Simpson Enterprises $1,500. Invoice no. 767, dated May 4, terms 2/15, n/30.
4	Issued check no. 751 in payment of telephone expense for the month of April, $200.
8	Sold merchandise for cash, $3,600, plus tax of $180.
9	Received payment from Cody Slaton in full settlement of account, $2,500.
10	Issued check no. 752 to Scanlan Wholesalers in payment of May 1 balance of $1,200.
12	Sold merchandise on account to Cody Slaton, $3,000 plus tax of $150. Sale no. 534.
12	Received payment from Kori Reynolds on account, $2,100.
13	Issued check no. 753 to Simpson Enterprises in payment of May 4 purchase. Invoice no. 767, less 2% discount.
13	Cody Slaton returned merchandise for a credit, $1,000 plus sales tax of $50.
17	Returned merchandise to Johnson Essentials for credit, $500.
22	Received payment from Natalie Gabbert on account, $1,555.
27	Sold merchandise on account to Natalie Gabbert, $2,000 plus tax of $100. Sale no. 535.

29   Issued check no. 754 in payment of wages (Wages Expense) for the four-week period ending May 30, $1,100.

Selected account balances as of May 1 were as follows:

Account	Account No.	Debit	Credit
Cash	101	$10,050.00	
Accounts Receivable	122	6,900.00	
Accounts Payable	202		4,550.00

David also had the following subsidiary ledger balances as of May 1.

Accounts Receivable:

Customer	Accounts Receivable Balance
Natalie Gabbert 12 Jude Lane Hartford, CT 06117	$1,821.00
Molly Mac 52 Juniper Road Hartford, CT 06118	279.00
Kori Reynolds 700 Hobbes Dr. Avon, CT 06108	2,300.00
Cody Slaton 5200 Hamilton Ave. Hartford, CT 06111	2,500.00

Accounts Payable:

Vendor	Accounts Payable Balance
Johnson Essentials 34 Harry Ave. East Hartford, CT 05234	$2,350.00
Kari Co. 1009 Drake Rd. Farmington, CT 06082	1,000.00
Scanlan Wholesalers 43 Lucky Lane Bristo, CT 06007	1,200.00
Simpson Enterprises 888 Anders Street Newington, CT 06789	—

REQUIRED

1. Record the transactions in the sales journal, cash receipts journal, purchases journal, cash payments journal, and general journal. Total, verify, and rule the columns where appropriate at the end of the month.

2. Post from the journals to the general ledger, accounts receivable ledger, and accounts payable ledger accounts. Use account numbers as shown in the chapter.

(continued)

SALES JOURNAL

PAGE 7

	DATE		SALE NO.	TO WHOM SOLD	POST REF.	ACCOUNTS RECEIVABLE DEBIT	SALES CREDIT	SALES TAX PAYABLE CREDIT	
1	20-- May	1	533	Molly Mac	✓	2 1 0 0 00	2 0 0 0 00	1 0 0 00	1
2		12	534	Cody Slaton	✓	3 1 5 0 00	3 0 0 0 00	1 5 0 00	2
3		27	535	Natalie Gabbert	✓	2 1 0 0 00	2 0 0 0 00	1 0 0 00	3
4						7 3 5 0 00	7 0 0 0 00	3 5 0 00	4
5						(1 2 2)	(4 0 1)	(2 3 1)	5

PURCHASES JOURNAL

PAGE 6

	DATE		INVOICE NO.	FROM WHOM PURCHASED	POST REF.	PURCHASES DEBIT/ACCOUNTS PAYABLE CREDIT	
1	20-- May	3	621	Scanlan Wholesalers	✓	2 0 0 0 00	1
2		4	767	Simpson Enterprises	✓	1 5 0 0 00	2
3						3 5 0 0 00	3
4						(50 1) (2 02)	4

JOURNAL

PAGE 5

	DATE		DESCRIPTION	POST REF.	DEBIT	CREDIT	
1	20-- May	13	Sales Returns and Allowances	401.1	1 0 0 0 00		1
2			Sales Tax Payable	231	5 0 00		2
3			Accounts Receivable/Cody Slaton	122/✓		1 0 5 0 00	3
4			Accepted returned merchandise				4
5							5
6		17	Accounts Payable/Johnson Essentials	202/✓	5 0 0 00		6
7			Purchases Returns and Allowances	501.1		5 0 0 00	7
8			Returned merchandise				8
9							9

CASH PAYMENTS JOURNAL

PAGE 11

	DATE		CK. NO.	ACCOUNT DEBITED	POST REF.	GENERAL DEBIT	ACCOUNTS PAYABLE DEBIT	PURCHASES DEBIT	PURCHASES DISCOUNTS CREDIT	CASH CREDIT	
1	20-- May	2	750	Kari Co.	✓		8 0 0 00		1 6 00	7 8 4 00	1
2		4	751	Telephone Expense	525	2 0 0 00				2 0 0 00	2
3		10	752	Scanlan Wholesalers	✓		1 2 0 0 00			1 2 0 0 00	3
4		13	753	Simpson Enterprises	✓		1 5 0 0 00		3 0 00	1 4 7 0 00	4
5		29	754	Wages Expense	511	1 1 0 0 00				1 1 0 0 00	5
6						1 3 0 0 00	3 5 0 0 00		4 6 00	4 7 5 4 00	6
7						(✓)	(2 0 2)		(5 0 1.2)	(1 0 1)	7

CASH RECEIPTS JOURNAL   PAGE 10

	DATE	ACCOUNT CREDITED	POST REF.	GENERAL CREDIT	ACCOUNTS RECEIVABLE CREDIT	SALES CREDIT	SALES TAX PAYABLE CREDIT	CASH DEBIT	
1	20-- May 8					3 6 0 0 00	1 8 0 00	3 7 8 0 00	1
2	9	C. Slaton	✓		2 5 0 0 00			2 5 0 0 00	2
3	12	K. Reynolds	✓		2 1 0 0 00			2 1 0 0 00	3
4	22	N. Gabbert	✓		1 5 5 5 00			1 5 5 5 00	4
5					6 1 5 5 00	3 6 0 0 00	1 8 0 00	9 9 3 5 00	5
6					(1 2 2)	(4 0 1)	(2 3 1)	(1 0 1)	6

2.

GENERAL LEDGER

ACCOUNT: Cash   ACCOUNT NO. 101

DATE	ITEM	POST REF.	DEBIT	CREDIT	BALANCE DEBIT	BALANCE CREDIT
20-- May 1	Balance	✓			10 0 5 0 00	
31		CR10	9 9 3 5 00		19 9 8 5 00	
31		CP11		4 7 5 4 00	15 2 3 1 00	

ACCOUNT: Accounts Receivable   ACCOUNT NO. 122

DATE	ITEM	POST REF.	DEBIT	CREDIT	BALANCE DEBIT	BALANCE CREDIT
20-- May 1	Balance	✓			6 9 0 0 00	
13		J5		1 0 5 0 00	5 8 5 0 00	
31		S7	7 3 5 0 00		13 2 0 0 00	
31		CR10		6 1 5 5 00	7 0 4 5 00	

ACCOUNT: Accounts Payable   ACCOUNT NO. 202

DATE	ITEM	POST REF.	DEBIT	CREDIT	BALANCE DEBIT	BALANCE CREDIT
20-- May 1	Balance	✓				4 5 5 0 00
17		J5	5 0 0 00			4 0 5 0 00
31		P6		3 5 0 0 00		7 5 5 0 00
31		CP11	3 5 0 0 00			4 0 5 0 00

ACCOUNT: Sales Tax Payable   ACCOUNT NO. 231

DATE	ITEM	POST REF.	DEBIT	CREDIT	BALANCE DEBIT	BALANCE CREDIT
20-- May 13		J5	5 0 00		5 0 00	
31		S7		3 5 0 00		3 0 0 00
31		CR10		1 8 0 00		4 8 0 00

ACCOUNT: Sales   ACCOUNT NO. 401

DATE	ITEM	POST REF.	DEBIT	CREDIT	BALANCE DEBIT	BALANCE CREDIT
20-- May 31		S7		7 0 0 0 00		7 0 0 0 00
31		CR10		3 6 0 0 00		10 6 0 0 00

(continued)

ACCOUNT: Sales Returns and Allowances   ACCOUNT NO. 401.1

DATE		ITEM	POST REF.	DEBIT	CREDIT	BALANCE	
						DEBIT	CREDIT
20-- May	13		J5	1 0 0 0 00		1 0 0 0 00	

ACCOUNT: Purchases   ACCOUNT NO. 501

DATE		ITEM	POST REF.	DEBIT	CREDIT	BALANCE	
						DEBIT	CREDIT
20-- May	31		P6	3 5 0 0 00		3 5 0 0 00	

ACCOUNT: Purchases Returns and Allowances   ACCOUNT NO. 501.1

DATE		ITEM	POST REF.	DEBIT	CREDIT	BALANCE	
						DEBIT	CREDIT
20-- May	17		J5		5 0 0 00		5 0 0 00

ACCOUNT: Purchases Discounts   ACCOUNT NO. 501.2

DATE		ITEM	POST REF.	DEBIT	CREDIT	BALANCE	
						DEBIT	CREDIT
20-- May	31		CP11		4 6 00		4 6 00

ACCOUNT: Wages Expense   ACCOUNT NO. 511

DATE		ITEM	POST REF.	DEBIT	CREDIT	BALANCE	
						DEBIT	CREDIT
20-- May	29		CP11	1 1 0 0 00		1 1 0 0 00	

ACCOUNT: Telephone Expense   ACCOUNT NO. 525

DATE		ITEM	POST REF.	DEBIT	CREDIT	BALANCE	
						DEBIT	CREDIT
20-- May	4		CP11	2 0 0 00		2 0 0 00	

ACCOUNTS RECEIVABLE LEDGER

NAME: Natalie Gabbert

ADDRESS: 12 Jude Lane Hartford, CT 06117

DATE		ITEM	POST REF.	DEBIT	CREDIT	BALANCE
20-- May	1	Balance	✓			1 8 2 1 00
	22		CR10		1 5 5 5 00	2 6 6 00
	27		S7	2 1 0 0 00		2 3 6 6 00

NAME: Molly Mac

ADDRESS: 52 Juniper Road Hartford, CT 06118

DATE		ITEM	POST REF.	DEBIT	CREDIT	BALANCE
20-- May	1	Balance	✓			2 7 9 00
	1		S7	2 1 0 0 00		2 3 7 9 00

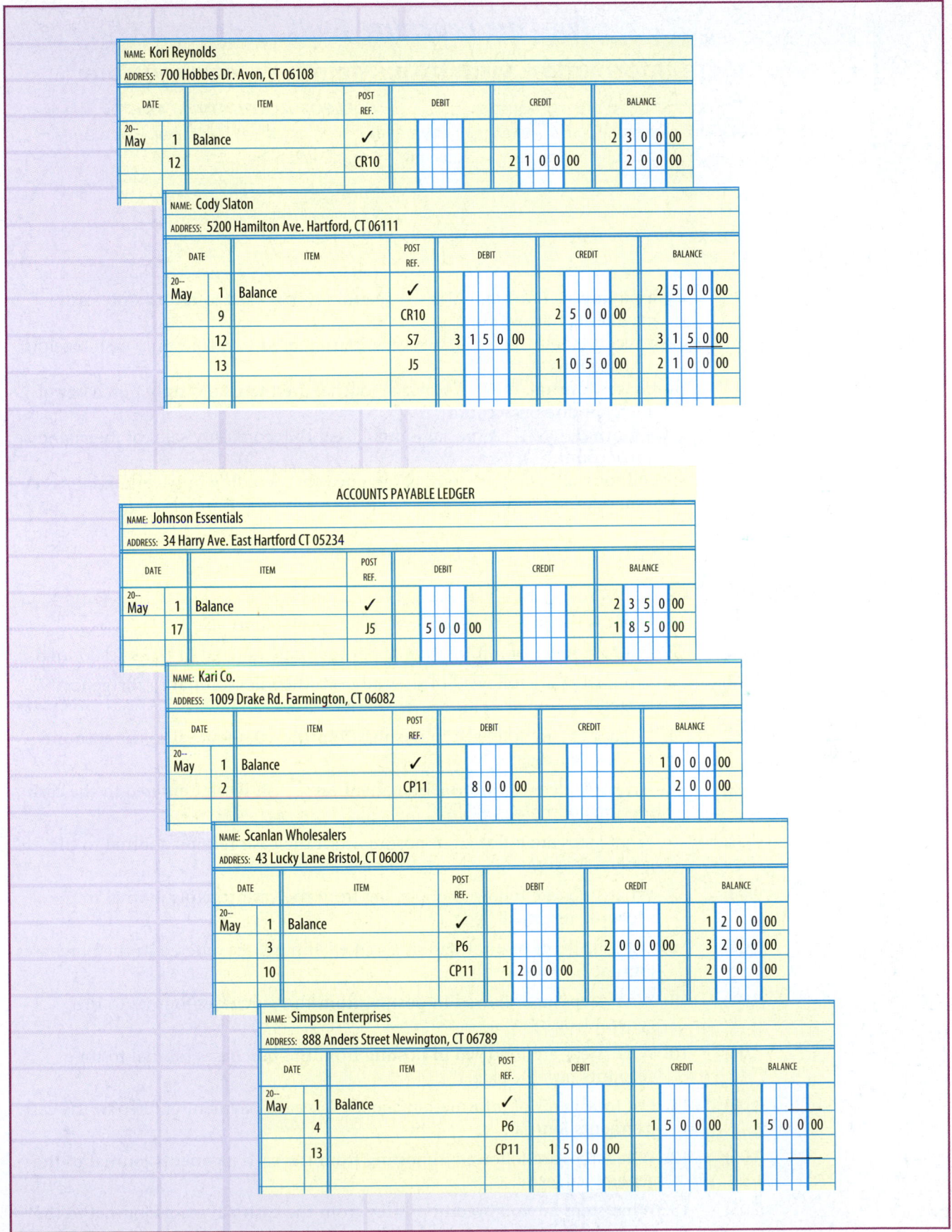

NAME: Kori Reynolds
ADDRESS: 700 Hobbes Dr. Avon, CT 06108

DATE		ITEM	POST REF.	DEBIT	CREDIT	BALANCE
20-- May	1	Balance	✓			2 3 0 0 00
	12		CR10		2 1 0 0 00	2 0 0 00

NAME: Cody Slaton
ADDRESS: 5200 Hamilton Ave. Hartford, CT 06111

DATE		ITEM	POST REF.	DEBIT	CREDIT	BALANCE
20-- May	1	Balance	✓			2 5 0 0 00
	9		CR10		2 5 0 0 00	
	12		S7	3 1 5 0 00		3 1 5 0 00
	13		J5		1 0 5 0 00	2 1 0 0 00

ACCOUNTS PAYABLE LEDGER

NAME: Johnson Essentials
ADDRESS: 34 Harry Ave. East Hartford CT 05234

DATE		ITEM	POST REF.	DEBIT	CREDIT	BALANCE
20-- May	1	Balance	✓			2 3 5 0 00
	17		J5	5 0 0 00		1 8 5 0 00

NAME: Kari Co.
ADDRESS: 1009 Drake Rd. Farmington, CT 06082

DATE		ITEM	POST REF.	DEBIT	CREDIT	BALANCE
20-- May	1	Balance	✓			1 0 0 0 00
	2		CP11	8 0 0 00		2 0 0 00

NAME: Scanlan Wholesalers
ADDRESS: 43 Lucky Lane Bristol, CT 06007

DATE		ITEM	POST REF.	DEBIT	CREDIT	BALANCE
20-- May	1	Balance	✓			1 2 0 0 00
	3		P6		2 0 0 0 00	3 2 0 0 00
	10		CP11	1 2 0 0 00		2 0 0 0 00

NAME: Simpson Enterprises
ADDRESS: 888 Anders Street Newington, CT 06789

DATE		ITEM	POST REF.	DEBIT	CREDIT	BALANCE
20-- May	1	Balance	✓			
	4		P6		1 5 0 0 00	1 5 0 0 00
	13		CP11	1 5 0 0 00		

On-Line Learning Tools

For more information, visit: http://heintz.swlearning.com

The Heintz & Parry product web site is designed specifically for **COLLEGE ACCOUNTING, 18e.** The features include downloadable student resources and an interactive study center, organized by chapter, which contains learning objectives, web links, on-line quizzes with automatic feedback, and more.

KEY TERMS

cash payments journal, (471)   A special journal used to record only cash payments transactions.

cash receipts journal, (460) A special journal used to record only cash receipts transactions.

purchases journal, (467)   A special journal used to record only purchases of merchandise on account.

sales journal, (457)   A special journal used to record only sales of merchandise on account.

special journal, (456)   A journal designed for recording only certain kinds of transactions.

REVIEW QUESTIONS

(LO1)   1. What is the primary purpose of using special journals?

(LO2)   2. List four items of information about each sale entered in the sales journal.

(LO2)   3. What steps are followed in posting from the sales journal to the general ledger?

(LO2)   4. What steps are followed in posting from the sales journal to the accounts receivable ledger?

(LO3)   5. List three items of information about each cash receipt entered in the cash receipts journal.

(LO3)   6. What steps are followed in posting from the cash receipts journal to the general ledger?

(LO3)   7. What steps are followed in posting from the cash receipts journal to the accounts receivable ledger?

(LO4)   8. List four items of information about each purchase entered in the purchases journal.

(LO4)   9. What steps are followed in posting from the purchases journal to the general ledger?

(LO4)   10. What steps are followed in posting from the purchases journal to the accounts payable ledger?

(LO5)   11. List four items of information about each cash payment entered in the cash payments journal.

(LO5)   12. What steps are followed in posting from the cash payments journal to the general ledger?

(LO5)   13. What steps are followed in posting from the cash payments journal to the accounts payable ledger?

Self-Study Test Questions

True/False

1. The types of special journals a business uses should depend on the types of transactions it has most frequently. _____

2. If a business uses special journals, it generally will not need a general journal. _____

3. All sales, for cash or on credit, are recorded in the sales journal. _____

4. A cash receipts journal is used to record all cash receipts transactions. _____

5. Purchases returns and allowances are recorded in the general journal. _____

Multiple Choice

1. In the cash receipts journal, each amount in the General Credit column is posted _____

   (a) daily.   (c) at the end of the month.
   (b) weekly.   (d) at the end of the year.

2. In the cash payments journal, each amount in the General Debit column is posted _____

   (a) daily.   (c) at the end of the month.
   (b) weekly.   (d) at the end of the year.

3. The journal that should be used to record the return of merchandise for credit is the _____

   (a) purchases journal.   (c) general journal.
   (b) cash payments journal.   (d) accounts payable journal.

4. A purchases journal is used to record all _____

   (a) purchases.   (c) purchases of merchandise on account.
   (b) cash purchases.   (d) purchases returns and allowances.

5. The first step in posting the sales journal to the general ledger is to _____

   (a) total and verify the equality of the amount columns.
   (b) enter the date in the Date column of the ledger account.
   (c) enter the new balance in the Balance columns of the ledger account.
   (d) enter the ledger account number below the column totals in the journal.

The answers to the Self-Study Test Questions are at the end of the text.

MANAGING YOUR WRITING

You have a part-time job as a bookkeeper at a local office supply store. The accounting records consist of a general journal and general ledger. The manager is concerned about efficiency and feels that too much time is spent recording transactions. In addition, there sometimes is difficulty determining the amount owed to specific suppliers. The manager knows you are an accounting student and asks for your suggestions to improve the accounting function.

Write a memo to the manager describing how to increase efficiency and accuracy by using different accounting records.

ETHICS CASE

Judy Baresford, the store manager of Comfort Futons, noticed that the amount of time the two bookkeepers were spending on accounts receivable, accounts payable, and cash receipts was increasing due to the store's increase in sales. A friend of Judy's who is also a store manager suggested that she might want to have some special journals designed that would reduce the amount of work involved in the day-to-day bookkeeping at her store. Judy approached Jon Fortner and Sue Stavio, the bookkeepers, and asked them to come up with a proposal for special journals. During lunch Jon told Sue he thought designing special journals would be a lot of work and it was not in his job description. Sue told him not to worry because she would just copy pages of special journals from her accounting textbook and they could submit these journals as their own design. Jon liked the idea and they agreed to meet the next night, scan the journals into Word, and submit them to Judy the following morning.

1. Do you think Sue's suggestion is unethical? Why or why not?

2. In using the generic special journals from Sue's accounting textbook, what possible problems can you foresee?

3. If you were Judy, how would you respond to Sue and Jon's "plan"?

SERIES A EXERCISE

EXERCISE 13-1A   **(LO1)**   **RECORDING TRANSACTIONS IN THE PROPER JOURNAL** Identify the journal (sales, cash receipts, purchases, cash payments, or general) in which each of the following transactions should be recorded.

a. Sold merchandise on account.

b. Purchased delivery truck on account for use in the business.

c. Received payment from customer on account.

d. Purchased merchandise on account.

e. Issued check in payment of electric bill.

f. Recorded depreciation on factory building.

EXERCISE 13-2A   **(LO2)**   **JOURNALIZING SALES TRANSACTIONS** Enter the following transactions in a sales journal. Use a 6% sales tax rate.

May 1: Dr. Accounts Receivable/J. Adams, $2,120

May 1   Sold merchandise on account to J. Adams, $2,000 plus sales tax. Sale no 488.

4   Sold merchandise on account to B. Clark, $1,800 plus sales tax. Sale no. 489.

8   Sold merchandise on account to A. Duck, $1,500 plus sales tax. Sale no. 490.

11   Sold merchandise on account to E. Hill, $1,950 plus sales tax. Sale no. 491.

EXERCISE 13-3A   **(LO3)**   **JOURNALIZING CASH RECEIPTS** Enter the following transactions in a cash receipts journal.

July 6: Cr. Accounts Receivable/J. Adler, $643

July 6   James Adler made payment on account, $643.

10   Cash sales for the week, $2,320.

14   Betty Havel made payment on account, $430.

15   J. L. Borg made payment on account, $117.

17   Cash sales for the week, $2,237.

EXERCISE 13-4A   (LO4)

May 9: Purchases Dr./
Accounts Payable Cr.,
$2,300

JOURNALIZING PURCHASES TRANSACTIONS   Enter the following transactions in a purchases journal like the one below.

May 3   Purchased merchandise from Cintron, $6,500. Invoice no. 321, dated May 1, terms n/30.

9   Purchased merchandise from Mitsui, $2,300. Invoice no. 614, dated May 8, terms 2/10, n/30.

18   Purchased merchandise from Aloha Distributors, $4,200. Invoice no. 180, dated May 15, terms 1/15, n/30.

23   Purchased merchandise from Soto, $6,300. Invoice no. 913, dated May 22, terms 1/10, n/30.

		PURCHASES JOURNAL		PAGE 5
DATE	INVOICE NO.	FROM WHOM PURCHASED	POST REF.	PURCHASES DEBIT/ACCOUNTS PAYABLE CREDIT

EXERCISE 13-5A   (LO5)

Sept. 12: Cash Cr., $6,930

JOURNALIZING CASH PAYMENTS Landmark Industries uses a cash payments journal. Prepare a cash payments journal using the same format and account titles as illustrated in the chapter. Record the following payments for merchandise purchased.

Sept. 5   Issued check no. 318 to Clinton Corp. for merchandise purchased August 28, $6,000, terms 2/10, n/30. Payment is made within the discount period.

12   Issued check no. 319 to Mitchell Company for merchandise purchased September 2, $7,500, terms 1/10, n/30. Received a credit memo from Mitchell Company for merchandise returned, $500. Payment is made within the discount period after deduction for the return dated September 8.

19   Issued check no. 320 to Expert Systems for merchandise purchased August 19, $4,100, terms n/30.

27   Issued check no. 321 to Graphic Data for merchandise purchased September 17, $9,000, terms 2/10, n/30. Payment is made within the discount period.

SERIES A PROBLEMS

PROBLEM 13-6A   (LO2)

Total Accounts Receivable
Dr.: $16,345.20

SALES JOURNAL J. K. Bijan owns a retail business and made the following sales during the month of August 20--. There is a 6% sales tax on all sales.

Aug. 1   Sale no. 213 to Jung Manufacturing Co., $1,200 plus sales tax.

3   Sale no. 214 to Hassad Co., $3,600 plus sales tax.

7   Sale no. 215 to Helsinki, Inc., $1,400 plus sales tax. (Open a new account for this customer. Address is 125 Fishers Dr., Noblesville, IN 47870-8867.)

11   Sale no. 216 to Ardis Myler, $1,280 plus sales tax.

18   Sale no. 217 to Hassad Co., $4,330 plus sales tax.

22   Sale no. 218 to Jung Manufacturing Co., $2,000 plus sales tax.

30   Sale no. 219 to Ardis Myler, $1,610 plus sales tax.

(continued)

REQUIRED

1. Record the transactions in the sales journal. Total and verify the column totals and rule the columns.

2. Post from the sales journal to the general ledger and accounts receivable ledger accounts. Use account numbers as shown in the chapter.

PROBLEM 13-7A   **(LO3)**

Total Accounts
Receivable Cr.:
$5,732

CASH RECEIPTS JOURNAL Zebra Imaginarium, a retail business, had the following cash receipts during December 20--. The sales tax is 6%.

Dec. 1	Received payment on account from Michael Anderson, $1,360.
2	Received payment on account from Ansel Manufacturing, $382.
7	Cash sales for the week, $3,160 plus tax. Bank credit card sales for the week, $1,000 plus tax. Bank credit card fee is 3%.
8	Received payment on account from J. Gorbea, $880.
11	Michael Anderson returned merchandise for a credit, $60 plus tax.
14	Cash sales for the week, $2,800 plus tax. Bank credit card sales for the week, $800 plus tax. Bank credit card fee is 3%.
20	Received payment on account from Tom Wilson, $1,110.
21	Ansel Manufacturing returned merchandise for a credit, $22 plus tax.
21	Cash sales for the week, $3,200 plus tax.
24	Received payment on account from Rachel Carson, $2,000.

Beginning general ledger account balances were:

Cash	$9,862
Accounts Receivable	$9,352

Beginning customer account balances were:

M. Anderson	$2,480
Ansel Manufacturing	982
J. Gorbea	880
R. Carson	3,200
T. Wilson	1,810

REQUIRED

1. Record the transactions in the cash receipts journal. Total and verify column totals and rule the columns. Use the general journal to record sales returns and allowances.

2. Post from the journals to the general ledger and accounts receivable ledger accounts. Use account numbers as shown in the chapter.

PROBLEM 13-8A   **(LO2/3)**

Total Accounts
Receivable Dr.:
$12,745.08

SALES JOURNAL, CASH RECEIPTS JOURNAL, AND GENERAL JOURNAL Owens Distributors is a retail business. The following sales, returns, and cash receipts occurred during March 20--. There is an 8% sales tax. Beginning general ledger account balances were Cash, $9,741.00; and Accounts Receivable, $1,058.25. Beginning customer account balances were Thompson Group, $1,058.25.

March 1	Sale no. 33C to Able & Co., $1,800 plus sales tax.
3	Sale no. 33D to R. J. Kalas, Inc., $2,240 plus sales tax.
5	Able & Co. returned merchandise from sale no. 33C for a credit (credit memo no. 66), $30 plus sales tax.
7	Cash sales for the week, $3,160 plus sales tax.
10	Received payment from Able & Co. for sale no. 33C less credit memo no. 66.
11	Sale no. 33E to Blevins Bakery, $1,210 plus sales tax.
13	Received payment from R. J. Kalas for sale no. 33D.
14	Cash sales for the week, $4,200 plus sales tax.
16	Blevins Bakery returned merchandise from sale no. 33E for a credit (credit memo no. 67), $44 plus sales tax.
18	Sale no. 33F to R. J. Kalas, Inc., $2,620 plus sales tax.
20	Received payment from Blevins Bakery for sale no. 33E less credit memo no. 67.
21	Cash sales for the week, $2,400 plus sales tax.
25	Sale no. 33G to Blevins Bakery, $1,915 plus sales tax.
27	Sale no. 33H to Thompson Group, $2,016 plus sales tax.
28	Cash sales for the week, $3,500 plus sales tax.

REQUIRED

1. Record the transactions in the sales journal, cash receipts journal, and general journal. Total, verify, and rule the columns where appropriate at the end of the month.

2. Post from the journals to the general ledger and accounts receivable ledger accounts. Use account numbers as shown in the chapter.

PROBLEM 13-9A   (LO4)
Total Purchases Dr.:
$20,790

PURCHASES JOURNAL J. B. Speck, owner of Speck's Galleria, made the following purchases of merchandise on account during the month of September.

Sept. 3	Purchase invoice no. 415, $2,650, from Smith Distributors.
8	Purchase invoice no. 132, $3,830, from Michaels Wholesaler.
11	Purchase invoice no. 614, $3,140, from J. B. Sanders & Co.
18	Purchase invoice no. 329, $2,250, from Bateman & Jones, Inc.
23	Purchase invoice no. 867, $4,160, from Smith Distributors.
27	Purchase invoice no. 744, $1,980, from Anderson Company.
30	Purchase invoice no. 652, $2,780, from Michaels Wholesaler.

REQUIRED

1. Record the transactions in the purchases journal. Total and rule the journal.

2. Post from the purchases journal to the general ledger and accounts payable ledger accounts. Use account numbers as shown in the chapter.

PROBLEM 13-10A (LO4)
Helmut's Hair Supply account balance: $4,240

PURCHASES JOURNAL, GENERAL LEDGER, AND ACCOUNTS PAYABLE LEDGER The purchases journal of Kevin's Kettle, a small retail business, is as follows:

	DATE		INVOICE NO.	FROM WHOM PURCHASED	POST REF.	PURCHASES DEBIT/ACCOUNTS PAYABLE CREDIT	
1	20-- Jan.	2	101	Ruiz Imports		3 0 0 0 00	1
2		3	621	Helmut's Hair Supply		2 4 8 0 00	2
3		7	195	Viola's Boutique		4 3 6 0 00	3
4		12	267	Royal Flush		1 9 5 0 00	4
5		18	903	Maria's Melodies		4 7 0 0 00	5
6		25	680	Helmut's Hair Supply		1 7 6 0 00	6
7						18 2 5 0 00	7

PURCHASES JOURNAL — PAGE 1

REQUIRED

1. Post the total of the purchases journal to the appropriate general ledger accounts. Use account numbers as shown in the chapter.

2. Post the individual purchase amounts to the accounts payable ledger.

PROBLEM 13-11A (LO5)
Total Cash Cr.: $30,984

CASH PAYMENTS JOURNAL Sam Santiago operates a retail variety store. The books include a cash payments journal and an accounts payable ledger. All cash payments (except petty cash) are entered in the cash payments journal.

Selected account balances on May 1 are as follows:

General Ledger

Cash	$40,000
Accounts Payable	20,000

Accounts Payable Ledger

Fantastic Toys	$5,200
Goya Outlet	3,800
Mueller's Distributors	3,600
Van Kooning	7,400

The following are the transactions related to cash payments for the month of May.

May 1 Issued check no. 426 in payment of May rent (Rent Expense), $2,400.

3 Issued check no. 427 to Mueller's Distributors in payment of merchandise purchased on account, $3,600 less a 3% discount. Check was written for $3,492.

7 Issued check no. 428 to Van Kooning in partial payment of merchandise purchased on account, $5,500. A cash discount was not allowed.

12 Issued check no. 429 to Fantastic Toys for merchandise purchased on account, $5,200, less a 1% discount. Check was written for $5,148.

15 Issued check no. 430 to City Power and Light (Utilities Expense), $1,720.

18 Issued check no. 431 to A-1 Warehouse for a cash purchase of merchandise, $4,800.

26   Issued check no. 432 to Goya Outlet for merchandise purchased on account, $3,800, less a 2% discount. Check was written for $3,724.

30   Issued check no. 433 to Mercury Transit Company for freight charges on merchandise purchased (Freight-In), $1,200.

31   Issued check no. 434 to Town Merchants for a cash purchase of merchandise, $3,000.

REQUIRED

1. Enter the transactions in a cash payments journal. Total, rule, and prove the cash payments journal.

2. Post from the cash payments journal to the general ledger and accounts payable ledger. Use general ledger account numbers as shown in the chapter.

PROBLEM 13-12A (LO4/5)

Total Cash Cr.: $11,170

PURCHASES JOURNAL, CASH PAYMENTS JOURNAL, AND GENERAL JOURNAL
Freddy Flint owns a small retail business called Flint's Fantasy. The cash account has a balance of $20,000 on July 1. The following transactions occurred during July.

July 1   Issued check no. 414 in payment of July rent, $1,500.

1   Purchased merchandise on account from Tang's Toys, invoice no. 311, $2,700, terms 2/10, n/30.

3   Purchased merchandise on account from Sillas & Company, invoice no. 812, $3,100, terms 1/10, n/30.

5   Returned merchandise purchased from Tang's Toys, receiving a credit memo on the amount owed, $500.

8   Purchased merchandise on account from Daisy's Dolls, invoice no. 139, $1,900, terms 2/10, n/30.

11   Issued check no. 415 to Tang's Toys for merchandise purchased on account, less return of July 5 and less 2% discount.

13   Issued a check no. 416 to Sillas & Company for merchandise purchased on account, less 1% discount.

15   Returned merchandise purchased from Daisy's Dolls, receiving a credit memo on the amount owed, $400.

18   Issued check no. 417 to Daisy's Dolls for merchandise purchased on account, less return of July 15 and less 2% discount.

25   Purchased merchandise on account from Allied Business, invoice no. 489, $2,450, terms n/30.

26   Purchased merchandise on account from Tang's Toys, invoice no. 375, $1,980, terms 2/10, n/30.

29   Purchased merchandise on account from Sillas & Company, invoice no. 883, $3,460, terms 1/10, n/30.

31   Freddy Flint withdrew cash for personal use, $2,000. Issued check no. 418.

31   Issued check no. 419 to Glisan Distributors for a cash purchase of merchandise, $975.

(continued)

REQUIRED

1. Record the transactions in the purchases journal, cash payments journal, and general journal. Total and rule the purchases and cash payments journals. Prove the cash payments journal.

2. Post from the journals to the general ledger and accounts payable ledger accounts. Use general ledger account numbers as shown in the chapter.

SERIES B EXERCISES

EXERCISE 13-1B   **(LO1)**   **RECORDING TRANSACTIONS IN THE PROPER JOURNAL** Identify the journal (sales, cash receipts, purchases, cash payments, or general) in which each of the following transactions should be recorded.

   a. Issued credit memo to customer for merchandise returned.

   b. Sold merchandise for cash.

   c. Purchased merchandise on account.

   d. Issued checks to employees in payment of wages.

   e. Purchased factory supplies on account.

   f. Sold merchandise on account.

EXERCISE 13-2B   **(LO2)**   **JOURNALIZING SALES TRANSACTIONS** Enter the following transactions in a sales journal. Use a 5% sales tax rate.

Sept. 1: Dr. Accounts Receivable/K. Smith, $1,890

Sept. 1	Sold merchandise on account to K. Smith, $1,800 plus sales tax. Sale no. 228.
3	Sold merchandise on account to J. Arnes, $3,100 plus sales tax. Sale no. 229.
5	Sold merchandise on account to M. Denison, $2,800 plus sales tax. Sale no. 230.
7	Sold merchandise on account to B. Marshall, $1,900 plus sales tax. Sale no. 231.

EXERCISE 13-3B   **(LO3)**   **JOURNALIZING CASH RECEIPTS** Enter the following transactions in a cash receipts journal.

Nov. 1: Cr. Accounts Receivable/ Jean Haghighat, $750

Nov. 1	Jean Haghighat made payment on account, $750.
12	Marc Antonoff made payment on account, $464.
15	Cash sales, $3,763.
18	Will Mossein made payment on account, $241.
25	Cash sales, $2,648.

EXERCISE 13-4B   **(LO4)**   **JOURNALIZING PURCHASES TRANSACTIONS** Enter the following transactions in a purchases journal like the one below.

Jan. 3: Purchases Dr./ Accounts Payable Cr., $6,000

Jan. 3	Purchased merchandise from Feng, $6,000. Invoice no. 416, dated January 1, terms 2/10, n/30.
12	Purchased merchandise from Miranda, $9,000. Invoice no. 624, dated January 10, terms n/30.
19	Purchased merchandise from J. B. Barba, $6,400. Invoice no. 190, dated January 18, terms 1/10, n/30.

26   Purchased merchandise from Ramirez, $3,700. Invoice no. 923, dated January 25, terms 1/15, n/30.

PURCHASES JOURNAL					PAGE 5
DATE	INVOICE NO.	FROM WHOM PURCHASED		POST REF.	PURCHASES DEBIT/ACCOUNTS PAYABLE CREDIT

EXERCISE 13-5B (LO5)
Apr. 19: Cash Cr., $4,950

JOURNALIZING CASH PAYMENTS Sandcastles Northwest uses a cash payments journal. Prepare a cash payments journal using the same format and account titles as illustrated in the chapter. Record the following payments for merchandise purchased.

April 5   Issued check no. 429 to Standard Industries for merchandise purchased April 3, $8,000, terms 2/10, n/30. Payment is made within the discount period.

19   Issued check no. 430 to Finest Company for merchandise purchased April 10, $5,300, terms 1/10, n/30. Received a credit memo from Finest Company for merchandise returned, $300. Payment is made within the discount period after deduction for the return dated April 12.

21   Issued check no. 431 to Funny Follies for merchandise purchased March 21, $3,250, terms n/30.

29   Issued check no. 432 to Classic Data for merchandise purchased April 20, $7,000, terms 2/10, n/30. Payment is made within the discount period.

SERIES B PROBLEMS

PROBLEM 13-6B (LO2)
Total Accounts Receivable Dr.: $13,072.50

SALES JOURNAL T. M. Maxwell owns a retail business and made the following sales during the month of July 20--. There is a 5% sales tax on all sales.

July 1   Sale no. 101 to Saga, Inc., $1,200 plus sales tax.

8   Sale no. 102 to Vinnie Ward, $2,100 plus sales tax.

15   Sale no. 103 to Dvorak Manufacturing, $4,300 plus sales tax.

21   Sale no. 104 to Vinnie Ward, $1,800 plus sales tax.

24   Sale no. 105 to Zapata Co., $1,600 plus sales tax. (Open a new account for this customer. Address is 789 N. Stafford Dr., Bloomington, IN 47401-6201.)

29   Sale no. 106 to Saga, Inc., $1,450 plus sales tax.

REQUIRED

1. Record the transactions in the sales journal. Total and verify the column totals and rule the columns.

2. Post the sales journal to the general ledger and accounts receivable ledger accounts. Use account numbers as shown in the chapter.

PROBLEM 13-7B (LO3)

Total Accounts Receivable Cr.: $3,481

CASH RECEIPTS JOURNAL Color Florists, a retail business, had the following cash receipts during January 20--. The sales tax is 5%.

Jan. 1   Received payment on account from Ray Boyd, $880.

3   Received payment on account from Clint Hassell, $271.

(continued)

5	Cash sales for the week, $2,800 plus tax. Bank credit card sales for the week, $1,200 plus tax. Bank credit card fee is 3%.
8	Received payment on account from Jan Sowada, $912.
11	Ray Boyd returned merchandise for a credit, $40 plus tax.
12	Cash sales for the week, $3,100 plus tax. Bank credit card sales for the week, $1,900 plus tax. Bank credit card fee is 3%.
15	Received payment on account from Robert Zehnle, $1,100.
18	Robert Zehnle returned merchandise for a credit, $31 plus tax.
19	Cash sales for the week, $2,230 plus tax.
25	Received payment on account from Dazai Manufacturing, $318.

Beginning general ledger account balances were:

Cash	$2,890.75
Accounts Receivable	6,300.00

Beginning customer account balances were:

R. Boyd	$1,400
Dazai Manufacturing	318
C. Hassell	815
J. Sowada	1,481
R. Zehnle	2,286

REQUIRED

1. Record the transactions in the cash receipts journal. Total and verify the column totals and rule the columns. Use the general journal to record sales returns and allowances.

2. Post from the journals to the general ledger and accounts receivable ledger accounts. Use account numbers as shown in the chapter.

PROBLEM 13-8B (LO2/3)

Power Accounting System Software®

Total Accounts Receivable Dr.: $7,853.80

SALES JOURNAL, CASH RECEIPTS JOURNAL, GENERAL JOURNAL Paul Jackson owns a retail business. The following sales, returns, and cash receipts are for April 20--. There is a 7% sales tax.

April 1	Sale no. 111 to O. L. Meyers, $2,100 plus sales tax.
3	Sale no. 112 to Andrew Plaa, $1,000 plus sales tax.
6	O. L. Meyers returned merchandise from sale no. 111 for a credit (credit memo no. 42), $50 plus sales tax.
7	Cash sales for the week, $3,240 plus sales tax.
9	Received payment from O. L. Meyers for sale no. 111 less credit memo no. 42.
12	Sale no. 113 to Melissa Richfield, $980 plus sales tax.
14	Cash sales for the week, $2,180 plus sales tax.
17	Melissa Richfield returned merchandise from sale no. 113 for a credit (credit memo no. 43), $40 plus sales tax.
19	Sale no. 114 to Kelsay Munkres, $1,020 plus sales tax.
21	Cash sales for the week, $2,600 plus sales tax.
24	Sale no. 115 to O. L. Meyers, $920 plus sales tax.

27   Sale no. 116 to Andrew Plaa, $1,320 plus sales tax.

28   Cash sales for the week, $2,800 plus sales tax.

Beginning general ledger account balances were:

Cash	$2,864.54
Accounts Receivable	2,726.25

Beginning customer account balances were:

O. L. Meyers	$2,186.00
K. Munkres	482.00
M. Richfield	58.25

REQUIRED

1. Record the transactions in the sales journal, cash receipts journal, and general journal. Total, verify, and rule the columns where appropriate at the end of the month.

2. Post from the journals to the general ledger and accounts receivable ledger accounts. Use account numbers as shown in the chapter.

PROBLEM 13-9B   (LO4)
Total Purchases Dr.:
$18,515

PURCHASES JOURNAL Ann Benton, owner of Benton's Galleria, made the following purchases of merchandise on account during the month of October.

Oct. 2   Purchase invoice no. 321, $1,950, from Boggs Distributors.

7   Purchase invoice no. 152, $2,915, from Wolfs Wholesaler.

10   Purchase invoice no. 634, $3,565, from Komuro & Co.

16   Purchase invoice no. 349, $2,845, from Fritz & McCord, Inc.

24   Purchase invoice no. 587, $3,370, from Boggs Distributors.

26   Purchase invoice no. 764, $2,240, from Sanderson Company.

31   Purchase invoice no. 672, $1,630, from Wolfs Wholesaler.

REQUIRED

1. Record the transactions in the purchases journal. Total and rule the journal.

2. Post from the purchases journal to the general ledger and accounts payable ledger accounts. Use account numbers as shown in the chapter.

PROBLEM 13-10B   (LO4)
Amelia & Vincente
account balance: $7,810

PURCHASES JOURNAL, GENERAL LEDGER, AND ACCOUNTS PAYABLE LEDGER The purchases journal of Ryan's Rats Nest, a small retail business, is as follows:

	PURCHASES JOURNAL				PAGE 1	
	DATE	INVOICE NO.	FROM WHOM PURCHASED	POST REF.	PURCHASES DEBIT/ACCOUNTS PAYABLE CREDIT	
1	20-- Jan. 3	121	Sandra's Sweets		4 4 9 0 00	1
2	5	641	Amelia & Vincente		5 9 2 0 00	2
3	9	215	Nobuko's Nature Store		2 6 8 0 00	3
4	15	227	Smith and Johnson Company		6 5 6 0 00	4
5	21	933	Hidemi Inc.		1 3 0 0 00	5
6	30	650	Amelia & Vincente		1 8 9 0 00	6
7					22 8 4 0 00	7

(continued)

REQUIRED

1. Post the total of the purchases journal to the appropriate general ledger accounts. Use account numbers as shown in the chapter.

2. Post the individual purchase amounts to the accounts payable ledger.

PROBLEM 13-11B   (LO5)

Total Cash Cr.: $29,890

CASH PAYMENTS JOURNAL Kay Zembrowski operates a retail variety store. The books include a cash payments journal and an accounts payable ledger. All cash payments (except petty cash) are entered in the cash payments journal. Selected account balances on May 1 are as follows:

General Ledger

Cash	$40,000
Accounts Payable	20,000

Accounts Payable Ledger

Cortez Distributors	$4,200
Indra & Velga	6,800
Toy Corner	4,600
Troutman Outlet	4,400

The following are the transactions related to cash payments for the month of May.

May 1   Issued check no. 326 in payment of May rent (Rent Expense), $2,600.

4   Issued check no. 327 to Cortez Distributors in payment of merchandise purchased on account, $4,200 less a 3% discount. Check was written for $4,074.

7   Issued check no. 328 to Indra & Velga in partial payment of merchandise purchased on account, $6,200. A cash discount was not allowed.

11   Issued check no. 329 to Toy Corner for merchandise purchased on account, $4,600 less a 1% discount. Check was written for $4,554.

15   Issued check no. 330 to County Power and Light (Utilities Expense), $1,500.

19   Issued check no. 331 to Builders Warehouse for a cash purchase of merchandise, $3,500.

25   Issued check no. 332 to Troutman Outlet for merchandise purchased on account, $4,400 less a 2% discount. Check was written for $4,312.

30   Issued check no. 333 to Rapid Transit Company for freight charges on merchandise purchased (Freight-In), $800.

31   Issued check no. 334 to City Merchants for a cash purchase of merchandise, $2,350.

REQUIRED

1. Enter the transactions in a cash payments journal. Total, rule, and prove the cash payments journal.

2. Post from the cash payments journal to the general ledger and accounts payable ledger. Use general ledger account numbers as shown in the chapter.

PROBLEM 13-12B **(LO4/5)**

Power Accounting System Software®

Total Cash Cr.: $10,760

PURCHASES JOURNAL, CASH PAYMENTS JOURNAL, AND GENERAL JOURNAL
Debbie Mueller owns a small retail business called Debbie's Doll House. The cash account has a balance of $20,000 on July 1. The following transactions occurred during July.

July 1	Issued check no. 314 for July rent, $1,400.
1	Purchased merchandise on account from Topper's Toys, invoice no. 211, $2,500, terms 2/10, n/30.
3	Purchased merchandise on account from Jones & Company, invoice no. 812, $2,800, terms 1/10, n/30.
5	Returned merchandise purchased from Topper's Toys receiving a credit memo on the amount owed, $400.
8	Purchased merchandise on account from Downtown Merchants, invoice no. 159, $1,600, terms 2/10, n/30.
11	Issued check no. 315 to Topper's Toys for merchandise purchased on account, less return of July 5 and less 2% discount.
13	Issued check no. 316 to Jones & Company for merchandise purchased on account, less 1% discount.
15	Returned merchandise purchased from Downtown Merchants receiving a credit memo on the amount owed, $600.
18	Issued check no. 317 to Downtown Merchants for merchandise purchased on account, less return of July 15 and less 2% discount.
25	Purchased merchandise on account from Columbia Products, invoice no. 468, $3,200, terms n/30.
26	Purchased merchandise on account from Topper's Toys, invoice no. 395, $1,430, terms 2/10, n/30.
29	Purchased merchandise on account from Jones & Company, invoice no. 853, $2,970, terms 1/10, n/30.
31	Mueller withdrew cash for personal use, $2,500. Issued check no. 318.
31	Issued check no. 319 to Burnside Warehouse for a cash purchase of merchandise, $1,050.

REQUIRED

1. Record the transactions in the purchases journal, cash payments journal, and general journal. Total and rule the purchases and cash payments journals. Prove the cash payments journal.

2. Post from the journals to the general ledger and accounts payable ledger accounts. Use general ledger account numbers as shown in the chapter.

MASTERY PROBLEM

**Total Accounts
Receivable Cr.: $7,235**

During the month of Oct, 20--, The Pink Petal flower shop engaged in the following transactions:

Oct. 1 Sold merchandise on account to Elizabeth Shoemaker, $1,000 plus tax of $50. Sale no. 222.

2 Issued check no. 190 to Jill Hand in payment of October 1 balance of $500, less 2% discount.

2 Purchased merchandise on account from Flower Wholesalers $4,000. Invoice no. 500, dated October 2, terms 2/10, n/30.

4 Purchased merchandise on account from Seidl Enterprises $700. Invoice no. 527, dated October 4, terms 2/15, n/30.

5 Issued check no. 191 in payment of telephone expense for the month of September, $150.

7 Sold merchandise for cash, $3,500, plus tax of $175.

9 Received payment from Leigh Summers in full settlement of account, $2,000.

11 Issued check no. 192 to Flower Wholesalers in payment of October 1 balance of $1,500.

12 Sold merchandise on account to Leigh Summers, $2,000 plus tax of $100. Sale no. 223.

12 Received payment from Meg Johnson on account, $3,100.

13 Issued check no. 193 to Seidl Enterprises in payment of October 4 purchase. Invoice no. 527, less 2% discount.

14 Meg Johnson returned merchandise for a credit, $300 plus sales tax of $15.

17 Returned merchandise to Vases Etc. for credit, $900.

24 Received payment from David's Decorating on account, $2,135.

27 Sold merchandise on account to David's Decorating, $3,000 plus tax of $150. Sale no. 224.

29 Issued check no. 194 in payment of wages (Wages Expense) for the four-week period ending October 30, $900.

Selected account balances as of October 1 were as follows:

Account	Account No.	Debit	Credit
Cash	101	$18,225.00	
Accounts Receivable	122	9,619.00	
Accounts Payable	202		$5,120.00

The Pink Petal also had the following subsidiary ledger balances as of October 1.

Accounts Receivable:

Customer	Accounts Receivable Balance
David's Decorating 12 Jude Lane Hartford, CT 06117	$3,340.00

Elizabeth Shoemaker
52 Juniper Road
Hartford, CT 06118   279.00

Meg Johnson
700 Hobbes Dr.
Avon, CT 06108   4,000.00

Leigh Summers
5200 Hamilton Ave.
Hartford, CT 06111   2,000.00

Accounts Payable:

Vendor	Accounts Payable Balance
Vases Etc. 34 Harry Ave. East Hartford, CT 05234	$3,120.00
Jill Hand 1009 Drake Rd. Farmington, CT 06082	500.00
Flower Wholesalers 43 Lucky Lane Bristo, CT 06007	1,500.00
Seidl Enterprises 888 Anders Street Newington, CT 06789	—

REQUIRED:

1. Record the transactions in a sales journal (p. 7), cash receipts journal (p. 10), purchases journal (p. 6), cash payments journal (p. 11), and general journal (p. 5). Total, verify, and rule the columns where appropriate at the end of the month.

2. Post from the journals to the general ledger, accounts receivable ledger, and accounts payable ledger accounts. Use account numbers as shown in the chapter.

CHALLENGE PROBLEM

This problem challenges you to apply your cumulative accounting knowledge to move a step beyond the material in the chapter.

June 3: Cr. City Sales Tax Payable, $4.22

Screpcap Co. had the following transactions during the first week of June.

June 1   Purchased merchandise on account from Acme Supply, $2,700 plus freight charges of $160.

1   Issued check no. 219 to Denver Wholesalers for merchandise purchased on account, $720 less 1% discount.

1   Sold merchandise on account to F. Colby, $246 plus 5% state sales tax plus 2% city sales tax.

2   Received cash on account from N. Dunlop, $315.

2   Made cash sale of $413 plus 5% state sales tax plus 2% city sales tax.

(continued)

2   Purchased merchandise on account from Permon Co., $3,200 plus freight charges of $190.

3   Sold merchandise on account to F. Ayres, $211 plus 5% state sales tax plus 2% city sales tax.

3   Issued check no. 220 to Ellis Co. for merchandise purchased on account, $847 less 1% discount.

3   Received cash on account from F. Graves, $463.

4   Issued check no. 221 to Penguin Warehouse for merchandise purchased on account, $950 less 1% discount.

4   Sold merchandise on account to K. Stanga, $318 plus 5% state sales tax plus 2% city sales tax.

4   Purchased merchandise on account from Mason Milling, $1,630 plus freight charges of $90.

4   Received cash on account from O. Alston, $381.

5   Made cash sale of $319 plus 5% state sales tax plus 2% city sales tax.

5   Issued check no. 222 to Acme Supply for merchandise purchased on account, $980 less 1% discount.

REQUIRED

1. Record the transactions in a general journal.

2. Assuming these are the types of transactions Screpcap Co. experiences on a regular basis, design the following special journals for Screpcap.
    (a) Sales journal
    (b) Cash receipts journal
    (c) Purchases journal
    (d) Cash payments journal

DIGITAL IMAGING GROUP

The Voucher System

By the end of the first year of operations of Parkway Pet Supplies, Evan Taylor finds that revenues and expenses have become much larger than in the early months. Evan feels comfortable with control over revenues. He has developed a good feel for what sales should be on a weekly and even a daily basis in most cases. All cash is deposited daily in the bank, and he regularly monitors his inventory.

For expenditures, Evan personally signs all checks after reviewing any bills or other supporting paper work. He is unaware of any errors having occurred. Still, Evan wonders whether he has adequate control over his expenditures. His bookkeeper says that she learned in one of her recent courses that a voucher system is a good way to control expenditures. Evan is interested in such a system. What is a voucher system? Would a voucher system be a good idea for Evan's business?

Careful study of this chapter should enable you to:

LO1 Describe how a voucher system is used to control expenditures.

LO2 Prepare a voucher.

LO3 Describe and use a voucher register.

LO4 Describe the payment process using a voucher system.

LO5 Describe and use a check register and prepare a schedule of vouchers payable.

LO6 Account for returns, allowances, and partial payments.

Chapter 13 demonstrated how merchandise purchased on account can be efficiently recorded in a purchases journal. In this chapter, we will learn to use a special journal for recording all purchases of assets and services of any kind. Chapter 13 also demonstrated how cash payments can be efficiently recorded in a cash payments journal. In this chapter, we will learn to use another type of journal for recording cash payments.

The two new journals introduced in this chapter provide more than an efficient way to record transactions. These journals are an important part of what is called a voucher system.

INTERNAL CONTROL OF EXPENDITURES

LO1 Describe how a voucher system is used to control expenditures.

Internal controls are important in every business, regardless of its size. The main effect of size on internal controls is that in larger businesses, the internal controls need to be more formal and tend to be more costly.

To be successful, management must have adequate control of the operations of the business. When we think of controlling business operations, most of us tend to emphasize ways to control revenues. For example, when a sale occurs, we want to be sure the sales clerk puts the cash in the register. In fact, it is just as important to control the expenditure process.

Management needs to see that expenditures are made only for goods and services needed by the business and at a fair price. In a small business, management does so by direct involvement with the expenditure process. But as a business grows larger, management cannot continue such direct involvement. Instead, in medium- and large-size businesses, management controls expenditures by using an appropriate internal control system.

Elements of Internal Control

Internal controls are the set of procedures used to ensure that there is proper accounting for all activities of the business. A full discussion of internal controls is a subject for an advanced text. Our attention will be limited to three elements of internal control that are particularly important for expenditures:

1. Segregation of duties

2. Authorization procedures and related responsibilities

3. Adequate documents and records

   Segregation of duties means that:

1. Different employees should be responsible for different parts of a transaction; and

2. Employees who account for transactions should not also have custody of the assets.

For example, one employee should be responsible for ordering goods and a different employee should be responsible for issuing the check to pay for them. Similarly, one employee should be responsible for recording the purchase of goods and a different employee should be responsible for receiving and placing the goods in inventory. This segregation of duties provides a built-in check by one employee on another. One employee cannot obtain goods for personal use without being caught by another employee.

Authorization procedures and related responsibilities means that every business activity should be properly authorized. In addition, it should be possible to identify who is responsible for every activity that has occurred. For example, to acquire new equipment, a signed document should authorize the purchase. After the purchase is made, this signed document shows who is responsible for the action.

Adequate documents and records means that accounting documents and records should be used so that all business transactions are recorded. For example, every purchase that occurs should be supported by a document. These documents should be prenumbered, used in sequence, and subsequently accounted for. In this way, the business can be sure that it has made a record of each transaction.

Voucher System

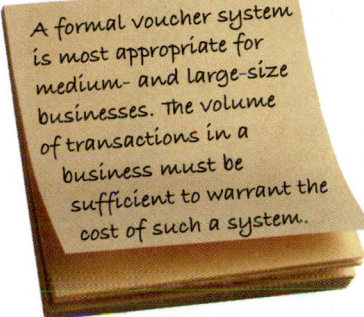

A formal voucher system is most appropriate for medium- and large-size businesses. The volume of transactions in a business must be sufficient to warrant the cost of such a system.

The three elements of internal control described above can be combined to control expenditures by using a voucher system. A **voucher system** is a control technique that requires that every acquisition and subsequent payment be supported by an approved voucher. A **voucher** is a document that shows that an acquisition is proper and that payment is authorized.

Figure 14-1 is a simplified illustration of how the purchasing portion of a voucher system operates. The purchase requisition, purchase order, receiving report, and purchase invoice were explained and illustrated in Chapter 12. Recall that an authorized person or department prepares a purchase requisition to indicate the need for goods. The purchasing department reviews and approves the purchase requisition and prepares a purchase order to send to the supplier. When the goods are received, a receiving report is prepared. A copy of each of these documents is sent to the vouchers payable section in the accounting department.

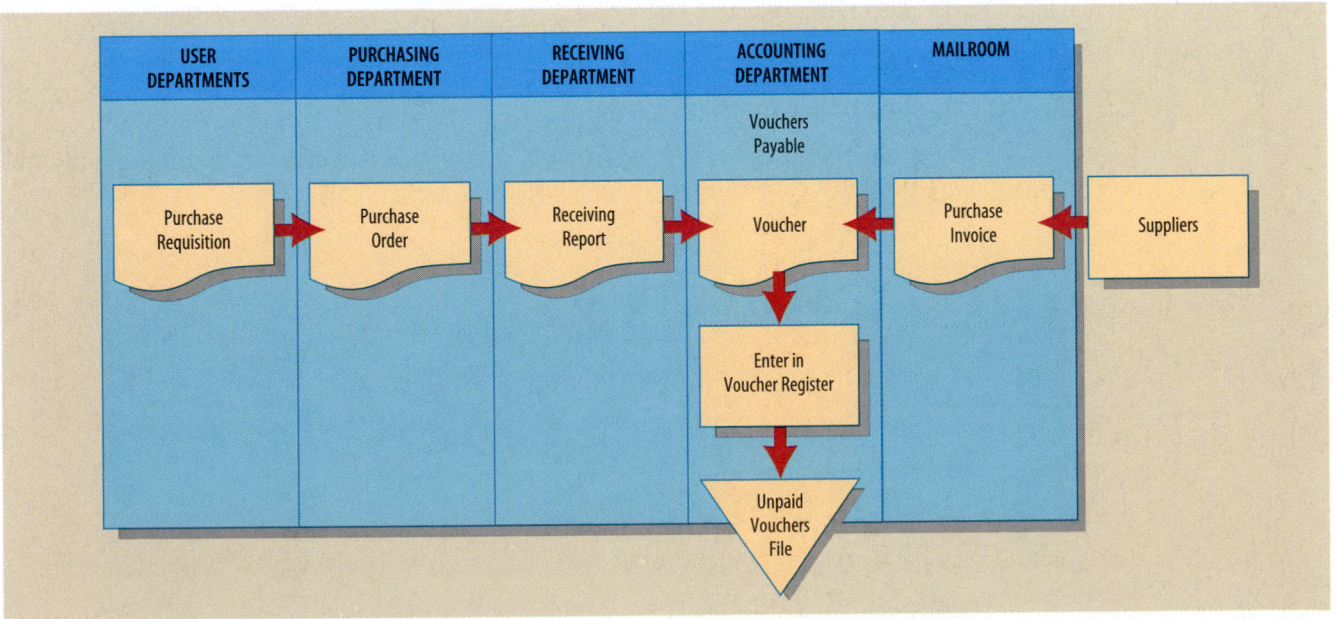

FIGURE 14-1 Voucher System—Purchasing Process

When the purchase invoice arrives, it is compared with the purchase requisition, purchase order, and receiving report. If the purchase invoice is

- for the goods ordered (purchase requisition and purchase order),
- at the correct price (purchase order),
- and for the correct quantity (receiving report),

then a voucher (see Figure 14-3, page 510) is prepared. This is the first key control provided by the voucher system. If any aspect of the purchase is improper, it will be caught when the voucher is prepared.

After the voucher is prepared and approved, it is entered in a special journal called a voucher register. It then is filed in an unpaid vouchers file by due date.

The completed voucher provides the basis for paying the supplier's invoice on the due date. This is the second key control provided by the voucher system. *No payment may be made without an approved voucher.* The payment process will be discussed later in this chapter.

LEARNING KEY: The voucher system contains elements of internal control such as segregation of duties, authorization to order the goods and prepare the voucher, and accounting procedures that require prenumbering and accounting for the supporting documents.

Notice how the three elements of internal control can be seen in this system. (1) *Duties are segregated* because different employees order, receive, and record the purchases. (2) *Authorization* is required to order the goods and to prepare the voucher. (3) The *documents and records* include purchase requisitions, purchase orders, receiving reports, and vouchers that are prenumbered and accounted for. This means that every recorded purchase is supported by the following five documents:

1. Voucher

2. Purchase invoice

3. Receiving report

4. Purchase order

5. Purchase requisition

This provides management with strong assurance that purchasing activities are properly controlled.

PREPARING A VOUCHER

LO2 Prepare a voucher.

To illustrate the preparation of a voucher and how a voucher system works, we extend the Northern Micro transactions used in Chapters 12 and 13. In this chapter, we assume that Northern Micro uses a voucher system, and several transactions are added.

When a purchase invoice (Figure 14-2) is received from a supplier, the following procedures are performed in the voucher section.

STEP 1   Compare the invoice with the purchase requisition, purchase order, and receiving report to determine that:

a.   the quantity was requisitioned (purchase requisition), ordered (purchase order), and received (receiving report)

b.   the price and credit terms are proper (purchase order)

STEP 2   Judge whether the purchase is appropriate for the business.

STEP 3   Verify all computations on the invoice (quantity × price, and any discounts).

Note how the voucher section thus provides a final, independent check on the entire purchasing process. If any aspect is improper, it can be caught before payment is made.

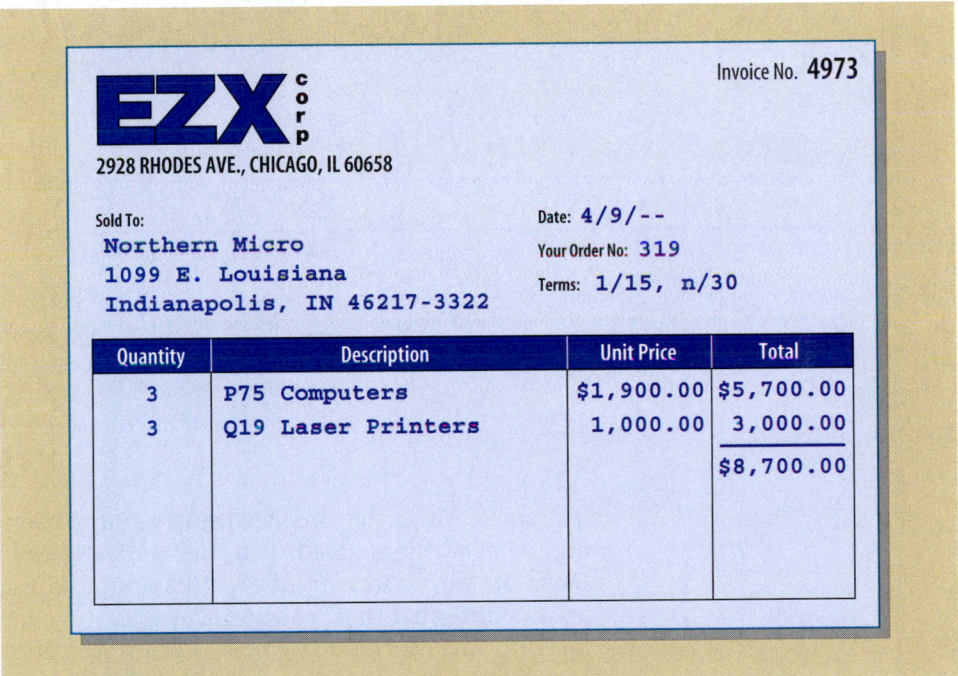

FIGURE 14-2 Purchase Invoice

After performing these procedures, the voucher is prepared. Many acceptable formats for vouchers can be used. Figure 14-3 illustrates a commonly used form. This voucher was prepared based on the purchase invoice in Figure 14-2.

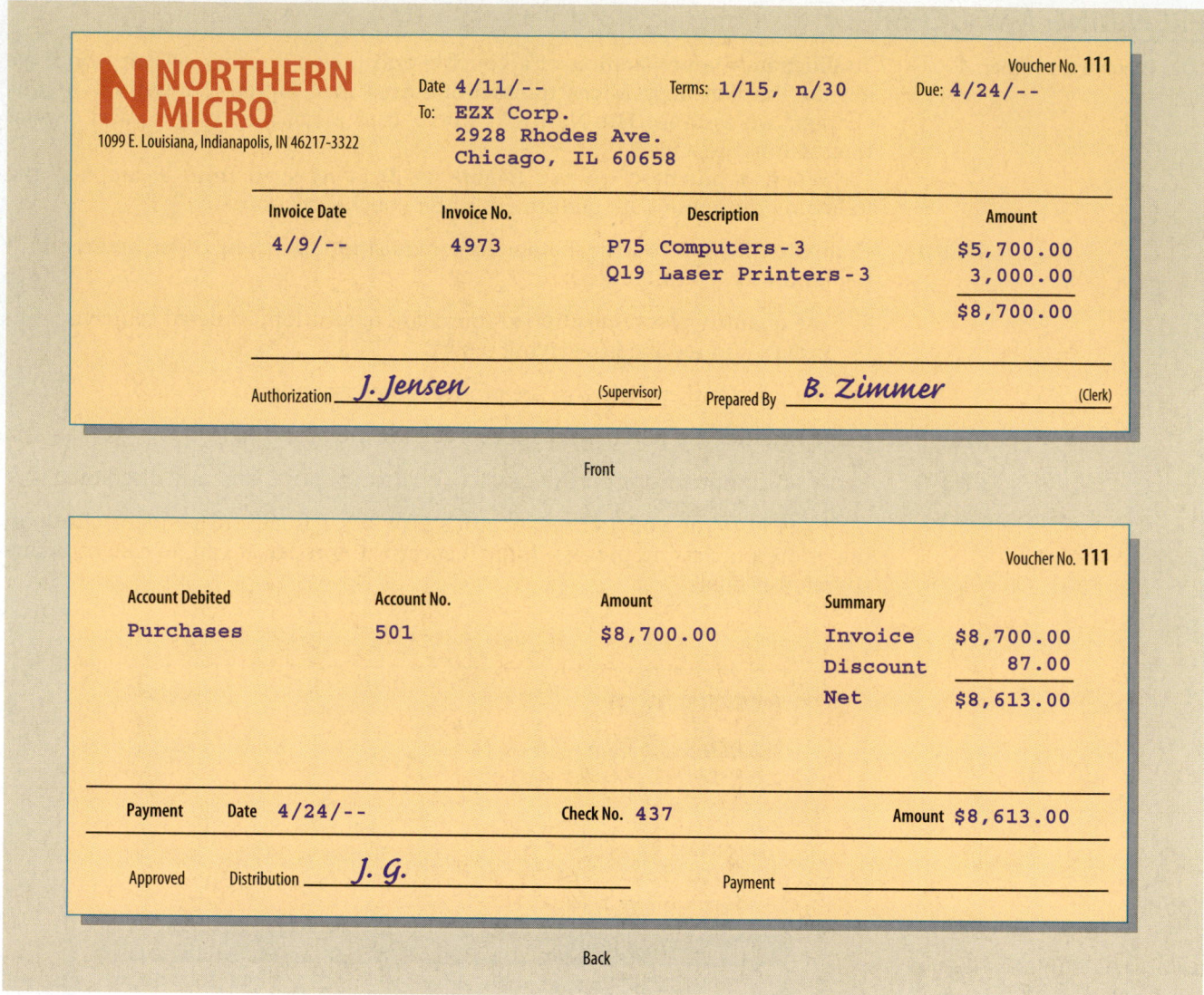

FIGURE 14-3 Voucher

The front of the voucher usually shows the voucher number, date, supplier, and what was purchased. The back indicates the accounts to be debited and the payment date, check number, and amount. If an expenditure requires a credit to an account other than Vouchers Payable, this can be shown as a separate notation beneath the Account Debited section on the back of the voucher. Payroll expenditures usually require this treatment because of the related liabilities for Employees Income Tax, Social Security Tax, Medicare Tax, etc.

The prenumbered voucher in Figure 14-3 was prepared using the following steps.

STEP 1   On the front of the voucher, insert

   a. voucher date

   b. invoice terms

   c. due date

   d. supplier name and address

   e. invoice date

   f. description of items purchased

   g. invoice amount

STEP 2   On the back, insert the accounts and amounts to be debited.

After these steps are completed, the voucher clerk (B. Zimmer) signs the voucher and has it approved by the voucher section supervisor (J. Jensen). On the back of the voucher, the "Distribution" (the accounts to which the expenditure is charged) is approved by the accounting supervisor (J.G.). The "Payment" approval is not completed until the voucher is paid on the due date. The $87 purchases discount will be recorded when the voucher is paid.

VOUCHER REGISTER

LO3 Describe and use a voucher register.

After the voucher is completed and approved, it is entered in a voucher register. A **voucher register** is a special journal used to record purchases of all types of assets and services. You can think of a voucher register as an expanded purchases journal like the one we saw in Chapter 13. In fact, if a voucher register is used, it replaces the purchases journal.

LEARNING KEY: Use the voucher register to record all types of purchases.

Figure 14-4 illustrates Northern Micro's voucher register. It has four debit columns—Purchases, Supplies, Wages Expense, and General Debit—and a credit column for Vouchers Payable. The General Debit column is used for transactions affecting account titles other than those with special column headings. To allow for credits to accounts other than Vouchers Payable, the General Debit column can be expanded to include General Debit and Credit columns. The additional accounts and amounts would be listed in these columns of the voucher register. The voucher register also has a Payment column that is used when the voucher is paid. As with any special journal, the exact number and types of debit and credit columns used depends on the nature of the business.

The transaction on 4/15/-- for payroll actually would require a debit to Payroll and credits to Vouchers Payable, Employee Income Tax Payable, Social Security Tax Payable, and Medicare Tax Payable. To simplify the illustrations in this chapter, all payroll transactions are shown as a debit to Wages Expense and a credit to Vouchers Payable for a single amount.

	DATE	VOUCHER NO.	ISSUED TO	PURCHASES DEBIT		
1	4/2/--	106	Triumph Leasing			1
2	4/4/--	107	Sam's Cyberware	1 4 0 0 00		2
3	4/4/--	108	Compucraft, Inc.	3 3 0 0 00		3
4	4/8/--	109	Datasoft	2 5 0 0 00		4
5	4/9/--	110	Bemon Office Supply			5
6	4/11/--	111	EZX Corp.	8 7 0 0 00		6
7	4/15/--	112	Payroll			7
15				23 5 6 0 00		15

VOUCHER REGISTER

FIGURE 14-4 Voucher Register (left side)

A voucher is recorded in the voucher register by entering the following information.

1. Date

2. Voucher number

3. Person or business to whom the voucher is issued

4. Dollar amounts of debits and credits (and the account name if the General Dr. column is used)

The entry for Voucher No. 111 (Figure 14-3) was made on April 11.

Filing Unpaid Vouchers

After the voucher is entered in the voucher register, the voucher and supporting documents (purchase requisition, purchase order, receiving report, and purchase invoice) are stapled together. This "voucher packet" is then filed in an **unpaid vouchers file**, normally by due date. Alternatively, vouchers can be filed by supplier name. Filing by due date is preferred because this helps management plan for cash needs. It also helps ensure that vouchers are paid on the due date and cash discounts are taken.

An additional benefit of a voucher system is that the unpaid vouchers file can function as an accounts payable ledger. This accounts payable ledger differs from the one described in Chapter 12 in that the payables are grouped by due date rather than by supplier.

LEARNING KEY: When a voucher system is used, the unpaid vouchers file can serve as an accounts payable ledger.

Posting from the Voucher Register

Both individual and summary postings are required from the voucher register to the general ledger. Figure 14-5 illustrates the posting process for Northern Micro's voucher register for April, as follows:

PAGE 4

	SUPPLIES DEBIT			WAGES EXPENSE DEBIT			GENERAL DEBIT					VOUCHERS PAYABLE CREDIT					PAYMENT		
							ACCOUNT	POST REF.	AMOUNT								DATE	CHECK NO.	
1							Rent Exp.		2	4	0	0	00	2	4	0	0	00	4/2/--	421	1
2														1	4	0	0	00	4/4/--	423	2
3														3	3	0	0	00			3
4														2	5	0	0	00			4
5	1	6	0	00										1	6	0	00		4/25/--	438	5
6														8	7	0	0	00	4/24/--	437	6
7				8	3	0	00							8	3	0	00		4/15/--	430	7
15	2	8	0	00	1	7	0	0	00			5	9	0	0	00	31	4	4	0	00			15

FIGURE 14-4 Voucher Register (right side)

On a daily basis:

STEP 1 Post each amount from the General Debit column to the appropriate general ledger account. (Note that only the first half of the month is shown in Figure 14-5. The rest of the month would be posted in a similar manner.)

STEP 2 Insert the date in the Date column and the initials "VR" and the voucher register page number in the Posting Reference column of each general ledger account.

STEP 3 Insert the general ledger account numbers in the Posting Reference column of the General Debit column of the voucher register.

At the end of each month:

STEP 4 Total the amount columns, verify that the total of the debit columns equals the total of the credit column, and rule the columns.

STEP 5 Post each column total except the General Debit column to the general ledger account indicated in the column headings.

STEP 6 Insert the date in the Date column and the initials "VR" and the voucher register page number in the Posting Reference column of each ledger account.

STEP 7 Insert the general ledger account numbers immediately below each column total except the General Debit column.

STEP 8 Insert a check mark (✓) immediately below the General Debit column total.

The payables account in Figure 14-5 may be called either Vouchers Payable or Accounts Payable. Even with a voucher system, many businesses still use the Accounts Payable title. On the balance sheet, the Accounts Payable title is almost always used.

No posting to an accounts payable ledger is necessary for Northern Micro. They use the unpaid vouchers file as their accounts payable ledger. The unpaid vouchers file was updated when the vouchers were filed after being entered in the voucher register.

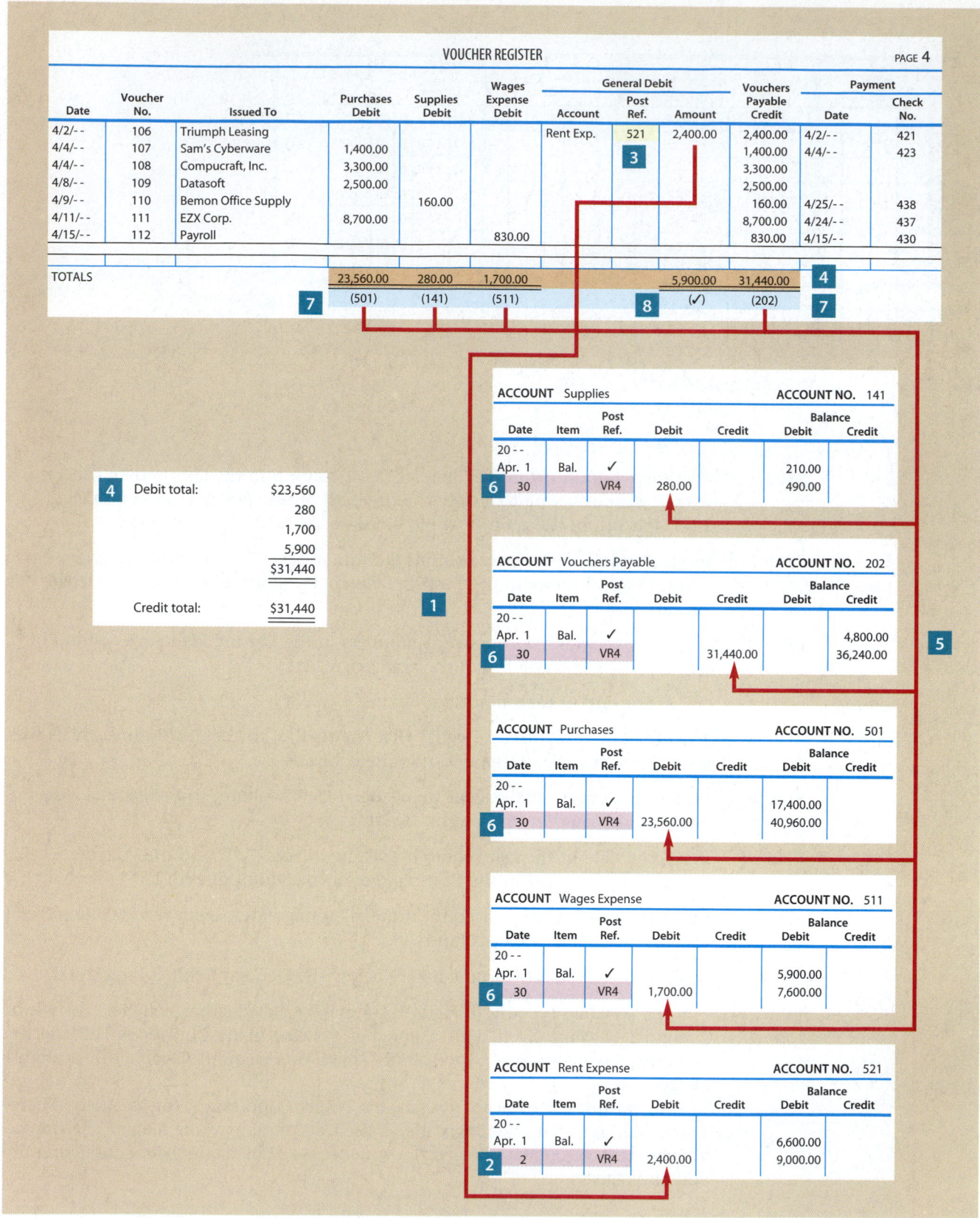

FIGURE 14-5 Posting Voucher Register to General Ledger

THE PAYMENT PROCESS USING A VOUCHER SYSTEM

LO4 **Describe the payment process using a voucher system.**

Figure 14-6 illustrates the payment process when a voucher system is used. On the due date, the voucher is pulled from the unpaid vouchers file. The voucher is given to the person responsible for preparing and signing checks (for Northern Micro, the cashier). The cashier reviews each voucher and supporting documents to see that the expenditure is proper. The cashier then prepares and signs the check and sends it to the supplier. It is important for internal control that no check be prepared without a supporting voucher and that the check be mailed as soon as it is signed.

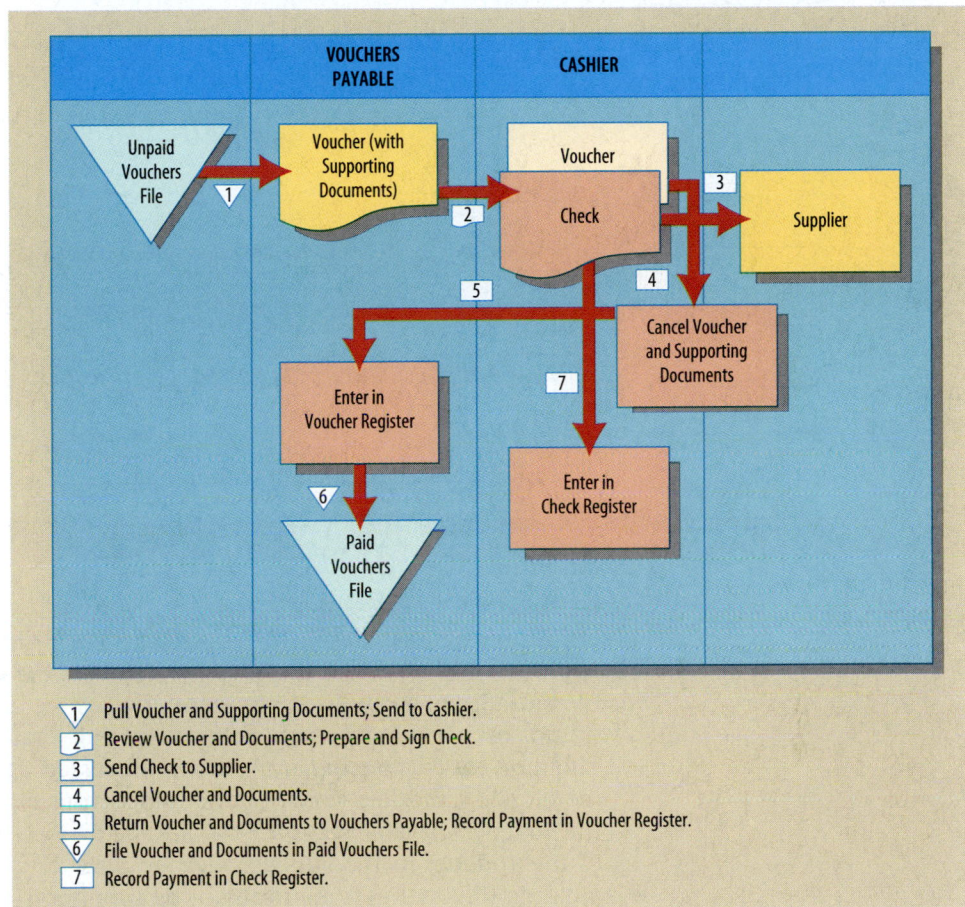

1. Pull Voucher and Supporting Documents; Send to Cashier.
2. Review Voucher and Documents; Prepare and Sign Check.
3. Send Check to Supplier.
4. Cancel Voucher and Documents.
5. Return Voucher and Documents to Vouchers Payable; Record Payment in Voucher Register.
6. File Voucher and Documents in Paid Vouchers File.
7. Record Payment in Check Register.

FIGURE 14-6   Voucher System—Payment Process

 LEARNING KEY: For good internal control of cash payments, it is important for the check to be mailed as soon as it is signed.

Ordinary checks may be used to make payments, but under the voucher system, voucher checks often are used. A **voucher check** is a check with space for entering data about the voucher being paid. Figure 14-7 shows Northern Micro's voucher check to pay Voucher No. 111 (Figure 14-3).

The voucher check has two parts:

1. The check itself, which is similar to an ordinary check, and

2. An attached statement, which indicates the invoice being paid and any deductions.

In addition, the voucher check stub identifies the voucher number being paid.

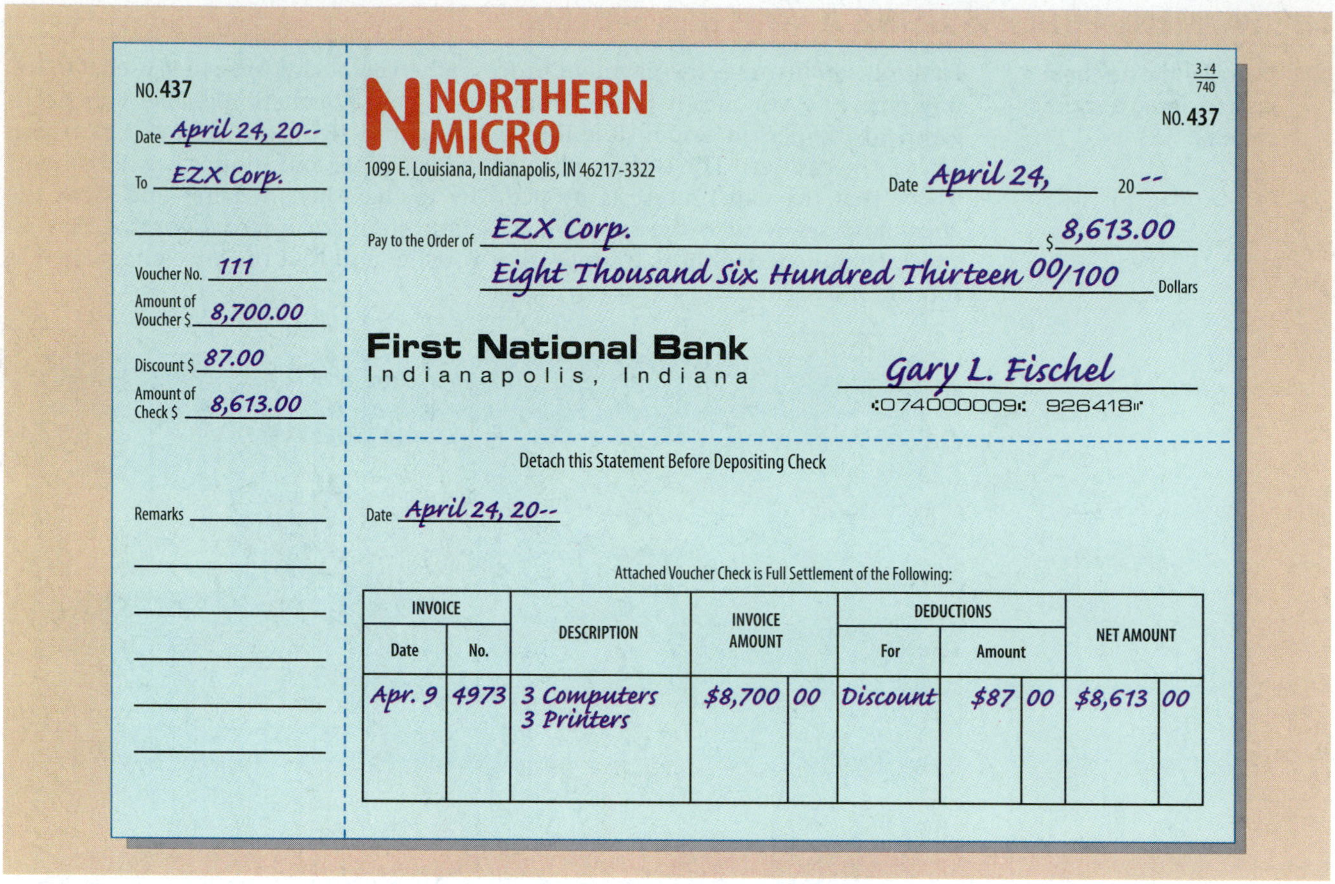
NO. 437
Date April 24, 20--
To EZX Corp.
Voucher No. 111
Amount of Voucher $ 8,700.00
Discount $ 87.00
Amount of Check $ 8,613.00
Remarks

NORTHERN MICRO
1099 E. Louisiana, Indianapolis, IN 46217-3322

3-4/740
NO. 437

Date April 24, 20--

Pay to the Order of EZX Corp. $ 8,613.00

Eight Thousand Six Hundred Thirteen 00/100 Dollars

First National Bank
Indianapolis, Indiana

Gary L. Fischel

⑆074000009⑆ 926418⑈

Detach this Statement Before Depositing Check

Date April 24, 20--

Attached Voucher Check is Full Settlement of the Following:

INVOICE		DESCRIPTION	INVOICE AMOUNT		DEDUCTIONS			NET AMOUNT	
Date	No.				For	Amount			
Apr. 9	4973	3 Computers 3 Printers	$8,700	00	Discount	$87	00	$8,613	00

FIGURE 14-7 Voucher Check

After the voucher has been paid, the cashier completes the "Payment" approval on the back of the voucher. The voucher and supporting documents are then cancelled to indicate payment. The cancelling can be done with a rubber stamp, by perforating, or by simply writing "paid" on all relevant documents. This prevents a voucher from being processed again to create a duplicate payment. The cancelled voucher and supporting documents are then returned to the vouchers payable section. The cancelled voucher is used to record the payment of the voucher in the voucher register. The voucher and supporting documents are then filed either numerically or by supplier in a **paid vouchers file**. In either case, the numerical sequence should be accounted for to identify possible missing or duplicate vouchers.

CHECK REGISTER

LO5 Describe and use a check register and prepare a schedule of vouchers payable.

A copy of the check is used to enter the payment in a check register. A **check register** is a special journal used to record all checks written in a voucher system. Figure 14-8 illustrates Northern Micro's check register.

A check register is similar to the cash payments journal we saw in Chapter 13 (Figure 13-15). A key difference is that the check register has only three amount columns—Vouchers Payable Debit, Purchases Discounts Credit, and Cash Credit. Recall that in a voucher system, every purchase of assets or services must be supported by a voucher. This means that every purchase has been recorded in a

A BROADER VIEW

Fraud Can Mean Expensive Supplies

©GETTY IMAGES/PHOTODISC

A computer systems worker at Mobil Chemical Co. in Stratford, Connecticut, stole $522,000 by paying for purchases of supplies that did not exist. First, the worker established a false company. At Mobil, he prepared purchase orders to purchase supplies from this company. He then prepared receiving reports for supplies that were never delivered. When he sent bills from the company to Mobil, they were paid based on the bogus receiving reports and purchase orders. Checks issued to pay for the supplies were sent to a post office box where the worker collected them.

This fraud shows the importance of segregation of duties and use of a voucher system as described in this chapter. This worker was able to control too many parts of this purchase transaction. In addition, payment was made without an approved voucher with all supporting documents.

voucher register before any payment can be made. Thus the debit in the check register is to Vouchers Payable, and the credits are to Purchases Discounts and Cash. When a business uses the voucher system and a voucher register, the check register replaces the cash payments journal.

	DATE	CHECK NO.	PAYEE	VOUCHERS PAYABLE DR.		PURCHASES DISCOUNTS CREDIT	CASH CREDIT	
				NO.	AMOUNT			
1	4/1/--	420	Payroll	105	8 7 0 0 00		8 7 0 0 00	1
2	4/2/--	421	Triumph Leasing	106	2 4 0 0 00		2 4 0 0 00	2
19	4/24/--	437	EZX Corp.	111	8 7 0 0 00	8 7 00	8 6 1 3 00	19
20	4/25/--	438	Bemon Office Supply	110	1 6 0 0 00		1 6 0 0 00	20
21	4/29/--	439	TTA Products	115	1 5 0 0 00		1 5 0 0 00	21
22	TOTALS				24 3 4 0 00	1 7 9 00	24 1 6 1 00	22

CHECK REGISTER — PAGE 4

FIGURE 14-8   Check Register

LEARNING KEY: There are only three amount columns in the check register: Vouchers Payable Debit, Purchases Discounts Credit, and Cash Credit.

	DATE	VOUCHER NO.	ISSUED TO	PURCHASES DEBIT	
6	4/11/- -	111	EZX Corp.	8 7 0 0 00	6
7					7
8					8

FIGURE 14-9 Partial Voucher Register (left side)

A check is recorded in the check register by entering the following information.

1. Date

2. Check number

3. Payee

4. Voucher number

5. Dollar amounts

The entry on April 24 is for the voucher check in Figure 14-7.

The check-entering process also affects the voucher register. As shown in the diagram in Figure 14-6, the canceled voucher is used to enter the payment of the vouchers in the voucher register. A portion of the voucher register in Figure 14-4 is reproduced in Figure 14-9, with the Payment column filled in for voucher no. 111. Both the date of payment and the check number are inserted to indicate that the voucher has been paid.

Posting from the Check Register

Only monthly summary postings are required from the check register to the general ledger. Figure 14-10 illustrates the posting process for Northern Micro's check register at the end of April, as follows:

STEP 1 Total the amount columns, verify that the total of the debit column equals the total of the credit columns, and rule the columns.

STEP 2 Post each column total to the general ledger account indicated in the column headings.

STEP 3 Insert the date in the Date column and the initials "CK" and the check register page number in the Posting Reference column of each ledger account.

STEP 4 Insert the general ledger account numbers immediately below each column total.

	SUPPLIES DEBIT		WAGES EXPENSE DEBIT		GENERAL DEBIT				VOUCHERS PAYABLE CREDIT		PAYMENT		
					ACCOUNT	POST REF.	AMOUNT				DATE	CHECK NO.	
6									8 7 0 0 00		4/24/--	437	6
7													7
8													8

PAGE 4

FIGURE 14-9   Partial Voucher Register (right side)

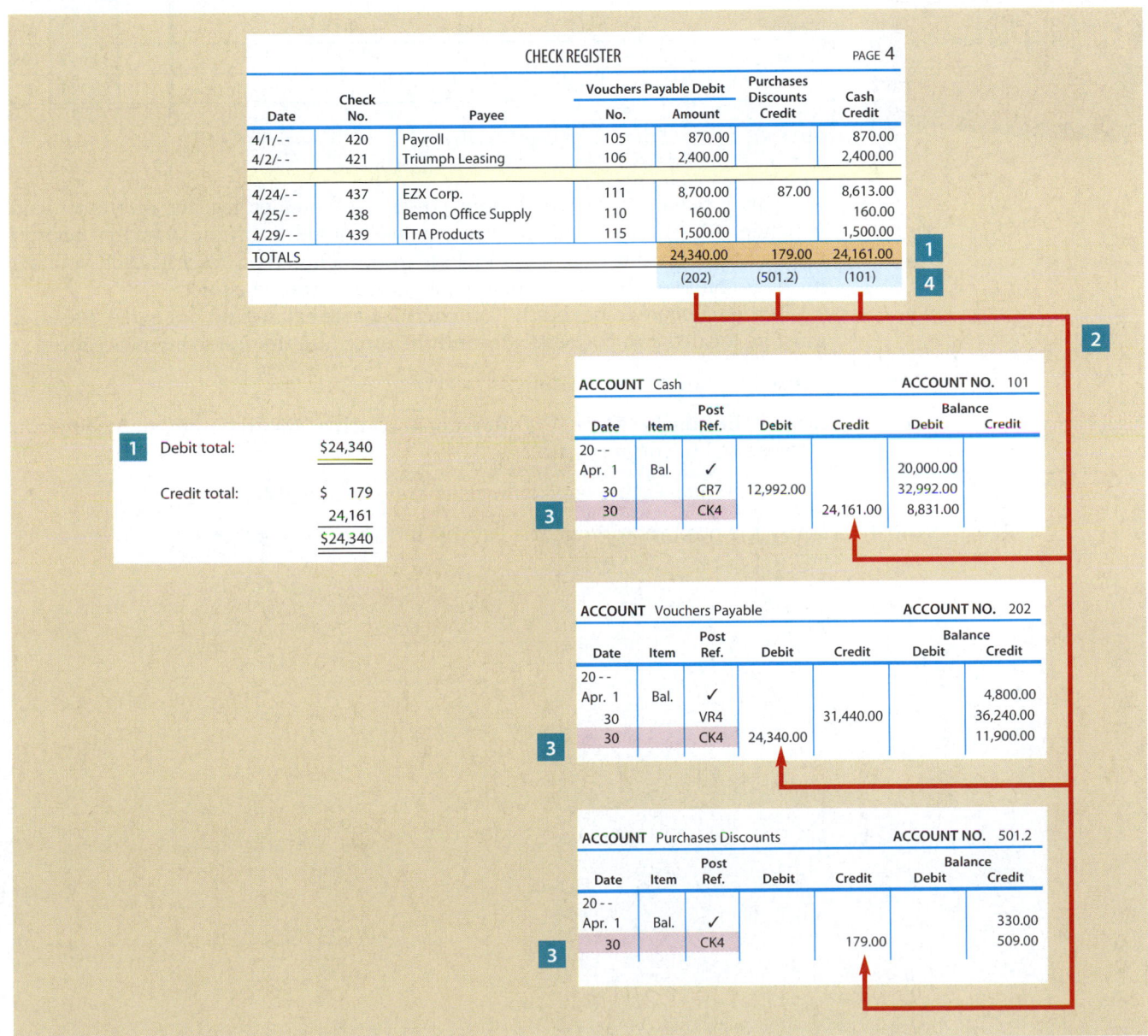

FIGURE 14-10   Posting Check Register to General Ledger

Schedule of Vouchers Payable

It was explained earlier that most businesses that use a voucher system do not keep an accounts payable ledger. It is still desirable, however, to verify each month that the sum of the individual amounts owed to creditors equals the Vouchers Payable balance. For this purpose, a schedule of vouchers payable (Figure 14-11) is prepared. Note that the $11,900 total listed in the schedule equals the vouchers payable balance shown in Figure 14-10.

The schedule of vouchers payable can also be prepared by due date. In this case, due dates would be listed in place of the supplier names.

Northern Micro Schedule of Vouchers Payable April 30, 20 - -					
Compucraft, Inc.	$ 3	3	0	0	00
Datasoft	2	5	0	0	00
Printpro		8	0	0	00
Televax	5	3	0	0	00
	$11	9	0	0	00

FIGURE 14-11 Schedule of Vouchers Payable

This schedule is prepared from either the voucher register or the unpaid vouchers file. Every blank in the Payment column of the voucher register represents an unpaid voucher to include in the schedule. Similarly, each voucher in the unpaid vouchers file should be included in the schedule.

If the schedule total and the Vouchers Payable balance do not agree, the error must be located and corrected. To find the error, use the following procedures.

STEP 1 Verify the total of the schedule.

STEP 2 Review the voucher register or the unpaid vouchers file to be sure no vouchers were missed or counted twice.

STEP 3 Verify the totals in the voucher register and check register.

STEP 4 Verify the postings to Vouchers Payable in the general ledger.

RETURNS, ALLOWANCES, AND PARTIAL PAYMENTS

LO6 Account for returns, allowances, and partial payments.

For a voucher system to provide good control of expenditures, vouchers must be carefully handled and recorded. This includes both the initial creation and recording of the voucher as well as its subsequent payment. Because the voucher is such an important control device, special procedures are needed when the amount of the voucher needs to be changed.

Purchases Returns and Allowances

If a complete return is made on May 9 of merchandise costing $670 and a credit memo is received from the supplier, the following procedures are performed.

1. Note the return on the voucher, attach the credit memo, and place the voucher in the paid vouchers file.

2. Note the return in the Payment column of the voucher register by inserting the date of the return and an R (for "Return") in the Check No. column.

	DATE	VOUCHER NO.	ISSUED TO	PURCHASES DEBIT	VOUCHERS PAYABLE CREDIT	PAYMENT DATE	CHECK NO.	
1	5/6/--	121	Compumax	6 7 0 00	6 7 0 00	5/9/--	R	1

3. Make a general journal entry to record the return.

5	May	9	Vouchers Payable/Compumax		6 7 0 00			5
6			Purchases Returns and Allowances			6 7 0 00		6
7			Returned merchandise					7

If a partial return is made on May 9 of $250 of merchandise costing $670 and a credit memo is received, the following procedures are performed.

1. Note the return on the voucher, attach the credit memo, and return the voucher to the unpaid vouchers file.

2. Note the return in the Payment column of the voucher register as follows:

	DATE	VOUCHER NO.	ISSUED TO	PURCHASES DEBIT	VOUCHERS PAYABLE CREDIT	PAYMENT DATE	CHECK NO.	
1	5/6/--	121	Compumax	6 7 0 00	6 7 0 00	5/9/--	R/250	1

Notice that both the return and the dollar amount are indicated. This distinguishes the partial return from a complete return.

3. Make a general journal entry to record the return.

8	May	9	Vouchers Payable/Compumax		2 5 0 00			8
9			Purchases Returns and Allowances			2 5 0 00		9
10			Returned merchandise					10

4. When the voucher is paid for the original amount less the return, note the payment in the Payment column of the voucher register, as follows:

	DATE	VOUCHER NO.	ISSUED TO	PURCHASES DEBIT	VOUCHERS PAYABLE CREDIT	PAYMENT DATE	PAYMENT CHECK NO.	
1	5/6/--	121	Compumax	6 7 0 00	6 7 0 00	5/9/-- 5/21/--	R/250 451	1

Partial Payments

If partial payments (installments) are planned at the time a purchase is made, a separate voucher is prepared for each payment. Each voucher and payment is then recorded in the voucher register and check register in the normal manner.

If a partial payment is made after a voucher is created and entered, the original voucher is canceled and new vouchers are created. Assume that merchandise is purchased on May 3 for $600. On May 7, a partial payment of only $200 is made. The following procedures are used to account for the partial payment.

1. Note the creation of two new vouchers in the Payment column of the voucher register, as follows:

	DATE	VOUCHER NO.	ISSUED TO	PURCHASES DEBIT	VOUCHERS PAYABLE CREDIT	PAYMENT DATE	PAYMENT CHECK NO.	
1	5/3/--	118	PC - Time	6 0 0 00	6 0 0 00	5/7/--	V122/ 123	1

Note that the three debits to Purchases in the voucher register on 5/3/-- ($600) and 5/7/-- ($200 and $400) are offset by the credit to Purchases in the general journal entry on May 7 ($600). Thus the correct net amount of Purchases of $600 is recorded.

2. Make a general journal entry to cancel the original voucher.

12	May	7	Vouchers Payable/PC -Time	6 0 0 00		12
13			Purchases		6 0 0 00	13
14			Canceled voucher			14

3. Prepare two new vouchers for $200 and $400 and enter them in the voucher register. Note the payment of the $200 voucher in the Payment column.

	DATE	VOUCHER NO.	ISSUED TO	PURCHASES DEBIT	VOUCHERS PAYABLE CREDIT	PAYMENT DATE	PAYMENT CHECK NO.	
1	5/7/--	122	PC - Time	2 0 0 00	2 0 0 00	5/7/--	447	1
2	5/7/--	123	PC - Time	4 0 0 00	4 0 0 00			2

Learning Objectives	Key Points to Remember
1 **Describe how a voucher system is used to control expenditures.**	The three elements of internal control that are combined to control expenditures in a voucher system are: 1. Segregation of duties 2. Authorization procedures and related responsibilities 3. Adequate documents and records
2 **Prepare a voucher.**	In a voucher system, every acquisition and subsequent payment must be supported by a voucher. When a purchase invoice arrives, the voucher section verifies the quantity, price, and computations on the invoice. In addition, the appropriateness of the purchase is evaluated before preparing the voucher.
3 **Describe and use a voucher register.**	A voucher is recorded in a voucher register by entering the following information. 1. Date 2. Voucher number 3. Person or business to whom the voucher is issued 4. Dollar amounts of debits and credits (and the account name if the General Dr. column is used). After entry in the voucher register, vouchers are filed in an unpaid vouchers file, normally by due date. The voucher register is posted to the general ledger as follows: On a daily basis: 1. Post General Debit amounts to the general ledger. 2. Insert the date and posting reference in the accounts. 3. Insert the account numbers in the posting reference column of the voucher register. At the end of each month: 4. Total, verify the equality of, and rule the amount columns. 5. Post specific account column totals to the general ledger accounts. 6. Insert the date and posting reference in the accounts. 7. Insert the account numbers below the specific account column totals in the voucher register. 8. Insert a check mark below the General Debit column.
4 **Describe the payment process using a voucher system.**	On the due date, the voucher and supporting documents are reviewed by the check signer, who prepares and signs the check and sends it to the supplier. After a voucher is paid, the voucher and supporting documents are cancelled to prevent processing them again to create a duplicate payment.
5 **Describe and use a check register and prepare a schedule of vouchers payable.**	A check is recorded in the check register by entering the following information. 1. Date 2. Check number 3. Payee 4. Voucher number 5. Dollar amounts The check register is posted to the general ledger as follows: 1. Total, verify the equality of, and rule the amount columns.

(continued)

Learning Objectives	Key Points to Remember
	2. Post column totals to the general ledger accounts.
	3. Insert the date and posting reference in the accounts.
	4. Insert the account numbers below the column totals in the check register.
	To verify that the sum of the individual amounts owed to creditors equals the Vouchers Payable balance, a schedule of vouchers payable is prepared.
6 **Account for returns, allowances, and partial payments.**	Special procedures are required when purchases returns and allowances or partial payments occur in a voucher system. In each case, entries are needed in both the voucher register and the general journal.

Reflection: Answering the Opening Question

A voucher system is a control technique requiring every acquisition and subsequent payment to be supported by an approved document called a voucher. A voucher system is most appropriate for medium- and large-size businesses. The volume of transactions in Evan's business probably is not sufficient to warrant the cost of a voucher system.

DEMONSTRATION PROBLEM

Harpo, Inc., is a retail novelty store. The following transactions relate to operations for the month of March.

March 2   Issued voucher no. 313 to Tremont Rental for March rent, $500.

2   Issued check no. 450 to Tremont Rental, $500. Voucher no. 313.

3   Purchased merchandise from Gail's Gags, $550, terms 2/15, n/60. Voucher no. 314.

4   Purchased merchandise from Silly Sam's, $200, terms 2/10, n/60. Voucher no. 315.

10   Issued check no. 451 to Jerry's Jokes, $500 less $10 discount. Voucher no. 310.

12   Received a credit memo from Silly Sam's for returned merchandise that was purchased on March 4, $100.

14   Issued check no. 452 to Resource Supplies, $250. Voucher no. 311.

16   Purchased merchandise from Giggles, $700, terms 2/10, n/30. Voucher no. 316.

18   Issued check no. 453 to Gail's Gags for purchase made on March 3 less 2% discount. Voucher no. 314.

19   Issued check no. 454 to Donnelley's, $750. Voucher no. 312.

21   Purchased merchandise from Creations, $870, terms 3/15, n/50. Voucher no. 317.

25   Purchased supplies from Hal's Supply, $120, terms 3/10, n/30. Voucher no. 318.

31   Issued check no. 455 to Silly Sam's for purchase made on March 4 less returns made on March 12. Voucher no. 315.

31   Issued voucher no. 319 to Payroll in payment of March wages, $1,250.

31   Issued check no. 456 to Payroll, $1,250. Voucher no. 319.

REQUIRED

Selected general ledger accounts and their opening balances as well as a portion of the voucher register for February follow.

1.   Enter the transactions in the voucher register, check register (page 6), and general journal (page 3). Total, rule, and prove the voucher register and check register.

2.   Post the transactions to the general ledger accounts.

3.   Prepare a schedule of vouchers payable and compare the March 31 balance to the balance of Vouchers Payable in the general ledger.

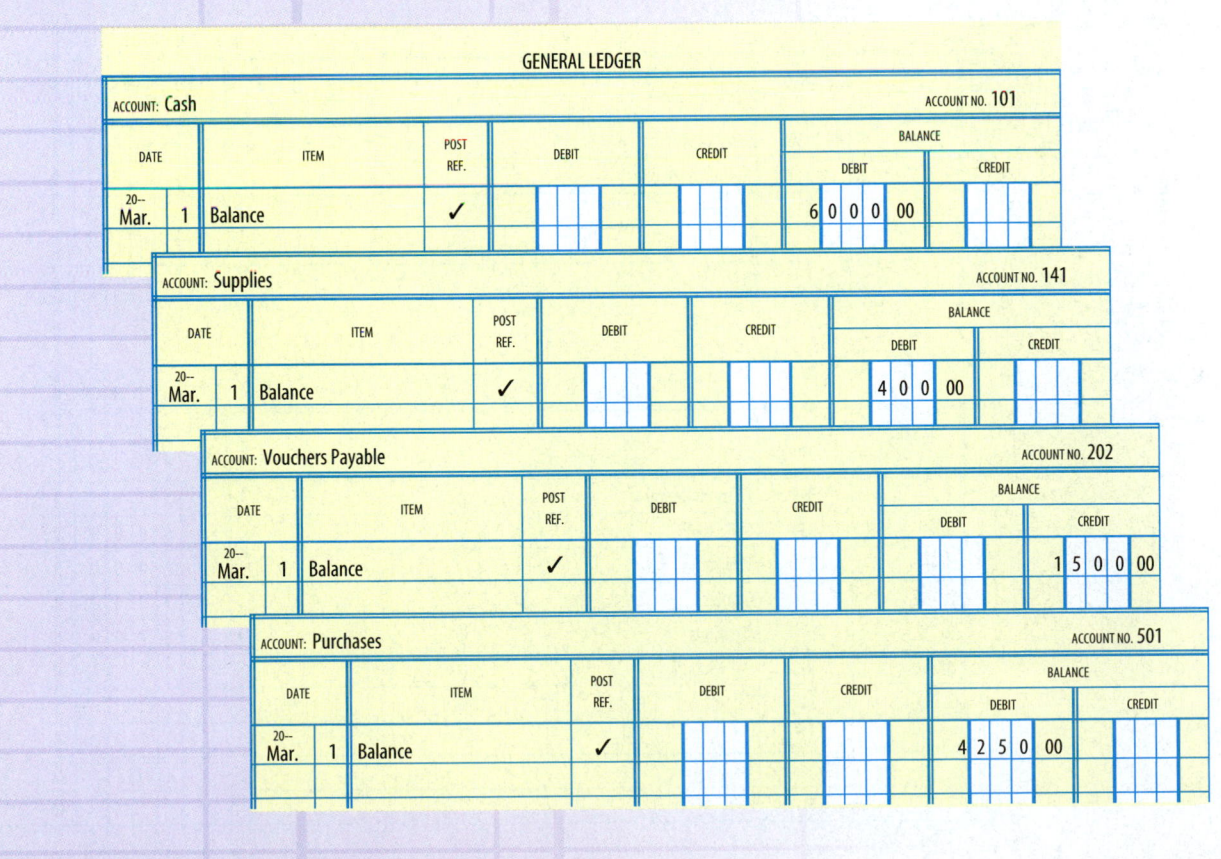

GENERAL LEDGER

ACCOUNT: Cash   ACCOUNT NO. 101

DATE		ITEM	POST REF.	DEBIT	CREDIT	BALANCE DEBIT	BALANCE CREDIT
20-- Mar.	1	Balance	✓			6 0 0 0 00	

ACCOUNT: Supplies   ACCOUNT NO. 141

DATE		ITEM	POST REF.	DEBIT	CREDIT	BALANCE DEBIT	BALANCE CREDIT
20-- Mar.	1	Balance	✓			4 0 0 00	

ACCOUNT: Vouchers Payable   ACCOUNT NO. 202

DATE		ITEM	POST REF.	DEBIT	CREDIT	BALANCE DEBIT	BALANCE CREDIT
20-- Mar.	1	Balance	✓				1 5 0 0 00

ACCOUNT: Purchases   ACCOUNT NO. 501

DATE		ITEM	POST REF.	DEBIT	CREDIT	BALANCE DEBIT	BALANCE CREDIT
20-- Mar.	1	Balance	✓			4 2 5 0 00	

(continued)

ACCOUNT: Purchases Returns and Allowances   ACCOUNT NO. 501.1

DATE		ITEM	POST REF.	DEBIT	CREDIT	BALANCE	
						DEBIT	CREDIT
20-- Mar.	1	Balance	✓				1 0 0 00

ACCOUNT: Purchases Discounts   ACCOUNT NO. 501.2

DATE		ITEM	POST REF.	DEBIT	CREDIT	BALANCE	
						DEBIT	CREDIT
20-- Mar.	1	Balance	✓				5 0 00

VOUCHER REGISTER

	DATE	VOUCHER NO.	ISSUED TO	PURCHASES DEBIT	
1	2/24/--	310	Jerry's Jokes	5 0 0 00	1
2	2/26/--	311	Resource Supplies		2
3	2/26/--	312	Donnelly's	7 5 0 00	3
4					4
5					5

Solution

1.

VOUCHER REGISTER

	DATE	VOUCHER NO.	ISSUED TO	PURCHASES DEBIT	
1	2/24/--	310	Jerry's Jokes	5 0 0 00	1
2	2/26/--	311	Resource Supplies		2
3	2/26/--	312	Donnelly's	7 5 0 00	3
4					4
5					5

VOUCHER REGISTER

	DATE	VOUCHER NO.	ISSUED TO	PURCHASES DEBIT	
1	3/2/--	313	Tremont Rental		1
2	3/3/--	314	Gail's Gags	5 5 0 00	2
3	3/4/--	315	Silly Sam's	2 0 0 00	3
4	3/16/--	316	Giggles	7 0 0 00	4
5	3/21/--	317	Creations	8 7 0 00	5
6	3/25/--	318	Hal's Supply		6
7	3/31/--	319	Payroll		7
8				2 3 2 0 00	8
9				(5 01)	9
10					10

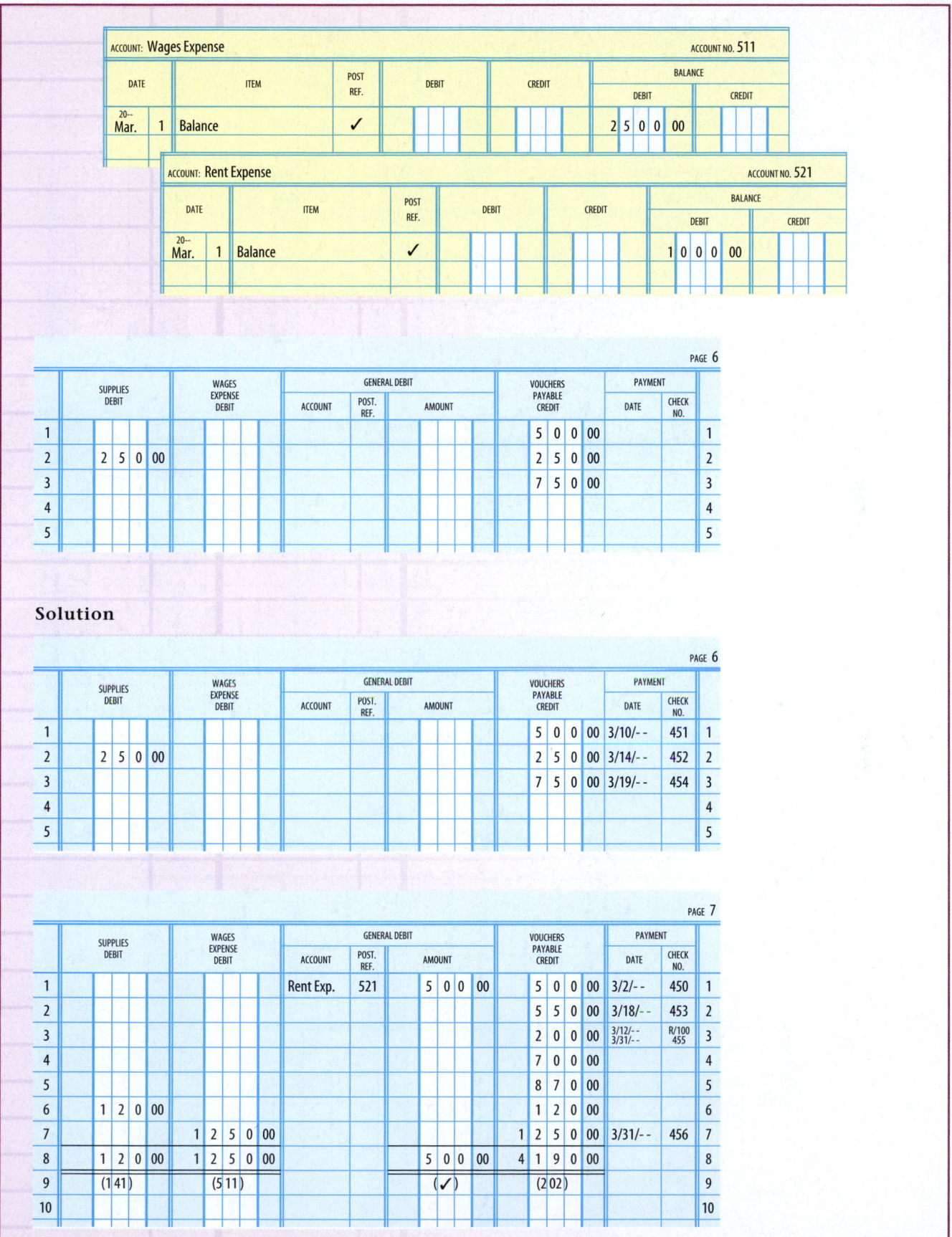

ACCOUNT: Wages Expense							ACCOUNT NO. 511
DATE	ITEM	POST REF.	DEBIT	CREDIT	BALANCE		
					DEBIT	CREDIT	
20-- Mar. 1	Balance	✓			2 5 0 0 00		

ACCOUNT: Rent Expense						ACCOUNT NO. 521
DATE	ITEM	POST REF.	DEBIT	CREDIT	BALANCE	
					DEBIT	CREDIT
20-- Mar. 1	Balance	✓			1 0 0 0 00	

PAGE 6

	SUPPLIES DEBIT	WAGES EXPENSE DEBIT	GENERAL DEBIT			VOUCHERS PAYABLE CREDIT	PAYMENT		
			ACCOUNT	POST. REF.	AMOUNT		DATE	CHECK NO.	
1						5 0 0 00			1
2	2 5 0 00					2 5 0 00			2
3						7 5 0 00			3
4									4
5									5

Solution

PAGE 6

	SUPPLIES DEBIT	WAGES EXPENSE DEBIT	GENERAL DEBIT			VOUCHERS PAYABLE CREDIT	PAYMENT		
			ACCOUNT	POST. REF.	AMOUNT		DATE	CHECK NO.	
1						5 0 0 00	3/10/--	451	1
2	2 5 0 00					2 5 0 00	3/14/--	452	2
3						7 5 0 00	3/19/--	454	3
4									4
5									5

PAGE 7

	SUPPLIES DEBIT	WAGES EXPENSE DEBIT	GENERAL DEBIT			VOUCHERS PAYABLE CREDIT	PAYMENT		
			ACCOUNT	POST. REF.	AMOUNT		DATE	CHECK NO.	
1			Rent Exp.	521	5 0 0 00	5 0 0 00	3/2/--	450	1
2						5 5 0 00	3/18/--	453	2
3						2 0 0 00	3/12/-- 3/31/--	R/100 455	3
4						7 0 0 00			4
5						8 7 0 00			5
6	1 2 0 00					1 2 0 00			6
7		1 2 5 0 00				1 2 5 0 00	3/31/--	456	7
8	1 2 0 00	1 2 5 0 00			5 0 0 00	4 1 9 0 00			8
9	(1 41)	(5 11)			(✓)	(2 02)			9
10									10

(continued)

1.

CHECK REGISTER
PAGE 6

	DATE	CHECK NO.	PAYEE	VOUCHERS PAYABLE DR.		PURCHASES DISCOUNTS CREDIT	CASH CREDIT	
				NO.	AMOUNT			
1	3/2/--	450	Tremont Rental	313	5 0 0 00		5 0 0 00	1
2	3/10/--	451	Jerry's Jokes	310	5 0 0 00	1 0 00	4 9 0 00	2
3	3/14/--	452	Resource Supplies	311	2 5 0 00		2 5 0 00	3
4	3/18/--	453	Gail's Gags	314	5 5 0 00	1 1 00	5 3 9 00	4
5	3/19/--	454	Donnelly's	312	7 5 0 00		7 5 0 00	5
6	3/31/--	455	Silly Sam's	315	1 0 0 00		1 0 0 00	6
7	3/31/--	456	Payroll	319	1 2 5 0 00		1 2 5 0 00	7
8					3 9 0 0 00	2 1 00	3 8 7 9 00	8
9					(202)	(501.2)	(101)	9

GENERAL JOURNAL
PAGE 3

	DATE		DESCRIPTION	POST REF.	DEBIT	CREDIT	
1	20-- Mar.	12	Vouchers Payable/Silly Sam's	202	1 0 0 00		1
2			Purchases Returns & Allowances	501.1		1 0 0 00	2
3			Received credit memo from Silly Sam's				3
4							4
5							5
6							6
7							7
8							8
9							9
10							10

2.

GENERAL LEDGER

ACCOUNT: Cash   ACCOUNT NO. 101

DATE		ITEM	POST REF.	DEBIT	CREDIT	BALANCE DEBIT	BALANCE CREDIT
20-- Mar.	1	Balance	✓			6 0 0 0 00	
	31		CK6		3 8 7 9 00	2 1 2 1 00	

ACCOUNT: Supplies   ACCOUNT NO. 141

DATE		ITEM	POST REF.	DEBIT	CREDIT	BALANCE DEBIT	BALANCE CREDIT
20-- Mar.	1	Balance	✓			4 0 0 00	
	31		VR7	1 2 0 00		5 2 0 00	

ACCOUNT: Vouchers Payable ACCOUNT NO. 202

DATE	ITEM	POST REF.	DEBIT	CREDIT	BALANCE DEBIT	BALANCE CREDIT
20-- Mar. 1	Balance	✓				1 5 0 0 00
12		J3	1 0 0 00			1 4 0 0 00
31		VR7		4 1 9 0 00		5 5 9 0 00
31		CK6	3 9 0 0 00			1 6 9 0 00

ACCOUNT: Purchases ACCOUNT NO. 501

DATE	ITEM	POST REF.	DEBIT	CREDIT	BALANCE DEBIT	BALANCE CREDIT
20-- Mar. 1	Balance	✓			4 2 5 0 00	
31		VR7	2 3 2 0 00		6 5 7 0 00	

ACCOUNT: Purchases Returns and Allowances ACCOUNT NO. 501.1

DATE	ITEM	POST REF.	DEBIT	CREDIT	BALANCE DEBIT	BALANCE CREDIT
20-- Mar. 1	Balance	✓				1 0 0 00
12		J3		1 0 0 00		2 0 0 00

ACCOUNT: Purchases Discounts ACCOUNT NO. 501.2

DATE	ITEM	POST REF.	DEBIT	CREDIT	BALANCE DEBIT	BALANCE CREDIT
20-- Mar. 1	Balance	✓				5 0 00
31		CK6		2 1 00		7 1 00

ACCOUNT: Wages Expense ACCOUNT NO. 511

DATE	ITEM	POST REF.	DEBIT	CREDIT	BALANCE DEBIT	BALANCE CREDIT
20-- Mar. 1	Balance	✓			2 5 0 0 00	
31		VR7	1 2 5 0 00		3 7 5 0 00	

ACCOUNT: Rent Expense ACCOUNT NO. 521

DATE	ITEM	POST REF.	DEBIT	CREDIT	BALANCE DEBIT	BALANCE CREDIT
20-- Mar. 1	Balance	✓			1 0 0 0 00	
2		VR7	5 0 0 00		1 5 0 0 00	

3.

Harpo, Inc.
Schedule of Vouchers Payable
March 31, 20 - -

Giggles	$ 7 0 0 00
Creations	8 7 0 00
Hal's Supply	1 2 0 00
	$1 6 9 0 00

KEY TERMS

check register, (516)   A special journal used to record all checks written in a voucher system.

internal controls, (506)   The set of procedures used to ensure that there is proper accounting for all activities of the business.

paid vouchers file, (516)   A file containing vouchers paid and cancelled and filed either numerically or by supplier.

unpaid vouchers file, (512)   A file containing vouchers and supporting documents stapled together and filed either by due date (preferred) or by supplier until paid.

voucher, (507)   A document that shows that an acquisition is proper and that payment is authorized.

voucher check, (515)   A check with space for entering data about the voucher being paid.

voucher register, (511)   A special journal used to record purchases of all types of assets and services.

voucher system, (507)   A control technique that requires that every acquisition and subsequent payment be supported by an approved voucher.

REVIEW QUESTIONS

(LO1)   1. What three elements of internal control are particularly important for controlling expenditures?

(LO1)   2. What two key controls over expenditures are provided by the voucher system?

(LO2)   3. When a purchase invoice is received from a supplier, what procedures are performed by the voucher section?

(LO3)   4. List four items of information about each voucher entered in the voucher register.

(LO3)   5. Why is it desirable to file unpaid vouchers by due date?

(LO3)   6. What steps are followed in posting from the voucher register to the general ledger?

(LO4)   7. After a voucher is paid, what should be done with the voucher and supporting documents? Why?

(LO5)   8. List five items of information about each check entered in the check register.

(LO5)   9. What steps are followed in posting from the check register to the general ledger?

(LO5)   10. If the total of the schedule of vouchers payable does not equal the Vouchers Payable balance, what procedures should be used to search for the error?

(LO6)   11. If a partial return of merchandise is made, what procedures are used in a voucher system?

(LO6)   12. If a partial payment is made after a voucher has been created and entered for the full amount of a purchase, what procedures are used in a voucher system?

Self-Study Test Questions

True/False

1. The voucher system is a control technique that requires every acquisition and subsequent payment to be supported by an approved voucher.   _____

2. A voucher is prepared after the check is issued for payment of an invoice.   _____

3. Segregation of duties, authorization procedures, and adequate documents and records are examples of internal controls.   _____

4. The total of the schedule of vouchers payable should be the same as the total of the vouchers with a blank in the Payment column of the voucher register.   _____

5. A voucher register is used together with a cash payments journal and a purchases journal.   _____

Multiple Choice

1. The check register takes the place of the   _____

   (a) voucher register.   (c) purchases journal.
   (b) cash payments journal.   (d) sales journal.

2. The unpaid vouchers file often replaces the   _____

   (a) voucher register.
   (b) purchases journal.
   (c) cash payments journal.
   (d) accounts payable ledger.

3. In the check register, _____ is always debited.   _____

   (a) Vouchers Payable   (c) Purchases
   (b) Accounts Payable   (d) Cash

4. When merchandise is returned and a credit memo is received and attached to the unpaid voucher, _____ is credited.   _____

   (a) Vouchers Payable
   (b) Accounts Payable
   (c) Purchases Returns and Allowances
   (d) Purchases Discounts

(continued)

Self-Study Test Questions *(continued)*

5. When a partial payment is made for merchandise, the original voucher is canceled, and _____ is credited.

    (a) Cash   (c) Accounts Payable
    (b) Purchases   (d) Vouchers Payable

The answers to the Self-Study Test Questions are at the end of the text.

MANAGING YOUR WRITING

The major fund-raiser for a local youth center traditionally has been a variety show put on by the members of the center. Tickets for the show are sold primarily by the members. The tickets are available in boxes at the center, and members simply take them as needed. Money is then turned in for whatever tickets are sold. The new manager of the center is concerned about whether all of the money from ticket sales is being turned in and is seeking your advice. Write a memo to the manager explaining how to control the tickets and money to ensure that both are being accounted for.

ETHICS CASE

Earl Farr, Mandy Wells, and Ron Good are clerks in a busy doctor's office. One of Earl's responsibilities is to reconcile the bank statement. (He isn't involved in authorizing payments, writing checks, or making deposits.) Ron is the accounts receivable clerk. He posts all payments and makes bank deposits. Occasionally, when he gets busy, Earl asks Ron to perform the monthly bank reconciliation. After it is reconciled, Earl initials it as though he had done it. Mandy, who is in charge of accounts payable, has been observing Earl and Ron and is considering saying something to their supervisor, the office manager. Mandy is sure the office manager is unaware of what is going on.

1. Is what Earl and Ron are doing unethical? Would your answer be different if Ron were stealing money?

2. If Mandy chooses not to say anything to the office manager, is she being unethical?

3. Write a short memo from the office manager to Earl, Mandy, and Ron explaining the importance of the segregation of duties.

4. In pairs, play the roles of Mandy and the office manager, assuming Mandy decides to tell the office manager about the situation.

WEB WORK

Vouchers are part of a system of checks and balances that reduce loss due to employee theft and embezzling.

   Where can loss occur, and what are possible preventative techniques? Visit the Interactive Study Center on our web site at **http://heintz.swlearning.com** for special hotlinks to assist you in this assignment.

Interactive Learning: **http://heintz.swlearning.com**

SERIES A EXERCISES

EXERCISE 14-1A   (LO1)   PURCHASING PROCESS USING A VOUCHER SYSTEM In the following flow-chart, identify the documents and records that illustrate the purchasing process in a voucher system.

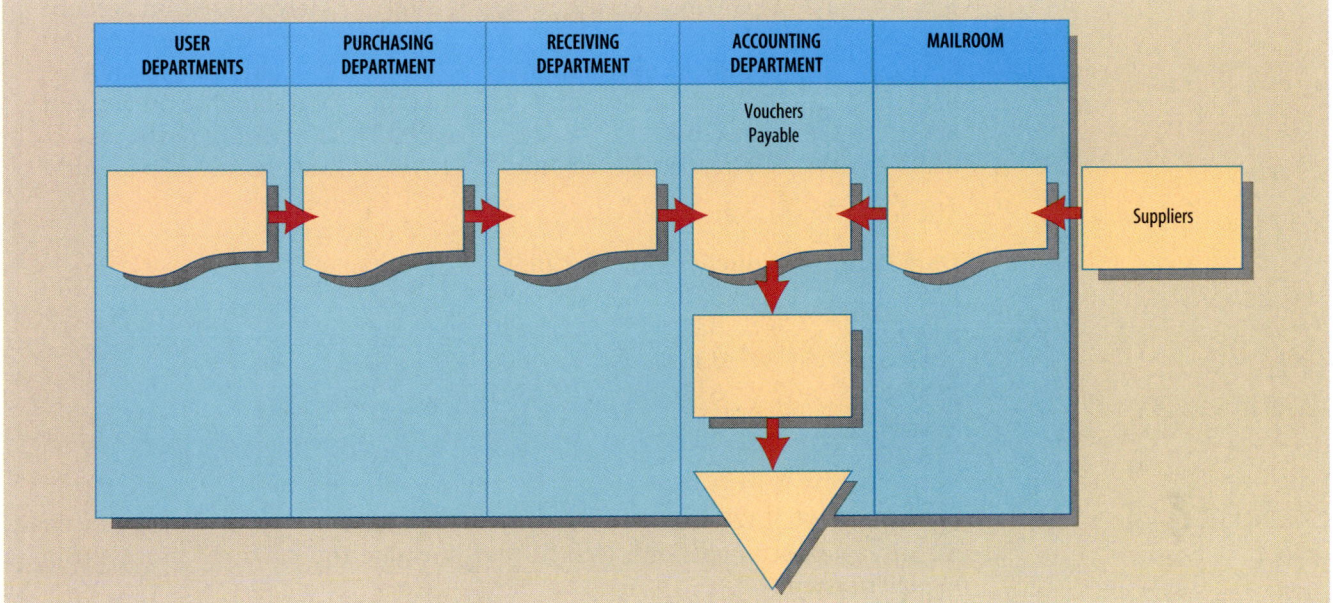

EXERCISE 14-2A   (LO2)   PREPARING A VOUCHER Prepare voucher no. 164 on May 8, similar to the one shown in Figure 14-3 in the chapter, from the purchase invoice shown below.

The supplier, Sportime Corp., sent 12 Prince Spectrum rackets with a unit price of $130 and 2 DuraLink nets with a unit price of $110. Assume that the cash discount will be taken. Indicate that the voucher was prepared by you and authorized by J. Jenkins and that distribution was approved by B. Zimmer.

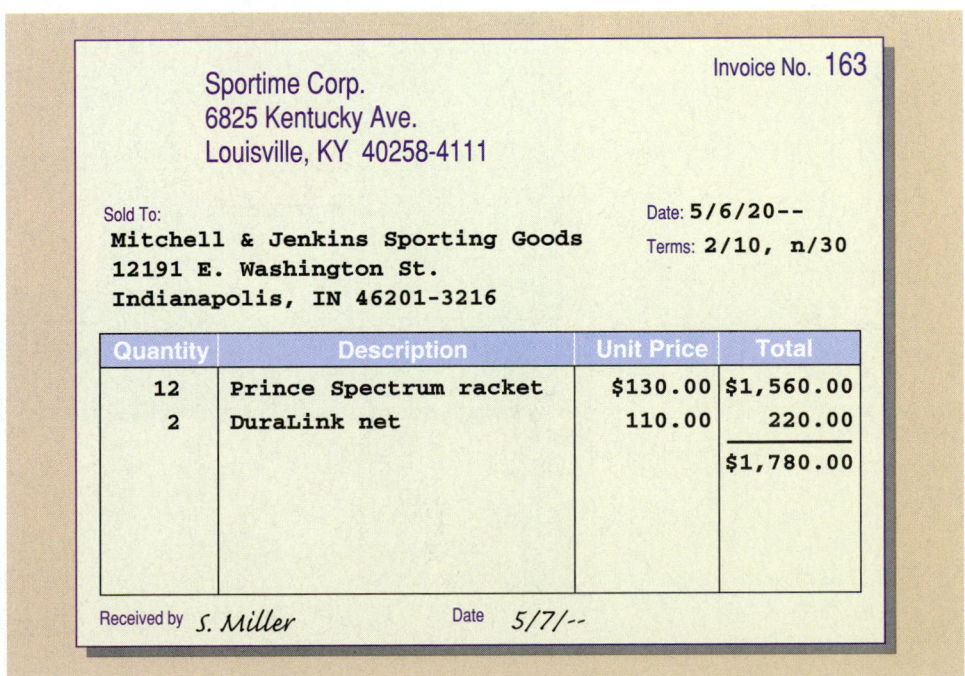

EXERCISE 14-3A   (LO3)

Voucher No. 334:
Supplies Dr., $244

VOUCHER REGISTER Enter the following vouchers and payments into a voucher register.

Date	Voucher No.	Issued To	Amount	Purpose
6/1	331	Middleton Assoc.	$1,200	June rent
6/5	332	Guzman Distributors	960	Merchandise on account
6/9	333	MicroLabs, Inc.	1,400	Merchandise on account
6/11	334	Miller Office Supply	244	Prepaid office supplies
6/13	335	Bradham Products	1,604	Merchandise on account
6/15	336	Payroll	6,000	Bimonthly paychecks
6/21	337	Guzman Distributors	1,700	Merchandise on account

The following vouchers were paid.

Date Paid	Voucher No.	Check No.
6/10	331	498
6/14	332	499
6/15	336	500
6/18	333	501
6/20	335	502
6/30	337	503

EXERCISE 14-4A   (LO4)

PAYMENT PROCESS USING A VOUCHER SYSTEM In the following flowchart, identify the documents and records that illustrate the payment process using a voucher system.

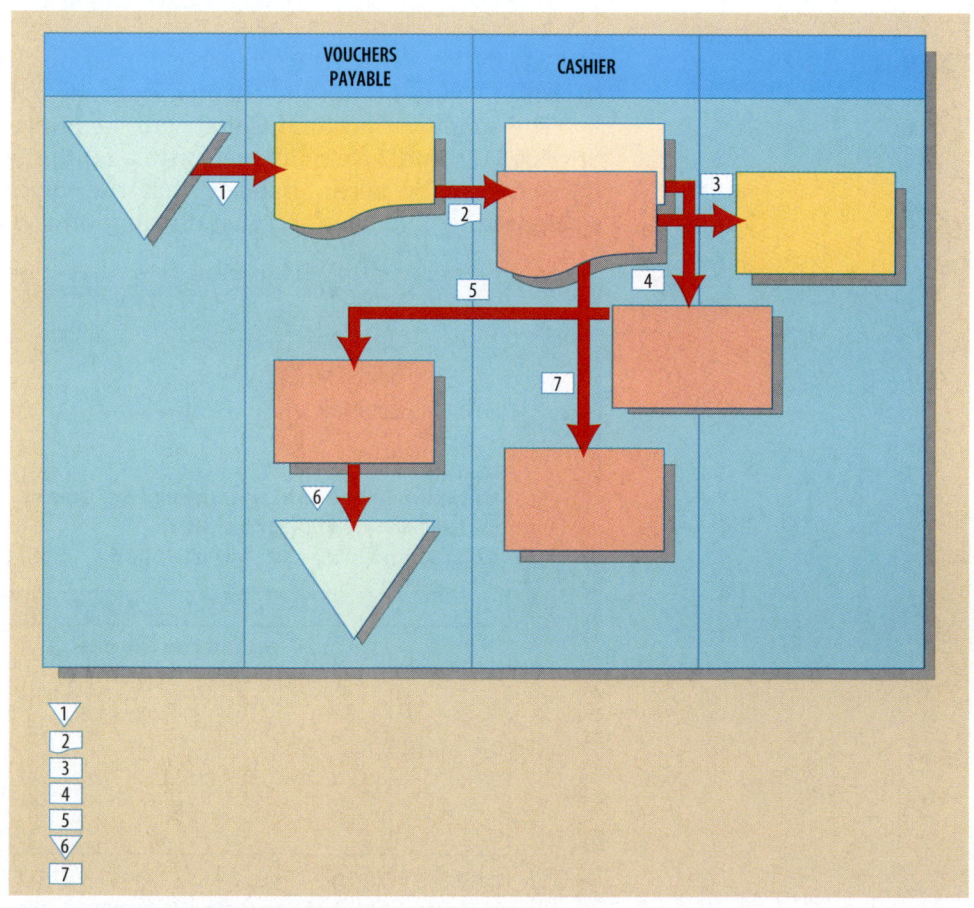

1
2
3
4
5
6
7

EXERCISE 14-5A   **(LO5)**
Total Cash Cr.: $14,823.68

CHECK REGISTER The following vouchers, taken from the voucher register, were paid during the month of August. Enter the appropriate information for payment of these vouchers into a check register. The discount amounts shown should be deducted from the voucher amounts. Total and rule the register.

Date	Voucher No.	Pay To	Amount	Check No.	Purpose	Discount Amount
8/5	111	Armos Bros.	$1,600	406	Merchandise on account	$16.00
8/7	108	H & L Realty	1,000	407	August rent	
8/11	113	Excel Products	760	408	Merchandise on account	15.20
8/13	109	Bell & Mason	1,280	409	Merchandise on account	25.60
8/15	115	Payroll	4,000	410	Bimonthly paychecks	
8/19	117	C. P. Delgado	1,776	411	Merchandise on account	35.52
8/25	119	Office Pro, Inc.	500	412	Office supplies	
8/31	120	Payroll	4,000	413	Bimonthly paychecks	

EXERCISE 14-6A   **(LO5)**
Total vouchers payable: $1,412

SCHEDULE OF VOUCHERS PAYABLE Prepare a schedule of vouchers payable for Randalls Appliances, based on information found in the following voucher register.

VOUCHER REGISTER

	DATE	VOUCHER NO.	ISSUED TO	PURCHASES DEBIT	
1	1/1/--	101	Alomar, Inc.	6 0 0 00	1
2	1/3/--	102	Bremer Office Supplies		2
3	1/6/--	103	Kettles and Kabrus	2 8 0 00	3
4	1/7/--	104	Moore & Johnson		4
5	1/11/--	105	Kitchen Kaboodle	3 0 0 00	5
6	1/13/--	106	Alomar, Inc.	3 7 5 00	6
7	1/16/--	107	Payroll		7
8	1/21/--	108	Rich & Associates	4 0 0 00	8
9	1/29/--	109	Darin Elwood Co.	2 1 9 00	9
10				2 1 7 4 00	10

Voucher Register—left side

PAGE **1**

	SUPPLIES DEBIT	WAGES EXPENSE DEBIT	GENERAL DEBIT			VOUCHERS PAYABLE CREDIT	PAYMENT		
			ACCOUNT	POST REF.	AMOUNT		DATE	CHECK NO.	
1						6 0 0 00	1/11/--	2	1
2	1 1 8 00					1 1 8 00			2
3						2 8 0 00	1/24/--	4	3
4			Rent Exp.		5 0 0 00	5 0 0 00	1/7/--	1	4
5						3 0 0 00			5
6						3 7 5 00			6
7		1 0 0 0 00				1 0 0 0 00	1/16/--	3	7
8						4 0 0 00			8
9						2 1 9 00			9
10	1 1 8 00	1 0 0 0 00			5 0 0 00	3 7 9 2 00			10

Voucher Register—right side

EXERCISE 14-7A   (LO6)
Gen. journal entry,
Sept. 24: Dr. Vouchers
Payable, $600

RETURN OF MERCHANDISE AND PARTIAL PAYMENTS Enter the following merchandise returns and partial payments in a general journal and in a voucher register like the one shown below, as appropriate.

Sept. 10 Merchandise purchased from XYZ Co. for $800, voucher no. 203, is returned. A credit memo is received, attached to the voucher, and the voucher is placed in the paid vouchers file.

20 A partial return of merchandise purchased from Trizon Suppliers is made for $200, voucher no. 206. A credit memo is received, attached to the voucher, and the voucher is returned to the unpaid vouchers file.

24 A partial payment for merchandise purchased from F. B. Jones Co. is made for $300 on voucher no. 208, which was for $600. Plan to pay the remaining $300 in two weeks (new vouchers are issued). Check no. 682.

28 A partial return of merchandise purchased from Arbiters, Inc. is made for $80, voucher no. 204. A credit memo is received, attached to the voucher, and the voucher is returned to the unpaid vouchers file.

VOUCHER REGISTER

	DATE	VOUCHER NO.	ISSUED TO	PURCHASES DEBIT	
1	9/6/--	202	Briggs Store	6 0 0 00	1
2	9/8/--	203	XYZ Co.	8 0 0 00	2
3	9/10/--	204	Arbiters, Inc.	7 0 0 00	3
4	9/11/--	205	Paper Traders		4
5	9/15/--	206	Trizon Suppliers	3 5 0 00	5
6	9/16/--	207	Payroll		6
7	9/18/--	208	F. B. Jones Co.	6 0 0 00	7
8					8

Voucher Register—left side

PAGE 1

	SUPPLIES DEBIT	WAGES EXPENSE DEBIT	GENERAL DEBIT			VOUCHERS PAYABLE CREDIT	PAYMENT		
			ACCOUNT	POST REF.	AMOUNT		DATE	CHECK NO.	
1						6 0 0 00	9/8/--	681	1
2						8 0 0 00			2
3						7 0 0 00			3
4	1 8 6 00					1 8 6 00			4
5						3 5 0 00			5
6		1 2 0 0 00				1 2 0 0 00			6
7						6 0 0 00			7
8									8

Voucher Register—right side

SERIES A PROBLEMS

PROBLEM 14-8A   **(LO3)**

Total Vouchers Payable Cr.:
$11,396

VOUCHER REGISTER AND POSTING TO GENERAL LEDGER Escribano Electronics had the following transactions for the month of July 20--.

Date	Voucher No.	Issued To	Amount	Purpose	Date Paid	Check No.
7/1	206	Parkhouse, Inc.	$ 600	July rent	7/1	318
7/3	207	G. B. Fiorucci	1,700	Merchandise	7/18	320
7/5	208	Richardson's	240	Office supplies		
7/9	209	Soto Supply	1,800	Merchandise	7/19	321
7/15	210	Payroll	2,000	Paychecks	7/15	319
7/21	211	Pressman's	1,160	Merchandise		
7/28	212	T. R. Canady Co.	1,240	Merchandise		
7/30	213	Excelsior Ltd.	656	Merchandise		
7/31	214	Payroll	2,000	Paychecks	7/31	322

REQUIRED

1. Enter the transactions for July 20-- on page 7 of the voucher register. Total, rule, and prove the register.

2. Post the voucher register to the general ledger. Use account numbers as shown in the chapter.

PROBLEM 14-9A   **(LO5)**

Total Cash Cr.: $7,736.20

CHECK REGISTER AND POSTING TO GENERAL LEDGER The following transactions occurred during August 20--. A voucher register is used. Assume terms of 2/10, n/30 for purchases on account and assume that all discounts are taken. General ledger account balances on August 1 were Cash, $9,862; and Vouchers Payable, $8,482.

Date	Check No.	Pay To	Voucher No.	Amount	Purpose
8/3	111	M. Pearson	108	$ 800	August rent
8/5	112	K. B. Adams Co.	109	550	Merchandise on account
8/8	113	Quality Paper	111	300	Office supplies
8/11	114	Paulson Group	113	600	Merchandise on account
8/15	115	Payroll	115	2,000	Bimonthly payroll
8/17	116	Peerson, Inc.	116	720	Merchandise on account
8/22	117	K. B. Adams Co.	118	380	Merchandise on account
8/25	118	Wilson's	121	440	Merchandise on account
8/31	119	Payroll	123	2,000	Bimonthly payroll

REQUIRED

1. Enter the transactions for August 20-- in the check register (page 8). Total, rule, and prove the register.

2. Post the check register totals to the general ledger. Use account numbers as shown in the chapter.

(continued)

PROBLEM 14-10A (LO3/5)

1. Total Vouchers Payable
Cr.: $6,450

VOUCHER REGISTER, CHECK REGISTER, POSTING, AND SCHEDULE OF VOUCHERS PAYABLE Betty Classic owns the Classic Candle Shop. The following transactions occurred during April 20--. The Classic Candle Shop uses a voucher register, a check register, and a general ledger. Unpaid vouchers are filed and listed at the end of the month. General ledger account balances on April 1 were Cash, $5,189; and Supplies, $408.

Date	Voucher No.	Issued To	Amount	Purpose	Terms
4/1	1101	Landmark Realty	$ 500	April rent	
4/3	1102	Wax House	280	Merchandise	2/10, n/30
4/5	1103	Designs West	490	Merchandise	2/10, n/30
4/9	1104	Crane Stationers	180	Office supplies	
4/11	1105	Magic Solutions	600	Merchandise	2/10, n/30
4/15	1106	Payroll	1,500	Bimonthly payroll	
4/23	1107	Wax House	510	Merchandise	1/10, n/30
4/25	1108	Baskets & More	440	Merchandise	2/10, n/30
4/28	1109	Magic Solutions	450	Merchandise	2/10, n/30
4/30	1110	Payroll	1,500	Bimonthly payroll	

Checks issued:

Date	Check No.	Payee	Voucher No.	Amount
4/1	928	Landmark Realty	1101	$ 500
4/9	929	Crane Stationers	1104	180
4/11	930	Wax House	1102	280
4/15	931	Payroll	1106	1,500
4/19	932	Designs West	1103	490
4/30	933	Payroll	1110	1,500

REQUIRED

1. Enter the transactions for April in the voucher register (page 4). Total, rule, and prove the register. Update the Payment column when vouchers are paid.

2. Enter the transactions for April in the check register (page 4). Be sure to take discounts where appropriate. Total, rule, and prove the register.

3. Post the voucher register and the check register to the general ledger. Use account numbers as shown in the chapter.

4. Prepare a schedule of vouchers payable.

PROBLEM 14-11A (LO3/5/6)
Total Cash Cr.: $4,194.60

VOUCHER REGISTER, CHECK REGISTER, AND GENERAL JOURNAL (RETURNS AND PARTIAL PAYMENTS) Richard Harris owns Harris's Appliance Store. The following transactions occurred during May 20--. Harris's Appliance Store uses a voucher register, a check register, and a general journal.

May 1   Issued voucher no. 208 to McPherson's Co. for May rent, $800.

1   Issued check no. 411 to McPherson's Co., $800. Voucher no. 208.

3   Purchased merchandise from Welding Supply Co., $280, terms 2/10, n/30. Voucher no. 209.

5   Received a credit memo from Welding Supply Co. for returned merchandise that was purchased on May 3, $40.

7   Purchased supplies from Quality Office Supply, $118. Voucher no. 210.

7   Issued check no. 412 to Quality Office Supply, $118. Voucher no. 210.

10   Purchased merchandise from Piper's Inc., $440, terms 2/10, n/30. Voucher no. 211.

10   Received a credit memo from Piper's Inc., for returned merchandise that was purchased on May 10, $440.

11   Issued check no. 413 to Welding Supply Co. for purchase made on May 3, less return made on May 5 less 2% discount. Voucher no. 209.

12   Purchased merchandise from Moreno's Wholesale, $620, terms 2/10, n/30. Voucher no. 212.

15   Issued voucher no. 213 to Payroll in payment of bimonthly wages, $1,000.

15   Issued check no. 414 to Payroll, $1,000. Voucher no. 213.

19   Purchased merchandise from Welding Supply Co., $860, terms 2/10, n/30. Voucher no. 214.

21   Issued check no. 415 to Welding Supply Co., in partial payment of goods purchased on May 19, $430 less 2% discount. Voucher no. 214. Issued new vouchers no. 215 and 216.

22   Purchased supplies from Quality Office Supply, $210. Voucher no. 217.

23   Issued check no. 416 to Moreno's Wholesale, $620. Voucher no. 212.

25   Purchased merchandise from Regional Distributors, $460, terms 1/10, n/30. Voucher no. 218.

28   Purchased merchandise from Pringle's & Co., $600, terms 2/10, n/30. Voucher no. 219.

31   Issued voucher no. 220 to Payroll in payment of bimonthly wages, $1,000.

31   Issued check no. 417 to Payroll, $1,000. Voucher no. 220.

REQUIRED

Enter the transactions in a voucher register (page 5), check register (page 5), or general journal (page 5), as appropriate. Total, rule, and prove the voucher register and check register.

SERIES B EXERCISES

EXERCISE 14-1B   **(LO1)**   **PURCHASING PROCESS USING A VOUCHER SYSTEM** In the following flow-chart, identify the departments and other sources of the documents and records that illustrate the purchasing process in a voucher system.

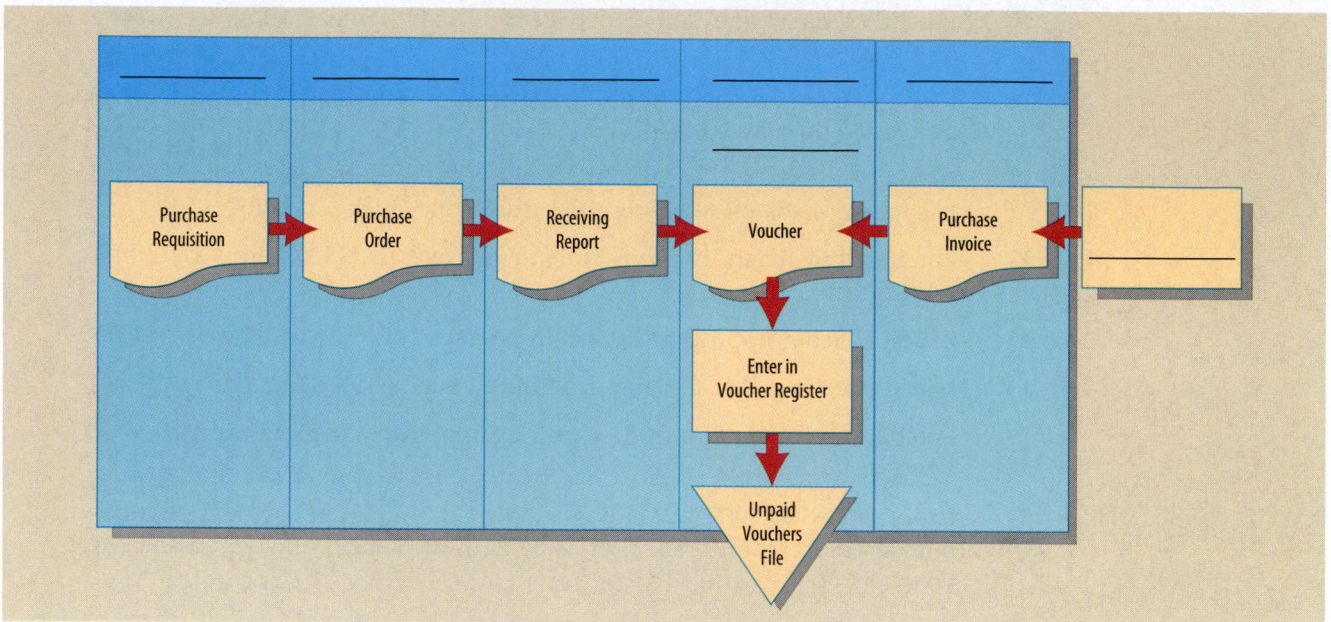

EXERCISE 14-2B   **(LO2)**   **PREPARING A VOUCHER** Prepare voucher no. 193 on May 18, similar to the one shown in Figure 14-3 in the chapter, from the purchase invoice shown below.

The supplier, Sportime Corp., sent 33 cases of Sport tennis balls at $30 a case and 14 Wilke racket covers at $25 each. Assume that the cash discount will be taken. Indicate that the voucher was prepared by you and authorized by J. Jenkins and that distribution was approved by B. Zimmer.

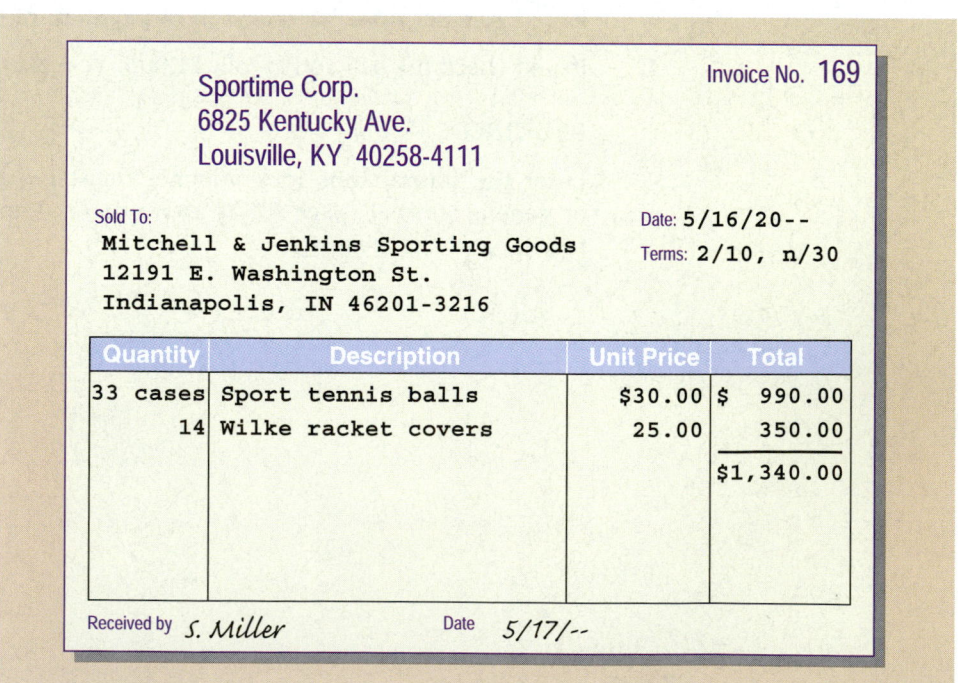

EXERCISE 14-3B   **(LO3)**   **VOUCHER REGISTER** Enter the following vouchers and payments into a
Voucher No. 434:   voucher register.
Supplies Dr., $55

Date	Voucher No.	Issued To	Amount	Purpose
7/1	431	Katz Management	$ 200	July rent
7/5	432	Garcia Distributors	340	Merchandise on account
7/9	433	Mirror Labs, Inc.	150	Merchandise on account
7/11	434	Owens Office Supply	55	Prepaid office supplies
7/13	435	Richards Products	176	Merchandise on account
7/15	436	Payroll	1,250	Bimonthly paychecks
7/21	437	Garcia Distributors	175	Merchandise on account

The following vouchers were paid.

Date Paid	Voucher No.	Check No.
7/10	431	598
7/14	432	599
7/15	436	600
7/18	433	601
7/20	435	602

EXERCISE 14-4B   **(LO4)**   **PAYMENT PROCESS USING A VOUCHER SYSTEM** The following flowchart
illustrates the payment process using a voucher system. Briefly describe each
document and file.

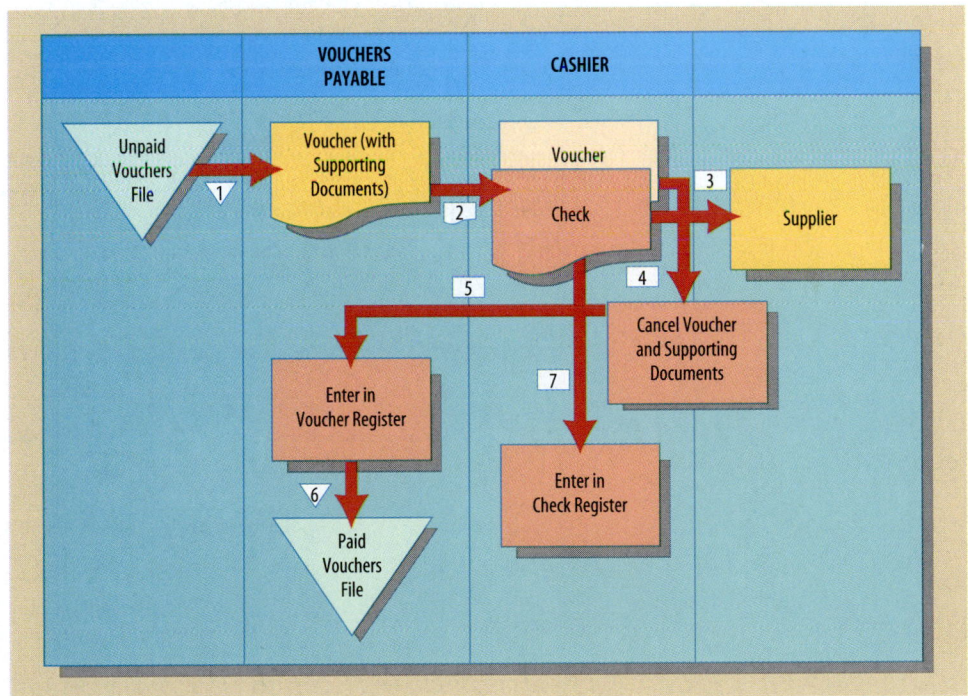

EXERCISE 14-5B   (LO5)
Total Cash Cr.: $3,415.36

CHECK REGISTER The following vouchers, taken from the voucher register, were paid during the month of September. Enter the appropriate information for payment of these vouchers into a check register. The discount amounts shown should be deducted from the voucher amounts. Total and rule the register.

Date	Voucher No.	Pay To	Amount	Check No.	Purpose	Discount Amount
9/5	1111	Mendel Bros.	$ 300	2814	Merchandise on account	$3.00
9/7	1108	B & J Realty	200	2815	September rent	
9/11	1113	Trycl Products	140	2816	Merchandise on account	$2.80
9/13	1114	Myro & Smith	270	2817	Merchandise on account	$5.40
9/15	1109	Payroll	1,100	2818	Bimonthly paychecks	
9/19	1117	T. M. Kingley	244	2819	Merchandise on account	$2.44
9/25	1123	Bly Stationers	75	2820	Office supplies	
9/30	1120	Payroll	1,100	2821	Bimonthly paychecks	

EXERCISE 14-6B   (LO5)
Total vouchers payable: $1,368

SCHEDULE OF VOUCHERS PAYABLE Prepare a schedule of vouchers payable for M. B. Jacobs, based on information found in the following voucher register.

VOUCHER REGISTER

	DATE	VOUCHER NO.	ISSUED TO	PURCHASES DEBIT	
1	3/1/--	306	Richland Associates		1
2	3/4/--	307	Carlson & Daughter	8 0 0 00	2
3	3/6/--	308	Wu Office Supplies		3
4	3/9/--	309	Black & Brewer	6 0 0 00	4
5	3/12/--	310	Kreklow Company	3 8 0 00	5
6	3/16/--	311	Payroll		6
7	3/21/--	312	Anderson Enterprises	2 6 0 00	7
8	3/24/--	313	Carlson & Daughter	4 1 0 00	8
9	3/28/--	314	Wu Office Supplies		9
10	3/31/--	315	Payroll		10
11				2 4 5 0 00	11

Voucher Register—left side

PAGE 3

	SUPPLIES DEBIT	WAGES EXPENSE DEBIT	GENERAL DEBIT			VOUCHERS PAYABLE CREDIT	PAYMENT		
			ACCOUNT	POST REF.	AMOUNT		DATE	CHECK NO.	
1			Rent Exp.		3 0 0 00	3 0 0 00	3/2/--	806	1
2						8 0 0 00	3/11/--	808	2
3	1 8 0 00					1 8 0 00	3/8/--	807	3
4						6 0 0 00			4
5						3 8 0 00	3/18/--	810	5
6		1 0 0 0 00				1 0 0 0 00	3/16/--	809	6
7						2 6 0 00			7
8						4 1 0 00			8
9	9 8 00					9 8 00			9
10		1 0 0 0 00				1 0 0 0 00	3/31/--	811	10
11	2 7 8 00	2 0 0 0 00			3 0 0 00	5 0 2 8 00			11

Voucher Register—right side

EXERCISE 14-7B   (LO6)
Gen. journal entry, Sept. 25:
Dr. Vouchers Payable, $350

RETURN OF MERCHANDISE AND PARTIAL PAYMENTS Enter the following merchandise returns and partial payments in a general journal and in a voucher register like the one below, as appropriate.

Sept. 15   Merchandise purchased from Arbiters, Inc. for $700, voucher no. 204, is returned. A credit memo is received, attached to the voucher, and the voucher is placed in the paid vouchers file.

20   A partial return of merchandise purchased from XYZ Co. is made for $300, voucher no. 203. A credit memo is received, attached to the voucher, and the voucher is returned to the unpaid vouchers file.

25   A partial payment for merchandise purchased from Trizon Suppliers is made for $150 on voucher no. 206, which was for $350. Plan to pay the remaining $200 in two weeks (new vouchers are issued). Check no. 682.

30   A partial return of merchandise purchased from F. B. Jones Co. is made for $20, voucher no. 208. A credit memo is received, attached to the voucher, and the voucher is returned to the unpaid vouchers file.

VOUCHER REGISTER

	DATE	VOUCHER NO.	ISSUED TO	PURCHASES DEBIT	
1	9/6/--	202	Briggs Store	6 0 0 00	1
2	9/8/--	203	XYZ Co.	8 0 0 00	2
3	9/10/--	204	Arbiters, Inc.	7 0 0 00	3
4	9/11/--	205	Paper Traders		4
5	9/15/--	206	Trizon Suppliers	3 5 0 00	5
6	9/16/--	207	Payroll		6
7	9/18/--	208	F. B. Jones Co.	6 0 0 00	7
8					8

Voucher Register—left side

PAGE 1

	SUPPLIES DEBIT	WAGES EXPENSE DEBIT	GENERAL DEBIT			VOUCHERS PAYABLE CREDIT	PAYMENT		
			ACCOUNT	POST REF.	AMOUNT		DATE	CHECK NO.	
1						6 0 0 00	9/8/--	681	1
2						8 0 0 00			2
3						7 0 0 00			3
4	1 8 6 00					1 8 6 00			4
5						3 5 0 00			5
6		1 2 0 0 00				1 2 0 0 00			6
7						6 0 0 00			7
8									8

Voucher Register—right side

(continued)

SERIES B PROBLEMS

PROBLEM 14-8B   (LO3)
Total Vouchers Payable Cr.:
$12,736

VOUCHER REGISTER AND POSTING TO GENERAL LEDGER Stodolski Sounds had the following transactions for the month of July 20--.

Date	Voucher No.	Issued To	Amount	Purpose	Date Paid	Check No.
7/1	771	Milltown Realty	$1,000	July rent	7/1	330
7/4	772	Khalaf Electronics	1,700	Merchandise	7/11	332
7/7	773	Phak's	640	Office supplies	7/8	331
7/11	774	Breck Sound Supply	760	Merchandise	7/21	334
7/15	775	Payroll	3,000	Bimonthly paychecks	7/15	333
7/21	776	Clear Tone Disks	1,360	Merchandise		
7/28	777	Khalaf Electronics	820	Merchandise		
7/29	778	Phak's	456	Office supplies		
7/31	779	Payroll	3,000	Bimonthly paychecks	7/31	335

REQUIRED

1. Enter the transactions for July 20-- in the voucher register (page 7). Total, rule, and prove the voucher register.

2. Post the voucher register to the general ledger. Use account numbers as shown in the chapter.

PROBLEM 14-9B   (LO5)
Total Cash Cr.: $5,054.04

CHECK REGISTER AND POSTING TO GENERAL LEDGER The following transactions occurred during August 20--. A voucher register is used. Assume terms of 2/10, n/30 for purchases on account, and assume that all discounts are taken. General ledger account balances on August 1 were Cash, $9,862; and Vouchers Payable, $8,482.

Date	Check No.	Pay To	Voucher No.	Amount	Purpose
8/2	211	Realty Co.	108	$600	August rent
8/5	212	Tri-Cities Co.	111	238	Merchandise on account
8/8	213	Miller's	112	412	Merchandise on account
8/10	214	A & E Office Co.	115	108	Office supplies
8/15	215	Payroll	114	900	Bimonthly payroll
8/18	216	Blythe Mill	118	620	Merchandise on account
8/22	217	Tri-Cities Co.	119	512	Merchandise on account
8/27	218	Miller's	122	816	Merchandise on account
8/31	219	Payroll	123	900	Bimonthly payroll

REQUIRED

1. Enter the transactions for August 20-- in the check register (page 8). Total, rule, and prove the register.

2. Post the check register totals to the general ledger. Use account numbers as shown in the chapter.

PROBLEM 14-10B   (LO3/5)

1. Total Vouchers Payable
Cr.: $4,827

VOUCHER REGISTER, CHECK REGISTER, POSTING, AND SCHEDULE OF VOUCHERS PAYABLE Jane Hledik is owner of Hledik Lawn Supply. The following transactions occurred during April 20--. Hledik Lawn Supply uses a voucher register, a check register, and a general ledger. Unpaid vouchers are filed and listed at the end of the month. General ledger account balances on April 1 were Cash, $5,189; and Supplies, $408.

Vouchers issued:

Date	Voucher No.	Issued To	Amount	Purpose	Terms
4/2	662	Brenner's	$600	April rent	
4/4	663	Lawn Care Wholesale	300	Merchandise	2/10, n/30
4/7	664	Southern Supply	128	Office supplies	
4/10	665	Clay's Chemicals	420	Merchandise	1/20, n/30
4/13	666	Mendel & Son	530	Merchandise	2/10, n/30
4/15	667	Payroll	950	Bimonthly payroll	
4/19	668	Lawn Care Wholesale	570	Merchandise	1/10, n/30
4/27	669	Southern Supply	99	Office supplies	
4/29	670	Lakeside Fertilizer	280	Merchandise	2/10, n/30
4/30	671	Payroll	950	Bimonthly payroll	

Checks issued:

Date	Check No.	Payee	Voucher No.	Amount
4/2	748	Brenner's	662	$600
4/7	749	Southern Supply	664	128
4/11	750	Lawn Care Wholesale	663	300
4/15	751	Payroll	667	950
4/20	752	Mendel & Son	666	530
4/30	753	Payroll	671	950

REQUIRED

1. Enter the transactions for April in the voucher register (page 4). Total, rule, and prove the register. Update the Payment column when vouchers are paid.

2. Enter the transactions for April in the check register (page 4). Be sure to take discounts where appropriate. Total, rule, and prove the register.

3. Post the voucher register and the check register to the general ledger. Use account numbers as shown in the chapter.

4. Prepare a schedule of vouchers payable.

PROBLEM 14-11B (LO3/5/6)
Total Cash Cr.: $4,004.80

VOUCHER REGISTER, CHECK REGISTER, AND GENERAL JOURNAL (RETURNS AND PARTIAL PAYMENTS) Michael Blake owns Blake's Appliance Store. The following transactions occurred during May 20--. Blake's Appliance Store uses a voucher register, a check register, and a general journal.

May 1 Issued voucher no. 308 to Johnson & Smith for May rent, $500.

1 Issued check no. 411 to Johnson & Smith in payment of May rent, $500. Voucher no. 308.

3 Purchased merchandise from Wilson Supply Co., $380, terms 2/10, n/30. Voucher no. 309.

5 Received a credit memo from Wilson Supply Co. for returned merchandise that was purchased May 3, $50.

7 Purchased supplies from B & J Office Supply, $138. Voucher no. 310.

7 Issued check no. 412 to B & J Office Supply, $138. Voucher no. 310.

10 Purchased merchandise from P. T. Benkley Co., $540, terms 2/10, n/30. Voucher no. 311.

11 Received a credit memo from P. T. Benkley Co. for returned merchandise that was purchased May 10, $540.

(continued)

11	Issued check no. 413 to Wilson Supply Co. for purchase made on May 3 less returns made on May 5 less 2% discount. Voucher no. 309.
12	Purchased merchandise from Wesley's Wholesale, $720, terms 2/10, n/30. Voucher no. 312.
15	Issued voucher no. 313 to Payroll in payment of bimonthly wages, $1,000.
15	Issued check no. 414 to Payroll, $1,000. Voucher no. 313.
19	Purchased merchandise from Wilson Supply Co., $660, terms 2/10, n/30. Voucher no. 314.
21	Issued check no. 415 to Wilson Supply Co. in partial payment for goods purchased on May 19, $330 less 2% discount. Voucher no. 314. Issued new vouchers no. 315 and 316.
22	Purchased supplies from B & J Office Supply, $120. Voucher no. 317.
23	Issued check no. 416 to Wesley's Wholesale, $720. Voucher no. 312.
25	Purchased merchandise from Eastern Distributors, $360, terms 1/10, n/30. Voucher no. 318.
28	Purchased merchandise from Torres & Co., $400, terms 2/10, n/30. Voucher no. 319.
31	Issued voucher no. 320 to Payroll in payment of bimonthly wages, $1,000.
31	Issued check no. 417 to Payroll, $1,000. Voucher no. 320.

REQUIRED

Enter the transactions in a voucher register (page 5), check register (page 5), or general journal (page 5), as appropriate. Total, rule, and prove the voucher register and check register.

MASTERY PROBLEM

1. Total Vouchers Payable Cr.: $4,853

Sunshine Flower Shop began operations in the month of July. The following transactions occurred during the first month of business.

July 1	Purchased merchandise from Thorny Wholesale, $600. Voucher no. 1.
2	Issued check no. 1 to Strongs Rental for July rent, $1,000. Voucher no. 2
3	Purchased merchandise from Flowerbed, Inc., $470, terms 2/15, n/60, FOB shipping point. Voucher no. 3.
7	Issued check no. 2 to Thorny Wholesale in partial payment for goods purchased on July 1, $300. Voucher no. 1. Issued new vouchers no. 4 and 5.
9	Issued check no. 3 to Charlie's Trucking for shipping charges, $20. Voucher no. 6.
15	Issued check no. 4 to Payroll for wages, $600. Voucher no. 7.
16	Purchased merchandise from Petals Co., $377, terms 2/15, n/30. Voucher no. 8.
17	Purchased merchandise from Weeds Plus, $436, terms 3/15, n/60. Voucher no. 9.
18	Issued check no. 5 to Flowerbed, Inc., for goods purchased on July 3 less discount. Voucher no. 3.

23   Purchased supplies from Staples Supply, $150. Voucher no. 10.

25   Received a credit memo from Weeds Plus for returned merchandise that was purchased on July 17, $80.

31   Issued check no. 6 to Petals Co. for goods purchased on July 16 less discount. Voucher no. 8.

31   Issued check no. 7 to Payroll for wages, $600. Voucher no. 11.

REQUIRED

The general ledger accounts are listed below. The $6,000 with which the Flower Shop began business is entered in the cash account. Only this account has a beginning balance.

Cash	101
Supplies	141
Vouchers Payable	202
Purchases	501
Purchases Returns and Allowances	501.1
Purchases Discounts	501.2
Freight-In	502
Wages Expense	511
Rent Expense	521

1. Enter all transactions in the voucher register (page 1), check register (page 1), and general journal (page 1). Total, rule, and prove the voucher register and check register.

2. Post the transactions to the general ledger.

3. Prepare a schedule of vouchers payable and compare the July 31 total to the balance of Vouchers Payable in the general ledger.

CHALLENGE PROBLEM

This problem challenges you to apply your cumulative accounting knowledge to move a step beyond the material in the chapter.

Voucher register, July 11: Fed. Inc. Tax Payable Cr., $608

Enter the following selected transactions in a voucher register like the one presented on the next page or in a general journal, as appropriate.

July 8   Merchandise purchased from Rebound Co. for $1,380. Voucher no. 105.

11   Employee wages and salaries for the week totaled $4,140. Amounts withheld were as follows: federal income tax payable, $608; state income tax payable, $62.10; social security tax payable, $248; medicare tax payable, $60.03. Voucher no. 106.

15   Issued check no. 413 to Rebound Co. for $300 in partial payment for merchandise purchased on July 8. Issued voucher nos. 110 and 111. Voucher no. 110 is paid.

18   Returned $230 of merchandise purchased from Rebound Co. on July 8 and received credit memo.

25   Issued check no. 430 to Rebound Co. in payment of the balance due for merchandise purchased on July 8.

(continued)

VOUCHER REGISTER

	DATE	VOUCHER NO.	ISSUED TO	PURCHASES DEBIT	SUPPLIES DEBIT	
1						1
2						2
3						3
4						4
5						5
6						6
7						7
8						8
9						9
10						10
11						11
12						12
13						13
14						14
15						15
16						16
17						17
18						18
19						19
20						20

Voucher Register—left side

	WAGES AND SALARIES EXPENSE DR.	GENERAL				VOUCHERS PAYABLE CREDIT	PAYMENT		
		ACCOUNT	POST REF.	DEBIT	CREDIT		DATE	CHECK NO.	
1									1
2									2
3									3
4									4
5									5
6									6
7									7
8									8
9									9
10									10
11									11
12									12
13									13
14									14
15									15
16									16
17									17
18									18
19									19
20									20

Voucher Register—right side

© GETTY IMAGES / PHOTODISC

Adjustments and the Work Sheet for a Merchandising Business

Often we are expected to pay in advance for goods and services. This is true for season tickets for sporting events, magazine subscriptions, or tickets for popular operas or rock concerts. In return, we expect to receive the goods or services. When customers place special orders, Evan Taylor requires them to pay a cash deposit of half of the total sales amount. How should these cash receipts be treated by his business?

Careful study of this chapter should enable you to:

LO1 Prepare an adjustment for merchandise inventory using the periodic inventory system.

LO2 Prepare an adjustment for unearned revenue.

LO3 Prepare a work sheet for a merchandising business.

LO4 Journalize adjusting entries for a merchandising business.

LO5 Prepare adjusting journal entries under the perpetual inventory system.

In Chapters 11 through 14, we learned how to account for the day-to-day transactions of a merchandising business. In this chapter, we focus on end-of-period adjustments and the preparation of the work sheet. Finally, in Chapter 16, we will complete the accounting cycle by preparing financial statements and closing entries.

A work sheet for a merchandising business is similar to the work sheet prepared for a service business (Chapter 5). It is used to prepare adjustments for supplies, prepaid insurance, wages earned but not paid, depreciation, and other necessary year-end adjustments. A merchandising business must also make an adjustment to properly report the amount of merchandise inventory held at the end of the accounting period. While revisiting the work sheet, we will also introduce a new adjustment for unearned revenue.

ADJUSTMENT FOR MERCHANDISE INVENTORY

LO1 Prepare an adjustment for merchandise inventory using the periodic inventory system.

As discussed in Chapters 11 and 12, when merchandise inventory is purchased, the purchases account is debited and cash or accounts payable is credited. When inventory is sold, cash or accounts receivable is debited and sales is credited. This method of accounting for inventory transactions is called the **periodic inventory system**. Figure 15-1 provides a review of these entries.

TRANSACTION	ENTRY		
Purchase of merchandise	Purchases	xxx	
	Accounts Payable or Cash		xxx
Sale of merchandise	Accounts Receivable or Cash	xxx	
	Sales		xxx

FIGURE 15-1 Review of Entries for Purchase and Sale of Merchandise

Note that the merchandise inventory account is not debited or credited in either of these entries. Since sales and purchases have taken place during the year, the beginning balance of the merchandise inventory account no longer provides an accurate picture of the inventory held at the end of the year. Thus, an adjustment must be made to remove the beginning inventory and enter the ending inventory in the merchandise inventory account. The quantity of inventory on hand at the end of the accounting period is determined by taking a physical count of the goods on hand. This process is referred to as a **physical inventory**. The cost of these goods is determined by reviewing the accounting records. Of course, this year's ending inventory becomes next year's beginning inventory.

To illustrate the adjustment for merchandise inventory, let's assume that Ponder's Bike Parts had a beginning merchandise inventory of $25,000. During

LEARNING KEY: To adjust the merchandise inventory account, take out the old and bring in the new.

the year, the entries shown in Figure 15-1 were made as merchandise was purchased and sold. At the end of the accounting period, a physical inventory of the merchandise determined that merchandise costing $30,000 was still on hand. This indicates that the cost of the merchandise purchased exceeded cost of goods sold by $5,000.

As shown in Figure 15-2, the inventory adjustment is made in two steps:

STEP 1   In adjustment (a), the beginning inventory ($25,000) is removed by crediting Merchandise Inventory. Income Summary is debited because this amount is used in the calculation of cost of goods sold. "Cost of goods sold" is an expense on the income statement.

STEP 2   In adjustment (b), the ending inventory ($30,000) is entered by debiting Merchandise Inventory. Income Summary is credited because this amount also is used in the calculation of cost of goods sold. After making the second adjustment, the balance of $30,000 in Merchandise Inventory reflects the inventory on hand at the end of the accounting period.

LEARNING KEY: Income Summary is used to adjust Merchandise Inventory. It is also used when closing the temporary owner's equity accounts.

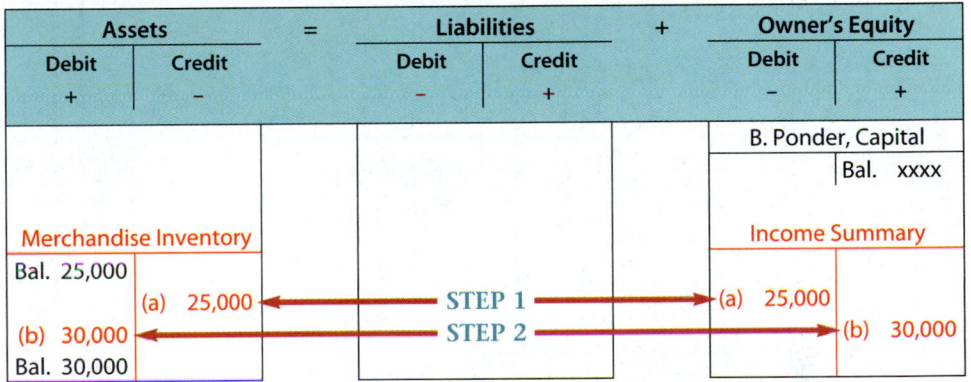

FIGURE 15-2   Two-Step Adjustment for Merchandise Inventory

The two-step adjustment process is a bit unusual. Perhaps the best way to explain the reason for this approach is by illustrating how these adjustments are made on the work sheet and how the work sheet information is used to prepare the income statement. Figure 15-3 illustrates a partial work sheet for Ponder's Bike Parts and the cost of goods sold section of the income statement.

The inventory adjustments are made following the two-step process described above.

Step 1	Income Summary	25,000	
	Merchandise Inventory		25,000
Step 2	Merchandise Inventory	30,000	
	Income Summary		30,000

Both the debit of $25,000 and the credit of $30,000 made to the income summary account are extended to the Adjusted Trial Balance and Income Statement columns. *This is the only time that the individual figures, rather than the net amount, are extended on the work sheet.* It is done in this case because the individual amounts are needed for the calculation of cost of goods sold on the

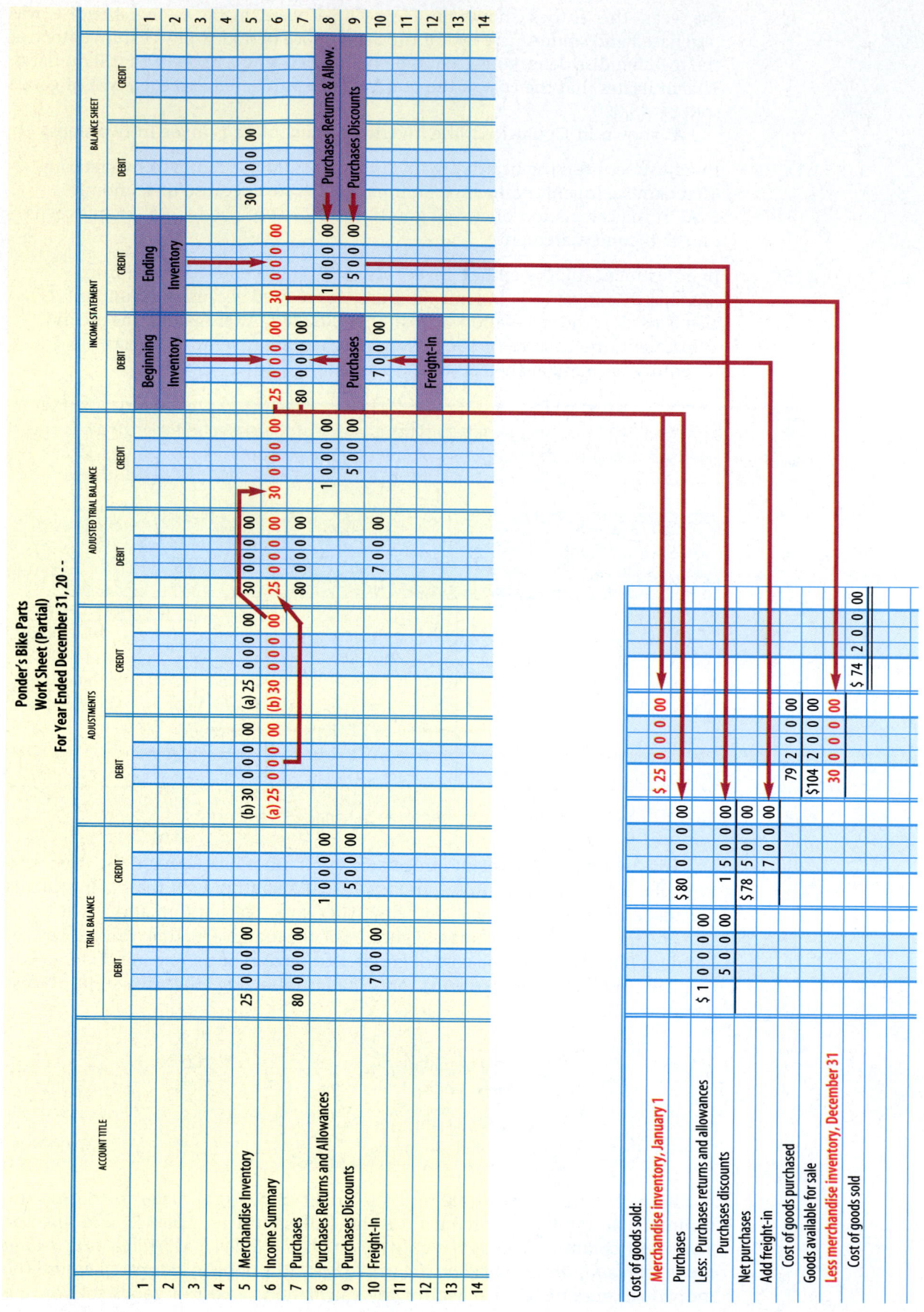

FIGURE 15-3   Calculation of Cost of Goods Sold Using Information in the Income Statement Columns of the Work Sheet

A BROADER VIEW

The Importance of Inventory

Note the important role of the ending inventory in the calculation of cost of goods sold in Figure 15-3. If the ending inventory is overstated for any reason, net income will also be overstated. Given this important relationship, auditors observe and verify the accuracy of the physical inventory. However, unethical managers, desperate to improve profits, have on occasion found ways to mislead auditors.

In one case, managers overstated inventory counts for items that the auditors had not physically verified. In another case, auditors found a barrel whose contents had been valued by management at thousands of dollars. It actually contained floor sweepings. Finally, there was a case where management called the auditor, the day after the inventory audit, to report that additional inventory had arrived and should be included in the inventory count. The auditor never verified that the inventory was real. It turned out to be a scam that helped the company double its reported profits for the year. These unfortunate events highlight the reason auditors must exercise great care when conducting an inventory audit.

income statement. As shown in Figure 15-3, all of the information needed for the preparation of the income statement is in the Income Statement columns of the work sheet. This is the result of using the two-step adjustment process for inventory and extending both the debit and credit made to Income Summary.

LEARNING KEY: Both the debit and credit amounts on the income summary line are extended. This is because both amounts are needed to prepare the income statement. The amount in the debit column is the beginning inventory. The amount in the credit column is the ending inventory.

ADJUSTMENT FOR UNEARNED REVENUE

LO2 Prepare an adjustment for unearned revenue.

Some businesses require payment before delivering a product or performing a service. Examples include insurance companies, magazine publishers, apartment complexes, college food services, and professional sports and theater companies that sell season tickets. The cash received in advance is called **unearned revenue**.

Since the cash has been received in advance, the company owes the customers the product or service, or must refund their money. Thus, unearned revenue is reported as a *liability* on the balance sheet.

 LEARNING KEY: Remember, under the accrual basis of accounting, revenue is recorded when *earned* regardless of when cash is received.

To illustrate, let's assume that the Brown County Playhouse sells season tickets for five plays produced throughout the year. Tickets sell for $10 for each play ($50 for a season ticket) and a maximum of 1,000 seats can be sold for each play. For simplicity, let's assume that all shows sell out during the first week that season tickets are available for sale. As shown below and in Figure 15-4, the sale of the tickets would be recorded as follows:

8	(1)	Cash	50 0 0 0 00		8
9		Unearned Ticket Revenue		50 0 0 0 00	9
10		Season ticket sales			10
11		($10 × 1,000 seats × 5 shows)			11

To prepare financial statements following production of the third show, an adjusting entry is needed to recognize that $30,000 ($10 × 1,000 seats × 3 shows) in ticket revenue has been earned. To do this, the following adjusting entry is made.

13		Adjusting Entries		13
14		Unearned Ticket Revenue	30 0 0 0 00	14
15		Ticket Revenue	30 0 0 0 00	15

The remaining balance of $20,000 in Unearned Ticket Revenue is reported as a current liability on the balance sheet.

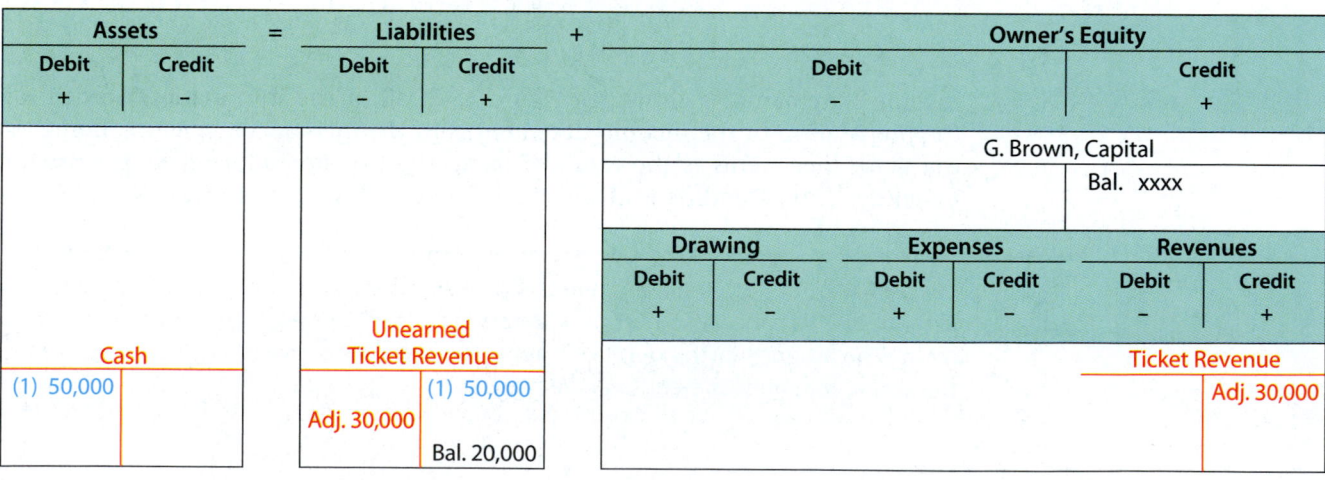

FIGURE 15-4 Entries for Unearned Revenue

Expanded Chart of Accounts

Let's take a look at where the new accounts for a merchandising business fit into a chart of accounts. Recall that the chart of accounts follows the form of the accounting equation (Assets = Liabilities + Owner's Equity + Revenues – Expenses).

A chart of accounts for Northern Micro is provided in Figure 15-5. Note the classification of the new accounts introduced in Chapters 11 and 12 for a merchandising firm.

Merchandise Inventory is listed as a current asset. Since Northern Micro sells subscriptions to a computer magazine that it produces, Unearned Subscriptions Revenue is listed as a current liability, and Subscriptions Revenue is listed as a revenue. Sales Returns and Allowances and Sales Discounts are **contra-revenue accounts**. Recall, however, that Northern Micro does not offer sales discounts.

Purchases, Purchases Returns and Allowances, Purchases Discounts, and Freight-In are used to compute cost of goods sold. Thus, they are listed under this heading. Purchases Returns and Allowances and Purchases Discounts are often called **contra-cost accounts** or contra-purchases accounts.

Interest Expense is classified as "Other Expense" instead of being listed under Operating Expenses. This is because it represents the expense of obtaining money to do business, rather than an expense directly associated with operating the business.

NORTHERN MICRO
CHART OF ACCOUNTS

Assets		Revenue	
Current Assets		401	Sales
101	Cash	401.1	Sales Returns and Allowances
122	Accounts Receivable		
131	Merchandise Inventory	**Other Revenue**	
141	Supplies	411	Interest Revenue
145	Prepaid Insurance	412	Rent Revenue
		413	Subscriptions Revenue
Property, Plant, and Equipment		**Expenses**	
161	Land	**Cost of Goods Sold**	
171	Building	501	Purchases
171.1	Accumulated Depreciation—Building	501.1	Purchases Returns and Allowances
181	Store Equipment	501.2	Purchases Discounts
181.1	Accumulated Depreciation—Store Equipment	502	Freight-In
Liabilities		**Operating Expenses**	
Current Liabilities		511	Wages Expense
201	Notes Payable	512	Advertising Expense
202	Accounts Payable	513	Bank Credit Card Expense
219	Wages Payable	521	Rent Expense
231	Sales Tax Payable	523	Supplies Expense
241	Unearned Subscriptions Revenue	525	Telephone Expense
		533	Utilities Expense
Long-Term Liabilities		535	Insurance Expense
251	Mortgage Payable	540	Depreciation Expense—Building
Owner's Equity		541	Depreciation Expense—Store Equipment
311	Gary L. Fishel, Capital	549	Miscellaneous Expense
312	Gary L. Fishel, Drawing	**Other Expenses**	
313	Income Summary	551	Interest Expense

FIGURE 15-5 Chart of Accounts for Northern Micro

PREPARING A WORK SHEET FOR A MERCHANDISING BUSINESS

LO3 Prepare a work sheet for a merchandising business.

The work sheet for a merchandising business is similar to the one shown in Chapter 5 for a service business. Recall the five steps taken to prepare a work sheet:

STEP 1 Prepare the trial balance.

STEP 2 Prepare the adjustments.

STEP 3 Prepare the adjusted trial balance.

STEP 4 Extend the adjusted trial balance to the Income Statement and Balance Sheet columns.

STEP 5 Complete the work sheet by totaling the Income Statement and Balance Sheet columns to compute the net income or net loss.

The work sheet format and the five steps taken when preparing the work sheet are illustrated in Figure 15-6. Note that the new accounts introduced for a merchandising firm and the unearned revenue account are highlighted so that you can see their proper placement and extensions. (The abbreviation BI stands for beginning inventory; EI stands for ending inventory.) Pay particular attention to the extension of Income Summary. Both the debit and credit amounts for this account must be extended.

Adjustments for Northern Micro

Before preparing a work sheet for Northern Micro, let's review the preparation of adjustments in T account form. Figure 15-7 provides year-end adjustment information for Northern Micro. Figure 15-8 shows adjusting entries based on this information. The unadjusted balances for these accounts were taken from Northern Micro's trial balance.

Preparing a Work Sheet for Northern Micro

Let's prepare a work sheet for Northern Micro following the five steps illustrated in Figure 15-6.

STEP 1 In Figure 15-9, the Trial Balance columns are completed by copying the balances of all accounts from the general ledger (not shown).

STEP 2 In Figure 15-10, the adjustments are entered. These entries are exactly the same as those made in T account form in Figure 15-8.

STEP 3 In Figure 15-11, extensions are made to the Adjusted Trial Balance columns. Note that both the debit and credit amounts for Income Summary are extended.

STEP 4 In Figure 15-12, the Adjusted Trial Balance amounts are extended to the Income Statement and Balance Sheet columns.

STEP 5 In Figure 15-12, the work sheet is completed by totaling the Income Statement and Balance Sheet columns. The difference between the debits and credits for each pair of columns represents the net income or net loss.

Name of Company
Work Sheet
For Year Ended December 31, 20 - -

ACCOUNT TITLE	TRIAL BALANCE DEBIT	TRIAL BALANCE CREDIT	ADJUSTMENTS DEBIT	ADJUSTMENTS CREDIT	ADJUSTED TRIAL BALANCE DEBIT	ADJUSTED TRIAL BALANCE CREDIT	INCOME STATEMENT DEBIT	INCOME STATEMENT CREDIT	BALANCE SHEET DEBIT	BALANCE SHEET CREDIT	
(Insert Ledger Account Titles)	**Step 1:** Prepare a Trial Balance		**Step 2:** Prepare the Adjustments		**Step 3:** Prepare the Adjusted Trial Balance		**Step 4:** Extend Adjusted Account Balances				
Assets	Assets				Assets				Assets		4
Mdse. Inv. (BI) / Mdse. Inv. (EI)	Mdse. Inv. (BI)		EI	BI	Mdse. Inv. (EI)				Mdse. Inv. (EI)		5
Liabilities		Liabilities				Liabilities				Liabilities	6
Unearned		Unearned				Unearned				Unearned	7
Revenues		Revenues				Revenues				Revenues	8
Capital		Capital				Capital				Capital	9
Drawing	Drawing				Drawing				Drawing		10
Income Summary			BI	EI	BI	EI	BI	EI			13
Revenues		Revenues				Revenues		Revenues			15
Sales		Sales				Sales		Sales			16
Sales R&A	Sales R&A				Sales R&A		Sales R&A				17
Sales Discounts	Sales Discounts				Sales Discounts		Sales Discounts				18
Expenses	Expenses				Expenses		Expenses				20
Purchases	Purchases				Purchases		Purchases				21
Purch. R&A		Purch. R&A				Purch. R&A		Purch. R&A			22
Purch. Discounts		Purch. Discounts				Purch. Discounts		Purch. Discounts			23
Freight-In	Freight-In				Freight-In		Freight-In				24
							Step 5: Complete the work sheet 1) Sum columns 2) Compute net income (loss)				25–28
							Net Income / Net Loss	**Net Loss / Net Income**	**Net Loss / Net Income**	**Net Income / Net Loss**	30–31

B I = Beginning Inventory
E I = Ending Inventory

FIGURE 15-6 Overview of Work Sheet for a Merchandising Business

YEAR-END ADJUSTMENT DATA FOR NORTHERN MICRO	
(a, b)	A physical count showed that merchandise inventory costing $18,000 is on hand as of December 31.
(c)	Supplies remaining at the end of the year, $400.
(d)	Unexpired insurance on December 31, $600.
(e)	Depreciation expense on the building for the year, $4,000.
(f)	Depreciation expense on the store equipment for the year, $3,000.
(g)	Wages earned but not paid as of December 31, $450.
(h)	Northern Micro publishes a computer magazine. Subscribers pay in advance. Unearned subscriptions revenue as of December 31, $2,000.

FIGURE 15-7 Year-End Adjustment Data for Northern Micro

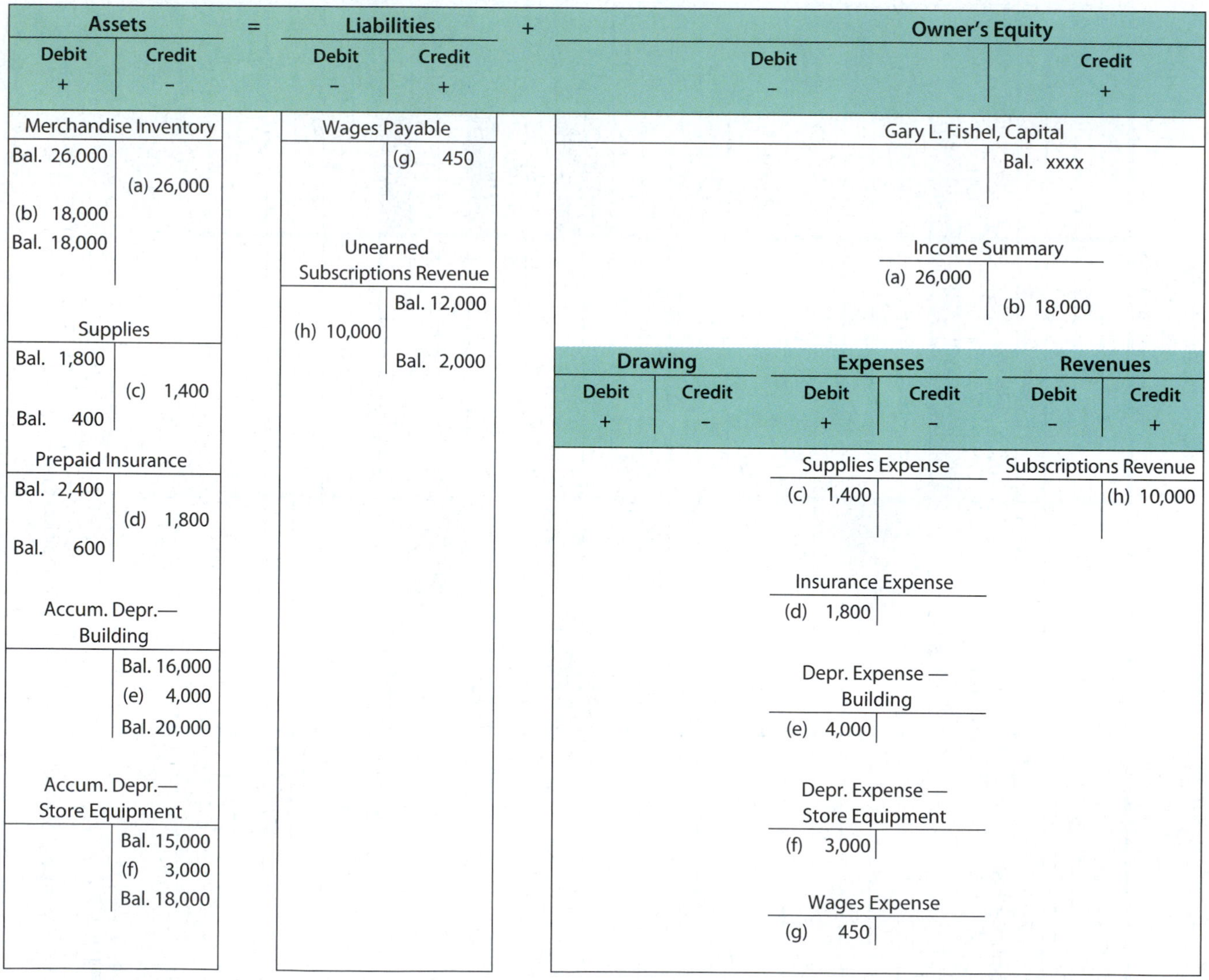

FIGURE 15-8 Adjusting Entries for Northern Micro

Northern Micro
Work Sheet
For Year Ended December 31, 20--

The work sheet is ruled with six paired Debit/Credit money columns — TRIAL BALANCE, ADJUSTMENTS, ADJUSTED TRIAL BALANCE, INCOME STATEMENT, and BALANCE SHEET. In this step only the Trial Balance columns are completed; all other columns are blank.

#	ACCOUNT TITLE	Trial Balance DEBIT	Trial Balance CREDIT
1	Cash	20 0 0 0 00	
2	Accounts Receivable	15 0 0 0 00	
3	Merchandise Inventory	26 0 0 0 00	
4	Supplies	1 8 0 0 00	
5	Prepaid Insurance	2 4 0 0 00	
6	Land	10 0 0 0 00	
7	Building	90 0 0 0 00	
8	Accum. Depr.—Building		16 0 0 0 00
9	Store Equipment	50 0 0 0 00	
10	Accum. Depr.—Store Equipment		15 0 0 0 00
11	Notes Payable		5 0 0 0 00
12	Accounts Payable		10 0 0 0 00
13	Wages Payable		
14	Sales Tax Payable		1 5 0 0 00
15	Unearned Subscriptions Revenue		12 0 0 0 00
16	Mortgage Payable		30 0 0 0 00
17	Gary L. Fishel, Capital		114 4 0 0 00
18	Gary L. Fishel, Drawing	20 0 0 0 00	
19	Income Summary		
20	Sales		214 0 0 0 00
21	Sales Returns and Allowances	1 2 0 0 00	
22	Interest Revenue		9 0 0 00
23	Rent Revenue		8 0 0 00
24	Subscriptions Revenue		
25	Purchases	105 0 0 0 00	
26	Purchases Returns and Allowances		8 0 0 00
27	Purchases Discounts		1 0 0 0 00
28	Freight-In	3 0 0 0 00	
29	Wages Expense	42 0 0 0 00	
30	Advertising Expense	2 5 0 0 00	
31	Bank Credit Card Expense	1 5 0 0 00	
32	Rent Expense	20 0 0 0 00	
33	Supplies Expense		
34	Telephone Expense	3 5 0 0 00	
35	Utilities Expense	12 0 0 0 00	
36	Insurance Expense		
37	Depr. Expense—Building		
38	Depr. Expense—Store Equipment		
39	Miscellaneous Expense	2 2 5 0 00	
40	Interest Expense	3 1 5 0 00	
41		428 6 0 0 00	428 6 0 0 00
42			

STEP 1

FIGURE 15-9 Step 1: Completion of the Trial Balance Columns

Northern Micro
Work Sheet
For Year Ended December 31, 20- -

#	ACCOUNT TITLE	TRIAL BALANCE DEBIT	TRIAL BALANCE CREDIT	ADJUSTMENTS DEBIT	ADJUSTMENTS CREDIT	ADJUSTED TRIAL BALANCE DEBIT	ADJUSTED TRIAL BALANCE CREDIT	INCOME STATEMENT DEBIT	INCOME STATEMENT CREDIT	BALANCE SHEET DEBIT	BALANCE SHEET CREDIT
1	Cash	20 0 0 0 00									
2	Accounts Receivable	15 0 0 0 00									
3	Merchandise Inventory	26 0 0 0 00		(b) 18 0 0 0 00	(a) 26 0 0 0 00						
4	Supplies	1 8 0 0 00			(c) 1 4 0 0 00						
5	Prepaid Insurance	2 4 0 0 00			(d) 1 8 0 0 00						
6	Land	10 0 0 0 00									
7	Building	90 0 0 0 00									
8	Accum. Depr.—Building		16 0 0 0 00		(e) 4 0 0 0 00						
9	Store Equipment	50 0 0 0 00									
10	Accum. Depr.—Store Equipment		15 0 0 0 00		(f) 3 0 0 0 00						
11	Notes Payable		5 0 0 0 00								
12	Accounts Payable		10 0 0 0 00								
13	Wages Payable				(g) 4 5 0 00						
14	Sales Tax Payable		1 5 0 0 00								
15	Unearned Subscriptions Revenue		12 0 0 0 00	(h) 10 0 0 0 00							
16	Mortgage Payable		30 0 0 0 00								
17	Gary L. Fishel, Capital		114 4 0 0 00								
18	Gary L. Fishel, Drawing	20 0 0 0 00									
19	Income Summary			(a) 26 0 0 0 00	(b) 18 0 0 0 00						
20	Sales		214 0 0 0 00								
21	Sales Returns and Allowances	1 2 0 0 00									
22	Interest Revenue		9 0 0 00								
23	Rent Revenue		8 0 0 0 00								
24	Subscriptions Revenue				(h) 10 0 0 0 00						
25	Purchases	105 0 0 0 00									
26	Purchases Returns and Allowances		8 0 0 00								
27	Purchases Discounts		1 0 0 0 00								
28	Freight-In	3 0 0 0 00									
29	Wages Expense	42 0 0 0 00		(g) 4 5 0 00							
30	Advertising Expense	2 5 0 0 00									
31	Bank Credit Card Expense	1 5 0 0 00									
32	Rent Expense	20 0 0 0 00									
33	Supplies Expense			(c) 1 4 0 0 00							
34	Telephone Expense	3 5 0 0 00									
35	Utilities Expense	12 0 0 0 00									
36	Insurance Expense			(d) 1 8 0 0 00							
37	Depr. Expense—Building			(e) 4 0 0 0 00							
38	Depr. Expense—Store Equipment			(f) 3 0 0 0 00							
39	Miscellaneous Expense	2 2 5 0 00									
40	Interest Expense	3 1 5 0 00									
41		428 6 0 0 00	428 6 0 0 00	64 6 5 0 00	64 6 5 0 00						
42											

STEP 1   STEP 2

FIGURE 15-10 Step 2: Preparation of the Adjustments

Northern Micro
Work Sheet
For Year Ended December 31, 20 - -

Row	Account Title	Trial Balance Debit	Trial Balance Credit	Adjustments Debit	Adjustments Credit	Adjusted Trial Balance Debit	Adjusted Trial Balance Credit	Income Statement Debit	Income Statement Credit	Balance Sheet Debit	Balance Sheet Credit
1	Cash	20 0 0 0 00				20 0 0 0 00					
2	Accounts Receivable	15 0 0 0 00				15 0 0 0 00					
3	Merchandise Inventory	26 0 0 0 00		(b) 18 0 0 0 00	(a) 26 0 0 0 00	18 0 0 0 00	18 0 0 0 00				
4	Supplies	1 8 0 0 00			(c) 1 4 0 0 00	4 0 0 00					
5	Prepaid Insurance	2 4 0 0 00			(d) 1 8 0 0 00	6 0 0 00					
6	Land	10 0 0 0 00				10 0 0 0 00					
7	Building	90 0 0 0 00				90 0 0 0 00					
8	Accum. Depr.—Building		16 0 0 0 00		(e) 4 0 0 0 00		20 0 0 0 00				
9	Store Equipment	50 0 0 0 00				50 0 0 0 00					
10	Accum. Depr.—Store Equipment		15 0 0 0 00		(f) 3 0 0 0 00		18 0 0 0 00				
11	Notes Payable		5 0 0 0 00				5 0 0 0 00				
12	Accounts Payable		10 0 0 0 00				10 0 0 0 00				
13	Wages Payable				(g) 4 5 0 00		4 5 0 00				
14	Sales Tax Payable		1 5 0 0 00				1 5 0 0 00				
15	Unearned Subscriptions Revenue		12 0 0 0 00	(h) 10 0 0 0 00			2 0 0 0 00				
16	Mortgage Payable		30 0 0 0 00				30 0 0 0 00				
17	Gary L. Fishel, Capital		114 4 0 0 00				114 4 0 0 00				
18	Gary L. Fishel, Drawing	20 0 0 0 00				20 0 0 0 00					
19	Income Summary			(a) 26 0 0 0 00	(b) 18 0 0 0 00	26 0 0 0 00	18 0 0 0 00				
20	Sales		214 0 0 0 00				214 0 0 0 00				
21	Sales Returns and Allowances	1 2 0 0 00				1 2 0 0 00					
22	Interest Revenue		9 0 0 00				9 0 0 00				
23	Rent Revenue		8 0 0 0 00				8 0 0 0 00				
24	Subscriptions Revenue				(h) 10 0 0 0 00		10 0 0 0 00				
25	Purchases	105 0 0 0 00				105 0 0 0 00					
26	Purchases Returns and Allowances		8 0 0 00				8 0 0 00				
27	Purchases Discounts		1 0 0 0 00				1 0 0 0 00				
28	Freight-In	3 0 0 0 00				3 0 0 0 00					
29	Wages Expense	42 0 0 0 00		(g) 4 5 0 00		42 4 5 0 00					
30	Advertising Expense	2 5 0 0 00				2 5 0 0 00					
31	Bank Credit Card Expense	1 5 0 0 00				1 5 0 0 00					
32	Rent Expense	20 0 0 0 00				20 0 0 0 00					
33	Supplies Expense			(c) 1 4 0 0 00		1 4 0 0 00					
34	Telephone Expense	3 5 0 0 00				3 5 0 0 00					
35	Utilities Expense	12 0 0 0 00				12 0 0 0 00					
36	Insurance Expense			(d) 1 8 0 0 00		1 8 0 0 00					
37	Depr. Expense—Building			(e) 4 0 0 0 00		4 0 0 0 00					
38	Depr. Expense—Store Equipment			(f) 3 0 0 0 00		3 0 0 0 00					
39	Miscellaneous Expense	2 2 5 0 00				2 2 5 0 00					
40	Interest Expense	3 1 5 0 00				3 1 5 0 00					
41		428 6 0 0 00	428 6 0 0 00	64 6 5 0 00	64 6 5 0 00	454 0 5 0 00	454 0 5 0 00				
42											

Annotations: "Ending Inventory" (Merchandise Inventory, Adjusted Trial Balance Debit); "Beginning Inventory" and "Ending Inventory" (Income Summary, Adjusted Trial Balance); "Both the debit and credit are extended."

STEP 1   STEP 2   STEP 3

FIGURE 15-11 Step 3: Extensions to the Adjusted Trial Balance Columns

Northern Micro
Work Sheet
For Year Ended December 31, 20- -

#	Account Title	Trial Balance Debit	Trial Balance Credit	Adjustments Debit	Adjustments Credit	Adjusted Trial Balance Debit	Adjusted Trial Balance Credit	Income Statement Debit	Income Statement Credit	Balance Sheet Debit	Balance Sheet Credit
1	Cash	20 000 00				20 000 00				20 000 00	
2	Accounts Receivable	15 000 00				15 000 00				15 000 00	
3	Merchandise Inventory	26 000 00		(b) 18 000 00	(a) 26 000 00	18 000 00				18 000 00	
4	Supplies	1 800 00			(c) 1 400 00	4 00 00				4 00 00	
5	Prepaid Insurance	2 400 00			(d) 1 800 00	6 00 00				6 00 00	
6	Land	10 000 00				10 000 00				10 000 00	
7	Building	90 000 00				90 000 00				90 000 00	
8	Accum. Depr.—Building		16 000 00		(e) 4 000 00		20 000 00				20 000 00
9	Store Equipment	50 000 00				50 000 00				50 000 00	
10	Accum. Depr.—Store Equipment		15 000 00		(f) 3 000 00		18 000 00				18 000 00
11	Notes Payable		5 000 00				5 000 00				5 000 00
12	Accounts Payable		10 000 00				10 000 00				10 000 00
13	Wages Payable				(g) 4 50 00		4 50 00				4 50 00
14	Sales Tax Payable		1 500 00				1 500 00				1 500 00
15	Unearned Subscriptions Revenue		12 000 00	(h) 10 000 00			2 000 00				2 000 00
16	Mortgage Payable		30 000 00				30 000 00				30 000 00
17	Gary L. Fishel, Capital		114 400 00				114 400 00				114 400 00
18	Gary L. Fishel, Drawing	20 000 00				20 000 00				20 000 00	
19	Income Summary			(a) 26 000 00	(b) 18 000 00	26 000 00	18 000 00	26 000 00	18 000 00		
20	Sales		214 000 00				214 000 00		214 000 00		
21	Sales Returns and Allowances	1 200 00				1 200 00		1 200 00			
22	Interest Revenue		9 00 00				9 00 00		9 00 00		
23	Rent Revenue		8 00 00				8 00 00		8 00 00		
24	Subscriptions Revenue				(h) 10 000 00		10 000 00		10 000 00		
25	Purchases	105 000 00				105 000 00		105 000 00			
26	Purchases Returns and Allowances		8 00 00				8 00 00		8 00 00		
27	Purchases Discounts		1 000 00				1 000 00		1 000 00		
28	Freight-In	3 000 00				3 000 00		3 000 00			
29	Wages Expense	42 000 00		(g) 4 50 00		42 450 00		42 450 00			
30	Advertising Expense	2 500 00				2 500 00		2 500 00			
31	Bank Credit Card Expense	1 500 00				1 500 00		1 500 00			
32	Rent Expense	20 000 00				20 000 00		20 000 00			
33	Supplies Expense			(c) 1 400 00		1 400 00		1 400 00			
34	Telephone Expense	3 500 00				3 500 00		3 500 00			
35	Utilities Expense	12 000 00				12 000 00		12 000 00			
36	Insurance Expense			(d) 1 800 00		1 800 00		1 800 00			
37	Depr. Expense—Building			(e) 4 000 00		4 000 00		4 000 00			
38	Depr. Expense—Store Equipment			(f) 3 000 00		3 000 00		3 000 00			
39	Miscellaneous Expense	2 250 00				2 250 00		2 250 00			
40	Interest Expense	3 150 00				3 150 00		3 150 00			
41		428 600 00	428 600 00	64 650 00	64 650 00	454 050 00	454 050 00	230 050 00	252 700 00	224 000 00	201 350 00
42	Net Income							22 650 00			22 650 00
43								252 700 00	252 700 00	224 000 00	224 000 00

STEP 1   STEP 2   STEP 3   STEPS 4 AND 5

FIGURE 15-12 Step 4: Extensions to the Income Statement and Balance Sheet Columns   Step 5: Completing the Work Sheet and Computing Net Income

ADJUSTING ENTRIES

LO4 Journalize adjusting entries for a merchandising business.

Recall that making the adjustments on the work sheet has no effect on the actual accounts in the general ledger. Journal entries must be made to enter the adjustments into the accounting system. Figure 15-13 shows the adjusting entries for Northern Micro.

 LEARNING KEY: Recall that the work sheet is just a planning tool. The adjusting entries must be entered in the general journal.

GENERAL JOURNAL   PAGE 3

	DATE		DESCRIPTION	POST REF.	DEBIT	CREDIT	
1			Adjusting Entries				1
2	20-- Dec.	31	Income Summary		26 0 0 0 00		2
3			Merchandise Inventory			26 0 0 0 00	3
4							4
5		31	Merchandise Inventory		18 0 0 0 00		5
6			Income Summary			18 0 0 0 00	6
7							7
8		31	Supplies Expense		1 4 0 0 00		8
9			Supplies			1 4 0 0 00	9
10							10
11		31	Insurance Expense		1 8 0 0 00		11
12			Prepaid Insurance			1 8 0 0 00	12
13							13
14		31	Depr. Expense—Building		4 0 0 0 00		14
15			Accumulated Depr.—Building			4 0 0 0 00	15
16							16
17		31	Depr. Expense—Store Equipment		3 0 0 0 00		17
18			Accumulated Depr.—Store Equipment			3 0 0 0 00	18
19							19
20		31	Wages Expense		4 5 0 00		20
21			Wages Payable			4 5 0 00	21
22							22
23		31	Unearned Subscriptions Revenue		10 0 0 0 00		23
24			Subscriptions Revenue			10 0 0 0 00	24
25							25

FIGURE 15-13 Adjusting Entries for Northern Micro

PREPARING AND JOURNALIZING ADJUSTING ENTRIES UNDER THE PERPETUAL INVENTORY SYSTEM

LO5 Prepare adjusting journal entries under the perpetual inventory system.

Under the **perpetual inventory system**, the merchandise inventory and cost of goods sold accounts are continually updated throughout the year to reflect purchases and sales of inventory. When inventory is purchased, the merchandise

Under the perpetual inventory method, two entries are required to record the sale of merchandise.

inventory account is debited and cash or accounts payable is credited. When inventory is sold, two entries are made:

1. Cash or accounts receivable is debited and sales is credited.

2. Cost of goods sold is debited and merchandise inventory is credited.

A comparison of the entries under the periodic and perpetual inventory systems is provided in Figure 15-14.

TRANSACTION	PERIODIC SYSTEM			PERPETUAL SYSTEM		
Purchased merchandise on account, $800	Purchases	800		Merchandise Inventory	800	
	Accounts Payable		800	Accounts Payable		800
Sold merchandise on account, $400. The cost of the merchandise sold was $300.	Accounts Receivable	400		Accounts Receivable	400	
	Sales		400	Sales		400
				Cost of Goods Sold	300	
				Merchandise Inventory		300

FIGURE 15-14 Entries for Periodic and Perpetual Inventory Systems

LEARNING KEY: Under the perpetual inventory system, cost of goods sold and the amount of merchandise inventory on hand are continually updated as merchandise is bought and sold.

With the increased use of computers and optical scanning devices, more and more businesses are using a perpetual inventory system. The primary advantage of this system is that the firm always knows the amount of inventory that should be on hand. This is very helpful when deciding when to replenish specific types of inventory. Of course, before preparing financial statements, it is important to take a physical count of the inventory to verify the accuracy of the inventory system. If the physical count confirms the accuracy of the ending inventory, no adjusting entry is necessary. However, clerical errors, breakage, spoilage, and shoplifting are likely to result in a physical count that is different from the amount currently reported in the inventory account. In this case, an adjustment is necessary.

For example, if the balance of the merchandise inventory account at the end of the accounting period is $500, but the physical count of the inventory is $450, the following adjusting entry would be made.

| 12 | Dec. 31 | Cost of Goods Sold | | | 5 0 00 | | | 12 |
| 13 | | Merchandise Inventory | | | | 5 0 00 | | 13 |

On the other hand, if the balance of the merchandise inventory account at the end of the accounting period is $500, but the physical count of the inventory is $540, the following adjusting entry would be made.

| 12 | Dec. 31 | Merchandise Inventory | | | 4 0 00 | | | 12 |
| 13 | | Cost of Goods Sold | | | | 4 0 00 | | 13 |

Learning Objectives	Key Points to Remember

1 **Prepare an adjustment for merchandise inventory using the periodic inventory sytem.**

Extra care is required for the end-of-period adjustment for merchandise inventory and the related extensions on the work sheet. The two-step adjustment process in T account form and the work sheet treatment for Northern Micro are reviewed in Figures 15-15 and 15-16 below and on the following page.

Assets		=	Liabilities		+	Owner's Equity	
Debit	Credit		Debit	Credit		Debit	Credit
+	–		–	+		–	+

						Gary L. Fishel, Capital	
							Bal. xxx
Merchandise Inventory						**Income Summary**	
Bal. 26,000							
	Adj. 26,000	← STEP 1 →				Adj. 26,000	
Adj. 18,000		← STEP 2 →					Adj. 18,000

FIGURE 15-15 Two-Step Adjustment for Merchandise Inventory in T Account Form

---

2 **Prepare an adjustment for unearned revenue.**

Some firms receive cash before providing a service or selling a product. The cash received in advance is considered a liability, unearned revenue, until earned. The adjusting entry to recognize that unearned revenue has become earned is:

Unearned Revenue	xxx	
Revenue		xxx

---

3 **Prepare a work sheet for a merchandising business.**

Steps to follow when preparing a work sheet:
1. Prepare the trial balance.
2. Prepare the adjustments.
3. Prepare the adjusted trial balance.
4. Extend the adjusted trial balance amounts to the Income Statement and Balance Sheet columns.
5. Total the Income Statement and Balance Sheet columns to compute the net income or net loss.

---

4 **Journalize adjusting entries for a merchandising business.**

The work sheet is a useful tool when preparing end-of-period adjustments and financial statements. Remember: The work sheet is NOT a formal part of the accounting system. Adjustments made on the work sheet must be entered in a journal and posted to the ledger.

---

5 **Prepare adjusting journal entries under the perpetual inventory system.**

Under the perpetual inventory system, the cost of goods sold and merchandise inventory acccounts are updated whenever merchandise is purchased or sold. Thus, the firm knows how much inventory should be on hand at any given point in time. However, the balance of the merchandise inventory account must be verified with an actual physical count of the inventory before issuing financial statements. If there is a difference, an adjusting entry is made. If the balance in the inventory account is greater than the physical count, the following entry is made.

Cost of Goods Sold	xxx	
Merchandise Inventory		xxx

If the balance in the inventory account is less than the physical count, the following entry is made.

Merchandise Inventory	xxx	
Cost of Goods Sold		xxx

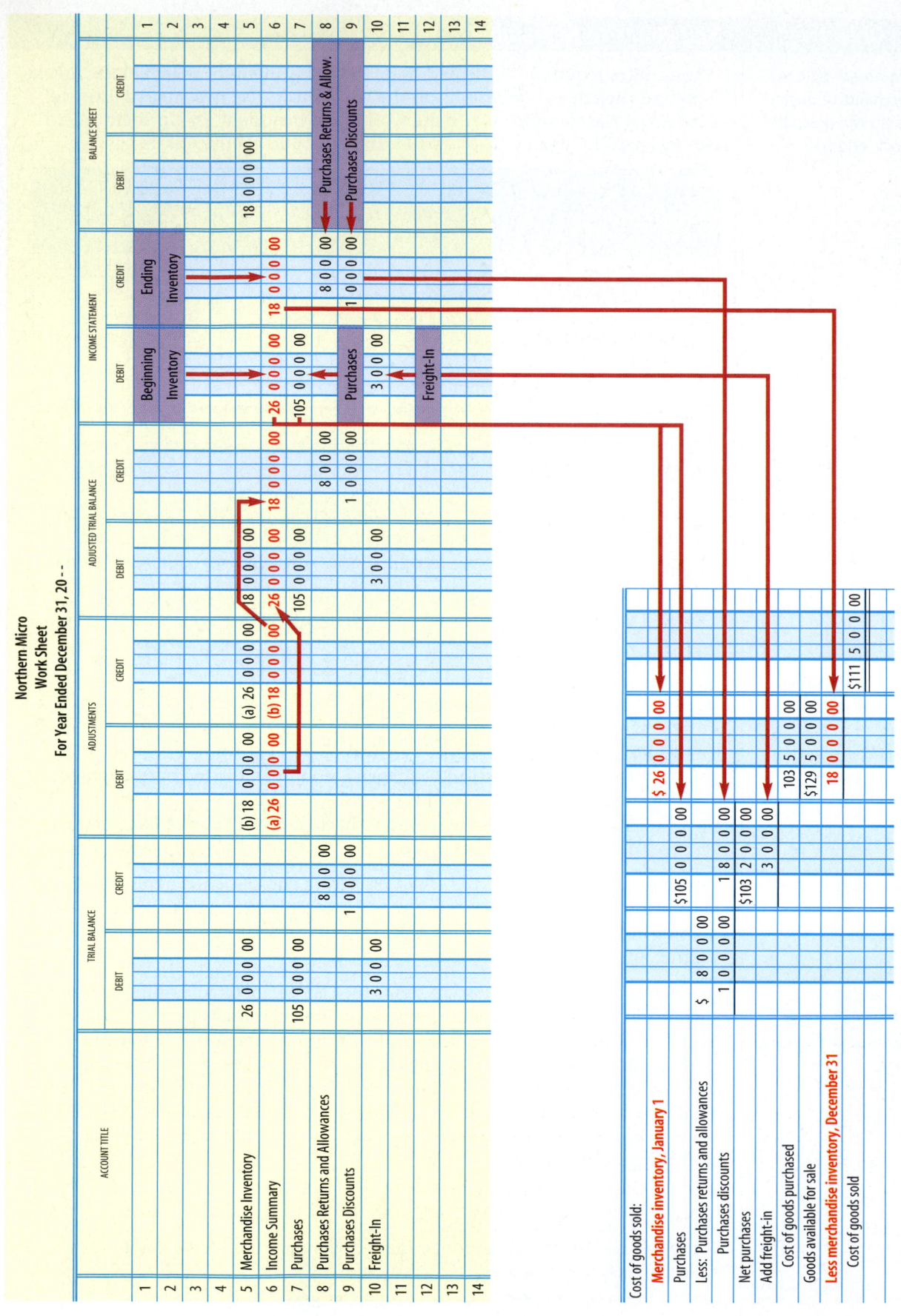

FIGURE 15-16 Work Sheet Adjustment and Extension for Merchandise Inventory and Calculation of Cost of Goods Sold Using Information in the Income Statement Columns of the Work Sheet

Reflection: Answering the Opening Question

Since cash is received, the cash account must be debited. However, since Evan has not yet delivered the merchandise, it is inappropriate to recognize revenue. Thus, a liability, unearned revenues, is credited. When Evan delivers the merchandise, the liability account is reduced and revenue is recognized.

DEMONSTRATION PROBLEM

WebTUTOR Advantage

Aaron Patton owns and operates Patton's Bait Shop and Boat Rental. A year-end trial balance is shown on the next page.

Year-end adjustment data for Patton's Bait Shop and Boat Rental is as follows:

(a, b)   A physical count shows that merchandise inventory costing $15,000 is on hand as of December 31, 20--.

(c)   Supplies remaining at the end of the year, $200.

(d)   Unexpired insurance on December 31, $300.

(e)   Depreciation expense on the building for 20--, $2,000.

(f)   Depreciation expense on the store equipment for 20--, $1,500.

(g)   Wages earned but not paid as of December 31, $225.

(h)   Unearned boat rental revenue as of December 31, $1,000.

REQUIRED

1.   Prepare a year-end work sheet.

2.   Journalize the adjusting entries.

Patton's Bait Shop and Boat Rental
Trial Balance
December 31, 20 - -

ACCOUNT TITLE	DEBIT BALANCE	CREDIT BALANCE
Cash	10 0 0 0 00	
Accounts Receivable	7 5 0 0 00	
Merchandise Inventory	19 0 0 0 00	
Supplies	9 0 0 00	
Prepaid Insurance	1 2 0 0 00	
Land	5 0 0 0 00	
Building	45 0 0 0 00	
Accumulated Depreciation—Building		8 0 0 0 00
Store Equipment	25 0 0 0 00	
Accumulated Depreciation—Store Equipment		7 5 0 0 00
Notes Payable		2 5 0 0 00
Accounts Payable		5 0 0 0 00
Wages Payable		
Unearned Boat Rental Revenue		11 0 0 0 00
Aaron Patton, Capital		77 9 0 0 00
Aaron Patton, Drawing	10 0 0 0 00	
Income Summary		
Sales		100 2 5 0 00
Sales Returns and Allowances	6 0 0 00	
Boat Rental Revenue		
Purchases	52 5 0 0 00	
Purchases Returns and Allowances		4 0 0 00
Purchases Discounts		5 0 0 00
Freight-In	1 5 0 00	
Wages Expense	21 0 0 0 00	
Advertising Expense	3 7 5 0 00	
Supplies Expense		
Telephone Expense	1 7 5 0 00	
Utilities Expense	6 0 0 0 00	
Insurance Expense		
Depreciation Expense —Building		
Depreciation Expense —Store Equipment		
Miscellaneous Expense	3 6 2 5 00	
Interest Expense	7 5 00	
	213 0 5 0 00	213 0 5 0 00

Solution

1.

Patton's Bait Shop and Boat Rental
Work Sheet
For Year Ended December 31, 20--

#	Account Title	Trial Balance Debit	Trial Balance Credit	Adjustments Debit	Adjustments Credit	Adj. Trial Balance Debit	Adj. Trial Balance Credit	Income Statement Debit	Income Statement Credit	Balance Sheet Debit	Balance Sheet Credit
1	Cash	10 000 00				10 000 00				10 000 00	
2	Accounts Receivable	7 500 00				7 500 00				7 500 00	
3	Merchandise Inventory	19 000 00		(b) 15 000 00	(a) 19 000 00	15 000 00				15 000 00	
4	Supplies	900 00			(c) 700 00	200 00				200 00	
5	Prepaid Insurance	1 200 00			(d) 900 00	300 00				300 00	
6	Land	5 000 00				5 000 00				5 000 00	
7	Building	45 000 00				45 000 00				45 000 00	
8	Accum. Depr.—Building		8 000 00		(e) 2 000 00		10 000 00				10 000 00
9	Store Equipment	25 000 00				25 000 00				25 000 00	
10	Accum. Depr.—Store Equipment		7 500 00		(f) 1 500 00		9 000 00				9 000 00
11	Notes Payable		2 500 00				2 500 00				2 500 00
12	Accounts Payable		5 000 00				5 000 00				5 000 00
13	Wages Payable				(g) 225 00		225 00				225 00
14	Unearned Boat Rental Revenue		11 000 00	(h) 10 000 00			1 000 00				1 000 00
15	Aaron Patton, Capital		77 900 00				77 900 00				77 900 00
16	Aaron Patton, Drawing	10 000 00				10 000 00				10 000 00	
17	Income Summary			(a) 19 000 00	(b) 15 000 00	19 000 00	15 000 00	19 000 00	15 000 00		
18	Sales		100 250 00				100 250 00		100 250 00		
19	Sales Returns and Allowances	600 00				600 00		600 00			
20	Boat Rental Revenue				(h) 10 000 00		10 000 00		10 000 00		
21	Purchases	52 500 00				52 500 00		52 500 00			
22	Purchases Returns and Allowances		400 00				400 00		400 00		
23	Purchases Discounts		500 00				500 00		500 00		
24	Freight-In	1 500 00				1 500 00		1 500 00			
25	Wages Expense	21 000 00		(g) 225 00		21 225 00		21 225 00			
26	Advertising Expense	3 750 00				3 750 00		3 750 00			
27	Supplies Expense			(c) 700 00		700 00		700 00			
28	Telephone Expense	1 750 00				1 750 00		1 750 00			
29	Utilities Expense	6 000 00				6 000 00		6 000 00			
30	Insurance Expense			(d) 900 00		900 00		900 00			
31	Depr. Expense—Building			(e) 2 000 00		2 000 00		2 000 00			
32	Depr. Expense—Store Equipment			(f) 1 500 00		1 500 00		1 500 00			
33	Miscellaneous Expense	1 600 00				1 600 00		1 600 00			
34	Interest Expense	750 00				750 00		750 00			
35		213 050 00	213 050 00	49 325 00	49 325 00	231 775 00	231 775 00	113 775 00	126 150 00	118 000 00	105 625 00
36	Net Income							12 375 00			12 375 00
37								126 150 00	126 150 00	118 000 00	118 000 00

(continued)

2.

	DATE		DESCRIPTION	POST REF.	DEBIT	CREDIT	
1			Adjusting Entries				1
2	20-- Dec.	31	Income Summary		19 0 0 0 00		2
3			Merchandise Inventory			19 0 0 0 00	3
4							4
5		31	Merchandise Inventory		15 0 0 0 00		5
6			Income Summary			15 0 0 0 00	6
7							7
8		31	Supplies Expense		7 0 0 00		8
9			Supplies			7 0 0 00	9
10							10
11		31	Insurance Expense		9 0 0 00		11
12			Prepaid Insurance			9 0 0 00	12
13							13
14		31	Depr. Expense—Building		2 0 0 0 00		14
15			Accumulated Depr.—Building			2 0 0 0 00	15
16							16
17		31	Depr. Expense—Store Equipment		1 5 0 0 00		17
18			Accumulated Depr.—Store Equipment			1 5 0 0 00	18
19							19
20		31	Wages Expense		2 2 5 00		20
21			Wages Payable			2 2 5 00	21
22							22
23		31	Unearned Boat Rental Revenue		10 0 0 0 00		23
24			Boat Rental Revenue			10 0 0 0 00	24
25							25

GENERAL JOURNAL — PAGE 3

On-Line Learning Tools

For more information, visit: http://heintz.swlearning.com

The Heintz & Parry product web site is designed specifically for **COLLEGE ACCOUNTING, 18e.** The features include downloadable student resources and an interactive study center, organized by chapter, which contains learning objectives, web links, on-line quizzes with automatic feedback, and more.

KEY TERMS

contra-cost accounts, (555)   Accounts that are deducted from the Purchases account when computing cost of goods sold—Purchases Returns and Allowances, and Purchases Discounts.

contra-revenue accounts, (555)   Accounts that are deducted from Sales on the income statement—Sales Returns and Allowances, and Sales Discounts.

periodic inventory system, (550)   Under this system, the ending inventory and cost of goods sold are determined at the end of the accounting period, when a physical inventory is taken.

perpetual inventory system, (563)   Under this system, the merchandise inventory and cost of goods sold accounts are updated when merchandise is bought and sold.

physical inventory, (550)   A physical count of the goods on hand.

unearned revenue, (553)   Cash received in advance of delivering a product or performing a service.

REVIEW QUESTIONS

(LO1)   1.   A firm is preparing to make adjusting entries at the end of the accounting period. The balance of the merchandise inventory account is $200,000. If the firm is using the periodic inventory system, what does this balance represent?

(LO1)   2.   What work sheet amounts are used to compute cost of goods sold?

(LO1)   3.   Why are both the debit and credit amounts in the Adjustments columns on the Income Summary line of the work sheet extended to the Adjusted Trial Balance columns?

(LO2)   4.   What is an unearned revenue?

(LO2)   5.   Give three examples of unearned revenues.

(LO3)   6.   List the five steps taken to prepare a work sheet.

(LO3)   7.   What does the difference between the totals of the Income Statement columns represent? What does the difference between the Balance Sheet column totals represent?

(LO5)   8.   A firm is preparing to make adjusting entries at the end of the accounting period. The balance of the merchandise inventory account is $100,000. If the firm is using the perpetual inventory system, what does this balance represent?

Self-Study Test Questions

True/False

1.   The beginning inventory is removed from the merchandise inventory account with a credit to Merchandise Inventory and a debit to Income Summary.   _____

2.   The ending inventory is entered by debiting Merchandise Inventory and crediting Income Summary.   _____

3.   The cash received in advance before delivering a product or performing a service is called unearned revenue.   _____

(continued)

Self-Study Test Questions *(continued)*

4. Unearned revenue is adjusted into an expense account at the end of the accounting period.   _____

5. Sales Returns and Allowances is classified as a contra-expense account on the income statement.   _____

Multiple Choice

1. Purchases Returns and Allowances and Purchases Discounts are classified as _____ on the income statement.   _____

   (a) expense accounts   (c) revenue accounts
   (b) contra-cost accounts   (d) contra-revenue accounts

2. The first step in preparing a work sheet is to   _____

   (a) prepare the trial balance.
   (b) prepare the income statement.
   (c) prepare the adjustments.
   (d) prepare the balance sheet.

3. The last step in preparing a work sheet is to   _____

   (a) prepare the adjusted trial balance.
   (b) total the Income Statement and Balance Sheet columns to compute net income or net loss.
   (c) prepare the adjustments.
   (d) extend the Adjusted Trial Balance columns.

4. Unearned Revenue is extended into the _____ on the work sheet.   _____

   (a) Adjustments columns   (c) Income Statement columns
   (b) Balance Sheet columns   (d) Trial Balance columns

5. The most useful tool in preparing end-of-period adjustments and financial statements is the   _____

   (a) general ledger.   (c) general journal.
   (b) work sheet.   (d) physical inventory.

The answers to the Self-Study Test Questions are at the end of the text.

MANAGING YOUR WRITING

A friend of yours recently opened Abracadabra, a sportswear shop specializing in monogrammed athletic gear. Most merchandise is special ordered for customers. However, a small inventory is on hand. Your friend does not understand why a physical inventory is necessary before preparing the financial statements. She knows how much she paid for all merchandise purchased. Why not simply use this amount for cost of goods sold? After all, it has been paid for. Write a brief memo explaining the purpose of the physical inventory and why she should not use the cost of purchases as cost of goods sold.

ETHICS CASE

Jason Tierro, an inventory clerk at Lexmar Company, is responsible for taking a physical count of the goods on hand at the end of the year. He has been performing this duty for several years. This year Jason was very busy due to a shortage of personnel at the company, so he decided to just estimate the amount of ending inventory instead of doing an accurate count. He reasoned that he could come very close to the true amount because of his past experience working with inventory. Besides, he was sure that the sophisticated computer program that Lexmar had just invested in kept an accurate record of inventory on hand.

1. What is your opinion of Jason's reasoning?

2. If Jason underestimates the dollar amount of ending inventory, what effect will it have on net income for the current accounting period?

3. Write a short paragraph explaining why a physical inventory should be taken at least once a year.

4. In groups of three or four make a list of possible reasons that the actual ending inventory might not agree with the ending inventory according to a computer system.

WEB WORK

Visit Sears' homepage for a look at their annual report. Start at their homepage and select "about Sears" from the column on the left. Then choose "for investors" to view the annual report. Notice that their inventory fluctuated over the last five years. What reasons could there be for the larger increases and decreases?

Visit the Interactive Study Center on our web site at **http://heintz.swlearning.com** for special hotlinks to assist you in this assignment.

SERIES A EXERCISES

EXERCISE 15-1A   **(LO1)**   **ADJUSTMENT FOR MERCHANDISE INVENTORY USING T ACCOUNTS: PERIODIC INVENTORY SYSTEM** Sam Baker owns a business called Sam's Sporting Goods. His beginning inventory as of January 1, 20--, was $47,000 and his ending inventory as of December 31, 20--, was $53,000. Set up T accounts for Merchandise Inventory and Income Summary and perform the year-end adjustment for Merchandise Inventory.

EXERCISE 15-2A   **(LO1)**
Cost of goods sold: $65,200

CALCULATION OF COST OF GOODS SOLD: PERIODIC INVENTORY SYSTEM Prepare the cost of goods sold section for Adams Gift Shop. The following amounts are known.

Beginning merchandise inventory	$26,000
Ending merchandise inventory	23,000
Purchases	71,000
Purchases returns and allowances	3,500
Purchases discounts	5,500
Freight-in	200

EXERCISE 15-3A **(LO2)** **ADJUSTMENT FOR UNEARNED REVENUES USING T ACCOUNTS** Set up T accounts for Cash, Unearned Ticket Revenue, and Ticket Revenue. Post the following two transactions to the appropriate accounts, indicating each transaction by letter.

(a) Sold 1,500 season tickets at $30 each, receiving cash of $45,000.

(b) An end-of-period adjustment is needed to recognize that $35,000 in ticket revenue has been earned.

EXERCISE 15-4A **(LO3)**
Cost of goods sold: $75,500

WORK SHEET EXTENSIONS FOR MERCHANDISE INVENTORY ADJUSTMENTS: PERIODIC INVENTORY SYSTEM The following partial work sheet is taken from Kevin's Gift Shop for the year ended December 31, 20--. The ending merchandise inventory is $50,000.

1. Complete the Adjustments columns for the merchandise inventory.

2. Extend the merchandise inventory to the Adjusted Trial Balance, Income Statement, and Balance Sheet columns.

3. Extend the remaining accounts to the Adjusted Trial Balance and Income Statement columns.

4. Prepare a cost of goods sold section from the partial work sheet.

Kevin's Gift Shop
Work Sheet (Partial)
For Year Ended December 31, 20 - -

	ACCOUNT TITLE	TRIAL BALANCE		ADJUSTMENTS		
		DEBIT	CREDIT	DEBIT	CREDIT	
1	Merchandise Inventory	40 0 0 0 00				1
12	Income Summary					12
13	Purchases	90 0 0 0 00				13
14	Purchases Returns and Allowances		2 0 0 0 00			14
15	Purchases Discounts		3 0 0 0 00			15
16	Freight-In	5 0 0 0 00				16
17						17
18						18

EXERCISE 15-5A **(LO3)**
Beg. inv.: $55,000

DETERMINING THE BEGINNING AND ENDING INVENTORY FROM A PARTIAL WORK SHEET: PERIODIC INVENTORY SYSTEM From the following partial work sheet, indicate the dollar amount of beginning and ending merchandise inventory.

	ACCOUNT TITLE	ADJUSTMENTS		ADJUSTED TRIAL BALANCE		INCOME STATEMENT		BALANCE SHEET		
		DEBIT	CREDIT	DEBIT	CREDIT	DEBIT	CREDIT	DEBIT	CREDIT	
1	Merchandise Inventory	(b) 60 0 0 0 00	(a) 55 0 0 0 00	60 0 0 0 00				60 0 0 0 00		1
2	Income Summary	(a) 55 0 0 0 00	(b) 60 0 0 0 00	55 0 0 0 00	60 0 0 0 00	55 0 0 0 00	60 0 0 0 00			2

EXERCISE 15-6A   (LO4)

(a) Inc. Sum: $45,000; Mdse. Inv.: $45,000

JOURNALIZE ADJUSTING ENTRIES FOR A MERCHANDISING BUSINESS The following partial work sheet is taken from the books of Kelly's Kittens, a local pet kennel, for the year ended December 31, 20--. Journalize the adjustments in a general journal.

Kelly's Kittens
Work Sheet (Partial)
For Year Ended December 31, 20 - -

	ACCOUNT TITLE	TRIAL BALANCE DEBIT	TRIAL BALANCE CREDIT	ADJUSTMENTS DEBIT	ADJUSTMENTS CREDIT	
1	Merchandise Inventory	45 0 0 0 00		(b) 50 0 0 0 00	(a) 45 0 0 0 00	1
2	Supplies	10 0 0 0 00			(d) 7 0 0 0 00	2
3	Building	60 0 0 0 00				3
4	Accum. Depr.—Building		15 0 0 0 00		(e) 5 0 0 0 00	4
5	Wages Payable				(f) 1 2 0 0 00	5
6	Unearned Grooming Revenue		3 0 0 0 00	(c) 2 0 0 0 00		6
7	Income Summary			(a) 45 0 0 0 00	(b) 50 0 0 0 00	7
8	Grooming Revenue		20 0 0 0 00		(c) 2 0 0 0 00	8
9	Wages Expense	37 0 0 0 00		(f) 1 2 0 0 00		9
10	Supplies Expense			(d) 7 0 0 0 00		10
11	Depr. Expense—Building			(e) 5 0 0 0 00		11
12				110 2 0 0 00	110 2 0 0 00	12
13						13

EXERCISE 15-7A   (LO5)

JOURNAL ENTRIES UNDER THE PERPETUAL INVENTORY SYSTEM Bhushan Building Supplies entered into the following transactions. Prepare journal entries under the perpetual inventory system.

June 1   Purchased merchandise on account from Brij Builder's Materials, $500,000.

3   Purchased merchandise for cash, $400,000.

5   Sold merchandise on account to Champa Construction for $20,000. The merchandise cost $15,000.

EXERCISE 15-8A   (LO5)

JOURNALIZE ADJUSTING ENTRY FOR A MERCHANDISING BUSINESS: PER-PETUAL INVENTORY SYSTEM On December 31, Anup Enterprises completed a physical count of its inventory. Although the merchandise inventory account shows a balance of $350,000, the physical count comes to $325,000. Prepare the appropriate adjusting entry under the perpetual inventory system.

SERIES A PROBLEMS

PROBLEM 15-9A (LO1/2/3/4)

Adj. Col. total: $78,600;
Net income: $39,390

COMPLETION OF A WORK SHEET SHOWING A NET INCOME The trial balance for the Seaside Kite Shop, a business owned by Joyce Kennington, is shown on page 576. Year-end adjustment information is as follows:

(a, b)   Merchandise inventory costing $30,000 is on hand as of December 31, 20--. (The periodic inventory system is used.)

(c)   Supplies remaining at the end of the year, $2,700.

(d)   Unexpired insurance on December 31, $2,900.

(e)   Depreciation expense on the building for 20--, $5,000.

(continued)

(f)   Depreciation expense on the store equipment for 20--, $3,200.

(g)   Unearned rent revenue as of December 31, $2,200.

(h)   Wages earned but not paid as of December 31, $900.

REQUIRED

1. Complete the Adjustments columns, identifying each adjustment with its corresponding letter.

2. Complete the work sheet.

3. Enter the adjustments in a general journal.

Seaside Kite Shop
Trial Balance
December 31, 20 - -

ACCOUNT TITLE	DEBIT BALANCE	CREDIT BALANCE
Cash	20 0 0 0 00	
Accounts Receivable	14 0 0 0 00	
Merchandise Inventory	25 0 0 0 00	
Supplies	8 0 0 0 00	
Prepaid Insurance	5 4 0 0 00	
Land	30 0 0 0 00	
Building	50 0 0 0 00	
Accumulated Depreciation—Building		20 0 0 0 00
Store Equipment	35 0 0 0 00	
Accumulated Depreciation—Store Equipment		14 0 0 0 00
Accounts Payable		9 6 0 0 00
Wages Payable		
Sales Tax Payable		5 9 0 0 00
Unearned Rent Revenue		8 9 0 0 00
Mortgage Payable		45 0 0 0 00
Joyce Kennington, Capital		65 4 1 0 00
Joyce Kennington, Drawing	26 0 0 0 00	
Income Summary		
Sales		118 0 0 0 00
Sales Returns and Allowances	1 7 0 0 00	
Rent Revenue		
Purchases	27 0 0 0 00	
Purchases Returns and Allowances		1 4 0 0 00
Purchases Discounts		1 8 0 0 00
Freight-In	2 1 0 0 00	
Wages Expense	32 0 0 0 00	
Advertising Expense	3 6 0 0 00	
Supplies Expense		
Telephone Expense	1 3 5 0 00	
Utilities Expense	8 0 0 0 00	
Insurance Expense		
Depreciation Expense —Building		
Depreciation Expense —Store Equipment		
Miscellaneous Expense	8 6 0 00	
	290 0 1 0 00	290 0 1 0 00

PROBLEM 15-10A (LO1/2/3/4)

Power Accounting System Software®

Adj. Col. total: $72,650;
Net loss: $45,760

COMPLETION OF A WORK SHEET SHOWING A NET LOSS The trial balance for Cascade Bicycle Shop, a business owned by David Lamond, is shown below. Year-end adjustment information is provided below.

(a, b) Merchandise inventory costing $22,000 is on hand as of December 31, 20--. (The periodic inventory system is used.)

(c) Supplies remaining at the end of the year, $2,400.

(d) Unexpired insurance on December 31, $1,750.

(e) Depreciation expense on the building for 20--, $4,000.

(f) Depreciation expense on the store equipment for 20--, $3,600.

(g) Unearned storage revenue as of December 31, $1,950.

(h) Wages earned but not paid as of December 31, $750.

Cascade Bicycle Shop
Trial Balance
December 31, 20 - -

ACCOUNT TITLE	DEBIT BALANCE	CREDIT BALANCE
Cash	23 0 0 0 00	
Accounts Receivable	15 0 0 0 00	
Merchandise Inventory	31 0 0 0 00	
Supplies	7 2 0 0 00	
Prepaid Insurance	4 6 0 0 00	
Land	28 0 0 0 00	
Building	53 0 0 0 00	
Accumulated Depreciation—Building		17 0 0 0 00
Store Equipment	27 0 0 0 00	
Accumulated Depreciation—Store Equipment		9 0 0 0 00
Accounts Payable		3 8 0 0 00
Wages Payable		
Sales Tax Payable		3 0 5 0 00
Unearned Storage Revenue		5 6 0 0 00
Mortgage Payable		42 0 0 0 00
David Lamond, Capital		165 7 6 0 00
David Lamond, Drawing	33 0 0 0 00	
Income Summary		
Sales		51 0 0 0 00
Sales Returns and Allowances	2 4 0 0 00	
Storage Revenue		
Purchases	21 0 0 0 00	
Purchases Returns and Allowances		1 3 0 0 00
Purchases Discounts		1 9 0 0 00
Freight-In	1 8 0 0 00	
Wages Expense	35 0 0 0 00	
Advertising Expense	5 7 0 0 00	
Supplies Expense		
Telephone Expense	2 2 0 0 00	
Utilities Expense	9 6 0 0 00	
Insurance Expense		
Depreciation Expense —Building		
Depreciation Expense —Store Equipment		
Miscellaneous Expense	9 1 0 00	
	300 4 1 0 00	300 4 1 0 00

(continued)

REQUIRED

1. Complete the Adjustments columns, identifying each adjustment with its corresponding letter.

2. Complete the work sheet.

3. Enter the adjustments in the general journal.

PROBLEM 15-11A (LO1/2/4)
Adj. Col. total: $88,155

WORKING BACKWARD FROM ADJUSTED TRIAL BALANCE TO DETERMINE ADJUSTING ENTRIES The partial work sheet shown on page 579 is taken from the books of Stark Street Computers, a business owned by Logan Cowart, for the year ended December 31, 20--.

REQUIRED

1. Determine the adjusting entries by analyzing the difference between the adjusted trial balance and the trial balance.

2. Journalize the adjusting entries in a general journal.

PROBLEM 15-12A (LO1/2/3/4)
Adj. Col. total: $92,335;
Cost of goods sold: $33,145

WORKING BACKWARD FROM THE INCOME STATEMENT AND BALANCE SHEET COLUMNS OF THE WORK SHEET TO DETERMINE ADJUSTED TRIAL BALANCE AND ADJUSTING ENTRIES The partially completed work sheet from the books of Lewis Music Store, a business owned by Hugo Lewis, for the year ended December 31, 20--, is shown on page 580.

REQUIRED

1. Analyze the work sheet and determine the adjusted trial balance and the adjusting entries by working backward from the Income Statement and Balance Sheet columns.

2. Journalize the adjusting entries in a general journal.

3. Prepare the cost of goods sold section of the income statement for Lewis Music Store.

SERIES B EXERCISES

EXERCISE 15-1B (LO1)

ADJUSTMENT FOR MERCHANDISE INVENTORY USING T ACCOUNTS: PERIODIC INVENTORY SYSTEM Sandra Owens owns a business called Sandra's Sporting Goods. Her beginning inventory as of January 1, 20--, was $33,000 and her ending inventory as of December 31, 20--, was $36,000. Set up T accounts for Merchandise Inventory and Income Summary and perform the year-end adjustment for Merchandise Inventory.

EXERCISE 15-2B (LO1)
Cost of goods sold: $58,100

CALCULATION OF COST OF GOODS SOLD: PERIODIC INVENTORY SYSTEM Prepare the cost of goods sold section for Havens Gift Shop. The following amounts are known.

Beginning merchandise inventory	$29,000
Ending merchandise inventory	27,000
Purchases	62,000
Purchases returns and allowances	2,800
Purchases discounts	3,400
Freight-in	300

Stark Street Computers
Work Sheet (Partial)
For Year Ended December 31, 20- -

	ACCOUNT TITLE	TRIAL BALANCE		ADJUSTMENTS		ADJUSTED TRIAL BALANCE		
		DEBIT	CREDIT	DEBIT	CREDIT	DEBIT	CREDIT	
1	Cash	18 0 0 0 00				18 0 0 0 00		1
2	Accounts Receivable	11 0 0 0 00				11 0 0 0 00		2
3	Merchandise Inventory	25 0 0 0 00				35 0 0 0 00		3
4	Supplies	8 0 0 0 00				2 8 2 0 00		4
5	Prepaid Insurance	5 4 0 0 00				1 2 2 5 00		5
6	Land	27 0 0 0 00				27 0 0 0 00		6
7	Building	48 0 0 0 00				48 0 0 0 00		7
8	Accum. Depr.—Building		20 0 0 0 00				27 0 0 0 00	8
9	Store Equipment	33 0 0 0 00				33 0 0 0 00		9
10	Accum. Depr.—Store Equipment		8 7 0 0 00				12 8 0 0 00	10
11	Accounts Payable		6 4 0 0 00				6 4 0 0 00	11
12	Wages Payable						1 3 0 0 00	12
13	Sales Tax Payable		5 7 0 0 00				5 7 0 0 00	13
14	Unearned Repair Revenue		8 2 0 0 00				1 8 0 0 00	14
15	Mortgage Payable		44 0 0 0 00				44 0 0 0 00	15
16	Logan Cowart, Capital		80 0 2 5 00				80 0 2 5 00	16
17	Logan Cowart, Drawing	35 0 0 0 00				35 0 0 0 00		17
18	Income Summary					25 0 0 0 00	35 0 0 0 00	18
19	Sales		122 0 0 0 00				122 0 0 0 00	19
20	Sales Returns and Allowances	2 2 5 0 00				2 2 5 0 00		20
21	Repair Revenue						6 4 0 0 00	21
22	Purchases	29 7 5 0 00				29 7 5 0 00		22
23	Purchases Returns and Allowances		1 8 5 0 00				1 8 5 0 00	23
24	Purchases Discounts		1 4 2 5 00				1 4 2 5 00	24
25	Freight-In	3 2 0 0 00				3 2 0 0 00		25
26	Wages Expense	37 0 0 0 00				38 3 0 0 00		26
27	Advertising Expense	4 1 2 5 00				4 1 2 5 00		27
28	Supplies Expense					5 1 8 0 00		28
29	Telephone Expense	1 6 5 0 00				1 6 5 0 00		29
30	Utilities Expense	9 1 5 0 00				9 1 5 0 00		30
31	Insurance Expense					4 1 7 5 00		31
32	Depr. Expense—Building					7 0 0 0 00		32
33	Depr. Expense—Store Equipment					4 1 0 0 00		33
34	Miscellaneous Expense	7 7 5 00				7 7 5 00		34
35		298 3 0 0 00	298 3 0 0 00			345 7 0 0 00	345 7 0 0 00	35

EXERCISE 15-3B   **(LO2)**   **ADJUSTMENT FOR UNEARNED REVENUES USING T ACCOUNTS** Set up T accounts for Cash, Unearned Ticket Revenue, and Ticket Revenue. Post the following two transactions to the appropriate accounts, indicating each transaction by letter.

(a) Sold 1,200 season tickets at $20 each, receiving cash of $24,000.

(b) An end-of-period adjustment is needed to recognize that $19,000 in ticket revenue has been earned.

(continued)

Lewis Music Store
Work Sheet
For Year Ended December 31, 20--

	ACCOUNT TITLE	TRIAL BALANCE DEBIT	TRIAL BALANCE CREDIT	ADJUSTMENTS DEBIT	ADJUSTMENTS CREDIT	ADJUSTED TRIAL BALANCE DEBIT	ADJUSTED TRIAL BALANCE CREDIT	INCOME STATEMENT DEBIT	INCOME STATEMENT CREDIT	BALANCE SHEET DEBIT	BALANCE SHEET CREDIT
1	Cash	27 0 0 0 00								27 0 0 0 00	
2	Accounts Receivable	13 3 0 0 00								13 3 0 0 00	
3	Merchandise Inventory	34 0 0 0 00								38 0 0 0 00	
4	Supplies	5 3 0 0 00								1 5 0 0 00	
5	Prepaid Insurance	6 1 0 0 00								1 7 8 5 00	
6	Land	31 0 0 0 00								31 0 0 0 00	
7	Building	52 0 0 0 00								52 0 0 0 00	
8	Accum. Depr.—Building		17 0 0 0 00								21 1 4 5 00
9	Store Equipment	39 0 0 0 00								39 0 0 0 00	
10	Accum. Depr.—Store Equipment		11 9 0 0 00								14 8 7 5 00
11	Accounts Payable		6 2 5 0 00								6 2 5 0 00
12	Wages Payable										8 7 5 00
13	Sales Tax Payable		6 2 0 0 00								6 2 0 0 00
14	Unearned Rent Revenue		7 4 0 0 00								3 1 7 5 00
15	Mortgage Payable		46 0 0 0 00								46 0 0 0 00
16	Hugo Lewis, Capital		111 6 2 0 00								111 6 2 0 00
17	Hugo Lewis, Drawing	37 0 0 0 00								37 0 0 0 00	
18	Income Summary							34 0 0 0 00	38 0 0 0 00		
19	Sales		136 0 0 0 00						136 0 0 0 00		
20	Sales Returns and Allowances	3 5 0 0 00						3 5 0 0 00			
21	Rent Revenue								4 2 2 5 00		
22	Purchases	39 0 0 0 00						39 0 0 0 00			
23	Purchases Returns and Allowances		2 5 3 0 00						2 5 3 0 00		
24	Purchases Discounts		1 9 7 5 00						1 9 7 5 00		
25	Freight-In	2 6 5 0 00						2 6 5 0 00			
26	Wages Expense	42 0 0 0 00						42 8 7 5 00			
27	Advertising Expense	4 1 7 5 00						4 1 7 5 00			
28	Supplies Expense							3 8 0 0 00			
29	Telephone Expense	1 9 8 0 00						1 9 8 0 00			
30	Utilities Expense	7 9 4 5 00						7 9 4 5 00			
31	Insurance Expense							4 3 1 5 00			
32	Depr. Expense—Building							4 1 4 5 00			
33	Depr. Expense—Store Equipment							2 9 7 5 00			
34	Miscellaneous Expense	9 2 5 00						9 2 5 00			
35		346 8 7 5 00	346 8 7 5 00					152 2 8 5 00	182 7 3 0 00	240 5 8 5 00	210 1 4 0 00
36	Net Income							30 4 4 5 00			30 4 4 5 00
37								182 7 3 0 00	182 7 3 0 00	240 5 8 5 00	240 5 8 5 00

PROBLEM 15-12A

EXERCISE 15-4B   (LO3)
Cost of goods sold: $73,400

WORK SHEET EXTENSIONS FOR MERCHANDISE INVENTORY ADJUSTMENTS: PERIODIC INVENTORY SYSTEM The following partial work sheet is taken from Nicole's Gift Shop for the year ended December 31, 20--. The ending merchandise inventory is $37,000.

1. Complete the Adjustments columns for the merchandise inventory.

2. Extend the merchandise inventory to the Adjusted Trial Balance, Income Statement, and Balance Sheet columns.

3. Extend the remaining accounts to the Adjusted Trial Balance and Income Statement columns.

4. Prepare a cost of goods sold section from the partial work sheet.

Nicole's Gift Shop
Work Sheet (Partial)
For Year Ended December 31, 20 - -

	ACCOUNT TITLE	TRIAL BALANCE DEBIT	TRIAL BALANCE CREDIT	ADJUSTMENTS DEBIT	ADJUSTMENTS CREDIT	
1	Merchandise Inventory	30 0 0 0 00				1
12	Income Summary					12
13	Purchases	85 0 0 0 00				13
14	Purchases Returns and Allowances		2 2 0 0 00			14
15	Purchases Discounts		2 5 0 0 00			15
16	Freight-In	1 0 0 00				16
17						17
18						18

EXERCISE 15-5B   (LO3)
Beg. inv.: $49,000

DETERMINING THE BEGINNING AND ENDING INVENTORY FROM A PARTIAL WORK SHEET: PERIODIC INVENTORY SYSTEM From the following partial work sheet, indicate the dollar amount of beginning and ending merchandise inventory.

	ACCOUNT TITLE	ADJUSTMENTS DEBIT	ADJUSTMENTS CREDIT	ADJUSTED TRIAL BALANCE DEBIT	ADJUSTED TRIAL BALANCE CREDIT	INCOME STATEMENT DEBIT	INCOME STATEMENT CREDIT	BALANCE SHEET DEBIT	BALANCE SHEET CREDIT	
1	Merchandise Inventory	(b) 45 0 0 0 00	(a) 49 0 0 0 00	45 0 0 0 00				45 0 0 0 00		1
2	Income Summary	(a) 49 0 0 0 00	(b) 45 0 0 0 00	49 0 0 0 00	45 0 0 0 00	49 0 0 0 00	45 0 0 0 00			2

EXERCISE 15-6B (LO4) **JOURNALIZE ADJUSTING ENTRIES FOR A MERCHANDISING BUSINESS** The following partial work sheet is taken from the books of Carmen's Collies, a local pet kennel, for the year ended December 31, 20--. Journalize the adjustments in a general journal.

Carmen's Collies
Work Sheet (Partial)
For Year Ended December 31, 20 - -

	ACCOUNT TITLE	TRIAL BALANCE DEBIT	TRIAL BALANCE CREDIT	ADJUSTMENTS DEBIT	ADJUSTMENTS CREDIT	
1	Merchandise Inventory	35 0 0 0 00		(b) 30 0 0 0 00	(a) 35 0 0 0 00	1
2	Supplies	4 5 0 0 00			(d) 3 1 0 0 00	2
3	Building	50 0 0 0 00				3
4	Accum. Depr.—Building		23 0 0 0 00		(e) 6 0 0 0 00	4
5	Wages Payable				(f) 1 3 0 0 00	5
6	Unearned Grooming Revenue		7 0 0 0 00	(c) 5 5 0 0 00		6
7	Income Summary			(a) 35 0 0 0 00	(b) 30 0 0 0 00	7
8	Grooming Revenue		24 0 0 0 00		(c) 5 5 0 0 00	8
9	Wages Expense	41 0 0 0 00		(f) 1 3 0 0 00		9
10	Supplies Expense			(d) 3 1 0 0 00		10
11	Depr. Expense—Building			(e) 6 0 0 0 00		11
12				80 9 0 0 00	80 9 0 0 00	12
13						13

EXERCISE 15-7B (LO5) **JOURNAL ENTRIES UNDER THE PERPETUAL INVENTORY SYSTEM** Sunita Computer Supplies entered into the following transactions. Prepare journal entries under the perpetual inventory system.

May 1 Purchased merchandise on account from Anju Enterprises, $200,000.

8 Purchased merchandise for cash, $100,000.

15 Sold merchandise on account to Salil's Pharmacy for $8,000. The merchandise cost $5,000.

EXERCISE 15-8B (LO5) **JOURNALIZE ADJUSTING ENTRY FOR A MERCHANDISING BUSINESS: PERPETUAL INVENTORY SYSTEM** On December 31, Anup Enterprises completed a physical count of its inventory. Although the merchandise inventory account shows a balance of $200,000, the physical count comes to $210,000. Prepare the appropriate adjusting entry under the perpetual inventory system.

SERIES B PROBLEMS

PROBLEM 15-9B (LO1/2/3/4)

Adj. Col. total: $76,500;
Net income: $13,950

COMPLETION OF A WORK SHEET SHOWING A NET INCOME A trial balance for the Basket Corner, a business owned by Linda Palermo, is shown on page 583. Year-end adjustment information is provided below.

(a, b) Merchandise inventory costing $24,000 is on hand as of December 31, 20--.

(c) Supplies remaining at the end of the year, $2,100.

(d) Unexpired insurance on December 31, $2,600.

(e) Depreciation expense on the building for 20--, $5,300.

(f) Depreciation expense on the store equipment for 20--, $3,800.

(g)   Unearned decorating revenue as of December 31, $1,650.

(h)   Wages earned but not paid as of December 31, $750.

REQUIRED

1. Complete the Adjustments columns, identifying each adjustment with its corresponding letter.

2. Complete the work sheet.

3. Enter the adjustments in a general journal.

Basket Corner Trial Balance December 31, 20 - -			
ACCOUNT TITLE	DEBIT BALANCE	CREDIT BALANCE	
Cash	25 0 0 0 00		
Accounts Receivable	8 1 0 0 00		
Merchandise Inventory	32 0 0 0 00		
Supplies	7 1 0 0 00		
Prepaid Insurance	3 6 0 0 00		
Land	40 0 0 0 00		
Building	45 0 0 0 00		
Accumulated Depreciation—Building		16 0 0 0 00	
Store Equipment	27 0 0 0 00		
Accumulated Depreciation—Store Equipment		5 5 0 0 00	
Accounts Payable		3 6 0 0 00	
Wages Payable			
Sales Tax Payable		6 2 0 0 00	
Unearned Decorating Revenue		6 3 0 0 00	
Mortgage Payable		36 0 0 0 00	
Linda Palermo, Capital		112 0 5 0 00	
Linda Palermo, Drawing	31 0 0 0 00		
Income Summary			
Sales		125 0 0 0 00	
Sales Returns and Allowances	2 6 0 0 00		
Decorating Revenue			
Purchases	38 0 0 0 00		
Purchases Returns and Allowances		2 2 0 0 00	
Purchases Discounts		1 7 0 0 00	
Freight-In	1 9 0 0 00		
Wages Expense	38 0 0 0 00		
Advertising Expense	4 2 0 0 00		
Supplies Expense			
Telephone Expense	1 8 7 0 00		
Utilities Expense	8 4 0 0 00		
Insurance Expense			
Depreciation Expense —Building			
Depreciation Expense —Store Equipment			
Miscellaneous Expense	7 8 0 00		
	314 5 5 0 00	314 5 5 0 00	

PROBLEM 15-10B (LO1/2/3/4)

Adj. Col. total: $86,730;
Net loss: $53,630

COMPLETION OF A WORK SHEET SHOWING A NET LOSS The trial balance for Oregon Bike Company, a business owned by Craig Moody, is shown below. Year-end adjustment information is provided below.

(a, b) Merchandise inventory costing $26,000 is on hand as of December 31, 20--.

(c) Supplies remaining at the end of the year, $2,500.

(d) Unexpired insurance on December 31, $1,820.

(e) Depreciation expense on the building for 20--, $6,400.

(f) Depreciation expense on the store equipment for 20--, $2,800.

(g) Unearned rent revenue as of December 31, $2,350.

(h) Wages earned but not paid as of December 31, $1,100.

Oregon Bike Company Trial Balance December 31, 20 - -									
ACCOUNT TITLE	DEBIT BALANCE					CREDIT BALANCE			
Cash	27	0	0	0	00				
Accounts Receivable	12	0	0	0	00				
Merchandise Inventory	39	0	0	0	00				
Supplies	6	2	0	0	00				
Prepaid Insurance	5	8	0	0	00				
Land	32	0	0	0	00				
Building	58	0	0	0	00				
Accumulated Depreciation—Building						27	0	0	0	00
Store Equipment	31	0	0	0	00				
Accumulated Depreciation—Store Equipment						14	0	0	0	00
Accounts Payable						4	9	0	0	00
Wages Payable									
Sales Tax Payable						2	9	0	0	00
Unearned Rent Revenue						6	1	0	0	00
Mortgage Payable						49	0	0	0	00
Craig Moody, Capital						169	5	0	0	00
Craig Moody, Drawing	36	0	0	0	00				
Income Summary									
Sales						58	0	0	0	00
Sales Returns and Allowances	3	3	0	0	00				
Rent Revenue									
Purchases	19	0	0	0	00				
Purchases Returns and Allowances							9	0	0	00
Purchases Discounts						1	4	5	0	00
Freight-In		8	0	0	00				
Wages Expense	47	0	0	0	00				
Advertising Expense	6	2	0	0	00				
Supplies Expense									
Telephone Expense	1	8	6	0	00				
Utilities Expense	8	1	0	0	00				
Insurance Expense									
Depreciation Expense —Building									
Depreciation Expense —Store Equipment									
Miscellaneous Expense		4	9	0	00				
	333	7	5	0	00	333	7	5	0	00

REQUIRED

1. Complete the Adjustments columns, identifying each adjustment with its corresponding letter.

2. Complete the work sheet.

3. Enter the adjustments in a general journal.

PROBLEM 15-11B (LO1/2/4)
Adj. Col. total: $88,805

WORKING BACKWARD FROM ADJUSTED TRIAL BALANCE TO DETERMINE ADJUSTING ENTRIES The partial work sheet shown below is taken from the books of Burnside Auto Parts, a business owned by Barbara Davis, for the year ended December 31, 20--.

Burnside Auto Parts
Work Sheet (Partial)
For Year Ended December 31, 20 - -

	ACCOUNT TITLE	TRIAL BALANCE DEBIT	TRIAL BALANCE CREDIT	ADJUSTMENTS DEBIT	ADJUSTMENTS CREDIT	ADJUSTED TRIAL BALANCE DEBIT	ADJUSTED TRIAL BALANCE CREDIT	
1	Cash	21 000 00				21 000 00		1
2	Accounts Receivable	8 300 00				8 300 00		2
3	Merchandise Inventory	32 000 00				36 000 00		3
4	Supplies	6 150 00				1 865 00		4
5	Prepaid Insurance	5 925 00				1 835 00		5
6	Land	41 750 00				41 750 00		6
7	Building	43 000 00				43 000 00		7
8	Accum. Depr.—Building		24 000 00				27 500 00	8
9	Store Equipment	25 400 00				25 400 00		9
10	Accum. Depr.—Store Equipment		12 400 00				14 750 00	10
11	Accounts Payable		8 100 00				8 100 00	11
12	Wages Payable						980 00	12
13	Sales Tax Payable		5 200 00				5 200 00	13
14	Unearned Rent-A-Junk Revenue		7 950 00				2 350 00	14
15	Mortgage Payable		26 000 00				26 000 00	15
16	Barbara Davis, Capital		109 130 00				109 130 00	16
17	Barbara Davis, Drawing	40 000 00				40 000 00		17
18	Income Summary					32 000 00	36 000 00	18
19	Sales		123 500 00				123 500 00	19
20	Sales Returns and Allowances	2 860 00				2 860 00		20
21	Rent-A-Junk Revenue						5 600 00	21
22	Purchases	32 525 00				32 525 00		22
23	Purchases Returns and Allowances		2 150 00				2 150 00	23
24	Purchases Discounts		2 400 00				2 400 00	24
25	Freight-In	3 175 00				3 175 00		25
26	Wages Expense	44 175 00				45 155 00		26
27	Advertising Expense	3 275 00				3 275 00		27
28	Supplies Expense					4 285 00		28
29	Telephone Expense	2 200 00				2 200 00		29
30	Utilities Expense	8 250 00				8 250 00		30
31	Insurance Expense					4 090 00		31
32	Depr. Expense—Building					3 500 00		32
33	Depr. Expense—Store Equipment					2 350 00		33
34	Miscellaneous Expense	845 00				845 00		34
35		320 830 00	320 830 00			363 660 00	363 660 00	35

(continued)

REQUIRED

1. Determine the adjusting entries by analyzing the difference between the adjusted trial balance and the trial balance.

2. Journalize the adjusting entries in a general journal.

PROBLEM 15-12B (LO1/2/3/4)
Adj. Col. total: $99,545;
Cost of goods sold: $31,975

WORKING BACKWARD FROM THE INCOME STATEMENT AND BALANCE SHEET COLUMNS OF THE WORK SHEET TO DETERMINE ADJUSTED TRIAL BALANCE AND ADJUSTING ENTRIES The partial work sheet shown on page 587 is taken from the books of Diamond Music Store, a business owned by Ned Diamond, for the year ended December 31, 20--.

REQUIRED

1. Analyze the work sheet and determine the adjusted trial balance and the adjusting entries by working backward from the Income Statement and Balance Sheet columns.

2. Journalize the adjusting entries in a general journal.

3. Prepare the cost of goods sold section of the income statement for Diamond Music Store.

MASTERY PROBLEM

Adj. T.B. Col. total: $695,325;
Net income: $37,125

John Neff owns and operates the Waikiki Surf Shop. A year-end trial balance is provided on page 588. Year-end adjustment data for the Waikiki Surf Shop is shown below.

(a, b) A physical count shows merchandise inventory costing $45,000 on hand as of December 31, 20--. Neff uses the periodic inventory system.

(c) Supplies remaining at the end of the year, $600.

(d) Unexpired insurance on December 31, $900.

(e) Depreciation expense on the building for 20--, $6,000.

(f) Depreciation expense on the store equipment for 20--, $4,500.

(g) Wages earned but not paid as of December 31, $675.

(h) Unearned boat rental revenue as of December 31, $3,000.

REQUIRED

1. Prepare a year-end work sheet.

2. Journalize the adjusting entries.

Diamond Music Store
Work Sheet
For Year Ended December 31, 20 --

#	ACCOUNT TITLE	TRIAL BALANCE DEBIT	TRIAL BALANCE CREDIT	ADJUSTMENTS DEBIT	ADJUSTMENTS CREDIT	ADJUSTED TRIAL BALANCE DEBIT	ADJUSTED TRIAL BALANCE CREDIT	INCOME STATEMENT DEBIT	INCOME STATEMENT CREDIT	BALANCE SHEET DEBIT	BALANCE SHEET CREDIT
1	Cash	31 000 00								31 000 00	
2	Accounts Receivable	11 980 00								11 980 00	
3	Merchandise Inventory	33 600 00								39 100 00	
4	Supplies	7 140 00								1 965 00	
5	Prepaid Insurance	5 985 00								1 235 00	
6	Land	36 200 00								36 200 00	
7	Building	51 850 00								51 850 00	
8	Accum. Depr.—Building		13 590 00								18 875 00
9	Store Equipment	32 675 00								32 675 00	
10	Accum. Depr.—Store Equipment		10 290 00								14 755 00
11	Accounts Payable		5 895 00								5 895 00
12	Wages Payable										1 250 00
13	Sales Tax Payable		6 375 00								6 375 00
14	Unearned Rent Revenue		8 850 00								2 930 00
15	Mortgage Payable		42 400 00								42 400 00
16	Ned Diamond, Capital		116 350 00								116 350 00
17	Ned Diamond, Drawing	39 500 00								39 500 00	
18	Income Summary							33 600 00	39 100 00		
19	Sales		148 000 00						148 000 00		
20	Sales Returns and Allowances	2 800 00						2 800 00			
21	Rent Revenue								5 920 00		
22	Purchases	40 700 00						40 700 00			
23	Purchases Returns and Allowances		2 775 00						2 775 00		
24	Purchases Discounts		2 325 00						2 325 00		
25	Freight-In	1 875 00						1 875 00			
26	Wages Expense	47 000 00						48 250 00			
27	Advertising Expense	4 695 00						4 695 00			
28	Supplies Expense							5 175 00			
29	Telephone Expense	2 250 00						2 250 00			
30	Utilities Expense	6 825 00						6 825 00			
31	Insurance Expense							4 750 00			
32	Depr. Expense—Building							5 285 00			
33	Depr. Expense—Store Equipment							4 465 00			
34	Miscellaneous Expense	775 00						775 00			
35		356 850 00	356 850 00					161 445 00	198 120 00	245 505 00	208 830 00
36	Net Income							36 675 00			36 675 00
37								198 120 00	198 120 00	245 505 00	245 505 00

PROBLEM 15-12B

Waikiki Surf Shop Trial Balance December 31, 20 - -										
ACCOUNT TITLE	**DEBIT BALANCE**					**CREDIT BALANCE**				
Cash	30	0	0	0	00					
Accounts Receivable	22	5	0	0	00					
Merchandise Inventory	57	0	0	0	00					
Supplies	2	7	0	0	00					
Prepaid Insurance	3	6	0	0	00					
Land	15	0	0	0	00					
Building	135	0	0	0	00					
Accumulated Depreciation—Building						24	0	0	0	00
Store Equipment	75	0	0	0	00					
Accumulated Depreciation—Store Equipment						22	5	0	0	00
Notes Payable						7	5	0	0	00
Accounts Payable						15	0	0	0	00
Wages Payable										
Unearned Boat Rental Revenue						33	0	0	0	00
John Neff, Capital						233	7	0	0	00
John Neff, Drawing	30	0	0	0	00					
Income Summary										
Sales						300	7	5	0	00
Sales Returns and Allowances	1	8	0	0	00					
Boat Rental Revenue										
Purchases	157	5	0	0	00					
Purchases Returns and Allowances						1	2	0	0	00
Purchases Discounts						1	5	0	0	00
Freight-In		4	5	0	00					
Wages Expense	63	0	0	0	00					
Advertising Expense	11	2	5	0	00					
Supplies Expense										
Telephone Expense	5	2	5	0	00					
Utilities Expense	18	0	0	0	00					
Insurance Expense										
Depreciation Expense —Building										
Depreciation Expense —Store Equipment										
Miscellaneous Expense	10	8	7	5	00					
Interest Expense		2	2	5	00					
	639	1	5	0	00	639	1	5	0	00

CHALLENGE PROBLEM

This problem challenges you to apply your cumulative accounting knowledge to move a step beyond the material in the chapter.

Net purchases in 20-1: $410,000

Block Food's, a retail grocery store, has agreed to purchase all of its merchandise from Square Wholesalers. In return, Block receives a special discount on purchases. Over recent months, Square noticed that purchases by Block had been falling off. At first, Square simply thought that business might be down for Block and was hopeful that their purchases would pick up. When business with Block did not return to a normal level, Square requested financial statements from Block. Square's records indicate that Block purchased $300,000 worth of merchandise during 20-1, the most recent year.

Selected information taken from Block's fianancial statements:

Balance Sheet	12/31/-1	12/31/-0
Inventory	$30,000	$20,000

Income Statement	
Cost of Goods Sold	$400,000

REQUIRED

Compute net purchases made by Block during 20-1. Does it appear that Block violated the agreement?

Chapter 15 Appendix
Expense Method of Accounting for Prepaid Expenses

Careful study of this appendix should enable you to:

LO1 Use the expense method of accounting for prepaid expenses.

LO2 Make the appropriate adjusting entries when the expense method is used for prepaid expenses.

THE EXPENSE METHOD

LO1 Use the expense method of accounting for prepaid expenses.

Under the **expense method** of accounting for prepaid expenses, supplies and other prepaid items are entered as expenses when purchased. Under this method, we must adjust the accounts at the end of each accounting period to record the unused portions as assets. To illustrate, let's assume that the following entry was made when office supplies were purchased.

4		Office Supplies Expense		4	2	5	00						4
5		Cash						4	2	5	00		5
6		Purchased office supplies											6

In the next section, we will illustrate the proper adjusting entry when using the expense method.

ADJUSTING ENTRIES UNDER THE EXPENSE METHOD

LO2 Make the appropriate adjusting entries when the expense method is used for prepaid expenses.

Office Supplies Expense was debited for a total of $425 during the period. An inventory taken at the end of the period shows that supplies on hand amounted to $150. The following adjusting entry is made for supplies on hand.

8		Office Supplies		1	5	0	00						8
9		Office Supplies Expense						1	5	0	00		9
10													10

As shown in the T accounts below, after this entry is posted, the office supplies expense account has a debit balance of $275. This amount is reported on the income statement as an operating expense. The office supplies account has a debit balance of $150. It is reported on the balance sheet as a current asset.

Office Supplies		Office Supplies Expense	
		425	
Adj. 150		Adj. 150	
		Bal. 275	

Let's consider another example of the use of the expense method. The following entry was made for the payment of $6,000 for a three-year insurance policy.

11		Insurance Expense		6 0 0 0 00		11
12		Cash			6 0 0 0 00	12
13		Paid insurance premium				13

At the end of the first year, one-third of the premium has expired and two-thirds remains. Thus, $2,000 for insurance expense should be reported on the income statement and $4,000 in prepaid insurance should be reported on the balance sheet. The following adjusting entry is made.

15		Prepaid Insurance		4 0 0 0 00		15
16		Insurance Expense			4 0 0 0 00	16
17						17

As shown in the T accounts below, after this entry is posted, the prepaid insurance account has a debit balance of $4,000. The insurance expense account has a debit balance of $2,000.

Prepaid Insurance		Insurance Expense	
		6,000	
Adj. 4,000			Adj. 4,000
		Bal. 2,000	

The asset and expense methods of accounting for prepaid expenses give the same final result. In the **asset method**, the prepaid item is first debited to an asset account. At the end of each period, the amount consumed is debited to an expense account. In the expense method, the original amount is debited to an expense account. At the end of each accounting period, the portion not consumed is debited to an asset account.

Learning Objectives	Key Points to Remember
1 Use the expense method of accounting for prepaid expenses.	Under the expense method, an expense account is debited when prepaid items are acquired.
2 Make the appropriate adjusting entries when the expense method is used for prepaid expenses.	At the end of the accounting period, an asset must be recognized for the amount of the prepaid item remaining. The expense account must be credited so that the ending balance represents the amount of the item consumed.

KEY TERMS

asset method, (592)   Under this method, the acquisition of a prepaid item is debited to an asset account.

expense method, (591)   Under this method, the acquisition of a prepaid item is debited to an expense account.

EXERCISES

EXERCISE 15Apx-1A   (LO2)   **EXPENSE METHOD OF ACCOUNTING FOR PREPAID EXPENSES** Davidson's Food Mart paid $1,200 in advance to the local newspaper for advertisements that will appear monthly. The following entry was made.

4		Advertising Expense	1 2 0 0 00		4
5		Cash		1 2 0 0 00	5
6		Paid prepaid advertising			6

At the end of the year, December 31, 20--, Davidson received notification that advertisements costing $800 had been run. Prepare the adjusting entry.

EXERCISE 15Apx-1B (LO1/2)   **EXPENSE METHOD OF ACCOUNTING FOR PREPAID EXPENSES** Ryan's Fish House purchased supplies costing $3,000 for cash. This amount was debited to the supplies expense account. At the end of the year, December 31, 20--, an inventory showed that supplies costing $500 remained. Prepare the entry for the purchase and year-end adjustment.

Financial Statements and Year-End Accounting for a Merchandising Business

After closing Parkway Pet Supplies' books for the year, Betty Jenkins, the book-keeper, went to Florida for a vacation. She plans to return during the second week of January. Before leaving, Betty gave Evan careful instructions on how to enter basic transactions while she is gone. Unfortunately, Evan is a bit confused about the proper entry for the first payroll of the new year. He knows that those first paychecks of the year cover wages earned at the end of last year, but not yet paid, as well as wages earned this year. Evan decides to check with Betty to get the proper allocation before he records the paychecks. Although he didn't want to interrupt Betty's vacation, he called her in Florida to get the information. Surprisingly, Betty said, "Don't worry about it. Just make the 'normal' entry by debiting Wages Expense and crediting Cash." Why is Betty not concerned about the proper allocation for the first payroll period?

Careful study of this chapter should enable you to:

LO1 Prepare a single-step and multiple-step income statement for a merchandising business.

LO2 Prepare a statement of owner's equity.

LO3 Prepare a classified balance sheet.

LO4 Compute standard financial ratios.

LO5 Prepare closing entries for a merchandising business.

LO6 Prepare reversing entries.

The first six chapters of this text illustrated the accounting cycle for a service business. Chapter 10 demonstrated accounting procedures for a professional enterprise. In this chapter we complete the accounting cycle for a merchandising business.

In Chapter 15, we prepared the year-end work sheet and adjusting entries for Northern Micro. In this chapter, we will prepare financial statements, closing and reversing entries, and look briefly at financial statement analysis.

THE INCOME STATEMENT

LO1 Prepare a single-step and multiple-step income statement for a merchandising business.

As you know, a primary purpose of the work sheet is to serve as an aid in preparing the financial statements. Figure 16-1 shows the completed work sheet for Northern Micro. We will use it to prepare financial statements.

The purpose of an income statement is to summarize the results of operations during an accounting period. The income statement shows the sources of revenue, types of expenses, and the amount of the net income or net loss for the period. Two forms of the income statement commonly used are the single step and the multiple step. The **single-step income statement** lists all revenue items and their total first, followed by all expense items and their total. The difference, which is either net income or net loss, is then calculated. A single-step income statement for Northern Micro is illustrated in Figure 16-2.

The **multiple-step income statement** is commonly used for merchandising businesses. The term "multiple-step" is used because the final net income is calculated on a step-by-step basis. Gross sales is shown first, less sales returns and allowances and sales discounts. This difference is called **net sales**. (Many published income statements begin with the amount of net sales.) Cost of goods sold is subtracted next to arrive at **gross profit** (sometimes called **gross margin**).

Operating expenses are then listed and subtracted from the gross profit to compute **income from operations** (sometimes called **operating income**). Operating expenses are directly associated with providing the primary goods and services of the business. Some companies divide operating expenses into the following subcategories.

Selling expenses. These expenses are directly associated with selling activities. Examples include:

- Sales Salaries Expense
- Sales Commissions Expense
- Advertising Expense
- Bank Credit Card Expense

Northern Micro
Work Sheet
For Year Ended December 31, 20 --

#	Account Title	Trial Balance Debit	Trial Balance Credit	Adjustments Debit	Adjustments Credit	Adjusted Trial Balance Debit	Adjusted Trial Balance Credit	Income Statement Debit	Income Statement Credit	Balance Sheet Debit	Balance Sheet Credit
1	Cash	20 0 0 0 00				20 0 0 0 00				20 0 0 0 00	
2	Accounts Receivable	15 0 0 0 00				15 0 0 0 00				15 0 0 0 00	
3	Merchandise Inventory	26 0 0 0 00		(b) 18 0 0 0 00	(a) 26 0 0 0 00	18 0 0 0 00				18 0 0 0 00	
4	Supplies	1 8 0 0 00			(c) 1 4 0 0 00	4 0 0 00				4 0 0 00	
5	Prepaid Insurance	2 4 0 0 00			(d) 1 8 0 0 00	6 0 0 00				6 0 0 00	
6	Land	10 0 0 0 00				10 0 0 0 00				10 0 0 0 00	
7	Building	90 0 0 0 00				90 0 0 0 00				90 0 0 0 00	
8	Accum. Depr.—Building		16 0 0 0 00		(e) 4 0 0 0 00		20 0 0 0 00				20 0 0 0 00
9	Store Equipment	50 0 0 0 00				50 0 0 0 00				50 0 0 0 00	
10	Accum. Depr.—Store Equipment		15 0 0 0 00		(f) 3 0 0 0 00		18 0 0 0 00				18 0 0 0 00
11	Notes Payable		5 0 0 0 00				5 0 0 0 00				5 0 0 0 00
12	Accounts Payable		10 0 0 0 00				10 0 0 0 00				10 0 0 0 00
13	Wages Payable				(g) 4 5 0 00		4 5 0 00				4 5 0 00
14	Sales Tax Payable		1 5 0 0 00				1 5 0 0 00				1 5 0 0 00
15	Unearned Subscriptions Revenue		12 0 0 0 00	(h) 10 0 0 0 00			2 0 0 0 00				2 0 0 0 00
16	Mortgage Payable		30 0 0 0 00				30 0 0 0 00				30 0 0 0 00
17	Gary L. Fishel, Capital		114 4 0 0 00				114 4 0 0 00				114 4 0 0 00
18	Gary L. Fishel, Drawing	20 0 0 0 00				20 0 0 0 00				20 0 0 0 00	
19	Income Summary			(a) 26 0 0 0 00	(b) 18 0 0 0 00	26 0 0 0 00	18 0 0 0 00	26 0 0 0 00	18 0 0 0 00		
20	Sales		214 0 0 0 00				214 0 0 0 00		214 0 0 0 00		
21	Sales Returns and Allowances	1 2 0 0 00				1 2 0 0 00		1 2 0 0 00			
22	Interest Revenue		9 0 0 0 00				9 0 0 0 00		9 0 0 0 00		
23	Rent Revenue		8 0 0 0 00				8 0 0 0 00		8 0 0 0 00		
24	Subscriptions Revenue				(h) 10 0 0 0 00		10 0 0 0 00		10 0 0 0 00		
25	Purchases	105 0 0 0 00				105 0 0 0 00		105 0 0 0 00			
26	Purchases Returns and Allowances		8 0 0 0 00				8 0 0 0 00		8 0 0 0 00		
27	Purchases Discounts		1 0 0 0 00				1 0 0 0 00		1 0 0 0 00		
28	Freight-In	3 0 0 0 00				3 0 0 0 00		3 0 0 0 00			
29	Wages Expense	42 0 0 0 00		(g) 4 5 0 00		42 4 5 0 00		42 4 5 0 00			
30	Advertising Expense	2 5 0 0 00				2 5 0 0 00		2 5 0 0 00			
31	Bank Credit Card Expense	1 5 0 0 00				1 5 0 0 00		1 5 0 0 00			
32	Rent Expense	20 0 0 0 00				20 0 0 0 00		20 0 0 0 00			
33	Supplies Expense			(c) 1 4 0 0 00		1 4 0 0 00		1 4 0 0 00			
34	Telephone Expense	3 5 0 0 00				3 5 0 0 00		3 5 0 0 00			
35	Utilities Expense	12 0 0 0 00				12 0 0 0 00		12 0 0 0 00			
36	Insurance Expense			(d) 1 8 0 0 00		1 8 0 0 00		1 8 0 0 00			
37	Depr. Expense—Building			(e) 4 0 0 0 00		4 0 0 0 00		4 0 0 0 00			
38	Depr. Expense—Store Equipment			(f) 3 0 0 0 00		3 0 0 0 00		3 0 0 0 00			
39	Miscellaneous Expense	2 2 5 0 00				2 2 5 0 00		2 2 5 0 00			
40	Interest Expense	3 1 5 0 00				3 1 5 0 00		3 1 5 0 00			
41		428 6 0 0 00	428 6 0 0 00	64 6 5 0 00	64 6 5 0 00	454 0 5 0 00	454 0 5 0 00	230 0 5 0 00	252 7 0 0 00	224 0 0 0 00	201 3 5 0 00
42	Net Income							22 6 5 0 00			22 6 5 0 00
43								252 7 0 0 00	252 7 0 0 00	224 0 0 0 00	224 0 0 0 00

FIGURE 16-1 Northern Micro Work Sheet

Northern Micro Income Statement For Year Ended December 31, 20 - -											
Revenues:											
Net sales	$212	8	0	0	00						
Interest revenue		9	0	0	00						
Rent revenue	8	0	0	0	00						
Subscriptions revenue	10	0	0	0	00						
Total revenues						$231	7	0	0	00	
Expenses:											
Cost of goods sold	$111	5	0	0	00						
Wages expense	42	4	5	0	00						
Advertising expense	2	5	0	0	00						
Bank credit card expense	1	5	0	0	00						
Rent expense	20	0	0	0	00						
Supplies expense	1	4	0	0	00						
Telephone expense	3	5	0	0	00						
Utilities expense	12	0	0	0	00						
Insurance expense	1	8	0	0	00						
Depreciation expense—building	4	0	0	0	00						
Depreciation expense—store equipment	3	0	0	0	00						
Miscellaneous expense	2	2	5	0	00						
Interest expense	3	1	5	0	00						
Total expenses						209	0	5	0	00	
Net income						$ 22	6	5	0	00	

FIGURE 16-2   Single-Step Income Statement

- Delivery Expense
- Depreciation Expense—Store Equipment and Fixtures

General expenses. These expenses are associated with administrative, office, or general operating activities. Examples include:

- Rent Expense
- Office Salaries Expense
- Office Supplies Expense
- Telephone Expense
- Utilities Expense
- Insurance Expense
- Depreciation Expense—Office Equipment

Finally, other revenues are added and other expenses are subtracted to arrive at net income (or net loss). A multiple-step income statement for Northern Micro is shown in Figure 16-3. Note that the operating expenses are arranged according to the order given in the chart of accounts. They could also be listed by descending amount, with Miscellaneous Expense last.

By showing other revenues and other expenses separately, it is possible to show income from operations. This makes it easier for the reader to see how the business is doing in its main activity.

Northern Micro Income Statement For Year Ended December 31, 20 - -							
Revenue from sales:							
Sales				$214 0 0 0 00			
Less sales returns and allowances				1 2 0 0 00			
Net sales						$212 8 0 0 00	
Cost of goods sold:							
Merchandise inventory, January 1, 20- -				$ 26 0 0 0 00			
Purchases		$105 0 0 0 00					
Less: Purchases returns and allowances	$ 8 0 0 0 00						
Purchases discounts	1 0 0 0 00	1 8 0 0 0 00					
Net purchases		$103 2 0 0 00					
Add freight-in		3 0 0 00					
Cost of goods purchased				103 5 0 0 00			
Goods available for sale				$129 5 0 0 00			
Less merchandise inventory, December 31, 20- -				18 0 0 0 00			
Cost of goods sold						111 5 0 0 00	
Gross profit						$101 3 0 0 00	
Operating expenses:							
Wages expense				$ 42 4 5 0 00			
Advertising expense				2 5 0 0 00			
Bank credit card expense				1 5 0 0 00			
Rent expense				20 0 0 0 00			
Supplies expense				1 4 0 0 00			
Telephone expense				3 5 0 0 00			
Utilities expense				12 0 0 0 00			
Insurance expense				1 8 0 0 00			
Depreciation expense—building				4 0 0 0 00			
Depreciation expense—store equipment				3 0 0 0 00			
Miscellaneous expense				2 2 5 0 00			
Total operating expenses						94 4 0 0 00	
Income from operations						$ 6 9 0 0 00	
Other revenues:							
Interest revenue				$ 9 0 0 00			
Rent revenue				8 0 0 0 00			
Subscriptions revenue				10 0 0 0 00			
Total other revenues				$ 18 9 0 0 00			
Other expenses:							
Interest expense				3 1 5 0 00		15 7 5 0 00	
Net income						$ 22 6 5 0 00	

FIGURE 16-3 Multiple-Step Income Statement

LEARNING KEY: Although the format for the single-step and multiple-step income statements are different, the reported net income is the same.

THE STATEMENT OF OWNER'S EQUITY

LO2 Prepare a statement of owner's equity.

The statement of owner's equity summarizes all changes in the owner's equity during the period. It includes the net income or loss and any additional investments or withdrawals by the owner. These changes result in the end-of-period balance shown on this statement and the balance sheet.

To prepare the statement of owner's equity for Northern Micro, two sources of information are needed: (1) the work sheet, and (2) Gary Fishel's capital account (no. 311) in the general ledger. The work sheet (Figure 16-1) shows net income of $22,650 and withdrawals of $20,000 during the year. Fishel's capital account (Figure 16-4) shows a beginning balance of $104,400. An additional $10,000 was invested in the business in February of the current year. The statement of owner's equity for Northern Micro for the year ended December 31, 20--, is shown in Figure 16-5.

ACCOUNT: Gary L. Fishel, Capital							ACCOUNT NO. 311	
DATE		ITEM	POST REF.	DEBIT	CREDIT	BALANCE		
						DEBIT	CREDIT	
20-- Jan.	1	Balance	✓				104 4 0 0 00	
Feb.	12		CR7		10 0 0 0 00		114 4 0 0 00	

FIGURE 16-4 Capital Account for Gary L. Fishel

> The statement of owner's equity is the same for service and merchandising businesses.

Northern Micro Statement of Owner's Equity For Year Ended December 31, 20 - -			
Gary L. Fishel, capital, January 1, 20 - -			$104 4 0 0 00
Add additional investments			10 0 0 0 00
Total investment			$114 4 0 0 00
Net income for the year	$22 6 5 0 00		
Less withdrawals for the year	20 0 0 0 00		
Increase in capital			2 6 5 0 00
Gary L. Fishel, capital, December 31, 20 - -			$117 0 5 0 00

FIGURE 16-5 Statement of Owner's Equity

THE BALANCE SHEET

LO3 Prepare a classified balance sheet.

The report form of a classified balance sheet is illustrated in Figure 16-6. The balance sheet classifications used by Northern Micro are explained below.

 LEARNING KEY: Note the use of the ending balance for merchandise inventory. It is reported on the income statement as part of the calculation of cost of goods sold. It also is reported on the balance sheet as a current asset.

Northern Micro
Balance Sheet
December 31, 20 - -

Assets				
Current assets:				
Cash		$20 0 0 0 00		
Accounts receivable		15 0 0 0 00		
Merchandise inventory		18 0 0 0 00		
Supplies		4 0 0 00		
Prepaid insurance		6 0 0 00		
Total current assets			$ 54 0 0 0 00	
Property, plant, and equipment:				
Land		$10 0 0 0 00		
Building	$90 0 0 0 00			
Less accumulated depreciation	20 0 0 0 00	70 0 0 0 00		
Store equipment	$50 0 0 0 00			
Less accumulated depreciation	18 0 0 0 00	32 0 0 0 00		
Total property, plant, and equipment			112 0 0 0 00	
Total assets			$166 0 0 0 00	
Liabilities				
Current liabilities:				
Notes payable	$ 5 0 0 0 00			
Accounts payable	10 0 0 0 00			
Wages payable	4 5 0 00			
Sales tax payable	1 5 0 0 00			
Unearned subscriptions revenue	2 0 0 0 00			
Mortgage payable (current portion)	5 0 0 00			
Total current liabilities		$19 4 5 0 00		
Long-term liabilities:				
Mortgage payable	$30 0 0 0 00			
Less current portion	5 0 0 00	29 5 0 0 00		
Total liabilities			$ 48 9 5 0 00	
Owner's Equity				
Gary L. Fishel, capital			117 0 5 0 00	
Total liabilities and owner's equity			$166 0 0 0 00	

FIGURE 16-6 Balance Sheet for Northern Micro

Current Assets

Current assets include cash and all other assets expected to be converted into cash or consumed within one year or the normal operating cycle of the business, whichever is longer. The **operating cycle** is the length of time generally required for a business to buy inventory, sell it, and collect the cash. This time period is generally less than a year. Thus, most firms use one year for classifying current assets. In a merchandising business, the current assets usually include cash, receivables (such as accounts receivable and notes receivable), and merchandise inventory. Since prepaid expenses, such as unused supplies and unexpired insurance, are likely to be consumed within a year, they also are reported as current assets.

Current assets are listed on the balance sheet from the most liquid to least liquid. **Liquidity** refers to the speed with which the company can convert the asset to cash. Cash is the most liquid asset and is always listed first. Notes Receivable, Accounts Receivable, and Merchandise Inventory often follow it on the balance sheet.

Property, Plant, and Equipment

Assets that are expected to be used for more than one year in the operation of a business are called **property, plant, and equipment**. Examples include land, buildings, office equipment, store equipment, and delivery equipment. Of these assets, only land is permanent; however, all of these assets have useful lives that are comparatively long. Typically, assets with longer useful lives are listed first.

The balance sheet of Northern Micro shows Land, Building, and Store Equipment. Land is not depreciated. Accumulated depreciation amounts are shown as deductions from the costs of the building and store equipment. The difference represents the **undepreciated cost**, or **book value**, of the assets. This amount less any salvage value will be written off as depreciation expense in future periods.

Current Liabilities

Current liabilities include those obligations that are due within one year or the normal operating cycle of the business, whichever is longer, and will require the use of current assets. As of December 31, the current liabilities of Northern Micro consist of Notes Payable, Accounts Payable, Wages Payable, Sales Tax Payable, Unearned Subscriptions Revenue, and the portion of Mortgage Payable that is due within the next year.

Long-Term Liabilities

Long-term liabilities include those obligations that will extend beyond one year or the normal operating cycle, whichever is longer. A common long-term liability is a mortgage payable.

A **mortgage** is a written agreement specifying that if the borrower does not repay a debt, the lender has the right to take over specific property to satisfy the debt. When the debt is paid, the mortgage becomes void. **Mortgage Payable** is an account that is used to reflect an obligation that is secured by a mortgage on certain property.

The current portion of long-term debt, the amount due within one year, is reported as a current liability. The remainder is reported under long-term liabilities.

Owner's Equity

The permanent owner's equity accounts reported on the balance sheet are determined by the type of organization. The accounts for a sole proprietorship, a partnership, and a corporation differ. Northern Micro is a sole proprietorship and reports one owner's equity account, Gary L. Fishel, Capital. The balance of this account is taken from the statement of owner's equity. Partnerships are illustrated in Chapter 21 and corporations are discussed in Chapters 22 and 23.

FINANCIAL STATEMENT ANALYSIS

LO4 Compute standard financial ratios.

Both management and creditors are interested in using the financial statements to evaluate the financial condition and profitability of the firm. This can be done by making a few simple calculations.

Balance Sheet Analysis

Recall the following:

1. Current assets include cash, items that will be converted to cash, and items that will be consumed within one year.

2. Current liabilities are obligations that will require the use of current assets.

    Thus, the difference between current assets and current liabilities represents the amount of capital the business has available for current operations. This is called **working capital**.

Working Capital = Current Assets − Current Liabilities

The balance sheet in Figure 16-6 shows that Northern Micro has current assets of $54,000 and current liabilities of $19,450. Thus, the working capital at year end is $34,550 ($54,000 − $19,450). This amount should be more than adequate to satisfy current operating requirements.

Two measures of the firm's ability to pay its current liabilities are the **current ratio** and **quick ratio**. The formulas for calculating these ratios are as follows:

Northern Micro

$$\text{Current Ratio} = \frac{\text{Current Assets}}{\text{Current Liabilities}} = \frac{\$54,000}{\$19,450} = 2.8 \text{ to } 1$$

$$\text{Quick Ratio} = \frac{\text{Quick Assets}}{\text{Current Liabilities}} = \frac{\$35,000}{\$19,450} = 1.8 \text{ to } 1$$

Northern Micro's current ratio of 2.8 to 1 is quite high, which indicates a favorable financial position. The traditional "rule of thumb" has been that a current ratio should be about 2 to 1, but many businesses operate successfully on a current ratio of 1.5 to 1. Although a rule of thumb is helpful, it is better to compare an individual company to industry averages, which are available in most public libraries.

 LEARNING KEY: Ratio analysis is most informative when the ratios are compared with past performance and with those of similar businesses.

Quick assets include cash and all other current assets that can be converted into cash quickly, such as accounts receivable and temporary investments. Temporary investments are discussed in more advanced textbooks. The balance sheet in Figure 16-6 shows total quick assets of $35,000 ($20,000 in cash + $15,000 in accounts receivable). This produces a quick ratio of 1.8 to 1. Quick assets appear to be more than adequate to meet current obligations. The traditional rule of thumb has been that a quick ratio should be about 1 to 1, but many businesses operate successfully on a quick ratio of 0.6 to 1.

Interstatement Analysis

Interstatement analysis provides a comparison of the relationships between selected income statement and balance sheet amounts. A good example of interstatement analysis is the ratio of net income to owner's equity in the business. This ratio is known as **return on owner's equity**.

$$\text{Return on Owner's Equity} = \frac{\text{Net Income}}{\text{Average Owner's Equity}} = \frac{\text{Northern Micro}}{(\$104,400 + \$117,050) \div 2}$$

$$= \frac{\$22,650}{\$110,725}$$

$$= 20.5\%$$

The statement of owner's equity in Figure 16-5 shows that the owner's equity of Northern Micro was $104,400 on January 1 and $117,050 on December 31. The net income for the year of $22,650 is 20.5% of the average owner's equity. A comparison of this ratio with the return on owner's equity in prior years should be of interest to the owner. It may also be of interest to compare the return on owner's equity of Northern Micro with the same ratio for other businesses of comparable nature and size.

A second ratio involving both income statement and balance sheet accounts is a measure of the time required to collect cash from credit customers. This financial measure is often computed in two ways. The **accounts receivable turnover** is the number of times the accounts receivable "turned over," or were collected, during the accounting period. Of course, a higher number indicates that cash is collected more quickly. This ratio is calculated as follows:

$$\text{Accounts Receivable Turnover} = \frac{\text{Net Credit Sales for the Period}}{\text{Average Accounts Receivable}}$$

The accounts receivable turnover for Northern Micro for the year ended December 31 is computed as follows.

Net credit sales for the year (determined from the accounting records)	$110,000
Accounts receivable balance, January 1, 20-- (taken from last year's balance sheet)	10,000
Accounts receivable balance, December 31, 20--	15,000

$$\text{Average Accounts Receivable} = \frac{\text{Beginning Balance} + \text{Ending Balance}}{2} = \frac{\text{Northern Micro}}{\$10,000 + \$15,000}$$

$$= \$12,500$$

$$\text{Accounts Receivable Turnover} = \frac{\text{Net Credit Sales for the Period}}{\text{Average Accounts Receivable}} = \frac{\$110,000}{\$12,500}$$

$$= 8.8$$

The **average collection period** is calculated by dividing the number of days in the year (365) by the rate of turnover to determine the number of days credit customers take to pay for their purchases. Northern Micro's customers are taking about 42 days.

$$365 \text{ days} \div 8.8 = 41.5 \text{ days}$$

Comparing the average collection period with a business's credit terms offers an indication of whether customers are paying within the terms. If Northern Micro allows credit terms of n/45, an average collection period of 41.5 days would suggest that customers are paying on a timely basis.

A third ratio involving both income statement and balance sheet accounts is the rate of **inventory turnover**. This is the number of times the merchandise inventory turned over, or was sold, during the accounting period. This ratio is calculated as follows:

$$\text{Inventory Turnover} = \frac{\text{Cost of Goods Sold for the Period}}{\text{Average Inventory}}$$

If inventory is taken only at the end of each accounting period, the average inventory for the period can be calculated by adding the beginning and ending inventories and dividing their sum by two. Northern Micro's turnover for the year ended December 31 is computed as follows:

Cost of goods sold for the period	$111,500
Beginning inventory	26,000
Ending inventory	18,000

$$\text{Average Inventory} = \frac{\text{Beginning Inventory} + \text{Ending Inventory}}{2} = \frac{\$26,000 + \$18,000}{2}$$

Northern Micro

$$= \$22,000$$

A BROADER VIEW

Who Cares About Tracking Financial Ratios?

Tracking a business's average collection period for receivables can help investors avoid making poor investments. Take the case of Kendall Square, a supercomputer maker. In an effort to increase sales and profits, Kendall Square recognized large amounts of revenues that had not actually been earned. Since no cash was received for these sales, accounts receivable increased dramatically (by 57%). Similarly, the average collection period increased to 157 days. Large increases in the average collection period should warn potential investors that something might be wrong. What happened at Kendall Square? Over $10 million of sales on account was never collected. This was equal to almost half of the revenues reported for the year. When eventually discovered, Kendall Square's stock price fell from $24.25 to $2.28 a share.

© DAVIDSON CHIGMAROFF / SUPERSTOCK

$$\underset{\text{Turnover}}{\text{Inventory}} = \frac{\text{Cost of Goods Sold for the Period}}{\text{Average Inventory}} = \frac{\$111,500}{\$22,000}$$

$$= 5.1$$

The **average days to sell inventory** can be computed by dividing the number of days in the year (365) by the inventory turnover. For Northern Micro it takes about two months.

365 days ÷ 5.1 = 71.6 days

The higher the rate of inventory turnover, the smaller the profit required on each dollar of sales to produce a satisfactory gross profit. This is because the increase in the number of units sold offsets the smaller amount of gross profit earned per unit. For example, grocery stores have a very small gross profit on each item sold, but make up for this with a rapid inventory turnover. Other types of businesses, jewelers for example, need a high gross profit on each item because their inventory turnover is quite slow. Evaluations of Northern Micro's rate of inventory turnover would require comparison with prior years, other companies, or its industry.

CLOSING ENTRIES

LO5 Prepare closing entries for a merchandising business.

Closing entries for a service business were illustrated in Chapter 6. The process is essentially the same for a merchandising business. All revenues and expenses reported on the income statement must be closed to Income Summary. Then, the income summary and drawing accounts are closed to the owner's capital account. Keep in mind, however, that a few new accounts were needed for a merchandising business. These include Sales Returns and Allowances, Sales Discounts, Purchases Returns and Allowances, and Purchases Discounts. Since these are temporary accounts reported on the income statement, they also must be closed. The easiest way to complete the closing process is by using the work sheet to prepare the closing entries in four basic steps, as illustrated in Figures 16-7 and 16-8.

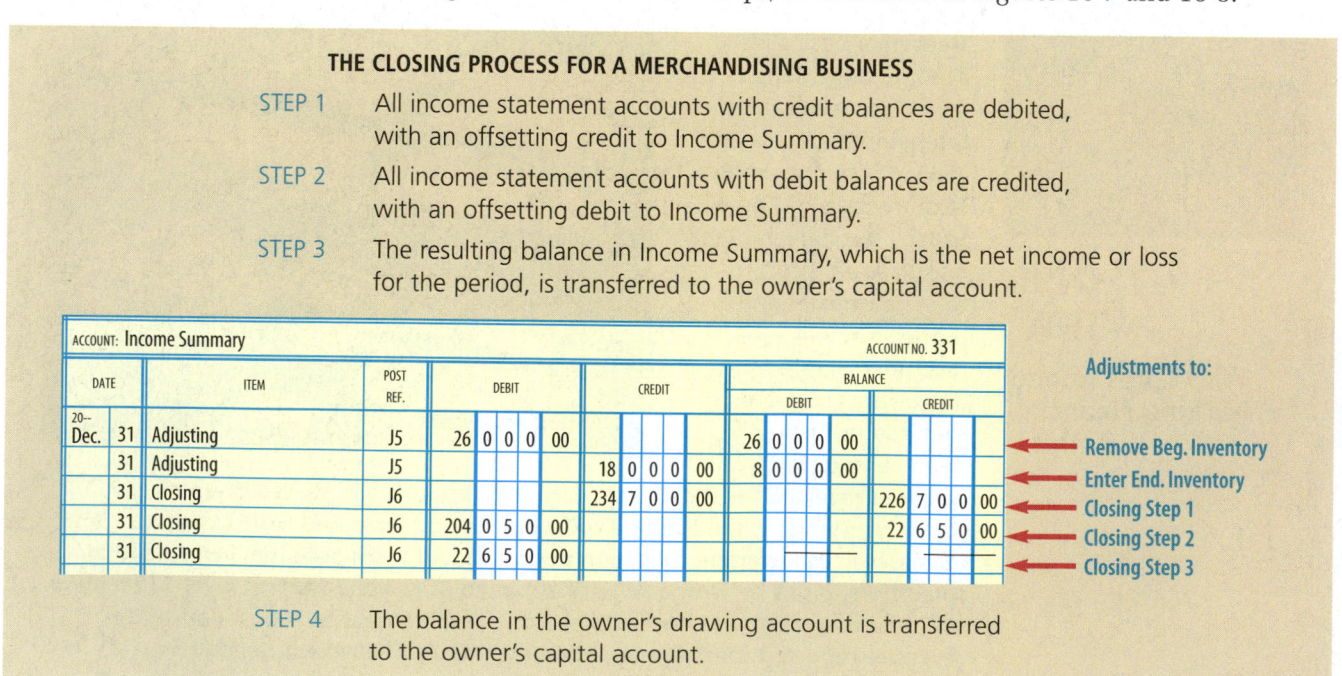

THE CLOSING PROCESS FOR A MERCHANDISING BUSINESS

STEP 1   All income statement accounts with credit balances are debited, with an offsetting credit to Income Summary.

STEP 2   All income statement accounts with debit balances are credited, with an offsetting debit to Income Summary.

STEP 3   The resulting balance in Income Summary, which is the net income or loss for the period, is transferred to the owner's capital account.

STEP 4   The balance in the owner's drawing account is transferred to the owner's capital account.

FIGURE 16-8 The Closing Process

Northern Micro
Work Sheet (Partial)
For Year Ended December 31, 20--

	ACCOUNT TITLE	INCOME STATEMENT DEBIT	INCOME STATEMENT CREDIT	BALANCE SHEET DEBIT	BALANCE SHEET CREDIT	
17	Gary L. Fishel, Capital				114 4 0 0 00	17
18	Gary L. Fishel, Drawing			20 0 0 0 00		18
19	Income Summary	26 0 0 0 00	18 0 0 0 00			19
20	Sales		214 0 0 0 00			20
21	Sales Returns and Allowances	1 2 0 0 0 00				21
22	Interest Revenue		9 0 0 00			22
23	Rent Revenue		8 0 0 0 00			23
24	Subscriptions Revenue		10 0 0 0 00			24
25	Purchases	105 0 0 0 00				25
26	Purchases Returns and Allow.		8 0 0 0 00			26
27	Purchases Discounts		1 0 0 0 00			27
28	Freight-In	3 0 0 0 00				28
29	Wages Expense	42 4 5 0 00				29
30	Advertising Expense	2 5 0 0 00				30
31	Bank Credit Card Expense	1 5 0 0 00				31
32	Rent Expense	20 0 0 0 00				32
33	Supplies Expense	1 4 0 0 00				33
34	Telephone Expense	3 5 0 0 00				34
35	Utilities Expense	12 0 0 0 00				35
36	Insurance Expense	1 8 0 0 00				36
37	Depr. Expense—Building	4 0 0 0 00				37
38	Depr. Expense—Store Equip.	3 0 0 0 00				38
39	Miscellaneous Expense	2 2 5 0 00				39
40	Interest Expense	3 1 5 0 00				40
41		230 0 5 0 00	252 7 0 0 00	224 0 0 0 00	201 3 5 0 00	41
42	Net Income	22 6 5 0 00			22 6 5 0 00	42
43		252 7 0 0 00	252 7 0 0 00	224 0 0 0 00	224 0 0 0 00	43
44						44

GENERAL JOURNAL   PAGE 6

	DATE	DESCRIPTION	POST REF.	DEBIT	CREDIT	
1	20--	Closing Entries				1
2	Dec. 31	Sales		214 0 0 0 00		2
3		Subscriptions Revenue		10 0 0 0 00		3
4		Interest Revenue		9 0 0 00		4
5		Rent Revenue		8 0 0 0 00		5
6		Purchases Returns and Allowances		8 0 0 0 00		6
7		Purchases Discounts		1 0 0 0 00		7
8		Income Summary			234 7 0 0 00	8
9						9
10		31 Income Summary		204 0 5 0 00		10
11		Sales Returns and Allowances			1 2 0 0 0 00	11
12		Purchases			105 0 0 0 00	12
13		Freight-In			3 0 0 0 00	13
14		Wages Expense			42 4 5 0 00	14
15		Advertising Expense			2 5 0 0 00	15
16		Bank Credit Card Expense			1 5 0 0 00	16
17		Rent Expense			20 0 0 0 00	17
18		Supplies Expense			1 4 0 0 00	18
19		Telephone Expense			3 5 0 0 00	19
20		Utilities Expense			12 0 0 0 00	20
21		Insurance Expense			1 8 0 0 00	21
22		Depreciation Exp.—Building			4 0 0 0 00	22
23		Depreciation Exp.—Store Equip.			3 0 0 0 00	23
24		Miscellaneous Expense			2 2 5 0 00	24
25		Interest Expense			3 1 5 0 00	25
26						26
27		31 Income Summary		22 6 5 0 00		27
28		Gary L. Fishel, Capital			22 6 5 0 00	28
29						29
30		31 Gary L. Fishel, Capital		20 0 0 0 00		30
31		Gary L. Fishel, Drawing			20 0 0 0 00	31
32						32

FIGURE 16-7   Closing Entries for a Merchandising Business

Post-Closing Trial Balance

A trial balance of the general ledger accounts taken after the temporary owner's equity accounts have been closed is called a **post-closing trial balance**. The purpose of the post-closing trial balance is to prove that the general ledger is in balance at the beginning of a new accounting period, before any transactions for the new accounting period are entered. Figure 16-9 shows a post-closing trial balance for Northern Micro.

> The post-closing trial balance must be prepared by taking the balances from the general ledger accounts. It should not be prepared from the balances on the work sheet. Using the general ledger accounts makes sure that all adjusting and closing entries were entered and posted correctly.

Northern Micro
Post-Closing Trial Balance
December 31, 20 - -

ACCOUNT TITLE	ACCOUNT NO.	DEBIT BALANCE	CREDIT BALANCE
Cash	101	20 0 0 0 00	
Accounts Receivable	122	15 0 0 0 00	
Merchandise Inventory	131	18 0 0 0 00	
Supplies	141	4 0 0 00	
Prepaid Insurance	145	6 0 0 00	
Land	161	10 0 0 0 00	
Building	171	90 0 0 0 00	
Accumulated Depreciation—Building	171.1		20 0 0 0 00
Store Equipment	181	50 0 0 0 00	
Accumulated Depreciation—Store Equipment	181.1		18 0 0 0 00
Notes Payable	201		5 0 0 0 00
Accounts Payable	202		10 0 0 0 00
Wages Payable	219		4 5 0 00
Sales Tax Payable	231		1 5 0 0 00
Unearned Subscriptions Revenue	241		2 0 0 0 00
Mortgage Payable	251		30 0 0 0 00
Gary L. Fishel, Capital	311		117 0 5 0 00
		204 0 0 0 00	204 0 0 0 00

FIGURE 16-9 Post-Closing Trial Balance

REVERSING ENTRIES

LO6 Prepare reversing entries.

Numerous adjusting entries are needed at the end of the accounting period to bring the account balances up to date for presentation in the financial statements. Although not required, some of these adjusting entries should be reversed at the beginning of the next accounting period. This is done to simplify the recording of transactions in the new accounting period. As its name implies, a **reversing entry** is the reverse or opposite of the adjusting entry.

ADJUSTING ENTRY

| 4 | Dec. | 31 | Wages Expense | | 4 5 0 00 | | 4 |
| 5 | | | Wages Payable | | | 4 5 0 00 | 5 |

REVERSING ENTRY (OPPOSITE)

| 7 | Jan. | 1 | Wages Payable | | 4 5 0 00 | | 7 |
| 8 | | | Wages Expense | | | 4 5 0 00 | 8 |

To see the advantage of using reversing entries, let's consider the effect of reversing Northern Micro's adjusting entry for wages earned, but not paid, at the end of the year. Figure 16-10 shows that accrued wages on December 31 were $450. These wages are for work performed by the employees on the last three days of the accounting period (150 × 3 = $450). The employees will be paid on Friday, January 2, the normal payday.

| | 20-1 | | | 20-2 | |
	12/29/-1 Monday	12/30/-1 Tuesday	12/31/-1 Wednesday	1/1/-2 Thursday	1/2/-2 Friday
Wages Earned	150	150	150	150	150
Wages Paid	0	0	0	0	750
Total Earned			450		300
Total Paid			0		750
Accrued Wages on 12/31/-1			450		

Date	Without Reversing Entry		With Reversing Entry	

12/31/-1 Adj. Entry	Wages Expense 450
	  Wages Payable 450
			Wages Expense 450
			  Wages Payable 450	

12/31/-1 Closing Entry	Income Summary 42,450
	  Wages Expense 42,450
			Income Summary 42,450
			  Wages Expense 42,450	

1/1/-2 Rev. Entry	No Entry		Wages Payable 450 Wages Expense 450	

1/2/-2 Payment of Payroll	Wages Expense 300
	Wages Payable 450
	  Cash 750
			Wages Expense 750
			  Cash 750	

Wages Expense

Description		Description
Bal.	42,000	
12/31/-1 Adj.	450	
	42,450	12/31/-1 Close
1/2/-2 Payroll	300	

Description		Description
Bal.	42,000	
12/31/-1 Adj.	450	
	42,450	12/31/-1 Close
	450	1/1/-2 Reversing
1/2/-2 Payroll	750	
Bal.	300	

Wages Payable

	450	12/31/-1 Adj.
1/2/-2 Payroll	450	

	450	12/31/-1 Adj.
1/1/-2 Reverse	450	

Cash

	750	1/2/-2 Payroll

	750	1/2/-2 Payroll

FIGURE 16-10 Adjusting, Closing, and Reversing Entries for Wages

Note that the adjusting and closing entries are the same, regardless of whether a reversing entry is made. However, the reversing entry on January 1 has an impact on the entry made when the employees are paid. **Without** a reversing entry, the payment on January 2, 20-2, must be split between reduction of the Wages Payable account for wages earned in 20-1 and Wages Expense for wages earned in 20-2. **With** a reversing entry, the bookkeeper simply debits Wages Expense and credits Cash, as is done on every other payday. Thus, the likelihood of error is reduced. Reversing entries are particularly important in large businesses where the individual recording the entry for wages may not even know what adjusting entries were made.

Not all adjusting entries should be reversed. To determine which adjusting entries to reverse, follow this rule: *Except for the first year of operations, reverse all adjusting entries that increase an asset or liability account from a zero balance.*

LEARNING KEY: Reverse all adjusting entries that increase an asset or liability account from a zero balance.

Except for the first year of operation, merchandise inventory, and contra-assets like accumulated depreciation, will have existing balances. Thus, they should never be reversed. The adjusting entries for Northern Micro are shown in Figure 16-11. Note that only the adjustment for accrued wages is reversed in Figure 16-12.

GENERAL JOURNAL   PAGE 5

	DATE	DESCRIPTION	POST REF.	DEBIT	CREDIT	SHOULD THE ADJUSTMENT BE REVERSED?
1		Adjusting Entries				
2	20-- Dec. 31	Income Summary		26 0 0 0 00		Never reverse adjustments for merchandise inventory.
3		Merchandise Inventory			26 0 0 0 00	
4						
5	31	Merchandise Inventory		18 0 0 0 00		Never reverse adjustments for merchandise inventory.
6		Income Summary			18 0 0 0 00	
7						
8	31	Supplies Expense		1 4 0 0 00		No. No asset or liability with a zero balance has been increased.
9		Supplies			1 4 0 0 00	
10						
11	31	Insurance Expense		1 8 0 0 00		No. No asset or liability with a zero balance has been increased.
12		Prepaid Insurance			1 8 0 0 00	
13						
14	31	Depr. Expense—Building		4 0 0 0 00		Never reverse adjustments for depreciation.
15		Accum. Depr.—Building			4 0 0 0 00	
16						
17	31	Depr. Expense—Store Equipment		3 0 0 0 00		Never reverse adjustments for depreciation.
18		Accum. Depr.—Store Equipment			3 0 0 0 00	
19						
20	31	Wages Expense		4 5 0 00		Yes. A liability account with a zero balance has been increased.
21		Wages Payable			4 5 0 00	
22						
23	31	Unearned Subscriptions Revenue		10 0 0 0 00		No. No asset or liability with a zero balance has been increased.
24		Subscriptions Revenue			10 0 0 0 00	
25						

FIGURE 16-11   Which Adjusting Entries to Reverse?

	GENERAL JOURNAL				PAGE 7
	DATE	DESCRIPTION	POST REF.	DEBIT	CREDIT
1		Reversing Entries			1
2	20-- Jan. 1	Wages Payable		4 5 0 00	2
3		Wages Expense			4 5 0 00	3
4					4
5					5

FIGURE 16-12   Reversing Entry for Northern Micro

Learning Objectives	Key Points to Remember
1 **Prepare a single-step and multiple-step income statement for a merchandising business.**	The general format for a single-step and multiple-step income statement is shown below.

Single-Step
Income Statement
For Year Ended December 31, 20--

Revenues:		
List all revenues	$xxx	
Total revenues		$xxx
Expenses:		
Cost of goods sold	$xxx	
List all other expenses	xxx	
Total expenses		xxx
Net income		$xxx

Multiple-Step
Income Statement
For Year Ended December 31, 20--

Revenue from sales:			
Sales		$xxx	
Less sales returns and allowances		xxx	
Net sales			$xxx
Cost of goods sold			xxx
Gross profit			$xxx
Operating expenses:			
List all operating expenses		$xxx	
Total operating expenses			xxx
Income from operations			$xxx
Other revenue:			
List all other revenue		$xxx	
Total other revenue		$xxx	
Other expenses:			
List all other expenses	$xxx		
Total other expenses		xxx	xxx
Net income			$xxx

Learning Objectives	Key Points to Remember
2 Prepare a statement of owner's equity.	A statement of owner's equity has the following format:

Business Name
Statement of Owner's Equity
For Year Ended December 31, 20--

Capital, January 1, 20--		$xxx
Add additional investments		xxx
Total investment		$xxx
Net income for the year	$xxx	
Less withdrawals	xxx	
Increase in capital		xxx
Capital, December 31, 20--		$xxx

3 Prepare a classified balance sheet.

A classified balance sheet has the following major headings:

Business Name
Balance Sheet
December 31, 20--

Assets

Current assets:			
All are listed		$xxx	
Total current assets			$xxx
Property, plant, and equipment:			
All are listed	$xxx		
Less accumulated depreciation (if appropriate)	xxx	$xxx	
Total property, plant, and equipment			xxx
Total assets			$xxx

Liabilities

Current liabilities:			
All are listed		$xxx	
Total current liabilities			$xxx
Long-term liabilities:			
All are listed		$xxx	
Total long-term liabilities			xxx
Total liabilities			$xxx

Owner's Equity

Owner's capital	xxx
Total liabilities and owner's equity	$xxx

4 Compute standard financial ratios.

The following measures of financial condition may be computed from financial statement information.

Working Capital	=	Current Assets − Current Liabilities
Current Ratio	=	Current Assets ÷ Current Liabilities
Quick Ratio	=	Quick Assets ÷ Current Liabilities
Return on Owner's Equity	=	Net Income ÷ Average Owner's Equity
Accounts Receivable Turnover	=	$\dfrac{\text{Net Credit Sales for the Period}}{\text{Average Accounts Receivable}}$
Average Collection Period	=	$\dfrac{365}{\text{Accounts Receivable Turnover}}$
Inventory Turnover	=	$\dfrac{\text{Cost of Goods Sold for the Period}}{\text{Average Inventory}}$

Learning Objectives	Key Points to Remember
	$$\text{Average Days to Sell Inventory} \quad = \quad \frac{365}{\text{Inventory Turnover}}$$
5 Prepare closing entries for a merchandising business.	There are four steps in the closing process for a merchandising business:
	STEP 1 All income statement accounts with credit balances are debited, with an offsetting credit to Income Summary.
	STEP 2 All income statement accounts with debit balances are credited, with an offsetting debit to Income Summary.
	STEP 3 The resulting balance in Income Summary, which is the net income or loss for the period, is transferred to the owner's capital account.
	STEP 4 The balance in the owner's drawing account is transferred to the owner's capital account.
6 Prepare reversing entries.	Use the following rule to determine which adjusting entries to reverse:
	Except for the first year of operations, reverse all adjusting entries that increase an asset or liability account from a zero balance.

Reflection: Answering the Opening Question

As discussed in this chapter, Betty has made reversing entries for the payroll. Thus, it is not necessary for Evan to be concerned about the proper payroll allocation between last year's and this year's financial statements.

DEMONSTRATION PROBLEM

Tom McKinney owns and operates McK's Home Electronics. He has a store where he sells and repairs televisions and stereo equipment. A completed work sheet for 20-1 is provided on page 615. McKinney made a $20,000 additional investment during 20-1. The current portion of Mortgage Payable is $1,000. Net credit sales for 20-1 were $200,000, and the balance of Accounts Receivable on January 1 was $26,000.

REQUIRED

1. Prepare a multiple-step income statement.

2. Prepare a statement of owner's equity.

(continued)

3. Prepare a balance sheet.

4. Compute the following measures of performance and financial condition for 20-1:

    a. current ratio

    b. quick ratio

    c. working capital

    d. return on owner's equity

    e. accounts receivable turnover and the average number of days required to collect receivables

    f. inventory turnover and the average number of days required to sell inventory

5. Prepare adjusting entries and indicate which should be reversed and why.

6. Prepare closing entries.

7. Prepare reversing entries for the adjustments where appropriate.

McK's Home Electronics
Work Sheet
For Year Ended December 31, 20-1

Account Title	Trial Balance Debit	Trial Balance Credit	Adjustments Debit	Adjustments Credit	Adjusted Trial Balance Debit	Adjusted Trial Balance Credit	Income Statement Debit	Income Statement Credit	Balance Sheet Debit	Balance Sheet Credit
Cash	10 000 00				10 000 00				10 000 00	
Accounts Receivable	22 500 00				22 500 00				22 500 00	
Merchandise Inventory	39 000 00		(b) 45 000 00	(a) 39 000 00	45 000 00				45 000 00	
Supplies	2 700 00			(c) 2 100 00	600 00				600 00	
Prepaid Insurance	3 600 00			(d) 2 700 00	900 00				900 00	
Land	15 000 00				15 000 00				15 000 00	
Building	135 000 00				135 000 00				135 000 00	
Accum. Depr.—Building		24 000 00		(e) 6 000 00		30 000 00				30 000 00
Store Equipment	75 000 00				75 000 00				75 000 00	
Accum. Depr.—Store Equipment		22 500 00		(f) 4 500 00		27 000 00				27 000 00
Notes Payable		7 500 00				7 500 00				7 500 00
Accounts Payable		15 000 00				15 000 00				15 000 00
Wages Payable				(g) 675 00		675 00				675 00
Sales Tax Payable		2 250 00				2 250 00				2 250 00
Unearned Repair Fees		18 000 00	(h) 15 000 00			3 000 00				3 000 00
Mortgage Payable		45 000 00				45 000 00				45 000 00
Tom McKinney, Capital		151 600 00				151 600 00				151 600 00
Tom McKinney, Drawing	30 000 00				30 000 00				30 000 00	
Income Summary			(a) 39 000 00	(b) 45 000 00	39 000 00	45 000 00	39 000 00	45 000 00		
Sales		300 750 00				300 750 00		300 750 00		
Sales Returns and Allowances	1 800 00				1 800 00		1 800 00			
Repair Fees				(h) 15 000 00		15 000 00		15 000 00		
Interest Revenue		1 350 00				1 350 00		1 350 00		
Purchases	157 500 00				157 500 00		157 500 00			
Purchases Returns and Allowances		1 200 00				1 200 00		1 200 00		
Purchases Discounts		1 500 00				1 500 00		1 500 00		
Freight-In	450 00				450 00		450 00			
Wages Expense	63 000 00		(g) 675 00		63 675 00		63 675 00			
Advertising Expense	3 750 00				3 750 00		3 750 00			
Supplies Expense			(c) 2 100 00		2 100 00		2 100 00			
Telephone Expense	5 250 00				5 250 00		5 250 00			
Utilities Expense	18 000 00				18 000 00		18 000 00			
Insurance Expense			(d) 2 700 00		2 700 00		2 700 00			
Depr. Expense—Building			(e) 6 000 00		6 000 00		6 000 00			
Depr. Expense—Store Equipment			(f) 4 500 00		4 500 00		4 500 00			
Miscellaneous Expense	3 375 00				3 375 00		3 375 00			
Interest Expense	4 725 00				4 725 00		4 725 00			
	590 650 00	590 650 00	114 975 00	114 975 00	646 825 00	646 825 00	312 825 00	364 800 00	334 000 00	282 025 00
Net Income							51 975 00			51 975 00
							364 800 00	364 800 00	334 000 00	334 000 00

(continued)

Solution

1.

McK's Home Electronics Income Statement For Year Ended December 31, 20 -1					
Revenue from sales:					
Sales			$300 7 5 0 00		
Less sales returns and allowances			1 8 0 0 00		
Net sales				$298 9 5 0 00	
Cost of goods sold:					
Merchandise inventory, January 1, 20-1			$ 39 0 0 0 00		
Purchases		$157 5 0 0 00			
Less: Purchases returns and allowances	$1 2 0 0 00				
Purchases discounts	1 5 0 0 00	2 7 0 0 00			
Net purchases		$154 8 0 0 00			
Add freight-in		4 5 0 00			
Cost of goods purchased			155 2 5 0 00		
Goods available for sale			$194 2 5 0 00		
Less merchandise inventory, December 31, 20-1			45 0 0 0 00		
Cost of goods sold				149 2 5 0 00	
Gross profit				$149 7 0 0 00	
Operating expenses:					
Wages expense			$ 63 6 7 5 00		
Advertising expense			3 7 5 0 00		
Supplies expense			2 1 0 0 00		
Telephone expense			5 2 5 0 00		
Utilities expense			18 0 0 0 00		
Insurance expense			2 7 0 0 00		
Depreciation expense—building			6 0 0 0 00		
Depreciation expense—store equipment			4 5 0 0 00		
Miscellaneous expense			3 3 7 5 00		
Total operating expenses				109 3 5 0 00	
Income from operations				$ 40 3 5 0 00	
Other revenues:					
Repair fees			$ 15 0 0 0 00		
Interest revenue			1 3 5 0 00		
Total other revenues			$ 16 3 5 0 00		
Other expenses:					
Interest expense			4 7 2 5 00	11 6 2 5 00	
Net income				$ 51 9 7 5 00	

2.

McK's Home Electronics Statement of Owner's Equity For Year Ended December 31, 20 -1			
Tom McKinney, capital, January 1, 20-1		$131 6 0 0 00	
Add additional investments		20 0 0 0 00	
Total investment		$151 6 0 0 00	
Net income for the year	$51 9 7 5 00		
Less withdrawals	30 0 0 0 00		
Increase in capital		21 9 7 5 00	
Tom McKinney, capital, December 31, 20-1		$173 5 7 5 00	

3.

McK's Home Electronics
Balance Sheet
December 31, 20 -1

Assets

Current assets:			
Cash	$ 10 0 0 0 00		
Accounts receivable	22 5 0 0 00		
Merchandise inventory	45 0 0 0 00		
Supplies	6 0 0 00		
Prepaid insurance	9 0 0 00		
Total current assets			$ 79 0 0 0 00
Property, plant and equipment:			
Land	$ 15 0 0 0 00		
Building	$135 0 0 0 00		
Less accumulated depreciation	30 0 0 0 00	105 0 0 0 00	
Store equipment	$ 75 0 0 0 00		
Less accumulated depreciation	27 0 0 0 00	48 0 0 0 00	
Total property, plant and equipment			168 0 0 0 00
Total assets			$247 0 0 0 00

Liabilities

Current liabilities:			
Notes payable	$ 7 5 0 0 00		
Accounts payable	15 0 0 0 00		
Wages payable	6 7 5 00		
Sales tax payable	2 2 5 0 00		
Unearned repair fees	3 0 0 0 00		
Mortgage payable (current portion)	1 0 0 0 00		
Total current liabilities		$ 29 4 2 5 00	
Long-term liabilities:			
Mortgage payable	$45 0 0 0 00		
Less current portion	1 0 0 0 00	44 0 0 0 00	
Total liabilities			$ 73 4 2 5 00

Owner's Equity

Tom McKinney, capital		173 5 7 5 00
Total liabilities and owner's equity		$247 0 0 0 00

4.

a. Current Ratio = Current Assets ÷ Current Liabilities
   = $79,000 ÷ $29,425 = 2.68 to 1

b. Quick Ratio = Quick Assets ÷ Current Liabilities
   = $32,500 ÷ $29,425 = 1.10 to 1

c. Working Capital = Current Assets − Current Liabilities
   = $79,000 − $29,425 = $49,575

d. Return on Owner's Equity = Net Income ÷ Average Owner's Equity

$$= \frac{\$51,975}{(\$131,600 + \$173,575) \div 2}$$

= $51,975 ÷ $152,587.50

= 34%

(continued)

e. Accounts Receivable Turnover $= \dfrac{\text{Net Credit Sales for the Period}}{\text{Average Accounts Receivable}}$

$$= \dfrac{\$200{,}000}{(\$26{,}000 + \$22{,}500) \div 2}$$

$$= \$200{,}000 \div \$24{,}250$$

$$= 8.25$$

Average number of days to collect an account receivable:
$365 \div 8.25 = 44.24$ days

f. Inventory Turnover $= \dfrac{\text{Cost of Goods Sold for the Period}}{\text{Average Inventory}}$

$$= \dfrac{\$149{,}250}{(\$39{,}000 + \$45{,}000) \div 2}$$

$$= \$149{,}250 \div \$42{,}000$$

$$= 3.6$$

Average number of days to sell inventory:
$365 \div 3.6 = 101.39$ days

5.

GENERAL JOURNAL PAGE 3

	DATE	DESCRIPTION	POST REF.	DEBIT	CREDIT	
1		Adjusting Entries				1
2	20-1 Dec. 31	Income Summary		39 0 0 0 00		2
3		Merchandise Inventory			39 0 0 0 00	3
4						4
5	31	Merchandise Inventory		45 0 0 0 00		5
6		Income Summary			45 0 0 0 00	6
7						7
8	31	Supplies Expense		2 1 0 0 00		8
9		Supplies			2 1 0 0 00	9
10						10
11	31	Insurance Expense		2 7 0 0 00		11
12		Prepaid Insurance			2 7 0 0 00	12
13						13
14	31	Depr. Expense—Building		6 0 0 0 00		14
15		Accum. Depr.—Building			6 0 0 0 00	15
16						16
17	31	Depr. Expense—Store Equipment		4 5 0 0 00		17
18		Accum. Depr.—Store Equipment			4 5 0 0 00	18
19						19
20	31	Wages Expense		6 7 5 00		20
21		Wages Payable			6 7 5 00	21
22						22
23	31	Unearned Repair Fees		15 0 0 0 00		23
24		Repair Fees			15 0 0 0 00	24
25						25

SHOULD THE ADJUSTMENT BE REVERSED?

Never reverse adjustments for merchandise inventory.

Never reverse adjustments for merchandise inventory.

No. No asset or liability with a zero balance has been increased.

No. No asset or liability with a zero balance has been increased.

Never reverse adjustments for depreciation.

Never reverse adjustments for depreciation.

Yes. A liability account with a zero balance has been increased.

No. No asset or liability with a zero balance has been increased.

6.

	GENERAL JOURNAL				PAGE 4	
	DATE	DESCRIPTION	POST. REF.	DEBIT	CREDIT	
1		Closing Entries				1
2	20-1 Dec. 31	Repair Fees		15 0 0 0 00		2
3		Sales		300 7 5 0 00		3
4		Interest Revenue		1 3 5 0 00		4
5		Purchases Returns and Allowances		1 2 0 0 00		5
6		Purchases Discounts		1 5 0 0 00		6
7		Income Summary			319 8 0 0 00	7
8						8
9	31	Income Summary		273 8 2 5 00		9
10		Sales Returns and Allowances			1 8 0 0 00	10
11		Purchases			157 5 0 0 00	11
12		Freight-In			4 5 0 00	12
13		Wages Expense			63 6 7 5 00	13
14		Advertising Expense			3 7 5 0 00	14
15		Supplies Expense			2 1 0 0 00	15
16		Telephone Expense			5 2 5 0 00	16
17		Utilities Expense			18 0 0 0 00	17
18		Insurance Expense			2 7 0 0 00	18
19		Depr. Expense—Building			6 0 0 0 00	19
20		Depr. Expense—Store Equipment			4 5 0 0 00	20
21		Miscellaneous Expense			3 3 7 5 00	21
22		Interest Expense			4 7 2 5 00	22
23						23
24	31	Income Summary		51 9 7 5 00		24
25		Tom McKinney, Capital			51 9 7 5 00	25
26						26
27	31	Tom McKinney, Capital		30 0 0 0 00		27
28		Tom McKinney, Drawing			30 0 0 0 00	28
29						29

7.

	GENERAL JOURNAL				PAGE 5	
	DATE	DESCRIPTION	POST. REF.	DEBIT	CREDIT	
1		Reversing Entries				1
2	20-2 Jan. 1	Wages Payable		6 7 5 00		2
3		Wages Expense			6 7 5 00	3
4						4

On-Line Learning Tools

For more information, visit: http://heintz.swlearning.com

The Heintz & Parry product web site is designed specifically for **COLLEGE ACCOUNTING, 18e.** The features include downloadable student resources and an interactive study center, organized by chapter, which contains learning objectives, web links, on-line quizzes with automatic feedback, and more.

KEY TERMS

accounts receivable turnover, (604)   The number of times the accounts receivable turned over, or were collected, during the accounting period. When 365 is divided by the turnover, this measure can be expressed in terms of the average number of days required to collect receivables.

average collection period, (605)   The number of days in the year (365) divided by the accounts receivable turnover. Provides an indication of the number of days credit customers take to pay for their purchases.

average days to sell inventory, (606)   The number of days in the year (365) divided by the inventory turnover. Provides an indication of the average number of days required to sell inventory.

book value, (602)   See undepreciated cost.

current assets, (602)   Cash and all other assets expected to be converted into cash or consumed within one year or the normal operating cycle of the business, whichever is longer.

current liabilities, (602)   Those obligations that are due within one year or the normal operating cycle of the business, whichever is longer, and will require the use of current assets.

current ratio, (603)   Current assets divided by current liabilities.

general expenses, (598)   Those expenses associated with administrative, office, or general operating activities.

gross margin, (596)   See gross profit.

gross profit, (596)   Net sales minus cost of goods sold.

income from operations, (596)   Gross profit minus operating expenses on a multiple-step income statement.

interstatement analysis, (604)   Compares the relationship between certain amounts in the income statement and balance sheet.

inventory turnover, (605)   The number of times the merchandise inventory turned over, or was sold, during the accounting period. When 365 is divided by the turnover, this measure can be expressed in terms of the average number of days required to sell inventory.

liquidity, (602)   Refers to the speed with which an asset can be converted to cash.

long-term liabilities, (602)   Those obligations that will extend beyond one year or the normal operating cycle, whichever is longer.

mortgage, (602)   A written agreement specifying that if the borrower does not repay a debt, the lender has the right to take over specific property to satisfy the debt.

Mortgage Payable, (602)   An account that is used to reflect an obligation that is secured by a mortgage on certain property.

multiple-step income statement, (596)   This statement shows a step-by-step calculation of net sales, cost of goods sold, gross profit, operating expenses, income from operations, other revenues and expenses, and net income.

net sales, (596)   Gross sales less sales returns and allowances and less sales discounts.

operating cycle, (602)   The length of time generally required for a business to buy inventory, sell it, and collect the cash.

operating income, (596)   See income from operations.

post-closing trial balance, (608)   A trial balance taken after the temporary owner's equity accounts have been closed.

property, plant, and equipment, (602)   Assets that are expected to be used for more than one year in the operation of a business.

quick assets, (604)   Cash and all other current assets that can be converted into cash quickly, such as accounts receivable and temporary investments.

quick ratio, (603)   Quick assets divided by current liabilities.

return on owner's equity, (604)   Net income divided by average owner's equity.

reversing entry, (608)   The opposite of the adjusting entry. It is made on the first day of the next accounting period and simplifies recording transactions in the new period.

selling expenses, (596)   Those expenses directly associated with selling activities.

single-step income statement, (596)   This statement lists all revenue items and their total first, followed by all expense items and their total.

undepreciated cost, (602)   Cost of plant and equipment less the accumulated depreciation amounts. Also called book value.

working capital, (603)   The difference between current assets and current liabilities, which represents the amount of capital the business has available for current operations.

REVIEW QUESTIONS

(LO1)   1.   Describe the nature of the two forms of an income statement.

(LO4)   2.   Name and describe the calculation of two measures that provide an indication of a business's ability to pay current obligations.

(LO4)   3.   Describe how to calculate the following ratios:

    a.   return on owner's equity

    b.   accounts receivable turnover

    c.   inventory turnover

(LO5)   4.   Where is the information obtained that is needed in journalizing the closing entries?

(LO5)   5.   Explain the function of each of the four closing entries made by Northern Micro.

(LO5)   6.   What is the purpose of a post-closing trial balance?

(LO6)   7.   What is the primary purpose of reversing entries?

(LO6)   8.   What is the customary date for reversing entries?

(LO6)   9.   What adjusting entries should be reversed?

Self-Study Test Questions

True/False

1.   A multiple-step form of income statement calculates gross profit, before subtracting operating expenses.   _____

2.   Current assets include cash, items expected to convert into cash, and items that will be consumed during a year or the normal operating cycle, whichever is shorter.   _____

3.   Current assets are listed on the balance sheet in order of liquidity.   _____

Interactive Learning: **http://heintz.swlearning.com**

Self-Study Test Questions *(continued)*

4. Working capital is the difference between current assets and current liabilities.   _____

5. Accounts receivable turnover is the number of times merchandise inventory turned over or was sold during the accounting period.   _____

Multiple Choice

1. Which of these assets is *not* a current asset?   _____

    (a) Cash   (c) Office Equipment
    (b) Accounts Receivable   (d) Merchandise Inventory

2. Which of these would be listed *first* on a balance sheet?   _____

    (a) Accounts Receivable   (c) Accounts Payable
    (b) Delivery Equipment   (d) Prepaid Insurance

3. Which of these is considered a *quick asset*?   _____

    (a) Merchandise Inventory   (c) Office Equipment
    (b) Accounts Receivable   (d) Prepaid Insurance

4. To calculate the accounts receivable turnover ratio, _____ is divided by average accounts receivable.   _____

    (a) Net sales   (c) Total sales
    (b) Cost of goods sold   (d) Net credit sales

5. Inventory turnover is calculated by dividing cost of goods sold by   _____

    (a) average accounts receivable.
    (b) average owner's equity.
    (c) average inventory.
    (d) accounts receivable turnover.

The answers to the Self-Study Test Questions are at the end of the text.

MANAGING YOUR WRITING

A friend of yours has the opportunity to invest in a small business. She has come to you for advice on how she might determine whether this would be a good investment. In particular, she is concerned about how long it takes to sell the merchandise and collect receivables. Draft a memo suggesting various ratios that should be computed to evaluate the business's profitability, ability to pay its current obligations, and time required to sell inventory and collect receivables.

ETHICS CASE

Brian Marlow recently was hired to prepare Louise Michener Consulting's year-end financial statements. Brian just earned his CPA certificate, and Louise Michener was one of his first clients. Louise employs a bookkeeper, Martha Halling, who does the daily journal entries and prepares a year-to-date trial balance at the end of each month. Martha gives the December 31 trial balance to a CPA to make the adjustments and generate the financial statements. As Brian was looking through Louise Michener's books he noticed two things. First, in each of the last three years a different CPA had prepared the financial statements. Second, the amount shown on the December 31 trial balance for miscellaneous expense was quite high this year compared to prior years. Brian called Martha to find out if she knew why miscellaneous expense had such a high balance. Martha's response was "I just do what Louise tells me to do. If she wants to charge personal expenses to the company, it's none of my business."

1. What should Brian do?

2. How might Brian's decision affect Martha? Has Martha done anything unethical?

3. Write a short letter from Brian to Louise explaining why personal items should not be charged to a business.

4. In small groups, discuss the ethical responsibilities of an accountant relating to a client's books.

WEB WORK

Annual reports show a variety of financial statements. Find two companies you are interested in, merchandising or otherwise, and study the formats used for their financial statements. Be prepared to discuss your findings in class. Visit the Interactive Study Center on our web site at **http://heintz.swlearning.com** for special hotlinks to assist you in this assignment.

SERIES A EXERCISES

EXERCISE 16-1A   **(LO1)**

Net sales: $133,700

REVENUE SECTION, MULTIPLE-STEP INCOME STATEMENT Based on the information that follows, prepare the revenue section of a multiple-step income statement.

Sales	$140,000
Sales Returns and Allowances	3,500
Sales Discounts	2,800

EXERCISE 16-2A   **(LO1)**

Cost of goods sold: $102,560

COST OF GOODS SOLD SECTION, MULTIPLE-STEP INCOME STATEMENT Based on the information that follows, prepare the cost of goods sold section of a multiple-step income statement.

Merchandise Inventory, January 1, 20--	$ 34,000
Purchases	102,000
Purchases Returns and Allowances	4,200
Purchases Discounts	2,040
Freight-In	800
Merchandise Inventory, December 31, 20--	28,000

EXERCISE 16-3A   **(LO1)**

Cost of goods sold: $87,860;
Net income: $15,634

MULTIPLE-STEP INCOME STATEMENT Use the following information to prepare a multiple-step income statement, including the revenue section and the cost of goods sold section, for Rau Office Supplies for the year ended December 31, 20--.

Sales	$148,300
Sales Returns and Allowances	1,380
Sales Discounts	2,166
Interest Revenue	240
Merchandise Inventory, January 1, 20--	26,500
Purchases	98,000
Purchases Returns and Allowances	2,180
Purchases Discounts	1,960
Freight-In	750
Merchandise Inventory, December 31, 20--	33,250
Wages Expense	23,800
Supplies Expense	900
Telephone Expense	1,100
Utilities Expense	7,000
Insurance Expense	1,000
Depreciation Expense—Equipment	3,100
Miscellaneous Expense	720
Interest Expense	3,880

EXERCISE 16-4A   **(LO5)**

CLOSING ENTRIES From the work sheet on page 625, prepare closing entries for Gimbel's Gifts and Gadgets in a general journal.

EXERCISE 16-5A   **(LO6)**

REVERSING ENTRIES From the work sheet used in Exercise 16-4A, identify the adjusting entry(ies) that should be reversed and prepare the reversing entry(ies).

EXERCISE 16-6A   **(LO5/6)**

ADJUSTING, CLOSING, AND REVERSING ENTRIES Based on the information that follows, prepare two sets of entries—one that will have a reversing entry and the other without a reversing entry. Enter existing balances and post all entries to two sets of T accounts for Wages Expense and Wages Payable.

a. Wages paid during 20-1 are $20,800.

b. Wages earned but not paid (accrued) as of December 31, 20-1, are $300.

c. On January 3, 20-2, payroll of $800 is paid, which includes the $300 of wages earned but not paid in December.

Gimbel's Gifts and Gadgets
Work Sheet
For Year Ended December 31, 20--

#	Account Title	Trial Balance Debit	Trial Balance Credit	Adjustments Debit	Adjustments Credit	Adjusted Trial Balance Debit	Adjusted Trial Balance Credit	Income Statement Debit	Income Statement Credit	Balance Sheet Debit	Balance Sheet Credit
1	Cash	8,214.00				8,214.00				8,214.00	
2	Accounts Receivable	6,720.00				6,720.00				6,720.00	
3	Merchandise Inventory	14,210.00		(b) 16,800.00	(a) 14,210.00	16,800.00				16,800.00	
4	Supplies	6,800.00			(c) 3,800.00	3,000.00				3,000.00	
5	Prepaid Insurance	8,000.00			(d) 2,000.00	6,000.00				6,000.00	
6	Building	71,900.00				71,900.00				71,900.00	
7	Accum. Depr.—Building		13,600.00		(e) 4,000.00		17,600.00				17,600.00
8	Accounts Payable		5,280.00				5,280.00				5,280.00
9	Wages Payable				(f) 280.00		280.00				280.00
10	Sales Tax Payable		326.00				326.00				326.00
11	J.M. Gimbel, Capital		87,883.00				87,883.00				87,883.00
12	J.M. Gimbel, Drawing	8,000.00				8,000.00				8,000.00	
13	Income Summary			(a) 14,210.00	(b) 16,800.00	14,210.00	16,800.00	14,210.00	16,800.00		
14	Sales		86,000.00				86,000.00		86,000.00		
15	Sales Returns and Allowances	1,840.00				1,840.00		1,840.00			
16	Purchases	50,870.00				50,870.00		50,870.00			
17	Purchases Returns and Allowances		2,813.00				2,813.00		2,813.00		
18	Purchases Discounts		1,084.00				1,084.00		1,084.00		
19	Freight-In	800.00				800.00		800.00			
20	Wages Expense	16,800.00		(f) 280.00		17,080.00		17,080.00			
21	Advertising Expense	784.00				784.00		784.00			
22	Supplies Expense			(c) 3,800.00		3,800.00		3,800.00			
23	Telephone Expense	210.00				210.00		210.00			
24	Utilities Expense	1,310.00				1,310.00		1,310.00			
25	Insurance Expense			(d) 2,000.00		2,000.00		2,000.00			
26	Depr. Expense—Building			(e) 4,000.00		4,000.00		4,000.00			
27	Miscellaneous Expense	386.00				386.00		386.00			
28	Interest Expense	142.00				142.00		142.00			
29		196,986.00	196,986.00	41,090.00	41,090.00	218,066.00	218,066.00	97,432.00	106,697.00	120,634.00	111,369.00
30	Net Income							9,265.00			9,265.00
31								106,697.00	106,697.00	120,634.00	120,634.00

EXERCISE 16-4A

EXERCISE 16-7A (LO4)
Current ratio: 4.64 to 1;
Return on owner's equity: 28.9%;
Inventory turnover: 3.13

FINANCIAL RATIOS Based on the financial statements for Jackson Enterprises (income statement, statement of owner's equity, and balance sheet) shown below and on the next page, prepare the following financial ratios. All sales are credit sales. The Accounts Receivable balance on January 1, 20--, was $21,600.

1. Working capital

2. Current ratio

3. Quick ratio

4. Return on owner's equity

5. Accounts receivable turnover and average number of days required to collect receivables

6. Inventory turnover and average number of days required to sell inventory

Jackson Enterprises
Income Statement
For Year Ended December 31, 20 - -

Revenue from sales:					
Sales			$184 2 0 0 00		
Less sales returns and allowances			2 1 0 0 00		
Net sales				$182 1 0 0 00	
Cost of goods sold:					
Merchandise inventory, January 1, 20- -			$ 31 3 0 0 00		
Purchases		$92 8 0 0 00			
Less: Purchases returns and allowances	$ 1 8 0 0 00				
Purchases discounts	1 8 5 6 00	3 6 5 6 00			
Net purchases		$89 1 4 4 00			
Add freight-in		9 3 3 00			
Cost of goods purchased			90 0 7 7 00		
Goods available for sale			$121 3 7 7 00		
Less merchandise inventory, December 31, 20- -			28 1 7 7 00		
Cost of goods sold				93 2 0 0 00	
Gross profit				$ 88 9 0 0 00	
Operating expenses:					
Wages expense			$ 38 0 0 0 00		
Advertising expense			1 1 8 0 00		
Supplies expense			3 8 0 00		
Telephone expense			2 2 1 0 00		
Utilities expense			11 0 0 0 00		
Insurance expense			9 0 0 00		
Depreciation expense—building			4 0 0 0 00		
Depreciation expense—equipment			3 8 0 0 00		
Miscellaneous expense			5 3 0 00		
Total operating expenses				62 0 0 0 00	
Income from operations				$ 26 9 0 0 00	
Other revenues:					
Interest revenue			$ 1 8 0 0 00		
Other expenses:					
Interest expense			9 0 0 00	9 0 0 00	
Net income				$ 27 8 0 0 00	

Jackson Enterprises Statement of Owner's Equity For Year Ended December 31, 20 - -											
J. B. Gray, capital, January 1, 20- -							$ 88	0	0	0	00
Net income for the year	$27	8	0	0	00						
Less withdrawals for the year	11	6	0	0	00						
Increase in capital							16	2	0	0	00
J. B. Gray, capital, December 31, 20- -							$104	2	0	0	00

Jackson Enterprises Balance Sheet December 31, 20 - -																
Assets																
Current assets:																
Cash						$20	8	0	0	00						
Accounts receivable						18	9	0	0	00						
Merchandise inventory						28	1	7	7	00						
Supplies						1	3	2	3	00						
Prepaid insurance							9	0	0	00						
Total current assets											$ 70	1	0	0	00
Property, plant, and equipment:																
Building	$90	0	0	0	00											
Less accumulated depreciation	28	0	0	0	00	$62	0	0	0	00						
Equipment	$33	0	0	0	00											
Less accumulated depreciation	7	5	0	0	00	25	5	0	0	00						
Total property, plant, and equipment											87	5	0	0	00
Total assets											$157	6	0	0	00
Liabilities																
Current liabilities:																
Accounts payable	$12	6	0	0	00											
Wages payable		5	0	0	00											
Sales tax payable	1	2	0	0	00											
Mortgage payable (current portion)		8	0	0	00											
Total current liabilities						$15	1	0	0	00						
Long-term liabilities:																
Mortgage payable	$39	1	0	0	00											
Less current portion		8	0	0	00	38	3	0	0	00						
Total liabilities											$53	4	0	0	00
Owner's Equity																
J. B. Gray, capital											104	2	0	0	00
Total liabilities and owner's equity											$157	6	0	0	00

SERIES A PROBLEMS

PROBLEM 16-8A   (LO5/6)

Net income: $10,610; Post-closing trial bal. col. totals: $79,650

WORK SHEET, ADJUSTING, CLOSING AND REVERSING ENTRIES Ellis Fabric Store shows the trial balance on the following page as of December 31, 20--.

At the end of the year, the following adjustments need to be made.

(a, b)   Merchandise Inventory as of December 31, $28,900.

(c)   Unused supplies on hand, $1,350.

(d)   Insurance expired, $300.

(e) Depreciation expense for the year, $500.

(f) Wages earned but not paid (Wages Payable), $480.

Ellis Fabric Store
Trial Balance
For Year Ended December 31, 20 - -

ACCOUNT TITLE	DEBIT BALANCE					CREDIT BALANCE				
Cash	28	0	0	0	00					
Accounts Receivable	14	2	0	0	00					
Merchandise Inventory	33	0	0	0	00					
Supplies	1	6	0	0	00					
Prepaid Insurance		9	0	0	00					
Equipment	6	6	0	0	00					
Accumulated Depreciation—Equipment						1	0	0	0	00
Accounts Payable						16	6	2	0	00
Wages Payable										
Sales Tax Payable							8	5	0	00
W. P. Ellis, Capital						71	2	0	0	00
W. P. Ellis, Drawing	21	6	1	0	00					
Income Summary										
Sales						78	5	0	0	00
Sales Returns and Allowances	1	8	5	0	00					
Interest Revenue						1	2	0	0	00
Purchases	41	5	0	0	00					
Purchases Returns and Allowances						1	8	0	0	00
Purchases Discounts							8	3	0	00
Freight-In		6	6	0	00					
Wages Expense	14	8	8	0	00					
Advertising Expense		8	1	0	00					
Supplies Expense										
Telephone Expense	1	2	1	0	00					
Utilities Expense	3	2	4	0	00					
Insurance Expense										
Depreciation Expense—Equipment										
Miscellaneous Expense		9	2	0	00					
Interest Expense	1	0	2	0	00					
	172	0	0	0	00	172	0	0	0	00

REQUIRED

1. Prepare a work sheet.

2. Prepare adjusting entries.

3. Prepare closing entries.

4. Prepare a post-closing trial balance.

5. Prepare reversing entries.

PROBLEM 16-9A (LO1/2/3)

Cost of goods sold: $37,740;
Total assets: $39,850

INCOME STATEMENT, STATEMENT OF OWNER'S EQUITY, AND BALANCE SHEET Paulson's Pet Store completed the work sheet on page 630 for the year ended December 31, 20--. Owner's equity as of January 1, 20--, was $21,900. The current portion of Mortgage Payable is $500.

REQUIRED

1. Prepare a multiple-step income statement.

2. Prepare a statement of owner's equity.

3. Prepare a balance sheet.

PROBLEM 16-10A   (LO4)
Working capital: $29,200;
Quick ratio: 2.78 to 1;
Accts. receivable turnover: 22.86

FINANCIAL RATIOS Use the work sheet and financial statements prepared in Problem 16-9A. All sales are credit sales. The Accounts Receivable balance on January 1, 20--, was $3,800.

REQUIRED

Prepare the following financial ratios:

a. Working capital

b. Current ratio

c. Quick ratio

d. Return on owner's equity

e. Accounts receivable turnover and average number of days required to collect receivables

f. Inventory turnover and average number of days required to sell inventory

SERIES B EXERCISES

EXERCISE 16-1B   (LO1)
Net sales: $82,196

REVENUE SECTION, MULTIPLE-STEP INCOME STATEMENT Based on the information that follows, prepare the revenue section of a multiple-step income statement.

Sales	$86,200
Sales Returns and Allowances	2,280
Sales Discounts	1,724

EXERCISE 16-2B   (LO1)
Cost of goods sold: $59,442

COST OF GOODS SOLD SECTION, MULTIPLE-STEP INCOME STATEMENT Based on the information that follows, prepare the cost of goods sold section of a multiple-step income statement.

Merchandise Inventory, January 1, 20--	$13,800
Purchases	71,300
Purchases Returns and Allowances	3,188
Purchases Discounts	1,460
Freight-In	390
Merchandise Inventory, December 31, 20--	21,400

Paulson's Pet Store
Work Sheet
For Year Ended December 31, 20 - -

#	ACCOUNT TITLE	TRIAL BALANCE Debit	TRIAL BALANCE Credit	ADJUSTMENTS Debit	ADJUSTMENTS Credit	ADJUSTED TRIAL BALANCE Debit	ADJUSTED TRIAL BALANCE Credit	INCOME STATEMENT Debit	INCOME STATEMENT Credit	BALANCE SHEET Debit	BALANCE SHEET Credit
1	Cash	15 8 6 0 00				15 8 6 0 00				15 8 6 0 00	
2	Accounts Receivable	2 3 4 0 00				2 3 4 0 00				2 3 4 0 00	
3	Merchandise Inventory	15 0 0 0 00		(b) 16 5 0 0 00	(a) 15 0 0 0 00	16 5 0 0 00				16 5 0 0 00	
4	Supplies	8 0 0 00			(c) 2 0 0 00	6 0 0 00				6 0 0 00	
5	Prepaid Insurance	6 0 0 00			(d) 1 5 0 00	4 5 0 00				4 5 0 00	
6	Equipment	5 0 0 0 00				5 0 0 0 00				5 0 0 0 00	
7	Accum. Depr.—Equipment		4 5 0 00		(e) 4 5 0 00		9 0 0 00				9 0 0 00
8	Accounts Payable		4 8 9 0 00				4 8 9 0 00				4 8 9 0 00
9	Wages Payable				(f) 3 0 0 00		3 0 0 00				3 0 0 00
10	Sales Tax Payable		8 6 0 00				8 6 0 00				8 6 0 00
11	Mortgage Payable		4 0 0 0 00				4 0 0 0 00				4 0 0 0 00
12	B. Paulson, Capital		23 9 0 0 00				23 9 0 0 00				23 9 0 0 00
13	B. Paulson, Drawing	1 2 0 0 00				1 2 0 0 00				1 2 0 0 00	
14	Income Summary			(a) 15 0 0 0 00	(b) 16 5 0 0 00	15 0 0 0 00	16 5 0 0 00	15 0 0 0 00	16 5 0 0 00		
15	Sales		71 5 1 0 00				71 5 1 0 00		71 5 1 0 00		
16	Sales Returns and Allowances	1 3 4 0 00				1 3 4 0 00		1 3 4 0 00			
17	Purchases	40 6 6 0 00				40 6 6 0 00		40 6 6 0 00			
18	Purchases Returns and Allowances		1 0 2 0 00				1 0 2 0 00		1 0 2 0 00		
19	Purchases Discounts		8 0 0 00				8 0 0 00		8 0 0 00		
20	Freight-In	4 0 0 00				4 0 0 00		4 0 0 00			
21	Wages Expense	22 3 0 0 00		(f) 3 0 0 00		22 6 0 0 00		22 6 0 0 00			
22	Advertising Expense	3 0 0 00				3 0 0 00		3 0 0 00			
23	Supplies Expense			(c) 2 0 0 00		2 0 0 00		2 0 0 00			
24	Telephone Expense	6 8 4 00				6 8 4 00		6 8 4 00			
25	Utilities Expense	7 1 6 00				7 1 6 00		7 1 6 00			
26	Insurance Expense			(d) 1 5 0 00		1 5 0 00		1 5 0 00			
27	Depr. Expense—Equipment			(e) 4 5 0 00		4 5 0 00		4 5 0 00			
28	Miscellaneous Expense	1 5 0 00				1 5 0 00		1 5 0 00			
29	Interest Expense	8 0 00				8 0 00		8 0 00			
30		107 4 3 0 00	107 4 3 0 00	32 6 0 0 00	32 6 0 0 00	124 6 8 0 00	124 6 8 0 00	82 7 3 0 00	89 8 3 0 00	41 9 5 0 00	34 8 5 0 00
31	Net Income							7 1 0 0 00			7 1 0 0 00
32								89 8 3 0 00	89 8 3 0 00	41 9 5 0 00	41 9 5 0 00

PROBLEM 16-9A

EXERCISE 16-3B (LO1)
Cost of goods sold: $109,714;
Net income: $12,040

MULTIPLE-STEP INCOME STATEMENT Use the following information to prepare a multiple-step income statement, including the revenue section and the cost of goods sold section, for Aeito's Plumbing Supplies for the year ended December 31, 20--.

Sales	$166,000
Sales Returns and Allowances	1,620
Sales Discounts	3,320
Interest Revenue	3,184
Merchandise Inventory, January 1, 20--	33,200
Purchases	111,300
Purchases Returns and Allowances	3,600
Purchases Discounts	2,226
Freight-In	640
Merchandise Inventory, December 31, 20--	29,600
Wages Expense	22,000
Supplies Expense	650
Telephone Expense	1,100
Utilities Expense	9,000
Insurance Expense	1,000
Depreciation Expense—Building	4,600
Depreciation Expense—Equipment	2,800
Miscellaneous Expense	214
Interest Expense	1,126

EXERCISE 16-4B (LO5)

CLOSING ENTRIES From the work sheet on page 632, prepare closing entries for Balloons and Baubbles in a general journal.

EXERCISE 16-5B (LO6)

REVERSING ENTRIES From the work sheet in Exercise 16-4B, identify the adjusting entry(ies) that should be reversed and prepare the reversing entry(ies).

EXERCISE 16-6B (LO5/6)

ADJUSTING, CLOSING, AND REVERSING ENTRIES Based on the information that follows, prepare two sets of entries—one that will have a reversing entry and the other without a reversing entry. Enter existing balances and post all entries to two sets of T accounts for Wages Expense and Wages Payable.

a. Wages paid during 20-1 are $20,080.

b. Wages earned but not paid (accrued) as of December 31, 20-1, are $280.

c. On January 3, 20-2, payroll of $840 is paid, which includes the $280 of wages earned but not paid in December.

Balloons and Baubbles
Work Sheet
For Year Ended December 31, 20- -

	Account Title	Trial Balance Debit	Trial Balance Credit	Adjustments Debit	Adjustments Credit	Adjusted Trial Balance Debit	Adjusted Trial Balance Credit	Income Statement Debit	Income Statement Credit	Balance Sheet Debit	Balance Sheet Credit
1	Cash	2 8 0 0 00				2 8 0 0 00				2 8 0 0 00	
2	Accounts Receivable	4 2 0 0 00				4 2 0 0 00				4 2 0 0 00	
3	Merchandise Inventory	8 6 0 0 00		(b) 7 5 0 0 00	(a) 8 6 0 0 00	7 5 0 0 00				7 5 0 0 00	
4	Supplies	7 8 0 0 00			(c) 2 8 0 00	5 0 0 0 00				5 0 0 0 00	
5	Prepaid Insurance	6 2 0 0 00			(d) 1 2 0 00	5 0 0 0 00				5 0 0 0 00	
6	Equipment	3 0 0 0 00				3 0 0 0 00				3 0 0 0 00	
7	Accum. Depr.—Equipment		6 0 0 00		(e) 3 0 0 00		9 0 0 00				9 0 0 00
8	Accounts Payable		1 8 0 0 00				1 8 0 0 00				1 8 0 0 00
9	Wages Payable				(f) 2 0 0 00		2 0 0 00				2 0 0 00
10	Sales Tax Payable		8 0 00				8 0 00				8 0 00
11	L. Marlow, Capital		12 2 0 0 00				12 2 0 0 00				12 2 0 0 00
12	L. Marlow, Drawing	2 0 0 0 00				2 0 0 0 00				2 0 0 0 00	
13	Income Summary			(a) 8 6 0 0 00	(b) 7 5 0 0 00	8 6 0 0 00	7 5 0 0 00	8 6 0 0 00	7 5 0 0 00		
14	Sales		31 0 0 0 00				31 0 0 0 00		31 0 0 0 00		
15	Sales Returns and Allowances	8 0 0 00				8 0 0 00		8 0 0 00			
16	Purchases	22 0 0 0 00				22 0 0 0 00		22 0 0 0 00			
17	Purchases Returns and Allowances		1 8 0 0 00				1 8 0 0 00		1 8 0 0 00		
18	Purchases Discounts		4 0 7 00				4 0 7 00		4 0 7 00		
19	Freight-In	2 0 0 0 00				2 0 0 0 00		2 0 0 0 00			
20	Wages Expense	1 2 0 0 00		(f) 2 0 0 00		1 4 0 0 00		1 4 0 0 00			
21	Advertising Expense	3 0 0 00				3 0 0 00		3 0 0 00			
22	Supplies Expense			(c) 2 8 0 00		2 8 0 00		2 8 0 00			
23	Telephone Expense	7 0 0 00				7 0 0 00		7 0 0 00			
24	Utilities Expense	4 8 0 00				4 8 0 00		4 8 0 00			
25	Insurance Expense			(d) 1 2 0 00		1 2 0 00		1 2 0 00			
26	Depr. Expense—Equipment			(e) 3 0 0 00		3 0 0 00		3 0 0 00			
27	Miscellaneous Expense	1 1 0 00				1 1 0 00		1 1 0 00			
28	Interest Expense	9 7 00				9 7 00		9 7 00			
29		47 8 8 7 00	47 8 8 7 00	17 0 0 0 00	17 0 0 0 00	55 8 8 7 00	55 8 8 7 00	35 3 8 7 00	40 7 0 7 00	20 5 0 0 00	15 1 8 0 00
30	Net Income							5 3 2 0 00			5 3 2 0 00
31								40 7 0 7 00	40 7 0 7 00	20 5 0 0 00	20 5 0 0 00

EXERCISE 16-4B

EXERCISE 16-7B   (LO4)

Current ratio: 3.68 to 1;
Return on owner's equity: 42.6%;
Inventory turnover: 3.42

FINANCIAL RATIOS Based on the financial statements shown below and on the next page for McDonald Carpeting Co. (income statement, statement of owner's equity, and balance sheet), prepare the following financial ratios. All sales are credit sales. The balance of accounts receivable on January 1, 20--, was $6,800.

1. Working capital

2. Current ratio

3. Quick ratio

4. Return on owner's equity

5. Accounts receivable turnover and the average number of days required to collect receivables

6. Inventory turnover and the average number of days required to sell inventory

McDonald Carpeting Co. Income Statement For Year Ended December 31, 20--				
Revenue from sales:				
Sales			$122 800 00	
Less sales returns and allowances			1 100 00	
Net sales				$121 700 00
Cost of goods sold:				
Merchandise inventory, January 1, 20--			$ 19 300 00	
Purchases		$62 800 00		
Less: Purchases returns and allowances	$2 800 00			
Purchases discounts	1 944 00	4 744 00		
Net purchases		$58 056 00		
Add freight-in		944 00		
Cost of goods purchased			59 000 00	
Goods available for sale			$ 78 300 00	
Less merchandise inventory, December 31, 20--			16 700 00	
Cost of goods sold				61 600 00
Gross profit				$ 60 100 00
Operating expenses:				
Wages expense			$ 18 000 00	
Advertising expense			9 80 00	
Supplies expense			3 20 00	
Telephone expense			1 200 00	
Utilities expense			8 000 00	
Insurance expense			800 00	
Depreciation expense—building			3 500 00	
Depreciation expense—equipment			2 500 00	
Miscellaneous expense			2 000 00	
Total operating expenses				35 500 00
Income from operations				$ 24 600 00
Other revenues:				
Interest revenue			$ 2 800 00	
Other expenses:				
Interest expense			2 100 00	700 00
Net income				$ 25 300 00

(continued)

McDonald Carpeting Co.
Statement of Owner's Equity
For Year Ended December 31, 20 - -

C. S. McDonald, capital, January 1, 20- -			$52 0 0 0 00
Net income for the year	$25 3 0 0 00		
Less withdrawals for the year	10 4 0 0 00		
Increase in capital			14 9 0 0 00
C. S. McDonald, capital, December 31, 20- -			$66 9 0 0 00

McDonald Carpeting Co.
Balance Sheet
December 31, 20 - -

Assets			
Current assets:			
Cash		$10 4 0 0 00	
Accounts receivable		8 9 0 0 00	
Merchandise inventory		16 7 0 0 00	
Supplies		1 2 0 0 00	
Prepaid insurance		7 0 0 00	
Total current assets			$37 9 0 0 00
Property, plant, and equipment:			
Building	$60 0 0 0 00		
Less accumulated depreciation—building	18 0 0 0 00	42 0 0 0 00	
Equipment	$22 0 0 0 00		
Less accumulated depreciation—equipment	6 2 0 0 00	15 8 0 0 00	
Total property, plant, and equipment			57 8 0 0 00
Total assets			$95 7 0 0 00
Liabilities			
Current liabilities:			
Accounts payable	$ 8 4 0 0 00		
Wages payable	3 0 0 00		
Sales tax payable	1 0 0 0 00		
Mortgage payable (current portion)	6 0 0 00		
Total current liabilities		$10 3 0 0 00	
Long-term liabilities:			
Mortgage payable	$19 1 0 0 00		
Less current portion	6 0 0 00	18 5 0 0 00	
Total liabilities			$28 8 0 0 00
Owner's Equity			
C. S. McDonald, capital			66 9 0 0 00
Total liabilities and owner's equity			$95 7 0 0 00

SERIES B PROBLEMS

PROBLEM 16-8B   (LO5/6)

Net income: $4,590; Post-closing
trial bal. columns: $53,500

WORK SHEET, ADJUSTING, CLOSING AND REVERSING ENTRIES The trial balance for Darby Kite Store as of December 31, 20-- is shown on the next page.

At the end of the year, the following adjustments need to be made.

(a, b)   Merchandise inventory as of December 31, $23,600.

(c)   Unused supplies on hand, $1,050.

(d)   Insurance expired, $250.

Darby Kite Store Trial Balance For Year Ended December 31, 20 - -										
ACCOUNT TITLE	\multicolumn{5}{c}{DEBIT BALANCE}	\multicolumn{5}{c}{CREDIT BALANCE}
Cash	11	7	0	0	00					
Accounts Receivable	11	2	0	0	00					
Merchandise Inventory	25	0	0	0	00					
Supplies	1	2	0	0	00					
Prepaid Insurance		8	0	0	00					
Equipment	5	4	0	0	00					
Accumulated Depreciation—Equipment							8	0	0	00
Accounts Payable						7	6	0	0	00
Wages Payable										
Sales Tax Payable							2	5	0	00
M. D. Akins, Capital						50	0	0	0	00
M. D. Akins, Drawing	10	5	0	0	00					
Income Summary										
Sales						57	9	9	0	00
Sales Returns and Allowances	1	4	5	0	00					
Purchases	34	5	0	0	00					
Purchases Returns and Allowances						1	1	0	0	00
Purchases Discounts							6	3	0	00
Freight-In		3	6	0	00					
Wages Expense	10	8	8	0	00					
Advertising Expense		7	4	0	00					
Supplies Expense										
Telephone Expense	1	1	0	0	00					
Utilities Expense	2	3	0	0	00					
Insurance Expense										
Depreciation Expense—Equipment										
Miscellaneous Expense		3	2	0	00					
Interest Expense		9	2	0	00					
	118	3	7	0	00	118	3	7	0	00

(e) Depreciation expense for the year, $400.

(f) Wages earned but not paid (Wages Payable), $360.

REQUIRED

1. Prepare a work sheet.
2. Prepare adjusting entries.
3. Prepare closing entries.
4. Prepare a post-closing trial balance.
5. Prepare reversing entries.

PROBLEM 16-9B (LO1/2/3)

Cost of goods sold: $75,350;
Total assets: $117,750

INCOME STATEMENT, STATEMENT OF OWNER'S EQUITY, AND BALANCE SHEET Backlund Farm Supply completed the work sheet on page 636 for the year ended December 31, 20--. Owner's equity as of January 1, 20--, was $50,000. The current portion of Mortgage Payable is $1,000.

REQUIRED

1. Prepare a multiple-step income statement.
2. Prepare a statement of owner's equity.
3. Prepare a balance sheet.

Backlund Farm Supply
Work Sheet
For Year Ended December 31, 20- -

	ACCOUNT TITLE	TRIAL BALANCE DEBIT	TRIAL BALANCE CREDIT	ADJUSTMENTS DEBIT	ADJUSTMENTS CREDIT	ADJUSTED TRIAL BALANCE DEBIT	ADJUSTED TRIAL BALANCE CREDIT	INCOME STATEMENT DEBIT	INCOME STATEMENT CREDIT	BALANCE SHEET DEBIT	BALANCE SHEET CREDIT
1	Cash	10 1 8 0 00				10 1 8 0 00				10 1 8 0 00	
2	Accounts Receivable	26 4 2 0 00				26 4 2 0 00				26 4 2 0 00	
3	Merchandise Inventory	42 1 6 0 00		(b) 44 3 0 0 00	(a) 42 1 6 0 00	44 3 0 0 00				44 3 0 0 00	
4	Supplies	4 3 6 0 00			(c) 8 6 0 00	3 5 0 0 00				3 5 0 0 00	
5	Prepaid Insurance	3 0 0 0 00			(d) 7 5 0 00	2 2 5 0 00				2 2 5 0 00	
6	Equipment	38 0 0 0 00				38 0 0 0 00				38 0 0 0 00	
7	Accum. Depr.—Equipment		6 0 0 0 00		(e) 9 0 0 00		6 9 0 0 00				6 9 0 0 00
8	Accounts Payable		41 2 0 0 00				41 2 0 0 00				41 2 0 0 00
9	Wages Payable				(f) 4 2 0 00		4 2 0 00				4 2 0 00
10	Sales Tax Payable		8 0 0 0 00				8 0 0 0 00				8 0 0 0 00
11	Mortgage Payable		8 0 0 0 00				8 0 0 0 00				8 0 0 0 00
12	J. Backlund, Capital		57 0 0 0 00				57 0 0 0 00				57 0 0 0 00
13	J. Backlund, Drawing	6 8 0 0 00				6 8 0 0 00				6 8 0 0 00	
14	Income Summary			(a) 42 1 6 0 00	(b) 44 3 0 0 00	42 1 6 0 00	44 3 0 0 00	42 1 6 0 00	44 3 0 0 00		
15	Sales		141 8 0 0 00				141 8 0 0 00		141 8 0 0 00		
16	Sales Returns and Allowances	1 3 1 0 00				1 3 1 0 00		1 3 1 0 00			
17	Purchases	81 3 0 0 00				81 3 0 0 00		81 3 0 0 00			
18	Purchases Returns and Allowances		2 9 0 0 00				2 9 0 0 00		2 9 0 0 00		
19	Purchases Discounts		1 5 1 0 00				1 5 1 0 00		1 5 1 0 00		
20	Freight-In	6 0 0 00				6 0 0 00		6 0 0 00			
21	Wages Expense	41 3 0 0 00		(f) 4 2 0 00		41 7 2 0 00		41 7 2 0 00			
22	Advertising Expense	4 0 0 0 00				4 0 0 0 00		4 0 0 0 00			
23	Supplies Expense			(c) 8 6 0 00		8 6 0 00		8 6 0 00			
24	Telephone Expense	8 0 0 00				8 0 0 00		8 0 0 00			
25	Utilities Expense	1 3 0 0 00				1 3 0 0 00		1 3 0 0 00			
26	Insurance Expense			(d) 7 5 0 00		7 5 0 00		7 5 0 00			
27	Depr. Expense—Equipment			(e) 9 0 0 00		9 0 0 00		9 0 0 00			
28	Miscellaneous Expense	2 0 0 00				2 0 0 00		2 0 0 00			
29	Interest Expense	1 0 8 0 00				1 0 8 0 00		1 0 8 0 00			
30		259 2 1 0 00	259 2 1 0 00	89 3 9 0 00	89 3 9 0 00	304 8 3 0 00	304 8 3 0 00	173 3 8 0 00	190 5 1 0 00	131 4 5 0 00	114 3 2 0 00
31	Net Income							17 1 3 0 00			17 1 3 0 00
32								190 5 1 0 00	190 5 1 0 00	131 4 5 0 00	131 4 5 0 00

PROBLEM 16-9B

PROBLEM 16-10B   (LO4)

Working capital: $43,230;
Quick ratio: .84 to 1;
Accts. receivable turnover: 4.35

FINANCIAL RATIOS Use the work sheet and financial statements prepared in Problem 16-9B. All sales are credit sales. The Accounts Receivable balance on January 1 was $38,200.

REQUIRED

Prepare the following financial ratios:

a. Working capital

b. Current ratio

c. Quick ratio

d. Return on owner's equity

e. Accounts receivable turnover and the average number of days required to collect receivables

f. Inventory turnover and the average number of days required to sell inventory

MASTERY PROBLEM

Net income: $21,350;
Total assets: $99,000;
Current ratio: 2.65 to 1;
Return on owner's equity: 28%

Dominique Fouque owns and operates Dominique's Doll House. She has a small shop in which she sells new and antique dolls. She is particularly well known for her collection of antique Ken and Barbie dolls. A completed work sheet for 20-3 is shown on the next page. Fouque made no additional investments during the year and the long-term note payable is due in 20-9. No portion of the long-term note is due within the next year. Net credit sales for 20-3 were $35,300 and receivables on January 1 were $2,500.

REQUIRED

1. Prepare a multiple-step income statement.

2. Prepare a statement of owner's equity.

3. Prepare a balance sheet.

4. Compute the following measures of performance and financial condition for 20-3:

    a.   Current ratio

    b.   Quick ratio

    c.   Working capital

    d.   Return on owner's equity

    e.   Accounts receivable turnover and average number of days required to collect receivables

    f.   Inventory turnover and the average number of days required to sell inventory

5. Prepare adjusting entries and indicate which should be reversed and why.

6. Prepare closing entries.

7. Prepare reversing entries for the adjustments where appropriate.

Dominique's Doll House
Work Sheet
For Year Ended December 31, 20-3

#	Account Title	Trial Balance Debit	Trial Balance Credit	Adjustments Debit	Adjustments Credit	Adjusted Trial Balance Debit	Adjusted Trial Balance Credit	Income Statement Debit	Income Statement Credit	Balance Sheet Debit	Balance Sheet Credit
1	Cash	5 2 0 0 00				5 2 0 0 00				5 2 0 0 00	
2	Accounts Receivable	3 2 0 0 00				3 2 0 0 00				3 2 0 0 00	
3	Merchandise Inventory	22 3 0 0 00		(b) 24 6 0 0 00	(a) 22 3 0 0 00	24 6 0 0 00				24 6 0 0 00	
4	Office Supplies	8 0 0 00			(c) 6 0 0 00	2 0 0 00				2 0 0 00	
5	Prepaid Insurance	1 2 0 0 00			(d) 4 0 0 00	8 0 0 00				8 0 0 00	
6	Store Equipment	85 0 0 0 00				85 0 0 0 00				85 0 0 0 00	
7	Accum. Depr.—Store Equipment		15 0 0 0 00		(e) 5 0 0 0 00		20 0 0 0 00				20 0 0 0 00
8	Notes Payable		6 0 0 0 00				6 0 0 0 00				6 0 0 0 00
9	Accounts Payable		5 5 0 0 00				5 5 0 0 00				5 5 0 0 00
10	Wages Payable				(g) 2 0 0 00		2 0 0 00				2 0 0 00
11	Sales Tax Payable		8 5 0 00				8 5 0 00				8 5 0 00
12	Unearned Rent Revenue		1 0 0 0 00	(f) 7 0 0 00			3 0 0 00				3 0 0 00
13	Long-Term Note Payable		10 0 0 0 00				10 0 0 0 00				10 0 0 0 00
14	Dominique Fouque, Capital		75 8 0 0 00				75 8 0 0 00				75 8 0 0 00
15	Dominique Fouque, Drawing	21 0 0 0 00				21 0 0 0 00				21 0 0 0 00	
16	Income Summary			(a) 22 3 0 0 00	(b) 24 6 0 0 00	22 3 0 0 00	24 6 0 0 00	22 3 0 0 00	24 6 0 0 00		
17	Sales		130 5 0 0 00				130 5 0 0 00		130 5 0 0 00		
18	Sales Returns and Allowances	9 0 0 00				9 0 0 00		9 0 0 00			
19	Rent Revenue		25 0 0 0 00		(f) 7 0 0 00		25 7 0 0 00		25 7 0 0 00		
20	Purchases	72 0 0 0 00				72 0 0 0 00		72 0 0 0 00			
21	Purchases Discounts		7 5 0 00				7 5 0 00		7 5 0 00		
22	Freight-In	1 2 0 0 00				1 2 0 0 00		1 2 0 0 00			
23	Wages Expense	42 0 0 0 00		(g) 2 0 0 00		42 2 0 0 00		42 2 0 0 00			
24	Rent Expense	6 0 0 0 00				6 0 0 0 00		6 0 0 0 00			
25	Office Supplies Expense			(c) 6 0 0 00		6 0 0 00		6 0 0 00			
26	Telephone Expense	1 5 0 0 00				1 5 0 0 00		1 5 0 0 00			
27	Utilities Expense	7 6 0 0 00				7 6 0 0 00		7 6 0 0 00			
28	Insurance Expense			(d) 4 0 0 00		4 0 0 00		4 0 0 00			
29	Depr. Expense—Store Equipment			(e) 5 0 0 0 00		5 0 0 0 00		5 0 0 0 00			
30	Interest Expense	5 0 0 00				5 0 0 00		5 0 0 00			
31		270 4 0 0 00	270 4 0 0 00	53 8 0 0 00	53 8 0 0 00	300 2 0 0 00	300 2 0 0 00	160 2 0 0 00	181 5 5 0 00	140 0 0 0 00	118 6 5 0 00
32	Net Income							21 3 5 0 00			21 3 5 0 00
33								181 5 5 0 00	181 5 5 0 00	140 0 0 0 00	140 0 0 0 00

MASTERY PROBLEM

CHALLENGE PROBLEM

This problem challenges you to apply your cumulative accounting knowledge to move a step beyond the material in the chapter.

Average days to convert inventory to cash: 45.0 days

John Byers owns and operates Byers Building Supplies. The following information was taken from his financial statements.

Balance Sheet	12/31/02	12/31/01
Accounts Receivable	$700	$500
Inventory	300	100

Income Statement

Credit Sales	$7,200
Cost of Goods Sold	5,000

All sales are made on account.

REQUIRED

Based on the above information, on average, approximately how many days pass from the time Byers purchases inventory until he receives cash from customers?

COMPREHENSIVE PROBLEM 2: ACCOUNTING CYCLE
WITH SUBSIDIARY LEDGERS, PART 1

During the month of December 20-1, TJ's Specialty Shop engaged in the following transactions.

Dec. 1 Sold merchandise on account to Anne Clark, $2,000 plus tax of $100. Sale no. 637.

2 Issued check no. 806 to Owen Enterprises in payment of December 1 balance of $1,600, less 2% discount.

3 Issued check no. 807 to Nathen Co. in payment of December 1 balance of $3,000, less 2% discount.

4 Purchased merchandise on account from Owen Enterprises, $1,550. Invoice no. 763, dated December 4, terms 2/10, n/30.

4 Issued check no. 808 in payment of telephone expense for the month of November, $180.

6 Purchased merchandise on account from Evans Essentials, $2,350. Invoice no. 621, dated December 5, terms net 30.

8 Sold merchandise for cash, $4,840, plus tax of $242.

9 Received payment from Heather Waters in full settlement of account, $490.

9 Sold merchandise on account to Lucy Greene, $800 plus tax of $40. Sale no. 638.

10 Issued check no. 809 to West Wholesalers in payment of December 1 balance of $1,000.

11 Issued check no. 810 in payment of advertising expense for the month of December, $400.

12 Sold merchandise on account to Martha Boyle, $1,260 plus tax of $63. Sale no. 639.

12 Received payment from Anne Clark on account, $1,340.

13 Issued check no. 811 to Owen Enterprises in payment of December 4 purchase. Invoice no. 763, less 2% discount.

13 Martha Boyle returned merchandise for a credit, $740 plus sales tax of $37.

15 Issued check no. 812 in payment of wages (Wages Expense) for the two-week period ending December 14, $1,100.

15 Received payment from Lucy Greene on account, $1,960.

16 Sold merchandise on account to Kim Fields, $160 plus sales tax of $8. Sale no. 640.

17 Returned merchandise to Evans Essentials for credit, $150.

18 Issued check no. 813 to Evans Essentials in payment of December 1 balance of $1,250 less the credit received on December 17.

19 Sold merchandise on account to Lucy Greene, $620 plus tax of $31. Sale no. 641.

22 Received payment from John Dempsey on account, $1,560.

23 Issued check no. 814 for the purchase of supplies, $120. (Debit Supplies)

24 Purchased merchandise on account from West Wholesalers, $1,200. Invoice no. 465, dated December 24, terms net 30.

26 Purchased merchandise on account from Nathen Co., $800. Invoice no. 817, dated December 26, terms 2/10, n/30.

27   Issued check no. 815 in payment of utilities expense for the month of November, $630.

27   Sold merchandise on account to John Dempsey, $2,020 plus tax of $101. Sale no. 642.

29   Received payment from Martha Boyle on account, $2,473.

29   Issued check no. 816 in payment of wages (Wages Expense) for the two-week period ending December 28, $1,100.

30   Issued check no. 817 to Meyers Trophy Shop for a cash purchase of merchandise, $200.

As of December 1, TJ's account balances were as follows:

Account	Account No.	Debit	Credit
Cash	101	$ 11,500	
Accounts Receivable	122	8,600	
Merchandise Inventory	131	21,800	
Supplies	141	1,035	
Prepaid Insurance	145	1,380	
Land	161	8,700	
Building	171	52,000	
Accum. Depr.—Building	171.1		$ 9,200
Store Equipment	181	28,750	
Accum. Depr.—Store Equipment	181.1		9,300
Accounts Payable	202		6,850
Wages Payable	219		
Sales Tax Payable	231		970
Mortgage Payable	251		12,525
Tom Jones, Capital	311		90,000
Tom Jones, Drawing	312	8,500	
Income Summary	313		
Sales	401		116,000
Sales Returns and Allowances	401.1	690	
Purchases	501	60,500	
Purchases Returns and Allowances	501.1		460
Purchases Discounts	501.2		575
Freight-In	502	175	
Wages Expense	511	25,000	
Advertising Expense	512	4,300	
Supplies Expense	524		
Telephone Expense	525	2,000	
Utilities Expense	533	6,900	
Insurance Expense	535		
Depr. Expense—Building	540		
Depr. Expense—Store Equipment	541		
Miscellaneous Expense	549	2,700	
Interest Expense	551	1,350	
		$245,880	$245,880

TJ also had the following subsidiary ledger balances as of December 1.

Accounts Receivable Ledger		*Accounts Payable Ledger*	
Customer	**Balance**	**Vendor**	**Balance**
Martha Boyle 12 Jude Lane Hartford, CT 06117	$3,250	Evans Essentials 34 Harry Ave. East Hartford, CT 05234	$1,250
Anne Clark 52 Juniper Road Hartford, CT 06118	1,340	Nathen Co. 1009 Drake Rd. Farmington, CT 06082	3,000
John Dempsey 700 Hobbes Dr. Avon, CT 06108	1,560	Owen Enterprises 43 Lucky Lane Bristol, CT 06007	1,600
Kim Fields 5200 Hamilton Ave. Hartford, CT 06117	—	West Wholesalers 888 Anders Street Newington, CT 06789	1,000
Lucy Greene 236 Bally Lane Simsbury, CT 06123	1,960		
Heather Waters 447 Drury Lane West Hartford, CT 06107	490		

At the end of the year, the following adjustments (a)–(g) need to be made.

(a, b) Merchandise inventory as of December 31, $19,700.

(c) Unused supplies on hand, $525.

(d) Unexpired insurance on December 31, $1,000.

(e) Depreciation expense on the building for the year, $800.

(f) Depreciation expense on the store equipment for the year, $450.

(g) Wages earned but not paid as of December 31, $330.

Requirements and working papers for this problem are provided in two versions: General Journal based and Special Journals based. Complete the version as directed by your instructor.

REQUIRED—GENERAL JOURNAL

1. If you are not using the working papers, open a general ledger, an accounts receivable ledger, and an accounts payable ledger as of December 1. Enter the December 1 balance of each of the accounts, with a check mark in the Post. Ref. Column.

2. Enter transactions for the month of December in the general journal. Post immediately to the accounts receivable and accounts payable ledgers.

3. Post from the journal to the general ledger.

4. Prepare schedules of accounts receivable and accounts payable.

REQUIRED—SPECIAL JOURNALS

1. If you are not using the working papers, open a general ledger, an accounts receivable ledger, and an accounts payable ledger as of December 1. Enter the December 1 balance of each of the accounts, with a check mark in the Post. Ref. Column.

2. Enter transactions for the month of December in the proper journals. Post immediately to the accounts receivable and accounts payable ledgers.

3. Post from the journals to the general ledger. Post the journals in the following order: general, sales, purchases, cash receipts, and cash payments.

4. Prepare schedules of accounts receivable and accounts payable.

REQUIRED—GENERAL JOURNAL (continued)

5. Prepare a year-end work sheet, an income statement, a statement of owner's equity, and a balance sheet. The mortgage payable includes $600 that is due within one year.

6. Journalize and post adjusting entries.

7. Journalize and post closing entries. (*Hint:* Close all expense and revenue account balances listed in the Income Statement columns of the work sheet. Then, close Income Summary and Tom Jones, Drawing to Tom Jones, Capital.)

8. Prepare a post-closing trial balance.

9. Journalize and post reversing entries for the adjustments where appropriate, as of January 1, 20-2.

REQUIRED—SPECIAL JOURNALS (continued)

5. Prepare a year-end work sheet, an income statement, a statement of owner's equity, and a balance sheet. The mortgage payable includes $600 that is due within one year.

6. Journalize and post adjusting entries.

7. Journalize and post closing entries. (*Hint:* Close all expense and revenue account balances listed in the Income Statement columns of the work sheet. Then, close Income Summary and Tom Jones, Drawing to Tom Jones, Capital.)

8. Prepare a post-closing trial balance.

9. Journalize and post reversing entries for the adjustments where appropriate, as of January 1, 20-2.

COMPREHENSIVE PROBLEM 2: ACCOUNTING CYCLE WITH SUBSIDIARY LEDGERS, PART 2

During the month of January 20-2, TJ's Specialty Shop engaged in the following transactions.

Jan. 1 Sold merchandise on account to Anne Clark, $3,000 plus tax of $150. Sale no. 643.

2 Issued check no. 818 to Nathen Co. in payment of January 1 balance of $800, less 2% discount.

3 Purchased merchandise on account from West Wholesalers, $1,500. Invoice no. 678, dated January 3, terms 2/15, n/30.

4 Purchased merchandise on account from Owen Enterprises, $2,000. Invoice no. 767, dated January 4, terms 2/10, n/30.

4 Issued check no. 819 in payment of telephone expense for the month of December, $180.

8 Sold merchandise for cash, $3,600, plus tax of $180.

9 Received payment from Lucy Greene in full settlement of account, $1,491.

10 Issued check no. 820 to West Wholesalers in payment of January 1 balance in amount of $1,200.

12 Sold merchandise on account to Martha Boyle, $1,000 plus tax of $50. Sale no. 644.

12 Received payment from Anne Clark on account, $2,100.

12 Issued check no. 821 in payment of wages (Wages Expense) for the two-week period ending January 11, $1,100.

13 Issued check no. 822 to Owen Enterprises in payment of January 4 purchase. Invoice no. 767, less 2% discount.

13 Martha Boyle returned merchandise for a credit, $800 plus sales tax of $40.

17 Returned merchandise to Evans Essentials for credit, $300.

22 Received payment from John Dempsey on account, $2,121.

26 Issued check no. 823 in payment of wages (Wages Expense) for the two-week period ending January 25, $1,100.

27 Issued check no. 824 in payment of utilities expense for the month of December, $630.

27 Sold merchandise on account to John Dempsey, $2,000 plus tax of $100. Sale no. 645.

Late in January, TJ agreed to sell the business to a competitor. To agree on a selling price, financial statements are needed as of January 31 and for the month of January 20-2. To prepare these financial statements, TJ's must perform the same procedures it normally does at year end.

At the end of January, the following adjustments (a)–(g) need to be made.

(a,b) Merchandise inventory as of January 31, $19,000.

(c) Unused supplies on hand, $115.

(d) Unexpired insurance on January 31, $968.

(e) Depreciation expense on the building for the month, $67.

(f) Depreciation expense on the store equipment for the month, $38.

(g) Wages earned but not paid as of January 31, $330.

REQUIRED—GENERAL JOURNAL

1. If you are not using the working papers, open a general ledger, accounts receivable ledger, and accounts payable ledger as of January 1. Enter the January 1 balance of each of the accounts, with a check mark in the Post. Ref. Column. The beginning balances for Part 2 are the same as the balances from your solution to Part 1 of Comprehensive Problem 2.

2. Enter transactions for the month of January in the general journal. Post immediately to the accounts receivable and accounts payable ledgers.

3. Post from the journal to the general ledger.

4. Prepare schedules of accounts receivable and accounts payable.

5. Prepare a month-end work sheet, income statement, statement of owner's equity, and balance sheet. The mortgage payable includes $600 that is due within one year.

6. Journalize and post adjusting entries.

7. Journalize and post closing entries. (*Hint:* Close all expense and revenue account balances listed in the Income Statement columns of the work sheet. Then close Income Summary and Tom Jones, Drawing to Tom Jones, Capital.)

8. Prepare a post-closing trial balance.

REQUIRED—SPECIAL JOURNALS

1. If you are not using the working papers, open a general ledger, accounts receivable ledger, and accounts payable ledger as of January 1. Enter the January 1 balance of each of the accounts, with a check mark in the Post. Ref. Column. The beginning balances for Part 2 are the same as the balances from your solution to Part 1 of Comprehensive Problem 2.

2. Enter transactions for the month of January in the proper journals. Post immediately to the accounts receivable and accounts payable ledgers.

3. Post from the journals to the general ledger. Post the journals in the following order: general, sales, purchases, cash receipts, and cash payments.

4. Prepare schedules of accounts receivable and accounts payable.

5. Prepare a month-end work sheet, income statement, statement of owner's equity, and balance sheet. The mortgage payable includes $600 that is due within one year.

6. Journalize and post adjusting entries.

7. Journalize and post closing entries. (*Hint:* Close all expense and revenue account balances listed in the Income Statement columns of the work sheet. Then close Income Summary and Tom Jones, Drawing to Tom Jones, Capital.)

8. Prepare a post-closing trial balance.

©GETTY IMAGES/PHOTODISC

Specialized Accounting Procedures for Merchandising Businesses and Partnerships

DIGITAL IMAGING GROUP

Accounting for Accounts Receivable

With the rapid growth of his pet supply business, Evan Taylor has opened a second store. One reason for the success of Parkway Pet Supplies is Evan's willingness to make some sales on account. When Evan makes these sales, he knows that some portion of the customers will not pay their accounts. He is puzzled as to how to account for this expense. The matching principle says expenses should be matched with the revenues they helped to produce. This implies Evan should write off some accounts receivable in the current period so that the expenses are matched with the related sales. But he doesn't know which accounts will prove uncollectible. How can he write them off before he knows which ones they are? He could wait until he knows which customers are not going to pay their bills, but this seems to violate the matching principle. What should Evan do?

Careful study of this chapter should enable you to:

LO1 Apply the allowance method of accounting for uncollectible accounts.

LO2 Estimate and write off uncollectible accounts using the percentage of sales method and the percentage of receivables method.

LO3 Apply the direct write-off method of accounting for uncollectible accounts.

Businesses generally are willing to sell goods and services on account. A major reason for doing so is to increase sales. Most of us simply tend to buy more if we can "charge it" rather than pay cash. In fact, one way a business can increase sales is to have easy credit policies and sell on account to virtually anyone. Unfortunately, some businesses and individuals who "charge it" then are unwilling or unable to "pay for it." Thus a cost to a business of selling goods and services on account is that some of the accounts receivable will be uncollectible or bad debts. The more willing a business is to make sales on account, the more uncollectible accounts it is likely to have.

There are two methods of accounting for uncollectible accounts: (1) the allowance method and (2) the direct write-off method. The purpose of this chapter is to learn how to use these methods.

ALLOWANCE METHOD

LO1 Apply the allowance method of accounting for uncollectible accounts.

Bad debt expense is a loss from failure to collect an account receivable. The **allowance method** is a technique that attempts to recognize bad debt expense in the same period that the related credit sales are made. This method is consistent with the **matching principle**, which states that expenses should be matched with the revenues they helped to produce.

Under the accrual basis of accounting, the allowance method is generally required for financial reporting purposes. To use the allowance method, three steps are followed:

STEP 1 At the end of each accounting period, the amount of uncollectible accounts is estimated.

STEP 2 An adjusting entry is made to recognize the bad debt expense and reduce reported receivables for the amount of estimated uncollectible accounts. For example, if the estimated amount at December 31 is $900, the entry is as shown below and in Figure 17-1:

LEARNING KEY: Under the allowance method, bad debt expense is recorded as a *year-end adjustment.*

4	Dec.	31	Bad Debt Expense		9 0 0 00			4
5			Allowance for Bad Debts			9 0 0 00		5
6								6

Assets		=	Liabilities		+	Owner's Equity			
Debit	**Credit**		**Debit**	**Credit**		**Debit**		**Credit**	
+	–		–	+		–		+	
						Drawing		**Expenses**	**Revenues**
						Debit / **Credit**		**Debit** / **Credit**	**Debit** / **Credit**
						+ / –		+ / –	– / +
Accounts Receivable							Bad Debt Expense		
Bal. 30,000.00							900.00		
Allowance for Bad Debts									
	900.00								

FIGURE 17-1 Adjusting Entry for Bad Debt Expense

Note that the credit is not to Accounts Receivable. This is because at this time we do not know which specific customers will fail to pay. Instead, a contra-asset account, Allowance for Bad Debts (also known as Allowance for Uncollectible Accounts or Allowance for Doubtful Accounts), is credited. The balance of this account is deducted from Accounts Receivable on the balance sheet. The remaining amount is known as the **net receivables** or **net realizable value** of accounts receivable because it is the amount the business expects to collect. Accounts receivable of $30,000 with an allowance of $900 would appear as follows:

Current assets:

Accounts receivable	$30,000	
Less allowance for bad debts	900	$29,100 ← Net receivables (Net realizable value)

STEP 3　In a subsequent period, when a specific uncollectible account is identified, an entry is made to write off the account and reduce the balance in Allowance for Bad Debts. For example, if the uncollectible account is $250, the entry is:

8		Allowance for Bad Debts		2 5 0 00		8
9		Accounts Receivable/Customer Name			2 5 0 00	9
10		Wrote off uncollectible account				10

ESTIMATING AND WRITING OFF UNCOLLECTIBLES

LO2 Estimate and write off uncollectible accounts using the percentage of sales method and the percentage of receivables method.

To use the allowance method, we need a way to estimate the amount of uncollectibles. Two basic methods are used: the percentage of sales method and the percentage of receivables method. A company chooses one method or the other and uses it consistently over time.

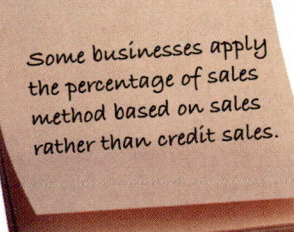

Percentage of Sales Method

The **percentage of sales method** is based on the relationship between the amount of credit sales and the amount of uncollectible accounts. Assume that during 20-1 and 20-2, Chris Co. had total credit sales of $200,000 and that $2,000 of those credit sales had become uncollectible. Based on this experience, Chris could estimate its uncollectible accounts at 1% of credit sales.

$$\frac{\text{Uncollectible Accounts}}{\text{Credit Sales}} = \frac{\$2,000}{\$200,000} = 1\%$$

If during 20-3 Chris had credit sales of $120,000, the estimate of uncollectible accounts would be made as follows:

Credit sales	$120,000
Estimated % uncollectible	× 1%
Estimated uncollectible accounts	$ 1,200

Thus, the following adjusting entry would be made on December 31, 20-3.

4	Dec.	31	Bad Debt Expense		1 2 0 0 00		4
5			Allowance for Bad Debts			1 2 0 0 00	5
6							6

In T account form, Allowance for Bad Debts would appear as follows:

Allowance for Bad Debts

	20-3
	12/31 1,200

Assume that during 20-4, uncollectible accounts totaling $1,100 were written off as follows:

8			Allowance for Bad Debts		1 1 0 0 00		8
9			Accounts Receivable/Customer Names			1 1 0 0 00	9
10			Wrote off uncollectible accounts				10

After posting this entry, Allowance for Bad Debts would have a credit balance of $100.

Allowance for Bad Debts

	20-3
	12/31 1,200
20-4 1,100	
	20-4 Bal. 100

Assume that during 20-4, Chris had credit sales of $130,000. Based on experience, Chris would still estimate its uncollectible accounts at 1% of credit sales. This would yield estimated uncollectible accounts of $1,300 (1% × $130,000), and the following adjusting entry would be made on December 31, 20-4.

4	Dec	31	Bad Debt Expense		1 3 0 0 00		4
5			Allowance for Bad Debts			1 3 0 0 00	5
6							6

This would increase the Allowance for Bad Debts balance to $1,400.

Allowance for Bad Debts

	20-3
	12/31 1,200
20-4 1,100	
	20-4 Bal. 100
	12/31 Adj. 1,300
	12/31 Bal. 1,400

LEARNING KEY: Percentage of Sales Method: When making the adjusting entry, ignore any existing balance in Allowance for Bad Debts.

This demonstrates an important feature of the percentage of sales method. Allowance for Bad Debts may have a debit or credit balance prior to adjustment. This is a normal result of underestimating or overestimating uncollectible accounts. Under the percentage of sales method, any balance in Allowance for Bad Debts prior to adjustment is generally *ignored* in making the current period's adjusting entry.

This is because the percentage of sales method focuses on the *current year's* credit sales. Any previous balance in the allowance account relates to credit sales and uncollectible accounts from *prior years*. In the above illustration, the balance was a credit of $100. This balance could have been a credit of $300 or a debit of $200, and it would not have mattered. The adjusting entry for uncollectible accounts would have been the same—$1,300.

There is one exception to ignoring the balance in Allowance for Bad Debts in making the adjustment. When a large debit or credit balance accumulates in the allowance account, the percentage of credit sales used to estimate uncollectible accounts should be increased or decreased. This provides a better estimate based on recent experience.

Percentage of Receivables Method

The **percentage of receivables method** is based on the relationship between the amount of accounts receivable and the amount of uncollectible accounts. The simplest form of this method involves computing uncollectible accounts as a percentage of the Accounts Receivable balance. Assume that Craft Co. had an average Accounts Receivable balance at the end of the past two years of $110,000, and average uncollectible accounts of $4,400. Craft would estimate its percentage of uncollectible accounts as follows:

$$\frac{\text{Average Uncollectible Accounts}}{\text{Average Accounts Receivable}} = \frac{\$4,400}{\$110,000} = 4\%$$

Assume that the Accounts Receivable balance at the end of the current year was $120,000. The estimate of uncollectible accounts would be made as follows:

Accounts receivable	$120,000
Estimated % uncollectible	× 4%
Estimated uncollectible accounts	$ 4,800

Assuming Allowance for Bad Debts has a zero balance prior to adjustment, the following adjusting entry would be made at year end.

4	Dec.	31	Bad Debt Expense			4 8 0 0 00			4
5			Allowance for Bad Debts				4 8 0 0 00	5
6								6

Although the above approach is simple, the estimate of uncollectible accounts is not very precise. Therefore, the percentage of receivables method usually is applied in a way that yields a better estimate. Instead of using the total accounts receivable in making the estimate, each customer's balance is analyzed to determine how long it has been outstanding. The probability that a customer's account will not be collected usually increases with the length of time the account has been outstanding. Because of the emphasis on the length of time the accounts have been outstanding, this process is called **aging the receivables**.

An aging schedule similar to the one in Figure 17-2 is often used to analyze the receivables and estimate the uncollectible amount. The following steps are used in preparing the aging schedule.

STEP 1   Categorize each account receivable according to the length of time the amounts have been outstanding.

STEP 2   Multiply the amount of receivables in each category by an estimate of the percent that will be uncollectible. This percentage is based on past experience and increases as the number of days past due increases.

STEP 3   Total the estimates for each category to determine the amount that is not expected to be collected.

AGING SCHEDULE OF ACCOUNTS RECEIVABLE — December 31, 20-1

CUSTOMER	TOTAL	NOT YET DUE	NUMBER OF DAYS PAST DUE					
			1–30	31–60	61–90	91–180	181–365	OVER 365
W. Billiard	$ 3 000 00	$ 2 500 00	$ 500 00					
K. Campbell	950 00			$ 650 00		$ 300 00		
J. Farley	4 325 00	3 800 00			$ 525 00			
L. Gilbert	1 900 00	1 500 00		400 00				
E. Rome	3 950 00	3 170 00					$ 780 00	
B. Zimmerman	200 00					200 00		
Total	$100 500 00	$65 000 00	$18 000 00	$8 250 00	$6 310 00	$1 810 00	$ 780 00	$ 350 00
Estimated percent uncollectible		2 %	5 %	10 %	20 %	30 %	50 %	80 %
Total est. uncollectible accounts	$ 5 500 00	$ 1 300 00	$ 900 00	$ 825 00	$1 262 00	$ 543 00	$ 390 00	$ 280 00
	($ 5 500 00	= 1 300 00	+ 900 00	+ 825 00	+ 1 262 00	+ 543 00	+ 390 00	+ 280 00)

FIGURE 17-2   Aging Schedule

Based on the aging schedule in Figure 17-2, uncollectible accounts would be estimated as $5,500 as indicated in the Total column. Thus, assuming Allowance for Bad Debts has a zero balance prior to adjustment, the following adjusting entry would be made at December 31, 20-1.

4	Dec.	31	Bad Debt Expense		5 5 0 0 00		4
5			Allowance for Bad Debts			5 5 0 0 00	5
6							6

In T account form, Allowance for Bad Debts would appear as follows:

Allowance for Bad Debts

```
                              |  20-1
                              |  12/31   Adj.      5,500
```

Assume that during 20-2, uncollectible accounts totaling $5,200 were written off as follows:

8		Allowance for Bad Debts		5 2 0 0 00		8
9		Accounts Receivable/Customer Names			5 2 0 0 00	9
10		Wrote off uncollectible accounts				10

Allowance for Bad Debts now would have a credit balance of $300.

Allowance for Bad Debts

```
                              |  20-1
                              |  12/31   Adj.      5,500
 20-2              5,200       |
                              |  20-2    Bal.       300
```

Accounts written off during 20-2

Assume that at the end of 20-2 another aging schedule like the one in Figure 17-2 is prepared, and that the estimated uncollectible amount is $5,700. To bring the credit balance in the allowance account to $5,700, an adjustment of $5,400 is needed.

Estimated uncollectible amount	$5,700
Current credit balance in account	– 300
Adjustment needed	$5,400

Thus the following adjusting entry would be made on December 31, 20-2:

4	Dec.	31	Bad Debt Expense		5 4 0 0 00		4
5			Allowance for Bad Debts			5 4 0 0 00	5
6							6

This would increase the Allowance for Bad Debts balance to $5,700.

Allowance for Bad Debts

			20-1			
			12/31	Adj.	5,500	Adjustment to increase the balance to $5,700
20-2		5,200				
			20-2	Bal.	300	
			12/31	Adj.	**5,400**	
			12/31	Bal.	5,700	

This demonstrates an important feature of the percentage of receivables method. Allowance for Bad Debts may have a debit or credit balance prior to adjustment. Under the percentage of receivables method, this balance must be considered in making the current period's adjusting entry.

LEARNING KEY: Percentage of receivables method: Unlike the percentage of sales method, consider the balance in Allowance for Bad Debts prior to adjustment when making the current period's adjusting entry.

This is because the percentage of receivables method focuses on the Accounts Receivable balance at the end of the year. That balance contains receivables from the current year and any remaining from prior years. The total Accounts Receivable balance consisting of current and prior year receivables is analyzed to determine the proper allowance account balance. The adjusting entry is then made to achieve that balance in the allowance account. In the above illustration, the balance prior to adjustment was a credit of $300. Therefore, the adjustment to bring the balance to $5,700 was $5,400 ($5,700 – $300). If the balance prior to adjustment had been a debit of $100, the necessary adjusting entry would have been $5,800:

Estimated uncollectible amount	$5,700
Current debit balance in account	+ 100
Adjustment needed	$5,800

Notice that the resulting credit balance in Allowance for Bad Debts after adjustment would once again be $5,700.

Allowance for Bad Debts

20-2	Bal.	100	20-2		
			12/31	Adj.	5,800
			12/31	Bal.	5,700

Comparison of Methods

Let's summarize the differences between the percentage of sales and percentage of receivables methods of estimating uncollectibles. Figure 17-3 identifies the key features of the two methods.

FEATURE	PERCENTAGE OF SALES	PERCENTAGE OF RECEIVABLES
1 Basis for estimate	% of credit sales	Aging (%) of accounts receivable
2 Amount of year-end adjustment	% of credit sales	Amount calculated by aging accounts receivable **Plus** debit balance in allowance account before adjustment or **Minus** credit balance in allowance account before adjustment
3 Balance after adjustment	% of credit sales **Plus** credit balance in allowance account before adjustment or **Minus** debit balance in allowance account before adjustment	Amount calculated by aging accounts receivable

FIGURE 17-3   Key Features of Allowance Methods

Write-off of Uncollectible Accounts

Recall that to write off a $250 uncollectible account, the following entry is made.

4		Allowance for Bad Debts			2	5	0	00					4
5		Accounts Receivable/Customer Name								2	5	0	00	5
6		Wrote off uncollectible account												6

LEARNING KEY: Under both allowance methods, the entry to write off an account is the same.

This entry is the same under both the percentage of sales and percentage of receivables methods.

Note the effect of this entry on the income statement and balance sheet. No income statement accounts are used in the entry, so clearly there is no effect on the income statement. Not so obviously, the balance sheet is not affected either. Since Allowance for Bad Debts is a contra-asset and Accounts Receivable is an asset, the effects offset each other. Let's look more closely at this perhaps surprising situation.

LEARNING KEY: Under the allowance method, the write-off of an account as uncollectible does not affect either the income statement or the balance sheet.

Effect of Entry on the Income Statement. First, how can we write off an account as uncollectible and have no income statement effect? The answer lies in the adjusting entry we made at year end for the estimated uncollectibles. Assume the entry was for $900.

9		Bad Debt Expense			9	0	0	00					9
10		Allowance for Bad Debts								9	0	0	00	10
11													11

A BROADER VIEW

Accounts Receivable and Management of Cash Flows

It is important to be aware of the difference between sales on account and cash inflows, particularly in running a small business. Green Co., a construction contractor in Connecticut, learned this distinction the hard way.

During a period of rapid growth, Green bid successfully on several municipal contracts. This led to major increases in revenue. Unfortunately, accounts receivable also increased dramatically because municipalities tend to be slow in paying their bills,

particularly on construction contracts. Thus, Green found itself facing payroll expenses and major bills from its suppliers that required prompt payment, but its cash was tied up in the accounts receivable.

Fortunately, with help from the Small Business Development Center, Green was able to obtain financing to make it through this "cash crunch." But it will long remember that accounts receivable are not the same as cash inflows.

The bad debt expense was already recognized with this adjusting entry. It would be double counting to recognize the expense again when the specific account is written off.

Effect of Entry on the Balance Sheet. Second, why is the balance sheet not affected? The best way to answer is with an example. Assume that on December 31, 20-1, the balance sheet showed the following information concerning Accounts Receivable.

Current assets:
Accounts receivable $100,500
Less allowance for bad debts   5,500   **$95,000** — Net receivables

On January 15, 20-2, Bill McDonald's account for $500 is written off by making the following entry.

14	Jan.	15	Allowance for Bad Debts			5 0 0 00			14
15			Accounts Receivable/B. McDonald				5 0 0 00	15
16			Wrote off uncollectible account					16

If the balance sheet was prepared immediately after posting the above transaction, the following information would be reported for Accounts Receivable.

Current assets:
Accounts receivable $100,000
Less allowance for bad debts   5,000   **$95,000** — Net receivables

Note that both Accounts Receivable and Allowance for Bad Debts have been reduced by $500. Thus, the reported net receivables are not changed. The business expected to collect $95,000 before writing off McDonald's account and still expects to collect $95,000 after writing off his account. Management knew that there would be some uncollectible accounts. Now they know that McDonald is one of them.

Recovery of Accounts Previously Written Off— Allowance Method

Occasionally an account that was written off is collected. For example, assume that a check for $500 was received on February 1 from Bill McDonald, whose account was written off on January 15. This requires two entries:

1. Reinstate the account.

2. Record the collection.

To reinstate an account, simply reverse the entry made to write off the account, as follows:

5	Feb.	1	Accounts Receivable/B. McDonald			5	0	0	00								5
6			Allowance for Bad Debts									5	0	0	00		6
7			Reinstated account receivable														7

To record the collection, the following entry is made.

9	Feb.	1	Cash			5	0	0	00								9
10			Accounts Receivable/B. McDonald									5	0	0	00		10
11			Collection on account														11

Instead of making these entries, it might be simpler to debit Cash and credit Allowance for Bad Debts. However, this shortcut should not be taken. Without the reinstatement, the subsidiary ledger will report only that McDonald's account was written off as uncollectible. With the reinstatement, the subsidiary ledger will reflect the fact that McDonald has paid his account. This information will be important to McDonald and the business should he desire credit in the future.

DIRECT WRITE-OFF METHOD

LO3 Apply the direct write-off method of accounting for uncollectible accounts.

Under the **direct write-off method** the bad debt expense is not recognized until it has been determined that an account is uncollectible. For example, assume that on August 15, John Lafollette's account for $500 is judged to be uncollectible. The following entry would be made.

5	Aug.	15	Bad Debt Expense			5	0	0	00								5
6			Accounts Receivable/J. Lafollette									5	0	0	00		6
7			Wrote off uncollectible account														7

Advantage and Disadvantages of Direct Method

The direct write-off method has one advantage. It is very simple to apply. However, there are three disadvantages of using this method. First, efforts to collect the account often extend over many months. Thus, the revenue from the sale might be recognized in one period and the bad debt expense recognized in another. This violates the matching principle.

Second, the amount of bad debt expense recognized in a given period can be manipulated by management. This occurs because there is no general rule for deciding when an account becomes uncollectible. Thus, management can use its subjective judgment in deciding when to recognize bad debt expense.

Third, the amount of accounts receivable reported on the balance sheet does not represent the amount of cash actually expected to be collected. Thus, the assets are overstated by the amount of uncollectible accounts included in accounts receivable. For these reasons, the direct write-off method is generally not

To deduct bad debt expense for income tax purposes, the taxpayer must have attempted unsuccessfully to collect the account.

acceptable for financial reporting purposes. It is acceptable only if the amount of uncollectible accounts cannot be reasonably estimated or if the estimated amount is very small. This method is required, however, for income tax purposes.

Recovery of Accounts Previously Written Off— Direct Write-off Method

Occasionally an account that was written off is collected. The proper entries for the recovery depend on the period in which the cash is collected.

Write-off and Recovery in Same Accounting Period. Assume the write-off and recovery are made in the same accounting period. In this case, first reinstate the account by reversing the entry for the write-off. Then record the collection in the usual manner as shown below.

To write off account:

5	Aug.	15	Bad Debt Expense	5 0 0 00		5
6			Accounts Receivable/J. Lafollette		5 0 0 00	6
7			Wrote off uncollectible account			7

To reinstate account:

35	Dec.	20	Accounts Receivable/J. Lafollette	5 0 0 00		35
36			Bad Debt Expense		5 0 0 00	36
37			Reinstated account receivable			37

To record collection:

39	Dec.	20	Cash	5 0 0 00		39
40			Accounts Receivable/J. Lafollette		5 0 0 00	40
41			Collection on account			41

Write-off and Recovery in Different Accounting Periods. Now assume that the write-off is made in one period and the recovery in the following accounting period. In this case, first reinstate the account by debiting Accounts Receivable and crediting Uncollectible Accounts Recovered. This revenue account is credited instead of Bad Debt Expense because a credit to the expense account would understate bad debt expense for the current year. Uncollectible Accounts Recovered is reported on the income statement as other revenue. The entries for the write-off and recovery are shown below.

To write off account:

5	Aug.	15	Bad Debt Expense	5 0 0 00		5
6			Accounts Receivable/J. Lafollette		5 0 0 00	6
7			Wrote off uncollectible account			7

To reinstate account:

35	Jan.	20	Accounts Receivable/J. Lafollette	5 0 0 00		35
36			Uncollectible Accounts Recovered		5 0 0 00	36
37			Reinstated account receivable			37

To record collection:

39	Jan.	20	Cash	5 0 0 00		39
40			Accounts Receivable/J. Lafollette		5 0 0 00	40
41			Collection on account			41

Learning Objectives	Key Points to Remember
1 **Apply the allowance method of accounting for uncollectible accounts.**	To use the allowance method, apply three steps:

STEP 1   At the end of the period, estimate the uncollectible amount.

STEP 2   Make the following adjusting entry:

4		Bad Debt Expense			x	x	x	xx						4
5		Allowance for Bad Debts								x	x	x	xx		5

STEP 3   When an uncollectible account is identified, make the following entry:

8		Allowance for Bad Debts			x	x	x	xx						8
9		Accounts Receivable/Customer Name								x	x	x	xx		9
10		Wrote off uncollectible account													10

| **2** **Estimate and write off uncollectible accounts using the percentage of sales method and the percentage of receivables method.** | The *percentage of sales method* is based on the relationship between the amount of credit sales and the amount of uncollectible accounts. Any balance in Allowance for Bad Debts prior to adjustment is ignored in making the current period's adjusting entry.

The *percentage of receivables method* is based on the relationship between the amount of accounts receivable and the amount of uncollectible accounts. The estimate of uncollectibles is usually based on an aging of receivables. Any balance in Allowance for Bad Debts prior to adjustment is considered in making the current period's adjusting entry.

Under the allowance method, the actual write-off of an uncollectible account does not affect either the income statement or the balance sheet.

When an account is collected that has been written off, the account is reinstated and then the collection is recorded. |
|---|---|
| **3** **Apply the direct write-off method of accounting for uncollectible accounts.** | Under the direct write-off method, bad debt expense is not recognized until an account is written off as uncollectible.

The entries for collection of an account previously written off depend on when the collection occurs. If the collection is in the same period as the write-off, the credit is to Bad Debt Expense. If the collection is in the following period, the credit is to Uncollectible Accounts Recovered. |

Reflection: Answering the Opening Questions

Until Evan has experience to provide a basis for estimating the percentage of his credit sales that will be uncollectible, he may want to use the direct write-off method. This method is not consistent with the matching principle, but it would be acceptable for Evan's situation. Alternatively, Evan could seek advice from owners of similar businesses. They might be able to share their experience with uncollectible accounts.

As soon as Evan is able to make a reasonable estimate of his uncollectible accounts, he should adopt the allowance method of accounting for uncollectible accounts. He could use either the percentage of sales or the percentage of receivables method but should be consistent in whichever method he chooses.

DEMONSTRATION PROBLEM

Budke and Budke, a landscaping service, uses the allowance method to record the following transactions related to accounts receivable. Adjusting and closing entries completed during the current year ended December 31, 20--, are also described below.

Mar. 6	Received 50% of the $12,000 balance owed by Columbia Gardens, a bankrupt business, and wrote off the remainder as uncollectible.
June 12	Reinstated the account of Ramon Burgos, which had been written off in the previous year, and received $2,250 cash in full settlement.
Sept. 19	Wrote off the $13,800 balance owed by Kelly Richeson, who has no assets.
Nov. 9	Reinstated the account of Jackie Kwas, which had been written off in the preceding year, and received $2,175 cash in full settlement.
Dec. 27	Wrote off the following accounts as uncollectible, in compound entry form: Blair & Smith, $10,480; Landscapes Unlimited, $8,570; Beekman Brothers, $22,500; B. J. McKay, $9,300.
31	Based on an aging analysis of $1,460,000 of accounts receivable, it was estimated that $73,500 will be uncollectible. Made the adjusting entry.
31	Made the entry to close the appropriate account to Income Summary.

Selected accounts and beginning balances on January 1, 20--, are as follows:

122.1	Allowance for Bad Debts	$95,000 credit
313	Income Summary	—
532	Bad Debt Expense	—

REQUIRED

1. Open the three selected accounts.

2. Enter the transactions and the adjusting and closing entries in general journal form (page 12 for the first 2 entries; page 13 for all others). After each entry, post to the three accounts named.

3. Determine the net realizable value as of December 31, 20--.

(continued)

Solution

1, 2.

GENERAL LEDGER

ACCOUNT: Allowance for Bad Debts — ACCOUNT NO. 122.1

DATE	ITEM	POST REF.	DEBIT	CREDIT	BALANCE DEBIT	BALANCE CREDIT
20-- Jan. 1	Balance	✓				95 0 0 0 00
Mar. 6		J12	6 0 0 0 00			89 0 0 0 00
June 12		J13		2 2 5 0 00		91 2 5 0 00
Sept. 19		J13	13 8 0 0 00			77 4 5 0 00
Nov. 9		J13		2 1 7 5 00		79 6 2 5 00
Dec. 27		J13	50 8 5 0 00			28 7 7 5 00
31		J13		44 7 2 5 00		73 5 0 0 00

ACCOUNT: Income Summary — ACCOUNT NO. 313

DATE	ITEM	POST REF.	DEBIT	CREDIT	BALANCE DEBIT	BALANCE CREDIT
20-- Dec. 31		J13	44 7 2 5 00		44 7 2 5 00	

ACCOUNT: Bad Debt Expense — ACCOUNT NO. 532

DATE	ITEM	POST REF.	DEBIT	CREDIT	BALANCE DEBIT	BALANCE CREDIT
20-- Dec. 31		J13	44 7 2 5 00		44 7 2 5 00	
31		J13		44 7 2 5 00		

GENERAL JOURNAL — PAGE 12

	DATE	DESCRIPTION	POST REF.	DEBIT	CREDIT	
1	20-- Mar. 6	Cash		6 0 0 0 00		1
2		Accounts Receivable/Columbia Gardens			6 0 0 0 00	2
3		Collection on account				3
4						4
5	6	Allowance for Bad Debts	122.1	6 0 0 0 00		5
6		Accounts Receivable/Columbia Gardens			6 0 0 0 00	6
7		Wrote off uncollectible account				7
8						8

	DATE		DESCRIPTION	POST. REF.	DEBIT					CREDIT					
			GENERAL JOURNAL										PAGE **13**		
1	20-- June	12	Accounts Receivable/R. Burgos		2	2	5	0	00						1
2			Allowance for Bad Debts	122.1						2	2	5	0	00	2
3			Reinstated account receivable												3
4															4
5		12	Cash		2	2	5	0	00						5
6			Accounts Receivable/R. Burgos							2	2	5	0	00	6
7			Collection on account												7
8															8
9	Sept.	19	Allowance for Bad Debts	122.1	13	8	0	0	00						9
10			Accounts Receivable/K. Richeson							13	8	0	0	00	10
11			Wrote off uncollectible account												11
12															12
13	Nov.	9	Accounts Receivable/J. Kwas		2	1	7	5	00						13
14			Allowance for Bad Debts	122.1						2	1	7	5	00	14
15			Reinstated account receivable												15
16															16
17		9	Cash		2	1	7	5	00						17
18			Accounts Receivable/J. Kwas							2	1	7	5	00	18
19			Collection on account												19
20															20
21	Dec.	27	Allowance for Bad Debts	122.1	50	8	5	0	00						21
22			Accounts Receivable/Blair & Smith							10	4	8	0	00	22
23			Accounts Receivable/Landscapes Unlimited							8	5	7	0	00	23
24			Accounts Receivable/Beekman Brothers							22	5	0	0	00	24
25			Accounts Receivable/B. J. McKay							9	3	0	0	00	25
26			Wrote off uncollectible accounts												26
27															27
28			**Adjusting Entry**												28
29		31	Bad Debt Expense	532	44	7	2	5	00						29
30			Allowance for Bad Debts	122.1						44	7	2	5	00	30
31															31
32			**Closing Entry**												32
33		31	Income Summary	313	44	7	2	5	00						33
34			Bad Debt Expense	532						44	7	2	5	00	34
35															35

3.

Accounts receivable, December 31, 20--	$1,460,000
Less allowance for bad debts	73,500
Net realizable value	$1,386,500

On-Line Learning Tools

For more information, visit: http://heintz.swlearning.com

The Heintz & Parry product web site is designed specifically for **COLLEGE ACCOUNTING, 18e.** The features include downloadable student resources and an interactive study center, organized by chapter, which contains learning objectives, web links, on-line quizzes with automatic feedback, and more.

KEY TERMS

aging the receivables, (651)   The process of estimating the uncollectible amount by analyzing account balances according to the length of time the accounts have been outstanding.

allowance method, (648)   A technique that attempts to recognize bad debt expense in the same period that the related credit sales are made.

bad debt expense, (648)   A loss from failure to collect an account receivable.

direct write-off method, (656)   A method in which the bad debt expense is not recognized until it has been determined that an account is uncollectible.

matching principle, (648)   A concept that requires expenses to be matched with the revenues they helped to produce.

net realizable value, (649)   The amount a business expects to collect from its accounts receivable; calculated as Accounts Receivable less Allowance for Bad Debts. Also called net receivables.

net receivables, (649)   See net realizable value.

percentage of receivables method, (651)   A method in which the current year's uncollectible accounts are estimated based on the relationship between the amount of accounts receivable and the amount of uncollectible accounts in prior years.

percentage of sales method, (649)   A method in which the current year's uncollectible accounts are estimated based on the relationship between the amount of credit sales and the amount of uncollectible accounts in prior years.

REVIEW QUESTIONS

(LO1)   1. What method of accounting for uncollectible accounts is generally required for financial reporting purposes?

(LO1)   2. Describe the steps to follow when using the allowance method to account for uncollectible accounts.

(LO1)   3. Explain how to compute net realizable value.

(LO2)   4. Describe the process followed when estimating uncollectible accounts under the percentage of sales method.

(LO2)   5. Describe the process followed when estimating uncollectible accounts under the percentage (aging) of receivables method.

(LO2)   6. How does the balance in Allowance for Bad Debts before adjustment affect the amount of the year-end adjustment under the percentage of sales method? under the percentage of receivables method?

(LO2)   7. Under the allowance method, what impact does the write-off of a customer's account have on the financial statements?

(LO2)   8. Under the allowance method, what journal entries are made if an account is collected that was previously written off?

(LO3)   9. Describe the accounting procedures when using the direct write-off method to account for uncollectible accounts.

(LO3)   10. What are three disadvantages of using the direct write-off method?

Self-Study Test Questions

True/False

1. There are two methods of accounting for uncollectible accounts: the allowance method and the direct write-off method. _____

2. The matching principle states that debits should be matched with credits. _____

3. Using the percentage of sales method, the balance in Allowance for Bad Debts must be taken into consideration before making the adjusting entry. _____

4. When an account is written off under the allowance method, there should be a debit to Bad Debt Expense. _____

5. Each time an account is written off under the direct write-off method, Bad Debt Expense is debited. _____

Multiple Choice

1. The dollar difference between Accounts Receivable and Allowance for Bad Debts is called _____
   - (a) book value.
   - (b) interest value.
   - (c) carrying value.
   - (d) net realizable value.

2. A business has an ending balance in Accounts Receivable of $35,000; credit sales for the year of $300,000; and a credit balance in Allowance for Bad Debts of $800. If the percentage of sales method is used and the percentage is estimated at 1% of credit sales, what is the amount to be entered for the adjusting entry? _____
   - (a) $3,000
   - (b) $3,800
   - (c) $2,200
   - (d) $1,150

3. A business has an ending balance in Accounts Receivable of $35,000; credit sales for the year of $300,000; and a credit balance in Allowance for Bad Debts of $800. If the percentage of sales method is used and the percentage is estimated at 1% of credit sales, what is the ending balance in Allowance for Bad Debts *after* the adjusting entry? _____
   - (a) $3,000
   - (b) $3,800
   - (c) $2,200
   - (d) $1,150

4. A business has an ending balance in Accounts Receivable of $40,000; credit sales for the year of $500,000; and a debit balance in Allowance for Bad Debts of $300. If an aging analysis indicates that $4,800 should be the balance in Allowance for Bad Debts, the amount to be entered for the adjusting entry is _____
   - (a) $4,800.
   - (b) $4,500.
   - (c) $5,000.
   - (d) $5,100.

5. Under the allowance method, when an account is determined to be worthless, the journal entry to write off the account will include a _____
   - (a) debit to Allowance for Bad Debts.
   - (b) debit to Bad Debt Expense.
   - (c) credit to Allowance for Bad Debts.
   - (d) debit to Accounts Receivable.

The answers to the Self-Study Test Questions are at the end of the text.

MANAGING YOUR WRITING

The heads of the marketing and finance areas at your business are arguing about tight versus easy credit policies. One feels the policy should be tightened and the other feels it should be eased. The division manager is concerned about which approach to use and asks for your advice. Prepare a memo to the division manager stating arguments for and against tight and easy credit policies. The manager will use this information to decide on which policy to establish.

ETHICS CASE

Preston Enterprises uses the direct write-off method of accounting for uncollectible accounts. On October 12 a very large account was written off. The amount was subsequently recovered on December 15. Ray Preston, the owner of the company, instructed the accountant to not make a journal entry for the recovery and to hold the check in his desk until after the first of the year "for tax purposes."

1. If you were the accountant, what would you think of Preston's request?

2. If the December 15 entry is not made, how will it affect Preston's current year financial statements?

3. Assume the amount of the charge-off and the subsequent recovery was $10,000. Prepare the proper journal entries for October 12 and December 15.

4. In groups of two or three, discuss the possible consequences for the accountant holding the check in his desk drawer for a couple of weeks.

WEB WORK

Although all businesses that give credit should expect some uncollectible accounts, there are ways to cut down on the number of such accounts. What strategies can businesses employ to minimize the number of accounts that become uncollectible? Visit the Interactive Study Center on our web site at **http://heintz.swlearning.com** for special hotlinks to assist you in this assignment.

SERIES A EXERCISES

EXERCISE 17-1A   (LO1)
1. Net realizable value: $42,000

CALCULATION OF NET REALIZABLE VALUE J. B. Bucks owns a department store that has a $45,000 balance in Accounts Receivable and a $3,000 credit balance in Allowance for Bad Debts.

1. Determine the net realizable value of the accounts receivable.

2. Assume that an account receivable in the amount of $400 was written off using the allowance method. Determine the net realizable value of the accounts receivable after the write-off.

EXERCISE 17-2A   (LO2)
1. Dr. Bad Debt Exp.: $5,400

UNCOLLECTIBLE ACCOUNTS—PERCENTAGE OF SALES Ryan's Express has total credit sales for the year of $180,000 and estimates that 3% of its credit sales will be uncollectible. Record the end-of-period adjusting entry on December 31, in general journal form, for the estimated bad debt expense. Assume the following independent conditions existed prior to the adjustment.

1. Allowance for Bad Debts has a credit balance of $925.

2. Allowance for Bad Debts has a debit balance of $385.

EXERCISE 17-3A   (LO2)
2. Dr. Bad Debt Exp.: $4,525

UNCOLLECTIBLE ACCOUNTS—PERCENTAGE OF RECEIVABLES Tammie's Toyota Sales and Service estimates the amount of uncollectible accounts using the percentage of receivables method. After aging the accounts, it is estimated that $4,250 will not be collected. Record the end-of-period adjusting entry on December 31, in general journal form, for the estimated bad debt expense. Assume the following independent conditions existed prior to the adjustment.

1. Allowance for Bad Debts has a credit balance of $690.

2. Allowance for Bad Debts has a debit balance of $275.

EXERCISE 17-4A   (LO2)
Sept. 27, Cr. Allow. for
Bad Debts: $5,350

COLLECTION OF ACCOUNTS WRITTEN OFF—ALLOWANCE METHOD Julia Alvarez, owner of Alvarez Rentals, uses the allowance method in accounting for uncollectible accounts. Record the following transactions in general journal form.

July 7   Wrote off $5,350 owed by Randy Dalzell, who has no assets.

Aug. 12   Wrote off $2,870 owed by Jason Flint, who declared bankruptcy.

Sept. 27   Reinstated the account of Randy Dalzell, which had been written off on July 7, and received $5,350 cash in full settlement.

EXERCISE 17-5A   (LO2)
1(b). Dr. Bad Debt Exp.:
$28,570

UNCOLLECTIBLE ACCOUNTS—PERCENTAGE OF SALES AND PERCENTAGE OF RECEIVABLES At the end of the current year, the accounts receivable account of Glenn's Nursery Supplies has a debit balance of $390,000. Credit sales are $2,800,000. Record the end-of-period adjusting entry on December 31, in general journal form, for the estimated bad debt expense. Assume the following independent conditions existed prior to the adjustment.

1. Allowance for Bad Debts has a credit balance of $1,760.

    a. The percentage of sales method is used and bad debt expense is estimated to be 1% of credit sales.

    b. The percentage of receivables method is used and an analysis of the accounts produces an estimate of $30,330 in uncollectible accounts.

2. Allowance for Bad Debts has a debit balance of $1,900.

    a. The percentage of sales method is used and bad debt expense is estimated to be ¾ of 1% of credit sales.

    b. The percentage of receivables method is used and an analysis of the accounts produces an estimate of $29,890 in uncollectible accounts.

EXERCISE 17-6A   (LO3)
July 20, Dr. Bad Debt Exp.:
$2,325

DIRECT WRITE-OFF METHOD Maria Rivera, owner of Rivera Pharmacy, uses the direct write-off method in accounting for uncollectible accounts. Record the following transactions in general journal form.

July 20   Wrote off $2,325 owed by Joe Balouka, who has no assets.

Oct. 15   Wrote off $1,675 owed by Alice Rose, who declared bankruptcy.

EXERCISE 17-7A   **(LO3)**   **COLLECTION OF ACCOUNT WRITTEN OFF—DIRECT WRITE-OFF METHOD**
Sept. 2, Cr. Bad Debt Exp.: Como's Music Store uses the direct write-off method in accounting for uncol-
$1,745   lectible accounts. Record the following transactions in general journal form.

20-1

May 8   Wrote off $1,745 owed by Vickie Lawrence, who has no assets.

July 15   Wrote off $1,300 owed by Dan Utter, who declared bankruptcy.

Sept. 2   Reinstated the account of Vickie Lawrence, which had been written off on May 8, and received $1,745 cash in full settlement.

20-2

May 15   Reinstated the account of Dan Utter, which had been written off in the previous year, and received $1,300 cash in full settlement.

SERIES A PROBLEMS

PROBLEM 17-8A   **(LO1/2)**   **UNCOLLECTIBLE ACCOUNTS—ALLOWANCE METHOD**   Emery Nurseries used the allowance method to record the following transactions, adjusting entries, and closing entries during the year ended December 31, 20--.

3. $921,300

Feb. 9   Received 60% of the $5,000 balance owed by Patty's Petunias, a bankrupt business, and wrote off the remainder as uncollectible.

May 28   Reinstated the account of Danielle Bell, which had been written off in the preceding year, and received $2,400 cash in full settlement.

Aug. 16   Wrote off the $8,200 balance owed by Rich Bouie as uncollectible.

Oct. 5   Reinstated the account of Bonnie McCelland, which had been written off in the preceding year, and received $3,600 cash in full settlement.

Dec. 28   Wrote off the following accounts as uncollectible, in compound entry form: Bloudeck & Rhodes, $14,450; Creative Landscapers, $16,100; Ramona Randol, $12,750.

31   Based on an aging analysis of the $980,000 of accounts receivable, it was estimated that $58,700 will be uncollectible. Made the adjusting entry.

31   Made the entry to close the appropriate account to Income Summary.

Selected accounts and beginning balances on January 1, 20--, are as follows:

122.1	Allowance for Bad Debts	$52,000 credit
313	Income Summary	—
532	Bad Debt Expense	—

REQUIRED

1.   Open the three selected accounts.

2.   Enter the transactions and the adjusting and closing entries in a general journal (page 6). After each entry, post to the three accounts named.

3.   Determine the net realizable value as of December 31.

PROBLEM 17-9A   (LO2)

1(b). Dr. Bad Debt Exp.: $6,620

UNCOLLECTIBLE ACCOUNTS—PERCENTAGE OF SALES AND PERCENTAGE OF RECEIVABLES At the completion of the current fiscal year ending December 31, the balance of Accounts Receivable for Yang's Gift Shop was $30,000. Credit sales for the year were $355,200.

REQUIRED

Make the necessary adjusting entry in general journal form under each of the following assumptions. Show calculations for the amount of each adjustment and the resulting net realizable value.

1. Allowance for Bad Debts has a credit balance of $330.

    a. The percentage of sales method is used and bad debt expense is estimated to be 2.0% of credit sales.

    b. The percentage of receivables method is used and an analysis of the accounts produces an estimate of $6,950 in uncollectible accounts.

2. Allowance for Bad Debts has a debit balance of $400.

    a. The percentage of sales method is used and bad debt expense is estimated to be 1.5% of credit sales.

    b. The percentage of receivables method is used and an analysis of the accounts produces an estimate of $5,685 in uncollectible accounts.

PROBLEM 17-10A   (LO2)

2. Dr. Bad Debt Exp.: $2,790

AGING ACCOUNTS RECEIVABLE An analysis of the accounts receivable of Johnson Company as of December 31, 20--, reveals the following.

Age Interval	Balance	Estimated Percent Uncollectible
Not yet due	$65,000	2%
1–30 days past due	4,500	5
31–60 days past due	3,550	10
61–90 days past due	1,650	25
91–180 days past due	1,200	35
181–365 days past due	650	55
Over 365 days past due	400	85
Total	$76,950	

REQUIRED

1. Prepare an aging schedule as of December 31, 20--, by adding the following column to the three columns shown above: Estimated Amount Uncollectible.

2. Assuming that Allowance for Bad Debts had a credit balance of $620 before adjustment, record the end-of-period adjusting entry in general journal form to enter the estimate for the bad debt expense.

PROBLEM 17-11A   (LO3)

PASS
PowerAccounting System Software®

Yr. 2, Jan. 17, Cr.
Uncoll. Accounts
Recovered: $6,300

DIRECT WRITE-OFF METHOD Williams & Hendricks Distributors uses the direct write-off method in accounting for uncollectible accounts.

20-1

Feb. 18   Sold merchandise on account to Merry Merchants, $17,500.

Mar. 22   Sold merchandise on account to Utter Unicorns, $14,300.

June 3   Received $10,000 from Merry Merchants and wrote off the remainder owed on the sale of February 18 as uncollectible.

(continued)

Sept. 9	Received $8,000 from Utter Unicorns and wrote off the remainder owed on the sale of March 22 as uncollectible.
Nov. 13	Reinstated the account of Merry Merchants, which had been written off on June 3, and received $7,500 cash in full settlement.

20-2

Jan. 17	Reinstated the account of Utter Unicorns, which had been written off on September 9 of the previous year, and received $6,300 cash in full settlement.

REQUIRED

Record the transactions in general journal form.

SERIES B EXERCISES

EXERCISE 17-1B   **(LO1)**
1. Net Realizable Value: $60,025

CALCULATION OF NET REALIZABLE VALUE Mary Martin owns a department store that has a $65,200 balance in Accounts Receivable and a $5,175 credit balance in Allowance for Bad Debts.

1. Determine the net realizable value of the accounts receivable.

2. Assume that an account receivable in the amount of $900 was written off using the allowance method. Determine the net realizable value of the accounts receivable after the write-off.

EXERCISE 17-2B   **(LO2)**
1. Dr. Bad Debt Exp.: $7,600

UNCOLLECTIBLE ACCOUNTS—PERCENTAGE OF SALES Nicole's Neckties has total credit sales for the year of $380,000 and estimates that 2% of its credit sales will be uncollectible. Record the end-of-period adjusting entry on December 31, in general journal form, for the estimated bad debt expense. Assume the following independent conditions existed prior to the adjustment.

1. Allowance for Bad Debts has a credit balance of $430.

2. Allowance for Bad Debts has a debit balance of $295.

EXERCISE 17-3B   **(LO2)**
2. Dr. Bad Debt Exp.: $4,495

UNCOLLECTIBLE ACCOUNTS—PERCENTAGE OF RECEIVABLES Charlie's Chevy Sales and Service estimates the amount of uncollectible accounts using the percentage of receivables method. After aging the accounts, it is estimated that $3,935 will not be collected. Record the end-of-period adjusting entry on December 31, in general journal form, for the estimated bad debt expense. Assume the following independent conditions existed prior to the adjustment.

1. Allowance for Bad Debts has a credit balance of $245.

2. Allowance for Bad Debts has a debit balance of $560.

EXERCISE 17-4B   **(LO2)**
Sept. 23, Cr. Allow. for Bad Debts: $6,040

COLLECTION OF ACCOUNT WRITTEN OFF—ALLOWANCE METHOD Raynette Ramos, owner of Ramos Rentals, uses the allowance method in accounting for uncollectible accounts. Record the following transactions in general journal form.

July 9	Wrote off $6,040 owed by Sue Sanchez, who has no assets.
Aug. 15	Wrote off $4,790 owed by Lonnie Jones, who declared bankruptcy.
Sept. 23	Reinstated the account of Sue Sanchez, which had been written off on July 9, and received $6,040 cash in full settlement.

EXERCISE 17-5B   **(LO2)**
1(b), Dr. Bad Debt Exp.: $22,640

UNCOLLECTIBLE ACCOUNTS—PERCENTAGE OF SALES AND PERCENTAGE OF RECEIVABLES At the end of the current year, the accounts receivable account of Parker's Nursery Supplies has a debit balance of $350,000. Credit sales are $2,300,000. Record the end-of-period adjusting entry on December 31, in general journal form, for the estimated bad debt expense. Assume the following independent conditions existed prior to the adjustment.

1. Allowance for Bad Debts has a credit balance of $1,920.

    a. The percentage of sales method is used and bad debt expense is estimated to be 1% of credit sales.

    b. The percentage of receivables method is used and an analysis of the accounts produces an estimate of $24,560 in uncollectible accounts.

2. Allowance for Bad Debts has a debit balance of $1,280.

    a. The percentage of sales method is used and bad debt expense is estimated to be ¾ of 1% of credit sales.

    b. The percentage of receivables method is used and an analysis of the accounts produces an estimate of $22,440 in uncollectible accounts.

EXERCISE 17-6B   **(LO3)**
July 19, Dr. Bad Debt Exp.: $1,935

DIRECT WRITE-OFF METHOD Brent Mussellman, owner of Brent's Barbells, uses the direct write-off method in accounting for uncollectible accounts. Record the following transactions in general journal form.

July 19   Wrote off $1,935 owed by Arnold Swartz, who has no assets.

Oct. 12   Wrote off $2,125 owed by Janice Strong, who declared bankruptcy.

EXERCISE 17-7B   **(LO3)**
Sept. 20, Cr. Bad Debt Exp.: $2,360

COLLECTION OF ACCOUNT WRITTEN OFF—DIRECT WRITE-OFF METHOD Madonna's Music Store uses the direct write-off method in accounting for uncollectible accounts. Record the following transactions in general journal form.

20-1

May 5   Wrote off $2,360 owed by Neal Dammond, who has no assets.

July 18   Wrote off $1,255 owed by Maxine Mouse, who declared bankruptcy.

Sept. 20   Reinstated the account of Neal Dammond, which had been written off on May 5, and received $2,360 cash in full settlement.

20-2

May 11   Reinstated the account of Maxine Mouse, which had been written off in the previous year, and received $1,255 cash in full settlement.

SERIES B PROBLEMS

PROBLEM 17-8B   **(LO1/2)**

3. $1,107,850

UNCOLLECTIBLE ACCOUNTS—ALLOWANCE METHOD Lewis Warehouse used the allowance method to record the following transactions, adjusting entries, and closing entries during the year ended December 31, 20--.

Feb. 7   Received 70% of the $8,000 balance owed by Luxury Sofas, a bankrupt business, and wrote off the remainder as uncollectible.

May 26   Reinstated the account of Sandy Johnson, which had been written off in the preceding year, and received $3,725 cash in full settlement.

(continued)

Aug. 15   Wrote off the $9,350 balance owed by Izumi Goto as uncollectible.

Oct. 6   Reinstated the account of Doreen Woods, which had been written off in the preceding year, and received $4,320 cash in full settlement.

Dec. 29   Wrote off the following accounts as uncollectible, in compound entry form: Schmidt & Yeager, $13,945; Economy Homes, $15,830; Davis Industries, $11,865.

31   Based on an aging analysis of the $1,175,000 of accounts receivable, it was estimated that $67,150 will be uncollectible. Made the adjusting entry.

31   Made the entry to close the appropriate account to Income Summary.

Selected accounts and beginning balances on January 1, 20--, are as follows:

122.1	Allowance for Bad Debts	$49,850 credit
313	Income Summary	—
532	Bad Debt Expense	—

REQUIRED

1. Open the three selected accounts.

2. Enter the transactions and the adjusting and closing entries in a general journal (page 6). After each entry, post to the three accounts named.

3. Determine the net realizable value as of December 31, 20--.

PROBLEM 17-9B   **(LO2)**
1(b). Dr. Bad Debt Exp.: $27,650

UNCOLLECTIBLE ACCOUNTS—PERCENTAGE OF SALES AND PERCENTAGE OF RECEIVABLES At the completion of the current fiscal year ending December 31, the balance of Accounts Receivable for Anderson's Greeting Cards was $180,000. Credit sales for the year were $1,950,000.

REQUIRED

Make the necessary adjusting entry in general journal form under each of the following assumptions. Show calculations for the amount of each adjustment and the resulting net realizable value.

1. Allowance for Bad Debts has a credit balance of $2,600.

    a. The percentage of sales method is used and bad debt expense is estimated to be 1.5% of credit sales.

    b. The percentage of receivables method is used and an analysis of the accounts produces an estimate of $30,250 in uncollectible accounts.

2. Allowance for Bad Debts has a debit balance of $1,900.

    a. The percentage of sales method is used and bad debt expense is estimated to be 1.0% of credit sales.

    b. The percentage of receivables method is used and an analysis of the accounts produces an estimate of $20,500 in uncollectible accounts.

PROBLEM 17-10B   (LO2)
2. Dr. Bad Debt Exp.: $9,792

AGING ACCOUNTS RECEIVABLE An analysis of the accounts receivable of Matsushita Company as of December 31, 20--, reveals the following.

Age Interval	Balance	Estimated Percent Uncollectible
Not yet due	$250,000	1.5%
1–30 days past due	17,000	4
31–60 days past due	12,800	9
61–90 days past due	8,200	20
91–180 days past due	4,600	30
181–365 days past due	4,200	45
over 365 days past due	1,400	75
Total	$298,200	

REQUIRED

1. Prepare an aging schedule as of December 31, 20--, by adding the following column to the three columns shown above: Estimated Amount Uncollectible.

2. Assuming that Allowance for Bad Debts had a credit balance of $1,750 before adjustment, record the end-of-period adjusting entry in general journal form to enter the estimate for the bad debt expense.

PROBLEM 17-11B   (LO3)

PASS
Power Accounting System Software®

Yr. 2, Jan. 11, Cr.
Uncoll. Accounts
Recovered: $5,800

DIRECT WRITE-OFF METHOD Lee and Chen Distributors uses the direct write-off method in accounting for uncollectible accounts.

20-1

Feb. 16   Sold merchandise on account to Biggs and Daughters, $16,000.

Mar. 23   Sold merchandise on account to Lloyd Place, $12,800.

June 8   Received $12,000 from Biggs and Daughters and wrote off the remainder owed on the sale of February 16 as uncollectible.

Sept. 27   Received $7,000 from Lloyd Place and wrote off the remainder owed on the sale of March 23 as uncollectible.

Nov. 18   Reinstated the account of Biggs and Daughters, which had been written off on June 8, and received $4,000 cash in full settlement.

20-2

Jan. 11   Reinstated the account of Lloyd Place, which had been written off on September 27 of the previous year, and received $5,800 cash in full settlement.

REQUIRED

Record the transactions in general journal form.

MASTERY PROBLEM

5. Net realizable value: $59,000

Sam and Robert are identical twins. They opened identical businesses and experienced identical transactions. However, they decided to estimate uncollectible accounts in different ways. Sam elected to use the percentage of sales method and Robert elected to use the percentage of receivables method. Listed below are the beginning balances of Cash, Accounts Receivable, and Allowance for Bad Debts (items a–c), and summary transactions that occurred during the year (items d–g) for both businesses. Remember, both businesses experienced the same events: credit sales, collections of receivables, and write-offs. The only difference between the businesses is the method of estimating uncollectible accounts.

	Sam	Robert
(a) Balance of Cash, January 1, 20--	$300,000	$300,000
(b) Balance of Accounts Receivable, January 1	50,000	50,000
(c) Balance of Allowance for Bad Debts, January 1	5,000	5,000
(d) Sales on account during 20--	550,000	550,000
(e) Collections on account during 20--	530,000	530,000
(f) Uncollectible accounts written off during 20--	4,500	4,500
(g) Collections made on accounts written off during 20--	500	500

REQUIRED

1. Enter items (a) through (c) in two sets of general ledger accounts: one for Sam and one for Robert.

For Sam:

2. Prepare entries in a general journal (page 4) for summary transactions (d) through (g) for Sam.

3. Post the entries to a general ledger for Sam, using the following accounts and numbers.

Cash	101
Accounts Receivable	122
Allowance for Bad Debts	122.1
Sales	401
Bad Debt Expense	532

4. Sam estimates that 1% of all sales on account will be uncollectible. Calculate the estimated bad debt expense and make the appropriate adjusting entry in a general journal. Post the entry to the general ledger accounts on December 31, 20--.

5. Compute the net realizable value of Sam's accounts receivable on December 31, 20--.

For Robert:

6. Prepare entries in a general journal (page 4) for summary transactions (d) through (g) for Robert.

7. Post the entries to a general ledger for Robert, using the same accounts and numbers as were used for Sam.

8. Robert bases the estimate of uncollectible accounts on an aging schedule of accounts receivable. Using the following information, compute the estimated uncollectible amounts and make the appropriate adjusting entry in a general journal. Post the entry to the general ledger accounts on December 31, 20--.

Customers	Invoice Dates and Amounts for Unpaid Invoices					
Beets, D.	10/7	$2,300	11/15	$1,200	12/18	$8,500
Cook, L.	6/1	1,200	8/15	2,500		
Hylton, D.	9/23	4,300	10/22	2,500	12/23	2,800
Martin, D.	10/15	5,400	11/12	3,200	12/15	1,500
Stokes, D.	9/9	200	12/15	9,500		
Taylor, T.	11/20	400	12/10	1,400		
Thomas, O.	12/2	5,500				
Tower, R.	12/15	2,300				
Williams, G.	11/18	2,800	12/8	8,000		

All sales are billed n/30. The following aging chart is used to estimate the uncollectibles using the percentage of receivables method.

Age Interval	Estimated Percent Uncollectible
Not yet due	2%
1–30 days	5
31–60 days	10
61–90 days	25
91–120 days	50
Over 120 days	80

9. Compute the net realizable value for Robert on December 31, 20--.

CHALLENGE PROBLEM

This problem challenges you to apply your cumulative accounting knowledge to move a step beyond the material in the chapter.

2. Dr. Bad Debt Exp.: $25,000

1. Martel Co. has $320,000 in Accounts Receivable on December 31, 20-1, the end of its first year of operations. The business is new, so it has no prior experience with uncollectible accounts. In Martel's overall industry, the percentage of uncollectible accounts receivable is about 3%. For companies similar to Martel in size and operations, the percentage is about 5%. Martel decides to use the overall industry experience as the basis for its estimate of uncollectible accounts.

REQUIRED

Prepare the adjusting entry on December 31, 20-1 for Martel Co.'s bad debt expense.

2. At the end of 20-2, Martel Co. had $380,000 in Accounts Receivable and a debit balance of $6,000 in Allowance for Bad Debts. Because it has been operating for only two years, Martel once again wants to base its estimate of uncollectible accounts on the industry average or the experience of similar companies. The industry and similar company percentages for the year were the same as in 20-1.

(continued)

REQUIRED

Based on Martel Co.'s experience in 20-2, select the most appropriate basis (industry or similar company) for estimating its uncollectible accounts for 20-2. Prepare the adjusting entry on December 31, 20-2 for Martel Co.'s bad debt expense.

3. At the end of 20-3, Martel Co. had $410,000 in Accounts Receivable and a credit balance of $300 in Allowance for Bad Debts. Martel has now been in business for three years and wants to base its estimate of uncollectible accounts on its own experience.

REQUIRED

Assume that Martel Co.'s adjusting entry for bad debt expense on December 31, 20-2 was a debit to Bad Debt Expense and a credit to Allowance for Bad Debts of $25,000.

a. Estimate Martel's uncollectible accounts percentage based on its actual bad debt experience during the past two years.

b. Prepare the adjusting entry on December 31, 20-3 for Martel Co.'s bad debt expense.

© GETTY IMAGES / PHOTODISC

Accounting for Notes and Interest

Evan Taylor recently arranged to borrow $3,000 from a bank. He plans to use this money to pay for new counters and shelving in one of his stores. The term of the loan is 12 months, and the stated interest rate is 9%. At the closing meeting on the loan, Evan signed a note for $3,000 but was given only $2,730. The loan officer explained that the bank had "deducted the interest of $270 in advance." Is the bank trying to cheat Evan? What interest rate is Evan really paying to borrow the $2,730 (rather than the $3,000 he wanted)?

Careful study of this chapter should enable you to:

LO1 Describe a promissory note.

LO2 Calculate interest on and determine the due date of promissory notes.

LO3 Account for notes receivable transactions and accrued interest.

LO4 Account for notes payable transactions and accrued interest.

In Chapter 17, we learned how to account for accounts receivable. Recall that an account receivable is an unwritten promise by a customer to pay for goods or services. In this chapter, we will learn how to account for a more formal, written type of receivable called a promissory note.

After completing our study of notes receivable, we will learn to account for notes payable. You will see that a note payable is very similar to a note receivable. Both are promissory notes. We simply look at the note from two different points of view. A note receivable is someone's promise to pay you. A note payable is your promise to pay someone else.

THE PROMISSORY NOTE

LO1 Describe a promissory note.

A **promissory note** (usually called a note) is a written promise to pay a specific sum at a definite future date. The note must be signed by the person or business agreeing to make the payment, known as the **maker** of the note. The note must be payable to a specific person or business, known as the **payee**.

Notes are often used when credit is extended for 60 days or more, or when large amounts of money are involved. Figure 18-1 shows one form of promissory note. Sara Morney, the maker of the note, promises to pay a specific amount of money ($2,500) at a definite future time (September 7). Central Bank, the payee of the note, is to receive the specified amount of money. Notice that to Morney it is a note payable while to Central Bank it is a note receivable.

PAYEE	MAKER	
Central Bank	Sarah Morney	Loan Number __2307__
711 Wakarusa	1123 Main	Date __6/9/20--__
Lawrence, KS 66049	Lecompton, KS 66050	Maturity Date __9/7/20--__
		Loan Amount __$2500.00__
LENDER	**BORROWER**	Renewal Of _____
"You" means the Lender, its successors and assigns.	"I" includes each Borrower above, jointly and severally.	

NOTE – For value received, I promise to pay to you, or your order, at your address above, the principal sum of:
__Two thousand five hundred and no/100__ – – – – – – – – – – – Dollars $ __2,500.00__
plus interest from __6/9/20--__ at the rate of __9.0__ % per year until paid in full.
Payment – I will pay this note as follows:
  Interest due: __9/7/20--__
  Principal due: __9/7/20--__
                                    Signature __Sarah Morney__

FIGURE 18-1 Promissory Note

Notes may be interest bearing or non-interest bearing. An **interest-bearing note** is one with an explicit interest rate stated on the face of the note. The note in Figure 18-1 is a 9% interest-bearing note. A **non-interest-bearing note** is one on which no rate of interest is specified, although the note does include an interest component. Notes signed when borrowing from a bank often are of this type. This type of transaction is illustrated later in the chapter.

CALCULATING INTEREST AND DETERMINING DUE DATE

LO2 Calculate interest on and determine the due date of promissory notes.

To calculate interest on notes, three factors are used:

1. Principal of the note

2. Rate of interest

3. Term of the note

The **principal of the note** is the face amount of the note that the maker promises to pay at maturity. The principal is the base on which the interest is calculated. The principal of the note in Figure 18-1 is $2,500.

The **rate of interest** usually is expressed as a percentage, such as 8% or 10%. Ordinarily an annual rate is used, but in some cases a monthly rate is quoted, such as 1½% a month. A rate of 1½% a month is equivalent to a rate of 18% a year payable monthly (1½% × 12 = 18%). The rate of interest on the note in Figure 18-1 is 9% per year.

The **term of the note** is the months or days from the date of issue to the date of maturity. The term of the note is used to calculate **time**, which is the term of the note stated as a fraction of a year. When the term of the note is specified in months, time is calculated on the basis of months. For example, a 3-month note issued on June 1 is payable on September 1, and time is calculated as follows:

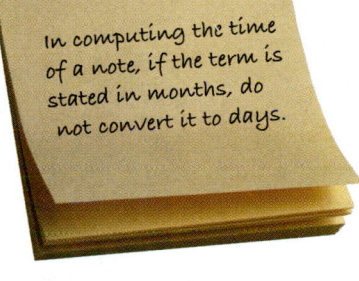

In computing the time of a note, if the term is stated in months, do not convert it to days.

Time
3 mos./12 mos. = 3/12 = ¼ year

When the term of a note is specified in days or when the due date is specified in a note, time is computed using the exact number of days from the date of the note to the date of its maturity. In making this computation, the maturity date is counted but the date of issue is not. For example, for a $1,000, 9% note dated March 1, with a due date of June 1, time is computed as follows:

Days in March	31	
Deduct date of note, March 1	1	
Days remaining in March		30
Add: Days in April		30
Days in May		31
Maturity date, June 1		1
Total time in days		92

Time = 92/360

LEARNING KEY: To compute the time of a note, count the maturity date; do *not* count the date of issue.

Notice the use of 360 in the denominator in the above calculation. In computing interest, it is common to use 360 days as a year. Many banks and business firms follow this practice, though all federal government agencies use 365 days as the base in computing daily interest.

The due date of the note in Figure 18-1 is September 7. The term of the note is ninety days, calculated as follows:

Days in June	30	
Deduct date of note, June 9	9	
Days remaining in June		21
Add: Days in July		31
Days in August		31
Maturity date, September 7		7
Total time in days		90

Calculating Interest

The principal, interest rate, and time of the note are used in the following formula to calculate interest:

$$\text{Interest} = \text{Principal} \times \text{Rate} \times \text{Time}$$

LEARNING KEY: I = P × R × T
I = amount of *interest*
P = amount of *principal*
R = *rate* of interest (annual)
T = *time*

For the $1,000, 9% note described on page 677, interest is calculated as follows:

$$
\begin{aligned}
I &= P \times R \times T \\
&= \$1,000 \times .09 \times 92/360 \\
&= \$23
\end{aligned}
$$

For a $2,000, 8% note due in 3 months, interest is calculated as follows:

$$
\begin{aligned}
I &= P \times R \times T \\
&= \$2,000 \times .08 \times 3/12 \\
&= \$40
\end{aligned}
$$

For the note in Figure 18-1, interest is calculated as follows:

$$
\begin{aligned}
I &= P \times R \times T \\
&= \$2,500 \times .09 \times 90/360 \\
&= \$56.25
\end{aligned}
$$

The principal of the note plus interest equals the **maturity value** of the note. For example, the maturity value of the $1,000 note above is $1,023. Similarly, the maturity value of the $2,000 note is $2,040. Figure 18-2 uses a time line to illustrate the gradual accumulation of interest on the $1,000 note to its $1,023 maturity value.

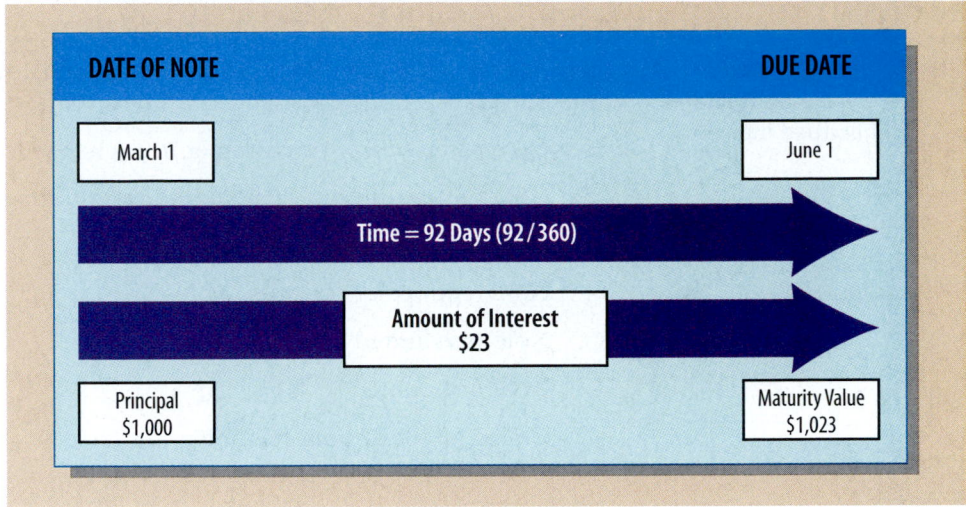

FIGURE 18-2 Accumulation of Interest Time Line

Determining the Due Date

As previously explained, the period of time between the date of issue and the maturity date of a note may be stated in either months or days. If the term of the note is stated in months, the due date is determined by counting the number of months from the date the note was issued. The note is due on the date in the month of maturity that corresponds with the date the note was issued. For example, a three-month note dated August 10 would be due November 10. If there is no date in the month of maturity corresponding to the issue date, the due date is the last day of the month. For example, a three-month note dated January 31 would be due April 30.

If the term of the note is stated in days, the due date is the specified number of days after the issue date. To determine the due date, apply these three steps:

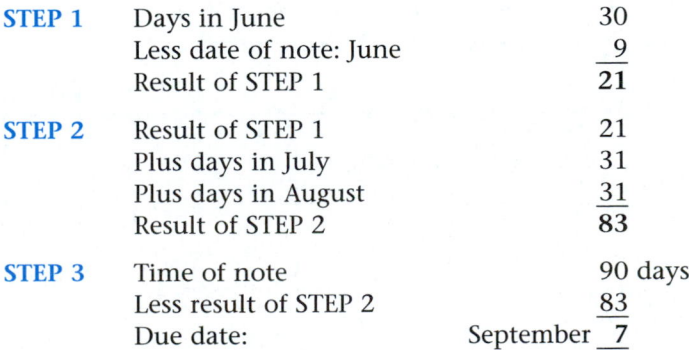

The examples throughout the chapter are for notes of 90 days and less. Notes can be for much longer periods of time—2 to 5 years is common with auto loans.

STEP 1   Subtract the date on which the note was issued from the number of days in the month of issuance.

STEP 2   Add to the result of STEP 1 the number of days in as many months as possible without exceeding the time of the note.

STEP 3   Subtract the result of STEP 2 from the time of the note. The result is the date of the month the note is due.

To calculate the due date of the note in Figure 18-1, a 90-day note dated June 9, apply the three steps as follows:

STEP 1
Days in June	30
Less date of note: June	9
Result of STEP 1	**21**

STEP 2
Result of STEP 1	21
Plus days in July	31
Plus days in August	31
Result of STEP 2	**83**

STEP 3
Time of note	90 days
Less result of STEP 2	83
Due date:	September 7

ACCOUNTING FOR NOTES RECEIVABLE TRANSACTIONS

LO3 Account for notes receivable transactions and accrued interest.

Businesses other than banks and savings and loans generally encounter seven types of transactions involving notes receivable:

1. Note received from a customer in exchange for assets sold

2. Note received from a customer to extend time for payment of an account

3. Note collected at maturity

4. Note renewed at maturity

5. Note discounted before maturity

6. Note dishonored

7. Collection of dishonored note

Note Received from a Customer in Exchange for Assets Sold

When a business makes a large sale, it may accept a note for the amount of the sale. A business may be willing to accept the note for two reasons. First, the note is a formal, written promise to pay. This note can be converted to cash at a bank if necessary. Second, the note is likely to bear interest.

Assume that on June 1 Linesch Hardware Co. sells an industrial mower to Williams Manufacturing for $8,500. Williams gives Linesch a 180-day, 9% note for $8,500 in exchange for the mower. This transaction is entered by Linesch as follows:

1	June	1	Notes Receivable		8 5 0 0 00		1
2			Sales			8 5 0 0 00	2
3			Received note for merchandise sale				3

Note Received from a Customer to Extend Time for Payment

When a customer's account is due, the customer may issue a note for all or part of the amount. Assume that Michael Putter owes Linesch Hardware Co. $2,000 on account. To settle the account, Putter gives Linesch a 90-day, 10% note dated June 8. This transaction is entered by Linesch as follows:

15	June	8	Notes Receivable		2 0 0 0 00		15
16			Accounts Receivable/M. Putter			2 0 0 0 00	16
17			Received note to settle account				17

If instead Putter gives a check for $250 and a note for $1,750 to settle the account, Linesch makes the following entry.

15	June	8	Cash		2 5 0 00		15
16			Notes Receivable		1 7 5 0 00		16
17			Accounts Receivable/M. Putter			2 0 0 0 00	17
18			Received cash and note to settle account				18

Note Collected at Maturity

When a note receivable matures, it may be collected:

1. By the payee (in Figure 18-1, Central Bank),

2. By the bank named in the note, or

3. By a bank where it was left for collection.

Assume that on September 6, Putter pays Linesch the $2,000 principal plus $50 interest on the note described above. Linesch makes the following entry.

31	Sept.	6	Cash		2 0 5 0 00		31
32			Notes Receivable			2 0 0 0 00	32
33			Interest Revenue			5 0 00	33
34			Received payment of note with interest				34

When a bank makes the collection, it notifies the payee that the net amount has been added to the payee's account. The bank uses a **credit advice** like the one in Figure 18-3 for this purpose.

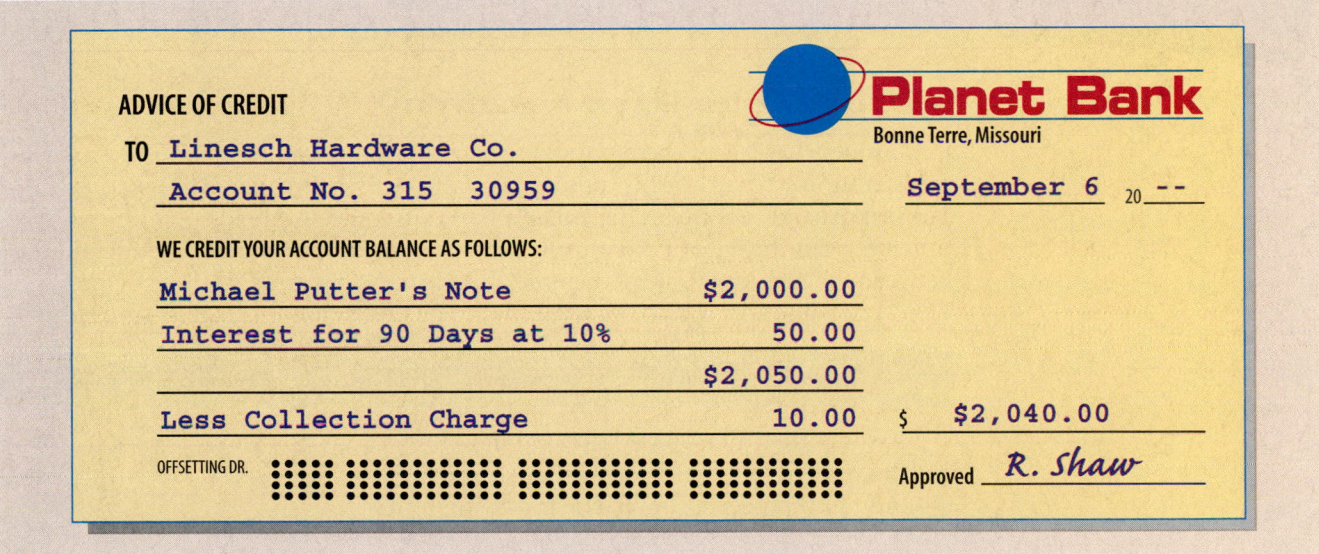

FIGURE 18-3   Credit Advice

Assume that Linesch left Putter's 90-day, 10% note for $2,000 at Planet Bank for collection. On September 6, the bank notifies Linesch that the note plus $50 interest have been collected. The bank fee for collecting the note was $10. Linesch enters this transaction as follows:

37	Sept.	6	Cash		2 0 4 0 00		37
38			Collection Expense		1 0 00		38
39			Notes Receivable			2 0 0 0 00	39
40			Interest Revenue			5 0 00	40
41			Received payment of note with interest				41
42			less collection fee				42

Note Renewed at Maturity

If the maker of a note is unable to pay the amount due at maturity, the payee may allow the maker to renew all or part of the note. Assume that at maturity of the $2,000 note, Putter pays only the $50 interest and gives a new 60-day, 10% note. Linesch enters this transaction as follows:

31	Sept.	6	Cash		5 0 00		31
32			Notes Receivable (new note)	2 0 0 0 00			32
33			Notes Receivable (old note)			2 0 0 0 00	33
34			Interest Revenue			5 0 00	34
35			Received new note plus interest on old note				35

If Putter pays $50 interest plus $500 on the principal and gives a new 90-day, 11% note for $1,500, Linesch makes the following entry:

31	Sept.	6	Cash		5 5 0 00		31
32			Notes Receivable (new note)	1 5 0 0 00			32
33			Notes Receivable (old note)			2 0 0 0 00	33
34			Interest Revenue			5 0 00	34
35			Received new note plus partial payment				35
36			and interest on old note				36

> One of the reasons a business might prefer a promissory note from a customer is that the business can obtain cash by discounting the note at the bank.

Note Discounted Before Maturity

If a business needs cash before the due date of a note, it can endorse the note and transfer it to a bank. This process is called **discounting a note receivable**. The bank charges an interest fee called a **bank discount** for the **discount period**, the time between the date of discounting and the due date of the note. The difference between the maturity value of the note and the bank discount is called the **proceeds**. This is the amount of cash received by the business discounting the note.

> Maturity Value − Discount = Proceeds

Assume that the $2,000, 10%, 90-day note receivable from Putter dated June 8 is discounted by Linesch at the bank on July 8 at a rate of 12%. To calculate the discount and proceeds, apply the following four steps.

STEP 1 Compute the maturity value of the note.

Face	+	Interest	=	**Maturity Value**
$2,000	+	$50	=	$2,050

STEP 2 Compute the number of days in the discount period—from the discount date to the due date.

Discount date	July 8	
Days in July		31
Less discount date	July	8
Remaining days in July		23
Plus days in August		31
Plus due date	September	6
Days in **discount period**		60

STEP 3 Compute the discount amount.

Maturity Value*	×	Discount Rate	×	Discount Period	=	**Discount Amount**
$2,050	×	12%	×	60/360	=	$41

*Note that in calculating the discount amount, the *maturity value* of the note is used, not the principal.

STEP 4   Compute the proceeds.

Maturity Value	–	Discount Amount	=	**Proceeds**
$2,050	–	$41	=	$2,009

 LEARNING KEY: To calculate the discount amount, use the maturity value of the note.

Figure 18-4 shows a time line illustration of this transaction.

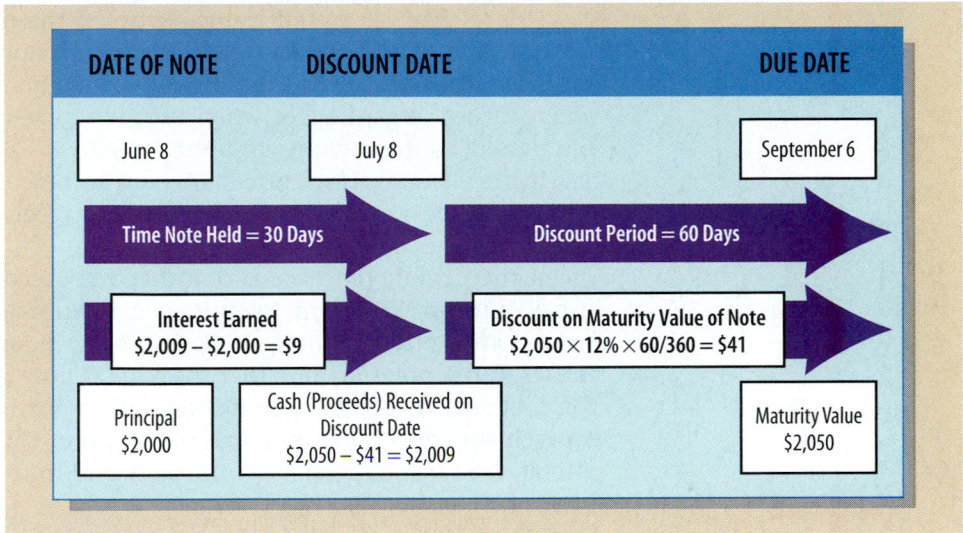

FIGURE 18-4   Discounted Note Receivable Time Line

The excess of the $2,009 proceeds over the $2,000 face value of the note represents interest revenue of $9. Linesch enters this transaction as follows:

26	July	8	Cash		2 0 0 9 00			26
27			Notes Receivable			2 0 0 0 00		27
28			Interest Revenue			9 00		28
29			Discounted note receivable					29

If the proceeds from discounting a note are less than the face value of the note, the difference represents interest expense. For example, if the proceeds from discounting Putter's $2,000 note were only $1,992, Linesch would make the following entry.

26	July	8	Cash		1 9 9 2 00			26
27			Interest Expense		8 00			27
28			Notes Receivable			2 0 0 0 00		28
29			Discounted note receivable					29

When a note receivable is discounted, the business that endorses the note becomes potentially liable to the bank. If the maker of the note does not pay it at maturity, the business that discounted the note must pay the maturity value and any bank fees to the bank. This kind of potential liability that may become a real liability, depending on future events, is called a **contingent liability**. A contingent liability does not affect the accounting records. It is disclosed in the notes to the financial statements.

Note Dishonored

If the maker of a note does not pay or renew it at maturity, the note is said to be **dishonored**. The maker of the note is still liable to the payee for the principal amount plus interest. But a dishonored note loses its legal status as a note receivable. Therefore, the payee transfers the amount due from Notes Receivable to Accounts Receivable. For example, if the $2,000, 10%, 90-day note from Putter is dishonored, Linesch makes the following entry.

16	Sept.	6	Accounts Receivable/M. Putter		2 0 5 0 00		16
17			Notes Receivable			2 0 0 0 00	17
18			Interest Revenue			5 0 00	18
19			Note receivable dishonored				19

Notice that the $50 difference between the maturity value and principal of the note is credited to Interest Revenue. This is done even though the amount has not been collected. Recall that under accrual accounting, revenue is recognized when earned, regardless of when cash is received. The time period of the note has passed, so the interest has been earned.

If the claim against Putter turns out to be completely worthless, the $2,050 will be treated as an uncollectible account receivable. Chapter 17 showed how to account for this type of transaction.

If the dishonored note is one that was discounted at a bank, the endorser usually must pay the bank the principal, interest, and any bank fees. The endorser records the total amount paid to the bank as an account receivable from the maker of the note. Assume that the $2,000 note receivable discounted on July 8 for proceeds of $2,009 was dishonored by Putter at maturity. The bank bills Linesch for the $2,000 principal of the note, $50 interest, and a $10 bank fee, a total of $2,060. Linesch pays the bank and makes the following journal entry.

23	Sept.	6	Accounts Receivable/M. Putter		2 0 6 0 00		23
24			Cash			2 0 6 0 00	24
25			Paid bank for dishonored note				25

Note that the $10 bank fee is included in the amount receivable from Putter. This is because the fee was incurred as a result of Putter's dishonoring of the note, and this is not Linesch's expense.

Collection of Dishonored Note

What if a note that has been dishonored eventually is collected? When that occurs, the payee records collection of the account receivable. In addition, interest usually is charged for the period from the due date of the original note to the final collection date. Interest is based on the maturity value of the note plus the bank fee, if any, incurred when the note was dishonored. Let's look again at Putter's $2,000 note that Linesch discounted at the bank on July 8. When this note was dishonored on September 6, the $2,000 principal of the note, $50 interest, and $10 bank fee were transferred to Accounts Receivable. Assume that on October 16, Putter pays the original maturity value of the note plus the bank fee ($2,060) and interest for the period from September 6 to October 16. Interest would be computed as follows.

Original Maturity Value Plus Bank Fee	×	Rate	×	Time		
$2,060	×	10%	×	40*/360	=	$22.89

* Days in September	30
Less original maturity date of note	6
Days remaining in September	24
Plus due date in October	16
Total days	40

Linesch would make the following journal entry.

Recall that $50 interest revenue on the $2,000 note was already recorded on September 6 when the note was dishonored.

16	Oct.	16	Cash			2	0	8	2	89									16
17			Accounts Receivable										2	0	6	0	00		17
18			Interest Revenue												2	2	89		18
19			Collected dishonored note with interest																19

Notes Receivable Register

When a business receives many notes, it may keep a **notes receivable register**. This is a detailed auxiliary record of notes receivable. Figure 18-5 shows an abbreviated version of a notes receivable register. A more complete register might also include the number of each note and where the note is payable. The information contained in the register is obtained directly from the notes.

NOTES RECEIVABLE REGISTER											PAGE 1	
DATE RECEIVED	MAKER	TIME	DUE DATE	AMOUNT	INTEREST		DISCOUNTED		DATE COLLECTED	REMARKS		
					RATE	AMOUNT	BANK	DATE				
20-- Apr. 4	L. Peters	60 day	June 3	4 0 0 00	8%	5 33			June 3			
21	J. Slaw	60 day	June 20	6 0 0 00	9%	9 00			June 20	Renewal for $500		
May 2	S. Alpart	30 day	June 1	7 0 0 00	9%	5 25			June 1	Sent for collection 5/30		
19	L. Shein	90 day	Aug. 17	8 0 0 00	9%	1 8 00						
June 20	J. Slaw	60 day	Aug. 19	5 0 0 00	9%	7 50				Renewal of 4/21 note		

FIGURE 18-5 Notes Receivable Register

A BROADER VIEW
Some Noteworthy Notes

A former branch manager of a bank in Bridgeport, Connecticut, pleaded guilty to defrauding the bank of $142,000 over a three-year period. The manager had approved ten loans to one customer, using notes with varying maturities. Based on these notes, the manager issued checks, money orders, credits, and cash to herself and the customer. The customer's accounts were credited for loan payments never received by the bank. The bogus loan activity was discovered as part of an FBI crackdown on fraud in the banking industry.

Accrued Interest Receivable

Under accrual accounting, revenue is recognized when it is earned. For notes receivable, interest literally is earned day by day. It would be impractical, however, to record the interest revenue each day. Instead, for notes that are received and due within a single accounting period, no entry is made for interest revenue until the note is due.

For notes that are received in one period and due in the following period, however, accrued interest must be recorded at the end of the period. **Accrued interest on notes receivable** is interest revenue that has been earned but not yet received. The amount of accrued interest can be computed from the notes themselves or from the notes receivable register. The notes receivable register in Figure 18-5 can be used as an example. At June 30, the end of this company's fiscal year, two notes are outstanding. Accrued interest on these notes is calculated as follows:

Principal	Date of Issue	Rate of Interest	Days from Issue Date to June 30	Accrued Interest June 30
$800.00	May 19	9%	42	$8.40
500.00	June 20	9%	10	1.25
Total accrued interest on notes receivable				$9.65

The following adjusting entry is made on June 30 for the accrued interest.

16	June	30	Accrued Interest Receivable				9	65					16
17			Interest Revenue							9	65	17
18			Interest accrued on notes receivable									18

Accrued interest receivable is reported as a current asset on the balance sheet. Interest revenue is reported as other revenue on the income statement.

ACCOUNTING FOR NOTES PAYABLE TRANSACTIONS

LO4 Account for notes payable transactions and accrued interest.

Businesses generally encounter five types of transactions involving notes payable:

1. Note issued to a supplier in exchange for assets purchased

2. Note issued to a supplier to extend time for payment of an account

3. Note issued as security for cash loan

4. Note paid at maturity

5. Note renewed at maturity

Note Issued to a Supplier in Exchange for Assets Purchased

When a business makes a large purchase, it may give a note for the amount of the purchase. Assume that on June 1 Linesch Hardware Co. purchases a truckload of trees and shrubs from Evergreen Enterprises for $4,000. Linesch gives Evergreen a 90-day, 9% note for $4,000 in exchange for the trees and shrubs. This transaction is entered by Linesch as follows:

5	June	1	Purchases		4	0	0	0	00						5
6			Notes Payable							4	0	0	0	00	6
7			Issued note for inventory purchase												7

Note Issued to a Supplier to Extend Time for Payment

When a firm's account with a supplier is due, the supplier may be willing to accept a note for all or part of the amount due. Assume that Linesch Hardware Co. owes Bella & Co. $700 on June 11. If Linesch issues Bella a 90-day, 10% note for $700, Linesch makes the following entry.

26	June	11	Accounts Payable/Bella & Co.		7	0	0	00						26
27			Notes Payable							7	0	0	00	27
28			Issued note to settle account											28

If instead, Linesch gives Bella a check for $200 and a 90-day, 10% note for $500, the entry by Linesch is:

26	June	11	Accounts Payable/Bella & Co.		7	0	0	00						26
27			Cash							2	0	0	00	27
28			Notes Payable							5	0	0	00	28
29			Made partial payment and issued note											29
30			to settle account											30

Note Issued as Security for Cash Loan

Businesses sometimes have brief periods during which receipts from customers are not adequate to finance operations. During such periods, businesses commonly borrow money from banks on short-term notes.

Interest-Bearing Notes. Assume that on June 16, Linesch borrows $6,000 from the Planet Bank on a 60-day, 10½% note. This transaction is entered as follows:

38	June	16	Cash		6	0	0	0	00						38
39			Notes Payable							6	0	0	0	00	39
40			Issued note for bank loan												40

LEARNING KEY: As with discounting notes receivable, to calculate the discount amount, use the maturity value of the note.

Non-Interest-Bearing Notes. When making a loan, banks often deduct interest in advance, using a procedure known as **discounting**. The nature of this transaction and the procedures for handling it are very similar to those for discounting notes receivable (see pages 682–683). To illustrate, suppose that Linesch borrowed $6,000 on a 60-day, non-interest-bearing note that the bank discounted at 10½%. No interest rate is stated on the face of a non-interest-bearing note, but clearly there is an interest component. In this case, it is the 10½% discount rate. The bank calculates the **bank discount** at 10½% and deducts this amount from the $6,000 face of the note. The amount of the discount and the proceeds to Linesch are calculated using three steps:

STEP 1   Compute the maturity value of the note.

Face	+	Interest	=	**Maturity Value**
$6,000	+	0	=	$6,000

STEP 2   Compute the discount amount.

Maturity Value*	×	Discount Rate	×	Discount Period	=	**Discount Amount**
$6,000	×	10½%	×	60/360	=	$105

* Note that in calculating the discount amount, the *maturity value* of the note is used.

STEP 3   Compute the proceeds.

Maturity Value	–	Discount Amount	=	**Proceeds**
$6,000	–	$105	=	$5,895

Figure 18-6 shows a time line illustration of this transaction.

DATE OF NOTE	DISCOUNT RATE	DUE DATE
June 16	10.5%	August 15

Discount Period = 60 Days

Proceeds $6,000 − $105 = $5,895	+	Discount $105	=	Maturity Value $6,000

FIGURE 18-6 Discounted Note Payable Time Line

Linesch records receipt of the $5,895 proceeds ($6,000 − $105) from the loan as shown below and in Figure 18-7.

14	June	16	Cash		5 8 9 5 00		14
15			Discount on Notes Payable		1 0 5 00		15
16			Notes Payable			6 0 0 0 00	16
17			Issued note for bank loan				17

Assets	=	Liabilities	+	Owner's Equity				
Debit + / **Credit** −		**Debit** − / **Credit** +		**Debit** −			**Credit** +	
				Drawing	**Expenses**	**Revenues**		
				Debit + / Credit −	Debit + / Credit −	Debit − / Credit +		

Cash		Notes Payable	
5,895.00			6,000.00
		Discount on Notes Payable	
		105.00	

FIGURE 18-7 Journal Entry for Discounted Note Payable

The $105 debit to Discount on Notes Payable is an offset to the $6,000 note payable. Linesch's liability at this time is only $5,895, which is the net amount or **proceeds** received from the bank. Discount on Notes Payable is a contra-liability account. As shown in Figure 18-8, it is reported as a deduction from Notes Payable on the balance sheet.

Current liabilities:			
Notes payable	$6 0 0 0 00		
Less: discount on notes payable	1 0 5 00	$5 8 9 5 00	

FIGURE 18-8 Notes Payable and Related Discount on the Balance Sheet

Stated Versus Effective Interest Rate. The stated rate of interest was 10½% on both the interest-bearing and discounted notes. Notice, however, that the real interest rates on the two notes are not the same. With the interest-bearing note, Linesch obtained $6,000 for 60 days at a cost of $105—exactly 10½%.

$$\begin{aligned}
\$105 \div \$6,000 &= 1.75\% \text{ for 60 days} \\
&\underline{\times\ 6} \quad (360 \div 60) \\
&= 10.5\% \text{ for 360 days}
\end{aligned}$$

With the discounted note, Linesch paid $105 for the use of only $5,895 for 60 days—a rate of nearly 10.7%. This rate is known as the **effective rate** of interest.

$$\begin{aligned}
\$105 \div \$5,895 &= 1.781\% \text{ for 60 days} \\
&\underline{\times\ 6} \quad (360 \div 60) \\
&= 10.686\% \text{ for 360 days}
\end{aligned}$$

Note Paid at Maturity

The proper entry to make when a note is paid at maturity depends on whether the note is interest bearing or non-interest bearing. For an interest-bearing note, the same entry is made for payment to a supplier or to a bank. For example, let's reconsider Linesch's $6,000, 60-day, 10½% note due August 15. When the note is paid on August 15, Linesch will make the following entry.

21	Aug.	15	Notes Payable	6 0 0 0 00			21
22			Interest Expense	1 0 5 00			22
23			Cash		6 1 0 5 00		23
24			Paid note with interest at maturity				24

For a non-interest-bearing note from a bank, the entry to record the payment of the note is different. This is because Discount on Notes Payable was debited when the money was borrowed. For example, recall Linesch's $6,000, 60-day, non-interest-bearing note discounted by the bank at 10½%. When the money was borrowed, the following entry was made.

14	June	16	Cash	5 8 9 5 00			14
15			Discount on Notes Payable	1 0 5 00			15
16			Notes Payable		6 0 0 0 00		16
17			Issued note for bank loan				17

The $105 discount gradually becomes interest expense. This expense is recognized when the $6,000 principal amount of the note is repaid on August 15, the due date. Linesch will enter the payment of the note at maturity as follows:

22	Aug.	15	Notes Payable	6 0 0 0 00			22
23			Interest Expense	1 0 5 00			23
24			Cash		6 0 0 0 00		24
25			Discount on Notes Payable		1 0 5 00		25
26			Paid note at maturity				26

Note Renewed at Maturity

The payee of a note may allow the maker to renew all or a part of the note at maturity. For example, let's reconsider the $6,000 interest-bearing note that Linesch issued to Planet Bank on June 16. Assume that on August 15 Linesch pays $105 interest and $1,000 on the principal of this note and gives a new 60-day, 10½% note for $5,000. Linesch enters this transaction as follows:

27	Aug.	15	Notes Payable (old note)	6 0 0 0 00		27
28			Interest Expense	1 0 5 00		28
29			Cash		1 1 0 5 00	29
30			Notes Payable (new note)		5 0 0 0 00	30
31			Paid interest and part of principal on			31
32			old note and issued new note			32

Notes Payable Register

When a business issues many notes, it may keep a **notes payable register**. This is a detailed auxiliary record of notes payable. An abbreviated version of a notes payable register is shown in Figure 18-9. A more complete register might also include the number of each note and where the note is payable. The information contained in the register is obtained directly from the notes.

NOTES PAYABLE REGISTER   PAGE 1

DATE ISSUED	PAYEE	TIME	DUE DATE	AMOUNT	INTEREST RATE	INTEREST AMOUNT	DATE PAID	REMARKS
20-- Apr. 14	L. Knoop	60 days	June 13	2 0 0 0 00	9%	3 0 00	June 13	Settled 2/14 invoice
May 13	Apex Bank	90 days	Aug. 11	8 0 0 0 00	10%	2 0 0 00		
June 2	S. Bront	30 days	July 2	1 5 0 0 00	11%	1 3 75		Settled 4/2 invoice

FIGURE 18-9 Notes Payable Register

Accrued Interest Payable

As with notes receivable, it also is necessary to record accrued interest on notes payable at the end of the period. For notes payable issued in one period and due in the following period, accrued interest payable must be recorded. **Accrued interest on notes payable** is interest expense that has been incurred but not paid. The amount of accrued interest can be computed from the notes themselves or from the notes payable register.

The proper entry for accrued interest on notes payable depends on whether the note is interest bearing or non-interest bearing. Assume that a $900, 60-day, 10% note was issued on May 31. On June 30, this company's fiscal year end, an adjusting entry for accrued interest of $7.50 ($900 \times 10\% \times 30/360$) is recorded as follows:

19	June	30	Interest Expense	7 50		19
20			Accrued Interest Payable		7 50	20
21			Interest accrued on note payable			21

Assume instead that the $900, 60-day note was non-interest bearing and discounted at the bank at 10%. When the money was borrowed, the following entry was made.

23	May	31	Cash				8	8	5	00								23
24			Discount on Notes Payable*					1	5	00								24
25			Notes Payable									9	0	0	00			25
26			Issued note for bank loan															26
27																		27

* $900 × 10% × 60/360 = $15

On June 30, part of the discount must be transferred from Discount on Notes Payable to Interest Expense. The note was issued on May 31, so 30 days of the 60-day life of the note have passed. Thus, half of the balance in Discount on Notes Payable should be recognized as interest expense. The following adjusting entry is made on June 30.

29	June	30	Interest Expense					7	50							29
30			Discount on Notes Payable									7	50			30
31			Interest accrued on note payable													31

Note that the credit is to Discount on Notes Payable rather than Accrued Interest Payable. This is because the bank already deducted the interest at the time the money was borrowed. Thus, there is no additional interest payable to recognize. There is an increase in a liability, but that liability is notes payable instead of accrued interest payable. As shown below, the credit to Discount on Notes Payable increases the carrying value of the notes payable.

Balance Sheet:	May 31	June 30
Notes payable	$900.00	$900.00
Less: Discount on notes payable	(15.00)	(7.50)
	$885.00	$892.50

> **LEARNING KEY:** The adjusting entry for accrued interest on an interest-bearing note payable differs from the adjusting entry for accrued interest on a non-interest-bearing note from a bank.

Interest expense is reported as other expense on the income statement. Accrued interest payable is reported as a current liability on the balance sheet. As previously illustrated in Figure 18-8 (page 688), discount on notes payable is reported as a contra-liability to notes payable on the balance sheet.

Learning Objectives	Key Points to Remember
1 **Describe a promissory note.**	A promissory note is a written promise to pay a specific sum at a future date. Notes are used when credit is extended for periods of 60 days or more, or when large amounts of money are involved. To the maker of a note, the note is a note payable. To the payee of a note, the note is a note receivable.
2 **Calculate interest on and determine the due date of promissory notes.**	The following formula is used to calculate interest on notes receivable and payable:

$$ I = P \times R \times T $$
$$ \text{Interest} = \text{Principal} \times \text{Rate} \times \text{Time} $$

To determine the due date of a note with a term stated in months, count the number of months from the issue date of the note. To determine the due date of a note with a term stated in days:

STEP 1 Subtract the issue date from the number of days in the month of issuance.

STEP 2 Add to STEP 1 the number of days in as many months as possible without exceeding the time of the note.

STEP 3 Subtract STEP 2 from the time of the note.

3 **Account for notes receivable transactions and accrued interest.**	Businesses generally encounter seven types of transactions involving notes receivable:

1. Note received from a customer in exchange for assets sold
2. Note received from a customer to extend time for payment
3. Note collected at maturity
4. Note renewed at maturity
5. Note discounted before maturity
6. Note dishonored
7. Collection of dishonored note

When a note receivable is discounted at a bank, four steps are applied to calculate the discount and proceeds:

STEP 1 Compute the maturity value of the note.

STEP 2 Compute the number of days in the discount period.

STEP 3 Compute the discount amount.

STEP 4 Compute the proceeds.

If a note receivable that was discounted at a bank is dishonored, the endorser of the note is liable to the bank for the maturity value of the note and any bank fees.

Notes that are received in one period and due in the following period require an adjustment for accrued interest at the end of the period.

4 **Account for notes payable transactions and accrued interest.**	Businesses generally encounter five types of transactions involving notes payable:

1. Note issued to a supplier in exchange for assets purchased
2. Note issued to a supplier to extend time for payment
3. Note issued as security for cash loan
4. Note paid at maturity

Learning Objectives	Key Points to Remember

5. Note renewed at maturity

When money is borrowed at a bank on a non-interest-bearing note that is discounted by the bank, three steps are used to calculate the discount and proceeds:

STEP 1   Compute the maturity value of the note.

STEP 2   Compute the discount amount.

STEP 3   Compute the proceeds.

Notes payable that are issued in one period and due in the following period require an adjustment for accrued interest at the end of the period. The proper entry depends on whether or not the note is interest bearing.

Reflection: Answering the Opening Questions

Evan apparently signed a non-interest-bearing note that was discounted at 9%. With this type of loan, banks often deduct the interest in advance using a procedure called discounting. The stated rate of interest on the loan is 9%, but the effective rate is 9.89%, calculated as follows:

$270 ÷ $2,730 = 9.89%

DEMONSTRATION PROBLEM

Barbar Brothers, partners in a wholesale hardware business, completed the following transactions involving notes and interest during the first half of 20--.

Jan. 11   Received a $900, 60-day, 10% note from Paul Heinsius in payment for sale of merchandise.

18   Borrowed $10,000 from Landmark Bank issuing a 90-day, 11% note.

Feb. 6   Received an $875, 30-day, 9% note from Ana Fuentes in payment of an account receivable.

21   Issued a $650, 60-day, 11% note to Swanson & Johnson, a supplier, in payment of an account payable.

Mar. 1   Received a $1,000, 90-day, 10% note from Steve Roberts, a customer, in payment of an account receivable.

9   Received a check for $881.56 from Ana Fuentes in payment of note due March 8, including interest.

12   Paul Heinsius dishonored his $900 note due March 12.

(continued)

31 Discounted the $1,000 note from Steve Roberts at Manchester Bank at a discount rate of 12%.

Apr. 11 Paul Heinsius paid the original maturity value of his note due March 12, plus interest at 10% on the maturity value for the 30 days from March 12 to April 11.

18 Paid Landmark Bank for $10,000 note due today, including interest. (See January 18 transaction.)

22 Paid Swanson & Johnson $61.92 on the note due today (interest of $11.92 plus $50 toward the principal), and issued a new $600, 60-day, 11% note.

May 31 Steve Roberts dishonored his $1,000 note due at the Manchester Bank yesterday. Paid Manchester Bank $1,000, plus interest, plus a $10 bank fee, for the dishonored note.

June 20 Issued a $750, 90-day, 9% note to Greene Acres, a supplier, for purchase of merchandise.

REQUIRED

Record each transaction in a general journal.

Solution

GENERAL JOURNAL   PAGE 5

	DATE		DESCRIPTION	POST REF.	DEBIT	CREDIT	
1	Jan.	11	Notes Receivable		9 0 0 00		1
2			Sales			9 0 0 00	2
3			Received note for merchandise sale				3
4							4
5		18	Cash		10 0 0 0 00		5
6			Notes Payable			10 0 0 0 00	6
7			Isssued note for bank loan				7
8							8
9	Feb.	6	Notes Receivable		8 7 5 00		9
10			Accounts Receivable/A. Fuentes			8 7 5 00	10
11			Received note to settle account				11
12							12
13		21	Accounts Payable/Swanson & Johnson		6 5 0 00		13
14			Notes Payable			6 5 0 00	14
15			Issued note to settle account				15
16							16
17	Mar.	1	Notes Receivable		1 0 0 0 00		17
18			Accounts Receivable/S. Roberts			1 0 0 0 00	18
19			Received note to settle account				19
20							20
21		9	Cash		8 8 1 56		21
22			Notes Receivable			8 7 5 00	22
23			Interest Revenue			6 56	23
24			Received payment of note with interest				24
25							25
26		12	Accounts Receivable/P. Heinsius		9 1 5 00		26
27			Notes Receivable			9 0 0 00	27
28			Interest Revenue			1 5 00	28
29			Note receivable dishonored				29
30							30

	DATE		DESCRIPTION	POST REF.	DEBIT					CREDIT					
	20--														
1	Mar.	31	Cash		1	0	0	4	50						1
2			Notes Receivable							1	0	0	0	00	2
3			Interest Revenue										4	50	3
4			Discounted note receivable												4
5															5
6			Principal	$1,000.00											6
7			Interest to maturity	25.00											7
8			Maturity value	$1,025.00											8
9			Less: Discount												9
10			($1,025 x 12% x 60/360)	20.50											10
11			Cash Proceeds	$1,004.50											11
12															12
13	Apr.	11	Cash			9	2	2	63						13
14			Accounts Receivable/P. Heinsius								9	1	5	00	14
15			Interest Revenue										7	63	15
16			Collected dishonored note with interest												16
17															17
18		18	Notes Payable		10	0	0	0	00						18
19			Interest Expense			2	7	5	00						19
20			Cash							10	2	7	5	00	20
21			Paid note with interest at maturity												21
22															22
23		22	Notes Payable (old note)			6	5	0	00						23
24			Interest Expense				1	1	92						24
25			Cash									6	1	92	25
26			Notes Payable (new note)								6	0	0	00	26
27			Paid interest and part of principal on old note												27
28			and issued new note												28
29															29
30	May	31	Accounts Receivable/S. Roberts		1	0	3	5	00						30
31			Cash							1	0	3	5	00	31
32			Paid bank for dishonored note												32
33															33
34			Principal	$1,000.00											34
35			Interest	25.00											35
36			Bank fee	10.00											36
37				$1,035.00											37
38															38
39	June	20	Purchases			7	5	0	00						39
40			Notes Payable								7	5	0	00	40
41			Issued note for inventory purchase												41
42															42

GENERAL JOURNAL   PAGE 6

On-Line Learning Tools

For more information, visit: http://heintz.swlearning.com

The Heintz & Parry product web site is designed specifically for **COLLEGE ACCOUNTING, 18e.** The features include downloadable student resources and an interactive study center, organized by chapter, which contains learning objectives, web links, on-line quizzes with automatic feedback, and more.

KEY TERMS

accrued interest on notes payable, (690)   Interest expense that has been incurred but not paid.

accrued interest on notes receivable, (686)   Interest revenue that has been earned but not yet received.

bank discount (note payable), (687)   The amount that the bank deducts from the face of a note.

bank discount (note receivable), (682)   An interest fee that the bank charges for the time between the date of discounting and the due date of the note.

contingent liability, (683)   A potential liability that may become a real liability depending on future events. In the case of a note discounted at a bank, the business that discounted the note must pay the maturity value and any bank fees if the maker of the note does not pay it at maturity.

credit advice, (681)   A notification to the payee that the bank has collected interest on a note and added the amount to the payee's account.

discount period, (682)   The time between the date of discounting and the due date of the note.

discounting (note payable), (687)   The procedure, which banks often use, of deducting interest in advance when making a loan.

discounting a note receivable, (682)   Transferring a note receivable to a bank for cash.

dishonored, (683)   A note which the maker does not pay or renew at maturity.

effective rate, (689)   The interest amount paid divided by the proceeds received on a discounted note. This amount will differ from the stated rate on a discounted note.

interest-bearing note, (676)   A note with an explicit interest rate stated on the face of the note.

maker, (676)   The person or business agreeing to make the payment on a note.

maturity value, (678)   The principal of the note plus interest equals the maturity value of the note.

non-interest-bearing note, (676)   A note on which no rate of interest is specified, although the note does include an interest component.

notes payable register, (690)   A detailed auxiliary record of notes payable.

notes receivable register, (685)   A detailed auxiliary record of notes receivable.

payee, (676)   The specific person or business to whom a note is payable.

principal of the note, (677)   The face amount of the note that the maker promises to pay at maturity. The principal is the base on which the interest is calculated.

proceeds (note payable), (688)   The net amount received from the bank.

proceeds (note receivable), (682)   The difference between the maturity value of the note and the bank discount. This is the amount of cash received by the business discounting the note.

promissory note, (676)   A written promise to pay a specific sum at a definite future date.

rate of interest, (677)   The rate at which interest is charged, usually expressed as an annual percentage, but in some cases a monthly rate is quoted.

term of the note, (677)   The months or days from the date of issue to the date of maturity.

time, (677)   The term of the note stated as a fraction of a year.

REVIEW QUESTIONS

(LO1)   1. How does a note receivable differ from an account receivable?

(LO2)   2. What is the formula for calculating interest on notes?

(LO2)   3. In the formula for calculating interest, how is time computed?

(LO2)   4. What number of days is considered as a year by most banks and businesses in computing interest?

(LO3)   5. What seven types of transactions involving notes receivable do businesses generally encounter?

(LO3)   6. If a note receivable is discounted at a bank, on what amount and for what time period does the bank compute the discount?

(LO3)   7. If a note receivable that was discounted at a bank is dishonored by its maker, what is the responsibility of the person or business discounting the note?

(LO3/4)   8. On which notes receivable and notes payable is it necessary to record accrued interest at the end of the period?

(LO4)   9. What five types of transactions involving notes payable do businesses generally encounter?

(LO4)   10. When a business borrows money from a bank on a non-interest-bearing note, how are the bank discount and proceeds calculated?

(LO4)   11. What kind of account is Discount on Notes Payable and how is it reported on the balance sheet?

(LO4)   12. What is the appropriate entry for accrued interest on notes payable for an interest-bearing note? for a non-interest-bearing note from a bank?

(LO3/4)   13. How are accrued interest receivable and accrued interest payable reported on the balance sheet?

Self-Study Test Questions

True/False

1. The maturity value of a note includes both principal and interest. _____

2. When a note is renewed at maturity, the old note is cancelled and a new note is issued. _____

3. The difference between the maturity value of a note and the net proceeds is called discounting. _____

4. When a note is dishonored, the interest is not credited to Interest Revenue because it is not earned. _____

5. When a dishonored note is collected, interest is collected for the time between date of maturity and date of collection. _____

Multiple Choice

1. Which account is debited for interest earned but not yet received? _____
   - (a) Interest Revenue
   - (b) Accrued Interest Receivable
   - (c) Accrued Interest Payable
   - (d) Interest Expense

2. When a note payable is paid at maturity, what account is debited for the amount of the interest? _____
   - (a) Interest Revenue
   - (b) Notes Payable
   - (c) Interest Expense
   - (d) Discount on Notes Payable

3. Accrued interest payable is reported as a _____ on the balance sheet. _____
   - (a) current asset
   - (b) long-term asset
   - (c) current liability
   - (d) long-term liability

4. Principal plus interest equals _____ of a note. _____
   - (a) discount
   - (b) net proceeds
   - (c) interest rate
   - (d) maturity value

5. The discount amount is calculated by multiplying the maturity value times _____ times the discount period. _____
   - (a) discount rate
   - (b) interest rate
   - (c) term of note
   - (d) net proceeds

The answers to the Self-Study Test Questions are at the end of the text.

MANAGING YOUR WRITING

You are purchasing a new car and plan to finance it through your employee credit union. The credit union has offered you two different promissory note plans, as follows:

Option 1: Three years at 9%, with interest payable annually.

Option 2: One year at 8%, renewable each year for up to three more years, at the then-current interest rate. Interest is payable at the end of each year.

Prepare a written report summarizing the advantages and disadvantages of each of these options.

ETHICS CASE

Rochelle needed to borrow $3,000 for three months in order to pay for college expenses while waiting for her scholarship to arrive. After Rochelle filled out the loan application, the loan officer at the bank asked her if she would like to pay the interest up front or at the maturity of the note. He went on to explain that it didn't make a difference, but he preferred that she pay it up front because it would make his paperwork easier. He also told Rochelle that the interest rate and amount would be the same. Rochelle agreed, signed the three-month, 12 percent, discounted note and left with a check for $2,910.

1. Did the loan officer offer Rochelle an acceptable explanation of the interest rate? Justify your answer.

2. What is the effective rate of interest on Rochelle's loan? Round to the nearest tenth of a percent.

3. In a short paragraph, explain the difference between an "interest-bearing" note and a "discounted" note.

4. In groups of two or three, discuss some common situations where the average person might misunderstand interest rate quotations.

WEB WORK

How could promissory notes be used to finance the start-up or improvement of your business? Visit the Interactive Study Center on our web site at **http://heintz.swlearning.com** for special hotlinks to assist you in this assignment.

SERIES A EXERCISES

EXERCISE 18-1A   **(LO2)**

May 4 note: 74 days

TERM OF A NOTE Calculate total time in days for the following notes. (Assume there are 28 days in February.)

Date of Note	Due Date	Time in Days
May 4	July 17	_____
August 17	October 1	_____
July 5	September 5	_____
December 11	February 5	_____
March 24	May 16	_____
January 6	March 18	_____

EXERCISE 18-2A   **(LO2)**

$5,000 note: $25

CALCULATING INTEREST Using 360 days as the denominator, calculate interest for the following notes using the formula $I = P \times R \times T$.

Principal	Rate	Time	Interest
$5,000	6.00%	30 days	_____
1,000	7.50	60	_____
4,500	8.00	120	_____
950	6.80	95	_____
1,250	7.25	102	_____
2,900	7.00	90	_____

EXERCISE 18-3A **(LO2)** **DETERMINING DUE DATE** Determine the due date for the following notes. (Assume there are 28 days in February.)

PASS
Power Accounting System Software®

Aug. 12 note = Nov. 10

Date of Note	Term of Note	Due Date
August 12	90 days	_____
September 1	60	_____
January 3	120	_____
March 18	88	_____
June 11	200	_____
May 17	38	_____

EXERCISE 18-4A **(LO3)** **JOURNAL ENTRIES (NOTE RECEIVED, RENEWED, AND COLLECTED)** Prepare general journal entries for the following transactions.

Feb. 15, Cr. Interest
Rev.: $150

Jan. 15   Received a 30-day, 9% note in payment for merchandise sale of $20,000.

Feb. 15   Received $150 (interest) on the old (January 15) note; the old note is renewed for 30 days at 11%.

Mar. 17   Received principal and interest on the new (February 15) note.

19   Received a 60-day, 9% note in payment for accounts receivable balance of $10,000.

May 6   Received $120 (interest) plus $1,000 principal on the old (March 19) note; the old note is renewed for 60 days (from May 6) at 9%.

July 5   Received principal and interest on the new (May 6) note.

EXERCISE 18-5A **(LO3)** **JOURNAL ENTRIES (NOTE RECEIVED, DISCOUNTED, DISHONORED, AND COLLECTED)** Prepare general journal entries for the following transactions.

June 2, Cr. Interest
Rev.: $7.50

Apr. 6   Received 120-day, 11% note in payment for accounts receivable balance of $3,000.

26   Discounted the note at a rate of 12%.

May 3   Received a 30-day, 10% note in payment for accounts receivable balance of $900.

June 2   The $900, 30-day, 10% note is dishonored.

5   The dishonored note is paid, plus interest at 10% on the maturity value.

EXERCISE 18-6A **(LO3)** **JOURNAL ENTRIES (ACCRUED INTEREST RECEIVABLE)** At the end of the year the following interest is earned, but not yet received. Record the adjusting entry in a general journal.

Cr. Interest Rev.: $58.50

Interest on $4,000, 90-day, 12% note (for 15 days)	$20.00
Interest on $7,000, 60-day, 11% note (for 18 days)	38.50
	$58.50

EXERCISE 18-7A **(LO4)** **JOURNAL ENTRIES (NOTE ISSUED, RENEWED, AND PAID)** Prepare general journal entries for the following transactions.

July 1, Dr. Interest
Exp.: $41.67

May 1   Purchased $5,000 worth of equipment from a supplier on account.

June 1   Issued a $5,000, 30-day, 10% note in payment of the account payable.

July 1   Paid $500 cash plus interest to the supplier, extending the note for 30 days from July 1.

31   Paid the note in full.

Aug. 10   Issued a $3,500, 60-day, 9% note to a supplier for purchase of merchandise.

EXERCISE 18-8A   (LO4)
Discount: $100

JOURNAL ENTRIES (NOTE ISSUED FOR BANK LOAN) Prepare general journal entries for the following transactions.

July 15   Borrowed $5,000 cash from the bank, giving a 60-day non-interest-bearing note. The note is discounted 12% by the bank.

Sept. 13   Paid the $5,000 note, recognizing the discount as interest expense.

EXERCISE 18-9A   (LO4)
Dr. Interest Exp.: $22.50

JOURNAL ENTRIES (ACCRUED INTEREST PAYABLE) At the end of the year the following interest is payable, but not yet paid. Record the adjusting entry in the general journal.

Interest on $5,000, 60-day, 9% note (for 12 days) $15.00
Interest on $2,500, 30-day, 12% note (for 9 days)   7.50
                                                         $22.50

SERIES A PROBLEMS

PROBLEM 18-10A (LO2/3)

Feb. 13, Cr. Interest
Rev.: $13.64

NOTES RECEIVABLE ENTRIES J. K. Pratt Co. had the following transactions.

20-1

July 20   Received a $750, 30-day, 10% note from J. Akita in payment for sale of merchandise.

Aug. 21   J. Akita paid note issued July 20 plus interest.

25   Sold merchandise on account to L. Beene, $1,100.

Sept. 5   L. Beene paid $100 and gave a $1,000, 30-day, 12% note to extend time for payment.

Oct. 5   L. Beene paid note issued September 5, plus interest.

10   Sold merchandise to R. Harris for $750: $50 plus a $700, 30-day, 11% note.

Nov. 9   R. Harris paid $200 plus interest on note issued October 10, and extended the note ($500) for 30 days.

Dec. 9   R. Harris paid note extended on November 9, plus interest.

10   Sold merchandise on account to B. Kraus, $1,500.

15   B. Kraus paid $150 on merchandise purchased on account, and gave a $1,350, 30-day, 12% note to extend time for payment.

20-2

Jan. 14   B. Kraus' note of December 15 is dishonored.

Feb. 13   Collected B. Kraus' dishonored note, plus interest at 12% on the maturity value.

REQUIRED

Record the transactions in a general journal.

PROBLEM 18-11A (LO2/3)

May 5, Cr. Interest
Rev.: $4.25

NOTES RECEIVABLE DISCOUNTING Movado Suppliers had the following transactions.

Mar. 1   Sold merchandise on account to R. Sticca, $5,000.

20   R. Sticca gave a $5,000, 90-day, 12% note to extend time for payment.

30   R. Sticca's note is discounted at Commerce Bank at a discount rate of 15%.

Apr. 20   Received a $3,000, 60-day, 10% note from K. Jones in payment for sale of merchandise.

May 5   K. Jones' note is discounted at Commerce Bank at a discount rate of 12%.

June 19   K. Jones' note is dishonored. The bank bills Movado for the maturity value of the note plus a $40 bank fee.

July 31   K. Jones' dishonored note is collected; Jones pays Movado the maturity value of the note, the $40 bank fee, and interest at 10% on the maturity value plus the bank fee.

Aug. 1   Sold merchandise on account to R. Brown, $5,600.

12   R. Brown paid $400 and gave a $5,200, 30-day, 12% note to extend time for payment.

Sept. 11   R. Brown paid $400, plus interest, and gave a new $4,800, 60-day, 14% note to extend time for payment.

26   R. Brown's note is discounted at Commerce Bank at a discount rate of 16%.

Nov. 10   R. Brown's note is dishonored. The bank bills Movado for the maturity value of the note plus a $40 bank fee.

Dec. 15   R. Brown's dishonored note is collected. Brown pays Movado the maturity value of the note, the $40 bank fee, and interest at 14% on the maturity value plus the bank fee.

REQUIRED

Record the transactions in a general journal.

PROBLEM 18-12A (LO3)

Accrued interest: $151.03

ACCRUED INTEREST RECEIVABLE The following is a list of outstanding notes receivable as of December 31, 20--.

Maker	Date of Note	Principal	Interest	Term	No. of Days
K. Savelin	12/15/--	$1,000	10%	60 days	16
R. Hillier	12/3/--	5,000	12	90	28
B. Miranda	11/30/--	2,800	8	90	31
R. Hansen	11/18/--	7,500	9	120	43

REQUIRED

1. Compute the accrued interest at the end of the year.

2. Prepare the adjusting entry in the general journal.

PROBLEM 18-13A (LO4)

June 4, Dr. Interest
Exp.: $33.33

NOTES PAYABLE ENTRIES Milo Radio Shop had the following notes payable transactions.

Apr. 1   Borrowed $5,000 from the Builder's Bank, signing a 90-day, 8% note.

5   Gave a $2,000, 60-day, 10% note to Breaker Parts Co. for purchase of merchandise.

10	Paid $500 cash and gave a $1,500, 30-day, 12% note to M. K. Reynolds in payment of an account payable.
May 10	Paid $500 cash, plus interest, and issued a new $1,000, 30-day, 14% note to M. K. Reynolds.
20	Borrowed $3,500 for 60 days from the Builder's Bank on a non-interest-bearing note. The discount rate is 12%.
June 4	Paid $500 cash, plus interest, to Breaker Parts Co. (see April 5) and gave a new $1,500, 30-day, 12% note to extend time for payment.
9	Paid the principal and interest due on the $1,000 note to M. K. Reynolds. (See May 10.)
30	Paid the principal and interest due on the $5,000 note to the Builder's Bank. (See April 1.)
July 4	Paid the principal and interest due on the $1,500 note to Breaker Parts Co. (See June 4.)
19	Paid the $3,500 non-interest-bearing note to Builder's Bank. (See May 20.)

REQUIRED

Record the transactions in a general journal.

PROBLEM 18-14A   (LO4)
Accrued interest: $75.37

ACCRUED INTEREST PAYABLE The following is a list of outstanding notes payable as of December 31, 20--.

Maker	Date of Note	Principal	Interest	Term	No. of Days
B. Jones	12/1/--	$1,000	11%	90 days	30
M. Aguilor	11/25/--	2,500	9	80	36
T. Plant	12/14/--	3,800	12	120	17
W. Brand	11/19/--	1,900	10	180	42

REQUIRED

1. Compute the accrued interest at the end of the year.

2. Prepare the adjusting entry in the general journal.

SERIES B EXERCISES

EXERCISE 18-1B   (LO2)

PASS
Power Accounting System Software®

Aug. 17 note: 54 days

TERM OF A NOTE Calculate total time in days for the following notes. (Assume there are 28 days in February.)

Date of Note	Due Date	Time in Days
August 17	October 10	_____
January 12	March 10	_____
July 15	September 13	_____
December 3	February 1	_____
April 11	July 6	_____
October 6	December 18	_____

EXERCISE 18-2B   **(LO2)**   **CALCULATING INTEREST** Using 360 days as the denominator, calculate interest for the following notes using the formula $I = P \times R \times T$.

$4,000 note: $46.67

Principal	Rate	Time	Interest
$4,000	7.00%	60 days	_____
3,000	9.50	30	_____
7,500	8.00	150	_____
850	7.90	99	_____
2,250	7.55	122	_____
1,900	8.80	82	_____

EXERCISE 18-3B   **(LO2)**   **DETERMINING DUE DATE** Determine the due date for the following notes. (Assume there are 28 days in February.)

July 11 note: Aug. 25

Date of Note	Term of Note	Due Date
July 11	45 days	_____
December 23	90	_____
April 18	120	_____
October 3	77	_____
January 1	180	_____
August 13	65	_____

EXERCISE 18-4B   **(LO3)**   **JOURNAL ENTRIES (NOTE RECEIVED, RENEWED, AND COLLECTED)** Prepare general journal entries for the following transactions.

June 21, Cr. Interest Rev.: $165

May 22   Received a 30-day, 9% note in payment for merchandise sale of $22,000.

June 21   Received $165.00 cash (interest) on the old (May 22) note; the old note is renewed for 30 days at 10%.

July 21   Received principal and interest on the new (June 21) note.

28   Received a 45-day, 7% note in payment for accounts receivable balance of $11,600.

Sept. 11   Received $101.50 cash (interest) plus $1,600 principal on the old (July 28) note; the old note is renewed for 60 days (from September 11) at 9%.

Nov. 10   Received principal and interest on the new (September 11) note.

EXERCISE 18-5B   **(LO3)**   **JOURNAL ENTRIES (NOTE RECEIVED, DISCOUNTED, DISHONORED, AND COLLECTED)** Prepare general journal entries for the following transactions.

Oct. 5, Cr. Interest Rev.: $11

Aug. 4   Received a 120-day, 12% note in payment for accounts receivable balance of $4,000.

14   Discounted the note at a rate of 14%.

Sept. 6   Received a 30-day, 11% note in payment for accounts receivable balance of $1,200.

Oct. 5   The $1,200, 30-day, 11% note is dishonored.

Nov. 4   The dishonored note is paid, plus interest at 11% on the maturity value.

EXERCISE 18-6B   **(LO3)**   **JOURNAL ENTRIES (ACCRUED INTEREST RECEIVABLE)** At the end of the year
Cr. Interest Rev.: $80   the following interest is earned, but not yet received. Record the adjusting entry
in a general journal.

Interest on $6,000, 60-day, 11% note (for 24 days) $44.00
Interest on $9,000, 90-day, 12% note (for 12 days)   ___36.00
$80.00

EXERCISE 18-7B   **(LO4)**   **JOURNAL ENTRIES (NOTE ISSUED, RENEWED, AND PAID)** Prepare general
Aug. 14, Dr. Interest   journal entries for the following transactions.
Exp.: $60

June 15   Purchased $6,000 worth of equipment from a supplier on account.

July 15   Issued a $6,000, 30-day, 12% note in payment of the account payable.

Aug. 14   Paid $600 cash plus interest to the supplier, extending the note for 30 days
from August 14.

Sept. 13   Paid the note in full.

Sept. 27   Issued at $5,000, 60-day, 10% note to a supplier for purchase of merchandise.

EXERCISE 18-8B   **(LO4)**   **JOURNAL ENTRIES (NOTE ISSUED FOR BANK LOAN)** Prepare general journal
Discount: $140   entries for the following transactions.

Sept. 15   Borrowed $7,000 cash from the bank, giving a 60-day non-interest-bearing note.
The note is discounted 12% by the bank.

Nov. 14   Paid the $7,000 note, recognizing the discount as interest expense.

EXERCISE 18-9B   **(LO4)**   **JOURNAL ENTRIES (ACCRUED INTEREST PAYABLE)** At the end of the year the
Dr. Interest Exp.: $40.75   following interest is payable, but not yet paid. Record the adjusting entry in the
general journal.

Interest on $8,000, 90-day, 8% note (for 18 days) $32.00
Interest on $4,500, 60-day, 10% note (for 7 days)   ___8.75
$40.75

SERIES B PROBLEMS

PROBLEM 18-10B   **(LO2/3)**   **NOTES RECEIVABLE ENTRIES** M. L. DiMaurizio had the following notes receivable transactions:

20-3

June 20   Received a $2,400, 30-day, 10% note from K. Lorenzo in payment for sale
of merchandise.

Jan. 13, Cr. Interest   July 20   K. Lorenzo paid the note plus interest.
Rev.: $25.59
25   Sold merchandise on account to R. Boone, $5,600.

Aug. 4   R. Boone paid $600 and gave a $5,000, 30-day, 12% note to extend time
for payment.

Sept. 3   R. Boone paid the note plus interest.

10   Sold merchandise to T. Akins for $3,000: $400 plus a $2,600, 30-day, 11% note.

Oct. 10   T. Akins paid $600, plus interest, and extended the note ($2,000) for 30 days.

(continued)

Nov. 9   T. Akins paid the note plus interest.

Nov. 10   Sold merchandise on account to J. Brown, $5,000.

25   J. Brown paid $1,000 and gave a $4,000, 30-day, 12% note to extend time for payment.

Dec. 25   J. Brown's note is dishonored.

20-4

Jan. 13   J. Brown's dishonored note is collected, plus interest at 12% on the maturity value.

REQUIRED

Record the transactions in a general journal.

PROBLEM 18-11B (LO2/3)
July 5, Cr. Interest
Rev.: $3.40

NOTES RECEIVABLE DISCOUNTING Madison Graphics had the following notes receivable transactions.

May 1   Sold merchandise on account to L. Carney, $5,600.

20   L. Carney gave a $5,600, 90-day, 12% note to extend time for payment.

30   L. Carney's note is discounted at Commercial Bank at a discount rate of 15%.

June 20   Received a $2,400, 60-day, 10% note from P. Arnst in payment for sale of merchandise.

July 5   P. Arnst's note is discounted at Commercial Bank at a discount rate of 12%.

Aug. 19   P. Arnst's note is dishonored. The bank bills Madison Graphics for the maturity value of the note plus a $30 bank fee.

31   P. Arnst's dishonored note is collected; Arnst pays Madison the maturity value of the note, the $30 bank fee, and interest at 10% on the maturity value plus the bank fee.

Sept. 1   Sold merchandise on account to B. Faust, $6,400.

12   B. Faust paid $400 and gave a $6,000, 30-day, 12% note to extend time for payment.

Oct. 12   B. Faust paid $400, plus interest, and gave a new $5,600, 60-day, 14% note to extend time for payment.

26   B. Faust's note is discounted at Commercial Bank at a discount rate of 14%.

Dec. 11   B. Faust's note is dishonored. The bank bills Madison Graphics for the maturity value of the note plus a $30 bank fee.

Dec. 27   B. Faust's dishonored note is collected. Faust pays Madison Graphics the maturity value of the note, the $30 bank fee, and interest at 14% on the maturity value plus the bank fee.

REQUIRED

Record the transactions in a general journal.

PROBLEM 18-12B   **(LO3)**
Accrued interest: $94.02

ACCRUED INTEREST RECEIVABLE The following is a list of outstanding notes receivable as of December 31, 20--.

Maker	Date of Note	Principal	Interest	Term	No. of Days
P. Harrison	12/17/--	$1,200	11.0%	60 days	14
T. Rieber	12/3/--	4,000	12.0	90	28
K. Burke	12/1/--	2,200	9.0	90	30
A. Pai	11/28/--	4,500	8.5	120	33

REQUIRED

1. Compute the accrued interest at the end of the year.

2. Prepare the adjusting entry in the general journal.

PROBLEM 18-13B   **(LO4)**
June 4, Dr. Interest
Exp.: $50

NOTES PAYABLE Mary's Travel Agency had the following notes payable transactions.

Apr. 1   Borrowed $4,000 from the Finance Bank, signing a 90-day, 8% note.

5   Gave a $3,000, 60-day, 10% note to Krenshaw Airline for purchase of merchandise.

10   Paid $400 cash and issued a $1,600, 30-day, 12% note to Andrew Adams in payment of an account payable.

May 10   Paid $400, plus interest, and gave a new $1,200, 30-day, 14% note to Andrew Adams.

20   Borrowed $4,500 for 60 days from Finance Bank on a non-interest-bearing note. The discount rate is 14%.

June 4   Paid $500, plus interest, to Krenshaw Airline (see April 5) and gave a new $2,500, 30-day, 12% note to extend time for payment.

9   Paid the principal and interest due on the $1,200 note to Andrew Adams. (See May 10.)

30   Paid the principal and interest due on the $4,000 note to Finance Bank. (See April 1.)

July 4   Paid the principal and interest due on the $2,500 note to Krenshaw Airline (See June 4.)

19   Paid the $4,500 non-interest-bearing note to Finance Bank. (See May 20.)

REQUIRED

Record the transactions in a general journal.

PROBLEM 18-14B   **(LO4)**
Accrued interest: $83.54

ACCRUED INTEREST PAYABLE The following is a list of outstanding notes payable as of December 31, 20--.

Payee	Date of Note	Principal	Interest	Term	No. of Days
X. Rayal	12/1/--	$1,200	11%	90 days	30
G. Richards	11/28/--	2,300	8	80	33
A. Gray	12/16/--	3,400	12	120	15
O. Hankins	11/13/--	2,900	10	180	48

REQUIRED

1. Compute the accrued interest at the end of the year.

2. Prepare the adjusting entry in the general journal.

MASTERY PROBLEM

Nov. 1, Cr. Interest
Rev.: $5.89

Eddie Edwards and Phil Bell own and operate The Second Hand Equipment Shop. The following transactions involving notes and interest were completed during the last three months of 20--.

Oct. 1   Issued a $6,800, 60-day, 10% note to Mac Farm Equipment for purchase of merchandise.

15   Received a $2,000, 60-day, 12% note from R. Chambers in payment for sale of merchandise.

Nov. 1   Discounted the note received from R. Chambers on October 15 at Merchants National Bank. The discount rate is 14%.

1   Borrowed $5,000 from First National Bank on a three-month, non-interest-bearing note that was discounted at 10%.

20   Received a $4,000, 90-day, 9% note from L. Revsine in payment of an account receivable.

30   Issued a check to Mac Farm Equipment in payment of the note issued on October 1, including interest.

Dec. 10   Issued a $3,000, 90-day, 9% note to Remak Tractors to extend time for payment of an account payable.

16   Received notification from Merchants National Bank that R. Chambers has dishonored his note. A check is issued to cover the note plus a $20 bank fee that must be paid to the bank.

REQUIRED

1. Prepare general journal entries for the transactions.

2. Prepare necessary adjusting entries for the notes outstanding on December 31.

CHALLENGE PROBLEM

This problem challenges you to apply your cumulative accounting knowledge to move a step beyond the material in the chapter.

July 1, Lawrence
Bank, Dr. Interest
Rec.: $13.50

REQUIRED

Prepare general journal entries on the books of both Mirror Co. and the other party (either Rosman Co., Kaw County Bank, or Lawrence Bank) for each of the following transactions.

June 1   Rosman Co. gave Mirror Co. a $3,000, 90-day, 10% note to extend the time for payment of its account.

20   Mirror Co. borrowed $2,000 for 60 days from Kaw County Bank on a non-interest-bearing note. The discount rate was 12%.

July 1   Mirror Co. discounted Rosman Co.'s note at Lawrence Bank at a discount rate of 12%.

Aug. 20   Mirror Co. paid the $2,000 non-interest-bearing note to Kaw County Bank.

30   Rosman Co.'s $3,000 note (see June 1 transaction) was collected by Lawrence Bank. (Treat Lawrence Bank as the other party.)

DIGITAL IMAGING GROUP

Accounting for Merchandise Inventory

As you walk through a grocery store, have you ever wondered what the store paid for each item? It would be nice to know which items really are "good buys" and which are "overpriced." What happens when management pays different amounts for identical products on the shelf? The selling price for each unit is the same. Otherwise, we could have customers arguing over the identical items marked with the different prices. Evan Taylor has a similar situation with his pet supplies inventory. Many of the product units are identical, but he paid different prices for them. If the units are identical, how does he know which unit was sold: the one with the higher or lower purchase price? Does it matter?

Careful study of this chapter should enable you to:

LO1 Explain the impact of merchandise inventory on the financial statements.

LO2 Describe the two principal systems of accounting for merchandise inventory —the periodic system and the perpetual system.

LO3 Compute the costs allocated to the ending inventory and cost of goods sold using different inventory methods.

LO4 Estimate the ending inventory and cost of goods sold by using the gross profit and retail inventory methods.

One of the major reasons for keeping accounting records is to determine the net income (or net loss) of a business. For a merchandising business, the cost of goods available for sale during the accounting period must be divided between the cost of goods (merchandise) sold and the ending merchandise inventory. (Recall that the terms "goods" and "merchandise" mean the same thing and are used interchangeably.) End-of-period adjustments for merchandise inventory were illustrated in earlier chapters. In those illustrations, the costs assigned to the cost of goods sold and ending inventory were provided. In this chapter, you will learn how to determine the dollar amounts assigned to the cost of goods sold and ending merchandise inventory.

THE IMPACT OF MERCHANDISE INVENTORY ON FINANCIAL STATEMENTS

LO1 Explain the impact of merchandise inventory on the financial statements.

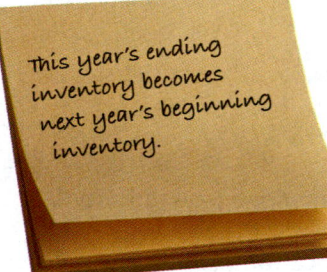

This year's ending inventory becomes next year's beginning inventory.

A company's ending inventory must be reported accurately. An error in the reported inventory will cause errors on the income statement, statement of owner's equity, and balance sheet. In addition, since this year's ending inventory becomes next year's beginning inventory, financial statements for the following year will also contain errors.

Figure 19-1 illustrates the impact of an error in the *ending inventory*. The first pair of columns presents partial financial statements when the ending inventory is correct. For this illustration, sales, cost of goods sold, and operating expenses are assumed to be the same for 20-1 and 20-2. Thus, the same net income of $30 and beginning and ending merchandise inventories of $20 are reported for both years.

The second pair of columns in Figure 19-1 illustrates the effects of understating the ending inventory. Understating the ending inventory for 20-1 by $5 causes the cost of goods sold to be overstated by $5 and net income to be understated by $5. Since net income is reported on the statement of owner's equity, Erv Bultman's capital on December 31 is understated by $5. The understated capital also appears in the owner's equity section of the balance sheet. The understated ending inventory is reported in the current assets section of the balance sheet.

Even if the ending inventory for 20-2 is accurately reported, we still have a problem with the income statement. Since the ending inventory for 20-1 was understated, the beginning inventory for 20-2 is understated also ($15 instead of $20). This error causes cost of goods sold to be understated by $5 and net income to be overstated by $5.

LEARNING KEY: If the ending inventory for 20-1 is understated, net income for 20-1 is understated and net income for 20-2 is overstated.

At this point, we can see that this inventory error "washes out" over the two-year period. The understated net income for 20-1 is offset by overstated net income in 20-2. Thus, Bultman's capital account as of December 31, 20-2, is reported accurately on the statement of owner's equity and balance sheet at $160. Assuming no future inventory errors, the financial statements for 20-3 and thereafter will be correct.

	ENDING INVENTORY FOR 20-1 IS CORRECT		ENDING INVENTORY FOR 20-1 IS UNDERSTATED		ENDING INVENTORY FOR 20-1 IS OVERSTATED	
	20-1	20-2	20-1	20-2	20-1	20-2
Income Statement						
Sales	80	80	80	80	80	80
Cost of goods sold:						
Beginning merchandise inventory	20	20	20	15	20	25
Add purchases (net)	40	40	40	40	40	40
Cost of goods available for sale	60	60	60	55	60	65
Less ending merchandise inventory	(20)	(20)	(15)	(20)	(25)	(20)
Cost of goods sold	(40)	(40)	(45)	(35)	(35)	(45)
Gross profit	40	40	35	45	45	35
Operating expenses	(10)	(10)	(10)	(10)	(10)	(10)
Net income	30	30	25	35	35	25
Statement of Owner's Equity						
Erv Bultman, capital, January 1	100	130	100	125	100	135
Net income	30	30	25	35	35	25
Erv Bultman, capital, December 31		130	160	125	160	135	160
Balance Sheet (Partial)						
Current assets:						
Merchandise inventory	20	20	15	20	25	20
Owner's equity:						
Erv Bultman, capital	130	160	125	160	135	160

FIGURE 19-1   Effect of Inventory Errors on Net Income

The third pair of columns in Figure 19-1 illustrates the effects of overstating the ending inventory in 20-1. This causes net income to be overstated in 20-1 and understated in 20-2. As previously discussed, these errors "wash out" by the end of 20-2. Thus, Bultman's capital account is correct in the 20-2 financial statements.

 LEARNING KEY: If the ending inventory for 20-1 is overstated, net income for 20-1 is overstated and net income for 20-2 is understated.

It is very important to have an accurate count and valuation for the ending inventory. Since errors in the ending inventory have a direct effect on net income for the period, managers may be tempted to manipulate this amount to achieve a desired result: to either increase net income to make the company look good, or decrease net income to reduce taxes or smooth earnings. For this reason, observing and verifying the ending inventory is an important aspect of an external auditor's job.

TYPES OF INVENTORY SYSTEMS: PERIODIC AND PERPETUAL

LO2 Describe the two principal systems of accounting for merchandise inventory—the periodic system and the perpetual system.

The two principal systems of accounting for merchandise inventory are the periodic and the perpetual systems. Under the periodic inventory system, the balance in the merchandise inventory account is merely a record of the most recent count of the physical inventory. The purchases account is debited for the cost of all goods purchased. The sales account is credited for the selling prices of all goods sold. Under this system, the current merchandise inventory and the cost of goods sold are not determined until the end of the accounting period, when a physical inventory is taken. At that time, the following formula is applied to calculate cost of goods sold.

	Beginning Inventory (last year's ending physical count)
+	Net Purchases (account balance at end of this year)
=	Cost of Goods Available for Sale
−	Ending Inventory (this year's ending physical count)
=	Cost of Goods Sold (for this year)

LEARNING KEY: Under the periodic inventory system, the ending inventory and cost of goods sold are determined at the end of the accounting period, when a physical inventory is taken.

Recall that adjusting entries are needed at the end of the fiscal year to update the merchandise inventory account. These entries are illustrated as Transaction 7 for the periodic system in Figure 19-2.

Under the perpetual inventory system, entries are made to the merchandise inventory and cost of goods sold accounts as transactions take place during the accounting period. The merchandise inventory account is debited for the cost of all goods purchased, including freight charges, and credited for the cost of all goods sold. In addition, this account is debited when customers return merchandise and is credited when suppliers grant returns, allowances, and discounts. Thus, the balance of the account represents the cost of goods on hand at all times. The cost of goods sold account is debited when merchandise is sold and credited when customers return merchandise. Thus, the balance of the account reflects the cost of goods sold at any point during the accounting period. No year-end adjusting entry is necessary as long as the physical inventory agrees with the amount reported in the merchandise inventory account. Figure 19-2 compares entries made under the periodic and perpetual inventory systems.

LEARNING KEY: Under the perpetual inventory system, cost of goods sold and the amount of merchandise inventory on hand are continually updated as merchandise is bought and sold.

TRANSACTION	PERIODIC SYSTEM		PERPETUAL SYSTEM	

1. Purchased merchandise on account, $100.	Purchases
	    Accounts Payable
		100
		  100
			Merchandise Inventory
			    Accounts Payable
				100
				  100

2. Paid freight charge, $30.	Freight-In
	    Cash
		30
		  30
			Merchandise Inventory
			    Cash
				30
				  30

3. Sold merchandise on account, $80. The cost of the merchandise was $50.	Accounts Receivable
	    Sales
		80
		  80
			Accounts Receivable
			    Sales
			Cost of Goods Sold
			    Merchandise Inventory
				80
				  80
				50
				  50

4. Merchandise costing $10 was returned to the supplier.	Accounts Payable
	    Purchases Ret. & Allow.
		10
		  10
			Accounts Payable
			    Merchandise Inventory
				10
				  10

5. Customers returned merchandise sold for $20. The cost of the merchandise was $15.	Sales Ret. and Allow.
	    Accounts Receivable
		20
		  20
			Sales Ret. and Allow.
			    Accounts Receivable
			Merchandise Inventory
			    Cost of Goods Sold
				20
				  20
				15
				  15

6. Paid for merchandise costing $100. The supplier granted a 2% discount for prompt payment.	Accounts Payable
	    Purchases Discounts
	    Cash
		100
		  2
		  98
			Accounts Payable
			    Merchandise Inventory
			    Cash
				100
				  2
				  98

7. Adjusting entries made at the end of the accounting period.	Income Summary
	    Merchandise Inventory
	
	Merchandise Inventory
	    Income Summary
		xx
		  xx
		
		xx
		  xx
			Not necessary if physical inventory agrees with amount reported in merchandise inventory account.	

FIGURE 19-2   Entries for Periodic and Perpetual Inventory Systems

Figure 19-3 provides a summary of the transactions that affect the merchandise inventory account during the year and adjustments made at year end under the periodic and perpetual systems.

PERIODIC INVENTORY SYSTEM		PERPETUAL INVENTORY SYSTEM	
Merchandise Inventory		**Merchandise Inventory**	

Entries made during year:
  NONE
		Entries made during year:
		  Purchases
		
		  Freight-In
		  Sales Returns
			Purchases Returns
			  & Allowances
			Purchases Discounts
			Cost of Goods Sold

Year-end adjustments:
  (2) Enter ending
      inventory
	(1) Remove beginning
	    inventory
		Year-end adjustments:
		  Adjust for differences
		  between physical count
		  and amount in account.
		  Debit if physical
		    inventory > Books
			Credit if physical inventory
			  < Books

FIGURE 19-3   Transactions and Adjustments Affecting Merchandise Inventory

ASSIGNING COST TO INVENTORY AND COST OF GOODS SOLD

LO3 Compute the costs allocated to the ending inventory and cost of goods sold using different inventory methods.

To determine the cost of goods sold and ending inventory, it is important to understand:

1. the purpose of a physical inventory,

2. the specific calculations used under the periodic and perpetual systems, and

3. the role of the lower-of-cost-or-market rule.

Taking a Physical Inventory

Under the periodic system, the goods on hand at the end of the period are counted to allocate merchandise costs between sold and unsold goods. This process is called taking a **physical inventory**. A physical inventory is also important under the perpetual system. It verifies that the amount of merchandise actually held agrees with what is reported in the accounting records.

Taking a physical inventory can be a sizable task. Frequently, it is done after regular business hours. Some companies even close for a few days to take inventory. The ideal time to count the goods is when the quantity on hand is at its lowest level. A fiscal year that starts and ends at the time the stock of goods is normally at its lowest level is known as a **natural business year**. Such a year is used by many businesses for accounting purposes.

Various procedures are followed in taking an inventory to be sure that no items are missed and that no items are included more than once. Frequently, persons taking inventory work in pairs: one counts the items and the other records the information. Usually this information is entered on a special form called an **inventory sheet**, like the one illustrated in Figure 19-4. The inventory sheet has columns for recording the description of each item, the quantity on hand, the cost per unit, and the extension.

> Even under the perpetual inventory system, there will be differences between the actual inventory on the floor and the amount on the books. These differences are the result of breakage, spoilage, and theft. Thieves rarely yell "Debit Loss Due to Theft and credit Merchandise Inventory" as they attempt to leave the store with merchandise under their coats.

Description	Quantity	Unit	Unit Cost	Extensions	
Table Lamp	20	ea.	62.80	1,256.00	
Wall Rack	18	ea.	19.70	354.60	
Bookcase	7	ea.	88.10	616.70	
End Table	13	ea.	53.20	691.60	
Desk	6	ea.	158.30	949.80	
Total					6,465.10

INVENTORY Aug. 31 20 -- Page 1
Sheet No. 1
Called by L.M.M.   Department A
Entered by K.N.   Location Storeroom
Costed by C.M.H.
Extended by C.M.H.
Examined by C.J.C.

FIGURE 19-4 Inventory Sheet

Only goods that are the property of the company should be included in a physical inventory. Two special situations that require care to determine ownership are (1) goods held for sale on **consignment** and (2) goods **in transit**. Sometimes one business will try to sell merchandise for another business or individual on a commission basis. This is called selling goods on consignment. Goods

A BROADER VIEW

The "Magic Wand" at Wal-Mart

At any given time, a typical Wal-Mart discount store has more than 70,000 standard items in stock. Every item must be inventoried and replenished in a timely way to avoid having too much or too little stock. Wal-Mart associates have the aid of the "Magic Wand," a handheld computer, linked by a radio-frequency network to in-store terminals. These high-tech devices provide up-to-the-minute information on inventory on hand, upcoming deliveries, and stock at Wal-Mart distribution centers.

MAGIC WAND

"Space age"

technology helps

keep Wal-Mart

in front on price

and service

WAL-MART

held on consignment remain the property of the shipper (**consignor**). They should not be included in the inventory of the company holding the goods (**consignee**).

To determine whether goods in transit at year end should be included in inventory, we must know the FOB (free on board) terms. If goods are shipped FOB shipping point, the buyer pays for shipping and the goods belong to the buyer as soon as they are shipped. If goods are shipped FOB destination, the seller pays for shipping and the goods belong to the seller until they are received by the buyer.

LEARNING KEY: Under FOB shipping point, the goods belong to the buyer as soon as they are shipped. Under FOB destination, the goods belong to the seller until they are received by the buyer.

After calculating the quantities of goods owned at the end of the period, the proper cost must be assigned to the inventory. In addition to the purchase price, we include delivery costs (freight-in), insurance, and, occasionally, storage fees. Therefore, cost means all necessary and reasonable costs incurred to get the goods to the buyer's place of business.

If all purchases of the same item were made at the same price per unit, computing the cost of the ending inventory would be simple. We would multiply the number of units by the cost per unit. In a world of changing prices, however, identical items are purchased at different times and at different costs per unit. Of the goods available for sale, how do we decide which units were sold and which units remain on the shelf? As shown in Figure 19-5, this decision affects the income statement and balance sheet. The following four inventory methods have become generally accepted for answering this question.

1. Specific identification

2. First-in, first-out (FIFO)

3. Weighted-average

4. Last-in, first-out (LIFO)

These methods may be applied under the periodic or perpetual inventory systems.

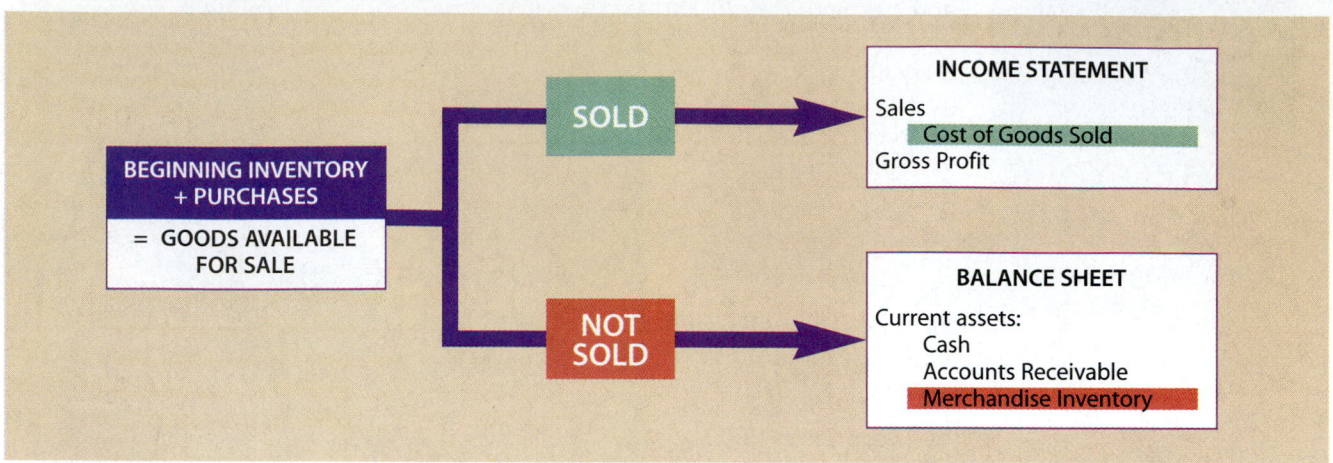

FIGURE 19-5 Allocation of Goods Available for Sale to Cost of Goods Sold and Ending Inventory

The Periodic Inventory System

Specific Identification Method. When each unit of inventory can be specifically identified, the **specific identification method** can be used. To use this method, inventory items must be physically different from each other, or they must have serial numbers. Examples include cars, motorcycles, furniture, appliances, and fine jewelry. When a unit is sold, its cost is determined from the supplier's invoice. This method is practical only for businesses in which sales volume is relatively low and inventory unit value is relatively high. Otherwise, record keeping becomes expensive and time consuming.

 LEARNING KEY: The specific identification method requires that each inventory item have a distinguishing feature or marking to assure proper identification.

To illustrate how specific identification costing works, assume the following data for an inventory of one specific model of children's bicycles.

Children's Bicycles (Model ZX007)

	Units	Unit Price	Total Cost
On hand at start of period	40	$62	$ 2,480
Purchased during period:			
1st purchase	60	65	3,900
2nd purchase	80	67	5,360
3rd purchase	70	68	4,760
Number of units available for sale	250		$16,500
On hand at end of period	50		
Number of units sold during period	200		

Of the 200 units sold during the period, the bicycle serial numbers show that 30 were from the beginning inventory, 50 were from the first purchase, 60 were from the second purchase, and 60 were from the last purchase. The cost of goods sold and the cost of inventory at the end of the period are determined as shown in Figure 19-6.

	COST OF GOODS SOLD			COST OF ENDING INVENTORY		
	Units	Unit Price	Total	Units	Unit Price	Total
Beginning inventory	30	$62	$ 1,860	10	$62	$ 620
1st purchase	50	65	3,250	10	65	650
2nd purchase	60	67	4,020	20	67	1,340
3rd purchase	60	68	4,080	10	68	680
Total	200		$13,210	50		$ 3,290
Alternative calculation given goods available for sale and cost of goods sold or ending inventory.	Cost of goods available for sale Less cost of ending inventory Cost of goods sold		$16,500 (3,290) $13,210	Cost of goods available for sale Less cost of goods sold Cost of ending inventory		$16,500 (13,210) $ 3,290

FIGURE 19-6   Specific Identification Inventory Method

First-In, First-Out (FIFO) Method. Another widely used method of allocating merchandise cost is called the **first-in, first-out,** or **FIFO, method.** This costing method assumes that the first goods purchased were the first goods sold. Therefore, the latest goods purchased remain in inventory.

LEARNING KEY: FIFO means First-In, First-Out.

Whenever possible, a business will attempt to sell the older goods first. This is particularly true of businesses that sell perishable items or merchandise that may become obsolete. Grocery stores, fresh fruit stands, and computer software businesses are good examples. These businesses must rotate their stock forward. They pull the oldest bread, milk, fruit, and vegetables to the front of the shelves and try to sell all copies of the current software before a new version arrives. FIFO costing is, therefore, widely used because it often follows the actual movement of goods. It assumes that the oldest units have been sold and the newest or freshest units are in the ending inventory.

Applying FIFO to the bicycle inventory data, the cost of goods sold and the cost of inventory at the end of the period are determined as shown in Figure 19-7.

	COST OF GOODS SOLD			COST OF ENDING INVENTORY		
	Units	Unit Price	Total	Units	Unit Price	Total
Beginning inventory	40	$62	$ 2,480		$62	$ 0
1st purchase	60	65	3,900		65	0
2nd purchase	80	67	5,360		67	0
3rd purchase	20	68	1,360	50	68	3,400
Total	200		$13,100	50		$ 3,400
Alternative calculation given goods available for sale and cost of goods sold or ending inventory.	Cost of goods available for sale Less cost of ending inventory Cost of goods sold		$16,500 (3,400) $13,100	Cost of goods available for sale Less cost of goods sold Cost of ending inventory		$16,500 (13,100) $ 3,400

FIGURE 19-7   FIFO Inventory Method

Note that the 50 items on hand at the end of the period are considered to be those most recently purchased.

FIFO costing is widely used because businesses have used this method for a long time. Accountants are reluctant to change a long-followed method of accounting when such a change would affect the comparability of their income calculations over a period of years. **Consistency** based on comparability is an important accounting principle.

LEARNING KEY: The consistency principle of accounting suggests that a business should use the same accounting techniques from year to year.

Weighted-Average Method. Another method of allocating merchandise cost is called the **weighted-average method**, or **average cost method**. This costing method is based on the average cost of identical units.

Consider the bicycle inventory data again. The average cost of identical units is determined by dividing the total cost of units available for sale ($16,500) by the total number of units available for sale (250).

$$\frac{\$16{,}500 \text{ (cost of units available for sale)}}{250 \text{ (units available for sale)}} = \$66 \text{ weighted-average cost per unit}$$

The cost of goods sold and the cost of the end-of-period inventory are calculated as follows:

Cost of goods sold	200	units @ $66 =	$13,200
Cost of ending inventory	50	units @ $66 =	3,300
Total	250	units	$16,500

There is a logical appeal to the weighted-average method of allocating cost between goods sold and goods on hand. In this example, one-fifth (50) of the total units available (250) were unsold. The weighted-average method assigns one-fifth ($3,300) of the total cost ($16,500) to these goods.

Last-In, First-Out (LIFO) Method. A fourth method of allocating merchandise cost is called the **last-in, first-out**, or **LIFO, method**. It assumes that the sales in the period were made from the most recently purchased goods. Therefore, the earliest goods purchased remain in inventory.

LEARNING KEY: LIFO means Last-In, First-Out.

This physical flow is associated with businesses selling products that are not perishable or likely to become obsolete, and may be difficult to handle. Imagine a large barrel of nails at a lumberyard. Customers take nails from the top of the barrel. When the supply gets low, new nails are simply piled on top of the old ones. There is no need to rotate the nails from the bottom to the top of the barrel.

Applying LIFO to the bicycle inventory data, the cost of goods sold and the cost of inventory at the end of the period are determined as shown in Figure 19-8.

	COST OF GOODS SOLD			COST OF ENDING INVENTORY		
	Units	Unit Price	Total	Units	Unit Price	Total
Beginning inventory	0	$62	$ 0	40	$62	$ 2,480
1st purchase	50	65	3,250	10	65	650
2nd purchase	80	67	5,360		67	0
3rd purchase	70	68	4,760		68	0
Total	200		$13,370	50		$ 3,130
Alternative calculation given goods available for sale and cost of goods sold or ending inventory.	Cost of goods available for sale		$16,500	Cost of goods available for sale		$16,500
	Less cost of ending inventory		(3,130)	Less cost of goods sold		(13,370)
	Cost of goods sold		$13,370	Cost of ending inventory		$ 3,130

FIGURE 19-8 LIFO Inventory Method

Note that the 50 units on hand at the end of the period are considered to be the 40 units in the beginning inventory plus 10 of the units from the first purchase.

The LIFO method has been justified on the grounds that the physical movement of goods in some businesses is actually last-in, first-out. This is rarely the case, but the method has become popular for other reasons. One persuasive argument for the use of the LIFO method is that it matches the most current cost of items purchased against the current sales revenue. When the most current costs of purchases are subtracted from sales revenue, the impact of changing prices on the resulting gross profit figure is minimized. In the opinion of many accountants, this is proper and desirable.

Another reason for the popularity of the LIFO method is its effect on income taxes. When prices are rising, net income calculated under the LIFO method is less than net income calculated under either the FIFO or the weighted-average method. Since the net income amount under LIFO is less, the related income tax will be less. The reverse would be true if prices were falling. However, periods of falling prices over the past two centuries have been few and brief.

Opponents of the LIFO method contend that its use causes old, out-of-date inventory costs to be shown on the balance sheet. The theoretical and practical merits of FIFO versus LIFO are the subject of much professional debate.

Physical Flows and Cost Flows. Of the four inventory costing methods described, only the specific identification costing method will necessarily reflect cost flows that match physical flows of goods. Each of the other three methods—FIFO, weighted-average, and LIFO—is based on assumed cost flows. The assumed cost flows *are not required to reflect the actual physical movement of goods* within the company. Any one of the three assumed cost flow methods could be used under any set of physical flow conditions. For example, a fresh fruit stand with an actual FIFO flow of inventory may use LIFO for accounting purposes. Similarly, a supplier of building materials that sells nails, lumber, and sand off the top of the pile may use FIFO even though the physical flow of goods is LIFO.

LEARNING KEY: The inventory method used does not have to match the physical flow of goods.

Comparison of Methods. To compare the results of the four inventory methods, let's assume that the 200 bicycle units in our example were sold for $18,000. Figure 19-9 contrasts the ending inventory, cost of goods sold, and gross profit under each of the four methods.

	SPECIFIC IDENTIFICATION		FIFO		WEIGHTED-AVERAGE		LIFO	
Sales		$18,000		$18,000		$18,000		$18,000
Cost of goods sold:								
Beginning inventory	$ 2,480		$ 2,480		$ 2,480		$ 2,480	
Purchases	14,020		14,020		14,020		14,020	
Goods available for sale	$16,500		$16,500		$16,500		$16,500	
Less ending inventory	3,290		3,400		3,300		3,130	
Cost of goods sold		13,210		13,100		13,200		13,370
Gross profit		$ 4,790		$ 4,900		$ 4,800		$ 4,630

FIGURE 19-9   Comparison of Inventory Methods

During periods of rising prices, we can observe the following:

LIFO generally produces the highest cost of goods sold, lowest gross profit, and lowest ending inventory. Since the most recent units purchased are assumed to have been sold, the most recent costs are matched against revenues and this provides the best measure of gross profit and net income. After all, the units sold must be replaced at current prices. However, under LIFO, the first units purchased are assumed to remain in inventory (FISH: First-In, Still Here). This means that units purchased many years ago may remain in the ending inventory. These dollar amounts are likely to have little meaning when measuring the firm's performance or financial health.

FIFO generally produces the lowest cost of goods sold, highest gross profit, and highest ending inventory. Since the last units purchased are assumed to be in ending inventory, these most recent costs provide the best inventory measure on the balance sheet (LISH: Last-In, Still Here). However, under FIFO, the first units purchased are assumed to have been sold. This means that somewhat older prices are used to compute cost of goods sold and gross profit than under LIFO. Thus, these measures are somewhat less useful than those computed under LIFO.

The weighted-average inventory method produces measures between LIFO and FIFO. The specific identification method will produce measures based on the actual units sold.

LEARNING KEY: In periods of rising prices, LIFO produces the lowest net income and FIFO produces the highest net income.

The Internal Revenue Service requires the use of the same inventory method for tax and financial reporting purposes. Since LIFO generally produces the highest cost of goods sold, lowest gross profit, and lowest tax liability, many firms use the LIFO inventory method to minimize federal income taxes. The tax dollars saved are then available for other purposes.

As discussed earlier, keep the following in mind when selecting the inventory method to be used by a business.

1. The physical flow of the inventory does not need to match the flow assumed by the inventory method.

2. The consistency principle requires that the same accounting methods be followed from period to period. Although it is acceptable to make changes, it is not appropriate to switch back and forth from FIFO to LIFO based on the desire to maximize or minimize earnings for a given year.

The Perpetual Inventory System

Under the perpetual inventory system, a continuous record is maintained for the quantities and costs of goods on hand at all times. The general ledger account for Merchandise Inventory under such a system is somewhat like the account for Cash. It provides a chronological record of each addition (purchase) and subtraction (sale). The balance of the account at any time shows the cost of goods that should be on hand.

When perpetual inventory records are kept, the merchandise inventory account in the general ledger is usually a controlling account. A subsidiary ledger is maintained with an account for each type of merchandise. These accounts are often recorded on cards or in computer files. As shown in Figure 19-10, the subsidiary accounts are designed to handle additions and subtractions and determine the new balance after each change. Goods sold usually are assigned cost on either a FIFO, moving-average, or LIFO basis. Procedures for applying the FIFO method in a perpetual inventory system are similar to those illustrated for a periodic system. The first merchandise purchased is treated as the first merchandise sold. The illustration in Figure 19-10 is based on the FIFO method. The specific techniques used to apply the moving-average and LIFO methods in a perpetual system are more complicated. They are illustrated in the appendix.

 LEARNING KEY: A controlling account and subsidiary ledger are maintained for inventory in much the same way as for accounts receivable and accounts payable.

DATE	PURCHASES			COST OF GOODS SOLD				INVENTORY ON HAND				
	Units	Cost/ Unit	Total	Units	Cost/ Unit	CGS	Cumulative CGS	Layer	Units	Cost/ Unit	Layer Cost	Total
Jan. 1 (BI)								(1)	40	$62.00	$2,480	$2,480.00
Feb. 15				30	$62.00	$1,860.00	$ 1,860.00	(1)	10	$62.00	620	$ 620.00
Mar. 1								(1)	10	$62.00	620	
	60	$ 65	$3,900					(2)	60	65.00	3,900	$4,520.00
April 1				10	$62.00	$ 620.00		(2)	30	$65.00	1,950	
				30	$65.00	1,950.00	$ 4,430.00					$1,950.00
May 15								(2)	30	$65.00	1,950	
	80	$ 67	$5,360					(3)	80	67.00	5,360	$7,310.00
June 30				30	$65.00	$1,950.00		(3)	20	$67.00	1,340	
				60	67.00	4,020.00	$10,400.00					$1,340.00
Aug. 28								(3)	20	$67.00	1,340	
	70	$ 68	$4,760					(4)	70	68.00	4,760	$6,100.00
Oct. 30				20	$67.00	$1,340.00		(4)	50	$68.00	3,400	
				20	68.00	1,360.00	$13,100.00					$3,400.00
Cost of Goods Sold during 20--							$13,100.00					

BI: Beginning Inventory

FIGURE 19-10   Perpetual Inventory Record: FIFO Method

As discussed in Chapter 15, the perpetual inventory system does not eliminate the need for taking physical inventories. The perpetual records must be compared with the physical inventory to discover and correct any errors or losses of merchandise from theft, breakage, or spoilage. If a difference is found between the physical count and the amount in the perpetual inventory records, the records must be corrected by an adjusting entry. As discussed in Chapter 15, many firms use Cost of Goods Sold to make this adjustment. A preferrable approach is to use an account called **Inventory Short and Over**. For example, if the book balance is $3,840 and the physical count shows $3,710 worth of merchandise, the $130 shortage would be entered as follows:

4		Inventory Short and Over			1	3	0	00						4
5		Merchandise Inventory								1	3	0	00	5
6		To adjust inventory per physical count												6

LEARNING KEY: A physical inventory is still important under the perpetual inventory method. It is used to verify the accuracy of the inventory records.

Similarly, if the book balance is $3,840 and the physical count shows $3,900 worth of merchandise, this $60 overage would be entered as follows:

4		Merchandise Inventory			6	0	00					4
5		Inventory Short and Over							6	0	00	5
6		To adjust inventory per physical count										6

If Inventory Short and Over has a debit balance, the account is listed with other expenses on the income statement. If it has a credit balance, the account is listed with other revenues on the income statement.

Using a separate account, Inventory Short and Over, makes it easier for management to track inventory problems associated with errors, theft, breakage, and spoilage. Further, it removes these items from the calculation of cost of goods sold and provides a better measure of the gross profit on sales.

LEARNING KEY: Inventory Short and Over is reported as other expense or other revenue on the income statement.

A business that sells a wide selection of low-cost goods may not find it practical to keep a perpetual inventory. In contrast, a business that sells a few high-cost items (cars, fine jewelry, stereo equipment) can maintain such a record without incurring excessive processing costs. The increasing use of computers and optical scanning devices at the point of sale has enabled more businesses to switch from the periodic to the perpetual inventory method.

Lower-of-Cost-or-Market Method of Inventory Valuation

It is a well-established tradition in accounting that gains should not be recognized unless a sale has occurred. If the value of an asset increases while it is being held, no formal entry of the gain is made on the books. On the other hand, if an asset's value declines while it is being held, it is generally considered proper to recognize a loss. This is in keeping with the accounting practice of **conservatism**, which states that when in doubt, the lower asset value and net income measure should be used. Thus, we should never anticipate gains, but we should always anticipate and account for losses.

LEARNING KEY: The accounting practice of conservatism states that when in doubt, the lower asset value and net income measure should be used. Thus, when in doubt, we should not record gains, but we should record losses.

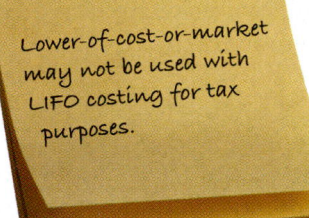

Lower-of-cost-or-market may not be used with LIFO costing for tax purposes.

As applied to inventory, conservatism means that if the value of inventory declines while it is being held, the loss should be recognized in the period of the decline. The purpose of the **lower-of-cost-or-market method** is to recognize such losses on the income statement and to report the lower inventory valuation on the balance sheet.

In applying the lower-of-cost-or-market method, "**cost**" means the dollar amount calculated using one of the four inventory costing methods. "**Market**" means the cost to replace the inventory. It is the price in the market in which goods are purchased by the business—not the price in the market in which they are normally sold by the business. The lower-of-cost-or-market method assumes that a decline in the purchase (replacement) price of inventory is accompanied by a decline in the selling price. In this sense, a decline in the purchase (replacement) price signals a decline in the value of the inventory.

LEARNING KEY: Under lower-of-cost-or-market, market represents the cost to replace the inventory item, not the selling price.

To illustrate the lower-of-cost-or-market method, assume the following end-of-period inventory data for three items.

Item	Recorded Purchase Cost	End-of-Period Market Value	Lower-of-Cost-or-Market
1	$ 8,000	$ 7,000	$ 7,000
2	9,000	10,000	9,000
3	7,000	6,500	6,500
	$24,000	$23,500	$22,500

The illustration shows two ways to calculate the lower-of-cost-or-market. First, the lower-of-cost-or-market method can be applied to the total inventory. This involves comparing the $24,000 total cost with the $23,500 *total end-of-period market value*. Under the second approach, the method is applied to each item in inventory. This involves comparing the $24,000 total cost with the $22,500 lower-of-cost-or-market value determined by comparing cost with market value for *each item*. Either approach is acceptable, but the one chosen should be applied consistently across periods.

The difference between the cost and market value is considered a loss due to holding inventory. Normally it is charged to an account such as Loss on Write-Down of Inventory. For example, based on application of the method to the total inventory in the previous illustration, a $500 loss ($24,000 – $23,500) is recognized as follows:

14		Loss on Write-Down of Inventory		5 0 0 00		14
15		Merchandise Inventory			5 0 0 00	15
16		To recognize loss in value of inventory held				16

The loss due to write-down of inventory should be reported on the income statement as an expense. Although not a preferred treatment, some businesses include it in cost of goods sold if the amounts are small.

ESTIMATING ENDING INVENTORY AND COST OF GOODS SOLD

LO4 **Estimate the ending inventory and cost of goods sold by using the gross profit and retail inventory methods.**

Many businesses prepare monthly or quarterly financial statements. To do this, the business must estimate the inventory at the end of the month or quarter and the cost of goods sold for the period. This is not a problem for businesses using the perpetual inventory method. Although these amounts need to be verified by a physical inventory at the end of the year, the unverified amounts are generally reliable estimates and can be used for these "interim" statements.

Businesses using the periodic inventory method must use other methods to estimate the ending inventory and cost of goods sold. Two generally accepted methods are the gross profit method and the retail inventory method.

Gross Profit Method of Estimating Inventory

Under the **gross profit method**, a business's normal gross profit (Net Sales – Cost of Goods Sold) is used to estimate the cost of goods sold and ending inventory. To illustrate the gross profit method, assume the following data with respect to Groomer Company:

Inventory, start of period	$80,000
Net purchases, first month	$70,000
Net sales, first month	$110,000
Normal gross profit as a percentage of sales	40%

The estimated cost of goods sold for the month and the estimated merchandise inventory at the end of the month would be determined as shown in Figure 19-11.

STEP 1	Compute the cost of goods available for sale.	Cost of goods available for sale:		
		Inventory, start of period	$ 80,000	
		Net purchases, first month	70,000	
		Cost of goods available for sale		$150,000
STEP 2	Estimate cost of goods sold by deducting the normal gross profit from net sales.	Estimated cost of goods sold:		
		Net sales	$110,000	
		Normal gross profit	44,000	
		($110,000 × 40%)		
		Estimated cost of goods sold		66,000
STEP 3	Estimate the ending inventory by deducting cost of goods sold from the cost of goods available for sale.	Estimated end-of-month inventory		$ 84,000

FIGURE 19-11   Steps for the Gross Profit Method

This calculation is appropriate only if the firm's normal gross profit as a percentage of net sales has been relatively stable over time. This type of calculation also can be used to test the reasonableness of the amount of inventory that was computed on the basis of a physical count. A large difference between the two amounts might indicate a mistake in the count, a mistake in the costing of the items, or a marked change in the gross profit rate. The gross profit procedure also can be used to estimate the cost of an inventory that was destroyed by fire or other casualty.

Retail Method of Estimating Inventory

Many retail businesses, such as department and clothing stores, use a variation of the gross profit method to calculate cost of goods sold and ending inventory. The procedure used, called the **retail method** of inventory, requires keeping records of both the cost and selling (retail) prices of all goods purchased. This information can be used to estimate cost of goods sold and ending inventory, as shown in Figure 19-12.

			COST	RETAIL
STEP 1	Compute the cost of goods available for sale at cost and retail.	Inventory, start of period	$ 60,000	$ 85,000
		Net purchases during period	126,000	163,000
		Goods available for sale	$186,000	$248,000
STEP 2	Compute the ending inventory at retail by subtracting sales at retail from goods available for sale at retail.	Less net sales for period		180,000
		Inventory, end of period, at retail		$ 68,000
STEP 3	Compute the cost-to-retail ratio by dividing the cost of goods available for sale by retail value of the goods available for sale.	Ratio of cost-to-retail prices of goods available for sale ($186,000 ÷ $248,000)		75%
STEP 4	Estimate the cost of the ending inventory by multiplying the ending inventory at retail (Step 2) by the cost-to-retail ratio.	Inventory, end of period, at estimated cost (75% of $68,000)	(51,000)	
STEP 5	Estimate cost of goods sold by a. multiplying sales at retail by the cost-to-retail ratio, or b. subtracting the estimated ending inventory from the cost of goods available for sale.	Estimated cost of goods sold (or, sales of $180,000 × 75% = $135,000)	$135,000	

FIGURE 19-12 Steps in the Retail Inventory Method

Learning Objectives	Key Points to Remember
1 Explain the impact of merchandise inventory on the financial statements.	The cost of goods available for sale during the accounting period must be divided between the cost of goods sold and the ending merchandise inventory. Cost of goods sold is reported on the income statement and used to determine the gross profit for the period. The ending merchandise inventory is reported as a current asset on the balance sheet. Figure 19-13 illustrates the allocation of cost of goods available for sale into cost of goods sold and ending inventory.

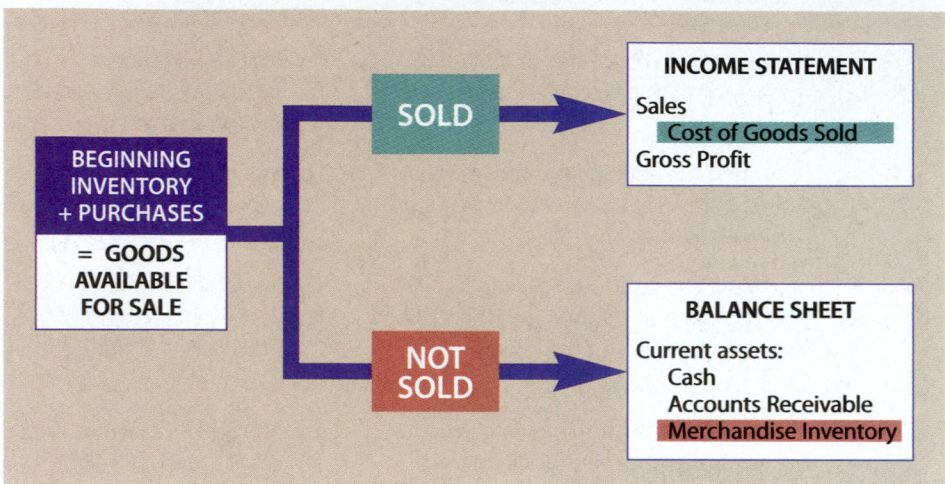

FIGURE 19-13 Allocation of Goods Available for Sale to Cost of Goods Sold and Ending Inventory

2 Describe the two principal systems of accounting for merchandise inventory—the periodic system and the perpetual system.	There are two systems of accounting for merchandise.

Periodic Inventory System
1. The purchases account is debited for the cost of all goods purchased.
2. The sales account is credited for the selling prices of all goods sold.
3. At the end of the accounting period, a physical inventory is taken and the following formula is applied to calculate cost of goods sold.

> Beginning Inventory (last year's ending physical count)
> + Net Purchases (account balance at end of this year)
> = Cost of Goods Available for Sale
> − Ending Inventory (this year's ending physical count)
> = Cost of Goods Sold (for this year)

Perpetual Inventory System
1. The merchandise inventory account is debited for all purchases.
2. The cost of goods sold account is debited and the merchandise inventory account is credited for all sales.
3. Thus, the merchandise inventory account provides a running balance of the goods on hand.

Learning Objectives	Key Points to Remember

3 **Compute the costs allocated to the ending inventory and cost of goods sold using different inventory methods.**

One of four inventory methods is generally used to determine the costs assigned to the goods sold and ending inventory:

- Specific identification
- FIFO: first-in, first-out
- Weighted-average
- LIFO: last-in, first-out

The actual physical flow of inventory does not have to match the method used. During periods of rising prices, LIFO produces the lowest net income and FIFO produces the highest net income.

4 **Estimate the ending inventory and cost of goods sold by using the gross profit and retail inventory methods.**

Firms using the periodic inventory method often need to estimate their inventory. Two methods are used for this purpose:

- **Gross Profit Method**—The firm's normal gross profit as a percentage of net sales is used to estimate cost of goods sold and ending inventory in three steps:
    1. Compute cost of goods available for sale.
    2. Estimate cost of goods sold by deducting the normal gross profit (net sales × normal gross profit as percentage of net sales) from net sales.
    3. Estimate the ending inventory by deducting cost of goods sold from the cost of goods available for sale.

- **Retail Inventory Method**—The firm's ratio of cost-to-retail prices of goods available for sale is used to estimate ending inventory and cost of goods sold in five basic steps:
    1. Compute the cost of goods available for sale at cost and retail.
    2. Compute the ending inventory at retail by subtracting sales at retail from goods available for sale at retail.
    3. Compute the cost-to-retail ratio by dividing the cost of goods available for sale by the retail value of the goods available for sale.
    4. Estimate the cost of ending inventory by multiplying the ending inventory at retail by the cost-to-retail ratio.
    5. Estimate cost of goods sold by:
        a. multiplying sales at retail by the cost-to-retail ratio, or
        b. subtracting the estimated ending inventory from the cost of goods available for sale.

REFLECTION

Reflection: Answering the Opening Questions

When a business sells many identical units with different costs, it can be difficult to determine which units were sold and which are still in inventory. Yes, it matters which units were sold. As discussed in the chapter, the cost of goods sold is deducted from net sales to compute gross profit. If all of the less costly units were sold, gross profit would be higher than if all of the more costly units were sold. Thus, Evan must make an assumption about the flow of inventory through the business. This assumption (FIFO, LIFO, etc.) does not have to match the actual physical flow of the inventory, but must be followed consistently from year to year.

DEMONSTRATION PROBLEM

WebTUTOR Advantage

Fialka Company's beginning inventory and purchases during the fiscal year ended October 31, 20-2, were as follows:

		Units	Unit Price	Total Cost
November 1, 20-1	Beginning inventory	500	$25.00	$ 12,500
November 12, 20-1	1st purchase	600	26.25	15,750
December 28, 20-1	2nd purchase	400	27.50	11,000
March 29, 20-2	3rd purchase	1,000	28.00	28,000
May 31, 20-2	4th purchase	750	28.50	21,375
July 29, 20-2	5th purchase	350	29.00	10,150
August 30, 20-2	6th purchase	675	30.00	20,250
October 21, 20-2	7th purchase	225	31.00	6,975
		4,500		$126,000

There are 1,600 units of inventory on hand on October 31, 20-2.

REQUIRED

1. Calculate the total amount to be assigned to cost of goods sold for the fiscal year and ending inventory on October 31, 20-2, under each of the following methods.

    a.   FIFO

    b.   LIFO

    c.   Weighted-average cost (round calculations to two decimal places)

2. Assume that the market price per unit (cost to replace) of Fialka's inventory on October 31, 20-2, was $29. Calculate the total amount to be assigned to the ending inventory on October 31, 20-2, under each of the following methods.

    a.   FIFO lower-of-cost-or-market

    b.   Weighted-average lower-of-cost-or-market

3. Assume that a fire destroyed Fialka's store and all inventory on October 31, just prior to taking a physical inventory. Thus, Fialka must estimate the ending inventory and cost of goods sold. During the fiscal year ended October 31, 20-2, net sales of $134,000 were made. The normal gross profit rate is 40%. Use the gross profit method to estimate the cost of goods sold for the fiscal year ended October 31, 20-2, and the inventory on October 31, 20-2.

Solution

1a.

DATE	FIFO INVENTORY METHOD COST OF GOODS SOLD			COST OF ENDING INVENTORY		
20-1/-2	**Units**	**Unit Price**	**Total**	**Units**	**Unit Price**	**Total**
Nov. 1 Beginning inventory	500	$25.00	$ 12,500		$25.00	$ 0
Nov. 12 1st purchase	600	26.25	15,750		26.25	0
Dec. 28 2nd purchase	400	27.50	11,000		27.50	0
Mar. 29 3rd purchase	1,000	28.00	28,000		28.00	0
May 31 4th purchase	400	28.50	11,400	350	28.50	9,975
July 29 5th purchase		29.00	0	350	29.00	10,150
Aug. 30 6th purchase		30.00	0	675	30.00	20,250
Oct. 21 7th purchase		31.00	0	225	31.00	6,975
Total	2,900		$ 78,650	1,600		$ 47,350

Alternative calculation given goods available for sale and cost of goods sold or ending inventory.						
	Cost of goods available for sale		$126,000	Cost of goods available for sale		$126,000
	Less cost of ending inventory		(47,350)	Less cost of goods sold		(78,650)
	Cost of goods sold		$ 78,650	Cost of ending inventory		$ 47,350

1b.

DATE	LIFO INVENTORY METHOD COST OF GOODS SOLD			COST OF ENDING INVENTORY		
20-1/-2	**Units**	**Unit Price**	**Total**	**Units**	**Unit Price**	**Total**
Nov. 1 Beginning inventory		$25.00	$ 0	500	$25.00	$ 12,500
Nov. 12 1st purchase		26.25	0	600	26.25	15,750
Dec. 28 2nd purchase		27.50	0	400	27.50	11,000
Mar. 29 3rd purchase	900	28.00	25,200	100	28.00	2,800
May 31 4th purchase	750	28.50	21,375		28.50	0
July 29 5th purchase	350	29.00	10,150		29.00	0
Aug. 30 6th purchase	675	30.00	20,250		30.00	0
Oct. 21 7th purchase	225	31.00	6,975		31.00	0
Total	2,900		$ 83,950	1,600		$ 42,050

Alternative calculation given goods available for sale and cost of goods sold or ending inventory.						
	Cost of goods available for sale		$126,000	Cost of goods available for sale		$126,000
	Less cost of ending inventory		(42,050)	Less cost of goods sold		(83,950)
	Cost of goods sold		$ 83,950	Cost of ending inventory		$ 42,050

(continued)

1c.	Weighted-average method:	
	Average cost per unit: $126,000 ÷ 4,500 units = $28.	
	Inventory, October 31, 20-2:	
	1,600 units @ $28 =	$44,800
	Cost of goods sold for 20-1/-2:	
	2,900 units @ $28 =	$81,200
2a.	FIFO lower-of-cost-or-market:	
	FIFO cost	$47,350
	Market 1,600 @ $29	$46,400
	Choose market	$46,400
2b.	Weighted-average lower-of-cost-or-market:	
	Weighted-average cost	$44,800
	Market 1,600 @ $29	$46,400
	Choose weighted-average cost	$44,800

3.	Estimated inventory on October 31, 20-2:			
	Inventory, November 1, 20-1		$ 12,500	
	Net purchases, November 1, 20-1			
	through October 31, 20-2		113,500	
	Cost of goods available for sale			$126,000
	Estimated cost of goods sold:			
	Net sales		$134,000	
	Normal gross profit ($134,000 × 40%)		53,600	
	Estimated cost of goods sold			80,400
	Estimated inventory on October 31, 20-2			$ 45,600

On-Line Learning Tools

For more information, visit: http://heintz.swlearning.com

The Heintz & Parry product web site is designed specifically for **COLLEGE ACCOUNTING, 18e.** The features include downloadable student resources and an interactive study center, organized by chapter, which contains learning objectives, web links, on-line quizzes with automatic feedback, and more.

KEY TERMS

average cost method, (718)   See weighted-average method.

conservatism, (722)   The accounting practice of conservatism states that we should never anticipate gains, but always anticipate and account for losses. As applied to inventory, conservatism means that if the value of inventory declines while it is being held, the loss should be recognized in the period of the decline.

consignee, (715)   The company holding the merchandise of another business to be sold.

consignment, (714)   Goods that are held by one business for sale but that are owned by another business.

consignor, (715)   The owner of the merchandise that is held by another business.

consistency, (718)   The principle that states that a business should use the same accounting methods from period to period. This improves the comparability of the financial statements over time.

cost, (723)   In applying the lower-of-cost-or-market method, cost means the dollar amount calculated using one of the four inventory costing methods.

first-in, first-out (FIFO) method, (717)   A method of allocating merchandise cost which assumes that the first goods purchased were the first goods sold and, therefore, that the latest goods purchased remain in inventory.

gross profit method, (724)   A method of estimating inventory in which a business's normal gross profit percentage is used to estimate the cost of goods sold and ending inventory.

in transit, (714)   Goods that are in the process of being shipped between the seller and the buyer.

inventory sheet, (714)   A form used for recording inventory items. It has columns for recording the description of each item, the quantity on hand, the cost per unit, and the extension.

Inventory Short and Over, (722)   An account used to adjust the perpetual inventory records when a difference exists between the physical count and the amount in the perpetual inventory records.

last-in, first-out (LIFO) method, (718)   A method of allocating merchandise cost which assumes that the sales in the period were made from the most recently purchased goods. Therefore, the earliest goods purchased remain in inventory.

lower-of-cost-or-market method, (723)   An inventory valuation method under which inventory is valued at the lower of cost or market value (replacement cost).

market, (723)   In applying the lower-of-cost-or-market method, market means the cost to replace the inventory. It is the prevailing price in the market in which goods are purchased—not the prevailing price in the market in which they are normally sold.

natural business year, (714)   A fiscal year that starts and ends at the time the stock of goods is normally at its lowest level.

physical inventory, (714)   Counting the goods on hand at the end of the period to allocate merchandise costs between sold and unsold goods.

retail method, (725)   A variation of the gross profit method that is used by many retail businesses, such as department and clothing stores, to estimate the cost of goods sold and ending inventory.

specific identification method, (716)   A method of allocating merchandise cost in which each unit of inventory is specifically identified.

weighted-average method, (718)   A method of allocating merchandise cost based on the average cost of identical units. The average cost of identical units is determined by dividing the total cost of units available for sale by the total number of units available for sale.

REVIEW QUESTIONS

(LO1)   1.   What financial statements are affected by an error in the ending inventory?

(LO2)   2.   What is the main difference between the periodic system of accounting for inventory and the perpetual system of accounting for inventory?

(LO3)   3.   Is a physical inventory necessary under the periodic system? Why or why not?

(LO3)   4. Is a physical inventory necessary under the perpetual system? Why or why not?

(LO3)   5. In a period of rising prices, which inventory method will result in:

    a.   the highest cost of goods sold?

    b.   the lowest cost of goods sold?

    c.   the highest ending inventory?

    d.   the lowest ending inventory?

    e.   the highest gross profit?

    f.   the lowest gross profit?

(LO3)   6. What two factors are taken into account by the weighted-average method of merchandise cost allocation?

(LO3)   7. Which inventory method always follows the actual physical flow of merchandise?

(LO3)   8. When lower-of-cost-or-market is assigned to the items that comprise the ending merchandise inventory, what does "cost" mean? What does "market" mean?

(LO4)   9. List the three steps followed under the gross profit method of estimating inventory.

(LO4)   10. List the five steps followed under the retail method of estimating inventory.

Self-Study Test Questions

True/False

1. An overstatement of ending inventory in the year 20-1 will cause net income to be overstated in the year 20-1. _____

2. An understatement of ending inventory in the year 20-1 will cause net income to be overstated in the year 20-2, assuming no other errors. _____

3. Under the perpetual system of accounting for inventory, the current merchandise inventory and the cost of goods sold are not determined until the end of the accounting period when a physical inventory is taken. _____

4. A fiscal year that starts and ends at the time the stock of goods is normally at its lowest level is known as a natural business year. _____

5. If goods are shipped FOB shipping point, the seller pays for the shipping costs. _____

Self-Study Test Questions (continued)

Multiple Choice

1. Goods held on consignment remain the property of the

   (a) consignee.
   (b) consignor.
   (c) buyer.
   (d) seller.
   _____

2. In times of rising prices, the inventory cost method that will yield the lowest net income is

   (a) FIFO.
   (b) weighted-average.
   (c) LIFO.
   (d) none of the above.
   _____

3. In times of rising prices, the inventory cost method that will yield the highest cost of goods sold is

   (a) LIFO.
   (b) weighted-average.
   (c) FIFO.
   (d) none of the above.
   _____

4. In the application of "lower-of-cost-or-market," market is the

   (a) lowest sales price.
   (b) highest sales price.
   (c) replacement cost.
   (d) average sales price.
   _____

5. An understatement of ending inventory in the year 20-1 will cause the owner's equity account at the end of the year 20-2, assuming no other errors, to be

   (a) understated.
   (b) correctly stated.
   (c) overstated.
   (d) none of the above.
   _____

The answers to the Self-Study Test Questions are at the end of the text.

MANAGING YOUR WRITING

Does your local grocery store have optical scanning devices at the checkout stands? Most major grocery chains have them and they certainly reduce the time required to check out. What benefits do they provide to the business? Next time you go to the grocery store, take a few minutes to chat with the manager. Ask the manager to describe the benefits of the scanning devices over the old machines that required the clerk to key in each purchase. Pay particular attention to the linkage between the scanning devices and the inventory systems. Be sure to ask whether the grocery store is on a periodic or perpetual system.

After your visit, write a memo to your instructor describing the benefits of the scanning devices and how they are linked with the inventory system.

ETHICS CASE

Electronics, Inc., is a high-volume, wholesale merchandising company. Most of its inventory turns over four or five times a year. The company has had 50 units of a particular brand of computers on hand for over a year. These computers have not sold and probably will not sell unless they are discounted 60 to 70 percent. The accountant is carrying them on the books at cost and intends to recognize

(continued)

the loss when they are sold. This way, she can avoid a significant write-down in inventory on the current year's financial statements.

1. Is the accountant correct in her treatment of the inventory? Why or why not?

2. If the computers cost $1,000 each and their market value is 40 percent of their cost, journalize the entry necessary for the write-down.

3. In a short paragraph, explain what is meant by conservatism and how it ties in with the lower-of-cost-or-market method of accounting for inventory.

4. In groups of three or four, make a list of reasons why inventories of electronic equipment might have to be written down.

WEB WORK

How big a difference in sales can a computerized inventory system make? Visit the Interactive Study Center on our web site at **http://heintz.swlearning.com** for special hotlinks to assist you in this assignment.

SERIES A EXERCISES

EXERCISE 19-1A **(LO1)** **INVENTORY ERRORS** Assume that in year 1, the ending merchandise inventory is overstated by $50,000. If this is the only error in years 1 and 2, indicate which items will be understated, overstated, or correctly stated for years 1 and 2.

	Year 1	Year 2
Ending merchandise inventory	_____	_____
Beginning merchandise inventory	_____	_____
Cost of goods sold	_____	_____
Gross profit	_____	_____
Net income	_____	_____
Ending owner's capital	_____	_____

EXERCISE 19-2A **(LO2)** **JOURNAL ENTRIES—PERIODIC INVENTORY** Bill Diamond owns a business called Diamond Distributors. The following transactions took place during January of the current year. Journalize the transactions in a general journal using the periodic inventory method.

Jan. 5 Purchased merchandise on account from Prestigious Jewelers, $3,700.

8 Paid freight charge on merchandise purchased, $200.

12 Sold merchandise on account to Diamonds Unlimited, $4,900.

15 Received a credit memo from Prestigious Jewelers for merchandise returned, $600.

22 Issued a credit memo to Diamonds Unlimited for merchandise returned, $800.

EXERCISE 19-3A **(LO2)** **JOURNAL ENTRIES—PERPETUAL INVENTORY** Sandy Johnson owns a small variety store. The following transactions took place during March of the current year. Journalize the transactions in a general journal using the perpetual inventory method.

Mar. 3 Purchased merchandise on account from City Galleria, $2,700.

7 Paid freight charge on merchandise purchased, $175.

13 Sold merchandise on account to Amber Specialties, $3,000. The cost of the merchandise was $1,800.

18   Received a credit memo from City Galleria for merchandise returned, $500.

22   Issued a credit memo to Amber Specialties for merchandise returned, $400.
The cost of the merchandise was $240.

EXERCISE 19-4A   (LO3)
End. inv.: $45,500

ENDING INVENTORY COSTS Sandy Chen owns a small specialty store, named Chen's Chattel, whose year end is June 30. Determine the total amount that should be included in Chen's Chattel's year-end inventory. A physical inventory taken on June 30 reveals the following:

Cost of merchandise on the showroom floor and in the warehouse	$37,800
Goods held on consignment (consignor is National Manufacturer)	6,400
Goods that Chen's Chattel, as the consignor, has for sale at the location of the Grand Avenue Vista	4,600
Sales invoices indicate that merchandise was shipped on June 29, terms FOB shipping point, delivered at buyer's receiving dock on July 3	3,800
Sales invoices indicate that merchandise was shipped on June 25, terms FOB destination, delivered at buyer's receiving dock on July 5	3,100

EXERCISE 19-5A   (LO3)
Case 1, Dr. Mdse. Inv.: $1,500

JOURNAL ENTRY—INVENTORY SHORT AND OVER Tiger Industries uses the perpetual inventory method in accounting for inventory. Prepare the necessary adjusting entry for each of the following independent cases, using the account Inventory Short and Over. How would Inventory Short and Over be reported on the income statement for each independent case?

Case 1:
Physical count as of April 30	$48,300
Perpetual inventory records as of April 30	46,800

Case 2:
Physical count as of April 30	$43,600
Perpetual inventory records as of April 30	45,200

EXERCISE 19-6A   (LO3)
1. End. inv., FIFO: $300.00;
Weighted-avg.: $242.50

LOWER-OF-COST-OR-MARKET Stalberg Company's beginning inventory and purchases during the fiscal year ended December 31, 20--, were as follows:

		Units	Unit Price	Total Cost
Jan. 1	Beginning inventory	10	$20	$200
Mar. 5	1st purchase	10	22	220
Sept. 9	2nd purchase	10	25	250
Dec. 8	3rd purchase	10	30	300
		40		$970

There are 10 units of inventory on hand on December 31.

1. Calculate the total amount to be assigned to the ending inventory under each of the following methods.

    a.   FIFO

    b.   Weighted-average (round calculations to two decimal places)

2. Assume that the market price per unit (cost to replace) of Stalberg's inventory on December 31, 20--, was $26. Calculate the total amount to be assigned to the ending inventory on December 31 under each of the following methods.

    a.   FIFO lower-of-cost-or-market

    b.   Weighted-average lower-of-cost-or-market

SERIES A PROBLEMS

PROBLEM 19-7A   (LO3)

1. Cost of goods sold, FIFO:
$77,100; LIFO: $81,150;
Weighted-avg.: $79,050;
Specific I.D.: $78,450

SPECIFIC IDENTIFICATION, FIFO, LIFO, AND WEIGHTED-AVERAGE Hamilton Company's beginning inventory and purchases during the fiscal year ended September 30, 20-2, were as follows:

		Units	Unit Price	Total Cost
October 1, 20-1	Beginning inventory	300	$20.00	$ 6,000
October 18	1st purchase	500	21.50	10,750
November 25	2nd purchase	400	22.00	8,800
January 12, 20-2	3rd purchase	800	23.00	18,400
March 17	4th purchase	900	23.50	21,150
June 2	5th purchase	600	24.00	14,400
August 21	6th purchase	500	25.00	12,500
September 27	7th purchase	400	25.75	10,300
		4,400		$102,300

There are 1,000 units of inventory on hand on September 30, 20-2. Of these 1,000 units:

100 are from the October 18, 20-1	1st purchase
300 are from the January 12, 20-2	3rd purchase
100 are from the March 17	4th purchase
200 are from the June 2	5th purchase
100 are from the August 21	6th purchase
200 are from the September 27	7th purchase

REQUIRED

Calculate the total amount to be assigned to cost of goods sold for 20-2 and ending inventory on September 30, 20-2, under each of the following methods.

1. FIFO

2. LIFO

3. Weighted-average (round calculations to two decimal places)

4. Specific identification

PROBLEM 19-8A   (LO3)

1. Ending inv., FIFO: $13,825;
LIFO: $8,000;
Weighted-avg.: $10,500

COST ALLOCATION AND LOWER-OF-COST-OR-MARKET Douglas Company's beginning inventory and purchases during the fiscal year ended December 31, 20--, were as follows:

		Units	Unit Price	Total Cost
January 1, 20--	Beginning inventory	1,100	$ 8.00	$ 8,800
March 5	1st purchase	900	9.00	8,100
April 16	2nd purchase	400	9.50	3,800
June 3	3rd purchase	700	10.25	7,175
August 18	4th purchase	600	11.00	6,600
September 13	5th purchase	800	12.00	9,600
November 14	6th purchase	400	14.00	5,600
December 3	7th purchase	500	14.05	7,025
		5,400		$56,700

There are 1,000 units of inventory on hand on December 31.

REQUIRED

1. Calculate the total amount to be assigned to the ending inventory and cost of goods sold on December 31 under each of the following methods.

    a. FIFO

    b. LIFO

    c. Weighted-average (round calculations to two decimal places)

2. Assume that the market price per unit (cost to replace) of Douglas' inventory on December 31 was $13. Calculate the total amount to be assigned to the ending inventory on December 31 under each of the following methods.

    a. FIFO lower-of-cost-or-market

    b. Weighted-average lower-of-cost-or-market

PROBLEM 19-9A   (LO4)
Est. ending inv.: $80,800

GROSS PROFIT METHOD A fire completely destroyed all the inventory of Glisan Lumber Yard on August 5, 20--. Fortunately, the books were not destroyed in the fire. The following information is taken from the books of Glisan Lumber Yard for the time period January 1 through August 5:

Beginning inventory, January 1, 20--	$100,000
Net purchases, January 1 through August 5	420,000
Net sales, January 1 through August 5	732,000
Normal gross profit as a percentage of sales	40%

REQUIRED

Estimate the amount of merchandise inventory destroyed in the fire on August 5 using the gross profit method.

PROBLEM 19-10A   (LO4)
Est. ending inv.: $39,000

RETAIL INVENTORY METHOD The following information is taken from the books of Raynette's Pharmacy for the last quarter of its fiscal year ending on March 31, 20--.

	Cost	Retail
Inventory, start of period, January 1, 20--	$ 32,000	$ 52,000
Net purchases during the period	176,000	268,000
Net sales for the period		260,000

REQUIRED

1. Estimate the ending inventory as of March 31 using the retail inventory method.

2. Estimate the cost of goods sold for the time period January 1 through March 31 using the retail inventory method.

SERIES B EXERCISES

EXERCISE 19-1B   **(LO1)**   **INVENTORY ERRORS** Assume that in year 1, the ending merchandise inventory is understated by $40,000. If this is the only error in years 1 and 2, indicate which items will be understated, overstated, or correctly stated for years 1 and 2.

	Year 1	Year 2
Ending merchandise inventory	_____	_____
Beginning merchandise inventory	_____	_____
Cost of goods sold	_____	_____
Gross profit	_____	_____
Net income	_____	_____
Ending owner's capital	_____	_____

EXERCISE 19-2B   **(LO2)**   **JOURNAL ENTRIES—PERIODIC INVENTORY** Amy Douglas owns a business called Douglas Distributors. The following transactions took place during January of the current year. Journalize the transactions in a general journal using the periodic inventory method.

Jan. 5   Purchased merchandise on account from Elite Warehouse, $4,100.

8   Paid freight charge on merchandise purchased, $300.

12   Sold merchandise on account to Memories Unlimited, $5,200.

15   Received a credit memo from Elite Warehouse for merchandise returned, $700.

22   Issued a credit memo to Memories Unlimited for merchandise returned, $400.

EXERCISE 19-3B   **(LO2)**   **JOURNAL ENTRIES—PERPETUAL INVENTORY** Doreen Woods owns a small variety store. The following transactions took place during March of the current year. Journalize the transactions in a general journal using the perpetual inventory method.

Mar. 3   Purchased merchandise on account from Corner Galleria, $3,500.

7   Paid freight charge on merchandise purchased, $200.

13   Sold merchandise on account to Sonya Specialties, $4,250. The cost of the merchandise was $2,550.

18   Received a credit memo from Corner Galleria for merchandise returned, $900.

22   Issued a credit memo to Sonya Specialties for merchandise returned, $500. The cost of the merchandise was $300.

EXERCISE 19-4B   **(LO3)**   **ENDING INVENTORY COSTS** Danny Steele owns a small specialty store, named
Ending inv.: $53,700   Steele's Storeroom, whose year end is June 30. Determine the total amount that should be included in Steele's Storeroom's year-end inventory. A physical inventory taken on June 30 reveals the following:

Cost of merchandise on the showroom floor and in the warehouse	$42,600
Goods held on consignment (consignor is Quality Manufacturer)	7,600
Goods that Steele's Storeroom, as the consignor, has for sale at the location of the Midtown Galleria	8,300
Sales invoices indicate that merchandise was shipped on June 28, terms FOB shipping point, delivered at buyer's receiving dock on July 6	4,350
Sales invoices indicate that merchandise was shipped on June 26, terms FOB destination, delivered at buyer's receiving dock on July 1	2,800

EXERCISE 19-5B   **(LO3)**

Case 1, Dr. Inv. Short
and Over: $3,150

JOURNAL ENTRY—INVENTORY SHORT AND OVER Hanson Industries uses the perpetual inventory method in accounting for inventory. Prepare the necessary adjusting entry for each of the following independent cases, using the account Inventory Short and Over. How would Inventory Short and Over be reported on the income statement for each independent case?

Case 1:
Physical count as of April 30 $44,150
Perpetual inventory records as of April 30   47,300

Case 2:
Physical count as of April 30 $38,400
Perpetual inventory records as of April 30   36,200

EXERCISE 19-6B   **(LO3)**

1. Ending inv., FIFO: $800;
Weighted-avg.: $697.20

LOWER-OF-COST-OR-MARKET Bouie Company's beginning inventory and purchases during the fiscal year ended December 31, 20--, were as follows:

		Units	Unit Price	Total Cost
Jan. 1	Beginning inventory	20	$30	$ 600
Mar. 5	1st purchase	22	34	748
Sept. 9	2nd purchase	24	35	840
Dec. 8	3rd purchase	22	40	880
		88		$3,068

There are 20 units of inventory on hand on December 31.

1. Calculate the total amount to be assigned to the ending inventory under each of the following methods.

    a.   FIFO

    b.   Weighted-average (round calculations to two decimal places)

2. Assume that the market price per unit (cost to replace) of Bouie's inventory on December 31, 20--, was $39. Calculate the total amount to be assigned to the ending inventory on December 31 under each of the following methods.

    a.   FIFO lower-of-cost-or-market

    b.   Weighted-average lower-of-cost-or-market

SERIES B PROBLEMS

PROBLEM 19-7B   **(LO3)**

1. Ending inv., FIFO: $19,075;
LIFO: $14,350;
Weighted-avg.: $16,290;
Specific I.D.: $17,000

SPECIFIC IDENTIFICATION, FIFO, LIFO, AND WEIGHTED-AVERAGE Boyce Company's beginning inventory and purchases during the fiscal year ended September 30, 20-2, were as follows:

		Units	Unit Price	Total Cost
October 1, 20-1	Beginning inventory	400	$15.00	$ 6,000
October 18	1st purchase	300	16.50	4,950
November 25	2nd purchase	600	17.00	10,200
January 12, 20-2	3rd purchase	700	17.25	12,075
March 17	4th purchase	800	18.00	14,400
June 2	5th purchase	400	19.00	7,600
August 21	6th purchase	300	21.00	6,300
September 27	7th purchase	500	21.75	10,875
		4,000		$72,400

There are 900 units of inventory on hand on September 30, 20-2. Of these 900 units:

50 are from the October 18, 20-1	1st purchase
300 are from the January 12, 20-2	3rd purchase
100 are from the March 17	4th purchase
200 are from the June 2	5th purchase
50 are from the August 21	6th purchase
200 are from the September 27	7th purchase

REQUIRED

Calculate the total amount to be assigned to the cost of goods sold for 20-2 and ending inventory on September 30, 20-2, under each of the following methods.

1. FIFO

2. LIFO

3. Weighted-average (round calculations to two decimal places)

4. Specific identification

PROBLEM 19-8B   (LO3)

1. Cost of goods sold, FIFO: $55,950; LIFO: $64,300; Weighted-avg.: $60,475

COST ALLOCATION AND LOWER-OF-COST-OR-MARKET Hall Company's beginning inventory and purchases during the fiscal year ended December 31, 20--, were as follows:

		Units	Unit Price	Total Cost
January 1	Beginning inventory	800	$11.00	$ 8,800
March 5	1st purchase	600	12.00	7,200
April 16	2nd purchase	500	12.50	6,250
June 3	3rd purchase	700	14.00	9,800
August 18	4th purchase	800	15.00	12,000
September 13	5th purchase	900	17.00	15,300
November 14	6th purchase	400	18.00	7,200
December 3	7th purchase	500	20.30	10,150
		5,200		$76,700

There are 1,100 units of inventory on hand on December 31.

REQUIRED

1. Calculate the total amount to be assigned to the ending inventory and cost of goods sold on December 31 under each of the following methods.

   a. FIFO

   b. LIFO

   c. Weighted-average (round calculations to two decimal places)

2. Assume that the market price per unit (cost to replace) of Hall's inventory on December 31 was $16. Calculate the total amount to be assigned to the ending inventory on December 31 under each of the following methods.

   a. FIFO lower-of-cost-or-market

   b. Weighted-average lower-of-cost-or-market

PROBLEM 19-9B   **(LO4)**

Est. inv.: $82,500

GROSS PROFIT METHOD A flood completely destroyed all the inventory of Bayside Waterworks Company on July 1, 20--. Fortunately, the books were not destroyed in the flood. The following information is taken from the books of Bayside Waterworks for the time period January 1 through July 1, 20--.

Beginning inventory, January 1, 20--	$ 60,000
Net purchases, January 1 through July 1	380,000
Net sales, January 1 through July 1	650,000
Normal gross profit as a percentage of sales	45%

REQUIRED

Estimate the amount of merchandise inventory destroyed in the flood on July 1 using the gross profit method.

PROBLEM 19-10B   **(LO4)**

Est. cost of goods sold: $193,750

RETAIL INVENTORY METHOD The following information is taken from the books of Beverly's Basket Corner for the last quarter of its fiscal year ending on March 31, 20--.

	Cost	Retail
Inventory, start of period, January 1, 20--	$ 50,000	$ 80,000
Net purchases during the period	220,000	352,000
Net sales for the period		310,000

REQUIRED

1. Estimate the ending inventory as of March 31 using the retail inventory method.

2. Estimate the cost of goods sold for the time period January 1 through March 31 using the retail inventory method.

MASTERY PROBLEM

1. Cost of goods sold, FIFO: $64,250; LIFO: $75,000; Weighted-avg.: $69,600

2. Ending inv., FIFO LCM: $21,600; Weighted-avg. LCM: $17,400

3. Estimated inv.: $22,000

Tiller Company's beginning inventory and purchases during the fiscal year ended December 31, 20-2, were as follows:

		Units	Unit Price	Total Cost
January 1, 20-2	Beginning inventory	1,500	$10.00	$15,000
January 12	1st purchase	500	11.50	5,750
February 28	2nd purchase	600	14.50	8,700
June 29	3rd purchase	1,200	15.00	18,000
August 31	4th purchase	800	16.50	13,200
October 29	5th purchase	300	18.00	5,400
November 30	6th purchase	700	18.50	12,950
December 21	7th purchase	400	20.00	8,000
		6,000		$87,000

There are 1,200 units of inventory on hand on December 31, 20-2.

REQUIRED   1. Calculate the total amount to be assigned to the cost of goods sold for 20-2 and ending inventory on December 31 under each of the following methods.

    a. FIFO

    b. LIFO

    c. Weighted-average (round calculations to two decimal places)

(continued)

2. Assume that the market price per unit (cost to replace) of Tiller's inventory on December 31 was $18. Calculate the total amount to be assigned to the ending inventory on December 31 under each of the following methods.

   a. FIFO lower-of-cost-or-market

   b. Weighted-average lower-of-cost-or-market

3. In addition to taking a physical inventory on December 31, Tiller decides to estimate the ending inventory and cost of goods sold. During the fiscal year ended December 31, 20-2, net sales of $100,000 were made at a normal gross profit rate of 35%. Use the gross profit method to estimate the cost of goods sold for the fiscal year ended December 31 and the inventory on December 31.

CHALLENGE PROBLEM

This problem challenges you to apply your cumulative accounting knowledge to move a step beyond the material in the chapter.

FIFO CGS 20-2: $4,250;
LIFO CGS 20-2: $4,200

Bhushan Company has been using LIFO for inventory purposes because it would prefer to keep gross profits low for tax purposes. In its second year of operation (20-2), the controller pointed out that this strategy did not appear to work and suggested that FIFO cost of goods sold would have been higher than LIFO cost of goods sold for 20-2. Is this possible?

20-1	Units	Cost/Unit
Purchase 1	100	$1.00
Purchase 2	200	$2.00
Purchase 3	300	$3.00
Ending Inventory	200	

20-2	Units	Cost/Unit
Beginning Inventory	200	
Purchase 4	150	$4.00
Purchase 5	250	$5.00
Purchase 6	350	$6.00
Ending Inventory	50	

REQUIRED

Using the information provided, compute the cost of goods sold for 20-1 and 20-2 comparing the LIFO and FIFO methods.

OBJECTIVES

Careful study of this appendix should enable you to:

LO1 Compute the costs allocated to the ending inventory and cost of goods sold using the perpetual LIFO inventory method.

LO2 Compute the costs allocated to the ending inventory and cost of goods sold using the perpetual moving-average inventory method.

Chapter 19 Appendix
Perpetual Inventory Method: LIFO and Moving-Average Methods

In Chapter 19, you learned how to apply the LIFO and weighted-averge inventory methods under the periodic inventory system. Recall that all calculations under the periodic system are done at the end of the accounting period. Under the perpetual system, costs are computed every time merchandise is purchased and sold. These costs are used to maintain a running record of the cost of goods sold to date and the balance of inventory on hand.

PERPETUAL LIFO

LO1 Compute the costs allocated to the ending inventory and cost of goods sold using the perpetual LIFO inventory method.

When using the perpetual LIFO inventory method, every time inventory is purchased a new layer is formed. When inventory is sold, we assume that the most recently purchased layer is sold first. As those units are used up, units are taken from the next most recently purchased layer. To illustrate, let's assume that Phaler's Fishing Supplies has the following beginning inventory, purchases, and sales of one type of bobber during the month of June. Note that the beginning inventory also has layers based on the prices paid in earlier periods.

Date	Beginning Inventory and Purchases		Sales
	Units	Cost/Unit	Units
June 1 (BI)	20	$0.80	
	160	1.00	
	20	1.20	
June 4	300	$1.50	
June 20			400
June 30	100	$1.80	

BI: Beginning Inventory

As shown in Figure 19A-1, the beginning inventory of 200 units forms Phaler's first three layers of inventory. The purchase on June 4 forms a fourth layer (300 units @ $1.50 = $450). At this point, Phaler has a total of 500 units at a total cost of $650. On June 20, Phaler sells 400 units. Under perpetual LIFO, we assume that the 300 units purchased on June 4 are sold first, followed by 20 that cost $1.20 each and 80 units that cost $1.00 each from the beginning inventory. The cost of goods sold on June 20 is $554. The cost of the inventory on hand is $96. At this point, Phaler has 100 units remaining from the beginning inventory.

On June 30, Phaler purchases 100 units at $1.80 each. This forms a new fifth layer (100 @ $1.80 = $180). This layer is added to the two layers remaining from the beginning inventory for a total of 200 units at a total cost of $276 of inventory on hand on June 30. Note that the third ($1.20 layer) and fourth ($1.50 layer) layers of inventory are gone. They will never reappear. If Phaler makes additional sales before buying more inventory, they will come from the fifth layer at $1.80 each, followed by units from the second ($1.00) and then the first ($0.80) layers.

DATE	PURCHASES			COST OF GOODS SOLD				INVENTORY ON HAND				
	Units	Cost/ Unit	Total	Units	Cost/ Unit	CGS	Cumulative CGS	Layer	Units	Cost/ Unit	Layer Cost	Total
June 1 (BI)								(1)	20	$0.80	$ 16.00	
								(2)	160	1.00	160.00	
								(3)	20	1.20	24.00	$200.00
June 4								(1)	20	$0.80	$16.00	
								(2)	160	1.00	160.00	
								(3)	20	1.20	24.00	
	300	$1.50	$450.00				→	(4)	300	1.50	450.00	$650.00
June 20				300	$1.50	$450.00		(1)	20	$0.80	$16.00	
				20	$1.20	24.00		(2)	80	1.00	80.00	$ 96.00
				80	$1.00	80.00	$554.00					
June 30								(1)	20	$0.80	$16.00	
								(2)	80	1.00	80.00	
	100	$1.80	$180.00				→	(5)	100	1.80	180.00	$276.00
Cost of Goods Sold for June							$554.00					

BI: Beginning Inventory

FIGURE 19A-1 Perpetual LIFO Inventory System

PERPETUAL MOVING-AVERAGE

LO2 Compute the costs allocated to the ending inventory and cost of goods sold using the perpetual moving-average inventory method.

When using the perpetual moving-average inventory method, every time inventory is purchased a new average cost per unit is calculated. When inventory is sold, the most recent average cost is used to measure cost of goods sold and the remaining inventory on hand. To illustrate, let's look again at the purchases and sales of Phaler's Fishing Supplies for the month of June.

Date	Beginning Inventory and Purchases		Sales
	Units	Cost/Unit	Units
June 1 (BI)	20	$0.80	
	160	1.00	
	20	1.20	
June 4	300	$1.50	
June 20			400
June 30	100	$1.80	

BI: Beginning Inventory

As shown in Figure 19A-2, a new average cost is calculated each time a purchase is made. The average cost of the June 1 beginning inventory is shown as $1.00 ($200 cost/200 units). To compute the average cost after buying more inventory on June 4, we take the cost of the inventory on hand ($200 + $450 = $650) and divide by the number of units on hand (200 + 300 = 500). Thus, the average cost of the inventory on hand on June 4 is $1.30 per unit. To compute the cost of the 400 units sold on June 20, multiply the 400 units by $1.30 to get the cost of goods sold of $520. The remaining cost of the inventory on hand is $130 ($650 – $520). The number of units on hand is reduced to 100 (500 – 400).

On June 30, 100 additional units are purchased. This increases the units on hand to 200 (100 + 100) and the cost of the inventory on hand to $310 ($130 + $180). Dividing the cost of the inventory on hand by the number of units on hand provides a new moving-average cost of $1.55 ($310 ÷ 200). If Phaler makes another sale before buying additional units, this average cost will be used to compute the cost of goods sold and determine the cost of the inventory remaining on hand. Note that selling inventory does not change the moving-average cost. This is because the units are being removed at the most recent average cost.

> When using the moving-average inventory method it is best to do the calculations on a calculator or computer spreadsheet. Carry each calculation out to the number of decimal places allowed by the technology used. This will reduce rounding errors.

DATE	PURCHASES			COST OF GOODS SOLD				INVENTORY ON HAND AND AVG. COST/UNIT			
	Units	Cost/ Unit	Total	Units	Cost/ Unit	CGS	Cumulative CGS	Cost of Purchase or (Sale)	Cost of Inventory on Hand	Units on Hand	Avg. Cost/Unit
June 1 (BI)									$200.00	200.00	$1.0000
June 4	300.00	$1.50	$450.00					$450.00	650.00	500.00	1.3000
June 20				400.00	$1.30	$520.00	$520.00	(520.00)	130.00	100.00	1.3000
June 30	100.00	1.80	180.00					180.00	310.00	200.00	1.5500
Cost of Goods Sold during January							$520.00				

BI: Beginning Inventory

FIGURE 19A-2   Perpetual Moving-Average Inventory System

SERIES A EXERCISE

EXERCISE 19Apx-1A **(LO1/2)** The beginning inventory, purchases and sales for Myrl Sign Company for the month of April follow.

CGS under perpetual LIFO: $3,345; CGS under perpetual moving average: $3,250

Date	Beginning Inventory and Purchases		Sales
	Units	Cost/Unit	Units
April 1 (BI)	100	$4.30	
	100	4.50	
	200	4.60	
April 20	400	$5.50	
April 30			650

BI: Beginning Inventory

REQUIRED

Calculate the total amount to be assigned to cost of goods sold for April and the ending inventory on April 30, under each of the following methods.

1. Perpetual LIFO inventory method

2. Perpetual moving-average inventory method

SERIES A PROBLEM

PROBLEM 19Apx-2A   **(LO1/2)**   **PERPETUAL—LIFO AND MOVING-AVERAGE** Kelley Company began business on January 1, 20-1. Purchases and sales during the month of January follow.

CGS under perpetual LIFO: $1,900; CGS under perpetual moving average: $1,856.64

Date	Purchases		Sales
	Units	Cost/Unit	Units
Jan. 1	100	$1.00	
Jan. 4	400	1.10	
Jan. 5			300
Jan. 10	300	1.30	
Jan. 12			200
Jan. 15	200	1.35	
Jan. 18	500	1.60	
Jan. 22			800
Jan. 27			100
Jan. 31	300	1.80	

REQUIRED

Calculate the total amount to be assigned to cost of goods sold for January and then ending inventory on January 31, under each of the following methods.

1. Perpetual LIFO inventory method
2. Perpetual moving-average inventory method

SERIES B EXERCISE

EXERCISE 19Apx-1B   **(LO1/2)**   The beginning inventory, purchases and sales for the Harrington Equipment Company for the month of August follow.

CGS under perpetual LIFO: $5,435; CGS under perpetual moving average: $5,395

Date	Beginning Inventory and Purchases		Sales
	Units	Cost/Unit	Units
Aug. 1	100	$8.00	
	150	8.10	
	250	8.30	
Aug. 15	300	$8.50	
Aug. 31			650

BI: Beginning Inventory

REQUIRED

Calculate the total amount to be assigned to cost of goods sold for August and the ending inventory on August 31, under each of the following methods.

1. Perpetual LIFO inventory method
2. Perpetual moving-average inventory method

SERIES B PROBLEM

PROBLEM 19Apx-2B   **(LO1/2)** **PERPETUAL—LIFO AND MOVING-AVERAGE** Vozniak Company began business

CGS under perpetual LIFO: on January 1, 20-1. Purchases and sales during the month of January follow.
$3,720; CGS under perpetual
moving average: $3,665.25

Date	Purchases		Sales
	Units	Cost/Unit	Units
Jan. 1	100	$2.00	
Jan. 5	500	2.30	
Jan. 7			300
Jan. 12	300	2.40	
Jan. 15			300
Jan. 17	200	2.50	
Jan. 19	500	2.70	
Jan. 24			800
Jan. 28			100
Jan. 31	200	2.90	

REQUIRED

Calculate the total amount to be assigned to cost of goods sold for January and
then ending inventory on January 31, under each of the following methods.

1. Perpetual LIFO inventory method

2. Perpetual moving-average inventory method

©DIGITAL IMAGING GROUP

Accounting for Long-Term Assets

Evan Taylor believes his business could be run more efficiently if he had a delivery van to pick up merchandise and make deliveries. In fact, he thinks the business needs two delivery vans, but he can afford only one at this time. The expected useful life of the van is four years, but it will be used especially heavily during the first year or two until Evan can purchase a second van. Betty Jenkins, his bookkeeper, has described straight-line depreciation to him, but he does not believe that this pattern of depreciation will match the way he plans to use the van. Are there other depreciation methods that could be used?

Assets that are expected to provide benefits for a number of accounting periods are called **long-term assets**. Long-term assets that are **tangible** (have physical substance) and that are used in the operations of the business are called **property, plant, and equipment; plant assets;** or **fixed assets**. Examples include land, buildings, furniture, and equipment. Assets whose physical substance consists of natural resources that are consumed in the operation of the business are often called **wasting assets**. Examples include mines (coal, salt, and gold), stands of timber, and oil and gas wells. Long-term assets that have no physical substance are called **intangible assets**. Common examples include patents, copyrights, and trademarks.

All long-term assets except land gradually wear out or are used up as time passes. As an asset's useful life expires, a portion of the asset's cost is recognized as an expense. This is often referred to as "writing off" the asset. A different term is used to describe this expense for the different types of long-term assets. For plant assets, the expense is called **depreciation**; for natural resources, it is called **depletion**; and for intangible assets, it is called **amortization**. In this chapter, proper accounting for property, plant, and equipment; natural resources; and intangible assets is described and illustrated.

 LEARNING KEY: Since land does not wear out, no depreciation is recognized.

ACQUISITION COST OF PROPERTY, PLANT, AND EQUIPMENT

LO1 Determine the cost of property, plant, and equipment.

The cost of a long-term asset includes all amounts spent to acquire the asset and prepare it for its intended use. Purchases of long-term assets are entered by debiting the proper asset account and crediting either the cash or the proper liability account.

Land

All costs incurred to purchase land and prepare it for its intended use are debited to the land account. These costs include legal and real estate fees as well as the cost of removing old buildings and grading the land to prepare it for its intended use. Special tax assessments for streets, sewers, or parks also are debited to the land account, because these items are viewed as permanent.

Land Improvements

Costs related to land that are not permanent in nature are normally debited to the land improvements account. Common examples include the costs of planting trees and shrubs, installing fences, and paving parking areas. Items debited to the land improvements account are depreciated over their expected useful lives.

Buildings

The cost of buildings that are purchased includes the purchase price, realtor and legal fees, and related taxes on the purchase. If the purchase price includes land, the cost of the land and building must be determined and accounted for separately. If the building is constructed, costs include all normal construction costs for material and labor and architectural and engineering fees. In addition, insurance premiums and interest on loans *while the building is being constructed* are considered part of the cost of the asset.

Equipment

The cost of equipment includes the purchase price, transportation charges, insurance while in transit, installation costs, and any other costs that are incurred up to the point of placing the asset in service.

Treatment of Interest when Acquiring or Constructing Assets

The proper treatment of interest depends on whether the asset is being purchased or constructed. Often, businesses must borrow money to buy major long-term assets. The method used to finance the *acquisition* of an asset should not affect its cost. For example, interest on a mortgage to purchase a building should not be included in the cost of the asset. We always use the **cash equivalent price**, which is the amount of cash that could have been paid for the asset on the date of purchase.

Interest costs are treated differently for assets being constructed. Interest incurred *while an asset is being constructed* should be included as part of the cost of the asset. Since the asset is not operational during the construction period, it is not generating revenues against which the interest could be matched. Thus, the interest is included in the cost of the asset and recognized as part of depreciation expense when the asset is placed in operation and begins generating revenues.

DEPRECIATION

LO2 Explain the nature and purpose of depreciation.

The purpose of depreciation is to match a plant asset's cost with the revenues it helps to produce. As discussed in earlier chapters, the following is a typical adjusting entry made at the end of each accounting period.

5	Dec.	31	Depr. Expense—Delivery Equipment	541		1	0	0	00							5
6			Accum. Depr.—Delivery Equipment	185.1							1	0	0	00		6
7																7

LEARNING KEY: Depreciation matches an asset's cost with the revenues it helps generate.

Recall that Depreciation Expense is reported on the income statement and Accumulated Depreciation is reported on the balance sheet as a contra-asset. Accumulated Depreciation is deducted from the asset account to report the book value, or undepreciated cost, of the asset. For example, a machine with a cost of

$3,000 and accumulated depreciation of $600 would be reported on the balance sheet as follows:

Property, Plant, and Equipment
Equipment $3,000
Less accumulated depreciation   600 $2,400

Keep in mind that depreciation is a process of *cost allocation*, not a process of valuation. Many factors cause the market values of plant assets to change over time. The recognition of depreciation is not intended to make the assets reflect their market values on the balance sheet. The net amounts reported on the balance sheet (book values) are merely the portions of the original costs that have not yet been allocated to expense.

LEARNING KEY: Market Value   =   Amount Asset Can Be Sold For
                      Book Value   =   Cost – Accumulated Depreciation

The recognition of depreciation is not intended to represent market values on the balance sheet.

The two major types of depreciation are physical and functional. **Physical depreciation** is the loss of usefulness because of deterioration from age and wear. **Functional depreciation** is the loss of usefulness because of inadequacy or obsolescence. As a business grows, some of its plant assets may become inadequate to handle the increased workload. As new manufacturing methods are developed, assets may become obsolete because there are faster, more efficient, or more effective assets that may be used to perform this work.

DEPRECIATION METHODS

LO3 Compute depreciation using the straight-line, declining-balance, sum-of-the-years'-digits, and units-of-production methods.

Before we discuss the methods of calculating depreciation, there are several terms to be defined.

Cost   The sum of all amounts spent to acquire an asset and prepare it for its intended use.

Useful Life   The amount of service expected to be obtained from an asset. It can be expressed in years, hours of operation, units of production, or miles driven. There is no way of knowing exactly how long an asset will last or exactly what its output will be. Therefore, estimates must be made based on past experience and information from trade associations and engineers.

LEARNING KEY: Recall the concepts of physical and functional depreciation. The useful life is based on an estimate of the period of time that an asset *will be useful* to the business, not necessarily the actual life of the asset.

Salvage Value   The estimated **scrap**, or market, **value** for the asset on its expected disposal date. This amount can be difficult to predict. Often a zero salvage value is used if the asset is expected to have little or no value at the end of its useful life.

Depreciable Cost (Base)   The original cost less salvage (or scrap) value.

Depreciable Cost = Original Cost − Salvage Value

Book Value   The undepreciated cost of the asset.

Book Value = Cost − Accumulated Depreciation

There are several different ways of calculating the amount of depreciation for each period. The most commonly used methods for financial reporting purposes are the following:

1.   Straight-line method

2.   Declining-balance method

3.   Sum-of-the-years'-digits method

4.   Units-of-production method

Straight-Line Method

Under the **straight-line method**, the depreciable cost of an asset is allocated equally over the years of the asset's useful life according to the following formula:

Straight-Line Method

$$\text{Annual Depreciation} = \frac{(\text{Cost} - \text{Salvage Value})}{\text{Estimated Useful Life}}$$

To illustrate, assume that a new asset costs $10,000, has an expected life of four years, and has a $1,000 estimated salvage value. Using the straight-line method, the amount of depreciation allocated to each year would be $2,250, computed as follows:

Original Cost	−	Salvage Value	=	Depreciable Cost
$10,000	−	$1,000	=	$9,000

$$\frac{\text{Depreciable Cost}}{\text{Estimated Useful Life}} = \frac{\$9,000}{4 \text{ years}} = \$2,250 \text{ annual depreciation}$$

The annual *rate* of depreciation is 25 percent (100% ÷ 4 years) of the depreciable cost.

LEARNING KEY: Under the straight-line method, the same amount of depreciation is recorded each period.

A month is usually the shortest period that is used in depreciation accounting. An asset purchased on or before the fifteenth of the month is considered to have been owned for the full month. An asset purchased after the fifteenth of the month is considered to have been acquired the first of the next month.

LEARNING KEY: An asset purchased on or before the fifteenth of the month is depreciated for the full month. An asset purchased after the fifteenth of the month is not depreciated until the next month.

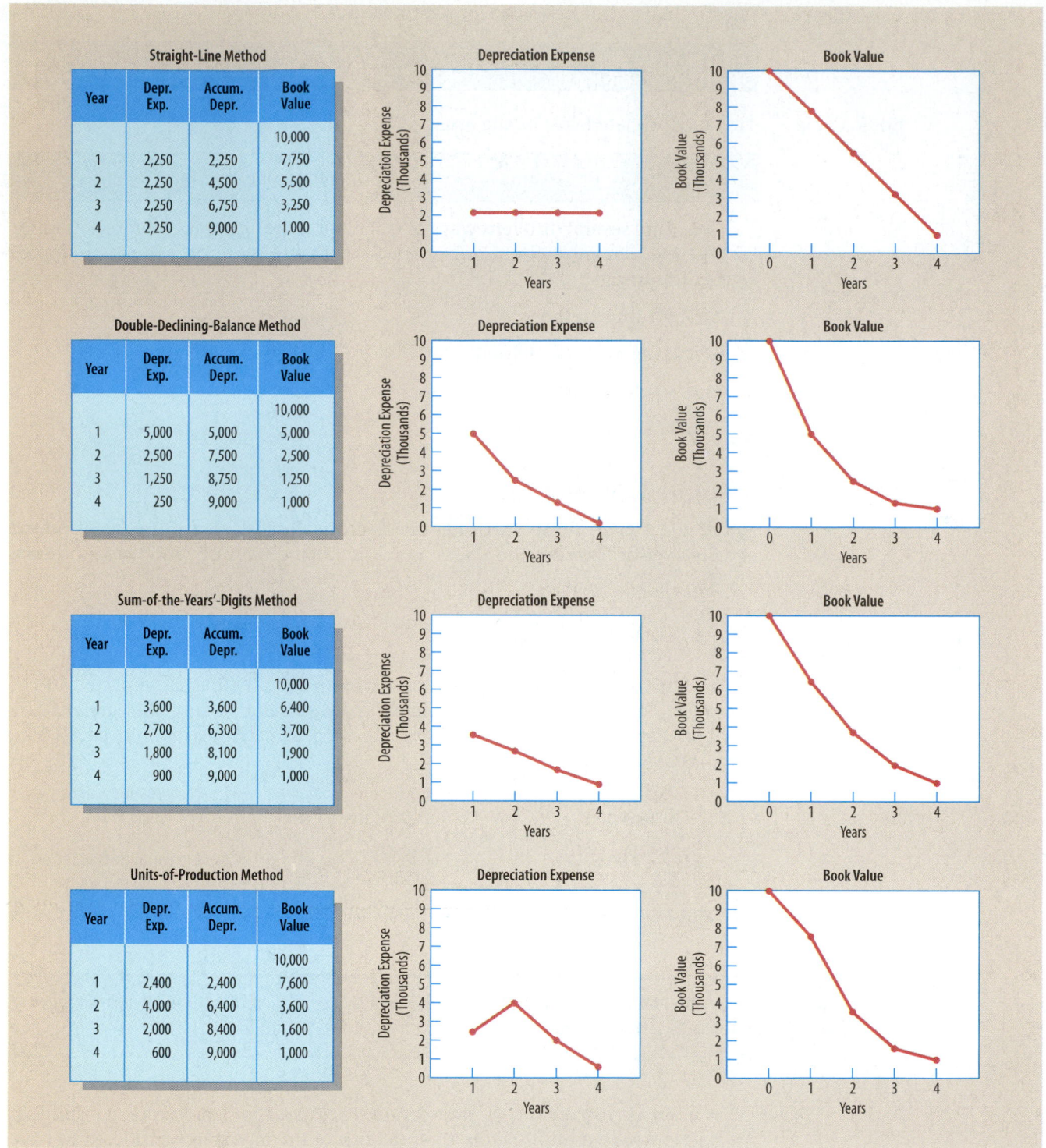

FIGURE 20-1 Comparison of Depreciation Methods

With the straight-line method, the book value of the asset decreases uniformly period by period. As shown in Figure 20-1, the book value over several periods is a downward-sloping, perfectly straight line. That is how the method got its name.

Declining-Balance Method

Many plant assets require repairs and replacement of parts to keep them in service. Such expenses usually increase as the assets get older. Some accountants believe that depreciation expense, therefore, should be higher in the early years to offset the higher repair and maintenance expenses of the later years. Others suggest that assets contribute more to the business when they are comparatively new. For these reasons, it may be desirable to calculate depreciation in a way that will give larger write-offs in the early years of the asset's life. Depreciation methods that provide for a higher depreciation charge in the first year of an asset's life and gradually decreasing charges in subsequent years are called **accelerated depreciation methods**.

One popular accelerated method is the **declining-balance method**. As shown in the following formula, under this method, the book value is multiplied by a fixed rate.

Declining-Balance Method

Annual Depreciation = Depreciation Rate × Book Value at Beginning of Year

This method results in successively smaller depreciation charges as the book value declines year by year. The most common rate used is double the straight-line rate. For this reason, this technique is sometimes referred to as the **double-declining-balance method**.

LEARNING KEY: "Double" means double the straight-line rate. "Declining balance" means that we should multiply the rate by the declining beginning book value balance.

To illustrate, let's use the same asset as for the straight-line method. The asset cost $10,000, has an expected life of four years, and has a $1,000 estimated salvage value. Using the double-declining-balance method, the depreciation rate to be applied to the book value of the asset each year is 50%, computed as follows:

Straight-line rate = 25% (100% ÷ 4 years)

Double-declining-balance rate = 50% (2 × 25%)

The annual depreciation and the book value at the end of each year are as follows:

Year	Book Value Beginning of Year	Rate	Annual Depreciation	Accumulated Depreciation End of Year	Book Value End of Year
1	$10,000	50%	$5,000	$5,000	$5,000
2	5,000	50	2,500	7,500	2,500
3	2,500	50	1,250	8,750	1,250
4	1,250	—	250*	9,000	1,000

*$250 = $1,250 (book value at beginning of year) − $1,000 (salvage value)

The salvage value is not considered in determining the annual depreciation. However, the asset's book value should not be allowed to fall below its estimated salvage value. Thus, the amount of depreciation actually recorded in the final year (year 4) is limited to $250 ($1,250 − $1,000). As shown in Figure 20-1, with the declining-balance method, the book value declines rapidly in the early years and more slowly in the later years of an asset's life.

LEARNING KEY: Do not subtract the salvage value from the original cost before multiplying by the declining-balance rate.

Declining-Balance Method For Partial Periods

If the asset was acquired at some time other than the beginning of the year, a change would be necessary in the computation of depreciation for the year. For example, if the asset was acquired on April 1, the depreciation for year 1 would be calculated as follows:

Year 1: $10,000 × 50% = $5,000 × 9/12 = $3,750

Depreciation for years 2 through 4 would then be calculated by applying the 50% depreciation rate to the book value of the asset at the beginning of each year, as follows:

Year	Book Value Beginning of Year	Rate	Annual Depreciation	Accumulated Depreciation End of Year	Book Value End of Year
2	$6,250*	50%	$3,125	$6,875	$3,125
3	3,125	50	1,563	8,438	1,562
4	1,562	—	562**	9,000	1,000

*$6,250 = $10,000 (cost) − $3,750 (depreciation for year 1)
**$562 = $1,562 (book value at beginning of year) − $1,000 (salvage value)

Depreciation in year 4 is limited to $562 because the asset should not be depreciated below its estimated salvage value. If the asset continued to be used in year 5, no depreciation would be recorded.

LEARNING KEY: An asset should not be depreciated below its estimated salvage value.

Sum-of-the-Years'-Digits Method

As shown in the following formula, under the **sum-of-the-years'-digits method**, the depreciation each year is determined by multiplying the depreciable cost by a schedule of fractions.

Sum-of-the-Years'-Digits Method

$$\text{Annual Depreciation} = (\text{Cost} - \text{Salvage Value}) \times \frac{\text{Remaining Useful Life}}{\text{Sum-of-the-Years'-Digits}}$$

The numerator in any year is the number of years of remaining life for the asset, measured from the beginning of the year. The denominator for all fractions is determined by listing the digits that represent the years of the estimated life of the asset and adding these digits. For example, suppose that the estimated life of an asset is four years. The sum of the digits (4 + 3 + 2 + 1) equals 10 (the denominator). The following formula can also be used to determine the denominator.

Calculating the Sum-of-the-Years'-Digits

$$S = N \times \frac{(N + 1)}{2}$$

S = sum of the digits
N = number of years of estimated life

If the life of the asset is four years:

$$S = 4 \times \frac{(4 + 1)}{2} = 4 \times (2.5) = 10$$

The denominator equals 10. Therefore, the fractions used for an asset with a four-year life would be 4/10, 3/10, 2/10, and 1/10. Applying these fractions to the asset in our illustration, the results are as follows:

Year	Depreciable Cost	Rate	Annual Depreciation	Accumulated Depreciation End of Year	Book Value End of Year
1	$9,000	4/10	$3,600	$3,600	$6,400
2	9,000	3/10	2,700	6,300	3,700
3	9,000	2/10	1,800	8,100	1,900
4	9,000	1/10	900	9,000	1,000

As shown in Figure 20-1, the pattern of decline in the book value using the sum-of-the-years'-digits method is accelerated. However, the write-off is not as rapid as it is with the double-declining-balance method.

Sum-of-the-Years'-Digits Method for Partial Periods

If the asset is acquired at some time other than the beginning of the year, a modification is necessary in the calculation. For example, if the asset is acquired on April 1, the depreciation for years 1 through 3 is calculated as follows:

Year 1: $9,000 × 4/10   = $3,600 × 9/12   = $2,700

Year 2: $9,000 × 4/10   = $3,600 × 3/12   = $ 900
        9,000 × 3/10   =   2,700 × 9/12   =   2,025
                                                    $2,925

Year 3: $9,000 × 3/10   = $2,700 × 3/12   = $ 675
        9,000 × 2/10   =   1,800 × 9/12   =   1,350
                                                    $2,025

Depreciation for years 4 and 5 is calculated in a similar manner.

Units-of-Production Method

Under the **units-of-production method**, depreciation is based on the extent to which the asset was used during the year. As shown below, annual depreciation is computed in two steps. First, a depreciation charge per unit produced or consumed is computed. Second, this unit rate is multiplied by the number of units produced or consumed during the year.

Units-of-Production Method

Step 1:   Depreciation per Unit $= \dfrac{\text{(Cost – Salvage Value)}}{\text{Estimated Useful Life in Units}}$

Step 2:   Annual Depreciation $=$ Depreciation per Unit $\times$ Number of Units Produced or Consumed this Year

This method can be used for certain types of machinery, equipment, and vehicles. It is most appropriate for assets that receive varying amounts of use over time. For example, assume that a company purchases a car at a cost of $10,000 and expects that it can be sold for $1,000 after 90,000 miles of service. The calculation of depreciation for the first year when the car was driven 24,000 miles follows:

Depreciable cost = $10,000 Original Cost − $1,000 Salvage Value = $9,000

$$\text{Depreciation per mile} = \frac{\$9,000 \text{ Depreciable Cost}}{90,000 \text{ Total Miles}} = \$.10$$

First-year depreciation = 24,000 miles × $.10/mile = $2,400

As shown in Figure 20-1, the depreciation expense and book value for each year do not follow a particular pattern. They are a function of the miles driven each year (24,000; 40,000; 20,000; and 6,000 in this illustration).

Depreciation for Federal Income Tax Purposes

A business is allowed to deduct depreciation expenses in calculating taxable income. Allowable depreciation methods for tax purposes vary depending on when the asset was acquired. For plant assets acquired before 1981, any of the four methods described in the previous sections is permitted. For plant assets acquired between 1981 and 1986, either the straight-line method or the **Accelerated Cost Recovery System (ACRS)** must be used. ACRS classifies all business plant assets into four different useful life categories. Most business assets fall into one of three categories: 3-year, 5-year, or 18-year property. For plant assets acquired after 1986, either the straight-line method or the **Modified Accelerated Cost Recovery System (MACRS)** must be used. MACRS identifies eight categories of useful life for plant assets. Most business assets other than real estate fall into one of two categories: 5-year or 7-year property. ACRS and MACRS define depreciation rates for various categories. For example, the rates for 5-year property follow. In using these rates, salvage value is ignored. Note that depreciation under MACRS for a 5-year asset must be spread over six years. This is because MACRS assumes one-half year's depreciation in year 1 and one-half year's depreciation in year 6. Note that MACRS offers an accelerated "write-off" of the asset and that both methods permit depreciating 100% of the cost of the asset.

Depreciation Rates for Five-Year Assets
ACRS and MACRS Depreciation

Year	ACRS	MACRS
1	15%	20.0%
2	22	32.0
3	21	19.2
4	21	11.5
5	21	11.5
6	——	5.8
	100%	100.0%

 LEARNING KEY: Under ACRS and MACRS, salvage value is ignored when computing the asset's depreciable cost.

REPAIRS, MAINTENANCE, ADDITIONS, AND IMPROVEMENTS TO PLANT AND EQUIPMENT

LO4 Account for repairs, maintenance, additions, and improvements to plant and equipment.

Plant and equipment require normal repairs and maintenance for proper operating efficiency and quality. Replacement of minor parts, lubrication, and cleaning are typical examples of normal repairs and maintenance. These expenditures are debited to Repairs Expense, as follows:

5		Repairs Expense				x	x	x	xx						5
6		Cash or Supplies Inventory								x	x	x	xx		6
7		Made repairs													7

LEARNING KEY: Repairs Expense is debited for normal repair and maintenance costs that do not extend the life of the asset or improve its usefulness.

Additions or improvements to plant and equipment are accounted for in two ways. All additions and some improvements increase the usefulness of the buildings or equipment and will provide benefits in future periods. For example, the addition of a wing to a building and improvements such as the installation of partitions, shelving, sprinkler systems, or air conditioning systems enhance the quality and efficiency of the building. These expenditures are debited to the building account and credited to either the cash or a liability account, as follows:

9		Building or Equipment				x	x	x	xx						9
10		Cash or Liability								x	x	x	xx		10
11		Made addition													11

Since these improvements will benefit future periods, depreciation will be recognized in future periods.

Some improvements extend the useful life of the asset, but do not increase its usefulness or efficiency. For example, a business may replace the engine in a truck. This extends the life of the truck, but it does not improve the truck's usefulness or efficiency. This expenditure is debited to Accumulated Depreciation and credited to either the cash or a liability account, as follows:

14		Accum. Depr.—Building or Equipment				x	x	x	xx						14
15		Cash or Liability								x	x	x	xx		15
16		Made improvement													16

Accumulated Depreciation is debited because the depreciation taken on the original engine has been recaptured by replacing it with a new one. The debit to Accumulated Depreciation increases the book value of the asset. Since the new engine will benefit future periods, additional depreciation will be taken in future periods.

LEARNING KEY: Expenditures on plant and equipment are accounted for in the following ways.

- If the expenditures simply maintain the asset's operating condition, debit the expense account.
- If the expenditures increase the asset's usefulness or efficiency, debit the asset account.
- If the expenditures extend the asset's useful life, but do not increase its usefulness or efficiency, debit the accumulated depreciation account.

Notice that the book value of the asset is increased regardless of whether we debit the asset account or the accumulated depreciation account. This increase in book value leads to an increase in the amount of depreciation recognized in future periods. To illustrate, assume that a business owns the following two computers that were purchased on January 1, 20-1.

	Computer A	Computer B
Cost	$6,500	$6,500
Salvage value	500	500
Depreciable base	$6,000	$6,000
Estimated life	3 years	3 years
Depreciation method	Straight-line	Straight-line
Depreciation expense		
20-1	$2,000	$2,000

At the beginning of 20-2, a disk drive is replaced on computer A and a new tape drive backup unit is added to computer B. Let's assume that the disk drive and tape backup units cost $400 each. The entries for the improvement to computer A, which extends its life but does not increase its usefulness, and the addition to computer B are shown in T account form as follows:

Computer A		Computer B	
6,500		6,500	
		Jan. 1, 20-2 400	
		Bal. 6,900	

Accum. Depr.—Computer A		Accum. Depr.—Computer B	
	Dec. 31, 20-1 2,000		Dec. 31, 20-1 2,000
Jan. 1, 20-2 400			
	Bal. 1,600		

Note that after recording the expenditures on January 1, 20-2, computers A and B both have book values of $4,900 as follows:

	Computer A	Computer B
Asset account balance	$6,500	$6,900
Accumulated depreciation	(1,600)	(2,000)
Book value	$4,900	$4,900

To compute depreciation expense for 20-2:

1. Compute the new depreciable base by deducting the salvage value from the book value of the computers after recording the expenditures.

2. Divide the new depreciable base by the remaining useful life, two years.

	Computer A	Computer B
Book value	$4,900	$4,900
Salvage value	(500)	(500)
New depreciable cost	$4,400	$4,400
Remaining useful life	2 years	2 years
Depreciation expense ($4,400/2)	$2,200	$2,200

Thus, depreciation expense is $2,200 for each computer in 20-2 and 20-3.

DISPOSAL OF PLANT ASSETS

LO5 Account for the disposition of property, plant, and equipment.

A plant asset can be disposed of in several ways:

1. It may be discarded or retired.

2. It may be sold.

3. It may be exchanged or traded in for another asset.

Regardless of the method of disposal, any gain or loss that occurred on the disposal must be determined. This is done by comparing the market and book values of the asset on the date of disposal. *To determine the book value on the date of disposal, an adjusting entry must be made to record depreciation from the end of the previous period to the disposal date.* Gains and losses are determined as follows:

Determining Gains and Losses on Disposal of Assets

Gain = Market Value greater than Book Value

Loss = Market Value less than Book Value

Gains are similar to revenue and increase net income. Losses are similar to expenses and reduce net income. They are reported on the income statement under Other Revenues and Other Expenses.

Discarding or Retiring Plant Assets

A plant asset may be discarded or retired at any time. If its book value on the disposal date is zero, no gain or loss will be realized. If it is greater than zero, the book value of the discarded asset will represent a loss.

To illustrate, assume that a printer with a cost of $800 and accumulated depreciation of $800 is discarded. Because the printer is fully depreciated, its book value is zero and no gain or loss results from this transaction. The removal of the asset and related accumulated depreciation is recorded as follows:

5		Accum. Depr.—Office Equipment			8 0 0 00		5
6		Office Equipment				8 0 0 00	6
7		Discarded printer					7

However, if at the time the printer is discarded, the accumulated depreciation is $720, the book value is $80 and a loss results. In this case, the discard of the asset and recognition of the loss are recorded as follows:

9		Accum. Depr.—Office Equipment			7 2 0 00		9
10		Loss on Discarded Office Equipment			8 0 00		10
11		Office Equipment				8 0 0 00	11
12		Discarded printer					12

Selling Plant Assets

Now let's assume that this same printer is sold for $80 at the time its book value is $80. This transaction is entered as follows:

5		Cash			8 0 00			5
6		Accum. Depr.—Office Equipment			7 2 0 00			6
7		Office Equipment				8 0 0 00		7
8		Sold printer						8

No gain or loss results from this transaction because the printer's selling price, or market value, is equal to its book value.

If the printer is sold for $120 at the time its book value is $80, there is a gain of $40. In this case, the journal entry is as follows:

5		Cash			1 2 0 00			5
6		Accum. Depr.—Office Equipment			7 2 0 00			6
7		Office Equipment				8 0 0 00		7
8		Gain on Sale of Printer				4 0 00		8
9		Sold printer						9

If, instead, the printer is sold for $50, there is a loss of $30. This transaction is recorded as follows:

5		Cash			5 0 00			5
6		Accum. Depr.—Office Equipment			7 2 0 00			6
7		Loss on Sale of Printer			3 0 00			7
8		Office Equipment				8 0 0 00		8
9		Sold printer						9

LEARNING KEY: Gains and losses are always computed by comparing the market and book values of the asset being sold or exchanged.

Exchange or Trade-In of Plant Assets

If one asset is traded in on the purchase of another similar asset, a **trade-in allowance** may be granted. This trade-in allowance may be greater than, less than, or equal to the book value of the asset traded in.

If you have ever traded in a car for a newer model, you know that trade-in allowances frequently are not equal to the fair market value. Therefore, the fair market value of the asset traded in must be determined to calculate the gain or loss on the exchange. For simplicity, however, we will assume in our illustrations that the trade-in allowance is equal to the market value of the old asset being traded.

To illustrate accounting for the exchange of similar assets, let's assume that an old delivery truck is traded for a new one. Relevant information for this transaction is as follows:

Old Delivery Truck		New Delivery Truck	
Cost	$8,000	Market value (new truck)	$30,000
Accumulated depreciation	6,900	Trade-in allowance (old truck)	1,000
Book value	$1,100	Cash required	$29,000

A BROADER VIEW

Value? Which Value?

©DAVID YOUNG-WOLFF/TONY STONE

Determining the market value of an asset is not always easy. For example, if you have ever traded your car for a newer one, you probably learned that the trade-in allowance is often different from what the dealer would "pay" for the car and different from what you might sell it for by advertising in the newspaper. To test this concept, try it. Next time you are shopping for a car, ask the dealer two questions. First, ask the dealer what trade-in allowance he or she would offer on your car. Then, ask what he or she would accept for the new car if you paid cash. The difference between the "cash price" and the cash that you must pay with a trade-in offers a measure of what the dealer is paying you for your old car. (See illustration below.) This amount probably is not the same as the trade-in allowance offered by the dealer and may not be the same as the amount you could sell the car for by advertising in the paper. Of course, you need this information to make a good decision on whether to trade your car or sell it yourself.

Sticker price of new car	$20,000	
Trade-in allowance	5,000	
Cash that must be paid	$15,000	Cash price for new car $18,000

The value of your old car to the dealer is $3,000. Compare this with what you might sell it for by advertising in the paper.

Gain or Loss on Exchange	
$1,100	Book value
(1,000)	Market value (trade-in allowance)
$ 100	Loss

If the new truck has a fair market value of $30,000 and the **trade-in value** of the old truck is $1,000, then $29,000 is due in cash ($30,000 − $1,000). As discussed earlier, the gain or loss on the exchange is determined by comparing the market value of the old asset ($1,000) with its book value ($1,100). In this case, there is a $100 loss. The transaction is entered as follows:

5		Delivery Equipment (new truck)	30	0	0	0	00						5
6		Accum. Depr.—Delivery Equipment	6	9	0	0	00						6
7		Loss on Exchange of Delivery Equipment		1	0	0	00						7
8		Delivery Equipment (old truck)						8	0	0	0	00	8
9		Cash						29	0	0	0	00	9
10		Purchased a new truck											10

The previous entry has the following effects on the accounting records:

1. The original cost ($8,000) and accumulated depreciation ($6,900) for the old truck are removed from the books.

2. Cash is credited to show the amount paid ($29,000).

3. The new delivery equipment is entered on the books at its market value ($30,000).

4. The loss on the exchange is recognized ($100).

Now let's assume the same event, except that the market value and trade-in allowance for the old truck is $1,500. As shown below, this means that only $28,500 in cash is required and there is a $400 gain on the exchange ($1,500 − $1,100 = $400).

Old Delivery Truck		New Delivery Truck	
Cost	$8,000	Market value (new truck)	$30,000
Accumulated depreciation	6,900	Trade-in allowance (old truck)	1,500
Book value	$1,100	Cash required	$28,500

Gain or Loss on Exchange	
$1,500	Market value (Trade-in allowance)
(1,100)	Book value
$ 400	Gain

Because of the practice of conservatism, we are not allowed to recognize this gain for financial reporting purposes. Conservatism states that *when in doubt we should choose the reporting technique that is least likely to overstate assets or net income*. Since an old delivery truck was replaced with a new delivery truck, the company intends to continue earning revenues by making deliveries. Thus, the earnings process of the delivery service has not been completed. This raises doubt about the amount of earnings to recognize at this time. As noted in Chapter 19, conservatism states that we should never anticipate gains. Thus, no gain should be recognized when recording this transaction. The proper entry is as follows:

5		Delivery Equipment (new truck)	29 6 0 0 00		5
6		Accum. Depr.—Delivery Equipment	6 9 0 0 00		6
7		Delivery Equipment (old truck)		8 0 0 0 00	7
8		Cash		28 5 0 0 00	8
9		Purchased a new truck			9

The previous entry has the following effects on the accounting records:

1. The original cost ($8,000) and accumulated depreciation ($6,900) for the old truck are removed from the books.

2. Cash is credited to show the amount paid ($28,500).

3. The new delivery equipment is entered on the books at its market value less the amount of the unrecognized gain ($30,000 − $400). This must be done to avoid the recognition of the gain.

For tax purposes, neither gains nor losses are recognized on the exchange of similar assets ("like-kind" exchanges).

Property, Plant, and Equipment Records

If a business has many depreciable assets, a summary general ledger account will be kept for each major class of assets. For example, separate accounts might be kept for buildings, equipment, and furniture. Each summary account has a related accumulated depreciation account. Subsidiary records in the form of cards or computer files support these summary accounts. A typical property, plant, and equipment record is shown in Figure 20-2.

Fully Depreciated Plant Assets

A plant asset is fully depreciated when the book value is equal to the salvage value. When an asset is fully depreciated, no further depreciation should be entered. Since the rate of depreciation is based on its *estimated* useful life, an asset may still be used after it is fully depreciated. In this case, the cost of the asset and the accumulated depreciation are left in the accounts. When the asset eventually is disposed of, the cost and accumulated depreciation should be removed from the accounts, as illustrated in previous sections.

PROPERTY, PLANT, AND EQUIPMENT RECORD

Description	Computer	Account	Office Equipment
Age when acquired	New	Estimated salvage value	$500
Estimated life	5 years	Rate of annual depreciation based on cost less salvage value	20%

COST				DEPRECIATION RECORD			
Date Purchased	Description	Amount		Year	Rate	Amount	Total To Date
20-2 Jan. 9	ABC DE/3 MODEL 50	5,000 00		20-2	20%	900 00	900 00
	Serial No. 8403637			20-3	20%	900 00	1800 00
	American Micro			20-4	20%	450 00	2250 00
	Less estimated salvage value	500 00		20			
	Depreciable cost	4,500 00		20			
				20			
				20			
				20			
				20			

SOLD, EXCHANGED, OR DISCARDED					20			
Date	Explanation	Amount Realized	Book Value on Disposal Date	Gain (Loss)	20			
20-4 July 1	Sold	2,500 00	2,250 00	250 00	20			
					20			
					20			
					20			

FIGURE 20-2 Property, Plant, and Equipment Record

NATURAL RESOURCES

LO6 Explain the nature of, purpose of, and accounting for depletion.

The consumption or exhaustion of *natural resources* is called *depletion*. The purpose of depletion is to allocate the cost of these assets to the periods in which they are consumed. Computing *cost depletion* is similar to computing depreciation using the units-of-production method. The cost of the property, less the estimated salvage or residual value, is divided by the estimated number of units that the property contains. The result is the depletion expense per unit. This amount times the number of units removed and sold during the period is the depletion expense for the period.

 LEARNING KEY: Depletion is the consumption or exhaustion of natural resources.

To illustrate, assume a coal mine is acquired at a cost of $1,000,000. No salvage value is expected. The estimated recoverable amount of coal in the mine is 1,000,000 tons. During the current year, 180,000 tons of coal are mined and sold. The computation of the amount of depletion expense is as follows:

$$\frac{\$1,000,000}{1,000,000 \text{ tons}} = \$1 \text{ per ton}$$

180,000 tons × $1 per ton = $180,000 depletion expense

An adjusting entry is made at the end of the accounting period to recognize the depletion expense. For the coal mine, this entry is as follows:

11		Depletion Expense—Coal Mine	180 0 0 0 00		11
12		Accum. Depletion—Coal Mine		180 0 0 0 00	12
13					13

The difference between the cost of the mine and the amount of the accumulated depletion is the undepleted cost of the property:

Cost of coal mine	$1,000,000
Less: Accumulated depletion	180,000
Undepleted cost of mine	$ 820,000

Depletion Expense is reported as an operating expense on the income statement. Accumulated Depletion is reported on the balance sheet as a deduction from the related asset account, with the difference identified as undepleted cost of the asset. As was explained for depreciation, this undepleted cost of the wasting asset simply represents the cost not yet charged to operations. It is not intended to reflect the market value of the asset.

INTANGIBLE ASSETS

LO7 Explain the nature of and account for intangible assets.

In an accounting sense, the term "intangible" has come to have a very restricted meaning. Intangible assets refers to a limited group of valuable legal or economic rights that a firm may acquire. All items classified as intangibles are considered to be long-term assets. Major examples of intangibles include patents, copyrights, and trademarks.

Patents

A **patent** is a grant by the federal government to an inventor giving the exclusive right to produce, use, and sell an invention for a period of twenty years. A firm may purchase a patent from a prior patent owner or may develop its own and acquire an original patent from the government. If purchased, the amount paid represents the cost of the patent.

If a company carries on regular research and development activities to develop its own patents, the costs of such activities are treated as current expenses. If the government grants a patent on an invention the company develops, the cost of this patent includes only the fees paid to the government and to patent attorneys for their services. This amount is debited to an asset account and amortized over the patent's useful life.

Since the life of a patent is specifically limited, any cost assigned to it is allocated over no more than the number of years that the patent right will exist. The greatest number of years would be twenty if the firm developed and applied for the patent. If the expected useful or economic life of a patent is less than its legal life, the cost should be allocated over the shorter period.

With the straight-line method, the amortization each year is determined by dividing the cost of the patent by its expected life. Let's assume that a patent with thirteen years to run is purchased at a cost of $12,000, and that the buyer expects the useful life of the patent to be only ten years. In that event, $1,200 ($12,000 ÷ 10 years) would be amortized as expense for each of the ten years. The adjusting entry for the amortization at the end of each year is as follows:

7		Patent Amortization	1 2 0 0 00				7
8		Patents			1 2 0 0 00		8

Patent amortization is usually treated as an operating expense. Since patents are assets, their unamortized cost is reported on the balance sheet as an intangible long-term asset.

Copyrights

A **copyright** is similar in many respects to a patent. It consists of a federal grant of the exclusive right to the reproduction and sale of a literary, artistic, or musical composition. A copyright is granted for life plus 50 years after the death of the holder. The cost of obtaining the initial copyright on a composition is nominal. It is treated as an ordinary expense. However, if an existing copyright is purchased, the cost may be large enough and the expected future value sufficient to warrant charging the cost to an asset account entitled Copyrights.

It is a rare case in which a copyright would have an economic life as long as its legal life. In most cases the cost of a copyright is written off in a very few years. The write-off can be on a straight-line basis or in the proportion of the actual sales of the copyrighted item during the period to the total expected sales of the item. The amount of the write-off for each period is debited to Copyright Amortization (or Copyright Expense) and credited to Copyrights. Copyright amortization is treated as an operating expense. Any unamortized portion of the cost of copyrights is reported on the balance sheet as an intangible long-term asset.

Trademarks

The practice of using a **trademark** or registered trade name to identify a firm's merchandise is widespread. Such designations can be legally protected by registering them with the United States Patent Office. As long as the trademark or trade name is continuously used, the trademark is legally enforceable.

Research and development costs incurred to develop a trademark are expensed as incurred. However, costs incurred to register a trademark are debited to an asset account and amortized over the trademark's useful life. These costs include attorney and registration fees.

If a trademark is acquired by purchase, its cost is debited to an asset account entitled Trademarks. The future value of a trademark or a trade name is highly uncertain. Conservatism suggests that any cost incurred in purchasing a trademark should be written off within a few years.

The amount written off each period is debited to Trademark Amortization and credited to Trademarks. The amount written off is reported as an operating expense in the income statement. Any unamortized portion of the cost of trademarks or trade names is reported on the balance sheet as an intangible long-term asset.

Learning Objectives	Key Points to Remember
1 **Determine the cost of property, plant, and equipment.**	The cost to acquire an asset includes the purchase price and all costs incurred to prepare the asset for its intended use.
2 **Explain the nature and purpose of depreciation.**	The purpose of depreciation is to match a plant asset's cost with the revenues it helps to produce.
3 **Compute depreciation using the straight-line, declining-balance, sum-of-the-years'-digits, and units-of-production methods.**	Depreciation methods for financial reporting purposes: *Straight-Line Method* $$\text{Annual Depreciation} = \frac{(\text{Cost} - \text{Salvage Value})}{\text{Estimated Useful Life}}$$ *Declining-Balance Method* $$\text{Annual Depreciation} = \text{Depreciation Rate} \times \text{Book Value at Beginning of Year}$$ *Sum-of-the-Years'-Digits Method* $$\text{Annual Depreciation} = (\text{Cost} - \text{Salvage Value}) \times \frac{\text{Remaining Useful Life}}{\text{Sum-of-the-Years'-Digits}}$$ *Units-of-Production Method* $$\text{Depreciation per Unit} = \frac{(\text{Cost} - \text{Salvage Value})}{\text{Estimated Useful Life in Units}}$$ $$\text{Annual Depreciation} = \text{Depreciation per Unit} \times \text{Number of Units Produced or Consumed this Year}$$

4 **Account for repairs, maintenance, additions, and improvements to plant and equipment.**	Entry for additions and improvements that increase the usefulness of equipment:
	
	Building or Equipment xxx
	    Cash or Liability account xxx
	
	Entry for improvements that extend the life of the asset, but do not improve usefulness or efficiency:
	
	Accumulated Depreciation—Building or Equipment xxx
	    Cash or Liability account xxx

Learning Objectives	Key Points to Remember
	To compute straight-line depreciation expense for the year following an addition or improvement:
	1. Compute the new depreciable base by deducting the salvage value from the book value of the asset following the expenditures for the addition or improvement.
	2. Divide the new depreciable base by the remaining useful life.
5 Account for the disposition of property, plant, and equipment.	**Disposal of Plant Assets**
	When an asset is discarded:
	1. Remove cost and accumulated depreciation from accounting records.
	2. If book value is greater than zero, recognize loss.
	When an asset is sold:
	1. Remove cost and accumulated depreciation from accounting records.
	2. Debit cash for amount received.
	3. Recognize gain or loss (Market Value – Book Value of asset sold).
	When an asset is traded in for another similar asset:
	1. Remove cost and accumulated depreciation for asset traded in from accounting records.
	2. Credit cash for amount paid.
	3. Treatment of gain or loss (Market Value – Book Value of asset traded in):
	a. Always recognize losses.
	b. Do not recognize gains on the exchange of similar assets.
	4. Valuation of new asset:
	a. When exchanged at a loss,
	Cost = Market Value of new asset.
	b. When similar assets are exchanged at a gain,
	Cost = Market Value of new asset – Gain.
6 Explain the nature of, purpose of, and accounting for depletion.	The consumption or exhaustion of natural resources is called depletion. The purpose of accounting for depletion is to allocate the cost of these assets to the periods in which they are consumed.
7 Explain the nature of and account for intangible assets.	The term intangible assets is used to refer to a limited group of valuable legal or economic rights (patent, copyright, and trademark) that a firm may acquire. Since the life of an intangible asset is limited, any cost assigned to it is allocated over no more than the number of years that the asset will exist.

REFLECTION

Reflection: Answering the Opening Question

Yes, there are three additional methods that may be used for financial reporting purposes: declining-balance, sum-of-the-years'-digits, and units-of-production. The most appropriate for the van would probably be the units-of-production method. Under this method, the depreciation would be based on the number of miles driven.

DEMONSTRATION PROBLEM

WebTUTOR Advantage

Stillman Company purchased a new machine at the start of their current year at a cost of $37,500. The machine is expected to serve for five years and to have a salvage value of $3,000. Ronald L. Stillman, the chief executive officer, has asked for information as to the effects of alternative depreciation methods.

REQUIRED

1. Calculate the annual depreciation expense for each of the five years of expected life of the machine, the accumulated depreciation at the end of each year, and the book value at the end of each year using the:

   a.   Straight-line method

   b.   Double-declining-balance method

   c.   Sum-of-the-years'-digits method

2. Assume that in year 2 and year 4 of the five-year life of this machine, revenues are $45,000 and costs and expenses other than depreciation are $25,000. Calculate the net income for year 2 and year 4 using the same three depreciation methods used in Requirement 1.

3. Assume that Stillman chose the double-declining-balance method of depreciation for this machine. Then, in the first week of year 5, the machine was exchanged (traded in) for similar equipment costing $45,000. The market value and trade-in allowance on the old machine was $4,000 and cash was paid for the balance. Prepare the necessary journal entry to record this exchange.

Solution

1.

	Year	Annual Depreciation Expense	Accumulated Depreciation End of Year	Book Value End of Year
a.	1	$6,900	$ 6,900	$30,600
	2	6,900	13,800	23,700
	3	6,900	20,700	16,800
	4	6,900	27,600	9,900
	5	6,900	34,500	3,000
b.	1	$15,000	$15,000	$22,500
	2	9,000	24,000	13,500
	3	5,400	29,400	8,100
	4	3,240	32,640	4,860
	5	1,860*	34,500	3,000
c.	1	$11,500	$11,500	$26,000
	2	9,200	20,700	16,800
	3	6,900	27,600	9,900
	4	4,600	32,200	5,300
	5	2,300	34,500	3,000

*The machine is not depreciated below its estimated salvage value of $3,000.

2.

Year 2	(a) Straight-Line Method	(b) Double-Declining-Balance Method	(c) Sum-of-the-Years'-Digits Method
Revenue	$45,000	$45,000	$45,000
Costs and expenses other than depreciation	25,000	25,000	25,000
Depreciation	6,900	9,000	9,200
Net income	$13,100	$11,000	$10,800
Year 4			
Revenue	$45,000	$45,000	$45,000
Costs and expenses other than depreciation	25,000	25,000	25,000
Depreciation	6,900	3,240	4,600
Net income	$13,100	$16,760	$15,400

3.

			Debit	Credit	
5		Equipment (new machine)	45 0 0 0 00		5
6		Accum. Depr.—Equipment	32 6 4 0 00		6
7		Loss on Exchange of Equipment	8 6 0 00		7
8		Equipment (old machine)		37 5 0 0 00	8
9		Cash		41 0 0 0 00	9
10		Purchased a new machine			10

Old Equipment		New Equipment	
Cost of old equipment	$37,500	Market value (new)	$45,000
Accumulated depreciation	32,640	Trade-in allowance (old)	4,000
Book value	$ 4,860	Cash required	$41,000
Book value	$ 4,860		
Trade-in (market value)	(4,000)		
Loss	$ 860		

On-Line Learning Tools

For more information, visit: http://heintz.swlearning.com

The Heintz & Parry product web site is designed specifically for **COLLEGE ACCOUNTING, 18e.** The features include downloadable student resources and an interactive study center, organized by chapter, which contains learning objectives, web links, on-line quizzes with automatic feedback, and more.

KEY TERMS

Accelerated Cost Recovery System (ACRS), (758)   A method of depreciation used for federal income tax purposes for plant assets acquired between 1981 and 1986.

accelerated depreciation methods, (755)   Depreciation methods that provide for a higher depreciation charge in the first year of an asset's life and gradually decreasing charges in subsequent years.

amortization, (750)   The portion of an intangible asset's cost that is recognized as expense.

book value, (753)   The undepreciated cost of the asset (Cost – Accumulated Depreciation).

cash equivalent price, (751)   The amount of cash that could have been paid for the asset on the date of purchase.

copyright, (767)   Similar to a patent, a copyright consists of a federal grant of the exclusive right to the reproduction and sale of a literary, artistic, or musical composition.

cost, (752)   The sum of all amounts spent to acquire an asset and prepare it for its intended use.

declining-balance method, (755)   An accelerated depreciation method in which the book value is multiplied by a fixed rate. A common rate is double the straight-line rate (the double-declining-balance method).

depletion, (750)   The consumption or exhaustion of natural resources.

depreciable cost (base), (753)   The original cost less salvage (or scrap) value.

depreciation, (750)   The portion of a plant asset's cost that is recognized as expense.

double-declining-balance method, (755)   An accelerated depreciation method in which the book value is multiplied by double the straight-line rate.

fixed assets, (750)   See property, plant, and equipment.

functional depreciation, (752)   The loss of usefulness because of inadequacy or obsolescence.

intangible assets, (750)   Long-term assets that have no physical substance (patents, copyrights, and trademarks).

long-term assets, (750)   Assets that are expected to provide benefits for a number of accounting periods.

Modified Accelerated Cost Recovery System (MACRS), (758)   A method of depreciation used for federal income tax purposes for plant assets acquired after 1986.

patent, (767)   A grant by the federal government to an inventor giving the exclusive right to produce, use, and sell an invention for a period of twenty years.

physical depreciation, (752)   The loss of usefulness because of deterioration from age and wear.

plant assets, (750)   See property, plant, and equipment.

property, plant, and equipment, (750)   Long-term tangible assets that are used in the operations of the business. Also called plant assets or fixed assets.

salvage value, (752)   The estimated market value of an asset on its expected disposal date.

scrap value, (752)   See salvage value.

straight-line method, (753)   A depreciation method in which the depreciable cost of an asset is allocated equally over the years of the asset's useful life.

sum-of-the-years'-digits method, (756)   A depreciation method in which the annual depreciation is determined by multiplying the depreciable cost by a schedule of fractions.

tangible assets, (750)   Long-term assets that have physical substance.

trade-in allowance, (762)   If one asset is traded in on the purchase of another similar asset, an allowance may be granted.

trade-in value, (763)   See trade-in allowance.

trademark, (768)   A registered trade name or symbol that identifies a firm's merchandise.

units-of-production method, (757)   A depreciation method in which depreciation is based on the extent to which the asset was used during the year.

useful life, (752)   The amount of service expected to be obtained from an asset.

wasting assets, (750)   Assets whose physical substance consists of natural resources that are consumed in the operation of the business.

REVIEW QUESTIONS

(LO1)   1. What costs should be included when measuring the total cost to acquire a long-term asset?

(LO1)   2. How should the cost of such activities as planting trees and shrubs be entered?

(LO2)   3. What are the two major types of depreciation?

(LO3)   4. What is meant by the "depreciable cost" of a plant asset?

(LO3)   5. What are the four most commonly used methods of calculating depreciation for financial reporting purposes? How do they differ in their application?

(LO3)   6. Which depreciation method provides the fastest write-off of an asset?

(LO3)   7. Explain how the depreciation method selected affects the balance sheet and income statement.

(LO3)   8. For assets acquired after 1986, what depreciation methods are allowed for federal income tax purposes?

(LO4)   9. How should additions or improvements representing an increase in the usefulness of plant assets be entered?

(LO4)   10. Explain what is meant by additions and identify the two types of improvements.

(LO5)   11. What are the three major ways of disposing of a plant asset?

(LO5)   12. For what time interval should depreciation be entered on the date of an asset's disposal?

(LO5)   13. When a plant asset is sold, what must be known about the asset in order to determine the proper amount of gain or loss on the sale?

(LO5)   14. What details about a particular asset are provided by a property, plant, and equipment record?

(LO6)   15. What is the purpose of depletion?

(LO3/6)   16. Which depreciation method is similar to the method used to compute depletion expense?

(LO7)   17. Over what period of time should the cost of a patent be allocated if its economic life is expected to be less than its legal life?

(LO7)   18. How should the unamortized portion of the cost of a copyright be reported on the balance sheet?

(continued)

(LO7)   19. How does conservatism suggest that the cost of a trademark or trade name be accounted for subsequent to acquisition?

Self-Study Test Questions

True/False

1. All long-term assets wear out gradually or are gradually used up entirely.

2. Intangible assets are depreciated; plant assets are amortized.

3. Depreciation is a process of asset valuation; that is, book value is the same as true asset value.

4. The straight-line method of depreciation allocates the cost of an asset more rapidly than the sum-of-the-years'-digits method.

5. The units-of-production method of depreciation allocates the cost of an asset equally over each year of the useful life.

Multiple Choice

1. Using the sum-of-the-years'-digits method, the denominator for a five-year useful life would be

   (a) 5.   (c) 12.
   (b) 7.   (d) 15.

2. A machine that cost $100 and had accumulated depreciation of $80 was sold for $20.

   (a) There was a $20 gain.   (c) There was no gain or loss.
   (b) There was a $20 loss.   (d) There was a $60 loss.

3. A computer was sold on April 1, 20-2, for $575. Its cost was $3,000, and accumulated depreciation as of December 31, 20-1, was $2,100 ($700 a year).

   (a) There was a gain of $150.   (c) There was a gain of $325.
   (b) There was a loss of $150.   (d) There was a loss of $325.

4. Cost depletion of natural resources is most like which of these depreciation methods?

   (a) straight-line   (c) declining balance
   (b) units-of-production   (d) sum-of-the-years'-digits

5. Which of these is granted for life plus 50 years after the death of the holder?

   (a) patent   (c) copyright
   (b) mineral rights   (d) trademark

The answers to the Self-Study Test Questions are at the end of the text.

MANAGING YOUR WRITING

A friend owns and operates her own business and is concerned about completing her tax return. She owns several assets and uses straight-line depreciation for business purposes. She intended to use straight-line depreciation for tax purposes also, but recently heard about another method called MACRS. She has asked for your advice on which method to use on her tax return. Write a brief memo recommending a depreciation method and explaining why you believe it should be used.

ETHICS CASE

Creative Solutions purchased a patent from Russell Lazarus, an inventor. At the time of the purchase, the patent had two years remaining. The president of Creative Solutions decided to have the accountant amortize the cost of the patent, $200,000, over ten years rather than two years. His reasoning was that the $200,000 has already been spent and stockholders might ask a lot of questions about a $100,000 expense showing up on the income statement but probably wouldn't pay much attention to a $20,000 expense.

1. What is Creative Solutions' ethical responsibility to the company's stockholders?

2. According to GAAP, how should the amortization of patents be treated?

3. Write a short paragraph explaining similarities and differences between plant assets and intangible assets.

4. In groups of two or three, determine an appropriate method of depreciation, depletion, or amortization of the following assets for financial reporting purposes: (1) a car used as a taxi, (2) a parcel of land that will be resold in a few years, (3) a computer that has a very short life and loses most of its value in the first year or two, (4) an ore mine, (5) research and development costs incurred to develop a trademark.

WEB WORK

Intellectual property is one of the most valuable resources a company can have. Whether it is the name "Coke," or the movie *Star Wars*, companies have many ways of using and protecting their properties. What problems come up with the Internet and fair use policies?

Visit the Interactive Study center on our web site at **http://heintz. swlearning.com** for special hotlinks to assist you in this assignment.

SERIES A EXERCISES

EXERCISE 20-1A   (LO1)   **COST OF PROPERTY, PLANT, AND EQUIPMENT** Consider the following list of expenditures and indicate whether each would be debited to Land, Building, or Equipment as part of the cost to purchase these assets. Place a check mark in the appropriate column.

	Yes	No
Debit Land?		
Real estate fees	_____	_____
Cost to remove old buildings	_____	_____
Cost to pave parking areas	_____	_____
Tax assessment for streets	_____	_____
Debit Building?		
Cost of land on which the building is located	_____	_____
Legal fees related to purchase	_____	_____
Taxes related to purchase	_____	_____
Realtor fees	_____	_____
Interest on construction loan while building was under construction	_____	_____
Debit Equipment?		
Transportation charges	_____	_____
Insurance while in transit	_____	_____
Installation costs	_____	_____
Interest on loan to buy equipment	_____	_____

EXERCISE 20-2A   (LO3)

Year 1: SL, $3,000, DDB, $6,750; SYD, $5,333.33

STRAIGHT-LINE, DECLINING-BALANCE, AND SUM-OF-THE-YEARS'-DIGITS METHODS A light truck is purchased on January 1 at a cost of $27,000. It is expected to serve for eight years and have a salvage value of $3,000. Calculate the depreciation expense for the first and third years of the truck's life using the:

1. Straight-line method

2. Double-declining-balance method (round to two decimal places)

3. Sum-of-the-years'-digits method (round to two decimal places)

EXERCISE 20-3A   (LO3)

Depr. for Year 1: $5,000

UNITS-OF-PRODUCTION METHOD The truck purchased in Exercise 20-2A is expected to be used for 96,000 miles over its eight-year useful life. Using the units-of-production method, calculate the depreciation expense for the first and third years of use if the truck is driven 20,000 miles in year 1 and 18,000 miles in year 3.

EXERCISE 20-4A   (LO4)   **JOURNAL ENTRIES: REPAIRS, MAINTENANCE, ADDITIONS, AND IMPROVE-MENTS** Prepare the entries for the following transactions for Stepanski's Food Mart using a general journal.

1. Replaced the checkout computer in checkout stand A for $2,000 cash. The computer is part of the checkout stand.

2. Added a laser scanner to checkout stand B for $3,000 cash to decrease checkout time.

3. Cleaned scanner window on checkout stand A for $20 cash (normal maintenance).

EXERCISE 20-5A   (LO5)

1(a) Loss, $500; 1(b) No gain/loss; 1(c) Gain, $50; 2(a) Loss, $2,000; 2(b) Cost of new drill press, $72,000.

JOURNAL ENTRIES: DISPOSITION OF PLANT ASSETS Prepare the entries for the following transactions using a general journal.

1. Discarding an asset.

    a. On January 4, shelving units, which had cost $6,400 and had accumulated depreciation of $5,900, were discarded.

    b. On June 15, a hand cart, which had cost $1,500 and had accumulated depreciation of $1,350, was sold for $150.

    c. On October 1, a copy machine, which had cost $7,200 and had accumulated depreciation of $6,800, was sold for $450.

2. Exchange or trade-in of assets.

    a. On December 31, a drill press, which had cost $60,000 and had accumulated depreciation of $48,000, was traded in for a new drill press with a fair market value of $75,000. The old drill press and $65,000 in cash were given for the new drill press.

    b. On December 31, the old drill press in (a) and $60,000 in cash were given for the new drill press.

EXERCISE 20-6A   (LO6)

1. Depletion Exp.: $25,000; 2. Depletion Exp.: $500,000

DEPLETION Prepare the following entries using a general journal.

1. A coal mine was acquired at a cost of $1,500,000 and estimated to contain 6,000,000 tons of ore. During the year, 100,000 tons were mined and sold. Prepare the journal entry for the year's depletion expense.

2. A silver mine was acquired at a cost of $3,000,000 and estimated to contain 750,000 tons of ore. During the year, 125,000 tons were mined and sold. Prepare the journal entry for the year's depletion expense.

SERIES A PROBLEMS

PROBLEM 20-7A   (LO3)

Depr. exp. for Year 8: (a) $7,000.00; (b) $1,968.89; (c) $1,555.56

STRAIGHT-LINE, DECLINING-BALANCE, AND SUM-OF-THE-YEARS'-DIGITS METHODS A machine is purchased January 1 at a cost of $59,000. It is expected to serve for eight years and have a salvage value of $3,000.

REQUIRED

Prepare a schedule showing depreciation for each year and the book value at the end of each year using the:

a. Straight-line method

b. Double-declining-balance method (round to two decimal places)

c. Sum-of-the-years'-digits method (round to two decimal places)

PROBLEM 20-8A   (LO3)

Depr. Year 1: $4,300

UNITS-OF-PRODUCTION METHOD A machine is purchased January 1 at a cost of $59,000. It is expected to produce 130,000 units and have a salvage value of $3,000 at the end of its useful life.

Units produced are as follows:

Year 1	10,000
Year 2	8,000
Year 3	12,000
Year 4	16,000
Year 5	11,000

(continued)

REQUIRED

Prepare a schedule showing depreciation for each year and the undepreciated cost at the end of each year using the units-of-production method (round calculations to two decimal places).

PROBLEM 20-9A   (LO3)

1. Depr. exp.: $8,075

CALCULATING AND JOURNALIZING DEPRECIATION Equipment records for Johnson Machine Co. for the year follow. Johnson Machine uses the straight-line method of depreciation. In the case of assets acquired by the fifteenth day of the month, depreciation should be computed for the entire month. In the case of assets acquired after the fifteenth day of the month, no depreciation should be considered for the month in which the asset was acquired.

Asset	Purchase Price	Useful Life	Salvage Value	Date Purchased
Truck #1	$20,000	8 years	$4,000	January 1
Truck #2	24,000	8	4,000	April 10
Tractor #1	18,000	5	3,000	May 1
Tractor #2	14,000	6	2,000	June 18
Forklift	40,000	10	4,000	September 1

REQUIRED

1. Calculate the depreciation expense for Johnson Machine as of December 31, 20--.

2. Prepare the entry for depreciation expense using a general journal.

PROBLEM 20-10A   (LO4)

1: Depr. exp. is $8,000 for each;
2: Sim. A—Dr. Accum. Depr., $3,000; 3: Sim. A—$8,428.57 per year

IMPACT OF IMPROVEMENTS ON THE CALCULATION OF DEPRECIATION On January 1, 20-1, two flight simulators were purchased by a space camp for $68,000 each with a salvage value of $4,000 each and estimated useful lives of eight years. On January 1, 20-2, the jacks supporting simulator A were replaced for $3,000 cash and an updated computer for more advanced students was installed in simulator B for $10,000 cash.

REQUIRED

1. Using the straight-line method, prepare general journal entries for depreciation on December 31, 20-1, for simulators A and B.

2. Enter the transactions for January 20-2 in a general journal.

3. Assuming no other additions or improvements, calculate the depreciation expense for each simulator for 20-2 through 20-8.

PROBLEM 20-11A   (LO5)

Jan. 8, Loss: $200;
Feb. 1, Motor
(new): $6,800

DISPOSITION OF ASSETS: JOURNALIZING Mitchell Parts Co. had the following plant asset transactions during the year.

1. Assets discarded or sold:

Jan. 1   Motor #12, which had cost $2,800 and had accumulated depreciation of $2,800, was discarded.

8   Motor #8, which had cost $4,400 and had accumulated depreciation of $4,000, was sold for $200.

14   Motor #16, which had cost $5,600 and had accumulated depreciation of $5,400, was sold for $450.

2. Assets exchanged or traded-in:

Feb. 1   Motor #6, which had cost $6,000 and had accumulated depreciation of $4,800, was traded in for a new motor (#22) with a fair market value of $7,000. The old motor and $5,600 in cash were given for the new motor.

9   Motor #9, which had cost $5,500 and had accumulated depreciation of $5,000, was traded in for a new motor (#23) with a fair market value of $6,500. The old motor and $6,200 in cash were given for the new motor.

REQUIRED

Prepare general journal entries for the transactions.

PROBLEM 20-12A   **(LO6)**   **DEPLETION: CALCULATING AND JOURNALIZING** Mineral Works Co. acquired a salt mine at a cost of $1,700,000. The estimated number of units available for production from the mine is 3,400,000 tons.

1. Depletion exp. for
Year 1: $100,000

a.   During the first year, 200,000 tons are mined and sold.

b.   During the second year, 600,000 tons are mined and sold.

REQUIRED

1.   Calculate the amount of depletion expense for both years.

2.   Prepare general journal entries for depletion expense.

PROBLEM 20-13A   **(LO7)**   **INTANGIBLE LONG-TERM ASSETS** Track Town Co. had the following trans-actions involving intangible assets.

1. Patent amortization: $1,000

Jan. 1   Purchased a patent for leather soles for $10,000 and estimated its useful life to be 10 years.

Apr. 1   Purchased a copyright for a design for $15,000 with a life left on the copyright of 25 years. The estimated remaining (economic) life of the copyright is 5 years.

July 1   Purchased a trademark at a cost of $50,000. The estimated economic life of the trademark is 25 years. However, conservatism suggests it should be written off in 5 years.

REQUIRED

1.   Using the straight-line method, calculate the amortization of the patent, copyright, and trademark.

2.   Prepare general journal entries to record the end-of-year amortizations.

SERIES B EXERCISES

EXERCISE 20-1B   **(LO1)**   **COST OF PROPERTY, PLANT, AND EQUIPMENT** Lam Company purchased the following long-term assets. Determine the purchase cost of each asset.

Cost of asset: (a) $61,400;
(b) $41,900; (c) $108,400

a.   Ten computers:

Purchase price	$60,000
Transportation costs	500
Insurance during transportation	100
Installation	800
Interest on loan to purchase computers	3,000

(continued)

b.   Three acres of land:

Purchase price	$30,000
Grading of land in preparation to build	10,000
Planting of trees around border	5,000
Fence on southern border	3,000
Tax assessment for sewer	1,000
Legal fees related to purchase	900

c.   Five-thousand square foot building:

Purchase price	$102,000
Real estate fees	5,000
Land on which building is located	10,000
Legal fees related to purchase	600
Taxes related to purchase	800
Interest on mortgage to buy building	300

EXERCISE 20-2B   **(LO3)**

Year 1: SL: $3,600;
DDB: $7,600; SYD: $6,000

STRAIGHT-LINE, DECLINING-BALANCE, AND SUM-OF-THE-YEARS'-DIGITS METHODS A light truck is purchased on January 1 at a cost of $19,000. It is expected to serve for five years and have a salvage value of $1,000. Calculate the depreciation expense for the first and third years of the truck's life using the:

1.   Straight-line method

2.   Double-declining-balance method

3.   Sum-of-the-years'-digits method

EXERCISE 20-3B   **(LO3)**

Depr. for Year 1: $3,240

UNITS-OF-PRODUCTION METHOD The truck purchased in Exercise 20-2B is expected to be used for 100,000 miles over its five-year useful life. Using the units-of-production method, calculate the depreciation expense for the first and third years of use if the truck is driven 18,000 miles in year 1 and 22,000 miles in year 3.

EXERCISE 20-4B   **(LO4)**

JOURNAL ENTRIES: REPAIRS, MAINTENANCE, ADDITIONS, AND IMPROVE- MENTS Enter the following transactions for Larry's Lawn Service in a general journal.

1.   Added a second mower deck to tractor A for $550 cash to decrease mowing time.

2.   Replaced the engine in mower D for $200 cash.

3.   Lubricated engine of tractor A for $25 cash (normal maintenance).

EXERCISE 20-5B   **(LO5)**

1(a): Loss, $300; 1(b): No gain/loss;
1(c): Gain, $100; 2(a): Cost of
new drill press, $52,500;
2(b): Loss, $2,500

JOURNAL ENTRIES: DISPOSITION OF PLANT ASSETS Prepare the entries for the following transactions using a general journal.

1.   Discarding an asset.

a.   On January 4, shelving units, which had cost $7,200 and had accumulated depreciation of $6,900, were discarded.

b.   On June 15, a hand cart, which had cost $2,500 and had accumulated depreciation of $2,250, was sold for $250.

c.   On October 1, a copy machine, which had cost $5,200 and had accumulated depreciation of $4,800, was sold for $500.

2. Exchange or trade-in of assets.

   a. On December 31, a drill press, which had cost $50,000 and had accumulated depreciation of $37,500, was traded in for a new drill press with a fair market value of $55,000. The old drill press and $40,000 in cash were given for the new drill press.

   b. On December 31, the old drill press in (a) and $45,000 in cash were given for the new drill press.

EXERCISE 20-6B   **(LO6)**

1. Depletion Exp.: $77,000;
2. Depletion Exp.: $300,000

DEPLETION Prepare the following entries using a general journal.

1. A coal mine was acquired at a cost of $1,750,000 and estimated to contain 2,500,000 tons of ore. During the year, 110,000 tons were mined and sold. Prepare the journal entry for the year's depletion expense.

2. A silver mine was acquired at a cost of $2,000,000 and estimated to contain 500,000 tons of ore. During the year, 75,000 tons were mined and sold. Prepare the journal entry for the year's depletion expense.

SERIES B PROBLEMS

PROBLEM 20-7B   **(LO3)**

Power Accounting System Software®

Depr. Exp. for Year 1: (a) $9,000;
(b) $19,250; (c) $16,000

STRAIGHT-LINE, DECLINING-BALANCE, AND SUM-OF-THE-YEARS'-DIGITS METHODS A machine is purchased January 1 at a cost of $77,000. It is expected to serve for eight years and have a salvage value of $5,000.

REQUIRED

Prepare a schedule showing depreciation for each year and the book value at the end of each year using the:

a. Straight-line method

b. Double-declining-balance method (round to two decimal places)

c. Sum-of-the-years'-digits method (round to two decimal places)

PROBLEM 20-8B   **(LO3)**

Depr. for Year 1: $9,000

UNITS-OF-PRODUCTION METHOD A machine is purchased January 1 at a cost of $58,000. It is expected to produce 110,000 units and have a salvage value of $3,000 at the end of its useful life.

Units produced are as follows:

Year 1	18,000
Year 2	16,000
Year 3	20,000
Year 4	16,000
Year 5	12,000

REQUIRED

Prepare a schedule showing depreciation for each year and the undepreciated cost at the end of each year using the units-of-production method.

PROBLEM 20-9B   **(LO3)**

Depr. exp.: $10,250

CALCULATING AND JOURNALIZING DEPRECIATION Equipment records for Byerly Construction Co. for the year follow. Byerly Construction uses the straight-line method of depreciation. In the case of assets acquired by the fifteenth day of the month, depreciation should be computed for the entire month. In the case of assets acquired after the fifteenth day of the month, no depreciation should be considered for the month in which the asset was acquired.

Asset	Purchase Price	Useful Life	Salvage Value	Date Purchased
Truck #1	$22,000	7 years	$1,000	January 17
Truck #2	24,000	5	4,000	March 23
Molding #1	18,000	5	3,000	May 14
Molding #2	24,000	6	6,000	July 1
Forklift	35,000	8	3,000	September 19

REQUIRED

1. Calculate the depreciation expense for Byerly Construction as of December 31, 20--.

2. Prepare the entry for depreciation expense using a general journal.

PROBLEM 20-10B   **(LO4)**

1: Depr. exp. is $600 each;
2: J–H A—Dr. Asset for $800;
J–H B—Dr. Accum. Depr. for $200;
3: J–H A—$866.67 per year;
J–H B—$666.67 per year

IMPACT OF IMPROVEMENTS ON THE CALCULATION OF DEPRECIATION On January 1, 20-1, Dan's Demolition purchased two jackhammers for $2,500 each with a salvage value of $100 each and estimated useful lives of four years. On January 1, 20-2, a stronger blade to improve performance was installed in jackhammer A for $800 cash and the compressor was replaced in jackhammer B for $200 cash.

REQUIRED

1. Using the straight-line method, prepare general journal entries for depreciation on December 31, 20-1, for jackhammers A and B.

2. Enter the transactions for January 20-2 in a general journal.

3. Assuming no other additions or improvements, calculate the depreciation expense for each jackhammer for 20-2 through 20-4.

PROBLEM 20-11B   **(LO5)**

Jan. 8, Loss: $200;
Feb. 1, Van #20: $12,700

DISPOSITION OF ASSETS: JOURNALIZING Mayer Delivery Co. had the following plant asset transactions during the year.

1. Assets discarded or sold:

Jan. 1   Van #11, which had cost $8,800 and had accumulated depreciation of $8,800, was discarded.

8   Van #7, which had cost $9,400 and had accumulated depreciation of $9,000, was sold for $200.

14   Van #13, which had cost $7,600 and had accumulated depreciation of $7,400, was sold for $250.

2. Assets exchanged or traded-in:

Feb. 1   Van #8, which had cost $11,000 and had accumulated depreciation of $8,800, was traded in for a new van (#20) with a fair market value of $13,000. The old van and $10,500 in cash were given for the new van.

9   Van #3, which had cost $7,500 and had accumulated depreciation of $7,000, was traded in for a new van (#21) with a fair market value of $9,500. The old van and $9,200 in cash were given for the new van.

REQUIRED

Prepare general journal entries for the transactions.

PROBLEM 20-12B   **(LO6)**   **DEPLETION: CALCULATING AND JOURNALIZING** Mining Works Co. acquired a copper mine at a cost of $1,200,000. The estimated number of units available for production from the mine is 3,000,000 tons.

1. Depletion exp. for
Year 1: $160,000

a.   During the first year, 400,000 tons are mined and sold.

b.   During the second year, 700,000 tons are mined and sold.

REQUIRED

1.   Calculate the amount of depletion expense for both years.

2.   Prepare general journal entries for depletion expense.

PROBLEM 20-13B   **(LO7)**   **INTANGIBLE LONG-TERM ASSETS** B. J. Bakery had the following transactions involving intangible assets.

1. Patent amortization:
$1,000

Jan. 1   Purchased a patent for a new pastry for $10,000 and estimated its useful life to be 10 years.

Apr. 1   Purchased a copyright for a cookie cutter design for $5,000 with a life left on the copyright of 15 years. Estimated that the future remaining (economic) life of the copyright is 5 years.

July 1   Purchased a trademark at a cost of $40,000. The estimated economic life on the trademark is 20 years. However, conservatism suggests it should be written off in 5 years.

REQUIRED

1.   Using the straight-line method, calculate the amortization of the patent, copyright, and trademark.

2.   Prepare journal entries to record the end-of-year amortizations using a general journal.

MASTERY PROBLEM

1(c). Loss on exchange: $4,750;
2(c). Cost of new copy
machine: $34,500

On April 1, 20-3, Kwik Kopy Printing purchased a copy machine for $50,000. The estimated life of the machine is five years and it has an estimated salvage value of $5,000. The machine was used until July 1, 20-6.

REQUIRED

1. Assume that Kwik Kopy uses straight-line depreciation and prepare the following entries.

   a. Adjusting entries for depreciation on December 31 of 20-3 through 20-5.

   b. Adjusting entry for depreciation on June 30, 20-6, just prior to trading in the asset.

   c. On July 1, 20-6, the copy machine was traded in for a new copy machine. The market value of the new machine is $38,000. Kwik Kopy must trade in the old copy machine and pay $22,000 for the new machine.

2. Assume that Kwik Kopy uses sum-of-the-years'-digits depreciation and prepare the following entries.

   a. Adjusting entries for depreciation on December 31, 20-3 through 20-5.

   b. Adjusting entry for depreciation on June 30, 20-6, just prior to trading in the asset.

   c. On July 1, 20-6, the copy machine was traded in for a new copy machine. The market value of the new machine is $38,000. Kwik Kopy must trade in the old copy machine and pay $22,000 for the new machine.

CHALLENGE PROBLEM

This problem challenges you to apply your cumulative accounting knowledge to move a step beyond the material in the chapter.

Cumulative tax savings over eight years: $841.20

Don Burnette is starting a new home planning business. For years, people have asked Don to draw up the blueprints for their homes and he has done so in his spare time. Don has decided to go into business full time and believes that he will need to add one new draftsman each year for the next five years as his business grows. Don believes that the best way to design homes is by using home designing software on a computer. Thus, he plans to buy himself a new computer and a computer for each new associate who joins the company.

Don has heard that using MACRS for tax purposes will save him taxes and has asked you to develop a schedule illustrating the depreciation expense that would be recognized using straight-line depreciation for his income statement and MACRS depreciation for his tax return over the next eight years under the following assumptions.

1. Don will start his business on July 1, 20-1 and will purchase a new computer on that date.

2. Don will hire four new associates, one on July 1 of each year for the next four years, 20-2 through 20-5. He will also buy each associate a computer.

3. The computers cost $4,000, have useful lives of five years, and no salvage value. Don will take a half-year's depreciation in the first and last year of each computer's life when computing straight-line depreciation. He will use

the MACRS rates shown below which also assume a half-year convention in the first and last years of the asset's life.

4. As each computer completes its five-year life, Don will buy a new one to replace it.

5. Don's tax rate is 30%.

REQUIRED

1. Prepare a depreciation schedule showing the straight-line depreciation expense for years 20-1 through 20-8.

2. Prepare a depreciation schedule showing the MACRS depreciation for years 20-1 through 20-8. The MACRS rates are shown below.

Depreciation Rates for Five-Year Assets
MACRS Depreciation

Year	MACRS
1	20.0%
2	32.0
3	19.2
4	11.5
5	11.5
6	5.8
	100.0%

3. Compute the difference between straight-line depreciation and MACRS depreciation for each year, 20-1 through 20-8.

4. The differences in part #3 represent the differences in Don's taxable income each year. By using MACRS, how much does Don save in taxes each year, and in total?

5. Under what conditions would Don lose the accumulated tax savings?

DIGITAL IMAGING GROUP

Accounting for Partnerships

E van Taylor was approached by a colleague, who owns a boarding kennel and pet grooming business, and asked to consider forming a partnership by combining their businesses. Evan has heard about partnerships, but he does not know the advantages and disadvantages of this form of ownership structure. Will he need to make an additional cash investment? Or, will each partner simply invest the assets from their current businesses? How will the assets be valued to measure each partner's investment? How will the profits be distributed? Will Evan have a regular salary to live on? Should any of these issues be placed in writing?

When two or more individuals engage in an enterprise as co-owners, the organization is known as a **partnership.** This form of organization is common to practically all types of enterprises. However, it is more popular among personal service enterprises than among merchandising businesses. For example, the partnership form of organization is quite common in the legal and public accounting professions. In this chapter, the important features of and accounting procedures for partnerships will be discussed and illustrated.

PARTNERSHIP FORMATION

LO1 Explain how a partnership is formed and account for the formation.

The Uniform Partnership Act states that "a partnership is an association of two or more persons who carry on, as co-owners, a business for profit." Partnerships are formed for many reasons. Primarily, however, they are formed on the belief that individuals with complementary resources and abilities can operate more profitably together than as individuals.

A BROADER VIEW

Partnerships: How Large Can They Go?

When we think of partnerships, we often picture small businesses with a few partners. This is often the case. However, some partnerships are quite large. Take Ernst & Young, an international accounting firm, as an example. This partnership has over 7,000 partners guiding the efforts of over 105,000 personnel in 670 offices located in 140 countries. Worldwide revenues exceed $10 billion. This is not what you might call a "mom and pop" operation.

The Partnership Agreement

A written agreement containing the various provisions for operating a partnership is known as a **partnership agreement**. There is no standard form of partnership agreement, but the following provisions are essential.

1. Date of agreement

2. Names of the partners

3. Kind of business to be conducted

4. Length of time the partnership is to run

5. Name and location of the business

6. Investment of each partner

7. Basis on which profits or losses are to be shared by the partners

8. Limitation of partners' rights and activities

9. Salary allowances to partners

10. Division of assets upon dissolution of the partnership

11. Signatures of the partners

    Figure 21-1 is an example of a partnership agreement.

LEARNING KEY: Forming a partnership may lead to a great working relationship where partners can pool their assets, talents, and enthusiasm for the business. However, it is important to have a clear understanding of the key elements of the partnership: expectations for each partner, payments to partners in various forms, sharing of profits and losses, and dissolution of the partnership. The best way to ensure a clear understanding is to put everything in writing.

Characteristics of Partnerships

The characteristics of a partnership are different from those of the sole proprietorships we have accounted for in previous chapters. Some of the more important of these characteristics are listed as follows:

Co-Ownership of Assets. All assets held by a partnership are co-owned by all partners. If one partner contributes an asset to the business, the asset is jointly owned by all partners.

Mutual Agency. Any partner can bind the other partners to a contract if he or she is acting within the general scope of the business. Thus, if Mitchell signs a contract to purchase merchandise for the business, Jenkins is bound by that contract. On the other hand, if Mitchell contracts to buy a personal automobile, this is not part of normal business operations, and Jenkins would not be bound by it.

Limited Life. A partnership has a limited life. It may be dissolved as the result of any change in the ownership. These include death, bankruptcy, incapacity, withdrawal of a partner, addition of a new partner, or expiration of the time specified in the partnership agreement.

PARTNERSHIP AGREEMENT

THIS CONTRACT, made and entered into on the first day of January 20--, by and between Sam Mitchell of Indianapolis, Indiana, and Lisa Jenkins of the same city and state.

WITNESSETH: That the said parties have this day formed a partnership for the purpose of engaging in and conducting a wholesale and retail business in the city of Indianapolis under the following stipulations which are a part of this contract:

FIRST: The said partnership is to continue for a term of twenty-five years from January 1, 20--.

SECOND: The business is to be conducted under the firm name of Mitchell & Jenkins, at 2200 East Washington Street, Indianapolis, Indiana.

THIRD: The investments are as follows: Sam Mitchell, cash, $350,000; Lisa Jenkins, cash, $200,000. These invested assets are partnership property.

FOURTH: Each partner is to devote his/her entire time and attention to the business and to engage in no other business enterprise without the written consent of the other partner.

FIFTH: During the operation of the partnership, neither partner is to become surety or bonding agent for anyone without the written consent of the other partner.

SIXTH: Sam Mitchell is to receive a salary allowance of $36,000 a year, payable $1,500 in cash on the fifteenth day and last business day of each month. Lisa Jenkins is to receive a salary allowance of $48,000 a year, payable $2,000 in cash on the fifteenth day and last business day of each month. At the end of each annual fiscal period, the net income or the net loss shown by the income statement after the salaries of the two partners have been allowed is to be shared as follows: Sam Mitchell, 60 percent; Lisa Jenkins, 40 percent.

SEVENTH: Neither partner is to withdraw assets in excess of his/her salary, any part of the assets invested, or assets in anticipation of net income to be earned, without the written consent of the other partner.

EIGHTH: In the case of the death or the legal disability of either partner, the other partner is to continue the operations of the business until the close of the annual fiscal period on the following December 31. At that time the continuing partner is to be given an option to buy the interest of the deceased or incapacitated partner at not more than 10 percent above the value of the deceased or incapacitated partner's proprietary interest as shown by the balance of his/her capital account after the books are closed on December 31. It is agreed that this purchase price is to be paid one half in cash and the balance in four equal installments payable quarterly.

NINTH: At the conclusion of this contract, unless it is mutually agreed to continue the operation of the business under a new contract, the assets of the partnership, after the liabilities are paid, are to be divided in proportion to the net credit of each partner's capital account on that date.

IN WITNESS WHEREOF, the parties aforesaid have hereunto set their hands and affixed their seals on the day and year above written.

Sam Mitchell (Seal)
Sam Mitchell

Lisa Jenkins (Seal)
Lisa Jenkins

FIGURE 21-1 Partnership Agreement

Unlimited Liability. Each partner is personally liable for all debts incurred by the partnership. If the partnership cannot pay a bill, creditors will expect payment from the personal assets of the partners.

Federal Income Taxes. Partnerships are not subject to federal income taxes. However, partnerships file federal income tax returns for informational purposes and notify partners of the amount of partnership income that must be reported on their individual federal (and state if appropriate) income tax returns. Note that partners are taxed on their share of net income, not the amount withdrawn.

Advantages and Disadvantages

In comparison with the sole proprietorship, the partnership form of business offers certain advantages.

1. The ability and experience of the partners are combined in one enterprise.

2. More capital may be raised because the resources of the partners are combined.

3. Credit may be improved because each general partner is personally liable for partnership debts.

    There also are some disadvantages of the partnership form of organization.

1. Unlimited liability is a major disadvantage of the partnership form of ownership. This means that a partner could lose not only the amount invested, but also personal assets. Although this is also true for a sole proprietorship, it is not true for the corporate form of ownership, which will be introduced in Chapters 22 and 23. Under the laws of some states, certain partners may limit their liability. At least one partner, however, must be a general partner who has unlimited liability.

2. Mutual agency can lead to serious problems if all partners do not act responsibly and consult each other before signing contracts. Yes, unwitting partners could be liable for swamp land purchased by another partner.

3. The interest of a partner in the partnership cannot be transferred without the consent of the other partners.

4. Termination of the partnership agreement, bankruptcy of the firm, death of one of the partners, or any change in partner membership dissolves the partnership.

Accounting for Initial Investments

Accounting for a partnership is basically the same as accounting for a sole proprietorship. The main difference is that separate capital and drawing accounts are maintained for each partner. Care should be used when preparing the opening entry and entering any transactions that affect the respective interests of the partners.

Cash Investments. A partnership may be formed by the investment of cash by the partners. In opening the books for a partnership, a separate journal entry is made for each partner's investment. The opening entries for Mitchell & Jenkins based on the partnership agreement shown in Figure 21-1 are as follows:

5	Cash		350	0	0	0	00					5
6	Sam Mitchell, Capital							350	0	0	0	00	6
7	S. Mitchell invested $350,000 in cash												7
8													8
9	Cash		200	0	0	0	00					9
10	Lisa Jenkins, Capital							200	0	0	0	00	10
11	L. Jenkins invested $200,000 in cash												11

Investment of Cash and Other Assets. A partnership may also be formed by the investment of cash and other assets by the partners. Certain liabilities also may be assumed by the partnership. Each partner's capital account should be credited for the difference between the market value of the assets invested and liabilities assumed.

Instead of investing $200,000 in cash, assume that Jenkins invested:

1 inventory valued at $47,500 on which $10,500 was owed,

2 office equipment valued at $40,000,

3 delivery equipment valued at $92,000, on which $19,000 was owed on a note, and

4 $50,000 in cash.

The following opening entry would be made.

Accountants generally focus on historical costs and book values. However, when forming a partnership, market values are used to measure the investment of each partner. This is reasonable.

Investing $1,000 in cash is equivalent to investing an asset that could be sold for $1,000. The book value of the asset is not useful in this situation.

5	Cash	4	50	0	0	0	00					5
6	Inventory	1	47	5	0	0	00					6
7	Office Equipment	2	40	0	0	0	00					7
8	Delivery Equipment	3	92	0	0	0	00					8
9	Notes Payable							3	19	0	0	0	00	9
10	Accounts Payable							1	10	5	0	0	00	10
11	Lisa Jenkins, Capital							200	0	0	0	00	11
12	L. Jenkins' investment in partnership												12

Partnerships Formed from Existing Businesses. Two or more sole proprietors may combine their businesses to form a partnership. Their respective balance sheets serve as the basis for the opening entries for the investments of such partners. For example, assume that on April 1, Donna Morning and Larry Knight form a partnership under the firm name of Morning & Knight Sports. The balance sheets shown in Figure 21-2 are made a part of the partnership agreement. They agree to invest their assets and that the partnership will assume the liabilities shown in their respective balance sheets. Each partner's investment is measured by the difference between the assets invested and the liabilities assumed. The profits and losses are to be shared on a 50-50 basis. In case of dissolution, the assets are to be distributed between the partners in the ratio of their capital interests at the time of dissolution.

LEARNING KEY: The difference between the assets invested and the liabilities assumed is each partner's investment.

Morning Sports
Balance Sheet
March 31, 20 - -

Assets				Liabilities			
Cash		$ 6 3 4 4 00		Notes payable	$4 6 0 0 00		
Accounts receivable	$5 5 2 4 00			Accounts payable	9 0 8 2 00		
Less allowance for bad debts	4 3 0 00	5 0 9 4 00		Total liabilities		$13 6 8 2 00	
Merchandise inventory		24 5 7 4 00					
Store equipment	$3 8 4 0 00			Owner's Equity			
Less accumulated depreciation	1 0 0 0 00	2 8 4 0 00		Donna Morning, capital		25 1 7 0 00	
Total assets		$38 8 5 2 00		Total liabilities and owner's equity		$38 8 5 2 00	

Knight Athletics
Balance Sheet
March 31, 20 - -

Assets				Liabilities			
Cash		$ 3 5 4 4 00		Notes payable	$ 6 0 0 0 00		
Accounts receivable	$5 2 8 0 00			Accounts payable	13 2 3 8 00		
Less allowance for bad debts	7 2 0 00	4 5 6 0 00		Total liabilities		$19 2 3 8 00	
Merchandise inventory		29 6 9 2 00					
Supplies		2 8 6 00					
Office equipment	$4 3 2 0 00						
Less accumulated depreciation	1 1 0 0 00	3 2 2 0 00					
Store equipment	$4 8 0 0 00			Owner's Equity			
Less accumulated depreciation	1 2 0 0 00	3 6 0 0 00		Larry Knight, capital		25 6 6 4 00	
Total assets		$44 9 0 2 00		Total liabilities and owner's equity		$44 9 0 2 00	

FIGURE 21-2   Balance Sheets for Morning Sports and Knight Athletics Prior to the Formation of the Partnership

When two sole proprietors decide to combine their businesses, assets should be recorded at their fair market values as of the date of formation of the partnership. For Morning and Knight, any accounts receivable known to be uncollectible as of March 31, 20--, should be written off. None were considered uncollectible in this case. The balance in Accounts Receivable is debited and the amount of the Allowance for Bad Debts is credited in the books of the partnership. In this way, the accounts receivable are entered at their approximate fair market value.

LEARNING KEY: Assets should be recorded at their fair market values as of the date a partnership is formed.

Both Morning and Knight had been using the first-in, first-out (FIFO) method of inventory costing. Recall that under FIFO, the most recently purchased inventory is considered to be on hand. Thus, the values shown for merchandise inventories on their respective balance sheets are close to their fair market values as of March 31, 20--. If Morning or Knight had been using some other inventory costing method, the merchandise inventory amounts might have required restatement to reflect fair market value.

The fair market value of Morning's store equipment as of March 31, 20--, is $3,600. This amount should be entered on the books of the new partnership rather than the book value of $2,840 shown on Morning's balance sheet in Figure 21-2. In like manner, the fair market values of Knight's office equipment and store equipment as of March 31, 20--, are $3,850 and $4,200, respectively. These amounts should be entered on the books of the new partnership, rather than the respective book values of $3,220 and $3,600 shown on Knight's balance sheet. Once again, the difference between assets invested and liabilities assumed is credited to each partner's capital account. The opening entries for Morning & Knight Sports are as follows:

	DATE		DESCRIPTION	POST REF.	DEBIT	CREDIT	
	20--						
1	Apr.	1	Cash		6 3 4 4 00		1
2			Accounts Receivable		5 5 2 4 00		2
3			Merchandise Inventory		24 5 7 4 00		3
4			Store Equipment		3 6 0 0 00		4
5			Allowance for Bad Debts			4 3 0 00	5
6			Notes Payable			4 6 0 0 00	6
7			Accounts Payable			9 0 8 2 00	7
8			Donna Morning, Capital			25 9 3 0 00	8
9			D. Morning's investment in partnership				9
10							10
11		1	Cash		3 5 4 4 00		11
12			Accounts Receivable		5 2 8 0 00		12
13			Merchandise Inventory		29 6 9 2 00		13
14			Supplies		2 8 6 00		14
15			Office Equipment		3 8 5 0 00		15
16			Store Equipment		4 2 0 0 00		16
17			Allowance for Bad Debts			7 2 0 00	17
18			Notes Payable			6 0 0 0 00	18
19			Accounts Payable			13 2 3 8 00	19
20			Larry Knight, Capital			26 8 9 4 00	20
21			L. Knight's investment in partnership				21
22							22

GENERAL JOURNAL — PAGE 1

PARTNER COMPENSATION AND THE ALLOCATION OF NET INCOME

LO2 Explain how partners are compensated and account for the allocation of net income.

In the absense of any agreement between the partners, profits and losses must be shared equally regardless of the partners' investments. Generally, however, the basis on which reported profits and losses are shared is a matter of agreement between the partners. If both partners invest similar amounts of assets in the business and devote the same amount of time to the operation of the business, they may elect to allocate profits and losses equally. However, if the contributions to the success of the business are not similar, they may agree to allocate profits and losses based on each partner's contribution. For example, one partner may contribute most of the assets but render no services, while the other partner may contribute less in assets but devote full time to operating the business. In this case, the partners may agree to allocate the net income or loss based on salary and interest allowances. One partner would have a higher salary allowance to reflect the greater number of hours devoted to running the business. The other partner would have a higher interest allowance to reflect the larger financial investment in the partnership.

Partner compensation is reported on the income statement but is not used to compute net income. Instead, salary and interest allowances indicate how net income is allocated to each partner's capital account. The **salary allowance** is generally based on the services provided by each partner to the operations of the business. The **interest allowance** is based on the balance of each partner's capital account.

Withdrawals in a partnership are essentially the same as discussed earlier for a sole proprietorship. In a partnership, however, the agreement sets limits on the amount a partner may withdraw. For example, the Mitchell and Jenkins partnership agreement limits withdrawals to the amount of the salary allowance. To make an additional withdrawal, the written consent of the other partner is required. These agreements vary across partnerships. Since partners must pay federal income taxes on their share of net income, many partnership agreements permit the withdrawal of a partner's entire share of net income.

Profits and Losses Shared Equally

If the Mitchell and Jenkins partnership agreement shown in Figure 21-1 did not specify how the partners would be compensated, the profits and losses would be shared equally. If net income for the year was $190,800, the allocation would be reported on the income statement as shown in Figure 21-3.

Mitchell and Jenkins Income Statement (Partial) For Year Ended December 31, 20 - -			
Net income			$190 8 0 0 00
	S. MITCHELL	L. JENKINS	TOTAL
Allocation of net income	$95 4 0 0 00	$95 4 0 0 00	$190 8 0 0 00

FIGURE 21-3   Allocation of Profit and Loss (Equal Division)

Maintaining a record of each partner's share of net income and the amount of drawing each year requires a minor change in the way closing entries are made. Recall that four closing entries are made for sole proprietorships at the end of the accounting period. For a partnership, separate capital and drawing accounts are maintained for each partner. Thus, entries three and four must be changed as shown in Figure 21-4.

	CLOSING ENTRIES—SOLE PROPRIETOR		CLOSING ENTRIES—PARTNERSHIP
1.	Close all revenues to Income Summary.	1.	Close all revenues to Income Summary.
2.	Close all expenses to Income Summary.	2.	Close all expenses to Income Summary.
3.	Close Income Summary to the owner's capital account.	3.	Close Income Summary *by allocating each partner's share of net income or loss to the individual capital accounts.*
4.	Close Drawing to the owner's capital account.	4.	Close *each partner's drawing account to the individual capital accounts.*

FIGURE 21-4 Closing Entries

Based on the net income allocation shown in Figure 21-3, the third closing entry is:

5		Income Summary	190 8 0 0 00		5
6		S. Mitchell, Capital		95 4 0 0 00	6
7		L. Jenkins, Capital		95 4 0 0 00	7

If Mitchell and Jenkins withdrew $36,000 and $48,000, respectively, the fourth closing entry would be:

9		S. Mitchell, Capital	36 0 0 0 00		9
10		S. Mitchell, Drawing		36 0 0 0 00	10
11					11
12		L. Jenkins, Capital	48 0 0 0 00		12
13		L. Jenkins, Drawing		48 0 0 0 00	13

The four closing entries for a partnership are summarized in T account form in Figure 21-5.

Allocation of Profits and Losses with Salary Allowances

Net Income Exceeds Salary Allowances. The partnership agreement in Figure 21-1 specifies that after providing for salary allowances of $36,000 for Mitchell and $48,000 for Jenkins, the remaining net income or loss is divided on a 60-40 basis. Recall that salary payments (or allowances) are debited to the partners' drawing accounts. They are not considered an expense and not included in the calculation of net income. Under these conditions, the allocation of net income would be reported on the income statement as shown in Figure 21-6.

LEARNING KEY: If net income is greater than the salary allowances, the remaining income is allocated according to the ratio specified in the partnership agreement.

Net income $190,800
Less total allowances   84,000
Remaining income $106,800
60% of $106,800 = $64,080
40% of $106,800 = $42,720

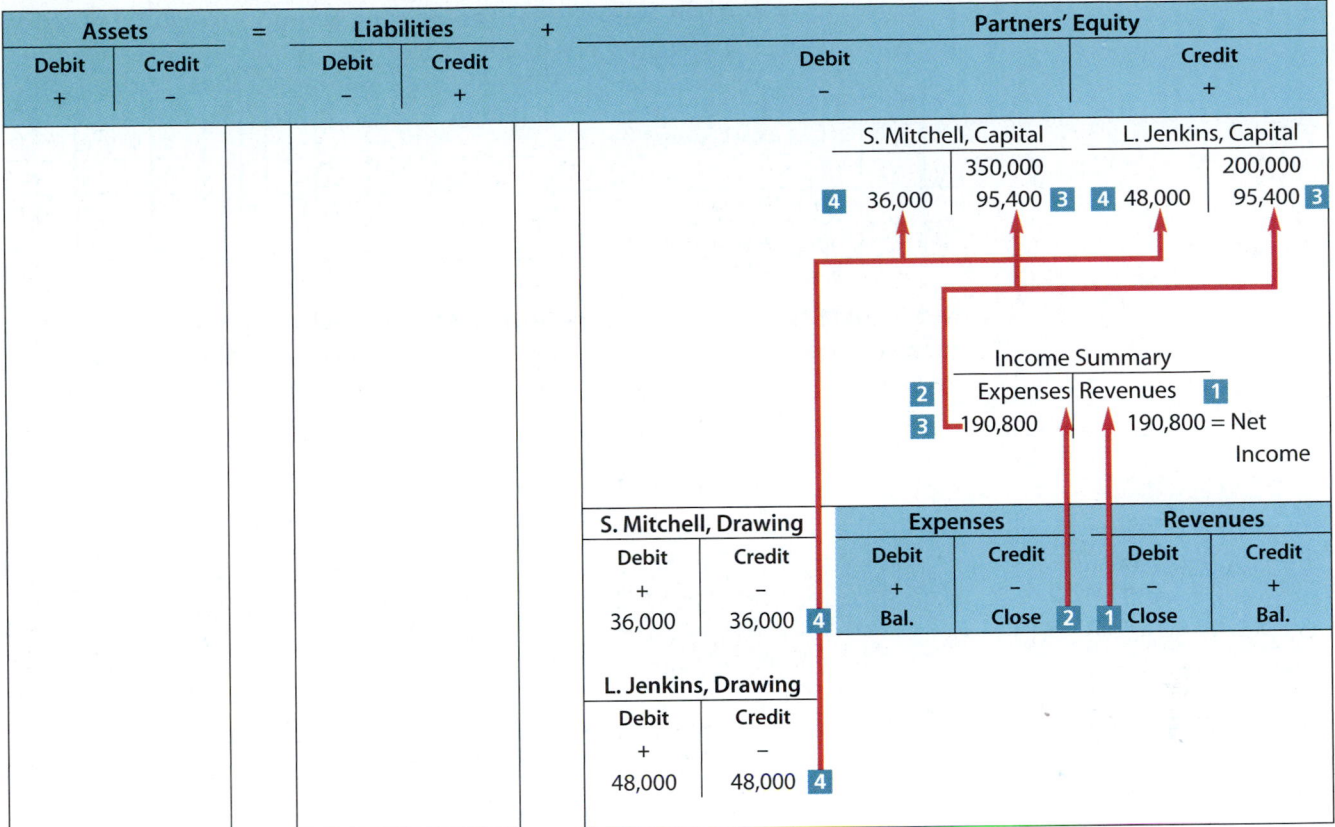

FIGURE 21-5 Closing Process for a Partnership

Mitchell and Jenkins				
Income Statement (Partial)				
For Year Ended December 31, 20 - -				
		S. MITCHELL	L. JENKINS	TOTAL
Net income				$190 8 0 0 00
Allocation of net income:				
Salary allowances		$ 36 0 0 0 00	$ 48 0 0 0 00	$ 84 0 0 0 00
Remaining income		64 0 8 0 00	42 7 2 0 00	106 8 0 0 00
Allocation of net income		$100 0 8 0 00	$ 90 7 2 0 00	$190 8 0 0 00

FIGURE 21-6 Allocation of Profit and Loss on Income Statement (60-40 Basis)

Based on the net income allocation shown above, the closing entry is:

5	Dec.	31	Income Summary		190 8 0 0 00		5
6			S. Mitchell, Capital			100 0 8 0 00	6
7			L. Jenkins, Capital			90 7 2 0 00	7

Assuming that Mitchell and Jenkins withdrew their salaries as described in the partnership agreement, the balances in the drawing accounts at year end would be \$36,000 and \$48,000, respectively. The drawing accounts would be closed to the partners' capital accounts at year end as follows:

9	Dec.	31	S. Mitchell, Capital	36 0 0 0 00		9
10			S. Mitchell, Drawing		36 0 0 0 00	10
11						11
12			L. Jenkins, Capital	48 0 0 0 00		12
13			L. Jenkins, Drawing		48 0 0 0 00	13

Net Income Is Less than Salary Allowances. If the salary allowances are greater than net income, the excess is allocated to the partners according to the ratio specified in the partnership agreement. If net income for Mitchell and Jenkins is \$44,000, the allocation is made as shown in Figure 21-7.

It may be helpful to think of the excess of salary allowances over net income as an economic loss to the partnership. Although net income of \$44,000 is reported on the income statement, the partnership did not generate enough revenues to cover expenses and the salary allowances for the partners. It is this economic loss (\$40,000) that is being allocated according to the profit/loss sharing ratio to determine the proper allocation of the reported net income.

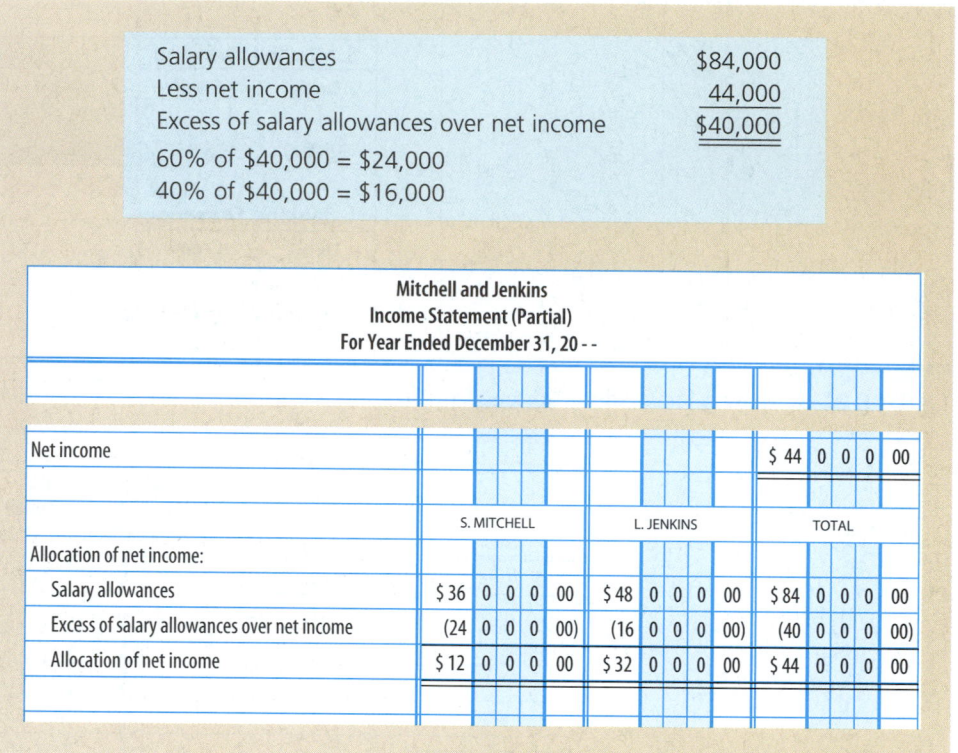

FIGURE 21-7   Allocation of Profit and Loss on Income Statement when Salary Allowances are Greater than Net Income

Given the lower profits of the partnership, let's assume in this case that Mitchell and Jenkins withdrew only \$30,000 and \$40,000 respectively, during this period. Based on the net income allocation in Figure 21-7, the closing entries are:

5	Dec.	31	Income Summary	44 0 0 0 00		5
6			S. Mitchell, Capital		12 0 0 0 00	6
7			L. Jenkins, Capital		32 0 0 0 00	7
8						8
9			S. Mitchell, Capital	30 0 0 0 00		9
10			S. Mitchell, Drawing		30 0 0 0 00	10
11						11
12			L. Jenkins, Capital	40 0 0 0 00		12
13			L. Jenkins, Drawing		40 0 0 0 00	13

Allocation of Profits and Losses with Salary and Interest Allowances

Net Income Exceeds Allowances. Partners may agree that the best method of allocating profits and losses is to base salaries on the services rendered by each partner and to provide interest on capital investments. The remainder is then shared equally, or according to a predefined ratio. Assume that B. K. Kelly and S. B. Arthur form a partnership on January 1 of the current year. Kelly will devote full time to operating the business, invest $50,000, and draw a salary of $35,000 per year. Arthur will devote about 10 hours per week, invest $150,000, and draw a salary of $10,000 per year. The partners will be allowed interest of 10 percent on capital balances on January 1 of each year and the balance of earnings will be divided equally. Net income of $80,000 in the first year of operation would be allocated as reported in Figure 21-8.

Kelly and Arthur Income Statement (Partial) For Year Ended December 31, 20 - -			
	B. K. KELLY	**S. B. ARTHUR**	**TOTAL**
Net income			$80 0 0 0 00
Allocation of net income:			
Salary allowances	$35 0 0 0 00	$10 0 0 0 00	$45 0 0 0 00
Interest allowances	5 0 0 0 00	15 0 0 0 00	20 0 0 0 00
Remaining income	7 5 0 0 00	7 5 0 0 00	15 0 0 0 00
Allocation of net income	$47 5 0 0 00	$32 5 0 0 00	$80 0 0 0 00

FIGURE 21-8   Allocation of Profit and Loss on Income Statement (Interest and Salary Allowances)

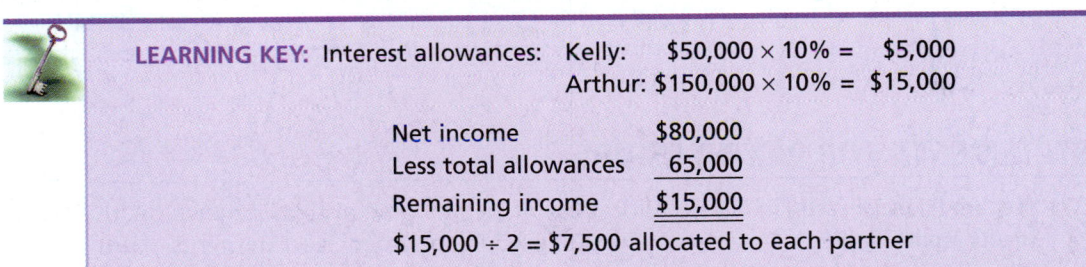

LEARNING KEY: Interest allowances: Kelly: $50,000 × 10% = $5,000
Arthur: $150,000 × 10% = $15,000

Net income	$80,000
Less total allowances	65,000
Remaining income	$15,000

$15,000 ÷ 2 = $7,500 allocated to each partner

Based on the net income allocation shown in Figure 21-8, the closing entry is:

5	Dec.	31	Income Summary	80 0 0 0 00		5
6			B. K. Kelly, Capital		47 5 0 0 00	6
7			S. B. Arthur, Capital		32 5 0 0 00	7

Net Income Is Less than Total Allowances. If Kelly and Arthur incurred a net loss of $20,000 in year 1, the allocation would be made as shown in Figure 21-9.

Kelly and Arthur Income Statement (Partial) For Year Ended December 31, 20 - -				
		B. K. KELLY	S. B. ARTHUR	TOTAL
Net loss				$(20 0 0 0 00)
Allocation of net loss:				
Salary allowances		$ 35 0 0 0 00	$ 10 0 0 0 00	$ 45 0 0 0 00
Interest allowances		5 0 0 0 00	15 0 0 0 00	20 0 0 0 00
Excess of allowances over income allocated equally		(42 5 0 0 00)	(42 5 0 0 00)	(85 0 0 0 00)
Allocation of net loss		$ (2 5 0 0 00)	$(17 5 0 0 00)	$(20 0 0 0 00)

FIGURE 21-9 Allocation of Net Loss on Income Statement

LEARNING KEY:

Net loss	$20,000
Plus total allowances	65,000
Excess of allowances over net income	$85,000

$85,000 ÷ 2 = $42,500 allocated to each partner

The following closing entry would be made to allocate the loss of $20,000.

5	Dec.	31	B. K. Kelly, Capital		2 5 0 0 00		5
6			S. B. Arthur, Capital		17 5 0 0 00		6
7			Income Summary			20 0 0 0 00	7

STATEMENTS FOR PARTNERSHIPS

LO3 Prepare financial statements reporting the allocation of net income and partnership equity.

The allocation of net income and its impact on the partners' capital balances should be disclosed in the financial statements. All three financial statements are affected: the income statement, statement of owners' (partners') equity, and balance sheet. As illustrated in the preceding section, the allocation is often reported in the lower portion of the income statement. In addition, the statement of partners' equity reflects the equity of each partner and summarizes the allocation of net income for the year.

LEARNING KEY: The allocation of net income and its impact on the partners' capital balances should be disclosed in the financial statements.

Recall that the capital balances for Kelly and Arthur on January 1, 20--, were $50,000 and $150,000, respectively. Let's assume that Arthur invested an additional $10,000, net income was $80,000 and allocated as reported in Figure 21-8, and the partners withdrew only the salary portion of their compensation ($35,000 and $10,000, respectively) during the first year of operation. As shown in Figure 21-10, the statement of partners' equity reports this information and the income allocations reported on the income statement.

Kelly and Arthur Statement of Partners' Equity For Year Ended December 31, 20 - -	B. K. KELLY	S. B. ARTHUR	TOTAL
Capital, January 1, 20 --	$50 0 0 0 00	$150 0 0 0 00	$200 0 0 0 00
Additional investments during the year		10 0 0 0 00	10 0 0 0 00
	$50 0 0 0 00	$160 0 0 0 00	$210 0 0 0 00
Net income for the year	47 5 0 0 00	32 5 0 0 00	80 0 0 0 00
	$97 5 0 0 00	$192 5 0 0 00	$290 0 0 0 00
Withdrawals (salaries during the year)	35 0 0 0 00	10 0 0 0 00	45 0 0 0 00
Capital, December 31, 20 --	$62 5 0 0 00	$182 5 0 0 00	$245 0 0 0 00

FIGURE 21-10   Statement of Partners' Equity

LEARNING KEY: Interest allowances for year 2 would be computed as follows:

Kelly: $62,500 × 10% = $6,250
Arthur: $182,500 × 10% = $18,250

The additional investment is reported in the same manner as for a sole proprietorship.

Finally, the partners' equity section of the balance sheet reports the equity of each partner. This is illustrated as follows.

Kelly and Arthur Balance Sheet (Partial) December 31, 20 - -		
Partners' Equity		
B. K. Kelly, capital	$ 62 5 0 0 00	
S. B. Arthur, capital	182 5 0 0 00	
Total partners' equity		$245 0 0 0 00

DISSOLUTION OF A PARTNERSHIP

LO4 **Describe the actions that result in the dissolution of a partnership and account for the dissolution.**

One of the primary characteristics of the partnership form of organization is its limited life. Any change in the members of the partnership results in **dissolution**. Dissolution of a partnership may occur because of the addition of a new partner, the death or withdrawal of one of the partners, or bankruptcy.

LEARNING KEY: The partnership is dissolved if there is any change in the members of the partnership.

Dissolution of the partnership does not necessarily imply that business operations will halt. It simply means that the partnership is dissolved. The business may continue with a new group of partners, or a different form of ownership. Any time the original partnership agreement is altered, a new partnership agreement must be prepared to replace the original agreement.

Admitting a New Partner

A new partner may be admitted by agreement among the existing partners. When this happens, the old partnership is dissolved and a new one is created. A new partner may buy into the business in three ways: (1) by purchasing an interest directly from existing partners, (2) by making a cash investment in the business, or (3) by contributing assets from an existing business.

Assume that Morning and Knight admit Sunny Noon as a new partner as of July 1, 20--, when Morning and Knight have capital interests of $30,000 and $20,000, respectively. Noon pays $12,000 to Morning for one-third of her interest and $12,000 to Knight for one-half of his interest. These cash payments go to the partners directly, not to the business. Thus, the following entry is made by the partnership.

	20--					
1	July	1	Donna Morning, Capital	10 0 0 0 00*		1
2			Larry Knight, Capital	10 0 0 0 00**		2
3			Sunny Noon, Capital		20 0 0 0 00	3
4			S. Noon admitted to partnership			4
5			*$30,000 × 1/3 = $10,000			5
6			**$20,000 × 1/2 = $10,000			6

The extra $2,000 ($12,000 – $10,000) paid to both Morning and Knight represents profit to them, but it has no effect on the *partnership's* financial statements.

Now, assume instead that Noon invested $25,000 cash in the new partnership. In this case, the following entry would be made to admit Noon.

	20--					
1	July	1	Cash	25 0 0 0 00		1
2			Sunny Noon, Capital		25 0 0 0 00	2
3			S. Noon admitted to partnership			3
4						4

Finally, let's assume that Noon had been operating her own business, which was then taken over by the new partnership. In this case the balance sheet for Sunny Noon's Golf, shown in Figure 21-11, would serve as a basis for preparing the opening entry. The assets listed in the balance sheet are taken over, the liabilities are assumed, and Noon's capital account is credited for the difference.

Sunny Noon's Golf
Balance Sheet
June 30, 20 - -

Assets			Liabilities		
Cash		$ 5 0 0 0 00	Notes payable	$9 0 4 8 00	
Accounts receivable	$14 2 9 0 00		Accounts payable	7 5 5 0 00	
Less allowance for bad debts	1 0 7 8 00	13 2 1 2 00	Total liabilities		$16 5 9 8 00
Merchandise inventory		27 2 9 0 00	Owner's Equity		
			Sunny Noon, capital		28 9 0 4 00
Total assets		$45 5 0 2 00	Total liabilities and owner's equity		$45 5 0 2 00

FIGURE 21-11 Balance Sheet for Sunny Noon's Golf

Noon has no knowledge of any uncollectible accounts receivable as of June 30, 20--, and has been using the FIFO method of inventory costing. Thus, the amounts reported on the balance sheet are reasonable approximations of market values. The entry to admit Noon as a partner, therefore, is as follows:

	20--														
1	July	1	Cash		5	0	0	0	00						1
2			Accounts Receivable		14	2	9	0	00						2
3			Merchandise Inventory		27	2	9	0	00						3
4			Allowance for Bad Debts							1	0	7	8	00	4
5			Notes Payable							9	0	4	8	00	5
6			Accounts Payable							7	5	5	0	00	6
7			Sunny Noon, Capital							28	9	0	4	00	7
8			S. Noon admitted to partnership												8
9															9

Withdrawal of Partner

By agreement, a partner may retire and be permitted to withdraw assets equal to, less than, or greater than the amount of his or her interest in the partnership. The book value of a partner's interest is shown by the credit balance of the partner's capital account. The balance is computed after all profits or losses have been allocated in accordance with the partnership agreement and the books closed. If a retiring partner withdraws cash or other assets equal to the credit balance of his or her capital account, the transaction will have no effect on the capital of the remaining partners.

To illustrate, assume that several years after the formation of Morning, Noon, and Knight Sports, Sunny Noon decided to retire. The partners agreed to the withdrawal of cash equal to the amount of Noon's equity in the assets of the partnership. After bringing all accounts up to date, assume that the partners' capital accounts had credit balances as follows:

Donna Morning	$55,000
Sunny Noon	40,000
Larry Knight	45,000

If Noon withdraws $40,000 in cash, the entry on the books of the partnership is as follows:

12			Sunny Noon, Capital		40	0	0	0	00						12
13			Cash							40	0	0	0	00	13
14			S. Noon retired, withdrawing												14
15			$40,000 in equity settlement												15

Note that this transaction decreases cash and decreases the total capital of the partnership, but it does not affect the equity of the remaining partners. Morning still has an equity of $55,000 and Knight an equity of $45,000 in the partnership assets.

If a retiring partner agrees to withdraw less than the amount in his or her capital account, the transaction will increase the capital accounts of the remaining partners. For example, if Noon withdraws only $30,000 in settlement of the interest, the entry in the books of the partnership is as follows:

12	Sunny Noon, Capital	40 0 0 0 00		12
13	Cash		30 0 0 0 00	13
14	Donna Morning, Capital		5 5 0 0 00	14
15	Larry Knight, Capital		4 5 0 0 00	15
16	S. Noon retired, withdrawing			16
17	$30,000 in equity settlement			17

The difference between Noon's equity in the assets of the partnership and the amount of cash withdrawn is $10,000 ($40,000 – $30,000). This difference is divided between the remaining partners on the basis stated in the partnership agreement. In this case it is divided according to the ratio of their capital interests after allocating net income and closing their drawing accounts. On this basis, Morning's capital account is credited for $5,500 and Knight's is credited for $4,500. The calculations are as follows:

Remaining Equity in Partnership

Morning	$55,000
Knight	45,000
Total	$100,000

Allocation to Morning: ($55,000 ÷ $100,000) × $10,000 = $5,500
Allocation to Knight: ($45,000 ÷ $100,000) × $10,000 = $4,500

If a retiring partner withdraws more than the amount in his or her capital account, the transaction will decrease the capital accounts of the remaining partners. Thus, if Morning and Knight allow Noon to withdraw $45,000 in settlement of Noon's interest, the entry in the books of the partnership is as follows:

12	Sunny Noon, Capital	40 0 0 0 00		12
13	Donna Morning, Capital	2 7 5 0 00		13
14	Larry Knight, Capital	2 2 5 0 00		14
15	Cash		45 0 0 0 00	15
16	S. Noon retired, withdrawing			16
17	$45,000 in equity settlement			17

The excess of the amount of cash withdrawn over Noon's equity in the partnership ($5,000) is divided between the remaining partners on the basis stated in the partnership agreement. Thus, Morning, Capital is debited for $2,750 (55/100 of $5,000), while Knight, Capital is debited for $2,250 (45/100 of $5,000).

When a partner retires from the business, the partner's interest may be purchased directly by one or more of the remaining partners or by an outside party. If the retiring partner's interest is sold to one of the remaining partners, the retiring partner's equity is merely transferred to the other partner. For example, assume that Noon's equity is sold to Morning. The entry for the transaction on the books of the partnership is as follows:

12	Sunny Noon, Capital	40 0 0 0 00		12
13	Donna Morning, Capital		40 0 0 0 00	13
14	D. Morning purchased S. Noon's			14
15	interest in partnership			15

The amount paid to Noon by Morning is a personal transaction and has no effect on the above entry. Any gain or loss resulting from the transaction is a personal gain or loss of the withdrawing partner and not of the business. Thus, whatever amount is involved, the credit in Noon's account is transferred to Morning's account.

Death of a Partner

The death of a partner dissolves the partnership. On the date of death, the accounts are closed and the net income for the year to date is allocated to the partners' capital accounts. Most agreements call for an audit and revaluation of the assets at this time. The balance of the deceased partner's capital account is then transferred to a liability account with the deceased's estate. The surviving partners may continue the business or liquidate. If the business continues, the procedures for settling with the estate are the same as those described earlier for the withdrawal of a partner. Liquidation procedures are described in the following section.

LIQUIDATION OF A PARTNERSHIP

LO5 Describe how a partnership is liquidated and prepare associated entries and a statement of partnership liquidation.

Liquidation of a partnership generally means that the assets are sold, liabilities are paid, and the remaining cash or other assets are distributed to the partners. When normal operations are discontinued, adjusting and closing entries are made. Thus, only the assets, liabilities, and partners' equity accounts remain open. As the assets are sold, the cash realized is applied first to the claims of creditors. Once all liabilities are paid, the remaining cash and other assets are distributed to the partners according to their ownership interests as indicated by their capital accounts.

LEARNING KEY: When a partnership is liquidated, the assets are sold, liabilities are paid, and the remaining cash or other assets are distributed to the partners.

To illustrate, assume that after several years of operations, the partnership of Morning, Noon, and Knight Sports is to be liquidated. After making closing entries on May 31, 20--, the following accounts remain open. For simplicity, "Other Assets" and "Liabilities" are used as account titles. In actual practice, several asset, contra-asset, and liability accounts would be involved.

	Account Balance	
Account Title	Debit	Credit
Cash	$ 10,000	
Inventory	120,000	
Other Assets	220,000	
Liabilities		$ 80,000
Donna Morning, Capital		95,000
Larry Knight, Capital		120,000
Sunny Noon, Capital		55,000

Using these account balances, accounting for the liquidation of the partnership is illustrated in Figure 21-12. For convenience, let's assume that all assets are sold in one transaction on June 1, 20--, and all liabilities are paid at once on June 15, 20--. On June 18, cash settlements are made with the partners who share equally in all profits and losses.

Gain on Sale of Assets

Assume that the noncash assets are sold for $370,000. Since these assets have a book value of $340,000, a gain of $30,000 on the sale is recognized. The gain is allocated to the partners' capital accounts according to the profit-and-loss sharing ratio. In this case, the gain is shared equally. Next, the liabilities are paid and the remaining cash distributed to the partners according to their capital account balances. A statement of partnership liquidation summarizing these transactions is provided in Figure 21-12.

	CASH	INVENTORY	OTHER ASSETS	LIABILITIES	CAPITAL D. MORNING	L. KNIGHT	S. NOON
Balance before sale of assets	$ 10 0 0 0 00	$120 0 0 0 00	$220 0 0 0 00	$ 80 0 0 0 00	$ 95 0 0 0 00	$120 0 0 0 00	$ 55 0 0 0 00
Sale of noncash assets and allocation of gain	370 0 0 0 00	(120 0 0 0 00)	(220 0 0 0 00)		10 0 0 0 00	10 0 0 0 00	10 0 0 0 00
Balance after sale	$380 0 0 0 00	0	0	$ 80 0 0 0 00	$105 0 0 0 00	$130 0 0 0 00	$ 65 0 0 0 00
Payment of liabilities	(80 0 0 0 00)			(80 0 0 0 00)			
Balance after payment of liabilities	$300 0 0 0 00	0	0	0	$105 0 0 0 00	$130 0 0 0 00	$ 65 0 0 0 00
Distribution of cash to partners	(300 0 0 0 00)				(105 0 0 0 00)	(130 0 0 0 00)	(65 0 0 0 00)
Final balance	0	0	0	0	0	0	0

Morning, Noon, and Knight Sports
Statement of Partnership Liquidation
For Period June 1–18, 20 - -

FIGURE 21-12 Statement of Partnership Liquidation

The entries for these transactions are as follows:

	20--					
1	June	1	Cash	370 0 0 0 00		1
2			Inventory		120 0 0 0 00	2
3			Other Assets		220 0 0 0 00	3
4			Gain on Sale of Assets		30 0 0 0 00	4
5			Sale of assets			5
6						6
7		1	Gain on Sale of Assets	30 0 0 0 00		7
8			Donna Morning, Capital		10 0 0 0 00	8
9			Larry Knight, Capital		10 0 0 0 00	9
10			Sunny Noon, Capital		10 0 0 0 00	10
11			Allocation of gain			11
12						12
13		15	Liabilities	80 0 0 0 00		13
14			Cash		80 0 0 0 00	14
15			Payment of liabilities			15
16						16
17		18	Donna Morning, Capital	105 0 0 0 00		17
18			Larry Knight, Capital	130 0 0 0 00		18
19			Sunny Noon, Capital	65 0 0 0 00		19
20			Cash		300 0 0 0 00	20
21			Distribution of cash to partners			21

Loss on Sale of Assets

Using the same information for Morning, Noon, and Knight as given on page 805, assume that the noncash assets are sold for $295,000, resulting in a loss of $45,000. A statement of partnership liquidation reflecting the equal allocation of the loss on the sale of assets, payment of the liabilities, and distribution of the cash to the partners is illustrated in Figure 21-13.

Morning, Noon, and Knight Sports
Statement of Partnership Liquidation
For Period June 1–18, 20 - -

	CASH	INVENTORY	OTHER ASSETS	LIABILITIES	CAPITAL D. MORNING	CAPITAL L. KNIGHT	CAPITAL S. NOON
Balance before sale of assets	$ 10 0 0 0 00	$120 0 0 0 00	$220 0 0 0 00	$ 80 0 0 0 00	$ 95 0 0 0 00	$120 0 0 0 00	$ 55 0 0 0 00
Sale of noncash assets and							
allocation of loss	295 0 0 0 00	(120 0 0 0 00)	(220 0 0 0 00)		(15 0 0 0 00)	(15 0 0 0 00)	(15 0 0 0 00)
Balance after sale	$305 0 0 0 00	0	0	$ 80 0 0 0 00	$ 80 0 0 0 00	$105 0 0 0 00	$ 40 0 0 0 00
Payment of liabilities	(80 0 0 0 00)			(80 0 0 0 00)			
Balance after payment of liabilities	$225 0 0 0 00	0	0	0	$ 80 0 0 0 00	$105 0 0 0 00	$ 40 0 0 0 00
Distribution of cash to partners	(225 0 0 0 00)				(80 0 0 0 00)	(105 0 0 0 00)	(40 0 0 0 00)
Final balance	0	0	0	0	0	0	0

FIGURE 21-13 Statement of Partnership Liquidation

The entries for these transactions are as follows:

	20 - -						
1	June	1	Cash	295 0 0 0 00			1
2			Loss on Sale of Assets	45 0 0 0 00			2
3			Inventory		120 0 0 0 00		3
4			Other Assets		220 0 0 0 00		4
5			Sale of assets				5
6							6
7		1	Donna Morning, Capital	15 0 0 0 00			7
8			Larry Knight, Capital	15 0 0 0 00			8
9			Sunny Noon, Capital	15 0 0 0 00			9
10			Loss on Sale of Assets		45 0 0 0 00		10
11			Allocation of loss				11
12							12
13		15	Liabilities	80 0 0 0 00			13
14			Cash		80 0 0 0 00		14
15			Payment of liabilities				15
16							16
17		18	Donna Morning, Capital	80 0 0 0 00			17
18			Larry Knight, Capital	105 0 0 0 00			18
19			Sunny Noon, Capital	40 0 0 0 00			19
20			Cash		225 0 0 0 00		20
21			Distribution of cash to partners				21

Learning Objectives	Key Points to Remember
1 **Explain how a partnership is formed and account for the formation.**	The proper accounting for the formation of a partnership depends on the type of investment made by each partner. Cash investments are recorded by recognizing the cash and an equal amount of partnership capital as follows:

5		Cash	50	0	0	0	00						5
6		Katherine Meisenheimer, Capital						50	0	0	0	00	6
7		K. Meisenheimer invested $50,000 in cash											7

If a partner invests cash and other assets, the assets are entered at their market values. The partner's capital account is credited for the sum of the cash and the market value of assets contributed as follows:

5		Cash	10	0	0	0	00						5
6		Inventory (market value)	20	0	0	0	00						6
7		Office Equipment (market value)	8	0	0	0	00						7
8		Delivery Equipment (market value)	15	0	0	0	00						8
9		Sara Bates, Capital						53	0	0	0	00	9
10		S. Bates investment in partnership											10

If existing sole proprietorships are combined, the balance sheets of the proprietorships are used to prepare the entry for the formation of the partnership. Each partner's investment is measured by the difference between the market value of the assets invested and the liabilities assumed by the partnership as shown below. Before transferring receivables to the partnership, any known uncollectible accounts must be written off by the proprietorship.

1	20-- Apr.	1	Cash	5	0	0	0	00						1
2			Accounts Receivable	20	0	0	0	00						2
3			Merchandise Inventory (market value)	50	0	0	0	00						3
4			Store Equipment (market value)	30	0	0	0	00						4
5			Allowance for Bad Debts							2	0	0	00	5
6			Notes Payable						10	0	0	0	00	6
7			Accounts Payable						12	0	0	0	00	7
8			Alex Von Rosenberger, Capital						82	8	0	0	00	8
9			A. Von Rosenberger's investment											9
10			in partnership											10

2 **Explain how partners are compensated and account for the allocation of net income.**	Partner compensation may be based on salary and interest allowances as well as an allocation of remaining profits as stated in the partnership agreement.
3 **Prepare financial statements reporting the allocation of net income and partnership equity.**	Partnership financial statements report the allocation of net income and partnership equity as shown in the statements on the next page.
4 **Describe the actions that result in the dissolution of a partnership and account for the dissolution.**	Any change in the members of the partnership results in its dissolution. Accounting for the dissolution varies depending on whether a new partner is admitted or a partner withdraws, and whether an additional investment is made in the partnership or payments are made directly to existing partners.

Learning Objectives	Key Points to Remember

5 **Describe how a partnership is liquidated and prepare associated entries and a statement of partnership liquidation.**

The steps in the liquidation process are:

1. Assets are sold.
2. Gains or losses are allocated to the partners.
3. Liabilities are paid.
4. Remaining cash and other assets are distributed to the partners according to their capital accounts.

3 **(continued)**

Prepare financial statements reporting the allocation of net income and partnership equity.

Kelly and Arthur
Income Statement (Partial)
For Year Ended December 31, 20 - -

	B. K. KELLY	S. B. ARTHUR	TOTAL
Net income			$80 000 00
Allocation of net income:			
Salary allowances	$35 000 00	$10 000 00	$45 000 00
Interest allowances	5 000 00	15 000 00	20 000 00
Remaining income	7 500 00	7 500 00	15 000 00
	$47 500 00	$32 500 00	$80 000 00

Kelly and Arthur
Statement of Partners' Equity
For Year Ended December 31, 20 - -

	B. K. KELLY	S. B. ARTHUR	TOTAL
Capital, January 1, 20 --	$50 000 00	$150 000 00	$200 000 00
Additional investments during the year	— — —	10 000 00	10 000 00
	$50 000 00	$160 000 00	$210 000 00
Net income for the year	47 500 00	32 500 00	80 000 00
	$97 500 00	$192 500 00	$290 000 00
Withdrawals (salaries during the year)	35 000 00	10 000 00	45 000 00
Capital, December 31, 20 --	$62 500 00	$182 500 00	$245 000 00

Kelly and Arthur
Balance Sheet (Partial)
December 31, 20 - -

Partners' Equity		
B. K. Kelly, capital	$ 62 500 00	
S. B. Arthur, capital	182 500 00	
Total partners' equity		$245 000 00

Reflection: Answering the Opening Question

As discussed in the chapter, advantages of a partnership include the increased capital and credit available to a partnership as well as the combined knowledge and experience that the partners bring to the operation of the business. Disadvantages include personal liability for each partner, non-transferability of a partnership interest without the consent of other partners, and the fact that a partnership dissolves with the termination of the partnership agreement, bankruptcy, or a change in the partners. Evan may be asked to make a cash investment. However, since the plan is to combine two existing businesses, he will probably be contributing his firm's assets. The assets are valued at market value. Distribution of profits and salary allowances will be determined through a negotiation between Evan and his potential partner. Of course, all of the essential aspects of the partnership should be clearly and openly discussed and then placed in writing in the form of a partnership agreement.

DEMONSTRATION PROBLEM

WebTUTOR Advantage

Mascha Schuurmans, Jolijn Brouwer, and Mirjam van Tuil are partners in Holland Law. They share profits and losses in a 50-30-20 ratio. The partnership agreement calls for annual salaries of $40,000, $35,000, and $30,000, respectively, and interest of 12 percent on their January 1 capital balances.* Any remaining net income (or net loss) is to be divided in accordance with the ratios used for sharing profits and losses.

The partners' capital balances as of January 1, 20-1, were Schuurmans, $120,000; Brouwer, $75,000; and van Tuil, $50,000. No additional investments were made during the year. The net income of the partnership for the year 20-1 was $160,000. Partners' withdrawals for the year were Schuurmans, $50,000; Brouwer, $40,000; and van Tuil, $35,000.

On March 4, 20-2, the partners decide to liquidate their law firm. On that date, the firm has a cash balance of $46,000, noncash assets of $274,000, and liabilities of $40,000. No additional investments or withdrawals were made in 20-2. Between March 5 and March 31, the noncash assets are sold for $290,000, the gain is divided according to the profit and loss sharing ratio, and the liabilities are paid. The remaining cash is then distributed to the partners.

*Salaries and interest are not recognized as expenses in the determination of net income.

REQUIRED

1. Prepare the lower portion of the income statement of Holland Law for the year ended December 31, 20-1, showing the division of the partnership net income for the year.

2. Prepare the general journal entry to close Income Summary to the partners' capital accounts as of December 31, 20-1.

3. Prepare a statement of partners' equity for Holland Law for the year ended December 31, 20-1.

4. Prepare a statement of partnership liquidation for Holland Law for the period March 5 through March 31, 20-2.

5. Prepare the general journal entries as of March 31, 20-2, for:

    a.   The sale of the noncash assets of the partnership

    b.   The division of any loss or gain on the sale of assets

    c.   The payment of partnership liabilities

    d.   The distribution of remaining cash to the partners

Solution

1.

Holland Law Income Statement (Partial) For Year Ended December 31, 20-1				
	M. SCHUURMANS	J. BROUWER	M. VAN TUIL	TOTAL
Net income				$160 000 00
Allocation of net income:				
Salary allowances	$40 000 00	$35 000 00	$30 000 00	$105 000 00
Interest allowances	14 400 00	9 000 00	6 000 00	29 400 00
Remaining income	12 800 00	7 680 00	5 120 00	25 600 00
	$67 200 00	$51 680 00	$41 120 00	$160 000 00

2.

4					4
5	Dec.	31	Income Summary	160 000 00	5
6			Mascha Schuurmans, Capital	67 200 00	6
7			Jolijn Brouwer, Capital	51 680 00	7
8			Mirjam van Tuil, Capital	41 120 00	8
9					9

3.

Holland Law Statement of Partners' Equity For Year Ended December 31, 20-1				
	M. SCHUURMANS	J. BROUWER	M. VAN TUIL	TOTAL
Capital, January 1, 20-1	$120 000 00	$ 75 000 00	$50 000 00	$245 000 00
Net income for the year	67 200 00	51 680 00	41 120 00	160 000 00
	$187 200 00	$126 680 00	$91 120 00	$405 000 00
Withdrawals	50 000 00	40 000 00	35 000 00	125 000 00
Capital, December 31, 20-1	$137 200 00	$ 86 680 00	$56 120 00	$280 000 00

(continued)

4.

Holland Law
Statement of Partnership Liquidation
For Period March 5–31, 20 - 2

	CASH	NONCASH ASSETS	LIABILITIES	CAPITAL M. SCHUURMANS	J. BROUWER	M. VAN TUIL
Balance before sale of assets	$ 46 0 0 0 00	$274 0 0 0 00	$ 40 0 0 0 00	$137 2 0 0 00	$ 86 6 8 0 00	$ 56 1 2 0 00
Sale of noncash assets and allocation of gain	290 0 0 0 00	(274 0 0 0 00)		8 0 0 0 00	4 8 0 0 00	3 2 0 0 00
Balance after sale	$336 0 0 0 00	0	$ 40 0 0 0 00	$145 2 0 0 00	$ 91 4 8 0 00	$ 59 3 2 0 00
Payment of liabilities	(40 0 0 0 00)		(40 0 0 0 00)			
Balance after payment of liabilities	$296 0 0 0 00	0	0	$145 2 0 0 00	$ 91 4 8 0 00	$ 59 3 2 0 00
Distribution of cash to partners	(296 0 0 0 00)			(145 2 0 0 00)	(91 4 8 0 00)	(59 3 2 0 00)
Final balance	0	0	0	0	0	0

5.

GENERAL JOURNAL   PAGE 1

	DATE	DESCRIPTION	POST REF.	DEBIT	CREDIT	
a.	1	20-2 Mar. 31 Cash		290 0 0 0 00		1
	2	Noncash Assets			274 0 0 0 00	2
	3	Gain on Sale of Assets			16 0 0 0 00	3
	4	Sale of assets				4
	5					5
b.	6	31 Gain on Sale of Assets		16 0 0 0 00		6
	7	Mascha Schuurmans, Capital			8 0 0 0 00	7
	8	Jolijn Brouwer, Capital			4 8 0 0 00	8
	9	Mirjam van Tuil, Capital			3 2 0 0 00	9
	10	Allocation of gain				10
	11					11
c.	12	31 Liabilities		40 0 0 0 00		12
	13	Cash			40 0 0 0 00	13
	14	Payment of liabilities				14
	15					15
d.	16	31 Mascha Schuurmans, Capital		145 2 0 0 00		16
	17	Jolijn Brouwer, Capital		91 4 8 0 00		17
	18	Mirjam van Tuil, Capital		59 3 2 0 00		18
	19	Cash			296 0 0 0 00	19
	20	Distribution of cash to partners				20

KEY TERMS

dissolution, (801)   Dissolving of the partnership resulting from any change in the members of the partnership.

interest allowance, (795)   A method of allocating partnership net income based on the balance of each partner's capital account.

liquidation, (805)   The process of selling the assets, paying the liabilities, and distributing the remaining cash or other assets to the partners.

partnership, (788)   The form of organization in which two or more individuals engage in an enterprise as co-owners.

partnership agreement, (789)   A written agreement containing the various provisions for operating a partnership.

salary allowance, (795)   A method of allocating partnership net income based on the services provided by each partner to the operations of the business.

REVIEW QUESTIONS

(LO1)   1.   Identify eleven essential provisions of a partnership agreement.

(LO1)   2.   Identify three advantages of a partnership as compared with a sole proprietorship.

(LO1)   3.   Identify four disadvantages of a partnership form of business organization.

(LO1)   4.   When two sole proprietors decide to combine their businesses, at what values should the noncash assets be taken over by the partnership?

(LO2)   5.   In the absence of any agreement between the partners, how must profits and losses be shared? If the partnership agreement specifies how profits are to be shared, but there is no agreement as to how losses are to be shared, what must be true with respect to losses?

(LO2)   6.   What factors generally are considered in determining the allocation of profits and losses?

(LO4)   7.   Identify three ways in which a partnership may be dissolved.

(LO4)   8.   When a new partner who has been the sole owner of a business is admitted to a partnership by having the partnership take over the old business, what usually serves as the basis for preparing the opening entry?

(LO5)   9.   Describe the four accounting entries for the liquidation of a partnership.

Self-Study Test Questions

True/False

1. When two or more individuals engage in an enterprise as co-owners, the organization is known as a proprietorship.

2. Mutual agency is a characteristic of a partnership in which any partner can bind the other partners to a contract if he/she is acting within the general scope of the business.

3. Limited life is a characteristic of a partnership in which each partner is personally liable for all debts incurred by the partners.

4. One advantage of a partnership is that the interest of a partner cannot be transferred without the consent of the other partners.

5. When two or more sole proprietors form a partnership, their respective balance sheets serve as the basis for the opening entries for the investments of such partners.

Multiple Choice

1. The basis on which profits and losses are to be shared among partners is

    (a) a matter of agreement among the partners. (c) the same as their investment ratio.
    (b) the same as their withdrawal ratio.   (d) always equal among all partners.

2. In the absence of any agreement among partners, profits and losses must be shared

    (a) equally among all partners.   (c) on the basis of their investment ratio.
    (b) on the basis of their withdrawals.   (d) in accordance with the Uniform
                                                      Partnership Act.

3. If the partnership agreement specifies how profits are to be shared but does not specify how losses are to be shared, the losses must be shared

    (a) equally among all partners.   (c) on the basis of their investment ratio.
    (b) on the basis of their withdrawals.   (d) none of the above.

4. After closing the temporary owner's equity accounts into Income Summary and after allocating the net income and closing the partners' drawing accounts, assume the partners' capital accounts had credit balances as follows: Abbott, $20,000; Barnes, $30,000; Costello, $45,000.
    If Abbott retired and withdrew $25,000 in settlement of her equity, the debit to her capital account would be in the amount of

    (a) $25,000.   (b) $55,000.   (c) $20,000.   (d) $45,000.

5. After closing the temporary owner's equity accounts into Income Summary and after allocating the net income and closing the partners' drawing accounts, assume the partners' capital accounts had credit balances as follows: Abbott, $20,000; Barnes, $30,000; Costello, $45,000. The difference between the withdrawing partner's equity and amount of cash withdrawn is divided according to the ratio of the remaining partners' capital interests.
    If Costello retired and withdrew $40,000 in settlement of his equity, the amount entered in Abbott's capital account would be a

    (a) $2,000 credit.   (b) $2,000 debit.   (c) $3,000 credit.   (d) $3,000 debit.

The answers to the Self-Study Test Questions are at the end of the text.

MANAGING YOUR WRITING

A friend, Joan Mellencamp, has mentioned that she is thinking about forming a partnership with a small group of colleagues. She is interested in learning about the advantages and disadvantages of the partnership form of ownership. In addition, she has asked for your advice on the kinds of issues that should be agreed upon in advance of the formation of the partnership. Write a memo to your friend explaining the advantages and disadvantages of a partnership and offer your advice on the issues that should be settled in advance.

ETHICS CASE

Kathy Lentz, Rob Snyder, and Tom Rohm were all general partners in a consulting business. Each partner owned one-third of the business. The partnership agreement stated that all three partners must approve vouchers for payments in amounts exceeding $5,000. While Tom was on vacation, Kathy and Rob decided to purchase a new computer system costing $6,800. A voucher was prepared and Rob signed both his and Tom's name. Kathy signed her name and gave the voucher to the accounts payable clerk who wrote the check for $6,800.

1. Why would a partnership agreement specify that all purchases over a certain amount be approved by all partners? Are there any circumstances that would warrant deviation from this policy?

2. What are the disadvantages of the partnership form of business ownership?

3. Write a short memo from Tom Rohm to Kathy Lentz and Rob Snyder expressing disapproval of the situation.

4. In groups of three or four, discuss some of the possible outcomes of this situation.

WEB WORK

The Internet contains many resources to assist those wishing to start a business or change the form of their business. Two of the most helpful, and free, resources are provided by the federal government. What are three specific ways these resources could help you if you are wanting to form a partnership?

Visit the Interactive Study Center on our web site at **http://heintz. swlearning.com** for special hotlinks to assist you in this assignment.

SERIES A EXERCISES

EXERCISE 21-1A   **(LO1)**   **PARTNERSHIP OPENING ENTRIES** Lisa Morris and Joyce Laski agreed on September 1 to go into business as partners. According to the agreement, Morris is to contribute $45,000 cash and Laski is to contribute $65,000 cash. Provide a separate journal entry for the investment of each partner.

EXERCISE 21-2A   (LO2)

4. Rhea: $42,000

ENTRIES FOR ALLOCATION OF NET INCOME Karen Rhea and Wayne Sellevaeg decided to form a partnership on July 1, 20-1. Rhea invested $100,000 and Sellevaeg invested $50,000. For the fiscal year ended June 30, 20-2, a net income of $90,000 was earned. Determine the amount of net income that Rhea and Sellevaeg would receive under each of the following independent assumptions.

1. There is no agreement concerning the distribution of net income.

2. Each partner is to receive 10% interest on their original investment. The remaining net income is to be divided equally.

3. Rhea and Sellevaeg are to receive a salary allowance of $30,000 and $40,000, respectively. The remaining net income is to be divided equally.

4. Each partner is to receive 10% interest on their original investment. Rhea and Sellevaeg are to receive a salary allowance of $30,000 and $40,000, respectively. The remaining net income is to be divided as follows: Rhea 40% and Sellevaeg 60%.

EXERCISE 21-3A   (LO3)

1. Allocation of net income:
   Cooper, $40,000;
2. Capital: Cooper, $110,000

PARTIAL FINANCIAL STATEMENTS Karen Cooper and Alex Orme formed a partnership on May 1, 20-1. Cooper contributed $80,000 and Orme contributed $50,000. During the year, Cooper contributed an additional $20,000. The partnership agreement states that Cooper is to receive $30,000 and Orme is to receive $60,000 as a salary allowance. Any remaining net income is to be divided as follows: Cooper 20% and Orme 80%. The partnership earned net income of $140,000 for the fiscal year ending April 30, 20-2. During the first year of operation, Cooper and Orme withdrew $30,000 and $50,000, respectively.

1. Prepare the lower portion of the income statement showing the allocation of net income between Cooper and Orme for the fiscal year ended April 30, 20-2.

2. Prepare a statement of partners' equity showing each individual partner's equity for the fiscal year ended April 30, 20-2.

EXERCISE 21-4A   (LO4)

2. Ending capital bal.:
   Bowman, $80,000;
   Emery, $45,000

ADMITTING NEW PARTNERS Jeff Bowman and Kristi Emery, who have ending capital balances of $100,000 and $60,000, respectively, agree to admit two new partners to their business on August 18, 20--. Dan Bridges will buy one-fifth of Bowman's capital interest for $30,000 and one-fourth of Emery's capital interest for $20,000. Payments will be made directly to the partners. Anna Terrell will invest $50,000 in the business, for which she will receive a $50,000 capital interest.

1. Prepare general journal entries showing the transactions admitting Bridges and Terrell to the partnership.

2. Calculate the ending capital balances of all four partners after the transactions.

EXERCISE 21-5A   (LO5)

Gain: $50,000

ENTRIES: PARTNERSHIP LIQUIDATION On liquidation of the partnership of J. Hui and K. Cline, as of November 1, 20--, inventory with a book value of $180,000 is sold for $230,000. Given that Hui and Cline share profits and losses equally, prepare the entries for the sale and the allocation of gain.

SERIES A PROBLEMS

PROBLEM 21-6A **(LO1)**

Cr. to
Woodworth,
Capital:
$29,010

PARTNERSHIP OPENING ENTRIES On July 1, 20--, Susan Woodworth and Barbara Holly combined their two businesses to form a partnership under the firm name of Woodworth and Holly. The balance sheets of the two sole proprietorships are as follows:

Woodworth's Antiques
Balance Sheet
June 30, 20 - -

Assets				Liabilities			
Cash		$ 7 1 0 0 00		Notes payable	$2 5 0 0 00		
Accounts receivable	$4 5 0 0 00			Accounts payable	8 4 0 0 00		
Less allowance for bad debts	6 2 0 00	3 8 8 0 00		Total liabilities		$10 9 0 0 00	
Merchandise inventory		21 4 3 0 00					
Store equipment	$8 2 0 0 00			Owner's Equity			
Less accumulated depreciation	1 3 0 0 00	6 9 0 0 00		Susan Woodworth, capital		28 4 1 0 00	
Total assets		$39 3 1 0 00		Total liabilities and owner's equity		$39 3 1 0 00	

Holly's Unfinished Furniture
Balance Sheet
June 30, 20 - -

Assets				Liabilities			
Cash		$ 4 5 2 0 00		Notes payable	$8 0 0 0 00		
Accounts receivable	$3 2 7 5 00			Accounts payable	6 3 0 0 00		
Less allowance for bad debts	4 7 5 00	2 8 0 0 00		Total liabilities		$14 3 0 0 00	
Merchandise inventory		28 1 9 0 00					
Supplies		9 6 0 00					
Office equipment	$7 4 0 0 00						
Less accumulated depreciation	1 8 0 0 00	5 6 0 0 00					
Store equipment	$7 7 0 0 00			Owner's Equity			
Less accumulated depreciation	1 5 0 0 00	6 2 0 0 00		Barbara Holly, capital		33 9 7 0 00	
Total assets		$48 2 7 0 00		Total liabilities and owner's equity		$48 2 7 0 00	

The balance sheets reflect fair market values except for the following:

a. The fair market value of Woodworth's store equipment is $7,500.

b. The fair market value of Holly's office equipment and store equipment are $6,100 and $6,800, respectively.

REQUIRED

Prepare the opening entry for the formation of the Woodworth and Holly partnership as of July 1, 20--, using fair market values. The difference between assets invested and liabilities assumed should be credited to each partner's capital account. Neither partner has knowledge of any uncollectible accounts receivable.

PROBLEM 21-7A   **(LO3)**

1. Allocation of net income:
   Hiller, $79,700;
2. Capital: Hiller, $69,100

PREPARING PARTIAL FINANCIAL STATEMENTS AND CLOSING ENTRIES The partnership of Hiller and Roundtree, CPAs, showed revenues of $195,000 and expenses of $52,000 on their year-end work sheet. Their capital balances as of January 1, 20--, were $52,000 for B. Hiller and $48,000 for O. Roundtree. No additional investments were made during the year. As stated in their partnership agreement, after withdrawing salary allowances of $60,000 for Hiller and $40,000 for Roundtree, the partners each withdrew 5% interest on their January 1 capital balances. No additional withdrawals were made. Any remaining net income is to be divided on a 45-55 basis.

REQUIRED

1. Prepare the lower portion of the income statement of the partnership for the year ended December 31, 20--, showing the division of the partnership net income for the year.

2. Prepare a statement of partners' equity for the year ended December 31, 20--, and the partners' equity section of the balance sheet on that date.

3. Prepare closing entries for the partnership as of December 31, 20--. (For simplicity, use the account titles "Revenues" for all revenues and "Expenses" for all expenses.)

PROBLEM 21-8A   **(LO4)**

1. Cr. to Mike Kelly,
   Capital: $5,000;
2. Dr. to Mike Kelly,
   Capital: $7,500

ENTRIES FOR DISSOLUTION OF PARTNERSHIP The Kelly and Kelly Wrecking Company, a partnership, operates a general demolition business. Ownership of the company is divided among the partners, Mike Kelly, Kim Kelly, Larry Dennis, and Jim Wheeles. Profits and losses are shared equally. The books are kept on a calendar year basis.

On September 15, after the business had been in operation for several years, Dennis died. Mrs. Dennis wished to sell her husband's interest in the partnership for $25,000. After the books were closed, the partners' capital accounts had credit balances as follows:

Mike Kelly	$50,000
Kim Kelly	25,000
Larry Dennis	35,000
Jim Wheeles	25,000

REQUIRED

1. Prepare the general journal entry required to enter the check issued to Mrs. Dennis in payment of her deceased husband's interest in the partnership. According to the partnership agreement, the difference between the amount paid to Mrs. Dennis and the book value of Larry Dennis' capital account is allocated to the remaining partners based on their ending capital account balances.

2. Assume instead that Mrs. Dennis is paid $50,000 for the book value of Larry Dennis' capital account. Prepare the necessary journal entry.

3. Assume instead that Jim Wheeles (with the consent of the remaining partners) purchased Dennis' interest for $40,000 and gave Mrs. Dennis a personal check for that amount. Prepare the general journal entry for the partnership only.

PROBLEM 21-9A   (LO5)

1. Cash distributed to partners:
   Baldwin, $55,000

STATEMENT OF PARTNERSHIP LIQUIDATION WITH GAIN After several years of operations, the partnership of Baldwin, Cowan, and Stewart is to be liquidated. After making closing entries on June 30, 20--, the following accounts remain open.

Account Title	Account Balance Debit	Credit
Cash	$ 5,000	
Inventory	55,000	
Other Assets	180,000	
Liabilities		$40,000
R. J. Baldwin, Capital		50,000
N. R. Cowan, Capital		90,000
K. M. Stewart, Capital		60,000

The noncash assets are sold for $250,000. Profits and losses are shared equally.

REQUIRED

1. Prepare a statement of partnership liquidation for the period July 1–20, 20--, showing the following:

   a. The sale of noncash assets on July 1

   b. The allocation of any gain or loss to the partners on July 1

   c. The payment of the liabilities on July 15

   d. The distribution of cash to the partners on July 20

2. Journalize these four transactions in a general journal.

PROBLEM 21-10A   (LO5)

1. Distribution of cash to partners: Nelson, $30,000

STATEMENT OF PARTNERSHIP LIQUIDATION WITH LOSS After several years of operations, the partnership of Nelson, Pope, and Williams is to be liquidated. After making closing entries on March 31, 20--, the following accounts remain open.

Account Title	Account Balance Debit	Credit
Cash	$ 15,000	
Inventory	40,000	
Other Assets	220,000	
Liabilities		$ 75,000
C. W. Nelson, Capital		40,000
J. R. Pope, Capital		60,000
M. L. Williams, Capital		100,000

The noncash assets are sold for $230,000. Profits and losses are shared equally.

REQUIRED

1. Prepare a statement of partnership liquidation for the period April 1–15, 20--, showing the following:

   a. The sale of the noncash assets on April 1

   b. The allocation of any gain or loss to the partners on April 1

   c. The payment of the liabilities on April 12

   d. The distribution of cash to the partners on April 15

2. Journalize these four transactions in a general journal.

SERIES B EXERCISES

EXERCISE 21-1B   **(LO1)**   **PARTNERSHIP OPENING ENTRIES** Sharon Usher and Leann Gomez agreed on September 1 to go into business as partners. According to the agreement, Usher is to contribute $30,000 cash and Gomez is to contribute $50,000 cash. Provide a separate journal entry for the investment of each partner.

EXERCISE 21-2B   **(LO2)**
4. Clark: $35,500

ENTRIES FOR ALLOCATION OF NET INCOME John Clark and David Haase decided to form a partnership on July 1, 20-6. Clark invested $60,000 and Haase invested $40,000. For the fiscal year ended June 30, 20-7, a net income of $80,000 was earned. Determine the amount of net income that Clark and Haase would receive under each of the following independent assumptions.

1. There is no agreement concerning the distribution of net income.

2. Each partner is to receive 10% interest on their original investment. The remaining net income is to be divided equally.

3. Clark and Haase are to receive a salary allowance of $25,000 and $30,000, respectively. The remaining net income is to be divided equally.

4. Each partner is to receive 10% interest on their original investment. Clark and Haase are to receive a salary allowance of $25,000 and $30,000, respectively. The remaining net income is to be divided as follows: Clark 30% and Haase 70%.

EXERCISE 21-3B   **(LO3)**
1. Allocation of net income:
   Nolan, $33,000;
2. Capital: Nolan, $78,000

PARTIAL FINANCIAL STATEMENTS Randy Nolan and Jill Brenton formed a partnership on May 1, 20-1. Nolan contributed $50,000 and Brenton contributed $25,000. During the year Nolan contributed an additional $10,000. The partnership agreement states that Nolan is to receive $15,000 and Brenton is to receive $50,000 as a salary allowance. Any remaining net income is to be divided as follows: Nolan 40% and Brenton 60%. The partnership earned net income of $110,000 for the fiscal year ending April 30, 20-2. During the first year of operation, Nolan and Brenton withdrew $15,000 and $40,000, respectively.

1. Prepare the lower portion of the income statement showing the allocation of net income between Nolan and Brenton for the fiscal year ended April 30, 20-2.

2. Prepare a statement of partners' equity, showing each individual partner's equity for the fiscal year ended April 30, 20-2.

EXERCISE 21-4B   **(LO4)**
2. Capital bal.: Rhodes, $60,000; Blair, $32,000

ADMITTING NEW PARTNERS Maria Rhodes and Craig Blair, who have ending capital balances of $90,000 and $40,000, respectively, agree to admit two new partners to their business on September 1, 20--. Lori Kinder will buy one-third of Rhodes' capital interest for $40,000 and one-fifth of Blair's capital interest for $12,000. Payments will be made directly to the partners. Todd Gilbert will invest $30,000 in the business for which he will receive a $30,000 capital interest.

1. Prepare general journal entries showing the transactions admitting Kinder and Gilbert to the partnership.

2. Calculate the ending capital balances of all four partners after the transactions.

EXERCISE 21-5B　　(LO5)
Loss: $16,000

ENTRIES: PARTNERSHIP LIQUIDATION On liquidation of the partnership of L. Straw and M. Maury, as of February 9, 20--, assets with a book value of $156,000 are sold for $140,000. Given that the profit-and-loss ratio is 60% for Straw and 40% for Maury, prepare the entries for the sale and the allocation of loss.

SERIES B PROBLEMS

PROBLEM 21-6B　　(LO1)
Cr. to Bush, Capital: $32,960

PARTNERSHIP OPENING ENTRIES On July 1, 20--, Lisa Bush and Wally Dodge combined their two businesses to form a partnership under the firm name of Bush and Dodge. The balance sheets of the two sole proprietorships are shown below. The balance sheets reflect fair market values except for the following:

a. The fair market value of Bush's store equipment is $7,350.

b. The fair market values of Dodge's office equipment and store equipment are $5,875 and $6,100, respectively.

REQUIRED

Prepare the opening entry for the formation of the Bush and Dodge partnership as of July 1, 20--, using fair market values. The difference between assets invested and liabilities assumed should be credited to each partner's capital account. Neither partner has knowledge of any uncollectible accounts receivable.

Bush's Grooming & Pet Supplies
Balance Sheet
June 30, 20 - -

Assets				Liabilities		
Cash		$ 4 6 0 0 00		Notes payable	$3 6 0 0 00	
Accounts receivable	$4 2 0 0 00			Accounts payable	7 6 9 0 00	
Less allowance for bad debts	4 8 0 00	3 7 2 0 00		Total liabilities		$11 2 9 0 00
Merchandise inventory		28 5 8 0 00				
Store equipment	$9 2 6 0 00			Owner's Equity		
Less accumulated depreciation	2 4 0 0 00	6 8 6 0 00		Lisa Bush, capital		32 4 7 0 00
Total assets		$43 7 6 0 00		Total liabilities and owner's equity		$43 7 6 0 00

Wally's Pet World
Balance Sheet
June 30, 20 - -

Assets				Liabilities		
Cash		$ 3 3 5 0 00		Notes payable	$6 0 0 0 00	
Accounts receivable	$4 1 5 0 00			Accounts payable	5 5 0 0 00	
Less allowance for bad debts	2 5 0 00	3 9 0 0 00		Total liabilities		$11 5 0 0 00
Merchandise inventory		27 2 4 0 00				
Supplies		8 4 5 00				
Office equipment	$8 8 3 0 00					
Less accumulated depreciation	3 4 0 0 00	5 4 3 0 00				
Store equipment	$9 1 7 5 00			Owner's Equity		
Less accumulated depreciation	4 2 5 0 00	4 9 2 5 00		Wally Dodge, capital		34 1 9 0 00
Total assets		$45 6 9 0 00		Total liabilities and owner's equity		$45 6 9 0 00

PROBLEM 21-7B   **(LO3)**

1. Allocation of net income:
   Rummel, $52,140;
2. Capital: Rummel, $46,040

PREPARING PARTIAL FINANCIAL STATEMENTS AND CLOSING ENTRIES The partnership of Rummel and Kang, Stonecutters, showed revenues of $133,000 and expenses of $41,000 on their year-end work sheet. Their capital balances as of January 1, 20--, were $41,000 for C. Rummel and $25,000 for V. Kang. No additional investments were made during the year. As stated in their partnership agreement, after withdrawing salary allowances of $43,000 for Rummel and $34,000 for Kang, the partners each withdrew 10% interest on their January 1 capital balances. No additional withdrawals were made. Any remaining net income is to be divided on a 60-40 basis.

REQUIRED

1. Prepare the lower portion of the income statement of the partnership for the year ended December 31, 20--, showing the division of the partnership net income for the year.

2. Prepare a statement of partners' equity for the year ended December 31, 20--, and the partners' equity section of the balance sheet on that date.

3. Prepare closing entries for the partnership as of December 31, 20--. (For simplicity, use the account titles "Revenues" for all revenues and "Expenses" for all expenses.)

PROBLEM 21-8B   **(LO4)**

1. Cr. to Cummings,
   Capital: $4,500;
2. Dr. to Cummings,
   Capital: $9,000

ENTRIES FOR DISSOLUTION OF PARTNERSHIP Cummings and Stickel Construction Company, a partnership, is operating a general contracting business. Ownership of the company is divided among the partners, Katie Cummings, Julie Stickel, Roy Hewson, and Patricia Weber. Profits and losses are shared equally. The books are kept on the calendar year basis.

On August 10, after the business had been in operation for several years, Patricia Weber died. Mr. Weber wished to sell his wife's interest for $30,000. After the books were closed, the partners' capital accounts had credit balances as follows:

Katie Cummings	$90,000
Julie Stickel	60,000
Roy Hewson	50,000
Patricia Weber	40,000

REQUIRED

1. Prepare the general journal entry required to enter the check issued to Mr. Weber in payment of his deceased wife's interest in the partnership. According to the partnership agreement, the difference between the amount paid to Mr. Weber and the book value of Patricia Weber's capital account is allocated to the remaining partners based on their ending capital account balances.

2. Assume instead that Mr. Weber is paid $60,000 for the book value of Patricia Weber's capital account. Prepare the necessary journal entry.

3. Assume instead that Julie Stickel (with the consent of the remaining partners) purchased Weber's interest for $70,000 and gave Mr. Weber a personal check for that amount. Prepare the general journal entry for the partnership only.

PROBLEM 21-9B   **(LO5)**

1. Cash distributed to partners:
   Leonard, $67,000

STATEMENT OF PARTNERSHIP LIQUIDATION WITH GAIN After several years of operations, the partnership of Leonard, Mitchell, and Swanson is to be liquidated. After making closing entries on June 30, 20--, the following accounts remain open.

Account Title	Account Balance Debit	Account Balance Credit
Cash	$ 4,000	
Inventory	40,000	
Other Assets	150,000	
Liabilities		$44,000
B. J. Leonard, Capital		60,000
W. T. Mitchell, Capital		15,000
J. C. Swanson, Capital		75,000

The noncash assets are sold for $211,000. Profits and losses are shared equally.

REQUIRED

1. Prepare a statement of partnership liquidation for the period July 1–20, 20--, showing the following:

   a. The sale of noncash assets on July 1

   b. The allocation of any gain or loss to the partners on July 1

   c. The payment of the liabilities on July 15

   d. The distribution of cash to the partners on July 20

2. Journalize these four transactions in a general journal.

PROBLEM 21-10B   **(LO5)**

1. Cash distributed to partners:
   Delco, $15,000

STATEMENT OF PARTNERSHIP LIQUIDATION WITH LOSS After several years of operations, the partnership of Delco, Smith, and Walker is to be liquidated. After making closing entries on March 31, 20--, the following accounts remain open.

Account Title	Account Balance Debit	Account Balance Credit
Cash	$ 7,000	
Inventory	25,000	
Other Assets	185,000	
Liabilities		$17,000
D. W. Delco, Capital		30,000
C. S. Smith, Capital		90,000
T. R. Walker, Capital		80,000

The noncash assets are sold for $165,000. Profits and losses are shared equally.

REQUIRED

1. Prepare a statement of partnership liquidation for the period April 1–15, 20--, showing the following:

   a. The sale of noncash assets on April 1

   b. The allocation of any gain or loss to the partners on April 1

   c. The payment of the liabilities on April 12

   d. The distribution of cash to the partners on April 15

2. Journalize these four transactions in a general journal.

MASTERY PROBLEM

2. Distribution of cash to partners: I. Fleming, $92,600

Jim Bond, a plumber, has been working for Fleming's Plumbing Supplies for several years. Based on his hard work and the fact that he recently married Ivan Fleming's daughter, Jim has been invited to enter into a partnership with Fleming. The new partnership will be called Fleming and Bond's Plumbing Supplies. The terms of the partnership are as follows:

a. Fleming will invest the assets of Fleming's Plumbing Supplies and the partnership will assume all liabilities. The market values of the office and store equipment are estimated to be $18,000 and $8,000, respectively. All other values reported on the balance sheet are reasonable approximations of market values. Fleming has no knowledge of any uncollectible accounts receivable.

b. Bond will invest $50,000 cash.

c. Fleming will draw a salary allowance of $50,000 per year and Bond will receive $30,000.

d. Each partner will receive 10% interest on the January 1 balance of his capital account.

e. Profits or losses remaining after allocating salaries and interest will be distributed as follows: Fleming 60% and Bond 40%.

Fleming's Plumbing Supplies
Balance Sheet
December 31, 20-1

Assets					Liabilities				
Cash			$ 13 5 4 4 00		Notes payable	$36 0 0 0 00			
Accounts receivable	$15 2 8 0 00				Accounts payable	18 0 8 2 00			
Less allowance for bad debts	1 7 2 0 00	13 5 6 0 00			Total liabilities			$ 54 0 8 2 00	
Merchandise inventory		89 6 9 2 00							
Supplies		1 2 8 6 00							
Office equipment	$14 3 2 0 00								
Less accumulated depreciation	1 1 0 0 00	13 2 2 0 00							
Store equipment	$ 8 8 0 0 00				**Owner's Equity**				
Less accumulated depreciation	2 2 0 0 00	6 6 0 0 00			Ivan Fleming, capital			83 8 2 0 00	
Total assets		$137 9 0 2 00			Total liabilities and owner's equity			$137 9 0 2 00	

REQUIRED

1. Prepare the entries on January 1, 20-2, for the formation of the partnership.

2. Net income for the partnership for 20-2 was $150,000. Prepare the lower portion of the income statement reporting the allocation of the profits to each partner.

3. In December, 20-4, Fleming's daughter, Penny, graduated from business college and asked to join the business as a partner. She has $30,000 to invest and it is agreed that Penny will be given a capital interest of $30,000. Profits and losses will be shared as follows: I. Fleming, 50%; J. Bond, 30%; P. Fleming, 20%. Prepare the entry for Penny's investment on January 1, 20-5.

4. After several years of operations, it is decided to liquidate the partnership. After making closing entries on July 31, 20-9, the following accounts remain open.

Cash	$ 20,000	
Inventory	150,000	
Office Equipment	30,000	
Accum. Depreciation—Office Equipment		$18,000
Store Equipment	22,000	
Accum. Depreciation—Store Equipment		15,000
Notes Payable		20,000
Ivan Fleming, Capital		80,000
Jim Bond, Capital		50,000
Penny Fleming, Capital		39,000

    a. On August 1, 20-9, the inventory is sold for $130,000.

    b. On August 3, the office equipment is sold for $10,000.

    c. On August 5, the store equipment is sold for $12,000.

    d. On August 10, the notes payable are paid.

    e. On August 15, the remaining cash is distributed to the partners according to the balances in their capital accounts.

    Prepare a statement of partnership liquidation and related journal entries for the period August 1–15, 20-9.

CHALLENGE PROBLEM

This problem challenges you to apply your cumulative accounting knowledge to move a step beyond the material in the chapter.

Allocation of net income:
Dewi, $122,500

The partnership agreement for the law firm of Dewi, Cheetem, and Howe states that net income should be allocated in the following manner:

1. Salaries are to be paid as follows:
    *   Dewi, $50,000 per year   *   Howe, $20,000 per year
    *   Cheetem, $40,000 per year

2. Each partner is to be paid a bonus of 25% of all revenues he or she generated. During 20-1, each partner generated the following revenues:
    *   Dewi, $250,000   *   Howe, $100,000
    *   Cheetem, $150,000

3. Each partner receives 10% interest on the beginning balance of his or her capital account. Beginning balances of the capital accounts are as follows:
    *   Dewi, $200,000   *   Howe, $50,000
    *   Cheetem, $100,000

Net income for the year ended December 31, 20-1, was $240,000.

REQUIRED

Prepare the lower portion of the income statement showing the allocation of net income to Dewi, Cheetem, and Howe.

COMPREHENSIVE PROBLEM 3: SPECIALIZED ACCOUNTING PROCEDURES

Siblings Jordan and Morgan Hartley are partners in a trendy toy store called ToyMania! Jordan, as senior partner, receives an annual salary allowance of $20,000 and 60 percent of all income/losses after salary and interest allowances are paid. Junior partner Morgan receives an annual salary allowance of $15,000 and 40 percent of all income/losses after salary and interest allowances are paid. The partners receive a 10 percent interest allowance at the end of the accounting period based on their respective January 1 capital account balances. Capital balances as of January 1 are $60,000 for Jordan Hartley and $40,000 for Morgan Hartley.

ToyMania! uses the allowance method for uncollectible accounts. Credit terms are 2/10, n/30. Longer payment terms are available by accepting interest-bearing notes receivable. Terms will vary depending on individual circumstances and will be provided in the related transactions. Notes under $1,000 are collected by ToyMania! while notes greater than $1,000 are collected by either Dean Bank or Marshall Bank. Interest is based on a 360-day year. Estimated uncollectibles are based on 3 percent of accounts receivable. Accounts are written off, as they are deemed uncollectible; however, efforts to collect all receivables continue for a two year period.

ToyMania! occasionally writes notes to finance larger purchases and to extend time on accounts payable. Terms will be specified in the related transactions. Again, interest is based on a 360-day year.

Plant assets are depreciated using one of the various GAAP methods for depreciation. Fully depreciated assets that are useful remain in service until a sale, trade, or disposal is necessary. ToyMania! holds a patent on a toy which is amortized during year-end adjustments. The $25,000 patent's economic life is 10 years although the legal life is 20 years.

A periodic inventory system is maintained valuing inventory using the First-In, First-Out (FIFO) method. The lower-of-cost-or-market rule is applied by recognizing a loss on write-down of inventory when necessary. Beginning merchandise inventory on January 1 was $91,250.

Transactions for 20-1 are provided below.

Jan. 5	Reinstated the account of Christine Roby, which had been written off in the preceding year, and received $500 cash in full settlement.
14	Issued a $3,000, 3-month, 6% note to Zekir Computer Systems to purchase a new computer system (*Computer System*). The system, with an expected life of four years and no salvage value, will be depreciated using the double-declining-balance method.
Feb. 15	Received a $2,500, 6-month, 7% note from Carol Reynolds for sale of merchandise.
Mar. 11	Morgan Hartley invested an additional $5,000 into the business.
Apr. 1	Disposed of a cash register (*Store Equipment*) originally costing $675 with a $75 salvage value. Depreciation is computed on a monthly basis with adjusting entries made at the end of each year. Depreciation after eight years of use was $480 as of December 31. The cash register had an estimated life of 10 years.
12	Borrowed $5,000 from Dean Bank signing a 75-day, 10% note.
14	Paid $500, plus interest, to Zekir Computer Systems (see January 14) and gave a new $2,500, 30-day, 8% note to extend time for payment.
May 1	Wrote off the $1,200 balance owed by Brenda Husband as uncollectible.
14	Paid the principal and interest due on the $2,500 note to Zekir Computer Systems. (See April 14.)
25	Paid $75 cash to Snowden Service Station for an oil change, tire rotation, and coolant flushing on the van.

June 1   Received a $1,700, 120-day, 8% note from Heidi Kruczkiewicz to settle an account receivable.

20   Reinstated the account of Brenda Husband, which had been written off last month, and received $1,200 cash in full settlement. (See May 1.)

22   Paid $30,000 cash to Klippi Construction for an addition (Addition) to the store so that more merchandise could be displayed. The addition has an estimated salvage value of $2,000 and an estimated life of 20 years. Depreciation is to be calculated using the straight-line method.

26   Paid the principal and interest due on the $5,000 note to Dean Bank. (See April 12.)

30   Upon opening the store, it was apparent that someone had entered the store illegally. Jordan and Morgan need to determine whether anything had been stolen. A physical inventory was taken and it was determined that approximately $67,500 in inventory was on hand, but they need to know how much inventory should have been on hand. Estimate the cost using the retail method based on the following information. Figures at cost: beginning inventory, $91,250; and net purchases, $70,000. Figures at retail: beginning inventory, $120,000; net purchases $95,000; and net sales, $125,000. Compare your estimate with the balance of $67,500. Does it appear that any inventory was stolen? *Space is provided for your calculations following the journal pages for the problem in your working papers.*

July 1   Heidi Kruczkiewicz's note (see June 1) is discounted at Marshall Bank at a discount rate of 12%.

8   Sold $4,250 in merchandise to Kim Sackett, terms 2/10, n/30.

10   Purchased merchandise on account for $15,000 from Dionis Distributing. Credit terms are 3/20, n/30.

18   Received payment in full from Kim Sackett, less discount, for merchandise sold on July 8.

30   Paid Dionis Distributing for merchandise purchased on account on July 10.

Aug. 1   Paid $500 to Snowden's Service Station to replace the exhaust system on the company van.

15   Received notification from Dean Bank that the principal and interest were collected on the note from Carol Reynolds. (See February 15.) The bank fee for collecting the note was $10.

22   Wrote off the $750 balance owed by Shelley Kozub as uncollectible.

Sept. 1   Traded the company car (Automobile) for a more stylish one at Plume Motors. The old car originally cost $13,000 and is depreciated up-to-date in the amount of $9,000. A trade-in allowance of $5,500 was given. The new car had a market value of $18,000 and the balance was paid in cash. The new car should last at least 100,000 miles and will be depreciated at $.375 per mile.

9   Received a $2,000, 60-day, 7.5% note from Tammy Jones in payment of an account receivable.

15   Purchased $3,500 worth of toys from Dennis Designs, terms n/30.

29   Received notification from Marshall Bank that Heidi Kruczkiewicz's note was dishonored. (See June 1 and July 1.) A check is issued to cover the maturity value plus a $50 bank fee that must be paid to the bank.

Oct. 15   Issued a $3,500, 90-day, 8% note to Dennis Designs to extend time for payment on an account payable.

20   Borrowed $10,000 for 180 days from Ohler-Cupplo Savings Association on a non-interest-bearing note. The discount rate is 7.5%.

31   Sold $125 of merchandise for cash to Melinda Miller.

Nov. 1   Received a $500, 30-day, 5% note from Laura Nottingham in payment of an account receivable.

8   Received notification from Marshall Bank that Tammy Jones dishonored her note. (See September 9.) No fee was charged.

30   Heidi Kruczkiewicz's dishonored note is collected; Kruczkiewicz pays ToyMania! the maturity value of the note, the $50 bank fee, and interest at 9% on the maturity value plus bank fee. (See September 29.)

Dec. 1   Laura Nottingham paid the interest due on her note (see November 1), and gave a new note ($500) for 45 days at 8%.

14   Paid $2,000 to landscape and improve a grassy area on the lot. There will be no salvage value after 5 years and the landscaping will be depreciated using the sum-of-the-years' digits method.

31   Sold building fixtures for $100. The original cost of the fixtures was $500 with an estimated 5-year life and no salvage value. Depreciation up-to-date is $300.

REQUIRED

1. Journalize the above transactions as needed.

2. Prepare selected adjusting entries using the following information.
    (a)   Accrued interest receivable. (See December 1.)
    (b)   Accrued interest payable. *Separate entries should be made for discounted and non-discounted notes.* (See October 15 and October 20.)
    (c)   Depreciation for the year on the computer system put into service on January 14.
    (d)   Depreciation for the year on the new car. 7,000 miles were traveled this period.
    (e)   Depreciation for the year on the addition completed June 22.
    (f)   Depreciation for the year on the landscaping recorded December 14.
    (g)   Annual amortization on the patent.
    (h)   Estimated uncollectibles are based on accounts receivable of $48,940. Current Allowance for Bad Debts balance is $375 credit.
    (i, j)   Ending inventory valued at cost on December 31 is $102,000.
    (k)   Ending inventory valued at market prices on December 31 is $100,500.

3. Prepare the following financial statements:
    (a)   Partial Income Statement showing the allocation of net income. ToyMania! had a net income of $84,000 for the year. Each partner made withdrawals equal to his/her salary and interest allowances as stated in the partnership agreement.
    (b)   Statement of Partners' Equity. No additional withdrawals were made after salary and interest allowances were allocated.

4. Prepare selected closing entries, referring to the financial statements as needed.
    (a)   Close Income Summary to the Capital accounts.
    (b)   Close Drawing accounts to the Capital accounts.

5. Prepare reversing entries when appropriate.

6. Journalize the following transactions that occurred in the subsequent year.

Jan. 13   Paid the principal and interest due on the $3,500 note to Dennis Designs. (See October 15.)

15   Laura Nottingham paid her note plus interest. (See December 1.)

Apr. 16   Paid the principal on the $10,000 non-interest-bearing note to Ohler-Cupplo Savings Association. (See October 20.)

©CORBIS

Accounting for Corporations and Manufacturing Businesses

Corporations: Organization and Capital Stock

Mike Finbar has produced upper-end, specialty acoustic guitars for ten years. Starting out as a small operation in Mike's basement, the business now produces a range of acoustic guitars, mandolins, and banjos at three production facilities. In response to customer inquiries, Mike is considering expanding by adding acoustic-electric and electric instruments. The problem is that this will require a major increase in capital for new kinds of production equipment. His new accountant, who just completed his college degree, suggests that Mike consider incorporating. He says this will solve the problem of raising capital and also provide other benefits. What would be the advantages and disadvantages for Mike to incorporate?

Careful study of this chapter should enable you to:

LO1 Describe the characteristics, formation, and organization of a corporation.

LO2 Describe stockholders' equity and the types of capital stock, and compute dividends on preferred and common stock.

LO3 Account for capital stock transactions.

LO4 Prepare the stockholders' equity section of the corporate balance sheet.

For most of this text we have studied accounting for sole proprietorships. In Chapter 21, we focused on the partnership form of business. In this chapter, we turn our attention to the third type of business organization—the corporation.

It is important to learn about corporations because they play a major role in the economy. More businesses are organized as sole proprietorships and partnerships than as corporations in the United States. But corporations sell more goods and services in total than do sole proprietorships and partnerships combined.

THE CORPORATION

LO1 Describe the characteristics, formation, and organization of a corporation.

A corporation is a legal entity that exists separate and distinct from its owners. This is the key difference between corporations, sole proprietorships, and partnerships. The assets of sole proprietorships and partnerships legally belong to the owners. The liabilities of such businesses are legal liabilities of the owners. In contrast, a corporation's assets and liabilities are those of the business, not the owners. A corporation can own property, enter into contracts, and incur debt in its own name. It can sue and be sued.

Advantages and Disadvantages

In comparison with sole proprietorships and partnerships, the corporate form of organization offers five advantages:

1. *Limited liability of owners.* The owners of a corporation generally have no personal liability for the debts of the corporation. Their financial responsibility is limited to the amount they have invested. The limited liability feature is a major reason for the popularity of the corporate form of organization.

2. *Transferable ownership units.* The owners' equity in a corporation is called **capital stock**. The capital stock is divided into **shares** representing ownership rights in the corporation. These shares can be transferred from one person to another without the consent of the other owners and without disturbing the corporation's normal activities.

3. *Ease of raising capital.* The limited liability and transferable ownership characteristics make the corporation an attractive investment for many people. Therefore, a corporation generally can obtain capital by selling additional shares of stock.

4. *No mutual agency.* **Mutual agency** means that each owner has the power to act as an agent and engage in contracts for a business. In a corporation, individual owners do *not* have such power, unless the other owners have granted it to them.

5. *Unlimited life.* A corporation's life is specified in its charter. The charter either states the life as perpetual or provides for renewal if a limit is indicated. Changes of ownership through transfer of shares or death of owners have no effect on the life of a corporation.

Two disadvantages of the corporate form of organization are:

1. *Taxation of earnings.* A major disadvantage is that corporations must pay income taxes. In contrast, sole proprietorships and partnerships do not pay income taxes. The earnings of sole proprietorships and partnerships are taxed only as the personal income of the owners.

   In addition to the corporate income tax, the corporation's owners pay personal income tax on dividends they receive. **Dividends** are distributions of corporate income to the owners. Taxing corporate income both to the company that earns it and to the owners who receive it is called **double taxation**.

2. *Government regulation.* The corporation's activities may be regulated by federal, state, and local laws. These laws may restrict the corporation's ownership of real property, the purchase of its own stock, and the retention of its earnings. If a corporation does business in several states, each state may impose its own financial and tax reporting requirements.

Forming a Corporation

In the United States, the power to create corporations rests largely with the states. To form a corporation, the **incorporators** file an application with the state in which the company is to be incorporated. After the application is approved, a legal document called a **charter**, or **articles of incorporation**, is prepared. The contents of the charter may vary, but it typically includes:

1. Name of the corporation

2. Location of the principal office

3. Purpose of the business

4. Description of the capital stock

5. Names and addresses of the incorporators

After the state approves the charter, the incorporators meet to elect a temporary board of directors and to prepare the corporation **bylaws**. The charter and bylaws provide the general guidelines for conducting the business.

Next, the corporation issues capital stock. Those who buy the stock become owners, and are known as **stockholders**. Each stockholder receives a form called a **stock certificate** that shows the name of the stockholder and the number of shares owned.

Organization of a Corporation

The stockholders elect a **board of directors**. The board of directors determines corporate policies and selects the corporate officers. The officers generally manage the corporation and are responsible to the board. The officers usually consist of the president, one or more vice presidents, a secretary, and a treasurer. Figure 22-1 illustrates a common corporate organization, from the owners/stockholders through the employees.

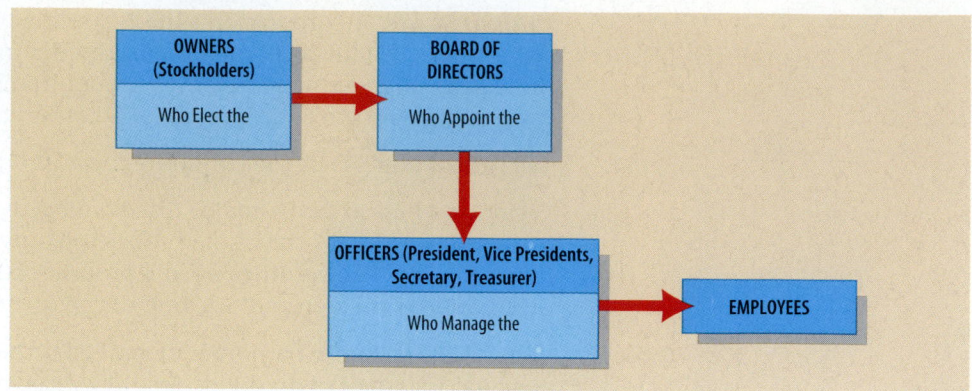

FIGURE 22-1   Corporate Organization

Organization Costs

The costs of organizing a corporation, such as incorporation fees, attorneys' fees, and promotion expenses, are called **organization costs**. Organization costs may be viewed as benefiting the entire life of a corporation, but accepted practice is to record them as expenses as they are incurred.

Assume that Neo Company was billed $8,000 for incorporation and attorney's fees. The journal entry for this transaction is as follows:

4	Organization Expenses	8 0 0 0 00		4
5	Accounts Payable		8 0 0 0 00	5
6	Corporate organization costs			6
7				7

Organization expenses are reported under Other Expenses on the income statement.

STOCKHOLDERS' EQUITY AND TYPES OF CAPITAL STOCK

LO2 Describe stockholders' equity and the types of capital stock, and compute dividends on preferred and common stock.

A corporation's asset, liability, revenue, and expense accounts are generally the same as those for a sole proprietorship or partnership. The owners' equity accounts, however, are quite different, as shown in T account form in Figure 22-2.

In sole proprietorships and partnerships, the owners' capital accounts are affected by three types of events, identified by number in Figure 22-2.

1. Initial and subsequent investments in the business

2. Net income or losses during the life of the business

3. Withdrawals by the owners

The only difference between the sole proprietorship and partnership accounts is that the partnership has multiple capital and drawing accounts. The drawing accounts represent the amount withdrawn from the business during a given accounting period. Recall that each partner's drawing account is closed to his or her capital account. This closing process is shown as item 4 in the T accounts.

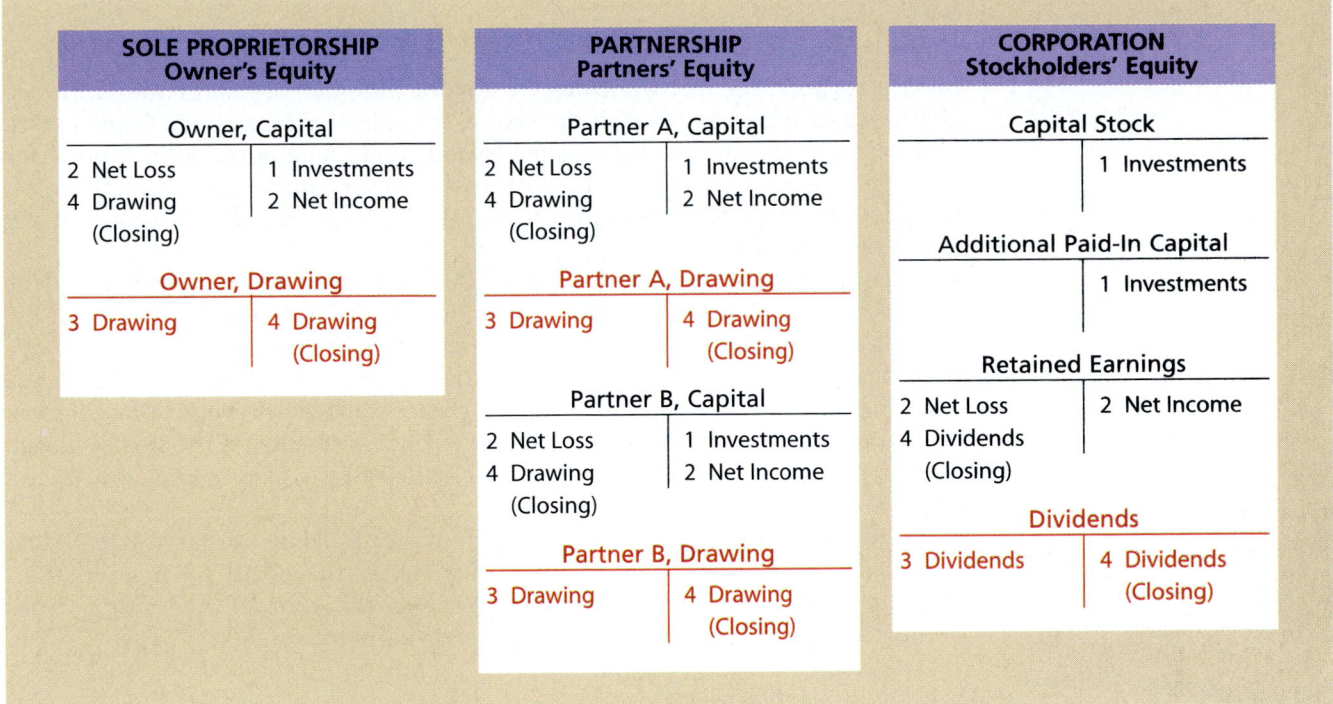

FIGURE 22-2 Owners' Equity Accounts

In a corporation, owners' equity is called **stockholders' equity**. More importantly, a distinction is made between capital invested by the owners and earnings retained in the business. The amount paid by the stockholders for their shares of stock is called **paid-in capital** and is generally recorded in two new types of accounts: Capital Stock and Additional Paid-In Capital. Both accounts are reported as part of stockholders' equity. These accounts will be explained in the following sections.

A corporation's net income (loss) is credited (debited) to Retained Earnings. Dividends are equivalent to withdrawals in a sole proprietorship or partnership. Dividends are debited to the dividends account in the same way that withdrawals are debited to Drawing in the sole proprietorship or partnership. Similarly, the dividends account is closed to Retained Earnings in the same way that Drawing is closed to the capital accounts in a sole proprietorship or partnership. Thus, **retained earnings** represents the accumulated earnings of the corporation that have not been paid out to stockholders as dividends.

We will look at a complete illustration of the stockholders' equity section of the corporate balance sheet near the end of the chapter. But to help you picture the paid-in capital and retained earnings accounts described here, Figure 22-3 illustrates the general format of the stockholders' equity section.

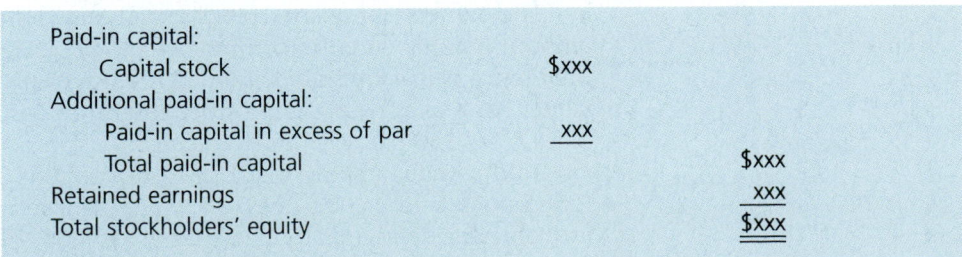

FIGURE 22-3 Stockholders' Equity Section Format

Capital Stock

Ownership rights in a corporation are represented by shares of capital stock issued by the corporation to the owners. The total number of shares the corporate charter authorizes a corporation to issue is called **authorized stock**. Capital stock that has been sold and issued is called **issued stock**. A corporation may buy back some of its own stock. This stock is known as **treasury stock**. The issued stock less treasury stock equals **outstanding stock**, which is the number of shares in the hands of stockholders.

Shares of stock commonly have a dollar amount per share printed on the stock certificate. This dollar amount is known as the **par value** of the stock. Par value is strictly a legal matter and has no direct relationship to the market value per share. **Market value** is the amount for which the stock can be sold on the open market. The par value has accounting importance, however, because it must be recorded in the capital stock account when stock is issued. If the stock is issued for more than its par value, the excess is credited to the paid-in capital in excess of par account.

Stock that has no dollar amount printed on it is called **no-par stock**. No-par stock sometimes is assigned a value per share by the board of directors. This amount is known as the **stated value** of the stock. From an accounting standpoint, par value and stated value stock are virtually the same.

A corporation must maintain detailed records of who owns all shares of its stock.

Common Stock

If a corporation issues only one class or type of stock, each share gives its owner the right to:

1. Vote at stockholders' meetings

2. Share in earnings distributions

3. Purchase additional shares in proportion to the owner's present holding, if more shares are issued by the corporation. (This is called a **preemptive right**.)

4. Share in the assets if the corporation liquidates

Such stock is called **common stock**.

Preferred Stock

Corporations sometimes issue two classes of stock—common stock and preferred stock. **Preferred stock** is stock that gives its owner certain preferences or rights superior to those of common stock. Usually these preferences pertain to dividends or to distribution of assets at liquidation. To obtain these preferences, owners of preferred stock usually do not have one or more of the four rights stated previously. For example, preferred stock owners typically have no voting rights.

The owners of preferred stock usually have the right to dividends of a certain amount before owners of common stock can receive any dividends. The dividend preference is usually stated as a dollar amount per share or as a percentage of par value. For example, preferred stock might be described as "$50 par, $4 preferred stock," or "$50 par, 8% preferred stock."

To illustrate, assume that Pref Company has 2,000 shares of $50 par, $4 preferred stock, and 2,000 shares of $10 par common stock outstanding. The amount available for dividends for the year is $14,000. This $14,000 would be allocated between the preferred and common shares as follows:

1. Total amount available for dividends $14,000
2. Dividend to preferred stock:
   2,000 shares × $4   8,000
3. Amount available for common stock $ 6,000

   Dividends per share:
   Preferred stock $4
   Common stock ($6,000 ÷ 2,000 shares) $3

Cumulative and Noncumulative Preferred Stock. Preferred stock on which any unpaid dividends accumulate from year to year is called **cumulative preferred stock**. The accumulated amounts and the current year preferred dividends must be paid to the preferred stockholders before the common stockholders can receive any dividends.

Preferred stock on which dividend claims do not accumulate from year to year is called **noncumulative preferred stock**. If in one year dividends are not declared, there is no carryover of dividends to the following years.

Assume that the Pref Company described in the previous illustration declared no dividends in Year 1 of operation and $22,000 in Year 2. Neither the preferred stock nor the common stock owners would receive any dividends in Year 1. The dividends in Year 2 for the cumulative and noncumulative preferred stock situations would be as follows:

	Year 2			
	Cumulative		Noncumulative	
Total amount available for dividends		$22,000		$22,000
Cumulative preferred dividend from prior year (2,000 shares × $4)	$8,000		$ 0	
Preferred dividend—current year (2,000 shares × $4)	8,000	16,000	8,000	8,000
Amount available for common stock		$ 6,000		$14,000
Dividends per share:				
Preferred		$8		$4
Common ($6,000 ÷ 2,000 shares)		$3		
($14,000 ÷ 2,000 shares)				$7

The cumulative feature of preferred stock is an important preference. Most preferred stock issued today is cumulative.

Participating and Nonparticipating Preferred Stock. Participating preferred stock gives its owners the right to share with common stock owners in dividends in excess of a stated dividend rate. If preferred dividends are limited to the stated dividend rate, the stock is called **nonparticipating**. It is unusual to find the participation feature in preferred stock today.

CAPITAL STOCK TRANSACTIONS

LO3 **Account for capital stock transactions.**

Corporations issue capital stock in exchange for cash and noncash assets. Issuance for cash is the most common transaction.

Issuing Par Value Stock at Par

If capital stock is issued at par for cash, Cash is debited and Common Stock or Preferred Stock is credited for the amount received. Assume that Linc Corp. issues 10,000 shares of $5 par common stock at par for $50,000 cash. The journal entry for this transaction is:

5	Cash	50 0 0 0 00		5
6	Common Stock		50 0 0 0 00	6
7	Issued common stock at par			7

LEARNING KEY: Record the sale of par value stock at a price above par by debiting Cash and by crediting Capital Stock and Paid-In Capital in Excess of Par.

Issuing Par Value Stock at a Premium

If stock is issued at a price above par, the amount received above par is known as a **premium**. Enter this transaction as follows:

1. Debit Cash for the amount received.

2. Credit Common Stock or Preferred Stock for the par amount.

3. Credit Paid-In Capital in Excess of Par for the amount above par.

©GETTY IMAGES/PHOTODISC

A BROADER VIEW

Did You Say Company or Country?

This chapter introduces the corporate form of business. Corporations tend to be the largest business enterprises. In fact, the size of some corporations can be difficult to imagine. One way to appreciate the magnitude of some of the largest corporations is to compare them with countries.

In economic terms, the gross domestic product of a country is comparable to the sales of a corporation. Based on these yardsticks, consider the following:

1. Based on sales, Wal-Mart Stores is the largest corporation in America. Its sales are larger than the gross domestic product of Austria or Sweden.

2. General Motors ranks second. Its sales are larger than the gross domestic product of Poland, Denmark, or Turkey.

3. Home Depot, which ranks 13th, has sales larger than the gross domestic product of New Zealand.

These comparisons give real meaning to the expression "big business."

Assume that Linc Corp. issues 10,000 shares of $5 par common stock for $60,000 cash. The journal entry for this transaction is:

5		Cash		60	0	0	0	00											5
6		Common Stock*								50	0	0	0	00					6
7		Paid-In Capital in Excess of Par—																	7
8		Common Stock**								10	0	0	0	00					8
9		Issued common stock at a premium																	9
10																			10
11		* 10,000 shares × $5 par																	11
12		**$60,000 cash received – $50,000 par value of stock																	12

As shown in Figure 22-3 on page 835, Paid-In Capital in Excess of Par is reported as an addition to paid-in capital on the balance sheet.

Issuing Par Value Stock at a Discount

If par value stock is issued at a price below par, the difference between the par amount and the amount received is called a **discount**. Enter this transaction as follows:

1. Debit Cash for the amount received.

2. Debit Discount on Common Stock or Discount on Preferred Stock for the difference between the par amount and the amount received.

3. Credit Common Stock or Preferred Stock for the par amount.

LEARNING KEY: Record the sale of par value stock at a price below par by debiting Cash and Discount on Capital Stock, and by crediting Capital Stock.

Assume that Linc Corp. issues 2,000 shares of $50 par, 8% preferred stock for $96,000 cash. The journal entry for this transaction is:

5		Cash		96	0	0	0	00										5
6		Discount on Preferred Stock*		4	0	0	0	00										6
7		Preferred Stock**								100	0	0	0	00				7
8		Issued preferred stock at a discount																8
9																		9
10		* $100,000 par value – $96,000 cash received																10
11		** 2,000 shares × $50 par																11

Discount on Preferred Stock is reported as a deduction from paid-in capital on the balance sheet.

Stock is seldom issued at a discount for three reasons:

1. Firms generally set very low par values.

2. The purchaser is liable to the corporation's creditors for the difference between the par value and the amount paid.

3. This practice is illegal in many states.

Issuing Stock with a Stated Value

If no-par stock has a stated value, this value is treated virtually the same as par value in the accounts. Only a slight change in account titles is needed.

LEARNING KEY: Record the sale of no-par stock with a stated value in virtually the same manner as the sale of par value stock.

Regardless of the amount for which par value or stated value stock is issued, the credit to Capital Stock is always for the par or stated value.

Assume that Stat Company issues 5,000 shares of no-par common stock with a stated value of $10 per share for $70,000 cash. The journal entry for this transaction is:

5	Cash	70	0	0	0	00	5
6	Common Stock*			50	0	0	0	00	6
7	Paid-In Capital in Excess of Stated Value—				7
8	Common Stock**			20	0	0	0	00	8
9	Issued common stock at a premium				9
10					10
11	* 5,000 shares × $10 stated value				11
12	** $70,000 cash received – $50,000 stated				12
13	value of stock				13

Like Paid-In Capital in Excess of Par, Paid-In Capital in Excess of Stated Value is reported as an addition to paid-in capital on the balance sheet.

Issuing No-Par Stock

Accounting for the issuance of no-par stock is generally simpler than for stock with a par or stated value. If no-par stock is issued, Cash is debited and Common Stock or Preferred Stock is credited for the amount received. No premium or discount is entered, regardless of the amount received.

LEARNING KEY: Record the sale of no-par stock by debiting Cash and crediting Capital Stock.

Assume that Noll Company issues 5,000 shares of no-par common stock for $70,000 cash. The journal entry for this transaction is:

5	Cash	70	0	0	0	00	5
6	Common Stock			70	0	0	0	00	6
7	Issued common stock				7

Similarly, if Noll issues 5,000 shares of no-par common stock for $40,000 cash, the journal entry is:

5	Cash	40	0	0	0	00	5
6	Common Stock			40	0	0	0	00	6
7	Issued common stock				7

Issuing Stock for Noncash Assets

Each transaction illustrated thus far has involved issuance of stock for cash. Corporations also sometimes issue stock for noncash assets. The accounting for this transaction can be more complicated because the value of the noncash assets received may need to be determined.

If stock is issued for noncash assets, follow this guideline:

The assets received are recorded at the fair market value of the assets or of the stock, whichever can be more clearly determined.

Once the value of the noncash assets or the stock is determined, the journal entry for the stock issuance is very similar to those involving cash. Assume that Linc Corp. issues 5,000 shares of $5 par common stock for a truck. Linc's stock is not actively traded, so its market value is difficult to determine, but the truck has a known fair market value of $30,000. Thus, the fair market value of the truck is used to record this transaction. The journal entry is:

11		Truck	30 0 0 0 00				11
12		Common Stock*		25 0 0 0 00			12
13		Paid-In Capital in Excess of Par—					13
14		Common Stock**		5 0 0 0 00			14
15		Issued common stock at a premium					15
16							16
17		* 5,000 shares × $5 par					17
18		**$30,000 fair market value of truck					18
19		received – $25,000 par value of stock					19

Assume instead that Linc Corp. issues 10,000 shares of $5 par common stock for a building with several different appraisal values. Linc's stock is actively traded and has a fair market value of $7 per share. In this case, the fair market value of the stock, $70,000 (10,000 shares × $7), is used to record this transaction. The journal entry is:

15		Building	70 0 0 0 00				15
16		Common Stock*		50 0 0 0 00			16
17		Paid-In Capital in Excess of Par—					17
18		Common Stock**		20 0 0 0 00			18
19		Issued common stock at a premium					19
20							20
21		* 10,000 shares × $5 par					21
22		**$70,000 fair market value of stock					22
23		– $50,000 par value of stock					23

Capital Stock Subscriptions

Corporations sometimes accept subscriptions for capital stock. A **capital stock subscription** is an agreement in which a buyer (**subscriber**) contracts to buy shares of stock from a corporation at a specific price. The subscriber generally agrees to pay the amount in full on a specified date or in installments. The corporation does not issue the stock until the subscriber makes the full payment.

Accounting for stock subscriptions requires the use of some new accounts. Assume that Linc Corp. received subscriptions for 10,000 shares of its $5 par common stock for $60,000. The journal entry for this transaction is:

8		Common Stock Subscriptions Receivable	60	0	0	0	00									8
9		Common Stock Subscribed*						50	0	0	0	00					9
10		Paid-In Capital in Excess of Par—															10
11		Common Stock**						10	0	0	0	00					11
12		Received subscriptions for common stock															12
13																	13
14		* 10,000 shares × $5 par															14
15		**$60,000 subscription amount −															15
16		$50,000 par value of stock															16

Common Stock Subscriptions Receivable looks like an asset, but current practice generally calls for treating it as a contra-equity account. It is reported as a deduction from the total of paid-in capital and retained earnings on the balance sheet. Common Stock Subscribed and Paid-In Capital in Excess of Par are reported as additions to paid-in capital on the balance sheet.

As the subscriber makes payments on the stock, the Common Stock Subscriptions Receivable balance is decreased. If the subscriber to Linc Corp.'s shares makes a payment of $40,000, the following journal entry is made.

25		Cash	40	0	0	0	00									25
26		Common Stock Subscriptions Receivable						40	0	0	0	00					26
27		Received subscription payment															27

> Controversy exists regarding the proper balance sheet presentation of Common Stock Subscriptions Receivable. Some sources say it is an asset; others say it is contra-owners' equity. The SEC generally requires the contra-owners' equity treatment.

When the stock subscription has been fully paid, the corporation issues the stock. At this point, Common Stock Subscribed is debited and Common Stock is credited for the par amount of $50,000. The $10,000 premium on the stock issuance was already credited to Paid-In Capital in Excess of Par—Common Stock at the time the subscription was recorded. Assume the subscriber to Linc Corp.'s shares makes the final payment of $20,000 and Linc issues the 10,000 shares. The following journal entries are made.

5		Cash	20	0	0	0	00									5
6		Common Stock Subscriptions Receivable						20	0	0	0	00					6
7		Received subscription payment															7
8																	8
9		Common Stock Subscribed	50	0	0	0	00									9
10		Common Stock						50	0	0	0	00					10
11		Issued common stock															11

Subscriptions at par or below par, for no-par stock, and for stated value stock are accounted for in a similar manner. The only new accounts that require special care are the same in each instance: Common (or Preferred) Stock Subscriptions Receivable and Common (or Preferred) Stock Subscribed.

Treasury Stock

When a company buys back some of its own shares of stock, these shares are called treasury stock. When a corporation purchases its own stock, Treasury Stock is debited for the cost of the stock, regardless of any par or stated value. Assume

Linc Corp. purchases 3,000 shares of its $5 par common stock for $6 per share, a total of $18,000. The journal entry for this transaction is:

5		Common Treasury Stock	18 0 0 0 00		5
6		Cash		18 0 0 0 00	6
7		Purchased treasury stock			7

If treasury stock is subsequently sold, the transaction is handled as follows:

1. Cash is debited for the amount received.

2. Treasury Stock is credited for its cost.

3. Any difference between the amount received and the cost is debited or credited to Paid-In Capital from Sale of Treasury Stock.

Assume that Linc Corp. sells 2,000 of the 3,000 treasury shares for $7 per share, a total of $14,000. The journal entry is:

15		Cash	14 0 0 0 00		15
16		Common Treasury Stock*		12 0 0 0 00	16
17		Paid-In Capital from Sale of Treasury Stock**		2 0 0 0 00	17
18		Sold treasury stock			18
19					19
20		* 2,000 shares × $6 cost per share			20
21		** $14,000 cash received − $12,000 cost			21
22		of treasury shares			22

Assume that Linc Corp. subsequently sells the remaining 1,000 treasury shares for $5.50 per share, a total of $5,500. The journal entry for this transaction is:

8		Cash	5 5 0 0 00		8
9		Paid-In Capital from Sale of Treasury Stock**	5 0 0 00		9
10		Common Treasury Stock*		6 0 0 0 00	10
11		Sold treasury stock			11
12					12
13		* 1,000 shares × $6 cost per share			13
14		** $6,000 cost of treasury shares			14
15		− $5,500 cash received			15

If treasury stock is sold for less than its cost and Paid-In Capital from Sale of Treasury Stock has a zero balance, the difference is debited to Retained Earnings.

Note that no gain or loss is recognized on treasury stock transactions. A corporation cannot realize a gain or incur a loss by dealing in its own shares.

Be careful in presenting treasury stock on the balance sheet. Treasury stock is *not* an asset. It is a contra-stockholders' equity account and is reported as a deduction from the total of paid-in capital and retained earnings. Paid-In Capital from Sale of Treasury Stock is reported as an addition to paid-in capital on the balance sheet.

Summary of Capital Stock Transaction Accounts

In recording capital stock transactions, we have been introduced to many new accounts. Figure 22-4 summarizes these new accounts by type, purpose, and balance sheet presentation. Refer to this figure as you work the exercises and problems for this chapter.

ACCOUNT	TYPE	PURPOSE	BALANCE SHEET PRESENTATION
Common Stock and Preferred Stock	Stockholders' Equity	If stock has par or stated value: Credited for par or stated value of stock issued If stock has no par or stated value: Credited for amount received for stock issued	Part of paid-in capital
Paid-In Capital in Excess of Par —Common and Preferred Stock Paid-In Capital in Excess of Stated Value —Common and Preferred Stock	Stockholders' Equity	Credited for amount by which issue price exceeds par or stated value of stock (Used only for stock with par or stated value)	Addition to paid-in capital
Discount on Common Stock and Preferred Stock	Stockholders' Equity	Debited for amount by which par or stated value exceeds issue price of stock	Deduction from paid-in capital
Common and Preferred Stock Subscriptions Receivable	Stockholders' Equity	Debited for subscription price of stock	Deduction from total of paid-in capital and retained earnings
Common and Preferred Stock Subscribed	Contra-Stockholders' Equity	If stock has par or stated value: Credited for par or stated value of stock subscribed If stock has no par or stated value: Credited for amount of stock subscription	Addition to paid-in capital
Treasury Stock—Common and Preferred	Contra-Stockholders' Equity	Debited for cost of stock purchased	Deduction from total of paid-in capital and retained earnings
Paid-In Capital from Sale of Treasury Stock	Stockholders' Equity	Credited for excess of selling price over cost of treasury stock or Debited for excess of cost over selling price of treasury stock (if a credit balance)	Addition to paid-in capital

FIGURE 22-4   Summary of Capital Stock Transaction Accounts

STOCKHOLDERS' EQUITY SECTION

LO4 Prepare the stockholders' equity section of a corporation balance sheet.

Now that we have seen the various accounts used in capital stock transactions, let's bring them together in a stockholders' equity section of the balance sheet. We will use the Roland Company for this purpose.

After closing its books on December 31, Roland Company's stockholders' equity accounts have the following balances.

Account	Balance	Additional Information
Preferred Stock Subscriptions Receivable	$ 20,000	
Common Stock Subscriptions Receivable	30,000	
Preferred Stock Subscribed	60,000	7%, $10 par, 6,000 shares
Common Stock Subscribed	40,000	no-par, 4,000 shares
Preferred Stock	140,000	7%, $10 par, 20,000 shares authorized, 14,000 shares issued
Common Stock	163,000	no-par, 40,000 shares authorized, 16,300 shares issued
Paid-In Capital in Excess of Par—Preferred Stock	56,000	
Paid-In Capital from Sale of Treasury Stock	600	
Common Treasury Stock	22,000 (Dr.)	no par, 2,000 shares, at cost
Retained Earnings	60,000	

Figure 22-5 shows the stockholders' equity section prepared from these accounts.

Stockholders' Equity			
Paid-in capital:			
Preferred stock, 7%, $10 par			
(20,000 shares authorized; 14,000 shares issued)	$140 0 0 0 00		
Preferred stock subscribed (6,000 shares)	60 0 0 0 00	$200 0 0 0 00	
Common stock, no par			
(40,000 shares authorized; 16,300 shares issued)	$163 0 0 0 00		
Common stock subscribed (4,000 shares)	40 0 0 0 00	203 0 0 0 00	
Additional paid-in capital:			
Paid-in capital in excess of par—preferred stock	$ 56 0 0 0 00		
Paid-in capital from sale of treasury stock	6 0 0 00	56 6 0 0 00	
Total paid-in capital		$459 6 0 0 00	
Retained earnings		60 0 0 0 00	
		$519 6 0 0 00	
Less: Preferred stock subscriptions receivable	$ 20 0 0 0 00		
Common stock subscriptions receivable	30 0 0 0 00		
Common treasury stock (2,000 shares at cost)	22 0 0 0 00	72 0 0 0 00	
Total stockholders' equity		$447 6 0 0 00	

FIGURE 22-5   Stockholders' Equity Section

Note the following characteristics of this stockholders' equity presentation.

1. Stockholders' equity is separated by source:
    Paid-in capital—amounts contributed by owners
    Retained earnings—accumulated, undistributed earnings

2. Paid-in capital is separated by source:
    Preferred stock
    Common stock
    Stock subscriptions
    Paid-in capital in excess of par
    Paid-in capital from sale of treasury stock

3. Stock characteristics are indicated:
    Dividend rate for preferred stock—7%
    Par or no-par value

4. Numbers of shares authorized, subscribed, issued, and held as treasury stock are indicated.

5. Preferred stock is listed first. (This is because of its preferred claim to dividends and assets.)

6. Retained earnings is listed after all paid-in capital.

7. Preferred stock subscriptions receivable, common stock subscriptions receivable, and treasury stock are subtracted from the total of paid-in capital and retained earnings.

Learning Objectives	Key Points to Remember
1 **Describe the characteristics, formation, and organization of a corporation.**	A corporation exists independently of its owners. Its assets and liabilities are those of the business. A corporation is formed according to the laws of the state in which it incorporates. It normally has a board of directors and four officers. Organization costs are expensed in the period they are incurred.
2 **Describe stockholders' equity and the types of capital stock, and compute dividends on preferred and common stock.**	A key characteristic of owners' equity in a corporation is the distinction between paid-in capital and retained earnings. Paid-in capital is the amount paid in by stockholders. Retained earnings is the accumulated earnings not paid out as dividends. Owners of capital stock generally have the right to: 1. Vote at stockholders' meetings 2. Share in earnings distributions 3. Purchase additional shares if more shares are issued by the corporation 4. Share in the assets if the corporation liquidates Owners of preferred stock generally give up the right to vote in order to have a preferential right to dividends and assets. Features such as cumulative and participating that may apply to preferred stock must be considered when calculating preferred stock and common stock dividends.
3 **Account for capital stock transactions.**	The accounting for par value and stated value stock is virtually the same. In each case, the difference between the par or stated value and the amount received at issuance is recorded as a premium or discount. ■ There is no premium or discount to account for when no-par stock is issued. ■ If stock is issued for noncash assets, the assets received are recorded at the fair market value of the assets or of the stock, whichever can be more clearly determined. ■ If capital stock subscriptions are received, the corporation does not issue the stock until the subscription is paid in full. ■ No gains or losses are recognized on treasury stock transactions.
4 **Prepare the stockholders' equity section of a corporation balance sheet.**	The stockholders' equity section of the corporate balance sheet has the following characteristics: 1. Stockholders' equity is separated into paid-in capital and retained earnings. 2. Paid-in capital is separated into preferred stock, common stock, stock subscriptions, paid-in capital in excess of par, and paid-in capital from sale of treasury stock. 3. The dividend rate for preferred stock and par or no-par value are indicated. 4. Numbers of shares authorized, subscribed, issued, and held as treasury stock are indicated. 5. Preferred stock is listed first. 6. Retained earnings is listed after all paid-in capital. 7. Preferred stock subscriptions receivable, common stock subscriptions receivable, and treasury stock are subtracted from the total of paid-in capital and retained earnings.

Reflection: Answering the Opening Question

Mike should consider the following advantages:

1. He would have limited liability rather than being personally liable for the debts of his business.
2. The ownership units would be transferable among the owners without affecting the operation of the business.
3. It would be easier to raise capital by selling additional ownership shares in the business.
4. There would be no mutual agency, so owners would not be able to engage in contracts for the business unless they were given specific power to do so.
5. The business would have unlimited life, so that death of an owner or transfer of ownership would not affect the business.

Mike also should be aware of the following disadvantages:

1. The earnings of the corporation are taxable to the corporation, and any dividends paid to Mike are also taxable to him.
2. The corporation is subject to federal, state, and local regulation.

DEMONSTRATION PROBLEM

Stockholders' equity accounts and other related accounts of the JKL Manufacturing Corporation as of October 1, 20-1, the beginning of its fiscal year, follow.

Preferred Stock Subscriptions Receivable	$ 80,000
Preferred Stock, 8%, $10 par (200,000 shares authorized,	
50,000 shares issued)	500,000
Preferred Stock Subscribed (10,000 shares)	100,000
Paid-In Capital in Excess of Par—Preferred Stock	50,000
Common Stock, $10 par (1,000,000 shares authorized,	
200,000 shares issued)	2,000,000
Paid-In Capital in Excess of Par— Common Stock	500,000
Retained Earnings	2,250,000

During the fiscal year ended September 30, 20-2, JKL Manufacturing completed the following transactions affecting stockholders' equity.

(a) Received the balance due on preferred stock subscriptions and issued the necessary certificates.

(b) Purchased 10,000 shares of common treasury stock for $120,000.

(c) Received subscriptions for 8,000 shares of 8% preferred stock at $12 each, collecting one-fourth of the subscription price.

(d) Sold 6,000 shares of common treasury stock for $78,000.

(e) Issued 80,000 shares of common stock at $15, receiving cash.

(f) Sold 2,000 shares of common treasury stock for $22,000.

(g) Issued 100,000 shares of common stock with a market value of $15 per share in exchange for land for business expansion.

REQUIRED

1. Prepare general journal entries for the transactions, identifying each transaction by the appropriate letter.

2. Prepare the stockholders' equity section of the balance sheet as of September 30, 20-2. The beginning retained earnings balance must be increased by the net income for the year, $720,000. The preferred stock was paid dividends at 8% on $600,000 par value of stock, and the common stock was paid dividends of $.80 per share on 378,000 outstanding shares.

Solution

1.

GENERAL JOURNAL PAGE 1

	DATE	DESCRIPTION	POST REF.	DEBIT	CREDIT	
1	(a)	Cash		80 0 0 0 00		1
2		Preferred Stock Subscriptions Rec.			80 0 0 0 00	2
3		Received subscription payments				3
4						4
5		Preferred Stock Subscribed		100 0 0 0 00		5
6		Preferred Stock			100 0 0 0 00	6
7		Issued preferred stock				7
8						8
9	(b)	Common Treasury Stock		120 0 0 0 00		9
10		Cash			120 0 0 0 00	10
11		Purchased treasury stock				11
12						12
13	(c)	Cash		24 0 0 0 00		13
14		Preferred Stock Subscriptions Rec.		72 0 0 0 00		14
15		Preferred Stock Subscribed			80 0 0 0 00	15
16		Paid-In Capital in Excess of Par—				16
17		Preferred Stock			16 0 0 0 00	17
18		Received subscriptions for preferred stock				18
19						19
20	(d)	Cash		78 0 0 0 00		20
21		Common Treasury Stock			72 0 0 0 00	21
22		Paid-In Capital from Sale of Treasury Stock			6 0 0 0 00	22
23		Sold treasury stock				23
24						24
25	(e)	Cash		1,200 0 0 0 00		25
26		Common Stock			800 0 0 0 00	26
27		Paid-In Capital in Excess of Par—				27
28		Common Stock			400 0 0 0 00	28
29		Issued common stock at a premium				29
30						30
31	(f)	Cash		22 0 0 0 00		31
32		Paid-In Capital from Sale of Treasury Stock		2 0 0 0 00		32
33		Common Treasury Stock			24 0 0 0 00	33
34		Sold treasury stock				34
35						35
36	(g)	Land		1,500 0 0 0 00		36
37		Common Stock			1,000 0 0 0 00	37
38		Paid-In Capital in Excess of Par—				38
39		Common Stock			500 0 0 0 00	39
40		Issued common stock at a premium				40

2.

Stockholders' Equity										
Paid-in capital:										
Preferred stock, 8%, $10 par (200,000 shares authorized; 60,000 shares issued)	$ 600	0	0	0	00					
Preferred stock subscribed (8,000 shares)	80	0	0	0	00	$ 680	0	0	0	00
Common stock, $10 par (1,000,000 shares authorized; 380,000 shares issued)						3,800	0	0	0	00
Additional paid-in capital:										
Paid-in capital in excess of par—preferred stock	$ 66	0	0	0	00					
Paid-in capital in excess of par—common stock	1,400	0	0	0	00					
Paid-in capital from sale of treasury stock	4	0	0	0	00	1,470	0	0	0	00
Total paid-in capital						$5,950	0	0	0	00
Retained earnings*						2,619	6	0	0	00
						$8,569	6	0	0	00
Less: Preferred stock subscriptions receivable	$ 72	0	0	0	00					
Common treasury stock (2,000 shares at cost)	24	0	0	0	00	96	0	0	0	00
Total stockholders' equity						$8,473	6	0	0	00

* $2,250,000 + $720,000 − $48,000 − $302,400 = $2,619,600

On-Line Learning Tools

For more information, visit: http://heintz.swlearning.com

The Heintz & Parry product web site is designed specifically for **COLLEGE ACCOUNTING, 18e.** The features include downloadable student resources and an interactive study center, organized by chapter, which contains learning objectives, web links, on-line quizzes with automatic feedback, and more.

KEY TERMS

articles of incorporation, (833)   See charter.

authorized stock, (836)   The total number of shares the corporate charter authorizes a corporation to issue.

board of directors, (833)   A group elected by the stockholders to determine corporate policies and to select corporate officers.

bylaws, (833)   Together with the charter, the bylaws provide the general guidelines for conducting the business.

capital stock, (832)   Represents ownership rights in a corporation. Generally broken down into common and preferred stock.

capital stock subscription, (841)   An agreement in which a buyer contracts to buy shares of a corporation at a specific price.

charter, (833)   Legal document that includes the name of the corporation, the location of the principal office, the purpose of the business, the description of the capital stock, and the names and addresses of the incorporators.

common stock, (836)   Stock that gives its owner the right to vote at stockholders' meetings, share in earnings distributions, purchase additional shares if more shares are issued by the corporation, and share in the assets if the corporation liquidates.

cumulative preferred stock, (837)   Preferred stock on which unpaid dividends accumulate from year to year.

discount, (839)   The difference between the par amount and the amount received when the par value stock is issued at a price below par.

dividends, (833)   The distributions of corporate income to the owners.

double taxation, (833)   The process of taxing corporate income both to the company that earns it and to the owners who receive it.

incorporators, (833)   Those who form a corporation by filing an application with the state in which the company is to be incorporated.

issued stock, (836)   Capital stock that has been sold and issued.

market value, (836)   The amount for which the stock can be sold on the open market.

mutual agency, (832)   The power of each owner to act as an agent and engage in contracts for a business.

noncumulative preferred stock, (837)   Preferred stock on which dividend claims do not accumulate from year to year.

nonparticipating, (837)   Preferred stock on which the dividends are limited to the stated dividend rate.

no-par stock, (836)   Stock that has no dollar amount printed on it.

organization costs, (834)   The costs of organizing a corporation, such as incorporation fees, attorneys' fees, and promotion expenses.

outstanding stock, (836)   The number of shares in the hands of stockholders.

paid-in capital, (835)   The amount paid by stockholders for their shares of stock.

par value, (836)   The dollar amount printed on the share of stock.

participating, (837)   Preferred stock that has a right to share with common stock in dividends in excess of a stated dividend rate.

preemptive right, (836)   The right to purchase additional shares in proportion to the owner's present holding, if more shares are issued by the corporation.

preferred stock, (836)   Stock that has certain preferences or rights superior to common stock.

premium, (838)   The difference between the par value and the price of a stock when the stock is issued at a price above par.

retained earnings, (835)   The accumulated earnings of the corporation that have not been paid out to stockholders as dividends.

shares, (832)   Capital stock is divided into shares that represent ownership rights in the corporation.

stated value, (836)   Value per share assigned to no-par stock by the board of directors.

stock certificate, (833)   A form received by each stockholder that shows the name of the stockholder and the number of shares owned.

stockholders, (833)   Owners of the corporation.

stockholders' equity, (835)   Owners' equity within a corporation.

subscriber, (841)   A buyer who contracts to purchase shares of stock from a corporation at a specific price.

treasury stock, (836)   Shares of stock that have been bought back by the issuing company.

REVIEW QUESTIONS

(L01)   1. Briefly describe five advantages of the corporate form of business organization. Describe two disadvantages.

(LO1)	2. What information usually is included in the charter?
(LO1)	3. Who elects the permanent board of directors?
(LO1)	4. Describe how to account for organization costs.
(LO2)	5. How do owners' equity accounts in a corporation differ from those in a sole proprietorship or partnership?
(LO2)	6. If a corporation issues only one class of stock, what four rights does each stockholder have?
(LO3/4)	7. How is Paid-In Capital in Excess of Par usually reported on the balance sheet? How is Discount on Capital Stock usually reported?
(LO3)	8. If stock is issued for noncash assets, at what amount should the assets be recorded?
(LO3/4)	9. How is Common Stock Subscriptions Receivable usually reported on the balance sheet?
(LO3/4)	10. How is Treasury Stock usually shown on the balance sheet?
(LO3/4)	11. How is Paid-In Capital from Sale of Treasury Stock usually shown on the balance sheet?

Self-Study Test Questions

True/False

1. Corporations do more dollar volume of business than sole proprietorships and partnerships combined.   _____

2. Owners of corporations have no personal liability for debts of the corporation.   _____

3. In a corporation, individual owners have mutual agency power.   _____

4. Dividends are not taxable because these earnings have already been taxed to the corporation.   _____

5. Organization costs are recorded as an intangible asset and are generally amortized over a period of five years.   _____

Multiple Choice

1. When par value stock is issued at a price above par, the amount above par is called a   _____

   (a) discount.   (c) stated value.
   (b) market value.   (d) premium.

2. When par value stock is issued at a price below par, the amount below par is called a   _____

   (a) discount.   (c) stated value.
   (b) market value.   (d) premium.

(continued)

Self-Study Test Questions *(continued)*

3. Shares of stock reacquired by the issuing company are called _____

   (a) par value stock.   (c) treasury stock.
   (b) no-par value stock.   (d) stock subscription.

4. Stock subscriptions receivable are listed as _____ on the balance sheet. _____

   (a) current liabilities   (c) long-term assets
   (b) current assets   (d) contra-stockholders' equity

5. Treasury stock is listed as a(n) _____ on the balance sheet. _____

   (a) current liability   (c) deduction from stockholders' equity
   (b) current asset   (d) addition to stockholders' equity

The answers to the Self-Study Test Questions are at the end of the text.

MANAGING YOUR WRITING

Your boss started a construction company as a partnership with several other contractors 20 years ago. Twelve years later, the partners incorporated to gain access to additional capital by issuing common stock. Forty percent of the shares were sold to the general public and 60 percent were acquired by the partners. In this way, the partners kept voting control of the business.

Now the company has an opportunity for a major expansion. To obtain additional capital to fund the expansion, the company is considering another stock offering. But the original partners do not want to lose voting control of the business. Your boss knows you are taking college business courses and asks whether there is a way the company can sell additional stock without the partners losing control of the business. Prepare a report for him describing the kinds of capital stock the company could issue that would accomplish his purpose.

ETHICS CASE

Tyler Corporation started its operations in March. During the first year of operation, a significant amount of money was spent on attorneys' fees and promotional expenses connected with organizing the corporation. The amount of revenue Tyler Corporation earned for the year was much higher than expected. Because of this, the accountant decided to charge the attorneys' fees and promotional expenses to advertising expense in the current year.

1. If the accountant simply was not aware of the proper treatment of these expenditures, were any ethical principles violated? Why or why not?

2. How would you have treated these expenditures?

3. Write a short memo from the accountant to the board of directors of Tyler Corporation explaining how costs of organizing a corporation are treated for accounting purposes.

4. In groups of two or three, discuss the difference between making unethical decisions and making careless decisions.

WEB WORK

What are some ways, other than the traditional, to raise money for a small business? Visit the Interactive Study Center on our web site at **http://heintz. swlearning.com** for special hotlinks to assist you in this assignment.

SERIES A EXERCISES

EXERCISE 22-1A   **(LO1)**

Dr. Organization
Expenses: $10,900

ORGANIZATION COSTS B&B Electric decided to incorporate and has incurred the following costs of organizing.

Incorporation fees	$ 400
Attorneys' fees	4,800
Promotion expenses	5,700

Prepare the entry to record payment of these organization costs for cash on January 31.

EXERCISE 22-2A   **(LO2)**

Situation 2. Div. per share,
common: $.20

DIVIDEND ALLOCATIONS

Situation 1   Akimoto Company has the following stock outstanding.

Common Stock	**Preferred Stock**
50,000 shares	5,000 shares
$1 par value	$40 par, $2 dividend

The amount available for dividends this year is $40,000. Prepare the dividend allocation between the preferred and common shares.

Situation 2   Benitez Company has the following stock outstanding.

Common Stock	**Preferred Stock**
70,000 shares	Cumulative: 1,500 shares
$1 par value	$50 par, $2 dividend
	Noncumulative: 4,000 shares
	$50 par, $2 dividend

No dividends were declared in year 1 of operation. In year 2, there is $28,000 available for dividends. Prepare the dividend allocation between the preferred and common shares.

EXERCISE 22-3A   **(LO3)**

(b) Cr. Paid-in Capital in Excess
of Par—Common: $5,000

STOCK ISSUANCE (PAR, NO-PAR, AND STATED VALUE) The following stock transactions occurred during January 20-- for the Bremer Corporation.

(a) Issued 5,000 shares of $10 par common stock for $50,000 cash.

(b) Issued 4,000 shares of $10 par common stock for $45,000 cash.

(c) Issued 4,000 shares of $10 par common stock for $37,500 cash.

(d) Issued 5,000 shares of no-par common stock for $60,000 cash.

(e) Issued 3,000 shares of no-par common stock for $40,000 cash.

(f) Issued 5,000 shares of no-par common stock with a stated value of $8 per share for $40,000 cash.

(g) Issued 2,000 shares of no-par common stock with a stated value of $8 per share for $15,000 cash.

(h) Issued 3,000 shares of no-par common stock with a stated value of $8 per share for $26,000 cash.

Prepare general journal entries to record the stock transactions, identifying each transaction by letter.

EXERCISE 22-4A   (LO3)

(b) Cr. Paid-in Capital in Excess of Par—Common: $7,500

STOCK ISSUANCE (NONCASH ASSETS, SUBSCRIPTION, AND TREASURY STOCK) Smith & Cline had the following stock transactions during the year.

(a) Issued 5,000 shares of common stock with a $5 par value in exchange for real estate (land) with a fair market value of $27,500.

(b) Issued 7,500 shares of common stock with a $5 par value and $6 fair market value in exchange for a building with an uncertain fair market value.

(c) Received subscriptions for 10,000 shares of $6 par common stock for $65,000.

(d) Received subscriptions for 5,000 shares of $6 par common stock for $28,000.

(e) Received a payment of $30,000 on the stock subscription in (c).

(f) Received the balance in full for the stock subscription in (c) and issued the stock.

(g) Received the balance in full for the stock subscription in (d) and issued the stock.

(h) Purchased 1,000 shares of its own $6 par common stock for $7 a share ($7,000).

(i) Sold 500 shares of the treasury stock in (h) for $7.50 a share.

(j) Sold 500 shares of the treasury stock in (h) for $6.75 a share.

Prepare general journal entries to record the transactions, identifying each by letter.

EXERCISE 22-5A   (LO4)

Total Paid-in Capital: $110,000

STOCKHOLDERS' EQUITY SECTION After closing its books on December 31, Pro Parts' stockholders' equity accounts had the following balances.

Common stock subscriptions receivable	$ 4,000
Common stock, $5 par, 10,000 shares	50,000
Preferred stock, $10 par, 5%, 5,000 shares	50,000
Common stock subscribed, $5 par, 2,000 shares	10,000
Retained earnings	25,000

Prepare the stockholders' equity section of the balance sheet.

SERIES A PROBLEMS

PROBLEM 22-6A   (LO3)

(e) Dr. Discount on Preferred Stock: $1,000

PAR AND NO-PAR, COMMON AND PREFERRED STOCK Hernandez Company had the following stock transactions during the year.

(a) Issued 25,000 shares of $1 par common stock for $25,000 cash.

(b) Issued 20,000 shares of $1 par common stock for $22,000 cash.

(c) Issued 22,000 shares of $1 par common stock for $21,000 cash.

(d) Issued 2,000 shares of $50 par, 8% preferred stock for $100,000 cash.

(e) Issued 1,000 shares of $50 par, 8% preferred stock for $49,000 cash.

(f) Issued 1,000 shares of $50 par, 8% preferred stock for $51,500 cash.

(g) Issued 2,500 shares of no-par common stock for $11,875 cash.

(h) Issued 1,500 shares of no-par, 7% preferred stock for $72,000 cash.

REQUIRED

Prepare general journal entries to record the transactions, identifying each transaction by letter.

PROBLEM 22-7A   **(LO3)**
(f) Dr. Building: $90,000

STATED VALUE, COMMON AND PREFERRED STOCK, AND NONCASH ASSETS Kris Kraft Stores had the following stock transactions during the year.

(a) Issued 4,000 shares of no-par common stock with a stated value of $10 per share for $40,000 cash.

(b) Issued 6,000 shares of no-par common stock with a stated value of $8 per share for $50,000 cash.

(c) Issued 5,000 shares of no-par, 6% preferred stock with a stated value of $15 per share for $75,000 cash.

(d) Issued 3,000 shares of no-par, 6% preferred stock with a stated value of $20 per share for $58,000 cash.

(e) Issued 10,000 shares of $5 par common stock for land with a fair market value of $50,000.

(f) Issued 10,000 shares of $8 par common stock with a $9 fair market value for a building with an uncertain fair market value.

(g) Issued 8,000 shares of $50 par, 8% preferred stock for land with a fair market value of $405,000.

REQUIRED

Prepare general journal entries to record the transactions, identifying each transaction by letter.

PROBLEM 22-8A   **(LO3)**

(c) Cr. Paid-in Capital in Excess of Par—Common: $5,000

STOCK SUBSCRIPTIONS Juneau & Associates had the following stock transactions during the year.

(a) Issued 100,000 shares of $1 par common stock for $105,000 cash.

(b) Issued 12,000 shares of $10 par, 8% preferred stock for $128,000 cash.

(c) Received subscriptions for 10,000 shares of $10 par common stock for $105,000.

(d) Received subscriptions for 5,000 shares of $15 par, 8% preferred stock for $80,000.

(e) Received a payment of $55,000 on the common stock subscription.

(f) Received a payment of $40,000 on the preferred stock subscription.

(g) Issued 40,000 shares of $1 par common stock in exchange for a truck with a fair market value of $48,000.

(h) Received the balance in full for the common stock subscription and issued the stock.

(i) Issued 2,500 shares of no-par common stock with a stated value of $8 per share for $21,500 cash.

(j) Received the balance in full for the preferred stock subscription and issued the stock.

REQUIRED

Prepare general journal entries to record the transactions, identifying each transaction by letter.

PROBLEM 22-9A   **(LO1/3)**

Sept. 18. Dr.
Common Stock
Subscribed:
$100,000

STOCK SUBSCRIPTIONS AND TREASURY STOCK Brown & Brown formed a corporation and had the following stock transactions during the year.

June 30   Incurred the following costs of incorporation:

Incorporation fees	$ 800
Attorneys' fees	5,000
Promotion fees	7,000

July 15   Issued 5,000 shares of $10 par common stock for $52,000 cash.

21   Issued 4,000 shares of $20 par, 8% preferred stock for $79,500 cash.

Aug. 1   Received subscriptions for 10,000 shares of $10 par common stock for $103,500.

15   Issued 10,000 shares of $10 par common stock in exchange for a building and fixtures with a fair market value of $110,000.

31   Received a payment of $53,500 for the common stock subscription.

Sept. 3   Purchased 1,000 shares of its own $10 par common stock for $11 a share.

12   Issued 3,500 shares of no-par common stock with a stated value of $8 per share for $30,000.

18   Received the balance in full for the common stock subscription and issued the stock.

30   Sold 500 shares of its treasury stock for $11.50 a share.

Oct. 15   Issued 5,000 shares of $20 par, 8% preferred stock in exchange for land with a fair market value of $108,000.

31   Sold 500 shares of its treasury stock for $10.75 a share.

REQUIRED

Prepare journal entries to record the transactions.

PROBLEM 22-10A   **(LO4)**
Total Paid-in Capital: $491,000

STOCKHOLDERS' EQUITY SECTION After closing its books on December 31, 20--, the Jackson Corporation's stockholders' equity accounts had the following balances.

Account	Balance	Additional Information
Preferred stock subscriptions receivable	$ 15,000	
Common stock subscriptions receivable	10,000	
Preferred Stock Subscribed	50,000	$4 dividend, $5 par, 10,000 shares
Common Stock Subscribed	30,000	$10 par, 3,000 shares
Preferred Stock	150,000	$4 dividend, $5 par, 30,000 shares
Common Stock	250,000	$10 par, 25,000 shares
Paid-In Capital in Excess of Par—Preferred Stock	10,000	
Paid-In Capital from Sale of Treasury Stock	1,000	
Common Treasury Stock	10,000	
Retained Earnings	75,000	

REQUIRED

Prepare the stockholders' equity section of the balance sheet for Jackson for the year ended December 31, 20--.

SERIES B EXERCISES

EXERCISE 22-1B   **(LO1)**

Dr. Organization
Expenses: $12,000

ORGANIZATION COSTS T&R TrackTown has decided to incorporate and has incurred the following costs of organizing.

Incorporation fees	$ 500
Attorneys' fees	6,800
Promotion fees	4,700

Prepare the entry to record payment of these organization costs for cash on January 20.

EXERCISE 22-2B   **(LO2)**

Situation 2. Div. per
share, common: $.75

DIVIDEND ALLOCATIONS

Situation 1   Espino Company has the following stock outstanding.

Common Stock	**Preferred Stock**
100,000 shares	9,000 shares
$.50 par value	$20 par, $2 dividend

The amount available for dividends this year is $50,000. Prepare the dividend allocation between the preferred and common shares.

Situation 2   Chiola Corporation has the following stock outstanding.

Common Stock	**Preferred Stock**
40,000 shares	Cumulative: 4,000 shares
$1 par value	$40 par, $2 dividend
	Noncumulative: 5,000 shares
	$40 par, $2 dividend

No dividends were declared in year 1 of operation. In year 2, there is $56,000 available for dividends. Prepare the dividend allocation between the preferred and common shares.

EXERCISE 22-3B   **(LO3)**

(b) Dr. Discount on
Common Stock: $5,000

STOCK ISSUANCE (PAR, NO-PAR, AND STATED VALUE) The following stock transactions occurred during January 20-- for Drexel Corporation.

(a) Issued 4,000 shares of $10 par common stock for $40,000 cash.

(b) Issued 5,000 shares of $10 par common stock for $45,000 cash.

(c) Issued 5,000 shares of $10 par common stock for $53,500 cash.

(d) Issued 6,000 shares of no-par common stock for $60,000 cash.

(e) Issued 4,000 shares of no-par common stock for $40,000 cash.

(f) Issued 6,000 shares of no-par common stock with a stated value of $8 per share for $48,000 cash.

(g) Issued 3,000 shares of no-par common stock with a stated value of $8 per share for $25,000 cash.

(h) Issued 4,000 shares of no-par common stock with a stated value of $8 per share for $30,500 cash.

Prepare general journal entries to record the stock transactions, identifying each transaction by letter.

EXERCISE 22-4B **(LO3)**

(b) Cr. Paid-in Capital in Excess of Par—Common: $5,500

STOCK ISSUANCE (NONCASH ASSETS, SUBSCRIPTION, AND TREASURY STOCK) Brant & Evans had the following stock transactions during the year.

(a) Issued 6,000 shares of common stock with a $5 par value in exchange for real estate (land) with a fair market value of $33,500.

(b) Issued 5,500 shares of common stock with a $6 par value and $7 fair market value in exchange for a building with an uncertain fair market value.

(c) Received subscriptions for 11,000 shares of $5 par common stock for $58,000.

(d) Received subscriptions for 8,000 shares of $5 par common stock for $38,000.

(e) Received a payment of $29,000 on the stock subscription in (c).

(f) Received the balance in full for the stock subscription in (c) and issued the stock.

(g) Received the balance in full for the stock subscription in (d) and issued the stock.

(h) Purchased 2,000 shares of its own $5 par common stock for $6 a share ($12,000).

(i) Sold 1,000 shares of the treasury stock in (h) for $6.50 a share.

(j) Sold 1,000 shares of the treasury stock in (h) for $5.75 a share.

Prepare general journal entries to record the transactions, identifying each transaction by letter.

EXERCISE 22-5B **(LO4)**

Total Paid-in Capital: $220,000

STOCKHOLDERS' EQUITY SECTION After closing its books on December 31, Mel Brothers' stockholders' equity accounts have the following balances.

Common stock subscriptions receivable	$ 6,000
Common stock, $6 par, 15,000 shares	90,000
Preferred stock, $10 par, 8%, 10,000 shares	100,000
Common stock subscribed, $6 par, 5,000 shares	30,000
Retained earnings	50,000

Prepare the stockholders' equity section of the balance sheet.

SERIES B PROBLEMS

PROBLEM 22-6B **(LO3)**

(e) Dr. Discount on Pref. Stock: $3,000

PAR AND NO-PAR, COMMON AND PREFERRED STOCK Valdez Company had the following stock transactions during the year.

(a) Issued 24,000 shares of $1 par common stock for $26,000 cash.

(b) Issued 20,000 shares of $1 par common stock for $19,000 cash.

(c) Issued 18,000 shares of $1 par common stock for $18,000 cash.

(d) Issued 3,000 shares of $10 par, 7% preferred stock for $30,000 cash.

(e) Issued 4,000 shares of $15 par, 7% preferred stock for $57,000 cash.

(f) Issued 4,500 shares of $10 par, 7% preferred stock for $46,500 cash.

(g) Issued 1,800 shares of no-par common stock for $10,475 cash.

(h) Issued 1,100 shares of no-par, 7% preferred stock for $32,000 cash.

REQUIRED

Prepare general journal entries to record the transactions, identifying each transaction by letter.

PROBLEM 22-7B   **(LO3)**
(f) Dr. Building: $99,000

STATED VALUE, COMMON AND PREFERRED STOCK, AND NONCASH ASSETS
Dan's Hobby Stores had the following stock transactions during the year.

(a) Issued 5,000 shares of no-par common stock with a stated value of $10 per share for $50,000 cash.

(b) Issued 6,000 shares of no-par common stock with a stated value of $7 per share for $43,000 cash.

(c) Issued 5,000 shares of no-par, 6% preferred stock with a stated value of $18 per share for $88,600 cash.

(d) Issued 3,500 shares of no-par, 6% preferred stock with a stated value of $22 per share for $77,000 cash.

(e) Issued 10,000 shares of $9 par common stock for land with a fair market value of $90,000.

(f) Issued 11,000 shares of $8 par common stock with a $9 fair market value for a building with an uncertain fair market value.

(g) Issued 8,000 shares of $30 par, 6% preferred stock for land with a fair market value of $243,000.

REQUIRED

Prepare general journal entries to record the transactions, identifying each transaction by letter.

PROBLEM 22-8B   **(LO3)**

(c) Dr. Discount on
Common Stock: $2,000

STOCK SUBSCRIPTIONS Athletics West had the following stock transactions during the year:

(a) Issued 140,000 shares of $1 par common stock for $145,000 cash.

(b) Issued 9,000 shares of $18 par, 7% preferred stock for $162,800 cash.

(c) Received subscriptions for 10,000 shares of $12 par common stock for $118,000.

(d) Received subscriptions for 5,000 shares of $18 par, 7% preferred stock for $92,000.

(e) Received a payment of $59,000 on the common stock subscription.

(f) Received a payment of $46,000 on the preferred stock subscription.

(g) Issued 60,000 shares of $1 par common stock in exchange for a truck with a fair market value of $66,000.

(h) Received the balance in full for the common stock subscription and issued the stock.

(i) Issued 3,500 shares of no-par common stock with a stated value of $6 per share for $21,500 cash.

(j) Received the balance in full for the preferred stock subscription and issued the stock.

REQUIRED

Prepare general journal entries to record the transactions, identifying each transaction by letter.

PROBLEM 22-9B **(LO1/3)**

PASS
Power Accounting System Software®

Sept. 18. Dr.
Common Stock
Subscribed:
$100,000

STOCK SUBSCRIPTIONS AND TREASURY STOCK Rogers & Hart formed a corporation and had the following stock transactions during the year.

June 30   Incurred the following costs of incorporation:

Incorporation fees	$ 900
Attorneys' fees	6,000
Promotion fees	8,000

July 15   Issued 8,000 shares of $10 par common stock for $82,000 cash.

21   Issued 5,000 shares of $25 par, 8% preferred stock for $124,500 cash.

Aug. 1   Received subscriptions for 10,000 shares of $10 par common stock for $101,500.

15   Issued 10,000 shares of $10 par common stock in exchange for a building and fixtures with a fair market value of $104,800.

31   Received a payment of $51,500 for the common stock subscription.

Sept. 3   Purchased 1,000 shares of its own $10 par common stock for $11 a share.

12   Issued 2,800 shares of no-par common stock with a stated value of $8 per share for $21,400.

18   Received the balance in full for the common stock subscription and issued the stock.

30   Sold 500 shares of its treasury stock for $11.50 a share.

Oct. 15   Issued 4,000 shares of $25 par, 8% preferred stock in exchange for land with a fair market value of $105,000.

31   Sold 500 shares of its treasury stock for $10.75 a share.

REQUIRED

Prepare journal entries to record the transactions.

PROBLEM 22-10B **(LO4)**
Total Paid-in Capital: $533,150

STOCKHOLDERS' EQUITY SECTION After closing its books on December 31, 20--, the Merrill Corporation's stockholders' equity accounts have the following balances.

Account	Balance	Additional Information
Preferred stock subscriptions receivable	$ 12,000	
Common stock subscriptions receivable	30,000	
Preferred Stock Subscribed	40,000	$4 dividend, $5 par, 8,000 shares
Common Stock Subscribed	80,000	$10 par, 8,000 shares
Preferred Stock	120,000	$4 dividend, $5 par, 24,000 shares
Common Stock	280,000	$10 par, 28,000 shares
Paid-In Capital in Excess of Par—Preferred Stock	12,000	
Paid-In Capital from Sale of Treasury Stock	1,150	
Common Treasury Stock	24,000	
Retained Earnings	88,000	

REQUIRED

Prepare the stockholders' equity section of the balance sheet for Merrill Corporation for the year ended December 31, 20--.

MASTERY PROBLEM

3. Total Paid-in Capital:
$1,756,000

Stockholders' equity accounts and other related accounts of the Gonzales Company as of January 1, 20--, the beginning of its fiscal year, are shown below.

Preferred Stock Subscriptions Receivable	$ 50,000
Preferred Stock, $10 par, 9%, (200,000 shares authorized; 20,000 shares issued)	200,000
Preferred Stock Subscribed (10,000 shares)	100,000
Paid-In Capital in Excess of Par—Preferred Stock	40,000
Common Stock, $10 par (100,000 shares authorized, 60,000 shares issued)	600,000
Paid-In Capital in Excess of Par—Common Stock	250,000
Retained Earnings	750,000

During 20--, the Gonzales Company completed the following transactions affecting stockholders' equity.

(a) Received $20,000 for the balance due on subscriptions for preferred stock with a par value of $40,000 and issued the stock.

(b) Purchased 10,000 shares of common treasury stock for $18 per share.

(c) Received subscriptions for 10,000 shares of common stock at $19 per share, collecting down payments of $45,000.

(d) Issued 15,000 shares of common stock in exchange for land with a fair market value of $290,000.

(e) Sold 5,000 shares of common treasury stock for $100,000.

(f) Issued 10,000 shares of preferred stock at $11.50 per share, receiving cash.

(g) Sold 3,000 shares of common treasury stock for $17 per share.

REQUIRED

1. Prepare general journal entries for the transactions, identifying each transaction by letter.

2. Post the journal entries to appropriate T accounts. The cash account has a beginning balance of $300,000.

3. Prepare the stockholders' equity section of the balance sheet as of December 31, 20--. Net income for the year was $825,000 and dividends of $400,000 were paid.

CHALLENGE PROBLEM

This problem challenges you to apply your cumulative accounting knowledge to move a step beyond the material in the chapter.

(e) Dr. Retained Earnings: $1,000

Prepare general journal entries for the following transactions, identifying each transaction by letter.

(a) Gnu Company issued 5,000 shares of $1 par common stock to the Prendergas law firm as partial payment of fees incurred to incorporate the business. Gnu was short of cash, so Prendergas agreed to accept $10,000 cash and the shares of common stock in full settlement of their bill for $55,000.

(b) Gnu issued 50,000 shares of $1 par common stock in exchange for a parcel of land for building a shopping plaza. (The list price for the land was $400,000; a similar parcel in the same area sold last week for $380,000. During the past month, the price at which Gnu's common stock has traded on the open market has ranged from $5 to $12 per share. Two trades occurred yesterday at $7 and $10 per share.)

(c) Gnu purchased 10,000 shares of $1 par value common treasury stock for $70,000. (This is the only treasury stock that Gnu holds.)

(d) Gnu sold 4,000 shares of common treasury stock for $32,000.

(e) Gnu sold 5,000 shares of common treasury stock for $30,000.

©GETTY IMAGES/PHOTODISC

Corporations: Earnings, Taxes, Distributions, and the Retained Earnings Statement

Mike Finbar incorporated the business described in Chapter 22, calling it Finny Co. The additional resources provided by the issuance of stock enabled the business to expand into electric instruments. With the new lines of instruments, the business has continued to grow in the four years since incorporating. In spite of its profitable operations, however, the business often is short of cash as it seeks to expand. Mike's accountant says the problem is that too much of the profits are paid out as cash dividends. He argues that the profits need to be retained in the business to finance the growth. If stockholders want distributions, he suggests issuing a stock dividend. How will issuing stock dividends instead of cash dividends enable Finny Co. to have more cash to expand? How will a stock dividend affect the stockholders' ownership in the business?

Careful study of this chapter should enable you to:

LO1 Explain the use of the retained earnings account and account for corporate income taxes.

LO2 Account for dividends and stock splits.

LO3 Account for appropriations of retained earnings.

LO4 Prepare a retained earnings statement.

In Chapter 22 we learned that stockholders' equity is separated into paid-in capital (amounts contributed by owners) and retained earnings (amounts of accumulated earnings not paid out to stockholders). The emphasis in Chapter 22 was on accounting for paid-in capital, primarily the issuance of capital stock. In this chapter, we focus on retained earnings.

THE RETAINED EARNINGS ACCOUNT

LO1 Explain the use of the retained earnings account and account for corporate income taxes.

Two major sources of capital for every type of business are:

1. Capital that results from investments by the owners

2. Capital that results from earnings retained in the business

In a corporation, capital resulting from the retention of earnings is entered in the retained earnings account. A corporation usually distributes only a portion of its earnings to stockholders. The balance is retained as additional capital to help finance the growth of the business.

Generally there are very few debits and credits to the retained earnings account. Typically the only credit to the account is for the net income of a period. The only debits are for a net loss, closing the dividends account, and appropriations (special restrictions) of retained earnings.

In this section, we will learn how to close the net income or net loss and the dividends for a period to the retained earnings account. Then, we will examine how to account for a new type of expense—corporate income taxes.

The Adjusting and Closing Process

The adjusting and closing process at the end of the period is virtually the same for corporations as for sole proprietorships and partnerships. The accounts are adjusted and all revenue and expense accounts are closed to Income Summary. A credit balance in Income Summary represents net income; a debit balance signifies a net loss. Beyond this point, however, the closing procedures for corporations differ from those for sole proprietorships and partnerships. The balance of the income summary account of a corporation is transferred to the retained earnings account. For example, if the corporation has net income of $337,000 for the period, the following closing entry is made.

18		Income Summary		337	0	0	0	00						18
19		Retained Earnings							337	0	0	0	00	19

If the corporation has a net loss of $52,000 for the period, the closing entry is:

18		Retained Earnings		52	0	0	0	00						18
19		Income Summary							52	0	0	0	00	19

LEARNING KEY: In a corporation, close Income Summary to Retained Earnings.

As noted in Chapter 22, the dividends account also is closed to Retained Earnings. If the corporation declares $30,000 in dividends, the closing entry is as shown below and in Figure 23-1.

| 18 | | Retained Earnings | 30 | 0 | 0 | 0 | 00 | | | | | | 18 |
| 19 | | Dividends | | | | | | 30 | 0 | 0 | 0 | 00 | 19 |

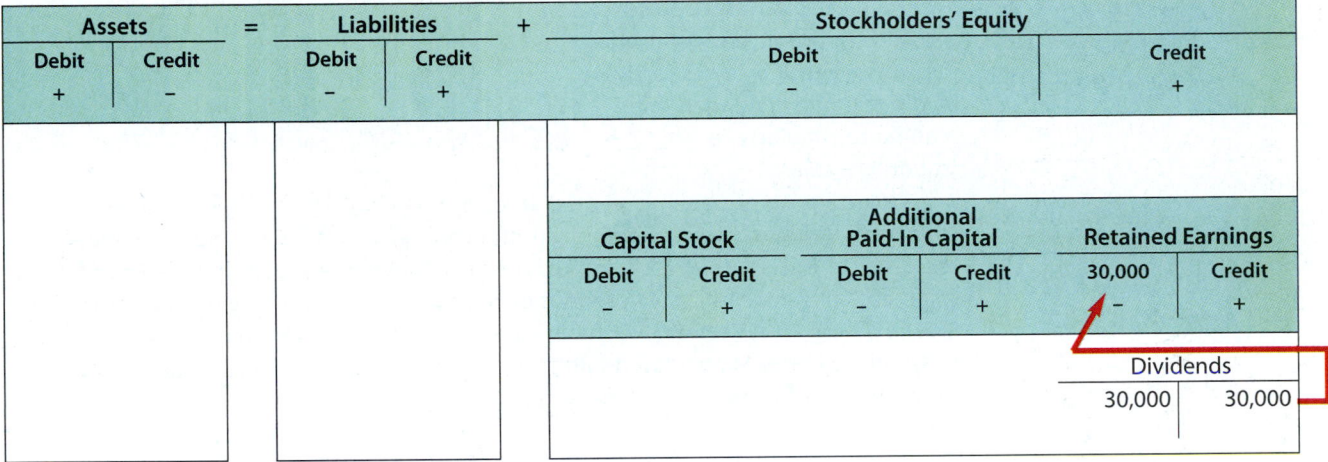

FIGURE 23-1   Closing the Dividends Account to Retained Earnings

Corporate Income Taxes

In accounting for sole proprietorships and partnerships, we did not need to deal with income taxes. Sole proprietorships and partnerships, as businesses, do not pay taxes. But, as noted in Chapter 22, a disadvantage of corporations is that they must pay income taxes.

Most corporations must estimate their annual income taxes and make quarterly payments. To illustrate, assume Boot Corp. estimates that its income taxes for 20-1 will be $160,000. Based on this estimate, Boot will have to pay $40,000 ($160,000 ÷ 4) on April 15, June 15, September 15, and December 15. The journal entry for each payment is:

5		Income Tax Expense	40	0	0	0	00						5
6		Cash						40	0	0	0	00	6
7		Made quarterly estimated tax payment											7

Corporations are subject to specific corporate tax rates different from those for individuals. Currently there are eight tax brackets ranging from 15% to 39%.

The actual amount of income taxes typically differs from the estimated amount. Thus, at year end, an adjusting entry is necessary to recognize the correct amount of income taxes for the year. Assume that as part of the year-end adjusting and closing process at Boot Corp., actual income taxes for the year are calculated as $163,000. The following adjusting journal entry would be made at December 31, 20-1.

5	Dec.	31	Income Tax Expense	3	0	0	0	00*						5
6			Income Tax Payable						3	0	0	0	00	6
7														7
8			* $163,000 actual − $160,000 estimated = $3,000											8

A BROADER VIEW

When Corporate Earnings Get Too Important

Earnings are important in virtually any business, but corporate managers sometimes become so focused on earnings growth that they "create" earnings that do not exist. This apparently is what happened at Kurzweil Applied Intelligence, Inc., a computerized speech recognition company based in Waltham, Massachusetts. Under pressure to produce consistently improving results, key executives at the company engaged in a scheme to regularly record fraudulent sales.

©CORBIS

According to generally accepted accounting principles, a sale should be counted when goods are shipped from the company to the customer. Kurzweil took a different approach. Millions of dollars of sales were recorded based on shipments of goods to local warehouses for storage until "real" sales could occur. Most of these "real" sales never happened. The fraud was uncovered when Kurzweil's auditor investigated bills from the warehouses for storage of goods supposedly sold nine months previously.

On March 15, 20-2, Boot Corp. would file its income tax return for the year ended December 31, 20-1, and pay the $3,000 income taxes due. The following entry would be made.

15	Mar.	15	Income Tax Payable		3 0 0 0 00			15
16			Cash			3 0 0 0 00		16
17			Made final 20-1 tax payment					17

Income taxes normally are reported as a separate expense item on the income statement, and are subtracted from income before income taxes. Assuming that Boot Corp. had income of $500,000 before considering income taxes, the bottom portion of Boot's income statement would appear as follows:

Income before income taxes	$500,000
Income tax expense	163,000
Net income	$337,000

ACCOUNTING FOR DIVIDENDS AND STOCK SPLITS

LO2 Account for dividends and stock splits.

A distribution of earnings by a corporation to its stockholders is known as a **dividend**. In this section, we consider two types of dividends: cash dividends and stock dividends.

Cash Dividends

A dividend payable in cash is known as a **cash dividend.** For a corporation to issue a cash dividend, three conditions are necessary.

1. Unrestricted retained earnings. In general, corporations can legally declare cash dividends only if the retained earnings balance is sufficient to cover the dividends.

2. Adequate cash balance. The retained earnings balance indicates whether a corporation can legally declare a dividend. But a corporation can pay a cash dividend only if an adequate amount of cash is available. Remember: retained earnings is not the same as cash.

3. Declaration of dividend. Only the board of directors can declare a dividend. Regardless of the amount of cash or other assets accumulated by a corporation, no dividend can be paid unless so declared by the board of directors.

Three dates are involved in the declaration and payment of dividends.

1. **Date of declaration**—the date on which the board of directors decides (declares) that a dividend is to be paid.

2. **Date of record**—the date on which the names of stockholders entitled to receive the dividend are determined.

3. **Date of payment**—the date on which the dividend is actually paid by the corporation.

For example, assume that on January 26 the board of directors declares a dividend of $2 a share on common stock, payable on February 16 to stockholders of record on February 6. In this case, the date of declaration, date of record, and date of payment are as shown in Figure 23-2. To be eligible to receive the dividend, a stockholder's ownership of stock must be entered in the records of the corporation not later than February 6.

> The most important dividend date is the date of declaration. This is the date when the corporation commits to paying the dividend.

FIGURE 23-2 Dividend Dates

Dividends on different classes of capital stock should be accounted for separately. To illustrate, assume that on February 1 the board of directors declares a dividend of $4 per share on 4,000 shares of preferred stock and a dividend of $2 per share on 10,000 shares of common stock. Both dividends are payable on February 20 to stockholders of record on February 10. These dividends are accounted for as follows:

Date of Declaration:

4	Feb.	1	Cash Dividends	16 0 0 0 00			4
5			Preferred Dividends Payable		16 0 0 0 00	5
6			Declared preferred stock cash dividend			6
7						7
8		1	Cash Dividends	20 0 0 0 00		8
9			Common Dividends Payable		20 0 0 0 00	9
10			Declared common stock cash dividend			10

Date of Record:

Feb. 10 No journal entry is made. The date of record has no effect on the corporation accounts. This date simply determines which stockholders receive the dividends.

Date of Payment:

18	Feb.	20	Preferred Dividends Payable		16	0	0	0	00							18
19			Cash								16	0	0	0	00	19
20			Paid preferred stock cash dividend													20
21																21
22			Common Dividends Payable		20	0	0	0	00							22
23			Cash								20	0	0	0	00	23
24			Paid common stock cash dividend													24

If a balance sheet is prepared between the date of declaration and date of payment, dividends payable accounts are reported as current liabilities.

Note that cash dividends reduce the stockholders' equity in the corporation. A cash dividend is a distribution of corporate assets to the stockholders. After Cash Dividends is closed to Retained Earnings, the retained earnings portion of stockholders' equity is reduced accordingly.

Stock Dividends

A **stock dividend** is a proportionate distribution of shares of a corporation's own stock to its stockholders. Corporations may distribute this type of dividend for several reasons:

1. The company may be short of cash.

2. The company may want to increase the marketability of its shares by lowering the price per share. A greater number of shares outstanding decreases the price per share and makes wider ownership possible.

3. The corporation may want to transfer a portion of retained earnings to a paid-in capital category to indicate that it is unavailable for dividends.

Stock dividends usually involve issuing additional common shares to current common stockholders. Stock dividends typically are stated as a percentage of common stock outstanding. For example, a 10% stock dividend means that a stockholder receives one additional share for each 10 shares owned. Thus, the owner of 100 shares of common stock receives an additional 10 shares (10% × 100 shares = 10 shares).

When a stock dividend is declared, the proper journal entry depends on the dividend percentage. If the stock dividend is for less than 20%–25% of the outstanding shares, Stock Dividends is debited for the *market value* of the stock to be distributed. If the stock has neither par nor stated value, Stock Dividends Distributable is credited for the market value of the shares. If the stock has a par or stated value, Stock Dividends Distributable is credited for the par or stated value of the shares. The excess of the market value over par or stated value is credited to Paid-In Capital in Excess of Par (or Stated) Value—Common Stock.

> Note that this 10% stock dividend does not give the stockholder any increased ownership in the corporation. <u>All</u> stockholders receive the 10% dividend, so
>
> everyone still owns the same portion of the corporation. Each stockholder owns 10% more shares, but each individual share is worth less.

LEARNING KEY: To record a stock dividend of less than 20%–25%, debit Retained Earnings for the *market value* of the shares distributed.

To illustrate, assume that Diven Corp. has 4,000 shares of $5 par common stock outstanding. Diven declares a 10% stock dividend on March 5, payable on March 27 to stockholders of record on March 14. The market value of Diven's common stock on the date of declaration is $12 per share. This means that Diven will issue a total of 400 shares of common stock (4,000 shares × 10% = 400 shares) with a market value of $4,800 (400 shares × $12 = $4,800).

We account for this stock dividend as follows:

Date of Declaration:

22	Mar.	5	Stock Dividends	4 8 0 0 00		22
23			Stock Dividends Distributable*		2 0 0 0 00	23
24			Paid-In Capital in Excess of Par—			24
25			Common Stock**		2 8 0 0 00	25
26			Declared Stock Dividend			26
27			* 400 shares × $5 par			27
28			** $4,800 market value − $2,000 par value			28

Date of Record:

Mar. 14   No journal entry. As with cash dividends, the date of record has no effect on the corporation accounts.

Date of Distribution:

14	Mar.	27	Stock Dividends Distributable	2 0 0 0 00		14
15			Common Stock		2 0 0 0 00	15
16			Distributed stock dividend			16

Stock Dividends Distributable is reported as an addition to common stock in the stockholders' equity section of the balance sheet. Stock Dividends Distributable is not a liability since no assets or services are owed.

If a stock dividend is more than 20%–25% of the outstanding shares, Stock Dividends is debited for the *par or stated value* rather than the market value of the shares to be distributed. Otherwise, the accounting is the same as that illustrated for stock dividends of less than 20%–25%.

Note that stock dividends do not affect the assets, liabilities, or total stockholders' equity of the corporation. As with cash dividends, the stock dividends account is closed to Retained Earnings. However, there is no distribution of corporate assets. Stock dividends merely transfer part of the balance of the retained earnings account to one or more paid-in capital accounts.

> For stock with no par or stated value, Retained Earnings usually is debited for the average amount of paid-in capital per share of outstanding stock.

Stock Splits

A **stock split** is an exchange of one share of an old issue of stock for multiple shares of a new issue with a reduced par or stated value. The usual purpose of a stock split is to improve the marketability of the shares by reducing the market price per share. Having a greater number of shares outstanding also makes it possible to have a wider ownership of the stock.

Accounting for a stock split differs from accounting for a stock dividend. A stock split requires no formal journal entry and may be recognized simply by a memorandum notation in the general journal and in the appropriate capital stock accounts. Thus, stock splits do not affect the assets, liabilities, or any component of stockholders' equity of a corporation.

LEARNING KEY: No formal journal entry is made for a stock split.

To illustrate, assume that Splice Corp. has 10,000 shares of $10 par common stock outstanding. Splice declares a two-for-one stock split. This means that Splice will issue a total of 20,000 shares of $5 par common stock in exchange for the 10,000 shares of $10 par common stock currently outstanding. Each stockholder will receive two shares of the new $5 par stock in exchange for one share of the old $10 par stock. The memorandum entry in the journal is as follows:

22		Declared two-for-one stock split. Exchanged							22
23		20,000 shares of $5 par common stock for 10,000							23
24		shares of $10 par common stock.							24

Summary of Dividend and Stock Split Transactions

We have seen that cash dividends, stock dividends, and stock splits affect stockholders' equity differently. Figure 23-3 briefly describes and summarizes the effects of these three transactions on the assets, paid-in capital, and retained earnings of the corporation. Refer to this figure as you work the exercises and problems for this chapter.

TRANS-ACTION	DESCRIPTION	JOURNAL ENTRIES			ASSETS	PAID-IN CAPITAL	RETAINED EARNINGS

Cash Dividend	Distribution of cash to stockholders	At declaration:
		Cash Dividends
		  Dividends Payable
		At payment:
		Dividends Payable
		  Cash
			xxx
			
			xxx
				
				xxx
				
				xxx
					Decrease by amount of dividend distributed	No effect	Decrease by amount of cash dividend*

Stock Dividend Less than 20%–25%	Distribution of corporation's stock to stockholders	At declaration:
		Stock Dividends
		  Stock Div. Distributable
		  Paid-In Capital in
		  Excess of Par
		At distribution:
		Stock Div. Distributable
		  Common Stock
			xxx
			
			xxx
				
				xxx
				
				xxx
				
				xxx
					No effect	Increase by market value of stock distributed	Decrease by market value of stock dividend*

More than 20%–25%	Distribution of corporation's stock to stockholders	At declaration:
		Stock Dividends
		  Stock Div. Distributable
		At distribution:
		Stock Div. Distributable
		  Common Stock
			xxx
			
			xxx
				
				xxx
				
				xxx
					No effect	Increase by par value of stock distributed	Decrease by par value of stock dividend*

Stock Split	Exchange of old stock for multiple shares of new stock	Memo notation			No effect	No effect	No effect

* Recall that Cash Dividends and Stock Dividends are closed to Retained Earnings at the end of the period.

FIGURE 23-3   Summary of Dividend and Split Transactions

APPROPRIATIONS OF RETAINED EARNINGS

LO3 Account for appropriations of retained earnings.

Thus far we have examined how net income, net loss, cash dividends, and stock dividends affect retained earnings. One other event that affects retained earnings is an appropriation. A **retained earnings appropriation** is a restriction of retained earnings by the board of directors for a specific purpose. Recall that corporations may pay dividends only if the retained earnings balance is sufficient to do so. A retained earnings appropriation is used primarily to limit the availability of retained earnings for paying dividends.

To illustrate, assume that Chem Corp. has decided to build a new waste treatment plant. Chem Corp. has a retained earnings balance of $900,000. To finance a portion of the plant (and to inform people of its concern for the environment), the board of directors decides to appropriate $600,000 of retained earnings over a three-year period. At the end of each year for three years, the following journal entry would be made.

1	Retained Earnings*	200 0 0 0 00				1
2	Retained Earnings Appropriated					2
3	for Treatment Plant		200 0 0 0 00			3
4	Appropriated retained earnings for					4
5	treatment plant					5
6	* $600,000 ÷ 3 = $200,000					6

Notice two important things about the appropriation of retained earnings. First, total retained earnings is unaffected. Retained earnings is simply separated into two categories: appropriated and unappropriated. Retained earnings would appear in the Chem Corp. balance sheet at the end of Year 1 as shown in Figure 23-4. The total retained earnings is $900,000, the same as it would be without the appropriation. Second, cash and other assets of the corporation are unaffected. Retained earnings is just a form of ownership interest in the assets of the corporation. All that a retained earnings appropriation does is restrict the corporation's ability to pay out its assets as dividends. In that sense, the *use* of corporate assets is restricted.

 LEARNING KEY: The appropriation of retained earnings does not affect either total retained earnings or the cash and other assets of the corporation.

Retained earnings:			
Appropriated for treatment plant	$200 0 0 0 00		
Unappropriated	700 0 0 0 00		
Total retained earnings		$900 0 0 0 00	

FIGURE 23-4   Retained Earnings Section of the Balance Sheet

After the retained earnings appropriation has served its purpose, the appropriated amount can be returned to retained earnings. To illustrate, let's return to the Chem Corp. example. At the end of three years, Retained Earnings Appropriated for Treatment Plant would have a balance of $600,000. Assume that the treatment plant is completed and that in Year 4 the board of directors decides that the appropriation is no longer needed. The following journal entry would be made.

11		Retained Earnings Appropriated											11
12		for Treatment Plant	600	0	0	0	00						12
13		Retained Earnings							600	0	0	0	00	13
14		Returned appropriation to												14
15		retained earnings												15

The practice of appropriating retained earnings is unusual today. Stockholders generally do not regard the retained earnings balance as the total amount likely to be distributed as dividends. Thus, it generally is unnecessary to make appropriations to advise balance sheet readers that retained earnings is not all available for dividends. Restrictions on dividends can be described just as well in a footnote to the financial statements.

RETAINED EARNINGS STATEMENT

LO4 Prepare a retained earnings statement.

A **retained earnings statement** explains the change in the amount of retained earnings during the year. All of the information necessary to prepare the retained earnings statement is contained in the dividends accounts and the unappropriated and appropriated retained earnings accounts in the general ledger. If there are no appropriated retained earnings, the statement begins with the beginning of the year retained earnings balance. Net income for the year is added (or net loss is subtracted). Any cash and stock dividends are then subtracted to yield the end of the year retained earnings balance. This balance is the same amount that appears in the stockholders' equity section of the year-end balance sheet. Figure 23-5 shows the format for a retained earnings statement with no appropriated retained earnings.

Sample Corporation Retained Earnings Statement For Year Ended December 31, 20 - -										
Retained earnings, January 1						$1,100	0	0	0	00
Add net income for the year						280	0	0	0	00
						$1,380	0	0	0	00
Less: Cash dividends	$30	0	0	0	00					
Stock dividends	20	0	0	0	00	50	0	0	0	00
Retained earnings, December 31						$1,330	0	0	0	00

FIGURE 23-5 Retained Earnings Statement without Appropriated Retained Earnings

If there are both appropriated and unappropriated retained earnings, each is shown separately in the retained earnings statement. To illustrate the preparation of this type of retained earnings statement, let's look again at Chem Corp. Assume that it is the end of the second year after beginning appropriations for the treatment plant. The appropriated and unappropriated retained earnings accounts from Chem's general ledger are shown as follows:

Retained Earnings Appropriated for Treatment Plant				Retained Earnings—Unappropriated				
	Jan. 1	Bal.	200,000	Mar. 15	30,000[3]	Jan. 1	Bal.	700,000
	Dec. 31		200,000[1]	June 15	20,000[4]	Dec. 31		280,000[2]
		Bal.	400,000	Dec. 31	200,000[1]			
							Bal.	730,000

[1] Current year appropriation for treatment plant
[2] Net income for the year
[3] Cash dividend
[4] Stock dividend

Figure 23-6 shows a retained earnings statement prepared from these accounts.

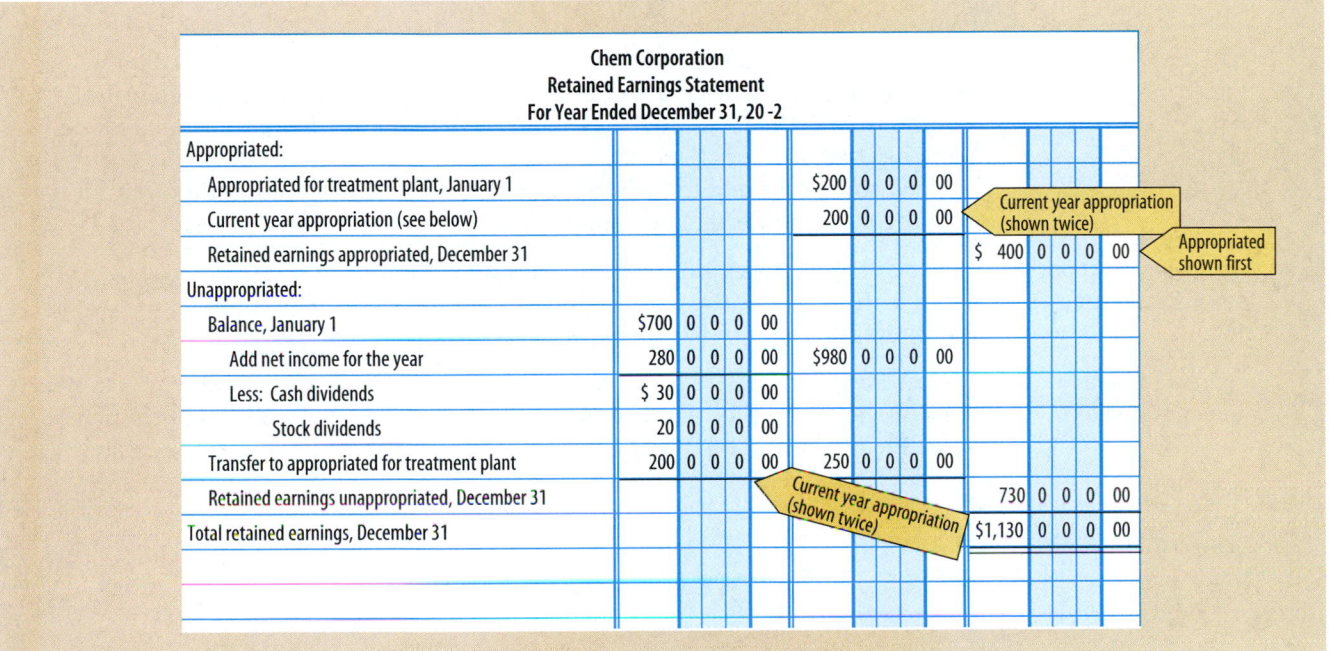

Chem Corporation
Retained Earnings Statement
For Year Ended December 31, 20 -2

Appropriated:			
Appropriated for treatment plant, January 1		$200 0 0 0 00	
Current year appropriation (see below)		200 0 0 0 00	*Current year appropriation (shown twice)*
Retained earnings appropriated, December 31			$ 400 0 0 0 00 *Appropriated shown first*
Unappropriated:			
Balance, January 1	$700 0 0 0 00		
Add net income for the year	280 0 0 0 00	$980 0 0 0 00	
Less: Cash dividends	$ 30 0 0 0 00		
Stock dividends	20 0 0 0 00		
Transfer to appropriated for treatment plant	200 0 0 0 00	250 0 0 0 00	*Current year appropriation (shown twice)*
Retained earnings unappropriated, December 31			730 0 0 0 00
Total retained earnings, December 31			$1,130 0 0 0 00

FIGURE 23-6   Retained Earnings Statement with Appropriated and Unappropriated Retained Earnings

Note the following characteristics of this retained earnings statement.

1. Appropriated retained earnings is presented first, followed by unappropriated retained earnings.

2. Changes in appropriated and unappropriated retained earnings are shown separately.

3. Current year appropriations of retained earnings are shown twice: as an increase in appropriated retained earnings and as a decrease in unappropriated retained earnings.

4. The ending unappropriated retained earnings balance is computed by adding net income for the year to the beginning-of-the-year balance, and then subtracting any dividends and current year appropriations.

5. Appropriated, unappropriated, and total retained earnings are shown separately.

Learning Objectives	Key Points to Remember
1 **Explain the use of the retained earnings account and account for corporate income taxes.**	Earnings retained in a corporation are recorded by closing the income summary account to the retained earnings account at the end of the period. Corporations must pay income taxes. Most corporations must estimate their annual income taxes and make quarterly payments.
2 **Account for dividends and stock splits.**	Three important dates in the declaration and payment of dividends are: 1. Date of declaration 2. Date of record 3. Date of payment Journal entries are necessary on the date of declaration and date of payment. For stock dividends of less than 20%–25%, Stock Dividends is debited for the market value of the shares to be distributed. For stock dividends of more than 20%–25%, Stock Dividends is debited for the par or stated value of the shares. A stock split requires no formal journal entry. A memorandum notation in the general journal and capital stock accounts is all that is necessary.
3 **Account for appropriations of retained earnings.**	A retained earnings appropriation has no effect on total retained earnings or on the assets of the corporation. An appropriation simply restricts the corporation's ability to pay out its assets as dividends.
4 **Prepare a retained earnings statement.**	A retained earnings statement explains the change in the amount of retained earnings during the year. If there are both appropriated and unappropriated retained earnings, each is shown separately on the retained earnings statement.

REFLECTION

Reflection: Answering the Opening Questions

With a cash dividend, cash is transferred from the business to the stockholders. In contrast, stock dividends involve distributing additional shares of stock rather than cash. The cash stays in the business and can be used for purposes such as expansion. As long as the stockholders do not sell the additional shares they receive, their ownership in the business is unaffected. They would have the same percentage ownership before and after the stock dividend.

DEMONSTRATION PROBLEM

On January 1, 20-1, Grant Company's retained earnings account had the following balances.

Appropriated for warehouse	$ 25,000
Unappropriated retained earnings	650,000
	$675,000

During the year ended December 31, 20-1, Grant completed the following selected transactions.

Apr. 15	Estimated that its 20-1 income tax will be $40,000. Based on this estimate, it will make four quarterly payments of $10,000 each on April 15, June 15, September 15, and December 15.
20	Declared semiannual dividend of $.30 per share on common stock to shareholders of record on May 5, payable May 15. Currently, 50,000 shares of $3 par stock are outstanding.
May 15	Paid the cash dividend.
June 15	Made estimated tax payment of $10,000.
Sept. 15	Made estimated tax payment of $10,000.
Oct. 20	Declared a semiannual dividend of $.30 per share on common stock to shareholders of record on November 5, payable on November 15.
Nov. 4	Last year, Grant's board of directors appropriated $50,000 for a warehouse over a two-year period. Made this year's appropriation for $25,000.
15	Paid the cash dividend.
16	Declared a 10% stock dividend to shareholders of record on December 2, distributable on December 10. Market value of the common stock was estimated at $7 per share.
Dec. 10	Issued certificates for common stock dividend.
15	Made estimated tax payment of $10,000.
	On December 31, the following adjusting and closing entries were made.
Dec. 31	Grant's actual 20-1 income tax is $44,000. This amount will be paid by March 15, 20-2. Made adjustment for the additional amount owed.
31	Net income for 20-1 was $98,000. Closed the income summary account.
31	Closed the cash dividends and stock dividends accounts.

REQUIRED

1. Prepare journal entries for the above transactions and for the adjusting and closing process.

2. Post all entries affecting the appropriated and unappropriated retained earnings accounts to T accounts.

3. Prepare a retained earnings statement for the year ended December 31, 20-1.

(continued)

Solution

1.

			GENERAL JOURNAL				PAGE 1		
	DATE		DESCRIPTION	POST REF.	DEBIT		CREDIT		
1	20-1 Apr.	15	Income Tax Expense		10 0 0 0 00				1
2			Cash				10 0 0 0 00		2
3			Made quarterly estimated tax payment						3
4									4
5		20	Cash Dividends		15 0 0 0 00				5
6			Common Dividends Payable				15 0 0 0 00		6
7			Declared common stock cash dividend						7
8									8
9	May	15	Common Dividends Payable		15 0 0 0 00				9
10			Cash				15 0 0 0 00		10
11			Paid common stock cash dividend						11
12									12
13	June	15	Income Tax Expense		10 0 0 0 00				13
14			Cash				10 0 0 0 00		14
15			Made quarterly estimated tax payment						15
16									16
17	Sept.	15	Income Tax Expense		10 0 0 0 00				17
18			Cash				10 0 0 0 00		18
19			Made quarterly estimated tax payment						19
20									20
21	Oct.	20	Cash Dividends		15 0 0 0 00				21
22			Common Dividends Payable				15 0 0 0 00		22
23			Declared common stock cash dividend						23
24									24
25	Nov.	4	Retained Earnings		25 0 0 0 00				25
26			Retained Earnings Appropriated for Warehouse				25 0 0 0 00		26
27			Appropriated retained earnings for warehouse						27
28									28
29		15	Common Dividends Payable		15 0 0 0 00				29
30			Cash				15 0 0 0 00		30
31			Paid common stock cash dividend						31

GENERAL JOURNAL PAGE 2

	DATE		DESCRIPTION	POST REF.	DEBIT	CREDIT	
1	20-1 Nov.	16	Stock Dividends		35 0 0 0 00		1
2			Stock Dividends Distributable ($3 × 5,000)			15 0 0 0 00	2
3			Paid-In Capital in Excess of Par—				3
4			Common Stock ($4 × 5,000)			20 0 0 0 00	4
5			Declared stock dividend				5
6							6
7	Dec.	10	Stock Dividends Distributable		15 0 0 0 00		7
8			Common Stock			15 0 0 0 00	8
9			Distributed stock dividend				9
10							10
11		15	Income Tax Expense		10 0 0 0 00		11
12			Cash			10 0 0 0 00	12
13			Made quarterly estimated tax payment				13
14							14
15			**Adjusting**				15
16		31	Income Tax Expense		4 0 0 0 00		16
17			Income Tax Payable			4 0 0 0 00	17
18							18
19			**Closing**				19
20		31	Income Summary		98 0 0 0 00		20
21			Retained Earnings			98 0 0 0 00	21
22							22
23		31	Retained Earnings		30 0 0 0 00		23
24			Cash Dividends			30 0 0 0 00	24
25							25
26		31	Retained Earnings		35 0 0 0 00		26
27			Stock Dividends			35 0 0 0 00	27
28							28
29							29

2.

Retained Earnings—Appropriated

Bal.	25,000		
Nov. 4	25,000		
Bal.	50,000		

Retained Earnings—Unappropriated

Nov. 4	25,000	Bal.	650,000
Dec. 31	30,000	Dec. 31	98,000
31	35,000		
		Bal.	658,000

3.

Grant Company
Retained Earnings Statement
For Year Ended December 31, 20 -1

Appropriated:				
Appropriated for warehouse, January 1			$ 25 0 0 0 00	
Current year appropriation (see below)			25 0 0 0 00	
Retained earnings appropriated, December 31				$ 50 0 0 0 00
Unappropriated:				
Balance, January 1	$650 0 0 0 00			
Add net income for the year	98 0 0 0 00	$748 0 0 0 00		
Less: Cash dividends	$ 30 0 0 0 00			
Stock dividends	35 0 0 0 00			
Transfer to appropriated for warehouse	25 0 0 0 00	90 0 0 0 00		
Retained earnings unappropriated, December 31				658 0 0 0 00
Total retained earnings, December 31				$708 0 0 0 00

On-Line Learning Tools

For more information, visit: http://heintz.swlearning.com

The Heintz & Parry product web site is designed specifically for **COLLEGE ACCOUNTING, 18e.** The features include downloadable student resources and an interactive study center, organized by chapter, which contains learning objectives, web links, on-line quizzes with automatic feedback, and more.

KEY TERMS

cash dividend, (866)   A dividend payable in cash.

date of declaration, (867)   The date on which the board of directors declares that a dividend is to be paid.

date of payment, (867)   The date on which the dividend is actually paid by the corporation.

date of record, (867)   The date on which the names of stockholders entitled to receive the dividend are determined.

dividend, (866)   A distribution of earnings by a corporation to its stockholders.

retained earnings appropriation, (871)   A restriction of retained earnings by the board of directors for a specific purpose.

retained earnings statement, (872)   A statement that explains the change in the amount of retained earnings during the year.

stock dividend, (868)   A proportionate distribution of shares of a corporation's own stock to its stockholders.

stock split, (869)   An exchange of one share of an old issue of stock for multiple shares of a new issue with a reduced par or stated value.

REVIEW QUESTIONS

(LO1)   1. What are the two major sources of capital for every type of business?

(LO1)   2. For what reason do corporations retain earnings in the business?

(LO1)   3. What expense do corporations incur that sole proprietorships and partnerships do not?

(LO1)   4. How do the procedures for closing Income Summary of a corporation differ from those of a sole proprietorship or partnership?

(LO2)   5. What are the three dates involved in the declaration and payment of dividends? What is the meaning of each date?

(LO2)   6. What is the effect of a cash dividend on the corporation accounts?

(LO2)   7. Give three reasons why a corporation may distribute a stock dividend.

(LO2)   8. Where should stock dividends distributable be reported on the balance sheet? Why?

(LO2)   9. What effect does a stock dividend have on the accounts of the corporation? a stock split?

(LO3)   10. What is the primary reason for appropriating retained earnings?

(LO4)   11. How are appropriated and unappropriated retained earnings shown on the retained earnings statement?

Self-Study Test Questions

True/False

1. Income taxes are a unique expense of the corporate form of business.

2. The adjusting and closing process at the end of the period is virtually the same for corporations as for sole proprietorships and partnerships.

3. A distribution of earnings by a corporation to its stockholders is known as a dividend.

4. A dividend payable in cash is known as a stock dividend.

5. When accounting for the declaration and payment of dividends, the date of record requires a journal entry.

Multiple Choice

1. A proportionate distribution of shares of a corporation's own stock to its stockholders is called a

    (a) stock dividend.   (c) stock split.
    (b) cash dividend.   (d) appropriation.

2. When a stock dividend is declared, the journal entry will include a credit to

    (a) Retained Earnings.   (c) Stock Dividends Payable.
    (b) Stock Dividends Distributable. (d) Stock Dividends Declared.

3. Stock Dividends Distributable is classified on the balance sheet as a(n)

    (a) asset.   (c) expense.
    (b) liability.   (d) stockholders' equity.

4. The payment of a cash dividend will include a

    (a) debit to Dividends Declared.   (c) credit to Cash.
    (b) credit to Dividends Payable.   (d) debit to Retained Earnings.

5. When retained earnings is appropriated, total retained earnings

    (a) remains the same.   (c) decreases.
    (b) increases.   (d) increases or decreases, depending on the amount.

The answers to the Self-Study Test Questions are at the end of the text.

MANAGING YOUR WRITING

The investments committee of your church has come to you for advice. One of the stocks held by the church has paid cash dividends for years. This year the company issued a 10% stock dividend, so that the church received additional shares rather than cash. The committee is concerned about whether this stock dividend is really worth anything. One committee member argues the stock dividend is as good as cash; another argues that the dividend is worthless.

Write a brief report to the committee explaining the difference between a cash dividend and a stock dividend. Evaluate the value of the stock dividend compared with the cash dividend the church has received in prior years.

ETHICS CASE

Richard Petri is the chief financial officer at Computer Electronics, Inc. In this capacity he attends all monthly board of directors meetings. A special meeting of the board of directors was called to discuss substantially increasing the amount of cash dividends paid to stockholders this year. The board voted unanimously to increase the dividend. Later that night Richard called his uncle and hinted around that Computer Electronics, Inc., was going to make its stockholders very happy. His uncle didn't own any stock in Computer Electronics but went out and purchased 500 shares the next day.

1. Did Richard do anything unethical? Would your answer be different if Richard specifically stated that the dividends on Computer Electronic, Inc., were being increased substantially?

2. What should Richard's boss do if he finds out what Richard said to his uncle?

3. Write a short paragraph explaining the difference between cash dividends and stock dividends.

4. In groups of two or three, discuss possible reasons why a corporation might want to pay a very low or high dividend in any given year.

WEB WORK

Wendy's International, Inc. went public in 1975 and since then has had seven stock splits.

1. Read about the history of Wendy's stock. Under Stock Information choose Stock Split History.

2. If you purchased 100 shares of Wendy's stock in 1975, how many would you have today?

Visit the Interactive Study Center on our web site at **http://heintz. swlearning.com** for special hotlinks to assist you in this assignment.

SERIES A EXERCISES

EXERCISE 23-1A **(LO1)**
Dec. 31. Dr. Income Tax
Expense, $6,000

CORPORATE INCOME TAX Stanton Company estimates that its 20-1 income tax will be $80,000. Based on this estimate, it will make four quarterly payments of $20,000 each on April 15, June 15, September 15, and December 15.

1. Prepare the journal entry for April 15.

2. Assume that all four quarterly payments have been entered in the general journal. On December 31, Stanton's actual income tax amounts to $86,000. This amount will be paid by March 15, 20-2. Prepare the journal entry to record the additional income tax owed.

EXERCISE 23-2A **(LO1)**
2. Cr. Stock Dividends, $18,000

CLOSING INCOME SUMMARY AND DIVIDENDS TO RETAINED EARNINGS Davidson Company had a net income of $120,000 and paid cash dividends of $24,000 for 20--. Wilson and Picket Company had a net loss of $30,000 and distributed a 10% stock dividend with a market value of $18,000.

1. Prepare the journal entries for Davidson as of December 31, 20--, to close Income Summary and Cash Dividends into Retained Earnings.

2. Prepare the journal entries for Wilson and Picket as of December 31, 20--, to close Income Summary and Stock Dividends into Retained Earnings.

EXERCISE 23-3A **(LO2)**
July 10. Dr. Cash
Dividends, $40,000

COMMON AND PREFERRED CASH DIVIDENDS Wakui Company currently has 100,000 shares of $1 par common stock outstanding and 1,000 shares of $100 par preferred stock outstanding. On July 10, the board of directors declared a semiannual dividend of $.40 per share on common stock to shareholders of record on August 1, payable on August 5.

On July 15, the board of directors declared a semiannual dividend of $10 per share on preferred stock to shareholders of record on August 5, payable on August 10.

Prepare journal entries for the declaration and payment of the common and preferred stock cash dividends.

EXERCISE 23-4A **(LO2)**
1. Mar. 15. Dr. Stock
Dividends, $60,000

STOCK DIVIDENDS Cruz Company currently has 100,000 shares of $1 par common stock outstanding. On March 15, a 10% stock dividend was declared to shareholders of record on April 2, distributable on April 14. Market value of the common stock was estimated at $6 per share.

1. Prepare journal entries for the declaration and distribution of the 10% common stock dividend.

2. Assume Cruz Company declared a stock dividend of 30% rather than 10%. Prepare journal entries for the declaration and distribution of the 30% common stock dividend.

EXERCISE 23-5A **(LO2)**
Memo entry only

STOCK SPLIT Goldstein Company has 100,000 shares of $10 par common stock outstanding. On July 1, the board of directors declared a two-for-one stock split. Prepare a memorandum entry in the general journal indicating the new par value and the total number of outstanding shares of common stock.

EXERCISE 23-6A **(LO3)**
Oct. 2. Dr. Retained
Earnings, $80,000

RETAINED EARNINGS APPROPRIATION On October 2, 20-1, the board of directors of Foxworth Company appropriated $80,000 of retained earnings for the purpose of buying a new sailboat (used for entertaining clients). On July 15, 20-2, the sailboat was purchased and the board of directors decided that the appropriation was no longer needed.

Prepare journal entries for the appropriation on October 2, 20-1, and the subsequent return on July 15, 20-2.

EXERCISE 23-7A   **(LO4)**   **RETAINED EARNINGS STATEMENT** McGregor Company had the following
Retained Earnings,   balances as of December 31, 20--.
Dec. 31: $75,000

Retained earnings, January 1	$60,000
Cash dividends declared	5,000
Net income for the year	20,000

Prepare a retained earnings statement for the year ended December 31, 20--.

SERIES A PROBLEMS

PROBLEM 23-8A   **(LO1/2)**   **CASH DIVIDENDS AND INCOME TAXES** During the year ended December 31,
1st Dec. 31 entry.   20-2, Bebeto Company completed the following selected transactions.
Dr. Income Tax
Expense, $5,000

Apr. 15   Estimated that its 20-2 income tax will be $30,000. Based on this estimate,
it will make four quarterly payments of $7,500 each on April 15, June 15,
September 15, and December 15. Made the first payment.

25   Declared a semiannual dividend of $.45 per share on common stock to
shareholders of record on May 10, payable May 20. Currently, 80,000 shares
of $1 par common stock are outstanding.

May 20   Paid the cash dividends.

June 15   Made estimated tax payment of $7,500.

Sept. 15   Made estimated tax payment of $7,500.

Oct. 25   Declared semiannual dividend of $.45 per share on common stock to
shareholders of record on November 10, payable on November 20.

Nov. 20   Paid the cash dividends.

Dec. 15   Made estimated tax payment of $7,500.

31   Bebeto's actual 20-2 income tax is $35,000. This amount will be paid by March
15, 20-3. Made adjustment for the additional amount owed.

31   Net income for 20-2 was $100,000. Closed the income summary account.

31   Closed the cash dividends account.

REQUIRED

Prepare journal entries for the transactions.

PROBLEM 23-9A   **(LO2)**   **CASH DIVIDENDS, STOCK DIVIDEND, AND STOCK SPLIT** During the year
ended December 31, 20--, Kuang-fu Company completed the following transactions.

Nov. 22. Dr. Stock
Dividends, $40,000

Apr. 15   Declared a semiannual dividend of $.80 per share on preferred stock and $.50
per share on common stock to shareholders of record on May 5, payable on
May 10. Currently, 4,000 shares of $100 par preferred stock and 50,000 shares
of $1 par common stock are outstanding.

May 10   Paid the cash dividends.

Oct. 15   Declared semiannual dividend of $.80 per share on preferred stock and $.50
per share on common stock to shareholders of record on November 5, payable
on November 20.

Nov. 20   Paid the cash dividends.

22   Declared a 10% stock dividend to shareholders of record on December 8,
distributable on December 16. Market value of the common stock was estimated
at $8 per share.

Dec. 16	Issued certificates for common stock dividend.
20	Board of directors declared a two-for-one common stock split.

REQUIRED

Prepare journal entries for the transactions.

PROBLEM 23-10A (LO2/3)
Nov. 12. Dr. Cash Dividends,
$19,500

CASH DIVIDEND AND APPROPRIATION OF RETAINED EARNINGS On January 1, 20--, MacMillan Company's retained earnings accounts had the following balances.

Appropriated for computer	$ 25,000
Appropriated for warehouse	80,000
Unappropriated retained earnings	600,000
	$705,000

During the year ended December 31, 20--, MacMillan completed the following selected transactions.

Mar. 16	Last year, MacMillan's board of directors appropriated $75,000 for a mainframe computer over a three-year period. Made this year's appropriation for $25,000.
Nov. 5	Purchased a new warehouse for $80,000, paying cash for the total amount.
5	The board of directors returned the amount of retained earnings set aside for the warehouse to unappropriated retained earnings.
12	Declared a cash dividend of $.65 per share on common stock to shareholders of record on December 8, payable on December 19. Currently, 30,000 shares of common stock are outstanding.
Dec. 19	Paid the cash dividends.

REQUIRED

Prepare journal entries for the transactions.

PROBLEM 23-11A (LO1/2/3/4)

3. Retained Earnings,
Dec. 31: $1,094,000

RETAINED EARNINGS ACCOUNTS AND STATEMENT On January 1, 20--, Glover Company's retained earnings accounts had the following balances.

Appropriated for land acquisition	$ 60,000
Unappropriated retained earnings	900,000
	$960,000

During the year ended December 31, 20--, Glover completed the following selected transactions.

Mar. 20	Declared a semiannual dividend of $.80 per share on preferred stock and $.25 per share on common stock to shareholders of record on April 10, payable on April 15. Currently, 10,000 shares of $50 par preferred stock and 100,000 shares of $5 par common stock are outstanding.
Apr. 15	Paid the cash dividends.
June 16	Last year, Glover's board of directors appropriated $180,000 for the purchase of land for a future building site over a three-year period. Made this year's appropriation for $60,000.
Oct. 10	Declared semiannual dividend of $.80 per share on preferred stock and $.25 per share on common stock to shareholders of record on November 5, payable on November 10.
Nov. 10	Paid the cash dividends.

(continued)

17	Declared a 5% stock dividend to shareholders of record on December 8, distributable on December 15. Market value of the common stock was estimated at $18 per share.
Dec. 15	Issued certificates for common stock dividend.
31	Net income for 20-- was $290,000. Closed the income summary account.
31	Closed the cash dividends and stock dividends accounts.

REQUIRED

1. Prepare journal entries for the transactions.

2. Post all entries affecting the appropriated and unappropriated retained earnings accounts to T accounts.

3. Prepare a retained earnings statement for the year ended December 31, 20--.

SERIES B EXERCISES

EXERCISE 23-1B (LO1)
Dec. 31. Dr. Income Tax
Expense, $12,000

CORPORATE INCOME TAX Regis Company estimates that its 20-1 income tax will be $100,000. Based on this estimate, it will make four quarterly payments of $25,000 each on April 15, June 15, September 15, and December 15.

1. Prepare the journal entry for April 15.

2. Assume that all four quarterly payments have been entered in the general journal. On December 31, Regis' actual income tax amounts to $112,000. This amount will be paid by March 15, 20-2. Prepare the journal entry to record the additional income tax owed.

EXERCISE 23-2B (LO1)
2. Cr. Stock Dividends, $15,000

CLOSING INCOME SUMMARY AND DIVIDENDS TO RETAINED EARNINGS Kennington Company had a net income of $90,000 and paid cash dividends of $18,000 for 20--. Mueller and Hanson Company had a net loss of $20,000 and distributed a 10% stock dividend with a market value of $15,000.

1. Prepare the journal entries for Kennington as of December 31, 20--, to close Income Summary and Cash Dividends into Retained Earnings.

2. Prepare the journal entries for Mueller and Hanson as of December 31, 20--, to close Income Summary and Stock Dividends into Retained Earnings.

EXERCISE 23-3B (LO2)
July 10. Dr. Cash
Dividends, $30,000

COMMON AND PREFERRED CASH DIVIDENDS Ramirez Company currently has 100,000 shares of $1 par common stock outstanding and 5,000 shares of $50 par preferred stock outstanding. On July 10, the board of directors declared a semiannual dividend of $.30 per share on common stock to shareholders of record on August 1, payable on August 5.

On July 15, the board of directors declared a semiannual dividend of $5 per share on preferred stock to shareholders of record on August 5, payable on August 10.

Prepare journal entries for the declaration and payment of the common and preferred stock cash dividends.

EXERCISE 23-4B (LO2)
1. Mar. 15. Dr. Stock
Dividends, $130,000

STOCK DIVIDENDS Martinez Company currently has 200,000 shares of $1 par common stock outstanding. On March 15, a 5% stock dividend was declared to shareholders of record on April 2, distributable on April 14. Market value of the common stock was estimated at $13 per share.

1. Prepare journal entries for the declaration and distribution of the 5% common stock dividend.

2. Assume Martinez Co. declared a stock dividend of 30% rather than 5%. Prepare journal entries for the declaration and distribution of the 30% common stock dividend.

EXERCISE 23-5B   **(LO2)**   **STOCK SPLIT** Rogerson Company has 40,000 shares of $2 par common stock
Memo entry only   outstanding. On July 1, the board of directors declared a two-for-one stock split.
    Prepare a memorandum entry in the general journal indicating the new par value and the total number of outstanding shares of common stock.

EXERCISE 23-6B   **(LO3)**   **RETAINED EARNINGS APPROPRIATION** On October 2, 20-1, the board of
Oct. 2. Dr. Retained   directors of Carr Company appropriated $400,000 of retained earnings for the
Earnings, $400,000   purpose of buying a new yacht (used for entertaining clients). On July 15, 20-2, the yacht was purchased and the board of directors decided that the appropriation was no longer needed.
    Prepare journal entries for the appropriation on October 2, 20-1, and the subsequent return on July 15, 20-2.

EXERCISE 23-7B   **(LO4)**   **RETAINED EARNINGS STATEMENT** Womack Company had the following
Retained Earnings,   balances as of December 31, 20--.
Dec. 31: $105,000

Retained earnings, January 1	$80,000
Cash dividends declared	15,000
Net income for the year	40,000

Prepare a retained earnings statement for the year ended December 31, 20--.

SERIES B PROBLEMS

PROBLEM 23-8B   **(LO1/2)**   **CASH DIVIDENDS AND INCOME TAXES** During the year ended December 31,
1st. Dec. 31 entry.   20-2, Tatu Company completed the following selected transactions.
Dr. Income Tax
Expense, $14,000

Apr. 15   Estimated that its 20-2 income tax will be $160,000. Based on this estimate, it will make four quarterly payments of $40,000 each on April 15, June 15, September 15, and December 15. Made the first payment.

25   Declared a semiannual dividend of $.50 per share on common stock to shareholders of record on May 10, payable May 20. Currently, 90,000 shares of $1 par common stock are outstanding.

May 20   Paid the cash dividends.

June 15   Made estimated tax payment of $40,000.

Sept. 15   Made estimated tax payment of $40,000.

Oct. 25   Declared semiannual dividend of $.50 per share on common stock to shareholders of record on November 10, payable on November 20.

Nov. 20   Paid the cash dividends.

Dec. 15   Made estimated tax payment of $40,000.

31   Tatu's actual 20-2 income tax amounts to $174,000. This amount will be paid by March 15, 20-3. Made adjustment for the additional amount owed.

31   Net income for 20-2 was $196,000. Closed the income summary account.

31   Closed the cash dividends account.

REQUIRED
Prepare journal entries for the transactions.

PROBLEM 23-9B   **(LO2)**

Nov. 22. Dr. Stock
Dividends, $105,000

CASH DIVIDENDS, STOCK DIVIDEND, AND STOCK SPLIT During the year ended December 31, 20--, Baggio Company completed the following transactions.

Apr. 15   Declared a semiannual dividend of $.65 per share on preferred stock and $.45 per share on common stock to shareholders of record on May 5, payable on May 10. Currently, 6,000 shares of $50 par preferred stock and 70,000 shares of $1 par common stock are outstanding.

May 10   Paid the cash dividends.

Oct. 15   Declared semiannual dividend of $.65 per share on preferred stock and $.45 per share on common stock to shareholders of record on November 5, payable on November 20.

Nov. 20   Paid the cash dividends.

22   Declared a 10% stock dividend to shareholders of record on December 8, distributable on December 16. Market value of the common stock was estimated at $15 per share.

Dec. 16   Issued certificates for common stock dividend.

20   Board of directors declared a two-for-one common stock split.

REQUIRED

Prepare journal entries for the transactions.

PROBLEM 23-10B   **(LO2/3)**

Nov. 12. Dr. Cash
Dividends, $36,000

CASH DIVIDEND AND APPROPRIATION OF RETAINED EARNINGS On January 1, 20--, Krausert Company's retained earnings accounts had the following balances.

Appropriated for computer	$ 50,000
Appropriated for warehouse	70,000
Unappropriated retained earnings	800,000
	$920,000

During the year ended December 31, 20--, Krausert completed the following selected transactions.

Mar. 16   Last year, Krausert's board of directors appropriated $100,000 for a mainframe computer over a two-year period. Made this year's appropriation for $50,000.

Nov. 5   Purchased a warehouse for $70,000, paying cash for the total amount.

5   The board of directors returned the amount of retained earnings set aside for the warehouse to unappropriated retained earnings.

12   Declared a cash dividend of $.90 per share on common stock to shareholders of record on December 8, payable on December 19. Currently, 40,000 shares of common stock are outstanding.

Dec. 19   Paid the cash dividends.

REQUIRED

Prepare journal entries for the transactions.

PROBLEM 23-11B   **(LO1/2/3/4)**

RETAINED EARNINGS ACCOUNTS AND STATEMENT On January 1, 20--, Nguyen Company's retained earnings accounts had the following balances.

Appropriated for land acquisition	$ 75,000
Unappropriated retained earnings	825,000
	$900,000

3. Retained Earnings, Dec. 31: $989,000

During the year ended December 31, 20--, Nguyen completed the following selected transactions.

Mar. 20   Declared a semiannual dividend of $.75 per share on preferred stock and $.20 per share on common stock to shareholders of record on April 10, payable on April 15. Currently, 12,000 shares of $50 par preferred stock and 90,000 shares of $2 par common stock are outstanding.

Apr. 15   Paid the cash dividends.

June 16   Last year, Nguyen's board of directors appropriated $150,000 for the purchase of land for a future building site over a two-year period. Made this year's appropriation for $75,000.

Oct. 10   Declared semiannual dividend of $.75 per share on preferred stock and $.20 per share on common stock to shareholders of record on November 5, payable on November 10.

Nov. 10   Paid the cash dividends.

17   Declared a 10% stock dividend to shareholders of record on December 8, distributable on December 15. Market value of the common stock was estimated at $13 per share.

Dec. 15   Issued certificates for common stock dividend.

31   Net income for 20-- was $260,000. Closed the income summary account.

31   Closed the cash dividends and stock dividends accounts.

REQUIRED

1. Prepare journal entries for the transactions.

2. Post all entries affecting the appropriated and unappropriated retained earnings accounts to T accounts.

3. Prepare a retained earnings statement for the year ended December 31, 20--.

MASTERY PROBLEM

On January 1, 20-1, Dover Company's retained earnings accounts had the following balances.

Appropriated for printing press	$ 50,000
Unappropriated retained earnings	800,000
	$850,000

3. Retained Earnings, Dec. 31: $958,000

During the year ended December 31, 20--, Dover completed the following selected transactions.

Mar. 15   Declared a semiannual dividend of $.30 per share on preferred stock and $.40 per share on common stock to shareholders of record on April 5, payable on April 10. Currently, 5,000 shares of $10 par preferred stock and 30,000 shares of $2 par common stock are outstanding.

Apr. 10   Paid the cash dividend.

July 2   Last year, Dover's board of directors appropriated $100,000 for a printing press over a two-year period. Made this year's appropriation for $50,000.

(continued)

Sept. 15	Declared semiannual dividend of $.30 per share on preferred stock and $.40 per share on common stock to shareholders of record on October 5, payable on October 10.
Oct. 10	Paid the cash dividend.
Nov. 10	Board of directors declared a two-for-one common stock split.
Dec. 31	Net income for 20-- was $135,000. Closed the income summary account.
31	Closed the cash dividends account.

REQUIRED

1. Prepare journal entries for the transactions.

2. Post all entries affecting the appropriated and unappropriated retained earnings accounts to T accounts.

3. Prepare a retained earnings statement for the year ended December 31, 20--.

CHALLENGE PROBLEM

This problem challenges you to apply your cumulative accounting knowledge to move a step beyond the material in the chapter.

1. (d). Dr. Cash Dividends, $57,200

LeeJin Corp. started a two-year period with 200,000 shares of $2 par common stock outstanding. During the two years, LeeJin had the following capital stock transactions.

(a) Declared a 10% common stock dividend. The market value of the common stock was estimated at $8 per share.

(b) Declared a cash dividend of $.20 per share on common stock

(c) Declared a 30% common stock dividend. The market value of the common stock was estimated at $9 per share.

(d) Declared a cash dividend of $.20 per share on common stock.

(e) Declared a two-for-one stock split.

(f) Declared a cash dividend of $.16 per share on common stock.

REQUIRED

1. Prepare general journal entries for each of the transactions. Identify each transaction by the appropriate letter. (Assume that any cash or share distributions have been completed and are a matter of record before the next transaction occurs.)

2. Compute the following:

    (a) Number of shares of common stock outstanding after all the transactions have been completed.

    (b) The par value per share of LeeJin's common stock after all the transactions have been completed.

©GETTY IMAGES/PHOTODISC

Corporations: Bonds

Several years have passed since Mike Finbar incorporated his business, and Finny Co. has an opportunity to expand its operations into nearby states. To do so, it needs substantial additional resources. After his experience dealing with stockholders who wanted too much of the company's profits paid out as cash dividends, Mike Finbar is reluctant to issue additional stock. Finny Co. has used promissory notes to borrow necessary funds several times, but the amount and duration of these are not what the company needs now.

Mike's accountant suggests that the company consider issuing bonds to obtain the additional resources. He says that bonds are different from notes. He warns that bonds can be riskier than stock, but that the risk should not be a problem for a successful company like Finny. How are bonds different from notes? How are bonds riskier than stock?

Careful study of this chapter should enable you to:

LO1 Describe the types of bonds and how their sales price is determined.

LO2 Account for bonds issued at face value.

LO3 Account for bonds issued at a premium.

LO4 Account for bonds issued at a discount.

LO5 Account for bond redemption and bond sinking funds.

In Chapters 22 and 23 we learned how to account for two major sources of funds for a corporation—capital stock and retained earnings. In this chapter, we turn our attention to a third major source of funds—bonds.

Bonds are similar to the promissory notes payable we saw in Chapter 18. Both are formal, written promises to pay an amount of money at a specified date. The main differences are that bonds are usually for larger sums of money and for longer time periods.

TYPES OF BONDS AND DETERMINATION OF SALES PRICE

LO1 Describe the types of bonds and how their sales price is determined.

A **bond** is a written promise to pay a specific sum of money at a specific future date. Bonds and stock often are mentioned in the same breath, but they are quite different. A bond is a debt of the corporation—a promise to pay certain amounts of money. If these payments are not made, the creditors can force the company into bankruptcy. Stock represents corporate ownership or equity; there is no promise to pay any definite amount of money. Bondholders are creditors of a corporation; stockholders are owners.

Bonds usually are issued in denominations of $1,000 each. For example, if a corporation issues $300,000 of bonds, this usually means it issues 300 individual bonds, each worth $1,000. This enables the issuing corporation to obtain large amounts of money by selling the bonds to many investors.

Classification of Bonds

To appeal to different types of investors, bonds come with many different features. Based on some of these features, bonds can be classified as to (1) security, (2) timing of payment of principal, and (3) identification of ownership.

Security. All bonds are either secured or unsecured. A **secured bond** is one that is backed by specific corporate assets. A common type of secured bond is a **mortgage bond**—a bond secured by a mortgage on corporate property such as real estate or equipment.

An **unsecured bond** is backed solely by the general credit of the corporation, rather than by any specific assets. These bonds are called **debenture bonds**.

Timing of Payment of Principal. The **principal** of a bond is the amount to be paid to the bondholder at maturity. Based on the provisions made for payment of the principal, four types of bonds can be identified.

1. **Term bonds**—bonds that all have the same maturity date.

2. **Serial bonds**—bonds issued in a series so that a specified amount of the bonds matures each year.

3. **Convertible bonds**—bonds that give the holder the option of exchanging the bonds for capital stock of the corporation.

4. **Callable bonds**—bonds that give the issuing corporation the option of calling the bonds for redemption before the maturity date.

Identification of Ownership. There are two types of bonds according to identification of ownership.

1. **Registered bonds**—bonds whose ownership is recorded (registered) in the corporate records. The corporation maintains a record of the name and address of each owner. Any change of ownership must be registered with the corporation.

2. **Coupon bonds (bearer bonds)**—bonds whose ownership generally is not recorded by the corporation. Change of ownership is accomplished simply by delivering the bond. A coupon bond has interest coupons attached, one for each interest period during the life of the bond. As each coupon comes due, the holder of the bond removes the coupon and presents it to a bank for payment. Today, corporations rarely issue coupon bonds, but old ones are still in circulation.

Determining Sales Price

At first glance, you would expect a $1,000 bond to sell for $1,000, its **face value**. But, for various reasons, bonds often do not sell at their face value. Two of the more important factors in determining the price at which bonds will sell are:

1. the rate of interest (**stated** or **coupon rate**) on the bonds, and

2. the current **market rate** of interest on similar investments.

The stated or coupon rate is the interest rate specified on the face of the bond. The market rate can be defined from two points of view. For the bond buyer, this is the rate that can be earned on similar investments. For the bond issuer, this is the rate that other companies in similar financial condition have to pay to borrow money.

To illustrate, assume that Watkin Corp. wants to sell $400,000 of 10%, 10-year bonds. If the current market rate on similar investments is 10 percent, the bonds will sell at their face value of $400,000. But if the current market rate is 11 percent, Watkin's bonds will sell at a **discount**, or at a price less than their face value of $400,000. This is because the lower interest rate (10% vs. 11%) on Watkin's bonds makes them less valuable. In simple terms, investors will not pay full price for Watkin's bonds with a 10 percent interest rate if they can get a similar investment with an 11 percent interest rate.

What if the current market rate is 9 percent? In this case, Watkin's bonds will sell at a **premium**, or at a price in excess of their face value of $400,000. This is because the higher interest rate (10% vs. 9%) on the bonds makes them more valuable.

Figure 24-1 summarizes the conditions in which bonds will sell at face value, premium, and discount.

LEARNING KEY: To determine whether a bond will sell at a price equal to, greater than, or less than face value, compare the stated and market interest rates.

INTEREST RATE			SELLING PRICE	
Stated rate	=	Market rate	=	Face value
Stated rate	>	Market rate	>	Face value (Premium)
Stated rate	<	Market rate	<	Face value (Discount)

FIGURE 24-1 Interest Rates and Bond Selling Prices

A BROADER VIEW

Debt Can Be Dangerous

©REUTERS NEW MEDIA INC./CORBIS

The independent auditors' report on the 2002 financial statement of American Airlines, Inc., included the following passage: "... the potential failure of the company to satisfy the liquidity requirements in certain of its credit agreements ... raise substantial doubt about the entity's ability to continue as a going concern." In other words, the independent auditors doubted that American would be able to survive as a business, in part because the company might not be able to meet its debt requirements.

This is a good example of the risk dimension of debt. By issuing stock, a company gives up ownership interest in the business. But when bonds and other types of debt are issued, a company runs the risk of going bankrupt if it cannot make the payments on its debts. Careful analysis and planning are needed in deciding how to finance a business.

Bond prices usually are stated using numbers such as 95, 99, or 102. These numbers are percentages of the face values of bond issues. Thus, a $100,000 bond issue sold at 95 has a market price of $95,000 ($100,000 × .95). A similar issue sold at 102 has a market price of $102,000. Numbers below 100 indicate discount issues. Numbers above 100 indicate premium issues.

ACCOUNTING FOR BONDS ISSUED AT FACE VALUE

LO2 Account for bonds issued at face value.

To illustrate the accounting for bonds, we will use bonds issued by Watkin Corp. Assume the following facts regarding these bonds.

Date of issue and sale:	April 1, 20-1
Principal amount:	$400,000
Denomination of each bond:	$1,000
Life of bonds:	10 years
Stated rate:	10%, payable semiannually each April 1 and October 1

Issuance

Assume that on April 1, 20-1, the stated rate of 10 percent on Watkin's bonds is the same as the current market rate. In this case, the bonds will sell at their face value. The journal entry for the sale and issuance of Watkin's bonds at face value on April 1, 20-1 is:

5	Apr.	1	Cash	400	0	0	0	00						5
6			Bonds Payable						400	0	0	0	00	6
7			Issued bonds at face value											7

Bonds payable is reported as a long-term liability on the corporation balance sheet.

Interest Expense

The journal entry for the first semiannual interest payment of $20,000 (10% × $400,000 × ½ year) on October 1, 20-1 is:

18	Oct.	1	Bond Interest Expense	20	0	0	0	00						18
19			Cash						20	0	0	0	00	19
20			Paid semiannual interest on bonds											20

On December 31, an adjusting entry is needed for interest accrued on the bonds since the last interest payment date, October 1, 20-1. Three months' interest has accrued (October 1–December 31), which amounts to $10,000 (10% × $400,000 × ¼ year). The adjusting entry therefore is:

| 25 | Dec. | 31 | Bond Interest Expense | 10 | 0 | 0 | 0 | 00 | | | | | | 25 |
| 26 | | | Bond Interest Payable | | | | | | 10 | 0 | 0 | 0 | 00 | 26 |

After the October 1 and December 31 entries are posted, Bond Interest Expense and Bond Interest Payable appear in T account form as follows:

Bond Interest Expense		Bond Interest Payable	
20-1		20-1	
Oct. 1	20,000	Dec. 31	10,000
Dec. 31	10,000		
	30,000		

The balance in the bond interest expense account is the total interest expense incurred from April 1 to December 31. Bond Interest Expense is reported as other expense on the income statement. The balance in the bond interest payable account is the accrued liability on December 31. Bond Interest Payable is reported as a current liability on the balance sheet.

The December 31, 20-1, adjusting entry normally is reversed as of January 1, 20-2, as follows:

| 8 | Jan. | 1 | Bond Interest Payable | 10 | 0 | 0 | 0 | 00 | | | | | | 8 |
| 9 | | | Bond Interest Expense | | | | | | 10 | 0 | 0 | 0 | 00 | 9 |

The next semiannual interest payment on April 1, 20-2, is made exactly like the entry on October 1, 20-1. After posting the reversing entry and the April 1 interest payment entry, Bond Interest Expense and Bond Interest Payable appear in T account form as follows:

Bond Interest Expense				Bond Interest Payable		
20-1				20-1		
Oct. 1	20,000			Dec. 31		10,000
Dec. 31	10,000	Dec. 31 Close	30,000			
20-2		20-2		20-2		
Apr. 1	20,000	Jan. 1 Rev.	10,000	Jan. 1 Rev. 10,000		

ACCOUNTING FOR BONDS ISSUED AT A PREMIUM

LO3 Account for bonds issued at a premium.

Recall that if the stated rate on bonds is greater than the current market rate, the bonds will sell at a premium. When bonds are issued at a premium, both bonds payable on the balance sheet and interest expense on the income statement are affected.

Issuance

Assume that on April 1, 20-1, the stated rate of 10 percent on Watkin's bonds is greater than the current market rate, so that the bonds sell for 106. This means that the bonds sell for $424,000 ($400,000 × 106%), a premium of $24,000. The journal entry for the sale and issuance of Watkin's bonds at a premium on April 1, 20-1, is:

5	Apr.	1	Cash	424 0 0 0 00		5
6			Bonds Payable		400 0 0 0 00	6
7			Premium on Bonds Payable		24 0 0 0 00	7
8			Issued bonds at a premium			8

Premium on Bonds Payable is an adjunct-liability account. It is added to bonds payable on the corporate balance sheet. On Watkin's balance sheet immediately after issuing the $400,000 of bonds for $424,000, the bonds payable and premium would appear as follows:

Long-term liabilities:		
Bonds payable	$400 0 0 0 00	
Premium on bonds payable	24 0 0 0 00	$424 0 0 0 00

The sum of bonds payable and premium on bonds payable is called the **carrying value** of the bonds.

Interest Expense and Premium Amortization

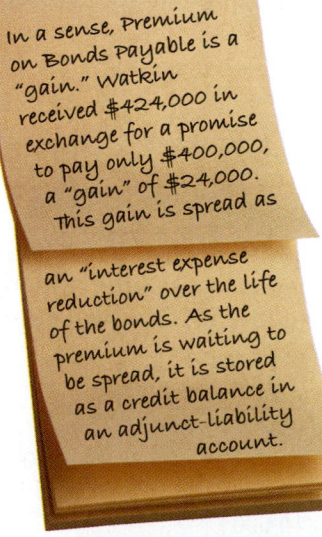

In a sense, Premium on Bonds Payable is a "gain." Watkin received $424,000 in exchange for a promise to pay only $400,000, a "gain" of $24,000. This gain is spread as an "interest expense reduction" over the life of the bonds. As the premium is waiting to be spread, it is stored as a credit balance in an adjunct-liability account.

When bonds are issued at a premium, the amount of interest actually paid is not the true interest expense. This is because the premium received when the bonds are issued effectively reduces the cost of borrowing. For example, Watkin received $424,000 for its bonds but will have to pay back only $400,000, the face value of the bonds. This $24,000 reduction ($424,000 – $400,000) in the cost of borrowing is spread over the life of the bond issue by adjusting interest expense on a regular basis.

The process of adjusting the bond interest expense account for any premium or discount is called **amortization** of the premium or discount. Two commonly used methods of amortizing premium (or discount) over the life of a bond are (1) effective interest and (2) straight-line. The effective interest method is recommended, but the straight-line method is much simpler to apply and generally provides acceptable results. We will use the straight-line method. The effective interest method is covered in the appendix.

Using the straight-line method, $1,200 of the premium on Watkin's bonds is amortized each semiannual interest period, calculated as follows:

$$\frac{\text{Premium}}{\text{Life of Bonds}} \quad \times \quad \tfrac{1}{2}\text{ Year} \quad = \quad \frac{\$24,000}{10\text{ Years}} \quad \times \quad \tfrac{1}{2}\text{ Year} \quad = \quad \$1,200$$

The entry for the first semiannual interest payment and amortization of bond premium on October 1, 20-1, is:

18	Oct.	1	Bond Interest Expense	18	8	0	0	00						18
19			Premium on Bonds Payable	1	2	0	0	00						19
20			Cash						20	0	0	0	00	20
21			Paid semiannual interest and											21
22			amortized premium on bonds											22

Note that the premium amortization does not affect the amount of cash paid. The amortization simply reduces the bond interest expense for the period and the carrying value of the bonds.

 LEARNING KEY: Premium amortization reduces the interest expense and carrying value of the bonds but has no effect on the amount of cash paid.

On December 31, an adjusting entry is needed both for accrued interest and for premium amortization for the period from October 1 through December 31. Three months' interest of $10,000 (10% × $400,000 × ¼ year) has accrued. Three months' premium of $600 ($24,000 ÷ 10 × ¼ year) should be amortized. The adjusting entry is:

25	Dec.	31	Bond Interest Expense	9	4	0	0	00						25
26			Premium on Bonds Payable		6	0	0	00						26
27			Bond Interest Payable						10	0	0	0	00	27

After the April 1, October 1, and December 31 entries are posted, Cash, Bond Interest Expense, Bonds Payable, Premium on Bonds Payable, and Bond Interest Payable appear in the accounting equation as shown in Figure 24-2.

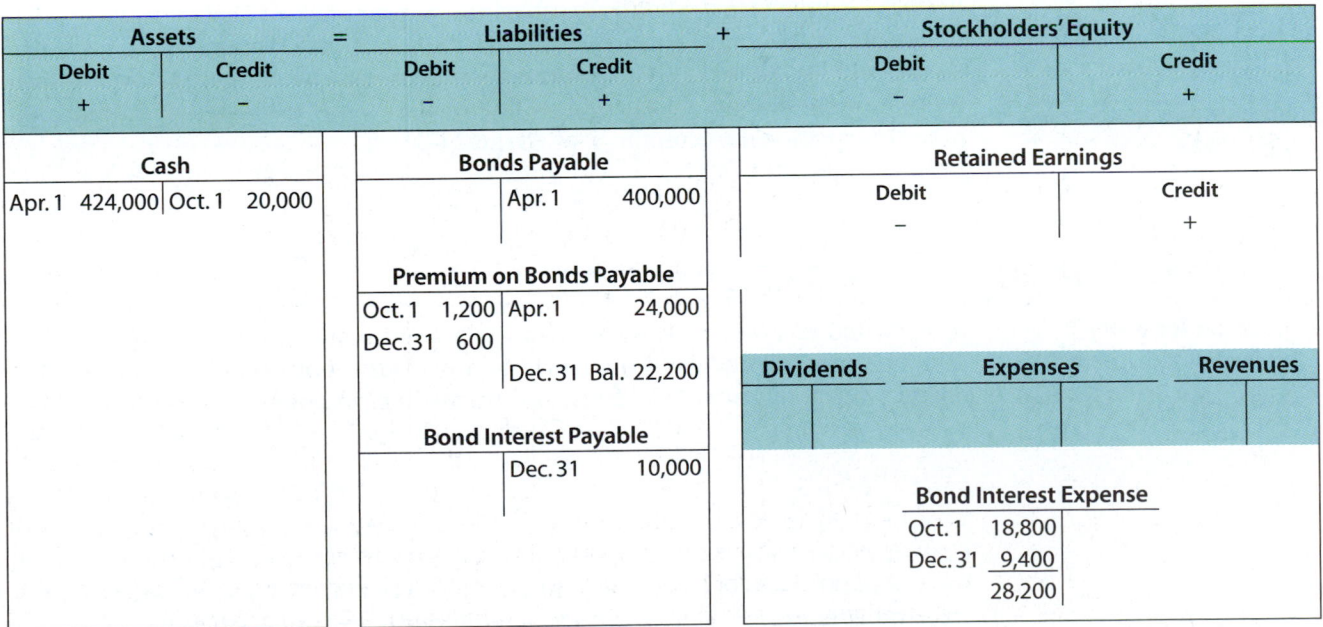

FIGURE 24-2 Bonds Payable and Related Accounts after Interest Accrual and Premium Amortization

The December 31, 20-1, adjusting entry normally is reversed as of January 1, 20-2. The next semiannual interest and premium amortization entry on April 1, 20-2, is made exactly like the entry on October 1, 20-1. Columns 2, 3, and 4 in Figure 24-3 summarize the semiannual interest and premium amortization entries for the life of the bonds.

	BOND PREMIUM AMORTIZATION SCHEDULE STRAIGHT-LINE METHOD					
(1)	(2)	(3)	(4)	(5)	(6)	(7)
Date	Interest Expense Debit	Premium on Bonds Payable Debit	Cash Credit	Bonds Payable Balance	Premium on Bonds Payable Balance	Carrying Value of Bonds [(5) + (6)]
4/1/-1				$400,000	$24,000	$424,000
10/1/-1	$18,800	$1,200	$20,000	400,000	22,800	422,800
4/1/-2*	18,800	1,200	20,000	400,000	21,600	421,600
10/1/-2	18,800	1,200	20,000	400,000	20,400	420,400
–	–	–	–	–	–	–
–	–	–	–	–	–	–
–	–	–	–	–	–	–
4/1/10	18,800	1,200	20,000	400,000	2,400	402,400
10/1/10	18,800	1,200	20,000	400,000	1,200	401,200
3/31/11	18,800	1,200	20,000	400,000	0	400,000

* The entry for the first interest payment each year assumes that the adjusting entry at December 31 of the preceding year was reversed.

FIGURE 24-3   Premium Amortization Schedule

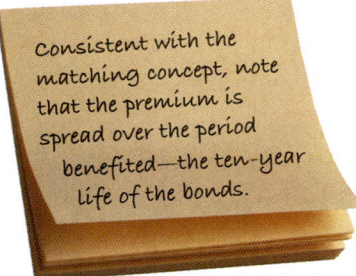

Consistent with the matching concept, note that the premium is spread over the period benefited—the ten-year life of the bonds.

Note that the effect of the premium amortization is to reduce both the interest expense for the period and the balance in the premium on bonds payable account. In fact, the premium on bonds payable account balance is gradually reduced to zero over the life of the bonds, as shown in column 6 of Figure 24-3. Recall that Premium on Bonds Payable is an adjunct-liability account. It is added to bonds payable on the balance sheet. The amount that Watkin will have to pay at maturity is $400,000. By amortizing the premium on bonds payable over the life of the bonds, the carrying value of the bonds decreases to $400,000 at maturity, as shown in column 7 of Figure 24-3.

ACCOUNTING FOR BONDS ISSUED AT A DISCOUNT

LO4 **Account for bonds issued at a discount.**

If the stated rate on bonds is less than the current market rate, the bonds will sell at a discount. When bonds are issued at a discount, both bonds payable on the balance sheet and interest expense on the income statement are affected.

Issuance

Assume that on April 1, 20-1, the stated rate on Watkin's bonds is less than the current market rate, so that the bonds sell for 96. This means that the bonds sell for $384,000 ($400,000 × 96%), a discount of $16,000. The journal entry for the sale and issuance of Watkin's bonds at a discount on April 1, 20-1, is:

5	Apr.	1	Cash		384	0	0	0	00						5
6			Discount on Bonds Payable		16	0	0	0	00						6
7			Bonds Payable							400	0	0	0	00	7
8			Issued bonds at a discount												8

Discount on Bonds Payable is a contra-liability account. It is deducted from bonds payable on the corporate balance sheet. On Watkin's balance sheet immediately after issuing the $400,000 of bonds for $384,000, the bonds payable and discount would appear as follows:

Long-term liabilities:										
Bonds payable	$400	0	0	0	00					
Discount on bonds payable	16	0	0	0	00	$384	0	0	0	00

Bonds payable less the discount on bonds payable is called the carrying value of the bonds.

Interest Expense and Discount Amortization

When bonds are sold at a discount, we have a situation similar to what we saw in the case of bonds sold at a premium. The interest actually paid is not the true interest expense. This is because the discount given when the bonds are issued effectively increases the cost of borrowing. For example, Watkin received only $384,000 for its bonds but will have to pay back $400,000, the face value of the bonds. This $16,000 increase ($400,000 – $384,000) in the cost of borrowing is amortized over the life of the bond issue by adjusting interest expense on a regular basis.

Using the straight-line method, $800 of the discount on Watkin's bonds is amortized each semiannual interest period, calculated as follows:

$$\frac{\text{Discount}}{\text{Life of Bonds}} \quad \times \quad \tfrac{1}{2}\ \text{Year} \quad = \quad \frac{\$16,000}{10\ \text{years}} \quad \times \quad \tfrac{1}{2}\ \text{Year} \quad = \quad \$800$$

The entry for the first semiannual interest payment and amortization of bond discount on October 1, 20-1, is:

18	Oct.	1	Bond Interest Expense		20	8	0	0	00						18
19			Discount on Bonds Payable								8	0	0	00	19
20			Cash							20	0	0	0	00	20
21			Paid semiannual interest and												21
22			amortized discount on bonds												22

Note that the discount amortization does not affect the amount of cash paid. The amortization simply increases the bond interest expense for the period and the carrying value of the bonds.

 LEARNING KEY: Discount amortization increases the interest expense and carrying value of the bonds but has no effect on the amount of cash paid.

In a sense, Discount on Bonds Payable is a "loss." Watkin received only $384,000 in exchange for a promise to pay $400,000, a "loss" of $16,000. This loss is spread as an "interest expense increase" over the life of the bonds. As the discount is waiting to be spread, it is stored as a debit balance in a contra-liability account.

On December 31, an adjusting entry is needed both for accrued interest and for discount amortization for the period from October 1 through December 31. Three months' interest of $10,000 (10% × $400,000 × ¼ year) has accrued. Three months' discount of $400 ($16,000 ÷ 10 × ¼ year) should be amortized. The adjusting entry is:

25	Dec.	31	Bond Interest Expense		10 4 0 0 00			25
26			Bond Interest Payable			10 0 0 0 00		26
27			Discount on Bonds Payable			4 0 0 00		27

After the October 1 and December 31 entries are posted, Cash, Bond Interest Expense, Bonds Payable, Discount on Bonds Payable, and Bond Interest Payable appear in the accounting equation as shown in Figure 24-4.

Assets		=	Liabilities		+	Stockholders' Equity	
Debit	Credit		Debit	Credit		Debit	Credit
+	−		−	+		−	+

Cash

Apr. 1 384,000 | Oct. 1 20,000

Bonds Payable

| | Apr. 1 400,000 |

Discount on Bonds Payable

Apr. 1 16,000	Oct. 1 800
	Dec. 31 400
Dec. 31 Bal. 14,800	

Bond Interest Payable

| | Dec. 31 10,000 |

Retained Earnings

| Debit | Credit |
| − | + |

Dividends | **Expenses** | **Revenues**

Bond Interest Expense

Oct. 1 20,800	
Dec. 31 10,400	
31,200	

FIGURE 24-4 Bonds Payable and Related Accounts after Interest Accrual and Discount Amortization

The December 31 adjusting entry normally is reversed as of January 1, 20-2. The next semiannual interest and discount amortization entry on April 1, 20-2, is made exactly like the entry on October 1, 20-1. Columns 2, 3, and 4 in Figure 24-5 summarize the semiannual interest and discount amortization entries for the life of the bonds.

Note that the effect of the discount amortization is to increase the interest expense for the period and to decrease the balance in the discount on bonds payable account. In fact, the discount on bonds payable account balance is gradually reduced to zero over the life of the bonds, as shown in column 6 of Figure 24-5. Recall that Discount on Bonds Payable is a contra-liability account. It is subtracted from bonds payable on the balance sheet. The amount that Watkin will have to pay at maturity is $400,000. By amortizing the discount on bonds payable over the life of the bonds, the carrying value of the bonds increases to $400,000 at maturity, as shown in column 7 of Figure 24-5.

Consistent with the matching concept, note that the discount is spread over the period benefited—the ten-year life of the bonds.

	(1)	(2)	(3)	(4)	(5)	(6)	(7)
	Date	Interest Expense Debit	Discount on Bonds Payable Credit	Cash Credit	Bonds Payable Balance	Discount on Bonds Payable Balance	Carrying Value of Bonds [(5) – (6)]
	4/1/-1				$400,000	$16,000	$384,000
	10/1/-1	$20,800	$800	$20,000	400,000	15,200	384,800
	4/1/-2*	20,800	800	20,000	400,000	14,400	385,600
	10/1/-2	20,800	800	20,000	400,000	13,600	386,400
	–	–	–	–	–	–	–
	–	–	–	–	–	–	–
	–	–	–	–	–	–	–
	4/1/10	20,800	800	20,000	400,000	1,600	398,400
	10/1/10	20,800	800	20,000	400,000	800	399,200
	3/31/11	20,800	800	20,000	400,000	0	400,000

BOND DISCOUNT AMORTIZATION SCHEDULE — STRAIGHT-LINE METHOD

* The entry for the first interest payment each year assumes that the adjusting entry at December 31 of the preceding year was reversed.

FIGURE 24-5 Discount Amortization Schedule

ACCOUNTING FOR BOND REDEMPTION AND SINKING FUNDS

LO5 Account for bond redemption and bond sinking funds.

Usually, bonds issued by a corporation are redeemed at face value at their maturity. By that date, the entire amount of any premium or discount should have been amortized. To enter the redemption, Bonds Payable is debited and Cash is credited for the face value of the bonds. For example, if the $400,000 of Watkin bonds are redeemed at maturity, the following journal entry is made.

22		Bonds Payable	400 0 0 0 00		22
23		Cash		400 0 0 0 00	23
24		Redeemed bonds at face value			24

Corporations may redeem part or all of a bond issue before maturity. If the bonds are callable, a corporation may call in the bonds before they mature. The call price is defined in the original bond agreement. If the bonds are not callable, a corporation can purchase its bonds in the open market at the market price. When bonds are redeemed before maturity, any accrued interest must be paid and the premium or discount amortization must be brought up to date. Entries for doing so are the same as those illustrated in previous sections of the chapter.

Redemption of Bonds at a Loss

Usually, there is a gain or loss involved when bonds are redeemed before maturity. The gain or loss is the difference between the amount paid to redeem the bonds and the carrying value of the bonds. When bonds are issued at face value, the carrying value equals the face value throughout the life of the bonds. When bonds are issued at a premium or discount, the carrying value changes over the life of the bonds, as the premium or discount is amortized.

LEARNING KEY: To determine the amount of gain or loss on redemption of bonds, compare the redemption price with the carrying value of the bonds.

To illustrate, consider the Watkin Corp. $400,000, 10% bonds that were sold at face value. If $40,000 of the bonds are redeemed at 103, there is a loss of $1,200 on redemption of the bonds, calculated as follows:

Cash paid ($40,000 × 103%)	$41,200
Less carrying value (= face value) of bonds	40,000
Loss on redemption	$ 1,200

The journal entry for this transaction is:

31		Bonds Payable	40 0 0 0 00			31
32		Loss on Bonds Redeemed	1 2 0 0 00			32
33		Cash		41 2 0 0 00		33
34		Redeemed bonds at a loss				34

Loss on Bonds Redeemed is reported as an extraordinary item near the bottom of the income statement. Extraordinary Loss on Early Extinguishment of Debt is an appropriate title.

Now consider the Watkin Corp. bonds that were sold at a premium (106) for $424,000. Assume that eight years after the issuance, Watkin redeems $40,000 of this issue at 103. The carrying value of these bonds is calculated as follows:

Issue price ($40,000 × 106)	$42,400	
Face value	40,000	
Premium received at issuance		$ 2,400
Premium amortized per year ($2,400 ÷ 10 yrs)	$ 240	
Number of years since issuance	× 8	
Total premium amortized in 8 years		1,920
Unamortized premium		$ 480
Face value		40,000
Carrying value		$40,480

Thus, after the interest payment and premium amortization have been entered on April 1, 20-9, the carrying value of the $40,000 of bonds is $40,480. There is a loss of $720 on redemption of the bonds, calculated as follows:

Cash paid ($40,000 × 103)	$41,200
Less carrying value	40,480
Loss on redemption	$ 720

The journal entry for this transaction is:

5	Apr.	1	Bonds Payable	40 0 0 0 00			5
6			Premium on Bonds Payable	4 8 0 00			6
7			Loss on Bonds Redeemed	7 2 0 00			7
8			Cash		41 2 0 0 00		8
9			Redeemed bonds at a loss				9

Redemption of Bonds at a Gain

To illustrate the redemption of bonds at a gain, let's look again at two examples. Assume that $40,000 of Watkin's bonds that were issued at face value are redeemed at 97. In this case, Watkin has a gain of $1,200 on redemption of the bonds, calculated as follows:

	Carrying value (= face value) of bonds	$40,000
Less cash paid ($40,000 × 97)	38,800
Gain on bonds redeemed	$ 1,200

The journal entry for this transaction is:

31	Bonds Payable	40 0 0 0 00		31
32	Gain on Bonds Redeemed		1 2 0 0 00	32
33	Cash		38 8 0 0 00	33
34	Redeemed bonds at a gain			34

Gain on Bonds Redeemed is reported as an extraordinary item on the income statement.

Now consider the Watkin Corp. bonds that were sold at a discount (96) for $384,000. Assume that six years after issuance, Watkin redeems $40,000 of this issue at 97. The carrying value of these bonds is calculated as follows:

Face value	$40,000	
Issue price ($40,000 × 96)	38,400	
Discount at issuance		$1,600
Discount amortized per year ($1,600 ÷ 10 yrs.)	$ 160	
Number of years since issuance	× 6	
Total discount amortized in 6 years		960
Unamortized discount		$ 640
Face value		$40,000
Less unamortized discount		640
Carrying value		$39,360

Thus, after the interest payment and discount amortization have been entered on April 1, 20-7, the carrying value of the $40,000 of bonds is $39,360. There is a gain of $560 on redemption of the bonds, calculated as follows:

Carrying value of bonds	$39,360
Less cash paid ($40,000 × 97)	38,800
Gain on redemption	$ 560

The journal entry for this redemption is:

5	Apr.	1	Bonds Payable	40 0 0 0 00		5
6			Discount on Bonds Payable		6 4 0 00	6
7			Gain on Bonds Redeemed		5 6 0 00	7
8			Cash		38 8 0 0 00	8
9			Redeemed bonds at a gain			9

Bond Sinking Funds

The formal written agreement for issuing bonds is called the **bond indenture**. Bond indentures for term bonds frequently require the accumulation and investment of money over a period of years. This is to provide the amount needed to redeem the bonds at maturity. Such accumulations are known as **bond sinking funds**. The sinking fund usually is administered by a trustee. The corporation makes periodic cash deposits with the trustee. The trustee is responsible for investing the cash and accumulating amounts necessary to redeem the bonds at maturity.

To illustrate, assume that the bond indenture for the Watkin bonds required Watkin to make deposits of $30,000 to a trustee each year. The entry for each deposit is:

12		Bond Sinking Fund		30 0 0 0 00		12
13		Cash			30 0 0 0 00	13
14		Made sinking fund deposit				14

The trustee invests the cash and adds any earnings on these investments to the sinking fund. Assume that Watkin's trustee reports sinking fund earnings of $2,800 for the year. The following entry is made.

26		Bond Sinking Fund		2 8 0 0 00		26
27		Sinking Fund Earnings			2 8 0 0 00	27
28		Annual sinking fund earnings				28

When the bonds mature, the trustee sells all of the sinking fund investments. The corporation then deposits additional cash with the trustee so that the sum of the periodic deposits, the sinking fund earnings, and the additional cash is sufficient to redeem the bonds. When the Watkin bonds are redeemed at maturity by the trustee, the following entry is made.

5		Bonds Payable		400 0 0 0 00		5
6		Bond Sinking Fund			400 0 0 0 00	6
7		Redeemed bonds at face value				7

If any cash is left in the sinking fund after all of the bonds are redeemed, the cash is returned to the corporation. Assume that the sinking fund has a balance of $960 after all the bonds are redeemed. The following entry is made.

18		Cash		9 6 0 00		18
19		Bond Sinking Fund			9 6 0 00	19
20		Received sinking fund balance				20

Sinking fund earnings are reported as other revenue on the corporation income statement. The bond sinking fund is reported under investments on the corporation balance sheet.

Learning Objectives	Key Points to Remember

1 Describe the types of bonds and how their sales price is determined.

Bonds can be classified as to (1) security, (2) timing of payment of principal, and (3) identification of ownership. If the bond and market interest rates are equal, bonds will sell at face value. If the bond interest rate is greater than the market rate, bonds will sell at a premium. If the bond interest rate is less than the market rate, bonds will sell at a discount.

2 Account for bonds issued at face value.

3 Account for bonds issued at a premium.

4 Account for bonds issued at a discount.

The journal entries for bond issuance, interest payments, premium or discount amortization, and redemption can be summarized as follows:

	BONDS ISSUED AT		
	FACE	**PREMIUM**	**DISCOUNT**

Issuance	Cash
	  Bonds Payable
		Cash
		  Bonds Payable
		  Premium on Bonds Payable
			Cash
			Discount on Bonds Payable
			  Bonds Payable

Interest Payment and Amortization	Interest Expense
	  Cash
		Interest Expense
		Premium on Bonds Payable
		  Cash
			Interest Expense
			  Discount on Bonds Payable
			  Cash

Redemption at:
  Carrying Value
	Bonds Payable
	  Cash
		Bonds Payable
		Premium on Bonds Payable
		  Cash
			Bonds Payable
			  Discount on Bonds Payable
			  Cash

< Carrying Value	Bonds Payable
	  Gain on Redemption
	  Cash
		Bonds Payable
		Premium on Bonds Payable
		  Gain on Redemption
		  Cash
			Bonds Payable
			  Discount on Bonds Payable
			  Gain on Redemption
			  Cash

> Carrying Value	Bonds Payable
	Loss on Redemption
	  Cash
		Bonds Payable
		Premium on Bonds Payable
		Loss on Redemption
		  Cash
			Bonds Payable
			Loss on Redemption
			  Discount on Bonds Payable
			  Cash

5 Account for bond redemption and bond sinking funds.

The gain or loss on redemption of bonds is the difference between the amount paid to redeem the bonds and the carrying value of the bonds. Gains and losses on bonds redeemed are reported as extraordinary items on the income statement. Bond sinking funds are used to accumulate the money needed for bond redemption. The sum of the amounts deposited in the sinking fund, sinking fund earnings, and any additional cash deposited in the sinking fund by the company when the bonds mature is used to redeem the bonds.

REFLECTION

Reflection: Answering the Opening Questions

Bonds are usually for larger sums of money and for longer periods of time than notes. Bonds are riskier than stock in the sense that bonds are debts of the company rather than ownership interests. The company promises to pay certain amounts of money to bondholders. If the payments are not made, the creditors can force the company into bankruptcy.

DEMONSTRATION PROBLEM

Brooks Inc.'s fiscal year ends December 31. Selected transactions for the period 20-1 through 20-8 involving bonds payable issued by Brooks are as follows:

20-1

Nov. 30	Issued $800,000 of ten-year, 9%, callable bonds dated November 30, 20-1, for $776,000. Interest is payable semiannually on November 30 and May 31. The bond indenture provides that Brooks is to pay to the trustee bank $30,000 by June 15 of each year (except the tenth year) as a sinking fund for the retirement of the bonds on call or at maturity.
Dec. 31	Made the adjusting entry for interest payable and amortized one month's discount on the bonds (straight-line method).

20-2

Jan. 2	Reversed the adjusting entry for interest payable and bond discount amortization.
May 31	Paid the semiannual interest on the bonds and amortized six months' discount.
June 15	Paid the sinking fund trustee $30,000.
Nov. 30	Paid the semiannual interest on the bonds and amortized six months' discount.
Dec. 31	Made the adjusting entry for interest payable and amortized one month's discount on the bonds.
31	Sinking fund earnings for the year were $1,100.

20-8

June 15	Paid the sinking fund trustee $30,000.
Nov. 30	Paid the semiannual interest on the bonds and amortized six months' discount.
30	Redeemed the bonds, which were called at 102.

The balance in the bond discount account is $7,200 after the payment of interest and amortization of discount have been entered. The cash balance in the sinking fund is $320,000 which is applied to the redemption. Paid the sinking fund trustee the additional cash needed to pay off the bonds. *(Hint: First make the entry for payment to the sinking fund, then make the entry for redemption of the bonds.)*

REQUIRED

1. Enter the transactions in general journal form.

2. Calculate the carrying value of the bonds as of December 31, 20-2.

Solution

1.

			GENERAL JOURNAL												PAGE 1	
	DATE		DESCRIPTION	POST REF.	DEBIT					CREDIT							
1	20-1 Nov.	30	Cash		776	0	0	0	00								1
2			Discount on Bonds Payable		24	0	0	0	00								2
3			Bonds Payable							800	0	0	0	00			3
4			Issued bonds at a discount														4
5																	5
6			Adjusting Entry														6
7	Dec.	31	Bond Interest Expense		6	2	0	0	00								7
8			Bond Interest Payable							6	0	0	0	00			8
9			Discount on Bonds Payable*								2	0	0	00			9
10																	10
11			Reversing Entry														11
12	20-2 Jan.	2	Bond Interest Payable		6	0	0	0	00								12
13			Discount on Bonds Payable			2	0	0	00								13
14			Bond Interest Expense							6	2	0	0	00			14
15																	15
16	May	31	Bond Interest Expense		37	2	0	0	00								16
17			Discount on Bonds Payable							1	2	0	0	00			17
18			Cash							36	0	0	0	00			18
19			Paid semiannual interest and														19
20			amortized discount on bonds														20
21																	21
22	June	15	Bond Sinking Fund		30	0	0	0	00								22
23			Cash							30	0	0	0	00			23
24			Made sinking fund deposit														24
25																	25
26	Nov.	30	Bond Interest Expense		37	2	0	0	00								26
27			Discount on Bonds Payable							1	2	0	0	00			27
28			Cash							36	0	0	0	00			28
29			Paid semiannual interest and														29
30			amortized discount on bonds														30
31																	31
32																	32

*Amortization rate = $24,000 original discount ÷ 10 years = $2,400/year ÷ 12 months = $200/month

(continued)

	DATE		DESCRIPTION	POST REF.	DEBIT	CREDIT	
			GENERAL JOURNAL			PAGE 2	
1			Adjusting Entry				1
2	20-2 Dec.	31	Bond Interest Expense		6 2 0 0 00		2
3			Bond Interest Payable			6 0 0 0 00	3
4			Discount on Bonds Payable			2 0 0 00	4
5							5
6		31	Bond Sinking Fund		1 1 0 0 00		6
7			Sinking Fund Earnings			1 1 0 0 00	7
8			Annual sinking fund earnings				8
9							9
10	20-8 June	15	Bond Sinking Fund		30 0 0 0 00		10
11			Cash			30 0 0 0 00	11
12			Made sinking fund deposit				12
13							13
14	Nov.	30	Bond Interest Expense		37 2 0 0 00		14
15			Discount on Bonds Payable			1 2 0 0 00	15
16			Cash			36 0 0 0 00	16
17			Paid semiannual interest and				17
18			amortized discount on bonds				18
19							19
20		30	Bond Sinking Fund		496 0 0 0 00		20
21			Cash			496 0 0 0 00	21
22			[(800,000 × 102%) − 320,000]				22
23			Made sinking fund deposit				23
24							24
25		30	Bonds Payable		800 0 0 0 00		25
26			Loss on Bonds Redeemed		23 2 0 0 00		26
27			Discount on Bonds Payable*			7 2 0 0 00	27
28			Bond Sinking Fund			816 0 0 0 00	28
29			Redeemed bonds at a loss				29

* Original discount on bonds payable	$24,000
Amortization for 7 years at $2,400/year	(16,800)
Unamortized discount on November 30, 20-8	$ 7,200

2.
Face value of bonds		$800,000
Original discount on bonds payable	$24,000	
Less:		
Discount amortized on December 31, 20-1	(200)	
Discount amortized during 20-2	(2,400)	
Balance of discount on bonds payable at December 31, 20-2		21,400
Carrying value of bonds, December 31, 20-2		$778,600

On-Line Learning Tools

For more information, visit: http://heintz.swlearning.com

The Heintz & Parry product web site is designed specifically for *COLLEGE ACCOUNTING, 18e.* The features include downloadable student resources and an interactive study center, organized by chapter, which contains learning objectives, web links, on-line quizzes with automatic feedback, and more.

KEY TERMS

amortization, (894)   The process of adjusting the bond interest expense account for any premium or discount.

bearer bonds, (891)   See coupon bonds.

bond, (890)   A written promise to pay a specific sum of money at a specific future date.

bond indenture, (901)   The formal written agreement for issuing bonds.

bond sinking funds, (901)   The accumulation and investment of money over a period of years to provide the amount needed for the redemption of bonds.

callable bonds, (891)   Bonds that give the issuing corporation the option of calling the bonds for redemption before the maturity date.

carrying value, (894)   Bonds payable plus the premium or less the discount on bonds payable.

convertible bonds, (890)   Bonds that give the holder the option of exchanging the bonds for capital stock of the corporation.

coupon bonds, (891)   Bonds whose ownership generally is not recorded by the corporation. These bonds have interest coupons attached.

coupon rate, (891)   See stated rate.

debenture bonds, (890)   See unsecured bonds.

discount, (891)   The difference between the face value and the price of a bond when the current market interest rate is greater than the stated rate of that bond.

face value, (891)   The amount written on the face of the bond certificate.

market rate, (891)   The interest rate that can be earned on similar investments or the rate that other companies in similar financial condition have to pay to borrow money.

mortgage bonds, (890)   Bonds secured by a mortgage on corporate property such as real estate or equipment.

premium, (891)   The difference between the face value and the price of a bond when the current market interest rate is less than the stated rate of that bond.

principal, (890)   The amount to be paid to the bondholder at maturity.

registered bonds, (891)   Bonds whose ownership is recorded in the corporate records.

secured bonds, (890)   Bonds that are backed by specific corporate assets.

serial bonds, (890)   Bonds issued in a series so that a specified amount of the bonds matures each year.

stated rate, (891)   The rate of interest specified on the face of the bond.

term bonds, (890)   Bonds that all have the same maturity date.

unsecured bonds, (890)   Bonds backed solely by the general credit of the corporation issuing the bonds.

REVIEW QUESTIONS

(LO1)	1. Explain the difference between corporate bonds and stock from the standpoint of the issuing corporation.
(LO1)	2. Will a bond sell at a discount or at a premium if the stated rate is greater than the market rate on the bond? If the stated rate is less than the market rate?
(LO1)	3. Explain the meaning of a bond price quotation of 95. Of 102.
(LO2)	4. What accounts are affected when bonds are issued at face value?
(LO3/4)	5. How is Premium on Bonds Payable shown on the balance sheet? How is Discount on Bonds Payable shown?
(LO3/4)	6. How is the amount of bond premium or discount to be amortized in a period determined using the straight-line method?
(LO3/4)	7. How is the periodic interest expense affected by the amortization of the premium on bonds payable?
(LO3/4)	8. How is the periodic interest expense affected by the amortization of the discount on bonds payable?
(LO5)	9. When bonds are redeemed before maturity, how is the gain or loss on redemption determined? Why does the calculation differ for bonds issued at face value, at a premium, and at a discount?
(LO5)	10. Who usually administers a bond sinking fund?
(LO5)	11. How should sinking fund earnings be reported on the corporation income statement?
(LO5)	12. How should the bond sinking fund be reported on the corporation balance sheet?

Self-Study Test Questions

True/False

1. A secured bond is one that is backed by specific corporate assets. _____

2. If the stated rate of interest on a bond is 9 percent and the current market rate on similar investments is 10 percent, the bond will sell at a premium. _____

3. When bonds are issued at face value, the debit to Cash and credit to Bonds Payable are for the same amount. _____

4. Amortization of the premium on bonds payable increases the bond interest expense and the carrying value of the bonds. _____

5. To determine the amount of gain or loss on redemption of bonds, compare the redemption price with the carrying value of the bonds. _____

Self-Study Test Questions *(continued)*

Multiple Choice

1. Bonds that give the holder the option of exchanging the bonds for capital stock in the corporation are called

   (a) debenture bonds.
   (b) serial bonds.
   (c) convertible bonds.
   (d) callable bonds.

   _____

2. If bonds with a face value of $200,000 are sold at 102, Cash is debited for

   (a) $200,000.
   (b) $202,000.
   (c) $204,000.
   (d) $196,000.

   _____

3. Ten-year bonds with a face value of $300,000 are sold at a premium of $6,000. If the premium is amortized using the straight-line method, each semiannual interest payment and amortization of bond premium will include a

   (a) debit to Premium on Bonds Payable.
   (b) credit to Premium on Bonds Payable.
   (c) debit to Cash.
   (d) credit to Bond Interest Expense.

   _____

4. If bonds are issued at a discount, the amortization of the discount over the life of the bonds causes the

   (a) interest expense to decrease each period.
   (b) interest expense to increase each period.
   (c) carrying value of the bonds to decrease.
   (d) carrying value of the bonds to increase.

   _____

5. Bond sinking fund earnings are

   (a) subtracted from the bond sinking fund.
   (b) added to the bond sinking fund.
   (c) subtracted from the current year interest expense.
   (d) added to the current year interest expense.

   _____

The answers to the Self-Study Test Questions are at the end of the text.

MANAGING YOUR WRITING

The business where you work is considering issuing bonds to finance a major expansion. Your boss has just come from a lengthy meeting regarding the bonds, including the interest rate the bonds should carry. This has irritated your boss, who feels that the interest rate to use is obvious—the lowest one possible. This would yield the lowest interest expense to borrow the money. It seems stupid to pay big fees to financial advisors and lawyers when the question is so simple.

Write a report to your boss explaining how the issue price of the bonds (the net amount borrowed) is affected by the stated interest rate on the bonds. Include an explanation of how interest costs consist of more than just periodic interest payments.

ETHICS CASE

Alva Reese is 65 years old and getting ready to retire. She called her investment broker to help her decide what to do with the $50,000 that she has in the stock market. Alva told him that she didn't want any risky investments but hoped for an investment that was relatively safe and offered steady income. She had heard that bonds were safer than stocks and asked the broker how he felt about bonds. Her broker said bonds were a good safe choice and the ones he had in mind would offer her a high yield. He recommended that she invest all $50,000 in corporate callable bonds. Alva asked him to explain what callable bonds were and he told her the explanation was too technical but they were a safe investment that would serve her needs.

1. What information should the investment broker have given Alva?

2. Are all bonds safe? Why or why not?

3. Write a short paragraph describing how to determine the sales (trading) price of a bond.

4. In groups of three or four, make a list of the factors that Alva and the investment broker should consider before deciding how to invest the $50,000.

WEB WORK

Bonds are commonly used to raise capital for expansion or to purchase new facilities. But what value do bonds offer investors? Why would an investor want a lower interest bond rather than a higher paying stock? Visit the Interactive Study Center on our web site at **http://heintz.swlearning.com** for special hotlinks to assist you in this assignment.

SERIES A EXERCISES

EXERCISE 24-1A   **(LO2)**
Dec. 31. Dr. Bond Interest
Expense, $10,000

BONDS ISSUED AT FACE VALUE R & R Collectibles issued the following bonds.

Date of issue and sale:	April 1, 20-1
Principal amount:	$500,000
Sale price of bonds:	100
Denomination of bonds:	$1,000
Life of bonds:	10 years
Stated rate:	8%, payable semiannually on September 30 and March 31

Prepare journal entries for:

(a) Issuance of the bonds.

(b) Interest payment on the bonds on September 30.

(c) Year-end adjustment on the bonds.

EXERCISE 24-2A   (LO3)
Dec. 31. Dr. Bond Interest
Expense, $12,000

BONDS ISSUED AT A PREMIUM Velez Entertainment Co. issued the following bonds at a premium.

Date of issue and sale:	April 1, 20-1
Principal amount:	$500,000
Sale price of bonds:	104
Denomination of bonds:	$1,000
Life of bonds:	10 years
Stated rate:	10%, payable semiannually on September 30 and March 31

Prepare journal entries for:

(a) Issuance of the bonds at a premium.

(b) Interest payment and premium amortization on the bonds on September 30.

(c) Year-end adjustment on the bonds.

EXERCISE 24-3A   (LO4)
Dec. 31. Dr. Bond Interest
Expense, $9,000

BONDS ISSUED AT A DISCOUNT Brenner's Home Club issued the following bonds at a discount.

Date of issue and sale:	April 1, 20-1
Principal amount:	$500,000
Sale price of bonds:	98
Denomination of bonds:	$1,000
Life of bonds:	10 years
Stated rate:	7%, payable semiannually on September 30 and March 31

Prepare journal entries for:

(a) Issuance of the bonds at a discount.

(b) Interest payment and discount amortization on the bonds on September 30.

(c) Year-end adjustment on the bonds.

EXERCISE 24-4A   (LO2/5)
(b). Dr. Loss on Bonds
Redeemed, $3,200

REDEMPTION OF BONDS ISSUED AT FACE VALUE Levesque Lumber Co. issued $800,000 in bonds at face value ten years ago and has paid semiannual interest payments through the years.

(a) Assume the bonds are redeemed at face value.

(b) Assume that $80,000 of the bonds are redeemed at 104.

(c) Assume that $80,000 of the bonds are redeemed at 96.

Prepare journal entries to record (a), (b), and (c).

EXERCISE 24-5A   (LO3/5)
(a). Cr. Gain on Bonds
Redeemed, $1,800

REDEMPTION OF BONDS ISSUED AT A PREMIUM Brighton Unlimited sold bonds at a premium for $630,000 (premium of $30,000) eight years ago.

(a) The corporation redeems $60,000 of this issue at 98. The unamortized premium is $600.

(b) The corporation redeems $90,000 of this issue at 102. The unamortized premium is $900.

Prepare journal entries to record the redemption in (a) and (b).

EXERCISE 24-6A **(LO4/5)**
(b). Dr. Loss on Bonds
Redeemed, $100

REDEMPTION OF BONDS ISSUED AT A DISCOUNT Martinez Manufacturing sold bonds at a discount for $240,000 (discount of $10,000) seven years ago.

(a) The corporation redeems $25,000 of this issue at 96. The unamortized discount is $375.

(b) The corporation redeems $20,000 of this issue at 99. The unamortized discount is $300.

Prepare journal entries to record the redemption in (a) and (b).

EXERCISE 24-7A **(LO5)**
(b). Cr. Sinking Fund
Earnings, $3,200

BOND SINKING FUNDS M. J. Adams Corporation pays $40,000 into a bond sinking fund each year for the future redemption of bonds. At the end of the first year, earnings on the sinking fund are $3,200. When the bonds mature, there is a balance in the sinking fund of $301,800, of which $300,000 is used to redeem the bonds.
Prepare journal entries to record:

(a) The initial sinking fund deposit.

(b) The first year's earnings.

(c) The redemption of the bonds.

(d) The return of excess cash to the corporation.

SERIES A PROBLEMS

PROBLEM 24-8A **(LO2)**

Dec. 31 entry: Dr. Bond
Interest Expense, $7,500

BONDS ISSUED AT FACE VALUE Ito Co. issued the following bonds.

Date of issue and sale:	April 1, 20-1
Principal amount:	$300,000
Sale price of bonds:	100
Denomination of bonds:	$5,000
Life of bonds:	5 years
Stated rate:	10%, payable semiannually on September 30 and March 31

REQUIRED

Prepare journal entries for:

(a) Issuance of the bonds.

(b) Interest payment on the bonds on September 30, 20-1.

(c) Year-end adjustment on the bonds for 20-1.

(d) Reversing entry for the beginning of 20-2.

(e) Interest payments on the bonds for 20-2 (March 31 and September 30).

(f) Redemption at maturity.

PROBLEM 24-9A **(LO3)**
Carrying value, Aug. 31,
Year 2: $820,400

BONDS ISSUED AT A PREMIUM Bunkichi Corporation issued the following bonds at a premium.

Date of issue and sale:	March 1, 20-1
Principal amount:	$800,000
Sale price of bonds:	103
Denomination of bonds:	$1,000
Life of bonds:	10 years
Stated rate:	8%, payable semiannually on August 31 and February 28

REQUIRED

1. Prepare journal entries for:

    (a)   Issuance of the bonds at a premium.

    (b)   Interest payment and premium amortization on the bonds on August 31, 20-1.

    (c)   Year-end adjustment on the bonds for 20-1.

    (d)   Reversing entry for the beginning of 20-2.

    (e)   Interest payments and premium amortization on the bonds for 20-2 (February 28 and August 31).

2. Calculate the carrying value of the bonds on August 31, 20-2.

PROBLEM 24-10A   (LO4)
Carrying value, Sept. 30,
Year 2: $487,250

BONDS ISSUED AT A DISCOUNT Emerald, Inc., issued the following bonds at a discount.

Date of issue and sale:	April 1, 20-1
Principal amount:	$500,000
Sale price of bonds:	97
Denomination of bonds:	$1,000
Life of bonds:	10 years
Stated rate:	8%, payable semiannually on September 30 and March 31

REQUIRED

1. Prepare journal entries for:

    (a)   Issuance of the bonds at a discount.

    (b)   Interest payment and discount amortization on the bonds on September 30, 20-1.

    (c)   Year-end adjustment on the bonds for 20-1.

    (d)   Reversing entry for the beginning of 20-2.

    (e)   Interest payments and discount amortization on the bonds for 20-2 (March 31 and September 30).

2. Calculate the carrying value of the bonds on September 30, 20-2.

PROBLEM 24-11A (LO3/5)
Mar. 1, 20-6 entry: Dr. Loss on
Bonds Redeemed, $2,250

BONDS ISSUED AT A PREMIUM, REDEEMED AT A LOSS Perez Company issued the following bonds at a premium.

Date of issue and sale:	March 1, 20-1
Principal amount:	$400,000
Sale price of bonds:	103
Denomination of bonds:	$1,000
Life of bonds:	10 years
Stated rate:	12%, payable semiannually on August 31 and February 28

REQUIRED

   Prepare journal entries for:

(a) Issuance of the bonds.

(b) Interest payment and premium amortization on the bonds on August 31, 20-1.

(continued)

(c) Year-end adjustment on the bonds for 20-1.

(d) Reversing entry for the beginning of 20-2.

(e) Redemption of $50,000 of the bonds on March 1, 20-6, at 106.

PROBLEM 24-12A (LO4/5)
Apr. 1, 20-4 entry: Cr. Gain on
Bonds Redeemed, $1,300

BONDS ISSUED AT A DISCOUNT, REDEEMED AT A GAIN Cline & Co. issued the following bonds at a discount.

Date of issue and sale:	April 1, 20-1
Principal amount:	$500,000
Sale price of bonds:	98
Denomination of bonds:	$1,000
Life of bonds:	10 years
Stated rate:	9%, payable semiannually on September 30 and March 31

REQUIRED

Prepare journal entries for:

(a) Issuance of the bonds.

(b) Interest payment and discount amortization on the bonds on September 30, 20-1.

(c) Year-end adjustment on the bonds for 20-1.

(d) Reversing entry for the beginning of 20-2.

(e) Redemption of $50,000 of the bonds on April 1, 20-4, at 96.

PROBLEM 24-13A (LO2/5)
2nd Dec. 31 entry: Dr. Bond
Interest Expense, $12,500

BONDS ISSUED AT FACE VALUE WITH SINKING FUND Martin Manufacturing issued the following bonds.

Date of issue and sale:	April 1, 20-1
Principal amount:	$500,000
Sale price of bonds:	100
Denomination of bonds:	$10,000
Life of bonds:	10 years
Stated rate:	10%, payable semiannually on September 30 and March 31
Annual sinking fund requirement:	$34,000, payable June 1

REQUIRED

Prepare journal entries for:

(a) Issuance of the bonds.

(b) Deposit to sinking fund on June 1.

(c) Interest payment on the bonds on September 30, 20-1.

(d) Earnings of $2,400 on the sinking fund in 20-1.

(e) Year-end adjustment on the bonds for 20-1.

(f) Reversing entry for the beginning of 20-2.

(g) Interest payments on the bonds for 20-2 (March 31 and September 30).

(h) Redemption at maturity from the sinking fund.

(i) Return of excess cash of $1,050 from the sinking fund to the corporation.

SERIES B EXERCISES

EXERCISE 24-1B (LO2)
Dec. 31 entry: Dr. Bond
Interest Expense, $9,000

BONDS ISSUED AT FACE VALUE L & L Underwriters issued the following bonds.

Date of issue and sale:	April 1, 20-1
Principal amount:	$400,000
Sale price of bonds:	100
Denomination of bonds:	$1,000
Life of bonds:	10 years
Stated rate:	9%, payable semiannually on September 30 and March 31

Prepare journal entries for:

(a) Issuance of the bonds.

(b) Interest payment on the bonds on September 30.

(c) Year-end adjustment on the bonds.

EXERCISE 24-2B (LO3)
Dec. 31 entry: Dr. Bond
Interest Expense, $9,750

BONDS ISSUED AT A PREMIUM Bryant and Nelson Company issued the following bonds at a premium.

Date of issue and sale:	May 1, 20-1
Principal amount:	$500,000
Sale price of bonds:	103
Denomination of bonds:	$1,000
Life of bonds:	10 years
Stated rate:	12%, payable semiannually on October 31 and April 30

Prepare journal entries for:

(a) Issuance of the bonds at a premium.

(b) Interest payment and premium amortization on the bonds on October 31.

(c) Year-end adjustment on the bonds.

EXERCISE 24-3B (LO4)
Dec. 31 entry: Dr. Bond
Interest Expense, $8,300

BONDS ISSUED AT A DISCOUNT Beilke's Supply Stores issued the following bonds at a discount.

Date of issue and sale:	April 1, 20-1
Principal amount:	$400,000
Sale price of bonds:	97
Denomination of bonds:	$1,000
Life of bonds:	10 years
Stated rate:	8%, payable semiannually on September 30 and March 31

Prepare journal entries for:

(a) Issuance of the bonds at a discount.

(b) Interest payment and discount amortization on the bonds on September 30.

(c) Year-end adjustment on the bonds.

Interactive Learning: http://heintz.swlearning.com

EXERCISE 24-4B   (LO2/5)

(b). Dr. Loss on Bonds
Redeemed, $750

REDEMPTION OF BONDS ISSUED AT FACE VALUE Okano Medical Lab issued $300,000 in bonds at face value ten years ago and has paid semiannual interest payments through the years.

(a) Assume the bonds are redeemed at face value.

(b) Assume that $25,000 of the bonds are redeemed at 103.

(c) Assume that $25,000 of the bonds are redeemed at 97.

Prepare the journal entries to record (a), (b), and (c).

EXERCISE 24-5B   (LO3/5)

(a). Cr. Gain on Bonds
Redeemed, $3,000

REDEMPTION OF BONDS ISSUED AT A PREMIUM Miller & Miller sold bonds at a premium for $525,000 (premium of $25,000) eight years ago.

(a) The corporation redeems $50,000 of this issue at 95. The unamortized premium is $500.

(b) The corporation redeems $75,000 of this issue at 103. The unamortized premium is $750.

Prepare journal entries to record the redemption in (a) and (b).

EXERCISE 24-6B   (LO4/5)

(b). Dr. Loss on Bonds
Redeemed, $600

REDEMPTION OF BONDS ISSUED AT A DISCOUNT Medina Optical Supply sold bonds at a discount for $420,000 (discount of $20,000) eight years ago.

(a) The corporation redeems $25,000 of this issue at 94. The unamortized discount is $250.

(b) The corporation redeems $30,000 of this issue at 101. The unamortized discount is $300.

Prepare journal entries to record the redemption in (a) and (b).

EXERCISE 24-7B   (LO5)

(b). Cr. Sinking Fund
Earnings, $4,750

BOND SINKING FUNDS Sheng Corporation pays $50,000 into a bond sinking fund each year for the future redemption of bonds. At the end of the first year, earnings on the sinking fund are $4,750. When the bonds mature, there is a balance in the sinking fund of $502,125, of which $500,000 is used to redeem the bonds.

Prepare journal entries to record:

(a) The initial sinking fund deposit.

(b) The first year's earnings.

(c) The redemption of the bonds.

(d) The return of excess cash to the corporation.

SERIES B PROBLEMS

PROBLEM 24-8B   (LO2)

Dec. 31 entry: Dr. Bond
Interest Expense, $5,625

BONDS ISSUED AT FACE VALUE Ramona Arroyo Co. issued the following bonds.

Date of issue and sale:	April 1, 20-1
Principal amount:	$250,000
Sale price of bonds:	100
Denomination of bonds:	$5,000
Life of bonds:	10 years
Stated rate:	9%, payable semiannually on September 30 and March 31

REQUIRED

Prepare journal entries for:

(a) Issuance of the bonds.

(b) Interest payment on the bonds on September 30, 20-1.

(c) Year-end adjustment on the bonds for 20-1.

(d) Reversing entry for the beginning of 20-2.

(e) Interest payments on the bonds for 20-2 (March 31 and September 30).

(f) Redemption at maturity.

PROBLEM 24-9B (LO3)

Carrying value, Aug. 31,
Year 2: $256,375

BONDS ISSUED AT A PREMIUM Wang Corporation issued the following bonds at a premium.

Date of issue and sale:	March 1, 20-1
Principal amount:	$250,000
Sale price of bonds:	103
Denomination of bonds:	$500
Life of bonds:	10 years
Stated rate:	12%, payable semiannually on August 31 and February 28

REQUIRED

1. Prepare journal entries for:

    (a) Issuance of the bonds at a premium.

    (b) Interest payment and premium amortization on the bonds on August 31, 20-1.

    (c) Year-end adjustment on the bonds for 20-1.

    (d) Reversing entry for the beginning of 20-2.

    (e) Interest payments and premium amortization on the bonds for 20-2 (February 28 and August 31).

2. Calculate the carrying value of the bonds on August 31, 20-2.

PROBLEM 24-10B (LO4)

Carrying value, Sept. 30,
Year 2: $579,600

BONDS ISSUED AT A DISCOUNT Brandon, Inc., issued the following bonds at a discount.

Date of issue and sale:	April 1, 20-1
Principal amount:	$600,000
Sale price of bonds:	96
Denomination of bonds:	$1,000
Life of bonds:	10 years
Stated rate:	7%, payable semiannually on September 30 and March 31

REQUIRED

1. Prepare journal entries for:

    (a) Issuance of the bonds at a discount.

    (b) Interest payment and discount amortization on the bonds on September 30, 20-1.

(continued)

    (c)   Year-end adjustment on the bonds for 20-1.

    (d)   Reversing entry for the beginning of 20-2.

    (e)   Interest payments and discount amortization on the bonds for 20-2 (March 31 and September 30).

2.   Calculate the carrying value of the bonds on September 30, 20-2.

PROBLEM 24-11B   (LO3/5)
Mar. 1, 20-6 entry: Dr. Loss on Bonds Redeemed, $2,250

BONDS ISSUED AT A PREMIUM, REDEEMED AT A LOSS Blackwell Company issued the following bonds at a premium.

Date of issue and sale:	March 1, 20-1
Principal amount:	$500,000
Sale price of bonds:	103
Denomination of bonds:	$1,000
Life of bonds:	10 years
Stated rate:	12%, payable semiannually on August 31 and February 28

REQUIRED

Prepare journal entries for:

(a) Issuance of the bonds.

(b) Interest payment and premium amortization on the bonds on August 31, 20-1.

(c) Year-end adjustment on the bonds for 20-1.

(d) Reversing entry for the beginning of 20-2.

(e) Redemption of $50,000 of the bonds on March 1, 20-6, at 106.

PROBLEM 24-12B   (LO4/5)
Apr. 1, 20-4 entry: Cr. Gain on Bonds Redeemed, $950

BONDS ISSUED AT A DISCOUNT, REDEEMED AT A GAIN Ellis & Co. issued the following bonds at a discount.

Date of issue and sale:	April 1, 20-1
Principal amount:	$400,000
Sale price of bonds:	97
Denomination of bonds:	$1,000
Life of bonds:	10 years
Stated rate:	8%, payable semiannually on September 30 and March 31

REQUIRED

Prepare journal entries for:

(a) Issuance of the bonds.

(b) Interest payment and discount amortization on the bonds on September 30, 20-1.

(c) Year-end adjustment on the bonds for 20-1.

(d) Reversing entry for the beginning of 20-2.

(e) Redemption of $50,000 of the bonds on April 1, 20-4, at 96.

PROBLEM 24-13B (LO2/5)
2nd Dec. 31 entry: Dr. Bond
Interest Expense, $12,000

BONDS ISSUED AT FACE VALUE WITH SINKING FUND Creswell Entertainment issued the following bonds.

Date of issue and sale:	April 1, 20-1
Principal amount:	$600,000
Sale price of bonds:	100
Denomination of bonds:	$10,000
Life of bonds:	10 years
Stated rate:	8%, payable semiannually on September 30 and March 31
Annual sinking fund requirement:	$40,000, payable on June 1

REQUIRED

Prepare journal entries for:

(a) Issuance of the bonds.

(b) Deposit to sinking fund on June 1.

(c) Interest payment on the bonds on September 30, 20-1.

(d) Earnings of $3,000 on the sinking fund in 20-1.

(e) Year-end adjustment on the bonds for 20-1.

(f) Reversing entry for the beginning of 20-2.

(g) Interest payments on the bonds for 20-2 (March 31 and September 30).

(h) Redemption at maturity from the sinking fund.

(i) Return of excess cash of $1,900 from the sinking fund to the corporation.

MASTERY PROBLEM

Jackson, Inc.'s fiscal year ends December 31. Selected transactions for the period 20-1 through 20-8 involving bonds payable issued by Jackson are as follows:

20-1

Carrying value, Dec. 31,
Year 2: $610,600

Oct. 30	Issued $600,000 of ten-year, 10%, callable bonds dated October 31, 20-1, for $612,000. Interest is payable semiannually on October 31 and April 30. The bond indenture provides that Jackson is to pay to the trustee bank $20,000 by May 15 of each year (except the tenth year) as a sinking fund for the retirement of the bonds on call or at maturity.
Dec. 31	Made the adjusting entry for interest payable and amortized two months' premium on the bonds (straight-line method).

20-2

Jan. 2	Reversed the adjusting entry for interest payable and bond premium amortization.
Apr. 30	Paid the semiannual interest on the bonds and amortized six months' premium.
May 15	Paid the sinking fund trustee $20,000.
Oct. 31	Paid the semiannual interest on the bonds and amortized six months' premium.
Dec. 31	Made the adjusting entry for interest payable and amortized two months' premium on the bonds.
31	Sinking fund earnings for the year were $900.

(continued)

20-8

May 15   Paid the sinking fund trustee $20,000.

Oct. 31   Paid the semiannual interest on the bonds and amortized six months' premium.

31   Redeemed the bonds, which were called at 97.
 The balance in the bond premium account is $3,600 after the payment of interest and amortization of premium have been entered. The cash balance in the sinking fund is $200,000, which is applied to the redemption. Paid the sinking fund trustee the additional cash needed to pay off the bonds. *(Hint:* First make the entry for payment to the sinking fund, then make the entry for redemption of the bonds.)

REQUIRED

1. Enter the preceding transactions in general journal form.

2. Calculate the carrying value of the bonds as of December 31, 20-2.

CHALLENGE PROBLEM

This problem challenges you to apply your cumulative accounting knowledge to move a step beyond the material in the chapter.

1. Net savings = $27,000

On April 1, 20-1, Rebound Co. issued $300,000 of 10%, ten-year bonds, callable at 105 after three years, at face value. On April 1, 20-4, after completing three years of interest payments on the bonds, Rebound is considering calling the bonds and issuing $300,000 of new 8%, ten-year bonds at face value. The current market interest rate is only 8%, so Rebound thinks it might save money by taking this action.

REQUIRED

1. Compute the net savings to Rebound over the life of the original bond issue if it calls the old bonds and issues the new bonds.

2. Assuming Rebound calls the original bond issue, prepare the journal entry for the bond redemption.

O B J E C T I V E S

Careful study of this appendix should enable you to:

LO1 Amortize premium on bonds payable using the effective interest method.

LO2 Amortize discount on bonds payable using the effective interest method.

Chapter 24 Appendix
Effective Interest Method

In Chapter 24, you learned how to amortize premium and discount on bonds payable using the straight-line method. In this appendix, the effective interest method of amortization is explained and illustrated.

The key to applying the effective interest method is the effective interest rate at which the bonds are issued. The **effective interest rate** is the market rate of interest on the date the bonds are issued. This rate is used to determine both the interest expense and the premium or discount amortization for the period.

Under the **effective interest method**, the beginning-of-period carrying value of the bonds multiplied by the effective interest rate is the **effective interest expense**. The difference between the effective interest expense and the cash interest payment is the amount of premium or discount to be amortized for the period.

LEARNING KEY: Under the effective interest method, the effective interest expense for the period is calculated by multiplying the *beginning-of-period* carrying value of the bonds by the effective interest rate.

AMORTIZATION OF PREMIUM USING THE EFFECTIVE INTEREST METHOD

LO1 Amortize premium on bonds payable using the effective interest method.

To illustrate the effective interest method of amortizing bond premium, assume the following bond issue for Prime Co.

Date of issue and sale	4/1/20-1
Principal amount	$400,000
Denomination	$1,000
Life	10 years
Stated rate	9%
Market rate at issue	8%

Because the stated rate exceeds the market rate, these bonds will sell at a premium, for $427,181. The effective interest expense for the first semiannual interest period is $17,087, the carrying value of the bonds, $427,181, times the semiannual effective interest rate of 4 percent. The amount of bond premium to be amortized for the period is $913, the difference between the effective interest expense ($17,087) and the cash interest payment ($18,000). The bond premium amortization schedule for the Prime Co. bonds for the first three and the last three interest periods is shown in Figure 24A-1.

LEARNING KEY: Under the effective interest method, the amount of premium or discount to be amortized for a period is the difference between the effective interest expense and the cash interest payment.

BOND PREMIUM AMORTIZATION SCHEDULE EFFECTIVE INTEREST METHOD					
(1)	(2)	(3)	(4)	(5)	(6)
Date	Cash Payment	Interest Expense [(6) in previous row × 4%]	Premium Amortization [(2) – (3)]	Unamortized Premium	Carrying Value of Bonds
4/1/-1				$27,181	$427,181
10/1/-1	$18,000	$17,087	$913	26,268	426,268
4/1/-2	18,000	17,051	949	25,319	425,319
10/1/-2	18,000	17,013	987	24,332	424,332
–	–	–	–	–	–
–	–	–	–	–	–
–	–	–	–	–	–
4/1/10	18,000	16,222	1,778	3,773	403,773
10/1/10	18,000	16,151	1,849	1,924	401,924
3/31/11	18,000	16,076*	1,924	0	400,000

* A one dollar adjustment was subtracted to correct for rounding error.

FIGURE 24A-1   Bond Premium Amortization Schedule

The amount in column (2) is the semiannual cash interest payment. Column (3) contains the semiannual effective interest expense. This amount is computed by multiplying the beginning-of-period carrying value of the bond, which appears in the previous row of column (6), by the semiannual effective interest rate (4%). The difference between columns (2) and (3) is shown in column (4), the semiannual premium amortization. The unamortized premium is shown in column (5). As with the straight-line method of amortization, over the life of the bond, the unamortized premium decreases to zero and the carrying value of the bond decreases to its face value.

AMORTIZATION OF DISCOUNT USING THE EFFECTIVE INTEREST METHOD

LO2 Amortize discount on bonds payable using the effective interest method.

To illustrate the effective interest method of amortizing bond discount, assume the following bond issue for Disco Co.

Date of issue and sale	4/1/20-1
Principal amount	$400,000
Denomination	$1,000
Life	10 years
Stated rate	9%
Market rate at issue	10%

Because the stated rate is less than the market rate, these bonds will sell at a discount, for $375,076. The effective interest expense for the first semiannual interest period is $18,754, the carrying value of the bonds, $375,076, times the semiannual effective interest rate of 5 percent. The amount of bond discount to be amortized for the period is $754, the difference between the effective interest expense ($18,754) and the cash interest payment ($18,000). The bond discount amortization schedule for the Disco Co. bonds for the first three and the last three interest periods is shown in Figure 24A-2.

BOND DISCOUNT AMORTIZATION SCHEDULE EFFECTIVE INTEREST METHOD					
(1)	(2)	(3) Interest Expense [(6) in previous row × 5%]	(4) Discount Amortization [(3) − (2)]	(5) Unamortized Discount	(6) Carrying Value of Bonds
Date	Cash Payment				
4/1/-1				$24,924	$375,076
10/1/-1	$18,000	$18,754	$754	24,170	375,830
4/1/-2	18,000	18,791	791	23,379	376,621
10/1/-2	18,000	18,831	831	22,548	377,452
–	–	–	–	–	–
–	–	–	–	–	–
–	–	–	–	–	–
4/1/10	18,000	19,728	1,728	3,717	396,283
10/1/10	18,000	19,814	1,814	1,903	398,097
3/31/11	18,000	19,903*	1,903	0	400,000

* A two dollar adjustment was subtracted to correct for rounding error.

FIGURE 24A-2 Bond Discount Amortization Schedule

The amount in column (2) is the semiannual cash interest payment. Column (3) contains the semiannual effective interest expense. This amount is computed by multiplying the beginning-of-period carrying value of the bond, which appears in the previous row of column (6), by the semiannual effective interest rate (5%). The difference between columns (2) and (3) is shown in column (4), the semiannual discount amortization. The unamortized discount is shown in column (5). As with the straight-line method of amortization, over the life of the bond, the unamortized discount decreases to zero and the carrying value of the bond increases to its face value.

KEY TERMS

effective interest expense, (921) The beginning-of-period carrying value of the bonds multipled by the effective interest rate.

effective interest method, (921) A method of amortizing bond discount or premium that uses the effective interest rate on the bonds.

effective interest rate, (921) The market rate of interest on the date the bonds are issued.

SERIES A EXERCISE

EXERCISE 24Apx-1A (LO1)
Dr. Premium on
Bonds Payable, $456

On May 1, Holiday Company issued $200,000, 9%, ten-year bonds for $213,591 when the market rate was 8%. Prepare the general journal entry for the first semiannual interest payment and bond premium amortization on November 1, using the effective interest method.

SERIES A PROBLEM

PROBLEM 24Apx-2A (LO1)
Dec. 31 entry: Dr. Premium
on Bonds Payable, $1,156

BOND PREMIUM AMORTIZATION Fields Company sold an issue of $800,000, 10%, ten-year bonds for $852,032 on March 1. The interest is payable semiannually on September 1 and March 1. The market rate of interest at the time the bonds were issued was 9%. Journalize the following transactions (round all amounts to the nearest dollar).

Sept. 1 Paid the first semiannual interest payment and amortized the bond premium, using the effective interest method.

Dec. 31 Made the adjusting entry for bond interest accrued and amortization of the bond premium from September 1. (*Hint:* Use the effective interest rate for the four-month period from September 1 – December 31.)

Jan. 2 Reversed the adjusting entry for bond interest accrued and bond premium amortization as of December 31.

Mar. 1 Paid the second semiannual interest payment and amortized the bond premium.

SERIES B EXERCISE

EXERCISE 24Apx-1B (LO2)
Cr. Discount on
Bonds Payable, $565

On May 1, Saxophone Corp. issued $300,000, 9%, ten-year bonds for $281,307 when the market rate was 10%. Prepare the general journal entry for the first semiannual interest payment and bond discount amortization on November 1, using the effective interest method.

SERIES B PROBLEM

PROBLEM 24Apx-2B (LO2)
Dec. 31 entry: Cr. Discount
on Bonds Payable, $495

BOND DISCOUNT AMORTIZATION Zee Company sold an issue of $500,000, 9%, ten-year bonds for $468,845 on April 1. The interest is payable semiannually on October 1 and April 1. The market rate of interest at the time the bonds were issued was 10%. Journalize the following transactions (round all amounts to the nearest dollar).

Oct. 1 Paid the first semiannual interest payment and amortized the bond discount, using the effective interest method.

Dec. 31 Made the adjusting entry for bond interest accrued and amortization of the bond discount from October 1. (*Hint:* Use the effective interest rate for the three-month period from October 1 – December 31.)

Jan. 2 Reversed the adjusting entry for bond interest accrued and bond discount amortization as of December 31.

Apr. 1 Paid the second semiannual interest payment and amortized the bond discount.

©THIRD EYE IMAGES/CORBIS

Statement of Cash Flows

Mike Finbar was puzzled after reading the recent income statement prepared by the company's accountant. For months the company has had difficulty meeting the payroll and paying suppliers within the discount periods. The company just never seems to have enough cash. Yet, the most recent income statement shows that the company is exceeding profit expectations. How can the company be highly profitable and not have enough cash to pay its bills on time?

A business must have an adequate amount of cash to operate. Without sufficient cash, suppliers and employees cannot be paid, debt cannot be retired, and dividends cannot be paid to stockholders. Managers, creditors, stockholders, and others pay close attention to a company's cash position and the economic events and transactions leading to changes in that position. The statement of cash flows provides information about the events that affect the cash position of a company.

NATURE AND PURPOSE OF THE STATEMENT OF CASH FLOWS

LO1 Explain the purpose of the statement of cash flows.

The managers of a business must generate net income (profitability) and keep the enterprise solvent (liquidity). The income statement reports on the company's profitability by matching revenues and expenses on an accrual basis. Revenues are recognized when earned, regardless of when the cash is received. Expenses are recognized as incurred, regardless of when the cash is paid. Although the accrual basis of accounting is an excellent method for measuring profitability, it does not explain why a company's liquidity has improved or worsened. The income statement does not explain, for example, why a company reporting substantial profits can have difficulty paying its bills on time.

It would seem logical that a profitable company would have plenty of cash. Net income brings in cash, either immediately or as soon as receivables are collected. However, the cash inflow resulting from profitable operations may be used to acquire long-term assets, to pay off long-term debt, or to pay stockholders in the form of dividends. Thus, an increase or decrease in cash results from a combination of operating, investing, and financing activities by management. The income statement alone does not adequately reflect all of these activities.

Management and outside users of the financial statements want to know how cash was generated and used during the period. The purpose of the **statement of cash flows** is to provide this information.

OPERATING, INVESTING, AND FINANCING ACTIVITIES

LO2 Define operating, investing, and financing activities and describe transactions for each type of activity.

The statement of cash flows categorizes all cash flows into three major types of activities: operating, investing, and financing.

Operating Activities

Operating activities include transactions and events associated with selling a product or providing a service and are related to the revenues and expenses reported on the income statement. Since interest revenue, interest expense, and dividend revenue are reported on the income statement, they are also considered cash flows from operating activities. Figure 25-1 shows cash inflows and outflows from operating activities.

Operating activities represent the company's primary source of cash over the life of the business. Ultimately, net cash inflows from operating activities must be used to purchase plant and equipment, repay loans, and pay dividends to stockholders.

 LEARNING KEY: Cash flows from operating activities are primarily related to the revenues and expenses reported on the income statement.

The proper reporting of dividends and interest on the statement of cash flows can be confusing. Here's an easy way to keep it straight. If the item is reported on the income statement (interest expense, interest revenue, and dividend revenue), it is classified as an operating activity on the statement of cash flows. If not (dividends), it is classified as a financing activity.

OPERATING ACTIVITIES	
Cash Inflows	**Cash Outflows**
1. Cash receipts from the sale of goods or services.	1. Payments for the acquisition of inventory.
2. Interest received on loans made to outside entities.	2. Payments to employees and the government.
3. Dividends received on investments made in the stock of other corporations.	3. Payments for interest on loans.
	4. Payments to other suppliers and for other expenses.

FIGURE 25-1   Cash Flows from Operating Activities

Investing Activities

Investing activities are those transactions involving the purchase and sale of long-term assets, investments in debt and equity securities, and lending money and collecting the principal on the related loans. Figure 25-2 shows typical transactions for cash inflows and outflows from investing activities.

 LEARNING KEY: Investing activities include buying and selling long-term assets, investing in debt and equity securities, and lending money and collecting the principal on the related loans.

INVESTING ACTIVITIES	
Cash Inflows	**Cash Outflows**
1. Proceeds from collection of principal amount of loans made to borrowers.*	1. Loans made by the company to other parties.
2. Proceeds from the sale of property, plant, and equipment; intangibles; and other productive assets.	2. Payments to acquire property, plant, and equipment; intangibles; and other productive assets.
3. Proceeds from the sale of investments in debt and equity securities.	3. Payments to acquire investments in debt and equity securities.
4. Proceeds from discounting notes receivable.	

* Note that interest received on loans is not included with investing activities. It is included with cash inflows from operating activities.

FIGURE 25-2   Cash Flows from Investing Activities

Financing Activities

Financing activities are those transactions dealing with the exchange of cash between the company and its owners (stockholders) and creditors. Cash inflows and outflows include the types of transactions listed in Figure 25-3.

LEARNING KEY: Financing activities deal with the exchange of cash between the company and its stockholders and creditors.

FINANCING ACTIVITIES	
Cash Inflows	**Cash Outflows**
1. Proceeds from additional investments by the owners or the issuance of stock.	1. Payments of dividends to stockholders or withdrawals by the owners.
2. Proceeds from borrowing money through the signing of a mortgage, issuing a bond, or other long- or short-term loans.	2. Payments to purchase treasury stock.
	3. Repayment of the principal on loans.*

* Note that interest payments on loans are not reported under financing activities. They are reported as cash outflows under operating activities.
Note: Amounts owed to suppliers of goods and services are not considered financing activities. They are used in the calculation of cash from operating activities.

FIGURE 25-3   Cash Flows from Financing Activities

INFORMATION NEEDED TO PREPARE A STATEMENT OF CASH FLOWS

LO3 Describe the information needed to prepare a statement of cash flows.

To prepare a statement of cash flows, the following statements are needed:

1. Balance sheets for the beginning and end of the period.

2. Income statement for the period.

3. Statement of retained earnings for the period.

Additional information on major cash transactions is useful. This information and an analysis of all noncash balance sheet accounts are used to identify transactions involving cash flows during the year.

The statement of cash flows is divided into three sections:

1. cash flows from operating activities,

2. cash flows from investing activities, and

3. cash flows from financing activities.

> **LEARNING KEY:** The three major sections of the statement of cash flows focus on:
>
> operating activities
> investing activities
> financing activities

The sum of the cash generated or used by each of the three activities should equal the difference between the beginning and ending balance of the cash account. For example, if $5,000 was generated from operations, $2,000 used for investing activities, and $3,000 provided by financing activities, the cash balance must have increased by $6,000 ($5,000 – $2,000 + $3,000) during the year. The accuracy of the statement can be verified by computing the change in the balance of the cash account.

> **LEARNING KEY:** Change in cash balance:
>
> | | Cash from operating activities |
> |---|---|
> | ± | Cash from investing activities |
> | ± | Cash from financing activities |
> | = | Change in cash balance |

PREPARING A STATEMENT OF CASH FLOWS: SIMPLEX

LO4 Prepare a schedule for the calculation of cash from operating activities under the direct method.

Most major corporations use the indirect method. However, the Financial Accounting Standards Board is encouraging these companies to switch to the direct method.

A sure sign of financial difficulty for a business is the continuing need to sell assets or issue long-term debt to pay operating expenses. Therefore, an important factor in evaluating a company's financial condition is the ability to generate positive cash flows from operating activities. Cash generated from operating activities may be computed and reported using one of two methods. Under the **direct method**, revenues and expenses reported on the income statement are adjusted to reflect the amount of cash received or paid for each item. Under the **indirect method**, net income is adjusted for transactions that affect net income and cash flows in different ways. For example, depreciation expense reduces net income, but has no effect on cash flows. The direct method is presented in this chapter. The indirect method is illustrated in the appendix to this chapter.

To illustrate the preparation of a simple statement of cash flows, the Simplex Company is used. Figure 25-4 shows the financial statements and additional information for Simplex.

Simplex Company
Income Statement
For Year Ended December 31, 20-3

Net sales						$900	0	0	0	00
Cost of goods sold						600	0	0	0	00
Gross profit						$300	0	0	0	00
Operating expenses						177	0	0	0	00
Income before taxes						$123	0	0	0	00
Income tax expense						43	0	0	0	00
Net income						$ 80	0	0	0	00

Simplex Company
Statement of Retained Earnings
For Year Ended December 31, 20-3

Retained earnings, January 1, 20-3						$ 50	0	0	0	00
Net income	$ 80	0	0	0	00					
Less dividends	20	0	0	0	00					
Net increase in retained earnings						60	0	0	0	00
Retained earnings, December 31, 20-3						$110	0	0	0	00

FIGURE 25-4   Financial Statements and Additional Information for Simplex

Cash Flows from Operating Activities: The Direct Method

To compute the cash generated from operating activities for the Simplex Company, a schedule like the one shown in Figure 25-5 is prepared. Revenues and expenses reported on the income statement are converted to cash received or paid for operating purposes. Column 1 reports the revenue or expense as reported on the income statement. Columns 2 and 3 are used to make additions or subtractions necessary to reflect the associated cash flows in column 4.

Cash Received from Customers. The income statement for Simplex reports $900,000 in sales during the year. Remember that revenues are recognized when earned, regardless of the amount of cash actually received. To prepare the statement of cash flows, these revenues must be converted to the amount of *cash received from customers during the year.*

If all sales were made for cash, it would not be necessary to adjust the sales reported on the income statement. However, the presence of Accounts Receivable on the balance sheet indicates that Simplex extends credit to its customers. The rate at which credit customers pay their bills affects the cash received from sales during the year. This relationship is most easily understood by observing changes in the balance of Accounts Receivable.

For example, assume that a company's sales for the year were $100 and the balance of Accounts Receivable went from $0 to $10. Since the amount owed by customers increased by $10, the company received only $90 in cash during the year. On the other hand, if the beginning balance of the receivables account was $10 and the ending balance was $0, cash of $110 was actually received, even though sales for the year were only $100. The latter situation indicates that cash was received for all sales made during the current year and $10 was received from

Simplex Company
Comparative Balance Sheet
December 31, 20-3 and 20-2

	20-3	20-2	INCREASE (DECREASE)
Assets			
Current assets:			
Cash	$ 90 0 0 0 00	$200 0 0 0 00	$(110 0 0 0 00)
Accounts receivable	160 0 0 0 00	190 0 0 0 00	(30 0 0 0 00)
Merchandise inventory	180 0 0 0 00	200 0 0 0 00	(20 0 0 0 00)
Total current assets	$430 0 0 0 00	$590 0 0 0 00	(160 0 0 0 00)
Property, plant, and equipment:			
Land	$ 40 0 0 0 00	$ 40 0 0 0 00	0 00
Building	140 0 0 0 00		140 0 0 0 00
Equipment	100 0 0 0 00		100 0 0 0 00
Total property, plant, and equipment	$280 0 0 0 00	$ 40 0 0 0 00	240 0 0 0 00
Total assets	$710 0 0 0 00	$630 0 0 0 00	80 0 0 0 00
Liabilities			
Current liabilities:			
Notes payable	$ 60 0 0 0 00	$ 50 0 0 0 00	10 0 0 0 00
Accounts payable	120 0 0 0 00	180 0 0 0 00	(60 0 0 0 00)
Total liabilities	$180 0 0 0 00	$230 0 0 0 00	(50 0 0 0 00)
Stockholders' Equity			
Common stock ($5 par, 100,000 shares authorized;			
Issued: 58,000 in 20-3, 50,000 in 20-2)	$290 0 0 0 00	$250 0 0 0 00	40 0 0 0 00
Paid-in capital in excess of par—common stock	130 0 0 0 00	100 0 0 0 00	30 0 0 0 00
Retained earnings	110 0 0 0 00	50 0 0 0 00	60 0 0 0 00
Total stockholders' equity	$530 0 0 0 00	$400 0 0 0 00	130 0 0 0 00
Total liabilities and stockholders' equity	$710 0 0 0 00	$630 0 0 0 00	80 0 0 0 00

Additional information for 20-3:

1. A building and equipment were acquired for cash just before the year end.

2. Issued 8,000 shares of common stock for $8.75 per share.

3. Declared and paid cash dividends of $20,000.

FIGURE 25-4   Financial Statements and Additional Information for Simplex *(continued)*

sales made on account in prior years. Thus, an increase in accounts receivable represents a reduction in the cash generated from sales and a decrease in accounts receivable represents an increase in the cash generated from sales.

LEARNING KEY: Cash received from customers:

Sales

(– ↑) or (+ ↓) in Accounts Receivable

= Cash received from customers

Simplex Company
Schedule for the Calculation of Cash Generated from Operating Activities
For Year Ended December 31, 20-3

INCOME STATEMENT		ADDITIONS		DEDUCTIONS		CASH FLOWS	
Net sales	$900,000	**1**	$30,000			$930,000	◁ Cash received from customers
Cost of goods sold	600,000	**3**	60,000	**2**	$(20,000)	640,000	◁ Cash paid for merchandise
Gross profit	$300,000					$290,000	
Operating expenses	177,000					177,000	◁ Cash paid for operating expenses
Income before taxes	$123,000					$113,000	
Income tax expense	43,000					43,000	◁ Cash paid for income taxes
Net income	$ 80,000					$ 70,000	◁ Cash generated from operating activities

1 The $30,000 reduction in receivables is added to sales to compute cash received from customers.

2 The $20,000 reduction in inventory is subtracted from cost of goods sold to compute the cost of merchandise purchased ($600,000 – $20,000 = $580,000).

3 Reducing the amount owed to suppliers (Accounts Payable) required the expenditure of additional cash. By adding the reduction in Accounts Payable to the cost of merchandise purchased, cash paid for merchandise is determined ($580,000 + $60,000 = $640,000).

FIGURE 25-5   Schedule for the Calculation of Cash Generated from Operating Activities for Simplex

The balance sheet for Simplex shows that the receivables decreased during 20-3 by $30,000 ($190,000 – $160,000). From this decrease, we know that the cash received from customers was $30,000 greater than the $900,000 in current sales reported on the income statement. Thus, on the schedule in Figure 25-5, $30,000 is added to the $900,000 in sales reported on the income statement to show that $930,000 was received from customers during the past year.

T accounts also may be used to compute the cash received from customers as follows:

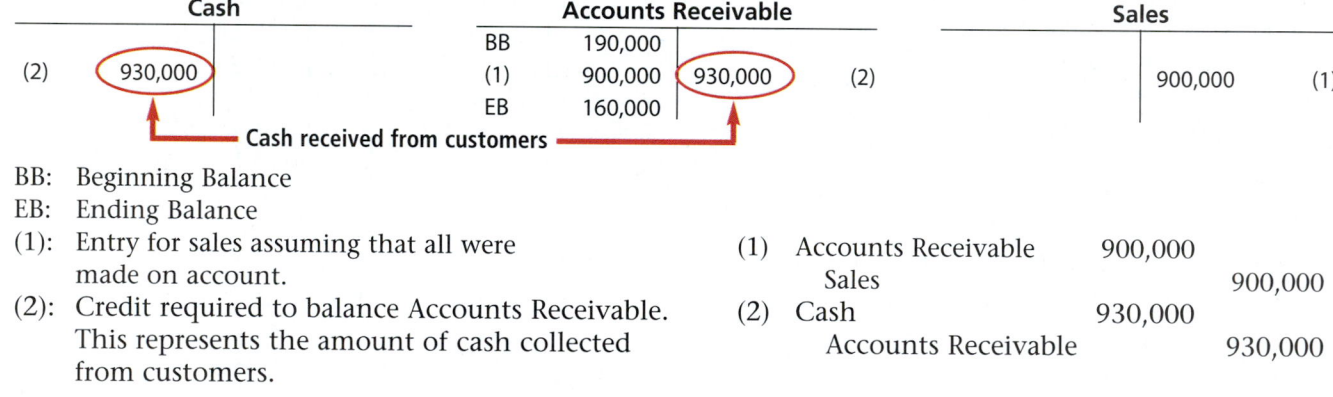

BB: Beginning Balance
EB: Ending Balance
(1): Entry for sales assuming that all were made on account.
(2): Credit required to balance Accounts Receivable. This represents the amount of cash collected from customers.

(1) Accounts Receivable	900,000	
Sales		900,000
(2) Cash	930,000	
Accounts Receivable		930,000

Cash Paid for Merchandise. Simplex reports cost of goods sold of $600,000 on the income statement. To determine cash generated from operating activities, cost of goods sold is adjusted to reflect cash paid to suppliers for merchandise. To do so, two steps are required:

STEP 1   Examine changes in the inventory account to determine the amount of merchandise purchased during the year.

STEP 2   Examine changes in the accounts payable account to determine the amount of cash actually paid to suppliers.

To determine the amount of inventory purchased during the year, examine the cost of goods sold and inventory accounts. An increase in inventory during the year indicates that merchandise purchases were greater than the cost of the merchandise sold. A decrease in inventory indicates that the company did not replace all of the inventory sold, and purchases were less than the cost of goods sold. Thus, purchases for the year can be determined by adjusting the cost of goods sold for changes in the inventory level.

For example, assume that the cost of goods sold is $80. If the inventory increased by $20, purchases would equal $100. If the inventory decreased by $20, purchases would equal $60.

Cost of goods sold	$ 80
Add increase in inventory	20
Cost of merchandise purchased	$100

Cost of goods sold	$ 80
Less decrease in inventory	(20)
Cost of merchandise purchased	$ 60

To determine the cash paid to suppliers, examine the cost of *merchandise* purchased, as computed above, and accounts payable. Accounts Payable is used primarily to record purchases of merchandise on account. When this is true, an increase in Accounts Payable indicates that the company has not yet paid for all of the goods purchased during the year. A decrease in Accounts Payable indicates that the company has paid for purchases made this year plus purchases made in prior years. Let's continue with the previous example for cost of merchandise purchased of $60. If Accounts Payable increased by $10, cash paid for merchandise would equal $50.

Cost of goods sold	$80
Less decrease in inventory	(20)
Cost of merchandise purchased	$60
Less increase in accounts payable	(10)
Cash paid for merchandise	$50

If Accounts Payable decreased by $10, cash paid for merchandise would equal $70.

Cost of goods sold	$80
Less decrease in inventory	(20)
Cost of merchandise purchased	$60
Add decrease in accounts payable	10
Cash paid for merchandise	$70

LEARNING KEY: Cash paid for merchandise:
Cost of goods sold
(+ ↑) or (– ↓) in Inventory
= Cost of merchandise purchased
(– ↑) or (+ ↓) in Accounts Payable
= Cash paid for merchandise

To compute the cash paid for merchandise by Simplex, consider the following three factors:

1. the cost of goods sold,

2. the change in Merchandise Inventory, and

3. the change in Accounts Payable.

Cost of goods sold, as reported on the income statement in Figure 25-4, was $600,000. However, the balance sheet reports that inventory decreased by $20,000 ($200,000 – $180,000). The cost of merchandise purchased by Simplex, therefore, was $580,000 ($600,000 – $20,000 [the decrease in inventory]). Thus, $20,000 is *deducted* from the cost of goods sold in column 3 of Figure 25-5.

The balance sheet shows that Accounts Payable decreased by $60,000 ($180,000 – $120,000). This indicates that in addition to paying for the purchases made this period, Simplex paid $60,000 for merchandise purchased in prior periods. Thus $60,000 must be *added* to the cost of goods sold in column 2 of Figure 25-5 to compute the cash paid for merchandise of $640,000.

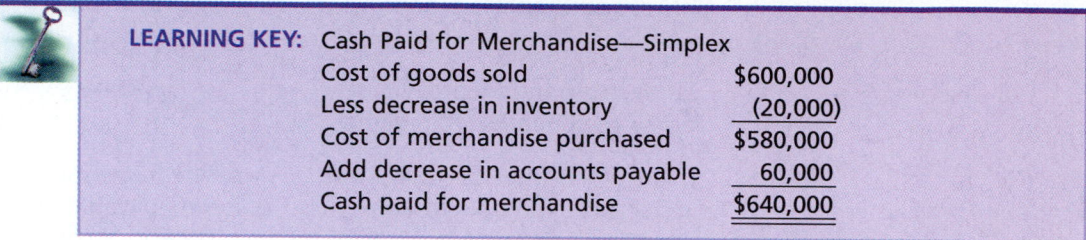

LEARNING KEY: Cash Paid for Merchandise—Simplex

Cost of goods sold	$600,000
Less decrease in inventory	(20,000)
Cost of merchandise purchased	$580,000
Add decrease in accounts payable	60,000
Cash paid for merchandise	$640,000

T accounts also may be used to compute cash paid for merchandise as follows:

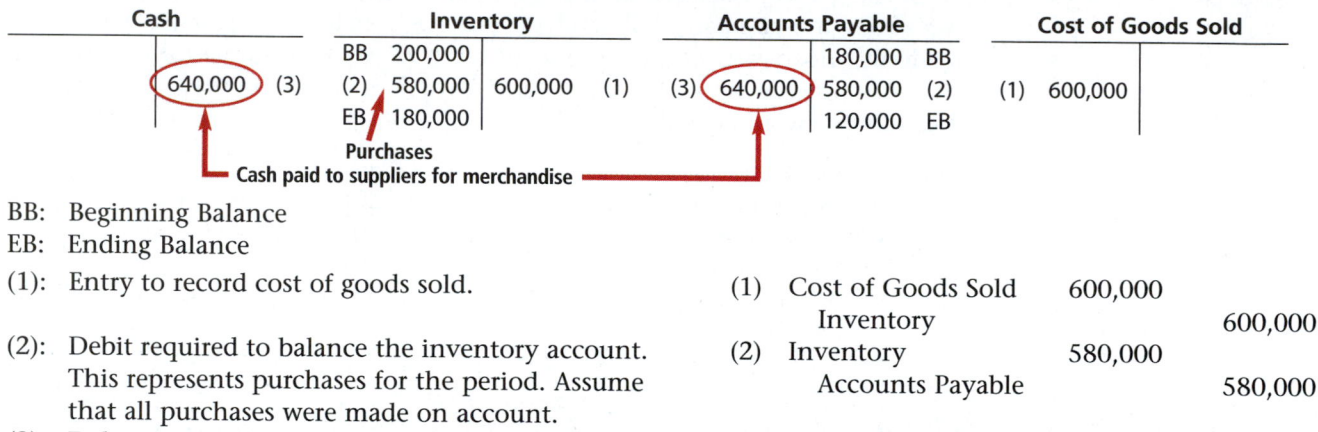

BB: Beginning Balance
EB: Ending Balance

(1): Entry to record cost of goods sold.

(2): Debit required to balance the inventory account. This represents purchases for the period. Assume that all purchases were made on account.

(3): Debit required to balance Accounts Payable. This represents the amount of cash paid for merchandise.

(1)	Cost of Goods Sold	600,000	
	Inventory		600,000
(2)	Inventory	580,000	
	Accounts Payable		580,000
(3)	Accounts Payable	640,000	
	Cash		640,000

Cash Paid for Operating Expenses. Adjustments to operating expenses generally are necessary for items such as prepaid expenses, accrued liabilities, or depreciation on plant and equipment. Simplex does not have any of these items, so there is no need to adjust operating expenses. The entire $177,000 of operating expenses is reported as a cash outflow. It is assumed that all of these expenses required cash outflows.

Cash Paid for Income Taxes. The balance sheet reports no receivables, payables, or other items related to income tax expense. Thus, tax expense reported on the income statement represents the amount of cash paid for taxes.

The schedule in Figure 25-5 demonstrates that net income was $80,000, but only $70,000 in cash was generated from operating activities. All of the information in column 4 is reported on the statement of cash flows illustrated in Figure 25-6.

Simplex Company
Statement of Cash Flows
For Year Ended December 31, 20-3

Cash flows from operating activities:		
Cash received from customers		$930 0 0 0 00
Cash paid for merchandise	$(640 0 0 0 00)	
Cash paid for operating expenses	(177 0 0 0 00)	
Cash paid for income taxes	(43 0 0 0 00)	
Total cash disbursed for operating activities		(860 0 0 0 00)
Net cash provided by operating activities		$ 70 0 0 0 00
Cash flows from investing activities:		
Purchased building	$(140 0 0 0 00)	
Purchased equipment	(100 0 0 0 00)	
Net cash used by investing activities		(240 0 0 0 00)
Cash flows from financing activities:		
Issued note payable	$ 10 0 0 0 00	
Issued common stock	70 0 0 0 00	
Paid cash dividends	(20 0 0 0 00)	
Net cash provided by financing activities		60 0 0 0 00
Net increase (decrease) in cash		$(110 0 0 0 00)
Cash balance, January 1, 20-3		200 0 0 0 00
Cash balance, December 31, 20-3		$ 90 0 0 0 00

FIGURE 25-6 Statement of Cash Flows for Simplex

A BROADER VIEW

Net Income Versus Cash from Operating Activities: Eli Lilly Company

Since cash from operating activities (CFO) is related to revenues and expenses on the income statement, many financial statement users assume that CFO and net income (NI) are similar in value and move in the same direction. This relationship holds, except for a few considerations. For example, depreciation and amortization

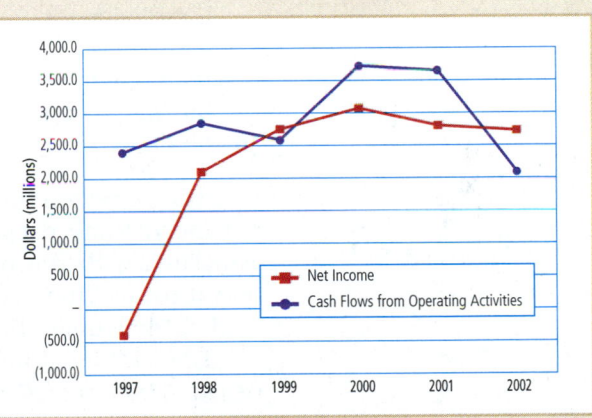

expense reduce net income, but do not reduce cash. Thus, over the life of the firm, you should expect CFO to be greater than NI by the amount of depreciation and amortization expenses. However, for specific years, major differences between CFO and NI are easy to observe. As shown above, Lilly reported a net loss of $385 million in 1997 while also reporting cash from operating activities of $2.4 billion. This occurred because Lilly reported a major expense associated with closing facilities that did not require the use of cash. In 2000, CFO increased substantially more than NI due to a $1.1 billion increase in accounts payable. By postponing payments to suppliers, Lilly effectively increased its CFO for 2000. In 2002, we see that cash from operating activities fell dramatically and dropped below NI. This was caused by major increases in receivables, inventories, other current assets, and a reduction in accounts payable for a combined reduction in CFO of $1.5 billion.

Cash Flows from Investing Activities

The second major section of the statement of cash flows reports investing activities. This section includes the purchase and sale of long-term assets as well as investments in the debt and equity securities of other businesses. Making loans and collecting the principal on loans are also reported in this section.

The balance sheet for Simplex reports that the building account increased from $0 to $140,000 and the equipment account increased from $0 to $100,000. As noted in the additional information in Figure 25-4, the building and equipment were acquired just before year end. As shown in Figure 25-6, the acquisition of the building and equipment are reported under investing activities. The amounts are reported in parentheses ( ) to indicate an outflow of cash. Since these are the only investing activities for the year, the net cash used by investing activities is $240,000.

Cash Flows from Financing Activities

This section of the statement reports exchanges of cash between the company and its stockholders and creditors. For Simplex, the only transaction with creditors is the $10,000 increase in Notes Payable. The proceeds from this financing activity are reported as a cash inflow from financing activities.

The balance sheet in Figure 25-4 shows that total stockholders' equity increased by $130,000. This can be broken down by analyzing the changes in the retained earnings and the capital stock accounts as follows:

Stockholders' equity, January 1, 20-3		$400,000
Retained earnings		
Net income	$80,000	
Less dividends	(20,000)	
Capital stock		
Issuance of common stock	70,000	
Increase in stockholders' equity		130,000
Stockholders' equity, December 31, 20-3		$530,000

As reported on the statement of retained earnings, Simplex earned $80,000 in net income and declared and paid cash dividends of $20,000. The cash flows associated with the net income have already been reported in the section on operating activities. However, the cash paid for dividends must be reported as a cash outflow under financing activities.

The additional information, reported in Figure 25-4, indicated that Simplex issued 8,000 shares of common stock for $70,000. This can be verified by examining the common stock and paid-in capital in excess of par—common stock accounts, shown in T account form as follows:

Common Stock		Paid-In Capital in Excess of Par—Common Stock	
	20-3		20-3
	Jan. 1 Bal. 250,000		Jan. 1 Bal. 100,000
	Issuance 40,000		Issuance 30,000
	Dec. 31 Bal. 290,000		Dec. 31 Bal. 130,000

40,000 + 30,000 = $70,000 cash received for common stock

The $70,000 in cash received from the issuance of common stock is reported as a cash inflow from financing activities.

Verifying the Accuracy of the Statement

The sum of the net cash inflow of $70,000 from operating activities, the net cash outflow of $240,000 from investing activities, and the net cash inflow of $60,000 from financing activities results in a net decrease in cash of $110,000. Simplex's balance sheet reports that cash decreased by $110,000 ($200,000 − $90,000) during the year. The fact that these numbers agree provides some assurance that all cash flow activities have been included in the statement. This reconciliation is generally reported at the bottom of the statement of cash flows.

PREPARING A STATEMENT OF CASH FLOWS: MULTIPLEX

LO5 Prepare a statement of cash flows under the following conditions:

a. the company defines cash as "cash and cash equivalents,"

b. the company reports depreciation expense,

c. the company has prepaid and accrued expenses, and

d. the company has non-cash investing and financing activities.

This section of the chapter shows how to prepare a statement of cash flows for a more complex business. Because of the increased complexity, a methodical approach is needed to identify all cash flows and to prepare the statement. This section provides step-by-step procedures for the preparation of the statement. In addition, four other aspects of a more complex environment are addressed. First, a more precise definition of cash is developed. Second, the treatment of depreciation expense is illustrated. Third, the effect of prepaid and accrued expenses is explained. Fourth, the reporting of noncash investing and financing activities is discussed.

To prepare a statement of cash flows under the direct method, use the information provided in Figure 25-7 and follow these steps:

Steps in Preparing the Statement of Cash Flows

STEP 1   Compute the change in cash and cash equivalents (defined in the following section) as reported on the balance sheet.

STEP 2   Prepare a schedule to calculate cash generated from operating activities by adjusting all income statement items for changes in current asset, current liability, and other related accounts as reported on the balance sheet.

STEP 3   Identify cash flows from investing activities by analyzing any additional information, as illustrated in Figure 25-7, and by reconciling balance sheet accounts related to long-term assets, investments in debt and equity securities, and loans made to parties outside the company.

STEP 4   Identify cash flows from financing activities by analyzing any additional information and reconciling balance sheet accounts related to transactions with stockholders and creditors.

NOTE: Upon completion of Steps 2–4, all noncash balance sheet accounts should have been analyzed in an attempt to identify cash flows. When performing the steps, check off each account to ensure that none is overlooked.

STEP 5   Sum the cash flows from operating, investing, and financing activities to determine the net increase or decrease in cash and cash equivalents. Compare this amount with the change in cash and cash equivalents computed in Step 1.

STEP 6   Prepare a schedule of noncash investing and financing activities.

Multiplex Corporation
Income Statement
For Year Ended December 31, 20-2

Net sales							$460	1	0	0	00
Cost of goods sold							270	1	0	0	00
Gross profit							$190	0	0	0	00
Operating expenses							120	7	5	0	00
Operating income							$ 69	2	5	0	00
Other revenues and expenses:											
Interest revenue	$	1	5	5	00						
Interest expense	(6	5	0	00)			(4	9	5	00)	
Income before taxes							$ 68	7	5	5	00
Income tax expense							24	0	0	0	00
Net income							$ 44	7	5	5	00

Multiplex Corporation
Statement of Retained Earnings
For Year Ended December 31, 20-2

Retained earnings, January 1, 20-2							$23	6	6	0	00
Net income	$44	7	5	5	00						
Less dividends	22	8	0	0	00						
Net increase in retained earnings							21	9	5	5	00
Retained earnings, December 31, 20-2							$45	6	1	5	00

Additional information:

1. Depreciation expense for the year was $10,400.

2. No equipment was sold during the period. The following cash purchases were made:

Store equipment	$ 9,200
Office equipment	4,000
	$13,200

3. A $13,000, three-year note was issued to acquire delivery equipment with a market value of $13,000.

4. Declared and paid cash dividends of $22,800.

5. Issued 200 shares of common stock for $15 per share.

FIGURE 25-7 Financial Statements and Additional Information for Multiplex

Multiplex Corporation
Comparative Balance Sheet
December 31, 20-2 and 20-1

	20-2		20-1		INCREASE (DECREASE)
Assets					
Current assets:					
Cash	$ 22 9 8 0 00		$20 0 0 0 00		$ 2 9 8 0 00
Government notes	1 8 0 0 00		3 2 0 0 00		(1 4 0 0 00)
Accrued interest receivable	1 0 0 00		3 0 0 00		(2 0 0 00)
Accounts receivable (net)	60 2 1 5 00		51 5 1 0 00		8 7 0 5 00
Merchandise inventory	64 5 7 0 00		67 5 0 0 00		(2 9 3 0 00)
Supplies and prepayments	4 0 0 0 00		2 7 5 0 00		1 2 5 0 00
Total current assets		$153 6 6 5 00		$145 2 6 0 00	8 4 0 5 00
Property, plant, and equipment:					
Store equipment	$ 48 0 0 0 00		$38 8 0 0 00		9 2 0 0 00
Less accumulated depreciation—store equipment	18 0 0 0 00	30 0 0 0 00	14 0 0 0 00	24 8 0 0 00	4 0 0 0 00
Delivery equipment	$ 45 0 0 0 00		$32 0 0 0 00		13 0 0 0 00
Less accumulated depreciation—delivery equip.	12 5 0 0 00	32 5 0 0 00	8 0 0 0 00	24 0 0 0 00	4 5 0 0 00
Office equipment	$ 38 0 0 0 00		$34 0 0 0 00		4 0 0 0 00
Less accumulated depreciation—office equipment	8 0 0 0 00	30 0 0 0 00	6 1 0 0 00	27 9 0 0 00	1 9 0 0 00
Total property, plant, and equipment		$ 92 5 0 0 00		$ 76 7 0 0 00	15 8 0 0 00
Total assets		$246 1 6 5 00		$221 9 6 0 00	24 2 0 5 00
Liabilities					
Current liabilities:					
Notes payable	$ 10 0 0 0 00		$11 8 0 0 00		(1 8 0 0 00)
Accounts payable	33 5 0 0 00		45 9 0 0 00		(12 4 0 0 00)
Income tax payable	3 0 0 0 00		2 0 0 0 00		1 0 0 0 00
Accrued and withheld payroll taxes	9 5 0 00		1 5 2 0 00		(5 7 0 00)
Accrued interest payable	1 0 0 00		8 0 00		2 0 00
Total current liabilities		$ 47 5 5 0 00		$ 61 3 0 0 00	(13 7 5 0 00)
Long-term liabilities:					
Note payable (3-year)		13 0 0 0 00			13 0 0 0 00
Total liabilities		$ 60 5 5 0 00		$ 61 3 0 0 00	(7 5 0 00)
Stockholders' Equity					
Common stock ($10 par, 100,000 shares authorized;					
Issued: 10,000 in 20-2 and 9,800 in 20-1)	$100 0 0 0 00		$98 0 0 0 00		2 0 0 0 00
Paid-in capital in excess of par—common stock	40 0 0 0 00		39 0 0 0 00		1 0 0 0 00
Retained earnings	45 6 1 5 00		23 6 6 0 00		21 9 5 5 00
Total stockholders' equity		185 6 1 5 00		160 6 6 0 00	24 9 5 5 00
Total liabilities and stockholders' equity		$246 1 6 5 00		$221 9 6 0 00	24 2 0 5 00

FIGURE 25-7 Financial Statements and Additional Information for Multiplex *(continued)*

Definition of Cash Equivalents

To earn a return on idle cash, many companies invest in short-term, highly liquid investments known as **cash equivalents**. To qualify as cash equivalents, the investments must be readily convertible to a *known* amount of cash, so that when cash is needed, the investments can be easily liquidated. Examples of cash equivalents include short-term investments in government notes and money market funds. These investments are considered the same as cash when preparing the statement of cash flows. Thus, the statement should explain the change in the amount of cash *and* cash equivalents held at the beginning and at the end of an accounting period.

> **LEARNING KEY:** A cash equivalent is a short-term, highly liquid investment that can be readily converted to a known amount of cash.

Multiplex has cash equivalents (government notes) of $1,800 and $3,200 on December 31, 20-2 and 20-1, respectively. Thus, the statement of cash flows must explain why cash and government notes increased by $1,580 during the year.

	20-2 Dec. 31	20-1 Dec. 31	Increase (Decrease)
Cash	$22,980	$20,000	$2,980
Government notes	1,800	3,200	(1,400)
Cash and cash equivalents	$24,780	$23,200	$1,580

Cash Flows from Operating Activities: The Direct Method

To compute the cash flows from operating activities, prepare a schedule converting the accrual basis income statement to cash flows, as shown in Figure 25-8. Following the same procedure used for Simplex, column 1 shows revenues and expenses as reported on the income statement. Columns 2 and 3 show additions and deductions to convert the accrual basis figures to the associated cash flows reported in column 4.

Cash Received from Customers. The abbreviated income statement for Multiplex in Figure 25-7 reports net sales of $460,100. The $8,705 increase in net receivables ($60,215 – $51,510) reported on the balance sheet means that cash was not received for all of the sales made during the year. As shown on the schedule in Figure 25-8, the increase in net receivables must be deducted from net sales to compute cash received from customers of $451,395.

Cash Paid for Merchandise. As discussed earlier, cost of goods sold must be adjusted for changes in Merchandise Inventory and Accounts Payable to compute cash paid for merchandise.

Merchandise Inventory. The balance sheet shows that inventory decreased by $2,930. This means that the cost of the goods sold exceeded the cost of the goods purchased during the year. Deduct the decrease in inventory from the cost of goods sold to compute net purchases, as shown in column 3 in Figure 25-8.

Accounts Payable. Multiplex reports a decrease in Accounts Payable of $12,400. This means that Multiplex paid for merchandise purchased this period *and* for merchandise purchased on account in prior periods. As shown in column 2 in

Multiplex Corporation
Schedule for the Calculation of Cash Generated from Operating Activities
For Year Ended December 31, 20-2

INCOME STATEMENT		ADDITIONS		DEDUCTIONS		CASH FLOWS	
Net sales	$460,100			1	$(8,705)	$451,395	Cash received from customers
Cost of goods sold	270,100	3	$12,400	2	(2,930)	279,570	Cash paid for merchandise
Gross profit	$190,000					$171,825	
Operating expenses	120,750	4	1,250	5	(10,400)		
		6	570			112,170	Cash paid for operating expenses
Operating income	$ 69,250					$ 59,655	
Interest revenue	155	7	200			355	Interest received
Interest expense	650			8	(20)	630	Interest paid
Income tax expense	24,000			9	(1,000)	23,000	Cash paid for income taxes
Net income	$ 44,755					$ 36,380	Cash generated from operating activities

1 The increase in Accounts Receivable reduced the amount of cash received from sales. Subtract this $8,705 increase from Sales to compute cash received from customers.

2 The $2,930 decrease in inventory indicates that Multiplex purchased less inventory than it sold. Subtract this decrease from cost of goods sold to compute the cost of merchandise purchased for the year ($270,100 − $2,930 = $267,170).

3 The $12,400 decrease in Accounts Payable means that Multiplex paid cash to suppliers in excess of amounts purchased. Add the decrease in the amount owed to suppliers to the cost of merchandise purchased to compute cash paid for merchandise ($267,170 + $12,400 = $279,570).

4 The increase in supplies and prepayments indicates that Multiplex not only replenished these items for the amounts used during the period, but also increased the supplies on hand and prepayments. Thus, the cash paid for these items is greater than the expense recognized for the period. Add the increase of $1,250 to compute cash paid for operating expenses.

5 Depreciation is an operating expense but requires no cash outflow. Subtract the $10,400 ($4,000 + $4,500 + $1,900) in depreciation expense from operating expenses to compute cash paid for operating expenses.

6 By making payments to the government and reducing Accrued and Withheld Payroll Taxes, the amount of cash paid to the government this period was increased. Add the reduction of $570 to operating expenses to compute cash paid for operating expenses.

7 Add the reduction in Accrued Interest Receivable of $200 to Interest Revenue to compute the amount of interest received in cash.

8 Deduct the increase in Accrued Interest Payable of $20 from Interest Expense to compute the amount of interest paid in cash.

9 Deduct the increase in Income Tax Payable of $1,000 to compute income taxes paid in cash.

FIGURE 25-8   Schedule for the Calculation of Cash Generated from Operating Activities for Multiplex

Figure 25-8, add the $12,400 decrease in the amount owed to suppliers to cost of goods sold. The adjustments for inventory and accounts payable result in $279,570 cash paid to suppliers for merchandise.

Cash Paid for Operating Expenses. The income statement shown in Figure 25-7 reports $120,750 in operating expenses. The balance sheet and additional information provided in Figure 25-7 are reviewed to identify necessary adjustments to compute cash paid for operating expenses.

Supplies and Prepayments. The balance sheet shows that Supplies and Prepayments increased by $1,250. Thus, the cash paid for these items was greater than the expense reported on the income statement. As shown in Figure 25-8, add the increase of $1,250 to operating expenses to compute cash paid for operating expenses.

> **LEARNING KEY:** Cash paid for supplies and prepayments:
> Expense reported for supplies and prepayments
> (+ ↑) or (– ↓) in supplies or prepayments
> = Cash paid for supplies and prepayments

Depreciation Expense. Accumulated depreciation on the various types of equipment increased by $10,400. The additional information in Figure 25-7 explains that this increase is the depreciation expense for the year. To recognize depreciation expense, Multiplex made the following adjusting entries at the end of the year:

4	Dec.	31	Depr. Expense—Store Equipment	4 0 0 0 00		4
5			Accum. Depr.—Store Equipment		4 0 0 0 00	5
6						6
7		31	Depr. Expense—Delivery Equipment	4 5 0 0 00		7
8			Accum. Depr.—Delivery Equipment		4 5 0 0 00	8
9						9
10		31	Depr. Expense—Office Equipment	1 9 0 0 00		10
11			Accum. Depr.—Office Equipment		1 9 0 0 00	11

These entries increase operating expenses and reduce net income, but do not require an outflow of cash. Therefore, the amount of depreciation expense must be deducted from the operating expenses to determine the cash paid for operating expenses, as shown in column 3 of Figure 25-8.

> **LEARNING KEY:** Depreciation Expense increases operating expenses, but requires no cash outflow. Therefore, deduct this amount from operating expenses to compute cash paid.

Accrued and Withheld Payroll Taxes. The balance sheet shows that Accrued and Withheld Payroll Taxes decreased by $570. This decrease means that payments made to the government by Multiplex exceeded the Payroll Tax Expense by $570. Thus, the $570 decrease in the accrued and withheld payroll taxes account must be added to operating expenses to compute cash paid for operating expenses.

> **LEARNING KEY:** Cash paid for accrued expenses:
> Accrued expenses reported on income statement (e.g., Payroll Tax Expense)
> (– ↑) or (+ ↓) in accrued liabilities (e.g., Payroll Tax Payable)
> = Cash paid for accrued expenses

As reported in column 4 of Figure 25-8, after completing the adjustments, cash paid for operating expenses is $112,170.

Cash Received from Interest. Review the balance sheet to determine whether Interest Revenue must be adjusted to reflect interest received in cash. Accrued Interest Receivable decreased by $200. This means that Multiplex received $200 in cash for interest earned in prior periods in addition to the cash received for interest earned this period. Add this amount to Interest Revenue to compute cash received from interest.

LEARNING KEY: Cash received from interest:
Interest revenue reported on income statement
(– ↑) or (+ ↓) in Interest Receivable
= Cash received from interest

Cash Paid for Interest. A similar procedure is applied for Interest Expense. As reported on the balance sheet, Accrued Interest Payable increased by $20. This means that Multiplex did not pay for all of the $650 of interest expense incurred this period. The $20 increase in the liability is deducted from Interest Expense to compute cash paid for interest.

LEARNING KEY: Cash paid for interest:
Interest expense reported on income statement
(– ↑) or (+ ↓) in Interest Payable
= Cash paid for interest

Cash Paid for Income Taxes. Income tax expense of $24,000 is reported on the income statement. The balance sheet reports that Income Tax Payable increased by $1,000. Postponing the payment for taxes reduces the cash paid for income taxes by $1,000. Thus, $1,000 is deducted from Income Tax Expense to compute the income taxes paid in cash ($24,000 – $1,000 = $23,000).

Once the accrual basis revenues and expenses are adjusted, cash from operating activities is determined to be $36,380. This amount is shown at the bottom of column 4. All of the information from column 4 is presented on the statement of cash flows, shown in Figure 25-9, under cash flows from operating activities.

Cash Flows from Investing Activities

Investing activities are transactions involving the purchase and sale of long-term assets, investments in debt and equity securities, and the lending of money and subsequent collection of the principal on those loans. Investing activities by Multiplex this past year included the purchase of store, delivery, and office equipment as disclosed under the additional information in Figure 25-7. These acquisitions explain the increase in store equipment of $9,200, delivery equipment of $13,000, and office equipment of $4,000 as reported on the balance sheet. Since cash was paid for the store and office equipment, these acquisitions are reported in parentheses on the statement of cash flows in Figure 25-9 to indicate a total outflow of cash for investing activities of $13,200. Since the delivery equipment was acquired by issuing a note payable, no cash outflow was required. This noncash investing and financing activity is reported in a separate schedule at the bottom of the statement.

Multiplex Corporation Statement of Cash Flows For Year Ended December 31, 20-2															
Cash flows from operating activities:															
Cash received from customers	$451	3	9	5	00										
Interest received		3	5	5	00										
Cash provided by operating activities						$451	7	5	0	00					
Cash paid for merchandise	$(279	5	7	0	00)										
Cash paid for operating expenses	(112	1	7	0	00)										
Interest paid		(6	3	0	00)										
Income taxes paid	(23	0	0	0	00)										
Total cash disbursed for operating activities						(415	3	7	0	00)					
Net cash provided by operating activities						$ 36	3	8	0	00					
Cash flows from investing activities:															
Purchased store equipment	$ (9	2	0	0	00)										
Purchased office equipment	(4	0	0	0	00)										
Net cash used by investing activities						(13	2	0	0	00)					
Cash flows from financing activities:															
Issued common stock	$ 3	0	0	0	00										
Paid cash dividends	(22	8	0	0	00)										
Retired note payable	(1	8	0	0	00)										
Net cash used by financing activities						(21	6	0	0	00)					
Net increase (decrease) in cash and cash equivalents						$ 1	5	8	0	00					
Cash and cash equivalents, January 1, 20-2						23	2	0	0	00					
Cash and cash equivalents, December 31, 20-2						$ 24	7	8	0	00					
Schedule of noncash investing and financing activities:															
Acquired delivery equipment by issuing a 3-year note.						$ 13	0	0	0	00					

FIGURE 25-9 Statement of Cash Flows for Multiplex

Cash Flows from Financing Activities

Financing activities include transactions with owners and creditors. The additional information in Figure 25-7 indicates that 200 shares of $10 par common stock were issued for $3,000. This explains the increases in Common Stock of $2,000 and in Paid-In Capital in Excess of Par—Common Stock of $1,000 as reported on the balance sheet. The $3,000 cash inflow is reported under financing activities.

The statement of retained earnings and additional information provided in Figure 25-7 indicate that $22,800 in dividends were declared and paid. These dividends represent an outflow of cash from financing activities and are reported in parentheses.

The reduction in the notes payable account (current) on the balance sheet indicates that a note of $1,800 was paid off. This additional outflow of cash is also reported in parentheses.

These three transactions resulted in a net cash outflow of $21,600 from financing activities. This amount also is reported on the statement of cash flows.

The long-term note payable was issued for the acquisition of delivery equipment, so no cash was received. This noncash investing and financing transaction is reported in the separate schedule at the bottom of the statement.

Schedule of Noncash Investing and Financing Activities

Some investing and financing activities involve no cash flows, but represent a significant change in the company's financial position. These events are called **noncash investing and financing activities**. An example of this type of transaction is the issuance of the $13,000 note payable to acquire delivery equipment. Multiplex entered this transaction as follows:

15		Delivery Equipment		13	0	0	0	00								15
16		Note Payable								13	0	0	0	00		16
17		Purchased delivery equipment by														17
18		issuing a note payable														18

> **LEARNING KEY:** Noncash investing and financing activities are investing and financing activities that involve no cash flows, but represent a significant change in the company's financial position.

Since no cash is involved in this transaction, it should not be included in any of the three main sections of the statement of cash flows. However, the acquisition of the delivery equipment is an investing activity and signing the note payable is a financing activity. Since this event is important in understanding changes in the company's financial position, it should be reported in a separate section of the statement as follows:

Schedule of noncash investing and financing activities:
  Acquired delivery equipment by issuing a note payable $13,000

Verifying the Accuracy of the Statement

At this point, the impact of changes in all noncash (and noncash equivalent) balance sheet accounts is reflected on the statement of cash flows. Therefore, the statement's accuracy should be verified. Summing the cash flows from operating, investing, and financing activities indicates that there was a net increase in cash and cash equivalents of $1,580. Since this agrees with the increase in the sum of the cash and government notes reported on the balance sheet in Figure 25-7, there is some assurance of the accuracy of the statement. Generally, this reconciliation is reported at the bottom of the statement of cash flows.

It is important to review all balance sheet accounts to identify transactions impacting cash. In more complex settings, it may be helpful to reconcile the balance of each account and record any impact on cash flows. This approach is illustrated in the appendix to this chapter.

INTERPRETING THE STATEMENT OF CASH FLOWS

LO6 Interpret the statement of cash flows.

The purpose of the statement of cash flows is to provide information on the sources and uses of cash. To do this, all cash-related activities are grouped into three categories: operating, investing, and financing. Probably the most important indicator of the financial health of a business is the net cash used or provided by operating activities. Both Simplex and Multiplex had positive cash flows from operations. This is important because these funds are needed to purchase property, plant, and equipment to upgrade or expand operations. Expansion and renewal can be financed through borrowing or through the issuance of capital stock. However, loans must be repaid with interest, and dividends will be paid to stockholders in proportion to the amount invested. Ultimately, these funds must be generated from operations. A chronic inability to generate positive cash flows from operations is a sure sign of financial instability.

 LEARNING KEY: Probably the most important indicator of the financial health of a business is the net cash used or provided by operating activities.

Information on investing and financing activities is also useful in evaluating the financial health of the company. For example, the statement of cash flows in Figure 25-9 shows that Multiplex generated $36,380 from operating activities. Of this amount, $15,000 ($13,200 + $1,800) was used to buy equipment and pay off debt. An additional $22,800 was paid out in dividends. Approximately 63 percent ($22,800 ÷ $36,380) of the cash generated from operating activities went to the stockholders. If dividends begin to exceed the cash generated from operating activities, it could imply that the company is planning to go out of business.

Modest increases or decreases in cash balances are normal. Major fluctuations should be investigated and can generally be explained by current and expected future investment and financing activities.

Learning Objectives	Key Points to Remember
1 **Explain the purpose of the statement of cash flows.**	The purpose of the statement of cash flows is to report how cash was generated and used throughout the accounting period.
2 **Define operating, investing, and financing activities and describe transactions for each type of activity.**	The statement has three major sections that report on cash flows from operating, investing, and financing activities. Operating activities include transactions and events associated with selling a product or providing a service and are related to the revenues and expenses reported on the income statement. Investing activities are those transactions involving the purchase and sale of long-term assets, investments in debt and equity securities, and lending money and collecting the principal on the related loans. Financing activities are those transactions dealing with the exchange of cash between the company and its stockholders and creditors. The inflows and outflows associated with these types of activities are as follows:

OPERATING ACTIVITIES	
Cash Inflows	**Cash Outflows**
1. Cash receipts from the sale of goods or services.	1. Payments for the acquisition of inventory.
2. Interest received on loans made to outside entities.	2. Payments to employees and the government.
3. Dividends received on investments made in the stock of other corporations.	3. Payments for interest on loans.
	4. Payments to other suppliers and for other expenses.

Learning Objectives	Key Points to Remember

INVESTING ACTIVITIES

Cash Inflows	Cash Outflows
1. Proceeds from collection of principal amount of loans made to borrowers.*	1. Loans made by the company to other parties.
2. Proceeds from the sale of property, plant, and equipment; intangibles; and other productive assets.	2. Payments to acquire property, plant, and equipment; intangibles; and other productive assets.
3. Proceeds from the sale of investments in debt and equity securities.	3. Payments to acquire investments in debt and equity securities.
4. Proceeds from discounting notes receivable.	

* Note that interest received on loans is not included with investing activities. It is included with cash inflows from operating activities.

FINANCING ACTIVITIES

Cash Inflows	Cash Outflows
1. Proceeds from additional investments by the owners or the issuance of stock.	1. Payments of dividends to stockholders or withdrawals by the owners.
2. Proceeds from borrowing money through the signing of a mortgage, issuing a bond, or other long- or short-term loans.	2. Payments to purchase treasury stock.
	3. Repayment of the principal on loans.*

* Interest payments on loans are not reported under financing activities. They are reported as cash outflows under operating activities.
Note: Amounts owed to suppliers of goods and services are not considered financing activities. They are used in the calculation of cash from operating activities.

3 Describe the information needed to prepare a statement of cash flows.

To prepare a statement of cash flows, the following information is needed:
1. balance sheets for the beginning and end of the period,
2. income statement,
3. statement of retained earnings, and
4. any additional information on major cash transactions.

4 Prepare a schedule for the calculation of cash generated from operating activities under the direct method.

Steps in preparing a schedule for the calculation of cash flows from operating activities under the direct method are as follows:

STEP 1 Convert sales to cash received from customers by adjusting for changes in accounts receivable.

STEP 2 Convert cost of goods sold to cash paid for merchandise by adjusting for changes in inventory and accounts payable.

STEP 3 Convert operating expenses to cash paid for operating expenses by adjusting for changes in current assets and current liabilities related to operating expenses and for noncash expenses.

STEP 4 Convert interest revenue and interest expense to cash received and paid for interest by adjusting for changes in interest receivable and interest payable.

Learning Objectives	Key Points to Remember

5 Prepare a statement of cash flows under the following conditions:

a. the company defines cash as "cash and cash equivalents,"

b. the company reports depreciation expense,

c. the company has prepaid and accrued expenses, and

d. the company has noncash investing and financing activities.

Steps in preparing a statement of cash flows are as follows:

STEP 1 Compute the change in cash and cash equivalents. Many companies define cash as "cash and cash equivalents" on the statement of cash flows. Cash equivalents are short-term, highly liquid investments that can be readily converted to a known amount of cash.

STEP 2 Prepare a schedule to calculate cash generated from operating activities under the direct method.

STEP 3 Identify cash flows from investing activities.

STEP 4 Identify cash flows from financing activities.

NOTE: All noncash balance sheet accounts should have been analyzed to identify cash flows. Check off each account so that none is overlooked.

STEP 5 Sum the cash flows from operating, investing, and financing activities to determine the net increase or decrease in cash and cash equivalents. Compare this amount with the change in the cash and cash equivalents computed in Step 1.

STEP 6 Prepare a schedule of noncash investing and financing activities. An example is the purchase of a machine by signing a note payable. Since no cash is exchanged, this transaction is reported in a separate section on the statement of cash flows.

6 Interpret the statement of cash flows.

Probably the most important indicator of the financial health of a company is the net cash used or provided by operating activities. These funds are needed to purchase property, plant, and equipment. Borrowing or the issuance of capital stock can be used to finance expansion, but loans must be repaid with interest and dividends must be paid to stockholders. These funds must ultimately be generated from operations.

R E F L E C T I O N

Reflection: Answering the Opening Question

The income statement is prepared under the accrual basis of accounting. Revenues are reported when earned, regardless of when cash is received, and expenses are reported when incurred, regardless of when paid. If customers are slow in paying and creditors expect prompt payment, cash balances may get low, even when the company reports adequate profits. In addition, the company may invest cash in additional plant and equipment, or repay loans faster than it is able to collect cash from customers. When this happens, it will be necessary for Mike to borrow cash from a bank or other creditor.

DEMONSTRATION PROBLEM

WebTUTOR Advantage

Financial statements and additional information for Megaproducts are provided below and on page 950.

Megaproducts, Inc.
Income Statement
For Year Ended December 31, 20-3

Net sales		$4,601 0 0 0 00
Cost of goods sold		2,701 0 0 0 00
Gross profit		$1,900 0 0 0 00
Operating expenses		1,207 5 0 4 00
Operating income		$ 692 4 9 6 00
Other revenues and expenses:		
Interest revenue	$1 5 5 0 00	
Interest expense	(6 4 4 0 00)	(4 8 9 0 00)
Income before taxes		$ 687 6 0 6 000
Income tax expense		$ 240 0 0 0 000
Net income		$ 447 6 0 6 00

Megaproducts, Inc.
Statement of Retained Earnings
For Year Ended December 31, 20-3

Retained earnings, January 1, 20-3		$236 6 2 2 00
Net income	$447 6 0 6 00	
Less dividends	128 0 0 0 00	
Net increase in retained earnings		319 6 0 6 00
Retained earnings, December 31, 20-3		$556 2 2 8 00

Additional information:

1. Depreciation expense for the year was $104,000.

2. No equipment was sold during the period. The following cash purchases were made:

Store equipment	$ 92,000
Delivery equipment	130,000
Office equipment	40,100
	$262,100

3. Declared and paid cash dividends of $128,000.

4. Issued 2,000 shares of $10 par common stock for $15 per share.

5. Retired notes payable for $17,200 and acquired additional office equipment by issuing a note payable for $12,000.

(continued)

Megaproducts, Inc.
Comparative Balance Sheet
December 31, 20-3 and 20-2

	20-3		20-2		INCREASE (DECREASE)
Assets					
Current assets:					
Cash	$ 211,786.00		$ 212,000.00		$ (214.00)
Government notes	26,000.00		20,000.00		6,000.00
Accrued interest receivable	3,000.00		7,000.00		(4,000.00)
Accounts receivable (net)	544,000.00		506,000.00		38,000.00
Merchandise inventory	645,678.00		675,120.00		(29,442.00)
Supplies and prepayments	40,150.00		27,356.00		12,794.00
Total current assets		$1,467,914.00		$1,441,176.00	26,738.00
Property, plant, and equipment:					
Store equipment	$ 480,000.00		$ 388,000.00		92,000.00
Less accumulated depreciation—store equip.	180,000.00	300,000.00	140,000.00	248,000.00	40,000.00
Delivery equipment	$ 450,000.00		$ 320,000.00		130,000.00
Less accumulated depreciation—delivery equip.	125,000.00	325,000.00	80,000.00	240,000.00	45,000.00
Office equipment	$ 392,000.00		$ 339,900.00		52,100.00
Less accumulated depreciation—office equip.	80,000.00	312,000.00	61,000.00	278,900.00	19,000.00
Total property, plant, and equipment		$ 937,000.00		$ 766,900.00	170,100.00
Total assets		$2,404,914.00		$2,208,076.00	196,838.00
Liabilities					
Current liabilities:					
Notes payable	$ 112,800.00		$ 118,000.00		(5,200.00)
Accounts payable	200,150.00		367,454.00		(167,304.00)
Income tax payable	125,000.00		100,000.00		25,000.00
Accrued and withheld payroll taxes	9,896.00		15,200.00		(5,304.00)
Accrued interest payable	840.00		800.00		40.00
Total liabilities		$ 448,686.00		$ 601,454.00	(152,768.00)
Stockholders' Equity					
Common stock ($10 par, 1,000,000 shares authorized; Issued: 100,000 in 20-3 and 98,000 in 20-2)	$1,000,000.00		$ 980,000.00		20,000.00
Paid-in capital in excess of par—common stock	400,000.00		390,000.00		10,000.00
Retained earnings	556,228.00		236,622.00		319,606.00
Total stockholders' equity		1,956,228.00		1,606,622.00	349,606.00
Total liabilities and stockholders' equity		$2,404,914.00		$2,208,076.00	196,838.00

REQUIRED

1. Prepare a schedule for the calculation of cash generated from operating activities for the year ended December 31, 20-3.

2. Prepare a statement of cash flows explaining the change in cash and cash equivalents for the year ended December 31, 20-3.

3. Reconcile the cash and cash equivalents at the bottom of the statement of cash flows.

Solution

1.

	Megaproducts, Inc. Schedule for the Calculation of Cash Generated from Operating Activities For Year Ended December 31, 20-3				
INCOME STATEMENT		**ADDITIONS**	**DEDUCTIONS**	**CASH FLOWS**	
Net sales	$4,601,000		☐1 $ (38,000)	$4,563,000	Cash received from customers
Cost of goods sold	2,701,000	☐3 $167,304	☐2 (29,442)	2,838,862	Cash paid for merchandise
Gross profit	$1,900,000			$1,724,138	
Operating expenses	1,207,504	☐4 12,794	☐5 $(104,000)		
		☐6 5,304		1,121,602	Cash paid for operating expenses
Operating income	$ 692,496			$ 602,536	
Interest revenue	1,550	☐7 400		1,950	Cash received from interest revenue
Interest expense	6,440		☐8 (40)	6,400	Cash paid for interest expense
Income tax expense	240,000		☐9 (25,000)	215,000	Cash paid for income taxes
Net income	$ 447,606			$ 383,086	Cash generated from operating activities

☐1 The increase in Accounts Receivable reduced the amount of cash received from sales. This $38,000 increase is subtracted from sales to compute cash received from customers.

☐2 The $29,442 decrease in inventory indicates that Megaproducts purchased less inventory than it sold. This decrease must be subtracted from the cost of goods sold to compute purchases for the year ($2,701,000 – $29,442 = $2,671,558).

☐3 The $167,304 decrease in Accounts Payable is added to the cost of merchandise purchased to compute cash paid for merchandise ($2,671,558 + $167,304 = $2,838,862).

☐4 The increase in Supplies and Prepayments indicates that Megaproducts not only replenished these items for the amounts used during the period, but also increased the supplies on hand and prepayments. Thus, the cash paid for these items is greater than the expense recognized for the period. The increase of $12,794 must be added in the calculation of cash paid for operating expenses.

☐5 Depreciation is an operating expense but requires no cash outflow. The $104,000 in Depreciation Expense is subtracted from operating expenses to compute cash paid for operating expenses.

☐6 By making payments to the government and reducing Accrued and Withheld Payroll Taxes, the amount of cash paid to the government this period was increased. This reduction of $5,304 is added to operating expenses to compute cash paid for operating expenses.

☐7 The $400 reduction in Accrued Interest Receivable is added to Interest Revenue to determine the amount of interest received.

☐8 The $40 increase in Accrued Interest Payable is deducted from Interest Expense to compute the amount of interest paid.

☐9 The increase in Income Tax Payable is deducted from Income Tax Expense to compute the amount of income taxes paid.

(continued)

2 and 3.   Megaproducts, Inc.'s statement of cash flows is shown below.

Megaproducts, Inc.
Statement of Cash Flows
For Year Ended December 31, 20-3

Cash flows from operating activities:										
Cash received from customers	$4,563	0	0	0	00					
Interest received	1	9	5	0	00					
Cash provided by operating activities						$4,564	9	5	0	00
Cash paid for merchandise	$(2,838	8	6	2	00)					
Cash paid for operating expenses	(1,121	6	0	2	00)					
Interest paid	(6	4	0	0	00)					
Income tax paid	(215	0	0	0	00)					
Total cash disbursed for operating activities						(4,181	8	6	4	00)
Net cash provided by operating activities						$ 383	0	8	6	00
Cash flows from investing activities:										
Purchased store equipment	$ (92	0	0	0	00)					
Purchased delivery equipment	(130	0	0	0	00)					
Purchased office equipment	(40	1	0	0	00)					
Net cash used by investing activities						(262	1	0	0	00)
Cash flows from financing activities:										
Paid cash dividends	$ (128	0	0	0	00)					
Issued common stock	30	0	0	0	00					
Retired note payable	(17	2	0	0	00)					
Net cash used by financing activities						(115	2	0	0	00)
Net increase (decrease) in cash and cash equivalents						$ 5	7	8	6	00
Cash and cash equivalents, January 1, 20-3						232	0	0	0	00
Cash and cash equivalents, December 31, 20-3						$ 237	7	8	6	00
Schedule of noncash investing and financing activities:										
Acquired office equipment by issuing a note payable.						$ 12	0	0	0	00

Note that Office Equipment and Notes Payable are affected by two transactions as follows:

Cash				Office Equipment				Notes Payable		
			BB	339,900					118,000	BB
17,200	(5a)		(5b)	12,000		(5a)	17,200	12,000	(5b)
40,100				40,100						
			EB	392,000					112,800	EB

KEY TERMS

cash equivalents, (940)   Short-term, highly liquid investments that are considered the same as cash when preparing the statement of cash flows.

direct method, (929)   A method of preparing the statement of cash flows in which the revenues and expenses reported on the income statement are adjusted to reflect the amount of cash received or paid for each item.

financing activities, (928)   Transactions dealing with the exchange of cash between the company and its owners (stockholders) and creditors.

indirect method, (929)   A method of reporting cash from operating activities in which net income is adjusted for transactions that affect both net income and cash from operating activities, but in different ways.

investing activities, (927)   Transactions involving the purchase and sale of long-term assets, investments in debt and equity securities, and lending money and collecting the principal on the related loans.

noncash investing and financing activities, (945)   Investing and financing activities that involve no cash flows, but represent a significant change in the company's financial position.

operating activities, (927)   Transactions and events associated with selling a product or providing a service. They are related to the revenues and expenses reported on the income statement.

statement of cash flows, (927)   Statement of the cash flows associated with the operating, investing, and financing activities of the company.

REVIEW QUESTIONS

(LO1)   1. What is the primary purpose of the statement of cash flows?

(LO1)   2. Name the four principal financial statements comprising a full set of financial statements.

(LO2)   3. What are the three categories of cash flows shown on a statement of cash flows?

(LO2)   4. Name the types of cash flows associated with financing activities.

(LO2)   5. Name the types of cash flows associated with investing activities.

(LO2)   6. Name the types of cash flows associated with operating activities under the direct method.

(LO2)   7. If a company pays cash dividends, where on the statement of cash flows should the payment be reported?

(LO3)   8. What information is needed to prepare a statement of cash flows?

(LO4)   9. What is meant by the direct method of reporting cash flows from operating activities?

(LO4)   10. What is meant by the indirect method of reporting cash flows from operating activities?

(LO5)   11. What are cash equivalents?

(LO5)   12. Provide an illustration of a noncash investing and financing activity.

(LO5)   13. Jones Company reported depreciation expense of $45,000 on its income statement. How much cash was paid for this expense?

(LO5)   14. Explain the step-by-step procedures to be followed when preparing a statement of cash flows.

(continued)

(LO5)   15. Where is cash received for interest reported on the statement of cash flows?

(LO5)   16. Explain the procedure for verifying the accuracy of the statement of cash flows.

Self-Study Test Questions

True/False

1. The purpose of the statement of cash flows is to provide information about total revenue and expenses.   _____

2. Investing activities are those transactions dealing with the exchange of cash between the company and its stockholders and creditors.   _____

3. A decrease in Accounts Receivable is added to Sales to determine the amount of cash received from customers.   _____

4. A decrease in Inventory is added to Cost of Goods Sold to determine the amount of cash paid for purchases.   _____

5. An increase in Accrued Interest Payable is deducted from Interest Expense to compute the cash paid for interest expense.   _____

Multiple Choice

1. The acquisition of a building by signing a mortgage note payable is included on the statement of cash flows as a(n)   _____

    (a) operating activity.   (c) financing activity.
    (b) investing activity.   (d) schedule of noncash investing and financing activities.

2. The receipt of dividends on an investment is included on the statement of cash flows as a(n)   _____

    (a) operating activity.   (c) financing activity.
    (b) investing activity.   (d) schedule of noncash investing and financing activities.

3. The purchase of new equipment is included on the statement of cash flows as a(n)   _____

    (a) operating activity.   (c) financing activity.
    (b) investing activity.   (d) schedule of noncash investing and financing activities.

4. The payment of interest on a note payable is classified on the statement of cash flows as a(n)   _____

    (a) operating activity.   (c) financing activity.
    (b) investing activity.   (d) schedule of noncash investing and financing activities.

5. The payment of a cash dividend to stockholders is classified on the statement of cash flows as a(n)   _____

    (a) operating activity.   (c) financing activity.
    (b) investing activity.   (d) schedule of noncash investing and financing activities.

Answers to the Self-Study Test Questions are at the end of the text.

MANAGING YOUR WRITING

Direct Method

A friend of yours was looking at a schedule for the calculation of cash generated from operating activities prepared under the direct method and asked why depreciation expense is deducted from operating expenses. He is curious why depreciation is not considered an expense. Write a brief memo that explains why Depreciation Expense is deducted from operating expenses when preparing this schedule.

Indirect Method

A friend of yours was reading a statement of cash flows prepared under the indirect method and saw that Depreciation Expense was added when computing cash from operating activities. She is curious why depreciation is considered a source of cash. Write a brief memo that explains why Depreciation Expense is added to net income on the statement of cash flows and why it certainly is not a source of cash.

ETHICS CASE

Lyle McGee had been the chief accountant at L & B Corporation for well over 20 years. He routinely omitted noncash investing and financing activities from the statement of cash flows, even when they were significant events. When a junior accountant who had just been hired questioned this practice, Lyle told her that it doesn't make any difference how significant an item is "if it doesn't involve cash. Besides, we're a small company and our stockholders are only interested in the bottom line."

1. Is it possible that Lyle thinks he is treating the significant noncash investing and financing activities properly?

2. If you were the junior accountant, what would you do?

3. Suppose that Lyle wants the junior accountant to give him a refresher course on the statement of cash flows. Write a brief memo to Lyle explaining the purpose of the statement of cash flows. Include a description of both the direct and indirect methods. Also, explain the importance of including significant noncash investing and financing activities.

4. In groups of two or three, discuss which method of preparing the statement of cash flows is easier for you to understand, the direct or the indirect, and why.

WEB WORK

Cash flow is tricky to predict in the best of situations, and for a seasonal business, like beekeeping and Christmas tree farms, it is even more difficult. What problems can you foresee in managing the cash flow of a seasonal business?

Visit the Interactive Study Center on our web site at **http://heintz. swlearning.com** for special hotlinks to assist you in this assignment.

SERIES A EXERCISES

EXERCISE 25-1A   (LO2)   **IDENTIFICATION OF OPERATING, INVESTING, AND FINANCING ACTIVITIES** The following activities took place during the current year. Indicate whether each activity is a cash inflow (+) or cash outflow (−), and whether it is an operating activity (O), investing activity (I), or financing activity (F).

a. Proceeds from collection of principal amount of loans made to borrowers

b. Cash receipts from the sale of goods

c. Payments for interest on loans

d. Payments of dividends to stockholders

e. Payments to acquire investments in debt securities

f. Dividends received on investments made in the stock of other corporations

g. Repayment of the principal on loans

h. Interest received on loans made to outside entities

i. Salaries paid to employees

j. Payments to acquire property, plant, and equipment and other productive assets

k. Payments to purchase treasury stock

l. Proceeds from the sale of equity securities

EXERCISE 25-2A   (LO4)
Cash received from customers: $815,000

CASH RECEIVED FROM CUSTOMERS Potts Company's sales for 20-2 were $800,000. The accounts receivable balance as of December 31, 20-1, was $90,000. This same account had a balance of $75,000 as of December 31, 20-2. Compute the amount of cash received from customers in 20-2.

EXERCISE 25-3A   (LO4)
Cash paid for merchandise: $420,000

CASH PAID FOR MERCHANDISE Douglas Company's cost of goods sold for 20-2 was $400,000. Compute the amount of cash paid for merchandise in 20-2. The December 31, 20-2 and 20-1, balances of Merchandise Inventory and Accounts Payable were as follows:

	20-2	20-1
Merchandise Inventory	$60,000	$80,000
Accounts Payable	30,000	70,000

EXERCISE 25-4A   (LO5)
Cash provided by financing activities: $60,000

CASH FLOWS FROM INVESTING AND FINANCING ACTIVITIES Rogerson Company's comparative balance sheet as of December 31, 20-2 and 20-1, showed the following with regard to investing and financing activities.

	20-2	20-1
Building	$130,000	$ 0
Equipment	90,000	0
Notes payable	30,000	20,000
Common stock at par	300,000	250,000
Paid-in capital in excess of par	80,000	50,000
Retained earnings	260,000	200,000

Net income for 20-2 was $90,000 and cash dividends of $30,000 were declared and paid. Determine the amount of cash received and paid for financing and investing activities and the cash flows as they would appear on Rogerson's statement of cash flows for the year ended December 31, 20-2.

EXERCISE 25-5A   (LO5)
Increase in cash and cash equivalents: $17,000

CHANGE IN CASH AND CASH EQUIVALENTS Himes Company's balance sheets as of December 31, 20-4 and 20-3, showed the following with regard to cash and cash equivalents.

	20-4	20-3
Cash	$70,000	$50,000
Government notes	2,000	5,000

Compute the amount of change in cash and cash equivalents and indicate whether it represented an increase or a decrease.

EXERCISE 25-6A   (LO5)
Cash paid for operating expenses: $332,200

CASH PAID FOR OPERATING EXPENSES The following information was obtained from Knox Company's income statement for 20-4, balance sheets as of December 31, 20-4 and 20-3, and auxiliary records.

Operating expenses for 20-4 $350,400
Depreciation expense for 20-4   22,000

	20-4	20-3
Supplies and prepayments	$9,600	$6,700
Accrued and withheld payroll taxes	2,900	3,800

Compute the amount of cash paid for operating expenses in 20-4.

EXERCISE 25-7A   (LO5)
Cash paid for interest: $1,500

CASH PAID FOR INTEREST Ball Company's income statement for 20-4 reported interest expense of $1,540. The comparative balance sheet as of December 31, 20-4 and 20-3, reported the following.

	20-4	20-3
Accrued interest payable	$260	$220

Compute the amount of cash paid for interest in 20-4.

EXERCISE 25-8A   (LO5)
Cash paid for interest: $470

CASH RECEIVED FOR INTEREST Eary Company's income statement for 20-4 reported interest revenue of $430. The comparative balance sheet as of December 31, 20-4 and 20-3, reported the following:

	20-4	20-3
Accrued interest receivable	$150	$190

Compute the amount of cash received for interest in 20-4.

EXERCISE 25-9A   (LO5)

NONCASH INVESTING AND FINANCING ACTIVITIES Norton's sign shop issued a $10,000, three-year note payable to acquire a new framing machine. Show how this transaction is reported on a statement of cash flows.

SERIES A PROBLEMS

PROBLEM 25-10A   (LO4)
Cash generated from operating expenses: $160,000

SCHEDULE FOR CALCULATION OF CASH GENERATED FROM OPERATING ACTIVITIES Mueller Company's condensed income statement for the year ended December 31, 20-2, was as follows:

Net sales	$900,000
Cost of goods sold	500,000
Gross profit	$400,000
Operating expenses	185,000
Income before taxes	$215,000
Income tax expense	75,000
Net income	$140,000

(continued)

Additional information obtained from Mueller's comparative balance sheets as of December 31, 20-2 and 20-1, was as follows:

	20-2	20-1
Cash and cash equivalents	$ 50,000	$ 10,000
Accounts receivable	80,000	90,000
Merchandise inventory	120,000	150,000
Accounts payable	60,000	80,000

REQUIRED

Prepare a schedule for the calculation of cash generated from operating activities for the year ended December 31, 20-2.

PROBLEM 25-11A **(LO5)**

Net increase in cash and cash equivalents: $40,000

STATEMENT OF CASH FLOWS Refer to Problem 25-10A. The following additional information was obtained from Mueller's financial statements and auxiliary records for the year ended December 31, 20-2.

Acquired a new warehouse	$120,000
Bought new warehouse equipment	80,000
Issued a note to the bank	40,000
Issued additional common stock:	
Par value	50,000
Paid-in capital in excess of par	20,000
Declared and paid cash dividends	30,000

REQUIRED

Prepare a statement of cash flows for Mueller for the year ended December 31, 20-2.

PROBLEM 25-12A **(LO5)**

Cash generated from operating activities: $206,070

SCHEDULE FOR CALCULATION OF CASH GENERATED FROM OPERATING ACTIVITIES Horn Company's condensed income statement for the year ended December 31, 20-4, was as follows:

Net sales		$1,220,000
Cost of goods sold		740,000
Gross profit		$ 480,000
Operating expenses		142,000
Operating income		$ 338,000
Other revenues and expenses:		
Interest revenue	$ 420	
Interest expense	(1,200)	(780)
Income before taxes		$ 337,220
Income tax expense		118,000
Net income		$ 219,220

Additional information obtained from Horn's comparative balance sheet and auxiliary records as of December 31, 20-4 and 20-3, was as follows:

	20-4	20-3
Accounts receivable	$135,000	$122,600
Merchandise inventory	145,300	158,900
Accounts payable	45,000	87,100
Income tax payable	2,000	1,000
Supplies and prepayments	11,300	6,800
Accrued and withheld payroll taxes	2,750	3,700
Accrued interest receivable	90	210
Accrued interest payable	240	160

Depreciation expense for 20-4, included in operating expenses on the income statement, was $32,000.

REQUIRED

Prepare a schedule for the calculation of cash generated from operating activities for the year ended December 31, 20-4.

PROBLEM 25-13A   (LO5)
Operating activities: $152,840;
Investing activities: $(234,000);
Financing activities: $80,000

EXPANDED STATEMENT OF CASH FLOWS Financial statements for McDowell Company as well as additional information relevant to cash flows during the period are below and on the next page.

McDowell Company
Income Statement
For Year Ended December 31, 20-4

Net sales		$1,890 0 0 0 00
Cost of goods sold		940 0 0 0 00
Gross profit		$ 950 0 0 0 00
Operating expenses		572 3 0 0 00
Operating income		$ 377 7 0 0 00
Other revenues and expenses:		
Interest revenue	$ 3 9 0 0 00	
Interest expense	(8 9 0 00)	3 0 1 0 00
Income before taxes		$ 380 7 1 0 00
Income tax expense		133 0 0 0 00
Net income		$ 247 7 1 0 00

McDowell Company
Statement of Retained Earnings
For Year Ended December 31, 20-4

Retained earnings, January 1, 20-4		$360 0 0 0 00
Net income	$ 247 7 1 0 00	
Less dividends	60 0 0 0 00	
Net increase in retained earnings		187 7 1 0 00
Retained earnings, December 31, 20-4		$547 7 1 0 00

Additional information:

1. Depreciation expense for the year was $112,000.

2. No equipment was sold during the period. The following purchases were made for cash.

Store equipment	$ 64,000
Delivery equipment	140,000
Office equipment	30,000
	$234,000

3. Declared and paid cash dividends of $60,000.

4. Issued 10,000 shares of $10 par common stock for $14 per share.

5. Acquired additional store equipment by issuing a note payable for $16,000.

(continued)

McDowell Company
Comparative Balance Sheet
December 31, 20-4 and 20-3

	20-4					20-3					INCREASE (DECREASE)				
Assets															
Current assets:															
Cash	$ 50	3	6	5	00	$ 40	3	2	5	00	$ 10	0	4	0	00
Government notes	6	8	0	0	00	18	0	0	0	00	(11	2	0	0	00)
Accrued interest receivable		7	2	0	00		6	1	0	00		1	1	0	00
Accounts receivable (net)	310	7	0	0	00	325	8	0	0	00	(15	1	0	0	00)
Merchandise inventory	685	4	0	0	00	540	2	0	0	00	145	2	0	0	00
Supplies and prepayments	27	0	0	0	00	39	0	0	0	00	(12	0	0	0	00)
Total current assets	$1,080	9	8	5	00	$ 963	9	3	5	00	117	0	5	0	00
Property, plant, and equipment:															
Store equipment	$ 540	0	0	0	00	$ 460	0	0	0	00	80	0	0	0	00
Less accumulated depreciation—store equipment	(210	0	0	0	00)	(150	0	0	0	00)	60	0	0	0	00
Delivery equipment	530	0	0	0	00	390	0	0	0	00	140	0	0	0	00
Less accumulated depreciation—delivery equipment	(140	0	0	0	00)	(100	0	0	0	00)	40	0	0	0	00
Office equipment	430	0	0	0	00	400	0	0	0	00	30	0	0	0	00
Less accumulated depreciation—office equipment	(88	0	0	0	00)	(76	0	0	0	00)	12	0	0	0	00
Total property, plant, and equipment	$1,062	0	0	0	00	$ 924	0	0	0	00	138	0	0	0	00
Total assets	$2,142	9	8	5	00	$1,887	9	3	5	00	255	0	5	0	00
Liabilities															
Current liabilities:															
Notes payable	$ 118	0	0	0	00	$ 102	0	0	0	00	16	0	0	0	00
Accounts payable	110	0	0	0	00	195	0	0	0	00	(85	0	0	0	00)
Income tax payable	20	0	0	0	00	25	0	0	0	00	(5	0	0	0	00)
Accrued and withheld payroll taxes	16	4	0	0	00	14	9	0	0	00	1	5	0	0	00
Accrued interest payable		8	7	5	00	1	0	3	5	00		(1	6	0	00)
Total liabilities	$ 265	2	7	5	00	$ 337	9	3	5	00	(72	6	6	0	00)
Stockholders' Equity															
Common stock ($10 par, 300,000 shares authorized;															
Issued: 90,000 in 20-4 and 80,000 in 20-3)	$ 900	0	0	0	00	$ 800	0	0	0	00	100	0	0	0	00
Paid-in capital in excess of par—common stock	430	0	0	0	00	390	0	0	0	00	40	0	0	0	00
Retained earnings	547	7	1	0	00	360	0	0	0	00	187	7	1	0	00
Total stockholders' equity	$1,877	7	1	0	00	$1,550	0	0	0	00	327	7	1	0	00
Total liabilities and stockholders' equity	$2,142	9	8	5	00	$1,887	9	3	5	00	255	0	5	0	00

REQUIRED

1. Prepare a schedule for the calculation of cash generated from operating activities for the year ended December 31, 20-4.

2. Prepare a statement of cash flows for the year ended December 31, 20-4.

3. Verify the accuracy of the statement of cash flows.

SERIES B EXERCISES

EXERCISE 25-1B **(LO2)** **IDENTIFICATION OF OPERATING, INVESTING, AND FINANCING ACTIVITIES** The following activities took place in Tomberlin Company during the most recent year. Indicate whether each activity is a cash inflow (+) or cash outflow (–), and whether it is an operating activity (O), investing activity (I), or financing activity (F).

   a. Payments to acquire productive assets

   b. Proceeds from the issuance of stock

   c. Interest received on loans made to outside entities

   d. Proceeds from the sale of productive assets

   e. Dividends received on investments made in the stock of other corporations

   f. Payments to other suppliers and for other expenses

   g. Payments of dividends to stockholders

   h. Payments to acquire investments in debt securities

   i. Payments for interest on loans

   j. Cash receipts from the sale of services

   k. Repayment of the principal on loans

   l. Payments for the acquisition of inventory

EXERCISE 25-2B **(LO4)**
Cash received from customers: $735,000

CASH RECEIVED FROM CUSTOMERS Boyd Company's sales for 20-2 were $760,000. The accounts receivable balance as of December 31, 20-1, was $60,000. This same account had a balance of $85,000 as of December 31, 20-2. Compute the amount of cash received from customers in 20-2.

EXERCISE 25-3B **(LO4)**
Cash paid for merchandise: $550,000

CASH PAID FOR MERCHANDISE Guild Company's cost of goods sold for 20-2 was $500,000. Compute the amount of cash paid for merchandise in 20-2. The December 31, 20-2 and 20-1, balances of Merchandise Inventory and Accounts Payable were as follows:

	20-2	20-1
Merchandise Inventory	$70,000	$50,000
Accounts Payable	60,000	90,000

EXERCISE 25-4B **(LO5)**
Net cash used by investing activities: $(230,000)

CASH FLOWS FROM INVESTING AND FINANCING ACTIVITIES Hansen Company's comparative balance sheets as of December 31, 20-2 and 20-1, showed the following with regard to investing and financing activities.

	20-2	20-1
Building	$160,000	$ 0
Equipment	70,000	0
Notes payable	20,000	30,000
Common stock at par	260,000	200,000
Paid-in capital in excess of par	60,000	40,000
Retained earnings	220,000	160,000

Net income for 20-2 was $80,000 and cash dividends of $20,000 were declared and paid. Determine the amount of cash received and paid for financing and investing activities and the cash flows as they would appear on Hansen's statement of cash flows for the year ended December 31, 20-2.

EXERCISE 25-5B   (LO5)
Increase in cash and cash
equivalents: $26,000

CHANGE IN CASH AND CASH EQUIVALENTS Pike Company's balance sheets as of December 31, 20-4 and 20-3, showed the following with regard to cash and cash equivalents.

	20-4	20-3
Cash	$90,000	$60,000
Government notes	4,000	8,000

Compute the amount of change in cash and cash equivalents and indicate whether it represented an increase or a decrease.

EXERCISE 25-6B   (LO5)
Cash paid for operating
expenses: $258,200

CASH PAID FOR OPERATING EXPENSES The following information was obtained from Busby Company's income statement for 20-4, balance sheets as of December 31, 20-4 and 20-3, and auxiliary records.

Operating expenses for 20-4	$290,500
Depreciation expense for 20-4	30,000

	20-4	20-3
Supplies and prepayments	$7,100	$8,300
Accrued and withheld payroll taxes	3,800	2,700

Compute the amount of cash paid for operating expenses in 20-4.

EXERCISE 25-7B   (LO5)
Cash paid for interest: $2,260

CASH PAID FOR INTEREST Mulligan Company's income statement for 20-4 reported interest expense of $2,190. The comparative balance sheet as of December 31, 20-4 and 20-3, reported the following.

	20-4	20-3
Accrued interest payable	$340	$410

Compute the amount of cash paid for interest in 20-4.

EXERCISE 25-8B   (LO5)
Cash received
for interest: $590

CASH RECEIVED FOR INTEREST Dowling Company's income statement for 20-4 reported interest revenue of $670. The comparative balance sheet as of December 31, 20-4 and 20-3, reported the following.

	20-4	20-3
Accrued interest receivable	$320	$240

Compute the amount of cash received for interest in 20-4.

EXERCISE 25-9B   (LO5)

NONCASH INVESTING AND FINANCING ACTIVITIES Murry's consulting services issued a two-year, $5,000 note payable to acquire new office furniture. Show how this transaction is reported on the statement of cash flows.

SERIES B PROBLEMS

PROBLEM 25-10B   (LO4)
Cash generated from operating
expenses: $155,000

SCHEDULE FOR CALCULATION OF CASH GENERATED FROM OPERATING ACTIVITIES Kennington Company's condensed income statement for the year ended December 31, 20-2 was as follows:

Net sales	$800,000
Cost of goods sold	475,000
Gross profit	$325,000
Operating expenses	148,000
Income before taxes	$177,000
Income tax expense	62,000
Net income	$115,000

Additional information obtained from Kennington's comparative balance sheet as of December 31, 20-2 and 20-1, was as follows:

	20-2	20-1
Cash and cash equivalents	$75,000	$20,000
Accounts receivable	50,000	75,000
Merchandise inventory	70,000	110,000
Accounts payable	25,000	50,000

REQUIRED

Prepare a schedule for the calculation of cash generated from operating activities for the year ended December 31, 20-2.

PROBLEM 25-11B   **(LO5)**

Net increase in cash and cash equivalents: $55,000

STATEMENT OF CASH FLOWS Refer to Problem 25-10B. The following additional information was obtained from Kennington's financial statements and auxiliary records for the year ended December 31, 20-2.

Acquired a new warehouse	$90,000
Bought new warehouse equipment	60,000
Issued a note to the bank	30,000
Issued additional common stock:	
Par value	30,000
Paid-in capital in excess of par	10,000
Declared and paid cash dividends	20,000

REQUIRED

Prepare a statement of cash flows for Kennington for the year ended December 31, 20-2.

PROBLEM 25-12B   **(LO5)**

Cash generated from operating activities: $179,395

SCHEDULE FOR CALCULATION OF CASH GENERATED FROM OPERATING ACTIVITIES Powell Company's condensed income statement for the year ended December 31, 20-4, was as follows:

Net sales		$1,160,000
Cost of goods sold		690,000
Gross profit		$ 470,000
Operating expenses		224,100
Operating income		$ 245,900
Other revenues and expenses:		
Interest revenue	$ 560	
Interest expense	(1,100)	(540)
Income before taxes		$ 245,360
Income tax expense		86,000
Net income		$ 159,360

Additional information obtained from Powell's comparative balance sheet and auxiliary records as of December 31, 20-4 and 20-3, was as follows:

	20-4	20-3
Accounts receivable	$122,700	$118,200
Merchandise inventory	116,800	139,300
Accounts payable	31,500	47,400
Income tax payable	10,000	15,000
Supplies and prepayments	10,900	5,200
Accrued and withheld payroll taxes	1,960	2,490
Accrued interest receivable	130	175
Accrued interest payable	230	110

(continued)

Depreciation expense for 20-4, included in operating expenses on the income statement, was $29,000.

REQUIRED

Prepare a schedule for the calculation of cash generated from operating activities for the year ended December 31, 20-4.

PROBLEM 25-13B   (LO5)

Operating activities: $99,300;
Investing activities: $(272,000);
Financing activities: $180,000

EXPANDED STATEMENT OF CASH FLOWS Financial statements for McGinnis Company as well as additional information relevant to cash flows during the period are as follows:

McGinnis Company Income Statement For Year Ended December 31, 20-4			
Net sales			$1,750 0 0 0 00
Cost of goods sold			890 0 0 0 00
Gross profit			$ 860 0 0 0 00
Operating expenses			590 6 0 0 00
Operating income			$ 269 4 0 0 00
Other revenues and expenses:			
Interest revenue	$2 7 0 0 00		
Interest expense	(7 5 0 00)	1 9 5 0 00	
Income before taxes			$ 271 3 5 0 00
Income tax expense			95 0 0 0 00
Net income			$ 176 3 5 0 00

McGinnis Company Statement of Retained Earnings For Year Ended December 31, 20-4		
Retained earnings, January 1, 20-4		$320 0 0 0 00
Net income	$176 3 5 0 00	
Less dividends	40 0 0 0 00	
Net increase in retained earnings		136 3 5 0 00
Retained earnings, December 31, 20-4		$456 3 5 0 00

Additional information:

1. Depreciation expense for the year was $70,000.

2. No equipment was sold during the period. The following purchases were made for cash.

Store equipment	$140,000
Delivery equipment	100,000
Office equipment	32,000
	$272,000

3. Declared and paid cash dividends of $40,000.

4. Issued 10,000 shares of $10 par common stock for $22 per share.

5. Acquired additional office equipment by issuing a note payable for $8,000.

McGinnis Company
Comparative Balance Sheet
December 31, 20-4 and 20-3

	20-4	20-3	INCREASE (DECREASE)
Assets			
Current assets:			
Cash	$ 68 4 2 0 00	$ 50 5 2 0 00	$ 17 9 0 0 00
Government notes	5 4 0 0 00	16 0 0 0 00	(10 6 0 0 00)
Accrued interest receivable	8 3 0 00	5 8 0 00	2 5 0 00
Accounts receivable (net)	300 6 0 0 00	309 2 0 0 00	(8 6 0 0 00)
Merchandise inventory	580 3 0 0 00	495 8 0 0 00	84 5 0 0 00
Supplies and prepayments	65 0 0 0 00	32 0 0 0 00	33 0 0 0 00
Total current assets	$1,020 5 5 0 00	$ 904 1 0 0 00	116 4 5 0 00
Property, plant, and equipment:			
Store equipment	$ 560 0 0 0 00	$ 420 0 0 0 00	140 0 0 0 00
Less accumulated depreciation—store equipment	(120 0 0 0 00)	(90 0 0 0 00)	30 0 0 0 00
Delivery equipment	430 0 0 0 00	330 0 0 0 00	100 0 0 0 00
Less accumulated depreciation—delivery equipment	(150 0 0 0 00)	(120 0 0 0 00)	30 0 0 0 00
Office equipment	420 0 0 0 00	380 0 0 0 00	40 0 0 0 00
Less accumulated depreciation—office equipment	(110 5 0 0 00)	(100 5 0 0 00)	10 0 0 0 00
Total property, plant, and equipment	$1,029 5 0 0 00	$ 819 5 0 0 00	210 0 0 0 00
Total assets	$2,050 0 5 0 00	$1,723 6 0 0 00	326 4 5 0 00
Liabilities			
Current liabilities:			
Notes payable	$ 117 0 0 0 00	$ 109 0 0 0 00	8 0 0 0 00
Accounts payable	135 0 0 0 00	185 0 0 0 00	(50 0 0 0 00)
Income tax payable	25 0 0 0 00	15 0 0 0 00	10 0 0 0 00
Accrued and withheld payroll taxes	15 8 0 0 00	13 4 0 0 00	2 4 0 0 00
Accrued interest payable	9 0 0 00	1 2 0 0 00	(3 0 0 00)
Total liabilities	$ 293 7 0 0 00	$ 323 6 0 0 00	(29 9 0 0 00)
Stockholders' Equity			
Common stock ($10 par, 400,000 shares authorized;			
Issued: 80,000 in 20-4 and 70,000 in 20-3)	$ 800 0 0 0 00	$ 700 0 0 0 00	100 0 0 0 00
Paid-in capital in excess of par—common stock	500 0 0 0 00	380 0 0 0 00	120 0 0 0 00
Retained earnings	456 3 5 0 00	320 0 0 0 00	136 3 5 0 00
Total stockholders' equity	$1,756 3 5 0 00	$1,400 0 0 0 00	356 3 5 0 00
Total liabilities and stockholders' equity	$2,050 0 5 0 00	$1,723 6 0 0 00	326 4 5 0 00

REQUIRED

1. Prepare a schedule for the calculation of cash generated from operating activities for the year ended December 31, 20-4.

2. Prepare a statement of cash flows for the year ended December 31, 20-4.

3. Verify the accuracy of the statement of cash flows.

MASTERY PROBLEM

Operating activities: $40,032;
Investing activities: $(157,260);
Financing activities: $108,700

Financial statements for Peachfield Corporation as well as additional information relevant to cash flows during the period follow.

Peachfield Corporation Income Statement For Year Ended December 31, 20-2		
Net sales		$985 0 0 0 00
Cost of goods sold		515 0 0 0 00
Gross profit		$470 0 0 0 00
Operating expenses		299 4 0 0 00
Operating income		$170 6 0 0 00
Other revenues and expenses:		
Interest revenue	$2 1 0 0 00	
Interest expense	(4 3 6 00)	1 6 6 4 00
Income before taxes		$172 2 6 4 00
Income tax expense		60 5 0 0 00
Net income		$111 7 6 4 00

Peachfield Corporation Statement of Retained Earnings For Year Ended December 31, 20 -2		
Retained earnings, January 1, 20-2		$141 9 7 3 00
Net income	$111 7 6 4 00	
Less dividends	20 0 0 0 00	
Net increase in retained earnings		91 7 6 4 00
Retained earnings, December 31, 20-2		$233 7 3 7 00

Additional information:

1. Depreciation expense for the year was $62,400.

2. No equipment was sold during the year. The following purchases were made for cash.

Store equipment	$ 55,200
Delivery equipment	78,000
Office equipment	24,060
	$157,260

3. Declared and paid cash dividends of $20,000.

4. Issued 11,200 shares of $10 par common stock for $118,000.

5. Issued a note payable for $10,700.

6. Additional store equipment was acquired by issuing a long-term note payable for $20,000.

Peachfield Corporation
Comparative Balance Sheet
December 31, 20-2 and 20-1

	20-2		20-1		INCREASE (DECREASE)
Assets					
Current assets:					
Cash	$ 27 072 00		$ 27 200 00		$ (1 28 00)
Government notes	3 600 00		12 000 00		(8 400 00)
Accrued interest receivable	3 20 00		2 50 00		7 0 00
Accounts receivable (net)	152 945 00		140 905 00		12 040 00
Merchandise inventory	355 490 00		295 400 00		60 090 00
Supplies and prepayments	14 500 00		21 500 00		(7 000 00)
Total current assets		$ 553 927 00		$497 255 00	56 672 00
Property, plant, and equipment:					
Store equipment	$308 000 00		$232 800 00		75 200 00
Less accumulated depreciation—store equipment	108 000 00	200 000 00	84 000 00	148 800 00	24 000 00
Delivery equipment	$270 000 00		$192 000 00		78 000 00
Less accumulated depreciation—delivery equipment	75 000 00	195 000 00	48 000 00	144 000 00	27 000 00
Office equipment	$228 000 00		$203 940 00		24 060 00
Less accumulated depreciation—office equipment	48 000 00	180 000 00	36 600 00	167 340 00	11 400 00
Total property, plant, and equipment		$ 575 000 00		$460 140 00	114 860 00
Total assets		$1,128 927 00		$957 395 00	171 532 00
Liabilities					
Current liabilities:					
Notes payable	$ 65 480 00		$ 54 780 00		10 700 00
Accounts payable	53 500 00		125 473 00		(71 973 00)
Income tax payable	7 000 00		5 000 00		2 000 00
Accrued and withheld payroll taxes	8 760 00		7 644 00		1 116 00
Accrued interest payable	4 50 00		5 25 00		(7 5 00)
Total current liabilities		$ 135 190 00		$193 422 00	(58 232 00)
Long-term liabilities:					
Notes payable		20 000 00		0	20 000 00
Total liabilities		$ 155 190 00		$193 422 00	(38 232 00)
Stockholders' Equity					
Common stock ($10 par, 100,000 shares authorized;					
Issued: 50,000 in 20-2 and 38,800 in 20-1)	$500 000 00		$388 000 00		112 000 00
Paid-in capital in excess of par—common stock	240 000 00		234 000 00		6 000 00
Retained earnings	233 737 00		141 973 00		91 764 00
Total stockholders' equity		973 737 00		763 973 00	209 764 00
Total liabilities and stockholders' equity		$1,128 927 00		$957 395 00	171 532 00

REQUIRED

1. Prepare a schedule for the calculation of cash generated from operating activities.

2. Prepare a statement of cash flows explaining the change in cash and cash equivalents.

3. Reconcile cash and cash equivalents at the bottom of the statement of cash flows.

CHALLENGE PROBLEM

The Long-Term Liability section of Guyton Enterprises follows. The bonds outstanding on January 1, 20-1, have an annual coupon rate of 4 percent and had been issued several years ago at a price to yield 5 percent per year. The discount is amortized using the effective interest method. On December 31, 20-1, $900,000, 5% bonds were issued at a price to yield 6 percent.

Long-Term Liabilities	December 31, 20-1	January 1, 20-1
Bonds Payable	$1,900,000	$1,000,000
Discount on Bonds	(202,461)	(104,651)
Total Long-Term Liabilities	$1,697,539	$895,349

REQUIRED

Compute the cash received from issuing the bonds on December 31, 20-1. (*Hint*: If you have not covered the effective interest method, assume that bond interest expense for 20-1 was $44,767.)

O B J E C T I V E S

Careful study of this appendix should enable you to:

LO1 Describe the indirect method of reporting cash flows from operating activities.

LO2 Prepare a statement of cash flows using the indirect method and a work sheet for reconciling balance sheet accounts.

Chapter 25 Appendix
Statement of Cash Flows:
The Indirect Method

This appendix illustrates the indirect method of reporting cash flows from operating activities. We also will show how to use a work sheet to prepare the statement of cash flows.

CASH FLOWS FROM OPERATING ACTIVITIES: INDIRECT METHOD

LO1 Describe the indirect method of reporting cash flows from operating activities.

The two methods of reporting *cash flows from operating activities* are the direct and indirect methods. The *direct method* was illustrated earlier in Chapter 25. Under the indirect method, net income is considered the primary source of cash from operating activities. Thus, net income is reported on the statement of cash flows under operating activities.

As you know, net income is measured using the accrual basis of accounting. Since increases and decreases in net income do not always increase or decrease cash, the following adjustments must be made to net income to report the cash flows from operating activities.

1. Changes in current assets related to operating activities.

2. Changes in current liabilities related to operating activities.

3. Noncash expenses.

4. Gains and losses on transactions not related to operating activities.

LEARNING KEY: Under the indirect method, net income is considered the primary source of cash from operating activities. However, it must be adjusted for transactions that affect both net income and cash from operating activities, but in different ways.

Although the direct and indirect methods result in different formats for reporting cash flows from operating activities, the two methods report the same amount. In addition, investing and financing activities are reported in the same manner under the direct and indirect methods. Thus, only the operating activities section is different.

Changes in Current Assets Related to Operating Activities

Accounts receivable, prepaid expenses, and inventories are examples of current assets related to operating activities. Increases in these assets reduce the cash generated from operating activities; decreases have the opposite effect. For example, if accounts receivable increased, the cash received from customers was less than the sales revenue reported on the income statement. This increase is deducted from net income when computing cash generated from operating activities. Similar adjustments are made for prepaid expenses. If prepaid expenses increased, the cash paid during the period exceeded the expense reported on the income statement. Again, the increase is deducted from net income. On the other hand, decreases in these assets increase cash from operating activities. Thus, decreases in current assets must be added to net income when computing cash flows from operating activities.

LEARNING KEY: If sales were $100,000 and Accounts Receivable increased by $5,000, think of the following entry.

Cash	95,000	
Accounts Receivable	5,000	
Sales		100,000

Since the revenue used to calculate net income is $5,000 greater than the cash received, $5,000 must be subtracted from net income to compute cash from operating activities.

LEARNING KEY: Adjustment for changes in current assets.
Net income
$(-\uparrow)$ or $(+\downarrow)$ in current assets related to operating activities
= Cash from operating activities

Changes in Current Liabilities Related to Operating Activities

Accounts Payable, Income Taxes Payable, and Salaries Payable are examples of current liabilities related to operating activities. Not all current liabilities are related to operating activities. The declaration of dividends, for example, is not an operating activity and has no effect on net income. Therefore, changes in Dividends Payable do not require an adjustment to net income.

Changes in current liabilities require an adjustment opposite that of current assets. By increasing the amount owed to others, the company increases cash from operating activities in the current period. Thus, increases in current liabilities are added to net income to compute cash from operating activities. Decreases in current liabilities are deducted from net income to compute cash from operating activities.

For example, an increase in Salaries Payable indicates that the expense recognized on the income statement for salaries is greater than the cash paid to employees. Thus, the increase in Salaries Payable must be added to net income to compute cash from operating activities. On the other hand, decreases in this account and other current liabilities reduce cash from operating activities and must be deducted from net income.

LEARNING KEY: If Salaries Expense was $5,000 and Salaries Payable increased by $500, think of the following entry.

Salaries Expense	5,000	
Salaries Payable		500
Cash		4,500

Since the expense is $500 greater than the cash paid, $500 must be added to net income to compute cash from operating activities.

LEARNING KEY: Adjustment for changes in current liabilities
Net income
(+ ↑) or (– ↓) in current liabilities related to operating activities
= Cash from operating activities

Noncash Expenses

Depreciation expense and the amortization of intangible assets are examples of **noncash expenses**. These expenses reduce net income, but do not require an outflow of cash during the period. Thus, they are added to net income to compute cash flows from operating activities.

LEARNING KEY: Adjustment for noncash expenses
Net income
+ Noncash expenses
= Cash from operating activities

Gains and Losses on the Sale of Long-Term Assets

Gains and losses on the sale of long-term assets are reported on the income statement and included in the calculation of net income. However, since these cash flows are not considered operating activities, the gains and losses should not be included in the calculation of cash from operating activities. Thus, net income must be adjusted on the statement of cash flows to compute cash from operating activities.

To illustrate, consider the financial statements for Stevie B's, shown in Figure 25A-1. Let's assume no income tax and that all revenues and expenses for the period were for cash. This means that the $300 of operating income reported on the income statement also reflects the net inflow of cash from operating activities. During the accounting period, Stevie B's sold land that cost $200 for $250. Since this is not an operating activity, the gain of $50 is reported separately on the income statement.

Stevie B's
Income Statement
For Year Ended December 31, 20-2

Sales (all cash)			$ 1 0 0 0	00
Wages expense (all cash)			7 0 0	00
Operating income			$ 3 0 0	00
Gain on sale of land			5 0	00
Net income			$ 3 5 0	00

Stevie B's
Balance Sheet
December 31, 20-2

Assets	12/31/-2	1/1/-2
Cash	$ 9 5 0 00	$ 4 0 0 00
Land	8 0 0 00	1 0 0 0 00
Total Assets	$1 7 5 0 00	$1 4 0 0 00
Stockholders' Equity		
Common stock	$1 2 0 0 00	$1 2 0 0 00
Retained earnings	5 5 0 00	2 0 0 00
Total Stockholders' Equity	$1 7 5 0 00	$1 4 0 0 00

Additional information:
Sold land that cost $200 for $250.

Stevie B's
Statement of Cash Flows
For Year Ended December 31, 20-2

Cash flows from operating activities:		
Net income	$ 3 5 0 00	
Less gain on sale of land	(5 0 00)	
Net cash provided by operating activities		$ 3 0 0 00
Investing activities:		
Sold land		2 5 0 00
Net increase in cash		$ 5 5 0 00

FIGURE 25A-1   Treatment of a Gain on the Statement of Cash Flows

On the statement of cash flows, this gain must be deducted from net income to compute cash from operating activities, $300. The entire amount of cash received from the sale of the land, $250, is reported as a cash inflow under investing activities.

LEARNING KEY: Adjustment for gains and losses
Net income
– Gains on the sale of plant and equipment
+ Losses on the sale of plant and equipment
= Cash from operating activities

STATEMENT OF CASH FLOWS: MULTIPLEX CORPORATION

LO2 **Prepare a statement of cash flows using the indirect method and a work sheet for reconciling balance sheet accounts.**

Follow these steps to prepare the statement of cash flows under the indirect method.

STEP 1   Compute the change in cash and cash equivalents reported on the comparative balance sheet.

STEP 2   Prepare a work sheet to identify all transactions affecting cash.

STEP 3   Compute cash flows from operating activities under the indirect method by adjusting net income for the following:

(a) Changes in current assets related to operating activities.

(b) Changes in current liabilities related to operating activities.

(c) Noncash expenses.

(d) Gains and losses on transactions not related to operating activities.

STEP 4   Identify cash flows from investing activities by analyzing any additional information and by reconciling balance sheet accounts related to long-term assets, investments in debt and equity securities, and loans made to parties outside the company.

STEP 5   Identify cash flows from financing activities by analyzing any additional information and by reconciling balance sheet accounts related to transactions with stockholders and creditors.

STEP 6   Sum cash flows from operating, investing, and financing activities to determine the net increase or decrease in cash. Compare this amount with the change in cash and cash equivalents computed in Step 1.

STEP 7   Prepare a schedule of noncash investing and financing activities.

STEP 8   Prepare supplemental disclosures of cash flow information, including cash paid during the year for interest and income taxes.

Figure 25-7 on pages 938–939 shows an income statement, statement of retained earnings, comparative balance sheet, and additional information about the cash flows for the period for Multiplex Corporation. This information is needed to prepare a statement of cash flows.

The purpose of the statement of cash flows is to report all transactions that resulted in cash receipts or payments. To provide a systematic method of searching for these transactions, all noncash (or cash equivalent) balance sheet accounts should be reconciled. The work sheet shown in Figure 25A-2 is helpful in accomplishing this task. Figure 25A-3 shows the statement of cash flows for Multiplex.

The beginning and ending balances reported on the comparative balance sheet in Figure 25-7 are inserted in columns 1 and 4 on the work sheet. The transactions and account changes for the year are entered in the reconciling columns. Once all transactions have been identified, the debits and/or credits in the reconciling columns should explain the difference between the beginning and ending balances. For example, Store Equipment had a beginning balance of $38,800. During the year, additional equipment of $9,200 was purchased (reconciling item number **11**). The beginning balance plus the equipment purchased during the year equals the ending balance of $48,000. The purchase of equipment is reported on the statement of cash flows under investing activities.

Multiplex Corporation
Work Sheet for Preparation of Statement of Cash Flows
December 31, 20-2 and 20-1

	DECEMBER 31, 20-1		20-2 RECONCILING DEBIT		20-2 RECONCILING CREDIT		DECEMBER 31, 20-2	
Assets								
Current assets:								
Cash		$ 20,000	16	$ 2,980				$ 22,980
Government notes		3,200			16	$ 1,400		1,800
Accrued interest receivable		300			2	200		100
Accounts receivable		51,510	3	8,705				60,215
Merchandise inventory		67,500			4	2,930		64,570
Supplies and prepayments		2,750	5	1,250				4,000
Total current assets		$145,260						$153,665
Property, plant, and equipment:								
Store equipment	$38,800		11	9,200			$48,000	
Less accumulated depreciation	(14,000)	24,800			10	4,000	(18,000)	30,000
Delivery equipment	$32,000		17	13,000			$45,000	
Less accumulated depreciation	(8,000)	24,000			10	4,500	(12,500)	32,500
Office equipment	$34,000		12	4,000			$38,000	
Less accumulated depreciation	(6,100)	27,900			10	1,900	(8,000)	30,000
Total property, plant, and equipment		$ 76,700						$ 92,500
Total assets		$221,960						$246,165
Liabilities								
Current liabilities:								
Notes payable	$11,800		15	1,800			$10,000	
Accounts payable	45,900		6	12,400			33,500	
Income tax payable	2,000				7	1,000	3,000	
Accrued and withheld payroll taxes	1,520		8	570			950	
Accrued interest payable	80				9	20	100	
Total current liabilities		$ 61,300						$ 47,550
Long-term liabilities:								
Note payable (3-year)					17	13,000		13,000
Total liabilities		$ 61,300						$ 60,550
Stockholders' Equity								
Common stock	$98,000				13	2,000	$100,000	
Paid-in capital in excess of par	39,000				13	1,000	40,000	
Retained earnings	23,660		14	22,800	1*	44,755	45,615	
Total stockholders' equity		$160,660						$185,615
Total liabilities and stockholders' equity		$221,960						$246,165

* Note: Numbers show the relationship between the reconciling entries on the work sheet and the items on the statement of cash flows.

FIGURE 25A-2   Work Sheet for the Preparation of the Statement of Cash Flows for Multiplex

Multiplex Corporation
Statement of Cash Flows
For Year Ended December 31, 20-2

Cash flows from operating activities:			
Net income	$44,755	1*	
Adjustments for changes in current assets and liabilities			
related to operating activities:			
Decrease in interest receivable	200	2	
Increase in accounts receivable	(8,705)	3	
Decrease in merchandise inventory	2,930	4	
Increase in supplies and prepayments	(1,250)	5	
Decrease in accounts payable	(12,400)	6	
Increase in income tax payable	1,000	7	
Decrease in accrued and withheld payroll taxes	(570)	8	
Increase in accrued interest payable	20	9	
Noncash expenses and other adjustments:			
Depreciation expense	10,400	10	
Net cash provided by operating activities			$36,380
Cash flows from investing activities:			
Purchase of store equipment	$ (9,200)	11	
Purchase of office equipment	(4,000)	12	
Total cash used by investing activities			(13,200)
Cash flows from financing activities:			
Issued common stock	$ 3,000	13	
Paid cash dividends	(22,800)	14	
Retired notes payable	(1,800)	15	
Total cash used by financing activities			(21,600)
Net increase in cash and cash equivalents		16	$ 1,580
Cash and cash equivalents, January 1, 20-2			23,200
Cash and cash equivalents, December 31, 20-2			$24,780
Schedule of noncash investing and financing activities:			
Purchased delivery equipment by issuing a 3-year note.		17	$13,000
Supplemental Disclosures of Cash Flow Information:			
Cash paid during the year for:			
Interest		18	$ 630
Income taxes		18	$23,000

* Note: Numbers show the relationship between the reconciling entries on the work sheet and the items on the statement of cash flows.

FIGURE 25A-3 Statement of Cash Flows for Multiplex

Each reconciling item has a debit and a credit. If a debit is made on the work sheet, an offsetting credit must be made either on the work sheet or on the statement of cash flows. Financial statements do not have debits and credits. However, cash receipts or additions to net income can be viewed as debits and cash payments or subtractions from net income as credits. Using this technique may help prevent errors when preparing the statement.

Cash Flows from Operating Activities

Under the indirect method, net income is considered the primary source of cash. Therefore, it is listed first on the statement of cash flows, followed by any necessary additions or subtractions. Since net income increases retained earnings, $44,755 is credited to the retained earnings account on the work sheet (see item number **1**). The credit on the work sheet (Figure 25A-2) is offset by a debit (cash inflow or addition to net income) on the statement of cash flows (Figure 25A-3).

Changes in Current Assets Related to Operating Activities. Items **2** and **4** represent decreases in current assets related to operating activities. These decreases represent increases in cash from operating activities. They are reported as credits on the work sheet to reconcile each account and as additions to net income (debits) on the statement of cash flows.

Items **3** and **5** represent increases in current assets related to operating activities. These increases represent reductions in cash from operating activities. They are reported as debits on the work sheet to reconcile each account and as subtractions from net income (credits) on the statement of cash flows.

Changes in Current Liabilities Related to Operating Activities. Items **6** and **8** represent decreases in current liabilities related to operating activities. These decreases reduce cash from operating activities. They are reported as debits on the work sheet to reconcile each account and as subtractions from net income (credits) on the statement of cash flows.

Items **7** and **9**, the increases in Income Tax Payable and Accrued Interest Payable, indicate that Multiplex did not pay all of the tax and interest expense incurred during the period. Thus, these increases are reported as additions to net income (debits) in the calculation of cash flows from operating activities and as credits on the work sheet to reconcile the accounts.

Noncash Expenses. Item **10** is for Depreciation Expense and represents noncash expenses. These expenses reduce net income on the income statement, but require no cash payments. Thus, they are added back to net income (debit) on the statement of cash flows. They are also entered as credits to Accumulated Depreciation—Store Equipment, Delivery Equipment, and Office Equipment to reconcile these accounts on the work sheet.

Cash Flows from Investing Activities

Items **11** and **12** are for purchases of equipment. These amounts are entered as debits on the work sheet to reconcile the equipment accounts and as outflows of cash (credits) under investing activities on the statement of cash flows.

Cash Flows from Financing Activities

Item **13** is for the issuance of common stock. Common Stock and Paid-In Capital are credited on the work sheet ($2,000 and $1,000, respectively) and the $3,000 is shown as an inflow of cash (debit) from financing activities on the statement of cash flows.

LEARNING KEY: Investing and financing activities are reported in the same manner under the direct and indirect methods.

The statement of retained earnings in Figure 25-7 shows cash dividends of $22,800 were declared and paid during the year. Since dividends reduce retained earnings, $22,800 is debited to Retained Earnings on the work sheet. The outflow of cash (credit) is reported under financing activities as item **14**.

Item **15** represents the decrease of $1,800 in current notes payable. Therefore, Notes Payable is debited on the work sheet and the $1,800 cash outflow (credit) is reported under financing activities on the statement of cash flows.

After accounting for the changes in all noncash balance sheet accounts, the net increase or decrease in cash as reported on the statement of cash flows is computed. This is done by taking the sum of net cash flows provided by operating activities ($36,380), cash used by investing activities ($13,200), and cash used by financing activities ($21,600). To verify the accuracy of the statement, sum the increase of $2,980 in Cash (item **16**) and decrease of $1,400 in Government Notes (item **16**) reported on the work sheet. This amount is the same as the $1,580 increase in cash and cash equivalents (item **16**) reported on the statement of cash flows.

Noncash Investing and Financing Activities

Item **17** represents the issuance of the $13,000, three-year note for the acquisition of delivery equipment. Since there is no cash involved in this transaction, no entries are made in the investing or financing sections of the statement of cash flows. Delivery Equipment is debited and Notes Payable is credited on the work sheet to reconcile these accounts. Note that all debits and credits are made on the work sheet. In addition, this event is noted in the schedule of noncash investing and financing activities on the statement of cash flows.

Supplemental Disclosures of Cash Flow Information

Companies using the indirect method are required to provide separate disclosure of the following information.

1. The change in accounts receivable.

2. The change in inventory.

3. The change in accounts payable.

4. Cash paid for interest (net of the amount capitalized).

5. Cash paid for income taxes.

These items are required so users of the financial statements can compute cash received from customers and cash paid to suppliers. The first three items have already been reported in the statement of cash flows. As we know from our calculations under the direct method, Multiplex paid $630 in interest and $23,000 for income taxes. The latter two items must be reported as supplemental disclosures on the face of the statement of cash flows, or in the notes to the financial statements. The items marked **18** represent the disclosure of this information on the face of the statement.

Learning Objectives	Key Points to Remember
1 Describe the indirect method of reporting cash flows from operating activities.	Under the indirect method, net income is considered the primary source of cash from operating activities. Thus, it is reported on the statement of cash flows under operating activities. Since increases and decreases in net income do not always increase or decrease cash, the following adjustments must be made to net income to report the cash flows from operating activities. 1. Changes in current assets related to operating activities. 2. Changes in current liabilities related to operating activities. 3. Noncash expenses. 4. Gains and losses on transactions not related to operating activities.
2 Prepare a statement of cash flows using the indirect method and a work sheet for reconciling balance sheet accounts.	Follow these steps to prepare the statement of cash flows under the indirect method. **STEP 1** Compute the change in cash and cash equivalents reported on the comparative balance sheet. **STEP 2** Prepare a work sheet to identify all transactions affecting cash. **STEP 3** Compute cash flows from operating activities under the indirect method by adjusting net income for the following: (a) Changes in current assets related to operating activities. (b) Changes in current liabilities related to operating activities. (c) Noncash expenses. (d) Gains and losses on transactions not related to operating activities. **STEP 4** Identify cash flows from investing activities by analyzing any additional information and by reconciling balance sheet accounts related to long-term assets, investments in debt and equity securities, and loans made to parties outside the company. **STEP 5** Identify cash flows from financing activities by analyzing any additional information and by reconciling balance sheet accounts related to transactions with stockholders and creditors. **STEP 6** Sum cash flows from operating, investing, and financing activities to determine the net increase or decrease in cash. Compare this amount with the change in the cash and cash equivalents computed in Step 1. **STEP 7** Prepare a schedule of noncash investing and financing activities. **STEP 8** Prepare supplemental disclosures of cash flow information, including cash paid during the year for interest and income taxes.

KEY TERMS

noncash expenses, (971)   Expenses that reduce net income, but do not require an outflow of cash during the period.

REVIEW QUESTIONS

(LO1) 1. Describe the indirect method of reporting cash flows from operating activities.

(LO1) 2. List the four major types of adjustments that must be made to net income when computing cash flows from operating activities.

(LO2) 3. What is the purpose of the work sheet for the preparation of the statement of cash flows?

(LO2) 4. List the seven major steps followed when preparing a statement of cash flows under the indirect method.

SERIES A EXERCISE

EXERCISE 25Apx-1A (LO1/2)
Operating activites: $400;
Net increase in cash: $900

GAINS AND LOSSES ON THE SALE OF LONG-TERM ASSETS The income statement for Hubbard's Professional Edge Tennis Camp follows. Assume that all revenues and expenses were for cash and that land was sold for $500. There were no other investing or financing activities during the year. The cash balances at the beginning and end of the year were $100 and $1,000, respectively. Prepare a statement of cash flows under the indirect method.

Hubbard's Professional Edge Tennis Camp Income Statement For Year Ended December 31, 20-2						
Sales (all cash)				$2	0	0	0	00
Wages expense (all cash)				1	6	0	0	00
Operating income				$	4	0	0	00
Gain on sale of land					1	0	0	00
Net income				$	5	0	0	00

SERIES A PROBLEMS

PROBLEM 25Apx-2A (LO2)
Operating activities: $160,000

CASH FLOWS FROM OPERATING ACTIVITIES Using the information provided in Problem 25-10A, compute net cash provided (used) by operating activities under the indirect method.

PROBLEM 25Apx-3A (LO2)
Operating activities: $206,070

CASH FLOWS FROM OPERATING ACTIVITIES Using the information provided in Problem 25-12A, compute net cash provided (used) by operating activities under the indirect method.

PROBLEM 25Apx-4A (LO2)
Operating activities: $152,840

CASH FLOWS FROM OPERATING ACTIVITIES Using the information provided in Problem 25-13A, prepare the following:

1. Net cash provided (used) by operating activities under the indirect method.

2. Supplemental disclosures of cash flow information required under the indirect method.

SERIES B EXERCISE

EXERCISE 25Apx-1B(LO1/2)
Operating activities: $2,000;
Net increase in cash: $2,600

GAINS AND LOSSES ON THE SALE OF LONG-TERM ASSETS The income statement for Leadbetter's Golf Camp follows. Assume that all revenues and expenses were for cash and that land was sold for $600. There were no other investing or financing activities during the year. The cash balances at the beginning and end of the year were $1,000 and $3,600, respectively. Prepare a statement of cash flows under the indirect method.

Leadbetter's Golf Camp Income Statement For Year Ended December 31, 20-2			
Sales (all cash)			$5 0 0 0 00
Wages expense (all cash)			3 0 0 0 00
Operating income			$2 0 0 0 00
Loss on sale of land			(2 0 0 00)
Net income			$1 8 0 0 00

SERIES B PROBLEMS

PROBLEM 25Apx-2B (LO2)
Operating activities: $155,000

CASH FLOWS FROM OPERATING ACTIVITIES Using the information provided in Problem 25-10B, compute net cash provided (used) by operating activities under the indirect method.

PROBLEM 25Apx-3B (LO2)
Operating activities: $179,395

CASH FLOWS FROM OPERATING ACTIVITIES Using the information provided in Problem 25-12B, compute net cash provided (used) by operating activities under the indirect method.

PROBLEM 25Apx-4B (LO2)
Operating activities: $99,300

CASH FLOWS FROM OPERATING ACTIVITIES Using the information provided in Problem 25-13B, prepare the following:

1. Net cash provided (used) by operating activities under the indirect method.

2. Supplemental disclosures of cash flow information required under the indirect method.

©GETTY IMAGES/PHOTODISC

Analysis of Financial Statements

Fiona Nairn has been working at Finny Co. for the past several years. Recently, Finny initiated an employee stock purchase program. All employees are given the opportunity to purchase a certain number of shares of stock at a price slightly below market. Given the company's excellent performance, and her support for employee ownership of the company, Fiona is considering buying stock. She has a copy of the most recent financial statements. The company reported net income of $300,000. This looks good to Fiona. What other factors should she consider when evaluating the financial health of the company?

Careful study of this chapter should enable you to:

LO1 Perform horizontal and vertical analyses of the income statement and balance sheet.

LO2 Compute and explain liquidity measures.

LO3 Compute and explain profitability measures.

LO4 Compute and explain leverage measures.

LO5 Explain the limitations of financial statement analysis.

This chapter demonstrates how to analyze financial statements to better understand the information obtained from them. Comparisons of financial statement variables over time and the calculation and interpretation of selected ratios will be presented.

COMPARATIVE ANALYSIS

LO1 Perform horizontal and vertical analyses of the income statement and balance sheet.

A business' financial statements supply information to management, present and potential owners and creditors, employees and their unions, government agencies, and sometimes the general public. Normally, interest centers on three aspects of the business.

1. **Liquidity**—the ability to pay current debts when they come due. Liquidity measures focus primarily on current liabilities.

2. **Profitability**—the ability to earn a satisfactory return on the investments in the business.

3. **Leverage**—the proportion of debt to stockholders' equity.

The financial statements can be much more informative if they are analyzed on a comparative basis. The following are four possible types of comparison:

1. with one or more previous periods

2. with data for the industry as a whole

3. with similar information for other businesses in the industry

4. with preset plans or goals (normally in the form of budgets)

We will use the financial statements of French Connection Importers (FCI) for the years ended December 31, 20-4 and 20-3, to illustrate the first type of analysis.

Horizontal Analysis

Comparing the amounts for the same item in the financial statements of two or more periods is called **horizontal analysis**. Figure 26-1 illustrates a horizontal analysis of the condensed comparative income statement of FCI for the two years under review, showing the amount and the percentage change in each item. In calculating the percentage change, the amount for the earlier year serves as the base. For example, to compute the percentage change in net sales, the increase or decrease in net sales for 20-4 is divided by net sales for 20-3.

LEARNING KEY: Horizontal analysis tracks the dollar and percentage change in financial statement amounts for the same company across accounting periods. Use the amount for the earlier year as the base when calculating the percentage change from year to year.

French Connection Importers
Comparative Income Statement
For Years Ended December 31, 20-4 and 20-3

	20-4	20-3	INCREASE (DECREASE)	PERCENT
Net sales	$835,950	$708,800	$127,150	17.9
Cost of goods sold	602,380	520,260	82,120	15.8
Gross profit	$233,570	$188,540	$ 45,030	23.9
Operating expenses	113,000	100,250	12,750	12.7
Operating income	$120,570	$ 88,290	$ 32,280	36.6
Other revenue	525	100	425	425.0
Other expenses	12,650	14,420	(1,770)	−12.3
Income before income taxes	$108,445	$ 73,970	$ 34,475	46.6
Income tax expense	36,600	19,210	17,390	90.5
Net income	$ 71,845	$ 54,760	$ 17,085	31.2

FIGURE 26-1   Comparative Income Statement—Horizontal Analysis

Net sales in 20-4 were 17.9% greater than in 20-3. Cost of goods sold increased only 15.8%. Because of the smaller percentage increase in cost of goods sold, the percentage increase in the gross profit (23.9%) was greater than that for sales. Operating expenses increased only 12.7%, which was much less than the growth in sales. These events caused an increase of 36.6% in operating income. Although the percentage increase in other revenue was enormous (425%), the amount of this revenue was small. Because other expenses decreased 12.3%, income before income tax was 46.6% greater. The relative amount of income tax increased significantly (90.5%), and net income increased by 31.2%.

This horizontal analysis of the income statement indicates a major improvement in FCI's operating results. A 17.9% increase in net sales accompanied by apparently successful cost control resulted in a 31.2% increase in net income.

The condensed comparative balance sheet as of December 31, 20-4 and 20-3, presented in Figure 26-2, illustrates horizontal analysis. The most noteworthy changes in the balance sheet follow (numbers correspond to those in the margin of Figure 26-2).

1 *Increase (18.4%) in current assets and decrease (38.3%) in current liabilities.*

The increase in current assets is due primarily to the increases in cash (30.4%) and receivables (23.5%). These increases probably were needed to support the higher level of operating activity indicated by the 17.9% increase in net sales noted previously.

The decrease in current liabilities is caused by the reduction in notes payable and accounts payable. FCI apparently used some of the funds from its successful operations during 20-4 to pay off a large portion of its current liabilities.

French Connection Importers
Comparative Balance Sheet
December 31, 20-4 and 20-3

	20-4	20-3	INCREASE (DECREASE)	PERCENT	
Assets					
Current assets:					
Cash	$ 25,695	$ 19,700	$ 5,995	30.4	
Government notes	5,000	1,000	4,000	400.0	
Accounts receivable (net)	61,750	50,000	11,750	23.5	
Merchandise inventory	55,500	54,250	1,250	2.3	
Supplies and prepayments	2,400	2,000	400	20.0	
Total current assets	$150,345	$126,950	$23,395	18.4	1
Property, plant, and equipment:					
Land	$ 40,000	$ 40,000	$ 0	0.0	
Building (net)	140,000	125,000	15,000	12.0	2
Store equipment (net)	100,000	90,000	10,000	11.1	2
Delivery and office equipment (net)	22,000	28,500	(6,500)	−22.8	
Organization costs	1,200	2,400	(1,200)	−50.0	
Total property, plant, and equipment	$303,200	$285,900	$17,300	6.1	
Total assets	$453,545	$412,850	$40,695	9.9	
Liabilities					
Current liabilities:					
Accrued and withheld payroll taxes	$ 2,500	$ 2,750	$ (250)	−9.1	
Notes payable	10,000	37,500	(27,500)	−73.3	
Accounts payable	40,000	59,000	(19,000)	−32.2	
Accrued interest payable	600	1,700	(1,100)	−64.7	
Income tax payable	13,600	13,400	200	1.5	
Dividends payable	7,500	6,000	1,500	25.0	
Total current liabilities	$ 74,200	$120,350	$(46,150)	−38.3	1
Long-term liabilities:					
Bonds payable	100,000	100,000	0	0.0	
Total liabilities	$174,200	$220,350	$(46,150)	−20.9	
Stockholders' Equity					
Common stock	$ 75,000	$ 60,000	$15,000	25.0	3
Paid-in capital in excess of par	20,000	12,500	7,500	60.0	3
Retained earnings	184,345	120,000	64,345	53.6	4
Total stockholders' equity	$279,345	$192,500	$86,845	45.1	
Total liabilities and stockholders' equity	$453,545	$412,850	$40,695	9.9	

FIGURE 26-2 Comparative Balance Sheet—Horizontal Analysis

2 *Increase in building (12.0%) and store equipment (11.1%).*

Increases in building and store equipment are important because they are signs of growth. It is common for long-term asset accounts to *decrease* simply because of depreciation and amortization. The decreases in delivery and office equipment and organization costs are examples of this tendency. *Increases* in the building and store equipment accounts mean that new long-term assets were acquired during 20-4.

3 *Increases in common stock (25.0%) and paid-in capital in excess of par (60.0%).*

Increases in common stock and paid-in capital in excess of par also indicate growth. Common stock with a par value of $15,000 was issued for $22,500 ($15,000 par + $7,500 paid-in capital in excess of par). Financing growth by issuing additional common stock is often desirable, particularly for a company carrying as much debt as FCI.

4 *Substantial increase (53.6%) in retained earnings.*

The large increase in retained earnings results from a highly profitable year (net income of $71,845) combined with a moderate dividend policy ($7,500). Retention of large amounts of earnings is another desirable way to finance corporate growth.

Vertical Analysis

Reporting the amount of each item in a statement as a percentage of some designated total is called **vertical analysis**. Vertical analysis is most helpful when statements relating to two or more periods are compared.

LEARNING KEY: Vertical analysis reports each financial statement amount as a percentage of a designated total.

Figure 26-3 shows FCI's condensed comparative income statement for the years ended December 31, 20-4 and 20-3. Each item is shown as a percentage of net sales for the year. This statement reveals that several factors contributed to FCI's increased profitability from 20-3 to 20-4. Both cost of goods sold and operating expenses decreased as a percentage of net sales. This allowed operating income to increase from 12.5% to 14.4% of net sales. Other expenses decreased from 2.0% to 1.5% of net sales, so that income before income taxes jumped from 10.4% to 13.0% of net sales. These positive factors were offset somewhat by the increase in taxes from 2.7% to 4.4% of net sales. However, net income as a percentage of net sales still increased from 7.7% to 8.6%.

LEARNING KEY: In vertical analysis of the income statement, each item is shown as a percentage of net sales for the year.

Vertical analysis of income statements automatically provides several important ratios. They include the following (numbers correspond to those in the margin of Figure 26-3).

1 **Cost of goods sold ratio**—ratio of cost of goods sold to net sales

2 **Gross profit ratio**—ratio of gross profit to net sales

3 **Operating expense ratio**—ratio of operating expenses to net sales

4 **Operating income ratio**—ratio of operating income to net sales

5 **Net income ratio**—(also called **profit margin**) ratio of net income to net sales

French Connection Importers
Comparative Income Statement
For Years Ended December 31, 20-4 and 20-3

	20-4	PERCENT*	20-3	PERCENT*	
Net sales	$835,950	100.0	$708,800	100.0	
Cost of goods sold	602,380	72.1	520,260	73.4	**1**
Gross profit	$233,570	27.9	$188,540	26.6	**2**
Operating expenses	113,000	13.5	100,250	14.1	**3**
Operating income	$120,570	14.4	$ 88,290	12.5	**4**
Other revenue	525	0.1	100	0.0	
Other expenses	12,650	1.5	14,420	2.0	
Income before income taxes	$108,445	13.0	$ 73,970	10.4	
Income tax expense	36,600	4.4	19,210	2.7	
Net income	$ 71,845	8.6	$ 54,760	7.7	**5**

* Percentages may not add due to rounding.

FIGURE 26-3   Comparative Income Statement—Vertical Analysis

Vertical analysis is also performed on balance sheets. For assets, each item is shown as a percentage of the total assets. For liabilities and stockholders' equity, each item is shown as a percentage of the total equities (liabilities and stockholders' equity). Figure 26-4 shows a comparative balance sheet for FCI using vertical analysis. This statement reveals that current assets were a somewhat larger share (33.1% versus 30.7%) of total assets on December 31, 20-4, than on the same date in 20-3. In addition, current liabilities decreased dramatically (16.4% versus 29.2%) as a percentage of total equities. These two factors reflect a major improvement in FCI's current position. Retained earnings increased significantly in amount and as a percentage of total equities. Finally, the combination of favorable changes in current liabilities, common stock, paid-in capital in excess of par, and retained earnings resulted in total liabilities being a much smaller share (38.4% versus 53.4%) of total equities.

LEARNING KEY: In vertical analysis of the balance sheet, assets are shown as a percentage of total assets. Liabilities and stockholders' equity are shown as a percentage of total liabilities and stockholders' equity.

French Connection Importers
Comparative Balance Sheet
December 31, 20-4 and 20-3

	20-4	PERCENT*	20-3	PERCENT*
Assets				
Current assets:				
Cash	$ 25,695	5.7	$ 19,700	4.8
Government notes	5,000	1.1	1,000	0.2
Accounts receivable (net)	61,750	13.6	50,000	12.1
Merchandise inventory	55,500	12.2	54,250	13.1
Supplies and prepayments	2,400	0.5	2,000	0.5
Total current assets	$150,345	33.1	$126,950	30.7
Property, plant, and equipment:				
Land	$ 40,000	8.8	$ 40,000	9.7
Building (net)	140,000	30.9	125,000	30.3
Store equipment (net)	100,000	22.0	90,000	21.8
Delivery and office equipment (net)	22,000	4.9	28,500	6.9
Organization costs	1,200	0.3	2,400	0.6
Total property, plant, and equipment	$303,200	66.9	$285,900	69.3
Total assets	$453,545	100.0	$412,850	100.0
Liabilities				
Current liabilities:				
Accrued and withheld payroll taxes	$ 2,500	0.6	$ 2,750	0.7
Notes payable	10,000	2.2	37,500	9.1
Accounts payable	40,000	8.8	59,000	14.3
Accrued interest payable	600	0.1	1,700	0.4
Income tax payable	13,600	3.0	13,400	3.2
Dividends payable	7,500	1.7	6,000	1.5
Total current liabilities	$ 74,200	16.4	$120,350	29.2
Long-term liabilities:				
Bonds payable	100,000	22.0	100,000	24.2
Total liabilities	$174,200	38.4	$220,350	53.4
Stockholders' Equity				
Common stock	$ 75,000	16.5	$ 60,000	14.5
Paid-in capital in excess of par	20,000	4.4	12,500	3.0
Retained earnings	184,345	40.6	120,000	29.1
Total stockholders' equity	$279,345	61.6	$192,500	46.6
Total liabilities and stockholders' equity	$453,545	100.0	$412,850	100.0

* Percentages may not add due to rounding.

FIGURE 26-4   Comparative Balance Sheet—Vertical Analysis

LIQUIDITY MEASURES

LO2 Compute and explain liquidity measures.

Liquidity measures indicate a company's ability to meet its current debts. These measures focus primarily on balance sheet amounts and on the company's ability to generate funds to liquidate current obligations.

Working Capital

LEARNING KEY Working Capital = Current Assets − Current Liabilities

Working capital is the excess of a company's current assets over current liabilities. This measures whether current assets are sufficient to pay off current liabilities. The calculation of working capital for FCI at the end of each year is shown in Figure 26-5.

Working Capital		20-4	20-3
	Current Assets	$150,345	$126,950
−	Current Liabilities	(74,200)	(120,350)
=	Working Capital	$ 76,145	$ 6,600

FIGURE 26-5 Calculation of Working Capital

FCI's working capital position improved dramatically between 20-3 and 20-4. Current assets were barely sufficient to cover current liabilities on December 31, 20-3, whereas there is a substantial margin of working capital at the end of 20-4.

Current Ratio

LEARNING KEY: Current Ratio $= \dfrac{\text{Current Assets}}{\text{Current Liabilities}}$

The **current ratio**, sometimes called **working capital ratio** because of its obvious linkage to working capital, is calculated by dividing current assets by current liabilities. The calculation of the current ratio for FCI at the end of each year is shown in Figure 26-6.

Current Ratio		20-4	20-3
$\dfrac{\text{Current Assets}}{\text{Current Liabilities}}$	=	$\dfrac{\$150,345}{\$74,200}$	$\dfrac{\$126,950}{\$120,350}$
		2.0 to 1	1.1 to 1

FIGURE 26-6 Calculation of Current Ratio

The current position of FCI improved greatly during the year ended December 31, 20-4. The general rule is that a current ratio of 2 to 1 or better is satisfactory, although this rule can be modified for certain types of businesses. FCI's current ratio was not acceptable in 20-3, but it improved to an acceptable level in 20-4.

Quick or Acid-Test Ratio

LEARNING KEY: Quick or Acid-Test Ratio $= \dfrac{\text{Quick Assets}}{\text{Current Liabilities}}$

Another frequently used measure of liquidity is the **quick** or **acid-test ratio**. This ratio is calculated by dividing "quick" assets—cash, temporary investments, and receivables—by current liabilities. The calculation of the quick ratio for FCI at the end of each year is shown in Figure 26-7.

			20-4	20-3
Quick or Acid-Test Ratio	$\dfrac{\text{Quick Assets}}{\text{Current Liabilities}}$ =		$92,445	$70,700
			$74,200	$120,350
			1.25 to 1	.59 to 1
Quick Assets	Cash		$25,695	$19,700
	Government Notes		5,000	1,000
	Accounts Receivable (net)		61,750	50,000
			$92,445	$70,700

FIGURE 26-7 Calculation of Quick Ratio

LEARNING KEY: Quick assets include cash, temporary investments, and receivables.

FCI's quick ratio improved during 20-4. As a general rule, the ratio should not be less than 1 to 1. FCI was far below that standard in 20-3, but the company's quick ratio at the end of 20-4 is acceptable.

While it is generally desirable that both the current ratio and the quick or acid-test ratio be high, it is possible for them to be too high. Cash and most receivables are not "earning assets" and the return on most temporary investments is not large. Inventories are expensive to hold. They take up costly space, tie up money, and are subject to loss of value from various causes. Management must try to maintain the ideal amount of each type of asset.

Accounts Receivable Turnover

LEARNING KEY: Accounts Receivable Turnover $= \dfrac{\text{Net Sales on Account}}{\text{Average Accounts Receivable (net)}}$

Also expressed in days: 365 ÷ Accounts Receivable Turnover

Since accounts receivable do not generally earn interest, and some receivables will never be collected, it is important to manage them carefully. The disadvantages of carrying receivables are accepted, however, because selling on account may generate greater sales and net income.

Accounts receivable turnover measures how promptly receivables are collected. It is calculated by dividing net sales on account by the average amount of net accounts receivable. It is preferable to calculate a monthly average of net receivables. However, if monthly figures are not available, averaging the beginning-of-year and end-of-year balances is acceptable if the receivables balance does not fluctuate widely. Only *accounts* receivable are considered. The calculations for FCI are shown in Figure 26-8. Note that beginning balances for 20-3 are not available on the current financial statements. These were taken from last year's financial statements.

> Net sales *on account* is used in this ratio. However, this information is not generally available on the financial statements. Net sales may be used if net sales on account is not available. Using net sales will provide a useful measure across time periods as long as the proportion of cash and credit sales remains relatively stable.

			20-4	20-3
Accounts Receivable Turnover	$\dfrac{\text{Net Sales on Account}}{\text{Average Accounts Receivable}}$	=	$\dfrac{\$668,760}{\$55,875}$	$\dfrac{\$567,040}{\$45,000}$
			11.97	12.6
Average Accounts Receivable	$\dfrac{\text{Beginning Accounts Receivable} + \text{Ending Accounts Receivable}}{2}$	=	$\dfrac{\$50,000 + \$61,750}{2}$	$\dfrac{\$40,000 + \$50,000}{2}$
			$\$55,875$	$\$45,000$
Average Collection Period	$\dfrac{365}{\text{Accounts Receivable Turnover}}$	=	$\dfrac{365}{11.97}$	$\dfrac{365}{12.6}$
			30.5 days	29 days

FIGURE 26-8   Calculation of Accounts Receivable Turnover

Another way of examining accounts receivable turnover is to divide 365 days by the turnover figure to get the average collection period. This shows the number of days it takes a business to convert receivables into cash. Fluctuations in the average collection period over time should be investigated.

For FCI, Figure 26-8 shows that the average collection period is 30.5 days and 29 days, respectively, for the years ended December 31, 20-4 and 20-3. Although the accounts receivable turnover decreased slightly, both rates are quite good. The average number of days that receivables are on the books should not be greater than 1½ times the regular length of the credit period. FCI offered 30 days' credit to more customers in 20-4, which probably explains the slight decrease in turnover.

Merchandise Inventory Turnover

LEARNING KEY: Merchandise Inventory Turnover = $\dfrac{\text{Cost of Goods Sold}}{\text{Average Merchandise Inventory}}$

Also expressed in days: 365 ÷ Merchandise Inventory Turnover

Every seller of goods would like to have maximum sales and a minimum inventory. **Merchandise inventory turnover** measures the relationship between sales and inventory. It is calculated by dividing cost of goods sold by average merchandise inventory. Again, calculating a monthly average of inventories is preferable. However, if monthly figures are not available, the average of the beginning-of-year and end-of-year inventories can be used. For FCI, the merchandise inventory turnover for each year is shown in Figure 26-9.

			20-4	20-3
Merchandise Inventory Turnover	$\dfrac{\text{Cost of Goods Sold}}{\text{Average Merchandise Inventory}}$	=	$\dfrac{\$602,380}{\$54,875}$ 10.98	$\dfrac{\$520,260}{\$52,500}$ 9.91
Average Merchandise Inventory	$\dfrac{\text{Beginning Merchandise Inventory} + \text{Ending Merchandise Inventory}}{2}$	=	$\dfrac{\$54,250 + \$55,500}{2}$ $\$54,875$	$\dfrac{\$50,750 + \$54,250}{2}$ $\$52,500$
Average Number of Days to Sell Inventory	$\dfrac{365}{\text{Merchandise Inventory Turnover}}$	=	$\dfrac{365}{10.98}$ 33.2 days	$\dfrac{365}{9.91}$ 36.8 days

FIGURE 26-9   Calculation of Merchandise Inventory Turnover

As with accounts receivable turnover, another way of examining merchandise inventory turnover is to divide 365 days by the turnover figure to get the average number of days required to sell the merchandise inventory. If all sales are made on account, this is the average number of days it takes FCI to convert merchandise inventory into accounts receivable. This number of days plus the number of days to collect accounts receivable indicates the number of days to convert inventory into cash. Figure 26-9 shows that merchandise remained in stock an average of 33 days and 37 days, respectively, for the years ended December 31, 20-4 and 20-3.

The turnover increased slightly from 20-3 to 20-4. Both years show acceptable inventory turnover rates. FCI maintained a reasonable inventory turnover while significantly increasing its sales volume.

PROFITABILITY MEASURES

LO3 Compute and explain profitability measures.

Profitability measures indicate a company's ability to earn income by operating efficiently. These measures focus primarily on the relationship between key income statement and balance sheet amounts.

Ratio of Net Sales to Assets

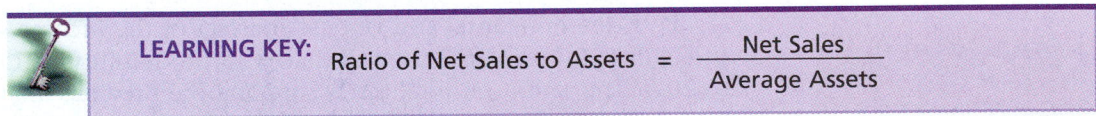

> **LEARNING KEY:**   Ratio of Net Sales to Assets $= \dfrac{\text{Net Sales}}{\text{Average Assets}}$

The **ratio of net sales to assets**, or **asset turnover ratio**, measures how efficiently a company used its assets to generate sales. The ratio is calculated by dividing net sales for the year by the average book value of the company's assets. The calculation for FCI is shown in Figure 26-10.

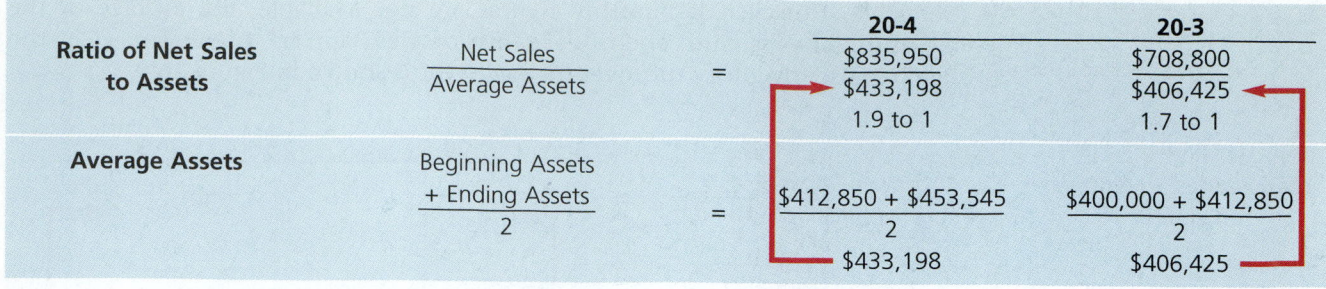

			20-4	20-3
Ratio of Net Sales to Assets	$\dfrac{\text{Net Sales}}{\text{Average Assets}}$	=	$\dfrac{\$835{,}950}{\$433{,}198}$	$\dfrac{\$708{,}800}{\$406{,}425}$
			1.9 to 1	1.7 to 1
Average Assets	$\dfrac{\text{Beginning Assets} + \text{Ending Assets}}{2}$	=	$\dfrac{\$412{,}850 + \$453{,}545}{2}$	$\dfrac{\$400{,}000 + \$412{,}850}{2}$
			$\$433{,}198$	$\$406{,}425$

FIGURE 26-10   Calculation of Net Sales to Assets

The ratio of net sales to assets increased modestly from 20-3 to 20-4. To evaluate FCI's efficiency in utilizing assets, this ratio can be compared with those of other companies in the same industry.

Return on Total Assets

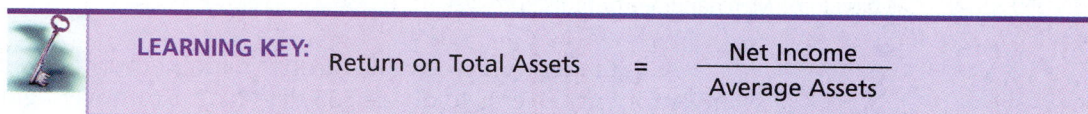

LEARNING KEY: Return on Total Assets   = $\dfrac{\text{Net Income}}{\text{Average Assets}}$

Owners or managers of most businesses strive to realize large earnings in relation to the company's resources. The return on total assets measures the success in achieving this objective. The **return on total assets** is calculated by dividing the net income for the year by the average assets for the year. For FCI, the ratio for each year is shown in Figure 26-11.

			20-4	20-3
Return on Total Assets	$\dfrac{\text{Net Income}}{\text{Average Assets}}$	=	$\dfrac{\$71{,}845}{\$433{,}198}$	$\dfrac{\$54{,}760}{\$406{,}425}$
			16.6%	13.5%
Average Assets	$\dfrac{\text{Beginning Assets} + \text{Ending Assets}}{2}$	=	$\dfrac{\$412{,}850 + \$453{,}545}{2}$	$\dfrac{\$400{,}000 + \$412{,}850}{2}$
			$\$433{,}198$	$\$406{,}425$

FIGURE 26-11   Calculation of Return on Total Assets

Many analysts prefer to add interest expense (net of taxes) to the numerator of return on total assets. This provides a measure of the efficient use of assets regardless of the method used to finance those assets.

Both the horizontal and vertical analyses of the income statement presented in Figures 26-1 and 26-3 showed that FCI's profitability had increased from 20-3 to 20-4. The return on total assets supports the previous analyses. The return on total assets increased from 13.5% in 20-3 to 16.6% in 20-4. This is a sign that management's performance improved during 20-4. To further evaluate management's performance, these results can be compared with those of similar companies or industry results.

A BROADER VIEW

Different Ways to Generate Return on Assets

Return on Assets	=	**Profit Margin**	x	**Asset Turnover**
$\dfrac{\text{Net Income}}{\text{Average Total Assets}}$	=	$\dfrac{\text{Net Income}}{\text{Net Sales}}$	×	$\dfrac{\text{Net Sales}}{\text{Average Total Assets}}$

Return on assets may be broken down into two major ratios, profit margin and asset turnover. This view of ROA helps illustrate that there are different ways to be profitable. Grocery stores, like The Kroger Company, have low profit margins and high asset turnover. For every dollar in net sales, net income is quite small, perhaps only a penny. However, these businesses are able to generate acceptable profits because they have many customers and must constantly restock the shelves. In contrast, companies like the Southern Natural Gas Company must make large investments in long-term assets to generate revenues. Thus, they must have high profit margins to compensate for low asset turnover.

As shown below, Kroger and Southern Natural Gas have a similar return on assets, but very different profit margins and asset turnovers.

©CORBIS

	Return on Assets	=	**Profit Margin**	x	**Asset Turnover**
Kroger	$\dfrac{\$1,043}{\$18,638.5}$ 5.6%	=	$\dfrac{\$1,043}{\$50,098}$ 2.08%	×	$\dfrac{\$50,098}{\$18,638.5}$ 2.69
Southern Natural Gas Company	$\dfrac{\$107}{\$1,818}$ 5.9%	=	$\dfrac{\$107}{\$402}$ 26.6%	×	$\dfrac{\$402}{\$1,818}$ 0.22

Source: 2001 Annual Reports for each company.   Dollars in millions.

Stockholders' equity includes Common Stock, Paid-in Capital in Excess of Par, and Retained Earnings. If FCI had preferred stock, the preferred dividends would be deducted from net income because these funds would not be available to common stockholders.

Return on Common Stockholders' Equity

Ultimately, the company must provide an adequate return to its common stockholders. Thus, **return on common stockholders' equity** is a very important performance measure. It is calculated by dividing net income available to common stockholders (net income less preferred dividends) for the year by the average common stockholders' equity during the year. For FCI, the calculation of the ratio for each year is shown in Figure 26-12.

LEARNING KEY: $\dfrac{\text{Return on Common}}{\text{Stockholders' Equity}} = \dfrac{\text{Net Income Available to Common Stockholders}}{\text{Average Common Stockholders' Equity}}$

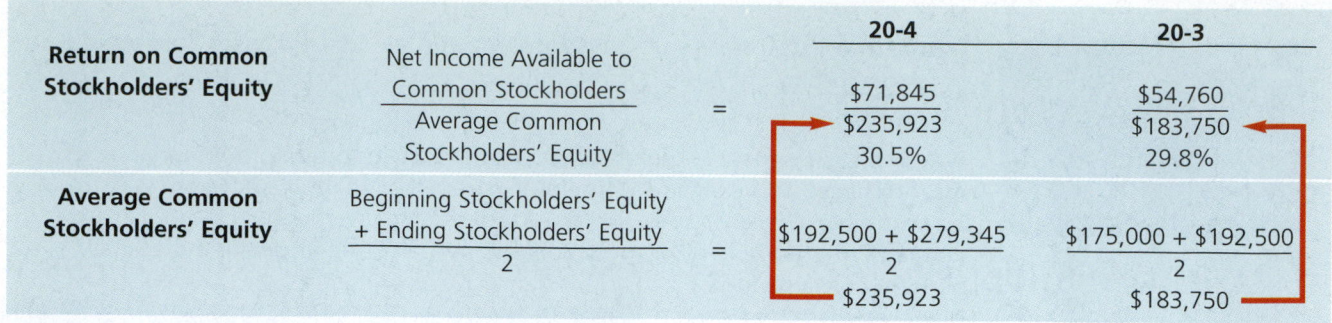

			20-4	20-3
Return on Common Stockholders' Equity	Net Income Available to Common Stockholders / Average Common Stockholders' Equity	=	$71,845 / $235,923 = 30.5%	$54,760 / $183,750 = 29.8%
Average Common Stockholders' Equity	Beginning Stockholders' Equity + Ending Stockholders' Equity / 2	=	$192,500 + $279,345 / 2 = $235,923	$175,000 + $192,500 / 2 = $183,750

FIGURE 26-12   Calculation of Return on Common Stockholders' Equity

Net income increased from $54,760 in 20-3 to $71,845 in 20-4, leading to an increase in the return on common stockholders' equity from 29.8% to 30.5%. These rates of return are quite strong.

Earnings Per Share of Common Stock

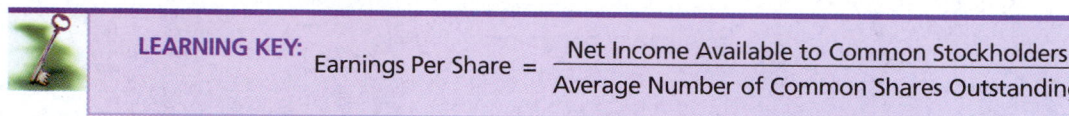

LEARNING KEY: Earnings Per Share = $\dfrac{\text{Net Income Available to Common Stockholders}}{\text{Average Number of Common Shares Outstanding}}$

One of the most important measures of profitability of the company is **earnings per share**. If only common stock is outstanding, earnings per share is calculated by dividing net income for the year by the average number of shares of common stock outstanding during the year. FCI had only common stock outstanding— 6,000 shares throughout 20-3, and 6,000 shares at the beginning and 7,500 shares at the end of 20-4. The 1,500 additional shares were issued in the middle of the year, so the average number of shares outstanding during 20-4 was 6,750 [(6,000 + 7,500) ÷ 2]. Therefore, FCI's earnings per share for each year is calculated in Figure 26-13.

			20-4	20-3
Earnings Per Share	Net Income Available to Common Stockholders / Average Number of Common Shares Outstanding	=	$71,845 / 6,750 = $10.64	$54,760 / 6,000 = $9.13
Average Number of Common Shares Outstanding	Beginning Shares Outstanding + Ending Shares Outstanding / 2	=	6,000 + 7,500 / 2 = 6,750	6,000 + 6,000 / 2 = 6,000

FIGURE 26-13   Calculation of Earnings Per Share of Common Stock

If preferred shares are outstanding, the earnings per share of common stock is calculated after deducting preferred dividend requirements. For example, if a corporation has 40,000 shares of $10 par, 8% preferred stock, $32,000 must be subtracted from net income before dividing by the average number of common shares outstanding. If net income is $310,000, and the average shares of common stock outstanding is 80,000, the earnings per share of common stock is computed as follows:

Net income	$310,000
Less preferred dividend requirements (40,000 × $10 × 8%)	32,000
Earnings available to common stockholders	$278,000
Average number of shares of common stock outstanding	80,000
Earnings per share of common stock	$ 3.48

> **LEARNING KEY:** Earnings per share means *per share of common stock.* Thus, we must focus on earnings available to common stockholders.

Book Value Per Share of Common Stock

> **LEARNING KEY:** $$\text{Book Value Per Share of Common Stock} = \frac{\text{Common Stockholders' Equity}}{\text{Number of Common Shares Outstanding at Year End}}$$

Book value per share is a measure of the ownership equity represented by each share. If a corporation has only common stock outstanding, book value per share is determined by dividing the total stockholders' equity as reported on the balance sheet by the number of shares outstanding at the end of the year. Book value per share means value per books, not the amount that stockholders would receive for their shares if sold or if the company liquidated.

FCI had 6,000 shares outstanding on December 31, 20-3, and 7,500 shares outstanding on December 31, 20-4. Therefore, the book value per share of common stock is calculated in Figure 26-14.

			20-4	20-3
Book Value Per Share	$\dfrac{\text{Common Stockholders' Equity}}{\text{Number of Common Shares Outstanding}} =$		$279,345	$192,500
			7,500	6,000
			$37.25	$32.08

FIGURE 26-14 Calculation of Book Value Per Share of Common Stock

When preferred shares are outstanding, the claims or equity of the preferred stock must be considered. These include liquidation values, dividends in arrears on cumulative preferred stock, and earnings available to participating preferred stock. For example, assume a corporation has 30,000 shares of $10 par, preferred stock with a liquidation value of $10.50 per share, and 60,000 shares of common stock outstanding. The total stockholders' equity in the company is $1,200,000. The book value per share of common stock is calculated as follows:

Total stockholders' equity	$1,200,000
Less liquidation claim of preferred stock ($10.50 × 30,000)	315,000
Balance applicable to common stock	$885,000
Number of shares outstanding	60,000
Book value per share of common stock	$14.75

LEVERAGE MEASURES

LO4 Compute and explain leverage measures.

Leverage measures indicate the extent to which a company is being financed by debt and the ability of the company to meet its debt obligations. One of these measures focuses on balance sheet relationships and the other focuses on the income statement.

Ratio of Liabilities to Stockholders' Equity

LEARNING KEY: Ratio of Liabilities to Stockholders' Equity = $\dfrac{\text{Total Liabilities}}{\text{Total Stockholders' Equity}}$

The **ratio of liabilities to stockholders' equity**, or **debt-to-equity ratio**, measures the extent of leverage, or proportion of borrowed capital, with which a business operates. This ratio is calculated by dividing total liabilities by total stockholders' equity. For FCI, the calculation of this ratio at the end of each year is shown in Figure 26-15.

			20-4	20-3
Liabilities to Stockholders' Equity	$\dfrac{\text{Total Liabilities}}{\text{Total Stockholders' Equity}}$ =		$\dfrac{\$174,200}{\$279,345}$	$\dfrac{\$220,350}{\$192,500}$
			0.62 to 1	1.14 to 1

FIGURE 26-15 Calculation of the Ratio of Liabilities to Stockholders' Equity

This ratio was much lower on December 31, 20-4, than it was on December 31, 20-3. The reduction in the ratio appears to have been caused by three factors.

1. Stockholders' equity increased by issuance of common stock for $22,500.

2. Stockholders' equity increased by keeping a large portion of 20-4's earnings.

3. Both notes payable and accounts payable were significantly reduced during 20-4, so that total liabilities decreased.

On December 31, 20-3, the majority of the financing for FCI came from debt. Companies in low-risk industries with fairly stable earnings can operate with a high ratio of liabilities to stockholders' equity. Comparing FCI's ratio with the industry average would be helpful in evaluating the degree of leverage.

Times Interest Earned Ratio

LEARNING KEY: Times Interest Earned Ratio = $\dfrac{\text{Income Before Taxes and Interest}}{\text{Interest Expense}}$

When a business has long-term liabilities such as bonds payable or mortgage payable, creditors want to know the amount of earnings available to pay interest. The ratio of earnings before taxes and interest to the interest expense is called the **times interest earned ratio**.

FCI had bonds payable of $100,000 outstanding on December 31, 20-4 and 20-3. The interest rate on the bonds was 10.5%. Interest expense in each year was

$10,500 ($100,000 × 10.5%). The calculation of the times interest earned ratio for each year is shown in Figure 26-16.

			20-4	20-3
Times Interest Earned	Income Before Taxes and Interest / Interest Expense	=	$118,945 / $10,500 = 11.3	$84,470 / $10,500 = 8.0
Income Before Taxes and Interest	Net Income		$71,845	$54,760
	Add: Income Tax		36,600	19,210
	Bond Interest		10,500	10,500
			$118,945	$84,470

FIGURE 26-16　Calculation of Times Interest Earned Ratio

These times interest earned ratios would be very satisfactory to the bond holders of FCI. In many businesses, a ratio of 2 or 3 is considered adequate.

LIMITATIONS OF FINANCIAL STATEMENT ANALYSIS

LO5 Explain the limitations of financial statement analysis.

Financial statement analysis can be a valuable tool in evaluating management performance. However, the methods of analysis need to be used cautiously and with an awareness of their limitations. The accounting system does not measure all aspects of operating a business. For example, the accounting numbers do not reflect the level of customer satisfaction with the company's products or the current employee morale. Further, the reported data are based on many estimates and approximations.

The period of time covered by the financial statements is another consideration. In this chapter, the analysis is based on only two years. A period of two consecutive years is not sufficient to establish a long-term trend. Many companies provide five- and ten-year summaries of operating results in published annual reports.

Comparison of FCI's financial results with other companies and with its industry as a whole can be difficult because generally accepted accounting principles allow different methods of accounting for similar events. For example, the choice of different inventory and depreciation methods can significantly impact both the income statement and the balance sheet. At a minimum, the accounting methods used by the other companies must be identified, so that their possible effects on comparisons can be considered.

Finally, in using ratios, remember that the observed number is simply an expression of the relationship between two other numbers. Either the numerator or the denominator can cause a ratio to provide a distorted message. For example, a company with the same net income in two consecutive years could show a higher rate of return in the second year, simply because the total assets in the second year are lower due to depreciation.

Computers and Accounting

Extensible Business Reporting Language—Gary P. Schneider, University of San Diego

In this chapter, you learned how to conduct financial analysis by using information from a company's financial statements to calculate ratios and trends that describe the profitability, liquidity, or financial strength of a company. Most of these ratios are more useful when compared with other companies in the same industry or of similar size. Thus, accountants need to obtain comparable numbers from the financial statements of other companies to do a complete analysis. Financial analysts that work for investment advisors and credit analysts at banks and other lenders also need comparative numbers from companies' financial statements to evaluate investment and lending risk. Accountants and financial analysts often develop complex models using spreadsheet software to perform ratio calculations for dozens or even hundreds of companies.

The task of entering numbers into the spreadsheet software one at a time from printed financial statements can be quite time consuming. Even if the financial statements are available in electronic form, such as a word-processing file or a web page, the process of copying and pasting each individual number is tedious. Automated approaches for capturing financial statement information displayed on web pages exist (the technique is called "screen scraping"); however, the variety of ways in which financial information can be displayed makes these efforts difficult.

Some accountants saw the need for a standardized way of presenting financial information on the Web. They worked to develop a markup language that companies could use for this purpose. In a text markup procedure, text is enclosed inside tags. The tags indicate the formatting or meaning of the text enclosed in them. A number of markup languages exist, including Hypertext Markup Language (HTML), which is used to create most web pages. Unfortunately, HTML does not provide the capabilities accountants need to create standardized presentations of financial information, because HTML tags are only capable of indicating the formatting of text they surround. HTML tags do not describe the content or meaning of the text.

Fortunately, a group of markup languages that have tags designed to indicate meaning does exist. The general name for this group is Extensible Markup Language (XML). XML allows users to create their own tags. You can learn more about XML at the http://www.xml.org and http://www.xml.com web sites. A number of industry groups have agreed on sets of XML tags that industry members can use to share information about inventory levels, inventory characteristics, and transactions such as orders and shipments. For example, the Chemistry Industry Data Exchange has created a standardized set of tags called Chemistry Markup Language (CML) for information sharing in the chemicals business. Accountants have developed similar XML implementations for the sharing of financial statement information between companies, investors, financial analysts, and other interested persons.

The most popular XML-based standard for financial reporting information is the Extensible Business Reporting Language (XBRL). The web site of XBRL International, the organization of the 170 companies and accounting firms that has sponsored the language, is http://www.xbrl.org. XBRL can be used to mark up financial statements, regulatory filings, internal accounting reports, and tax returns so they can be read and analyzed easily by recipients.

XBRL files can be placed on web pages for easy download by the general public or they can be attached to e-mail messages and sent to specific recipients. Most accounting reports and tax returns are still prepared on paper; however, technologies such as XBRL promise to turn these paper reports into electronic streams of information in the near future.

Learning Objectives	Key Points to Remember

1 Perform horizontal and vertical analyses of the income statement and balance sheet.

The financial statements can be much more informative and meaningful if they are analyzed on a comparative basis. The following are four possible types of comparisons:

1. with one or more previous periods
2. with data for the industry as a whole
3. with similar information for other businesses in the industry
4. with preset plans or goals (normally in the form of budgets)

A comparison of the amounts for the same item in the financial statements of two or more periods is called *horizontal analysis*.

Reporting the amount of each item in a statement as a percentage of some designated total is called *vertical analysis*.

**2
3
4 Compute and explain liquidity, profitability, and leverage measures.**

The following illustration summarizes the liquidity, profitability, and leverage measures.

LIQUIDITY MEASURES

Working Capital	Current Assets − Current Liabilities
Current Ratio	$\dfrac{\text{Current Assets}}{\text{Current Liabilities}}$
Quick Ratio	$\dfrac{\text{Quick Assets}}{\text{Current Liabilities}}$
Accounts Receivable Turnover	$\dfrac{\text{Net Sales on Account}}{\text{Average Accounts Receivable (net)}}$
Also expressed in days	365 ÷ Accounts Receivable Turnover
Merchandise Inventory Turnover	$\dfrac{\text{Cost of Goods Sold}}{\text{Average Merchandise Inventory}}$
Also expressed in days	365 ÷ Merchandise Inventory Turnover

PROFITABILITY MEASURES

Ratio of Net Sales to Assets	$\dfrac{\text{Net Sales}}{\text{Average Assets}}$
Return on Total Assets	$\dfrac{\text{Net Income}}{\text{Average Assets}}$
Return on Common Stockholders' Equity	$\dfrac{\text{Net Income Available to Common Stockholders}}{\text{Average Common Stockholders' Equity}}$
Earnings Per Share of Common Stock	$\dfrac{\text{Net Income Available to Common Stockholders}}{\text{Average Number of Common Shares Outstanding}}$
Book Value Per Share of Common Stock	$\dfrac{\text{Common Stockholders' Equity}}{\text{Number of Common Shares Outstanding at Year End}}$

LEVERAGE MEASURES

Ratio of Liabilities to Stockholders' Equity	$\dfrac{\text{Total Liabilities}}{\text{Total Stockholders' Equity}}$
Times Interest Earned Ratio	$\dfrac{\text{Income Before Taxes and Interest}}{\text{Interest Expense}}$

Learning Objectives	Key Points to Remember
5 Explain the limitations of financial statement analysis.	Limitations of financial statement analysis include the following: 1. Factors not reported on the financial statements are also important in evaluating the financial health of a company. 2. Financial statement information is based on many estimates. 3. Statements from many years should be considered before drawing conclusions about long-term trends. 4. Comparisons across companies are difficult due to the possible use of different accounting techniques. 5. The cause of changes in key ratios must be investigated before drawing conclusions.

Reflection: Answering the Opening Question

As discussed in this chapter, Fiona needs to consider more than the most recent net income figure. She should compute liquidity, profitability, and leverage measures for the past several years to see if there is an upward or downward trend in the company's financial health. These measures should also be compared with those of other companies in the same type of business.

DEMONSTRATION PROBLEM

Garfinkle Inc.'s comparative financial statements for the years ending December 31, 20-2 and 20-1, are shown on page 1001.

REQUIRED

1. Prepare a horizontal analysis of Garfinkle's comparative income statement for 20-2 and 20-1.

2. Prepare a vertical analysis of Garfinkle's comparative income statement for 20-2 and 20-1.

3. Prepare a horizontal analysis of Garfinkle's comparative balance sheet for 20-2 and 20-1.

4. Prepare a vertical analysis of Garfinkle's comparative balance sheet for 20-2 and 20-1.

5. Determine the following measures for 20-2 (round all calculations to two decimal places):

   (a)   working capital

   (b)   current ratio

   (c)   quick ratio

   (d)   accounts receivable turnover

(e) average collection period for accounts receivable

(f) merchandise inventory turnover

(g) average number of days required to sell merchandise inventory

(h) ratio of net sales to assets

(i) return on total assets

(j) return on common stockholders' equity

(k) earnings per share of common stock

(l) book value per share of common stock

(m) ratio of liabilities to stockholders' equity

(n) times interest earned ratio

Garfinkle Inc.
Comparative Income Statement
For Years Ended December 31, 20-2 and 20-1

	20-2	20-1
Sales (all on account)	$10,250,000	$6,515,200
Sales returns and allowances	250,000	115,200
Net sales	$10,000,000	$6,400,000
Cost of goods sold	6,800,000	4,160,000
Gross profit	$ 3,200,000	$2,240,000
Administrative expenses	$ 650,000	$ 448,000
Selling expenses	1,300,000	928,000
Total operating expenses	$ 1,950,000	$1,376,000
Operating income	$ 1,250,000	$ 864,000
Other expense (interest)	160,000	89,600
Income before income taxes	$ 1,090,000	$ 774,400
Income tax expense	390,000	234,400
Net income	$ 700,000	$ 540,000

Garfinkle Inc.
Comparative Balance Sheet
December 31, 20-2 and 20-1

	20-2	20-1
Assets		
Current assets:		
Cash	$ 350,000	$ 250,000
Accounts receivable (net)	1,150,000	750,000
Inventories	1,440,000	960,000
Supplies and prepayments	60,000	40,000
Total current assets	$3,000,000	$2,000,000
Plant assets (net)	4,686,000	4,346,000
Total assets	$7,686,000	$6,346,000
Liabilities		
Current liabilities	$1,500,000	$1,300,000
Stockholders' Equity		
Common stock, $10 par	$4,500,000	$4,000,000
Retained earnings	1,686,000	1,046,000
Total stockholders' equity	$6,186,000	$5,046,000
Total liabilities and stockholders' equity	$7,686,000	$6,346,000

(continued)

Solution

1. Horizontal analysis:

Garfinkle Inc.
Comparative Income Statement
For Years Ended December 31, 20-2 and 20-1

	20-2	20-1	INCREASE (DECREASE)	PERCENT
Sales (all on account)	$10,250,000	$6,515,200	$3,734,800	57.3
Sales returns and allowances	250,000	115,200	134,800	117.0
Net sales	$10,000,000	$6,400,000	$3,600,000	56.3
Cost of goods sold	6,800,000	4,160,000	2,640,000	63.5
Gross profit	$ 3,200,000	$2,240,000	$ 960,000	42.9
Administrative expenses	$ 650,000	$ 448,000	$ 202,000	45.1
Selling expenses	1,300,000	928,000	372,000	40.1
Total operating expenses	$ 1,950,000	$1,376,000	$ 574,000	41.7
Operating income	$ 1,250,000	$ 864,000	$ 386,000	44.7
Other expense (interest)	160,000	89,600	70,400	78.6
Income before income taxes	$ 1,090,000	$ 774,400	$ 315,600	40.8
Income tax expense	390,000	234,400	155,600	66.4
Net income	$ 700,000	$ 540,000	$ 160,000	29.6

2. Vertical analysis:

Garfinkle Inc.
Comparative Income Statement
For Years Ended December 31, 20-2 and 20-1

	20-2	PERCENT	20-1	PERCENT
Sales (all on account)	$10,250,000	102.5	$6,515,200	101.8
Sales returns and allowances	250,000	2.5	115,200	1.8
Net sales	$10,000,000	100.0	$6,400,000	100.0
Cost of goods sold	6,800,000	68.0	4,160,000	65.0
Gross profit	$ 3,200,000	32.0	$2,240,000	35.0
Administrative expenses	$ 650,000	6.5	$ 448,000	7.0
Selling expenses	1,300,000	13.0	928,000	14.5
Total operating expenses	$ 1,950,000	19.5	$1,376,000	21.5
Operating income	$ 1,250,000	12.5	$ 864,000	13.5
Other expense (interest)	160,000	1.6	89,600	1.4
Income before income taxes	$ 1,090,000	10.9	$ 774,400	12.1
Income tax expense	390,000	3.9	234,400	3.7
Net income	$ 700,000	7.0	$ 540,000	8.4

3.   Horizontal analysis:

Garfinkle Inc.
Comparative Balance Sheet
December 31, 20-2 and 20-1

	20-2	20-1	INCREASE (DECREASE)	PERCENT
Assets				
Current assets:				
Cash	$ 350,000	$ 250,000	$ 100,000	40.0
Accounts receivable (net)	1,150,000	750,000	400,000	53.3
Inventories	1,440,000	960,000	480,000	50.0
Supplies and prepayments	60,000	40,000	20,000	50.0
Total current assets	$3,000,000	$2,000,000	$1,000,000	50.0
Plant assets (net)	4,686,000	4,346,000	340,000	7.8
Total assets	$7,686,000	$6,346,000	$1,340,000	21.1
Liabilities				
Current liabilities	$1,500,000	$1,300,000	$ 200,000	15.4
Stockholders' Equity				
Common stock, $10 par	$4,500,000	$4,000,000	$ 500,000	12.5
Retained earnings	1,686,000	1,046,000	640,000	61.2
Total stockholders' equity	$6,186,000	$5,046,000	$1,140,000	22.6
Total liabilities and stockholders' equity	$7,686,000	$6,346,000	$1,340,000	21.1

4.   Vertical analysis:

Garfinkle Inc.
Comparative Balance Sheet
December 31, 20-2 and 20-1

	20-2	PERCENT*	20-1	PERCENT*
Assets				
Current assets:				
Cash	$ 350,000	4.6	$ 250,000	3.9
Accounts receivable (net)	1,150,000	15.0	750,000	11.8
Inventories	1,440,000	18.7	960,000	15.1
Supplies and prepayments	60,000	0.8	40,000	0.6
Total current assets	$3,000,000	39.0	$2,000,000	31.5
Plant assets (net)	4,686,000	61.0	4,346,000	68.5
Total assets	$7,686,000	100.0	$6,346,000	100.0
Liabilities				
Current liabilities	$1,500,000	19.5	$1,300,000	20.5
Stockholders' Equity				
Common stock, $10 par	$4,500,000	58.5	$4,000,000	63.0
Retained earnings	1,686,000	21.9	1,046,000	16.5
Total stockholders' equity	$6,186,000	80.5	$5,046,000	79.5
Total liabilities and stockholders' equity	$7,686,000	100.0	$6,346,000	100.0

* Percentages may not add due to rounding.

(continued)

5. (a) Working capital:

Current assets $3,000,000

− Current liabilities   (1,500,000)

     $1,500,000

(b) Current ratio:

$$\frac{\text{Current assets}}{\text{Current liabilities}} = \frac{\$3,000,000}{\$1,500,000} = \text{2.00 to 1}$$

(c) Quick ratio:

$$\frac{\text{Quick assets}}{\text{Current liabilities}} = \frac{\$1,500,000}{\$1,500,000} = \text{1.00 to 1}$$

(d) Accounts receivable turnover:

$$\frac{\text{Net sales on account}}{\text{Average accounts receivable}} = \frac{\$10,000,000}{(\$1,150,000 + \$750,000) \div 2} = 10.53$$

(e) Average collection period:

$$\frac{365}{10.53} = \text{34.66 days}$$

(f) Merchandise inventory turnover:

$$\frac{\text{Cost of goods sold}}{\text{Avg. merchandise inventory}} = \frac{\$6,800,000}{(\$1,440,000 + \$960,000) \div 2} = 5.67$$

(g) Average number of days to sell inventory:

$(365 \div 5.67) = \underline{\text{64.37 days}}$

(h) Ratio of net sales to assets:

$$\frac{\text{Net sales}}{\text{Average assets}} = \frac{\$10,000,000}{(\$7,686,000 + \$6,346,000) \div 2} = \text{1.43 to 1}$$

(i) Return on total assets:

$$\frac{\text{Net income}}{\text{Average assets}} = \frac{\$700,000}{(\$7,686,000 + \$6,346,000) \div 2} = 9.98\%$$

(j) Return on stockholders' equity:

$$\frac{\text{Net income}}{\text{Avg. stockholders' equity}} = \frac{\$700,000}{(\$6,186,000 + \$5,046,000) \div 2} = 12.46\%$$

(k) Earnings per share of common stock

$$\frac{\text{Net income}}{\text{Avg. no. of common shares outstanding}} = \frac{\$700,000}{(450,000 \text{ shares} + 400,000 \text{ shares}) \div 2} = \$1.65$$

(l) Book value per share of common stock:

$$\frac{\text{Common stockholders' equity}}{\text{No. of common shares outstanding}} = \frac{\$6,186,000}{450,000 \text{ shares}} = \$13.75$$

(m) Ratio of liabilities to stockholders' equity:

$$\frac{\text{Total liabilities}}{\text{Total stockholders' equity}} = \frac{\$1,500,000}{\$6,186,000} = \text{0.24 to 1}$$

(n) Times interest earned ratio:

Net income	$ 700,000
Corporate income taxes	390,000
Interest expense	160,000
Income before interest and taxes	$1,250,000

$$\frac{\text{Income before taxes and interest}}{\text{Interest expense}} = \frac{\$1,250,000}{\$160,000} = \text{7.81 times}$$

On-Line Learning Tools

For more information, visit: http://heintz.swlearning.com

The Heintz & Parry product web site is designed specifically for **COLLEGE ACCOUNTING, 18e.** The features include downloadable student resources and an interactive study center, organized by chapter, which contains learning objectives, web links, on-line quizzes with automatic feedback, and more.

KEY TERMS

accounts receivable turnover, (990)   The ratio of net sales on account to the average amount of net accounts receivable.

acid-test ratio, (989)   See quick ratio.

asset turnover ratio, (991)   See ratio of net sales to assets.

book value per share, (995)   The ratio of common stockholders' equity to the number of common shares outstanding at the end of the year.

cost of goods sold ratio, (986)   The ratio of cost of goods sold to net sales.

current ratio, (988)   The ratio of current assets to current liabilities. Also called working capital ratio.

debt-to-equity ratio, (996)   See ratio of liabilities to stockholders' equity.

earnings per share, (994)   The ratio of net income available to common stockholders to the average number of shares of common stock outstanding during the year.

gross profit ratio, (986)   The ratio of gross profit to net sales.

horizontal analysis, (982)   A comparison of the amounts for the same item in the financial statements of two periods.

leverage, (982) The proportion of debt to stockholders' equity.

leverage measures, (996)   Measures that indicate the extent to which a company is being financed by debt, and the ability of the company to meet its debt obligations.

liquidity, (982)   The ability to pay current debts when they come due.

liquidity measures, (988)   Measures that indicate a company's ability to meet its current debts as they come due.

merchandise inventory turnover, (990)   The ratio of cost of goods sold to the average merchandise inventory.

net income ratio, (986)   The ratio of net income to net sales.

operating expense ratio, (986)   The ratio of operating expenses to net sales.

operating income ratio, (986)   The ratio of operating income to net sales.

profit margin, (986)   See net income ratio.

profitability, (982)   The ability to earn a satisfactory return on the investments in the business.

profitability measures, (991)   Measures that indicate a company's ability to earn income by operating efficiently.

quick ratio, (989)   The ratio of quick assets to current liabilities. Also called the acid-test ratio.

ratio of liabilities to stockholders' equity, (996)   The ratio of total liabilities to total stockholders' equity. It is a measure of the extent of overall leverage, or proportion of borrowed capital, with which a business operates. Also called debt-to-equity ratio.

ratio of net sales to assets, (991)   A measure of how efficiently a company used its assets to generate sales. Also called asset turnover ratio.

(continued)

    return on common stockholders' equity, (993)   The ratio of net income available to common stockholders for the year to the average common stockholders' equity during the year.

    return on total assets, (992)   The ratio of net income for the year to the average assets for the year.

    times interest earned ratio, (996)   The ratio of earnings before interest and taxes to interest expense.

    vertical analysis, (985)   Reporting the amount of each item in a statement as a percentage of some designated total.

    working capital, (988)   The excess of a company's current assets over current liabilities.

    working capital ratio, (988)   See current ratio.

REVIEW QUESTIONS

(LO1)   1.   Financial statement analysis generally focuses on three main aspects of the business's financial health. What are they?

(LO1)   2.   Describe four possible types of comparisons that may be made in financial statement analysis.

(LO1)   3.   Why was the increase in FCI's operating income so much greater than the increase in its net sales?

(LO1)   4.   What were the main causes of the decrease in FCI's current liabilities?

(LO1)   5.   List five ratios that are automatically provided by the vertical analysis of income statements.

(LO2)   6.   Identify five measures of liquidity calculated by FCI.

(LO3)   7.   Identify five measures of profitability calculated by FCI.

(LO4)   8.   Identify two measures of the extent of leverage calculated by FCI.

(LO5)   9.   Briefly describe five limitations of financial statement analysis.

Self-Study Test Questions

True/False

1. Leverage is the ability to pay debts when they come due.   _____

2. A comparison of amounts for the same item in the financial statements of two or more periods is horizontal analysis.   _____

3. It is common for long-term asset accounts to show a decrease in the net balance from year to year.   _____

4. Working capital is calculated by dividing current assets by current liabilities.   _____

5. In calculating accounts receivable turnover, only accounts receivable are considered; others, such as accrued interest receivable, are not included.   _____

Self-Study Test Questions *(continued)*

Multiple Choice

1. The ability to earn a satisfactory return on investments is called

    (a) liquidity.   (c) leverage.
    (b) profitability.

    _____

2. Working capital is a measure of

    (a) liquidity.   (c) leverage.
    (b) profitability.

    _____

3. The times interest earned ratio is a measure of

    (a) liquidity.   (c) leverage.
    (b) profitability.

    _____

4. Financial statements are usually compared with

    (a) one or more previous periods.
    (b) data from the industry as a whole.
    (c) similar businesses in the industry.
    (d) all of the above.

    _____

5. Which of these is *not* a measure of liquidity?

    (a) working capital   (c) quick ratio
    (b) current ratio   (d) return on total assets

    _____

The answers to the Self-Study Test Questions are at the end of the text.

MANAGING YOUR WRITING

Many libraries have corporate annual reports and reports on the financial health of companies by financial analysts and rating agencies such as Standard and Poor's and Moody's. Go to the library and review financial information on two corporations in your favorite industry. Write a brief memo describing the information available and how it can be used to evaluate the financial health of a company.

ETHICS CASE

Jim Tennison, L & B Corporation's president, called the company's chief financial officer, Fred Harden, into his office late Friday afternoon. Jim had been reviewing the projected financial statements of L & B Corporation that would be issued as of year end. Jim told Fred he was worried that the company's liquidity position had been declining over the past two years. Fred assured Jim that the company still had sufficient liquidity and they had been steadily decreasing their debt. Jim said that there were three or four major stockholders who were very conservative and would raise lots of questions about the company's declining liquidity ratios. Jim and Fred then decided to take out a two-year loan secured by some land L & B Corporation owned, put the cash in the bank, and pay the loan off after January 1. Jim told Fred to account for the transaction as a long-term liability for

(continued)

financial reporting purposes. They agreed that this measure would solve the problem of liquidity at the annual stockholders' meeting because the company's ratios would be almost identical to last year. Jim was sure that most of the stockholders were only concerned with net income and ratios.

1. If you were a stockholder of L & B Corporation, how would you feel about Jim & Fred's idea? Have any ethical principles been violated?

2. If the transaction is booked as a debit to Cash and a credit to Long-Term Notes Payable, how will it affect the company's key current ratios and debt ratios?

3. Suppose Jim and Fred decide not to take out the loan. Write a brief note to the stockholders justifying a decrease in liquidity measures. Assure them that the company is still in the "safe range."

4. In groups of two or three, list as many reasons as possible, both positive and negative, for a decrease in net working capital.

WEB WORK

Look at the annual report for McDonald's. Be prepared to discuss both horizontal and vertical analysis of McDonald's financial statements. Visit the Interactive Study Center on our web site at **http://heintz.swlearning.com** for special hotlinks to assist you in this assignment.

SERIES A EXERCISES

EXERCISE 26-1A **(LO2)**

(a) 2.17 to 1; (b) 3.82 to 1;
(c) $1,716,800;
(d) 3.15 or 115.87 days;
(e) 2.05 or 178.05 days

ANALYSIS OF LIQUIDITY Based on the comparative income statement and balance sheet of Ace Kitchen Works, Inc., that follow, compute the following liquidity measures for 20-2 (round all calculations to two decimal places).

(a) Quick or acid-test ratio

(b) Current ratio

(c) Working capital

(d) Accounts receivable turnover

(e) Merchandise inventory turnover

Ace Kitchen Works, Inc.
Comparative Income Statement
For Years Ended December 31, 20-2 and 20-1

	20-2	20-1
Net sales (on account)	$2,643,000	$2,176,400
Cost of goods sold	1,868,200	1,614,200
Gross profit	$ 774,800	$ 562,200
Operating expenses	244,600	221,800
Other expense (interest)	24,200	24,200
Income tax expense	161,900	101,200
Net income	$ 344,100	$ 215,000

Ace Kitchen Works, Inc.
Comparative Balance Sheet
December 31, 20-2 and 20-1

	20-2	20-1
Cash	$ 129,000	$ 106,800
Government notes	300,000	300,000
Accounts receivable (net)	892,400	787,400
Merchandise inventory	952,800	866,200
Supplies and prepayments	50,600	46,600
Land	108,200	108,200
Building (net)	330,000	390,600
Office equipment (net)	13,600	15,000
Total assets	$2,776,600	$2,620,800
Current liabilities (accounts payable)	$ 608,000	$ 507,200
Bonds payable	200,000	220,000
Total liabilities	$ 808,000	$ 727,200
Common stock ($10 par, 170,000 shares)	$1,700,000	$1,700,000
Retained earnings	268,600	193,600
Total stockholders' equity	$1,968,600	$1,893,600
Total liabilities and stockholders' equity	$2,776,600	$2,620,800

EXERCISE 26-2A   **(LO3)**

(a) .98 to 1; (b) 12.75%;
(c) 17.82%; (d) $2.02;
(e) $11.58

ANALYSIS OF PROFITABILITY Based on the financial statement data in Exercise 26-1A, compute the following profitability measures for 20-2 (round all calculations to two decimal places).

(a) Ratio of net sales to assets

(b) Return on total assets

(c) Return on common stockholders' equity

(d) Earnings per share of common stock

(e) Book value per share of common stock

EXERCISE 26-3A   **(LO4)**

(a) .41 to 1; (b) 21.91 times

ANALYSIS OF LEVERAGE Based on the financial statement data in Exercise 26-1A, compute the following leverage measures (round all calculations to two decimal places).

(a) Ratio of liabilities to stockholders' equity

(b) Times interest earned ratio (Bond interest is $24,200.)

SERIES A PROBLEMS

PROBLEM 26-4A **(LO1)** **HORIZONTAL ANALYSIS OF COMPARATIVE FINANCIAL STATEMENTS**
Balances from the comparative income statement and balance sheet of Miller Electronics Corporation for the last two years are as follows:

Miller Electronics Corporation		
	(Dec.)	%
NI	$32,139	52.8
Cash	$20,894	94.9
RE	$95,018	126.5

Miller Electronics Corporation
Comparative Income Statement
For Years Ended December 31, 20-2 and 20-1

	20-2	20-1
Net sales (on account)	$650,220	$420,600
Cost of goods sold	395,410	258,668
Gross profit	$254,810	$161,932
Administrative expenses	$ 63,518	$ 42,288
Selling expenses	65,992	43,936
Total operating expenses	$129,510	$ 86,224
Operating income	$125,300	$ 75,708
Interest expense	1,282	1,204
Income before income taxes	$124,018	$ 74,504
Income tax expense	31,005	13,630
Net income	$ 93,013	$ 60,874

Miller Electronics Corporation
Comparative Balance Sheet
December 31, 20-2 and 20-1

	20-2	20-1
Assets		
Current assets:		
Cash	$ 42,900	$ 22,006
Receivables (net)	73,642	47,510
Merchandise inventory	92,060	50,396
Supplies and prepayments	3,788	1,158
Total current assets	$212,390	$121,070
Property, plant, and equipment:		
Office equipment (net)	12,150	8,490
Factory equipment (net)	105,360	71,190
Total property, plant, and equipment	$117,510	$ 79,680
Total assets	$329,900	$200,750
Liabilities		
Current liabilities:		
Notes payable	$ 10,000	$ 6,000
Accounts payable	43,524	30,242
Accrued and withheld payroll taxes	6,250	5,400
Total current liabilities	$ 59,774	$ 41,642
Stockholders' Equity		
Common stock ($10 par)	100,000	84,000
Retained earnings	170,126	75,108
Total stockholders' equity	$270,126	$159,108
Total liabilities and stockholders' equity	$329,900	$200,750

REQUIRED

Prepare a horizontal analysis. Add columns to show the amount of increase (decrease) and the percentage change. Round percentages to one decimal place.

PROBLEM 26-5A   **(LO1)**

PowerAccountingSystemSoftware®

	20-1
CGS	61.5
Cash	11.0

VERTICAL ANALYSIS OF COMPARATIVE FINANCIAL STATEMENTS Refer to the financial statements in Problem 26-4A.

REQUIRED

Prepare a vertical analysis of the income statement and balance sheet. Show each item on the income statement as a percentage of the net sales for each year. On the balance sheet, show each asset item as a percentage of the total assets and each liability and equity item as a percentage of the total liabilities and stockholders' equity. Round percentages to one decimal place.

PROBLEM 26-6A (LO2/3/4)

	20-1
(a)	32.34%
(c)	$7.25
(e)	1.67 to 1
(g)	$79,428
(i)	5.21 or 70.06 days
(j)	.26 to 1
(k)	2.23 to 1

RATIO ANALYSIS OF COMPARATIVE FINANCIAL STATEMENTS Refer to the financial statements in Problem 26-4A.

REQUIRED

Calculate the following ratios and amounts for 20-1 and 20-2 (round all calculations to two decimal places).

(a) Return on total assets (Total assets on January 1, 20-1, were $175,750.)

(b) Return on common stockholders' equity (Total common stockholders' equity on January 1, 20-1, was $106,944.)

(c) Earnings per share of common stock (The average numbers of shares outstanding were 8,400 shares in 20-1 and 9,200 in 20-2.)

(d) Book value per share of common stock

(e) Quick ratio

(f) Current ratio

(g) Working capital

(h) Receivables turnover (Net receivables on January 1, 20-1, were $39,800.)

(i) Merchandise inventory turnover (Merchandise Inventory on January 1, 20-1, was $48,970.)

(j) Ratio of liabilities to stockholders' equity

(k) Ratio of net sales to assets (Assets on January 1, 20-1, were $175,750.)

(l) Times interest earned ratio

SERIES B EXERCISES

EXERCISE 26-1B   **(LO2)**
(a) 2.25 to 1; (b) 3.87 to 1;
(c) $1,193,300;
(d) 3.06 or 119.28 days
(e) 1.81 or 201.66 days

ANALYSIS OF LIQUIDITY Based on the comparative income statement and balance sheet for Falcon Designers, Inc., given on the next page, compute the following liquidity measures for 20-2 (round all calculations to two decimal places).

(a) Quick or acid-test ratio

(b) Current ratio

(c) Working capital

(d) Accounts receivable turnover

(e) Merchandise inventory turnover

(continued)

Falcon Designers, Inc.
Comparative Income Statement
For Years Ended December 31, 20-2 and 20-1

	20-2	20-1
Net sales (on account)	$1,850,800	$1,532,600
Cost of goods sold	1,150,400	1,010,500
Gross profit	$ 700,400	$ 522,100
Operating expenses	180,300	156,600
Other expenses (interest)	18,200	18,200
Income tax expense	160,600	107,600
Net income	$ 341,300	$ 239,700

Falcon Designers, Inc.
Comparative Balance Sheet
December 31, 20-2 and 20-1

	20-2	20-1
Cash	$ 95,500	$ 79,700
Government notes	200,000	200,000
Accounts receivable (net)	639,300	570,600
Merchandise inventory	634,900	639,500
Supplies and prepayments	39,600	29,900
Land	81,900	78,400
Building (net)	227,500	289,300
Office equipment (net)	10,400	10,800
Total assets	$1,929,100	$1,898,200
Current liabilities (accounts payable)	$ 416,000	$ 394,500
Bonds payable	150,000	150,000
Total liabilities	$ 566,000	$ 544,500
Common stock ($10 par, 125,000 shares)	$1,250,000	$1,250,000
Retained earnings	113,100	103,700
Total stockholders' equity	$1,363,100	$1,353,700
Total liabilities and stockholders' equity	$1,929,100	$1,898,200

EXERCISE 26-2B   (LO3)
(a) .97 to 1; (b) 17.84%;
(c) 25.13%; (d) $2.73;
(e) $10.90

ANALYSIS OF PROFITABILITY Based on the financial statement data in Exercise 26-1B, compute the following profitability measures for 20-2 (round all calculations to two decimal places).

(a) Ratio of net sales to assets

(b) Return on total assets

(c) Return on common stockholders' equity

(d) Earnings per share of common stock

(e) Book value per share of common stock

EXERCISE 26-3B   (LO4)
(a) .42 to 1; (b) 28.58 times

ANALYSIS OF LEVERAGE Based on the financial statement data in Exercise 26-1B, compute the following leverage measures for 20-2 (round all calculations to two decimal places).

(a) Ratio of liabilities to stockholders' equity

(b) Times interest earned ratio (bond interest is $18,200)

SERIES B PROBLEMS

PROBLEM 26-4B   (LO1)

Johnson Stores, Inc.		
	(Dec.)	%
NI	$17,497	23.9
Cash	$14,671	94.0
RE	$39,148	70.2

HORIZONTAL ANALYSIS OF COMPARATIVE FINANCIAL STATEMENTS
Balances from the comparative income statement and balance sheet of Johnson Stores, Inc., for the last two years are as follows:

Johnson Stores, Inc.
Comparative Income Statement
For Years Ended December 31, 20-2 and 20-1

	20-2	20-1
Net sales (on account)	$467,865	$305,145
Cost of goods sold	256,955	149,005
Gross profit	$210,910	$156,140
Administrative expenses	$ 43,876	$ 30,617
Selling expenses	44,994	31,293
Total operating expenses	$ 88,870	$ 61,910
Operating income	$122,040	$ 94,230
Interest expense	916	903
Income before income taxes	$121,124	$ 93,327
Income tax expense	30,280	19,980
Net income	$ 90,844	$ 73,347

Johnson Stores, Inc.
Comparative Balance Sheet
December 31, 20-2 and 20-1

	20-2	20-1
Assets		
Current assets:		
Cash	$ 30,275	$ 15,604
Receivables (net)	42,441	33,565
Merchandise inventory	49,460	34,636
Supplies and prepayments	7,119	6,403
Total current assets	$129,295	$ 90,208
Property, plant, and equipment:		
Office equipment (net)	9,025	6,062
Factory equipment (net)	72,090	52,930
Total property, plant, and equipment	$ 81,115	$ 58,992
Total assets	$210,410	$149,200
Liabilities		
Current liabilities:		
Notes payable	$ 4,000	$ 8,000
Accounts payable	30,233	14,821
Accrued and withheld payroll taxes	6,250	7,600
Total liabilities	$ 40,483	$ 30,421
Stockholders' Equity		
Common stock ($10 par)	75,000	63,000
Retained earnings	94,927	55,779
Total stockholders' equity	$169,927	$118,779
Total liabilities and stockholders' equity	$210,410	$149,200

REQUIRED

Prepare a horizontal analysis of the statements. Add columns to show the amount of increase (decrease) and the percentage change. Round percentages to one decimal place.

PROBLEM 26-5B   **(LO1)**

	20-2	20-1
CGS	54.9	48.8
Cash	14.4	10.5

VERTICAL ANALYSIS OF COMPARATIVE FINANCIAL STATEMENTS Refer to the financial statements in Problem 26-4B.

REQUIRED

Prepare a vertical analysis of the income statement and balance sheet. Show each item on the income statement as a percentage of the net sales for each year. On the balance sheet, show each asset item as a percentage of the total assets and each liability and equity item as a percentage of the total liabilities and stockholders' equity. Round percentages to one decimal place.

PROBLEM 26-6B **(LO2/3/4)**

	20-1
(b)	73.06%
(d)	$18.85
(f)	2.97 to 1
(h)	9.76 or 37.40 days
(i)	4.44 or 82.21 days
(j)	.26 to 1
(k)	2.34 to 1

RATIO ANALYSIS OF COMPARATIVE FINANCIAL STATEMENTS Refer to the financial statements in Problem 26-4B.

REQUIRED

Calculate the following ratios and amounts for 20-1 and 20-2 (round all calculations to two decimal places).

(a) Return on total assets (Total assets on January 1, 20-1, were $111,325.)

(b) Return on common stockholders' equity (Total common stockholders' equity on January 1, 20-1, was $82,008.)

(c) Earnings per share of common stock (The average numbers of shares outstanding were 6,300 shares in 20-1 and 6,900 in 20-2.)

(d) Book value per share of common stock

(e) Quick ratio

(f) Current ratio

(g) Working capital

(h) Receivables turnover (Net receivables on January 1, 20-1, were $28,995.)

(i) Merchandise inventory turnover (Merchandise Inventory on January 1, 20-1, was $32,425.)

(j) Ratio of liabilities to stockholders' equity

(k) Ratio of net sales to assets (Assets on January 1, 20-1, were $111,325.)

(l) Times interest earned ratio

MASTERY PROBLEM

3(a) $41,800; 3(c) .58 to 1;
3(e) 6.59 or 55.39 days;
4(b) 11.53%; 4(d) $1.65
per share; 5(a) .35 to 1

Comparative financial statements for the Na Pali Coast Company for the years ending December 31, 20-1 and 20-2 are provided.

REQUIRED

1. Perform horizontal analysis of the comparative income statement and balance sheet. Round percentages to one decimal place.

2. Perform vertical analysis of the comparative income statement and balance sheet. Round percentages to one decimal place.

3. Compute the following liquidity measures for 20-2 (round all calculations to two decimal places).

  (a) Working capital

  (b) Current ratio

  (c) Quick or acid-test ratio

  (d) Accounts receivable turnover and average number of days to collect receivables (Assume that sales on account for 20-2 were $120,000.)

  (e) Merchandise inventory turnover and average number of days to sell inventory

4. Compute the following profitability measures for 20-2 (round all calculations to two decimal places):

  (a) Ratio of net sales to assets

  (b) Return on total assets

  (c) Return on common stockholders' equity

  (d) Earnings per share of common stock

  (e) Book value per share of common stock

5. Compute the following leverage measures for 20-2 (round all calculations to two decimal places):

  (a) Ratio of liabilities to stockholders' equity

  (b) Times interest earned ratio (Assume interest expense for 20-2 was $1,200.)

Na Pali Coast Company
Comparative Income Statement
For Years Ended December 31, 20-2 and 20-1

	20-2	20-1
Net sales	$466,451	$291,613
Cost of goods sold	285,889	188,626
Gross profit	$180,562	$102,987
Operating expenses	125,650	78,200
Operating income	$ 54,912	$ 24,787
Other expenses	1,200	500
Income before income taxes	$ 53,712	$ 24,287
Income tax expense	18,250	7,285
Net income	$ 35,462	$ 17,002

(continued)

Na Pali Coast Company
Comparative Balance Sheet
December 31, 20-2 and 20-1

	20-2	20-1
Assets		
Current assets:		
Cash	$ 8,600	$ 7,500
Government notes	3,000	2,000
Accounts receivable (net)	10,500	8,600
Merchandise inventory	53,600	33,200
Supplies and prepayments	4,500	3,200
Total current assets	$ 80,200	$ 54,500
Property, plant, and equipment:		
Land	$ 40,000	$ 40,000
Building (net)	200,000	150,000
Delivery equipment (net)	13,000	15,000
Office equipment (net)	5,400	6,000
Organization costs	5,000	6,000
Total property, plant, and equipment	$263,400	$217,000
Total assets	$343,600	$271,500
Liabilities		
Current liabilities:		
Notes payable	$ 5,000	$ 3,000
Accounts payable	28,700	22,300
Accrued and withheld payroll taxes	4,200	5,600
Accrued interest payable	500	1,700
Total current liabilities	$ 38,400	$ 32,600
Long-term liabilities:		
Bonds payable	50,000	20,000
Total liabilities	$ 88,400	$ 52,600
Stockholders' Equity		
Common stock ($5 par)	$115,000	$100,000
Paid-in capital in excess of par	65,000	60,000
Retained earnings	75,200	58,900
Total stockholders' equity	$255,200	$218,900
Total liabilities and stockholders' equity	$343,600	$271,500

CHALLENGE PROBLEM

This problem challenges you to apply your cumulative accounting knowledge to move a step beyond the material in the chapter.

Days cash is outstanding for merchandise: 54.05 days

Combining the information provided by various ratios can enhance your understanding of the financial condition of a business. Review the information provided for the Na Pali Coast Company in the Mastery Problem. Using this information, respond to the following questions.

REQUIRED

1. Compute the average number of days required to sell inventory and collect cash from customers buying on account.

2. Note that Na Pali Coast Company also buys inventory on account. On average, how many days pass before Na Pali pays its creditors?

3. Using the information from your answers to questions 1 and 2, compute the number of days from the time Na Pali Coast pays for inventory until it receives cash from customers on account.

©GETTY IMAGES/PHOTODISC

Departmental Accounting

Finny Co. has continued to enjoy profitable operations. Both the electric and acoustic instruments are known for their high quality. Mike Finbar is happy with the overall success of the business, but he has a gut feeling that the electric instruments are much more profitable than the acoustic. Unfortunately, the accounting reports for the business as a whole give him no evidence to support his feeling. Mike's accountant says that departmental reports could be prepared showing various measures of profitability of different product lines. What measures of departmental profitability can be prepared? Are any judgments and estimates necessary in order to prepare departmental reports? Is there a need for special care in interpreting the departmental profit measures?

Careful study of this chapter should enable you to:

LO1 Explain the nature and purpose of departmental accounting.

LO2 Describe and compute departmental gross profit.

LO3 Describe and compute departmental operating income.

LO4 Describe and compute departmental direct operating margin.

Companies often engage in different types of profit-making activities. For example, a merchandiser might sell different products, such as lawn mowers and bicycles. A service business might provide different services, such as auditing and management consulting. Such businesses are often organized into separate segments called departments. In this chapter, we will examine how to account for a business organized into departments.

DEPARTMENTAL ACCOUNTING

LO1 Explain the nature and purpose of departmental accounting.

When a business sells several products or services, it can be difficult to obtain useful and accurate information about the business. An income statement prepared for the business as a whole might show that the business is reasonably profitable. This statement would not show that one portion of the business is highly successful while another portion is operating at a loss. Departmental accounting overcomes this problem by providing separate information about the revenues and expenses of each department.

Departmental reports are useful to management for three purposes: (1) planning, (2) control, and (3) performance evaluation.

1. Planning—Successful managers set goals and develop plans for achieving these goals. An important part of planning is identifying the strengths and weaknesses of the different parts of the firm. Departmental reports can be very helpful for this purpose.

2. Control—To properly control operations, managers must be able to identify revenues and expenses that are out of line. Departmental reports help management focus attention on problem areas or departments.

3. Performance evaluation—When a business is organized into departments, responsibility for each department can be assigned to a specific manager. Departmental reports can then be used to evaluate each manager's performance.

Departmental reports are usually not part of the basic financial statements. These reports are for internal management use only. This means the accounting rules for external reporting do not apply. Department reports can be prepared in whatever form management finds useful. Generally, only a departmental income statement is prepared. In the following sections, we will look at departmental income statements for Annie's Sporting Goods, which sells golf and tennis equipment. These income statements will be extended through three different levels: gross profit, operating income, and direct operating margin.

DEPARTMENTAL GROSS PROFIT

LO2 Describe and compute departmental gross profit.

Departmental gross profit is the difference between a department's net sales and cost of goods sold. Each element used to compute gross profit must be determined for each department. Recall that the following elements are used to compute gross profit:

Sales
Sales returns and allowances
Inventory
Purchases
Purchases returns and allowances
Purchases discounts
Freight-in

Two ways of accumulating this information are:

1. Maintain separate general ledger accounts by department for each element (account) making up gross profit.

2. Maintain a single general ledger account for each element. The total in each account is assigned to the appropriate departments at the end of the accounting period.

Departmental Income Statement Showing Gross Profit

Figure 27-1 shows Annie's departmental income statement for the year 20--. The gross profit section is presented in condensed form. Gross profit is shown by department and in total.

Annie's Sporting Goods Income Statement For Year Ended December 31, 20 - -	GOLF					TENNIS					TOTAL				
Net sales	$1,075	0	0	0	00	$640	3	0	0	00	$1,715	3	0	0	00
Cost of goods sold	545	2	8	0	00	420	9	0	0	00	966	1	8	0	00
Gross profit	$ 529	7	2	0	00	$219	4	0	0	00	$ 749	1	2	0	00
Operating expenses:															
Store clerks' wages expense											$ 80	2	5	0	00
Truck drivers' wages expense											83	9	0	0	00
Advertising expense											79	5	0	0	00
Store rent expense											22	8	0	0	00
Bad debt expense											17	9	0	0	00
Depreciation expense—delivery equipment											24	0	0	0	00
Other operating expenses											350	4	3	0	00
Total operating expenses											$ 658	7	8	0	00
Operating income											$ 90	3	4	0	00

FIGURE 27-1   Income Statement Showing Departmental Gross Profit

This report shows that the golf department provides the majority of Annie's sales and gross profit. The report also reveals a large difference in the gross profit percentages of the two departments.

Golf department gross profit percentage: ($529,720 ÷ $1,075,000)	**49.3%**
Tennis department gross profit percentage: ($219,400 ÷ $640,300)	**34.3%**

Management should determine the causes of this difference and take appropriate action. Perhaps the normal retail markup on golf equipment is higher than that on tennis equipment. If so, management might want to emphasize selling golf equipment. If the normal retail markup on the two products is similar, the pricing policies for tennis equipment should be evaluated. The tennis department may be using an inadequate markup percentage. Another possibility is that the purchase prices for tennis equipment are too high. If so, the purchasing department should try to obtain better prices from vendors.

LEARNING KEY: An income statement showing departmental gross profit enables management to see whether each of its departments is earning an adequate gross profit.

A higher gross profit or gross profit percentage does not necessarily mean that a department is more profitable overall. Departmental operating expenses must also be considered.

DEPARTMENTAL OPERATING INCOME

LO3 Describe and compute departmental operating income.

Departmental operating income is the difference between a department's gross profit and its operating expenses. As with departmental gross profit, separate departmental accounts may be maintained for each operating expense. This approach is not common, however, because many operating expenses cannot be directly related to specific departments. Instead, a single general ledger account is maintained for each operating expense. The total is assigned or allocated to departments at the end of the period.

Direct and Indirect Operating Expenses

Departmental operating expenses can be classified as direct and indirect. **Direct expenses** are incurred for the sole benefit of and are traceable directly to a specific department. **Indirect expenses** are incurred for the benefit of the business as a whole and cannot be traced directly to a specific department. Figure 27-2 provides examples of direct and indirect expenses for Annie's Sporting Goods.

DIRECT EXPENSES	INDIRECT EXPENSES
Wages of golf department sales clerk	Cost of renting store space
Cost of advertising tennis equipment	Cost of advertising Annie's Sporting Goods store
Wages of driver who delivers golf equipment	Store manager's salary

FIGURE 27-2   Sample Direct and Indirect Expenses

To compute departmental operating income, direct expenses are *assigned* to departments based on the actual expenses incurred. If separate departmental accounts are used, the expenses are accumulated there. If separate departmental accounts are not used, the expenses are assigned to departments based on information contained in supporting records. For example, personnel records would show the departments in which employees work, and wages would be assigned accordingly. Indirect expenses are *allocated* to departments on some reasonable basis, such as relative sales, cost of goods sold, or floor space, or the estimated time spent serving a given department. There are no rules like generally accepted accounting principles. The key is to use a "reasonable basis."

Assigning and Allocating Departmental Expenses

To illustrate the computation of departmental operating income, we will assign and allocate the operating expenses of Annie's Sporting Goods. Annie's does not maintain separate general ledger departmental operating expense accounts.

Store Clerks' Wages Expense. Annie's employs five store clerks: two work solely in the golf department, one works in the tennis department, and two assist customers in both departments. Their wages are as follows:

EMPLOYEE NUMBER	DEPT.	WAGES	
1	Golf	$19,000	} $36,000
2	Golf	17,000	
3	Tennis	15,250	
4	Both	13,000	} $29,000
5	Both	16,000	
Total		$80,250	

Wages of $36,000 ($19,000 + $17,000) for the golf department clerks are assigned to golf. Wages of $15,250 for the tennis department clerk are assigned to tennis. Wages of $29,000 ($13,000 + $16,000) for the other two clerks are allocated between the departments based on the percentage of total net sales represented by each department.

Another reasonable basis for allocating the clerks' wages might be the percentage of total cost of goods sold. This is a good example of the judgment that must be made any time expenses need to be allocated.

$$\frac{\text{Golf net sales}}{\text{Total net sales}} = \frac{\$1,075,000}{\$1,715,300} = 62.7\%$$

$$\frac{\text{Tennis net sales}}{\text{Total net sales}} = \frac{\$640,300}{\$1,715,300} = 37.3\%$$

The total store clerks' wages expense is divided between the departments as follows:

		GOLF	TENNIS	TOTAL
Direct expense		$36,000	$15,250	$51,250
Indirect expense allocation:				
%	Total expense			
62.7% ×	$29,000	18,183		18,183
37.3% ×	$29,000		10,817	10,817
		$54,183	$26,067	$80,250

Truck Drivers' Wages Expenses. Annie's employs three delivery truck drivers, one of whom delivers only golf equipment. Their wages are as follows:

DRIVER NUMBER	PRODUCT DELIVERED	WAGES	
1	Golf	$29,000	
2	Both	26,500 }	
3	Both	28,400 }	$54,900
Total		$83,900	

> *Other reasonable bases for allocating the drivers' wages might be the cost of the equipment delivered or the number of units delivered.*

Wages of the driver who delivers only golf equipment ($29,000) are assigned to that department. Wages of the other two drivers ($54,900) are allocated based on the relative dollar amount of golf and tennis equipment delivered by the drivers. Shipping and delivery records are used to estimate the percentages as approximately 70% golf and 30% tennis. The total drivers' wages expense is divided between the departments as follows:

		GOLF	TENNIS	TOTAL
Direct expense		$29,000		$29,000
Indirect expense allocation:				
% × Total expense				
70% × $54,900		38,430		38,430
30% × $54,900			$16,470	16,470
		$67,430	$16,470	$83,900

Advertising Expense. Annie's total advertising expense is $79,500: $45,000 for newspaper advertising and $34,500 for radio. Newspaper advertising is classified as golf, tennis, or "mixed" based on the number of inches of copy space. The $45,000 of newspaper advertising is $17,000 for golf, $12,000 for tennis, and $16,000 mixed. All radio advertising is classified as mixed. The total mixed expense for advertising of $50,500 ($16,000 + $34,500) is allocated between departments based on the percentage of total net sales represented by each department. These percentages are 62.7% golf and 37.3% tennis, as calculated for store clerks' wages expense. The total advertising expense is divided between the departments as follows:

		GOLF	TENNIS	TOTAL
Direct expense		$17,000	$12,000	$29,000
Indirect expense allocation:				
% × Total expense				
62.7% × $50,500		31,664		31,664
37.3% × $50,500			18,836	18,836
		$48,664	$30,836	$79,500

Store Rent Expense. Annie's rents 5,000 square feet of store space for $22,800 per year. This entire expense is an indirect expense, allocated on the basis of the relative number of square feet of floor space occupied by each department. The golf department occupies 3,200 square feet, or 64% of the floor space. The tennis department occupies the remaining 36% of floor space. The rent expense is divided between the departments as follows:

	GOLF	TENNIS	TOTAL
Indirect expense allocation:			
% × Total expense			
64% × $22,800	$14,592		$14,592
36% × $22,800		$8,208	8,208
	$14,592	$8,208	$22,800

Bad Debt Expense. Annie's bad debt expense of $17,900 is treated as a direct expense. It is assigned to the departments based on experience with accounts written off. For the current year, $9,000 is assigned to golf and $8,900 to tennis.

Depreciation Expense—Delivery Equipment. Annie's has three delivery trucks, one of which is used to deliver only golf equipment. Total depreciation on the delivery equipment is $24,000 for the year, $9,000 of which relates to the golf delivery truck. The other $15,000 of depreciation is allocated on the basis of the relative dollar amount of golf and tennis equipment delivered with the other two trucks. These percentages are 70% golf and 30% tennis, as explained for the truck drivers' wages expense. The total depreciation expense on the delivery equipment is divided between the departments as follows:

	GOLF	TENNIS	TOTAL
Direct expense	$ 9,000		$ 9,000
Indirect expense allocation:			
% × Total expense			
70% × $15,000	10,500		10,500
30% × $15,000		$4,500	4,500
	$19,500	$4,500	$24,000

Other Operating Expenses. Annie's other operating expenses totaled $350,430. This total includes a broad range of expenses, from managers' salaries to postage expense. These expenses are assigned and allocated using methods like those used for the various expenses previously described. A summary of the amounts assigned and allocated for other operating expenses is as follows:

	GOLF	TENNIS	TOTAL
Direct expense	$ 84,420	$ 31,980	$116,400
Indirect expense allocation	159,380	74,650	234,030
	$243,800	$106,630	$350,430

Departmental Operating Expense Summary

The assignment and allocation of departmental operating expenses can be summarized in a **departmental operating expense summary**. The summary in Figure 27-3 shows the following:

1. Classification of each operating expense as direct or indirect

2. Amount assigned or allocated to each department

3. Total operating expenses for each department

Annie's Sporting Goods
Departmental Operating Expense Summary
For Year Ended December 31, 20--

	TOTAL	GOLF DIRECT	GOLF INDIRECT	GOLF TOTAL	TENNIS DIRECT	TENNIS INDIRECT	TENNIS TOTAL
Store clerks' wages expense	$ 80 2 5 0 00	$ 36 0 0 0 00	$ 18 1 8 3 00	$ 54 1 8 3 00	$15 2 5 0 00	$ 10 8 1 7 00	$ 26 0 6 7 00
Truck drivers' wages expense	83 9 0 0 00	29 0 0 0 00	38 4 3 0 00	67 4 3 0 00		16 4 7 0 00	16 4 7 0 00
Advertising expense	79 5 0 0 00	17 0 0 0 00	31 6 6 4 00	48 6 6 4 00	12 0 0 0 00	18 8 3 6 00	30 8 3 6 00
Store rent expense	22 8 0 0 00		14 5 9 2 00	14 5 9 2 00		8 2 0 8 00	8 2 0 8 00
Bad debt expense	17 9 0 0 00	9 0 0 0 00		9 0 0 0 00	8 9 0 0 00		8 9 0 0 00
Depreciation expense—delivery equipment	24 0 0 0 00	9 0 0 0 00	10 5 0 0 00	19 5 0 0 00		4 5 0 0 00	4 5 0 0 00
Other operating expenses	350 4 3 0 00	84 4 2 0 00	159 3 8 0 00	243 8 0 0 00	31 9 8 0 00	74 6 5 0 00	106 6 3 0 00
Total	$658 7 8 0 00	$184 4 2 0 00	$272 7 4 9 00	$457 1 6 9 00	$68 1 3 0 00	$133 4 8 1 00	$201 6 1 1 00

FIGURE 27-3 Departmental Operating Expense Summary

Departmental Income Statement Showing Operating Income

Figure 27-4 shows Annie's departmental income statement for the year 20--, with operating income by department and in total. Operating expense data on the statement were obtained from the departmental operating expense summary in Figure 27-3.

Compare this income statement with the one in Figure 27-1. Notice that the departmental gross profit, total operating expenses, and total operating income are the same in both statements. The difference is that Figure 27-4 shows operating expenses and operating income for each department.

Annie's Sporting Goods
Income Statement
For Year Ended December 31, 20 - -

	GOLF	TENNIS	TOTAL
Net sales	$1,075 0 0 0 00	$640 3 0 0 00	$1,715 3 0 0 00
Cost of goods sold	545 2 8 0 00	420 9 0 0 00	$ 966 1 8 0 00
Gross profit	$ 529 7 2 0 00	$219 4 0 0 00	$ 749 1 2 0 00
Operating expenses:			
Store clerks' wages expense	$ 54 1 8 3 00	$ 26 0 6 7 00	$ 80 2 5 0 00
Truck drivers' wages expense	67 4 3 0 00	16 4 7 0 00	83 9 0 0 00
Advertising expense	48 6 6 4 00	30 8 3 6 00	79 5 0 0 00
Store rent expense	14 5 9 2 00	8 2 0 8 00	22 8 0 0 00
Bad debt expense	9 0 0 0 00	8 9 0 0 00	17 9 0 0 00
Depreciated expense—delivery equipment	19 5 0 0 00	4 5 0 0 00	24 0 0 0 00
Other operating expenses	243 8 0 0 00	106 6 3 0 00	350 4 3 0 00
Total operating expenses	$ 457 1 6 9 00	$201 6 1 1 00	$ 658 7 8 0 00
Operating income	$ 72 5 5 1 00	$ 17 7 8 9 00	$ 90 3 4 0 00

FIGURE 27-4 Departmental Income Statement Showing Operating Income

Management can use this income statement to evaluate the overall perform-ance of the two departments. For example, the income statement shows that the operating income and operating income percentage of the golf department are much higher than those of the tennis department.

Golf department operating income percentage: **6.7%**
($72,551 ÷ $1,075,000)

Tennis department operating income percentage: **2.8%**
($17,789 ÷ $640,300)

Remember, however, that the golf department's gross profit and gross profit percentage are much higher than those of the tennis department. The golf department's operating income might be higher simply because the gross profit is higher. Further analysis shows that this is the case. As shown below, the operating expense percentage is lower for the tennis department than for the golf department.

		Golf	**Tennis**
Operating expenses	=	$457,169	$201,611
Net sales		$1,075,000	$640,300
Operating expense percentage		42.5%	31.5%

Management must be cautious in interpreting departmental operating income results. Most of Annie's operating expenses for both departments are indirect. They therefore are allocated between departments based on estimates. Indirect expenses, by definition, are incurred for the benefit of the business as a whole and cannot be traced directly to any department. Thus, the departments have no control over such expenses. Further, it might be possible to reduce some indirect expenses by eliminating a department, but most of these expenses would continue to be incurred. Many accountants argue that to properly evaluate departmental performance, an income measure should be used that considers only the direct expenses of each department.

A BROADER VIEW

The Supply Chain—Reaching Beyond Your Department or Business

Businesses face increasing demands from their customers for higher quality, faster service, and lower costs. One way companies are responding to these demands is through supply-chain management. The supply chain includes all of the purchasing, production, storage, delivery, and sales functions across a set of businesses. Supply-chain management requires focusing on the entire supply chain across businesses instead of just on one's own department or business. By coordinating and participating with other companies, all partners in the chain can operate more efficiently. These arrangements can lead to some new challenges in measuring department performance.

©JEFF ZARUBA/CORBIS

DEPARTMENTAL DIRECT OPERATING MARGIN

LO4 Describe and compute departmental direct operating margin.

Departmental direct operating margin is the difference between a department's gross profit and its direct operating expenses. To compute departmental direct operating margin, the elements of gross profit and the direct operating expenses are needed for each department. For Annie's, this information was developed in the previous section. We can use it to prepare a departmental income statement showing departmental direct operating margin. The information in the departmental operating expense summary (Figure 27-3) and in the income statement (Figure 27-4) simply needs to be reorganized.

Annie's income statement for the year 20--, showing departmental direct operating margins, appears in Figure 27-5. To determine the departmental direct operating margins, the direct operating expenses listed in the departmental operating expense summary (Figure 27-3) are subtracted from the departmental gross profits.

Departmental Gross Profit – Direct Operating Expenses = Direct Operating Margin

Indirect expenses are then subtracted from the total direct operating margin to calculate total operating income. Note that the indirect expenses that are separated by department in the departmental operating expense summary (Figure 27-3) are combined in Figure 27-5. Indirect expenses are not allocated to specific departments in preparing this departmental income statement.

Annie's Sporting Goods Income Statement For Year Ended December 31, 20 - -	GOLF	TENNIS	TOTAL
Net sales	$1,075 0 0 0 00	$640 3 0 0 00	$1,715 3 0 0 00
Cost of goods sold	545 2 8 0 00	420 9 0 0 00	966 1 8 0 00
Gross profit	$ 529 7 2 0 00	$219 4 0 0 00	$ 749 1 2 0 00
Direct operating expenses:			
Store clerks' wages expense	$ 36 0 0 0 00	$ 15 2 5 0 00	$ 51 2 5 0 00
Truck drivers' wages expense	29 0 0 0 00		29 0 0 0 00
Advertising expense	17 0 0 0 00	12 0 0 0 00	29 0 0 0 00
Bad debt expense	9 0 0 0 00	8 9 0 0 00	17 9 0 0 00
Depreciation expense—delivery equipment	9 0 0 0 00		9 0 0 0 00
Other operating expenses	84 4 2 0 00	31 9 8 0 00	116 4 0 0 00
Total direct operating expenses	$ 184 4 2 0 00	$ 68 1 3 0 00	$ 252 5 5 0 00
Departmental direct operating margin	$ 345 3 0 0 00	$151 2 7 0 00	$ 496 5 7 0 00
Indirect operating expenses:			
Store clerks' wages expense			$ 29 0 0 0 00
Truck drivers' wages expense			54 9 0 0 00
Advertising expense			50 5 0 0 00
Store rent expense			22 8 0 0 00
Depreciation expense—delivery equipment			15 0 0 0 00
Other operating expenses			234 0 3 0 00
Total indirect operating expenses			$ 406 2 3 0 00
Operating income			$ 90 3 4 0 00

FIGURE 27-5 Departmental Income Statement Showing Direct Operating Margin

In Figure 27-5:
Total direct
   operating
   expenses $252,550
Total indirect
   operating
   expenses   406,230
Total operating
   expenses $658,780

Compare this income statement with the one in Figure 27-4. Notice that the departmental gross profit ($529,720 and $219,400), total operating expenses ($252,550 + 406,230 = $658,780), and total operating income ($90,340) are the same in each statement. The key difference between the statements is that only direct operating expenses are split between departments in Figure 27-5. This permits calculation of the direct operating margin for each department.

Interpretation and Use of Direct Operating Margin

Management can use this form of income statement in several ways.

1. To evaluate departmental performance.

2. To determine the contribution a department makes to the overall operating income of the company.

3. To decide whether to discontinue a department.

Performance Evaluation. Recall that direct expenses are operating expenses that are traceable directly to a specific department. Departmental direct operating margin is calculated by subtracting only direct operating expenses from departmental gross profit. Thus, direct operating margin can be used to evaluate a department on the basis of only those expenses that it can control and for which it is directly responsible. The income statement in Figure 27-5 shows that the golf department's direct operating margin percentage is higher than that of the tennis department.

Golf department direct operating margin percentage: ($345,300 ÷ $1,075,000)	**32.1%**
Tennis department direct operating margin percentage: ($151,270 ÷ $640,300)	**23.6%**

LEARNING KEY: Direct operating margin is a performance measure that focuses on the revenues and expenses that a department can control.

Further analysis, however, shows that this is the case only because of the golf department's higher gross profit. In fact, the tennis department is controlling direct operating expenses more effectively than the golf department. The tennis department's direct operating expenses are only 10.6% ($68,130 ÷ $640,300) of net sales. The golf department's direct operating expenses are 17.2% ($184,420 ÷ $1,075,000) of net sales.

Contribution to Overall Operating Income. Departmental direct operating margin also shows a department's contribution to the company's overall operating income. The conventional operating income in Figure 27-4 implies that the tennis department contributes only $17,789 to overall profits. In contrast, the departmental direct operating margin in Figure 27-5 shows that the tennis department contributes $151,270. This amount is available to cover the company's indirect operating expenses and operating income.

It can be difficult to determine which expenses will change if a department is discontinued. Part of the plan to discontinue a department might be

to expand in some other area. The effects of other changes on departmental expenses must be considered.

Decision to Discontinue. A third possible use of the departmental direct operating margin data is in deciding whether to discontinue a department. In making this decision, management must focus on the revenues and expenses that will be eliminated if a department is discontinued. This means focusing on departmental direct operating margin, not on operating income. Remember that the indirect expenses that are subtracted in calculating conventional operating income are expenses incurred for the business as a whole. Unless management can reduce these expenses by eliminating a department, such expenses will be incurred even if a department is discontinued.

To illustrate, assume that R & R Co. is deciding whether to discontinue one of its three departments. Operating results for the current year for each department, for the business as a whole, and for departments A and B only are shown in Figure 27-6.

	DEPARTMENT A	DEPARTMENT B	DEPARTMENT C	TOTAL	DEPARTMENTS A & B ONLY
Net sales	$210 0 0 0 00	$185 0 0 0 00	$170 0 0 0 00	$565 0 0 0 00	$395 0 0 0 00
Cost of goods sold	115 0 0 0 00	110 0 0 0 00	96 0 0 0 00	321 0 0 0 00	225 0 0 0 00
Gross margin	$ 95 0 0 0 00	$ 75 0 0 0 00	$ 74 0 0 0 00	$244 0 0 0 00	$170 0 0 0 00
Direct operating expenses	55 0 0 0 00	45 0 0 0 00	54 0 0 0 00	154 0 0 0 00	100 0 0 0 00
Departmental direct operating margin	$ 40 0 0 0 00	$ 30 0 0 0 00	$ 20 0 0 0 00	$ 90 0 0 0 00	$ 70 0 0 0 00
Indirect operating expenses	27 0 0 0 00	22 0 0 0 00	25 0 0 0 00	74 0 0 0 00	74 0 0 0 00
Operating income (loss)	$ 13 0 0 0 00	$ 8 0 0 0 00	$ (5 0 0 0 00)	$ 16 0 0 0 00	$ (4 0 0 0 00)

FIGURE 27-6 R & R Company

Operating income results show that Department C is operating at a $5,000 loss. However, eliminating Department C would actually reduce rather than increase R & R's total operating income, as shown in the last column for departments A and B only. This reduction in operating income would occur because Department C's direct operating margin is $20,000. This $20,000 is available to cover the indirect operating expenses and add to the operating income of the firm. If Department C is eliminated, the remaining departments must absorb the indirect operating expenses of $25,000 allocated to Department C. Thus, the schedule lists indirect operating expenses as $74,000 both in the total column and in the Departments A and B only column.

Note in Figure 27-6 that the difference between the total operating income of $16,000 and the operating loss of $4,000 for departments A and B only is $20,000. This $20,000 is Department C's departmental direct operating margin. This amount would be lost if the department were eliminated. In general, if a department has a positive departmental direct operating margin, it should not be discontinued. The only exception would be when management has a plan to reduce indirect expenses by at least the amount of that department's direct operating margin.

LEARNING KEY: If a department has a positive direct operating margin, it usually should not be discontinued.

Learning Objectives	Key Points to Remember
1 **Explain the nature and purpose of departmental accounting.**	Departmental reports provide information about the revenues and expenses of each department. These reports are useful to management for planning, control, and performance evaluation.
2 **Describe and compute departmental gross profit.**	Departmental gross profit is the difference between a department's net sales and cost of goods sold. A departmental income statement showing gross profit can help management identify problems with both the sales prices and purchase prices of its products.
3 **Describe and compute departmental operating income.**	Departmental operating income is the difference between a department's gross profit and its operating expenses. Departmental operating expenses are either direct or indirect. Direct expenses are incurred for the sole benefit of a specific department. Indirect expenses are incurred for the benefit of the business as a whole.

Direct expenses are assigned to departments based on actual expenses incurred. Indirect expenses are allocated to departments on various reasonable bases. A departmental income statement showing departmental operating income permits evaluation of both the gross profit and operating expense performance of a department. |
| 4 **Describe and compute departmental direct operating margin.** | Departmental direct operating margin is the difference between a department's gross profit and its direct operating expenses. A departmental income statement showing departmental direct operating margin focuses attention on revenues and expenses under the control of a department manager. Such a statement can be very useful for performance evaluation, evaluating contribution to overall operating income, and deciding whether to discontinue a department. |

REFLECTION

Reflection: Answering the Opening Questions

Three measures of departmental profitability can be prepared for Finny Co.: gross profit, operating income, and direct operating margin. Gross profit must be carefully interpreted because it measures the excess of net sales over cost of goods sold, but not the overall profitability of a department. Departmental operating income measures overall profitability but includes indirect expenses that cannot be traced to specific departments and cannot be controlled by the departments. Estimates must be made to allocate the indirect expenses to different departments. Departmental direct operating margin focuses on only revenues and expenses under the control of a department manager. To compute direct operating margin, judgment is necessary to classify operating expenses as direct or indirect.

DEMONSTRATION PROBLEM

WebTUTOR Advantage

Kristen Owen and Stephen Kaplan are partners who own OK Cycling. They sell outdoor bicycles and exercise bicycles. They keep accounts and prepare reports on a departmental basis. Direct expenses are assigned and indirect expenses are allocated to departments by various means. Selected operating information for the year ended December 31, 20--, is as follows:

	Outdoor Bicycles	Exercise Bicycles
Net sales	$1,612,500	$1,150,600
Cost of goods sold	935,420	791,800
Direct operating expenses:		
Store clerks' wages expense	45,000	19,500
Truck drivers' wages expense	26,000	10,000
Advertising expense	16,000	20,000
Depreciation expense—delivery equipment	12,000	0
Bad debt expense	12,000	11,700
Other operating expenses	92,080	44,840
Indirect operating expenses:		
Store clerks' wages expense	26,400	14,850
Truck drivers' wages expense	62,800	22,250
Advertising expense	48,200	20,500
Depreciation expense—delivery equipment	13,800	5,700
Store rent expense	21,600	14,400
Other operating expenses	197,360	111,190

REQUIRED

1. Prepare an income statement showing departmental operating income.

2. Prepare another income statement showing departmental and total direct operating margins.

3. For the first statement, determine which department has the higher operating income percentage.

4. For the second statement, determine which department has the higher direct operating margin percentage.

5. Which of the two measures is more meaningful for decision-making purposes? Why?

Solution

1.

OK Cycling
Income Statement
For Year Ended December 31, 20 - -

	OUTDOOR BICYCLES	EXERCISE BICYCLES	TOTAL
Net sales	$1,612,500.00	$1,150,600.00	$2,763,100.00
Cost of goods sold	935,420.00	791,800.00	1,727,220.00
Gross profit	$ 677,080.00	$ 358,800.00	$1,035,880.00
Operating expenses:			
Store clerks' wages expense	$ 71,400.00	$ 34,350.00	$ 105,750.00
Truck drivers' wages expense	88,800.00	32,250.00	121,050.00
Advertising expense	64,200.00	40,500.00	104,700.00
Depreciation expense—delivery equipment	25,800.00	5,700.00	31,500.00
Store rent expense	21,600.00	14,400.00	36,000.00
Bad debt expense	12,000.00	11,700.00	23,700.00
Other operating expenses	289,440.00	156,030.00	445,470.00
Total operating expenses	$ 573,240.00	$ 294,930.00	$ 868,170.00
Operating income	$ 103,840.00	$ 63,870.00	$ 167,710.00

2.

OK Cycling
Income Statement
For Year Ended December 31, 20 - -

	OUTDOOR BICYCLES	EXERCISE BICYCLES	TOTAL
Net sales	$1,612,500.00	$1,150,600.00	$2,763,100.00
Cost of goods sold	935,420.00	791,800.00	1,727,220.00
Gross profit	$ 677,080.00	$ 358,800.00	$1,035,880.00
Direct operating expenses:			
Store clerks' wages expense	$ 45,000.00	$ 19,500.00	$ 64,500.00
Truck drivers' wages expense	26,000.00	10,000.00	36,000.00
Advertising expense	16,000.00	20,000.00	36,000.00
Depreciation expense—delivery equipment	12,000.00	0.00	12,000.00
Bad debt expense	12,000.00	11,700.00	23,700.00
Other operating expenses	92,080.00	44,840.00	136,920.00
Total direct operating expenses	$ 203,080.00	$ 106,040.00	$ 309,120.00
Departmental direct operating margin	$ 474,000.00	$ 252,760.00	$ 726,760.00
Indirect operating expenses:			
Store clerks' wages expense			$ 41,250.00
Truck drivers' wages expense			85,050.00
Advertising expense			68,700.00
Depreciation expense—delivery equipment			19,500.00
Store rent expense			36,000.00
Other operating expenses			308,550.00
Total indirect operating expenses			$ 559,050.00
Operating income			$ 167,710.00

(continued)

3. Operating income percentage:

For outdoor bicycles:

$$\frac{\text{Operating Income}}{\text{Net Sales}} = \frac{\$103,840}{\$1,612,500} = 6.4\%$$

For exercise bicycles:

$$\frac{\text{Operating Income}}{\text{Net Sales}} = \frac{\$63,870}{\$1,150,600} = 5.6\%$$

Outdoor bicycles has the higher operating income percentage.

4. Direct operating margin percentage:

For outdoor bicycles:

$$\frac{\text{Direct Operating Margin}}{\text{Net Sales}} = \frac{\$474,000}{\$1,612,500} = 29.4\%$$

For exercise bicycles:

$$\frac{\text{Direct Operating Margin}}{\text{Net Sales}} = \frac{\$252,760}{\$1,150,600} = 22.0\%$$

Outdoor bicycles has the higher direct operating margin percentage.

5. Most accountants believe that the departmental direct operating margin is more meaningful for decision-making purposes than departmental operating income. This is because the direct operating margin takes into account only the direct expenses of operating each department, while departmental operating income is affected by various allocations of indirect operating expenses.

OK Cycling's results demonstrate the importance of the direct operating margin. The answers to requirements 3 and 4 clearly show that the exercise bicycle department is less profitable than the outdoor bicycle department. Yet, the exercise bicycle department is still making a major contribution to the business. Its operating income is $63,870. More importantly, its direct operating margin is $252,760. Without the exercise bicycle department, OK Cycling would be operating at a loss of $85,050 ($167,710, the present total operating income, minus $252,760, the exercise bicycle department's direct operating margin).

On-Line Learning Tools

For more information, visit: http://heintz.swlearning.com

The Heintz & Parry product web site is designed specifically for **COLLEGE ACCOUNTING, 18e.** The features include downloadable student resources and an interactive study center, organized by chapter, which contains learning objectives, web links, on-line quizzes with automatic feedback, and more.

KEY TERMS

departmental direct operating margin, (1026) The difference between a department's gross profit and its direct operating expenses.

departmental gross profit, (1019) The difference between a department's net sales and cost of goods sold.

departmental operating expense summary, (1023) A summary of the assignment and allocation of departmental operating expenses which shows the classification of each operating expense as direct or indirect, the amount assigned or allocated to each department, and total operating expenses for each department.

departmental operating income, (1020) The difference between a department's gross profit and its operating expenses.

direct expenses, (1020) Operating expenses that are incurred for the sole benefit of and are traceable directly to a specific department.

indirect expenses, (1020) Operating expenses that are incurred for the benefit of the business as a whole.

REVIEW QUESTIONS

(LO1)   1. For what purposes are departmental reports useful to management?

(LO2)   2. In what two ways can the information necessary to compute departmental gross profit be accumulated?

(LO2)   3. In what two ways can departmental operating expense data be accumulated?

(LO3)   4. What is the difference between direct and indirect operating expenses?

(LO3)   5. On what basis are direct expenses assigned to departments?

(LO3)   6. On what basis are indirect expenses allocated to departments?

(LO3)   7. What information is contained in a departmental operating expense summary?

(LO3)   8. Why must management be cautious in interpreting departmental operating income results?

(LO4)   9. Distinguish between departmental gross profit, departmental operating income, and departmental direct operating margin.

(LO4)   10. In what ways can an income statement showing departmental direct operating margin be used by management?

Self-Study Test Questions

True/False

1. Departmental gross profit is the difference between a department's net sales and operating expenses.

    _____

2. The gross profit percentage can be computed by dividing gross profit by net sales.

    _____

3. Departmental operating income is the difference between a department's gross profit and its operating expenses.

    _____

4. Direct expenses are operating expenses incurred for the benefit of the business as a whole and untraceable directly to a specific department.

    _____

5. Departmental direct operating margin is the difference between a department's gross profit and its direct operating expenses.

    _____

Multiple Choice

1. The difference between a department's net sales and cost of goods sold is called

    _____

    (a) departmental gross profit.   (c) departmental operating income.
    (b) departmental direct operating income.   (d) net income.

2. Operating expenses incurred for the sole benefit of and traceable directly to a specific department are called

    _____

    (a) budgeted expenses.   (c) indirect expenses.
    (b) normal expenses.   (d) direct expenses.

3. A base used in the text to allocate store rent expense to specific departments is

    _____

    (a) net sales.   (c) number of employees.
    (b) square footage.   (d) number of customers.

4. The difference between a department's gross profit and its direct operating expenses is called

    _____

    (a) departmental gross profit.   (c) departmental operating income.
    (b) departmental direct operating margin. (d) net income.

5. The difference between a department's gross profit and its operating expenses is called

    _____

    (a) departmental gross profit.   (c) departmental operating income.
    (b) departmental direct operating margin. (d) net income.

The answers to the Self-Study Test Questions are at the end of the text.

MANAGING YOUR WRITING

Two department heads are engaging in an argument. The head of department A argues that department A makes a greater contribution to profits, having produced a higher operating income for three years. The business probably would be better off if department B were discontinued. In fact, department income statements from the last three years show department A had higher operating income than department B. Department B had an operating loss in two of the three years.

Write a memo addressing two issues:

1. What are the proper accounting measures to use to determine which department is making a greater contribution to the profits of the business?

2. What are the proper accounting measures to use to decide whether to discontinue one of the departments?

ETHICS CASE

Melanie Sanders and Joyce O'Dell were department heads at Hobgood's Toy and Hobby Store. They had been friends for a long time. Mr. Hobgood, the owner of the store, let the department heads make all decisions relating to the store's operations. During the summer the Hobby Department usually had a higher gross profit, but during the holidays the Toy Department usually caught up. This year the Toy Department wasn't doing well at all mainly because a new discount toy store had opened less than a mile away. In early December Melanie, the Toy Department manager, asked Joyce if she would mind charging all the remaining year's advertising and shipping expenses to the Hobby Department. Melanie went on to explain that she was afraid Mr. Hobgood would get upset if he found out the Toy Department wasn't doing well during the last quarter. She said she had a plan for next year to earn more revenue but was vague on what it involved. Joyce knew the Hobby Department's year-to-date earnings were above average but she felt uncomfortable with what Melanie had asked her to do.

1. What is your reaction to Melanie's idea?

2. If Joyce decides to let Melanie charge all advertising and shipping expenses to the Hobby Department in December, what impact will it have on the financial statements?

3. Write a short paragraph stating both the short- and long-run implications of Melanie's idea.

4. In groups of three or four, make a list of some suggestions to help Hobgood's Toy and Hobby Store earn more revenue.

WEB WORK

Time Warner owns a vast array of cable networks, movie studios, publishers, and other businesses. The information about all of the businesses must be kept separately as well as viewed as one large unit. Look at Time Warner's annual report by visiting the Financial Information section of their homepage. Try to determine where most of their profit comes from. Visit the Interactive Study Center on our web site at **http://heintz.swlearning.com** for special hotlinks to assist you in this assignment.

SERIES A EXERCISES

EXERCISE 27-1A (LO2)
Gross profit, Running Shoes
Dept.: $12,600

GROSS PROFIT SECTION OF DEPARTMENTAL INCOME STATEMENT Bill Walters and Alice Jennings are partners in a business called Walters and Jennings Sportswear that sells athletic footwear. They have organized the business on a departmental basis as follows: Running Shoes, Walking Shoes, and Specialty Shoes. At the end of the first year of operation, the sales and cost of goods sold for the three departments are as follows:

	Running Shoes	Walking Shoes	Specialty Shoes
Sales	$36,000	$42,000	$12,000
Cost of goods sold	23,400	23,520	7,680

Prepare the gross profit section of a departmental income statement for the year ended December 31, 20--. Show the gross profit for each department and for the business in total.

EXERCISE 27-2A (LO3)
Rent expense, Dept. A: $5,216

ALLOCATING OPERATING EXPENSE—SQUARE FEET Wray Company rents 10,000 square feet of store space for $32,600 per year. The amount of square footage by department is as follows:

Department A:	1,600 sq. ft.
Department B:	2,200 sq. ft.
Department C:	3,800 sq. ft.
Department D:	2,400 sq. ft.

Allocate the annual rent expense among the four departments on the basis of relative square feet of floor space occupied.

EXERCISE 27-3A (LO3)
Advertising expense,
Deluxe: $7,200

ALLOCATING OPERATING EXPENSE—RELATIVE NET SALES Tina Domingo owns a car stereo store. She has divided her store into three departments. Net sales for the month of July are as follows:

Deluxe:	$36,000
Standard:	30,000
Economy:	54,000

Advertising expense for July was $24,000.

Allocate the advertising expense among the three departments on the basis of relative net sales.

EXERCISE 27-4A (LO3)
Truck expense, Dept. 1: $5,760

ALLOCATING OPERATING EXPENSE—MILES DRIVEN Mercado Lopez owns a furniture store that offers free delivery of merchandise delivered within the local area. Mileage records for the three sales departments are as follows:

Department 1:	36,000 miles
Department 2:	48,000 miles
Department 3:	16,000 miles

The cost of using the truck for the last year, including depreciation, was $16,000.

Allocate the cost of the truck among the three departments on the basis of miles driven.

EXERCISE 27-5A   (LO3)
Purchasing dept. expense,
West Division: $6,600

ALLOCATING OPERATING EXPENSE—PURCHASE ORDERS   The purchasing department of Brindley Company performs the purchasing function for the entire business. The numbers of purchase orders processed during the most recent month are as follows:

West Division: 33 purchase orders
East Division: 47 purchase orders
Central Division: 20 purchase orders

The monthly cost of operating the purchasing department, including personnel, was $20,000.

Allocate the cost of the purchasing department using the number of purchase orders processed as an allocation base.

EXERCISE 27-6A   (LO4)
Direct operating margin,
Dept. A: $48,000

DEPARTMENTAL DIRECT OPERATING MARGIN AND DIRECT OPERATING MARGIN PERCENTAGE The sales, gross profit, and condensed direct and indirect operating expenses of Departments A and B of Pan Fei International are as follows:

	Dept. A	Dept. B	Total
Sales	$200,000	$300,000	$500,000
Gross profit	70,000	140,000	210,000
Direct operating expenses	22,000	53,000	75,000
Indirect operating expenses			50,000

Compute the departmental direct operating margin and direct operating margin percentage for each department.

SERIES A PROBLEMS

PROBLEM 27-7A   (LO2/3)

2. Gross profit %,
Commercial Sales: 40%

INCOME STATEMENT WITH DEPARTMENTAL GROSS PROFIT AND OPERATING INCOME Thomas and Hill Distributors has divided its business into two departments: Commercial Sales and Industrial Sales. The following information is provided for the year ended December 31, 20--.

Net sales, Commercial Sales Department	$630,000
Net sales, Industrial Sales Department	470,000
Cost of goods sold, Commercial Sales Department	378,000
Cost of goods sold, Industrial Sales Department	188,000
Warehouse wages expense	99,400
Truck drivers' wages expense	88,200
Advertising expense	66,000
Warehouse lease expense	30,000
Depreciation expense—delivery equipment	11,000
Other operating expenses	115,000

REQUIRED

1. Prepare an income statement showing departmental gross profit and total operating income.

2. Calculate departmental gross profit percentages.

PROBLEM 27-8A   **(LO2/3)**
2. Operating income %,
Breads: 21.5%

INCOME STATEMENT WITH DEPARTMENTAL OPERATING INCOME AND TOTAL OPERATING INCOME Carmella Campillo owns a business called Campillo's Bakery. She has divided her business into two departments: Breads and Pastries. The following information is provided for the fiscal year ended June 30, 20--.

	Breads	Pastries
Net sales	$182,000	$98,000
Cost of goods sold	72,800	58,800
Wages expense	30,000	20,000
Advertising expense	16,000	4,000
Other operating expenses	24,000	10,000

REQUIRED

1. Prepare an income statement showing departmental operating income and total operating income.

2. Calculate departmental operating expense and operating income percentages.

PROBLEM 27-9A **(LO2/3/4)**
2. Direct operating margin %,
Commercial property: 15.4%

INCOME STATEMENT WITH DEPARTMENTAL DIRECT OPERATING MARGIN AND TOTAL OPERATING INCOME Durwood Thomas operates the business Thomas Security that sells security equipment for commercial property and residential homes. The following information is provided for the year ended December 31, 20--.

	Commercial Property	Residential Homes
Net sales	$465,000	$135,000
Cost of goods sold	279,250	54,000
Direct operating expenses:		
Advertising expense	35,000	20,000
Store clerks' wages expense	30,000	18,000
Truck drivers' wages expense	15,000	15,000
Bad debt expense	8,000	3,000
Depreciation expense—delivery equipment	6,000	4,000
Other operating expenses	20,000	10,000

Indirect operating expenses:	
Store clerks' wages expense	$10,000
Advertising expense	15,000
Store rent expense	20,000
Other operating expenses	10,000

REQUIRED

1. Prepare an income statement showing departmental direct operating margin and total operating income.

2. Calculate departmental direct operating margin percentages.

PROBLEM 27-10A   (LO4)
1. Operating income, Depts.
A & C only: $5,000

WHETHER TO DISCONTINUE A DEPARTMENT Williams and Lloyd Company is trying to decide whether to discontinue department B. Operating results for the year just ended for each of the company's three departments and for the entire operation are as follows:

	Dept. A	Dept. B	Dept. C	Total
Net sales	$380,000	$260,000	$290,000	$930,000
Cost of goods sold	210,000	140,000	160,000	510,000
Gross profit	$170,000	$120,000	$130,000	$420,000
Direct operating expenses	100,000	90,000	80,000	270,000
Departmental direct operating margin	$ 70,000	$ 30,000	$ 50,000	$150,000
Indirect operating expenses	40,000	35,000	40,000	115,000
Operating income (loss)	$ 30,000	$ (5,000)	$ 10,000	$ 35,000

REQUIRED

1. Prepare an additional column that combines departments A and C only.

2. Review all data and decide if department B should be discontinued. Defend your decision.

SERIES B EXERCISES

EXERCISE 27-1B   (LO2)
Gross profit, Letters
Dept.: $1,600

GROSS PROFIT SECTION OF DEPARTMENTAL INCOME STATEMENT Nicole Lawrence and Josh Doyle are partners in a business that sells cheerleading uniforms. They have organized the business, called L and D Uniforms, on a departmental basis as follows: Letters, Sweaters, and Skirts. At the end of the first year of operation, the sales and cost of goods sold for the three departments are as follows:

	Letters	Sweaters	Skirts
Sales	$3,000	$12,000	$8,000
Cost of goods sold	1,400	5,900	4,750

Prepare the gross profit section of a departmental income statement for the year ended December 31, 20--. Show the gross profit for each department and for the business in total.

EXERCISE 27-2B   (LO3)
Rent expense, Dept. A: $9,600

ALLOCATING OPERATING EXPENSE—SQUARE FEET Johnson Company rents 5,000 square feet of store space for $40,000 per year. The amount of square footage by department is as follows:

Department A:	1,200 sq. ft.
Department B:	1,400 sq. ft.
Department C:	1,500 sq. ft.
Department D:	900 sq. ft.

Allocate the annual rent expense among the four departments on the basis of relative square feet of floor space occupied.

EXERCISE 27-3B **(LO3)**
Advertising expense,
Football: $2,000

ALLOCATING OPERATING EXPENSE—RELATIVE NET SALES Amelia Diaz owns a sporting goods store. She has divided her store into three departments. Net sales for the month of July are as follows:

Football:	$10,000
Basketball:	6,000
Baseball:	9,000

Advertising expense for July was $5,000.

Allocate the advertising expense among the three departments on the basis of relative net sales.

EXERCISE 27-4B **(LO3)**
Truck expense, Dept. 1: $800

ALLOCATING OPERATING EXPENSE—MILES DRIVEN Herbert Quiong owns a furniture store that offers free delivery of merchandise delivered within the local area. Mileage records for the three sales departments are as follows:

Department 1:	4,000 miles
Department 2:	13,000 miles
Department 3:	8,000 miles

The cost of using the truck for the last year, including depreciation, was $5,000.

Allocate the cost of the truck among the three departments on the basis of miles driven.

EXERCISE 27-5B **(LO3)**
Purchasing dept. expense,
West Division: $8,700

ALLOCATING OPERATING EXPENSE—PURCHASE ORDERS The purchasing department of Stokes Company performs the purchasing function for the entire business. The numbers of purchase orders processed during the most recent month are as follows:

West Division:	29 purchase orders
East Division:	37 purchase orders
Central Division:	34 purchase orders

The monthly cost of operating the purchasing department, including personnel, was $30,000.

Allocate the cost of the purchasing department using the number of purchase orders processed as an allocation base.

EXERCISE 27-6B **(LO4)**
Direct operatng margin,
Dept. A: $75,000

DEPARTMENTAL DIRECT OPERATING MARGIN AND DIRECT OPERATING MARGIN PERCENTAGE The sales, gross profit, and condensed direct and indirect operating expenses of Departments A and B of Robin Sun Enterprises are as follows:

	Dept. A	Dept. B	Total
Sales	$300,000	$400,000	$700,000
Gross profit	110,000	180,000	290,000
Direct operating expenses	35,000	72,000	107,000
Indirect operating expenses			78,000

Compute the departmental direct operating margin and direct operating margin percentage for each department.

SERIES B PROBLEMS

PROBLEM 27-7B   **(LO2/3)**

2. Gross profit %,
Retail Sales: 44%

INCOME STATEMENT WITH DEPARTMENTAL GROSS PROFIT AND OPERATING INCOME Bacon and Hand Distributors has divided its business into two departments: Retail Sales and Wholesale Sales. The following information is provided for the year ended December 31, 20--.

Net sales, Retail Sales Department	$570,000
Net sales, Wholesale Sales Department	830,000
Cost of goods sold, Retail Sales Department	319,200
Cost of goods sold, Wholesale Sales Department	398,400
Warehouse wages expense	110,000
Truck drivers' wages expense	90,500
Advertising expense	70,000
Warehouse lease expense	40,000
Depreciation expense—delivery equipment	12,000
Other operating expenses	130,000

REQUIRED

1. Prepare an income statement showing departmental gross profit and total operating income.

2. Calculate departmental gross profit percentages.

PROBLEM 27-8B   **(LO2/3)**

2. Operating income %,
Domestic Yarn: 10.5%

INCOME STATEMENT WITH DEPARTMENTAL OPERATING INCOME AND TOTAL OPERATING INCOME Sonya McDowell owns a business called The Knitting Chamber. She has divided her business into two departments: Domestic Yarn and International Yarn. The following information is provided for the fiscal year ended June 30, 20--.

	Domestic Yarn	International Yarn
Net sales	$60,000	$40,000
Cost of goods sold	37,200	28,000
Wages expense	10,000	5,000
Advertising expense	2,500	1,500
Other operating expenses	4,000	1,000

REQUIRED

1. Prepare an income statement showing departmental operating income and total operating income.

2. Calculate departmental operating expense and operating income percentages.

PROBLEM 27-9B (LO2/3/4)
2. Direct operating margin %,
Furniture: 7.2%

INCOME STATEMENT WITH DEPARTMENTAL DIRECT OPERATING MARGIN AND TOTAL OPERATING INCOME Tom Peterson owns the business Peterson's Furniture and Appliances. The following information is provided for the year ended December 31, 20--.

	Furniture Department	Appliance Department
Net sales	$390,000	$810,000
Cost of goods sold	234,000	405,000
Direct operating expenses:		
Advertising expense	30,000	60,000
Store clerks' wages expense	40,000	90,000
Truck drivers' wages expense	35,000	65,000
Bad debt expense	4,000	9,000
Depreciation expense—delivery equipment	4,000	8,000
Other operating expenses	15,000	50,000
Indirect operating expenses:		
Store clerks' wages expense	$20,000	
Advertising expense	15,000	
Store rent expense	50,000	
Other operating expenses	25,000	

REQUIRED

1. Prepare an income statement showing departmental direct operating margin and total operating income.

2. Calculate departmental direct operating margin percentages.

PROBLEM 27-10B   (LO4)
1. Operating income, Depts.
B & C only: $20,000

WHETHER TO DISCONTINUE A DEPARTMENT Mueller and Kenington Company is trying to decide whether to discontinue department A. Operating results for the year just ended for each of the company's three departments and for the entire operation are as follows:

	Dept. A	Dept. B	Dept. C	Total
Net sales	$680,000	$730,000	$690,000	$2,100,000
Cost of goods sold	400,000	380,000	360,000	1,140,000
Gross profit	$280,000	$350,000	$330,000	$960,000
Direct operating expenses	230,000	240,000	210,000	680,000
Departmental direct operating margin	$ 50,000	$110,000	$120,000	$280,000
Indirect operating expenses	70,000	70,000	70,000	210,000
Operating income (loss)	$ (20,000)	$ 40,000	$ 50,000	$ 70,000

REQUIRED

1. Prepare an additional column that combines departments B and C only.

2. Review all data and decide if department A should be discontinued. Defend your decision.

MASTERY PROBLEM

2b. Direct operating margin %, Grocery: 11%

Bob's Acme Supermarket has been in operation for many years offering high-quality groceries, produce, and meat at reasonable prices. Accounting records are maintained on a departmental basis with assignment of direct expenses and allocation of indirect expenses through the use of various procedures. Selected operating information for the year ended December 31, 20--, is as follows:

	Grocery	Meat	Produce	Total
Net sales	$2,104,890	$660,500	$345,800	$3,111,190
Cost of goods sold	1,683,912	462,350	207,480	2,353,742
Direct operating expenses:				
Store clerks' wages expense	125,000	58,000	38,500	221,500
Advertising expense	25,000	38,500	18,400	81,900
Depreciation expense—				
store equipment	10,800	15,000	12,000	37,800
Other operating expenses	28,200	28,540	35,600	92,340
Indirect operating expenses:				
Store clerks' wages expense	12,000	5,000	4,000	21,000
Advertising expense	7,000	2,000	1,000	10,000
Depreciation expense—				
store equipment	35,000	10,000	5,000	50,000
Store rent	60,000	20,000	20,000	100,000
Other operating expenses	25,500	4,500	18,450	48,450

REQUIRED

1. a. Prepare an income statement showing departmental operating income.

   b. Compute the gross profit percentage and operating income percentage for each department.

2. a. Prepare an income statement showing departmental and total direct operating margins.

   b. Compute the departmental direct operating margin percentage for each department.

3. Should Bob be concerned about the profitability of the three departments? Should any of the departments be discontinued?

CHALLENGE PROBLEM

This problem challenges you to apply your cumulative accounting knowledge to move a step beyond the material in the chapter.

Total operating income, Depts. A, B & D: $60,250

The results of the operating activities of Kobe Co. for the current year are as follows:

	Dept. A	Dept. B	Dept. C	Total
Net sales	$590,000	$735,000	$450,000	$1,775,000
Cost of goods sold	365,000	545,750	267,000	1,177,750
Gross margin	$225,000	$189,250	$183,000	$ 597,250
Direct operating expenses	127,000	97,000	209,000	433,000
Direct operating margin	$ 98,000	$ 92,250	$ (26,000)	$ 164,250
Indirect operating expenses	61,000	52,000	20,000	133,000
Operating income (loss)	$ 37,000	$ 40,250	$ (46,000)	$ 31,250

(continued)

Based on these results, Kobe is considering discontinuing Department C and establishing a new Department D. The estimated revenues and expenses of the new department are as follows:

	Dept. D
Net sales	$480,000
Cost of goods sold	270,000
Direct operating expenses	185,000

In addition, the proposed change will cause total indirect operating expenses to increase by $22,000.

REQUIRED

Determine whether Kobe should discontinue Department C and establish Department D.

©GETTY IMAGES/PHOTODISC

Manufacturing Accounting:
The Job Order Cost System

Finny Co. has obtained a large order to produce a complete set of string instruments for a high school music department. All instruments would have the same face and the school's initials on the neck. Mike Finbar is pleased with this new type of business but is not sure how to estimate the cost for a special order like this. His accountant says a job order cost system ought to work. A few estimates will be necessary, but the basic idea is simply to accumulate the costs of manufacturing that specific order of instruments. Mike is encouraged by his accountant's reaction, but he still has several questions. Exactly what is a job order cost system? What manufacturing costs should be accumulated? What estimates will be necessary?

Careful study of this chapter should enable you to:

LO1 Describe the three manufacturing costs.

LO2 Describe the three inventories of a manufacturing business.

LO3 Describe and illustrate how manufacturing costs and inventories affect the financial statements of a manufacturing business.

LO4 Define and describe how to operate a job order cost accounting system.

LO5 Describe a process cost accounting system.

In the final two chapters of this book, we will study how to account for a manufacturing business. From an accounting standpoint, the key difference between a manufacturing and a merchandising business involves inventory. The manufacturer makes the items it sells; the merchandiser purchases inventory in final form for resale. This makes accounting for a manufacturer more complicated. Special cost accounting systems are needed to accumulate the costs of manufacturing the products. Multiple inventory accounts must be kept. Both the income statement and balance sheet are affected by these accounting changes.

MANUFACTURING COSTS

LO1 Describe the three manufacturing costs.

The costs incurred to manufacture a product can be classified into three primary elements of manufacturing cost:

1. Materials

2. Labor

3. Factory overhead

As illustrated in Figure 28-1, these costs come together in a conversion process that produces completed products, commonly called finished goods.

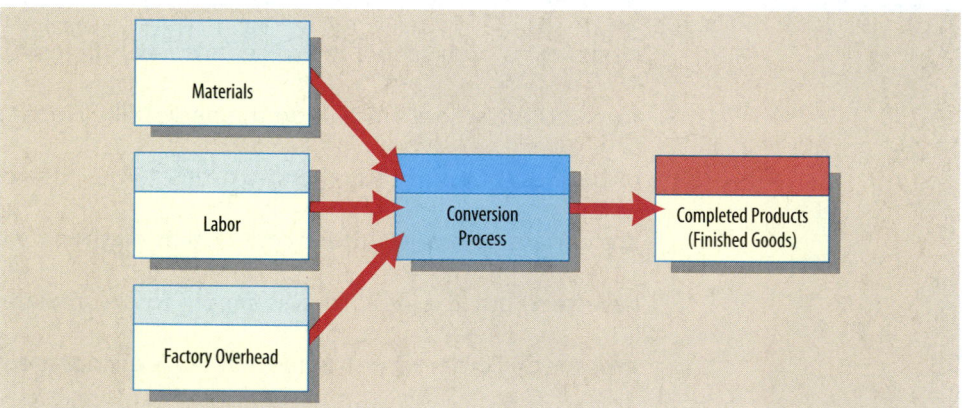

FIGURE 28-1 The Manufacturing Process

Materials

Various materials are needed to manufacture a product. A manufacturer of automobiles requires items such as sheet metal, bar steel, plastic, fabric, and tires. A manufacturer of electric guitars requires wood, plastic, electrical wire, magnets, nuts, and screws. In many instances, the only distinction between materials and finished goods is their relationship to a particular manufacturer. The finished goods of one manufacturer may be the materials of another. For example, flour is finished goods to a miller but materials to a baker. Similarly, silver may be finished goods to a mining company but materials to a manufacturer of silverware. Materials used in manufacturing are classified as:

1. Direct materials

2. Indirect materials

Direct materials enter into and become a major part of the finished product. Thus, the leather and linings used in the manufacture of shoes are direct materials. Similarly, the sheet metal, bar steel, fabric, and many other materials used in the manufacture of an automobile are direct materials.

Indirect materials are used in the manufacturing process but do not become a major part of the finished product. Thus, oil and grease used in the operation of machinery are indirect materials. Such materials are often called **factory supplies**. Indirect materials also may include inexpensive items such as nails, screws, and washers. These items may become a part of the finished product, but their small cost is most easily accounted for as part of indirect materials.

Labor

Wages and salaries paid to factory workers and supervisors are part of the cost of manufacturing a product. These wages and salaries are classified as:

1. Direct labor

2. Indirect labor

Direct labor includes the wages of employees who are directly involved in converting materials into finished goods. Such workers may do assembly work or operate factory machinery. These wages are charged directly to the cost of the products being manufactured.

Indirect labor includes the wages and salaries of employees who devote their time to supervision or to work of a general nature. Such workers may include superintendents, inspectors, timekeepers, receiving clerks, and janitors. The costs of these employees cannot be charged directly to the cost of the products being manufactured. They must be included in the indirect costs of the factory operation.

Factory Overhead

All manufacturing costs other than direct materials and direct labor are classified as **factory overhead**. This group of costs is sometimes described as **manufacturing overhead**, **indirect manufacturing cost**, or **factory burden**. Factory overhead consists of:

1. Indirect materials

2. Indirect labor

3. Other factory overhead

Indirect materials and indirect labor have already been discussed. Other factory overhead includes a variety of items, such as:

- Depreciation of factory buildings and equipment
- Repairs to factory buildings and equipment
- Insurance on factory buildings and equipment
- Property taxes on factory buildings and equipment
- Heat, light, and power

INVENTORIES

LO2 Describe the three inventories of a manufacturing business.

In accounting for a merchandising business, we used only a single inventory account, Merchandise Inventory. Because a manufacturing business acquires materials in one form and converts them into a different form for final sale, we need three inventory accounts:

1. Materials Inventory

2. Work in Process Inventory

3. Finished Goods Inventory

Materials Inventory consists of the materials acquired to be used in production. This account includes both direct and indirect materials.

Work in Process Inventory consists of products on which work has been started but is not yet finished at the end of the accounting period. Materials, labor, and overhead costs of producing a product are accumulated in this account until the product is completed.

Finished Goods Inventory contains products that have been completed and are ready for sale. All materials, labor, and overhead costs of completed products are accumulated in this account until the products are sold.

Flow of Manufacturing Costs

The flow of the three manufacturing costs through the three inventory accounts is illustrated in Figure 28-2. The figure shows how direct materials and direct labor flow directly into Work in Process. Indirect materials and indirect labor become part of Factory Overhead, which flows into Work in Process.

 LEARNING KEY: Direct materials and direct labor go directly into Work in Process. Indirect materials and indirect labor go through Factory Overhead, and then into Work in Process.

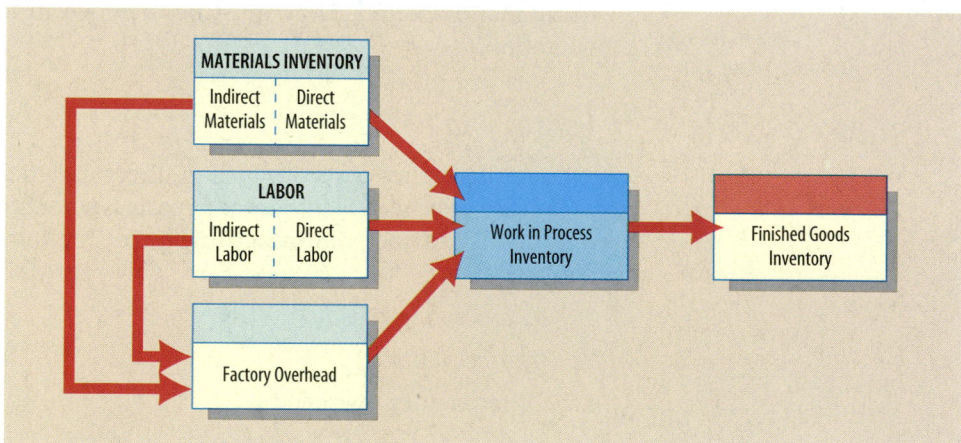

FIGURE 28-2 Flow of Manufacturing Costs

FINANCIAL STATEMENT EFFECTS

LO3 Describe and illustrate how manufacturing costs and inventories affect the financial statements of a manufacturing business.

The financial statements of a manufacturing business are very similar to those of a merchandiser. The main differences are in the cost of goods sold section of the income statement and the inventories on the balance sheet.

Income Statement

The key difference between the manufacturing and merchandising company income statements is highlighted in Figure 28-3. The purchases made by a merchandiser are the goods that eventually are sold. In contrast, the purchases made by a manufacturer are merely purchases of materials. The cost of manufacturing a product includes not only materials, but also labor and overhead. Thus, *cost of goods manufactured* on the manufacturer's income statement replaces *purchases* on the merchandiser's income statement.

MERCHANDISING COMPANY PARTIAL INCOME STATEMENT		MANUFACTURING COMPANY PARTIAL INCOME STATEMENT	
Cost of goods sold:		Cost of goods sold:	
Merchandise inventory, January 1, 20--	$10,000	Finished goods inventory, January 1, 20--	$10,000
Purchases	42,000	Cost of goods manufactured	42,000
Merchandise available for sale	$52,000	Goods available for sale	$52,000
Merchandise inventory, December 31, 20--	8,000	Finished goods inventory, December 31, 20--	8,000
Cost of goods sold	$44,000	Cost of goods sold	$44,000

FIGURE 28-3 Cost of Goods Sold Sections

The cost of goods sold section of the manufacturer's income statement is commonly supplemented by a schedule of cost of goods manufactured (see Figure 28-4). This schedule shows:

1 Beginning work in process.

2 Materials, labor, and overhead costs added to work in process during the period.

3 Ending work in process.

4 Cost of goods manufactured (cost of goods completed during the period).

1 Work in process, Jan. 1, 20--				$7,000 00
Materials inventory, Jan. 1, 20--	$3,000 00			
Materials purchases	15,000 00			
Materials available for use	$18,000 00			
Materials inventory, Dec. 31, 20--	2,500 00			
Cost of materials used		$15,500 00		
2 Direct labor		16,500 00		
Overhead		8,000 00		
Total manufacturing costs			40,000 00	
Total work in process during the period			$47,000 00	
3 Work in process, Dec. 31, 20--			5,000 00	
4 Cost of goods manufactured			$42,000 00	

FIGURE 28-4 Schedule of Cost of Goods Manufactured

The *cost of materials used* is calculated in the same way the cost of goods sold is calculated in a merchandiser's income statement. Beginning inventory of materials plus purchases equals materials available. This amount less the ending inventory of materials equals cost of materials used.

The cost of goods manufactured of $42,000 represents:

1 The amount *transferred out* of work in process during the period.

2 The amount *added to* finished goods during the period.

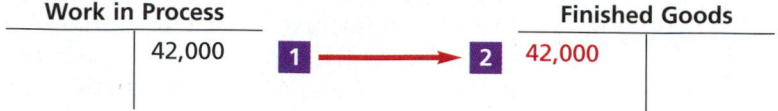

Balance Sheet

A manufacturer's balance sheet has three inventory accounts rather than the single merchandise inventory account used by a merchandiser. The current assets section of the manufacturer's balance sheet might appear as shown in Figure 28-5. The three inventories are listed in decreasing order of liquidity, with finished goods first and materials last.

Current assets:			
Cash			$17 0 0 0 00
Accounts receivable (net)			12 0 0 0 00
Inventories:			
Finished goods	$8 0 0 0 00		
Work in process	5 0 0 0 00		
Materials	2 5 0 0 00	15 5 0 0 00	
Supplies		2 3 0 0 00	
Total current assets			$46 8 0 0 00

FIGURE 28-5 Current Assets Section of Manufacturer's Balance Sheet

JOB ORDER COST ACCOUNTING

LO4 Define and describe how to operate a job order cost accounting system.

A **cost accounting system** is a system for accumulating detailed information about the cost of producing a product. Product cost information is needed for three purposes:

1. To assist in setting selling prices. A product's selling price must be sufficient to provide a gross profit and contribute to net income.

2. To assist in controlling production costs. If the actual costs of producing a product exceed the planned costs, management can take corrective action.

3. To assist in determining the net income or loss. When products are manufactured, the manufacturing costs must be accumulated to determine inventories, cost of goods sold, and net income or loss.

The two basic types of inventory cost accounting systems are:

1. Job order cost system.

2. Process cost system.

A **job order cost system** provides a separate record of the cost of producing each individual product or group of products. If products are made to customers' orders or in separately identifiable "lots" or "batches," a job order cost system is appropriate. A printing shop, custom cabinet maker, or consulting firm would use such a system.

A **process cost system** accumulates manufacturing costs by process, such as cutting, painting, or finishing. Each unit of product passing through the process during a period of time is assigned a share of the costs. A business that manufactures cement, chemicals, or flour would use such a system.

Perpetual Inventories

A cost accounting system uses perpetual inventories. To understand the journal entries and flow of information in a cost accounting system, we need to recall how a perpetual inventory system works.

A BROADER VIEW

Job Cost Systems— So Common You Find Them by Accident

Throughout this book we have seen the accounting side of many items we regularly encounter in our everyday lives: managing our checking account, deductions for taxes on our paychecks, purchases we make with our credit cards, and use of promissory notes to borrow money. In this chapter, we see yet another accounting item that is far more common than we probably realize—the job order cost system.

Presented to the right is Job Order #120898 used by City Chevrolet to repair Terry Garnet's car. If you ever had your car repaired or serviced, even something as minor as an oil change, you probably were a job order. In fact, any repairs or servicing of any kind—on TVs, computers, lawn tractors, etc.—usually are based on a job order system. You can see accounting issues almost everywhere. It is indeed an important language to learn.

Chapter 19 demonstrated how a perpetual inventory system works for a merchandising business. The merchandise inventory account is increased for each purchase and decreased for each sale.

A manufacturing business has three inventory accounts: Materials, Work in Process, and Finished Goods. This makes a manufacturing business' perpetual inventory system more complex than that of a merchandising business. The following four inventory movements and journal entries are illustrated in Figure 28-6.

INVENTORY MOVEMENTS		JOURNAL ENTRIES
1	Materials are purchased	Increase Materials
2	Materials are put into the manufacturing process	Decrease Materials Increase Work in Process
3	Product is completed	Decrease Work in Process Increase Finished Goods
4	Completed product is sold	Decrease Finished Goods Increase Cost of Goods Sold

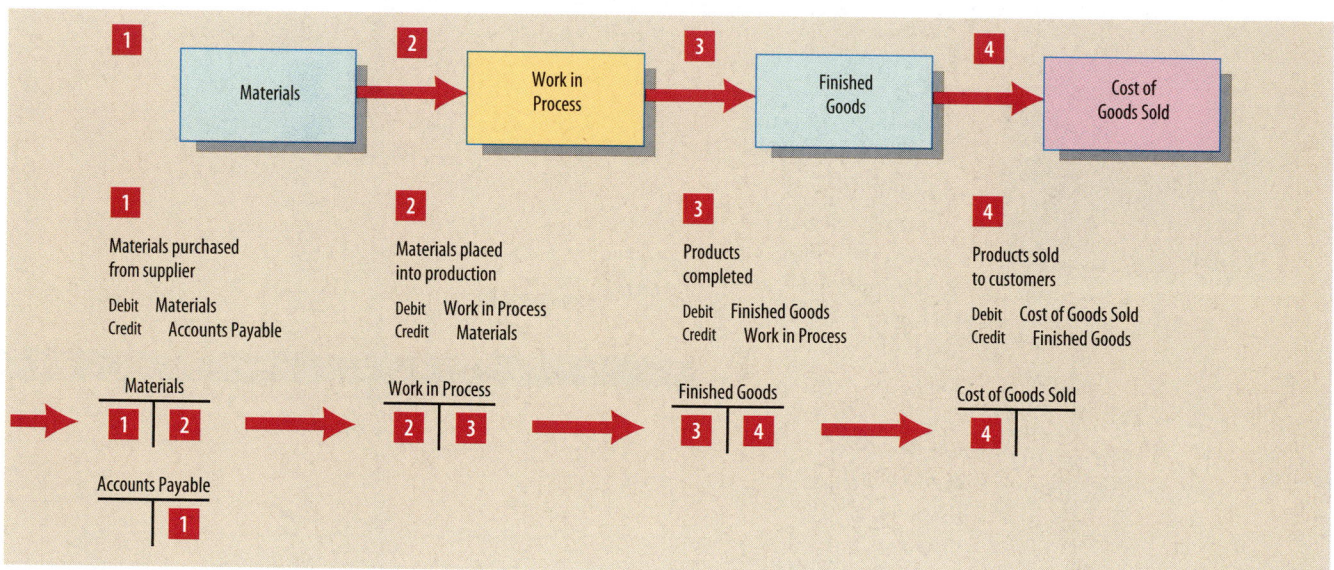

FIGURE 28-6 Flow of Costs Through Manufacturing Inventory Accounts

Accounting for Materials

When materials are purchased, their cost is debited to Materials. If materials costing $1,300 are purchased on account, the following journal entry is made.

4		Materials			1	3	0	0	00					4
5		Accounts Payable								1	3	0	0	00	5
6		Purchased materials on account													6

The materials account in the general ledger is a control account. A separate account for each type of material is kept in a subsidiary ledger called a **materials ledger** or **stores ledger**. Each subsidiary account shows the quantity and cost of the material received and issued and the resulting balance.

Materials are issued from the storeroom to production based on a form called a **materials requisition**. This form is both an authorization to the storekeeper to issue materials and a source document showing the movement of materials. Figure 28-7 illustrates one form of materials requisition. If these are direct materials, the following journal entry is made.

8	Work in Process (Job No. 319)	2 1 0 0 00		8
9	Materials		2 1 0 0 00	9
10	Issued direct materials to production			10

Note that the debit to Work in Process also indicates the job to which the materials are charged.

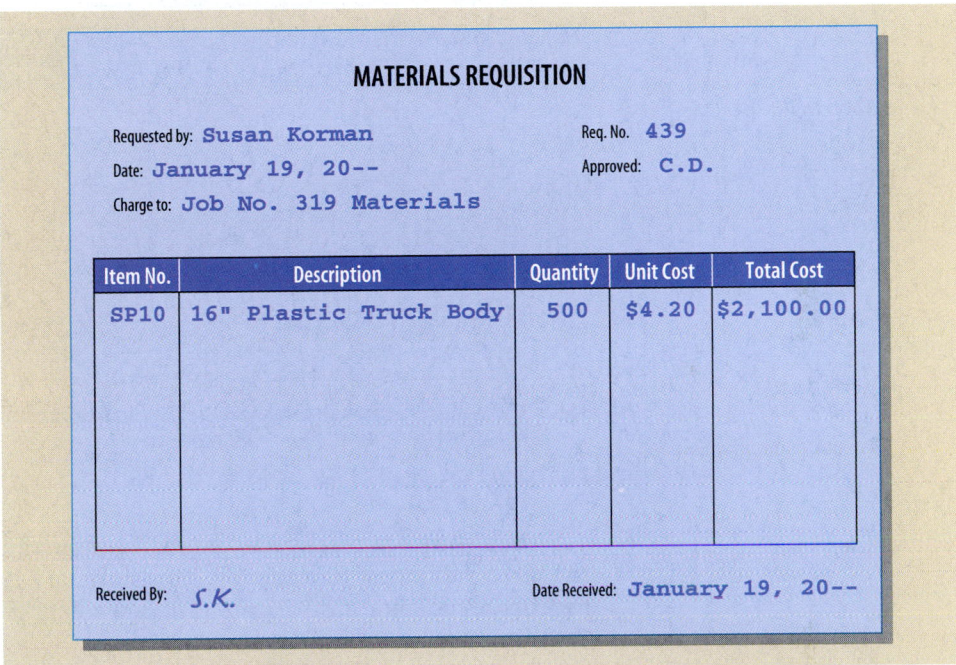

MATERIALS REQUISITION

Requested by: **Susan Korman**   Req. No. **439**

Date: **January 19, 20--**   Approved: **C.D.**

Charge to: **Job No. 319 Materials**

Item No.	Description	Quantity	Unit Cost	Total Cost
SP10	16" Plastic Truck Body	500	$4.20	$2,100.00

Received By: *S.K.*   Date Received: **January 19, 20--**

FIGURE 28-7 Materials Requisition

Materials requisitions also are used to issue indirect materials. Since indirect materials are part of overhead, the following journal entry is made to issue $250 of indirect materials to production.

13	Factory Overhead	2 5 0 00		13
14	Materials		2 5 0 00	14
15	Issued indirect materials to production			15

Notice that no job number is indicated for these overhead costs. This is because overhead costs relate to many different jobs. The application of these costs to specific jobs is illustrated later in the chapter.

Accounting for Labor

Chapter 8 showed how to account for employee earnings and payroll deductions. A job order cost accounting system uses the same procedures, except more detail is involved. The earnings of workers whose services are direct labor are charged to the jobs on which they worked. The earnings of workers whose services are indirect labor are charged to the proper factory overhead accounts. This requires keeping a record of the time worked and labor cost incurred on each job. One way of doing so is to require the direct labor employees to complete a **daily time sheet** or **time ticket** like the one in Figure 28-8.

In businesses with computer-based timekeeping systems, a record of time and labor costs on each job can be generated automatically. Employees' barcode time cards (Chapter 8, Figure 8-2) are inserted into a computer at their workstations. The labor costs are then distributed by the computer system.

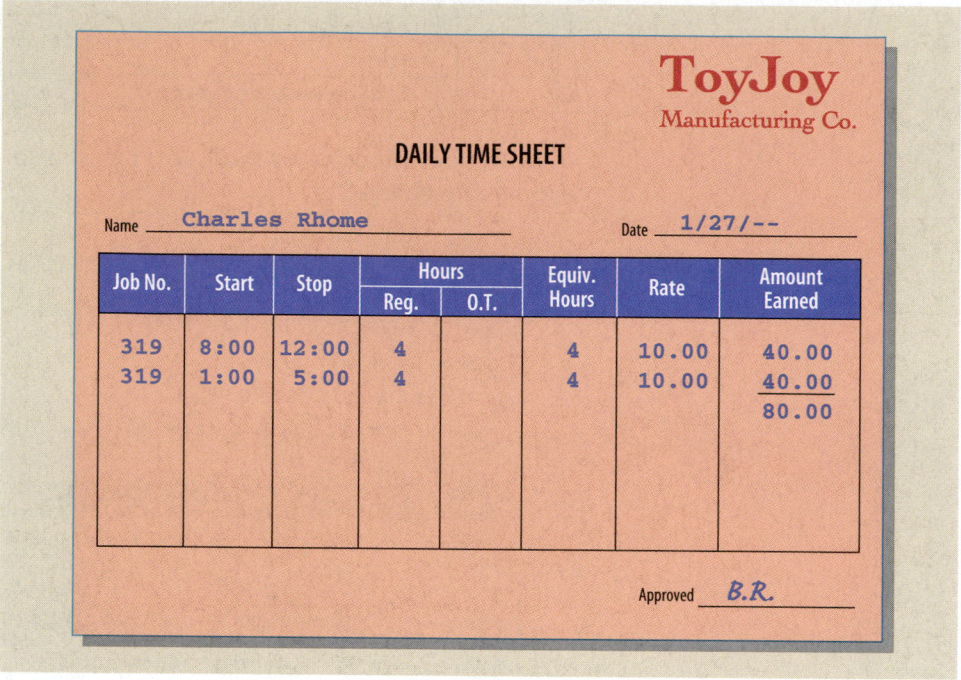

ToyJoy
Manufacturing Co.

DAILY TIME SHEET

Name ___Charles Rhome___   Date ___1/27/--___

Job No.	Start	Stop	Hours Reg.	Hours O.T.	Equiv. Hours	Rate	Amount Earned
319	8:00	12:00	4		4	10.00	40.00
319	1:00	5:00	4		4	10.00	40.00
							80.00

Approved ___B.R.___

FIGURE 28-8 Daily Time Sheet

Time sheets normally are summarized by days, weeks, or months to provide the direct labor cost for each job. This summary is used to make the journal entry for the direct labor costs incurred. Based solely on the time sheet in Figure 28-8, the entry is:

4		Work in Process (Job No. 319)			8	0	00					4
5		Wages Payable							8	0	00	5
6		Incurred direct labor costs										6

The debit to Work in Process also indicates the job to which the direct labor is charged.

Employees who perform indirect labor also use time sheets. Since indirect labor is part of overhead, the following journal entry is made if indirect labor costs of $110 are incurred.

As we saw with indirect materials, notice that no job number is indicated for these indirect labor overhead costs. These and other overhead costs are accumulated and will be applied to specific jobs.

8		Factory Overhead			1	1	0	00					8
9		Wages Payable							1	1	0	00	9
10		Incurred indirect labor costs											10

Accounting for Factory Overhead

Factory overhead includes all manufacturing costs other than direct materials and direct labor. The previous two sections showed how to charge indirect materials and indirect labor to Factory Overhead. Similarly, other overhead costs such as depreciation of factory buildings, utilities, and repairs are charged to Factory Overhead. For example, the factory lighting bill of $870 is recorded as follows:

12		Factory Overhead			8 7 0 00				12
13		Accounts Payable				8 7 0 00			13
14		Incurred factory lighting costs							14

The factory overhead account generally is a control account in the general ledger. Details of the different types of factory overhead costs are accumulated in a **factory overhead subsidiary ledger**. This ledger contains separate accounts for indirect materials, indirect labor, utilities, repairs, and other costs.

By using a factory overhead control account and subsidiary ledger, we can readily accumulate actual factory overhead costs. The major problem in a job order cost accounting system, however, is assigning a reasonable amount of overhead costs to each job. The nature of many factory overhead costs complicates the problem. Most factory overhead costs, such as depreciation of factory buildings, do not vary with the volume of production. Further, some types of overhead, such as heating costs, vacation pay, and repairs, are incurred irregularly throughout the year. These costs do not apply solely to the products manufactured in the months in which the costs occurred.

Predetermined Overhead Rate. Because of the difficulties of relating actual overhead costs to specific jobs, overhead is applied to jobs based on a **predetermined overhead rate**. The basic idea is that we estimate the total overhead costs and total production activity for the year. The overhead is then spread among the jobs based on the amount of production activity on each job. Common measures of production activity are direct labor hours, direct labor costs, and machine hours.

LEARNING KEY: Actual overhead costs are accumulated in factory overhead accounts. Overhead costs are applied to jobs using a predetermined overhead rate.

To illustrate, assume that ToyJoy Manufacturing Co. estimates its factory overhead costs at $366,000 and direct labor costs at $610,000 for the coming year. ToyJoy's predetermined overhead application rate based on direct labor costs is 60%.

$$\frac{\text{Estimated factory overhead costs}}{\text{Estimated direct labor costs}} = \frac{\$366,000}{\$610,000} = 60\%$$

As each job is completed during the year, 60% of the direct labor cost incurred on the job is added as the job's share of factory overhead. Assume that Job No. 319 had total direct labor costs of $5,040. Factory overhead applied to this job is $3,024.

Direct labor cost	$5,040
Application rate	× 60%
Overhead cost applied	$3,024

The entry to apply the overhead cost to Job No. 319 is:

4		Work in Process (Job No. 319)	3 0 2 4 00				4
5		Factory Overhead			3 0 2 4 00		5
6		Applied overhead to work in process					6

The debit to Work in Process also indicates the job to which the overhead is charged.

Accounting for Work in Process—The Job Cost Sheet

In the three previous sections, we saw materials, labor, and overhead costs charged to a specific job (No. 319) that was part of work in process. In a job order cost accounting system, Work in Process is a control account with a subsidiary ledger (**job cost ledger**). This ledger is made up of job cost sheets. A **job cost sheet** is a document for recording the direct materials and direct labor costs incurred and factory overhead costs applied on a specific job. The job cost sheet for Job No. 319 is illustrated in Figure 28-9. As the direct materials and direct labor costs are incurred on a specific job, they are entered on a cost sheet. When the job is completed, factory overhead is applied at the predetermined rate.

 LEARNING KEY: Direct materials, direct labor, and applied factory overhead costs are accumulated on a job cost sheet.

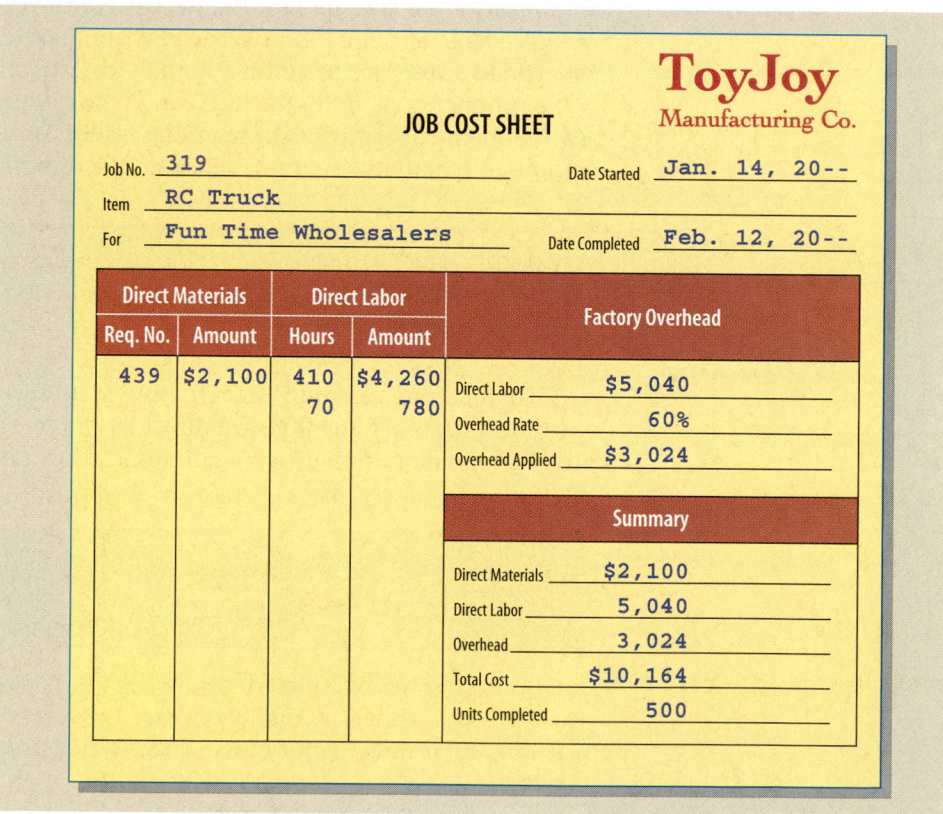

FIGURE 28-9 Job Cost Sheet

Accounting for Completed Jobs

After a job has been completed, all of the costs accumulated on the job cost sheet are transferred to finished goods. For Job No. 319 (Figure 28-9), the entry is:

9		Finished Goods (No. R4)	10	1	6	4	00				9
10		Work in Process (Job No. 319)						10	1	6	4	00	10
11		Transferred work in process to finished goods										11

The credit to Work in Process indicates the job that has been completed (Job No. 319). The debit to Finished Goods indicates the completed product number (R4). Finished Goods is a control account in the general ledger. A separate account for each product is kept in a subsidiary ledger called a **finished goods ledger**.

In T account form, product R4 would appear in the finished goods ledger as follows:

Product R4

Job #297	13,400	
Job #319	10,164	

Notice that the finished goods subsidiary ledger account shows the costs both by product and by job. Remember that in a job cost system, costs are accumulated by job.

At this point, the job has been completed and the costs have been transferred from Work in Process to Finished Goods. Since the costs are no longer in Work in Process, the job cost sheet is removed from the job cost ledger and filed for future reference.

Accounting for Sales

Each time a sale occurs, both the sale and the cost of the goods sold are recorded. Assume that the 500 RC trucks produced in Job No. 319 are sold to RC Time for $13,900 on account. The entry for this sale is:

4		Accounts Receivable	13	9	0	0	00				4
5		Sales						13	9	0	0	00	5
6												6
7		Cost of Goods Sold	10	1	6	4	00				7
8		Finished Goods (No. R4)						10	1	6	4	00	8
9		Made sale on account										9

The credit to Finished Goods also indicates the completed product that was sold (No. R4).

Flow of Job Order Cost Through the Accounts

In the preceding sections, we have made journal entries for events ranging from the purchase of materials through the sale of a finished product. We also used three different subsidiary ledgers. It might be helpful at this point to review the flow of costs in a job order cost system. Figure 28-10 summarizes the journal entries in T account form and ties in the subsidiary ledgers with the related control accounts for the following nine events.

1 Materials purchased from suppliers.

2 Direct materials issued to production (work in process).

3 Indirect materials issued to production (overhead).

4 Direct labor costs incurred (work in process).

5 Indirect labor costs incurred (overhead).

6 Other factory overhead costs incurred (e.g., utilities, depreciation).

7 Overhead applied to completed jobs at predetermined rate.

8 Jobs completed.

9 Finished goods sold to customers.

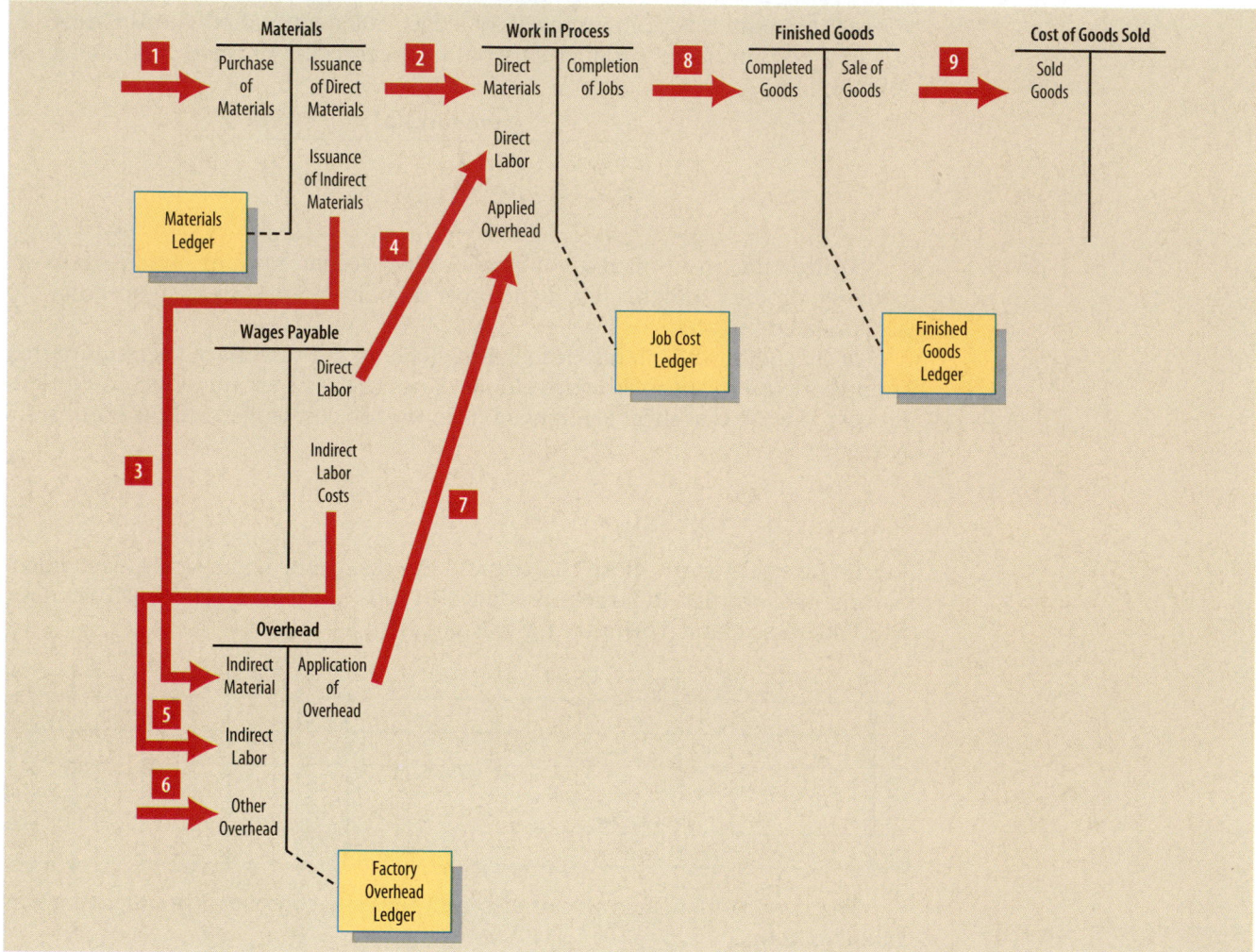

FIGURE 28-10 Flow of Job Order Costs

Note the linkage between each of the control accounts and its related subsidiary ledger. Each time an entry affects one of these control accounts, the related subsidiary ledger must be updated accordingly. All nine events require entries in both a control account and a subsidiary ledger.

Underapplied and Overapplied Factory Overhead

We apply factory overhead to completed jobs based on a predetermined rate. This rate is based on *estimates* of the total factory overhead costs and total production activity for the year. It is unlikely that these estimates will be exactly correct.

When either estimate is too high or too low, the amount of factory overhead cost actually incurred will differ from the amount applied. If the amount of applied overhead is greater than actual overhead cost incurred, the difference is called **overapplied overhead**. If the amount applied is less than actual overhead cost incurred, the difference is called **underapplied overhead**.

Figure 28-11 shows two versions of ToyJoy's factory overhead account after entries for actual and applied overhead have been made for the year. In Case 1, factory overhead is *under*applied by $900 ($185,000 – $184,100). Overhead costs of $900 were incurred that were not applied to goods produced. In Case 2, factory overhead is *over*applied by $1,000 ($185,000 – $186,000). Overhead costs of $1,000 more than were actually incurred were applied to goods produced.

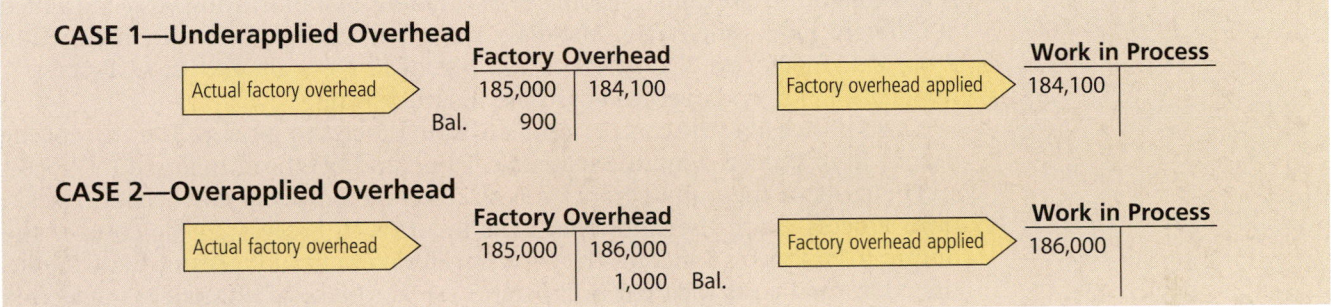

FIGURE 28-11   Factory Overhead Account

If underapplied or over-applied overhead is a large amount, it should be spread among the work in process, finished goods, and cost of goods sold accounts, based on the relative size of these accounts. Usually the amount is small, so the transfer to Cost of Goods Sold is acceptable.

What should we do with the underapplied or overapplied balance in the factory overhead account? Three accounts were affected by the overhead applications during the year: Work in Process, Finished Goods, and Cost of Goods Sold. We could spread the balance among these three accounts. This would require considerable cost and effort, and the accuracy achieved is generally viewed as not worth the trouble. Instead, the underapplied or overapplied overhead commonly is transferred to Cost of Goods Sold by an adjusting entry. The adjusting entries for each case shown in Figure 28-11 would be:

CASE 1—Underapplied Overhead

4		Cost of Goods Sold	9 0 0 00			4
5		Factory Overhead		9 0 0 00		5

CASE 2—Overapplied Overhead

7		Factory Overhead	1 0 0 0 00			7
8		Cost of Goods Sold		1 0 0 0 00		8

LEARNING KEY: Underapplied or overapplied overhead normally is transferred to Cost of Goods Sold.

PROCESS COST ACCOUNTING

LO5   Describe a process cost accounting system.

The job order cost system described in the previous section accumulates costs by job. This system is useful for costing separately identifiable products or batches of product. In a process cost system, costs are accumulated by process or department.

This system is useful for costing similar or identical products. Good examples include basic models of most automobiles, or wooden bookshelves.

As products move through the manufacturing process in a process cost system, costs of processing "attach" to the products. These costs are then passed on to the next processing operation where additional costs attach to the product. This sequence continues through the final production of finished goods.

 LEARNING KEY: In a process cost system, costs attach to products as the products move from one process to another.

The production of unassembled wooden bookshelves in a process cost system is illustrated in Figure 28-12. Notice how different manufacturing costs are added at different processing stages. Materials, labor, and overhead costs are incurred in Process 1. In Process 2, only labor and overhead costs are added. In Process 3, materials, labor, and overhead costs are incurred again.

Also notice how the costs accumulate from process to process. The costs of the output from Process 1 are the materials, labor, and overhead incurred in Process 1. The costs of the output from Process 2 include both the costs transferred in from Process 1 and the additional costs incurred in Process 2. The costs of the output from Process 3 include the costs transferred in from Processes 1 and 2, plus the additional costs incurred in Process 3. Thus, the costs ultimately transferred to Finished Goods include costs incurred in and transferred through three different processing operations.

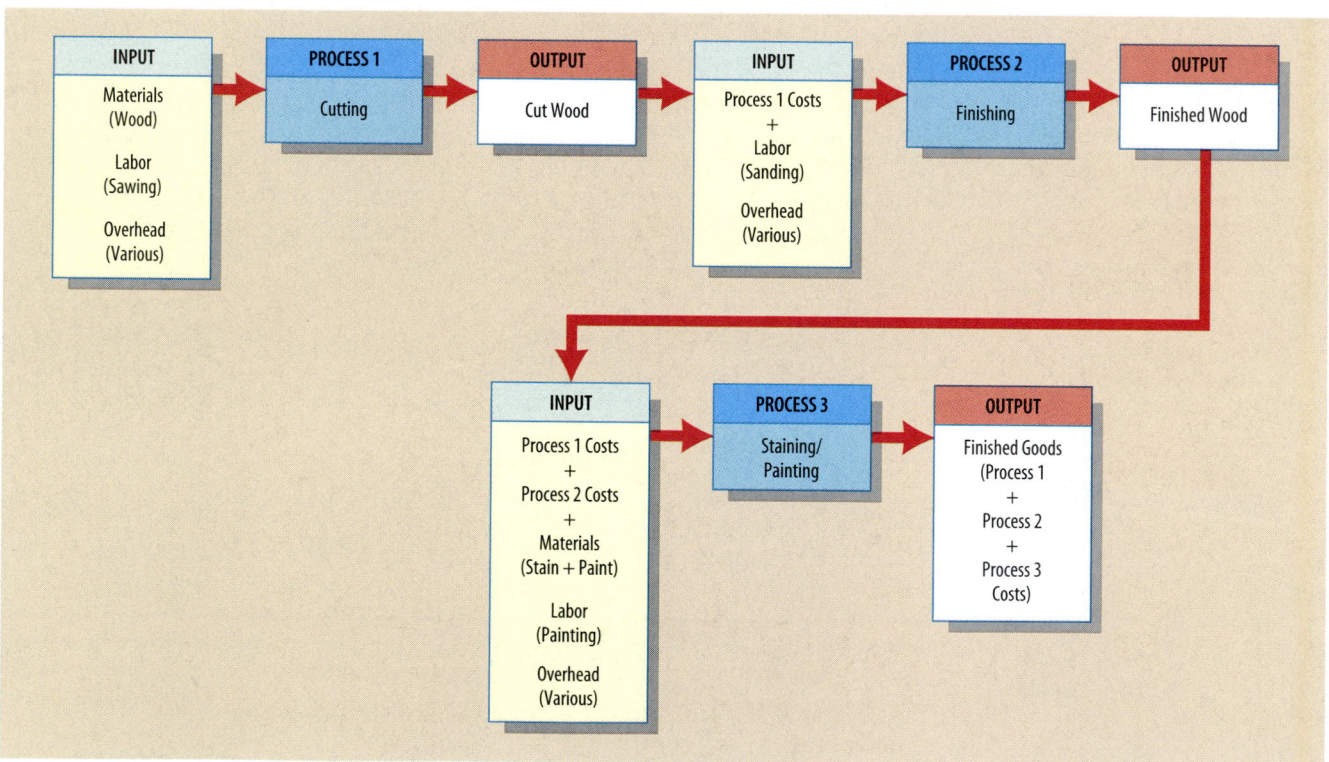

FIGURE 28-12 Process Cost System

To function effectively, a process cost system must also have the following features.

■ Work in process accounts. Each processing department has a separate work in process account.

- Overhead application rates. Each processing department has a separate pre-determined overhead application rate.
- Costs per unit. Costs are calculated per unit to allocate costs to products moving through the processes.

The number of units is computed for each process based on:

1. units in process at the beginning of the period,

2. units started and completed during the period, and

3. units still in process at the end of the period.

The cost per unit must be computed separately for materials, labor, and overhead.

In general, process cost systems are more complicated than job order cost systems. Process cost systems are fully explained and illustrated in more advanced texts.

Learning Objectives	Key Points to Remember
1 Describe the three manufacturing costs.	The three primary elements of manufacturing cost are materials, labor, and factory overhead. These three costs come together in a conversion process to produce completed products, as shown in Figure 28-1.
2 Describe the three inventories of a manufacturing business.	Three inventories are needed in a manufacturing business: materials, work in process, and finished goods. Materials inventory consists of materials acquired to be used in production. Work in process inventory consists of products started but not yet finished. Finished goods inventory contains completed products.
3 Describe and illustrate how manufacturing costs and inventories affect the financial statements of a manufacturing business.	There are two main differences in the financial statements of a manufacturer and a merchandiser: (1) cost of goods sold on the income statement and (2) inventories on the balance sheet. Purchases on the merchandiser's income statement is replaced by cost of goods manufactured on the manufacturer's income statement. The manufacturer's balance sheet has three inventory accounts: Finished Goods, Work in Process, and Materials.
4 Define and describe how to operate a job order cost accounting system.	A job order cost system provides a separate record of the cost of each product or group of products that is produced. A cost accounting system with perpetual inventories is used to accumulate information about the cost of producing each product. Under this system, at least one of the three inventory accounts is affected every time (1) materials are purchased, (2) materials are placed in production, (3) products are completed, or (4) products are sold, as shown in Figure 28-6.

Three important documents used in a job order cost system are the materials requisition, daily time sheet, and job cost sheet.

Overhead is applied to jobs based on a predetermined overhead rate. Underapplied or overapplied overhead normally is transferred to Cost of Goods Sold.

Four subsidiary ledgers are used in a job cost system: the materials ledger, factory overhead ledger, job cost ledger, and finished goods ledger. Figure 28-10 shows the use of these four ledgers. |
| 5 Describe a process cost accounting system. | In a process cost system, costs are accumulated by process or department rather than by job. |

R E F L E C T I O N

Reflection: Answering the Opening Questions

A job order cost system is an inventory costing system that provides a separate record of the cost of each product or group of products that is produced. The manufacturing costs to accumulate are the direct materials, direct labor, and overhead. Estimates must be made of the expected total overhead costs and total manufacturing activity for the period. These estimates are important in allocating an appropriate amount of overhead to each job.

DEMONSTRATION PROBLEM

WebTUTOR Advantage

Mantel Manufacturing Company uses a job order cost accounting system. The following is a summary of transactions completed during its first year of operations.

(a)   Purchased materials on account, $435,000.

(b) (1) Issued *direct materials* to production.

Job No. 1	$ 55,000	Job No. 4	119,000
Job No. 2	76,000	Job No. 5	65,000
Job No. 3	59,800	Job No. 6	18,000

   (2) Issued *indirect materials* to production, $11,900.

(c) (1) Incurred factory labor costs:

Job No. 1	$34,000	Job No. 4	76,000
Job No. 2	40,000	Job No. 5	38,000
Job No. 3	29,000	Job No. 6	12,000

   (2) Incurred indirect labor costs, $10,000.

(d)   Incurred other factory overhead costs, $96,000.

(e)   Depreciation expense on factory equipment, $29,000.

(f)   Applied factory overhead, 65% of direct labor cost incurred on jobs.

(g)   Finished Job Nos. 1, 2, 4, and 5 as products A, B, D, and E, respectively.

(h)   Shipped products A, B, and D and billed customers for $158,000, $210,000, and $362,000, respectively.

REQUIRED

1. Prepare general journal entries for the foregoing transactions. Make compound entries for (b), (c), and (f), but with separate debits for each job. (Use journal page numbers 7 and 8.)

2. Post the entries to the general ledger T accounts for Work in Process and Finished Goods, and determine the ending balances in these accounts.

3. Determine the balances in the job cost ledger to support the balance in the work in process account.

4. Determine the balances in the finished goods ledger to support the balance in the finished goods account.

5. Determine the amount of underapplied or overapplied overhead.

Solution

1.

		GENERAL JOURNAL					PAGE 7	
	DATE	DESCRIPTION	POST. REF.	DEBIT	CREDIT	

(a)

Line	Description	Debit	Credit	Line
1	Materials	435 0 0 0 00		1
2	Accounts Payable		435 0 0 0 00	2
3				3
4	Work in Process (Job No. 1)	55 0 0 0 00		4
5	Work in Process (Job No. 2)	76 0 0 0 00		5
6	Work in Process (Job No. 3)	59 8 0 0 00		6
7	Work in Process (Job No. 4)	119 0 0 0 00		7
8	Work in Process (Job No. 5)	65 0 0 0 00		8
9	Work in Process (Job No. 6)	18 0 0 0 00		9
10	Materials		392 8 0 0 00	10
11				11
12	Factory Overhead	11 9 0 0 00		12
13	Materials		11 9 0 0 00	13
14				14
15	Work in Process (Job No. 1)	34 0 0 0 00		15
16	Work in Process (Job No. 2)	40 0 0 0 00		16
17	Work in Process (Job No. 3)	29 0 0 0 00		17
18	Work in Process (Job No. 4)	76 0 0 0 00		18
19	Work in Process (Job No. 5)	38 0 0 0 00		19
20	Work in Process (Job No. 6)	12 0 0 0 00		20
21	Wages Payable		229 0 0 0 00	21
22				22
23	Factory Overhead	10 0 0 0 00		23
24	Wages Payable		10 0 0 0 00	24
25				25
26	Factory Overhead	96 0 0 0 00		26
27	Accounts Payable		96 0 0 0 00	27
28				28
29	Factory Overhead	29 0 0 0 00		29
30	Accumulated Depreciation		29 0 0 0 00	30
31				31
32	Work in Process (Job No. 1)	22 1 0 0 00		32
33	Work in Process (Job No. 2)	26 0 0 0 00		33
34	Work in Process (Job No. 3)	18 8 5 0 00		34
35	Work in Process (Job No. 4)	49 4 0 0 00		35
36	Work in Process (Job No. 5)	24 7 0 0 00		36
37	Work in Process (Job No. 6)	7 8 0 0 00		37
38	Factory Overhead		148 8 5 0 00	38
39				39
40	Finished Goods (Product A)	111 1 0 0 00		40
41	Work in Process (Job No. 1)		111 1 0 0 00	41
42				42
43	Finished Goods (Product B)	142 0 0 0 00		43
44	Work in Process (Job No. 2)		142 0 0 0 00	44

Row groupings: (a) lines 1–2; (b) lines 4–13; (c) lines 15–24; (d) lines 26–27; (e) lines 29–30; (f) lines 32–38; (g) lines 40–44.

(continued)

		DESCRIPTION		DEBIT					CREDIT					
45														45
46		Finished Goods (Product D)		244	4	0	0	00						46
47		Work in Process (Job No. 4)							244	4	0	0	00	47
48														48
49		Finished Goods (Product E)		127	7	0	0	00						49
50		Work in Process (Job No. 5)							127	7	0	0	00	50

GENERAL JOURNAL PAGE 8

	DATE	DESCRIPTION	POST REF.	DEBIT					CREDIT					
(h) 1		Accounts Receivable		158	0	0	0	00						1
2		Sales							158	0	0	0	00	2
3														3
4		Cost of Goods Sold		111	1	0	0	00						4
5		Finished Goods (Product A)							111	1	0	0	00	5
6														6
7		Accounts Receivable		210	0	0	0	00						7
8		Sales							210	0	0	0	00	8
9														9
10		Cost of Goods Sold		142	0	0	0	00						10
11		Finished Goods (Product B)							142	0	0	0	00	11
12														12
13		Accounts Receivable		362	0	0	0	00						13
14		Sales							362	0	0	0	00	14
15														15
16		Cost of Goods Sold		244	4	0	0	00						16
17		Finished Goods (Product D)							244	4	0	0	00	17
18														18

2.

Work in Process		Finished Goods	
55,000	111,100	111,100	111,100
76,000	142,000	142,000	142,000
59,800	244,400	244,400	244,400
119,000	127,700	127,700	127,700
65,000	625,200	625,200	497,500
18,000		Bal. 127,700	
34,000			
40,000			
29,000			
76,000			
38,000			
12,000			
22,100			
26,000			
18,850			
49,400			
24,700			
7,800			
770,650			
Bal. 145,450			

3. In job cost ledger: Job No. 3 $107,650
                         Job No. 6   37,800
                                            $145,450

4. Product E: $127,700

5.
Factory Overhead

11,900	148,850
10,000	
96,000	
29,000	
146,900	148,850
	1,950 (Overapplied overhead)

On-Line Learning Tools

For more information, visit: http://heintz.swlearning.com

The Heintz & Parry product web site is designed specifically for **COLLEGE ACCOUNTING, 18e.** The features include downloadable student resources and an interactive study center, organized by chapter, which contains learning objectives, web links, on-line quizzes with automatic feedback, and more.

KEY TERMS

cost accounting system, (1050)   A system for accumulating detailed information regarding the cost of producing a product.

daily time sheet, (1053)   A record of the time worked and labor cost incurred on each job.

direct labor, (1047)   The wages of employees who are directly involved in converting materials into finished goods.

direct materials , (1047)   Those materials that enter into and become a major part of the finished product.

factory burden, (1047)   See factory overhead.

factory overhead, (1047)   All manufacturing costs other than direct materials and direct labor.

factory overhead subsidiary ledger, (1055)   The ledger in which details of the different types of factory overhead costs are accumulated.

factory supplies, (1047)   See indirect materials.

Finished Goods Inventory, (1048)   The account that contains the costs of products that have been completed and are ready for sale.

finished goods ledger, (1057)   The subsidiary ledger in which a separate account for each product is kept.

indirect labor, (1047)   The wages and salaries of employees who devote their time to supervision or to work of a general nature.

indirect manufacturing cost, (1047)   See factory overhead.

indirect materials, (1047)   Those materials used in the manufacturing process that do not become a major part of the finished product.

job cost ledger, (1056)   A subsidiary ledger for the work in process control account that is made up of job cost sheets.

(continued)

job cost sheet, (1056)   A document for recording the direct materials, direct labor, and factory overhead costs incurred on a specific job.

job order cost system, (1051)   The system that provides a separate record of the cost of each individual product or group of products that is produced.

manufacturing overhead, (1047)   See factory overhead.

Materials Inventory, (1048)   The account that includes all the materials (both direct and indirect) acquired to be used in production.

materials ledger, (1052)   The subsidiary ledger that shows the quantity and cost of material received and issued, and the resulting balance for each type of material.

materials requisition, (1053)   A form used to issue materials from the storeroom to production.

overapplied overhead, (1059)   The excess of applied overhead over the actual overhead cost incurred.

predetermined overhead rate, (1055)   The rate used to apply overhead, based on production activity such as direct labor hours, direct labor costs, or machine hours; used because of the difficulties of relating specific overhead costs to specific jobs.

process cost system, (1051)   The system that accumulates manufacturing costs by process, such as cutting, painting, or finishing, and assigns each unit of product passing through the process a share of the costs.

stores ledger, (1052)   See materials ledger.

time ticket, (1053)   See daily time sheet.

underapplied overhead, (1059)   The excess of the actual overhead cost incurred over applied overhead.

Work in Process Inventory, (1048)   The account in which materials, labor, and overhead costs of producing a product are accumulated until the product is completed.

REVIEW QUESTIONS

(LO1)   1. Why is the accounting for a manufacturing business more complicated than that for a merchandising business?

(LO1)   2. What are the three primary elements of manufacturing cost?

(LO1)   3. What are the two major types of materials and how do they differ?

(LO1)   4. Distinguish between direct and indirect labor.

(LO1)   5. Describe and give three examples of factory overhead.

(LO2)   6. What are the three inventories needed in a manufacturing business?

(LO2)   7. Describe the flow of materials, labor, and overhead into Work in Process.

(LO3)   8. What are the main differences between the financial statements of a manufacturing and a merchandising business?

(LO4)   9. For what three reasons is product cost information needed by a manufacturing business?

(LO4)   10. What two purposes are served by a materials requisition?

(LO4)   11. What information is provided by the daily time sheet?

(LO4)   12. Explain how to calculate a predetermined overhead rate.

(LO4)   13. What costs are entered on the job cost sheet?

(LO4)   14. Describe underapplied and overapplied overhead. What is commonly done with the underapplied or overapplied balance in the factory overhead account?

(LO5)   15. Briefly describe the difference between a job order cost system and a process cost system.

Self-Study Test Questions

True/False

1. Both direct and indirect materials enter into and become major parts of the finished product.   _____

2. Factory overhead is also known as manufacturing overhead, indirect manufacturing cost, or factory burden.   _____

3. Work in Process Inventory consists of three items: materials, labor, and factory overhead.   _____

4. Finished Goods Inventory consists of only those items finished and sold during the period.   _____

5. Most cost accounting systems use perpetual inventories.   _____

Multiple Choice

1. Which of these would most likely be treated as an *indirect* material? (Assume you are manufacturing tables.)   _____

   (a) wood   (c) glue
   (b) lacquer   (d) table legs

2. The cost of goods sold section of the income statement for a manufacturing company would contain which of the following?   _____

   (a) purchases   (c) direct labor
   (b) cost of goods manufactured   (d) no inventory account

3. When total anticipated factory overhead is $500,000 and budgeted direct labor hours are 200,000, what is the predetermined factory overhead rate based on direct labor hours?   _____

   (a) $2.50/hour   (c) $10/hour
   (b) $5.00/hour   (d) It cannot be determined.

4. When direct labor hours for Job 101 are 30 and the predetermined factory overhead rate is $5/direct labor hour, what is the applied factory overhead amount?   _____

   (a) $250   (c) $150
   (b) $500   (d) It cannot be determined.

5. Underapplied or overapplied factory overhead is normally charged or credited to which account?   _____

   (a) Materials   (c) Finished Goods
   (b) Work in Process   (d) Cost of Goods Sold

The answers to the Self-Study Test Questions are at the end of the text.

MANAGING YOUR WRITING

Joan owns a print shop and has a difficult time figuring out what to bid on jobs. She knows how to estimate the cost of materials and labor on different jobs but is confused about how to handle many other costs she knows she incurs to run the shop. These include utilities, cleaning staff, property taxes on the building, and other expenses. Many of these types of costs vary from month to month. In addition, she often does not know the amounts until some time after jobs are completed.

Write a memo to Joan explaining how she should apply her overhead costs in developing bids on her jobs.

ETHICS CASE

Ben Reese is a painter for a small manufacturing plant. Sometimes he works directly on the product and sometimes he performs routine maintenance on the plant's three buildings. He is paid $11.50 an hour and fills out a time sheet at the end of each week. His supervisor then fills in the specific jobs that will be charged with Ben's time. On Friday afternoon, Ben's supervisor, Ralph Brooks, said he needed Ben to do a job off the plant site. Ralph explained that he had just installed a wooden garage door on his house and needed it painted. He told Ben to leave a couple of hours early and "just sign out as though you had stayed until quitting time." Even though this request made Ben uncomfortable, he did what the boss said.

1. What would you have done if you were Ben? Justify your answer.

2. How do you suppose Ralph will account for Ben's hours away from the plant?

3. Write a short paragraph explaining the difference between direct labor and indirect labor. Include how each is assigned to specific jobs.

4. In groups of two or three, come up with some suggestions on measures a company can take to prevent a situation like this from happening.

WEB WORK

Think of a pair of manufacturing competitors (such as Ford and General Motors or Coke and Pepsi), then look up their annual reports. Find out who is more profitable and who spends more on overhead, labor, and materials. Use the Annual Report Gallery as a starting point. Visit the Interactive Study Center on our web site at **http://heintz.swlearning.com** for special hotlinks to assist you in this assignment.

SERIES A EXERCISES

EXERCISE 28-1A   (LO3)
Cost of goods sold: $49,000

COST OF GOODS SOLD SECTION The following information is supplied for R&D Manufacturing Co. and WP West Co. (a merchandising company). Prepare the cost of goods sold sections for the income statements of both companies.

	R&D Manufacturing	WP West
Merchandise inventory, Jan. 1		$57,000
Finished goods inventory, Jan. 1	$57,000	
Merchandise purchases		36,000
Cost of goods manufactured	36,000	
Merchandise inventory, Dec. 31		44,000
Finished goods inventory, Dec. 31	44,000	

EXERCISE 28-2A   (LO3)
Total manufacturing costs: $98,000

SCHEDULE OF COST OF GOODS MANUFACTURED The following information is supplied for Morales Mining and Manufacturing Company. Prepare a schedule of cost of goods manufactured for the year ended December 31, 20--.

Work in Process, Jan. 1	$70,000
Materials inventory, Jan. 1	28,000
Materials purchases	32,000
Materials inventory, Dec. 31	24,000
Direct labor	44,000
Overhead	18,000
Work in Process, Dec. 31	56,000

EXERCISE 28-3A   (LO4)
Jan. 20 entry: Dr. Factory Overhead (Indirect Mats.), $4,000

JOURNAL ENTRIES FOR MATERIAL, LABOR, AND OVERHEAD Jones Manufacturing Corporation had the following transactions for their job order costing operation. Prepare general journal entries to record these transactions.

Jan. 1   Purchased materials on account, $15,000.

15   Issued direct materials to Job No. 101, $10,000.

20   Issued indirect materials (factory overhead), $4,000.

31   Incurred direct labor, Job No. 101, $8,000.

31   Incurred indirect labor (factory overhead), $2,000.

31   Incurred other indirect costs, (factory overhead; credit Accounts Payable), $1,500.

EXERCISE 28-4A   (LO4)
Entry for underapplied factory overhead: Dr. Cost of Goods Sold, $200

JOURNAL ENTRIES FOR FACTORY OVERHEAD Huang Company manufactures toys. They keep a factory overhead account where actual factory overhead costs are recorded as a debit and factory overhead applied is recorded as a credit. At the end of the month, underapplied or overapplied factory overhead is calculated and transferred to the cost of goods sold account. For the month of January, Huang had the following overhead transactions. Make appropriate general journal entries to record factory overhead and factory overhead applied, and to close the underapplied or overapplied factory overhead to the cost of goods sold account.

Jan. 1   Paid rent, $1,000.

10   Paid electricity bill, $250.

15   Paid repair expense, $1,500.

21   Vacation pay for machine operator, $500 (Wages Payable).

31   Depreciation expense for the month, $450.

Factory overhead applied was $3,500.

EXERCISE 28-5A **(LO4)**
(1) $10/direct labor hour

PREDETERMINED FACTORY OVERHEAD RATE Lovejoy Enterprises calculates a predetermined factory overhead rate so that factory overhead may be applied to production during the month. They calculate the overhead using three different methods and then decide which one to use. Total estimated factory overhead costs are $500,000. Total estimated direct labor hours are 50,000. Total estimated direct labor costs are $800,000. Total machine hours are estimated to be 100,000.

Calculate the predetermined overhead application rates based on (1) direct labor hours, (2) direct labor costs, and (3) machine hours.

EXERCISE 28-6A **(LO4)**
1st Apr. 30 entry: Dr. Finished Goods, $48,300

JOURNAL ENTRIES FOR MATERIAL, LABOR, OVERHEAD, AND SALES Micro Enterprises had the following job order transactions during the month of April. Record the transactions in the general journal, including issuance of materials, labor, and factory overhead applied; completed jobs sent to finished goods inventory; closing of the underapplied or overapplied factory overhead to the cost of goods sold account; and sale of finished goods.

Apr. 1	Purchased materials on account, $35,000.
10	Issued direct materials to Job No. 33, $10,000.
11	Issued direct materials to Job No. 34, $8,000.
12	Issued direct materials to Job No. 35, $11,000.
25	Incurred direct labor:
	On Job No. 33, $6,000
	On Job No. 34, $4,000
	On Job No. 35, $5,000
25	Applied factory overhead:
	To Job No. 33, $1,500
	To Job No. 34, $1,200
	To Job No. 35, $1,600
30	Transferred Job Nos. 33–35 to the finished goods inventory account.
30	Sold Job Nos. 33–35.
30	Actual factory overhead for Job Nos. 33–35, $4,220.

SERIES A PROBLEMS

PROBLEM 28-7A **(LO4)**

(d): Dr. Work in Process: (Job 300), $8,000

JOURNAL ENTRIES FOR MATERIAL, LABOR, AND OVERHEAD Eto Manufacturing had the following transactions during the month.

(a) Purchased raw materials on account, $70,000.

(b) Issued direct materials to Job No. 300, $25,000.

(c) Issued indirect materials to production, $10,000.

(d) Paid biweekly payroll and charged direct labor to Job No. 300, $8,000.

(e) Paid biweekly payroll and charged indirect labor to production, $3,000.

(f) Issued direct materials to Job No. 301, $20,000.

(g) Issued indirect materials to production, $4,000.

(h) Paid miscellaneous factory overhead charges, $6,000.

(i) Paid biweekly payroll and charged direct labor to Job No. 301, $10,000.

(j) Paid biweekly payroll and charged indirect labor to production, $2,000.

REQUIRED

Prepare general journal entries for transactions (a) through (j).

PROBLEM 28-8A   **(LO4)**

1. (h): Dr. Finished Goods, $64,500

JOB ORDER COSTING TRANSACTIONS B & L Enterprises makes garage doors. During the month of February, the company had four job orders: 303, 304, 305, and 306. Overhead was applied at predetermined rates, while actual factory overhead was recorded as incurred. All four jobs were completed.

(a) Purchased raw materials on account, $40,000.

(b) Issued direct materials to production:

Job No. 303:	$8,000
Job No. 304:	9,000
Job No. 305:	7,000
Job No. 306:	8,500

(c) Issued indirect materials to production, $5,000.

(d) Incurred direct labor costs:

Job No. 303:	$5,000
Job No. 304:	4,000
Job No. 305:	4,800
Job No. 306:	5,200

(e) Charged indirect labor to production, $3,100.

(f) Paid electricity, heating oil, and repair bills for the factory and charged to production, $4,900.

(g) Applied factory overhead to each of the jobs using a predetermined factory overhead rate as follows:

Job No. 303:	$3,000
Job No. 304:	3,500
Job No. 305:	3,000
Job No. 306:	3,500

(h) Finished Job Nos. 303–306 and transferred to the finished goods inventory account.

(i) Sold Job Nos. 303–306.

REQUIRED

1. Prepare general journal entries to record transactions (a) through (i).

2. Post the entries to the work in process and finished goods accounts only.

PROBLEM 28-9A   **(LO4)**

3: Balance in job cost ledger, $66,600

JOB ORDER COSTING WITH UNDERAPPLIED AND OVERAPPLIED FACTORY OVERHEAD M. Evans & Sons manufactures parts for radios. For each job order, they maintain ledger sheets on which they record direct labor, direct materials, and factory overhead applied. The factory overhead control account contains postings of actual overhead costs. At the end of the month, the underapplied or overapplied factory overhead is charged to the cost of goods sold account.

Factory overhead is applied on the basis of direct labor hours. For Job Nos. 101, 102, 103, and 104, direct labor hours are 12,000, 10,000, 11,000, and 18,000, respectively. The overhead application rate is $1.20/direct labor hour.

(a) Purchased raw materials on account, $50,000.

(b) Issued direct materials:

Job No. 101:	$10,000
Job No. 102:	8,000
Job No. 103:	9,000
Job No. 104:	15,000

(continued)

(c) Issued indirect materials to production, $8,000.

(d) Incurred direct labor costs:

Job No. 101:	$22,000
Job No. 102:	19,000
Job No. 103:	20,500
Job No. 104:	30,000

(e) Charged indirect labor to production, $15,000.

(f) Paid electricity bill, taxes, and repair fees for the factory and charged to production, $8,000.

(g) Depreciation expense on factory equipment, $30,000.

(h) Applied factory overhead to each of the jobs using the predetermined factory overhead rate (see above).

(i) Finished Job Nos. 101–103 and transferred to the finished goods inventory account.

(j) Sold Job Nos. 101 and 102.

(k) Transferred underapplied or overapplied factory overhead balance to the cost of goods sold account.

REQUIRED

1. Prepare general journal entries to record transactions (a) through (k).

2. Post the entries to the work in process and finished goods accounts only and determine the ending balances in these accounts.

3. Compute the balance in the job cost ledger and make certain this balance agrees with that in the work in process control account.

SERIES B EXERCISES

EXERCISE 28-1B **(LO3)**
Cost of goods sold: $13,750

COST OF GOODS SOLD SECTION The following information is supplied for A&B Manufacturing Co. and JC Yoshino Co. (a merchandising company). Prepare the cost of goods sold sections for the income statements of both companies.

	A&B Manufacturing	JC Yoshino
Merchandise inventory, Jan. 1		$15,750
Finished goods inventory, Jan. 1	$15,750	
Merchandise purchases		11,000
Cost of goods manufactured	11,000	
Merchandise inventory, Dec. 31		13,000
Finished goods inventory, Dec. 31	13,000	

EXERCISE 28-2B **(LO3)**
Total manufacturing costs: $25,000

SCHEDULE OF COST OF GOODS MANUFACTURED The following information is supplied for Sanchez Welding and Manufacturing Company. Prepare a schedule of cost of goods manufactured for the year ended December 31, 20--.

Work in process, Jan. 1	$20,500
Materials inventory, Jan. 1	11,000
Materials purchases	12,000
Materials inventory, Dec. 31	13,000
Direct labor	9,500
Overhead	5,500
Work in process, Dec. 31	10,500

EXERCISE 28-3B   (LO4)
Jan. 20 entry: Dr. Factory
Overhead (Indirect Mats),
$3,000

JOURNAL ENTRIES FOR MATERIAL, LABOR, AND OVERHEAD Rich Manufacturing Corporation had the following transactions for their job order costing operation. Prepare general journal entries to record these transactions.

Jan. 1   Purchased materials on account, $22,000.

15   Issued direct materials to Job No. 1, $18,000.

20   Issued indirect materials (factory overhead), $3,000.

31   Incurred direct labor, Job No. 1, $11,000.

31   Incurred indirect labor (factory overhead), $4,000.

31   Incurred other indirect costs, (factory overhead; credit Accounts Payable), $1,500.

EXERCISE 28-4B   (LO4)
Entry for underapplied factory
overhead: Dr. Cost of Goods
Sold, $500

JOURNAL ENTRIES FOR FACTORY OVERHEAD Bandy Company manufactures toys. They keep a factory overhead account where actual factory overhead costs are recorded as a debit and factory overhead applied is recorded as a credit. At the end of the month, underapplied or overapplied factory overhead is calculated and transferred to the cost of goods sold account. For the month of January, Bandy had the following overhead transactions. Make appropriate general journal entries to record factory overhead and factory overhead applied, and to close the underapplied or overapplied factory overhead to the cost of goods sold account.

Jan. 1   Paid rent, $2,000.

10   Paid electricity bill, $500.

15   Paid repair expense, $3,000.

21   Vacation pay for machine operator, $500 (Wages Payable).

31   Depreciation expense for the month, $500.

Factory overhead applied was $6,000.

EXERCISE 28-5B   (LO4)
(1) $20/direct labor hour

PREDETERMINED FACTORY OVERHEAD RATE Marston Enterprises calculates a predetermined factory overhead rate so that factory overhead may be applied to production during the month. They calculate the overhead using three different methods and then decide which one to use. Total estimated factory overhead costs are $600,000. Total estimated direct labor hours are 30,000. Total estimated direct labor costs are $1,200,000. Total machine hours are estimated to be 200,000.

Calculate the predetermined overhead application rates based on (1) direct labor hours, (2) direct labor costs, and (3) machine hours.

EXERCISE 28-6B   (LO4)
1st Apr. 30 entry: Dr. Finished
Goods, $46,700

JOURNAL ENTRIES FOR MATERIAL, LABOR, OVERHEAD, AND SALES Alert Enterprises had the following job order transactions during the month of April. Record the transactions in the general journal, including issuance of materials, labor, and factory overhead applied; completed jobs sent to finished goods inventory; closing of the underapplied or overapplied factory overhead to the cost of goods sold account; and sale of finished goods.

Apr. 1   Purchased materials on account, $28,000.

10   Issued direct materials to Job No. 26, $11,000.

11   Issued direct materials to Job No. 27, $9,000.

12   Issued direct materials to Job No. 28, $7,000.

(continued)

25   Incurred direct labor:
       On Job No. 26, $6,000
       On Job No. 27, $4,000
       On Job No. 28, $5,000

25   Applied factory overhead:
       To Job No. 26, $1,800
       To Job No. 27, $1,500
       To Job No. 28, $1,400

30   Transferred Job Nos. 26–28 to the finished goods inventory account.

30   Sold Job Nos. 26–28.

30   Actual factory overhead for Job Nos. 26–28, $4,500.

SERIES B PROBLEMS

PROBLEM 28-7B   (LO4)

(d): Dr. Work in Process
(Job 200), $4,500

JOURNAL ENTRIES FOR MATERIAL, LABOR, AND OVERHEAD   Shiar Manufacturing had the following transactions during the month.

(a) Purchased raw materials on account, $22,500.

(b) Issued direct materials to Job No. 200, $11,250.

(c) Issued indirect materials to production, $4,000.

(d) Paid biweekly payroll and charged direct labor to Job No. 200, $4,500.

(e) Paid biweekly payroll and charged indirect labor to production, $1,250.

(f) Issued direct materials to Job No. 201, $10,000.

(g) Issued indirect materials to production, $2,500.

(h) Paid miscellaneous factory overhead charges, $4,500.

(i) Paid biweekly payroll and charged direct labor to Job No. 201, $4,250.

(j) Paid biweekly payroll and charged indirect labor to production, $900.

REQUIRED

Prepare general journal entries for transactions (a) through (j).

PROBLEM 28-8B   (LO4)

1. (h): Dr. Finished Goods, $65,300

JOB ORDER COSTING TRANSACTIONS D & K Enterprises makes wicker baskets. During the month of August, the company had four job orders: 501, 502, 503, and 504. Overhead was applied at predetermined rates, while actual factory overhead was recorded as incurred. All four jobs were completed.

(a) Purchased raw materials on account, $44,000.

(b) Issued direct materials to production:
      Job No. 501: $8,200
      Job No. 502:   9,100
      Job No. 503:   7,300
      Job No. 504:   8,500

(c) Issued indirect materials to production, $5,000.

(d) Incurred direct labor costs:

Job No. 501:	$4,800
Job No. 502:	4,100
Job No. 503:	4,800
Job No. 504:	5,000

(e) Charged indirect labor to production, $3,300.

(f) Paid electricity, heating oil, and repair bills for the factory and charged to production, $5,200.

(g) Applied factory overhead to each of the jobs using a predetermined factory overhead rate as follows:

Job No. 501:	$3,100
Job No. 502:	3,300
Job No. 503:	3,300
Job No. 504:	3,800

(h) Finished Job Nos. 501–504 and transferred to the finished goods inventory account.

(i) Sold Job Nos. 501–504.

REQUIRED

1. Prepare general journal entries to record transactions (a) through (i).

2. Post the entries to the work in process and finished goods accounts only.

PROBLEM 28-9B   (LO4)

3: Balance in job cost ledger, $47,700

JOB ORDER COSTING WITH UNDERAPPLIED AND OVERAPPLIED FACTORY OVERHEAD   J. Bowen & Co. manufactures screen doors. For each job order, they maintain ledger sheets on which they record direct labor, direct materials, and factory overhead applied. The factory overhead control account contains postings of actual overhead costs. At the end of the month, the underapplied or over-applied factory overhead is charged to the cost of goods sold account.

Factory overhead is applied on the basis of direct labor hours. For Job Nos. 201, 202, 203, and 204, direct labor hours are 10,000, 11,000, 11,000, and 12,000, respectively. The overhead application rate is $1.50/direct labor hour.

(a) Purchased raw materials on account, $45,000.

(b) Issued direct materials:

Job No. 201:	$10,000
Job No. 202:	11,000
Job No. 203:	9,500
Job No. 204:	12,200

(c) Issued indirect materials to production, $7,500.

(d) Incurred direct labor costs:

Job No. 201:	$18,000
Job No. 202:	19,000
Job No. 203:	20,500
Job No. 204:	17,500

(e) Charged indirect labor to production, $11,000.

(f) Paid electricity bill, taxes, and repair fees for the factory and charged to production, $7,000.

(g) Depreciation expense on factory equipment, $40,000.

(continued)

(h) Applied factory overhead to each of the jobs using the predetermined factory overhead rate (see above).

(i) Finished Job Nos. 201–203 and transferred to the finished goods inventory account.

(j) Sold Job Nos. 201 and 202.

(k) Transferred underapplied or overapplied factory overhead balance to the cost of goods sold account.

REQUIRED

1. Prepare general journal entries to record transactions (a) through (k).

2. Post the entries to the work in process and finished goods accounts only and determine the ending balances in these accounts.

3. Compute the balance in the job cost ledger and make certain this balance agrees with that in the work in process control account.

MASTERY PROBLEM

3: Balance in job cost ledger, $97,260

Forester Manufacturing Company uses a job order cost accounting system to keep track of finished jobs and jobs in process. All production is either to customer order or to specification. The following is a summary of transactions completed during the month of August.

(a) Purchased materials (direct and indirect) on account, $158,000.

(b) Requisitioned materials from storerooms, $149,000 (direct materials, $122,000; indirect materials, $27,000). Charged to jobs as follows:

Job No. 805:	$34,000
Job No. 806:	44,000
Job No. 807:	20,000
Job No. 808:	24,000

(c) Incurred factory labor cost for the month, $211,800 (direct labor, $150,000; indirect labor, $61,800). Charged to jobs as follows:

Job No. 805:	$25,500
Job No. 806:	39,800
Job No. 807:	51,400
Job No. 808:	33,300

(d) Incurred other factory overhead costs, $85,000 (depreciation expense, $10,000; miscellaneous factory expense on account, $75,000).

(e) Applied factory overhead, 120% of direct labor cost incurred on jobs. (Make a separate debit for each job.)

(f) Finished Job Nos. 805, 806, and 807 and placed them in stock as products X, Y, and Z, respectively.

(g) Sold products X, Y, and Z on account for $123,000, $150,000, and $168,000, respectively. Costs of products sold were $90,100, $122,000, and $140,000, respectively. (Products Y and Z included some items from the beginning inventory of finished goods and some from the current period's production.)

The beginning balances in the inventory accounts were as follows:

Work in Process $0
Finished Goods $76,000 (Product Y, $46,000; Product Z, $30,000).

REQUIRED

1. Prepare general journal entries for the foregoing transactions.

2. Post the entries to the general ledger T accounts for Work in Process and Finished Goods, and compute the ending balances in these accounts.

3. Determine the job cost ledger balance to support the balance in the work in process account.

4. Determine the amount of underapplied or overapplied factory overhead.

CHALLENGE PROBLEM

This problem challenges you to apply your cumulative accounting knowledge to move a step beyond the material in the chapter.

2: Net Income = $75,750

For its most recent year of operations, Unovap Co. had sales of $950,000, cost of goods sold of $680,000, and operating expenses of $190,000. Its ending inventories were as follows:

Raw material $30,000
Work in process   88,000
Finished goods   32,000

In addition, it has $5,000 of underapplied overhead which has not yet been transferred to any other accounts.

REQUIRED

1. Transfer the underapplied overhead to Cost of Goods Sold and calculate the net income for the year.

2. Spread the underapplied overhead among Work in Process, Finished Goods, and Cost of Goods Sold, and calculate the net income for the year.

3. (a)   What is the difference in the net income based on the two different approaches to accounting for the underapplied overhead?

    (b)   How would you recommend accounting for the underapplied overhead in this case?

©CORBIS

Manufacturing Accounting: The Work Sheet and Financial Statements

Finny Co. completed the order for the set of instruments for the high school described in Chapter 28. Subsequently, that area of the business has expanded so that special orders are in process for several other high schools and two colleges. According to Mike's accountant, material, labor, and overhead costs will be accumulated for these jobs in the same manner as for the first special order. Mike's understanding of this cost system is that overhead is applied to each job when the job is completed. But it is now the end of the year and Mike once again has an accounting question. Should any overhead costs be applied to the ending work in process, even though these jobs are not finished?

LO1 Prepare a ten-column work sheet for a manufacturing company.

LO2 Prepare work sheet adjusting entries to (1) apply factory overhead to ending work in process, (2) record additional actual factory overhead, (3) record underapplied or overapplied overhead, (4) record other expenses not involving overhead, and (5) provide for corporate income taxes.

LO3 Prepare financial statements for a manufacturing company.

LO4 Prepare adjusting, closing, and reversing journal entries for a manufacturing company.

In Chapters 15 and 16, we learned how to use the work sheet to prepare financial statements for a merchandising company. In this chapter, we use a work sheet to prepare financial statements for a manufacturing company. Both the work sheet and financial statements of a manufacturer differ from those of a merchandiser.

THE WORK SHEET FOR A MANUFACTURING COMPANY

LO1 Prepare a ten-column work sheet for a manufacturing company.

The work sheet for a manufacturing company is similar to the one illustrated in Chapter 15 for a merchandising company. The same five steps are used to prepare both work sheets.

STEP 1 Prepare the trial balance.

STEP 2 Prepare the adjustments.

STEP 3 Prepare the adjusted trial balance.

STEP 4 Extend the adjusted trial balance amounts to the Income Statement and Balance Sheet columns.

STEP 5 Total the Income Statement and Balance Sheet columns to compute the net income or net loss.

Figure 29-1 shows the Trial Balance and Adjustments columns of ToyJoy Manufacturing Co.'s work sheet. The Trial Balance columns were completed by copying the balances of all accounts from the general ledger (not shown). The following accounts and related adjustments are different from the Chapter 15 illustration and are highlighted in the work sheet:

1 Finished Goods Inventory, Work in Process Inventory, and Materials Inventory

2 Cost of Goods Sold

3 Factory Overhead

4 Income Tax Expense and Income Tax Payable

ToyJoy Manufacturing Co.
Work Sheet (Partial)
For Year Ended December 31, 20 --

	ACCOUNT TITLE	Trial Balance Debit	Trial Balance Credit	Adjustments Debit	Adjustments Credit	
1	Cash	25 7 6 3 00				1
2	Government Notes	5 0 0 0 00				2
3	Accounts Receivable	66 4 8 5 00				3
4	Allowance for Bad Debts		4 6 0 00		(g) 1 4 0 5 00	4
5	Finished Goods Inventory	35 6 1 4 00				5
6	Work in Process Inventory [1]	9 9 9 0 00		(a) 2 7 0 0 00		6
7	Materials Inventory	9 2 7 5 00				7
8	Factory Supplies	5 5 4 2 00			(b) 5 0 2 0 00	8
9	Prepaid Insurance	8 0 6 0 00			(c) 6 5 2 0 00	9
10	Land	40 0 0 0 00				10
11	Factory Building	178 0 0 0 00				11
12	Accumulated Depreciation—Factory Building		30 0 0 0 00		(d) 7 5 0 0 00	12
13	Factory Equipment	155 0 0 0 00				13
14	Accumulated Depreciation—Factory Equipment		40 6 4 0 00		(d) 13 5 0 0 00	14
15	Office Equipment	21 3 0 0 00				15
16	Accumulated Depreciation—Office Equipment		4 9 2 5 00		(h) 2 0 0 0 00	16
17	Interest Payable				(f) 8 0 0 00	17
18	Accounts Payable		39 6 8 5 00			18
19	Income Tax Payable [4]				(i) 7 3 0 0 00	19
20	Bonds Payable		100 0 0 0 00			20
21	Capital Stock		75 0 0 0 00			21
22	Paid-In Capital in Excess of Par		20 0 0 0 00			22
23	Retained Earnings		132 6 9 0 00			23
24	Cash Dividends	15 0 0 0 00				24
25	Sales		835 9 4 8 00			25
26	Interest Revenue		4 3 0 00			26
27	Factory Overhead [3]	155 0 8 0 00	185 9 8 2 00	(b) 5 0 2 0 00	(a) 2 7 0 0 00	27
28				(c) 6 5 2 0 00		28
29				(d) 21 0 0 0 00		29
30				(e) 1 0 6 2 00		30
31	Cost of Goods Sold [2]	601 5 8 1 00			(e) 1 0 6 2 00	31
32	Wages Expense	91 3 1 6 00				32
33	Advertising Expense	5 2 6 4 00				33
34	Bad Debt Expense			(g) 1 4 0 5 00		34
35	Utilities Expense—Office	5 6 9 0 00				35
36	Depreciation Expense—Office Equipment			(h) 2 0 0 0 00		36
37	Interest Expense	8 8 0 0 00		(f) 8 0 0 00		37
38	Income Tax Expense [4]	23 0 0 0 00		(i) 7 3 0 0 00		38
39		1,465 7 6 0 00	1,465 7 6 0 00	47 8 0 7 00	47 8 0 7 00	39

FIGURE 29-1 Partial Work Sheet

Inventories

Instead of a single merchandise inventory account, the manufacturer has three inventory accounts—Finished Goods, Work in Process, and Materials. The manufacturer purchases materials (Materials Inventory) and converts them (Work in Process Inventory) to completed products (Finished Goods Inventory) for sale to customers.

Cost of Goods Sold

The cost of goods sold account is related to the inventory accounts. Cost of Goods Sold appears on the work sheet because ToyJoy uses a perpetual inventory system. With a perpetual inventory system, the movement of goods from materials to work in process to finished goods to cost of goods sold is recorded as the movement occurs. This has two important effects on ToyJoy's work sheet compared with the one presented in Chapter 15 for a business using the periodic inventory method.

1. The costs of goods sold are accumulated in Cost of Goods Sold as sales occur during the year. Thus, Cost of Goods Sold is not computed by means of an adjustment process at the end of the period as we did in Chapter 15.

2. The inventory accounts (Materials, Work in Process, and Finished Goods) reflect ending rather than beginning balances.

LEARNING KEY: Because ToyJoy uses a perpetual inventory system, Cost of Goods Sold contains the costs recorded as sales were made during the year. The inventory accounts reflect the ending balances.

Factory Overhead

The factory overhead account appears solely because ToyJoy is a manufacturer. Factory overhead exists as part of the cost of manufacturing products. Both the debit ($155,080) and credit ($185,982) totals are shown for this account.

The debit represents the actual overhead costs incurred. The credit represents overhead applied to production. Both the debit and credit balances are shown for completeness of presentation, and because both amounts are useful in preparing financial statements.

Income Tax

Income Tax Expense and Income Tax Payable appear because ToyJoy is a corporation. As explained in Chapter 22, income taxes are an expense of doing business as a corporation.

ADJUSTING ENTRIES

LO2 Prepare work sheet adjusting entries to (1) apply factory overhead to ending work in process, (2) record additional actual factory overhead, (3) record underapplied or overapplied overhead, (4) record other expenses not involving overhead, and (5) provide for corporate income taxes.

The second pair of amount columns in Figure 29-1 contains the adjustments. Data for adjusting the accounts are as follows:

(a) Factory overhead to be applied to work in process
       ending inventory $ 2,700

(b) Factory supplies consumed   5,020

(c) Insurance expired on factory building and equipment   6,520

(d) Depreciation on:
        factory building   7,500
        factory equipment   13,500

(e) Overapplied factory overhead   1,062

(f) Accrual of interest payable   800

(g) Estimate of uncollectible accounts, based on an aging
       of accounts receivable   1,865

(h) Depreciation on office equipment   2,000

(i) Provision for corporate income taxes   7,300

The adjustments that are similar to those illustrated in Chapter 15 will be explained very briefly. Adjustments (a), (b), (c), (d), (e), and (i) are new and will be explained more fully.

Apply Factory Overhead to Ending Work in Process

Adjustment (a)

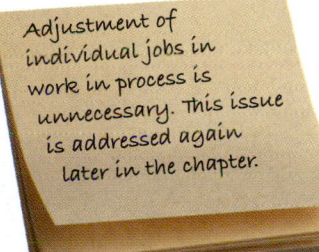

Adjustment of individual jobs in work in process is unnecessary. This issue is addressed again later in the chapter.

As jobs were completed during the year, factory overhead was applied to them at a rate of 60% of direct labor costs. At the end of the year, several jobs are still in process. To correctly state the work in process ending inventory, factory overhead must be applied to these jobs. The job cost ledger (not shown here) shows total direct labor costs of $4,500 on jobs in process at December 31. An adjustment is needed to apply $2,700 (60% of the direct labor costs) to work in process. Debit Work in Process Inventory and credit Factory Overhead.

LEARNING KEY: Factory overhead must be applied to Work in Process at the end of the year.

Record Additional Actual Factory Overhead

Adjustment (b)

A physical count of factory supplies at the end of the year shows that $5,020 of factory supplies were used during the year. Since factory supplies expense is part of factory overhead, debit Factory Overhead and credit Factory Supplies for $5,020. The factory supplies expense account in the factory overhead ledger (not shown here) also is debited for this amount.

Adjustment (c)

A review of the insurance policy files shows that $6,520 of insurance on the factory building and equipment has expired. Since factory building and equipment insurance expense is part of factory overhead, debit Factory Overhead and credit Prepaid Insurance for $6,520. Also debit the factory building and equipment insurance expense account in the factory overhead ledger.

Adjustment (d)

Depreciation expense for the year was $7,500 on the factory building and $13,500 on the factory equipment, a total of $21,000. Depreciation expense on the factory building and factory equipment is part of factory overhead. Therefore, debit Factory Overhead for $21,000, and credit Accumulated Depreciation—Factory Building for $7,500 and Accumulated Depreciation—Factory Equipment for $13,500. Also debit the depreciation expense—factory building and equipment account in the factory overhead ledger for $21,000.

Notice that adjustments (b), (c), and (d) are *debited* to Factory Overhead. Recall from Chapter 28 that actual factory overhead expenses are debited to Factory Overhead.

Record Underapplied or Overapplied Overhead

Adjustment (e)

This adjustment is needed because overhead was overapplied during the year. Figure 29-2 shows the factory overhead account in T account form. The amounts shown are:

1 debit and credit "balances" from the December 31 trial balance

2 debits for adjustments (b), (c), and (d)

3 credit for adjustment (a)

4 total actual overhead and overhead applied

5 debit for adjustment (e), which makes the total debits and credits equal in the account

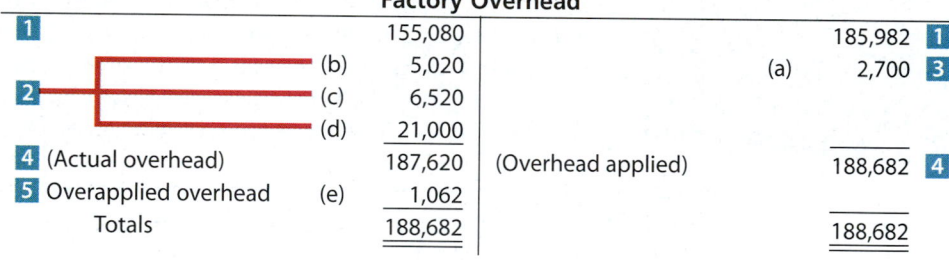

FIGURE 29-2   Factory Overhead T Account

The two item **4** amounts in Figure 29-2 show that actual overhead for the year was $187,620, while overhead applied was $188,682. Thus overhead was *overapplied* by $1,062. Debit Factory Overhead and credit Cost of Goods Sold for $1,062 to adjust for overapplied overhead.

 LEARNING KEY: After all adjustments are made for actual and applied overhead, an adjustment for underapplied or overapplied overhead is needed.

Record Other Expenses Not Involving Overhead

Adjustment (f)

Interest of $800 is accrued at the end of the year on the bonds payable. Debit Interest Expense and credit Interest Payable.

Adjustment (g)

The estimated amount of uncollectible accounts at the end of the year, based on an aging of accounts receivable, is $1,865. Allowance for Bad Debts had a credit balance of $460, so the necessary adjustment is $1,405 ($1,865 – $460). Debit Bad Debt Expense and credit Allowance for Bad Debts.

Adjustment (h)

Depreciation expense for the year on the office equipment was $2,000. Debit Depreciation Expense—Office Equipment and credit Accumulated Depreciation—Office Equipment.

Provide for Corporate Income Taxes

Adjustment (i)

Corporate income tax for the year is $30,300. Since income tax expense of $23,000 was recorded during the year, an adjustment of $7,300 is needed ($30,300 – $23,000 = $7,300). Debit Income Tax Expense and credit Income Tax Payable.

A BROADER VIEW

Work in Process Inventory—This Stuff Really Matters

When you study the year-end accounting procedures for a manufacturing company, you might question whether all the adjustments really matter in the real world. One way to answer that question is to consider the financial statements of a real company.

Boeing Co., a leading aircraft manufacturer, reported 2002 net income of $492 million. At the end of 2002, Boeing's ending inventory included $17 billion of work in process. Think about the accounting implications of these figures. Boeing's work in process inventory is more than 34 times ($17 billion ÷ $492 million = 34.55) the size of its net income. This means that a relatively small percentage error in work in process inventory could have a significant effect on the net income. Clearly, the year-end adjustments can be quite important for a company like Boeing.

©MATTHEW NEAL MCVAY/TONY STONE

Completing the Work Sheet

Figure 29-3 on page 1087 shows ToyJoy's full ten-column work sheet. Note the handling of the factory overhead account. The total debits and total credits of $188,682 appear in the Adjusted Trial Balance columns. But neither of these amounts is extended to the Income Statement or Balance Sheet columns. Figure 29-4 shows why this is so. Factory overhead costs are (1) incurred, (2) applied to Work in Process, (3) transferred to Finished Goods with completed products, and (4) transferred to Cost of Goods Sold when goods are sold.

 LEARNING KEY: The factory overhead account balances are not extended to the Income Statement or Balance Sheet columns.

The factory overhead amounts are not extended because they have already been transferred to Work in Process, Finished Goods, and Cost of Goods Sold. These three account balances are extended to the appropriate Income Statement and Balance Sheet columns.

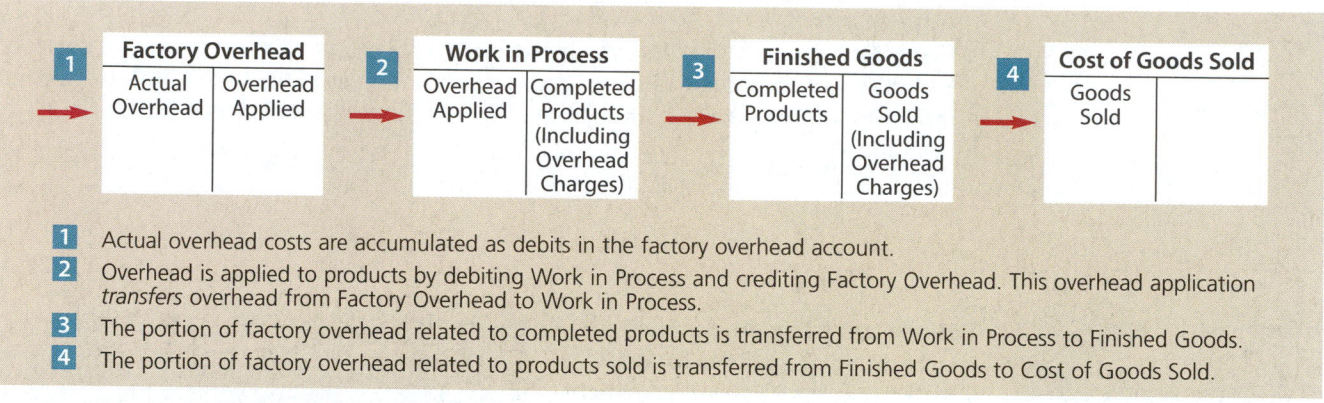

1 Actual overhead costs are accumulated as debits in the factory overhead account.
2 Overhead is applied to products by debiting Work in Process and crediting Factory Overhead. This overhead application *transfers* overhead from Factory Overhead to Work in Process.
3 The portion of factory overhead related to completed products is transferred from Work in Process to Finished Goods.
4 The portion of factory overhead related to products sold is transferred from Finished Goods to Cost of Goods Sold.

FIGURE 29-4 Flow of Overhead Costs in a Manufacturing Accounting System

FINANCIAL STATEMENTS

LO3 Prepare financial statements for a manufacturing company.

ToyJoy's financial statements include an income statement, retained earnings statement, balance sheet, and statement of cash flows. The statement of cash flows is essentially the same in format as the one illustrated in Chapter 25, so it is not presented here. We will focus on the statements prepared from the enhanced work sheet for a manufacturing business.

Income Statement

ToyJoy uses a perpetual inventory system, so cost of goods sold is already known, as shown in the worksheet in Figure 29-3. The procedures described here are simply to show the calculation of cost of goods sold on the income statement.

ToyJoy's income statement is presented in Figure 29-5 on page 1088. All income statement data were obtained from the Income Statement columns of the work sheet, except for the cost of goods sold section. To prepare this section, the beginning finished goods inventory was taken from the finished goods account in the general ledger (not shown). The cost of goods manufactured was taken from the schedule of cost of goods manufactured (Figure 29-6, page 1089). The ending finished goods inventory is from the Balance Sheet columns of the work sheet.

ToyJoy Manufacturing Co.
Work Sheet
For Year Ended December 31, 20 --

#	ACCOUNT TITLE	TRIAL BALANCE Debit	TRIAL BALANCE Credit	ADJUSTMENTS Debit	ADJUSTMENTS Credit	ADJUSTED TRIAL BALANCE Debit	ADJUSTED TRIAL BALANCE Credit	INCOME STATEMENT Debit	INCOME STATEMENT Credit	BALANCE SHEET Debit	BALANCE SHEET Credit
1	Cash	25 7 6 3 00				25 7 6 3 00				25 7 6 3 00	
2	Government Notes	5 0 0 0 00				5 0 0 0 00				5 0 0 0 00	
3	Accounts Receivable	66 4 8 5 00				66 4 8 5 00				66 4 8 5 00	
4	Allowance for Bad Debts		4 6 0 00		(g) 1 4 0 5 00		1 8 6 5 00				1 8 6 5 00
5	Finished Goods Inventory	35 6 1 4 00				35 6 1 4 00				35 6 1 4 00	
6	Work in Process Inventory	9 9 9 0 00		(a) 2 7 0 0 00		12 6 9 0 00				12 6 9 0 00	
7	Materials Inventory	9 2 7 5 00				9 2 7 5 00				9 2 7 5 00	
8	Factory Supplies	5 5 4 2 00			(b) 5 0 2 0 00	5 2 2 00				5 2 2 00	
9	Prepaid Insurance	8 0 6 0 00			(c) 6 5 2 0 00	1 5 4 0 00				1 5 4 0 00	
10	Land	40 0 0 0 00				40 0 0 0 00				40 0 0 0 00	
11	Factory Building	178 0 0 0 00				178 0 0 0 00				178 0 0 0 00	
12	Accum. Depr.—Factory Building		30 0 0 0 00		(d) 7 5 0 0 00		37 5 0 0 00				37 5 0 0 00
13	Factory Equipment	155 0 0 0 00				155 0 0 0 00				155 0 0 0 00	
14	Accum. Depr.—Factory Equip.		40 6 4 0 00		(d) 13 5 0 0 00		54 1 4 0 00				54 1 4 0 00
15	Office Equipment	21 3 0 0 00				21 3 0 0 00				21 3 0 0 00	
16	Accum. Depr.—Office Equipment		4 9 2 5 00		(h) 2 0 0 0 00		6 9 2 5 00				6 9 2 5 00
17	Interest Payable				(f) 8 0 0 00		8 0 0 00				8 0 0 00
18	Accounts Payable		39 6 8 5 00				39 6 8 5 00				39 6 8 5 00
19	Income Tax Payable				(i) 7 3 0 0 00		7 3 0 0 00				7 3 0 0 00
20	Bonds Payable		100 0 0 0 00				100 0 0 0 00				100 0 0 0 00
21	Capital Stock		75 0 0 0 00				75 0 0 0 00				75 0 0 0 00
22	Paid-in Capital in Excess of Par		20 0 0 0 00				20 0 0 0 00				20 0 0 0 00
23	Retained Earnings		132 6 9 0 00				132 6 9 0 00				132 6 9 0 00
24	Cash Dividends	15 0 0 0 00				15 0 0 0 00				15 0 0 0 00	
25	Sales		835 9 4 8 00				835 9 4 8 00		835 9 4 8 00		
26	Interest Revenue		4 3 0 00				4 3 0 00		4 3 0 00		
27	Factory Overhead	155 0 8 0 00	185 9 8 2 00	(b) 5 0 2 0 00	(a) 2 7 0 0 00	188 6 8 2 00	188 6 8 2 00	Not extended			
28				(c) 6 5 2 0 00							
29				(d) 21 0 0 0 00							
30				(e) 1 0 6 2 00							
31	Cost of Goods Sold	601 5 8 1 00			(e) 1 0 6 2 00	600 5 1 9 00		600 5 1 9 00			
32	Wages Expense	91 3 1 6 00				91 3 1 6 00		91 3 1 6 00			
33	Advertising Expense	5 2 6 4 00				5 2 6 4 00		5 2 6 4 00			
34	Bad Debt Expense			(g) 1 4 0 5 00		1 4 0 5 00		1 4 0 5 00			
35	Utilities Expense—Office	5 6 9 0 00				5 6 9 0 00		5 6 9 0 00			
36	Depr. Expense—Office Equip.			(h) 2 0 0 0 00		2 0 0 0 00		2 0 0 0 00			
37	Interest Expense	8 8 0 0 00		(f) 8 0 0 00		9 6 0 0 00		9 6 0 0 00			
38	Income Tax Expense	23 0 0 0 00		(i) 7 3 0 0 00		30 3 0 0 00		30 3 0 0 00			
39		1,465 7 6 0 00	1,465 7 6 0 00	47 8 0 7 00	47 8 0 7 00	1,500 9 6 5 00	1,500 9 6 5 00	746 0 9 4 00	836 3 7 8 00	566 1 8 9 00	475 9 0 5 00
40	Net Income							90 2 8 4 00			90 2 8 4 00
41								836 3 7 8 00	836 3 7 8 00	566 1 8 9 00	566 1 8 9 00

FIGURE 29-3 Work Sheet

A manufacturer's income statement is commonly supported by a schedule of cost of goods manufactured like the one in Figure 29-6. The ending materials and work in process inventories are from the Balance Sheet columns of the work sheet. Other data for this schedule, listed in the order in which they appear, were obtained from the following sources.

DATA	SOURCE OF DATA
Work in process inventory, Jan. 1	Work in process account in general ledger
Materials inventory, Jan. 1	Materials inventory account in general ledger
Purchases	Materials inventory account in general ledger
Direct labor	Work in process account in general ledger
Overhead	Factory overhead account in general ledger
Work in process inventory, Dec. 31	Balance Sheet columns of the work sheet

ToyJoy Manufacturing Co.
Income Statement
For Year Ended December 31, 20 --

Net sales			$835 9 4 8 00
Less cost of goods sold:			
Finished goods inventory, January 1	$ 24 5 6 9 00		
Cost of goods manufactured	611 5 6 4 00	◁ From Schedule	
Cost of goods available for sale	$636 1 3 3 00		
Finished goods inventory, December 31	35 6 1 4 00		
Cost of goods sold			600 5 1 9 00
Gross profit			$235 4 2 9 00
Operating expenses:			
Wages expense	$ 91 3 1 6 00		
Advertising expense	5 2 6 4 00		
Bad debt expense	1 4 0 5 00		
Utilities expense—office	5 6 9 0 00		
Depreciation expense—office equipment	2 0 0 0 00		
Total operating expenses			105 6 7 5 00
Operating income			$129 7 5 4 00
Other revenue:			
Interest revenue			4 3 0 00
			$130 1 8 4 00
Other expense:			
Interest expense			9 6 0 0 00
Income before income taxes			$120 5 8 4 00
Income tax			30 3 0 0 00
Net income	To Retained Earnings Statement ▷		$ 90 2 8 4 00

FIGURE 29-5 Income Statement

ToyJoy Manufacturing Co. Schedule of Cost of Goods Manufactured For Year Ended December 31, 20 --			
Work in process, January 1			$ 11 9 4 0 00
Materials inventory, January 1	$ 12 9 9 2 00		
Materials purchases	121 3 8 0 00		
Materials available for use	$134 3 7 2 00		
Materials inventory, December 31	9 2 7 5 00		
Cost of materials used		$125 0 9 7 00	
Direct labor		299 5 9 7 00	
Factory overhead		187 6 2 0 00	
Total manufacturing costs			612 3 1 4 00
Total work in process during the period			$624 2 5 4 00
Work in process, December 31			12 6 9 0 00
Cost of goods manufactured		To Income Statement	$611 5 6 4 00

FIGURE 29-6 Schedule of Cost of Goods Manufactured

Retained Earnings Statement

The retained earnings statement appears in Figure 29-7. The retained earnings balance at January 1 and the cash dividends for the year are taken from the Balance Sheet columns of the worksheet. The net income for the year can be taken from the Income Statement columns of the worksheet or from the income statement. The only distinctive feature of the retained earnings statement arises from ToyJoy being organized as a corporation. As a corporation, ToyJoy pays dividends, in this case, $15,000.

ToyJoy Manufacturing Co. Retained Earnings Statement For Year Ended December 31, 20 --		
Retained earnings, January 1		$132 6 9 0 00
Net income for the year (after provision for income taxes of $30,300)		90 2 8 4 00	From Income Statement
		$222 9 7 4 00
Less cash dividends ($1.00 per share) Corporate Dividends		15 0 0 0 00
Retained earnings, December 31		$207 9 7 4 00	To Balance Sheet

FIGURE 29-7 Retained Earnings Statement

Balance Sheet

ToyJoy's balance sheet is presented in Figure 29-8. Data for this statement were taken from the Balance Sheet columns of the work sheet, except for the retained earnings. This amount was taken from the retained earnings statement. Note that the retained earnings amount on the balance sheet ($207,974) also can be calculated from the work sheet. It is the sum of the retained earnings balance shown on the work sheet ($132,690) plus the net income for the year ($90,284) less the cash dividends for the year ($15,000).

Two main differences in this balance sheet compared with those for merchandising companies are:

1. Since this is a manufacturing company, there are three inventory accounts listed: Finished Goods, Work in Process, and Materials.

2. Since ToyJoy is a corporation, the stockholders' equity section contains information regarding capital stock, paid-in capital in excess of par, and retained earnings.

JOURNAL ENTRIES

LO4 Prepare adjusting, closing, and reversing journal entries for a manufacturing company.

Most of ToyJoy's adjusting, closing, and reversing entries are similar to those illustrated in Chapters 15 and 16 for a merchandising company. We will comment only on selected adjustments.

Adjusting Entries

The entries appearing in the Adjustments columns of the work sheet are journalized as shown in Figure 29-9 on page 1092. For ease of identification, each entry includes the coding letter from the work sheet.

Notice two things about these adjusting entries.

Aggregate work in process must be adjusted so that it is reported correctly on the financial statements. The individual jobs require no adjustment because they are not reported on any financial statements.

1. In adjustment (a), the application of factory overhead to ending work in process, no entries are made to the individual jobs in the job cost ledger. Only the aggregate work in process needs to be adjusted for financial reporting purposes at year end, not the individual jobs in process. The aggregate adjustment will be reversed at the beginning of the following period.

2. In adjustments (b), (c), and (d), the factory overhead account and the related subsidiary accounts are identified. Both the general ledger and subsidiary ledger accounts are adjusted for these actual overhead amounts.

ToyJoy Manufacturing Co. Balance Sheet December 31, 20--															
Assets															
Current assets:															
Cash							$ 25	7	6	3	00					
Government notes							5	0	0	0	00					
Accounts receivable	$ 66	4	8	5	00											
Less allowance for bad debts	1	8	6	5	00		64	6	2	0	00					
Inventories:															
Finished goods	$ 35	6	1	4	00											
Work in process	12	6	9	0	00											
Materials	9	2	7	5	00		57	5	7	9	00					
Factory supplies								5	2	2	00					
Prepaid insurance							1	5	4	0	00					
Total current assets												$155	0	2	4	00
Property, plant, and equipment:															
Land							$ 40	0	0	0	00					
Factory building	$178	0	0	0	00											
Less accumulated depreciation	37	5	0	0	00		140	5	0	0	00					
Factory equipment	$155	0	0	0	00											
Less accumulated depreciation	54	1	4	0	00		100	8	6	0	00					
Office equipment	$ 21	3	0	0	00											
Less accumulated depreciation	6	9	2	5	00		14	3	7	5	00					
Total property, plant, and equipment												295	7	3	5	00
Total assets												$450	7	5	9	00
Liabilities															
Current liabilities:															
Interest payable							$	8	0	0	00					
Accounts payable							39	6	8	5	00					
Income tax payable							7	3	0	0	00					
Total current liabilities												$ 47	7	8	5	00
Long-term liabilities:															
Bonds payable												100	0	0	0	00
Total liabilities												$147	7	8	5	00
Stockholders' Equity															
Common stock ($5 par value, 50,000 shares authorized;															
15,000 shares issued)							$ 75	0	0	0	00					
Paid-in capital in excess of par							20	0	0	0	00					
Retained earnings							207	9	7	4	00					
Total stockholders' equity												302	9	7	4	00
Total liabilities and stockholders' equity												$450	7	5	9	00

Three inventories

Corporate section

From Retained Earnings Statement

FIGURE 29-8 Balance Sheet

	DATE		DESCRIPTION	POST REF.	DEBIT					CREDIT					
			GENERAL JOURNAL												
1			Adjusting Entries												1
2	20— Dec.	31	Work in Process Inventory		2	7	0	0	00						2
3	(a)		Factory Overhead							2	7	0	0	00	3
4															4
5	(b)	31	Factory Overhead (Factory Supplies Expense)		5	0	2	0	00						5
6			Factory Supplies							5	0	2	0	00	6
7															7
8	(c)	31	Factory Overhead (Factory Building and Equipment,												8
9			Insurance Expense)		6	5	2	0	00						9
10			Prepaid Insurance							6	5	2	0	00	10
11															11
12	(d)	31	Factory Overhead (Depreciation Expense—												12
13			Factory Building and Equipment)		21	0	0	0	00						13
14			Accumulated Depreciation—Factory Equipment							13	5	0	0	00	14
15			Accumulated Depreciation—Factory Building							7	5	0	0	00	15
16															16
17	(e)	31	Factory Overhead		1	0	6	2	00						17
18			Cost of Goods Sold							1	0	6	2	00	18
19															19
20	(f)	31	Interest Expense			8	0	0	00						20
21			Interest Payable								8	0	0	00	21
22															22
23	(g)	31	Bad Debt Expense		1	4	0	5	00						23
24			Allowance for Bad Debts							1	4	0	5	00	24
25															25
26	(h)	31	Depreciation Expense—Office Equipment		2	0	0	0	00						26
27			Accumulated Depreciation—Office Equipment							2	0	0	0	00	27
28															28
29	(i)	31	Income Tax Expense		7	3	0	0	00						29
30			Income Tax Payable							7	3	0	0	00	30
31															31
32															32
33															33
34															34
35															35
36															36
37															37
38															38
39															39

Aggregate

Identify subsidiary

Identify subsidiary

Identify subsidiary

FIGURE 29-9 Adjusting Entries

Closing Entries

Six steps are used to close ToyJoy's temporary accounts.

STEP 1   Transfer the debit balance in the factory overhead account to Income Summary and close the subsidiary factory overhead accounts.

STEP 2   Transfer the credit balance in the factory overhead account to Income Summary.

STEP 3   Transfer the balances of the sales and interest revenue accounts to Income Summary.

STEP 4   Transfer the balances of the cost of goods sold and all expense accounts to Income Summary.

STEP 5   Transfer the balance of Income Summary to Retained Earnings.

STEP 6   Transfer the balance of Cash Dividends to Retained Earnings.

Figure 29-10 shows the journal entries corresponding to these six steps. Entries (3), (4), (5), and (6) are essentially the same as they would be for a merchandising company. Entries (1) and (2) require explanation.

GENERAL JOURNAL

	DATE		DESCRIPTION	POST REF.	DEBIT	CREDIT		
1			Closing Entries				1	
2	Dec. 20--	31	Income Summary		188 6 8 2 00		2	STEP 1
3	(1)		Factory Overhead (Subsidiary ledger accounts)			188 6 8 2 00	3	
4							4	
5	(2)	31	Factory Overhead		188 6 8 2 00		5	STEP 2
6			Income Summary			188 6 8 2 00	6	
7							7	
8	(3)	31	Sales		835 9 4 8 00		8	STEP 3
9			Interest Revenue		4 3 0 00		9	
10			Income Summary			836 3 7 8 00	10	
11							11	
12	(4)	31	Income Summary		746 0 9 4 00		12	STEP 4
13			Cost of Goods Sold			600 5 1 9 00	13	
14			Wages Expense			91 3 1 6 00	14	
15			Advertising Expense			5 2 6 4 00	15	
16			Bad Debt Expense			1 4 0 5 00	16	
17			Utilities Expense—Office			5 6 9 0 00	17	
18			Depreciation Expense—Office Equipment			2 0 0 0 00	18	
19			Interest Expense			9 6 0 0 00	19	
20			Income Tax Expense			30 3 0 0 00	20	
21							21	
22	(5)	31	Income Summary		90 2 8 4 00		22	STEP 5
23			Retained Earnings			90 2 8 4 00	23	
24							24	
25	(6)	31	Retained Earnings		15 0 0 0 00		25	STEP 6
26			Cash Dividends			15 0 0 0 00	26	

FIGURE 29-10   Closing Entries

The T account in Figure 29-2 on page 1084 shows that the factory overhead account has a zero balance after all adjustments are entered. This account must still be "closed" to close the factory overhead subsidiary ledger accounts. This is the purpose of entries (1) and (2) in Figure 29-10.

Entry (1) closes the total debit amount in the factory overhead account to Income Summary. At the same time, the related factory overhead subsidiary ledger accounts are closed. (The detail for each subsidiary ledger account is omitted here.) Entry (2) closes the total credit amount in factory overhead to Income Summary.

Reversing Entries

The purpose of reversing entries is to simplify the recording of routine transactions. Corporate income taxes are a specialized rather than routine transaction, so this adjustment is not reversed.

ToyJoy reverses two of the adjusting entries made on December 31. Entry (1) in Figure 29-11 is related to the accrued interest on bonds payable. The purpose of this type of reversing entry was explained in Chapter 16. Entry (2) is unique to a manufacturing company. This entry reverses the adjusting entry to apply factory overhead to Work in Process. This reversal facilitates applying factory overhead to completed jobs in the following year. Recall that factory overhead is applied at a predetermined rate when a job is completed. If this reversing entry were not made, it would be necessary to keep track of which jobs already had a partial overhead application from a prior year's adjustment.

 LEARNING KEY: Reverse the adjusting entry to apply overhead to Work in Process.

			GENERAL JOURNAL										
	DATE		DESCRIPTION	POST. REF.		DEBIT				CREDIT			
1			Reversing Entries										1
2	20-- Jan.	1	Interest Payable			8	0	0	00				2
3	(1)		Interest Expense							8	0	0	00	3
4													4
5	(2)	1	Factory Overhead		2	7	0	0	00				5
6			Work in Process Inventory							2	7	0	0	00	6
7													7

FIGURE 29-11   Reversing Entries

Computers and Accounting

Integrated Accounting Systems for Manufacturing—Gary P. Schneider, University of San Diego

As you have learned in this chapter, accounting for manufacturing companies can be significantly more complicated than for service and merchandising businesses. Manufacturers must keep track of materials inventory going into finished products, the labor (direct and indirect) that creates those finished products, and the overhead costs that support the manufacturing activity.

One of the first things that large manufacturing companies did to make their accounting systems more efficient was to remove paper from the process. Starting in the mid-1960s, companies began using data transmissions instead of sending paper purchase orders, invoices, and freight bills. This process, called electronic data interchange (EDI), was very successful in reducing paper-handling costs and reducing errors for large companies. Unfortunately, the cost of leasing telephone lines to transfer the data was very expensive and smaller companies often could not afford to participate in EDI. In recent years, the Internet and more powerful personal computers have given smaller businesses the ability to participate in EDI.

Larger companies use computers to automate and streamline all kinds of business activities. For example, most large companies have a computer generate the materials requisition form you learned about in this chapter. The computer can create this form automatically when a customer order is received. Inventory systems that accomplish this are called manufacturing resources planning systems (MRPs).

More advanced systems, called materials requirements planning (MRP II) systems, do far more than just generate a materials requisition form. These systems can plan the entire production process. When a customer order is received, an MRP II system can schedule time on production machinery, order needed materials, and even arrange workers' schedules to ensure that the item the customer ordered is manufactured and shipped on time. As MRP II systems have become more refined, they have begun to include design engineering. Some truly amazing things can be accomplished with a highly integrated MRP II system. For example, Boeing designed its 777 aircraft completely on computer. When a customer orders a 777, Boeing's MRP II system uses the electronic "blueprints" to create a production schedule and order all materials needed to build the airplane to meet the customer's specifications exactly. Dell Computer also uses a highly integrated system. Dell can build a computer to match a customer's order in less than four hours. MRP and MRP II systems are built using large databases that store the detailed information and provide software tools that accountants, plant managers, and operations staff can use to extract the information in a variety of formats.

Some large companies take information integration beyond the limits of MRP and MRP II systems. They combine all of their information processing functions into one massive system that managers can use to run the entire company. These enterprise-wide systems include all information processing functions for accounting, human resources management, manufacturing, design, engineering, and distribution in one database. The largest of these integrated systems are called enterprise resource planning (ERP) systems and can cost many millions of dollars to implement. The computer hardware for these large systems is expensive, but the software and the fees paid to outside consultants are even more costly. The main providers of ERP software include Baan (a Dutch company), Oracle, PeopleSoft, and SAP (a German company). The advantage of these systems is that they integrate the information flows throughout the company. This makes it easier for accountants to create comprehensive reports for management about how the business is doing.

As more companies integrate their accounting systems with the other computer systems in their organizations, it has become important for accountants to know more about computers in general. However, all companies—even those with ERP software—need people who understand how accounting works and what accounting reports mean.

Learning Objectives	Key Points to Remember
1 **Prepare a ten-column work sheet for a manufacturing company.**	Five steps are used to prepare a ten-column work sheet for a manufacturing company: 1. Prepare the trial balance. 2. Prepare the adjustments. 3. Prepare the adjusted trial balance. 4. Extend the adjusted trial balance amounts to the Income Statement and Balance Sheet columns. 5. Total the Income Statement and Balance Sheet columns to compute the net income or net loss. The new accounts and related adjustments on the work sheet are Finished Goods Inventory, Work in Process Inventory, Materials Inventory, Cost of Goods Sold, Factory Overhead, Income Tax Expense, and Corporate Income Tax Payable.
2 **Prepare work sheet adjusting entries to (1) apply factory overhead to ending work in process, (2) record additional actual factory overhead, (3) record underapplied or overapplied overhead, (4) record other expenses not involving overhead, and (5) provide for corporate income taxes.**	Overhead must be applied to work in process at year end. Adjustments for additional amounts of actual overhead are debited to Factory Overhead on the work sheet. After all adjustments are made for actual and applied overhead, an adjustment must be made for underapplied or overapplied overhead. An adjustment also is necessary for corporate income taxes. 　　The factory overhead account balances are extended to the Adjusted Trial Balance columns but not to the Income Statement or Balance Sheet columns on the work sheet.
3 **Prepare financial statements for a manufacturing company.**	The main differences between a manufacturer's income statement and that of a merchandiser are the cost of goods sold section and the supplementary schedule of cost of goods manufactured. 　　The only distinctive feature of ToyJoy's retained earnings statement is the deduction for dividends, because ToyJoy is a corporation. 　　Two main differences in ToyJoy's balance sheet are the three inventory accounts and the stockholders' equity section.
4 **Prepare adjusting, closing, and reversing journal entries for a manufacturing company.**	Each of the adjustments on the work sheet must be journalized. 　　All revenue and expense accounts and both the debit and credit totals of the Factory Overhead must be closed to Income Summary. Income Summary and Cash Dividends must be closed to Retained Earnings. 　　Reverse the adjusting entry for Interest Expense and the adjustment to apply factory overhead to work in process.

Reflection: Answering the Opening Question

To correctly state work in process ending inventory, factory overhead must be applied to jobs in process at the end of the year. The overhead should be applied on the same basis as it is applied to finished jobs.

DEMONSTRATION PROBLEM

WebTUTOR Advantage

The Montgomery Manufacturing Company manufactures and sells a limited line of products per customer order. Nothing is purchased for resale in its original form. The company rents offices and a factory building, and it owns neither real estate nor delivery equipment. It does have its own office and factory equipment. The company uses a perpetual inventory system and keeps its accounts on the calendar year basis. The trial balance of the general ledger as of December 31, 20--, is illustrated below. Data for the year-end adjustment of the accounts follows the trial balance.

Montgomery Manufacturing Co.
Trial Balance
December 31, 20 - -

ACCOUNT TITLE	DEBIT BALANCE	CREDIT BALANCE
Cash	56 1 1 5 00	
Accounts Receivable	90 9 2 8 00	
Allowance for Bad Debts		1 8 0 0 00
Finished Goods Inventory	63 1 8 0 00	
Work in Process Inventory	41 2 5 6 00	
Materials Inventory	46 8 4 5 00	
Office Supplies	2 9 1 6 00	
Factory Supplies	4 6 3 3 00	
Prepaid Insurance	5 5 8 9 00	
Factory Equipment	185 0 2 2 00	
Accumulated Depreciation—Factory Equipment		34 9 5 6 00
Office Equipment	19 5 3 0 00	
Accumulated Depreciation—Office Equipment		2 4 2 1 00
Notes Payable		27 0 0 0 00
Interest Payable		
Accounts Payable		38 5 9 0 00
Income Tax Payable		
Capital Stock		135 0 0 0 00
Retained Earnings		38 1 3 1 00
Cash Dividends	10 0 0 0 00	
Sales		842 1 5 7 00
Factory Overhead	44 2 1 2 00	60 5 8 5 00
Cost of Goods Sold	455 3 9 3 00	
Wages Expense	115 6 6 3 00	
Advertising Expense	24 6 8 0 00	
Office Rent Expense	13 1 8 0 00	
Office Supplies Expense		
Bad Debt Expense		
Insurance Expense—Office Equipment		
Depreciation Expense—Office Equipment		
Interest Expense	1 4 9 8 00	
Income Tax Expense		
	1,180 6 4 0 00	1,180 6 4 0 00

(continued)

Data for year-end adjustments are as follows:

(a)	Interest payable		$ 168
(b)	Office supplies expense		900
(c)	Factory supplies expense		1,870
(d)	Depreciation of office equipment		960
(e)	Depreciation of factory equipment		22,560
(f)	Insurance expense:		
	On office equipment	$ 120	
	On factory equipment	1,590	$ 1,710
(g)	Provision for uncollectible accounts (based on percentage of sales)		1,000
(h)	Provision for corporate income taxes		60,560
(i)	Factory overhead to be applied to work in process		4,729

Additional information needed to prepare the income statement and schedule of cost of goods manufactured is as follows:

Finished goods inventory, January 1	$219,692
Materials inventory, January 1	23,000
Purchases for the year	110,000
Direct labor	156,897
Work in process inventory, January 1	36,500

REQUIRED

1. Prepare a ten-column work sheet for the year ended December 31, 20--. After the factory overhead account is adjusted, the total debits will differ from the total credits. Enter the underapplied or overapplied overhead on the work sheet by transferring it to Cost of Goods Sold. (Label this adjustment (j).)

2. Prepare an income statement with a supporting schedule of cost of goods manufactured.

3. Journalize the adjusting journal entries from the work sheet. (For parts 3, 4, and 5, use journal page numbers 15–17.)

4. Prepare closing entries.

5. Prepare reversing entries.

Solution

1.

Montgomery Manufacturing Co.
Work Sheet
For Year Ended December 31, 20--

	ACCOUNT TITLE	TRIAL BALANCE Debit	TRIAL BALANCE Credit	ADJUSTMENTS Debit	ADJUSTMENTS Credit	ADJUSTED TRIAL BALANCE Debit	ADJUSTED TRIAL BALANCE Credit	INCOME STATEMENT Debit	INCOME STATEMENT Credit	BALANCE SHEET Debit	BALANCE SHEET Credit
1	Cash	56 115 00				56 115 00				56 115 00	
2	Accounts Receivable	90 928 00				90 928 00				90 928 00	
3	Allowance for Bad Debts		1 800 00		(g) 1 000 00		2 800 00				2 800 00
4	Finished Goods Inventory	63 180 00				63 180 00				63 180 00	
5	Work in Process Inventory	41 256 00		(i) 4 729 00		45 985 00				45 985 00	
6	Materials Inventory	46 845 00				46 845 00				46 845 00	
7	Office Supplies	2 916 00			(b) 900 00	2 016 00				2 016 00	
8	Factory Supplies	4 633 00			(c) 1 870 00	2 763 00				2 763 00	
9	Prepaid Insurance	5 589 00			(f) 1 710 00	3 879 00				3 879 00	
10	Factory Equipment	185 022 00				185 022 00				185 022 00	
11	Accum. Depr.—Factory Equip.		34 956 00		(e) 22 560 00		57 516 00				57 516 00
12	Office Equipment	19 530 00				19 530 00				19 530 00	
13	Accum. Depr.—Office Equip.		2 421 00		(d) 960 00		3 381 00				3 381 00
14	Notes Payable		27 000 00				27 000 00				27 000 00
15	Interest Payable				(a) 168 00		168 00				168 00
16	Accounts Payable		38 590 00				38 590 00				38 590 00
17	Income Tax Payable				(h) 60 560 00		60 560 00				60 560 00
18	Capital Stock		135 000 00				135 000 00				135 000 00
19	Retained Earnings		38 131 00				38 131 00				38 131 00
20	Cash Dividends	10 000 00				10 000 00				10 000 00	
21	Sales		842 157 00				842 157 00		842 157 00		
22	Factory Overhead	44 212 00	60 585 00	(c) 1 870 00 (e) 22 560 00 (f) 1 590 00	(i) 4 729 00 (j) 4 918 00	70 232 00	70 232 00				
23											
24											
25	Cost of Goods Sold	455 393 00		(j) 4 918 00		460 311 00		460 311 00			
26	Wages Expense	115 663 00				115 663 00		115 663 00			
27	Advertising Expense	24 680 00				24 680 00		24 680 00			
28	Office Rent Expense	13 180 00				13 180 00		13 180 00			
29	Office Supplies Expense			(b) 900 00		900 00		900 00			
30	Bad Debt Expense			(g) 1 000 00		1 000 00		1 000 00			
31	Insurance Exp.—Office Equip.			(f) 120 00		120 00		120 00			
32	Depr. Expense—Office Equip.			(d) 960 00		960 00		960 00			
33	Interest Expense	1 498 00		(a) 168 00		1 666 00		1 666 00			
34	Income Tax Expense			(h) 60 560 00		60 560 00		60 560 00			
35		1,180 640 00	1,180 640 00	99 375 00	99 375 00	1,275 535 00	1,275 535 00	679 040 00	842 157 00	526 263 00	363 146 00
36	Net Income							163 117 00			163 117 00
37								842 157 00	842 157 00	526 263 00	526 263 00

(continued)

2.

Montgomery Manufacturing Co.
Schedule of Cost of Goods Manufactured
For Year Ended December 31, 20 --

Work in process, January 1			$ 36 5 0 0 00
Materials inventory, January 1	$ 23 0 0 0 00		
Materials purchases	110 0 0 0 00		
Materials available for use	$133 0 0 0 00		
Materials inventory, December 31	46 8 4 5 00		
Cost of materials used		$ 86 1 5 5 00	
Direct labor		156 8 9 7 00	
Factory overhead		70 2 3 2 00	
Total manufacturing costs			313 2 8 4 00
Total work in process during the period			$349 7 8 4 00
Work in process, December 31			45 9 8 5 00
Cost of goods manufactured			$303 7 9 9 00

Montgomery Manufacturing Co.
Income Statement
For Year Ended December 31, 20 --

Net sales			$842 1 5 7 00
Less cost of goods sold:			
Finished goods inventory, January 1	$219 6 9 2 00		
Cost of goods manufactured	303 7 9 9 00		
Cost of goods available for sale	$523 4 9 1 00		
Finished goods inventory, December 31	63 1 8 0 00		
Cost of goods sold			460 3 1 1 00
Gross profit			$381 8 4 6 00
Operating expenses:			
Wages expense	$115 6 6 3 00		
Advertising expense	24 6 8 0 00		
Office rent expense	13 1 8 0 00		
Office supplies expense	9 0 0 00		
Bad debt expense	1 0 0 0 00		
Insurance expense—office equipment	1 2 0 00		
Depreciation expense—office equipment	9 6 0 00		
Total operating expenses			156 5 0 3 00
Operating income			$225 3 4 3 00
Other expense:			
Interest expense			1 6 6 6 00
Income before income taxes			$223 6 7 7 00
Income tax			60 5 6 0 00
Net income			$163 1 1 7 00

3.

	DATE		DESCRIPTION	POST REF.	DEBIT					CREDIT					
			GENERAL JOURNAL								PAGE 15				
1			Adjusting Entries												1
2	Dec.²⁰⁻⁻	31	Interest Expense			1	6	8	00						2
3	(a)		Interest Payable								1	6	8	00	3
4															4
5	(b)	31	Office Supplies Expense			9	0	0	00						5
6			Office Supplies								9	0	0	00	6
7															7
8	(c)	31	Factory Overhead		1	8	7	0	00						8
9			Factory Supplies							1	8	7	0	00	9
10															10
11	(d)	31	Depr. Expense—Office Equipment			9	6	0	00						11
12			Accum. Depr.—Office Equipment								9	6	0	00	12
13															13
14	(e)	31	Factory Overhead (Depr. Expense—Factory Equip.)		22	5	6	0	00						14
15			Accum. Depr.—Factory Equipment							22	5	6	0	00	15
16															16
17	(f)	31	Factory Overhead (Insurance Expense)		1	5	9	0	00						17
18			Insurance Expense—Office Equipment			1	2	0	00						18
19			Prepaid Insurance							1	7	1	0	00	19
20															20
21	(g)	31	Bad Debt Expense		1	0	0	0	00						21
22			Allowance for Bad Debts							1	0	0	0	00	22
23															23
24	(h)	31	Income Tax Expense		60	5	6	0	00						24
25			Income Tax Payable							60	5	6	0	00	25
26															26
27	(i)	31	Work in Process Inventory		4	7	2	9	00						27
28			Factory Overhead							4	7	2	9	00	28
29															29
30	(j)	31	Cost of Goods Sold		4	9	1	8	00						30
31			Factory Overhead							4	9	1	8	00	31

(continued)

4.

	GENERAL JOURNAL												PAGE 16	
	DATE		DESCRIPTION	POST REF.	DEBIT					CREDIT					
1			Closing Entries												1
2	Dec. 20--	31	Income Summary		70	2	3	2	00						2
3			Factory Overhead							70	2	3	2	00	3
4															4
5		31	Factory Overhead		70	2	3	2	00						5
6			Income Summary							70	2	3	2	00	6
7															7
8		31	Sales		842	1	5	7	00						8
9			Income Summary							842	1	5	7	00	9
10															10
11		31	Income Summary		679	0	4	0	00						11
12			Cost of Goods Sold							460	3	1	1	00	12
13			Wages Expense							115	6	6	3	00	13
14			Advertising Expense							24	6	8	0	00	14
15			Office Rent Expense							13	1	8	0	00	15
16			Office Supplies Expense								9	0	0	00	16
17			Bad Debt Expense							1	0	0	0	00	17
18			Insurance Expense—Office Equipment								1	2	0	00	18
19			Depr. Expense—Office Equipment								9	6	0	00	19
20			Interest Expense							1	6	6	6	00	20
21			Income Tax Expense							60	5	6	0	00	21
22															22
23		31	Income Summary		163	1	1	7	00						23
24			Retained Earnings							163	1	1	7	00	24
25															25
26		31	Retained Earnings		10	0	0	0	00						26
27			Cash Dividends							10	0	0	0	00	27
28															28

5.

	GENERAL JOURNAL												PAGE 17	
	DATE		DESCRIPTION	POST REF.	DEBIT					CREDIT					
1			Reversing Entries												1
2	Jan. 20--	1	Interest Payable			1	6	8	00						2
3			Interest Expense								1	6	8	00	3
4															4
5		1	Factory Overhead			4	7	2	9	00					5
6			Work in Process Inventory								4	7	2	9	00	6
7															7

On-Line Learning Tools

For more information, visit: http://heintz.swlearning.com

The Heintz & Parry product web site is designed specifically for **COLLEGE ACCOUNTING, 18e.** The features include downloadable student resources and an interactive study center, organized by chapter, which contains learning objectives, web links, on-line quizzes with automatic feedback, and more.

REVIEW QUESTIONS

(LO1)   1. What accounts and related adjustments are new in the work sheet of ToyJoy Manufacturing Co.?

(LO1)   2. How does the use of a perpetual inventory system affect the accounts on the work sheet?

(LO2)   3. Why must the Work in Process Inventory be adjusted for factory overhead applied at year end?

(LO2)   4. What is the relationship between the debit and credit balances in the factory overhead account when the overhead is said to be underapplied? overapplied?

(LO2)   5. Why are the balances in the factory overhead account not extended to the Income Statement and Balance Sheet columns of the work sheet?

(LO3)   6. What are the distinctive features of ToyJoy's income statement? its retained earnings statement? its balance sheet?

(LO4)   7. When the adjustment is made to apply overhead to ending work in process, why are no entries made in the job cost ledger?

(LO4)   8. Describe the procedures for closing the factory overhead account.

(LO4)   9. Which adjusting entries are reversed by ToyJoy?

Self-Study Test Questions

True/False

1. The ToyJoy Company in Chapter 29 uses a periodic inventory system.

2. Under the perpetual inventory system, Cost of Goods Sold is debited each time the finished goods inventory is sold.

3. On the work sheet, the factory overhead account shows both debit and credit totals in the Trial Balance columns.

4. The credit total of Factory Overhead represents actual factory overhead costs.

(continued)

Self-Study Test Questions (continued)

5. The adjustment for factory overhead applied to work in process at the end of the accounting period includes a debit to the factory overhead account.　　_____

Multiple Choice

1. The adjustment for the amount of factory supplies used during the year includes a　　_____

   (a) debit to Factory Supplies.
   (b) debit to Factory Overhead.
   (c) credit to Factory Overhead.
   (d) debit to Supplies Expense.

2. The adjustment for depreciation expense for the year on the factory building includes a　　_____

   (a) debit to Depreciation Expense.
   (b) credit to Factory Overhead.
   (c) credit to Accumulated Depreciation.
   (d) debit to Accumulated Depreciation.

3. At the end of the accounting period, a credit balance in the factory overhead account represents　　_____

   (a) overapplied factory overhead.
   (b) actual factory overhead.
   (c) underapplied factory overhead.
   (d) revenue earned.

4. During the closing process, the credit total in the factory overhead account is debited to　　_____

   (a) Work in Process Inventory.
   (b) Factory Overhead Expense.
   (c) Cost of Goods Sold.
   (d) Income Summary.

5. The adjusting entry to apply factory overhead to Work in Process is reversed at the beginning of the next accounting period and includes a　　_____

   (a) debit to Work in Process Inventory.
   (b) debit to Factory Overhead.
   (c) credit to Factory Overhead.
   (d) credit to Cost of Goods Sold.

The answers to the Self-Study Test Questions are at the end of the text.

MANAGING YOUR WRITING

You and a fellow student are arguing about the "value" of Chapter 29. She says that the chapter is mostly review. The work sheet and financial statements were fully covered in Chapter 16. Chapter 29 is a similar story with some cosmetic differences. You have just begun an impressive defense of Chapter 29 when your professor overhears the argument and decides to give the entire class the following assignment.

Prepare a report describing (1) the ways in which the manufacturer's work sheet differs from the merchandiser's and (2) the differences between the merchandiser's financial statements in Chapter 16 and the manufacturer's financial statements in Chapter 29.

ETHICS CASE

Kevin Ryan is an accountant for Warick Corporation, a medium-size manufacturing firm. One of his responsibilities is to review the adjusting entries at the end of each accounting period. Mary Sellers is a new accountant at Warick Corporation.

She is a recent graduate and this is her first accounting job. One of the duties Kevin assigned Mary was to prepare the adjusting entries. After reviewing Mary's work, Kevin came to the conclusion that Mary did not understand the adjusting process for a manufacturing company. During their review meeting, Kevin told Mary that he was concerned about her ability to do the job. Mary admitted not having a sound knowledge of the adjusting and closing process but asked Kevin to give her another month to catch on. Kevin said he would have to think about it over the weekend and he would get back to her on Monday. That weekend, Kevin was offered a much better paying job with a large manufacturing company in the same city. He immediately accepted the position. When he gave his boss notice that he would be leaving Warick, his boss asked him how Mary was doing. Kevin said he thought she'd do just fine.

1. Do you think Kevin should have told his boss about Mary's poor performance? Why or why not?

2. How will Kevin's decision to not say anything affect Mary?

3. Write a short incident report concerning Mary's poor job performance and subsequent conference with Kevin. Assume Kevin writes the report and it will be placed in Mary's personnel file.

4. In groups of two or three, discuss what alternatives Kevin had in this situation. Come to a group consensus on the best alternative.

WEB WORK

Find a major manufacturer (such as GE, Whirlpool, or General Dynamics) and determine what percentage of its assets are tied up in inventory. Visit the Interactive Study Center on our web site at **http://heintz.swlearning.com** for special hotlinks to assist you in this assignment.

SERIES A EXERCISES

EXERCISE 29-1A **(LO2)**
Factory overhead
overapplied: $4,400

ADJUSTING ENTRIES INCLUDING ADJUSTMENT FOR UNDERAPPLIED/ OVERAPPLIED FACTORY OVERHEAD Prepare the December 31 adjusting journal entries for Johnson Company. Data are as follows:

(a) Factory overhead is applied at a rate of 60% of direct labor costs. At the end of the year, the direct labor costs associated with the jobs still in process amounted to $6,000.

(b) A physical count of factory supplies at the end of the year shows that $4,630 of factory supplies were used during the year.

(c) A review of the insurance policy files shows that $5,190 of insurance on the factory building and equipment has expired.

(d) Depreciation expense for the year on the factory building was $8,200 and on factory equipment was $12,400, a total of $20,600.

(e) The factory overhead account has a debit balance of $178,300 and a credit balance of $182,700 (after recording adjustments (a) through (d)).

Was factory overhead underapplied or overapplied for the year?

EXERCISE 29-2A **(LO3)**

Cost of goods manufactured: $287,500

SCHEDULE OF COST OF GOODS MANUFACTURED Prepare a schedule of cost of goods manufactured for Tomas Company for the year ended June 30, 20-2. Information to prepare the schedule is as follows:

Work in process, July 1, 20-1	$ 6,400
Materials inventory, July 1, 20-1	4,875
Materials purchases	65,350
Direct labor	140,300
Actual factory overhead	85,225
Work in process, June 30, 20-2	7,700
Materials inventory, June 30, 20-2	6,950

EXERCISE 29-3A **(LO4)**

Factory supplies adjustment, Dr. Factory Overhead (Factory Supplies Expense): $3,400

ADJUSTING JOURNAL ENTRIES Prepare the December 31 adjusting journal entries for Hanna Company. Data for the end of the year adjustments are as follows:

Factory overhead to be applied to work in process ending inventory	$8,200
Interest receivable	680
Provision for uncollectible accounts	4,100
Office supplies consumed	960
Factory supplies consumed	3,400
Insurance expired on factory building and equipment	2,500
Depreciation on factory building	7,300
Depreciation on factory equipment	3,700

EXERCISE 29-4A **(LO4)**

Final closing entry, Dr. Income Summary: $119,660

CLOSING JOURNAL ENTRIES Prepare closing journal entries for Medina Company for the year ended December 31. Data for the closing entries are as follows:

Factory overhead, debit and credit balance	$193,460
Sales for the year	840,300
Interest revenue	800
Cost of goods sold	560,400
Salaries expense	93,800
Office supplies expense	2,200
Depreciation expense—office equipment	5,800
Utilities expense—office	6,100
Bad debt expense	1,940
Advertising expense	8,700
Interest expense	9,600
Income tax expense	32,900

EXERCISE 29-5A **(LO4)**

Final reversing entry, Dr. Factory Overhead: $3,180

REVERSING JOURNAL ENTRIES Prepare reversing journal entries for Rogerson Company on January 1, 20-2. The following year-end adjustments were made.

20-1

Dec. 31	Interest Receivable		140	
		Interest Revenue		140
	31	Interest Expense	930	
		Interest Payable		930
	31	Work in Process Inventory	3,180	
		Factory Overhead		3,180

SERIES A PROBLEMS

PROBLEM 29-6A (LO1/2/3)
Net income: $104,845

WORK SHEET, ADJUSTING ENTRIES, AND FINANCIAL STATEMENTS Herrera Company had the following trial balance.

Herrera Company
Trial Balance
December 31, 20 - -

ACCOUNT TITLE	DEBIT BALANCE	CREDIT BALANCE
Cash	30 3 0 0 00	
Government Notes	5 0 0 0 00	
Interest Receivable		
Accounts Receivable	34 0 0 0 00	
Allowance for Bad Debts		5 3 0 00
Finished Goods Inventory	24 0 0 0 00	
Work in Process Inventory	9 0 0 0 00	
Materials Inventory	8 5 0 0 00	
Office Supplies	3 1 0 0 00	
Factory Supplies	3 8 0 0 00	
Land	100 0 0 0 00	
Factory Building	120 0 0 0 00	
Accumulated Depreciation—Factory Building		10 0 0 0 00
Factory Equipment	40 0 0 0 00	
Accumulated Depreciation—Factory Equipment		5 0 0 0 00
Interest Payable		
Accounts Payable		13 8 0 0 00
Income Tax Payable		
Bonds Payable		80 0 0 0 00
Capital Stock		50 0 0 0 00
Paid-In Capital in Excess of Par		30 0 0 0 00
Retained Earnings		92 4 0 0 00
Cash Dividends	30 0 0 0 00	
Sales		405 1 0 0 00
Interest Revenue		3 0 0 00
Factory Overhead	78 6 3 0 00	89 3 0 0 00
Cost of Goods Sold	190 7 0 0 00	
Wages Expense	70 0 0 0 00	
Office Supplies Expense		
Bad Debt Expense		
Utilities Expense—Office	4 4 0 0 00	
Interest Expense	7 0 0 0 00	
Income Tax Expense	18 0 0 0 00	
	776 4 3 0 00	776 4 3 0 00

Data for adjusting the accounts are as follows:

(a) Factory overhead to be applied to work in process
    ending inventory $3,100

(b) Interest receivable   75

(continued)

(c)	Interest payable	$ 600
(d)	Estimate of uncollectible accounts, based on an aging of accounts receivable	2,930
(e)	Office supplies consumed	2,900
(f)	Factory supplies consumed	3,300
(g)	Factory building depreciation	5,000
(h)	Factory equipment depreciation	4,000
(i)	Overapplied factory overhead	1,470
(j)	Provision for corporate income taxes	6,100

Additional information needed to prepare the financial statements is as follows:

Beginning inventories:

Finished goods, January 1	$18,000
Work in process, January 1	7,300
Materials inventory, January 1	9,500
Materials purchases for the year	48,100
Direct labor	60,000
Actual factory overhead	90,930

REQUIRED

1. Prepare a work sheet.

2. Prepare the following financial statements and schedule:

    (a) income statement

    (b) schedule of cost of goods manufactured

    (c) retained earnings statement

    (d) balance sheet

PROBLEM 29-7A   (LO1/3)
2. Retained Earnings,
Dec. 31: $93,810

FINANCIAL STATEMENTS The Income Statement and Balance Sheet columns of Endo Company's work sheet are shown on the next page.

Additional information needed to prepare the financial statements is as follows:

Materials inventory, January 1	$ 3,760
Work in process inventory, January 1	5,315
Finished goods inventory, January 1	16,225
Materials purchases	130,040
Direct labor	75,000
Actual factory overhead	92,000

REQUIRED

1. Prepare an income statement and a schedule of cost of goods manufactured for the year ended December 31, 20--.

2. Prepare a retained earnings statement for the year ended December 31, 20--.

3. Prepare a balance sheet as of December 31, 20--.

PROBLEM 29-7A *(continued)*

Endo Company
Work Sheet (Partial)
For Year Ended December 31, 20 --

	ACCOUNT TITLE	INCOME STATEMENT DEBIT	INCOME STATEMENT CREDIT	BALANCE SHEET DEBIT	BALANCE SHEET CREDIT	
1	Cash			13 3 5 0 00		1
2	Government Notes			3 5 0 0 00		2
3	Interest Receivable			6 5 00		3
4	Accounts Receivable			24 1 0 0 00		4
5	Allowance for Bad Debts				1 2 2 5 00	5
6	Finished Goods Inventory			18 8 0 0 00		6
7	Work in Process Inventory			6 7 4 0 00		7
8	Materials Inventory			4 3 0 0 00		8
9	Office Supplies			3 2 0 00		9
10	Factory Supplies			4 1 0 00		10
11	Prepaid Insurance			6 0 0 00		11
12	Land			25 0 0 0 00		12
13	Factory Building			80 0 0 0 00		13
14	Accum. Depr.—Factory Building				20 1 5 0 00	14
15	Factory Equipment			90 0 0 0 00		15
16	Accum. Depr.—Factory Equipment				27 0 0 0 00	16
17	Interest Payable				4 5 0 00	17
18	Accounts Payable				16 0 0 0 00	18
19	Income Tax Payable				3 5 5 0 00	19
20	Bonds Payable				50 0 0 0 00	20
21	Capital Stock				40 0 0 0 00	21
22	Paid-In Capital in Excess of Par				15 0 0 0 00	22
23	Retained Earnings				80 2 2 5 00	23
24	Cash Dividends			25 0 0 0 00		24
25	Sales		397 1 1 0 00			25
26	Interest Revenue		3 2 5 00			26
27	Factory Overhead					27
28						28
29	Cost of Goods Sold	292 5 0 0 00				29
30	Wages Expense	44 2 0 0 00				30
31	Office Supplies Expense	1 2 0 0 00				31
32	Bad Debt Expense	2 4 5 0 00				32
33	Utilities Expense—Office	1 5 0 0 00				33
34	Interest Expense	2 5 5 0 00				34
35	Income Tax Expense	14 4 5 0 00				35
36		358 8 5 0 00	397 4 3 5 00	292 1 8 5 00	253 6 0 0 00	36
37	Net Income	38 5 8 5 00			38 5 8 5 00	37
38		397 4 3 5 00	397 4 3 5 00	292 1 8 5 00	292 1 8 5 00	38
39						39
40						40

PROBLEM 29-8A (LO1/2/4)

2. Final closing entry, Dr. Income Summary: $76,090

ADJUSTING ENTRIES, CLOSING ENTRIES, AND REVERSING ENTRIES A partial work sheet for Baldwin Company is shown on the next page.

Data for adjusting the accounts are as follows:

(a)	Factory overhead to be applied to work in process ending inventory	$3,600
(b)	Interest receivable	140
(c)	Interest payable	1,200
(d)	Estimate of uncollectible accounts, based on an aging of accounts receivable	2,370
(e)	Office supplies consumed	3,700
(f)	Factory supplies consumed	4,200
(g)	Insurance on factory building and equipment expired	5,100
(h)	Factory building depreciation	5,000
(i)	Factory equipment depreciation	4,000
(j)	Underapplied factory overhead	1,300
(k)	Provision for corporate income taxes	5,900

REQUIRED

1. Journalize the adjusting entries in the general journal.

2. Journalize the closing entries in the general journal.

3. Journalize the reversing entries as of January 1, 20-2, in the general journal.

SERIES B EXERCISES

EXERCISE 29-1B   (LO2)

Factory overhead underapplied: $3,500

ADJUSTING ENTRIES INCLUDING ADJUSTMENT FOR UNDERAPPLIED/ OVERAPPLIED FACTORY OVERHEAD Prepare the December 31 adjusting journal entries for Keiser Company. Data are as follows:

(a) Factory overhead is applied at a rate of 80% of direct labor costs. At the end of the year, the direct labor costs associated with the jobs still in process amounted to $7,000.

(b) A physical count of factory supplies at the end of the year shows that $3,750 of factory supplies were used during the year.

(c) A review of the insurance policy files shows that $4,360 of insurance on the factory building and equipment has expired.

(d) Depreciation expense for the year on the factory building was $9,400 and on factory equipment was $11,600, a total of $21,000.

(e) The factory overhead account has a debit balance of $146,700 and a credit balance of $143,200 (after recording adjustments (a) through (d)).

Was factory overhead underapplied or overapplied for the year?

PROBLEM 29-8A (continued)

Baldwin Company
Work Sheet (Partial)
For Year Ended December 31, 20-1

ACCOUNT TITLE	TRIAL BALANCE DEBIT	TRIAL BALANCE CREDIT	ADJUSTMENTS DEBIT	ADJUSTMENTS CREDIT	ADJUSTED TRIAL BALANCE DEBIT	ADJUSTED TRIAL BALANCE CREDIT	INCOME STATEMENT DEBIT	INCOME STATEMENT CREDIT	BALANCE SHEET DEBIT	BALANCE SHEET CREDIT
1 Cash	41 2 0 0 00				41 2 0 0 00					
2 Government Notes	6 0 0 0 00				6 0 0 0 00					
3 Interest Receivable			(b) 1 4 0 00		1 4 0 00					
4 Accounts Receivable	32 0 0 0 00				32 0 0 0 00					
5 Allowance for Bad Debts		9 2 0 00		(d) 1 4 5 0 00		2 3 7 0 00				
6 Finished Goods Inventory	21 0 0 0 00				21 0 0 0 00					
7 Work in Process Inventory	10 2 0 0 00		(a) 3 6 0 0 00		13 8 0 0 00					
8 Materials Inventory	9 1 0 0 00				9 1 0 0 00					
9 Office Supplies	4 2 0 0 00			(e) 3 7 0 0 00	5 0 0 00					
10 Factory Supplies	5 1 0 0 00			(f) 4 2 0 0 00	9 0 0 00					
11 Prepaid Insurance	6 2 0 0 00			(g) 5 1 0 0 00	1 1 0 0 00					
12 Land	80 0 0 0 00				80 0 0 0 00					
13 Factory Building	120 0 0 0 00				120 0 0 0 00					
14 Accum. Depr.—Factory Building		20 0 0 0 00		(h) 5 0 0 0 00		25 0 0 0 00				
15 Factory Equipment	50 0 0 0 00				50 0 0 0 00					
16 Accum. Depr.—Factory Equip.		8 0 0 0 00		(i) 4 0 0 0 00		12 0 0 0 00				
17 Interest Payable				(c) 1 2 0 0 00		1 2 0 0 00				
18 Accounts Payable		16 4 0 0 00				16 4 0 0 00				
19 Income Tax Payable				(k) 5 9 0 0 00		5 9 0 0 00				
20 Bonds Payable		90 0 0 0 00				90 0 0 0 00				
21 Capital Stock		60 0 0 0 00				60 0 0 0 00				
22 Paid-In Capital in Excess of Par		40 0 0 0 00				40 0 0 0 00				
23 Retained Earnings		46 7 8 0 00				46 7 8 0 00				
24 Sales		410 2 0 0 00				410 2 0 0 00				
25 Interest Revenue		5 0 0 00		(b) 1 4 0 00		6 4 0 00				
26 Factory Overhead	91 8 0 0 00	105 2 0 0 00	(f) 4 2 0 0 00	(a) 3 6 0 0 00	110 1 0 0 00	110 1 0 0 00				
27			(g) 5 1 0 0 00	(j) 1 3 0 0 00						
28			(h) 5 0 0 0 00							
29			(i) 4 0 0 0 00							
30 Cost of Goods Sold	203 5 0 0 00		(j) 1 3 0 0 00		204 8 0 0 00					
31 Salaries Expense	80 0 0 0 00				80 0 0 0 00					
32 Office Supplies Expense			(e) 3 7 0 0 00		3 7 0 0 00					
33 Bad Debt Expense			(d) 1 4 5 0 00		1 4 5 0 00					
34 Utilities Expense—Office	6 7 0 0 00				6 7 0 0 00					
35 Interest Expense	8 0 0 0 00		(c) 1 2 0 0 00		9 2 0 0 00					
36 Income Tax Expense	23 0 0 0 00		(k) 5 9 0 0 00		28 9 0 0 00					
37	798 0 0 0 00	798 0 0 0 00	35 5 9 0 00	35 5 9 0 00	820 5 9 0 00	820 5 9 0 00				
38										

EXERCISE 29-2B **(LO3)**
Cost of goods manufactured:
$685,956

SCHEDULE OF COST OF GOODS MANUFACTURED Prepare a schedule of cost of goods manufactured for Verdi Company for the year ended June 30, 20-2. Information to prepare the schedule is as follows:

Work in process, July 1, 20-1	$ 20,760
Materials inventory, July 1, 20-1	12,348
Materials purchases	154,008
Direct labor	330,576
Actual factory overhead	201,384
Work in process, June 30, 20-2	17,940
Materials inventory, June 30, 20-2	15,180

EXERCISE 29-3B **(LO4)**
Factory Supplies adjustment,
Dr. Factory Overhead (Factory
Supplies Expense): $4,160

ADJUSTING JOURNAL ENTRIES FOR A MANUFACTURING BUSINESS Prepare the December 31 adjusting journal entries for Ortiz Company. Data for the end of the year adjustments are as follows:

Factory overhead to be applied to work in process ending inventory	$7,780
Interest receivable	435
Provision for uncollectible accounts	3,876
Office supplies consumed	750
Factory supplies consumed	4,160
Insurance expired on factory building and equipment	3,200
Depreciation on factory building	6,800
Depreciation on factory equipment	4,200

EXERCISE 29-4B **(LO4)**
Final closing entry, Dr. Income
Summary: $44,655

CLOSING JOURNAL ENTRIES Prepare closing journal entries for Armour Company for the year ended December 31. Data for the closing entries are as follows:

Factory overhead, debit and credit balance	$186,250
Sales for the year	930,600
Interest revenue	920
Cost of goods sold	710,500
Salaries expense	98,100
Office supplies expense	3,500
Depreciation expense—office equipment	6,130
Utilities expense—office	7,460
Bad debt expense	2,275
Advertising expense	9,250
Interest expense	8,300
Income tax expense	41,350

EXERCISE 29-5B **(LO4)**
Final reversing entry, Dr.
Factory Overhead: $4,250

REVERSING ENTRIES Prepare reversing journal entries for Hendrix Company on January 1, 20-2. The following year-end adjustments were made.

20-1

Dec. 31	Interest Receivable		230	
		Interest Revenue		230
	31	Interest Expense	875	
		Interest Payable		875
	31	Work in Process Inventory	4,250	
		Factory Overhead		4,250

SERIES B PROBLEMS

PROBLEM 29-6B (LO1/2/3)

Net income: $73,790

WORK SHEET, ADJUSTING ENTRIES, AND FINANCIAL STATEMENTS Woods Company's trial balance is shown on the next page. Data for adjusting the accounts are as follows:

(a) Factory overhead to be applied to work in process ending inventory	$ 4,300
(b) Interest receivable	100
(c) Interest payable	700
(d) Estimate of uncollectible accounts, based on an aging of accounts receivable	4,110
(e) Office supplies consumed	3,200
(f) Factory supplies consumed	6,700
(g) Factory building depreciation	10,000
(h) Factory equipment depreciation	6,000
(i) Underapplied factory overhead	7,690
(j) Provision for corporate income taxes	8,100

Additional information needed to prepare the financial statements is as follows:

Beginning inventories:	
Finished goods, January 1	$ 22,300
Work in process, January 1	12,400
Materials inventory, January 1	7,900
Materials purchases for the year	18,700
Direct labor	90,300
Actual factory overhead	104,290

REQUIRED

1. Prepare a work sheet.

2. Prepare the following financial statements and schedule:
   - (a) income statement
   - (b) schedule of cost of goods manufactured
   - (c) retained earnings statement
   - (d) balance sheet

(continued)

PROBLEM 29-6B *(continued)*

	Woods Company								
	Trial Balance								
	December 31, 20 - -								

ACCOUNT TITLE	DEBIT BALANCE					CREDIT BALANCE			
Cash	28	4	0	0	00				
Government Notes	6	0	0	0	00				
Interest Receivable									
Accounts Receivable	32	8	0	0	00				
Allowance for Bad Debts							6	1	0	00
Finished Goods Inventory	26	1	0	0	00				
Work in Process Inventory	10	2	0	0	00				
Materials Inventory	9	3	0	0	00				
Office Supplies	4	2	0	0	00				
Factory Supplies	8	6	0	0	00				
Land	80	0	0	0	00				
Factory Building	160	0	0	0	00				
Accumulated Depreciation—Factory Building						30	0	0	0	00
Factory Equipment	60	0	0	0	00				
Accumulated Depreciation—Factory Equipment						20	0	0	0	00
Interest Payable									
Accounts Payable						16	0	0	0	00
Income Tax Payable									
Bonds Payable						100	0	0	0	00
Capital Stock						60	0	0	0	00
Paid-In Capital in Excess of Par						20	0	0	0	00
Retained Earnings						111	4	0	0	00
Cash Dividends	40	0	0	0	00				
Sales						410	7	0	0	00
Interest Revenue							5	0	0	00
Factory Overhead	81	5	9	0	00	92	3	0	0	00
Cost of Goods Sold	198	3	0	0	00				
Wages Expense	78	7	0	0	00				
Office Supplies Expense									
Bad Debt Expense									
Utilities Expense—Office	4	9	0	0	00				
Interest Expense	9	0	0	0	00				
Income Tax Expense	23	4	2	0	00				
	861	5	1	0	00	861	5	1	0	00

PROBLEM 29-7B **(LO1/3)**

2. Retained Earnings,
Dec. 31: $99,270

FINANCIAL STATEMENTS The Income Statement and Balance Sheet columns of Wen Company's work sheet are shown on the next page.

Additional information needed to prepare the financial statements is as follows:

Materials inventory, January 1	$ 4,750
Work in process inventory, January 1	3,600
Finished goods inventory, January 1	14,560
Materials purchases	110,990
Direct labor	110,000
Actual factory overhead	96,850

PROBLEM 29-7B *(continued)*

Wen Company
Work Sheet (Partial)
For Year Ended December 31, 20 --

	ACCOUNT TITLE	INCOME STATEMENT		BALANCE SHEET		
		DEBIT	CREDIT	DEBIT	CREDIT	
1	Cash			16 4 5 0 00		1
2	Government Notes			6 0 0 0 00		2
3	Interest Receivable			2 1 0 00		3
4	Accounts Receivable			19 7 0 0 00		4
5	Allowance for Bad Debts				1 6 0 0 00	5
6	Finished Goods Inventory			16 2 5 0 00		6
7	Work in Process Inventory			7 6 0 0 00		7
8	Materials Inventory			4 5 5 0 00		8
9	Office Supplies			4 6 5 00		9
10	Factory Supplies			3 7 5 00		10
11	Prepaid Insurance			7 0 0 00		11
12	Land			30 0 0 0 00		12
13	Factory Building			60 0 0 0 00		13
14	Accum. Depr.—Factory Building				15 2 3 0 00	14
15	Factory Equipment			85 0 0 0 00		15
16	Accum. Depr.—Factory Equipment				23 0 0 0 00	16
17	Interest Payable				6 0 0 00	17
18	Accounts Payable				14 4 5 0 00	18
19	Income Tax Payable				3 1 5 0 00	19
20	Bonds Payable				40 0 0 0 00	20
21	Capital Stock				30 0 0 0 00	21
22	Paid-In Capital in Excess of Par				20 0 0 0 00	22
23	Retained Earnings				83 0 2 0 00	23
24	Cash Dividends			12 5 0 0 00		24
25	Sales		410 1 5 0 00			25
26	Interest Revenue		6 5 0 00			26
27	Factory Overhead					27
28						28
29	Cost of Goods Sold	312 3 5 0 00				29
30	Wages Expense	43 1 0 0 00				30
31	Office Supplies Expense	2 2 5 0 00				31
32	Bad Debt Expense	1 7 5 0 00				32
33	Utilities Expense—Office	4 0 0 0 00				33
34	Interest Expense	3 1 0 0 00				34
35	Income Tax Expense	15 5 0 0 00				35
36		382 0 5 0 00	410 8 0 0 00	259 8 0 0 00	231 0 5 0 00	36
37	Net Income	28 7 5 0 00			28 7 5 0 00	37
38		410 8 0 0 00	410 8 0 0 00	259 8 0 0 00	259 8 0 0 00	38
39						39

REQUIRED

1. Prepare an income statement and a schedule of cost of goods manufactured for the year ended December 31, 20--.

2. Prepare a retained earnings statement for the year ended December 31, 20--.

3. Prepare a balance sheet as of December 31, 20--.

PROBLEM 29-8B (LO1/2/4)

Power Accounting System Software®

2. Final closing entry, Dr.
Income Summary: $65,510

ADJUSTING ENTRIES, CLOSING ENTRIES, AND REVERSING ENTRIES A partial work sheet for Milnor Company is shown on the next page.

Data for adjusting the accounts are as follows:

(a)	Factory overhead to be applied to work in process ending inventory	$4,400
(b)	Interest receivable	190
(c)	Interest payable	1,420
(d)	Estimate of uncollectible accounts, based on an aging of accounts receivable	4,450
(e)	Office supplies consumed	4,200
(f)	Factory supplies consumed	3,800
(g)	Insurance on factory building and equipment expired	6,800
(h)	Factory building depreciation	8,000
(i)	Factory equipment depreciation	5,000
(j)	Overapplied factory overhead	4,340
(k)	Provision for corporate income taxes	6,400

REQUIRED

1. Journalize the adjusting entries in the general journal.

2. Journalize the closing entries in the general journal.

3. Journalize the reversing entries as of January 1, 20-2, in the general journal.

PROBLEM 29-8B (continued)

Milnor Company
Work Sheet (Partial)
For Year Ended December 31, 20-1

ACCOUNT TITLE	TRIAL BALANCE DEBIT	TRIAL BALANCE CREDIT	ADJUSTMENTS DEBIT	ADJUSTMENTS CREDIT	ADJUSTED TRIAL BALANCE DEBIT	ADJUSTED TRIAL BALANCE CREDIT	INCOME STATEMENT DEBIT	INCOME STATEMENT CREDIT	BALANCE SHEET DEBIT	BALANCE SHEET CREDIT
1 Cash	39 6 0 0 00				39 6 0 0 00					
2 Government Notes	8 0 0 0 00				8 0 0 0 00					
3 Interest Receivable			(b) 1 9 0 00		1 9 0 00					
4 Accounts Receivable	40 0 0 0 00				40 0 0 0 00					
5 Allowance for Bad Debts		1 2 5 0 00		(d) 3 2 0 0 00		4 4 5 0 00				
6 Finished Goods Inventory	24 0 0 0 00				24 0 0 0 00					
7 Work in Process Inventory	12 3 0 0 00		(a) 4 4 0 0 00		16 7 0 0 00					
8 Materials Inventory	8 7 0 0 00				8 7 0 0 00					
9 Office Supplies	5 5 0 0 00			(e) 4 2 0 0 00	1 3 0 0 00					
10 Factory Supplies	4 9 5 0 00			(f) 3 8 0 0 00	1 1 5 0 00					
11 Prepaid Insurance	7 4 5 0 00			(g) 6 8 0 0 00	6 5 0 00					
12 Land	90 0 0 0 00				90 0 0 0 00					
13 Factory Building	130 0 0 0 00				130 0 0 0 00					
14 Accum. Depr.—Factory Building		40 0 0 0 00		(h) 8 0 0 0 00		48 0 0 0 00				
15 Factory Equipment	70 0 0 0 00				70 0 0 0 00					
16 Accum. Depr.—Factory Equip.		10 0 0 0 00		(i) 5 0 0 0 00		15 0 0 0 00				
17 Interest Payable				(c) 1 4 2 0 00		1 4 2 0 00				
18 Accounts Payable		17 2 0 0 00				17 2 0 0 00				
19 Income Tax Payable				(k) 6 4 0 0 00		6 4 0 0 00				
20 Bonds Payable		120 0 0 0 00				120 0 0 0 00				
21 Capital Stock		50 0 0 0 00				50 0 0 0 00				
22 Paid-In Capital in Excess of Par		30 0 0 0 00				30 0 0 0 00				
23 Retained Earnings		72 3 1 0 00				72 3 1 0 00				
24 Sales		395 2 0 0 00				395 2 0 0 00				
25 Interest Revenue		8 0 0 00		(b) 1 9 0 00		9 9 0 00				
26 Factory Overhead	84 5 6 0 00	108 1 0 0 00	(f) 3 8 0 0 00	(a) 4 4 0 0 00	112 5 0 0 00	112 5 0 0 00				
27			(g) 6 8 0 0 00							
28			(h) 8 0 0 0 00							
29			(i) 5 0 0 0 00							
30			(j) 4 3 4 0 00							
31 Cost of Goods Sold	194 6 0 0 00			(j) 4 3 4 0 00	190 2 6 0 00					
32 Wages Expense	90 0 0 0 00				90 0 0 0 00					
33 Office Supplies Expense			(e) 4 2 0 0 00		4 2 0 0 00					
34 Bad Debt Expense			(d) 3 2 0 0 00		3 2 0 0 00					
35 Utilities Expense—Office	7 2 0 0 00				7 2 0 0 00					
36 Interest Expense	9 0 0 0 00		(c) 1 4 2 0 00		10 4 2 0 00					
37 Income Tax Expense	19 0 0 0 00		(k) 6 4 0 0 00		25 4 0 0 00					
38	844 8 6 0 00	844 8 6 0 00	47 7 5 0 00	47 7 5 0 00	873 4 7 0 00	873 4 7 0 00				
39										

MASTERY PROBLEM

**2. Retained Earnings,
Dec. 31: $284,124**

Reese Manufacturing Company manufactures and sells a limited line of products made to customer order. The company uses a perpetual inventory system and keeps its accounts on a calendar year basis. A ten-column work sheet is presented on page 1119.

Additional information needed to prepare the income statement and schedule of cost of goods manufactured is as follows:

Finished goods inventory, January 1	$ 85,454
Materials inventory, January 1	11,633
Purchases for the year	93,237
Direct labor	107,740
Work in process inventory, January 1	22,600

REQUIRED

1. Prepare an income statement and schedule of cost of goods manufactured for the year ended December 31, 20--.

2. Prepare a retained earnings statement for the year ended December 31, 20--.

3. Prepare a balance sheet as of December 31, 20--.

4. Prepare the adjusting, closing, and reversing entries.

MASTERY PROBLEM (continued)

Reese Manufacturing Co.
Work Sheet
For Year Ended December 31, 20--

#	Account Title	Trial Balance Debit	Trial Balance Credit	Adjustments Debit	Adjustments Credit	Adjusted Trial Balance Debit	Adjusted Trial Balance Credit	Income Statement Debit	Income Statement Credit	Balance Sheet Debit	Balance Sheet Credit
1	Cash	49 423 00				49 423 00				49 423 00	
2	Accounts Receivable	78 096 00				78 096 00				78 096 00	
3	Allowance for Bad Debts		5 074 00		(g) 956 00		6 030 00				6 030 00
4	Finished Goods Inventory	42 675 00				42 675 00				42 675 00	
5	Work in Process Inventory	39 675 00		(i) 1 567 00		41 242 00				41 242 00	
6	Materials Inventory	22 353 00				22 353 00				22 353 00	
7	Office Supplies	3 546 00			(b) 800 00	2 746 00				2 746 00	
8	Factory Supplies	1 878 00			(c) 1 389 00	489 00				489 00	
9	Prepaid Insurance	1 500 00			(f) 1 454 00	46 00				46 00	
10	Factory Equipment	186 674 00				186 674 00				186 674 00	
11	Accum. Depr.—Factory Equip.		23 501 00		(e) 12 553 00		36 054 00				36 054 00
12	Office Equipment	46 986 00				46 986 00				46 986 00	
13	Accum. Depr.—Office Equip.		2 916 00		(d) 923 00		3 839 00				3 839 00
14	Notes Payable		12 470 00				12 470 00				12 470 00
15	Interest Payable				(a) 132 00		132 00				132 00
16	Accounts Payable		10 356 00				10 356 00				10 356 00
17	Income Tax Payable				(h) 45 725 00		45 725 00				45 725 00
18	Capital Stock		72 000 00				72 000 00				72 000 00
19	Retained Earnings		195 341 00				195 341 00				195 341 00
20	Cash Dividends	36 000 00				36 000 00				36 000 00	
21	Sales		532 027 00				532 027 00		532 027 00		
22	Factory Overhead	52 356 00	65 446 00	(c) 1 389 00 (e) 12 553 00 (f) 1 356 00	(i) 1 567 00 (j) 641 00	67 654 00	67 654 00				
23											
24											
25	Cost of Goods Sold	281 407 00		(j) 641 00		282 048 00		282 048 00			
26	Wages Expense	58 380 00				58 380 00		58 380 00			
27	Advertising Expense	11 450 00				11 450 00		11 450 00			
28	Office Rent Expense	5 443 00				5 443 00		5 443 00			
29	Office Supplies Expense			(b) 800 00		800 00		800 00			
30	Bad Debt Expense			(g) 956 00		956 00		956 00			
31	Insurance Exp.—Office Equip.			(f) 98 00		98 00		98 00			
32	Depr. Expense—Office Equip.			(d) 923 00		923 00		923 00			
33	Interest Expense	1 289 00		(a) 132 00		1 421 00		1 421 00			
34	Income Tax Expense			(h) 45 725 00		45 725 00		45 725 00			
35		919 131 00	919 131 00	66 140 00	66 140 00	981 628 00	981 628 00	407 244 00	532 027 00	506 730 00	381 947 00
36	Net Income							124 783 00			124 783 00
37								532 027 00	532 027 00	506 730 00	506 730 00

CHALLENGE PROBLEM

This problem challenges you to apply your cumulative accounting knowledge to move a step beyond the material in the chapter.

2. Revised net income: $56,670

Drafts of the condensed income statement and balance sheet of Allofe Co. for the current year are shown below. Shortly after preparing these draft financial statements, Allofe discovered that an error had been made in the year-end adjustment process. Overhead of $2,500 had not been applied to the ending work in process.

Allofe Co.
Condensed Income Statement
For Year Ended December 31, 20--

Net sales	$501,570
Cost of goods sold	360,312
Gross profit	$141,258
Operating expenses	87,088
Net income	$ 54,170

Allofe Co.
Condensed Balance Sheet
December 31, 20--

Assets	
Current assets	$ 93,014
Property, plant and equipment (net)	177,441
Total assets	$270,455
Liabilities	
Current liabilities	$ 28,671
Long-term liabilities	60,000
Total liabilities	$ 88,671
Stockholders' Equity	
Paid-in capital	$ 57,000
Retained earnings	124,784
Total stockholders' equity	181,784
Total liabilities and stockholders' equity	$270,455

REQUIRED

1. Identify all adjusting and closing entries that would be affected by this error and prepare the missing portions of the entries.

2. Prepare a revised condensed income statement and balance sheet for Allofe.

(In solving this problem, assume that corporate income tax is not affected by the error.)

CHAPTER 2

True/False

1. T   2. F (A/P is a liability)

3. T   4. T

5. F (other changes could occur: capital could increase, revenue could increase, etc.)

6. F (net income)   7. T

Multiple Choice

1. c   2. a   3. b   4. d   5. c

CHAPTER 3

True/False

1. T

2. F (liability accounts normally have credit balances)

3. T   4. F (credit balances)

5. T   6. F (increase)

Multiple Choice

1. c   2. c   3. b   4. d   5. a

CHAPTER 4

True/False

1. T   2. T   3. T

4. F (A, L, OE, R, E)   5. T

Multiple Choice

1. b   2. c   3. b   4. a   5. d

CHAPTER 5

True/False

1. F (match revenues and expenses)

2. F (to bring accounts up-to-date)

3. T

4. F (depreciable cost = cost – salvage value)

5. F (to match cost of asset against revenues it will help generate)

Multiple Choice

1. a   2. c   3. d   4. c   5. a

CHAPTER 6

True/False

1. T

2. F (additional investments are added to the beginning balance)

3. F   4. T   5. T

Multiple Choice

1. b   2. d   3. a   4. c   5. b

CHAPTER 7

True/False

1. F (primary purpose is to reconcile book balance with bank balance)

2. F (deducted from book balance)   3. T

4. F (deducted from book balance)

5. F (entries are not posted from petty cash record to general ledger)

Multiple Choice

1. b   2. a   3. c   4. b   5. d

CHAPTER 8

True/False

1. F (does *not* work under control and direction)

2. T   3. F (is called wages)

4. T   5. T

Multiple Choice

1. c   2. b   3. d   4. a   5. d

CHAPTER 9

True/False

1. F (these taxes are paid by the employer)

2. T   3. T

4. F (FUTA tax is levied on employers)

5. F (this form is W-2)

Multiple Choice

1. b   2. d   3. b   4. d   5. a

CHAPTER 10

True/False

1. T

2. F (large businesses use the accrual basis)

3. F (see Figure 7-2) 4. T   5. T

Multiple Choice

1. c   2. b   3. d   4. a   5. b

CHAPTER 11

True/False

1. T   2. T   3. T

4. F (the debit *excludes* the sales tax)   5. T

Multiple Choice

1. d   2. c   3. b   4. b   5. a

CHAPTER 12

True/False

1. F (purchase requisition)   2. T

3. T   4. F (credited)   5. F (buyer)

Multiple Choice

1. d   2. a   3. a   4. d   5. b

CHAPTER 13

True/False

1. T   2. F (general journal is still needed)

3. F (only credit sales)   4. T   5. T

Multiple Choice

1. a   2. a   3. c   4. c   5. a

CHAPTER 14

True/False

1. T   2. F (prepared before check is issued)

3. T   4. T

5. F (used with a check register)

Multiple Choice

1. b   2. d   3. a   4. c   5. b

CHAPTER 15

True/False

1. T   2. T   3. T

4. F (revenue is recognized)

5. F (contra-revenue account)

Multiple Choice

1. b   2. a   3. b   4. b   5. b

CHAPTER 16

True/False

1. T   2. F (whichever is longer)

3. T   4. T

5. F (number of times accounts receivable turned over)

Multiple Choice

1. c   2. a   3. b   4. d   5. c

CHAPTER 17

True/False

1. T   2. F (expenses matched with revenues)

3. F (balance in Allowance for Bad Debts is ignored)

4. F (debit to Allowance for Bad Debts)   5. T

Multiple Choice

1. d   2. a   3. b   4. d   5. a

CHAPTER 18

True/False

1. T   2. T

3. F (Difference is called the discount.)

4. F (Interest is credited to Interest Revenue; time has passed and the interest has been earned.)

5. T

Multiple Choice

1. b   2. c   3. c   4. d   5. a

CHAPTER 19

True/False

1. T   2. T

3. F (this is true for the periodic method)

4. T   5. F (the buyer pays)

Multiple Choice

1. b   2. c   3. a   4. c   5. b

CHAPTER 20

True/False

1. F (land)   2. F (reverse is true)

3. F (depreciation is a method of cost allocation)

4. F (the opposite is true)

5. F (the units-of-production method is based on the usage or output of the asset)

Multiple Choice

1. d   2. c   3. b   4. b   5. c

CHAPTER 21

True/False

1. F (partnership)   2. T

3. F (limited life is a characteristic of a partnership because the partnership is dissolved with any change in the partners)

4. F (this is a disadvantage)   5. T

Multiple Choice

1. a   2. a   3. d   4. c   5. a

CHAPTER 22

True/False

1. T   2. T

3. F (they do not have this power)

4. F (dividends are taxable to the recipients)

5. F (they are expensed when incurred)

Multiple Choice

1. d   2. a   3. c   4. d   5. c

CHAPTER 23

True/False

1. T   2. T   3. T

4. F (it is known as a cash dividend)

5. F (dates of declaration and payment require journal entries)

Multiple Choice

1. a   2. b   3. d   4. c   5. a

CHAPTER 24

True/False

1. T   2. F (discount)   3. T

4. F (decreases)   5. T

Multiple Choice

1. c   2. c   3. a   4. d   5. b

CHAPTER 25

True/False

1. F (cash flows)

2. F (buying and selling assets)   3. T

4. F (subtracted)   5. T

Multiple Choice

1. d   2. a   3. b   4. a   5. c

CHAPTER 26

True/False

1. F (leverage is a measure of the extent to which debt is used to finance the business)

2. T   3. T   4. F (WC = CA – CL)   5. T

Multiple Choice

1. b   2. a   3. c   4. d   5. d

CHAPTER 27

True/False

1. F (net sales and cost of goods sold)   2. T

3. T   4. F (indirect expenses)   5. T

Multiple Choice

1. a   2. d   3. b   4. b   5. c

CHAPTER 28

True/False

1. F (only direct materials)   2. T   3. T

4. F (items finished and not sold)   5. T

Multiple Choice

1. c   2. b   3. a   4. c   5. d

CHAPTER 29

True/False

1. F (perpetual)   2. T   3. T

4. F (debit total)   5. F (credit)

Multiple Choice

1. b   2. c   3. a   4. d   5. b

*Page references in bold indicate defined terms.

Note: While for a specific company each account number used would have only one title, titles vary from company to company as needed.

Assets (100–199)

100s—Cash Related Accounts
101 Cash
105 Petty Cash

120s—Receivables
121 Notes Receivable
122 Accounts Receivable
122.1 Allowance for Bad Debts
123 Interest Receivable (Also Accrued Interest Receivable)

130s—Inventories
131 Merchandise Inventory
132 Raw Materials
133 Work in Process
134 Finished Goods

140s—Prepaid Items
141 Supplies (Specialty items like Medical, Bicycle, Tailoring, etc.)
142 Office Supplies
144 Food Supplies
145 Prepaid Insurance

150s—Long-Term Investments
153 Bond Sinking Fund

160s—Land
161 Land
162 Natural Resources
162.1 Accumulated Depletion

170s—Buildings
171 Buildings
171.1 Accumulated Depreciation—Buildings

180s—Equipment
181 Office Equipment (Also Store Equipment)
181.1 Accumulated Depreciation—Office Equipment (Also Store Equipment)
182 Office Furniture
182.1 Accumulated Depreciation—Office Furniture
183 Athletic Equipment (Also Tailoring, Lawn, Cleaning)
183.1 Accumulated Depreciation—Athletic Equipment (Also Tailoring, Lawn, Cleaning)
184 Tennis Facilities (Also Basketball Facilities)
184.1 Accumulated Depreciation—Tennis Facilities (Also Basketball Facilities)
185 Delivery Equipment (Also Medical, Van)
185.1 Accumulated Depreciation—Delivery Equipment (Also Medical, Van)
186 Exercise Equipment
186.1 Accumulated Depreciation—Exercise Equipment
187 Computer Equipment
187.1 Accumulated Depreciation—Computer Equipment

190s—Intangibles
191 Patents
192 Copyrights

Liabilities (200–299)

200s—Short-Term Payables
201 Notes Payable
201.1 Discount on Notes Payable
202 Accounts Payable (Also Vouchers Payable)
203 United Way Contribution Payable
204 Income Tax Payable
205 Common Dividends Payable
206 Preferred Dividends Payable
207 Interest Payable (Also Bond Interest Payable)

210s—Employee Payroll Related Payables
211 Employee Income Tax Payable
212 Social Security Tax Payable
213 Medicare Tax Payable
215 City Earnings Tax Payable
216 Health Insurance Premiums Payable
217 Credit Union Payable
218 Savings Bond Deductions Payable
219 Wages Payable

220s—Employer Payroll Related Payables
221 FUTA Tax Payable
222 SUTA Tax Payable
223 Workers' Compensation Insurance Payable

230s—Sales Tax
231 Sales Tax Payable

240s—Deferred Revenues and Current Portion of Long-Term Debt
241 Unearned Subscription Revenue (Also Unearned Ticket Revenue, Unearned Repair Fees)
242 Current Portion of Mortgage Payable

250s—Long-Term Liabilities
251 Mortgage Payable
252 Bonds Payable
252.1 Discount on Bonds Payable
253 Premium on Bonds Payable